THE ROUGH GUIDE TO

California

There are more than one hundred and fifty Rough Guide titles
covering destinations from Amsterdam to Zimbabwe

Forthcoming titles include
Alaska • Copenhagen • Ibiza & Formentera • Iceland

Rough Guide Reference Series
Classical Music • Country Music • Drum 'n' bass • English Football
European Football • House • The Internet • Jazz • Music USA • Opera
Reggae • Rock Music • Techno • Unexplained Phenomena • World Music

Rough Guide Phrasebooks
Czech • Dutch • Egyptian Arabic • European Languages • French • German
Greek • Hindi & Urdu • Hungarian • Indonesian • Italian • Japanese
Mandarin Chinese • Mexican Spanish • Polish • Portuguese • Russian
Spanish • Swahili • Thai • Turkish • Vietnamese

Rough Guides on the Internet
www.roughguides.com

ROUGH GUIDE CREDITS

Text editor: Stephen Timblin
Series editor: Mark Ellingham
Editorial: Martin Dunford, Jonathan Buckley, Jo Mead, Kate Berens, Amanda Tomlin, Ann-Marie Shaw, Paul Gray, Helena Smith, Judith Bamber, Orla Duane, Olivia Eccleshall, Ruth Blackmore, Geoff Howard, Claire Saunders, Gavin Thomas, Alexander Mark Rogers, Polly Thomas, Joe Staines, Lisa Nellis, Andrew Tomičić, Richard Lim, Duncan Clark, Peter Buckley, Sam Thorne (UK); Andrew Rosenberg, Mary Beth Maioli, Don Bapst (US)
Production: Susanne Hillen, Andy Hilliard, Link Hall, Helen Ostick, Julia Bovis, Michelle Draycott,

Katie Pringle, Robert Evers, Mike Hancock, Robert McKinlay
Cartography: Melissa Baker, Maxine Repath, Nichola Goodliffe, Ed Wright
Picture research: Louise Boulton, Sharon Martins
Online: Kelly Cross, Anja Mutic-Blessing (US)
Finance: John Fisher, Gary Singh, Edward Downey, Mark Hall, Tim Bill
Marketing & Publicity: Richard Trillo, Niki Smith, David Wearn, Jemima Broadbridge (UK); Jean Marie Kelly, Simon Carloss, David Wechsler (US)
Administration: Tania Hummel, Demelza Dallow, Julie Sanderson

ACKNOWLEDGMENTS

Don Bapst: I would like to thank Suzen Brasile, Steve Hayes, Beverly Loranger, Amy Herzog, Sharon Malone Esler, Julie A. Webster, and Bill and Doreen Thornhill; **Jeff Dickey**: thanks to my wife, Brenna; **Mike Meyer**: thanks to Feng Dan, the K, the rangers of the National Park Service, *Mike and Tony's* in Shasta, the seal woman with clam chowder in Jenner and the streetfolk of Arcata and the Bay Area; **Paul Whitfield**: thanks to Toby Pyle at HI-AYH, Douglas Lochhead, Philip Silverton, and Susan Walton.

The editor would like to thank all those who contributed to this edition; Julia Bovis, Rob Evers and Susanne Hillen for smooth production, Gillian Armstrong for proof-reading, Sharon Martins for her photo research, Melissa Baker and Maxine Repath for putting together such useful maps, Antonia Hebbert and Paul Whitfield for Basics research, and both Andrew Rosenberg and Martin Dunford for support.

PUBLISHING INFORMATION

This sixth edition published September 2000 by Rough Guides Ltd, 62–70 Shorts Gardens, London WC2H 9AH.
Distributed by the Penguin Group:
Penguin Books Ltd, 27 Wrights Lane, London W8 5TZ
Penguin Putnam, Inc. 375 Hudson Street, NY 10014, USA
Penguin Books Australia Ltd, 487 Maroondah Highway, PO Box 257, Ringwood, Victoria 3134, Australia
Penguin Books Canada Ltd, 10 Alcorn Avenue, Toronto, Ontario, Canada M4V 1E4
Penguin Books (NZ) Ltd, 182–190 Wairau Road, Auckland 10, New Zealand
Typeset in Linotron Univers and Century Old Style to an original design by Andrew Oliver.
Printed in England by Clays Ltd, St Ives Plc
Illustrations in Part One and Part Three by Edward Briant.

Illustration on p.1 by Cathie Folstcad; illustration on p.647 by Sally Davies
© The Rough Guides Ltd 2000
No part of this book may be reproduced in any form without permission from the publisher except for the quotation of brief passages in reviews.
720pp – Includes index
A catalog record for this book is available from the British Library
ISBN 1-85828-539-9

The publishers and authors have done their best to ensure the accuracy and currency of all the information in *The Rough Guide to California*, however, they can accept no responsibility for any loss, injury, or inconvenience sustained by any traveler as a result of information or advice contained in the guide.

THE ROUGH GUIDE TO

California

written and researched by

Don Bapst, Deborah Bosley, Adrian Curry,
Jeff Dickey, Jamie Jensen, Olivia Mandel,
Mike Meyer, Ken Miller, Mick Sinclair,
Greg Ward and Paul Whitfield

ROUGH
GUIDES

We set out to do something different when the first Rough Guide was published in 1982. Mark Ellingham, just out of university, was traveling in Greece. He brought along the popular guides of the day, but found they were all lacking in some way. They were either strong on ruins and museums but went on for pages without mentioning a beach or taverna. Or they were so conscious of the need to save money that they lost sight of Greece's cultural and historical significance. Also, none of the books told him anything about Greece's contemporary life – its politics, its culture, its people, and how they lived.

So with no job in prospect, Mark decided to write his own guidebook, one which aimed to provide practical information that was second to none, detailing the best beaches and the hottest clubs and restaurants, while also giving hard-hitting accounts of every sight, both famous and obscure, and providing up-to-the-minute information on contemporary culture. It was a guide that encouraged independent travelers to find the best of Greece, and was a great success, getting shortlisted for the Thomas Cook travel guide award, and encouraging Mark, along with three friends, to expand the series.

The Rough Guide list grew rapidly and the letters flooded in, indicating a much broader readership than had been anticipated, but one which uniformly appreciated the Rough Guide mix of practical detail and humor, irreverence and enthusiasm. Things haven't changed. The same four friends who began the series are still the caretakers of the Rough Guide mission today: to provide the most reliable, up-to-date and entertaining information to independent-minded travelers of all ages, on all budgets.

We now publish more than 150 titles and have offices in London and New York. The travel guides are written and researched by a dedicated team of more than 100 authors, based in Britain, Europe, the USA and Australia. We have also created a unique series of phrasebooks to accompany the travel series, along with an acclaimed series of music guides, and a best-selling pocket guide to the Internet and World Wide Web. We also publish comprehensive travel information on our Web site:

www.roughguides.com

HELP US UPDATE

We've gone to a lot of effort to ensure that the sixth edition of *The Rough Guide to California* is accurate and up-to-date. However, things change – places get "discovered," opening hours are notoriously fickle, restaurants and rooms raise prices or lower standards. If you feel we've got it wrong or left something out, we'd like to know, and if you can remember the address, the price, the time, the phone number, so much the better.

We'll credit all contributions, and send a copy of the next edition (or any other Rough Guide if you prefer) for the best letters. Please mark letters: "Rough Guide California Update" and send to:
Rough Guides, 62–70 Shorts Gardens, London WC2H 9AH, or Rough Guides, 4th Floor, 345 Hudson St, New York, NY 10014.
Or send email to: mail@roughguides.co.uk
Online updates about this book can be found on Rough Guides' Web site at **www.roughguides.com**

READERS' LETTERS

Many thanks go to the readers who have taken the time to contact us with comments and suggestions. These include:

Cassie Antin, Jan Austin, Michael Beech, Christoph Bergemann, Jen Ceely, Philip Chklar, Trevor Chubb, Philip Clarke, Edward Coyle, D.L. Dang, Craig Dudley, Peter Eustance, Robert French, Randy Glessner, Pamela Hattingh, Auva Hartley, Jeremy Hughes, Jackie Hymers, Frank Keogh, Sonia Kolesoco, Steven Leigh, Douglas Lochhead, B. Lou, Paul MacDermott, Claire Mortimer, Jason Numez, Adrian Palmer, Justin Rupric, Gavin Scott, Elaine Simer, Alex Skinner, Gerrie Smits, Jonathan Stewart, Otto Stutgartner, Neville Walker, Susan Walton, John Yates, Kiri Yourchik and the many folks who contacted us via email but preferred to remain anonymous.

CONTENTS

PART THREE ░ CONTEXTS   647

LIST OF MAPS

MAP SYMBOLS

▭(80)▭	Interstate	⛷	Ski resort	〰	Gorge/cutting
(30)	U.S. Highway	⛳	Golf course	⋔	Waterfall
(1)	Highway	⛺	Campsite	⸬	Marshland
═════	4WD track	⛱	Picnic area	◆	General point of interest
———	Unpaved road	†	Church (regional maps)	ⓘ	Information centre
- - - -	Path/trail	🏛	Historic house	⊠	Post office
▬▬▬	Railway	🗼	Lighthouse	ℂ	Telephone
— —	Ferry route	⸫	Ruins	★	Public transport stop
▪▫▪▫	International border	◠	Caves	🅿	Parking
▬ ▫ ▬ ▫	State border	🌴	Oasis	■	Building
— — —	Chapter division boundary	�	Spring/spa	✚	Church
———	River	�	Viewpoint	╬	Cemetery
✈	Airport	峯	Mountain range	▨	National Park
◉	Hotel	▲	Mountain peak	▨	Park
▣	Restaurant	⤳	Pass	⋱	Beach

INTRODUCTION

California is America squared. It's the place you go to find more America than you ever thought possible.

What's Wrong with America by Scott Bradfield

No region of the world, perhaps, has been as publicized, and idealized, as **California**, and none lives up to the hype to quite the same degree. A terrestrial paradise of sun, sand, surf and sea, it has a whole lot more besides: high mountain ranges, fast-paced glitzy cities, deep primeval forests, and hot dry deserts.

Having zoomed from the Stone Age to Silicon Valley in little more than a couple of centuries, California doesn't dwell on the past. In some ways this part of America represents the ultimate "now" society, with all that entails – life is lived very much in the fast lane, and conspicuous consumption is emphasized to the exclusion of almost everything else. But this is only one side of the coin, and the deeper sense of age here often gets skimmed over. Provided you get out of the cities, it is readily apparent in the landscape: dense groves of ancient trees, primitive rock carvings left by the aboriginal Native American culture, and the eerie ghost towns of the Gold Rush pioneers. A land of superlatives, California really is full of the oldest, the tallest, the largest, the most spectacular, all of which goes far beyond local bravura.

It's important to bear in mind, too, that the supposed "superficiality" of California is largely a myth, an image promoted as much by Americans on the East Coast as by foreigners – even if the area's endeavors to gain cultural credibility can sometimes seem brash. Politically, it's probably the USA's most schizophrenic region, home state of some of its most reactionary figures – Ronald Reagan and Richard Nixon to name just two – yet also the source of some of the country's most progressive political movements. Some of the fiercest protests of the Sixties emanated from here, and in many ways this is still the heart of liberal America. Consider the level of environmental awareness, which puts the smoky East to shame, and the fact that California has set *the* standard for the rest of the US (and the world) regarding gay pride and social permissiveness. Economically, too, the region is crucial. The computer industries of Silicon Valley have led the American economy to new heights, the cash-flush entertainment field is dominated by California's film industry and recently ascendant music business, and even in the increasingly important financial markets, Los Angeles has become a major player.

Where to go

California is the third largest state in the US, covering nearly 160,000 square miles: keep in mind that distances between the main destinations can be huge, and that you won't, unless you're here for an extended period, be able to see everything on one trip.

In an area so varied it's hard to pick out specific highlights. You may well start off in **Los Angeles**, far and away the biggest and most stimulating city: a maddening collection of freeways and beaches, seedy suburbs and high-gloss neighborhoods and extreme lifestyles that you should see at least once, even if you make a quick exit for more relaxed locales. From Los Angeles you have a number of choices. You can head south to **San Diego**, the seventh largest city in America, complete with broad, welcoming beaches and a handy position close to the Mexican border, or you could push inland to the Californian **desert** areas, notably **Death Valley** – as its name suggests, a barren inhospitable landscape of volcanic craters and windswept sand dunes that in summer (when you can fry an egg on your car bonnet) becomes the hottest place on earth. It's a logical trip from here across to the **Grand Canyon** via **Las Vegas**; though not in California, we've included these last two in Chapter Three of the guide. An alternative is to make the steady journey up the **Central Coast**, a gorgeous run following the shoreline north through some of the state's most dramatic scenery, and taking in some of its liveliest small towns, notably Santa Barbara and Santa Cruz.

The Central Coast makes the transition from Southern to Northern California – a break that's more than just geographical. **San Francisco**, at the top end, is California's second city, and quite different from LA: the coast's oldest, most European-looking city, it's set compactly over a series of steep hills, with wooden houses tumbling down to water on both sides. San Francisco also gives access to some of the state's most extraordinary scenery, not least in the national parks to the east, especially **Yosemite**, where

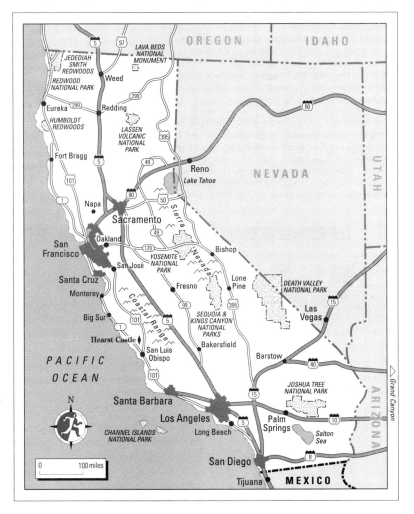

powerful waterfalls cascade into a sheer glacial valley that's been immortalized by Ansel Adams and countless others in search of the definitive landscape photograph.

North of San Francisco, the population thins and the physical look changes yet again. The climate is wetter up here, the valleys that much greener, flanked by a jagged coastline shadowed by mighty redwoods, the tallest trees in the world. Though many visitors choose to venture no further than the **Wine Country** and the Russian River Valley on weekend forays from the city, it's well worth taking time out to explore the state's northernmost regions, a volcano-scarred desolation that's as different from the popular image of California as it's possible to be.

When to go

California's climate comes close to its subtropical ideal. In **Southern California** in particular you can count on endless days of sunshine from May to October, and warm dry nights – though **LA**'s notorious smog is at its worst when the temperatures are highest, in August and September.

Right along the **coast** mornings can be hazily overcast, especially in May and June, though you can still get a suntan – or sunburn – even under grayish skies. In winter temperatures drop somewhat, but more importantly it can rain for weeks on end, causing massive mudslides that wipe out roads and hillside homes. Inland, the deserts are warm in winter and unbearably hot (120°F is not unusual) in summer; desert nights can be freezing in winter, when, strangely but beautifully, it can even snow. For serious **snow**, head to the mountains, where hiking trails at the higher elevations are blocked from November to June every year: skiers can take advantage of well-groomed slopes along the Sierra Nevada mountains and around Lake Tahoe.

The coast of **Northern California** is wetter and cooler than the south, its summers tempered by sea-breezes and fog, and its winters mild but wet. **San Francisco**, because of its exposed position at the tip of a peninsula, can be chilly all year, with summer fogs tending to roll in to ruin what may have started off as a pleasant sunny day. Head a mile inland, and you're back in the sun.

DAYTIME TEMPERATURES (MAX & MIN °F)							
	Jan		April		July		Oct
San Diego	66	46	69	54	76	63	73	58
Los Angeles	65	47	72	53	83	63	77	57
Fresno	55	36	75	47	99	63	80	48
San Francisco	56	45	62	49	65	54	68	54
Death Valley	65	37	91	61	116	87	91	51

PART ONE

THE
BASICS

GETTING THERE FROM BRITAIN AND EUROPE

Though flying to California from Europe is pretty straightforward, choosing the best route can be more complicated than you might think, with prices fluctuating wildly according to how and when you go. The majority of budget options involve non-stop services from Britain, although many others turn out to be so-called "direct" flights, which can land several times, waiting an hour or so at each stop – a flight is called direct as long as it keeps the same flight number throughout its journey. The first place the plane lands is your point of entry into the US, which means you'll have to collect your bags and go through customs and immigration formalities there, even if you're continuing on to California on the same plane. This can be a real pain after a ten-hour journey, so it's worth finding out before you book a ticket.

FARES, ROUTES AND AGENTS

Although you can fly to the US from any of the regional airports, the only **non-stop flights** from Britain to California are from London. Most of these land at LA, the hub of the region's air travel. Fewer travel non-stop to San Francisco, and you can't fly non-stop at all to San Diego. The non-stop **flight time** is around eleven hours from London to San Francisco or LA; add an hour at least for each intervening stop on direct flights, twice that if you have to change planes. Following winds ensure that return flights are always an hour or two shorter than outward journeys. Because of the time difference between Britain and the West Coast (eight hours almost all year), flights usually leave Britain mid-morning, while flights back from the US tend to arrive in Britain early in the morning.

Britain remains one of the best places in Europe to obtain flight bargains, though **fares** vary widely according to season, availability and the current level of inter-airline competition. The comments that follow can only act as a general guide, so be sure to shop around carefully for the best offers by checking the **travel ads** in the weekend papers, on the **holiday pages** of ITV's *Teletext* and, in London, scouring *Time Out* and the *Evening Standard*. Giveaway magazines aimed at young travelers, like *TNT*, are also useful resources. The **Internet** is another valuable resource, and you'll often find good deals on one of the many travel-based sites, including *www.ebookers.com*, *www.expedia.com* and *www.travelocity.com*.

Stand-by deals (open-dated tickets which you pay for and then decide later when you want

SAMPLE AIR FARES FROM BRITAIN

The prices given below (in £ sterling) are a general indication of the minimum transatlantic **air fares** currently obtainable from specialist companies; youth discount fares are cheaper, especially for one-way tickets. Remember to add £50–60 airport tax to these figures. Each airline decides the exact dates of its seasons. Prices are for departures from London to LA. (Flights from London to San Francisco are in the same price range).

	LOW Nov–Mar (except Christmas)		SHOULDER April, May, Sept, Oct		HIGH June–Aug, Christmas	
	one-way	round-trip	one-way	round-trip	one-way	round-trip
Los Angeles	179	185	206	250	256	437

One word of **warning**: it's not a good idea to buy a **one-way** ticket to the States. Not only are they rarely good value compared to a round-trip ticket, but US immigration officials usually take them as a sign that you aren't planning to go home, and may refuse your entry.

to fly – if there's room on the plane) are few and far between, and don't give great savings: in general you're better off with an **Apex** ticket. The conditions on these are pretty standard whoever you fly with – seats must be purchased seven days or more in advance, and you must stay for at least one Saturday night; tickets are normally valid for up to six months. Some airlines also do less expensive **Super-Apex** tickets, which fall into two categories: the first are approximately £150 cheaper than an ordinary Apex but must be bought 21 days in advance and require a minimum stay of seven days and a maximum stay of one month; the second are around £100 less than an Apex, must be purchased fourteen days in advance and entail a minimum stay of a week and a maximum stay of two months – such tickets are usually non-refundable or changeable. **"Open-jaw"** tickets can be a good idea, allowing you to fly into LA, for example, and back from San Francisco for little or no extra charge; fares are calculated by halving the return fares to each destination and adding the two figures together. This makes a convenient option for those who want a fly-drive holiday (see below).

Generally, the most expensive time to fly is **high season**, roughly between June and August and around Christmas. May and September are slightly less pricey, and the rest of the year is considered low season and is cheaper still. Keep an eye out for slack season bargains, and, additionally, make sure to check the exact dates of the seasons with your operator or airline; you might be able to make major savings by shifting your departure date by a week – or even a day. **Weekend rates** for all return flights tend to be around £20 more expensive than those in the week.

For an overview of the various offers, and unofficially discounted tickets, go straight to an **agent** specializing in low-cost flights (we've listed some on p.6). Especially if you're under 26 or a student, they may be able to knock up to thirty percent off the regular Apex fares when there are no special airline deals. Agents will usually offer non-stop

flights, or "direct" flights via another airport in the USA, although you may be offered other, stranger combinations (London–Los Angeles via Amsterdam, Manchester–Los Angeles via Paris for example) – all worth considering if the price is right.

The same agents also offer cut-price seats on **charter flights**. These are particularly good value if you're traveling from a British city other than London, although they tend to be limited to the summer season, be restricted to so-called "holiday destinations" and have fixed departure and return dates. Brochures are available in most high street travel agents, or contact the specialists direct.

Finally, if you've got a bit more time, or want to see a bit more of the USA, it's often possible to stop over in another city – **New York** especially – and fly on from there for little more than the cost of a direct flight to California. Also, with increased competition on the **London–Los Angeles** route, thanks to Virgin Atlantic among others and price wars between US carriers, the cost of a connecting flight from LA to San Francisco has been brought down to less than £40. Many airlines also offer **air passes**, which allow foreign travelers to fly between a given number of US cities for one discounted price. For more details on long-distance travel within the US see p.8.

COURIER FLIGHTS

It's still possible, if not as common as it used to be, for those on a very tight budget to travel as **couriers**. Courier firms offer opportunities to travel at discounted rates (for example £200 return to the West Coast) in return for delivering a package or escorting a cargo. There'll be someone to check you in and to meet you at your destination, which minimizes any red-tape hassle. You may have to travel light (but not necessarily, if you're escorting a cargo of several tons), and accept tight restrictions on travel dates. For phone numbers, check the *Yellow Pages*, as these businesses come and go.

PACKAGES

Packages – fly-drive, flight/accommodation deals and guided tours (or a combination of all three) – can work out cheaper than arranging the same trip yourself, especially for a short-term stay. The obvious drawbacks are the loss of flexibility and the fact that most schemes use hotels in the mid-range bracket, but there is a wide variety of options available. High-street travel agents have plenty of brochures and information about the various combinations.

FLY-DRIVE

Fly-drive deals, which give cut-rate (sometimes free) car rental when buying a transatlantic ticket, always work out cheaper than renting on the spot and give especially great value if you intend to do a lot of driving. On the other hand, you'll probably have to pay more for the flight than if you booked it through a discount agent. Competition between airlines (especially Northwest and TWA) and tour operators means that it's well worth phoning to check on current special promotions.

Northwest Flydrive offers excellent deals for not much more than an ordinary Apex fare; for example, a return flight to LA or San Francisco and a week's car rental (including insurance) might cost less than £300 per person in low season. Several of the other companies listed in the box on p.7 offer similar, and sometimes cheaper, packages.

Watch out for hidden extras, such as local taxes, and "drop-off" charges, which can be as much as a week's rental, and Collision Damage Waiver insurance (see p.31). Remember, too, that while you can drive in the States with a British license, there can be problems renting vehicles if you're under 25. For complete car-rental and driveaway details, see "Getting Around California" (p.29).

FLIGHTS FROM BRITAIN

The following carriers operate **non-stop flights** from London to California
(all from Heathrow unless otherwise stated):

Air New Zealand, daily from Heathrow to Los Angeles.
American Airlines, daily to Los Angeles.
British Airways, daily to Los Angeles and San Francisco.

United Airlines, daily to Los Angeles and San Francisco.
Virgin Atlantic, daily to Los Angeles and San Francisco, and in summer five times a week from Gatwick to San Francisco.

The following carriers operate **one-stop direct flights** from London to California
(all from Gatwick unless otherwise stated):

American Airlines, daily via Dallas to San Francisco, and daily from Heathrow via New York, Chicago or Los Angeles to San Francisco.
British Airways, daily via Phoenix to San Diego.
Continental, daily via Denver, Miami, Houston or Newark to Los Angeles, San Francisco and San Diego.

Delta, daily via Cincinnati or Atlanta to Los Angeles, San Francisco and San Diego.
Northwest, daily via Detroit or Minneapolis to Los Angeles and San Francisco.
TWA, daily via St Louis to Los Angeles and San Francisco.

The following carriers operate direct flights from **regional airports** to the US:

American Airlines, from Manchester to Chicago; May to October also from Glasgow to Chicago.
British Airways, from Manchester to New York.
Continental, from Glasgow, Birmingham and

Manchester to Newark.
Delta, from Manchester to Atlanta.
Northwest, from Glasgow to Boston.
Virgin Atlantic, from Manchester to Orlando.

AIRLINES

Air New Zealand ☎020/8741 2299;
www.airnz.co.nz
American Airlines ☎0345/789789;
www.aa.com
British Airways ☎0345/222111;
www.britishairways.com
Continental ☎01293/776464;

www.flycontinental.com
Delta ☎0800/414767; *www.delta-air.com*
Northwest ☎01424 /224400; *www.nwa.com*
TWA ☎0345/333333; *www.twa.com*
United ☎0845/844 4777; *www.ual.com*
Virgin Atlantic ☎01293/747747; *www. fly.virgin.com*

LOW-COST FLIGHT AGENTS FROM BRITAIN

Bridge The World, 47 Chalk Farm Rd, London NW1 8AN (☎020/7916 0990; *www.b-t-w.co.uk*).
Destination Group, 14 Greville Street, London EC1N 8SB (☎020/7400 7000; *www.destination-group.com*).
STA Travel, 86 Old Brompton Rd, London SW7 (☎0870/160 6070; *www.statravel.com*); branches nationwide.
Trailfinders, 42–50 Earls Court Rd, London W8 (☎020/7937 5400; *www.trailfinders.com*); branches nationwide.

Travel Bug, 597 Cheetham Hill Rd, Manchester M8 5EJ (☎0161/721 4000); 125 Gloucester Road, London SW7 (☎020/7835 2000; *www.flynow.com*).
Travel Cuts, 295a Regent St, London W1 (☎020/7255 2082; *www.travelcuts.com*).
Usit Campus, 52 Grosvenor Gardens, London SW1 (☎020 7730 2101; national call center 0870 240 1010; *www.usitcampus.co.uk*)
Usit Council, 28a Poland St, London W1V 3DB (☎020/7287 3337).

FLIGHT AND ACCOMMODATION DEALS

There's really no end of combined **flight and accommodation deals** to California, and although you can often do things cheaper independently, you won't be able to do the same things cheaper – in fact, the equivalent room booked separately will normally be a lot more expensive – and you can leave the organizational hassles to someone else. Drawbacks include the loss of flexibility and the fact that you'll probably have to stay in hotels in the mid-range to expensive bracket, even though less expensive accommodation is almost always available.

A handful of tour operators (see box) offer quite deluxe packages, of which Virgin Holidays are among the least expensive: for example, seven nights in San Francisco plus return flight costs around £559 in low season, £849 per person in high season. Discount agents can set up more basic packages for around £500 each. Pre-booked accommodation schemes, under which you buy vouchers for use in a specific group of hotels, are not normally good value – see p.37.

TOURING AND ADVENTURE PACKAGES

A simple and exciting way to see a chunk of California's extensive wilderness, without being hassled by too many practical considerations, is to take a specialist **touring and adventure package**, which includes transportation, accommodation, food and a guide. Some of the more adventurous carry small groups around on minibuses and use a combination of budget hotels and camping (equipment, except a sleeping bag, is provided). Most also have a food kitty of around £25 per week, with many meals cooked and eaten communally, although there's plenty of time to leave the group and do your own thing.

Trek America is one UK-based company to offer such deals; a typical package would be ten days in California and the "Wild West" for £425 or so excluding flights. Other operators are listed opposite. If you're interested in **backcountry hiking**, the San Francisco-based Sierra Club (see p.54) offers a range of tours that take you into parts of the state that most people never see.

FLIGHTS FROM IRELAND

Aer Lingus fly daily **direct** to Los Angeles from Dublin and Shannon. Delta has no direct flights to California, but flies daily to Atlanta and New York from Dublin. The **cheapest flights** from Ireland – if you're under 26 or a student – are available from USIT. Student-only return fares to San Francisco or Los Angeles direct range from IR£359 to IR£525. Flights via London may cost less, but you pay slightly more tax. Ordinary Apex fares are only marginally higher.

USIT can be contacted at Aston Quay, O'Connell Bridge, Dublin 2 (☎01/677 8117). Aer Lingus is at 40 O'Connell St, Dublin 1 and Dublin Airport (☎01/886 8888; *www.aerlingus.ie*), and Delta Airlines is at 24 Merrion Square, Dublin 2 (☎01/676 8080 or 1-800/768080).

FLIGHTS FROM EUROPE

It is generally far cheaper to fly non-stop to California from London than any other European city. However, for the **best deals** to New York from Brussels and Paris, contact Nouvelles Frontières, 87 boulevard de Grenelle, 75015 Paris (☎41.41.58.58) and 2 boulevard M. Lemonnier, 1000 Brussels (☎02/547 4444).

Other options are the cut-price charter flights occasionally offered from major European cities; ask at your nearest travel agent for details. In

Germany, look for discount **youth fare** deals which United offers (to those under 26 booking 72 hours or less in advance) from Frankfurt, its continental hub (☎069/605020).

SPECIALIST HOLIDAY OPERATORS

Airtours, Wavell House, Helmshore, Rossendale, Lancs BB4 4NB (☎01706/240033; www.airtours.co.uk). Multi-center holidays including combinations of Los Angeles, San Francisco and Las Vegas.

American Adventures, 64 Mount Pleasant Ave, Tunbridge Wells, Kent TN1 1QY (☎01892/512700; www.americanadventures.com). Small-group touring and adventure holidays on the West Coast; also hostelling with Road Runner International (see below).

American Airlines Holidays, PO Box 5, 12 Coningsby Rd, Peterborough PE3 8XP (☎0870/605 0506). Flight plus accommodation and fly-drive deals.

Bon Voyage, 18 Bellevue Rd, Southampton, Hants SO15 2AY (☎023/8024 8248). Flight-plus-accommodation deals in San Francisco, Los Angeles and Palm Springs.

Bridge Travel Service, Bridge House, Broxbourne, Herts EN10 7DT (☎01992/456600; www.bridgetravel.co.uk). City breaks in Los Angeles; accommodation only.

British Airways Holidays, Astral Towers, Bettsway, London Road, Crawley, West Sussex RH10 2XA (☎01293/723121). City breaks in Los Angeles, San Diego and San Francisco, and fly-drive deals (including motorhomes).

Connections, 10 York Way, Lancaster Rd, High Wycombe, Bucks HP12 3PY (☎01494/473173; www.connectionsworldwide.net). Tailor-mades, including short breaks in Los Angeles and San Francisco.

Contiki Travel, Wells House, 15 Elmfield Rd, Bromley, Kent BR1 1LS (☎020/8290 6777). West Coast coach tours.

Cosmos, Tourama House, 17 Homesdale Rd, Bromley, Kent BR2 9LX (☎020/8464 3444). Coach tours, including Los Angeles and San Diego.

Destination Group, 14 Greville Street, London EC1N 8SB (☎020/7400 7000; www.destination-group.com). Tailor-mades; can arrange accommodation and fly-drive deals.

Explore Worldwide, 1 Frederick St, Aldershot, Hants GU11 1LQ (☎01252/760000; www.explore.co.uk). Small-group walking tours, camping or staying in hotels.

Flydrive, USA PO Box 45, Bexhill-on-Sea, East Sussex TN40 1PY (☎01424/224400). Flight-plus-accommodation and fly-drive combinations.

Funway Holidays, 1 Elmfield Park, Bromley, Kent BR1 1LU (☎020/8466 0222). Tailor-mades in Los Angeles, San Diego, San Francisco and Palm Springs.

Kuoni, Kuoni House, Dorking, Surrey RH5 4AZ (☎01306/742888; www.kuoni.co.uk). Multi-center flight-plus-accommodation-plus-car deals featuring Los Angeles, San Francisco and San Diego.

North America Travel Service, 7 Albion St, Leeds LS1 5ER (☎0113/246 1466); 241 Kensington High Street, London W8 (☎020/7938 3737). Also branches in Nottingham, Manchester and Barnsley. Tailor-mades: flights, accommodation, car hire, and so on.

Premier Holidays, Westbrook, Milton Road, Cambridge CB4 1YQ (☎01223/516516; www.premierholidays.co.uk). Flight-plus-accommodation deals throughout California.

Road Runner, 64 Mount Pleasant Ave, Tunbridge Wells, Kent TN1 1QY (☎01892/512700). Hostelling version of American Adventures touring and adventure packages (see above).

Travelpack, Clarendon House, Clarendon Road, Eccles, Manchester M30 9TR (☎08705 747101). Escorted tours and tailor-made holidays throughout California.

Top Deck Travel, 131 Earls Court Rd, London SW5 (☎020/7370 4555; www.topdecktravel.co.uk). Agents for numerous adventure touring specialists.

Trek America, Malvern House, 4 Waterperry Court, Middleton Road, Banbury, OX16 4QB (☎01295 256777; www.trekamerica.com). Touring adventure holidays.

United Vacations, PO Box 377, Bromley, Kent (☎020/8313 0999). City breaks, tailor-mades and fly-drives.

Up & Away, 19 The Mall, Bromley, Kent BR1 1LY (☎020/8289 5050). Tailor-mades and fly-drives to Los Angeles and Californian National Parks.

Virgin Holidays, The Galleria, Station Road, Crawley, West Sussex RH10 1WW (☎01293/456789; www.virginholidays.co.uk). Packages to a wide range of California destinations.

GETTING THERE FROM NORTH AMERICA

Getting to California from anywhere else in North America is never a problem; the region is well served by air, rail and road networks. All the main airlines operate daily scheduled flights to San Francisco and LA from across the country, and there are daily flights from Toronto and Vancouver as well. Flying remains the best but most expensive way to travel; taking a train comes a slow second. Traveling by bus is the least expensive method, but again is slow, and is much less comfortable than either train or plane.

BY AIR

To Los Angeles, many domestic flights land at the city's international **LAX** airport, as well as the smaller airports at Burbank, Long Beach, Ontario and John Wayne in Orange County. For San Francisco, besides the main **San Francisco International Airport** (known as SFO), two others, both in the Bay Area, may be useful – particularly **Oakland International** (OAK), across the bay but easily accessible. The third Bay Area airport, **San Jose Municipal** (SJO), forty miles south, is a bit out of the way but has good connections with the western US, LA especially. Some carriers also fly to **San Diego**'s Lindbergh airport non-stop.

AIRLINES IN THE USA AND CANADA

Aer Lingus ☎1-800/223-6537; *www.aerlingus.ie*
Aeromexico ☎1-800/237-6639; *www.aeromexico.com*
Air Canada ☎1-800/776-3000; *www.aircanada.ca*
Air France ☎1-800/237-2747; in Canada ☎1-800/667-2747; *www.airfrance.com*
Alaska Airlines ☎1-800/426-0333; *www.alaska-air.com*
America West ☎1-800/2FLYAWA; *www.americawest.com*
American Airlines ☎1-800/433-7300; *www.americanair.com*
British Airways ☎1-800/247-9297; in Canada ☎1-800/668-1059; *www.british-airways.com*
Canadian ☎1-800/426-7000; in Canada ☎1-800/665-1177; *www.cdnair.ca*
Continental ☎1-800/525-0280; *www.flycontinental.com*
Delta Airlines ☎1-800/221-1212; in Canada, call directory inquiries for local toll-free number; *www.delta-air.com*
Hawaiian Airlines ☎1-800/367-5320; *www.hawaiianair.com*

Iberia ☎1-800/772-4642; *www.iberia.com/ingles/home.html*
Icelandair ☎1-800/223-5500; *www.icelandair.com*
KLM ☎1-800/374-7747; in Canada ☎1-800/361-5073; *www.klm.nl*
Lufthansa ☎1-800/645-3880; in Canada ☎1-800/563-5954; *www.lufthansa-usa.com*
Northwest ☎1-800/225-2525; *www.nwa.com*
Scandinavian Airlines ☎1-800/221-2350; *www.scandinavian.net*
Southwest ☎1-800/435-9792; *www.iflyswa.com*
Tower Air ☎1-800/221-2500; *www.towerair.com*
Trans World Airlines ☎1-800/221-2000; *www.twa.com*
United Airlines ☎1-800/241-6522; *www.ual.com*
US Airways ☎1-800/428-4322; *www.usairways.com*
Virgin Atlantic Airways ☎1-800/862-8621; *www.virginatlantic.com*

As airlines tend to match each other's prices, there's generally little difference in the quoted fares. Barring another fare war, round-trip prices start at around $350 from New York, slightly less from Midwest cities and slightly more from Toronto and Montréal. What makes more difference than your choice of carrier are the conditions governing the ticket – whether it's fully refundable, the time and day and most importantly the **time of year** you travel. Least expensive of all is a non-summer-season midweek flight, booked and paid for at least three weeks in advance. Also keep in mind that one-way tickets are sometimes more expensive than round-trip tickets. While it's good to call the airlines directly to get a sense of their official fares, it's also worth checking with a reputable **travel agent** to find out about any **special deals** or student/youth fares that may be available.

In addition to the big-name scheduled airlines, a few lesser-known carriers run no-frills flights, which can prove to be very good value, especially if you have a flexible schedule and can put up with a few delays. Tower Air, the New York-based charter operator, has flights from New York to Los Angeles for about $310 round-trip. Southwest flies from a host of Midwestern and Western cities at rock-bottom prices; four daily flights leave Salt Lake City for Oakland (they don't go directly to San Francisco) from $150 round-trip ($82 one way). Their lowest fare out of Seattle to Oakland is $148 round-trip ($83 one way), while LA to Oakland goes for as low as $112 round-trip ($68 one way).

Travelers intending to fly from **Canada** are likely to find that, with less competition on these routes (Canadian flies to San Francisco only from Vancouver; most other routes are monopolized by Air Canada), fares are somewhat higher than they are for flights wholly within the US. You may well find that it's worth the effort to get to a US city first, and fly on to California from there.

If you have a bit more money and hanker after a few more creature comforts (all the trains have private cabins and dining cars), or simply have the time and inclination to take in some of the rest of the US on your way to California, then an Amtrak **train** may be just the ticket for you. The most spectacular train journey of all has to be the *California Zephyr*, which runs all the way

> For all information on **Amtrak fares and schedules**, and to make reservations, use the toll-free number ☎1-800/USA-RAIL or Web site (*www.amtrak.com*). Do not call individual stations.

from Chicago to San Francisco (53 hours; departs 3.35pm daily) and comes into its own during the ride through the Rockies west of Denver. After climbing alongside raging rivers through gorgeous **mountain scenery**, the route drops down the west flank of the Rockies and races across the Utah and Nevada deserts by night, stopping at Salt Lake City and Reno. The next day the train climbs up and over the mighty Sierra Nevada, following the route of the first transcontinental railroad on its way into Oakland, where you change to a bus for the ride into San Francisco.

The major southern route, the 3000-mile *Sunset Limited*, originates in Miami, Florida, and stops at New Orleans, Houston, San Antonio and Flagstaff (where a connecting buses heads to the Grand Canyon) before eventually arriving in Los Angeles.

Amtrak **fares** are often more expensive than flying, though off-peak discounts and special deals can make the train an economical as well as an aesthetic choice. One-way cross-country fares are around $285, though if you're traveling round-trip you can take advantage of what they call **"Explore America"** fares, which are zone-based and allow three stopovers – within 45 days – between your origin and eventual return. Travel within the West (from Denver to the Pacific) costs $229 between September and May or $259 from June to August); within the West and Midwest (west of Chicago) costs $299/359; and for the entire USA the cost is $359/419. While Amtrak's basic fares are decent value, if you want to travel in a bit more comfort the cost rises quickly. **Sleeping compartments**, which include meals, small toilets and showers, start at around $150 per night for one or two people.

Bus travel is the most tedious and time-consuming way to get to California, and, for all the discomfort, won't really save you much money. **Greyhound** (☎1-800/231-2222) is the sole long-distance operator and has an extensive network of destinations in California. A one-way ticket from New York to San Francisco, bought 14 days in advance, costs $69, while tickets purchased on the day of travel go for $125.

The only reason to go Greyhound is if you're planning to visit a number of other places en route; Greyhound's **Ameripass** is good for unlimited travel within a certain time, and costs $169 for seven days, $249 for fifteen days, $349 for thirty days, and $479 for sixty days. **Foreign visitors** can buy Ameripasses before leaving home; see p.33 for details.

An alternative, in every sense, is the San Francisco-based **Green Tortoise** bus company; see p.34 for details.

BY CAR

Driving your own car gives the greatest freedom and flexibility, but if you don't have one (or don't trust the one you do have), one option worth considering is a **driveaway**. Companies operate in most major cities, and are paid to find drivers to take a customer's car from one place to another — most commonly between California and New York. The company will normally pay for your insurance and your first tank of gas; after that, you'll be expected to drive along the most direct route and to average 400 miles a day. Many driveaway companies are keen to use foreign travelers (German tourists are ideal, it seems), but if you can convince them you are a safe bet they'll take something like a $250 deposit, which you get back after delivering the car in good condition. It makes obvious sense to get in touch in

advance, to spare yourself a week's wait for a car to turn up. Look under "Automobile transporters and driveaway companies" in the *Yellow Pages* and phone around for the latest offers; or try one of the ninety branches of Auto Driveaway, based in Chicago (☎312/341-1900).

Renting a car is the usual story of phoning your local branch of one of the majors (Avis, Hertz, Budget, Thrifty, etc — listed on p.29), of which Thrifty tends to be the cheapest. Most have offices at destination airports, and addresses and phone numbers are comprehensively documented in the *Yellow Pages*.

Also worth considering are fly-drive deals, which give cut-rate (and sometimes free) car rental when buying an air ticket. They usually work out cheaper than renting on the spot and are especially good value if you intend to do a lot of driving.

PACKAGE TOURS

Many operators run all-inclusive packages which combine plane tickets and hotel accommodation with (for example) sightseeing, wining and dining, or excursions to tourist sites. Even if the "package" aspect doesn't thrill you to pieces, these deals can still be more convenient and sometimes even work out to be more economical than arranging the same thing yourself, providing you don't mind losing a little flexibility. With such a vast range of packages available, it's impossible to give an overview — major travel agents will have brochures detailing what's available.

GETTING THERE FROM AUSTRALIA AND NEW ZEALAND

From Australia and New Zealand there's very little price difference between airlines and no shortage of flights, via the Pacific or Asia, to Los Angeles and San Francisco. Via the Pacific most flights are non-stop, with traveling time between Auckland/Sydney and LA twelve to fourteen hours, though some allow stopovers in Honolulu and a number of the South Pacific islands. If you go via Asia (a slightly more roundabout route that can work out a little cheaper), you'll usually have to spend a night, or the best part of a day, in the airline's home city.

Various **coupon deals** – available with your international ticket for discounted flights within the US – are good value if California is part of a wider US trip. A minimum purchase of three coupons usually applies. For example, United Airlines' **Coupon Pass** costs US$389 for the first three, and US$60–100 for subsequent tickets (maximum of twelve in total). Tickets purchased direct from the airlines are usually at published

---

SPECIALIST AGENTS AND OPERATORS

If you prefer to have all the arrangements made for you before you leave, then the specialist agents below can help you plan your trip. Unfortunately there are few pre-packaged tours that include airfares from Australia and New Zealand, however, most specialist agents will also be able to assist with flight arrangements. In turn many of the tours below can also be arranged through your local travel agent.

Adventure Specialists 69 Liverpool St, Sydney (☎02/9261 2927). A good selection of adventure treks and tours.
Adventure World 73 Walker St, Sydney (☎02/9956 7766); 8 Victoria Ave, Perth (☎09/9221 2300); 101 Great South Rd, Auckland (☎09/524 5118). Individual and small-group exploratory tours and treks.
American Travel Centre Seventh Floor, 333 Adelaide St, Brisbane (☎07/3221 4788). All US travel arrangements.
Creative Tours Bookings through travel agents only. Escorted bus tours, air passes, accommodation and Disneyland packages.
Insight Bookings through travel agents only. Offers first class city accommodation, Disneyland packages, car rental and bus tours.
Peregrine Adventures 258 Lonsdale St, Melbourne (☎03/9662 2700); offices in

Brisbane, Sydney, Adelaide and Perth. Small-group active holidays from short walking and camping to longer overland trips through California.
Sydney International Travel Centre (*www.sydneytravel.com.au*) 75 King St, Sydney (☎1-800/251 911 or 02/9299 8000, fax 9299 1337). Individually tailored holidays, Disneyland passes, flights, bus and rail tours.
The Surf Travel Co 2/25 Cronulla Plaza, Cronulla Beach, NSW (☎02/9527 4722); 7 Danbury Drive, Torbay, Auckland (☎09/473 8388). Lake Tahoe snowboarding and ski trips.
Travel Plan 72 Chandos St, St Leonards, Sydney (☎02/9438 1333). Ski holiday packages in the Lake Tahoe region.
Wiltrans 10/189 Kent St, Sydney (☎02/9255 0899). Five-star all-inclusive escorted Californian sightseeing holidays.

GAY AND LESBIAN

Pride Travel 254 Bay St, Brighton, Melbourne (☎03/9596 3566).

Silke's Travel 263 Oxford St, Darlinghurst, Sydney (☎02/9380 5835).

AIRLINES

Air New Zealand (*www.airnz.co.nz*) Quay House, 29 Customs St W, Auckland (☎09/357-3000); in Australia call tollfree ☎13 2476. Daily flights to LA from major cities in Australia and New Zealand, via transfers in Auckland, or several times a week via either Auckland and Honolulu/Papeete, or Auckland, Fiji/Tonga and Honolulu.

Air Pacific (*www.airpacific.com*) Australia ☎1-800/230 150; New Zealand ☎09/379 2404. Once a week to LA from Sydney, Melbourne, Brisbane and major New Zealand cities via a stopover in Nadi (Fiji).

Cathay Pacific (*www.cathaypacific.com*) Australia ☎13 1747; New Zealand ☎09/379 0861. Daily to LA from major cities in Australia and New Zealand via a transfer or stopover in Hong Kong.

Delta Air Lines (*www.delta-air.com*) Australia ☎1-800/500 992; New Zealand ☎09/379 3370. Coupons for extended travel in the US.

Garuda Australia ☎1-300/365 330; New Zealand ☎09/366 1862. Several flights a week to LA from major cities in Australia and New Zealand via either a transfer or overnight stopover in Jakarta/Denpasar.

JAL Japan Airlines (*www.jal.co.jp/english*) Australia ☎02/9272 1111 in Sydney; New Zealand ☎09/379 9906. Several flights a week to LA from Sydney, Brisbane, Cairns and Auckland with an overnight stopover in either Tokyo or Osaka included in the fare.

Korean Air (*www.koreanair.com*) Auckland ☎ 09/307 3687; Brisbane ☎07/3226 6000; Sydney ☎02/9262 2041. Several flights per week from Auckland, Brisbane and Sydney to LA and San Francisco via Seoul.

Qantas (*www.qantas.com.au*), Australia ☎13 1313; New Zealand ☎ 0-800/808 767 or 09/357 8900. Daily to LA from major Australian cities, either non-stop or via Auckland or Nadi, and daily from Auckland via Sydney, Nadi or Papeete.

Singapore Airlines Australia ☎13 1011; New Zealand ☎09/379 3209. Daily to LA from major Australian cities and Auckland, all via Singapore.

United Airlines (*www.ual.com*) Australia ☎13 1777; New Zealand ☎09/379 3800. Daily to LA and San Francisco from Sydney, Melbourne and Auckland.

AUSTRALIAN DISCOUNT AGENTS

Anywhere Travel, 345 Anzac Parade, Kingsford, Sydney (☎02/9663 0411, fax 9662 2860; email: *anywhere@aussiemail.com.au*). Local agency specializing in cheap airfares to anywhere.

Australian Travel & Information Centre, 350 Kent St, Sydney, 2000 NSW (☎02/9262 4755, fax 9290 1905, *goway@goway.com.au*). Mainly geared towards travel around Australia but budget fares are frequently available.

Flight Centre (*www.flightcentre.com*) 1 MacQuarie Place, Sydney (☎02/9241 2422); 19 Bourke St, Melbourne (☎03/9650 2899), plus dozens of branches` nationwide. Call ☎131600 to find your closest branch. Near ubiquitous High Street agency frequently offering some of the lowest fares around.

Harvey World Travel. Franchised organization with agencies all over Australia. The nearest can be found with a local call ☎132757.

Northern Gateway, 22 Cavenagh St, Darwin (☎08/8941 1394, fax 8941 2815, *oztravel@norgate.com.au*). Local discount agent.

STA Travel (*www.statravel.com.au*) Shop 6, 127-139 Macleay St, Kings Cross, Sydney 2011 (☎02/9368 1111, fax 9368 1609, *traveller@statravel.com.au*); 273 Little Collins St, Melbourne 3000 (☎03/9654 8722, fax 9654 8919); plus other offices in Cairns, state capitals and major universities. (nearest branch ☎13 1776, fastfare telesales ☎1300/360 960). Major player in student, youth and budget travel.

Trailfinders (*www.trailfinders.com/australia*), 91 Elizabeth St, Brisbane 4000 (☎07/3229 0887); 3 Hides Corner, Lake St, Cairns 4870 (☎07/4041 1199); 8 Spring St, Sydney 2000 (☎02/9247 7666). Australian outposts of British specialists in tailor-made itineraries. Knowledgeable staff skilled at turning up odd itineraries and good prices.

Travel.com.au (*www.travel.com.au*), 80 Clarence St, Sydney, 2000 NSW (☎02/9290 1500). Youth-oriented centre with an efficient travel agency offering good fares, a travel bookshop and Internet café.

rates, which are often more expensive than a round-the-world fare. Travel agents offer the best deals on fares and have the latest information on limited special offers, such as free stopovers, fly-drive-accommodation and Disneyland packages.

Flight Centres and STA (which offer fare reductions for ISIC card holders and under-26s) generally offer the lowest fares. Airfares vary throughout the year, with seasonal differences generally working out between A/NZ$200. For

NEW ZEALAND DISCOUNT AGENTS

Budget Travel (*www.budgettravel.co.nz*). Major countrywide flight discounter. Call ☎0800/808040 to find your nearest agency.

Harvey World Travel. Franchised organization with agencies all over New Zealand.

Flight Centre, National Bank Towers, cnr Queen St & Darby St, Auckland (☎09/309-6171); Shop 1M, National Mutual Arcade, 418 Colombo St, Christchurch (☎03/379 6396); 50–52 Willis St, Wellington (☎04/472-8101); plus other branches countrywide; associated with its Australian counterparts.

STA Travel (*www.statravel.com.au*)10 High St, Auckland (☎09/309-9995, fax 309 2059); 130 Cuba St, Wellington (☎04/385-0561, fax 385 8170); 90 Cashel St, Christchurch (☎03/379-6372, fax365 7220); plus other offices in Dunedin, Palmerston North and universities. Major player in student, youth and budget travel.

Usit Beyond (*www.usitbeyond.co.nz*), cnr Shortland St & Jean Batten Place, Auckland (☎09/379 4224, fax 366 6275); cnr Courtenay Place and Taranaki St, Wellington (☎04/801 7238, fax 801 9432) and offices in Hamilton, Palmerston North and Christchurch. Youth-oriented travel agency incorporating YHA travel and your first stop for ISIC student cards. Nationwide freephone ☎0800/359 8748.

most airlines, **low season** is from mid-January to the end of February and October to the end of November; **high season** mid-May to the end of August and December to mid-January; **shoulder seasons** cover the rest of the year, though all of this is complicated by periodic high prices during school holidays. Seat availability on most international flights out of Australia and New Zealand is limited, so it's best to book several weeks ahead.

Traveling from **Australia**, fares to LA and San Francisco from eastern cities cost the same, while from Perth they're about A$400 more. There are daily non-stop flights from Sydney, to LA and San Francisco on United Airlines and to LA on Qantas, for around A$1899 low season.

In addition there are several airlines that fly via Asia, which involves either a transfer or stopover in their home cities. The best deal is on JAL (A$1550–1880), which includes a night's stopover accommodation in Tokyo or Osaka in the fare, while Garuda via either Jakarta or Denpasar, both start around A$1750. If you don't want to spend the night, Cathay Pacific and Singapore Airlines can get you there, via a transfer in the home cities of Hong Kong and Singapore, for around A$1880, and Korean Air (via Seoul) are sometimes a few dollars cheaper.

From **New Zealand**, most flights are out of **Auckland** (add about NZ$200–250 for Christchurch and Wellington departures), with the best deals on Air New Zealand, to Los Angeles either non-stop or via Honolulu, Fiji, Tonga or Papeete – or United Airlines, also non-stop to LA or San Francisco (both cost around NZ$2099–2499). Air Pacific via Fiji, and Qantas via Sydney (though direct is cheaper) both start around NZ$1800–2000. Via Asia, Singapore Airlines offers the best connecting service to LA and San Francisco from NZ$2099, while the best value for money (around NZ$1850–2250) is on JAL via either a transfer or stopover in Tokyo.

If you intend to take in California as part of a world trip, a round-the-world (**RTW**) ticket offers the greatest flexibility. Over the last couple of years, many of the major international airlines have aligned themselves with one of two globe-spanning networks: the "Star Alliance," which links Air New Zealand, Ansett Australia, United, Lufthansa, Thai, SAS, Varig and Air Canada; and "One World," which combines routes run by American, British Airways, Canadian Airlines, Cathay Pacific, LAN Chile and Qantas. Both offer RTW deals with three stopovers in each continental sector you visit, with the option of adding additional sectors relatively cheaply. Fares depend on the number of sectors required, but start at around A$2200 (low season) for a US–Europe–Asia and home itinerary. If this is more flexibility than you need, you can save $200–300 by going with an individual airline (in concert with code-share partners) and accepting fewer stops.

ENTRY REQUIREMENTS FOR FOREIGN VISITORS

VISAS

Under the **Visa Waiver Scheme**, designed to speed up lengthy immigration procedures, citizens of Andorra, Argentina, Australia, Austria, Belgium, Brunei, Denmark, Finland, France, Germany, Iceland, Ireland, Italy, Japan, Liechtenstein, Luxembourg, Monaco, the Netherlands, New Zealand, Norway, San Marino, Spain, Sweden, Switzerland, and the United Kingdom visiting the United States for a period of less than ninety days only need a **passport** and a **visa waiver form**. The latter will be provided either by your travel agency, or by the airline during check-in or on the plane, and must be presented to immigration on arrival. The same form covers entry across the land borders with Canada and Mexico as well as by air. However, those eligible for the scheme must apply for a visa if they intend to work, study, or stay in the country for more than ninety days.

Prospective visitors from parts of the world not mentioned above require a valid passport and a **non-immigrant visitor's visa**. How you'll obtain a visa depends on what country you're in and your status when you apply, so telephone the nearest US embassy or consulate (listed in box opposite). You'll need a passport valid six months beyond your intended stay, two passport photos and will be charged the equivalent of US$45. Expect it to take up to three weeks, though it could be substantially quicker. More information can be found at *http://travel.state.gov/visa_services.html*.

In **Britain**, only British or EU citizens, and those from other countries eligible for the visa

waiver scheme, can apply by post – fill in the application form available at most travel agents and send it with your passport and a SAE to the nearest US embassy or consulate. Expect a wait of one to three weeks before your passport is returned. All others must apply in person, making an appointment in advance. Visa application fees in Britain are currently US$20.

Australian and **New Zealand** passport holders staying less than ninety days do not require a visa, providing they arrive on a commercial flight with an onward or return ticket. For longer stays, US multiple entry visas cost the local equivalent of US$45. You'll need an application form, available from a US embassy or consulate (see box opposite), one signed passport photo and your passport, and either post it or personally lodge it at one of the US embassies or consulates. Processing takes about ten working days for postal applications; personal lodgements take two days – but check details with the consulate first.

Whatever your nationality, visas are not issued to convicted felons and anybody who owns up to being a communist, fascist or drug dealer.

IMMIGRATION CONTROLS

The standard immigration regulations apply to all visitors, whether or not they are using the Visa Waiver Scheme. During the flight, you'll be handed an **immigration form** (and a customs declaration; see p.16), which must be given up at immigration control once you land. The form requires details of where you are staying on your first night (if you

---

Canadian citizens are in a particularly privileged position when it comes to crossing the border into the US. Though it is possible to enter the States without your passport, you should really have it with you on any trip that brings you as far as California. Only if you plan to stay for more than ninety days do you need a visa. Bear in mind that if you cross into the States in your car, trunks and passenger compartments are subject to spot searches by US Customs personnel, though this sort of surveillance is likely to decrease as remaining tariff barriers fall over the next few years. Remember too, that without the proper paperwork, Canadians are legally barred from seeking gainful employment in the US.

US EMBASSY AND CONSULATES IN CANADA

Embassy:
100 Wellington St, Ottawa, ON K1P 5T1
(☎613/238-5335, fax 238-5720).

Consulates:
Suite 1050, 615 Macleod Trail SE, Calgary, AB
T2G 4T8 (☎403/266-8962, fax 264-6630).
Suite 910, Cogswell Tower, Scotia Square,

Halifax, NS B3J 3K1 (☎902/429-2480, fax 423-6861).
P.O. Box 65, Postal Station Desjardins, Montréal,
H5B 1G1 (☎514/398-9695, fax 398-0973).
360 University Ave, Toronto, ON M5G 1S4
(☎416/595-1700, fax 595-0051).
1095 West Pender St.Vancouver, BC V6E 2M6
(☎604/685-4311, fax 685-5285).

US EMBASSIES AND CONSULATES ELSEWHERE

Australia
US Embassy, Moonah Place, Canberra, ACT 2600
(☎02/6214 5600, fax 6214-5970, *usaemb@
cs.net.au*).
US Consulate, 553 St. Kilda Road, PO Box 6722,
Melbourne, Vic 3004 (☎03/9625-1583, fax 9510-4646, *uscgmelb@labyrinth.net.au*).
US Consulate, 59th Floor, MLC Centre, 19–29
Martin Place, Sydney NSW 2000 (☎02/9373-9200, fax 9221-0573, *usconsyd@ozemail.com.au*)
US Consulate, 13th floor, 16 St. George's Terrace,
Perth, WA 6000 (☎08/9231-9400, fax 9231-9444,
usgperth@starwon.com.au).

Denmark
Dag Hammerskjöld Allé 24, 2100 Copenhagen
(☎3555-3144, fax 3543-0223, *www.usis.dk*).

Ireland
42 Elgin Rd, Ballsbridge, Dublin (☎01/668 8777,
fax 668-9946, *aedublin@indigo.ie*).

Netherlands
Museumplein 19, 1071 DJ Amsterdam
(☎020/575 5309).
Lange Voorhout 102,2514 EJ, Den Hague
(☎070/310 9209, fax 361-4688).

New Zealand
US Embassy, 29 Fitzherbert Terr, Thorndon,
Wellington (☎04/472 2068, fax 471-2380,
www.usia.gov/posts/wellington).

US Consulate, Yorkshire General Building, 29
Shortland St, Fourth Floor, Auckland (☎09/303
2724, fax 366 0870, *amcongen@ihug.co.nz*).

Norway
US Embasssy, Drammensveien 18, 0244 Oslo
(☎22/44 85 50, fax 44-33-63, *http://www.
usembassy.no*).

South Africa
US Embassy, 877 Pretorius St, Arcadia 0083,
Pretoria (☎12/342 1048, fax 342-2244).
US Consulate, Durban Bay House, 29th Floor, 333
Smith St, Durban (☎31/304-4737, fax 301-8206).
US Consulate, Broadway Industries Centre,
Heerengracht, Foreshore, Capetown (☎21/21
4280, *gsocapetown@pixie.co.za*).
US Consulate, 1 River Street, c/o Riviera,
Killarney, Johannesburg (☎11/646-6900, fax 646-6913, *amcongen.jhb@pixie.co.za*).

Sweden
Strandvägen 101, Stockholm (☎08/783 5300, fax
661 1964).

UK
24/31 Upper Grosvenor Square, London W1A 1AE
(☎020/7499 9000; visa hotline ☎0891/200290).
3 Regent Terr, Edinburgh EH7 5BW (☎0131/556
8315, fax 557-6023).
Queens House, 14 Queen St, Belfast BT1 6EQ
(☎028/9032 8239, fax 248 482).

don't know, write "touring") and the date you
intend to **leave** the US. You probably won't be
asked unless you look disreputable in the eyes of
the official on duty, but you should be able to prove
that you have enough money to support yourself
while in the US – $300–400 a week is usually con-
sidered sufficient – as anyone revealing the slight-

est intention of working while in the country is likely to be refused admission. You may also experience difficulties if you admit to being HIV positive
or having AIDS or TB. Part of the immigration form
will be attached to your passport, where it must
stay until you leave, when an immigration or airline
official will detach it.

BRITISH CONSULATES IN CALIFORNIA

11766 Wilshire Blvd, Suite 400, Los Angeles, CA 90025 (☎310/477-3322, fax 575-1450). 1 Sansome St, Suite 850, San Francisco, CA 94101 (☎415/981-3030, fax 434-2018).

CUSTOMS

Customs officers will relieve you of your customs declaration and check whether you're carrying any fresh foods. You'll also be asked if you've visited a farm in the last month: if you have, you may well have your shoes taken away for inspection. The duty-free allowance if you're over 17 is 200 cigarettes or 50 cigars (*not* Cuban), a liter of spirits (if you're over 21), and $100 worth of gifts, which can include an additional 100 cigars. As well as foods and anything agricultural, it's prohibited to carry into the country any articles from North Korea, Iran, Iraq, Libya, Sudan or Cuba, obscene publications, drug paraphernalia, lottery tickets, chocolate liqueurs or pre-Columbian artifacts. Anyone caught carrying drugs into the country will not only face prosecution, but be entered in the records as an undesirable and probably denied entry for all time.

EXTENSIONS AND LEAVING

The date stamped on your passport is the latest you're legally allowed to stay. Leaving a few days later may not matter, especially if you're heading home, but more than a week or so can result in a protracted, rather unpleasant interrogation from officials, which may cause you to miss your flight and be denied entry to the US in the future. Your American hosts and/or employers could also face legal proceedings.

To get an **extension** before your time is up, apply at the nearest **US Immigration and Naturalization Service** (INS) office; the address will be under the Federal Government Offices listings at the front of the phone book. They will automatically assume that you're working illegally and it's up to you to convince them otherwise. Do this by providing evidence of ample finances, and, if you can, bring along an upstanding American citizen to vouch for you. You'll also have to explain why you didn't plan for the extra time initially.

STAYING ON

Anyone planning an extended legal stay in the United States should apply for a special **working visa** at any American Embassy *before* setting off. Different types of visas are issued, depending on your skills and length of stay, but unless you've got relatives (parents or children over 21) or a prospective employer to sponsor you, your chances are slim at best.

Illegal work is not as easy to find as it used to be, now that the government has introduced fines as high as $10,000 for companies caught employing anyone without a **social security number** (which effectively proves you're part of the legal workforce). Even in the traditionally more casual establishments, like restaurants and bars, things have really tightened up, and if you do find work it's likely to be of the less visible, poorly paid kind – dishwasher rather than waiter. Making up a social security number, or borrowing one from somebody else, is of course completely illegal, as are **marriages of convenience**, which are usually inconvenient for all concerned and with a lower success rate than is claimed.

Foreign students have a slightly better chance of a prolonged stay in California, especially those who can arrange a "year abroad" through their university at home. Otherwise you can apply directly to a university; if they admit you (and you can afford the painfully expensive fees charged to overseas students) it can be a great way to get to know the country, and maybe even learn something useful. The US grants more or less unlimited visas to those enrolled in full-time further education. Another possibility for students is to get onto an **Exchange Visitor Program**, for which participants are given a J-1 visa that entitles them to accept paid summer employment and apply for a social security number. However, most of these visas are issued for jobs in American **summer camps**, which aren't everybody's idea of a good time; they fly you over, and after a couple of months' work you end up with around $500 and a month to six weeks to blow it in. If you live in Britain and are interested, contact BUNAC (16 Bowling Green Lane, London EC1R 0QH, ☎020/7251 3472, fax 251 0215, *www.bunac.org.uk*), or Camp America (37 Queens' Gate, London SW7; ☎020/7581 7373, *http://globetrotter.nu/gjd*).

INSURANCE, HEALTH AND PERSONAL SAFETY

A typical travel insurance policy usually provides cover for the loss of baggage, tickets and – up to a certain limit – cash or checks, as well as cancellation or curtailment of your journey. Most of them exclude so-called dangerous sports unless an extra premium is paid: in California this can mean mountain climbing, whitewater rafting and windsurfing. Read the small print and benefits tables of prospective policies carefully; coverage can vary wildly for roughly similar premiums. Many policies can be chopped and changed to exclude coverage you don't need – for example, sickness and accident benefits can often be excluded or included at will. If you do take medical coverage, ascertain whether benefits will be paid as treatment proceeds or only after return home, and whether there is a 24-hour medical emergency number. When securing baggage cover, make sure that the per-article limit – typically under £500 equivalent – will cover your most valuable possession. If you need to make a claim, you should keep receipts for medicines and medical treatment, and in the event you have anything stolen, you must obtain an official statement from the police. Bank and credit cards often have certain levels of medical or other insurance included and you may automatically get travel insurance if you use a major credit card to pay for your trip.

Most travel agents and tour operators in the UK are likely to require some sort of insurance when you book a package holiday, though according to UK law they can't make you buy their own (other than a £1 premium for "schedule airline failure"). If you have a good all-risks home insurance policy it *may* cover your possessions against loss or theft even when overseas. Many private medical schemes, such as BUPA or PPP, also offer coverage plans for abroad, including baggage loss, cancellation or curtailment and cash replacement as well as sickness or accident.

Americans and **Canadians** should also check that they're not already covered, although Canadian provincial health plans should provide coverage for medical mishaps in the US.

ROUGH GUIDES TRAVEL INSURANCE

Rough Guides now offer their own **travel insurance**, customized for our readers by a leading UK broker and backed by a Lloyds underwriter. It's available for anyone, of any nationality, traveling anywhere in the world, and we are convinced that this is the best-value scheme you'll find.

There are two main Rough Guide insurance plans: **Essential**, for effective, no-frills cover, starting at £11.75 for 2 weeks; and **Premier** – more expensive but with more generous and extensive benefits. Each offer European or Worldwide cover, and can be supplemented with a "Hazardous Activities Premium" if you plan to indulge in sports considered dangerous, such as skiing or scuba-diving. Unlike many policies, the Rough Guides schemes are calculated by the day, so if you're traveling for 27 days rather than a month, that's all you pay for. You can alternatively take out annual **multi-trip insurance**, which covers you for all your travel throughout the year (with a maximum of 60 days for any one trip).

For a policy quote, call the Rough Guides Insurance Line on UK freefone ☎0800 015 0906, or, if you're calling from outside Britain on (+44) 1243 621-046. Alternatively, get an online quote at *www.roughguides.com/insurance*.

HEALTH ADVICE FOR FOREIGN TRAVELERS

If you have a serious **accident** while in the US, emergency medical services will get to you quickly and charge you later. For emergencies or ambulances, dial ☎**911**, the nationwide emergency number (or whatever variant may be on the information plate of the payphone).

Should you need to see a doctor, lists can be found in the *Yellow Pages* under "Clinics" or "Physicians and Surgeons." A basic consultation fee is $50–100, payable in advance. Medications aren't cheap either – keep all your receipts for later claims on your insurance policy.

Many **minor ailments** can be remedied using the fabulous array of potions and lotions available in **drugstores**. Foreign visitors should bear in mind that many pills available over the counter at home need a prescription in the US – most codeine-based painkillers, for example. Local brand names can be confusing; ask for advice at the **pharmacy** in any drugstore.

Travelers from Europe do not require **inoculations** to enter the US.

CRIME AND PERSONAL SAFETY

No one can pretend that California is trouble-free, although away from the urban centers, crime is often remarkably low-key. Even the lawless reputation of Los Angeles is far in excess of the truth, and most of the city, by day at least, is fairly safe; at night, though, a few areas – notably Compton, Inglewood, and East LA – are completely off limits. Members of the notorious **LA gangs** are a rare sight outside their own territories (which are usually well away from where you're likely to be), and they tend to kill each other rather than tourists. By being careful, planning ahead and taking care of your possessions, you should have few real problems.

MUGGING AND THEFT

The biggest problem for most travelers is the threat of **mugging**. It's impossible to give hard and fast rules about what to do if you're confronted by a mugger. Whether to run, scream or fight depends on the situation – but most locals would just hand over their money.

Of course, the best thing is simply to avoid being mugged, and a few obvious **basic rules** are worth remembering: don't flash money around; don't peer at your map (or this book) at

POLICE AND PASSPORTS

Foreign visitors tend to report that the police are helpful and obliging when things go wrong, although they'll be less sympathetic if they think you brought the trouble on yourself through carelessness. One way non-Americans might accidentally break the law is by **jaywalking**. If you cross the road on a red light or anywhere except an intersection, and are spotted by a cop, you're likely to get a stiff talking-to – and possibly a ticket, leading to a $20 fine. You might also fall foul of America's puritanical **drinking laws** which prohibit drinking in most public places – parks, beaches and the like.

Needless to say, having bags snatched that contain travel documents can be a big headache, none more so than **losing your passport**. If the worst happens, the British consulates in both Los Angeles and San Francisco (see p.16) will issue emergency passports, provided you have sufficient ID, for the current equivalent of £20. The process takes about thirty minutes (longer if you have trouble establishing your identity), but the resulting emergency passport is only a one-way travel document, good for return home. In non-emergency situations, the only way to get a new passport is through the British Embassy in Washington, DC (☎202/588-7800). If you aren't near one of the consulates in California, call and give an address where they can mail you an application form. When you return the filled out application, you'll need to include a notarized (ie specially stamped at any major bank) photocopy of any ID you might still have plus a $38 reissuing fee. The passport issuing process normally takes two weeks, but can take as long as six weeks. If you're in a real hurry, let them know and they will usually be as accommodating as possible.

every street corner, thereby announcing that you're a lost stranger; even if you're terrified or drunk (or both), try not to appear so; avoid dark streets, especially ones you can't see the end of; and in the early hours, stick to the roadside edge of the pavement so it's easier to run into the road to attract attention. If you have to ask for directions, choose your target carefully. Another idea is to carry a wad of cash, perhaps $50 or so, separate from the bulk of your holdings so that if you do get confronted you can hand over something of value without it costing you everything.

STOLEN TRAVELERS' CHECKS AND CREDIT CARDS

Keep a record of the numbers of your **travelers' checks** separately from the actual checks; if you lose them, ring the issuing company on the toll-free number below.

They'll ask you for the check numbers, the place you bought them, when and how you lost them and whether it's been reported to the police. All being well, you should get the missing checks reissued within a couple of days – and perhaps an emergency advance to tide you over.

EMERGENCY NUMBERS

American Express (TCs) ☎1-800/221-7282; (credit cards) ☎1-800/528-4800
Citicorp ☎1-800/645-6556
Diners Club ☎1-800/234-6377

Mastercard ☎1-800/307-7309
Thomas Cook ☎1-800/223-7373
Visa ☎1-800/227-6811

If the worst happens and your assailant is toting a gun or (more likely) a knife, try to stay calm: remember that he (for this is generally a male pursuit) is probably scared too. Keep still, don't make any sudden movements – and hand over your money. When he's gone, you should, despite your shock, try to find a phone and dial ☎**911**, or head to the nearest police station. Here, report the theft and get a reference number on the report to claim insurance and travelers' check refunds. If you're in a big city, ring the local Travelers Aid (their numbers are listed in the phone book) for sympathy and practical advice. For specific advice for women in case of mugging or attack, see p.46.

Another potential source of trouble is having your **hotel room burglarized**. Always store valuables in the hotel safe when you go out; when inside, keep your door locked and don't open it to anyone you don't trust. If they claim to be hotel staff and you don't believe them, call reception to check.

CAR CRIME

Crimes committed against tourists driving **rental cars** in the US have garnered headlines around the world in recent years. In major urbanized areas, any car you rent should have nothing on it – such as a particular license plate – that makes it easy to spot as a rental car. When driving, under no circumstances stop in any unlit or seemingly deserted urban area – and especially not if someone is waving you down and suggesting that there is something wrong with your car. Similarly, if you are "accidentally" rammed by the driver behind you, do not stop immediately but drive on to the nearest well-lit, busy area and **phone ☎911** for assistance. Keep your doors locked and windows never more than slightly open. Do not open your door or window if someone approaches your car on the pretext of asking directions. Hide any valuables out of sight, preferably locked in the trunk or in the glove compartment (any valuables you don't need for your journey should be left in your hotel safe).

COSTS, MONEY AND BANKS

To help with planning your vacation in California, this book contains detailed price information for lodging and eating. Unless otherwise stated, the hotel price codes (explained on p.36) are for the cheapest double room throughout most of the year. Note, though, that the price codes do not include local hotel taxes, which usually range from eight to twelve percent, but can soar as high as twenty percent. Meal prices listed include food only and not drinks or tip. For museums and similar attractions, the prices we quote are generally for adults; you can assume that children get in half-price. Naturally, costs will increase slightly overall during the life of this edition, but the relative comparisons should remain valid.

COSTS

Accommodation is likely to be your biggest single expense. Few hotel or motel rooms cost under $30; it's more usual to pay between $40 and $80 for anything halfway decent in a city, and rates in rural areas are not much cheaper. Although hostels offering dorm beds – usually for $12–15 – are reasonably common, they are by no means everywhere, besides which they save little money for two or more people traveling together. Camping, of course, is cheap, ranging from free to about $18 a night per site, but is rarely practical in or around the big cities.

As for **food**, $15 a day is enough to get an adequate life-support diet, while for a daily total of around $30 you can dine pretty well. Beyond this, everything hinges on how much sightseeing, taxi-taking, drinking and socializing you do. Much of any of these – especially in the major cities – and you're likely to go through upwards of $50 a day.

The rates for **traveling around**, especially on buses, and to a lesser extent on trains and even planes, may look inexpensive on paper, but the distances involved mean that costs soon mount up. For a group of two or more, **renting a car** can be a very good investment, not least because it enables you to camp or stay in the ubiquitous budget motels along the Interstate highways instead of relying on expensive downtown hotels.

Remember that a **sales tax** of 8.5 percent is added to virtually everything you buy in stores except for groceries.

PLASTIC MONEY AND CASH MACHINES

If you don't already have a **credit card**, you should think seriously about getting one before you set off. For many services, it's simply taken for granted that you'll be paying with plastic. When renting a car (or even a bike) or checking into a hotel, you may well be asked to show a credit card to establish your creditworthiness – even if you intend to settle the bill in cash. **Visa**, **Mastercard**, **Diners Club**, **American Express** and **Discover** are the most widely used.

With Mastercard or Visa it is also possible to **withdraw cash** at any bank displaying relevant stickers, or from appropriate automatic teller machines (**ATMs**). Diners Club cards can be used to cash personal checks at Citibank branches. American Express cards can only get cash, or buy travelers' checks, at American Express offices (check the *Yellow Pages*) or from the travelers' check dispensers at most major airports. Most **Canadian** credit cards issued by hometown banks are honored in the US.

ATMs are everywhere in California – in addition to banks, many supermarkets, convenience stores, and drug stores now have outlets where you can withdraw cash for a small transaction fee (usually around $2). ATM cards held by visitors from other states usually work in Californian

Each of the two main networks operates a toll-free line to let customers know the location of their nearest ATM; **Plus System** is ☎1-800/THE-PLUS, **Cirrus** is ☎1-800/4CI-RRUS.

machines – check with your bank before you leave home.

Most major credit cards issued by **foreign banks** are accepted in the US, as well as cash-dispensing cards linked to international networks such as Cirrus, Plus, and Star – once again, check before you set off, as otherwise the machine may simply reject your card. Overseas visitors should also bear in mind that fluctuating exchange rates may result in spending more (or less) than expected when the item eventually shows up on a statement.

BANKS AND TRAVELERS' CHECKS

It is worth carrying a second major credit card as a back-up, but you may feel more comfortable with a wad of **US dollar travelers' checks**. These are the best way, for both American and foreign visitors, to carry money; they offer the great security of knowing that lost or stolen checks will be replaced. You should have no problem using the better-known checks, such as American Express and Visa, in the same way as cash in shops, restaurants and gas stations (don't be put off by "no checks" signs, which only refer to personal checks). Be sure to have plenty of the $10 and $20 denominations for everyday transactions.

With credit cards, cash cards and travelers' checks you may never need to visit **banks**, which are generally open from 9am until 5pm Monday to Thursday, and 9am to 6pm on Friday. Most major banks **change foreign travelers' checks** and **currency**; though exchange bureaus, always found at airports, tend to charge less commission: Thomas Cook or American Express are the biggest names. Rarely, if ever, do hotels change foreign currency. **Emergency phone numbers** to call if your checks and/or credit cards are stolen are on p.19.

To find the nearest bank that sells a particular brand of travelers' check, or to buy checks by phone, call the following numbers: American Express (☎1-800/673-3782), Citicorp (☎1-800/645-6556), Mastercard International/Thomas Cook (☎1-800/223-7373) and Visa (☎1-800/227-6811).

FINANCIAL EMERGENCIES

Assuming you know someone who is prepared to send you money in a crisis, the quickest way is to have them take the cash to the nearest **Western Union** office (information on ☎1-800/325-6000 in the US; ☎0800/833833 in the UK; ☎1800/649565 in Australia; and ☎0800/270000 in New Zealand)

MONEY: A NOTE FOR FOREIGN TRAVELERS

With the current boom in the US economy and the continued strength of the dollar, California is becoming an increasingly expensive place to travel. It is true that car rental, gas, clothes and consumer goods are usually somewhat cheaper than in western Europe and Australasia, but the benefit is often less than it seems once you've factored in the additional 8.5 percent sales tax. At first, eating and drinking seem a bargain, and fast food joints are. But in more upscale establishments, you'll be adding close to 25 percent to your expected total to cover taxes and tips. It soon mounts up.

Regular upheaval in the world money markets causes the relative value of the US dollar against the currencies of the rest of the world to vary considerably. Generally speaking, one Canadian dollar is worth between 70¢ and 90¢; one Australian dollar is worth between 62¢ and 88¢; and one New Zealand dollar is worth between 50¢ and 72¢. Over the last five years, the dollar/sterling rate has remained remarkably stable at between $1.55 and $1.65 to the pound.

BILLS AND COINS

US currency comes in bills of $1, $5, $10, $20, $50 and $100, plus various larger (and rarer) denominations. It is necessary to check each bill carefully, as all are the same size and color, despite the opportunity to change the design afforded by the recent introduction of newer, harder-to-counterfeit bills. The dollar is made up of 100 cents with coins of 1 cent (known as a penny, and regarded as worthless), 5 cents (a nickel), 10 cents (a dime) and 25 cents (a quarter). Quarters are very useful for buses, vending machines, parking meters and telephones, so always carry plenty. Coin fans might want to look out for the new "state" quarter designs being introduced over the next few years, and also the new golden "Sacagawea" dollar coin, named after the Native American women who assisted Lewis and Clark on their expeditions through the uncharted West. Very occasionally you might come across JFK half-dollars (50¢), Susan B. Anthony dollar coins, or a two-dollar bill.

and have it instantaneously **wired** to the office nearest you, subject to the deduction of five to ten percent commission: the bigger the transaction, the lower the percentage. **American Express Moneygram** (☎1-800/543-4080) offers a similar service.

It's also possible to have money wired directly from a bank in your home country to a bank in the US, although this is somewhat less reliable because it involves two separate institutions. If you go this route, the person wiring the funds to you will need to know the telex number of the bank the funds are being wired to. Having money wired from home is never convenient or cheap, and should be considered a last resort.

If you have a few days' leeway, sending a postal money order, exchangeable at any post office through the mail is a cheaper option. The equivalent for foreign travelers is the **international money order**, for which you need to allow up to seven days in the international air mail before arrival. An ordinary check sent from overseas takes two to three weeks to clear.

Foreign travelers in difficulties have the final option of throwing themselves on the mercy of their nearest national **consulate**, which will – in worst cases only – repatriate you, but will never, under any circumstances, lend you money. See p.16 for the addresses of British consulates in LA and San Francisco.

TELEPHONES, MAIL AND EMAIL

Visitors from overseas tend to be impressed by the speed and efficiency of communications in the US. California largely lives up to this high standard, partly at least because its major cities are important business hubs that depend upon reliable links to the East Coast, as well as being able to keep in touch with the many isolated settlements in the state itself. In rural areas you may find it frustrating just getting to the nearest public phone – which may be many miles away – but in general keeping in touch is easy.

TELEPHONES

Californian **telephones** are run by a huge variety of companies, many of which were hived off from

TELEPHONE AREA CODES

Los Angeles 213
Hollywood and East Los Angeles 323
West Los Angeles 310
East Los Angeles and Long Beach 562
Pasadena and the San Gabriel Valley 626
Burbank and the San Fernando Valley 818
Northern Orange County 714
Southern Orange County and
   Newport Beach 949
San Bernardino and Riverside area 909
San Diego 619
Northern San Diego County 858
Southeastern California 760
Santa Barbara and San Luis Obispo 805
Monterey, Santa Cruz and Big Sur 831
Bakersfield and the southern
   San Joaquin Valley 661
Fresno and the central San Joaquin Valley 559
San Francisco and Marin County 415
East Bay and Oakland 510
The San Mateo Peninsula 650
San Jose 408
Wine Country and North Coast 707
Sacramento 916
Gold Country, Stockton and Yosemite 209
Lake Tahoe and northeastern California 530

INTERNATIONAL TELEPHONE CALLS

International calls can be dialed direct from private or (more expensively) public phones. You can get assistance from the **international operator** (☎00), who may also interrupt every three minutes, asking for more money, if you're on a public phone. The **lowest rates** for international calls to Europe are between 6pm and 7am, when a direct-dialed three-minute call will cost roughly $5.

In **Britain**, it's possible to obtain a free **BT Chargecard** (☎0800/345144), with which all calls from overseas can be charged to your quarterly domestic account. To use these cards in the US, or to make a **collect call** (to "reverse the charges") using a BT operator, contact the carrier: AT&T ☎1-800/445-5667; MCI ☎1-800/444-2162; or Sprint ☎1-800/800-0008. To avoid the international operator fee, BT credit card calls can be made directly using an automated system: AT&T ☎1-800/445-5688; MCI ☎1-800/854-4826; or Sprint ☎1-800/825-4904.

British visitors who are going to be making a number of calls to the US, and who want to be able to call ☎1-800 numbers, otherwise inaccessible from outside the country, should take advantage of the **Swiftcall** telephone club. Call your nearest office between 8am and midnight (in UK ☎0800/769 0800, Ireland ☎0800/409278, USA ☎1-800/513-7325), and once you've paid by credit card for however many units you want, you are given a PIN. Any time you want to get an international line, simply dial ☎0171/488-0800, punch in your PIN, and then dial as you would were you in the US, putting a 1 before the area code, followed by the number. Calls to the USA – including ☎1-800 numbers – cost about 14p per minute, a **saving** of over fifty percent. In New Zealand, ☎1-800 numbers can be accessed by first dialing 0168 followed by 1-800 and the number: these are charged at normal international rates.

Telephone cards such as Australia's Telstra Telecard or Optus Calling Card and New Zealand Telecom's Calling Card can be used to make calls abroad, which are charged back to a domestic account or credit card. Apply to Telstra ☎1-800/038 000, Optus ☎1300/300300, or NZ Telecom ☎123.

The telephone code to dial **TO the US** from the outside world (excluding Canada) is 1.

To make international calls **FROM the US**, dial 011 followed by the country code:

Australia 61	**Denmark** 45	**Germany** 49	**Ireland** 353
Netherlands 31	**New Zealand** 64	**Sweden** 46	**United Kingdom** 44

the previous Bell System monopoly – the successor to which is the nationwide AT&T network.

Public telephones invariably work, and in cities at any rate can be found everywhere – on street corners, in train and bus stations, hotels, bars and restaurants. They take 5¢, 10¢ and 25¢ coins. The cost of a **local call** from a public phone (generally one within the same area code) varies from a minimum of 25¢, and is usually 35¢; when necessary, a voice comes on the line telling you to pay more.

Some numbers covered by the same area code are considered so far apart that calls between them count as non-local (zone) calls and cost much more. Pricier still are long-distance calls (ie to a different area code, and always preceded by a 1), for which you'll need plenty of change. Non-local calls and long-distance calls are much less expensive if made between 6pm and 8am – the cheapest rates are after 11pm and at weekends – and calls from private phones are always much cheaper than those from public phones. Detailed rates are listed at the front of the telephone directory (the *White Pages*, a copious source of information on many matters).

For a fee, almost all phones will let you charge your call to your **credit card**, while anyone who has a US billing address can obtain an **AT&T calling card** (information on ☎1-800/451-4341). Foreign visitors will have to make do with **phone cards** – in denominations of $5, $10 and $20 – bought from general stores and some hostels. These provide you with a temporary account (just tap in the number printed on the card), and are a

---

USEFUL NUMBERS

Emergencies ☎911; ask for the appropriate emergency service: fire, police or ambulance

Directory information ☎411

Directory inquiries for toll-free numbers ☎1-800/555-1212

Long-distance directory information ☎1- (Area Code)/555-1212

lot cheaper than feeding coins into a payphone, especially if calling abroad.

Making telephone calls from **hotel rooms** is usually more expensive than from a payphone, though some budget hotels offer free local calls from rooms – ask when you check in.

Many government agencies, car rental firms, hotels and so on have **toll-free numbers**, which always have the prefix ☎1-800, ☎1-888 or ☎1-877. Within the US, you can dial any number starting with those digits free of charge, though some numbers only operate inside California: it isn't apparent from the number until you try. Numbers with the prefix ☎1-900 are pay-per-call lines, generally quite expensive and almost always involving either sports, phone psychics or phone sex. Some numbers, particularly those of consumer services, employ letters as part of their number. The letters are on the phone's number buttons, thus for example, ☎1-800/TAXI becomes ☎1-800/8294.

California has numerous area codes – three-digit numbers which must precede the seven-figure number if you're calling from abroad or from a region with a different area code. In this book, we've included the local area code with every phone number. With an ever increasing number of phones and phone numbers, new area codes in California are popping up every year. If you have trouble getting through, contact the operator or call Pacific Bell at ☎1-800/310-2355 for new area code information.

EMAIL AND INTERNET ACCESS

Email is often the cheapest and most convenient way to keep in touch. **Cybercafés** are found in most towns of any size, though their heyday has now passed and many travelers resort to the **free Internet access** provided by almost all public libraries. Generally you just reserve a half-hour slot and away you go, but high demand has forced some libraries either to charge for using email or ban it altogether. If neither of these options fit the bill, or you just need a fast machine with assorted peripherals, then find a commercial photocopying and printing shop (look under "Copying" in the *Yellow Pages*). They'll charge around 20¢ a minute for use of their computers, but you're guaranteed fast access. Most upscale hotels also offer email and Internet access – though again at a price.

By far the easiest way to collect and send email on the road is to sign up with one of the advertisement-funded **free email accounts**. Any of the major search engines will take you straight to one – *www.hotmail.com*, *www.excite.com* and *www.yahoo.com* to name just a few – and all can be accessed from any Net-linked computer. To sign up with one, all you need to do is pick a site and fill out a few forms. When you want to send or check your email, just go to the Web page and enter your name and password. Emails are kept indefinitely, but you are typically limited to a total of 2Mb of disk space and if you fail to use the account for three or six months (depending on the service supplier) you'll be closed down.

MAIL SERVICES, TELEGRAMS AND FAXES

Post offices are usually open Monday to Friday from 9am until 5pm, and Saturday from 9am to noon (sometimes 4pm), and there are blue **mail boxes** on many street corners. **Ordinary mail** within the US costs 33¢ for letters weighing up to an ounce; addresses must include the **zip code**, and a return address should be written in the upper left corner of the envelope. **Air mail** from California to Europe generally takes about a week. Aerograms and letters weighing up to half an ounce (a single sheet) cost 60¢, and postcards cost 55¢.

The last line of the address is made up of the city name, an abbreviation denoting the state (in California "CA") and a five-digit number – the **zip code** – denoting the local post office. (The additional four digits you will sometimes see appended to zip codes are not essential.) Letters which don't carry the zip code are liable to get lost or at least delayed; if you don't know it, phone books carry a list for their service area, and post offices – even in Britain – have directories.

Letters can be sent c/o **General Delivery** (what's known elsewhere as **poste restante**) to the one relevant post office in each city, but must include the zip code and will only be held for thirty days before being returned to sender – so make sure there's a return address on the envelope. If you're receiving mail at someone else's address, it should include "c/o" and the regular occupant's name, or it is likely to be returned.

Rules on sending **parcels** are very rigid: packages must be sealed according to the instructions given at the start of the *Yellow Pages*. To send anything out of the country, you'll need a green **customs declaration form**, available from the post office. **Postal rates** for sending a parcel weighing up to 1lb to Europe, Australia and New Zealand are $10.20.

To send a **telegram** (also known as a wire), don't go to a post office but to a Western Union office (listed in the *Yellow Pages*). Credit card holders can dictate messages over the phone. **International telegrams** cost slightly less than the cheapest international phone call: one sent in the morning from California should arrive at its destination the following day. For domestic telegrams ask for a **mailgram**, which will be delivered to any address in the country the next morning.

Public **fax** machines, which may require your credit card to be "swiped" through an attached device, are found at photocopy centers and, occasionally, bookstores.

INFORMATION AND MAPS

Advance information for a trip to California can be obtained by post from the California Office of Tourism, 801 K St, Suite 1600, Sacramento, CA 95814-3520 (☎1-800/862-2543 or 916/322-2881). Once you've arrived in the state, you'll find most towns have visitor centers of some description – often called the Convention and Visitors Bureau (CVB) or Chamber of Commerce: all are listed in the guide. These will give out detailed information on the local area and can often help with finding accommodation. Free newspapers in most areas carry news of events and entertainment.

Most of the tourist offices we've mentioned can supply you with good **maps**, either free or for a small charge, and, supplemented with our own, these should be enough for general sightseeing and touring. Rand McNally (*www.randmcnallystore. com*), produces a decent low-cost ($2.95) map of the state, and its *Road Atlas* ($6.95) covering the whole country plus Mexico and Canada, is a worthwhile investment if you're traveling further afield. For driving or cycling through rural areas, the *Atlas & Gazetteer: Northern California* and *Atlas & Gazetteer: Southern and Central California* ($16.95 each; published by DeLorme, *www.delorme.com*) are valuable companions, with detailed city plans, marked campsites and reams of national park and forest information. For something more detailed, say for **hiking** purposes, ranger stations in parks and wilderness areas all sell good-quality local hiking maps for $1–3, and camping stores generally have a good selection too. The American Automobile Association (*www.aaa.com*; ☎1-800/272-2155 in Northern CA, ☎1-800/678-3839 in Southern CA), has offices in most large cities and provides excellent free maps and travel assistance to its members, and to British members of the AA and RAC.

Most bookstores will have a range of local trail guides, the best of which we've listed in "Contexts," p.679.

MAP AND TRAVEL BOOK SUPPLIERS

UK

London
Daunt Books, 83 Marylebone High St, London
W1 (☎020/7224 2295).
National Map Centre, 22–24 Caxton St, London
SW1 (☎020/7222 2466, *www.mapsworld.com*).
Stanfords, 12–14 Long Acre, London WC2E 9LH
(☎020/7836 1321); 52 Grosvenor Gardens,
London SW1W 0AG; 156 Regent St, London W1R

5TA (☎020/7434 4744). Maps by mail or phone
order also available: ☎020/7836 1321.
The Travel Bookshop, 13–15 Blenheim Crescent,
London W11 2EE (☎020/7229 5260).
Glasgow
John Smith and Sons, 57–61 St Vincent St,
Glasgow G2 5TB (☎0141/221 7472).

IRELAND

Dublin
Easons Bookshop, 80 Middle Abbey St, Dublin 1
(☎01/873 3811).
Fred Hanna's Bookshop, 27–29 Nassau St, Dublin
2 (☎01/677 1255).

Hodges Figgis Bookshop, 56–58 Dawson St,
Dublin 2 (☎01/677 4754).
Belfast
Waterstone's, Queens Building, 8 Royal Ave,
Belfast BT1 1DA (☎028/9024 7355).

US

The Complete Traveler, 199 Madison Ave at
35th St, New York, NY 10016 (☎212/685-9007);
3207 Fillmore St, San Francisco, CA 92123
(☎1-800/950-3514 or 415/923-1511, fax 922-
5338, *info@completetraveler.com*).
Forsyth Travel Library, 226 Westchester Ave,
White Plains, NY 10604 (☎1-800/367-7984, fax
914/681-7251, *www.forsyth.com*).
Phileas Fogg's Books & Maps, 87 Stanford
Shopping Center, Palo Alto, CA 94304 (☎1-
800/533-3644).
Rand McNally, 444 N Michigan Ave, Chicago,
IL 60611 (☎312/321-1751); 150 E 52nd St, New

York, NY 10022 (☎212/758-7488); 595 Market St,
San Francisco, CA 94105 (☎415/777-3131);
10250 Santa Monica Blvd, Suite 681, Los
Angeles, CA 90067 (☎310/556-2202); and 19
other stores across the country (*www.
randmcnallystore.com*). Call ☎1-800/333-0136
(ext 2111) for the location of your nearest store,
or for direct mail maps.
The Savvy Traveller, 310 S Michigan Ave,
Chicago, IL 60604 (☎312/913-9800, *www.
thesavvytraveller.com*).
Sierra Club Bookstore, 85 Second St, San
Francisco, CA 94105 (☎415/977-5600).

CANADA

Open Air Books and Maps, 25 Toronto St,
Toronto, ON M5C 2R1 (☎416/363-0719).
Ulysses Travel Publications, 4176 St-Denis,
Montréal (☎514/843-9882, fax 843-9448,
guiduly@ulysses.ca).

World Wide Books and Maps, 552 Seymour
St, Vancouver, BC (☎604/687-3320).

AUSTRALIA

Adelaide
The Map Shop, 6–10 Peel St, SA 5000
(☎08/8231- 2033, fax 8231-2373, *mapshop. net.au*).
Brisbane
Worldwide Maps and Guides, 187 George St
(☎07/3221 4330, fax 3211 3684, *wwmaps@
powerup.com.au*).
Melbourne
Melbourne Map Centre, 738-740 Waverley
Road, Chadstone, Victoria and PO Box 55,
Holmesglen, Victoria, 3148 (03/9569-5472, fax
9569-8000, *melbmap.com.au*).
Map Land, 372 Little Bourke Street (☎03/9670
4383, fax 9670 7779, *mapland@lexicon.net.au*).

Sydney
Dymocks, 350 George St, New South Wales
(☎02/9223 5974, fax 9232 3061).
Travel Bookshop, 6 Bridge St, NSW 2000
(☎02/9241-3554, fax 9241-3159, *www.blueskies.
com.au/travelbook*).
USA Travel Service, 75 King Street, Sydney
(☎02/9299 1222).
Perth
Perth Map Centre, First Floor Shaft Lane, 884
Hay St, WA 6000 (☎09/8322-5733, fax 9322
5733, *www.q-net.net.au/-perthmap*).

NEW ZEALAND

Map Shop, 193 Vivian Street, PO Box 22-185,
Wellington (☎04/385 1462, fax 385 7941,
www.mapshop.co.nz).
Map Shop, 544 Grey St, Hamilton (☎07/856
4450, fax 856 4450).

Mapworld NZ, 173 Gloucester Street,
Christchurch (☎03/374 5399, fax374 5633,
maps@mapworld.co.nz).
Specialty Maps, 58 Albert St, Auckland
(☎09/307 2217, fax 526 6313).

THE MEDIA

The only newspaper that's read all over California is the *Los Angeles Times*, which gives probably the best coverage of state, national and world events in the country. Otherwise newspapers tend to excel at reporting their own area but generally rely on agencies for their foreign – and even some national – reports. Major newspapers from other parts of the US, such as the *New York Times*, and some overseas newspapers, can be found in the vending machines, newsstands and bookstores of major cities; and *USA Today* is, of course, ubiquitous.

Every community has at least a few **free newspapers**, found in street distribution bins, cafés and bars, or just lying around in piles. It's a good idea to pick up a full assortment: some simply cover local goings-on, others provide specialist coverage of interests ranging from long-distance cycling to getting ahead in business – and the classified and personal ads can provide hours of entertainment. Many of them are also excellent sources for bar, restaurant and nightlife information; the most useful titles are mentioned throughout the guide.

TELEVISION

Californian **TV** is pretty much the standard network barrage of sitcoms, newscasts and talk shows. A number of Spanish-language cable channels serve the state's large Hispanic population; a smaller number are aimed at other, particularly Asian, ethnic groups. **PBS**, the national public television station, broadcasts a steady stream of interesting documentaries, informative (if slightly dry) news programs, and educational children's television.

There's hardly a motel room in the state that's not hooked up to **cable**. The number of channels available to guests varies from place to place, but fifty is common and eighty isn't unheard of. Most cable stations are no better than the major networks (ABC, CBS, NBC, and FOX), though some of the more specialized channels are consistently interesting. The ARTS channel broadcasts enjoyable, if po-faced, arts features, imported TV plays and the like. CNN offers round-the-clock news, HBO shows recent big-bucks movies, AMC shows old black-and-white films, and ESPN exclusively covers sport. Finally, there's MTV (seemingly absent from the menu of most chain hotels), the thirty-something VH-1 and a number of other music stations.

To watch publicity-hyped pay-per-view events like world heavyweight boxing bouts, you may have to pay as much as $40, either to your motel or to a bar that's putting on a live screening. Many larger hotels and motels offer a choice of movies that have just finished their cinema run, for around $7 each.

RADIO

Radio stations are even more abundant than TV channels, and the majority, again, stick to a bland commercial format. Except for news and chat, stations on the **AM** band are best avoided in favor of **FM**, in particular the nationally funded public (NPR) and college stations, found between 88 and 92 FM. These provide diverse and listenable programming, and they're also good sources for information on local nightlife.

In the larger cities you are spoilt for choice, with dozens of good music stations, all specializing in a narrow (often astoundingly limited) playlist – pop, jazz, classical, classic rock, classic oldies, Eighties... you get the idea. However, driving through rural areas can be frustrating, since you might only be able to receive a few (very dull) stations for hundreds of miles. And you'd better like country music, or you'll have to resort to scanning up and down the frequencies, skipping between re-run Eagles tracks, fire-and-brimstone Bible thumpers and crazed phone-in chat shows. Weekday mornings (between 6am and 10am) bring relief with several stations carrying nationally syndicated talk shows; Howard Stern is the current king of the time slot. On Saturday mornings, listen out for the entertaining "Car Talk" (typically on NPR stations), even if you haven't the slightest interest in car maintenance.

Finally, **Mexican stations** – most local, but some broadcasting from very powerful transmitters located south of the border – provide an enjoyable, alternative flavor of Southern California, even if you don't speak Spanish.

USEFUL CALIFORNIA WEB SITES

TRAVEL

California Travel & Tourism *www.gocalif. ca.gov*
Stylishly designed and accessible, California's official travel and tourism site claims to suit you, whether you're traveling for "Family, Romance, Nature, or Recreation."

Caltran: The California Department of Transportation *www.dot.ca.gov/*
Straightforward and informative, the Caltran homepage contains current highway conditions, public transit schedules, information on traveling by bike and more.

Rough Guides *www.roughguides.com*
Post any of your pre-trip questions – or post-trip suggestions – in Travel Talk, our online forum for travelers.

ENTERTAINMENT & HOLLYWOOD

Ain't it Cool News *www.aint-it-cool-news.com*
Self-confessed geek Harry Knowles has attracted huge numbers of readers to his site, which consists of rambling film reviews and Hollywood insider secrets.

E! Online *www.eonline.com*
Breathless, gossipy and visually gorgeous site with pages full of star profiles and movie reviews.

Variety *www.variety.com*
The daily morning read of Hollywood insiders, full of news, review, previews and the latest Tinseltown tales.

DAILY NEWSPAPERS

For information on both local and national news, weather updates, sports scores and entertainment happenings, check out the following sites:

LA Times *www.latimes.com*

Sacramento Bee *www.sacbee.com*

San Diego Union Tribune *www. signonsandiego.com*

San Francisco Chronicle & Examiner *www. sfgate.com*

San Jose Mercury *www.sjmercury.com*

OUTDOOR PURSUITS

Backcountry Resource Center *www.jps.net/ prichins/backcountry_resource_center.htm*
Superb non-commercial site laden with valuable information on backcountry skiing, climbing and general outdoor interest with plenty of useful links.

SkiMaps *www.skimaps.com*
The latest snowfall reports, plus the snow-base depth and trail maps for all the major skiing and snowboarding resorts in California.

Surf Scene Magazine & Southern California Surf Report *www.surfscene.net/surf/index.html*
Hot California surfing news, with daily surf reports, as well as surfing links and a photo gallery.

MUSEUMS

Surf here to get the latest on the current and future shows for each museums, as well as any upcoming special events:

The Getty Museum (Los Angeles) *www.getty.edu*

Los Angeles County Museum of Art *www. lacma.org*

Los Angeles Museum of Contemporary Art *www.moca-la.org*

San Diego Museum of Contemporary Art *www.mcasandiego.org*

San Diego Museum of Art *www.sdmart.com*

San Francisco Museum of Modern Art *www. sfmoma.org*

San Francisco Art Institute *www.sfai-art.com*

LIBATIONS

The California Beerpage *www.beerpage.com*
Accessible guide to California's microbreweries and beer festivals.

The Napa Valley Tourist Guide *www. napasonomatourist.com*
Comprehensive list of hundreds of Napa Valley wineries, including tour-hours, wine selections and maps.

GETTING AROUND CALIFORNIA

Although distances can be great, getting around California is seldom much of a problem. Certainly, things are always easier if you have a car, but between the major cities there are good bus links and a reasonable train service. The only regions where things are more difficult using public transportation are the isolated rural areas, though even here, by adroit forward-planning, you can usually get to the main points of interest on local buses and charter services, details of which are in the relevant sections of the guide.

BY CAR

Driving is by far the best way to get around California. Los Angeles, for example, grew up and assumed its present shape after cars were invented, sprawling for so many miles in all directions that your hotel may be fifteen or twenty miles from the sights you came to see. Away from the cities, points of interest are much harder to reach without your own transportation; most national and state parks are only served by infrequent public transportation as far as the main visitor center, if that. What's more, if you are planning on doing a fair amount of camping, renting a car can save you money by allowing access to less expensive, out-of-the-way campgrounds.

Drivers wishing to **rent** cars are supposed to have held their licenses for at least one year (though this is rarely checked); people under 25 years old may encounter problems, and will probably get lumbered with a higher than normal insurance premium. Car rental companies (listed below) will also expect you to have a credit card; if you don't they may let you leave a hefty

CAR RENTAL COMPANIES

IN THE US AND CANADA

Alamo ☎1-800/354-2322
www.goalamo.com
Avis ☎1-800/331-1212
www.avis.com
Budget ☎1-800/527-0700
www.budgetrentacar.com
Dollar ☎1-800/421-6868
www.dollarcar.com
Enterprise ☎1-800/325-8007
www.pickenterprise.com
Hertz ☎1-800/654-3131;
in Canada ☎416/620-9620
www.hertz.com
Holiday Autos ☎1-800/422-7737
National ☎1-800/CAR-RENT
www.nationalcar.com
Payless ☎1-800/729-5377
www.paylesscar.com
Rent-A-Wreck ☎1-800/535-1391
www.rent-a-wreck.com
Thrifty ☎1-800/367-2277
www.thrifty.com

IN THE UK

Alamo ☎0990/994000
Avis ☎0870/6060100
Budget ☎ 0541/565656
Hertz ☎0990/996699
Holiday Autos ☎0171/491 1111
www.holidayautos.co.uk
National ☎0990/994000

IN AUSTRALIA

Avis ☎1-800/225 533
Budget ☎1-300/36 2848
Hertz ☎13/3039
National ☎13/1045

IN NEW ZEALAND

Avis ☎0-800/655 111 or 09/526-2847
Budget ☎0-800/652 227
Hertz ☎0-800/655 955
National ☎0-800/800 115

ROAD CONDITIONS

The California Department of Transportation (CalTrans) operates a toll-free **24-hour information line** (☎1-800/427-ROAD) giving up-to-the-minute details of road conditions throughout the state. On a touch-tone phone, simply input the number of the road ("5" for I-5, "299" for Hwy-299, etc) and a recorded voice will tell you about any relevant weather conditions, delays, detours, snow closures and so on. From out of state, or without a touch-tone phone, road information is also available on ☎916/445-1534. Nevada Highways has a similar system on ☎775/793-1313.

deposit (at least $200), but don't count on it. The likeliest tactic for getting a good deal is to phone

the major firms' toll-free numbers and ask for their best rate – most will try to beat the offers of their competitors, so it's worth haggling.

In general, the lowest rates are available at the airport branches – $149 a week for a sub-compact is a fairly standard budget rate. Always be sure to get free unlimited mileage, and be aware that leaving the car in a different city to the one in which you rent it will incur a **drop-off charge** that can be $200 or more – however, many companies do not charge drop-off fees within California itself so check before you book if you plan a one-way drive. If you are planning to venture outside California, inquire if there are any limitations; some companies don't allow travel beyond Reno or into Mexico, while others simply ramp up their insurance charges. Also,

DRIVING FOR FOREIGN VISITORS

UK nationals can **drive** in the US on a full UK driving license (International Driving Permits are not always regarded as sufficient). Fly-drive deals are good value if you want to **rent a car**, though you can save up to sixty percent simply by booking in advance with a major firm. If you choose not to pay until you arrive, be sure you take a written confirmation of the price with you. Remember that it's safer not to rent a car straight off a long transatlantic flight; and that standard rental cars have **automatic transmissions**.

It's also easier and cheaper to book **RVs** in advance from Britain. Most travel agents who specialize in the US can arrange RV rental, and usually do it cheaper if you book a flight through them as well. Once you have a vehicle, you'll find that **petrol** (US "gasoline") is fairly cheap; a self-served US gallon (3.8 liters) of **unleaded** – which most cars use – costs between $1.30 and $1.90, depending on the location of the gas station. In California most gas stations are self-service – when removing the nozzle from the pump, remember to lift or turn the lever to activate it – and you can often pay at the pump using your credit or ATM card. If you insist on having someone else pump your gas, you'll pay for it; full service pumps often charge upwards of $0.30 extra per gallon.

American **miles** are the same as British miles but sometimes **distances** are given in **hours** – the length of time it should take to drive between any two places. There are obviously other differences between driving in the US and in Britain, not least the fact that rules and regulations aren't always nationally fixed. Many foreign travelers have problems at first adjusting to **driving on the right**. This can be remarkably easy to forget – some people draw a cross or tie a ribbon on their right hand to remind them.

There are several **types of road**. The best for covering long distances quickly are the wide, straight and fast **Interstate highways**, usually at least six-lane motorways and always prefixed by "I" (eg I-5) – marked on maps by a red, white and blue shield bearing the number. Even-numbered Interstates usually run east–west and those with odd numbers north–south. Driving on these roads is easier than it first appears, but you need to adapt quickly to the American habit of **changing lanes**: US drivers do this frequently, and overtake on both sides. In California you are also permitted to stay in the fast lane while being overtaken on the inside, although common courtesy dictates that slower drivers stay to the right. All these roads are free: there are none of the turnpikes found in the east. Big overhead signs warn you if the road is about to split towards two different destinations (this happens quite often), or an exit's coming up. Sometimes a lane *must* exit, and if you lose concentration you're liable to leave the Interstate accidentally – no great calamity as it's easy enough to get back on again. **Missing an exit** is more annoying – U-turns are strictly illegal, and you have to continue to the next exit. In urban areas during **rush hour**, freeway traffic can often slow to a maddening halt. Your best bet is to entirely avoid freeway driving in the Bay Area and Los Angeles in the early morning and evening.

don't automatically go for the cheapest rate, as there's a big difference in the quality of cars from company to company; industry leaders like Hertz and Avis tend to have newer, lower-mileage cars, often with air-conditioning and stereo cassette decks or CD players as standard equipment – no small consideration on a 2000-mile desert drive.

Alternatively, various **local** companies rent out new – and not so new (try Rent-a-Heap or Rent-a-Wreck) – vehicles. They are certainly cheaper than the big chains if you just want to spin around a city for a day, but you have to drop them back where you picked them up, and free mileage is seldom included, so they can work out more costly for long-distance travel. Addresses and phone numbers are listed in the *Yellow Pages*.

When you rent a car, read the small print carefully for details on the **Collision Damage Waiver (CDW)** – sometimes called a Liability Damage Waiver (LDW) or a Physical Damage Waiver (PDW) – a form of insurance which usually isn't included in the initial rental charge but is well worth considering. Americans who have their own car insurance policy may already be covered (check before you leave home) but foreign visitors should definitely consider taking this option. It specifically covers the car that you are driving, as you are in any case insured for damage to other vehicles. At $9–13 a day, it can add twenty to forty percent to the daily rental fee, but without it you're liable for every scratch to the car – even those that aren't your fault. Some credit card companies offer automatic CDW coverage to anyone

---

A grade down, and broadly similar to British dual carriageways and main roads, are the **State highways** (eg Hwy-1) and the **US highways** (eg US-395). Some major roads in cities are technically state highways but are better known by their local name. Hwy-2 in Los Angeles, for instance, is better known as Santa Monica Boulevard. In rural areas, you'll also find much smaller **county roads**; their number is preceded by a letter denoting their county. In built-up areas **streets** are arranged on a grid system and labeled at each junction.

Although the law says that drivers must keep up with the flow of traffic, which is often hurtling along at 75mph, the maximum **speed limit** in California is 70mph, with lower signposted limits – usually around 35–45mph – in built-up areas, and 20mph near schools when children are present. There are no **spot fines**, but if given a ticket for **speeding**, your case will come to court and the size of the fine will be at the discretion of the judge; $90 is a rough minimum. If the **police** do flag you down, don't get out of the car, and don't reach into the glove compartment as the cops may think you have a gun. Simply sit still with your hands on the wheel; when questioned, be polite and don't attempt to make jokes.

As for other possible violations, US law requires that any **alcohol** be carried unopened in the boot (US "trunk") of the car, and it can't be stressed enough that **driving while intoxicated (DWI)** is a very serious offense. If a police officer smells alcohol on your breath or has reason to believe that you are under the influence, he/she is entitled to administer a breath, saliva or urine test. If you fail, you'll be locked up with other inebriates in the drunk tank of the nearest jail until you sober up. Your case will later be heard by a judge, who can fine you as much as $1000, or in extreme (or repeat) cases, imprison you for thirty days. Less serious offenses include making a **U-turn** on an Interstate or anywhere where a single unbroken line runs along the middle of the road; driving in **car pool lanes** with fewer than two people in the vehicle; **parking on a highway**; and riding without fastened **seatbelts** in the front seat. At **junctions**, one rule is crucially different from the UK: you can turn right on a red light (having first come to a halt) if there is no traffic approaching from the left; otherwise red means stop. Stopping is also compulsory, in both directions, when you come upon a school bus disgorging passengers with its lights flashing. Blinking red lights should be treated as a stop sign, and blinking yellow lights indicate that you should cross the intersection with caution, but do not need to come to a complete stop. And at any intersection with more than one **stop sign**, cars proceed in the order in which they arrived.

Once at your destination, you'll find in cities at least that **parking meters** are commonplace. Charges for an hour range from 25¢–$1. **Car parks** (US "parking lots") charge up to $15 a day. If you park in the wrong place (such as within 10ft of a fire hydrant) your car is likely to be towed away or **wheel-clamped**; a ticket on the windshield tells you where to pay the $25 fine. Watch out for signs indicating the **street cleaning** schedule, as you mustn't park overnight before an early-morning clean. **Validated parking**, where your fee for parking in, say, a shopping mall's lot is waived if one of the stores has stamped your parking stub (just ask), is common, as is **valet parking** at even quite modest restaurants, for which a small tip is expected.

using their card; read the fine print beforehand in any case. Smaller companies may offer low-cost CDW that still leaves you liable for, say, the first $500 of any claim. Before stumping up for their optional Personal Accident Coverage (or similar), consult your travel insurance policy, which may cover you for a certain amount of rental vehicle excess, eliminating the need for this extra cost.

You should also check your **third-party liability**. The standard policy often only covers you for the first $15,000 of the third party's claim against you, a paltry sum in litigation-conscious America. Companies strongly advise taking out third-party insurance, which costs a further $10–12 a day but indemnifies the driver for up to $2,000,000.

If you **break down** in a rented car, there will be an emergency number pinned to the dashboard or tucked away in the glove compartment. You can summon the highway patrol on one of the new emergency phones stationed along freeways (usually at half-mile intervals) and many other remote highways (mostly every two miles) – although since the highway patrol and state police cruise by regularly, you can just sit tight and wait. Raising your car hood is recognized as a call for assistance, although women traveling alone should be wary of doing this.

Another tip is to rent a **mobile telephone** from the car rental agency (or from outlets at major airports) – you often only have to pay a nominal amount until you actually use it, and in larger cities they increasingly come built into the car. Having a phone can be reassuring at least, and a potential lifesaver should something go terribly wrong.

One variation on renting is a **driveaway**, whereby you drive a car from one place to another on behalf of the owner, paying only for the gas you use. The same rules as for renting apply, but look the car over before you take it, as you'll be lumbered with any repair costs, and a large fuel bill if the vehicle's a big drinker. The most common routes are between California and New York, although there's a fair chance you'll find something that needs shifting up the coast, from Los Angeles to San Francisco. See p.10 for further details.

RENTING AN RV

Besides cars, Recreational Vehicles or **RVs** (camper vans) can be rented for around $500 a week, although outlets are surprisingly rare, as people tend to own their RVs: in LA try El Monte RVs, 12061 E Valley Blvd, El Monte, CA 91732 (☎1-800/367-6511 or 818/443-6158, *www.elmonte.com*) who also have a Bay Area branch at 4901 Coliseum Way, Oakland, CA 94601 (☎1-800/332-7878). The Recreational Vehicle Rental Association, 3930 University Drive, Fairfax, VA 22030 (☎1-800/336-0355 or 703/591-7130, fax 591-0734, *www.rvra.org*), publishes a directory of rental firms in the US and Canada ($10, $15 outside North America). Some of the larger companies offering RV rentals are Cruise America (☎1-800/327-7799, *www.cruiseamerica.com*) and Moturis (☎1-877/668 8747, *www.moturis.com*).

On top of the rental fees, take into account the cost of gas (some RVs do twelve miles to the gallon or less) and any drop-off charges, in case you plan to do a one-way trip across the country. Also, it is rarely legal simply to pull up in an RV and spend the night at the roadside – you are expected to stay in designated parks that cost up to $20 per night.

BY PLANE

A **plane** is obviously the quickest way of getting around California, and much less expensive than you may think; by keeping up to date with the ever-changing deals being offered by airlines – check with your local travel agent, read the ads in local newspapers or search the Internet – you may be able to take advantage of heavily discounted fares.

Airlines with a strong route structure in the state include Alaska, American, Continental, Delta, Northwest, Reno Air, Southwest, TWA and United. Phone the airlines for routes and schedules, then buy your ticket from a travel agent using the computerized Fare Assurance Program, which processes all the available ticket options and searches for the lowest fare, taking into account the special needs of individual travelers. One agent using the service is Travel Avenue (☎1-800/333-3335).

At **off-peak times**, flights between Los Angeles and San Francisco can cost as little as $50 one-way (only slightly more than the equivalent train fare), though may require a booking to be made 21 days in advance.

BY TRAIN

Unlike elsewhere in the US, traveling on the Amtrak **rail** network is a viable way of getting

RAIL, BUS AND AIR PASSES

AMTRAK RAIL PASSES

Foreign travelers have a choice of four rail passes; including the Coastal Pass, which permits unlimited train travel on the east and west coasts, but not between the two.

	15-day (June–Aug)	15-day (Sept–May)	30-day (June–Aug)	30-day (Sept–May)
Far West	$240	$185	$310	$240
West	$315	$195	$395	$260
Coastal	–	–	$275	$225
National	$425	$285	$535	$375

On production of a passport issued outside the US or Canada, the passes can be bought at travel agents, or at Amtrak stations in the US. In the **UK**, you can buy them from Destination Marketing, 14 Greville St, London EC1 N8SB (☎0171/400 7099); in **Ireland**, contact Usit Now (☎01/602 1600); in **Australia**, Amtrak Rail USA, 4 Davies St, Surry Hills (☎02/9318 1044); and in **New Zealand** passes can be purchased from almost any travel agent.

In addition, **Explore America** fares – available to anyone within a 45-day period – allow up to three stops on a round-trip ticket.

GREYHOUND AMERIPASSES

Foreign visitors and US and Canadian nationals can all buy a **Greyhound Ameripass**, offering unlimited travel within a set time limit: most travel agents can oblige or you can order online at www.greyhound.com. They come in several durations and the fare for international visitors is slightly less. A seven-day pass costs $149 for foreign visitors ($169 for North Americans), ten days go for $199 ($219), fifteen days for $229 ($249), thirty days for $319 ($349), forty-five days for $339 ($439), and the longest, a sixty-day pass, is $429 ($479). All kids under 12 go half price, and there are discounts of around seven percent for North American students and seniors (62+). No daily extensions are available. The first time you use your pass, it will be dated by the ticket clerk (which becomes the commencement date of the ticket), and your destination is written on a page which the driver will tear out and keep as you board the bus. Repeat this procedure for every subsequent journey.

AIR PASSES

All the main American airlines offer **air passes** for visitors who plan to fly a lot within the US. These must be purchased in advance, and comprise between three and eight **coupons**, each valid for a flight of any duration in the US, though in many cases only one flight can be transcontinental. Rates start at around US$400 for three coupons, and $60 for each additional coupon; a little more if you are not traveling to the States with that airline.

There are also **Visit USA** fares only available to non-US residents. These can be substantially less than the standard fare for that flight, and it is certainly worth asking your travel agent, but in many cases there are discount fares available which undercut the Visit USA fare. If you just plan to buy one flight, good low-season fares from New York, Washington and Boston to California are $300–350 round-trip; LA is marginally less expensive than San Francisco.

---

about California, thanks in great measure to the growing number of Amtrak Thruway buses, which bring passengers from the many rail-less parts of the state to the trains. Traveling by train is slightly more expensive than Greyhound, $48 one-way between Los Angeles and San Francisco, for example, but unlike on a bus, a smooth journey with few if any delays is a near certainty. All the major cities are connected and the carriages clean, comfortable and rarely crowded. Probably the prettiest route is the *Coast Starlight*, which

For all information on Amtrak fares and schedules in the US, use the toll-free number ☎1-800/USA-RAIL, or use the reservation facility on their Web site www.amtrak.com; do not phone individual stations.

winds along the coast between Santa Barbara and San Luis Obispo, a 100-mile coastline ride during which it's not unusual to see seals, dolphins or even whales in the waters offshore. The other LA-to-SF Amtrak routes head inland, by bus to Bakersfield then by rail north through the dull San Joaquin Valley. Avoid these unless you are making for Yosemite National Park.

If California is part of wider travels, it may be economic to buy one of Amtrak's rail passes (see box overleaf).

BY BUS

If you're traveling on your own, and making a lot of stops, **buses** are by far the cheapest way to get around. The main long-distance service is **Greyhound** (*www.greyhound.com*), which links all major cities and many smaller towns. Out in the country, buses are fairly scarce, sometimes appearing only once a day, and here you'll need to plot your route with care. But along the main highways, buses run around the clock to a fairly full timetable, stopping only for meal breaks (almost always fast-food dives) and driver changeovers. Greyhound buses are slightly less uncomfortable than you might expect, and it's feasible to save on a night's accommodation by traveling overnight and sleeping on the bus – though you may not feel up to much the next day.

To avoid possible hassle, lone female travelers in particular should take care to sit as near to the driver as possible, and arrive during daylight hours, as many bus stations are in fairly dodgy areas. It used to be that any sizeable community would have a Greyhound station; in some places, the post office or a gas station now doubles as the bus stop and ticket office, and in many others the bus service has been canceled altogether. Reservations, either in person at the station or on the toll-free number, are not essential but recommended – if a bus is full you may be forced to wait until the next one, sometimes overnight or longer.

Fares average 10¢ a mile, which can add up quickly; for example, $36 from Los Angeles to San Francisco one-way. For long-trip travel, riding the

Greyhound's nationwide toll-free **information service** can give you routes and times, plus phone numbers and addresses of local terminals. You can also make reservations: ☎1-800/231-2222.

GREEN TORTOISE

One alternative to long-distance bus hell is the slightly countercultural Green Tortoise (*www.greentortoise.com*), whose buses, furnished with foam cushions, bunks, fridges and rock music, ply the major Californian cities, running between Los Angeles, San Francisco and on into the Pacific Northwest. In summer, they also cross the country to New York and Boston, transcontinental trips which amount to mini-tours of the nation, taking 10–14 days (at a current cost of $349–389, not including contributions to the food fund which amount to around $10 a day), and allowing plenty of stops for hiking, river-rafting and hot springs. Other Green Tortoise trips include excursions to the major national parks (in 16 days for $499), south to Mexico and Central America and north to Alaska.

Main Office: 494 Broadway, San Francisco, CA 94133; ☎1-800/867-8647 or 415/956-7500.

bus costs about the same as the train; considering the time (75 hours coast-to-coast, if you eat and sleep on the bus) it's not that much cheaper than flying. However, the bus is the best deal if you plan to visit a lot of places, and Greyhound's **Ameripasses** (see box overleaf) can work out to be good value. There are also assorted three-, seven- fourteen- and twenty one-day advance purchase discounts, which can be useful for longer trips, though they seldom offer savings within California.

Greyhound produces a condensed **timetable** of major country-wide routes, but does not distribute it to travelers; to plan your route, pick up the free route-by-route timetables from larger stations, or consult Greyhound's Web site.

Smaller companies catering specifically to tourists come and go with alarming frequency. One currently operational is **AmeriBus** (1-800/685-7716), which uses buses and mini-vans on a circuit from LA up the coast to San Francisco, inland to Yosemite, down to Las Vegas and then back to LA. Services leave the major cities daily, so if you fork out $129 you've got unlimited travel around this loop for one month. They also have a series of short tours, as well as combined AmeriBus passes taking in a loop around Washington DC, New York City and Toronto, and another through southern Florida.

Bear in mind that fair distances can be covered for very little money (if also very slowly) using

local buses, which connect neighboring districts. It's possible, for example, to travel from San Diego to Los Angeles for $4, but it'll take all day and at least three changes of bus to do it. And of course, there's always the hippyish Green Tortoise, which runs between the major Californian cities (see box).

CYCLING

In general, **cycling** is a cheap and healthy method of getting around all the big **cities**, some of which have cycle lanes and local buses equipped to carry bikes, strapped to the outside. In **country areas**, certainly, there's much scenic and largely level land, especially around Sacramento and the Wine Country.

Bikes can be **rented** for $25 a day, and $90–100 a week from most bike stores; the local visitor center will have details (we've listed rental options where applicable throughout the guide). Apart from the coastal fog, which tends to clear by midday, you'll encounter few **weather** problems (except perhaps sunburn), but remember that the further north you go, the lower the temperatures and the more frequent the rains become.

For **long-distance cycling**, you'll need maps, spare tires, tools, panniers, a helmet (not a legal necessity, but a very good idea), and a good quality multi-speed bike. Don't immediately splurge on a mountain bike, unless you are planning a lot of off-road use – good road conditions and trail restrictions in National Parks make a touring bike an equally good or better choice. A route avoiding the Interstates (on which cycling is illegal) is essential, and it's also wise to cycle north to south, as the wind blows this way in the summer

HITCHING

The usual advice given to **hitchhikers** is that they should use their common sense; in fact, common sense should tell anyone that hitchhiking in the US is a **bad idea**. We do not recommend it, though it is practiced commonly enough by hikers seeking access to Sierra trailheads.

and can make all the difference between a pleasant trip and a journey full of acute leg-ache. The main **problem** you'll encounter is traffic: wide, cumbersome recreational vehicles spew unpleasant exhaust in your face and, in Northern California, enormous logging trucks have slipstreams that will pull you towards the middle of the road. Be particularly careful if you're planning to cycle along Hwy-1 on the central coast, since besides heavy traffic, it has tight curves, dangerous precipices, and is prone to fog.

If you're camping as well as cycling, look out for **hiker/biker campgrounds** ($3 per person per night), which are free of cars and RVs, dotted across California's state parks and beaches. Many of them were set up in 1976 as part of the **Pacific Coast Bicentennial Bike Route**, running 1825 miles from the Mexican border to Vancouver, Canada. Sites are allotted on a first-come-first-served basis, and all offer water and toilet facilities but seldom showers. For more information, call ☎1-800/444-7275 or write to Hostelling International – USA (see p.39); the Adventure Cycling Association (formerly Bikecentennial), PO Box 8308, Missoula, MT 59807 (☎1-800/755-2453 or 406/721-1776, fax 721-8754, *www.adv-cycling.org*); or the Sierra Club (address on p.54).

ACCOMMODATION

Accommodation standards in California – as in the rest of the US – are high, and costs inevitably form a significant proportion of the expenses for any trip to the state. It is possible to haggle, however, especially in the chain motels, and if you're on your own, you can possibly pare costs by sleeping in dormitory-style hostels, where a bed will cost $12–15. However, groups of two or more will find it only a little more expensive to stay in the far more plentiful motels and hotels, where basic rooms away from the major cities typically cost around $30 per night. Many hotels will set up a third single bed for around $5 to $10 on top of the regular price, reducing costs for three people sharing. By contrast, the lone traveler will have a hard time of it: "singles" are usually double rooms at an only slightly reduced rate. Prices quoted by hotels and motels are almost always for the actual room rather than for each person using it.

Motels are plentiful on the main approach roads to cities, around beaches and by the main road junctions in country areas. High-rise **hotels** predominate along the popular sections of the coast and are sometimes the only accommodation in city centers. In major cities, **campgrounds** tend to be on the outskirts, if they exist at all.

Wherever you stay, you'll be expected to **pay in advance**, at least for the first night and perhaps for further nights too, particularly if it's high season and the hotel's expecting to be busy. Payment can be in cash or in dollar travelers' checks, though it's more common to give your credit card number and sign for everything when you leave. **Reservations** are only held until 5pm or 6pm unless you've told them you'll be arriving late. Most of the larger chains have an advance booking form in their brochures and will make reservations at another of their premises for you.

Since cheap accommodation in the cities, on the popular sections of the coast and close to the major national parks is snapped up fast, **book ahead** whenever possible, using the suggestions in this book.

HOTELS AND MOTELS

Hotels and **motels** are essentially the same thing, although motels tend to be located beside the main roads away from city centers – and thus

ACCOMMODATION PRICE CODES

Throughout this book, **accommodation** has been price-coded according to the cost of the least expensive **double room** throughout most of the year; we have given individual dollar prices for **hostels** and whole apartments. Expect prices in most places to jump into the next highest category on Friday and Saturday nights.

However, with the exception of the budget Interstate motels, there's rarely such a thing as a set rate for a room. A basic motel in a seaside or mountain resort may double its prices according to the season, while a big-city hotel which charges $200 per room during the week will often slash its tariff at the weekend when all the business types have gone home. Particularly in scenic areas, prices might leap into the next higher category at weekends. As the high and low seasons for tourists vary widely across the state, astute planning can save a lot of money. Watch out also for local events, which can raise rates far above normal.

Only where we explicitly say so do these room rates include local taxes, which usually range from eight to twelve percent, but can be as high as twenty percent. Fees quoted for state and federally-run campgrounds include taxes.

① up to $30	④ $60–80	⑦ $130–175
② $30–45	⑤ $80–100	⑧ $175–250
③ $45–60	⑥ $100–130	⑨ $250+

HOTEL DISCOUNT VOUCHERS

For the benefit of overseas travelers, many of the higher-rung hotel chains offer pre-paid **discount vouchers**, which in theory save you money if you're prepared to pay in advance. To take advantage of such schemes, British travelers must purchase the vouchers in the UK, at a usual cost of £30–60 per night for a minimum of two people sharing. However, it's hard to think of a good reason to buy them; you may save a nominal amount on the fixed rates, but better-value accommodation is not exactly difficult to find in the US, and you may well regret the inflexibility imposed upon your travels. Most UK travel agents will have details of the various voucher schemes.

are much more accessible to drivers. The budget ones are pretty basic affairs, but in general there's a uniform standard of comfort everywhere – double rooms with bathroom, TV and phone – and you don't get a much better deal by paying, say, $50 instead of $35. Over $50, the room and its fittings get bigger and more luxurious, and there'll probably be a swimming pool which guests can use for free. Paying over $100 brings you into the realms of the en-suite jacuzzi.

While inexpensive diners may be everywhere, a growing number of Californian hotels are providing a **complimentary breakfast**. Sometimes this will be no more than a cup of coffee and a sticky bun, but increasingly it is a sit-down affair likely to comprise fruit, cereals, muffins and toast. In the pricier places, you may also be offered made-to-order omelets.

In most places you'll be able to find cheap one-off hotels and motels simply by keeping your eyes open – they're usually advertised by enormous roadside signs. Alternatively, there are a number of budget-priced **chains**, such as *Econolodge*, *Days Inn* and *Motel 6*, whose rooms cost $28–45. Mid-priced options include *Best Western, Howard Johnson, Travelodge* and *Ramada* – though if you can afford to pay this much ($50–100) there's normally somewhere nicer to stay. When it's worth blowing a hunk of cash on somewhere really atmospheric we've said as much in the guide. Bear in mind that the most upscale establishments have all manner of services which may appear to be free but for which you'll be expected to **tip** in a style commensurate with the hotel's status – ie big. For more on tipping see p.43 and p.60.

DISCOUNTS AND RESERVATIONS

During **off-peak periods**, many motels and hotels struggle to fill their rooms and it's worth **haggling** to get a few dollars off the asking price. Staying in the same place for more than one night will bring further reductions. Motels in particular also offer small but worthwhile discounts for seniors and members of various organizations, particularly the American Automobile Association (AAA). Additionally, pick up the many **discount coupons** which fill tourist information offices and look out for the free *Traveler Discount Guide*. Read the small print, though: what appears to be an amazingly cheap room rate sometimes turns out to be a per-person charge for two people sharing, and limited to midweek.

B&B INNS AND HOTELS

Bed and breakfast in California is a luxury – even the mattresses have to conform to a standard of comfort far higher than those in hotels. Typically, the bed-and-breakfast inns, as they're usually known, are restored buildings in the smaller cities and more rural areas – although the big cities also have a few, especially San Francisco. Even the larger establishments – often distinguished by being called B&B Hotels – tend to have no more than ten rooms, often without TV and phone but with plentiful flowers, stuffed cushions and a contrived homey atmosphere; others may just be a couple of furnished rooms in someone's home, or an entire apartment where you won't even see your host. Victorian and Romantic are dominant themes; while selecting the best in that vein, we've also gone out of our way to seek out those which don't conform.

While always including a huge and wholesome breakfast (five courses is not unheard of), prices vary greatly: anything from $70 to $250 depending on location and season. Most fall between $85 and $125 per night for a double, a little more for a whole apartment. Bear in mind, too, that they are frequently booked well in advance, and even if they're not full, the cheaper rooms which determine our price code may be already taken.

YS AND HOSTELS

At an average of $15 per night per person, **hostels** are clearly the cheapest accommodation option in California other than camping. There are three main kinds of hostel-type accommodation in

NATIONAL HOTEL, HOSTEL AND MOTEL CHAINS

Most of the hotel and lodging chains listed below publish handy free directories (with maps and illustrations of their properties). Although we have indicated typical room rates (using the codes explained opposite), bear in mind that the location of a particular hotel or motel has a huge impact on price.

Best Western (③–⑥) ☎1-800/528-1234
www.bestwestern.com

Clarion (④–⑥) ☎1-800/252-7466
www.hotelchoice.com

Comfort Inns (③–⑤) ☎1-800/228-5150
www.hotelchoice.com

Courtyard by Marriott (④–⑥) ☎1-800/321-2211
www.marriot.com

Days Inn (③–⑤) ☎1-800/325-2525
www.daysinn.com

Econolodge (①–③) ☎1-800/553-2666
www.econolodge.com

Embassy Suites Hotels (⑥–⑦) ☎1-800/362-2779
www.embassysuites.com

Fairfield Inns (③) ☎1-800/228-2800
www.marriot.com

Friendship Inns (④) ☎1-800/424-4777
www.roadway.com

Hampton Inns (④–⑤) ☎1-800/426-7866
www.hampton-inn.com

Hilton Hotels (⑤ and up) ☎1-800/445-8667
www.hilton.com

Holiday Inns (⑤ and up) ☎1-800/465-4329
www.holiday-inn.com

Hostelling International – American Youth Hostels ($12–18) ☎202/783-6161
www.hiayh.org

Howard Johnson (②–⑤) ☎1-800/654-2000
www.hojo.com

Hyatt Hotels (⑧–⑨) ☎1-800/233-1234
www.hyatt.com

Marriott Hotels (⑥ and up) ☎1-800/228-9290
www.marriott.com

Motel 6 (②–③) ☎1-800/466-8356
www.motel6.com

Quality Inn (③–⑤) ☎1-800/228-5151
www.hotelchoice.com

La Quinta Inns (④) ☎1-800/531-5900
www.laquinta.com

Radisson Hotels (⑥) ☎1-800/333-3333
www.raddison.com

Ramada Inns (④ and up) ☎1-800/272-6232
www.ramada.com

Red Carpet Inns (②) ☎1-800/251-1962
www.reservahost.com

Red Roof Inns (②–③) ☎1-800/843-7663
www.redroof.com

Renaissance Hotels (⑧–⑨) ☎1-800/468-3571
www.renaissancehotels.com

Rodeway Inns (④) ☎1-800/228-2000
www.hotelchoice.com

Scottish Inns (②) ☎1-800/251-1962
www.reservahost.com

Sheraton (⑤ and up) ☎1-800/325-3535
www.sheraton.com

Sleep Inns (③) ☎1-800/753-3746
www.sleepinn.com

Super 8 Motels (③–④) ☎1-800/800-8000
www.super8.com

Travelodge (②–③) ☎1-800/255-3050
www.travelodge.com

YMCA ($12–18) ☎1-800/872-9622
www.ymca.com

---

the US: YMCA/YWCA hostels (known as "Ys") offering accommodation for both sexes, or in a few cases, women-only accommodation; HI–AYH hostels; and a growing number of independent hostels variously affiliated to assorted umbrella organizations.

Prices in YMCAs range from around $12 for a dormitory bed to $18 for a single or double room. Some Ys are basically health clubs and do not offer accommodation. Those that do are often in older buildings in less than ideal neighborhoods, but facilities may include a gymnasium, a swimming pool, and an inexpensive cafeteria.

You'll find **HI-AYH** (*www.hiayh.com*) hostels (the prefix is usually shortened to HI in "Listings") in major cities and popular hiking areas, including national and state parks, across California. Most urban hostels have 24-hour access, while rural ones may have a curfew and limited daytime hours. HI also operates a couple of small "home hostels" in the state; though similar to other hostels you need to reserve in advance or there may be no one there to receive you. Rates at HI hostels range from $12 to $18 for HI members; non-members generally pay an additional $3 per night.

For a list of **B&Bs** throughout the state and in specific areas, contact one or more of the following:

Bed and Breakfast International (☎408/867-9662, *www.bbintl.com*).

California Office of Tourism. Ask for the brochure *Californian Bed and Breakfast Inns*.

Colby International, 139 Round Hey, Liverpool L28 1RG (☎0151/220 5848) For bed-and-breakfast rooms and apartments in the main cities and along the Central Coast.

Useful Web sites covering B&Bs in California include the B&B Channel (*www.bbchannel.com*), Inn Site (*www.innsite.com/browse-CA.html*), and the California B&B Travel Directory (*www2.bbtravel.com/bbtravel/*).

Particularly if you're traveling in high season, it's advisable to **book ahead**. Within North America you can call toll-free at 1-800/909-4776, followed by a two-digit code for the required hostel, which is published in the *Hostelling International Guide to North America* and is listed on the HI Web site. For a small fee you can also reserve on ☎202/783-6161, and when booking from outside North America you can use the IBN booking service (for local numbers see "Hostel Information" box below). Some HI hostels will allow you to use a **sleeping bag**, though offi-

cially they should (and many do) insist on a **sheet sleeping bag**, which can usually be rented at the hostel. The maximum stay at each hostel is technically three days, though this is again a rule which is often ignored if there's space. Few hostels provide meals, but most have **cooking** facilities. Alcohol, smoking and, of course, drugs are banned.

Independent hostels are usually a little less expensive than their HI counterparts, and have fewer rules. The quality is not as consistent; some can be quite poor, while others, which we've included in this book, are absolutely wonderful. In popular areas, especially LA, San Francisco and San Diego, they compete fiercely for your business with airport and train station pick-ups, free breakfasts and free bike hire. There is often no curfew and, at some, a party atmosphere is encouraged at barbecues and keg parties. Their independent status may be due to a failure to come up to the HI's (fairly rigid) criteria, but often it's simply because the owners prefer not to be tied down by HI regulations. Many have now loosely affiliated themselves under an assortment of bodies, mostly designed to encourage you to move on to a sister hostel.

All the information in this book was accurate at the time of going to press; however, hostels are often shoestring organizations, prone to changing address or closing down altogether. Similarly,

---

YOUTH HOSTEL INFORMATION

Local **youth hostel** information can be found at the following HI–AYH council offices:

Central CA Council, PO Box 3645, Merced, CA 95344 (☎209/383-0686).
Golden Gate Council, 425 Divisadero St #307, San Francisco, CA 94117 (☎415/788-2525).

Los Angeles Council, 1434 Second St, Santa Monica, CA 94010 (☎310/393-3413).
San Diego Council, 655 Fourth Ave, Suite 46, San Diego, CA 92101 (☎619/338-9981).

Hostelling International Guide to North America, the HI guide to hostels in the USA and Canada, is available free of charge to any overnight guest at HI-AYH hostels or direct for $3 from the **HI National Office**, 733 15th St NW, Suite 840, Washington DC 20005 (☎202/783-6161, fax 783-6171, *hiayhserv@hiayh.org*). For **overseas hostellers**, the two-volume *Hostelling International Guide* provides a full list of hostels. In Britain, it's available from the Youth Hostel Association shop, 14 Southampton St, London WC2 (☎0171/836 1036), where you can also buy a year's IYHF **membership** for £11 (£5.50 if you're under 18).

To make hostel reservations from outside the US using the IBN system, call your nearest credit card Booking Center:

Australia ☎02/9261-1111
Canada ☎1-800/663-5777
England ☎0171/836-1036
New Zealand ☎09/379-4224

Northern Ireland ☎0232/324-733
Republic of Ireland ☎01/301-766
Scotland ☎041/332-3004

new ones appear each year; check the notice-boards of other hostels for news.

CAMPING

California **campgrounds** range from the primitive (a flat piece of ground that may or may not have a water tap) to others which are more like open-air hotels, with shops, restaurants and washing facilities. When camping in national and state parks, as well as national forests, you can typically expect a large site designed to accommodate up to two vehicles, six people and all the paraphernalia that Americans like to take with them. There'll be a picnic table and fire pit on the site, with a short walk to an outhouse and a drinking water tap.

Naturally enough, prices vary accordingly, ranging from nothing for the most basic plots, up to $20 a night for something comparatively luxurious. There are plenty of campgrounds but often plenty of people intending to use them as well: take care over plotting your route if you're intending to camp in the big National Parks, or anywhere at all during national holidays or the summer, when many grounds will be either full or very crowded. Vacancies often exist in the grounds outside the parks – where the facilities are usually marginally better – and by contrast, some of the more basic campgrounds in isolated areas will often be empty whatever time of year you're there, and if there's any charge at all you'll need to pay by posting the money in the slot provided.

Look out too for **hiker/biker** or **walk-in** campgrounds, which, at $3 per person per night, are much cheaper than most sites but only available if you are traveling under your own steam (see p.40).

Much of California is in the public domain, and, if you're backpacking, you can **camp rough** pretty much anywhere you want in the gaping **wilderness areas** and **deserts**. However, in the more heavily hiked areas (we've indicated the relevant areas in the text), you must first get a **wilderness permit** (almost always free), and usually a free **campfire permit** (even if you are using a cooking stove). Campfire permits are available from park rangers' offices and once obtained are usually valid for a year. You should also take the proper precautions: carry sufficient food and drink to cover emergencies, inform the park ranger of your travel plans, and watch out for bears and rattlesnakes, as well as the effect *your* presence can have on *their* environment; see "Backcountry Camping, Hiking and Wildlife" on p.51.

LONG-TERM ACCOMMODATION

Excluding San Francisco, **apartment-hunting** in California is not the nightmare it is in, say, New York: accommodation is plentiful and not always expensive, although the absence of housing associations and co-ops means that there is very little really cheap accommodation anywhere except in very isolated country areas. Accommodation is

---

CAMPGROUND RESERVATIONS

Campgrounds in popular National Parks, State Parks and National Forests soon fill up in summer, especially during the July and August school vacation, so it pays to reserve as far in advance as you can. Phone and Web site reservations can often be made several months in advance, but must be lodged a minimum of two days before you plan to arrive. When making reservations, be sure to have dates, locations, number of people, a mailing address, and alternative sites picked out.

Reservations can be made on the following numbers and Web sites:

National Parks except Yosemite: ☎1-800/365-2267, *reservations.nps.gov*

Yosemite National Park: ☎1-800/436-7275, *reservations.nps.gov*

State Parks: call Destinet ☎1-800/444-7275 or 916/638-5883, *www.reserveamerica.com/usa/ca*

National Forests: contact the National Recreation Reservation Service ☎1-877/444-6777, *ReserveUSA.com*

Two private companies oversee a multitude of campgrounds all over California, although these are almost exclusively for RVs. For their brochures and lists, contact **California Travel Parks Association**, PO Box 5578, Auburn, CA 95604 (☎530/823-1076, fax 823-6331, *www.campground.com*) and **Kampgrounds of America (KOA)**, PO Box 30558, Billings, MT 59114 (☎406/248-7444, *www.koa.com*).

almost always rented unfurnished, so you'll have to buy furniture; expect to pay at least $700 a month for a studio or one-bedroom apartment and upwards of $2000 per month for two to three bedrooms in Los Angeles or San Francisco. Most landlords will expect one month's rent as a deposit, plus one month in advance.

There is no statewide organization for accommodation so you'll have to check out the options in each place. By far the best way to find somewhere is to ask around – particularly near universities or college campuses, where apartment turnover is unusually frequent. Otherwise rooms for rent are often advertised in the windows of houses and local papers have "Apartments For Rent" sections. In **Los Angeles** the best source is the *LA Weekly*, although you should also scan the *LA Times* classifieds. In **San Francisco** check out the *Chronicle* and the free *Bay Area Guardian, East Bay Express* – and, for women, *Bay Area Women's News*.

FOOD AND DRINK

It's not too much of an exaggeration to say that in California – its cities, at least – you can eat whatever you want, whenever you want. On every main street, a mass of restaurants, fast-food places and coffee shops try to outdo one another with bargains and special offers. Be warned, though, that in rural areas you might go for days finding little more than diners and cheap Mexican joints.

California's cornucopia stems largely from its being one of the most agriculturally rich parts of the country. Junk food is as common as anywhere else in the US, but the state also produces its own range of highly nutritious goodies: apples, avocados, dates, grapes, kiwifruit, melons, oranges and peaches are everywhere, plus abundant fish and seafood and high-quality meat and dairy goods. You'll rarely find anything that's not fresh, be it a bagel or a spinach-in-Mornay-sauce croissant

(California's mix'n'match food concoctions can be as anarchic as its architecture), and even fast food won't necessarily be rubbish.

California is also one of the most health-conscious states in the union, and the supermarket shelves are chock-full of products which if not fat-free, are low-fat, low-sodium, caffeine-free and dairy-free. Much the same ethic runs through the menu of most restaurants, though you needn't worry about going hungry: portions are as huge as elsewhere in the States, and what you don't eat can always be "boxed up" for later consumption.

BREAKFASTS

For the price, on average $4–7, breakfast is the best-value and most filling meal of the day. Go to a diner, or, slightly smarter, a café or coffee shop, all of which serve breakfast until at least 11am, with some diners serving them all day. There are often special deals at earlier times too, say 6–8am, when the price may be even lower.

The breakfasts themselves are pretty much what you'd find all over the country. **Eggs** are the staple ingredient, and are served in a variety of styles: "sunny side up" (fried on one side, leaving a runny yolk), "over" (flipped over in the pan to stiffen the yolk), "over easy" (flipped for a few seconds giving just a hint of solidity to the yolk), or scrambled (just that). **Omelets** are popular, usually made with three eggs and available with a range of exotic fillings (avocado, for instance). There is usually also some form of **meat** available: ham or bacon, streaky and fried to a crisp; or sausages, skinless and spicy, sometimes shaped as disc-like "sausage patties."

Many breakfasts come with **toast**: rye, white or whole-wheat bread generally, though tangy **sourdough bread** is also common. Alternatives are an **English muffin** (a toasted bread roll) or an **American muffin**, a fruitcake traditionally made with bran and sugar, often flavored with blueberries, poppyseed or chocolate chips. If you wish, you can add **waffles**, **pancakes** or **French toast** to the combination, consumed swamped in butter with lashings of sickly-sweet syrup, flavored to mimic the more delicate and expensive maple syrup. A concession to California's love of light food is the option of **fruit**: typically apple, banana, orange, pineapple or strawberry, wonderfully styled and served on their own or with pancakes, though costing as much as a full-blown fry-up.

Wherever you eat, a dollar or so will entitle you to wash the meal down with as much **coffee** as you can stomach; **tea** is less common, but isn't hard to find. Be warned, though, that anything called "English tea" will be a poor-quality brew made with weak tea bags or an inferior Earl Grey. Better to try the wide range of **herbal teas** (don't pronounce the "h"): apple and cinnamon, blackcurrant, emperors (a very spicy herb) and ginseng, peppermint and camomile, and a huge selection of others are available. A cup will cost upwards of $1, and is served straight rather than with milk.

LUNCH AND SNACKS

Most Californian workers take their lunch break between 11.30am and 1.30pm, and during these hours you should look for the low-cost **set menus** on offer – generally excellent value. Chinese restaurants, for example, frequently have help-yourself rice and noodles or dim sum feasts for $5–8, and many Japanese restaurants give you a chance to eat sushi much more cheaply ($8–12) than usual. Most Mexican restaurants are exceptionally well priced all the time: you can get a good-sized lunch for $5–7. In Northern California, watch out for seafood restaurants selling **fish and chips**: the fish is breaded and then fried – a vast improvement on English batter – and the chips are real chipped potatoes rather than the French fries you normally find. A plateful is about $5. Look, too, for **clam chowder**, a thick, creamy shellfish soup served almost everywhere for $3–4, sometimes using a hollowed-out sourdough cottage loaf as a bowl.

As you'd expect, there's also **pizza**, available from chains like *Pizza Hut*, *Round Table* and *Shakey's*, or local, more personalized restaurants. Most are dependable and have a similar range of offerings; count on paying around $10 for a basic two-person pizza. If it's a warm day and you can't face hot food, delis (see below) usually serve a broad range of salads for about $4. Consider also California's favorite healthy fast food: **frozen yogurt**, which is sold in most places by the tub for $2.

For **quick snacks**, you'll find many **delis** do ready-cooked meals for $4–5 as well as a range of **sandwiches "to go,"** which can be meals in themselves: huge French rolls filled with a custom-built combination of meat, cheese, and vegetables. *Subway*, the international chain, makes sandwiches fast-food style, but bear in mind that you'll often pay the same for higher quality, less processed ingredients. **Bagels** are also everywhere: thick, chewy rolls with a hole in the middle, filled with anything you fancy. **Street stands** sell hot dogs, burgers, tacos, or a slice of pizza for around $1.50, and most shopping malls have ethnic fast-food stalls, often pricier than their equivalent outside, but usually edible and filling. Be a little wary of the grottier **Mexican fast-food** stands if you're buying meat, although they're generally filling, cheap and more authentic than the Tex-Mex outlets. There are chains, too, like *El Pollo Loco*, *Del Taco* and *Taco Bell*, which sell swift tacos and burritos for around $1. And of course the **burger chains** are as ubiquitous here as anywhere in the US: *Wendy's*, *Burger King* and *McDonald's* are the familiar names, along with *Jack-in-the-Box* – a drive-through takeout where you place your order by talking to a plastic clown.

Finally, just about any of these places will serve **sodas**. Each brand is available in caffeine-free and sugar-free varieties. You can buy sodas

---

FREE FOOD

Some **bars** are used as much by diners as drinkers, who turn up in droves to fill up on the free **hors d'oeuvres** laid out by a lot of city bars between 5pm and 7pm Monday to Friday during **"happy hour"** – an attempt to nab the commuting classes before they head off to the suburbs. For the price of a drink you can stuff yourself silly on chili, seafood or pasta, though bear in mind that the food is more often than not downright unappetizing until you've had at least three drinks.

from vending machines and in supermarkets for about 65¢ a can, or from a fast-food outlet in three sizes – large, larger and gargantuan – for between 75¢ and $1.50, each with ice added by the shovelful.

RESTAURANTS

Even if it often seems swamped by the more fashionable regional and ethnic cuisines, traditional **American cooking** – juicy burgers, steaks, fries, salads (invariably served before the main dish) and baked potatoes – is found all over California. Cheapest of the food chains is the California-wide *Denny's*, although you'll rarely need to spend more than $10 for a solid blowout anywhere.

By contrast, though, it's **California cuisine**, geared towards health and aesthetics, that's raved about by foodies on the West Coast – and rightly so. Basically a development of French *nouvelle cuisine*, utilizing the wide mix of fresh, locally available ingredients, California cuisine is based on physiological efficiency – eating only what you need to and what your body can process. Vegetables are harvested before maturity and steamed to preserve a high concentration of vitamins, with a strong flavor – and to look better on the plate. Seafood comes from oyster farms and the catches of small-time fishermen, and what little meat there is on the menu tends to come from animals reared on organic farms. The result is small but beautifully presented portions, and high, high prices: it's not unusual to spend

TIPPING

Foreign visitors to the US are generally impressed by the fact that whatever you eat and wherever you eat, **service** will always be efficient and enthusiastic (sometimes overly so), mainly due to the American system of **tipping**, on which the staff depend for the bulk of their earnings. You should always top up the bill by fifteen or twenty percent; not to tip at all is severely frowned upon. Many (not all) restaurants accept payment in the form of credit/charge cards: if you use one, a space will be left to fill in the appropriate tip. Travelers' checks are also widely accepted with ID (see p.21). For more on tipping, see "Directory for Overseas Visitors" at the end of "Basics."

$40 a head (or much more) for a full dinner with wine; the minimum you'll need for a sample is $15, which will buy an entrée. To whet your appetite, starters include mussels in jalapeño and sesame vinaigrette, snails in puff pastry with mushroom purée, and, among main courses, roasted goat cheese salad with walnuts, swordfish with herb butter and ahi tuna with cactus ratatouille.

Restaurants serving California cuisine build their reputation by word of mouth; if you can, ask a local enthusiast for recommendations, or simply follow our suggestions in the guide, especially in Berkeley, the recognized birthplace of California cuisine. Of other American regional cooking, **Cajun** remains in vogue. Also known as

MEXICAN SPECIALTIES

Burritos	Refried beans, meat, and grated cheese wrapped in a flour tortilla	*Nachos*	Tortilla chips topped with melted cheese
Chiles rellenos	Green chilies stuffed with cheese and fried in egg batter	*Quesadilla*	Folded soft tortilla containing melted cheese
Enchiladas	Soft tortillas filled with meat and cheese or chili and baked	*Salsa*	Diced chilies, tomato, onion and cilantro
Fajitas	Like tacos but a soft flour tortilla stuffed with shrimp, chicken, beef and grilled onions	*Tacos*	Folded corn tortillas, stuffed with chicken, beef or (occasionally) cow's brains
Frijoles	Beans, either regular or mashed and fried	*Tamales*	Corn meal dough with meat and chili, wrapped in a corn husk and baked
Guacamole	Thick sauce made from avocado, garlic, onion and chili, used as a topping	*Tortillas*	Corn or wheat flour pancakes
Mariscos	Seafood	*Tostada*	Fried, flat tortillas, smothered with meat and vegetables

"Creole," it originated in Louisiana as a way of saving money by cooking up leftovers. It is centered on black beans, rice and seafood, and is always highly spiced. There are a few relatively inexpensive places to find it (charging around $10 per entrée), but its cachet has pushed prices up tremendously.

Although technically ethnic, **Mexican** food is so common that it often seems like (and, historically, often is) an indigenous cuisine, especially in Southern California. What's more, day or night, it's the cheapest type of food to eat: even a full dinner with a few drinks will rarely be over $12 anywhere except in the most upmarket establishments. In the main, Mexican food here is different from what you'll find in Mexico, making more use of fresh vegetables and fruit, but the essentials are the same: lots of rice and pinto beans, often served refried (ie boiled, mashed and fried), with variations on the **tortilla**, a thin maize or flour dough pancake. You can eat it as an accompaniment to your main dish; wrapped around the food and eaten by hand (a **burrito**); filled and folded (a **taco**); rolled, filled and baked (an **enchilada**); or fried flat and topped with a stack of food (a **tostada**). One of the few options for vegetarians in this meat-oriented cuisine is the **chile relleno**, a green pepper stuffed with cheese, dipped in egg batter and fried. Veggie burritos, filled with beans, rice, lettuce, avocado, cheese and sour cream are another prevalent option for those averse to meat.

Other ethnic cuisines are plentiful too. **Chinese** food is everywhere, and during lunchtime can often be as cheap as Mexican. **Japanese** is more expensive and fashionable – sushi is worshipped by some Californians. **Italian** food is very popular, but can be expensive once you leave the simple pizzas and pastas to explore the specialist Italian regional cooking that's fast catching on. **French** food, too, is widely available, though always pricey, and the cuisine of social climbers and power-lunchers, rarely found outside the larger cities. **Thai**, **Korean**, **Vietnamese** and **Indonesian** food is similarly city-based, though usually cheaper; **Indian** restaurants, on the other hand, are thin on the ground just about everywhere and often very expensive – although as Indian cuisine catches on the situation is gradually changing for the better, with a sprinkling of moderately priced Southern Indian food outlets.

DRINKING

As elsewhere in the States, in California you'll find typical **bars** and **cocktail lounges**, long dimly lit counters with a few punters perched on stools before a bartender-cum-guru, and tables and booths for those who don't want to join in the drunken bar-side debates. But in freeway-dominated Los Angeles, the traditional neighborhood bar is as rare as the traditional neighborhood. There are exceptions, but LA bars tend to be either extremely pretentious or extremely seedy, neither good for long bouts of social drinking. On the other hand, San Francisco is the consummate boozing town, still with a strong contingent of old-fashioned, get-drunk bars that are fun to spend an evening in even if you don't plan to get legless.

To **buy and consume alcohol** in California you need to be 21, and could well be asked for ID even if you look much older. **Licensing laws** and **drinking hours** are, however, among the most liberal in the country (though laws on drinking and driving are not; see p.31). Alcohol can be bought and drunk any time between 6am and 2am, seven days a week; and, as well as bars, nightclubs and restaurants are nearly always fully licensed. In addition, it is permitted by California law to take your own bottled wine into a restaurant, where the corkage fee will be $5–10. You can buy beer, wine or spirits more cheaply and easily in supermarkets, many delis, and, of course, liquor stores.

American **beers** fall into two diametrically opposite categories: wonderful and tasteless. You'll probably be familiar with the latter, which are found everywhere: light, fizzy brands such as Budweiser, Miller, Schlitz and Michelob, the only nationally sold variety likely to find fans among British beer drinkers. The alternative is a fabulous range of **"microbrewed" beers**, the product of a wave of backyard and in-house operations that swelled about ten years ago and has now matured to the point that many pump out over 150,000 barrels a year and are classed as "regional breweries." Head for one of the **brewpubs** (many are listed in the guide along with breweries you can visit; see also the California Beerpage Web site listed on p.28) and you'll find handcrafted beers such as crisp pilsners, wheat beers and stouts on tap, at prices only marginally above those of the national brews. Bottled microbrews, like Chico's hoppy Sierra Nevada Pale Ale and the full-bodied, San Francisco-brewed Anchor Steam Beer, are sold throughout the state, while Red Tail Ale is found throughout Northern California.

Alternatively, do what many locals do and stick to **imported** beers, especially the Mexican brands Bohemia, Corona, Dos Equis, and Tecate. Expect to fork out $3 for a glass of draught beer, about the same for a bottle of imported beer. Taste aside, imported beers gain advocates for their comparative alcoholic strength.

Don't forget that in all but the most pretentious bars, several people can save money by buying a half-gallon **"pitcher"** of beer for $6–8. If bar prices are a problem, you can stock up with **six-packs** from a supermarket ($3–5 for domestic, $5–8 for imported brews).

If you're partial to the internationally known Californian **wines**, like Gallo and Paul Masson, you may be surprised to learn that they are held in low regard on the West Coast, and produced in plants resembling oil refineries. Most people prefer the produce of California's innumerable, and invariably good, smaller wineries. The Napa and Sonoma Valleys – which produce predominantly dry wines made from French-strain grapes – are widely, and rightly, regarded as the cradle of the Californian wine industry. Wines are categorized by grape-type rather than place of origin: Cabernet Sauvignon is probably the most popular, a fruity and palatable red. Also widespread are the heavier reds – Burgundy, Merlot and Pinot Noir. Among the whites, Chardonnay is very dry and flavorful, and generally preferred to Sauvignon Blanc or Fumé Blanc, though these have their devotees.

The most unusual is the strongly flavored Zinfandel, which comes in white (mocked by wine snobs, but popular nonetheless), red or rosé.

You can learn a lot about Californian wine by taking a **winery tour**, mostly including free tastings (although some charge $4–5 for a full glass or two), a number of which we've mentioned in the guide. Alternatively, the visitor centers in popular wine-producing areas produce informative regional directories. The best lesson of all, of course, is simply to buy the stuff. It's fairly inexpensive: a decent glass of wine in a bar or restaurant costs about $4, a bottle $10–20. Buying from a supermarket is better still – a quality bottle can be purchased for as little as $7.

Cocktails are extremely popular, especially during **happy hours** (usually any time between 5pm and 7pm) when drinks are half-price and there's often a buffet thrown in. Varieties are innumerable, sometimes specific to a single bar or cocktail lounge, and they cost anything between $3 and $6.

An increasing alternative to drinking dens, **coffee shops** (look out for any joint with "Java" in the title) play a vibrant part in California's social scene, and are havens of high-quality coffee far removed from the stuff served in diners and convenience stores. In larger towns and cities, cafés will boast of the quality of the roast, and offer a full array of espressos, cappuccinos, lattes and the like, served straight, iced, organic or flavored with syrups. Herbal teas and light snacks are often also on the menu.

WOMEN TRAVELERS

Practically speaking, though a woman traveling alone is certainly not the attention-grabbing spectacle in California that she might be elsewhere in the world (or even elsewhere in the US), you're likely to come across some sort of harassment. More serious than the odd offensive comment, rape statistics in the US are high, and it goes without saying that, even more than anyone else, women should never hitch alone – this is widely interpreted as an invitation for trouble, and there's no shortage of weirdos to give it. Similarly, if you have a car, be careful whom you pick up: just because you're in the driver's seat doesn't mean you're safe. If you can, avoid traveling at night by public transportation – deserted bus stations, while not necessarily threatening, will do little to make you feel secure, and where possible you should team up with another woman. On Greyhound buses, follow the example of other lone women and sit as near to the front – and the driver – as possible.

Californian **cities**, especially San Francisco, can feel surprisingly safe, and **muggings** are an uncommon occurrence. But as with anywhere, particular care has to be taken at night, and a modicum of common sense can often avert disas-

ters. Walking through unlit, empty streets is never a good idea, and you should take cabs wherever possible. The advice that women who look confident tend not to encounter trouble is, like all home truths, grounded in fact but not written in stone; those who stand around looking lost and a bit scared are prime targets, but nobody is immune. Provided you listen to advice, though, and stick to the better parts of a town, going into **bars** and **clubs** alone should pose no problems, especially in San Francisco and LA, where there's generally a pretty healthy attitude towards women who choose to do so and whose privacy will be respected – only extremely unevolved specimens will assume you're available. If in doubt, gay and lesbian bars are usually a trouble-free alternative.

Small towns in rural areas are not blessed with the same liberal attitudes toward lone women travelers that you'll find in the cities. If you have a **vehicle breakdown** in a country area, walk to the nearest house or town for help; don't wait by the vehicle in the middle of nowhere hoping for somebody to stop – they will, but it may not be the kind of help you're looking for. Should disaster strike, all major towns have some kind of rape counseling service available; if not, the local sheriff's office will make adequate arrangements for you to get help, counseling, and, if necessary, get you home.

The National Organization for Women (*www.now.org*) is a women's issues group whose lobbying has done much to affect positive legislation. NOW branches, listed in local phone directories and on their Web site, can provide referrals for specific concerns, such as rape crisis centers and counseling services, feminist bookstores and lesbian bars. Further back-up material can be found in Women's Travel in Your Pocket ($14; Ferrari Publications, PO Box 37887, Phoenix, AZ 85069; ☎602/863-2408), an annual guide for women travelers. Specific women's contacts are listed where applicable in the city sections of the guide.

TRAVELERS WITH DISABILITIES

Travelers with mobility problems or other physical disabilities are likely to find California – as with the US in general – to be much more in tune with their needs than anywhere else in the world. All public buildings must be wheelchair-accessible and have suitable toilets; most city street corners have dropped curbs; subways have elevators, and most city buses are able to kneel to make access easier and are built with space and handgrips for wheelchair users. Most hotels, restaurants and theaters (certainly any built in the last ten years or so) have excellent wheelchair access.

GETTING TO AND FROM CALIFORNIA

Most airlines, transatlantic and within the US, do whatever they can to ease your journey, and will usually let attendants of people with serious disabilities accompany them at no extra charge. The Air Carriers Access Act of 1986 obliged all domestic air carriers to make the majority of their services accessible to travelers with disabilities.

Almost every **Amtrak train** includes one or more coaches with accommodation for disabled passengers. Guide dogs travel free, and Amtrak will provide wheelchair assistance at its train stations, adapted seating on board and a fifteen percent discount on the regular fare, all provided 24 hours' notice is given. Passengers with hearing impairment can get information on ☎1-800/523-6590.

Traveling by **Greyhound** and **Amtrak Thruway** buses, however, is not to be recommended. Buses are not equipped with lifts for wheelchairs, though staff will assist with boarding (intercity carriers are required by law to do this), and the "Helping Hand" scheme offers two-for-the-price-of-one tickets to passengers unable to travel alone (carry a doctor's certificate). For assistance on Greyhound, call ☎1-800/752-4841 at least 48 hours before you intend to travel.

The major **car rental** firms can, given sufficient notice, provide vehicles with hand controls (though these are usually only available on the more expensive models, and you'll need to reserve well in advance). The American Automobile Association (see p.25) produces the *Handicapped Driver's Mobility Guide* for **drivers with disabilities** (available free from AAA, Traffic Safety Dept, 150 Van Ness Ave, San Francisco, CA 94102; ☎415/565-2012). There are no longer differences in state **parking regulations** for disabled motorists; the Department of Transportation has decreed that all state licenses issued to disabled persons must carry a three-inch square international access symbol, and each state must provide placards bearing this symbol to be hung from the rear-view mirror – the placards are blue for permanent disabilities, red for temporary (maximum of six months). More information can be obtained from state motor vehicle offices.

As in other parts of the world, the rise of the **self-service gas station** is unwelcome for many disabled drivers. The state of California has addressed this by changing its laws so that most service stations are required to provide full service to disabled drivers at self-service prices.

INFORMATION

The California Office of Tourism's free *California State Visitor's Guide* (available at *www.gocalif.ca.gov*) lists handicap facilities at places of accommodation and attractions. The *San Francisco Lodging Guide* (free from the San Francisco CVB, 201 Third Street, Suite 900, San Francisco, CA 94103 (☎415/391-2000, fax 974-1992) lists many wheelchair-accessible properties – hotels, motels, apartments, B&Bs, hostels, RV parks – in the city and surrounding counties; as always, travelers should call to confirm details. The Center for Independent Living, 2539 Telegraph Ave in Berkeley (☎510/841-4776, *www.cilberkeley.org*) has long been one of the most effective organizations for people with disabilities in the world; it has a variety of counseling services.

National organizations facilitating travel for people with disabilities include SATH, the Society for the Advancement of Travelers with Handicaps (347 Fifth Ave, Suite 610, New York, NY 10016; ☎212/447-7284, *www.sath.org*), a nonprofit travel-industry grouping which includes travel agents, tour operators, hotel and airline management for people with disabilities. They will pass on any inquiry to the appropriate member; allow plenty of time for a response. Mobility International USA (PO Box 10767, Eugene, OR 97440; ☎541/343-1284, *www.miusa.org*) answers transportation queries and operates an exchange program for people with disabilities.

Other useful resources are *Travel for the Disabled*, *Wheelchair Vagabond* and *Directory for Travel Agencies for the Disabled*, all produced by **Twin Peaks Press**, PO Box 129, Vancouver, WA 98666 (☎1-800/637-2256 or 360/694-2462). Information-packed Web sites include Accessible San Diego at *www.accessandiego.org*, and Access-Able Travel Source at *www.access-able.com*.

ACCOMMODATION

The big motel and hotel chains are often the safest bet for accessible **accommodation**; there are plenty of excellent local alternatives, of course, but with a chain at least you'll know what to expect. At the higher end of the scale, *Embassy Suites* (☎1-800/362-2779, voice; 1-800/458-4708, TDD) have been working to implement new standards of access which meet and exceed ADA requirements, involving both new construction and the retrofitting of their one hundred existing hotels, and providing special training to all employees. Although the President of **Hyatt International Corporation** (☎1-800/233-1234) summed up the hotel industry's initial reaction to the ADA as "the end of the world as we know it," Hyatt has also committed itself to extensive redesign to improve accessibility.

THE GREAT OUTDOORS

Citizens or permanent residents of the US who have been "medically determined to be blind or permanently disabled" can obtain the **Golden Access Passport**, a free lifetime entrance pass to those federally operated parks, monuments, historic sites, recreation areas and wildlife refuges which charge entrance fees. The pass must be picked up in person, from the areas described, and it also provides a fifty percent discount on fees charged for facilities such as camping, boat launching and parking. The **Golden Bear Pass** (free to the disabled) offers similar concessions to state-run parks, beaches and historic sites.

For visitors to **national and state parks** the somewhat outdated *California Parks Access: A Complete Guide to the State and National Parks for Visitors With Limited Mobility* (Cougar Pass Pub Co]) is a great buy, with detailed descriptions of trails, sights and their access limitations.

Yosemite National Park (PO Box 577, Yosemite, CA 95389; ☎209/372-0296, voice; 209/372-4726, TDD) can supply general information direct, and wheelchairs are available to rent at the medical clinic (☎209/372-4637).

The **state parks** service also offers reduced rates for permanently disabled people who apply by mail for a Disabled Discount Pass ($3.50 once-only payment) to the California State Parks Store, PO Box 942896 Sacramento, CA 94296 (☎916/653-4000). The pass gives a fifty percent discount on all parking and camping fees above $3, except at Hearst Castle.

PACKAGES

Many US **tour companies** cater for disabled travelers or specialize in organizing disabled group tours. State tourist departments should be able to provide lists of such companies; failing that, ask the National Tour Association, 546 E Main St, PO Box 3071, Lexington, KY 40596 (☎1-800/755-8687 or 606/226-4444, fax 226-4414, *www.ntaonline.com*). They can put you in touch with operators whose tours match your needs.

TRAVELING WITH CHILDREN

Traveling with kids in California is relatively problem-free; children are readily accepted – indeed welcomed – in public places everywhere. Hotels and motels are well used to them (although some bed and breakfasts have a minimum age requirement of twelve – ask when making reservations), most state and national parks organize children's activities, every town or city has clean and safe playgrounds, and of course LA's Disneyland is the ultimate in kids' entertainment. Restaurants make considerable efforts to encourage parents to bring their offspring. All the national chains offer bolster chairs and a special kids' menu, packed with huge, excellent-value (though not necessarily healthy) meals – cheeseburger and fries for $2, and so on.

Local tourist offices (see p.25) can provide specific information on what California has to offer children, and various **guidebooks** have been written for parents traveling with children – try *The Unofficial Guide to California With Kids* ($17), in the Frommer's Family Guides list, and the very helpful *Trouble Free Travel with Children* ($6.95), available through Publishers MJF Books. John Muir Publications puts out a series of books for children, called *Kidding Around*, which tell about the history and describe the various sights of major US cities.

GETTING AROUND

Most families choose to travel **by car**, and while this is the least problematic way to get around, it's worth planning ahead to assure a pleasant trip. Don't set yourself unrealistic targets if you're hoping to enjoy a driving vacation with your kids – those long, boring journeys on the Interstate can be disastrous. If you're on a fly-drive vacation, note that when **renting a car** the company is legally obliged to provide free car seats for kids. RVs are also a good option for family travel, combining the convenience of built-in kitchens and bedrooms with the freedom of the road (see "Getting Around" on p.29 for details).

Children under 2 years old **fly** free on domestic routes, and for ten percent of the adult fare on international flights – though that doesn't mean they get a seat, let alone frequent-flier miles. When aged from 2 to 12 they are usually entitled to half-price tickets.

Traveling **by bus** may be the cheapest way to go, but it's also the most uncomfortable for kids. Under-2s travel (on your lap) for free; ages 2 to 11 are charged half the standard fare.

Taking the train is by far the best option for long journeys – not only does everyone get to enjoy the scenery, but you can get up and walk around, relieving pent-up energy. Most cross-country trains have sleeping compartments, which may be quite expensive but are likely to be seen as a great adventure. On Amtrak, two children aged between 2 and 15 can travel at half fare with each adult passenger.

SENIOR TRAVELERS

For many senior citizens, retirement brings the opportunity to explore the world in a style and at a pace that is the envy of younger travelers. As well as the obvious advantages of being free to travel for longer periods during the quieter, more congenial and less expensive seasons, anyone over the age of 62 can enjoy the tremendous variety of discounts available, but must produce suitable ID. Both Amtrak and Greyhound, for example, and many US airlines, offer (small-ish) percentage reductions on fares to older passengers.

Any US citizen or permanent resident aged 62 or over is entitled to free admission for life to all national parks, monuments and historic sites using a **Golden Age Passport**, for which a once-only $10 fee is charged; it can be issued at any such site. This free entry also applies to any accompanying car passengers in their car or, for those hiking or cycling, the passport-holder's immediate family. It also gives a fifty percent reduction on fees for camping, parking and boat launching.

The annual **Golden Bear Pass** ($5 to those 62 and over) offers a fifty percent discount on admission to state-run parks, beaches and historic sites, subject to a means test. There is also a Senior Citizen Discount (based on proof of age only) giving $1 off parking and $2 off family camping, except where the fee is less than $3.

Transport is cheaper too, with Amtrak giving a discount of fifteen percent on standard fares and Greyhound offering ten percent.

Museums, art galleries and even **hotels** offer small discounts, and since the definition of Senior can drop as low as 55, it is always worth asking.

The **American Association of Retired Persons**, 601 E St NW, Washington DC 20049 (☎1-800/424-3410 or 202/434-2277, *www.aarp.org*), membership of which is open to US residents aged 50 or over for an annual fee of $8, organizes group travel for senior citizens and can provide discounts on accommodation and vehicle rental.

GAY AND LESBIAN CALIFORNIA

The gay scene in California is huge, albeit heavily concentrated in the major cities. San Francisco, where between a quarter and a third of the voting population is reckoned to be gay or lesbian, is arguably the premier gay city of the world; Los Angeles and San Diego also have large gay populations, and up and down the coast gay men and women enjoy the kind of visibility and influence those in other places can only dream about. Gay politicians, and even police officers, are more than a novelty here and representation at every level is for real. Resources, places, facilities and organizations are endless.

In Los Angeles, the gay population has been growing steadily since the earliest days of the movie industry – a job which gave considerably greater freedom of lifestyle than most others at the time. Later, during World War II, the military purged suspected homosexuals at their point of embarkation. For those expecting to serve in the Pacific war zone, this meant they got off in San Francisco – where, unable to face the stigma of a return home, many remained, their ranks later swelled by gays who lost their government jobs during McCarthy's swipes of the 1950s.

In both these cities, the activism of the 1960s succeeded in highlighting gay issues, but they only developed into fully mainstream topics dur-

ing the 1970s, when, particularly in San Francisco, gays organized themselves into the largest and most influential minority group in the city. Politicians realized that the gay vote was the difference between winning and losing and quickly got on the case. In 1977, San Francisco got its first city official on the Board of Supervisors, the openly gay Harvey Milk. In 1978, he was assassinated by a former councilor, the conservative Dan White. After White received only a light jail sentence on the conviction of manslaughter, gays outraged over the verdict rioted around City Hall, torching several police cars during the process.

After the heady Seventies, however, and in the face of the AIDS crisis, the energies of gay men and women have been directed to the protection of existing rights and helping people affected by the disease. California has lost many to AIDS, but the state, perhaps more than anywhere else, has responded quickly and with compassion and intelligence: public health programs have had hitherto unheard of sums of money pumped into them, and attitudes across the board are broad-minded and supportive.

And nowadays, in San Francisco at least, to be an openly gay politician or businessperson is no more shocking than being a straight one. In the 1999 San Francisco mayoral race, gay politician Tom Ammiano captured a spot on the ballot with incumbent Willie Brown thanks to a write-in cam-

GAY AND LESBIAN PUBLICATIONS

National **publications** to look out for, most of which are available from any good bookstore, include the range of guides produced by The Damron Company (☎1-800/462-6654 or 415/255-0404; *www. damron.com*). These include the *Address Book* ($15.95), a pocket-sized yearbook full of listings of hotels, bars, clubs and resources for gay men; and the *Women's Traveler*, which provides similar listings for lesbians ($12.95). Other works to check out are the travel books published by **Ferrari** (☎602/863-2408; *www.q-net.com*). Also, keep a look out for the free *Columbia Fun Maps* (*www.funmaps.com*) – available at bars, clubs and bookstores in the US, Britain, France and Germany – that highlight gay-friendly establishments in California's larger cities.

The Advocate ($3.95; *www.advocate.com*) is a bimonthly national gay news magazine, with features, general info and classified ads (not to be confused with *Advocate Men*, which is a soft-porn magazine). The nation's most widely circulated gay and lesbian publication, *Out* ($4.95), is more progressive, though since it has recently been purchased by *The Advocate*, it remains to be seen how editorial content will be affected. *Instinct* (*www.instinctmag.com*) and *Genre* (*www.genremag.com*) are two more popular (if somewhat fluffy) nationals for gay men. For women, *Curve* (*www.curve.com*) is the leader, with *Girlfriends* (*www.gfriends.com*) running not far behind. Another useful lesbian publication is *Gaia's Guide* (132 W 24th St, New York, NY 10014; $6.95), a yearly international directory with a lot of US information.

paign, in which 25% of city voters wrote Ammiano's name on the ballot. Even though he lost the election a month later, the widespread popularity of the candidate showed that attitudes had improved dramatically since the days of Harvey Milk. In West Hollywood down the coast, an openly gay mayor, John Heilman, was elected; he is also the president of the Gay, Lesbian and Bisexual local official organization.

Ghettoization, then, is no longer a problem for Californian gays, although there are size-able, predominantly **gay areas** in almost all the major cities – San Diego's Hillcrest, Los Angeles' West Hollywood, San Francisco's Castro district – and both Guerneville and Palm Springs have earned gay resort status. However, although tolerance is high everywhere, the liberal attitudes of the major cities are not always reflected in the more isolated areas. For a complete rundown on local **resources**, **bars** and **clubs**, see the relevant city chapters of the guide.

BACKCOUNTRY CAMPING, HIKING AND WILDLIFE

California has some fabulous backcountry and wilderness areas, coated by dense forests and capped by great mountains. Unfortunately, while still immensely rewarding – California's landscape is one of *the* compelling reasons for coming – it isn't all as wild as it once was, thanks to the thousands who tramp through each year. If you're intending to do the same, you can help preserve the special qualities of the environment by observing a few simple rules. For practical information on traveling through the deserts, see the box on p.218.

The US's protected backcountry areas fall into a number of potentially confusing categories. Most numerous are **state parks**, owned and operated by the individual states. They include state beaches, state historic parks and state recreational areas, often around sites of geological or historical importance and not necessarily in rural areas. Daily fees are usually $4–6, though a $75 **annual pass** gives free access to most sites for a year.

National parks – such as Yosemite and Death Valley – are large, federally controlled and preserved areas of great natural beauty comprising

BACKCOUNTRY DANGERS AND WILDLIFE

You're likely to meet many kinds of **wildlife** and come upon unexpected **hazards** on your travels through the wilderness, but only a few are likely to cause problems. With due care, many potential difficulties can be avoided.

Hiking in the **foothills** should not be problematic, but you should check your clothes frequently for **ticks** – pesky bloodsucking burrowing insects which are known to carry Lyme disease. If you have been bitten, and especially if you get flu-like symptoms, get advice from a park ranger. Also annoying around water are **mosquitoes**; carry candles scented with citronella or insect repellent to keep them at bay.

Other than in a National Park, you're highly unlikely to encounter a **bear**. Even there, it's rare to stumble across one in the wilderness, and if you do it will be a black bear – the last California grizzly was shot in 1922. To reduce the likelihood of an unwanted encounter, make noise as you walk. If you see a bear before it detects you (they've got poor eyesight but an acute sense of smell), give it a wide berth; but if a bear visits your camp, scare it off by yelling and banging pots and pans. Basically, the bear isn't interested in you but your food, and you should do everything you can to prevent them from getting it – bears who successfully raid campsites can become dependent on human food. Bears within state and national parks are protected, but if they spend too much time around people the park rangers are, depressingly, left with no option but to shoot them. Some campgrounds are equipped with steel **bear lockers**, which you are obliged to use for storing food when not preparing or eating it. In the backcountry, you are strongly advised to store food in your pack within a hard plastic **bear-resistant food canister**. These can be purchased ($65–75) or rented (usually $3 a day) from camp stores in Yosemite, Kings Canyon and Sequoia National Parks. The alternatives are far inferior. Hanging food in a tree is a disaster, as Sierra bears simply chew through the supporting rope. The recommended variation is the **counterbalance method** (where food is balanced over a high tree branch in two equally weighted sacks on the opposite ends of a rope – see park literature for more information), but your chances of finding a suitable tree after a long days' hike are slim. Finally, never feed a bear or get between a mother and her cubs. Young animals are cute; irate mothers are not.

Rattlesnakes, which live in the desert areas and drier foothills up to around 6000ft, seldom attack unless provoked: do not tease or try to handle them. Rattlesnake bites are rarely fatal but you might suffer severe tissue damage (see p.219 for advice on what to do if bitten).

several different features or ecosystems; entry fees range from $5 for Death Valley to $20 for Yosemite. These are supplemented by the smaller **national monuments** (free to $5), like Devil's Postpile, with just one major feature, and **national seashores**. If you plan on visiting a few of these, invest in a **Golden Eagle Passport** ($50 cash from any national park entrance), which grants both driver and passengers (or if cycling or hiking, the holder's immediate family) twelve months' access to all the national parks, monuments and seashores across the country. Excellent free **ranger programs** – such as guided walks or slide shows – are held throughout the year. The federal government also operates **national recreation areas**, often huge hydro dams where you can jetski or windsurf free from the necessarily restrictive laws of the national parks. Campgrounds and equipment-rental outlets are always abundant.

California's eighteen **national forests** cover twenty percent of the state's surface area. Most of them border the national parks, and are also federally administered (by the US Forest Service), but with much less protection. More roads run through national forests, and often there is some limited logging and other land-based industry operated on a supposedly sustainable basis.

All the above forms of protected land can contain **wilderness areas**, which aim to protect natural resources in their most native state. In practice this means there's no commercial activity at all; buildings, motorized vehicles and bicycles are not permitted, nor are firearms and pets. Overnight camping is allowed, but **wilderness permits** (free–$1) must be obtained in advance from the land management agency responsible. In California, Lava Beds, Lassen, Death Valley, Sequoia-Kings Canyon, Joshua Tree, Pinnacles, Point Reyes and Yosemite all have large wilder-

Mountain lions (cougars, panthers or pumas) are being hard hit by increasing urban expansion into former habitats (from deserts to coastal and sub-alpine forests). Sightings are rare in the newly suburbanized areas, and there have been few attacks on pedestrians. But to reduce the already slim chance of an unwanted encounter, avoid walking by yourself, especially after dark, when lions tend to hunt. Make noise as you walk, wield a stick and keep children close to you. If you encounter one, don't run. Instead, face the lion and make yourself appear larger by raising your arms, or holding your coat above you, and it will probably back away. If not, throw rocks and sticks in its vicinity.

Campsite critters – ground squirrels, chipmunks and raccoons – are usually just a nuisance, though they tend to carry diseases and you should avoid contact. Only the marmot is a real pest, as it likes to chew through radiator hoses and car electrics to reach a warm engine on a cold night. Before setting off in the morning, check the motor for gnawed components, otherwise you might find yourself with a seized engine and a cooked or, at best, terrified marmot as a passenger. Boots and rucksacks also can fall prey to marmot scrutiny.

Poison oak is one thing that isn't going to come and get you, though you may come up against it. Recognized by its shiny configuration of three dark-green veined leaves (turning red or yellow in autumn) that secrete an oily juice, this twiggy shrub or climbing vine is found in open woods or along stream banks throughout much of California. It's highly allergenic, so avoid touching it. If you do, washing with strong soap, taking frequent dips in the sea and applying cortisone cream usually helps relieve the symptoms in mild cases; in extreme cases, see a doctor.

In the mountains, your biggest dangers have nothing to do with the flora or fauna. Late **snows** are common, giving rise to the possibility of avalanches and meltwaters, which make otherwise simple stream crossings hazardous. **Drowning** in fast-flowing meltwater rivers is the single biggest cause of death in the Kings Canyon and Sequoia National Parks. The riverbanks are strewn with large, slippery boulders – keep well clear unless you are specifically there for river activities.

With much of the High Sierra above 10,000ft, **Acute Mountain Sickness** (aka altitude sickness) is always a possibility. Only those planning to bag one of the 14,000-foot peaks are likely to have to contend with much more than a slight headache, but it pays to be on the alert and to acclimatize slowly. Try to limit your exertions for the first day or so, drink plenty of fluids, eat little and often, and note any nausea, headaches or double vision. If you experience any of these symptoms, the only solution is to descend until they ease, then ascend more gradually.

For more on the hazards of snakes and spiders, see Chapter Three, p.219, and for more on Californian wildlife generally, see p.657 of "Contexts."

ness areas – 94 percent of Yosemite – with only the regions near roads, visitor centers and buildings designated as less stringently regulated "front country."

CAMPING

When **camping rough**, check that fires are permitted before you start one; if they are, use a stove in preference to local materials – in some places firewood is scarce, although you may be allowed to use deadwood. No open fires are allowed in wilderness areas, where you should also try to camp on previously used sites. Where there are no toilets, **bury human waste** at least four inches into the ground and a hundred feet from the nearest water supply and camp. Always **pack out what you pack in** (or more if you come across some other inconsiderate soul's litter), and avoid the old advice to burn rubbish; wildfires have been started in this way. A growing problem is Giardia, a water-borne protozoan causing an intestinal disease, symptoms of which are chronic diarrhea, abdominal cramps, fatigue and loss of weight, that requires treatment. To avoid catching it, **never drink** directly from rivers and streams, no matter how clear and inviting they may look (you never know what unspeakable acts people – or animals – further upstream have performed in them). Before you drink **water** that isn't from taps, it should be boiled for at least five minutes, or cleansed with an iodine-based purifier (such as Potable Aqua) or a Giardia-rated filter, available from camping and sports shops.

Finally, don't use **soaps or detergents** (even special ecological or biodegradable soaps) anywhere near lakes and streams; folk using water purifiers or filters downstream won't thank you at all. Instead carry water at least a hundred feet (preferably two hundred) from the water's edge before washing.

CAMPING EQUIPMENT

Choose your tent wisely. Many Sierra sites are on rock with only a thin covering of soil, so driving pegs in can be a problem. Free-standing dome-style tents are therefore preferable. Go for one with a large area of mosquito netting and a removable fly sheet: tents designed for harsh European winters can get horribly sweaty once the sun rises.

Most developed campgrounds are equipped with fire rings with some form of grill for cooking, but many people prefer a **Coleman stove**, powered by white gas (a kind of super-clean gasoline). Both stoves and white gas (also used for MSR backcountry stoves) are widely available in camping stores. Other camping stoves are less common. Equipment using butane and propane – Camping Gaz and, to a lesser extent, EPI gas, Scorpion and Optimus – is on the rise, though outside of major camping areas you'll be pushed to find supplies: stock up when you can. If you need methylated spirits for your Trangia, go to a hardware store and ask for denatured alcohol.

HIKING

Wilderness areas start close to the main areas of national parks. There is normally no problem entering the wilderness for day walks, but overnight trips require **wilderness permits** (see above). In peak periods, a quota system operates for the most popular paths, so if there's a hike you specifically want to do, obtain your permit well ahead of time (at least two weeks, more for popular hikes). When completing the form for your permit, be sure to ask a park ranger for weather conditions and general information about the hike you're undertaking.

Hikes covered in the guide (usually appearing in boxes) are given with length and estimated walking time for a healthy, but not especially fit, adult. **State parks** have graded trails designed for people who drive to the corner store, so anyone used to walking and with a moderate degree of fitness will find these ratings conservative.

In California, the **Sierra Club** (c/o Outings Dept, 85 Second St, Second Floor, San Francisco, CA 94105, ☎415/977-5500, *www.sierraclub.org*) offers a range of backcountry hikes into otherwise barely accessible parts of the High Sierra wilderness, with food and guide provided. The tours are summer-only, and are heavily subscribed, making it essential to book at least three months in advance. You can expect to pay $500–600 for seven to ten days and will also have to pay $35 to join the club.

SPORTS AND OUTDOOR PURSUITS

Nowhere in the country do the various forms of athletic activity and competition have a higher profile than in California. The big cities generally have at least one team in each of the major professional sports – football (though LA lost its last football team to Oakland in 1995), baseball and basketball – as well as supporting teams in soccer, volleyball, ice hockey, wrestling and even roller derby.

For foreign visitors, American sports can appear something of a mystery, not least the passion for **intercollegiate sports** – college and university teams, competing against one another in the Pacific-10 Conference, usually with an enthusiasm fueled by passionate local rivalries. In Los Angeles, USC and UCLA have an intense and high-powered sporting enmity, with fans on each side as vociferous as any European soccer crowd, and in the San Francisco Bay Area, the rivalry between UC Berkeley and Stanford is akin to that of Britain's Oxford and Cambridge.

And in California, where being physically fit and adventurous often appears to be a condition of state citizenship, the locals are passionate about their outdoor pursuits; the most popular include surfing, cycling and skiing. When and where to enjoy any of California's most popular outdoor pursuits are detailed in the relevant chapters of the guide, along with listings of guides and facilities.

FOOTBALL

Football in America attracts the most obsessive and devoted fans of any sport, perhaps because there are fewer games played – only sixteen in a season, which lasts throughout the fall and culminates in the **Super Bowl** at the end of January. With many quick skirmishes and military-like movements up and down the field, it's ideal for television, and nowhere is this more apparent than during the **televised games** which are a feature of many bars on Monday nights – though most games are played on Sundays.

The game lasts for four fifteen-minute quarters, with a fifteen-minute break at half-time. But since time is only counted when play is in progress, matches can take up to three hours to complete, mainly due to interruptions for TV advertising. Commentators will discuss the game throughout to help your comprehension, though they use such a barrage of statistics to illustrate their remarks that you may feel hopelessly confused. Not that it matters – the spectacle of American football is fun to experience, even if you haven't a clue what's going on. Players tend to be huge, averaging about six foot five and weighing upwards of three hundred pounds; they look even bigger when they're suited up for battle in shoulder pads and helmets. The best players become nationally known celebrities, raking in millions of dollars in fees for product endorsements on top of astronomical salaries.

TEAMS AND TICKETS

All major teams play in the **National Football League** (NFL), the sport's governing body, which divides the teams into two conferences of equal stature, the **National Football Conference** (NFC) and the **American Football Conference** (AFC). In turn, each conference is split into three divisions, East, Central and West. For the end of season playoffs, the best team in each of the six divisions, plus three wildcards from each conference, fight it out for the title.

The Californian teams are the Oakland Raiders and the San Diego Chargers – neither of which do tremendously well – and the San Francisco 49ers, usually near the top of the NFL though currently languishing with an ageing team. There are no second division equivalents, though the college teams, particularly USC and UCLA, serve as a training ground for future NFL stars.

Tickets cost $20–80 for professional games, and college games can be as low as $5. To **book tickets** call:

NFL	☎212/450-2000
(*www.nfl.com*)	
San Diego Chargers	☎619/280-2112
(*www.chargers.com*)	
San Francisco 49ers	☎415/656-4900
(*www.sf49ers.com*)	
Oakland Raiders	☎1-888/44-RAIDERS
(*www.raiders.com*)	

BASEBALL

Baseball, much like cricket in its relaxed, summertime pace and seemingly Byzantine rules, is often called "America's pastime." Its image was somewhat tarnished by the bitter players' strike which shortened the 1994 season and saw the unthinkable canceling of the **World Series**. But the sheen was restored in 1998, when the back-slapping rivalry between Mark McGwire and Sammy Sosa captured the nation as they both closed on Roger Maris' home-run record. McGwire smashed the record with an astounding seventy home runs.

Games are played – 162 each season– all over the US almost every day from April to September, with the league championships and the World Series, the final best-of-seven play-off, lasting through October. Watching a game, even if you don't understand what's going on, can be at the least a pleasant day out, drinking beer and eating hot dogs in the bleachers (unshaded benches) beyond the outfield; tickets in this area are cheap and the crowds usually friendly and sociable.

TEAMS AND TICKETS

All Major League Baseball teams play in either the **National League** or the **American League**, each of equal stature and split into three divisions, East, Central and West. For the end of season playoffs and the World Series, the best team in each of the six divisions plus a second-place wildcard from each conference fight it out for the title.

California's Major League clubs are the **Oakland A's, Los Angeles Dodgers, San Diego Padres, Anaheim Angels** and the **San Francisco Giants**. In addition, there are also numerous **minor league** clubs, known as **farm teams** because they supply the top clubs with talent. Details are included in relevant chapters of the guide.

Tickets for games cost $5–75 per seat, and are generally available on the day of the game. To book tickets call:

Major League	☎212/931-7800
(*www.majorleaguebaseball.com*)	
National League	☎212/931-7700
American League	☎212/931-7600
Los Angeles Dodgers	☎323/224-1448
(*www.dodgers.com*)	
San Diego Padres	☎619/297-2373
(*www.padres.com*)	
San Francisco Giants	☎510/762-2255
(*www.sfgiants.com*)	
Anaheim Angels	☎714/663-9000
(*www.angelsbaseball.com*)	
Oakland A's	☎510/762-2255
(*www.oaklandathletics.com*)	

BASKETBALL

Basketball is one of the few professional sports that is also actually played by many ordinary Americans, since all you need is a ball and a hoop. It's a particularly popular sport in low-income, inner-city areas, where school playgrounds are packed with young hopefuls.

The professional game is governed by the National Basketball Association (NBA), who oversee a season running from November until the playoffs in May. It is played by athletes of phenomenal agility; seven-foot-tall giants who float through the air over a wall of equally tall defenders, seeming to change direction in mid-flight before slam-dunking the ball (smashing it through the hoop with such force that the backboard sometimes shatters) to score two points. Games last for an exhausting 48 minutes of playing time, around two hours total.

TEAMS AND TICKETS

California's basketball teams include the **Los Angeles Lakers**, the Golden State **Warriors** (who play in Oakland), the Sacramento **Kings** and the Los Angeles **Clippers**. LA's **UCLA** dominated the college game, winning national championships throughout the 1960s; they emerged to win again in 1995. **USC**, **UC Berkeley** and **Stanford** also field perpetually competitive intercollegiate teams, the latter victorious in 1999.

Tickets cost $15–80 for professional games, $4–10 for college games. To book tickets call:

NBA	☎212/407-8000
(*www.nba.com*)	
Golden State Warriors	☎510/986-2200
(*www.nba.com/warriors*)	
Los Angeles Clippers)	☎213/745-0400
(*www.nba.com/clippers*)	
Los Angeles Lakers	☎310/419-3865
(*www.nba.com/lakers*)	
Sacramento Kings	☎916/928-0000
(*www.nba.com/kings*)	

WOMEN'S BASKETBALL

Two **women's basketball** leagues, the **WNBA** and the **ABL** (American Basketball League) were launched amidst a media blitz in late 1996. Both leagues enjoyed considerable success in their inaugural seasons, but the financial and marketing support from the NBA has left the WNBA dominant.

TEAMS AND TICKETS

Starting at about $8, tickets are much more reasonable than their NBA counterparts, and if you don't mind rooting for a bunch of talented players who you've probably never heard of, the action can be quite exciting. The WNBA's season takes place in the summer.

WNBA	☎212/688-9622
(*www.wnba.com*)	
Los Angeles Sparks	☎310/330-2434
(*www.wnba.com/sparks*)	
Sacramento Monarchs	☎916/928-3650
(*www.wnba.com/monarchs*)	

ICE HOCKEY

Despite California's sun and sand reputation, **ice hockey** enjoys considerable popularity in the state, although most of the players are imported from more traditionally hockey-centric regions in Canada, Eastern Europe and Scandinavia. A considerable rivalry has developed over the years between players from the United States and Canada, owing largely to Canada's fear of losing their long-time claim as the world's premier hockey nation. As heavy favorites in the 1998 Winter Olympics, however, the over-confident US and Canadian national teams were both humiliated by the Czech Republic, Russia, and Finland.

THE RULES OF FOOTBALL

The rules of **American football** are fairly simple: the **field** is 100 yards long by 40 yards wide, with **end-zones** at each end. There are two teams of eleven men actually on the field, but the freedom to swap players at will means that each side might have up to eighty players arranged into offensive, defensive, kicking and other specialist teams. The game begins with a **kickoff**, after which the team in possession of the ball tries to move downfield to score a **touchdown**, while the opposing team tries to stop them. The attacking team has four chances to move the ball forward ten yards and gain a **first down**; otherwise they forfeit possession to the opposition. After the kickoff, the **quarterback**, the leader of the attack, either hands the ball off to a **running back**, or throws the ball through the air downfield to a **receiver**. Play ends when the man with the ball is tackled to the ground (or runs out of bounds), or if the pass attempt falls incomplete.

A **touchdown**, worth six points, is made when a player crosses into the defending team's end-zone carrying the ball; unlike in rugby, no actual touching down is necessary, it is enough just to carry the ball over the line. After a touchdown, the scoring team has one attempt at an "extra point" by either kicking a field goal (1 point) or crossing into the endzone (2 points) from three yards out. A regular **field goal**, worth three points, is scored when the **place-kicker** – always the smallest man on the team and often the lone foreigner – kicks the ball, as in rugby, through the **goalposts** that stand in the endzone. If the attacking team has failed to move the ball within scoring range, and seems unlikely to gain the required ten yards for another first down, they can elect to **punt** the ball, kicking it to the other.

A change of possession can also occur if the opposition players manage to **intercept** an attempted pass or force a **fumble**, taking the ball away from a runner.

THE RULES OF BASEBALL

The setup for **baseball** looks like the English game of rounders, with four **bases** set at the corners of a 90-foot diamond. The base at the bottom corner is called **home plate**, and serves much the same purpose as do the stumps in cricket. Play begins when the **pitcher**, standing on a pitcher's mound in the middle of the diamond, throws the ball at speeds up to a hundred miles an hour, making it curve and bend as it travels towards the **catcher**, who crouches behind home plate; seven other defensive players take up **positions**, one at each base and the others spread out around the field of play.

A **batter** from the opposing team stands beside home plate and tries to hit the ball. If the batter swings and misses, or if the pitched ball crosses the plate above the batter's knees and below his chest, it counts as a **strike**; if he doesn't swing and the ball passes outside this **strike zone**, it counts as a **ball** – equivalent to a "no ball" in cricket. If the batter gets **three strikes** against him he is **out**; four balls and he gets a free **walk**, and takes his place as a runner on first base. Foul balls, hit out of the field of play count as a strike, but a player cannot strike out (get a third strike) on a foul ball.

If he succeeds in hitting the pitched ball into **fair territory** (the wedge between the first and third bases), the batter runs toward first base; if the opposing players catch the ball before it hits the ground, the batter is **out**. Otherwise they field the ball and attempt to relay it to first base before the batter gets there; if they fail he is **safe** – and stays there, being moved along by subsequent batters until he makes a complete circuit and scores a **run**. The most exciting moment in baseball is the **home run**, when a batter hits the ball over the outfield fences, a boundary some 400 feet away from home plate; he and any runners on base when he hits the ball each score a run. If there are runners on all three bases it's called a **grand slam**.

The nine players per side bat in rotation; each side gets three outs per innings, and there are nine innings per game – the "top" of the innings is when the first team (always the visiting team) is batting, or is about to bat; the "bottom" of the innings is during the second team's turn. Games normally last two to three hours, and are never tied; if the scores are level after nine innings, extra innings are played until one side pulls ahead and wins.

TEAMS AND TICKETS

California boasts three **NHL** (National Hockey League) teams, and although all are mediocre, they still manage to draw considerable crowds; the **San Jose Sharks** sell out nearly every game. **Tickets** start at about $15. Call on the following numbers:

NHL (*www.nhl.com*)	☎212/789-2000
San Jose Sharks (*www.sj-sharks.com*)	☎408/287-7070
Los Angeles Kings (*www.lakings.com*)	☎310/419-3160
Mighty Ducks of Anaheim (*www.mightyducks.com*)	☎714/704-2700

SOCCER

In the main, the traditional American sports rule, but **soccer** is quickly gaining ground. At the professional level, the successful US bid to host the **1994 World Cup** led to the establishment of **Major League Soccer** (MLS; *www.mlsnet.com*) in 1996. The game continues to get injections of exposure with the national men's team earning a place in the **1998 World Cup** finals in France (though they didn't progress beyond the first round), and the US Women's team beating China in a nail-biting penalty shoot-out to win the **1999 Women's World Cup** in Anaheim. President Clinton was in the stands, and the win made the headlines across the nation.

The Los Angeles Galaxy and San Jose Clash both play in the Western Conference of the MSL; LA having twice reached the MSL Cup final, only to be beaten by DC United on both occasions. The season runs through the summer and tickets cost $8–30. To book tickets, call:

Los Angeles Galaxy (*www.lagalaxy.com*)	☎1-888/657-5425
San Jose Clash) (*www.clash.com*)	☎408/985-4625

OUTDOOR PURSUITS

Surfing is probably the best-known Californian pastime, immortalized in the songs of the Beach Boys and Frankie Avalon. The Southern California coast up to San Francisco is dotted with excellent surfing beaches. Some of the finest places to catch a wave, with or without a board, are at Tourmaline Beach near San Diego,

Huntington Beach and Malibu in Los Angeles, along the coast north of Santa Barbara, and at Santa Cruz – where there's a small but worthy surfing museum.

Cycling is an extremely popular outdoor pursuit, with California home to some highly competitive, world-class road races, particularly around the Wine Country. The heavy-duty, all-terrain **mountain bike** was invented here, designed to tackle the slopes of Mount Tamalpais in Marin County. Weekend enthusiasts now put their knobby tires to use on the countless trails that weave throughout California's beautiful backcountry. Special mountain bike parks, most of them operating in summer only, exploit the groomed, snowfree runs of the Sierra ski bowls of Lake Tahoe and Mammoth. In such places, and throughout California, you can rent bikes for $20–30 a day; see "Getting Around," p.35, for more on general cycling.

Skiing and **snowboarding** are also wildly popular, with downhill resorts all over eastern California – where, believe it or not, it snows heavily most winters. In fact, the Sierra Nevada mountains offer some of the best skiing in the US, particularly around Lake Tahoe, where the 1960 Winter Olympics were held (see p.574). You can rent equipment for about $40 a weekend, plus another $35 to $55 a day for lift tickets.

A cheaper option is **cross-country skiing**, or ski-touring. A number of backcountry ski lodges in the Sierra Nevada offer a range of rustic accommodation, equipment rental and lessons, from as little as $20 a day for skis, boots and poles, up to about $200 for an all-inclusive weekend tour.

California also has some of the world's best **rafting** rivers, the best of which cascade off the western side of the Sierra Nevada. Most rivers are highly seasonal, normally running best from mid-April to the end of June. Rivers and rapids are classed according to a grading system, ranging from a Class I, which is painstakingly easy, to a Class VI, which is literally dicing with death. Trips can be as short as a couple of hours, taking in the best a river has to offer (or just the most accessible section), or can extend up to several days, allowing more time to hike up side canyons, swim or just laze about on the bank. You might typically expect to pay around $100 for a four- to six-hour trip, going up to $130–150 a day for longer outings, including food and camping equipment rental.

FESTIVALS AND PUBLIC HOLIDAYS

Someone, somewhere is always celebrating something in California, although apart from national holidays, few festivities are shared throughout the entire state. Instead, there is a disparate multitude of local events: art and craft shows, county fairs, ethnic celebrations, music festivals, rodeos, sandcastle building competitions, and many others of every hue and shade.

Among California's major annual events are the **gay and lesbian freedom** parades held in June in LA and, particularly, San Francisco; the **Academy Awards** in LA in March, and the world-class **Monterey Jazz Festival** in September. These and other local highlights are covered in the text. In addition, California tourist offices can provide full lists, or you can just phone the visitor center in a particular region ahead of your arrival and ask what's coming up.

PUBLIC HOLIDAYS

The biggest and most all-American of the **national festivals and holidays** is **Independence Day** on the Fourth of July, when the entire country grinds to a standstill as people get drunk, salute the flag and take part in firework displays, marches, beauty pageants and more, all in commemoration of the signing of the Declaration of Independence in 1776. **Halloween** (October 31) lacks any such patriotic overtones, and is not a public holiday despite being one of the most popular yearly flings. Traditionally, kids run around the streets banging on doors demanding "trick or treat," and are given pieces of candy. These days that sort of activity is mostly confined to rural and suburban areas, while in bigger cities Halloween has grown into a massive gay celebration: in West Hollywood in LA and San Francisco's Castro district, the night is marked by mass crossdressing, huge block parties and general licentiousness. More sedate is **Thanksgiving Day**, on the last Thursday in November. The third big event of the year is essentially a domestic affair, when relatives return to the familial nest to stuff themselves with roast turkey, and (supposedly) fondly recall the first harvest of the Pilgrims in Massachusetts – though in fact Thanksgiving was already a national holiday before anyone thought to make that connection.

On the national **public holidays** listed below, banks and offices are liable to be closed all day, and shops may reduce their hours. The traditional **summer season** for tourism runs from **Memorial Day to Labor Day**, though California's benign weather extends that considerably, and the desert areas have their peak season through the winter.

January 1 **New Year's Day**

January 15 **Martin Luther King Jr's Birthday**

Third Monday in February **Presidents' Day**

Varies (usually early April) **Easter Monday**

Last Monday in May **Memorial Day**

July 4 **Independence Day**

First Monday in September **Labor Day**

Second Monday in October **Columbus Day**

November 11 **Veterans' Day**

Last Thursday in November **Thanksgiving Day**

December 25 **Christmas Day**

DIRECTORY FOR OVERSEAS VISITORS

ADDRESSES Though initially confusing for overseas visitors, American addresses are masterpieces of logical thinking. Generally speaking, roads in built-up areas are laid out to a grid system, creating "blocks" of buildings: addresses of buildings refer to the block, which will be numbered in sequence, from a central point usually downtown; for example, 620 S Cedar will be six blocks south of downtown. In small towns, and parts of larger cities, "streets" and "avenues" often run north–south and east–west respectively; streets are usually named (sometimes alphabetically), avenues generally numbered.

CIGARETTES AND SMOKING Smoking is a much-frowned-upon activity in the US, and especially so in California which recently banned smoking in all indoor public places, including bars and restaurants. In fact, it's quite possible to spend a month in the States without ever smelling tobacco. Cigarettes are sold in virtually any food shop, drugstore or bar, and also from vending machines. A packet of twenty costs around $2.50 – much cheaper than in Britain – though many smokers buy cigarettes by the carton for around $18.

DEPARTURE TAX All airport, customs and security taxes are included in the price of your ticket.

DRUGS Possession of under an ounce of the widely consumed marijuana is a misdemeanor in California, and the worst you'll get is a $200 fine. Being caught with more than an ounce, however, means facing a criminal charge for dealing, and a possible prison sentence – stiffer if caught anywhere near a school. Other drugs are, of course, completely illegal and it's a much more serious offense if you're caught with any.

ELECTRICITY 110V AC. The insubstantial two-pronged plugs have now largely been replaced by a more sturdy three-pronged affair. Some travel plug adapters don't fit American sockets.

FLOORS In the US, what would be the ground floor in Britain is the first floor, the first floor the second floor and so on.

ID Should be carried at all times. Two pieces should diffuse any suspicion, one of which should have a photo: driving license, passport and credit card(s) are your best bets.

MEASUREMENTS AND SIZES The US has yet to go metric, so measurements are in inches, feet, yards and miles; weight in ounces, pounds and tons. American pints and gallons are about four-fifths of Imperial ones. Clothing sizes are always two figures less what they would be in Britain – a British women's size 12 is a US size 10 – while British shoe sizes are half a size below American ones for women, and one size below for men.

TIME California runs on Pacific Standard Time (PST), eight hours behind GMT in winter and three hours behind the East Coast. British Summer Time runs almost concurrent with US Daylight Saving Time – implemented from the last Sunday in April to the last Sunday in October – causing a seven-hour time difference for two weeks of the year.

TIPPING You really shouldn't leave a bar or restaurant without leaving a tip of at least fifteen percent and about the same should be added to taxi fares. A hotel porter should get roughly $1 for each bag carried to your room. When paying by credit card you're expected to add the tip to the total bill before filling in the amount and signing.

VIDEOS The standard format used for video cassettes in the US is different from that used in Britain and Australasia, though many modern VCRs will play both formats. You cannot buy videos in the US compatible with a video camera bought in Britain.

WHALE-WATCHING During November and December, Californian gray whales migrate from the Arctic to their breeding grounds off the coast of Baja California, making their return journey during February and March. Along the coast in these months you'll often find open-air whale-themed events, generally with a display or talk about the whales, and with food, drink and even music supplied, as people peer out to the ocean hoping for (and usually getting) a glimpse of the great creatures.

PART TWO

THE
GUIDE

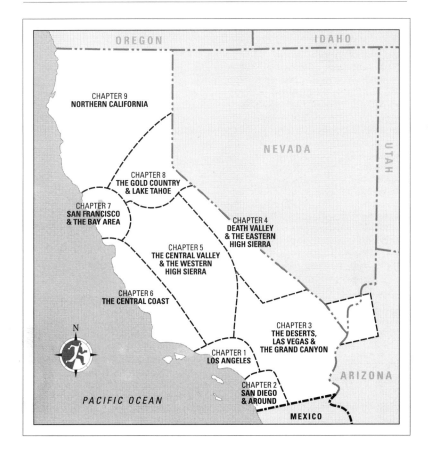

CHAPTER 9
NORTHERN CALIFORNIA

OREGON

IDAHO

NEVADA

UTAH

CHAPTER 8
**THE GOLD COUNTRY
& LAKE TAHOE**

CHAPTER 7
**SAN FRANCISCO
& THE BAY AREA**

CHAPTER 4
**DEATH VALLEY
& THE EASTERN
HIGH SIERRA**

CHAPTER 5
**THE CENTRAL VALLEY
& THE WESTERN
HIGH SIERRA**

CHAPTER 6
THE CENTRAL COAST

N

CHAPTER 3
**THE DESERTS,
LAS VEGAS &
THE GRAND CANYON**

CHAPTER 1
LOS ANGELES

ARIZONA

CHAPTER 2
**SAN DIEGO
& AROUND**

PACIFIC OCEAN

MEXICO

CHAPTER ONE

LOS ANGELES

T he rambling metropolis of **LOS ANGELES** sprawls across the floor of a great desert basin in a colorful jangle of fast-food joints, shopping malls, palm trees and swimming pools, bordered by snowcapped mountains and the Pacific Ocean, and stitched together by an intricate network of high-speed freeways rising above a thousand square miles of architectural anarchy. It's an extremely visual, often voyeuristic, city, and famously hard to make sense of – understandable, in F. Scott Fitzgerald's phrase, "only dimly, and in flashes."

For all that, LA can surprise you with a powerful sense of familiarity. The entertainment industry has been popularizing the city ever since filmmakers arrived in the 1910s, attracted by a climate that allowed them to film outdoors year-round, plenty of open land on which to build elaborate sets, nearby landscapes varied enough to form an imaginary backdrop to just about anywhere in the world, and of course, the ever-popular lures of cheap labor and low taxes. Since then, the money and glamour of Hollywood have enticed countless thousands of would-be actors, writers, designers and, more recently, rock stars. The myth of overnight success is intrinsic to the LA mind-set, but so is the reality of sudden disaster: floods, fires and earthquakes are facts of life here, and the coexistence of both extremes lends a perilous, almost unhinged personality to the city. Simply put, LA is like nowhere else on earth. Mud-wrestling venues and porn cinemas stand next door to quality bookstores and trendy restaurants, in a relentless but strangely addictive assault on the senses that can make everywhere else seem somehow tame and predictable.

Originally settled by Chumash and Tongva native tribes a thousand years before the arrival of eighteenth-century Spanish settlers, the LA region soon became a staging ground for part of Junipero Serra's string of 21 Franciscan missions. Later subdivided into Mexican "ranchos" and usurped by the expanding United States, until just over a century ago LA was a multicultural community of white American immigrants, poor Chinese laborers and wealthy Mexican ranchers, with a population of under fifty thousand. Only on completion of the transcontinental railroad in the 1880s did the city really begin to grow, consistently doubling in population every ten years. Hundreds of thousands descended upon the basin, drawn by the prospect of living in a subtropical paradise. Ranches were subdivided into innumerable suburban lots and scores of new towns, and land speculators marketed an enduring image of Los Angeles, epitomized by the family-sized suburban house (with swimming pool and two-car garage) set amid the orange groves in a glorious land of sunshine. The boom years came after World War II when many of the veterans who had passed through on their way to the South Pacific came back to stay, buying government-subsidized houses and finding well-paid work in the mushrooming aeronautics industry.

After the Cold War, though, Southern California was hit very hard by cutbacks in defense spending, particularly in the aeronautics industry. Unemployment reached a peak of ten percent, with crime rocketing as a result. Joblessness is now back down around five percent in the region, but the conservative suburb of Orange County, also known as the Orange Curtain, is still in a state of shock nicknamed White Fright. Despite the local crime rate improving along with the late-1990s economy (mostly reflecting national trends instead of any real improvement), suburban residents continue to fear the

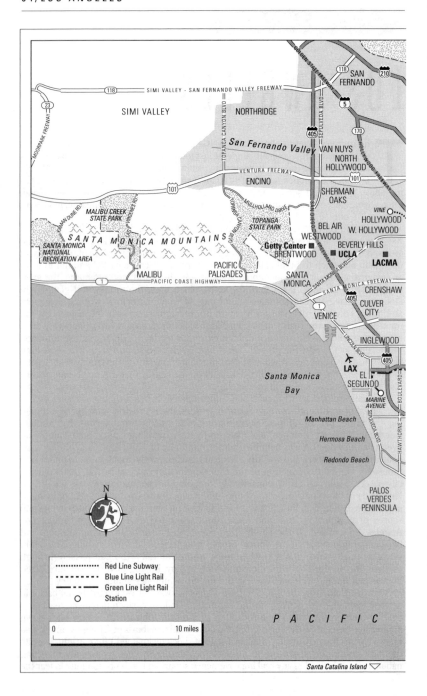

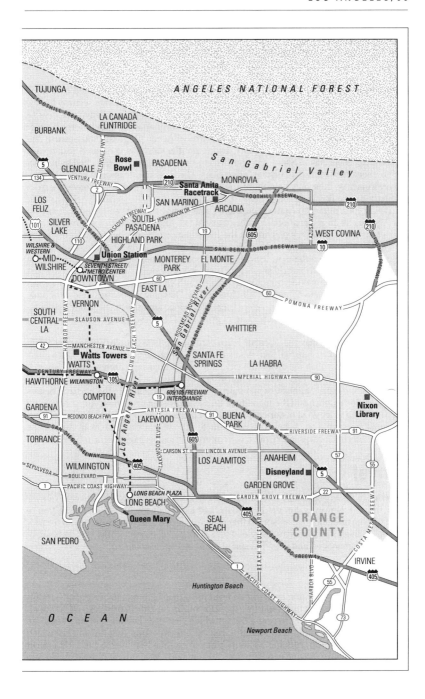

> Because the Los Angeles region has eight telephone **area codes** – ☎213, ☎310, ☎323, ☎562, ☎626, ☎714, ☎818 and ☎949 – we have included the code before each number.

lurking menace of LA crime, so much so that they have retreated into "gated communities," housing estates with boundary fences and roads patrolled by private security forces. Safely locked in, they voted in 1994 for Proposition 187, a state law denying access to health and education services to illegal (mostly Latino) immigrants, and more recently for ballot measures designed to undercut Affirmative Action programs and Spanish language instruction. Despite the hostility, Latino immigration has continued to increase dramatically, especially in Santa Ana and Garden Grove, and once-entrenched suburbanites now seek new refuges in distant "edge cities" like Rancho Cucamonga and Palmdale, where, ironically, their only neighbors are state prisons stocked with LA convicts – from whom they once fled in terror.

In LA proper, numerous glossy museums, built during the last two decades, maintain Los Angeles as an international center of visual art, and the forest of Downtown skyscrapers is proof of its key position as the high-finance gateway between America and the Far East. But the extent of the contradictions involved in dwelling in – and visiting – a metropolis that contains at least 100,000 homeless alongside some of the highest standards of living in the world are never far away. Race rioting has been as much a part of LA history as filmmaking. Eight years on in South Central, the underlying social factors behind 1992's riots continue to be ignored by Downtown's political and economic powerbrokers. Empty lots stand where there were once supermarkets, and it's still easier to buy a quart of whiskey than a bag of groceries. The psychological scars go much deeper.

When he chose to play the so-called "race card" in the 1995 double-murder trial of fallen football hero O.J. Simpson, lead defense attorney Johnnie Cochran tapped into questions and emotions that still divide the city and, some would say, contemporary America as well. Although "The Trial of the Century" is now long past, its legacy continues in the form of abiding racial animosities and outright hostility, especially in the barbaric behavior of some local police and the inability of LA's leaders even to acknowledge or respond to it. Unwilling to let go of historical prejudices, and its geographical, political, social and economic ghettos, Los Angeles may be in for more trouble. But in a city whose dynamism seems forever intertwined with internal strife, perhaps this is to be expected.

Arrival

Arriving in LA is potentially one of the most nerve-wracking experiences you're ever likely to have. However you get to the city, and especially if you're not driving, you're faced with an unending urban sprawl that can be a source of bewilderment even for people who've lived in it for years. Provided you don't panic, however, this savage beast of a city can be managed and even navigated, if not necessarily tamed.

By plane

All European and many domestic **flights** use Los Angeles International Airport – always known as **LAX** – sixteen miles southwest of Downtown LA (☎310/646-5252). If you're on a budget, and not planning to rent a car (in which case see "Driving and car rental" on p.69), the cheapest option is to take the free **"C" shuttle bus** (not "A" or "B," which serve the parking lots), running 24 hours a day from each terminal, to the LAX Transit Center at Vicksburg Avenue and 96th Street. From here, local **buses** (the MTA and others) leave for different parts of LA – see "City transportation" on p.68 for more details.

The most convenient way into town is to ride a minibus service such as **LAX Chequer Shuttle** (☎1-800/545-7745) or **SuperShuttle** (☎1-800/554-3146 or 310/782-6600), which run to Downtown, Hollywood, West LA and Santa Monica (the SuperShuttle also goes to Long Beach and Disneyland) and deliver you to your door; most have flashing signs on their fronts advertising their general destination. If you're heading to Santa Monica or the South Bay, another possibility is **Coast Shuttle** (☎310/417-3988). Fares vary depending on your destination, but are generally around $20–30. The shuttles run around the clock from outside the baggage reclaim areas, and you should never have to wait more than fifteen or twenty minutes; pay the fare when you board.

Taxis from the airport are always expensive: reckon on at least $25 to Downtown and West LA, $30 to Hollywood and $90 to Disneyland. Unlicensed taxi operators may approach you and offer flat fares to your destination; generally, such offers are best avoided. Don't even consider using the **Metro** system to get to your destination from LAX. The nearest light-rail train, the Green Line, stops miles from the airport, and the overall journey involves three time-consuming transfers (very difficult with luggage) before you even arrive in Downtown Los Angeles. Other destinations are completely inaccessible by rail.

The vast majority of flights into LA use LAX, but if you're arriving from elsewhere in the US or Mexico, you can land at one of the **other airports** in the LA area – at Burbank, Long Beach, Ontario or Orange County's John Wayne Airport. These are similarly well served by car rental firms; if you want to use public transportation phone the MTA Regional Information Network on arrival (Mon–Fri 6am–7pm, Sat 8am–6pm; ☎1-800/COMMUTE (outside LA 1-800/2LA-RIDE) or 213/626-4455), and tell them where you are and where you want to go.

By bus

The main **Greyhound** bus terminal, at 1716 E Seventh St (☎213/629-8401), is in a seedy section of Downtown – though access is restricted to ticket holders and it's safe enough inside. There are other Greyhound terminals elsewhere in LA handling fewer services: in Hollywood at 1409 Vine St; in Pasadena at 645 E Walnut St; North Hollywood at 11239 Magnolia Blvd; Long Beach at 464 W 3rd St; and Anaheim at 101 W Winston Rd. Only the Downtown terminal is open around the clock; all have toilets and left luggage lockers.

Green Tortoise (☎1-800/TORTOISE) offers one-way fares to LA from San Francisco ($35) and the Pacific Northwest ($60–80) with stops in Hollywood, at *McDonald's* on Vine Street, a block south of Sunset Boulevard; Downtown, across from Union Station; and Santa Monica, at the AYH Youth Hostel, 1436 2nd St at Santa Monica Boulevard.

By train

Arriving in LA by **train**, you'll be greeted with the expansive architecture of Union Station, on the north side of Downtown at 800 N Alameda St (☎213/624-0171; you can also access the nearby Gateway Transit Center, which offers connections to bus lines). Amtrak trains also stop at outlying stations in the LA area; for all listings call Amtrak (☎1-800/USA-RAIL).

By car

The main routes by **car** into Los Angeles are the Interstate highways, all of which pass through Downtown. From the east, I-10, the San Bernardino Freeway, and I-210, the

Foothill Freeway, have replaced the legendary Route 66; from the north and south, I-5 connects LA with Sacramento and San Diego. Of the non-Interstate routes into the city, US-101, the scenic route from San Francisco, cuts across the San Fernando Valley and Hollywood into Downtown, and Hwy-1, or the Pacific Coast Highway (PCH), follows the entire coast of California and takes surface streets through Santa Monica, the South Bay and Orange County.

Information

For free maps, accommodation suggestions and general information, the **Convention and Visitors Bureau (CVB)** operates two **visitor centers**: Downtown at 685 S Figueroa St (Mon–Fri 8am–5pm, Sat 8.30am–5pm; ☎213/689-8822), and in Hollywood at the Janes House, 6541 Hollywood Blvd (Mon–Fri 9am–5pm; ☎323/689-8822). You can also call toll-free for information on ☎1-800/228-2452.

Other LA suburbs have their own bureaux: in Santa Monica at 1400 Ocean Ave (daily 10am–4pm; ☎310/393-7593); Anaheim near Disneyland at 800 W Katella Ave (daily 9am–5pm; ☎714/999-8999); Beverly Hills, 239 S Beverly Dr (☎310/248-1015); and Long Beach, 1 World Trade Center, Suite 300 (☎562/436-3645).

All the centers offer free **maps** of their area, but you'd do better to purchase Gousha Publications' fully indexed *Los Angeles City Map* ($2.95), available from vending machines in visitor centers and most hotel lobbies. If you're in LA for a considerable period of time, consider investing in the thick, comprehensive *LA County Thomas Guide* ($30), the city's definitive **road atlas**. It's no good if you're absolutely lost and have no idea of the city compass (use a freeway map, local streetguides and ring ahead to your destination for directions instead), but for a meticulous, up-to-date guide of hard-to-find streets in unfamiliar neighborhoods, every driver in the city should have one. There are also similarly good *Thomas Guides* covering Orange, Riverside, and San Bernardino counties.

Newspapers and magazines

LA has just one **daily newspaper** of consequence: the *Los Angeles Times*, available from street corner racks all over Southern California (35¢). The Sunday edition ($2) is huge, and its *Calendar* section contains the most complete listings of what's on and where, as well as reviews and gossip of the city's arts and entertainment worlds. Of the city's many **free papers**, the fullest and most useful is the free *LA Weekly*, with over a hundred pages of trendier-than-thou news, reviews and listings. Numerous small local papers covering individual neighborhoods, musical scenes and political activism are available all over LA, especially at cafés and record- and bookstores.

To get a sense of how style-conscious LA sees itself, thumb through a copy of the monthly *Los Angeles* magazine ($3) or the younger and hipper *Buzz* ($4). Both are packed with gossipy news and profiles of local movers and shakers, as well as reviews of the city's trendiest restaurants and clubs. There are also dozens of less glossy, more erratic 'zines – including *Spunk, Planet Homo* and *The Edge* – focusing on LA's diverse gay and lesbian culture and nightclubs.

City transportation

The only certainty when it comes to **getting around** LA is that wherever and however you're going, you should allow plenty of time to get there. Obviously, this is partly due to the sheer size of the city, but the confusing entanglements of freeways and the gridlock common during rush hours can make car trips lengthy undertakings – and the fact that most local buses stop on every corner hardly makes bus travel a speedy alternative.

Driving and car rental

The best way to get around LA – though by no means the only way – is to **drive**. Despite the traffic being bumper-to-bumper much of the day, the **freeways** are the only way to cover long distances quickly. The system, however, can be confusing, especially since each stretch can have two or three names (often derived from their eventual destination, however far away) as well as a number. Four major freeways fan out from the Downtown: the Hollywood Freeway (a section of US-101) heads northwest through Hollywood into the San Fernando Valley; the Santa Monica Freeway (I-10) crosses West LA to Santa Monica; the Harbor Freeway (I-110) runs south to San Pedro – heading northeast it's called the Pasadena Freeway; and the Santa Ana Freeway (I-5) passes Disneyland and continues through Orange County. **Other area freeways** include the San Diego Freeway (I-405), which roughly follows the coast through West LA and the South Bay; the Ventura Freeway (Hwy-134), which links Burbank, Glendale and Pasadena to US-101 in the San Fernando Valley; and the Long Beach Freeway (I-710), which connects East LA and Long Beach. For **shorter journeys**, especially between Hollywood and West LA, the wide avenues and boulevards are a better option (sometimes the only option), not least because you get to see more of the city.

All the major **car rental** firms have branches throughout the city (simply look in the phone book for the nearest office or call one of the toll-free numbers listed on p.29), and most have their main office close to LAX, linked to each terminal by a free shuttle bus. A number of smaller rental companies specialize in everything from Gremlins to Bentleys. The best-known is Rent-a-Wreck (☎1-800/995-0994 or 310/826-7555), at 12333 W Pico Blvd in West LA and other area locations, with mid-1960s Mustang convertibles and other, less appealing, vehicles. Expect to pay in the region of $50 per day.

Parking is a particular problem Downtown, along Melrose Avenue's trendy Westside shopping streets, and in Beverly Hills and Westwood. Anywhere else is less troublesome, but watch out for restrictions – some lampposts boast as many as four placards listing dos and don'ts. Sometimes it's better to shell out $5 for valet parking than get stuck with a $30 ticket for parking in a residential zone.

Public transportation

The bulk of LA's public transportation is operated by the LA County Metropolitan Transit Authority (**MTA** or **"Metro"**), which is still sometimes abbreviated to its old name, the RTD. Its massive **Gateway Transit Center**, to the east of Union Station on Chavez Ave at Vignes Street, may eventually serve 100,000 commuters a day traveling by Metrorail, light rail, Metrolink commuter rail, Amtrak and the regional bus systems. The Center comprises **Patsaouras Transit Plaza**, from which you can hop on a bus; the glass-domed **East Portal**, through which you can connect to a train; and the 26-story **Gateway Tower**, at which you can find an MTA customer service office on the ground floor.

Metrorail
Hampered by a series of construction scandals and budget difficulties, LA's **Metrorail** subway and light-rail system has been struggling even to come into partial use. A successful local ballot measure ensures the system will not expand beyond its current plans, which are narrowly limited in scope and only involve three lines. The

---

MTA OFFICES AND INFORMATION

For **MTA route and transfer information,** phone ☎1-800-COMMUTE or 213/626-4455 (Mon–Fri 7.30am–3.30pm); be prepared to wait, and be ready to give precise details of where you are and where you want to go. Otherwise, you can go in person to Downtown's Gateway Transit Center, Chavez Ave at Vignes St (Mon–Fri 6am–6.30pm), or to three other centrally located offices: at 515 S Flower St, on level C of Arco Plaza (Mon–Fri 7.30am–3.30pm); 5301 Wilshire Blvd (Mon–Fri 9am–5pm); or 6249 Hollywood Blvd (Mon–Fri 10am–6pm).

---

underground **Red Line** as yet stretches only from the Transit Center northwest to the intersection of Hollywood and Vine, though it may eventually reach the San Fernando Valley. Of more use to residents than tourists, the **Green Line** runs between industrial El Segundo and colorless Norwalk, along the middle of the Century Freeway. Tantalizingly close to LAX, but in practical terms absolutely useless if you are in a hurry, the placing of the line has attracted much just criticism. Currently the most complete route, the **Blue Line** leaves Downtown and heads overland through South Central to Long Beach. It's a fairly safe journey through some of the most economically depressed areas of the city, and highlights the normality of everyday commuters' lives rather than the gangs and guns of media repute. **Fares** on all journeys are $1.35 one way. Peak-hour trains run at five- to six-minute intervals, at other times every ten to fifteen minutes. Don't bring takeaway refreshments on the trains – the fine is $250.

Buses

Car-less Angelenos are still most at ease with **buses**. Although initially bewildering, the gist of the MTA bus network is quite simple: the main routes run east–west (ie between Downtown and the coast) and north–south (between Downtown and the South Bay). Establishing the best transfer point if you need to change buses can be difficult, but with a bit of planning you should have few real problems – though you must always allow plenty of time.

Area brochures are available free from MTA offices, and you can pick up diagrams and timetables for individual bus routes, as well as regional bus maps showing larger sections of the metropolis. Buses on the major arteries between Downtown and the coast run roughly every fifteen minutes between 5am and 2am; other routes, and the **all-night services** along the major thoroughfares, are less frequent, usually every thirty minutes or hourly. At night be careful not to get stranded Downtown waiting for connecting buses.

The standard **one-way fare** is $1.35; **transfers**, which can be used in one direction within the time marked on the ticket (usually three hours), cost 25¢ more; **express buses** (a limited commuter service), and any others using a freeway, are usually $1.85, but can be as much as $3.85. Put the correct money (coins or notes) into the slot when getting on. If you're staying a while, you can save some money with a **monthly pass**, which costs $42 (with monthly student passes for $30) and also gives reductions at selected shops and travel agents. If you're staying about two weeks, consider a **semi-monthly pass**, which is sold for $21.

There are also the mini **DASH** buses, which operate as LADOT lines, with a flat fare of 25¢. Several lines ply a circuit around Hollywood, and five routes through the center of Downtown roughly every ten minutes between 6.30am and 6pm on weekdays, every fifteen minutes between 10am and 5pm on Saturday, but not at all on Sunday. Other DASH routes travel through the mid-Wilshire area, Pacific Palisades, Venice and several sections of South Central LA.

MTA BUS ROUTES

MTA's **buses** fall into six categories, as outlined below. Some of the routes can be characterized by their passengers; the early morning east–west route along Wilshire Boulevard is full of Latin American service workers, whereas tourists dominate the route west along Santa Monica Boulevard to the beach and pier. The drivers add to the atmosphere too; some deliver a chirpy running commentary, others are sour and abrupt. Whatever bus you're on, if traveling alone, especially at night, sit up front near the driver. Try and sit near a ventilation hatch, too, as the air conditioning can emit a rather sickly-sweet odor.

#1–99 – local routes to and from Downtown.

#100–299 – local routes to other areas.

#300–399 – limited-stop routes (usually rush hours only).

#400–499 – express routes to and from Downtown.

#500–599 – express routes, other areas.

#600–699 – special service routes (for sports events and the like).

MAJOR LA BUS SERVICES

From LAX to:
Downtown #42, #439.
Long Beach #232.
San Fernando Valley/Getty Center #561.
San Pedro #225.
Watts Towers #117.
West Hollywood #220 (for Hollywood change to #4 along Santa Monica Boulevard).

To and from Downtown:
Along Hollywood Blvd #1.
Along Sunset Blvd #2, #3, #302.
Along Santa Monica Blvd #4, #304.
Along Melrose Ave #10, #11.
Along Wilshire Blvd #20, #21, #22, #320.

From Downtown to:
Santa Monica #20, #22, #434.
Venice #33, #333, #436.
Forest Lawn Cemetery, Glendale #90, #91.
East LA #68.
Exposition Park #38, #81.
Huntington Library #79.
Burbank Studios #96.
San Pedro #445, #446, #447, transfer to LADOT #142 for Catalina.
Manhattan Beach/Hermosa Beach/Redondo Beach #439.
Palos Verdes #444.
Long Beach #60.
Orange County, Knott's Berry Farm, Disneyland #460.

Other **local bus services** include: Orange County (OCTD) ☎714/636-7433; Long Beach (LBTD) ☎562/591-2301; Culver City ☎310/253-6500; and Santa Monica ☎310/451-5444.

Taxis

You can find **taxis** at most terminals and major hotels. Otherwise phone – among the more reliable companies are Independent Cab Co (☎1-800/521-8294), LA Taxi (☎1-800/200-1085) and United Independent Taxi (☎1-800/411-0303). The typical fare is $1.90, plus $1.60 for each mile, with a $2.50 surcharge if you're picked up at LAX: the driver won't know every street in LA but will know the major ones; ask for the nearest junction and give directions from there.

Cycling

Cycling in LA may sound perverse, but in some areas it can be one of the better ways of getting around. There are beach bike-paths between Santa Monica and Redondo Beach, and from Long Beach to Newport Beach, and many equally enjoyable inland routes, notably around Griffith Park and the grand mansions of Pasadena. Contact the

GUIDED TOURS OF LA

One quick and easy way to see different sides of LA is from the window of a **guided bus tour**. These vary greatly in cost and quality. The **mainstream tours** carrying large bus-loads around the major sights are only worth considering if you're very pushed for time – none cover anything that you couldn't see for yourself at less cost. **Specialist tours** tailored to suit particular interests, which usually carry smaller groups of people, are often better value. **Studio tours** of film and TV production areas are covered on day-trips by most of the mainstream operators, though again you'll save money by turning up independently.

MAINSTREAM TOURS

By far the most popular of the mainstream tours is the half-day **"stars' homes"** jaunt. Usually including the Farmer's Market, Sunset Strip, Rodeo Drive, and the Hollywood Bowl, as well as, of course, the "stars' homes," this is much less tempting than it sounds – frequently no more than a view of the gate at the end of the driveway of the house of some has-been TV or celluloid celebrity. These tours are typically the most visible to newcomers, and the area around the Chinese Theatre is thick with tourists queueing for their tickets. Other programs include tours around the Westside at night, to the beach areas, the *Queen Mary*, day-long excursions to Disneyland and shopping trips to the Mexican border city of Tijuana.

Costs are $30 minimum per person; assorted leaflets are strewn over hotel lobbies and visitor centers. You can make reservations at (and be picked up from) most hotels. Otherwise contact one of the following booking offices:

Casablanca Tours, 6362 Hollywood Blvd (☎323/461-0156).

Tour Coach, 6922 Hollywood Blvd (☎323/463-3333).

Hollywood Fantasy Tours, 6671 Hollywood Blvd (☎323/469-8184).

SPECIALIST TOURS

The typical specialist tours listed are also generally $30+ per person. For more sugges-tions, pick up the free *LA Visitors Guide* from hotels and visitor centers.

Black LA Tours (☎323/750-9267). Black historical and entertainment tours.

The California Native, 6701 W 87th Place (☎1-800/926-1140 or 310/642-1140). Sea kayaking and adventure hikes. Tour uninhabited islands off the coast of California for $175 and up.

Googie Tours (☎323/980-3480). Pilgrimages to Southern California's remaining space-age glass and formica diners. Choose between the six-hour "San Gabriel Valley" and "Behind the Orange Curtain" tours, the three hour "Coffee Shop Modern & More" jaunt, or the four-hour, night-time "Cocktails 'n' Coffee Shops" trip – each an impressive pop-cul-ture journey, and a good deal for $35.

Grave Line Tours, PO Box 931694, Hollywood (by reservation only at ☎323/782-9652). Two-and-a-half hours in the back of a 1969 Cadillac hearse paus-ing at the scene of many, though by no means all, of the eventful deaths, scan-dals, perverted sex acts and drugs orgies that have tainted Hollywood and the surrounding area. Leaves daily 10am and 1pm. $40.

SPARC tours: the Murals of LA, 685 Venice Blvd, Venice (☎310/822-9560). Public art in LA is alive and well in the tradition of Diego Rivera, and this is a thoroughly enlight-ening tour of the "mural capital of the world."

STUDIO TOURS

For some small insight into how a film or TV show is made, or just to admire the special effects, there are guided tours at Warner Bros Studios ($30), NBC Television Studios ($7) and Universal Studios ($38), all in or near Burbank; see p.142. If you want to be part of the **audience** in a TV show, the street just outside the Chinese Theatre is the major solicita-tion spot: TV company reps regularly appear handing out free tickets, and they'll bus you to the studio and back. All you have to do once there is be willing to laugh and clap on cue.

AAA (☎213/741-3686) or the LA office of the state Department of Transportation (☎213/897-3656) for maps and information. The best place to **rent a bike** for the beaches is on Washington Street around Venice Pier, where numerous outlets include Spokes'n'Stuff, 4175 Admiralty Way (☎310/306-3332) and 1700 Ocean Ave (☎310/395-4748); in summer, bike rental stands line the beach. Prices range from $8 a day for a clunker to $15 a day or more for a mountain bike. For similar cost, many beachside stores also rent **roller skates** and **rollerblades**.

Walking and hiking

Although some people are surprised to find sidewalks in LA, let alone pedestrians, **walking** is in fact the best way to see much of Downtown and a number of other districts. You can structure your stroll by taking a **guided walking tour**, the best of which are organized by the Los Angeles Conservancy (☎213/623-CITY), whose treks around Downtown's battered but still beating heart are full of heyday Art Deco movie palaces, once-opulent financial monuments and architectural gems like the Bradbury Building (see p.86). Among many alternatives, it runs Downtown tours every Saturday, leaving the *Biltmore Hotel* on Olive Street at 10am (reservations required; $5). (See the box overleaf for details of other tour operators.) You can also take guided **hikes** through the wilds of the Santa Monica Mountains and Hollywood Hills free of charge every weekend with a variety of organizations, including the Sierra Club (☎323/387-4287), the State Parks Department (☎818/880-0350) and the Santa Monica Mountains National Recreation Area (☎818/597-1036).

Accommodation

Since LA has 100,000-plus rooms, finding **accommodation** is easy. Whether you're looking for a budget place to rest your head, or a world-class hotel where you can hob-nob with Hollywood stars and entertainment industry tycoons, LA has something for everyone, even though prices have been rising with LA's recent economic recovery.

Finding somewhere that's low-priced and well-located can sometimes be difficult, though not impossible. If you're driving, of course, you needn't worry about staying in a less than ideal location – a freeway is never far away. Otherwise you'll need to be more choosy about the district you plump for, as getting across town can be a time-consuming business.

Motels and the lower-end hotels start at around $40 for a double, but many are situated in seedy or out-of-the-way areas and often you'll find you gain by paying a little more for a decent location in any of a number of other non-chain, mid-range hotels. **Bed and breakfast inns** are rare in LA, and tend to be quite expensive and frequently fully booked. For those on a tight budget, **hostels** are dotted all over the city, many in good locations, though at some stays are limited to a few nights. Camping, perhaps surprisingly, is also an option: there are a few **campgrounds** on the edge of the metropolitan area – along the beach north of Malibu and in the San Gabriel mountains, for example – but you'll need a car to get to them. (Hostels and campgrounds are listed at the end of this section.) **College rooms** are also sometimes available for rent during student vacation time: contact **UCLA** Interfraternity Council (☎310/825-7878) for more information.

LA is so big that if you want to see it all without constantly having to cross huge expanses, it makes sense to divide your stay between several districts. Prices – and options – vary by area. Downtown has expensive and mid-range hotels; Hollywood has similar options, with motels providing cheaper accommodation; more salubrious West LA, Santa Monica, Venice and Malibu are predominantly mid-to-upper-range territory, with the odd hostel here and there. Among options further out, the South Bay and

Harbor area, well connected with other parts of town, carry a good selection of low- to mid-range hotels (and a hostel) strung mostly along the Pacific Coast Highway. It's only worth staying in Orange County, thirty miles southeast of Downtown, if you're aiming for Disneyland or are traveling along the coast: hotels under $70 a night are a rarity and you must book at least a week in advance, especially if a convention is in town. Unfortunately, many of the plentiful rooms along Katella Avenue and Harbor Boulevard in Anaheim are decrepit and depressing, even though they charge up to $100 a night. By far a better alternative are the hostels and coastal campgrounds in easy reach.

Since there are no **booking agencies** and visitor centers don't make accommodation reservations (though they will offer information and advice), you can only book a room through a travel agent or by phoning the hotel directly. Ask if there are special weekend or midweek rates. Especially at the lower end of the price scale, hotels are cheaper if booked by the week than the night, and don't be afraid to **haggle**.

Hotels are listed below by neighborhood, with specific accommodation options for gay and lesbian travelers listed on p.166. In case you're arriving on a late flight, or leaving on an early one, we've also listed a few places to stay near the airport: cheap hotels near LAX are blandly similar and generally around $40–60, but most have complimentary transportation to and from the terminals.

Downtown and around

See the map on p.82 for hotel locations.

Biltmore Hotel, 506 S Grand Ave at Fifth St (☎1-800/222-8888 or 213/624-1011). Classical 1920's architecture combined with modern luxury to make your head swim. ⑧.

City Center Motel, 1135 W Seventh St at Lucas Ave (☎213/628-7141). Bare but clean Sixties-style decor, with free continental breakfast and airport shuttle bus. ②.

Figueroa Hotel, 939 S Figueroa St at Olympic Blvd (☎1-800/421-9092 or 213/627-8971). Mid-range hotel on the south side of Downtown, with a jacuzzi-equipped pool and 24-hour coffee shop. ④.

Holiday Inn Downtown, 750 Garland Ave at Eighth St (☎1-800/628-5240 or 213/628-5242). On the western fringe of Downtown beside the Harbor Freeway. ⑤.

Hotel Inter-Continental, 251 S Olive St at Fourth St (☎1-800/327-0200 or 213/617-3300). Bunker Hill home to financial kingpins and Academy Award attendees. Very plush, adjacent to MOCA and the Music Center. ⑧.

Kawada Hotel, 200 S Hill St at Second St (☎1-800/752-9232 or 213/621-4455). Comfortable and clean if drab rooms in renovated, medium-sized hotel near the Civic Center. Popular with value-oriented business travelers. ④.

New Otani Hotel, 120 S Los Angeles St (☎213/629-1200). Luxury hotel mainly for business travelers, with comfortable rooms and an appealing and authentic Japanese garden. ⑦.

Orchid Hotel, 819 S Flower St (☎213/624-5855). The best deal in the heart of Downtown, near the Red Line subway station at Seventh and Flower. Clean, comfortable and safe. Weekly rates. ②.

Park Plaza, 607 S Park View St, between Sixth St and Wilshire Blvd (☎213/384-5281). Facing dicey MacArthur Park, with a stunning marble floor and sumptuous lobby popular with filmmakers – but ordinary rooms. ⑧.

Westin Bonaventure, 404 S Figueroa St, between Fourth and Fifth (☎1-800/228-3000 or 213/624-1000). Luxury postmodern masterpiece or oversized nightmare, depending on your point of view. Five glass towers, six-story lobby with a "lake." Breathtaking exterior elevator – featured in the climax of Clint Eastwood's *In the Line of Fire* – ascends to a rotating cocktail lounge which averages seven proposals of marriage a week. ⑧.

Hollywood
See the map on p.98 for hotel locations.

Best Western Hollywood Hills, 6141 Franklin Ave (☎323/464-5181). Part of the nationwide chain, with cable TV and pool, at the foot of the Hollywood Hills. ④.

Dunes Sunset Motel, 5625 Sunset Blvd (☎323/467-5171). On the dingy eastern side of Hollywood, but far enough away from the weirdness of Hollywood Boulevard to feel safe; adequate rooms, and decent for the location. ③.

Holiday Inn Hollywood, 1755 N Highland Ave (☎1-800/465-4329 or 323/462-7181). Massive, but perfectly placed. The price becomes reasonable with triple occupancy. ⑤.

Hollywood Metropolitan Hotel, 5825 Sunset Blvd (☎1-800/962-5800 or 323/962-5800). Sleek high-rise in central Hollywood. Good value for the area. ⑤.

Hollywood Roosevelt, 7000 Hollywood Blvd, between Highland and La Brea (☎323/466-7000). The first hotel built for the movie greats, now in the Clarion chain. The rooms are plain, but the place reeks atmosphere, with a History of Hollywood exhibit on the second floor. ⑥.

Hollywood Towne House Hotel, 6055 Sunset Blvd (☎323/462-3221). Hotel with decayed exterior and 1920s-era phones that connect to the front desk only. The rooms themselves are clean and comfortable enough. ③.

Saharan Motor Hotel, 7212 Sunset Blvd (☎323/874-6700). Unexciting but functional, and comparatively good value, considering its central location. ③.

Sunset 8 Motel, 6516 Sunset Blvd (☎323/461-2748). Many of the rooms on this strip rent by the hour, vibrating bed included. This place, though downtrodden, is a cut above; if you see a clean room, grab it for a brief stay near Hollywood's traditional sights. Across from the former Hollywood Athletic Club. ②.

West LA
See the map on p.107 for hotel locations.

Beverly Hills Hotel, 9641 Sunset Blvd (☎1-800/283-8885 or 310/276-2251). Painted bold pink and green and surrounded by its own exotic gardens, this famous hotel to the stars is pretty hard to miss. Marilyn Monroe once stayed here, and one of the bungalows is decorated in her honor. ⑨.

Beverly Laurel Motor Hotel, 8018 Beverly Blvd (☎323/651-2441). The hotel coffee shop, *Swingers* (see p.145), attracts the most attention here, primarily as a hang-out for locals and inquisitive tourists. Stylish, reasonable and friendly, with a good location. ④.

Bevonshire Lodge Motel, 7575 Beverly Blvd (☎323/936-6154). Well situated for both West LA and Hollywood. All of the functionally decorated rooms come with a refrigerator, and for a few dollars more you can have a kitchenette. ③.

Chateau Marmont, 8221 Sunset Blvd (☎323/626-1010). Exclusive French-style hotel – one-time haunt of John and Yoko; earlier saw the likes of Boris Karloff, Greta Garbo, Errol Flynn, Jean Harlow and, tragically, John Belushi. ⑧.

Claremont Hotel, 1044 Tiverton Ave (☎310/208-5957). Cheerful and inexpensive small hotel very close to UCLA and Westwood Village. ③.

Hotel Bel Air, 701 Stone Canyon Rd (☎1-800/648-1097 or 310/472-1211). LA's nicest hotel bar none, and the only hotel in Bel Air, in a lushly overgrown canyon above Beverly Hills. Go for a beautiful brunch by the Swan pond if you can't afford the rooms, which reach a dizzying $435 a night. ⑨.

Hotel Del Flores, 409 N Crescent Drive at Little Santa Monica (☎310/274-5115). Three blocks from Rodeo Drive, this place is small, pleasant and an excellent value. ④.

Le Montrose, 900 Hammond St (☎310/855-1115). West Hollywood hotel with Art Nouveau stylings, featuring rooftop tennis courts, pool and jacuzzi. Most rooms are suites with full amenities. ⑧.

Le Parc, 733 N West Knoll (☎1-800/578-4837 or 310/855-8888). West Hollywood apartment hotel with studios, one- and two-bedroom suites, rooftop pool and jacuzzi with view of the hills. A British rock star hangout. ⑧.

AIRPORT HOTELS

Days Inn, 901 W Manchester Blvd (☎1-800/231-2508 or 310/649-0800). Outdoor pool, free parking, free LAX shuttle. ③–⑤.

Howard Johnson, 8620 Airport Blvd (☎310/645-7700). A mile northeast of LAX, with a swimming pool and complimentary airport shuttle. ③.

Quality Inn, 5249 W Century Blvd (☎1-800/228-5151 or 310/645-2200). Featuring ten floors of comfortable, well-equipped rooms and a restaurant and bar, this motel also offers free LAX shuttles every fifteen minutes. ③.

Renaissance Hotel, 9620 Airport Blvd (☎310/337-2800). The best of the higher-end hotels close to LAX. With wood-and-marble decor, ample rooms, and luxurious suites with jacuzzis. ⑧–⑨.

Travelodge LAX South, 1804 E Sycamore Ave (☎310/615-1073). Just five minutes south of LAX; convenient for the South Bay. Rates include use of the pool and free tea, coffee and breakfast. ③.

Le Reve Hotel, 8822 Cynthia St (☎1-800/835-7997 or 310/854-1111). Gay-friendly place a few blocks north of Santa Monica Blvd, in residential West Hollywood. Suites in the style of a French provincial inn. ⑥.

The Standard, 8300 Sunset Blvd (☎323/654-2800). The latest youth-oriented hotel on the strip, designed for Sunset Strip hipsters with retro-1970s rooms, AstroTurf floors, and shag carpeting everywhere. ⑥.

Santa Monica, Venice and Malibu

See the map on p.119 for hotel locations.

Bayside Hotel, 2001 Ocean Ave, Santa Monica (☎310/396-6000). Just a block from Santa Monica beach and the Sixties-style café scene of Main Street, to which the original psychedelic bathroom tiles pay tribute. Bland exterior and no phones, but generally comfortable, with ocean views from the more expensive rooms. ④.

Cadillac Hotel, 8 Dudley Ave, Venice (☎310/399-8876). Stylishly restored Art Deco hotel/hostel on the Venice Boardwalk. Its private rooms are spartan and have few amenities, but given the location and price, there are few better deals in town. Nine additional dorm rooms cost only a third as much as private rooms. Sundeck, pool, gym and sauna. ①–④.

Channel Road Inn, 219 W Channel Rd, Pacific Palisades (☎310/459-1920). Fourteen rooms in a romantic getaway nestled in lower Santa Monica Canyon, with ocean views, a hot tub and free bike rental. Eat free grapes and sip champagne in the sumptuous rooms, each priced according to its view. ⑥–⑧.

Hotel Carmel, 201 Broadway, Santa Monica (☎310/451-2469). The best bet for lodging near the beach, with the ocean two blocks away and the Third Street Promenade a block in the other direction. ⑤.

Hotel Shangri-La, 1301 Ocean Ave, Santa Monica (☎310/394-2791). Wonderfully restored Art Deco treasure overlooking Palisades Park and the beach. ⑥.

Loew's Santa Monica Beach Hotel, 1700 Ocean Ave, Santa Monica (☎310/458-6700). A deluxe affair overlooking the ocean and the Santa Monica pier, often in demand as a film set. The best rooms top $400. ⑧.

Malibu Riviera Motel, 28920 PCH (☎310/457-9503). Quiet place outside town, less than a mile from the beach, with a sundeck and jacuzzi. Fairly isolated from the rest of the city. ④.

Malibu Surfer Motel, 22541 PCH (☎310/456-6169). Frightful decor, but located across from the beach and boasting king-size beds, refrigerators and TVs. Sufficient parking, too. ④.

Pacific Shore Hotel, 1819 Ocean Ave, Santa Monica (☎310/451-8711). A popular stop for package-tour Europeans, with great bay views. ⑤.

Santa Monica-Pico Blvd Travelodge, 3102 Pico Blvd, Santa Monica (☎310/450-5766). Predictably clean lodging at the eastern edge of town, a mile from the beach. ④.

Santa Monica Beach Travelodge, 1525 Ocean Ave (☎310/451-0761). Another of the reliable nationwide chain, this one a bit pricier due to beach proximity. ⑤.

The South Bay and Harbor Area

Barnabey's, 3501 N Sepulveda Blvd, Manhattan Beach (☎310/545-8466). One of the finest hotels in the area, with clean and spacious rooms, whirlpool, and LAX airport transit. ⑦.

Hotel Hermosa, 2515 PCH, Hermosa Beach (☎310/318-6000). Plush hotel at moderate prices, a short walk to the beach. ④–⑥.

Motel 6, 5665 E 7th St, Long Beach (☎562/597-1311). Decent rooms at cheap prices; good mainly for travelers on their way south to Orange County or San Diego. ③.

Rodeway Inn, 50 Atlantic Ave, Long Beach (☎562/435-8369). Inoffensive chain-motel accommodation not far from the marina and convention center. ③.

Seahorse Inn, 233 N Sepulveda Blvd, Manhattan Beach (☎1-800/233-8050 or 310/376-7951). Faded pastel exterior but clean and simple rooms. Further from the beach than others, but with a pool. ②.

Sea Sprite Ocean Front Apartment Motel, 1016 Strand, Hermosa Beach (☎310/376-6933). Right next to the beach along a popular strip. Ask the manager what's available as there are several different room options with varying prices. ④.

Vagabond Inn, 6226 PCH, Redondo Beach (☎310/378-8555). Clean and inexpensive lodging in a beachside tourist zone. ②.

Disneyland and around

Desert Palm Inn and Suites, 631 W Katella Ave, Anaheim (☎1-800/635-5423). Very comfortable and spacious rooms with refrigerators, microwaves, VCRs and continental breakfast. Conventions in town make prices jump. ④.

Disneyland Hotel, 1150 W Cerritos Ave, Anaheim (☎714/956-6400). The place to go for a pricey Disney-themed wedding with Mickey in attendance. Quite a bit overpriced (theme park admission is separate), but the Disneyland monorail does stop right outside. ⑧.

Holiday Inn, 1221 S Harbor Blvd, Anaheim (☎714/758-0900). Safe, clean lodging not far from the Magic Kingdom. ⑤.

Motel 6, 100 W Freedman Way, Anaheim (☎714/520-9696). Given the surrounding options, the best bargain in the area. ②.

Stovall's Inn, 1110 W Katella Ave, Anaheim (☎714/778-1880). Along with *Pavilions* at 1176 W Katella Ave (☎714/776-0140) and *Park Place Inn* at 1544 S Harbor Blvd (☎714/776-4800), a reliable member of the Best Western chain. ③–⑤.

The Orange County Coast

Hotel Laguna, 425 S Coast Hwy, Laguna Beach (☎949/494-1151). If you have the cash, this is the place to spend it; atmospheric and comfortable, and nearly every room has a sea view. In the center of Laguna Beach. ⑦.

Little Inn at the Bay, 2627 Newport Blvd (☎949/673-8800). Eighteen nice, comfortable rooms near Newport beach; the least pricey accommodations in the area, at this range. Close to Balboa Peninsula. ④.

Mission Inn – San Juan, 26891 Ortega Hwy, at I-5 (☎949/493-1151). Rooms at this reasonably priced place come with use of jacuzzi and pool. Located in distant San Juan Capistrano. ③.

Ocean View Motel, 16196 PCH, Huntington Beach (☎562/592-2700). Family-run establishment with clean rooms. Get a jacuzzi in your room for an extra $15. ②–③.

Seacliff Motor Hotel, 1661 S Coast Hwy, Laguna Beach (☎949-494-9717). Right on the ocean with cheap, decent rooms. ④.

Seal Beach Inn and Gardens, 212 Fifth St, Seal Beach (☎562/493-2416). Bed-and-breakfast establishment offering sumptuous furnishings two blocks from the sands. ⑥.

The San Gabriel and San Fernando valleys

The Artists Inn, 1038 Magnolia St, South Pasadena (☎626/799-5668). A themed bed-and-breakfast with five different rooms honoring various painters and styles – best of all is the Italian Suite, with rich, dark colors and a sun porch. ⑥.

Best Western Colorado Inn, 2156 E Colorado Blvd, Pasadena (☎626/793-9339). Affordable accommodation just north of San Marino's Huntington Museum. ④.

Ritz-Carlton Huntington Hotel, 1401 S Knoll, Pasadena (☎626/568-3900). Utterly luxurious and refurbished landmark 1906 hotel, discreetly tucked away in residential southern Pasadena. Suites start at $350. Rooms ⑨.

Sheraton Universal, 333 Universal Terrace, Burbank (☎1-800/325-3535 or 818/980-1212). With the neighboring *Universal City Hilton*, 555 Universal Terrace (☎818/506-2500), a large and luxurious hotel on the Universal Studios lot, with health club and elegant restaurant. Both ⑨.

Vagabond Inn Hotel, 1203 E Colorado Blvd at Michigan, Pasadena (☎626/449-3170). Friendly budget chain motel, usefully placed for exploring Pasadena. Also at 120 W Colorado St, Glendale (☎818/240-1700). ③.

Hostels

Banana Bungalow-Hollywood Hotel, 2775 Cahuenga Blvd West, in Cahuenga Pass (☎1-800/446-7835 or 323/851-1129). Popular large hostel near Universal City and US-101, with free airport shuttles, city tours to Venice Beach and Magic Mountain, and a relaxed atmosphere. Outdoor pool, free parking, and as much beer as you can drink every second night for $3. Dorms $18–20, and more expensive private singles and doubles $55+.

HI-Anaheim/Fullerton, 1700 N Harbor Blvd at Brea, Fullerton (☎714/738-3721). Convenient and comfortable, five miles north of Disneyland on the site of a former dairy farm. The hostel's excellent facilities include a grass volleyball court, golf driving range and picnic area. There are only 22 beds, so reservations are a must. Summer check-in 5–11pm, rest of year 4–11pm. Mornings open 7.10–noon. OCTA bus #43 stops outside. Members $11, others $13.

HI-LA/Santa Monica, 1436 Second St at Broadway, Santa Monica (☎310/393-9913). A few blocks from the beach and pier, the building was LA's Town Hall from 1887 to 1889, and retains its historic

---

LA AREA CAMPGROUNDS

A company called Destinet (☎1-800/444-7275) processes reservations at many of the **campgrounds** listed below and can look for an alternative if your chosen site is full. It charges a $6.75 fee per reservation per night up to a maximum of eight people per site, including one vehicle.

Bolsa Chica Campground (☎714/846-3460). Facing the ocean in Huntington Beach, near a wildlife sanctuary and birdwatchers' paradise. $14 for campers with a self-contained vehicle. No tent camping.

Chilao Flat, on Hwy-2 twenty miles northeast of Pasadena (☎626/574-1613). The only campground in the San Gabriel Mountains reachable by car, though there are many others accessible on foot. For more details contact the Angeles National Forest Ranger Station at 701 N Santa Anita Ave, Arcadia (☎626/574-1613). $17.

Dockweiler Beach County Park (☎310/305-9545 or via Destinet on ☎1-800/444-7275). On a noisy stretch of Vista del Mar, almost at the western end of the LAX runways. Mainly for RVs, tent sites by reservation only. $17–25.

Doheny State Beach Campground (☎949/496-6171 or via Destinet on ☎1-800/444-7275). Often packed with families, especially at weekends. Located

at southern end of Orange County. $16–21 per site.

Leo Carrillo State Beach Park, Malibu (☎818/706-1310 or via Destinet on ☎1-800/444-7275). Near one of LA's best beaches, 25 miles northwest of Santa Monica on Pacific Coast Hwy, and served twice an hour in summer by MTA bus #434. $16.

Malibu Creek State Park 1925 Las Virgenes Rd, in the Santa Monica Mountains (☎818/706-8809). A rustic campground in a park which can become crowded at times. Sixty sites in the shade of huge oak trees, almost all with fire pits, solar-heated showers and flush toilets. One-time filming location for TV show *M*A*S*H*. $15–21.

San Clemente State Beach Campground, two miles south of San Clemente (☎714/492-7146 or via Destinet on ☎1-800/444-7275). $20 hook-up sites, $16 others.

charm, with a pleasant inner courtyard, ivy-covered walls and a skylight. Members $18, others $20 – the price includes laundry machines and huge kitchens. Smoking and drinking are prohibited. Reservations essential in summer; open 24hr.

HI-LA/South Bay, 3601 S Gaffey St, building no. 613, San Pedro (☎310/831-8109). Sixty beds in old US Army barracks, with a panoramic view of the Pacific Ocean. Ideal for seeing San Pedro, Palos Verdes and the whole Harbor area. Open 7am–midnight. $11 members, $13 others; private rooms $27 per person. MTA bus #446 passes close by, but it's a two-hour journey from Downtown. You can also take the SuperShuttle from LAX.

Hostel California, 2221 Lincoln Blvd, Venice (☎310/305-0250). Twelve six-bed dorms with kitchens, pool table, big-screen TV, linen and parking. Cheap shuttle bus to and from LAX. $12 members, $14 others, or $84 a week.

Huntington Beach Colonial Inn Hostel, 421 Eighth St, Huntington Beach (☎714/536-3315). Four blocks from the beach and mostly double rooms. Sleeping bags allowed. Open 8am–11pm. Key rental after 1pm, $1 (plus $20 deposit). Dorms $14, private rooms $16.50 per person.

Jim's at the Beach, 17 Brooks Ave at Speedway, Venice (☎310/399-4018). Disorganized hostel near beach. Dorm accommodation on production of a passport. $17 per night or $120 per week, including free breakfast.

Orange Drive Manor, 1764 N Orange Dr, Hollywood (☎323/850-0350). Centrally located hostel (right behind the Chinese Theatre) offering tours of film studios, theme parks and houses of the stars. $15, private rooms $30.

Share-Tel Apartments, 20 Brooks Ave, Venice (☎310/392-0325). Apartments, each with 6–8 people sharing facilities and bedrooms. $15, including breakfast and dinner Mon–Fri.

Venice Beach Cotel, 25 Windward Ave, Venice (☎310/399-7649). Located in historic, colonnaded beachside building; dorm rooms $14–17, private rooms $32–44.

Orientation

Spilling over a vast, flat basin and often lacking well-defined divisions, LA is not a city in the usual sense. Instead, it's a massive conglomeration of interconnected districts, not all of which have that much in common. Traveling from one side to the other takes you through virtually every social extreme imaginable, from mind-boggling beachside luxury to some of the most severe inner-city poverty in the US – both resulting from the city's dizzying growth within a confined area. With the basin bordered by desert to the east, mountains to the north and ocean to the southwest, the millions of new arrivals who have poured in have had to fill the spaces between what were once small, geographically isolated communities, creating a metropolis on a mammoth scale.

If LA has a heart, however, it's **Downtown**. Located in the center of the basin, its towering office blocks punctuate what's for the most part a very low and level skyline. With everything from avant-garde art to the abject dereliction of Skid Row, Downtown offers a taste of almost everything you'll find elsewhere around the city, compressed (unusually for LA) into an area of small, easily walkable blocks. It's a good place to get your initial bearings, and the hub of the transportation network.

Around Downtown, a serviceable label for an assortment of areas with little in common except for being adjacent to or fanning out from Downtown, demonstrates still more of LA's diversity: from the decaying Victorian relics of the turn-of-the-century suburbs, and the later Art Deco buildings that characterized the city in the 1920s, to the center of LA's enormous Hispanic population, home to some rare sights of authentic street life, and the sprawl of impoverished neighborhoods that make up South Central LA.

Away from Downtown, you'll probably spend most of your time in the broad corridor that runs 25 miles west to the coast. Here are LA's best-known and most interesting districts, the first of which, **Hollywood**, has streets caked with movie legend – even if the genuine glamour is long gone. Tourists flock here, and it's also where some of LA's most eccentric street people choose to parade themselves. Neighboring **West LA**, also called the Westside, is home to the city's newest money, shown off in the incredibly expensive shops of Beverly Hills and the posey restaurants and nightspots of the Sunset Strip, and on its western edge merges into **Santa Monica** and **Venice** – the quintessential coastal LA of palm trees, white sands, and laid-back living. The coastline itself is the major draw, stretching north from here twenty miles to the northern edge of LA and **Malibu**, noted for its celebrity residences and their keenly guarded privacy – and for the wildfires that have destroyed many of those residences.

South along the coast from Venice, the three beach cities of the **South Bay** – Manhattan Beach, Hermosa Beach and Redondo Beach – are quieter, mostly inhabited by middle-class commuters, and a long way in spirit from the more bustling and fad-conscious portions of the city. The beaches are the sole focus of attention here, their bluffs and coves leading on to the **Harbor Area** – though, again, despite recent facelifts and some mildly enjoyable resort areas, there's nothing to detain you for more than half a day.

Orange County, southeast of the Harbor Area, is mainly lifeless suburban sprawl, and almost the only reason most people come here is to visit **Disneyland**, the city's biggest single tourist attraction and the granddaddy of all theme parks. If you're not keen on see-

LA'S MUSEUMS

Aerospace Hall	p.91	Japanese-American National Museum .	p.87
Aquarium of the Pacific	p.127	LA County Museum of Art	p.108
Armand Hammer Museum	p.116	Laguna Art Museum	p.136
Avalon Casino Museum	p.128	Lindhurst Galleries – USC	p.90
Avila Adobe museums	p.83	Long Beach Museum of Art	p.127
Bergamot Station	p.120	Malibu Lagoon Museum	p.123
Bowers Museum of Cultural Art	p.132	Maritime Museum – San Pedro	p.126
Cabrillo Marine Museum	p.126	Mission San Juan Capistrano Museum	p.136
California African-American Museum	p.91	Movieland Wax Museum	p.132
California Heritage Museum	p.121	Municipal Art Gallery – Hollywood	p.100
California Science Center	p.91	Museum of Contemporary Art (MOCA)	p.84
Carol and Barry Kaye Museum of Miniatures	p.110	Museum of Flying	p.120
Children's Museum	p.83	Museum of Jurassic Technology	p.109
Drum Barracks and Civil War Museum	p.126	Museum of Latin American Art	p.127
Fantasy Foundation	p.100	Museum of Neon Art	p.87
Fisher Gallery – USC	p.90	Museum of Television and Radio	p.114
Forest Lawn Museum	p.141	Museum of Tolerance	p.115
Frederick's of Hollywood Lingerie Museum	p.101	Natural History Museum of LA County	p.91
Geffen Contemporary	p.87	Norton Simon Museum	p.138
Gene Autry Western Heritage Museum	p.105	Orange County Museum of Art	p.135
George C Page Museum	p.109	Pacific Asia Museum	p.138
Getty Center	p.117	Peterson Automotive Museum	p.110
Griffith Observatory/Hall of Science	p.104	Richard Nixon Library and Birthplace	p.132
Hollywood Bowl Museum	p.106	Skirball Cultural Center	p.117
Hollywood Entertainment Museum	p.102	Southwest Museum	p.96
Hollywood Wax Museum	p.101	Wells Fargo Museum	p.85
Huntington Library and Gardens	p.140	Wight Art Gallery	p.116
International Surf Museum	p.134	Will Rogers Museum	p.123

ing "the happiest place on Earth" – as Disneyland calls itself – it's best to hug the coast and continue south, along the **Orange County Coast**, whose string of individualistic, libertarian communities provides for a few days' exploration on the way to San Diego.

In the opposite direction, LA has also grown on the other side of the hills that make up the northern wall of the basin to the **San Gabriel** and **San Fernando valleys**, which stretch east and west until LA fades into desert, mountains and ocean. The valleys are distanced from mainstream LA life socially as well as geographically, their inhabitants the butt of most Angeleno hick jokes and constantly threatening to secede from the city. The chief reasons for venturing here include a number of worthwhile art collections and a couple of working (and tourable) film studios, as well as the most famous of LA's cemeteries.

Downtown LA

From the homeless families on the steps of City Hall to the phallic towers of multinational finance, nowhere else do the social, economic and ethnic divisions of LA clash quite as loudly and visibly as in the square mile that makes up **DOWNTOWN LA**. In the space of a few short blocks, adobe buildings and Mexican market stalls give way to Japanese-style shopping plazas and avant-garde art galleries, and you're as likely to rub shoulders with a high-flying yuppie as with a down-and-out drunk. Though it's long been the commercial focus of the city, and always the seat of local government, as businesses spread out across the basin in the postwar boom years, the area became more dilapidated. Things picked up in the 1980s, when revitalization initiatives created museums, theaters and a rash of plush new condos for young professionals, but these have ultimately only served to intensify the extremes, and despite the development money that flows freely from city coffers, Downtown is unlikely to usurp the Westside as the focus of tourism or cultural activity. Still, it remains the city's most changed – and changing – neighborhood.

Each part of Downtown has its own share of history, museums and architecture, and it makes most sense to divide the area into simple geographic segments and see it on foot, starting with LA's historic and governmental heart at the **Civic Center**, crossing into the brasher and more modern corporate-tower-dominated **Bunker Hill**, continuing through the chaotic streets and historic movie theaters of **Broadway**, and finally, if you have the nerve, stepping into the strange combination of street people (an estimated 15,000 homeless live on Downtown's streets), warehouses and diminishing experimental art galleries that makes up the **Eastside**.

Downtown can easily be seen in a day, and if your feet get tired you can hop aboard the **DASH buses** which run every ten minutes on five loop systems through key areas (look for the silver-signed bus stops). Parking is expensive on weekdays (around $5–8 per hour), but on weekends is quite affordable (a flat $3–8); in any case, Downtown is the hub of the MTA networks and easily accessible by public transportation.

El Pueblo de Los Angeles and Chinatown

Although the bland municipal buildings of LA government form the focus of the **Civic Center**, the general area also includes **Chinatown** to the north and **Union Station** to the northeast. Just across US-101 from the current seat of local government, you can get a glimpse of LA's earlier days. **El Pueblo de Los Angeles**, at 845 N Alameda Street, was the site of the original late-eighteenth-century Mexican settlement of Los Angeles, and the few early buildings that remain evoke a strong sense of LA's Spanish and Mexican origins. The plaza church, **La Placita**, is the city's oldest and has long served as a sanctuary for illegal Central American refugees (with immigration again becoming a potent political issue). Try and squeeze in during one of the Mariachi Masses (Sun 11.30am & 4.30pm), held completely in Spanish and accompanied by a six-piece mariachi band.

Along with its Mexican heritage, the pueblo also features the remnants of Chinese, Italian, and even French settlement. With restoration work continuing on the turn-of-the-century Italian Hall and a Chinese museum, the zone may soon have more to offer than just a few old facades and shuttered buildings. The city's first **firehouse**, with a small but intriguing roomful of fire-fighting gear, is now open for free viewing, though the handsome, mission-style **Pico House**, LA's most luxurious hotel when it opened in 1870, remains closed. **Olvera Street**, which runs north from the plaza, is a curious attempt at restoration, contrived in part as a pseudo-Mexican village market. Taken over for numerous festivals throughout the year, like November's Day of the Dead, when Mexicans traditionally honor the spirits of the departed (see p.161), the street is at its best on such communal occasions.

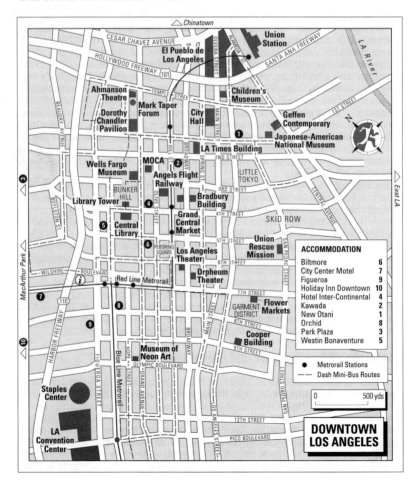

DOWNTOWN LOS ANGELES

ACCOMMODATION

Biltmore	6
City Center Motel	7
Figueroa	9
Holiday Inn Downtown	10
Hotel Inter-Continental	4
Kawada	2
New Otani	1
Orchid	8
Park Plaza	3
Westin Bonaventure	5

● Metrorail Stations
— — Dash Mini-Bus Routes

0   500 yds

Like other historic districts around the country, especially Virginia's Williamsburg, Olvera Street is not simply a charming vestige that just happened to thwart ruin. Rather, its re-emergence was the work of one Christine Sterling, who, with other powerful citizens and help from the city government, tore down the slum she found here in 1926 and built much of what you see today, incorporating some of the salvageable historic structures. For the next twenty years she organized fiestas and worked to popularize the city's Mexican heritage while living in the early nineteenth-century **Avila Adobe** at 10 Olvera St – touted as the oldest structure in Los Angeles, although almost entirely rebuilt out of reinforced concrete following the 1971 Sylmar earthquake. Inside the house are two **museums** (Mon–Sat 10am–5pm; free): one featuring an idealized view of pueblo-era domestic life; the other, across the landscaped courtyard, telling the sanitized official version of how the LA authorities connived to secure a water supply for the city (for the real story, see p.142).

Across the street, the **Sepulveda House** (Mon–Sat 10am–3pm, closed on holidays; ☎213/628-1274) is an 1887 Eastlake structure that offers rooms highlighting different periods in Mexican-American cultural history, and shows an informative free film (Mon–Sat 11am & 2pm) on the history of Los Angeles. For a more detailed look at the pueblo, there are also free **guided walking tours** (on the hour Tues–Sat 10am–1pm) from the information booth at 130 Paseo de la Plaza.

Union Station, across from Olvera Street at 800 N Alameda Street, echoes LA's roots in a rather different way: it is a striking mix of monumental Art Deco and mission-style architecture, finished in 1939. It is also the site of the original Chinatown, whose residents were forced to relocate when construction on the station began. Currently, with the country's national rail system – Amtrak – crippled by budget cuts and mismanagement, the building is no longer the evocative point of arrival and departure it once was. However, the structure itself is in fine condition, with a spacious vaulted lobby, heavy wooden benches and intact Art Deco signs, surrounded by courtyards planted in informal combinations of fig trees and jacarandas. Once thronged with passengers, it now sees just a few trains each day, although the nearby **Gateway Transit Center** has been built with the intention of somehow bringing back the crowds.

What's now **CHINATOWN** was established by 1938 along North Broadway and North Spring streets. It's not the bustling affair you'll find in a number of other US cities, however, and unless it's Chinese New Year, when there's a parade of dragons and firework celebrations, there's little point in turning up here except to eat in one of the restaurants. (To get a truer sense of contemporary Chinese culture, visit **Alhambra** or **Monterey Park**, both lively ethnic suburbs located just beyond LA's eastern boundary.)

South of the Santa Ana Freeway from Olvera Street, the central part of the **Civic Center** is a collection of plodding bureaucratic office buildings around a lifeless plaza. The exception to this, the Art Deco **City Hall**, known to the world through LA cop badges seen in TV shows ever since *Dragnet*, was until 1960 the city's tallest structure. The building's crown is as close as most visitors will ever get to seeing the Mausoleum at Halicarnassus, one of the seven ancient wonders of the world, which provided a curious, only-in-LA architectural inspiration. You can still get a good look at the inside of the building on the free tours, which include its 28th-story 360° observation deck (daily 10am & 11am; reserve on ☎213/485-4423).

Northeast of City Hall, at 310 N Main St, the **Children's Museum** (summer Tues–Fri 9.15am–1pm, Sat & Sun 10am–5pm; rest of year varied weekday hours, Sat & Sun 10am–5pm; $5, children $3, free for all weekdays in winter; ☎213/687-8801) is largely uninspired, but does offer mildly interesting science exhibits and high-tech toys for the kids. More edifying, on the south side of the Civic Center plaza, are the free tours of the **Los Angeles Times** building (Mon–Fri 11.15am; ☎213/237-5757) which show how the West Coast's biggest newspaper is put together.

Bunker Hill

Up until a century ago the area south of the Civic Center, **BUNKER HILL**, was LA's most elegant neighborhood, its elaborate mansions and houses connected by funicular railroad to the growing business district down below on Spring Street. As with all of Downtown, though, the population soon moved to new, outlying suburbs and many of the old homes were converted to boarding houses, later providing the seedy *film noir* backdrop for detective films, notably the apocalyptic 1955 Mike Hammer movie *Kiss Me Deadly*.

The **Angel's Flight** funicular, removed in 1969 but newly restored and repainted, is a bright and colorful memory of a long-departed era. Hop aboard one of the two trains near the corner of Hill and Fourth streets and, for a mere 25¢, ascend to the top of Bunker Hill and be dwarfed by office blocks, which have in the last three decades taken the place of the old Victorians. Once you arrive, the **FINANCIAL DISTRICT** looms above you with sleek modernity. Most of the fifty-story towers have a concourse of shops and restaurants at their base, high-style shopping malls intended to provide a synthetic street life for the brokers and traders, jaded from the day-to-day routine of setting up megabuck deals. The most striking structure is the **Gas Company Tower**, 555 W 5th St, a metallic blue building whose crown symbolizes a natural gas flame on its side.

The Museum of Contemporary Art

The largest and most ambitious development in the district is the **California Plaza** on Grand Avenue, a billion-dollar complex of offices and luxury condos centering on the **Museum of Contemporary Art (MOCA)** (Tues–Wed & Fri–Sun 11am–5pm, Thurs 11am–8pm; $6, students $4, free Thurs 5–8pm; *www.moca-la.org*). Funded by a one-percent tax on the value of all new Downtown construction, MOCA opened at the end of 1986 in an effort to raise the cultural stature of the area, and of the whole city. Designed by showman architect Arata Isozaki as a "small village in the valley of the skyscrapers," it justifies a visit for the building alone, its playful exterior a welcome splash of color among the dour Downtown skyscrapers. You may recognize its geometric red shapes from the occasional television commercials that are filmed here.

A barrel-vaulted entrance pavilion on Grand Avenue opens out to an outdoor sculpture plaza, off which are the ticket booth, the **museum store** and the entrance to the administration wing, covered in diamond-shaped green aluminum panels with bright pink joints. Stairs lead down from the upper plaza to a smaller courtyard, between the café and the main entrance to the galleries.

The brainchild of the high-rollers of the LA art world, MOCA was put together as a gesture of goodwill – and, cynics say, to raise the value of the works they loan for display. Much of the gallery is used for temporary exhibitions, and the bulk of the permanent collection is from the Abstract Expressionist period, including work by Franz Kline and Mark Rothko. You'll also find plenty of Pop Art, in Robert Rauschenberg's urban junk and Claes Oldenburg's papier-mâché representations of hamburgers and gaudy fast foods. Don't be surprised to find a few minimalist creations, either, such as Donald Judd's mind-numbing, machine-produced metallic boxes.

Unfortunately, there are few singularly great pieces among the established names, and most of the compelling ideas are expressed amid the paintings and sculpture of the rising stars in the stock bequeathed by collector Barry Lowen. Hard to categorize, these are something of a greatest hits collection of work by artists you're likely to come across in the trendier city galleries – Jennifer Bartlett, David Salle, Anselm Kiefer and

Eric Fischl, to name a famous few. The museum is also strong on photography, and features the two-thousand-print collection of New York dealer Robert Freidhaus, exhibiting the work of Diane Arbus, Larry Clark, Robert Frank, Lee Friedlander, John Pfahl and Gerry Winograd, among many others.

The theater on the lower floor of MOCA hosts some bizarre multimedia shows and performances, as well as the more standard lectures and seminars (☎213/621-2766 for details). The best time to visit MOCA is on a Thursday evening in summer, when entry is free, and concerts, usually jazz or classical and also free, are played. At other times, a ticket to MOCA also entitles you to same-day entrance to the Geffen Contemporary (see p.87), the museum's warehouse-like exhibition space on the east side of Downtown.

Around MOCA

The shallow but amusing **Wells Fargo Museum** (Mon–Fri 9am–5pm; free), at the base of the shiny towers of the Wells Fargo Center, provides relief from the rigors of MOCA's modern art. It tells the history of Wells Fargo & Co, the bank of Gold Rush California, with among other things a two-pound nugget of gold, some mining equipment and a simulated stagecoach journey from St Louis to San Francisco.

A block away, the shining glass tubes of the **Westin Bonaventure Hotel** (see "Accommodation," p.75) have become one of LA's most unusual landmarks. Although it is the only LA building by modernist architect John Portman, it doesn't fully live up to its billing. The disappointing interior doubles as a shopping mall and office complex – an M.C. Escher-style labyrinth of spiraling ramps and balconies that is disorientating enough to make it necessary to consult a color-coded map every twenty yards or so. But brace yourself and step inside for a ride in the glass elevators that run up and down the outside of the building (famously showcased in the Clint Eastwood action flick, *In the Line of Fire*), giving views over much of Downtown and beyond.

From the *Bonaventure*'s rotating skyline bar you'll get a bird's-eye view of one of LA's finest buildings, the Los Angeles **Central Library** across the street, restored after an arson attack many years back. The concrete walls and piers of the lower floors, enlivened by Lee Laurie's figurative sculptures symbolizing the "Virtues of Philosophy" and the "Arts," form a pedestal for the squat central tower, which is topped by a brilliantly colored pyramid roof. The library, built in 1926, was the last work of architect Bertram Goodhue, and its pared-down, angular lines set the tone for many LA buildings, most obviously the City Hall. Keep in mind that not all the interior design is original to Goodhue, especially the grand atrium added by the renovators, which seems to appear out of nowhere after you step off the escalators to the upper floors.

In exchange for planning permission and air rights, the developers of the **Library Tower** across Fifth Street – the tallest building west of Chicago – agreed to pay some fifty million dollars toward the restoration of the library. Now owned by Wells Fargo, the tower features Lawrence Halprin's huge **Bunker Hill Steps**, modeled after the Spanish Steps in Rome, which curve up Bunker Hill between a series of terraces with outdoor cafés and boutiques, and ultimately stop at the **Source Figure**, one of Robert Graham's creepy sculptures, at the top. Somewhat anticlimactic, the trip is still as good a way to ascend the hill as any.

Broadway and Pershing Square

Though it's hard to picture now, **Broadway** once formed the core of Los Angeles' most fashionable shopping and entertainment district, lively with movie palaces and department stores. Today it's largely taken over by the clothing and jewelry stores of a bustling Hispanic community, a cash-rich environment where pesos and dollars change hands to the sound of salsa music blaring from ghetto blasters nailed to the walls. The most vivid taste of the area is to be had amid the pickled pigs' feet, sheep's brains and other delicacies inside the newly renovated **Grand Central Market**, on Broadway between Third and Fourth. It's a real scrum but without doubt the best place (at least for carnivores) to enter the spirit of things.

The **Bradbury Building** (Mon–Sat 9am–5pm; free) across the street marks a break from the mayhem of the market, its magnificent sunlit atrium surrounded by wrought-iron balconies, and open-cage elevators alternating up and down on opposite sides of the narrow court, with elaborate open staircases at either end. The whole place is an art director's dream – not surprisingly, most of the income for this 1893 office building is generated by film shoots: *Blade Runner* and *Citizen Kane* were both filmed here. Tourists are now only permitted in the lobby, but it's a great view up. (Los Angeles Conservancy tours often begin here; see p.72 for more information.)

Aside from the street life, the best things about Broadway are the great movie palaces of the **THEATER DISTRICT**, some of whose "enchanted realms" still function today, if not exactly as their builders intended. Two are especially noteworthy: next to the Grand Central Market, the opulent 1918 **Million Dollar Theater**, its whimsical ter-racotta facade mixing buffalo heads with bald eagles in typical Hollywood Spanish Baroque style, is a theatrical icon and was originally built by theater magnate Sid Grauman, who went on to build the Egyptian and Chinese theaters in Hollywood (see p.101). It's now a South American-style evangelical meeting hall and entry is of course, free to all. The **Los Angeles Theater**, at 615 S Broadway, is even more extravagant, built in ninety days for the world premiere of Charlie Chaplin's *City Lights* in 1931, and crowning what had become the largest concentration of movie palaces in the world. The plush lobby behind the triumphal arch facade is lined by marble columns sup-porting an intricate mosaic ceiling, while the 1800-seat auditorium is enveloped by trompe l'oeil murals and lighting effects. Many think this theater to be the era's finest in LA, if not the West Coast altogether. In June, a program called Last Remaining Seats draws huge crowds to these and the nearby **Orpheum Theater**, 630 S Broadway, to watch revivals of classic Hollywood films, many from the silent era. If you're in town at the time, don't miss it.

With the advent of TV, the rise of the car and LA's drift to the suburbs, the movie palaces lost their customers and fell into decline. An underground parking lot was built in **Pershing Square** in an attempt to bring the punters back – a task for which it failed, and many of the movie houses these days show exploitation films to sadly depleted numbers. The redesign of Pershing Square itself, unfortunately, has turned the public park into a bleakly synthetic space only a bureaucrat could love. Inspired by the work of Mexican architect Luis Barragan, the square's bright purple campanile is its only highlight, towering as it does over charmless concrete benches and a dearth of grass and other plants. Needless to say, local street people and random lunatics are abundant.

Yet, some of the buildings around the square have – albeit after years of neglect – emerged in fine form. The most prominent of these, the **Biltmore Hotel**, stands over the west side of the square, its three brick towers rising from a Renaissance Revival arcade along Olive Street. Inside, the grand old lobby that was the original main entrance has an intricately painted Spanish-beamed ceiling that you can admire over a pricey glass of wine. A block south, at 617 S Olive St, the Art Deco **Oviatt Building** is another sumptuous survivor. The ground floor housed LA's most elegant haberdashery, catering to dapper types such as Clark Gable and John Barrymore, and has since been converted into the exquisitely expensive *Cicada* restaurant. If you can't afford the Italian food, the elevators, which open onto the street level exterior lobby, are still worth a look, featuring hand-carved oak paneling designed and executed by Parisian craftsman René Lalique. If you don't wish to go inside, marvel at the intricate 1928 design of the struc-ture's exterior, especially the building's grand sign and its looming clock above. Finally, four blocks to the south at 501 W Olympic Blvd, you can find the adulterated visage of Mona Lisa smiling at you through blue-and-yellow tubing at the **Museum of Neon Art** (Wed–Sat 11am–5pm, Sun noon–5pm; $5.00; *www.museneon.org*). Recently relocated next to the pleasant **Grand Hope Park**, the museum offers a small exhibition space featuring classic neon signs, more modern interpretations of the noble gas and a range of bizarre kinetic art. If you're in town, don't miss the museum's monthly bus tours of LA's best neon sights (reserve at ☎213/489-9918; $40).

The Eastside

A block east of Broadway, take a daring step into LA's old financial district along **Spring Street** between Fourth and Seventh Streets. Once at the center of the city's commerce and banking, the area has since been reduced to a virtual ghost town, with barren Neoclassical facades and shuttered entrances. Its only denizens are either homeless or mentally ill, or both. Despite the decay, the street is definitely worth a look for its departed glory.

Nearby, Downtown takes a further downturn in LA's **SKID ROW**: a shabby, down-trodden area around Los Angeles Street south from City Hall that has a more than slightly threatening air. A seedy neighborhood for decades, Skid Row has the dubiously arty associations to match. The Doors posed here for the cover of their album, *Morrison Hotel*, and Charles Bukowski is just one luminary of the booze'n'broads school of writers who've used the bars and poolrooms as a source of inspiration.

To the south of Skid Row, the lively **GARMENT DISTRICT**, with its Mexican-food wagons and cut-rate shops, is a respite from the bleak streets and attracts a lively multi-ethnic crowd. The **Cooper Building**, which takes up most of the Ninth Street block between Santee and Los Angeles streets, is famous for its infrequent designer sample sales. It also houses at least fifty stores where you'll find big markdowns on outfits that may normally be out of your price range. At the atmospheric early-morning **Flower Market** (Mon, Wed & Fri 1–9am, Tues, Thurs & Sat 5.30–10am, closed Sun) on Wall Street between Seventh and Eighth Streets, you can mingle with the wholesalers and buy flowers for a fraction of the high street prices.

Over the last ten years, the northern boundaries of Skid Row have been pushed back by the colorful shopping precincts of **LITTLE TOKYO** – the clearest evidence of the Japanese money that accounted for most of the new construction in LA during the 1980s, and then diminished with economic declines in both LA and Japan. For a closer look into the community, head for the **Japanese-American Cultural and Community Center**, 244 S San Pedro St, whose **Doizaki Gallery** (Tues–Fri noon–5pm, Sat & Sun 11am–4pm; free), shows traditional and contemporary Japanese art and calligraphy. The center also includes the **Japan America Theater**, which regularly hosts Kabuki theater groups. Improbably shoehorned between the two and easy to miss, the stunning **James Irvine Garden**, with a 170-foot stream running along its sloping hillside, is a real cultural treasure. Although named after its biggest financial contributor, it really owes its existence to the efforts of two hundred Japanese-American volunteers who gave up their Sundays to carve the space out of a flat lot, turning it into the "garden of the clear stream," and making the area seem a world away from LA's outside expanse of asphalt and concrete. From the cultural center, a zigzagging pathway takes you through the Shoji screens, sushi bars, shops and Zen rock gardens of the **Japanese Village Plaza** and along to the new **Japanese-American National Museum** at First and Central (Tues–Sun 10am–5pm, Thurs closes at 8pm; $6; *www.lausd.k12.ca.us/janm*), a converted Buddhist temple now housing exhibits on everything from origami to the internment of Japanese-Americans during World War II.

Across the street from Little Tokyo is the **Geffen Contemporary** at 152 N Central Ave (hours and prices as for MOCA, to which a ticket also entitles same-day entrance, see p.85) – an exhibition space in a converted police garage that shows edgy works by contemporary artists other LA museums won't touch. Designed by local maverick Frank Gehry, the museum was initially developed as the temporary home of the Museum of Contemporary Art, but the success of the gallery was such that it was kept on as an alternative exhibition space to its more mainstream sibling.

Around Downtown

When you leave Downtown you enter the LA sprawl, the diverse environs of which tend to be forgotten quarters, scythed by freeways, with large distances separating their points of interest. Cumulatively, there's quite a bit worth seeing, in areas either on the perimeter of Downtown or simply beginning here and continuing for many miles north or west. The districts immediately northwest of Downtown, around **Angelino Heights** and **Echo Park**, are where the upper crust of LA society luxuriously relocated itself at the turn of the century in groupings of wooden Victorian houses (now mostly in various states of preservation), vivid indicators of the prosperity of their time, just as the nondescript drabness surrounding them now evidences the blight which later befell the area. Much the same applies to the zone around **MacArthur Park**, though it still contains some of the impressive commercial architecture that set the stylistic tone for the city in the 1920s.

The other areas that surround Downtown are too far apart for it to make sense to try to see them consecutively; each is a ten- to thirty-minute drive away from the next. Directly south of Downtown, the long succession of unimaginative low-rent housing developments is interrupted only by the contrast of the **USC campus**, populated by conservative, well-coddled students, and the neighboring **Exposition Park**, with acres of gardens and several museums, several of which merit going out of your way to see. Beyond here, the deprivation resumes, leading into one of LA's most depressed areas – the vast urban bleakness of **South Central LA**. A counterpoint to the commercial vibrancy of Downtown, this district surrounds the main route (I-110) between Downtown and the Harbor Area, and it's generally a place to visit with caution or with someone who knows the area. More appealing is the Hispanic-dominated **East LA**, the largest Mexican enclave outside Mexico, and a buzzing district of markets, shops and street-corner music that gives a tangible insight into the other, relatively unacknowledged, side of LA. More recent arrivals from Central America often end up in the **Temple-Beaudry** and **Pico-Union** barrios, located to the immediate west of Downtown. These areas have a reputation as LA's most dangerous, but as long as you stick to the main thoroughfares and travel during daylight, you're unlikely to encounter any trouble. It's less hectic northeast of Downtown, where, amid the preserved homes of **Highland Park**, the **Southwest Museum** holds a fine and extremely comprehensive collection of Native American artifacts.

Angelino Heights and Echo Park

Long before there was a Malibu or a Beverly Hills, some of the most desirable addresses in Los Angeles were in **ANGELINO HEIGHTS**, LA's first suburb, laid out in the flush of a property boom at the end of the 1880s on a hilltop a little way northwest of Downtown. Though the boom soon went bust, the elaborate houses that were built here, especially along **Carroll Avenue**, have survived and been recently restored as reminders of the optimism and energy of the city's early years. There's a dozen or so in all, and most repay a look for their catalog of late-Victorian details – wraparound verandas, turrets and pediments, set oddly against the Downtown skyline; one, with a weird Great Pyramid roof, was used as the set for the haunted house in Michael Jackson's *Thriller* video.

At the foot of the hill, to the west of Angelino Heights, **Echo Park** is a tiny park of palm trees set around a lake. In the large white **Angelus Temple** on the northern side of the lake, the evangelist **Aimee Semple McPherson** used to preach fire and brimstone sermons to five thousand people, with thousands more listening in on the radio. The first in a long line of media evangelists, "Sister Aimee" died in mysterious circumstances in 1944, but the building is still used for services by her Four Square Gospel ministry, who dunk converts in the huge water tank during mass baptisms. Roman Polanski's film *Chinatown* pays homage to the park by having detective Jake Gittes follow the town water boss to clandestine meetings amid the palms and lotuses.

MacArthur Park and around

Wilshire Boulevard leaves Downtown between Sixth and Seventh streets as the main surface route across 25 miles of Los Angeles to Santa Monica's beachside Palisades Park. It was named by and for oil baron and entrepreneur Gaylord Wilshire, who, aside from his petroleum profits, made a fortune selling an electrical device that claimed to restore graying hair to its original color. Wilshire used his money to buy up a large plot of land west of Westlake Park, later renamed **MacArthur Park**, through the center of which ran the wide thoroughfare, previously known as the "Old Road." When the property market collapsed in 1888, Gaylord discovered politics, ran for Congress (and lost), and later moved to England, where he made friends with George Bernard Shaw and the Fabian Socialists.

A century later, the park has fallen into disrepair and, despite police efforts, remains a venue for drug deals after dark. But the nearest Red Line Metrorail connection has turned its patches of green and large lake into the nearest visual relief from the sidewalks of Downtown – though not aurally, as the ambient soundtrack frequently includes the rantings of mad street preachers and other assorted characters. Don't miss the overhead sign for the Westlake Theater, though, which proudly advertises a classic moviehouse that has since become a grungy swap meet, or flea market.

Half a mile west, the **Bullocks Wilshire** department store, 3050 Wilshire Blvd, is a stunning monument of 1920s Los Angeles, the most complete and unaltered example of Zigzag Art Deco architecture in the city. Built in 1929, in what was then a beanfield in the suburbs, Bullocks was the first department store in LA to be built outside Downtown, and the first to build its main entrance at the back of the structure, adjacent to the parking lot – catering for the automobile in a way that was to become the norm in this car-obsessed city. Transportation was the spirit of the time, and throughout the building, mural and mosaic images of planes and ocean liners glow with activity in a studied celebration of the modern world. The building was badly vandalized during the 1992 riots, and was closed for five years. It has since reopened as the law library of adjacent **Southwestern University**, but is still off-limits to the general public, unless you can get someone, perhaps a student, to give you an impromptu tour.

The **Ambassador Hotel**, just past Vermont Avenue at 3400 Wilshire Blvd, is another landmark of the boulevard's golden age. From the early 1920s to the late 1940s, when the hotel was the winter home of transient Hollywood celebrities, its *Cocoanut Grove* club was a favorite LA nightspot. The large ballroom hosted some of the early Academy Award ceremonies, and was featured in the first two versions of *A Star is Born* – though the hotel's most notorious event occurred on June 5, 1968, when **Bobby Kennedy** was fatally shot in the hotel kitchen while trying to avoid the press after winning the California Presidential Primary. Now closed to public view, the building's demolition was held up for years as a result of a legal feud between LA's school district and Donald Trump. While still standing, it's nevertheless clearly doomed, and has attracted few architectural preservationists to champion its cause. Across the street, another of LA's landmarks has been bizarrely reconstructed. The **Brown Derby** restaurant, once the city's prime example of programmatic architecture (or buildings shaped like objects – in this case, a hat), has now been relocated to the roof of a Korean mini-mall. Brimless and painted silver, it has become a curious nightclub called *Xcess*.

From the *Ambassador* you can either continue west up the so-called "Miracle Mile" (see p.108) or, two blocks south of Wilshire, between Vermont and Western, look in on **KOREATOWN**, the largest concentration of Koreans outside Korea and five times bigger than Chinatown and Little Tokyo combined. In reality, the comparison is unfair, for Koreatown is an active residential and commercial district, not just a tourist sight. The more fruitful comparison would be with the vibrant enclave of **Monterey Park**, east of LA, which is the focus of regional Chinese culture just as surely as Koreatown is of Korean culture.

The USC Campus

The **USC** (University of Southern California) **CAMPUS**, a few minutes south of Downtown, is an enclave of wealth in one of the city's poorer neighborhoods. USC, or the "University of Spoiled Children," is one of the most expensive universities in the country, its undergraduates thought of as more likely to have rich parents than fertile brains. Indeed, the stereotype is often borne out, both by their easy-going, suntanned, beach-bumming nature, and by USC being more famous for sporting prowess than academic achievement. Alumni include O.J. Simpson, who collected college football's highest honor, the Heisman Trophy, when he played for the school. There have been attempts to integrate the campus population more closely with the local community, but USC continues to be something of an elitist island, right down to its own fast-food outlet, and its students are cheerfully oblivious to the blight around them.

Though sizable, the campus is reasonably easy to get around. If you do want to visit, however, you might find it easiest to take the free hour-long **walking tour** (Mon–Fri 10am–2pm by appointment; ☎213/743-2183). Without a guide, a good place to start is in the **Doheny Library** (during academic year Mon–Thurs 8.30am–10pm, Fri 8.30am–5pm, Sat 9am–5pm, Sun 1–10pm; free), where you can pick up a campus map and pass an hour or so investigating the large stock of overseas newspapers and magazines on the second floor, although they tend to be at least three weeks behind the times and UCLA (see p.116) has a better selection. Another good place for general information is the **Student Union** building, just across from the library and straight out of *Beverly Hills 90210*. Food is priced to make the college money, and the **bar** is an under-used and claustrophobic room with mirrored walls and terrible beer. A **café** under the Wolfgang Puck banner, featuring nouveau pizzas and salads, provides some respite, however.

Of things to see, USC's art collection is housed in the **Fisher Gallery** on Exposition Boulevard (during academic year Tues–Fri noon–5pm, Sat 11am–3pm; free), which stages several major international exhibitions each year, and has a broad permanent stock. Elsewhere, you can see smaller shows of students' creative efforts in the **Helen Lindhurst Architecture Gallery** (Mon–Fri noon–6pm, Sat noon–5pm; free) and **Helen Lindhurst Fine Arts Gallery** (Mon–Fri 9am–5pm; free).

The campus is also home to the **School of Cinema-Television**, a decidedly mainstream rival to the UCLA film school in Westwood. Ironically, **Steven Spielberg**, one of the biggest box-office directors in history, couldn't get in to USC when he applied as an aspiring director. Now, his name is hallowed here, and writ large on the wall of the large and expensive sound-mixing center he later funded. A short walk away, the **Arnold Schoenberg Institute** (Mon–Fri 9am–5pm; free) is a study center devoted to the pioneering composer whose wide influence on modern musical thought – largely through his experiments with atonal and twelve-tone structures – is even more remarkable when you consider that he had no formal training. Schoenberg, born in Austria in 1871, came to the US to escape the Nazis, and spent the fourteen years before his death in 1951 in LA, sadly unappreciated and jealous of the affection showered on fellow expatriates like Igor Stravinsky – his longtime rival. The reception area holds a mock-up of his studio, while the small auditorium displays his personal mementos. During the academic year, students often give free lunchtime concerts of the great man's music, which can still sound rather thorny to the uninitiated.

Between USC and Exposition Park, sports fans may want to stop at the **Coliseum** on Hoover Boulevard. The site of the 1932 and 1984 Olympic Games has fallen on hard times lately, with the Los Angeles Raiders relocating to Oakland and a possible deal to land a new American football franchise ultimately failing amid corporate infighting. However, USC home games are still played here, and the imposing grand arch on the facade and muscular, headless commemorative statues create enough visual interest to make the place worth a look.

Exposition Park

Across Exposition Boulevard from the campus, **EXPOSITION PARK** is, given the grim nature of the surrounding area, one of the most appreciated parks in LA, incorporating lush landscaped gardens, a sports stadium and a number of decent museums. It's large by any standards, but the park retains a sense of community – a feeling bolstered by its function as a lunchtime picnic place for school kids. After eating, their favorite spot tends to be the **California Science Center** (*www.casciencectr.org*), set among a cluster of **museums** off Figueroa Street at 700 State Drive (unless otherwise stated, all daily 10am–5pm; free), a nicely renovated, multimillion-dollar showcase for scientific education, not unlike other such museums elsewhere in the US. With scores of working models and thousands of pressable buttons, some of the museum's highlights include a walk-in microscope, an assortment of displays on human anatomy and physics, and a giant talking robot that offers simple biology instruction. Although most of the simulations are fairly lightweight and geared for children, the institution does fulfill its mission of making science interesting and, on occasion, fun.

In the vicinity, an **IMAX Theater** plays a range of eye-popping documentaries on a gigantic curved screen. Because of the general lack of storytelling in many of the films, one screening (most are around 30min) is usually enough to get a sense of the unusual moviehouse. The **Aerospace Hall**, marked by the DC10 parked outside and the sleek jet stuck to its facade, is rather bland: a few models and displays pertaining to space and weather prediction. However, the building itself is something of a landmark, designed by Frank Gehry and prefiguring some of his later, better work. Nearby, head for the stimulating **California African-American Museum** (*www.caam.ca.gov*), which has diverse, temporary exhibitions on the history, art and culture of black people in the Americas.

Not far away, the **Natural History Museum of Los Angeles County** (Mon–Fri 9.30am–5pm, Sat–Sun 10am–5pm; $8; *www.nhm.org*) has much appeal as the home of the park's biggest collection, as well as its most striking building – an explosion of Spanish Revival with echoing domes, travertine columns and a marble floor. Foremost among the exhibits is a tremendous stock of dinosaur bones and fossils, and some individually imposing skeletons (usually casts) including the crested "duck-billed" dinosaur, the skull of a Tyrannosaurus Rex, and the astonishing frame of a Diatryma – a huge bird incapable of flight. But there's a lot beyond strictly natural history in the museum, and you should allow several hours at least for a comprehensive look around. In the fascinating pre-Columbian Hall are Mayan pyramid murals and the complete contents of a Mexican tomb (albeit a reconstruction), while the Californian history sections usefully document the early (white) settlement of the region during the Gold Rush era and after, with some amazing photos of Los Angeles in the 1920s. Topping the whole place off is the gem collection: several breathtaking roomfuls of crystals, their

THE LA RIOTS

The unexpected acquittal in 1992 of five white Los Angeles police officers, charged with using excessive force after they were videotaped kicking and beating black motorist Rodney King, could almost have been calculated to provoke a **violent backlash** in LA's poverty-stricken ghettos. What few predicted, however, was the sheer scale of the response to the verdict. The violence and anger far surpassed the Watts Riots of 1965 (see opposite), beginning in South Central LA with motorists being pulled from their cars and attacked, and quickly escalating into a chaos of arson, shooting and looting that spread across the city from Long Beach to Hollywood. Downtown police headquarters were surrounded by a mixed crowd of blacks, Hispanics and whites, chanting "No Justice, No Peace," as state governor Pete Wilson appealed for calm on live TV. Before long, the firebugs gave way to looters, who became the focus of the local media's attention, openly stealing stereos, appliances, and even diapers from large and small retail stores. Ultimately, it took the imposition of a four-day dusk-to-dawn curfew, and the presence on LA's streets of several thousand well-armed US National Guard troops, to restore calm – whereupon the full extent of the rioting became apparent. The worst urban violence seen in the US this century (second only to the bloody, Civil War-era New York draft riots) had left 58 dead, nearly 2000 injured, and caused an estimated $1 billion worth of damage. With much of the devastation in the city's poorest areas, a relief operation of Third World dimensions was mounted to feed and clothe those most severely affected by the carnage. A second trial, on charges that the officers violated Mr King's civil rights, resulted in prison sentences for two of the officers.

Though ignited by a single incident, the riots were a very real indication of the **tensions** in a city whose controllers and affluent inhabitants have traditionally been all too ready to turn a blind eye to social problems. Prompted by the Rodney King case, the Christopher Commission was set up to investigate racial prejudice within the LAPD. Sadly, its recommendations had all too blatantly not been implemented by the time of the O.J. Simpson trial in 1995, when the world was once again reminded that race is always an issue in Los Angeles.

qualities enhanced by special lighting. On a sunny day, spare some time for walking through Exposition Park's **Rose Garden** (daily 10am–5pm; free). The flowers are at their most fragrant in April and May, when the bulk of the 45,000 annual visitors come by to admire the 16,000 rose bushes and the overall prettiness of their setting.

South Central LA

Lacking the scenic splendor of the coast, the glamour of West LA and the history of Downtown, **SOUTH CENTRAL LA** hardly ranks on the tourist circuit – especially since it burst onto the world's TV screens as the focal point of the April 1992 **riots** (see box below). However much wealthy white LA would like to pretend South Central doesn't exist, it's an integral part of the city, especially in terms of size: a big, roughly circular chunk reaching from the southern edge of Downtown to the northern fringe of the Harbor Area. The population was once mostly black, but is increasingly Hispanic and Asian, interspersed here and there by elderly and working-poor whites. The dislocations occasioned by immigration have made for surprising trends and more than a little racial hostility. **Watts**, for example, once overwhelmingly black, now has a Hispanic majority. As a whole, South Central doesn't look so terribly run-down at first sight, mostly made up of detached bungalows enjoying their own patch of palm-shaded lawn. But this picture is deceptive, and doesn't conceal for long the fact that many residents are poor, get an abysmal deal at school and at work, and have very limited chances of climbing the social ladder and escaping to the more affluent parts of the city.

What will immediately strike you in South Central LA is the sheer monotony of the place: every block for twenty-odd miles looks much like the last, enlivened periodically by fast-food outlets, dingy liquor stores and abandoned factory sites. Like most commuters, you'll see almost nothing of the area by driving through on the Harbor Freeway (I-110), which is largely confined to its own isolated, walled-off channel.

Watts

The district of **WATTS**, on the eastern side of South Central, achieved notoriety as the scene of the six-day **Watts Riots** of August 1965. The arrest of a 21-year-old unemployed black man, Marquette Frye, on suspicion of drunken driving, gave rise to charges of police brutality and led to bricks, bottles and slabs of concrete being hurled at police and passing motorists during the night. The situation had calmed by the next morning, but the following evening, both young and old black people were on the streets, giving vent to an anger generated by years of what they felt to be less than even-handed treatment by the police and other white-dominated institutions. Weapons were looted from stores and many buildings set alight (though few residential buildings, black-owned businesses or community services, such as libraries and schools, were touched); street barricades were erected, and the events took a more serious turn. By the fifth day, the insurgents were approaching Downtown, which – along with the fear spreading through white LA – led to the call-out of the National Guard: 13,000 troops arrived, set up machine-gun placements and road blocks, and imposed an 8pm-to-dawn curfew, causing the rebellion to subside.

In the aftermath of the uprising, which left 36 dead, one German reporter said of Watts, "it looks like Germany during the last months of World War II." Much of it still does – Watts is by far the ugliest part of South Central LA. The promises of investment made after 1965 never amounted to much; indeed any forward strides made during the 1970s have long since been wiped out by wider economic decline, and eclipsed by the events of 1992. Although city politicians continue to pontificate about helping out the area, and business leaders occasionally promise to build a supermarket here or a bank there, this is still LA's economic ground zero.

Watts hit the headlines for a second time in 1975, when members of the Symbionese Liberation Army (SLA), who had kidnapped publishing heiress Patti Hearst, fought a lengthy – and televised – gun battle with police until the house they were trapped in burned to the ground. The site of the battle, at 1466 E 54th St, is now a vacant lot, though the surrounding houses are still riddled with bullet holes, visible reminders of another unpleasant chapter in local history.

The one valid reason to come here is to see the Gaudi-esque **Watts Towers**, sometimes called the Rodia Towers, at 1765 E 107th St. Constructed from iron, stainless steel, old bedsteads and cement, and decorated with fragments of bottles and around 70,000 crushed seashells, these striking pieces of street art are surrounded by more than a little mystery. Their maker, Simon Rodia, had no artistic background or training at all, but labored over the towers' construction from 1921 to 1954, refusing offers of help and unable to explain either their meaning or why on earth he was building them. Once finished, Rodia left the area, refused to talk about the towers, and faded into complete obscurity. The towers managed to stave off bureaucratic hostility and structural condemnation for many decades; finally, they were declared a cultural landmark. However, 1994's earthquake left the towers shrouded in scaffolding, and the while the bandages have mostly been removed, opening hours are erratic, though the Towers are sometimes open for Saturday tours; call the adjacent Watts Tower Arts Center, 1727 E 107th St (☎323/847-4646) to check on their condition.

The **Dunbar Hotel**, at 4225 S Central Ave, marks the first US hotel built specifically for blacks and patronized by almost every prominent African-American during the 1930s through the 1950s. Unfortunately, you can only see the hotel's restored lobby and facade, as it is now a home for the elderly. For information call the Dunbar Hotel Economic Development Corporation at ☎323/234-7882.

Compton and Inglewood
Between Watts and the Harbor Area, only a few districts are of passing interest. Despite its fame as the home of many of LA's rappers – NWA, for example, sang venomously of its ills on their album *Straight Outta Compton* – and of tennis phenoms Serena and Venus Williams, **COMPTON** is not a place where strangers should attempt to sniff out the local music scene. History buffs secure in their cars, however, might enjoy a stop at the **Dominguez Ranch Adobe**, 18127 S Alameda St (Tues & Wed 1–4pm, second & third Sun of each month 1–4pm; free conducted tour ☎310/631-5981). Now restored, the mission chronicles the social ascent of its founder, Juan Jose Dominguez – one of the soldiers who left Mexico with Padre Junipero Serra's expedition to found the California missions, whose long military service was acknowledged in 1782 by the granting of these 75,000 acres of land. As the importance of the area

---

THE GANGS OF LOS ANGELES

South Central LA is the heartland of the city's infamous **gangs**, said to have more than one hundred thousand members between them and which have existed for more than forty years, often encompassing several generations of a family. The black gangs known as Crips and Bloods are the most famous, but there are also many burgeoning Hispanic gangs as well, most prominently the 18th Street Gang, who despite their name operate all over the LA basin and in the San Fernando Valley. The characteristic violence associated with these groups often stems from territorial fights over drug-dealing, with many gangs staking claim to certain neighborhoods through their monikers (for example, the "Shoreline Gangster Crips" denotes a local gang active in the central ghetto of Venice). The larger gangs employ sophisticated schemes involving protection rackets, money laundering, and expansion into legitimate businesses from small retail operations to, it is rumored, the music industry – all tactics reminiscent not of common street thugs, but of old-style Italian mobsters.

Each new wave of immigration adds to the roster of gangs, which usually, though not always, organize themselves by ethnicity. With a massive influx of drug money, violence has escalated and automatic weaponry (not least Uzi machine guns) has become commonplace. Although most fatalities (there are about 350 a year) are a direct result of drug-trade rivalry, in recent decades there's been an increase in "drive-by shootings," the vast majority of which take place in established gangland areas and occasionally involve the death of bystanders. It was indicative of LA's entrenched racial and social divisions that the death of a white professional woman during a freak shootout in West LA in 1987 was one of the few gang-related deaths to excite widespread publicity and led to major anti-gang initiatives on the part of the police. The resulting clampdowns have seen a thousand arrests made on a single night, South Central homes invaded by the occasional LAPD tank, and the creation of a full-scale prison-industrial complex to house "drug kingpins," but on the whole they have made little headway in tackling the real problem: the desperate economic conditions in LA's poorer sections.

Despite the violence, an outsider is unlikely to see much evidence of the gangs beyond the occasional blue or red scarf (the colors of the Crips and Bloods) tied around a street sign to denote territory and, in some areas, the presence of widespread graffiti consisting of various letters and symbols that are almost always indecipherable. Don't expect to witness any inter-gang warfare, unless you do something foolish like cruising down Vermont Avenue on a Saturday night. As for personal danger, driving through South Central LA by day is generally safe, but be wary of delays at traffic lights, avoid the area after dusk unless you're with people who know their way around, and try to avoid using hand signals of any sort – tantamount to swearing in an unfamiliar language.

grew, so did the influence of Dominguez's descendants, who became powerful in local politics.

On the other side of the Harbor Freeway, closer to LAX, **INGLEWOOD**, unenticing in itself, is home to the **Hollywood Park Racetrack**, a landscaped track with lagoons and tropical vegetation, and a state-of-the-art computer-operated screen to give punters a view of the otherwise obscured back straight. Next door are the white pillars which ring **The Forum**, the 17,000-seat stadium that was the former headquarters of both the LA Lakers (basketball) and the LA Kings (hockey), and is now mostly a concert venue; see "Listings" on p.172.

Crenshaw

As a general rule, it's not a good idea to venture into South Central looking for entertainment, unless you're with a local. The **CRENSHAW** district and adjacent **Leimert Park**, on its western fringe, may be an exception. Where the old center of African-American culture was once along Central Avenue, the location of many nightclubs and the focus of a thriving big-name jazz scene, it is now here. Crenshaw and Leimert Park feature a number of restaurants, fine book and record stores, the flagship moviehouse of Magic Johnson's theater chain, and a multimillion-dollar shopping mall created with community-redevelopment money that acts as the real commercial center of the area. Beyond Crenshaw, the black upper-middle class resides in **BALDWIN HILLS**, a picturesque district marred by a slew of oil wells.

East LA

You can't visit LA without being made aware of the Hispanic influence on the city's demography and culture, whether it be through the thousands of Mexican restaurants, the innumerable Spanish street names, or, most obviously, through the sheer volume of Spanish spoken by people on the streets. None of this is surprising given LA's proximity to Mexico, but equally apparent are the clear distinctions between the Latino community and white LA. As a rule, it's the former who do the menial jobs for the latter. And although a great number live in the US lawfully, they're also the people who suffer most from the repeated drives against illegal immigration. During the 1992 riots, there were charges of brutality and racism against Immigration and Naturalization Service agents, who may have used the chaos as an opportunity to hunt down undocumented foreign workers.

Of the many Hispanic neighborhoods all over LA, the key one is **EAST LA**, which begins two miles east of Downtown, across the concrete-clad dribble of the Los Angeles river. There was a Mexican population here long before the white settlers arrived, and from the late nineteenth century onward millions more arrived, coming here chiefly to work on the land. As the white inhabitants gradually moved west towards the coast, the Mexicans stayed, creating a vast Spanish-speaking community that's more like a self-contained Hispanic city than part of a sprawling North American metropolis.

Activity in East LA (commonly abbreviated to "ELA" or "East Los") tends to be outdoors, in cluttered markets and busy shops. Non-Hispanic visitors are comparatively thin on the ground, but you are unlikely to meet any hostility on the streets during the day – though you should steer clear of the rough and very male-dominated bars, and avoid the whole area after dark. **Guadalupe**, the Mexican image of the Virgin Mary, appears in mural art all over East LA, nowhere better than at the junction of Mednik and Cesar Chavez avenues. When a housing project across the street was demolished in the early 1970s, one wall, bearing a particularly remarkable image of Mary surrounded by a rich band of rainbow colors, was saved from the wrecking ball and reinstated across the street. Lined with blue tile, it now forms an unofficial shrine where worshippers place fresh flowers and candles.

Other than the street life and murals, there are few specific "sights" in East LA. The best plan is just to turn up on a Saturday afternoon (the liveliest part of the week) and stroll along **Cesar Chavez Avenue**, formerly Brooklyn Avenue, going eastward from Indiana Street and look at the wild pet shops, with free-roaming parrots and cases of boa constrictors, and at the **botanicas shops**, which cater to practitioners of Santeria – a religion that is equal parts voodoo and Catholicism. Browse amid the shark's teeth, dried devil fish and plastic statuettes of Catholic saints and buy magical herbs, ointments or candles after consulting the shopkeeper and explaining (in Spanish) what ails you. Only slightly less exotic fare can be found in **El Mercado de Los Angeles**, 3425 E First St, an indoor market similar to Olvera Street (see p.82) but much more authentic.

Afterwards, head through the LA district of **Boyle Heights**, which through the 1940s was a center for Jewish culture but has since become a solid Hispanic enclave. Go to the junction of **Soto** and **Cesar Chavez**, where at 5pm each afternoon, *Norteños* combos (upright bass, accordion, guitar and banjo sexto) showcase their talents for free, hoping to be booked for weddings; failing that, listen to the mariachi bands that strike up at 6.30pm outside the Olympic Donut Shop, at First and Boyle, four blocks south of Cesar Chavez Avenue.

Highland Park

North of Downtown, the **Pasadena Freeway** curves along a dry riverbed towards the foothill community whose name it bears. The freeway, LA's first, was completed in 1941 as the Arroyo Seco Parkway. Highway engineers have since learned their lessons, but be aware that this antiquated roadway has "stop" signs on the on-ramps and exit ramps so short and sharp that the speed limit is 5mph.

Beside the freeway, two miles from Downtown, **HIGHLAND PARK** has a number of exuberantly detailed Victorian houses brought together from around the city to form **Heritage Square**, a fenced-off ten-acre park at 3800 Homer St (Sat–Sun noon–4pm; $5), which some critics have derided as an architectural "petting zoo." Just beyond the next freeway exit, at 200 E Ave 43, the **Lummis House** (Fri–Sun 1–4pm) is the well-preserved home of Charles F. Lummis, a publicist who was at the heart of LA's nineteenth-century boom. Unlike many of the real-estate speculators and journalists who did little more than publicize and glorify aspects of the Southern California good life, Lummis did some genuinely good deeds: he was an early champion of civil rights for Native Americans, and worked to save and preserve many of the missions, which were then in ruin. His house was a cultural center of turn-of-the-century Los Angeles, where the literati of the day would meet to discuss poetry and the art and architecture of the Southwest. Lummis built this house for himself in an ad hoc mixture of mission and medieval styles, naming it *El Alisal* after the many large sycamore trees (*alisal* in Spanish) that shade the gardens. He constructed the thick walls out of rounded granite boulders taken from the nearby riverbed, and the beams over the living room of old telephone poles. The solid wooden front doors are similarly built to last, reinforced with iron and weighing tons, while the plaster-and-tile interior features rustic, hand-cut timber ceilings and homemade furniture.

The Southwest Museum

Although people in LA scarcely know about it, the **Southwest Museum** (Tues–Sun 11am–5pm; $5, $3 students; *www.southwestmuseum.org*), which rises castle-like below Mount Washington, was Charles F. Lummis' most enduring achievement and is well worth an afternoon's visit. Half a mile north of the Lummis House (take the #81 or #83 bus from Downtown), the recently renovated museum is the oldest in Los Angeles, and was founded in 1907. Its name is a bit deceptive – there are displays of Native American artifacts from all over North America, with exhibits of pre-Columbian pottery, coastal

Chumash rock art and a full-size Plains Indian Cheyenne teepee. The museum also hosts traveling exhibitions, and its educational program of lectures, films and theatrical events has made it an international center for indigenous American cultures. The Braun Research Library has an unmatched collection of recordings and photographs of Native Americans from the Bering Straits to Mexico, and the museum shop features Navajo rugs, kachina dolls and turquoise jewelry, as well as an extensive selection of books and specialist publications. Nearby, the Casa de Adobe, administered by the museum, is a 1917 attempt to recreate a Mexican hacienda. It contains a small museum of its own detailing LA history into the nineteenth century. Call 323/221-2163 for more information.

Hollywood

If a single place name epitomizes the LA dream of glamour, money and overnight success, it's **HOLLYWOOD**. Ever since American movies and their stars became international symbols of the good life, Hollywood has been a magnet to millions of tourists on once-in-a-lifetime pilgrimages and an equally massive assortment of hopefuls drawn by the thought of riches and glory. Even if the real prospects of success were one in a million, enough people were taken in by the dream to make Hollywood what it is today – a weird combination of insatiable optimism and total despair. It may be a cliché, but Hollywood really does blur the edges of fact and fiction, simply because so much seems possible here – and yet so little, for most residents, actually is.

The truth is that Hollywood was more a center of corruption and scandal than the city of dreams the studio-made legend suggests. Successful Hollywood residents actually spent little time here – they left as soon as they could afford to for the privacy of the hills or coast. Although the area continues to be a secondary center for the film business, with technical service companies like prop shops and equipment suppliers abundant, the big film companies relocated long ago, leaving Hollywood in isolation, with prostitution, drug dealing and seedy adult bookstores becoming the reality behind the fantasy. Things have brightened up a little in the last few years, however, with public and private capital beginning to pour in to finance the construction of new shopping malls and tourist plazas – one of which, a reconstruction of the Babylonian facade from D.W. Griffith's 1918 film *Intolerance*, will lead the visitor to a fancy auditorium slated to host the Academy Awards beginning in 2002.

Orientation

Approaching from Downtown, **East Hollywood** is the first taste of the district, an assortment of cheap housing and low-rent businesses with only a few interesting sights. Things pick up in **Central Hollywood**, a compact area that's the real movie history territory, swamped by an eccentric street mix of social derelicts and star-struck tourists. Whether the memories have been turned into bizarre shrines, or forgotten and paved over by parking lots, Central Hollywood has them in quantity, and you'd have to be avidly uninterested in filmlore to find the place dull. Protecting Hollywood from the outside world, the rising slopes of the Santa Monica Mountains contain **Griffith Park** – several thousand acres of nature offering rugged hiking trails and busy sports and picnic grounds, which form a scenic northern edge to the area. Beyond the park, the more southerly of the slopes comprise the high ground known as the **Hollywood Hills**: exclusive homes perched on snaking driveways that are the most tangible reminders of the wealth generated in the city – and the incredible roll call of household names which has sprung from it. A small intermediary area between the park and East Hollywood, **Los Feliz** has become a trendy place to live and socialize, so much so that some pop stars have opened boutiques here.

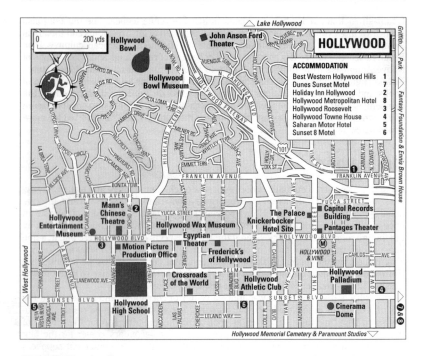

HOLLYWOOD

ACCOMMODATION

Best Western Hollywood Hills	1
Dunes Sunset Motel	7
Holiday Inn Hollywood	2
Hollywood Metropolitan Hotel	8
Hollywood Roosevelt	3
Hollywood Towne House	4
Saharan Motor Hotel	5
Sunset 8 Motel	6

East Hollywood

By night seedy, by day vibrant, **EAST HOLLYWOOD** is mostly inhabited by Hispanic immigrants who have yet to fulfill the American dream. The area between Downtown and Central Hollywood can be particularly unpleasant: this end of Sunset Boulevard is a notorious red-light strip, along whose length Hugh Grant famously encountered Divine Brown in 1995. But as ever in Los Angeles, where perimeter neighborhoods bordering the hills are highly sought after, the streets around Beachwood Avenue and at the foot of Griffith Park, have evolved into popular places to live and hang out, and Mediterranean-style homes now litter the hillside.

Four blocks north of Sunset Boulevard, the **SILVER LAKE** neighborhood was home to some of Hollywood's first studios, now converted into restaurants and galleries, or at least warehouses and storage units. Walt Disney opened his first studio at 2719 Hyperion Avenue in 1926 (now a grocery store), and the Keystone Kops were dreamt up in Mack Sennett's studio at 1712 Glendale Blvd, when the zone was known as **Edendale**, and where just a single sound studio now remains. Another faded bit of movie history can be found in the vicinity of 930 Vendome Street, where a lengthy stairway was a location for Laurel and Hardy's 1932 flick *The Music Box*, in which the lads tried to haul a piano up the many steps, to humorous effect. This is the only point of interest in an otherwise decrepit and unappealing neighborhood.

Nearby **LOS FELIZ** is home to many different communities, with fair-sized Hispanic and gay contingents, as with Silver Lake. On summer nights its bars are full of students from the local **American Film Institute** campus (Los Feliz Blvd at Western Ave), USC party animals, and slumming arty types from the Hollywood Hills. Johnny Depp's *Ed Wood* was partly shot, and premiered, at the architecturally impressive **Vista** movie theater, just off Hollywood Boulevard near Virgil – across from the former site of D.W. Griffith's *Intolerance* film set, which featured giant pillars and elephant statues, among many other curiosities. **Hollyhock House**, on a small hill close to the junction of Hollywood Boulevard and Vermont Avenue (Tues–Sun noon–3pm; $2), was the first of architect Frank Lloyd Wright's contributions to LA and was largely supervised by his student, Rudolf Schindler, later one of LA's pre-eminent architects. Completed in 1921, covered with Mayan motifs and imbued with an Art Deco flavor, it's an intriguingly obsessive dwelling, whose original furniture (now replaced by detailed reconstructions) continued the conceptual flow. The bizarre quality of the building was obviously too much for its oil heiress – and socialist – owner, Aline Barnsdall, who lived here only for a short time before donating both the house and the surrounding land to the city

A HISTORY OF HOLLYWOOD

Given its racy character, it's odd to think that Hollywood started life as a **temperance colony**, intended to provide a sober God-fearing alternative to raunchy Downtown LA, eight miles away by rough country road. Purchased and named by a pair of devout Methodists in 1887, the district remained autonomous until 1911, when residents were forced, in return for a regular water supply, to affiliate their city to LA as a suburb. The film industry, meanwhile, gathering momentum on the East Coast, needed a place with guaranteed sunshine and a diverse assortment of natural backdrops to enable pictures to be made quickly, and most importantly, a distant spot to dodge Thomas Edison's patent trust, which had restricted filmmaking in the East. Southern California, with its climate, scenery and isolation, was the perfect spot. A few offices affiliated to Eastern film companies appeared Downtown from 1906 and the first true studios opened in nearby Silver Lake, but independent hopefuls soon discovered the cheaper rents on offer in Hollywood. Soon, the first **Hollywood studio** opened in 1911, and within three years the place was packed with filmmakers – many of them, like **Cecil B. DeMille** who shared his barn-converted office space with a horse, destined to be the big names of the future.

The ramshackle industry expanded fast, bringing instant profits and fame, and the hopefuls who arrived eager for a slice of both soon swamped the original inhabitants, outraging them with their hedonistic lifestyles. Yet movie-making was far from being a financially secure business, and it wasn't until the release of D.W. Griffith's **The Birth of a Nation** in 1915 that the power of film was demonstrated. The film's right-wing and racist account of the Civil War caused riots outside cinemas and months of critical debate in the newspapers (President Woodrow Wilson approvingly described it as "writing history with lightning"), and for the first time drew the middle classes to moviehouses – despite the exorbitant $2 ticket price. It was also the movie which first perfected the narrative style and production techniques that gradually became standard in classic Hollywood cinema – close-ups, cross-cutting, etc.

Modern Hollywood took shape from the 1920s on, when film production grew more specialized and many small companies either went bust or were incorporated into one of the handful of bigger studios that came to dominate filmmaking. The **Golden Age** of the studio system was at its peak from the 1930s through the early 1950s, when a Supreme Court ruling put an end to studio monopolies controlling their exhibitors. Despite lean years from the later 1950s until the 1970s, and the onslaught of competition from television, Hollywood's enduring success is in making slick, pleasurable movies that sell – from the hard-bitten *film noir* of the 1940s to the new creativity of filmmakers such as David Lynch, Quentin Tarantino and Paul Thomas Anderson.

Ultimately, though, no matter how much lip service Hollywood pays to the "independent cinema" (mainly by purchasing brash upstarts like Miramax), it's been big names, big bucks and conservatism that have kept the town alive. With its profits gnawed into by TV and rock music, the film industry today rarely even thinks about taking artistic risks, even as it regularly takes unnecessary financial ones.

authorities for use as a cultural center. In keeping with this wish, the grounds of the house became known as **Barnsdall Art Park**, in which the **Municipal Art Gallery** (Wed–Sun 12.30–5pm, Fri until 8.30pm; $1.50) was erected to give exposure to new Southern Californian artists. If you've no interest in art or architecture, the park is still worth a visit as one of the few quiet spots around here to enjoy a view: the Hollywood Hills in one direction, all of Downtown and beyond in the other.

Another Wright building, the 1924 **Ennis-Brown House**, looms over Los Feliz at 2655 Glendower Avenue. One of four of his local structures to feature "textile" concrete block, its ominous, pre-Columbian appearance has added atmosphere to over thirty movies, from Vincent Price's *The House on Haunted Hill* to *Blade Runner*, and the house is open for bimonthly tours (reserve at ☎323/668-0234; $10, $5 students). Nearby, at 2495 Glendower, the **Fantasy Foundation** (daily 10am–4pm; free; call ☎323/MOON-FAN before arriving) boasts a truly amazing hoard of more than 300,000 items of horror, fantasy and sci-fi memorabilia. Forrest J. Ackerman, former editor of *Famous Monsters of Filmland* magazine and winner of science fiction's first Hugo award, has filled eighteen rooms of the "Ackermansion" with such delights as the fake breasts worn by Jane Fonda in *Barbarella*, the robot from *Metropolis* and the life masks of Boris Karloff, Bela Lugosi and Lon Chaney. Sixty-nine years in the making, this unique collection is enhanced by the draw of the man himself: numerous personal anecdotes and bits of gossip make his one-on-one tour a must.

Central Hollywood

The myths, magic, fable and fantasy splattered throughout the few short blocks of **CENTRAL HOLLYWOOD** would put a medieval fairytale to shame. With the densest concentration of faded glamour and film mythology in the world, a pervasive sense of nostalgia makes the area deeply appealing in a way no measure of commercialism can diminish. Although you're much more likely to find a porno theater than spot a star, the decline that blighted the area from the early 1960s is slowly receding in the face of prolonged efforts by local authorities – including repaving Hollywood Boulevard with a special glass-laden tarmac that sparkles in the streetlights. Nevertheless the place still gets hairy after dark, when the effects of homelessness, drug addiction and prostitution are more evident, and petty thieves go hunting for the odd purse or wallet.

Along Hollywood Boulevard

Following Hollywood Boulevard west, you'll come to the junction of **Hollywood and Vine**, a juxtaposition of street names that still tingles the spines of dedicated Hollywood-philes, some of whom can be spotted standing in respectful silence before crossing the road. During the early golden years, the rumor spread that any budding star had only to parade around this junction to be "spotted" by big-name film directors (the major studios were in those days all concentrated nearby), who nursed coffees behind the windows of neighboring restaurants. In typical Hollywood style the whole tale was blown wildly out of proportion, and while many real stars did pass by, it was only briefly on their way to and from work, and the crossing did nothing but earn a fabulous reputation. The only thing marking the legend today, apart from disappointed tourists, is a small plaque on the wall of the *New York Pizza Express*.

The junction is also the current terminus of the Red Line subway, so if you feel inclined to make a trip back Downtown or to MacArthur Park, this is the spot – an underground station decorated with film reels and familiar Hollywood imagery that is one of the few artistically interesting stops in LA's mass transit network. Above ground, at 1750 N Vine St, the **Capitol Records Tower** resembles a stack of 45rpm records and serves as the music company's headquarters, its 1950s design supposedly inspired by an offhand Johnny Mercer remark. Nearby, at 6233 Hollywood Blvd, the **Pantages**

Theater has a bland facade but one of the city's greatest interiors, a melange of Baroque styling that mainly highlights touring stage productions these days.

The bulky **Knickerbocker Hotel**, 1714 Ivar Ave, now a retirement center, was where the widow of legendary escapologist Harry Houdini conducted a rooftop seance in an attempt to assist her late spouse in his greatest escape of all. During the 1930s and 1940s, the hotel had a reputation for rooming some of Hollywood's more unstable characters, and a number of lesser-name suicides plunged from its high windows. At 1817 Ivar Street is the flea-bag boarding house where author and screenwriter **Nathanael West** lived during the 1930s, after coming west to revive his flagging financial situation – and ultimately failing. Gazing over the street's parade of extras, hustlers and make-believe cowboys, West penned the dark satirical portrait of Hollywood, *The Day of the Locust*, the apocalyptic finale of which was inspired by Hollywood Hills wildfires in the summer of 1935 (and which includes a character with the oddly prescient name of Homer Simpson). Back on Hollywood Boulevard, at no. 6608, the purple-and-pink **Frederick's of Hollywood** is a local landmark. Opened in 1947, it has been (under-)clothing Hollywood's sex goddesses ever since, and many more mortal bodies all over the world through its mail-order outlet. Inside, the **lingerie museum** (Mon–Sat 10am–6pm, Sun noon–5pm; free) displays some of the company's best corsets, bras and panties, donated by a host of big-name wearers, ranging from Liz Taylor and Lana Turner to Cher and Madonna.

A little further on, at no. 6708, the very first Hollywood premiere (*Robin Hood*, an epic swashbuckler starring Douglas Fairbanks Sr), took place in 1922 at the **Egyptian Theater**. Financed by impresario Sid Grauman, in its heyday the Egyptian was a glorious fantasy, modestly seeking to re-create the Temple of Thebes, with usherettes dressed as Cleopatra. This great old building was shattered in the 1994 earthquake, but has since been lovingly restored by the American Cinematheque film foundation, and now plays an assortment of Hollywood classics, avant-garde flicks, and foreign films to small but appreciative crowds. Your visit to the theater, however, may well be for a viewing of a short documentary, presented hourly, chronicling the rise of Hollywood as America's movie capital. Much less inspired, the **Hollywood Wax Museum**, 6767 Hollywood Blvd (daily 10am–midnight, Fri–Sat closes at 2am; $8.25) is a tawdry selection of over two hundred charmless dummies. Besides Spock's ears, Marilyn's backside and Dolly's breasts, there's a replica of Leonardo da Vinci's *The Last Supper* and other "greatest hits" of the art world, like Michelangelo's *Pietà*.

Much of the pavement along this stretch of Hollywood Boulevard is marked by the brass nameplates that make up the **Walk of Fame** (officially beginning at Hollywood and Vine). The laying of the plates began in 1960, instigated by the local Chamber of Commerce, which thought that by enshrining the big names in radio, television, movies, music and theater, it could somehow restore the boulevard's faded glamour and boost tourism. However, oversights have often been made; the Rolling Stones, for example, took decades to gain a star, long after they were past their prime. Selected stars have to part with several thousand dollars for the privilege of being included: among them are Marlon Brando (1717 Vine St), Marlene Dietrich (6400 Hollywood Blvd), Michael Jackson (6927 Hollywood Blvd), Elvis Presley (6777 Hollywood Blvd) and Ronald Reagan (6374 Hollywood Blvd).

Nothing as vulgar as money can taint the appeal of the foot- and handprints embedded in the concrete concourse of **Mann's Chinese Theatre** at 6925 Hollywood Blvd, opened in 1927 as a lavish setting for premieres of swanky new productions. Through the halcyon decades, this was *the* spot for movie first-nights, and the public crowded behind the rope barriers in the thousands to watch the movie aristocrats arriving for the screenings. The foot-and-hand-prints-in-concrete idea came about when actress Norma Talmadge accidentally (though some say it was a deliberate publicity stunt) trod in wet cement while visiting the construction site with owner Sid Grauman. The first formally to leave their marks were Mary Pickford and Douglas Fairbanks Sr, who ceremoniously dipped their digits when arriving for the opening of *King of Kings*, and the practice continues today – Richard Gere was a recent inductee. It's certainly fun to work out the actual dimensions of your favorite film stars, and to discover if your hands are smaller than Julie Andrews' or your feet are bigger than Rock Hudson's (or both). As for the building, it's an odd version of a classical Chinese temple, replete with dubious Chinese motifs and upturned dragon tail flanks. Try to catch a movie here when a spectacle isn't taking place out front; the Art Deco splendor of the lobby and the grand chinoiserie of the auditorium make for interesting viewing. Afterward, you may wish to hop aboard a tour bus for a look at the "homes of the stars" (see p.72), along with hundreds of other sightseers.

To catch a movie in the making, cross the road to the **Motion Picture Production Office**, Room 602, 6922 Hollywood Blvd (Mon–Fri 8am–5pm), which issues a free "shoot sheet" every weekday from 10.30am, detailing exactly what's being filmed around town that day. Most film shoots hire a couple of off-duty LAPD officers for security, but not all sets are impenetrable. A few doors down, 7000 Hollywood Blvd, the **Hollywood Roosevelt** was movieland's first luxury hotel. Opened in the same year as the Chinese Theatre, it fast became the meeting place of top actors and screenwriters, its *Cinegrill* restaurant feeding and watering the likes of W.C. Fields, Ernest Hemingway and F. Scott Fitzgerald, not to mention legions of hangers-on. In 1929 the first Oscars were presented here, beginning the long tradition of Hollywood rewarding itself in the absence of honors from elsewhere. Look inside for a view of the splashing fountains and elegantly weighty wrought-iron chandeliers of its marble-floored lobby, and for the intelligently compiled pictorial **History of Hollywood** on the second floor. The place is thick with legend: on the staircase from the lobby to the mezzanine Bill "Bojangles" Robinson taught Shirley Temple to dance; and the ghost of Montgomery Clift (who stayed here while filming *From Here to Eternity*) apparently haunts the place, announcing his presence by blowing a bugle. Surviving lounge divas like Eartha Kitt still put on the occasional show at the *Cinegrill* cabaret.

Across the street, the **Hollywood Entertainment Museum**, 7021 Hollywood Blvd (Tues–Sun 10am–6pm; $7.50, students $4.50), occupies a lower level of the crudely "futuristic" Hollywood Galaxy theater building. Although it contains the full set of the TV show *Cheers* and of the bridge of the Enterprise from *Star Trek*, along with rotating exhibitions and various antiques and curios from Hollywood history, the museum's real jewel is the **Max Factor Collection**, a display of beauty artifacts from Hollywood's Golden Age, which was formerly housed in its own building on Highland Avenue. The kissing machine, used to test the endurance of Factor's potions, and the calibration machine, invented to determine which features needed equalizing, are both memorable relics from a long-gone era.

Along Sunset Boulevard

There's more Hollywood nostalgia directly south of the central section of Hollywood Boulevard, on and around the less touristy **Sunset Boulevard**, which runs parallel. You might start your explorations at the corner of Sunset Boulevard and **Gower Street**. During the industry's formative years, when unemployed movie extras hopeful of a few days' work with one of the small local B-movie studios would hang around here, the junction earned the nicknames "Gower gulch" and "poverty row."

The delectable Spanish Revival-style building at 6525 Sunset Blvd was, from the 1920s until the 1950s, known as the **Hollywood Athletic Club**. Another of Hollywood's legendary watering holes, the likes of Charlie Chaplin, Clark Gable and Tarzan himself lounged beside its Olympic-sized pool, while Johns Barrymore and Wayne held drinking parties in the apartment levels above. After standing empty for 25 years, the building re-opened in 1990 as a billiards club, bar and restaurant, frequented by throngs of pouting bad-boy actors and assorted would-be stars.

The grouping of shops at the **Crossroads of the World**, 6672 Sunset Blvd, isn't much to look at now, but when finished in 1936, this was one of LA's major tourist attractions and one of the very first local malls. The central plaza supposedly resembles a ship, surrounded by shops designed with Tudor, French, Italian and Spanish motifs – the idea being that the shops are the ports into which the shopper would sail. Oddly enough, time has been kind to this place, and considering the more recent and far brasher architecture found in the city, this has a definite, if muted, charm. However, it can be seen in its full glory in the 1997 cop film *LA Confidential*, which also uses the nearby *Formosa Café* (see p.155) and *Frolic Room* as period emblems of 1950s LA swagger. Finally, for a closer look into the movie biz, nearby **Paramount Studios** (Mon–Fri 9am–2pm; hourly tours $15), at 5555 Melrose Ave, provides a very limited trek around the soundstages and offices of its sizable complex. Don't expect Universal-style theme rides or a lengthy Warner Brothers-meander, however; this is mainly for tourists who can't tell the difference between a close-up and a long-shot.

The Hollywood Memorial Cemetery

Despite the beliefs of some of their loopiest fans, even the biggest Hollywood stars are mortal, and the many LA cemeteries that hold their tombs get at least as many visitors as the city's museums. One of the most unheralded and least dramatically landscaped, though with more than its fair share of big names, is the **Hollywood Memorial Cemetery** (daily 8am–5pm; free), close to the junction of Santa Monica Boulevard and Gower Street and overlooked by the famous water tower of the neighboring Paramount Studios (whose even more famous gates are just around the corner on Santa Monica Boulevard). In the southeastern corner of the cemetery, the cathedral mausoleum sets the tone for the place, a solemn collection of tombs that includes, at no. 1205, the resting place of **Rudolph Valentino**. In 1926 10,000 people packed the cemetery when the celebrated screen lover died aged just 31, and to this day on each anniversary of his passing (23 August), at least one "Lady in Black" will likely be found mourning – a tradition that started as a publicity stunt in 1931 (the first weeping damsel claimed to be a former paramour of Valentino's but was exposed as a hired actress) and has continued ever since. While here, spare a thought for the more contemporary screen star, Peter Finch, who died in 1977. His crypt is opposite Valentino's and tourists often lean their rears unknowingly against it while photographing Rudolph's marker.

Fittingly, outside the mausoleum, the most pompous grave in the cemetery belongs to **Douglas Fairbanks Sr**, who, with his wife Mary Pickford, did much to introduce social snobbery to Hollywood. Even in death Fairbanks keeps a snooty distance from the pack, his ostentatious memorial, complete with sculptured pond, only reachable by a shrubbery-lined path from the mausoleum. If you revel in Tinseltown's post-life pretension, there are countless self-important obelisks and grandiose grave-markers throughout the park, under which LA's somebodies and nobodies finally, in death, mix. One of the cemetery's more recent arrivals was **Mel Blanc**, "the man of a thousand voices" – among them Bugs Bunny, Porky Pig, Tweety Pie and Sylvester – whose epitaph simply reads "That's All, Folks."

Despite its morbid glamour, the cemetery also has a contemporary function. As you enter, you will notice the many tightly packed rows of glossy black headstones with Orthodox crosses and Cyrillic lettering. These mark the resting places of Russian and Armenian immigrants, who increasingly populate the graveyard just as their living counterparts populate Central and West Hollywood.

Griffith Park

Vast **GRIFFITH PARK**, between Hollywood and the San Fernando Valley (daily 5am–10.30pm, mountain roads close at dusk; free), is a combination of gentle greenery

HIKING IN GRIFFITH PARK

The steeper parts of **Griffith Park**, which blend into the foothills of the Santa Monica Mountains, are the focus of a variety of **hikes**. You can get maps from the **ranger station**, at 4730 Crystal Springs Rd (☎323/655-5188) – also the starting point for guided hikes and atmospheric evening hikes, held whenever there's a full moon. The rangers also have maps for drivers that detail the best vantage points for views over the whole of Los Angeles, not least from the highest place in the park – the summit of Mount Hollywood.

and rugged mountain slopes that offers a welcome escape from the mind-numbing hubbub almost everywhere else in the city. The largest municipal park in the country, it's also one of the few places where LA's multitude of racial and social groups at least go through the motions of mixing together. Above the landscaped flat sections, where the crowds assemble to picnic, play sports or visit the fixed attractions, the hillsides are rough and wild, marked only by foot and bridle paths, leading into desolate but appealingly unspoiled terrain that gives great views over the LA basin and out towards the ocean. Bear in mind, though, that while the park is safe by day, its reputation for after-dark violence is well founded.

Around the park

There are four **main entrances** to Griffith Park. Western Canyon Road, north of Los Feliz Boulevard, enters the park through the **Ferndell** – as the name suggests, a lush glade of ferns, from which numerous trails run deeper into the park – continuing up to the **Observatory** (summer daily 12.30–10pm; rest of year Tues–Fri 2–10pm, Sat & Sun 12.30–10pm; free), familiar from its use as a backdrop in *Rebel Without A Cause* and numerous low-budget sci-fi flicks, and with moderately interesting science displays and shows in its **Hall of Science**. The astronomically minded will enjoy the array of heavenly bodies displayed in the **Planetarium** (Tues–Fri 3pm–7.30pm, Sat & Sun 1.30–7.30pm; shows every 90min; $4), while fans of rock and pop music can take in the beams in the adjacent **Laserium** (Sun–Thurs 6pm & 8.45pm, Fri–Sat & various holidays 6pm, 8.45pm & 9.45pm; $6.50). More enticingly, on clear nights there are brilliant views of the cosmos through the powerful **telescope** mounted on the roof (daily 7–10pm; free). One Saturday a month, the LA Astronomical Society gathers on the front lawn. Thirty or forty telescopes and their knowledgeable owners set up at 1pm to see the sun through filters and stay until the area closes, happy to discuss the planets and stars with passersby.

Descending from the observatory by way of Vermont Canyon Road (effectively the continuation of Western Canyon Road) brings you to the small **bird sanctuary**, set within a modest-sized wooded canyon. Various species have been encouraged to nest here, but as the birds aren't in captivity you might not see them. Across the road is the **Greek Theatre**, an open-air amphitheater that seats nearly five thousand beneath its Greek-style columns – though if you're not going in for a show (the *Greek* is a venue for big-name rock, jazz and country music concerts during the summer) you'll see just the bland exterior.

Crystal Springs Drive, off Riverside Drive, takes you to the ranger station. And the **northern end** of the park, over the hills in the San Fernando Valley, is best reached directly by car from the Golden State Freeway, although you can take the park roads (or explore the labyrinth of hiking trails) that climb the park's hilly core. At the end of the journey, don't bother with the cramped and dismal **LA Zoo** (daily 10am–5pm; $8.25, kids $3.25) or the unkempt old locomotives of **Travel Town** (daily 10am–5pm; free).

The Gene Autry Western Heritage Museum

Sharing a parking lot with the zoo, the **Gene Autry Western Heritage Museum** (Tues–Sun 10am–5pm; $7, students $5; *www.autry-museum.org*), at the northeastern corner of Griffith Park near the junction of the Ventura and Golden State freeways, bears the name of the "singing cowboy" who cut over six hundred discs from 1929, starred in blockbuster Hollywood Westerns during the 1930s and 1940s, became even more of a household name through his TV show in the 1950s, and died in 1999 after a very lengthy career – which included a stint as owner of baseball's California Angels franchise in Anaheim.

Autry fans hoping for a shrine to the man who penned the immortal *That Silver-Haired Daddy of Mine*, are in for a shock, however: the **collection** – from buckskin jackets and branding irons to Frederic Remington's sculptures of turn-of-the-century Western life and the truth about the shoot-out at the OK Corral – is a serious and credible attempt to explore the mindset and culture of those who participated in the US's colonization of the West. It also contains a nod to Hollywood, with a sizable collection of movie artifacts, posters and assorted memorabilia, much of it also discussed in an analytical, non-jingoistic fashion.

The Hollywood Hills

Quite apart from giving the chance to appreciate just how flat the LA basin is, the views from the **Hollywood Hills** feature perhaps the oddest, most opulent, selection of properties to be found anywhere. Around these canyons and slopes, which run from Hollywood itself into Benedict Canyon above Beverly Hills, mansions are so commonplace that only the half-dozen fully blown castles (at least, Hollywood-style castles) really stand out.

Mulholland Drive, named after LA's most famous engineer, runs along the crest, passing some of the most notorious sites – Rudolph Valentino's extravagant **Falcon Lair** (1436 Bella Dr), Errol Flynn's **Mulholland House** (7740 Mulholland Dr), and the former home of actress Sharon Tate, where some of the Manson family killings took place. Plus, there's a number of run-of-the-mill million-dollar residences belonging to an

---

THE HOLLYWOOD SIGN

One thing you can see from more or less anywhere in Hollywood is the **Hollywood Sign**, erected on Mount Lee to spell "Hollywoodland" in 1923 as a promotional device to sell property at the foot of the hills. The "land" part was removed in 1949, leaving the rest as a world-renowned symbol of the entertainment industry here. It has also (unjustifiably) gained a reputation as a suicide spot, ever since would-be movie star Peg Entwistle terminated her career and life here in 1932, aged 24. It was no mean feat – the sign being as difficult to reach then as it is now: from the end of Beachwood Drive she picked a path slowly upward through the thick brush and climbed the fifty-foot-high "H," eventually leaping from it to her death. Stories that this act led to a line of failed starlets desperate to make their final exit from Tinseltown's best known marker are untrue however – though many troubled souls may have died of exhaustion while trying to get to it. Less fatal mischief has been practiced by students of nearby Caltech, who on one occasion renamed the sign for their school. More unsavory acts of sign desecration have also occurred, most of them too juvenile and numerous to mention. Because of this history, there's no public road to the sign (Beachwood Drive comes nearest, but ends at a closed gate) and you'll incur minor cuts and bruises while scrambling to get anywhere near. In any case, infrared cameras and radar-activated zoom lenses have been installed to catch graffiti writers, and innocent tourists who can't resist a close look are also liable for the $107 fine. It's simply not worth the bother.

assortment of luminaries, visionaries, former politicians and movie moguls, some of whom have helped forge LA's reputation for ostentatious and utterly decadent living. Doubtless the most bizarre sight is the **Chemosphere**, at 776 Torreyson Dr, a giant UFO house hovering above the canyon on a long pedestal. Unfortunately, most of the area's other houses are hidden away, and there's no real way to explore in depth without your own car and a knowledgeable friend to help pinpoint the sights, spread widely across every hillside. You could use one of the guided tours (see p.72), but for the most part you're better off doing your own exploring, preferably with a copy of the latest *Thomas Guide* map and, if possible, a detailed and updated guide to LA architecture.

Lake Hollywood

Hemmed in among the hills between Griffith Park and the Hollywood Freeway, **Lake Hollywood** feels like a piece of open country in the heart of the city. The clear, calm waters, actually a reservoir intended to lubricate the whole of LA in times of drought, make a delightful spot, surrounded by clumps of pines in which squirrels, lizards and a few scurrying skunks and coyotes easily outnumber humans. You can't get too near the water, as metal fences protect it from the general public, but the footpaths that encircle it are pleasant for a stroll, especially for a glimpse of the stone bear heads that decorate the reservoir's curving front wall. There's no social kudos associated with being seen trotting around the footpath – which may explain why so few Angelenos deem it worthy of their presence. Nevertheless, the lake has figured in a few Hollywood films, notably the disaster epic *Earthquake*, which showed the dam bursting and flooding the basin to devastating effect. Of course, apocalypse is a constant theme in stories about LA.

You can only reach the lake by car. Although opening and closing times vary widely throughout the year, the lake **access road** is generally open from 7am until noon and 2pm until 7pm on weekdays, and 7am until 7.30pm on weekends: to get to it, go north on Cahuenga Boulevard past Franklin Avenue and turn right onto Dix Street, left into Holly Drive and climb to Deep Dell Place; from there it's a sharp left on Weidlake Drive. Follow the winding little street to the main gate.

The Hollywood Bowl

Where Highland Avenue hits the Hollywood Freeway, the **Hollywood Bowl** is an open-air auditorium that opened in 1921, and has since gained more fame than it deserves. The Beatles played here in the mid-1960s, but the Bowl's principal function is as home to the Los Angeles Philharmonic, which gives evening concerts from July to September. These are far less highbrow than you might imagine, many of them featuring popular pieces like *Victory at Sea* and the *1812 Overture*. It's long been the chic thing to eat a picnic in the grounds before making the climb to your seat, and nowadays the consumption tends to continue throughout the show, often rendering the music barely audible above the crunching of popcorn and fried chicken and the clink of empty wine bottles rolling down the steps. If that racket alone doesn't bother you, there's also the constant drone of jumbo jets flying above the Bowl on their long final descent toward LAX. Although not a choice spot for lovers of fine music, the venue can still be fun, with ticket prices starting at $1. If you're really broke, come to the Bowl Tuesday through Friday between 9.30am and noon to listen to rehearsals for free.

More about the Bowl's history can be gleaned from the video show inside the **Hollywood Bowl Museum** (summer 10am–8.30pm; rest of year Tues–Sat 10am–4pm; free) near the entrance, which has recently been refurbished. It's not an essential stop by any means, but it's worth a visit if you have any affection for the grand old concrete structure. With a collection of musical instruments from around the world, the museum also features recordings of notable symphonic moments in the Bowl's history and architectural drawings by Lloyd Wright, Frank's son (more famous for his Wayfarer's Chapel; see p.125), who contributed a design for one of the Bowl's many shells.

West LA

LA's Westside begins immediately beyond Hollywood in **WEST LA**, which contains some of the city's most expensive, and exclusive, neighborhoods. Bordered by the foothills of the Santa Monica Mountains to the north and the Santa Monica Freeway to the south, West LA, perhaps more than anywhere else, embodies the stylish images that the city projects to the outside world. Actually, once you're there, the reality is often less dazzling: away from the showcase streets are the usual long, residential blocks, only marginally less drab than normal with their better tended lawns, more upscale supermarkets, cleaner gas stations and tastier fast-food.

One of the best reasons to come to West LA is the engrossing collection of the **LA County Museum of Art (LACMA)**, on the eastern perimeter of the still firmly Jewish **Fairfax District**, and forming the centerpiece of the resurgent cultural zone known as the **Museum Mile**. It's not until you cross west of Fairfax Avenue and north of Beverly Boulevard that West LA truly reveals itself in **West Hollywood** – known for its art and

ACCOMMODATION

Beverly Hills Hotel	8
Beverly Laurel Motel	10
Bevonshire Lodge Motel	9
Chateau Marmont	3
Claremont	1
Hotel Bel Air	2
Hotel Des Flores	11
Le Montrose	5
Le Parc	7
Le Reve	6
The Standard	4

WEST LA

design, clogged by posey restaurants and boutiques, and surprisingly small-scale, except for a giant design center at its core. **Beverly Hills**, a little way west, is less gregarious but more affluent: you may need an expense account to buy a sandwich but it's a matchless place to indulge in window shopping on the way to the more roundly appealing **Westwood**. The main activity in this low-rise, Spanish Revival, fairly pedestrianized area has always been movies – seeing them rather than making them. The original Art Deco palaces still remain, a short way from the **UCLA Campus** – the second of LA's university sites, home to a number of galleries and museums and altogether more appealing for visitors than the fortress atmosphere of USC. The **Sepulveda Pass** forms the western edge of West LA and leads the visitor to two museums that have relocated to the area: the **Getty Center** and the **Skirball Cultural Center**, both positioned high above the basin's turmoil.

The Fairfax District and Miracle Mile

The West LA section of **Fairfax Avenue**, between Santa Monica and Wilshire, is the backbone of the city's Jewish culture. Apart from temples, yeshivas, kosher butcher shops and delicatessens there's little actually to see here, but by local standards it's a refreshingly vibrant neighborhood, and easily explored on foot. Fairfax continues down to the lackluster wooden structures of **Farmer's Market**, at the junction with Third Street (June–Sept Mon–Sat 9am–8pm; Oct–May Mon–Sat 9am–6.30pm, Sun 10am–5pm; free). The market is a rabbit warren of fast-food stalls and produce stands, the former offering greasy treats and the latter more natural delights. To the east on Third Street, **Pan Pacific Park** once featured the wondrous Streamline Moderne Pan Pacific Auditorium, a masterpiece of late Art Deco architecture. However, the structure burned in a 1989 fire, and only a pleasant park of the same name remains. Further on, the **May Company** department store on Wilshire Boulevard, at Fairfax Avenue, was built in 1934 and has been compared to an oversized, golden perfume bottle ever since; its main contemporary function is to show the work of local artists in its ground-floor display windows, with the art provided courtesy of LACMA. The store was placed here to announce the western entrance to the premier property development of the time, **Miracle Mile**, as it was named, which stretched along Wilshire eastward to La Brea Avenue and is still lined with faded Art Deco monuments. The department stores have long since closed, but an unprecedented number of museums, including LACMA, now create an impressive "Museum Mile" in their place. Although many of the office blocks are empty, look out for the old site of **Desmond's**, a former department store at no. 5514 consisting of a Zigzag Moderne tower stepping up from a streamlined two-story pedestal, and, just east of La Brea Avenue, the 1929 black-and-gold **Security Pacific Bank**. The bank gives you a hint of what LA's greatest Art Deco structure, the **Richfield Building** Downtown, must have looked like before it was summarily destroyed in 1968.

The Museum Mile

Oddly enough, the **LA County Museum of Art** (Mon–Tues 10am–5pm, Thurs noon–8pm, Fri noon–9pm, Sat–Sun 11am–8pm; $6, students $4; *www.lacma.org*) is an unimpressive series of buildings along Miracle Mile that was plopped down in 1965 in a fit of municipal-mindedness that has never really taken root. The buildings aside, some of the collections of applied art here are among the best in the world, and despite the loss of Armand Hammer's stock of paintings to his own museum in Westwood (see p.116), it justifies a lengthy visit. If you arrive on a Wednesday before 1pm, check out the schedule of films playing in the **Leo S. Bing Theater**, where you can see anything from a Hitchcock classic to a screwball comedy for only $2.

LACMA is enormous, and there's no way you could see the lot in one go; you're best off either focusing on the contemporary art and traveling exhibitions in the **Anderson Building** (the concrete block on Wilshire Blvd) or diving into the fine selection of Old Masters and world art in the **Ahmanson Building** (the concrete block on Ogden Drive). Get a **map** of the complex from the information desk in the central courtyard. Alongside many excellent collections of Southeast Asian sculpture and Middle Eastern decorative arts in the Ahmanson Building, the **Fearing Collection** consists of funeral masks and sculpted guardian figures from the ancient civilizations of pre-Columbian Mexico. Where the museum really excels, however, is in its specializations, notably the prints and drawings in the **Rifkind Center for German Expressionist Studies**, which includes a library of magazines and tracts from Weimar Germany, and the **Pavilion for Japanese Art**. This is a recent addition to the museum and the only effective building on the site; it was created by iconoclastic architect Bruce Goff and built to resemble the effects of traditional *shoji* screens, filtering varying levels and qualities of light through to the interior. Displays include painted screens and scrolls, ceramics, and lacquerware, rivaling the collection of the late Emperor Hirohito as the most extensive in the world, and viewable on a gently sloping ramp that spirals down to a small, ground-floor waterfall that trickles pleasantly amid the near-silence of the gallery.

The roof combs of the pavilion make a playful reference to the tusks of a model mastodon sinking slowly into the adjacent **La Brea Tar Pits**, a large pool of smelly tar ("*la brea*" in Spanish). Tens of thousands of years ago, such creatures tried to drink from the thin layer of water covering the tar in the pits, only to become stuck fast and preserved for modern science. Millions of bones belonging to the animals (and one set of human bones) have been found here and reconstructed in the adjacent **George C.**

A TRIP TO CULVER CITY

South of West LA and east of Venice you can find one of LA's most overlooked spots, **CULVER CITY** – one of the towns that helped give rise to the American movie industry in the 1910s. Much of this tradition is still visible at the gates of the old Triangle Pictures, 10202 Washington Blvd (now part of the off-limits Sony lot), where film pioneer and producer **Thomas Ince** began building his LA operation. Fans of *Gone with the Wind* may recognize Ince's other former studio complex up the road at 9336 Washington Blvd – predictably, this Colonial Revival "mansion" is no more than a facade.

While you're in the area, jump on the Culver City Trolley (Mon–Fri 11.30am–3pm; 25¢) and take a ride to the **Hayden Tract**. LA's premiere showplace for deconstructivist architecture, the Tract lies near Hayden Ave and National Blvd, and features much stunning work by avant-garde master-builder Eric Owen Moss. A few of his more striking works include Pittard Sullivan, 3535 Hayden Ave, a giant gray box with massive wooden ribs poking out; 8522 National, at that same address, featuring a jangled-up facade with a white staircase leading to nowhere; The Box, just to the east, another gray box, this one with a riveted cubic window that looks ready to tumble down to the street below; and the huge Samitaur, 3457 S La Cienega Blvd, massive gray warehouse-like offices with gnarled, jagged points and a truly freakish sense of geometry.

If movie history and weird architecture aren't enough for you, top off your trip with a visit to the always-bizarre **Museum of Jurassic Technology**, 9341 Venice Blvd (Thurs 2–8pm, Fri–Sun noon–6pm; $4; *www.mjt.org*). As much an art museum as a science center, this institution has little to do with distant history or roving dinosaurs. Rather, it features a great range of oddities from the pseudo-scientific to the paranormal to the just plain creepy, including trailer-park artworks, exhibitions of folk superstitions, narrative rants by crank scientists, and displays of unearthly Amazonian insects. The ultimate effect is quite unnerving, as these vivid, eerie exhibits are shown in dark rooms without windows or sunlight.

Page Discovery Center (Tues–Sat 10am–5pm; $6, students $3.50), where you can spot the skeletons of your favorite extinct Ice Age-era creatures, from giant ground sloths to menacing saber-tooth tigers. Tar still seeps from the ground, but most of the sticky goo oozes behind chain link fences.

At 6060 Wilshire Blvd, the **Peterson Automotive Museum** (Tues–Sun 10am–6pm; Fri until 9pm; $7) is the baby of media mogul Robert Peterson, with three floors paying sumptuous if superficial homage to the automobile, featuring special exhibits of movie stars' cars, customized low-riders and vintage footage of land-speed record attempts in the desert. It fails to explain the reasons behind the collapse of LA's early public transportation system and is not critical by any means, but it does have enough mint-condition classic models to render the car-crazy delirious with joy.

The next museum along the road is the curious **Carol and Barry Kaye Museum of Miniatures**, 5900 Wilshire Blvd (Tues–Sat 10am–5pm, Sun 11am–5pm; $7.50, students $5; *www.museumofminiatures.com*), housing the world's most comprehensive collection of miniatures, numbering over two-hundred works and offering tiny, elaborate reconstructions of such spots as Fontainebleau and Hampton Court. Other exhibits include Roman emperor Domitian's palace, a Japanese garden and the Hollywood Bowl, complete with pint-sized Ella, Satchmo and Dizzy. Further south, a mile from Wilshire down La Brea Ave, **St Elmo's Village**, at 4836 St Elmo Dr, (☎323/931-3409), is a popular version of community art-in-action. An arts project now more than twenty years old, the colorful murals and sculptures here grew out of efforts to foster a constructive and supportive environment for local youth. It's now also the site of the **Festival of the Art of Survival**, an annual celebration of hippie-flavored folk and popular art and music held each Memorial Day.

West Hollywood

Between Fairfax Avenue and Beverly Hills, **WEST HOLLYWOOD** is the newest of LA's constituent cities. Thanks to various legal technicalities, it was for many years a separate administrative entity from the rest of Los Angeles, notorious for its after-hours vice clubs and general debauchery. Things changed in 1983, however, when the autonomous city of West Hollywood was established, partly to clean up the place and partly to represent the interests of the gay community, elderly residents and property renters. There are still sleazy rent-boy areas around La Brea Avenue in the east, but much of the rest has smartened up considerably, from the new sculpture garden down the median of **Santa Monica Boulevard**, the district's main drag, to the flashy dance clubs and designer clothing stores appearing over the rest of the neighborhood. In front of the **Tomkat Theater**, beneath a marquee that has proclaimed everything from *Deep Throat* to *In Thrust We Trust*, the alternative **Porno Walk of Fame** is devoted entirely to X-rated film stars. By way of contrast, the eastern end of the boulevard has become home to a large and growing contingent of Russians, many of whom don't mesh well with the gay scene around them.

Melrose Avenue, LA's trendiest shopping street, runs parallel to Santa Monica Boulevard four blocks south, a streetscape that at times resembles nothing more than a low-budget 1950s sci-fi feature: neon and Art Deco abound among a fluorescent rash of designer and second-hand boutiques, exotic antique shops, avant-garde galleries, record shops and high-attitude restaurants. The west end of Melrose is more upmarket, with furniture shops and art galleries spread out around the hulking, bright blue glass mass of the **Pacific Design Center**, a furniture marketplace near San Vicente Boulevard known as the "Blue Whale" for the way it dwarfs its low-rise neighbors – along with a newer "Green Giant" addition.

The stylistic extremes of Melrose Avenue are also reflected in the area's domestic architecture. Four blocks east of La Cienega Boulevard, the 1922 **Schindler House**,

835 N King's Rd (Wed–Sun 11am–6pm, tours Sat–Sun 1–5pm, and by appointment; ☎323/651-1510; $5 donation), was for years the blueprint of California Modernist architecture, with sliding canvas panels designed to be removed in summer, exposed roof rafters, and open-plan rooms facing onto outdoor terraces – banal in replication but compelling in the original. Coming from his native Austria via Frank Lloyd Wright's studio to work on the Hollyhock House (p.99), Schindler was so pleased with the California climate that he built this house without any bedrooms, romantically planning to sleep outdoors year-round in covered sleeping baskets on the roof; he misjudged the weather, however, and soon moved inside.

Four blocks west, **La Cienega Boulevard** divides West Hollywood roughly down the middle, separating the next-wave trendies on the Hollywood side from the establishment couturiers on the Beverly Hills border. La Cienega ("the swamp" in Spanish) holds a mixture of LA's best and most expensive restaurants and art galleries, and continues south, passing the huge **Beverly Center** shopping mall at Beverly Boulevard – a nightmarish fortress of brown plaster that was thrown up in 1982 on top of the fun-but-faded **Beverlyland** amusement park. Another landmark structure, and one that managed to survive the wrecking ball by some adroit repositioning, is the **Tail o' the Pup**, the world-famous hot-dog stand shaped like a (mostly bun) hot dog, which was moved a block away from La Cienega to 329 San Vicente Blvd to make way for the garish *Sofitel* hotel.

Further south, right on the Beverly Hills border at 333 S La Cienega, the Academy of Motion Picture Arts and Sciences' **Margaret Herrick Library** (Mon–Tues & Thurs–Fri 10am–6pm) is a non-circulating research library that holds a huge hoard of film memorabilia and scripts inside a Moorish-style building that used to be a water treatment plant.

Sunset Strip

Above western Hollywood, on either side of La Cienega Boulevard, the roughly two-mile long conglomeration of restaurants, plush hotels and nightclubs on Sunset Boulevard has long been known as **Sunset Strip**. These establishments first began to appear during the early 1920s, along what was then a dusty dirt road serving as the main route between the Hollywood movie studios and the West LA "homes of the stars." F. Scott Fitzgerald and friends spent many leisurely afternoons over drinks here, around the swimming pool of the long-demolished *Garden of Allah* hotel, and the nearby *Ciro's* nightclub was *the* place to be seen in the swinging 1940s, surviving today as the original *Comedy Store* (see p.164). With the rise of TV, the Strip declined, only reviving in the 1960s when a scene developed around the landmark *Whisky-a-Go-Go* club, which featured seminal psychedelic rock bands such as Love and Buffalo Springfield during the heyday of West Coast flower power, as well as the manic theatrics of Jim Morrison and the Doors. Since the incorporation of West Hollywood, the striptease clubs and "head shops" have been phased out, and this fashionable area now rivals Beverly Hills for entertainment-industry executives per square foot. Some tourists come to the strip just to see the enormous **billboards**. The ruddy-faced and reassuring Marlboro Man is now a fixture, but there are many more along the strip that consistently re-invent the medium: fantastic commercial murals animated with eye-catching gimmicks, movie ads with names like "Schwarzenegger" in gargantuan letters and self-promotions for unknown actors whose dream is to loom over Tinseltown in Day-Glo splendor.

Greta Garbo was only one of many stars and starlets to appreciate the quirky character of the huge Norman castle that is the **Chateau Marmont Hotel**, towering over the east end of Sunset Strip at no. 8221. Built in 1927 as luxury apartments, this stodgy block of white concrete has long been a Hollywood favorite. Howard Hughes used to rent the entire penthouse so he could keep an eye on the bathing beauties around the

WEST HOLLYWOOD AND
THE MUSEUM MILE

0   500 yds

RESTAURANTS

Barefoot	46
Barney's Beanery	7
Ca' Brea	53
Campanile	56
Canter's Deli	36
Cava	50
Chianti	27
Chin Chin	6
Citrus	29
Duke's	10
East India Grill	35
Eat A Pita	34
Ed Debevic's	54
El Coyote	44
Erewhon	43
Figs	14
French Market Place	12
Georgia	31
The Gumbo Pot	51
Hard Rock Café	41
Inaka	45
India's Oven	57
Jerry's Famous Deli	39
Johnie's	58
Johnny Rockets	26
Kate Mantilini	52
Katsu	48
La Masia	25
Locanda Veneta	47
L'Orangerie	19
Mark's	21
Mishima	49
Noura	30
Pink's Hot Dogs	24
Spago	5
Swingers	42
Tail o' the Pup	38
Tommy Tang's	28
Yukon Mining Company	15

BARS & NIGHTCLUBS

Coconut Teaszer	2
The Conga Room	59
Doug Weston's Troubadour	32
Formosa Café	16
House of Blues	4
Key Club	8
King's Road Espresso House	40
Largo	37
Lava Lounge	1
Little Frida's	20
Lanapark	33
Molly Malone's	55
The Palms	18
The Plaza	23
Rage	22
The Roxy	9
7969	13
Tom Bergin's	60
Union	3
The Viper Room	17
Whisky-a-Go-Go	11

For reviews of all the above places, see "Eating", "Drinking: bars, pubs and cafés" and "Nightlife" listings starting on p.143.

pool below, and the hotel made the headlines in 1982 when comedian John Belushi died of a heroin overdose in the hotel bungalow that he used as his LA home. Belushi's spirit lives on across the street at no. 8430: the corrugated tin shack of the **House of Blues**, in which his estate and one-time partner Dan Aykroyd are prime investors, is a bar in the *Hard Rock Café/Planet Hollywood* mold (see p.162), and plays much of the man's music.

Beverly Hills and Century City

Probably the most famous small city in the world, **BEVERLY HILLS** has over the years sucked in more than its fair share of wealthy residents (the local pawnbrokers have an Oscar and a Ferrari for sale). It's not a particularly welcoming place, especially if your clothes don't match the elegant attire of the residents – the pets in Beverly Hills are better dressed and groomed than some of the people elsewhere in LA. It can be fun, though, to stroll the designer stores of Rodeo Drive and, if driving, take a spin by the mansions up in the canyons before the cops (Beverly Hills has more police per capita than anywhere else in the US) ask for your ID.

Beverly Hills divides into two distinct halves, separated by the old train line down Santa Monica Boulevard. Below the tracks are the flatlands of modest houses on rectangular blocks, set around the "Golden Triangle" business district that fills the wedge between Santa Monica and Wilshire boulevards. **Rodeo Drive** cuts through the triangle in a two-block-long, concentrated showcase of the most expensive names in international fashion. It's an intimidatingly stylish area, each boutique trying to outshine the rest: none as yet charges for admission, though some require an invitation. Look out for the tourist trap of **Two Rodeo** nearby, a *faux* European shopping alley that is the height of pretentious kitsch. For a complete overview of the shopping scene, including Rodeo Drive and beyond, take a trip on the Beverly Hills Trolley (daily noon-5pm summer, noon-4pm Saturday rest of year; $5), which offers tourists a 45-minute glimpse of the town's highlights, departing hourly from the corner of Rodeo and Dayton Way. Much more worthwhile is the newly opened **Museum of Television and Radio** at 465 N Beverly Drive (Wed–Sun noon–5pm, Thurs until 9pm; $6, students $4), which features a collection of more than 75,000 TV and radio programs and is LA's first real attempt at providing a media museum of scholarly value. The city still awaits a decent film museum, however.

Above Santa Monica Boulevard is the upmarket part of residential Beverly Hills, its gently curving drives converging on the gorgeous and gauche pink plaster **Beverly Hills Hotel**, on Sunset and Rodeo. Built in 1913 to attract wealthy settlers to what was then a town of just five hundred people, and currently owned by the Sultan of Brunei, the hotel's social cachet makes its *Polo Lounge* a prime spot for movie execs to power-lunch. In the verdant canyons and foothills above Sunset, a number of palatial estates lie hidden away behind landscaped security gates. **Benedict Canyon Drive** climbs from the hotel up past many of them. Further up Benedict Canyon, at 1740 Green Acres Drive, Harold Lloyd's **Green Acres**, where he lived for forty years, with its secret passageways and large private screening room, survives intact, though the grounds, which contained a waterfall and a nine-hole golf course, have since been broken up into smaller lots.

The grounds of the biggest house in Beverly Hills, **Greystone Mansion**, are now maintained as a public park by the city, which uses it to disguise a massive underground reservoir. The fifty-thousand-square-foot manor house was once the property of oil titan Edward Doheny, who was not only a huge figure in LA history, but was also a major player in the Teapot Dome scandal of the 1920s – it was Doheny's bribe to Interior Secretary Albert Fall for prime Wyoming real estate that got the debacle started. Although the house itself is rarely open (except for filming music videos by the likes of Meatloaf and movies like *The Big Lebowski*), you can visit the sixteen-acre **Greystone Park** (daily 10am–5pm) at 905 Loma Vista, which affords fine views of the LA sprawl and its attendant pollution.

Century City

The gleaming boxes of **CENTURY CITY**, just west of Beverly Hills, were erected during the Sixties on the backlot of the 20th Century Fox film studio. The plate-glass office towers aren't at all inviting, rising sharply and inhospitably skywards from sidewalks that are rarely used – a perhaps typically Sixties disaster, planned at a time when pedestrian concerns were considered irrelevant. The massive **ABC Entertainment Center** complex, at 2040 Avenue of the Stars, might conceivably bring you here – its Shubert Theater (see p.165) is one of LA's leading live theaters, specializing in touring productions of the latest Andrew Lloyd Webber hit. Along the southern edge of Century City, **Pico Boulevard** is quintessential LA: mile after mile of single-story shop fronts, auto-parts stores and delis, with a mini-mall on every other corner. To the west, look through the front gates of the still-working **20th Century Fox** film and TV studios to catch a glimpse of the intact New York City street set used for the filming of *Hello Dolly!* – though don't bother trying to get inside the place unless your cousin's a production assistant.

Less frivolously, just east of Century City, below Beverly Hills, an inauspicious white building houses the **Simon Wiesenthal Center for Holocaust Studies** at 9786 West Pico Blvd. The US headquarters of the organization devoted to tracking down ex-Nazis, the center has an extensive library of Holocaust-related documents, photographs and accounts – but the main draw for visitors is the affecting **Beit HaShoa Museum of Tolerance** (Mon–Thurs 10am–4pm, Fri 10am–3pm, Sun 11am–4pm; $8.50, students $5.50), an extraordinary interactive resource center aimed at exposing the lies of revisionist historians. The most technologically advanced institution of its kind, it uses videotaped interviews to provide LA's frankest examination of the 1992 riots, and leads the visitor through re-enactments outlining the rise of Nazism to a harrowing conclusion in a replica gas chamber.

Westwood, UCLA and the Sepulveda Pass

Just west of Beverly Hills, on the north side of Wilshire Boulevard, **WESTWOOD**, at one time known as Westwood Village, is one of LA's more user-friendly neighborhoods, a grouping of low-slung redbrick buildings that went up in the late 1920s, along with the nearby campus of the nascent University of California at Los Angeles (UCLA). It's an area that's easily explored on foot, and one very much shaped by the proximity of the university campus, which is really the lifeblood of the area. Because of its ease for pedestrians, the neighborhood has limited parking; for minimum frustration, find a cheap parking lot and dump your vehicle there for a few hours while you explore.

Broxton Avenue, Westwood's main drag, was for many years the weekend cruising strip of choice for West LA's teenagers. Following a gang-related shooting outside on Broxton in the late-1980s, the popularity of the area waned, although it still attracts students making the circuit of record stores, video-game arcades and diners. It's also a big movie-going district, with thirty or so cinema screens within a quarter-mile radius. Much of the original Spanish Revival design has survived the intervening years of less imaginative construction, though the ordinary businesses of the old days have been replaced by fancy boutiques and designer novelty shops. The spire at the end of the street, at 961 Broxton Ave, belongs to the 1931 **Fox Village** theater, which, together with the neon-signed **Bruin** across the street, is sometimes used by movie studios for "sneak" previews of films to gauge audience reaction, and is now part of the Mann theater chain. South of the village, Westwood Boulevard has a few more cinemas, some interesting shops and a number of specialist bookstores below Wilshire Boulevard. This section of Wilshire exploded in the 1970s and 1980s with oil-rich high-rise developments, leading to a change of scale that would seem bizarre anywhere outside of LA. Modest detached houses sit next to twenty-story condo towers in which penthouses with private heliports sell for upwards of $12 million.

Inside one of the towers, on the corner with Westwood Boulevard, the **Armand Hammer Museum of Art and Culture** (Tues–Wed & Fri–Sat 11am–7pm, Thurs 11am–9pm, Sun 11am–5pm; $4.50, students $3, Thurs 6–9pm free; *www.hammer. ucla.edu*) is one of the city's most debated art stashes, amassed over seven decades by the flamboyant and ultra-wealthy boss of the Occidental Petroleum Corporation. Art critic Robert Hughes called the paintings here "a mishmash of second or third-rate works by famous names," but while the Rembrandts and Rubenses may be less than stunning, the nineteenth-century pieces like Van Gogh's intense and radiant *Hospital at Saint Remy* more than make amends. In any case, with assistance from neighboring UCLA, the institution has recently shifted gears to focus on more contemporary, avant-garde works. Across Wilshire from the museum, at the end of the driveway behind the tiny Avco cinema, you'll find Hammer's speckled marble tomb, sharing the tiny cemetery of **Westwood Memorial Park** with the likes of movie stars Peter Lorre and Natalie Wood, wildman jazz drummer Buddy Rich, and, to the left of the entrance in the far northeast corner, the lipstick-covered plaque that marks the resting place of Marilyn Monroe.

The UCLA campus

The **UCLA campus** is the dominant feature in Westwood, a group of Romanesque buildings spread generously over well-landscaped grounds. It's worth a wander if you've time to kill, particularly for a couple of good exhibition spaces. The Student Union building, at the north end of Westwood Boulevard, half a mile north of Westwood, has a bowling alley, a good bookstore and a "rideboard" offering shared-expense car rides, and there's also a decent coffeehouse in Kerckhoff Hall, just behind.

Before embarking on your exploration, pick up a **map** from various information kiosks scattered around campus. Of things to see, the spacious rotunda of the **Powell Library**, on one side of the central quadrangle, was where Aldous Huxley put in long hours at the card catalogs in the late 1930s, researching his novel *After Many a Summer*, based on the life and legend of William Randolph Hearst. At the northern end of campus – fronted by the large **Franklin D. Murphy Sculpture Garden** (always open; free) which contains work by Rodin, Maillol, Moore and other modern artists, shaded by jacaranda trees – the **Wight Art Gallery** holds a variety of top-quality visiting exhibitions (Mon–Fri 9am–5pm; free).

Nearby, UCLA's **film school** is less mainstream and industry-oriented than USC's film school, and has produced offbeat film-makers like Francis Ford Coppola, Alison Anders and Alex Cox; it also has one of the most extensive collections of old films and TV programs in the world, examples of which are shown daily, often for free, in the large auditorium in **Melnitz Hall**. Check the bulletin board in the lobby or phone ☎310/206-FILM for the current schedule.

The Sepulveda Pass

The gap through the Santa Monica Mountains known as the **Sepulveda Pass** was, like the boulevard and nearby community, named for Mexican soldier Francisco Sepúlveda, who gained ownership in 1839 of the Rancho San Vicente y Santa Monica, which once encompassed the surrounding area. Now, the pass is best known for the 405 Freeway that cuts through it, but it also contains part of Sepulveda Boulevard, the longest road in the city or county of Los Angeles, which leads from Long Beach into the San

Fernando Valley. Recently, the pass has become more important as it connects several key museums in LA.

Starting at Sunset Boulevard just northwest of UCLA, you can follow the pass as it divides several of LA's most exclusive residential zones. **Brentwood** to the west is an insular enclave best known for being the former home of O.J. Simpson; to the east, **Bel Air** is a hillside community that is similarly well-heeled and boasts a particularly fine hotel, the *Bel Air* (see p.75), which is a prime spot to see the snooty hauteur of the city's self-anointed beautiful ones in full flower. A short distance away is Getty Center Drive, which leads up to the monumental **Getty Center** (Tues–Wed 11am–7pm, Thurs–Fri 11am–9pm, Sat–Sun 10am–6pm; free; *www.getty.edu*), a gleaming complex that towers over the city as oil baron J. Paul Getty once towered over his competitors. You cannot stop at the Center on a whim, however. Reservations for parking, which costs $5, are always made in advance and are difficult to get on weekends or holidays. However, if you arrive by cab or bus (the #561 line, which you can pick up at LAX), you are assured entry.

Designed by arch-modernist Richard Meier, the center was built for around $1 billion and was a decade in the making. Originally, Meier planned for the whole museum complex to be constructed from white metallic panels – his signature style – but protests from the Brentwood neighbors below forced him to re-design part of it in travertine, in the end a good aesthetic choice. Although the Getty foundation plunked down a ten-figure sum for the Center, it still has billions in reserve and must, by law, spend hundreds of millions each year from its endowment. Thus, it plays an elephantine role on the international art scene and can freely outbid its competitors for anything it wants. If he were still around, J. Paul would have been proud.

Getty started building his massive collection in the 1930s, storing much of it in his house until the Getty Museum opened in 1974, on a bluff overlooking the Pacific Ocean. That site is now closed, but will reopen in the next century as a showcase for the foundation's antiquities, few of which will then be shown here. As the collection is, not surprisingly, determined by the enthusiasms of Getty himself, there's a formidable array of ornate furniture and decorative arts, with clocks, chandeliers, tapestries and gilt-edged commodes, designed for the French nobility from the reign of Louis XIV, filling several overwhelmingly opulent rooms. Getty was much less interested in painting – although he did scoop up a very fine stash from the Renaissance and Baroque periods, including works by Rembrandt, Rubens, La Tour and more – but a large collection has been amassed since his death, featuring all the major names from the thirteenth century to the present: drawings by Raphael and Bernini, paintings of the Dutch Golden Age and a handful of French Impressionists, to name just a few. The museum's biggest catch is probably Van Gogh's *Irises*, which was originally in the possession of an Australian financier until he defaulted on his payments, after which the Getty foundation swooped in and snatched it up for a still-undisclosed sum. Elsewhere in the museum, there's also an extensive and highly absorbing collection of photographs by Man Ray, Laszlo Moholy-Nagy and notable others, along with a respectable assortment of sculpture from the seventeenth to the nineteenth century.

From the museum, continue up the Sepulveda Pass until you come to the **Skirball Cultural Center** at 2701 N Sepulveda Blvd (Tues–Fri 10am–4pm, Sat noon–5pm, Sun 10am–5pm; $7, students $5). The Center has in recent years taken the same step as the Getty Museum and relocated to a more isolated setting, removing itself from the limited confines of **Hebrew Union College** near USC. Devoting its attention to describing some of the history, beliefs and rituals of Judaism, the Center concentrates on the more mystical elements of the faith and is fairly absorbing. It also hosts a range of exhibitions and lectures designed to illuminate the American Jewish experience and offers a good, incisive overview of Judaic history and culture.

Santa Monica, Venice and Malibu

Set along an unbroken, twenty-mile strand of clean, white-sand beaches, and home to a diverse assortment of LA's finest stores, restaurants and art galleries, the small, self-contained communities that line the **Santa Monica Bay** feature some of the best of what Los Angeles has to offer, with none of the smog or searing heat that can make the rest of the metropolis unbearable. The entire area is well served by public transportation, near (but not too near) the airport, and there's a wide selection of accommodation, making the area an ideal base for seeing the rest of LA.

Santa Monica, set on palm-tree-shaded bluffs above the Pacific Ocean, is the oldest, biggest and best-known of the resort areas. Once a wild beachfront playground, and the memorable location for many scenes from the underworld stories of Raymond Chandler, it's now a self-consciously healthy and liberal community, which has enticed a large expatriate British community of writers and rock stars, ranging from Rod Stewart to John Lydon. In recent years, however, once-liberal policies towards homeless people have become more severe, as have rent-control laws, courtesy of a state effort to keep landlords and property owners happy. Directly south, **Venice**'s once-expansive network of canals and the beachfront boardwalk bring together a lively mixture of street performers, roller skaters and casual voyeurs.

North from Santa Monica along the Pacific Coast Highway, **Pacific Palisades** is a gathering of hugely expensive houses clinging to the lower foothills of the nearby mountains. Aside from some pioneering postwar architecture, however, there's nothing much to see, though you could push a few miles inland to **Will Rogers State Park**, home and museum of one of the legends of the American West, and with some rewarding hiking paths leading into the neighboring canyons. A few miles further along the coastal road, **Topanga Canyon** has more hiking, its reputation as haven of back-to-nature hippiedom gone, but still with a surprisingly wild set of trails leading into the deep, wooded canyons and sculptured rock outcrops of the Santa Monica Mountains.

Malibu, at the top of the bay, twenty miles from Santa Monica and the northern- and westernmost edge of the LA region, is a whole other world, studded with beach colony houses owned by those who are famous enough to need privacy and rich enough to afford it, despite the constant threat of hillside wildfires. However, you don't have to be a millionaire to enjoy its fine surfing beaches, or the birds, seals and – in migrating season – whales, for which this part of the coast is noted.

Santa Monica

As little as a century ago, most of the land between **SANTA MONICA** and what was then Los Angeles was covered by beanfields and citrus groves, interrupted by the occasional outposts of Hollywood and Beverly Hills. Like so much of the state, the land was owned by Collis Huntington's Southern Pacific Railroad, which tried – and failed – to make Santa Monica into the port of Los Angeles, losing out to other interests who dredged the harbor at Wilmington, near Long Beach. The linking of the beachfront with the rest of Los Angeles by the suburban streetcar system meant the town instead grew into one of LA's premier resorts – a giant funfair city that was the inspiration for Raymond Chandler's anything-goes "Bay City," described in *Farewell My Lovely*. Today Chandler wouldn't recognize the place: changes in the gaming laws and the advent of the private swimming pool have led to the removal of the offshore gambling ships and many of the bathing clubs, and Santa Monica is among the city's more elegant seaside towns. It's also well known for its rent control and stringent planning and development regulations, for which perceived infractions, local right-wingers refer sneeringly to the city as the "People's Republic."

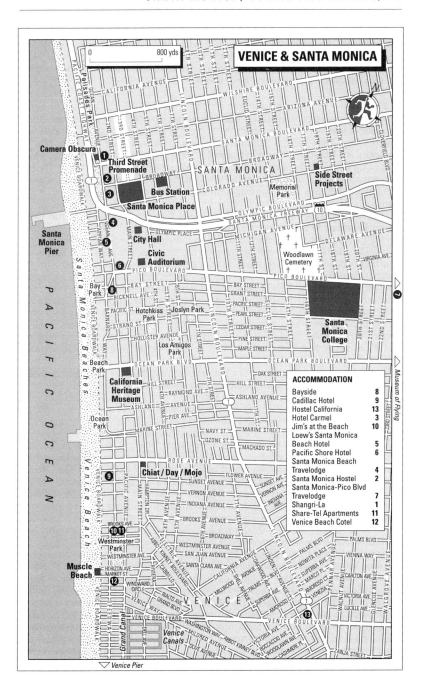

VENICE & SANTA MONICA

0   800 yds

Camera Obscura
Third Street Promenade
Bus Station
Santa Monica Place
Side Street Projects
City Hall
Civic Auditorium
Santa Monica Pier
Santa Monica College
Bay Park
Hotchkiss Park
Joslyn Park
Los Amigos Park
Beach Park
California Heritage Museum
Ocean Park
Chiat / Day / Mojo
Westminster Park
Muscle Beach
Woodlawn Cemetery
Memorial Park
Museum of Flying

PACIFIC OCEAN

Santa Monica Beaches

Venice Beach

Grand Canal

Venice Canals

Venice Pier

ACCOMMODATION

Bayside	8
Cadillac Hotel	9
Hostel California	13
Hotel Carmel	3
Jim's at the Beach	10
Loew's Santa Monica Beach Hotel	5
Pacific Shore Hotel	6
Santa Monica Beach Travelodge	4
Santa Monica Hostel	2
Santa Monica-Pico Blvd Travelodge	7
Shangri-La	1
Share-Tel Apartments	11
Venice Beach Cotel	12

Santa Monica lies across Centinela Avenue from West LA, and splits into three distinct portions. The town itself, holding a fair slab of Santa Monica's history and its day-to-day business, sits on the coastal bluffs; below there's the pier and beach; while Main Street, running south from close to the pier towards Venice, is a style-conscious quarter, with designer restaurants and fancy shops.

The Town

Santa Monica reaches nearly three miles inland, but most things of interest are situated within a few blocks of the beach. Make your first stop the **Visitor Information Office** (daily 10am–4pm; ☎310/393-7593), in a kiosk just south of Santa Monica Boulevard at 1400 Ocean Avenue in **Palisades Park**, the cypress-tree-lined strip which runs along the top of the bluffs and makes for striking views of the surf below. The visitor center's handy free map shows the whole of the town and the routes of the Santa Monica Big Blue Bus transit system, a useful Westside complement to the MTA network.

Two blocks east of Ocean Boulevard, between Wilshire and Broadway, the **Third Street Promenade** is the closest LA comes to energetic street life. A pedestrianized stretch long popular with buskers and itinerant evangelists, and lined by a variety of fashionable clothing outlets and restaurants, the promenade underwent a successful refurbishment several years ago and now attracts a lively crowd of characters. It's fun simply to hang out in the cafés, pubs and nightclubs, play a game of pool, or browse through the many secondhand and fine-art book shops – independent businesses which are becoming increasingly uncommon under the onslaught of chain retailers like The Gap and Barnes & Noble. The mall is anchored at its southern end by the expensive **Santa Monica Place**, a white stucco shopping precinct that is among architect Frank Gehry's less inspired work. It has the usual assortment of upmarket chain stores and a mandatory food court, all executed in an exhausted postmodern idiom, with faded pastel colors and gloomy chain-link fencing.

Santa Monica has a number of fine **galleries** selling works by emerging local and international artists. **Bergamot Station**, a collection of former tramcar sheds at 2525 Michigan Ave near the intersection of 26th and Cloverfield, houses a multitude of small art galleries (most open Tues–Fri 11am–5.30pm). Many of LA's latest generation of artists – such as Lari Pittman, Manuel Ocampo, Robert Williams and Erika Rothenberg – have shown here, and the construction of two small theater stages in adjoining warehouses will no doubt draw comparably rising stars of the performing arts. Don't miss the Gallery of Functional Art, which offers an array of mechanical gizmos and eccentric furniture like cubist lamps and neon-lit chairs. The **Side Street Projects**, 1629 18th St (hours vary; information at ☎310/829-0779) is another of the town's ambitious young art spaces and forms a part of the **18th Street Arts Complex**, Santa Monica's attempt to create a hip and modern center for various types of art, much of it experimental. The performance space Highways is one such example in the complex (see p.164), showcasing edgy political and gender-based work. Further inland, it's less easy to stumble upon Santa Monica's worthwhile sights. On the northern border, **San Vicente Boulevard's** grassy tree-lined strip is a joggers' freeway; south of San Vicente, the flashy novelty and clothing shops of **Montana Avenue** reflect the upward mobility of the area. At the southeast corner of Santa Monica Boulevard, Ocean Park Boulevard heads off to another place you'd be unlikely ever to stumble upon by chance, the **Museum of Flying** (Wed–Sun 10am–5pm; $7), at the Santa Monica Municipal Airport (now used only by private planes). The major employer in the early years of Santa Monica, the Donald Douglas Aircraft Company, had its main factory here – birthplace of the DC-3 and other planes which pioneered commercial aviation. The old premises display a number of vintage aircraft, of interest primarily to aeronautics buffs.

Santa Monica pier and beach

Despite the many attractions on top of the bluffs, the real focal point of Santa Monica life is down below, on the **beach** and around **Santa Monica pier**, the only reminder that the city was ever anything but a quiet coastal suburb. Jutting out into the bay at the foot of Colorado Avenue, the pier is a great example of its kind, recently having cleaned up its grungy appearance with new rides, a giant helter-skelter and a restored 1922 wooden **carousel** (daily 9am–6pm; 50¢ a ride). The pier has also opened a new carnival center, **Pacific Park**, featuring a roller coaster and various other thrill rides designed to attract the family crowd back from the suburbs.

The grand beach houses just north of the pier were known as the "Gold Coast," because of the many Hollywood personalities who lived in them. The largest, now the **Sand and Sea** beach club, was built as the servants' quarters of a massive 120-room house, now demolished, that belonged to William Randolph Hearst. MGM boss Louis B. Mayer owned the adjacent Mediterranean-style villa, where the Kennedy brothers were later rumored to have had their liaisons with Marilyn Monroe. If you're not intending to stretch out on the sands, you can follow the **bike path**, which begins at the pier, twenty miles south to Palos Verdes. Or, on foot, wander south along the beach to Pico Boulevard and head two blocks inland to Main Street.

Main Street

Santa Monica underwent a major change following completion of the Santa Monica Freeway in 1965, which brought the beachfront homes within a fifteen-minute drive of Downtown and isolated the bulk of the town from **Main Street**, five minutes' walk from the pier – where the collection of novelty shops, kite stores and classy restaurants is now one of the most popular shopping districts on the Westside.

Beyond shopping, eating and drinking, though, there's not much to do or see. **California Heritage Museum**, on Main Street at Ocean Park Boulevard (Wed–Sat 11am–4pm, Sun noon–4pm; $3), is the city's effort to preserve some of its architectural past in the face of new money. Two houses were moved here to escape demolition. One hosts temporary displays on Californian cultural topics like the reign of the Dodgers, and has several rooms restored to variously evoke the years 1890–1930. The other is known as the *Victorian Restaurant* and serves tea on its patio at weekends (reserve on ☎310/392-8537). Not all of Santa Monica has been so lucky, however. Ocean Park Boulevard was one of the main routes to the coast via the old streetcars of the Pacific Electric, and the entire beachfront between here and the Venice border, now overshadowed by massive gray condominiums, used to be the site of the largest and wildest of the amusement piers, the fantastic **Pacific Ocean Park**. "P-O-P," as it was known, had a huge roller coaster, a giant funhouse and a boisterous midway arcade, described by architectural historian Reyner Banham as a "fantasy in stucco and every known style of architecture and human ecology." Sadly, not a trace remains.

Venice

Immediately south of Santa Monica, **VENICE** was laid out in the marshlands of Ballona Creek in 1905 by developer Abbot Kinney as a romantic replica of the northern Italian city. Intended to attract artsy folk from Los Angeles to sample its sub-European bohemian air, this twenty-mile network of canals, lined by sham palazzos and waterfront homes, never really caught on, although a later remodel into a low-grade version of Coney Island postponed its demise for a few decades. With the coming of the automobile, many of the canals were filled in, and the area, now part of the city of Los Angeles, fell into disrepair, with most of the home sites being taken over by oil wells. This era features in Orson Welles' film *Touch of Evil*, in which derelict Venice stars as a seedy Mexican border town.

Kinney was, however, ahead of his time. A fair bit of the original plan survives, and the pseudo-European atmosphere has since proved just right for pulling in the artistic community he was aiming at, making Venice one of the coast's trendier spots. Main Street, for instance, is home to the offices of advertising firm **Chiat Day Mojo**. Marked by Claes Oldenburg's huge pair of binoculars at the entrance, the Frank Gehry-designed offices have no assigned desks, leaving employees to roam free with laptops and mobile phones, through spartan rooms lined with original modern art. Just to the north, the frightening *Ballerina Clown*, a gargantuan sculpture by Jonathan Borofsky, looms over a nearby intersection, its clown face and tutu creating one of the most disturbing pieces of public art in recent memory. Elsewhere, a strong alternative arts scene centers around the **Beyond Baroque Literary Arts Center and Bookshop** in the old City Hall at 681 Venice Blvd (Tues–Fri 10am–5pm, Sat noon–5pm; ☎310/822-3006), which holds regular readings and workshops of poetry, prose and drama.

Windward Avenue is the town's main artery, running from the beach into what was the Grand Circle of the canal system – where the curvaceous, roller-coaster facade of the Race Through the Clouds building pays tribute to the old theme park – now paved over and ringed by a number of galleries and the Venice post office, inside which a mural depicts the early layout. Leading to the beach, the original Romanesque **arcade**, around the intersection with Pacific Avenue, is alive with health-food shops, used-record stores and roller-skate rental stands, but sadly, less and less of it remains with passing years. Here and there colorful and portentous giant **murals** cover the whitewashed walls of the original hotels, and of the Venice Pavilion on the beach. The few remaining **canals** are just a few blocks south (enter on Dell Avenue west from Washington Boulevard), where the original quaint little bridges survive, and you can sit and watch the ducks paddle around in the still waters.

It's **Venice Beach** that draws most people to the town. Nowhere else does LA parade itself quite so openly and as sensuously as it does along the **Venice Boardwalk**, a wide pathway also known as Ocean Front Walk. Year-round at weekends and every day in summer it's packed with people and people-watchers, jugglers, fire-eaters, Hare Krishnas and roller-skating guitar players. You can buy anything you might need to look like a local without ever leaving the beach: cheap sunglasses, T-shirts, personal stereos and tennis shoes. South of Windward is **Muscle Beach**, a legendary weightlifting center where serious hunks of muscle pump serious iron, and high-flying gymnasts swing on the adjacent rings and bars. Incidentally, be warned that Venice Beach at **night** is a dangerous place, taken over by street gangs, drug dealers and assorted psychos. Even walking on the beach after dark is illegal, and anywhere in the immediate vicinity you should take great care.

Pacific Palisades and Will Rogers State Park

The district of **PACIFIC PALISADES**, which rises on the bluffs two miles north of Santa Monica pier, is slowly but very surely falling away into the bay, most noticeably on the point above Chautauqua Boulevard and Pacific Coast Highway, otherwise known as "PCH." With each winter's rains, a little bit more of the bluffs gets washed away in mud slides, blocking traffic on PCH, and gradually shrinking the backyards of the clifftop homes. There are few places of interest among the suburban ranch houses, although some of the most influential buildings of post-war LA were constructed here – the **Eames house**, for example, at 203 Chautauqua St, was fashioned out of prefabricated industrial parts in 1947 but is now generally inaccessible to the public.

In complete contrast, a mile east along Sunset Boulevard from the top of Chautauqua is the **Will Rogers State Historic Park** (summer daily 8am–7pm; rest of year daily 8am–6pm; free, parking $6), a steep climb from the MTA bus (#2, #302, #576) stop. This was the home and ranch of the Depression-era cowboy philosopher and journalist Will

Rogers, one of America's most popular figures of the time – after his death in a plane crash in 1935, there was a nationwide thirty-minute silence – and renowned for his down-home, common-sense thinking, and the saying that he "never met a man he didn't like." The overgrown ranch-style house serves as an informal **museum** (daily 10am–5pm; free), filled to overflowing with cowboy gear and Native American art; and the 200-acre park has miles of foot and bridle paths, including polo grounds where matches take place during the spring and summer. Just north of Sunset Boulevard's intersection with PCH, the **Getty Villa** sits on a picturesque bluff overlooking the ocean. Once the site of the Getty Museum (now in West LA; see p.117), the villa is closed to the public but is due to reopen as an antiquities center in 2001.

Topanga Canyon

In complete and surprising contrast to the turmoil of LA, **Topanga Canyon** provides an excellent natural refuge. With hillsides covered in golden poppies and wildflowers, a hundred and fifty thousand acres of these mountains and the seashore have been protected as the Santa Monica Mountains National Recreation Area, but as yet very few people take advantage of the fine views and fresh air, thus missing out on the sight of the deer, coyotes and the odd mountain lion that still live here. Like LA itself, the area is not without its element of danger, especially in winter and early spring, when mudslides threaten houses and waterfalls cascade down the cliffs. Park rangers offer free guided hikes throughout the mountains most weekends (information and reservations ☎818/597-9192), and there are self-guided trails through the canyon's Topanga State Park, off Old Topanga Canyon Road at the crest of the mountains, with spectacular views out over the Pacific.

Beyond Topanga Canyon, the beaches and ocean-views are blocked off by mile after mile of private homes all the way to Malibu. There are a few sign-posted beach-access points, but most of the rock stars and others who can afford to live here treat the sands and seas as their own. Although any bit of land below the high-tide line is legally in the public domain, you're sure to feel like a trespasser.

Malibu

Everyone has heard of **MALIBU**: the very name conjures up images of beautiful people sunbathing on a palm-fringed beach and lazily consuming cocktails. And the image is not so very far from the truth – even though you might not think so on arrival. As you enter the small town, the succession of ramshackle surf shops and fast-food stands scattered along both sides of PCH around the graceful Malibu Pier don't exactly reek of money, but the secluded estates just inland are as valuable as any in the entire US, even though many are subject to being battered by hillside wildfires that destroy anything in their path.

The south-facing beach next to the pier, Surfrider Beach, was the surfing capital of the world in the 1950s and early 1960s, popularized by the many Beach Blanket Bingo movies filmed here, starring Annette Funicello and Frankie Avalon. It's still a big surfing spot: the waves are best in late summer, when storms off Mexico cause them to reach upwards of eight feet. Just beyond is **Malibu Lagoon State Park** (parking $6), a nature reserve and bird refuge; birdwatching walks around the lagoon are offered some weekends, and there's a small **museum** (Wed–Sat 11am–3pm; $2) detailing the history of the area.

Most Malibu residents live in the houses and small ranches that hide away in the narrow canyons on the edges of the town, together forming a well-off, insular community with a long-established dread of outsiders. Up until the 1920s all of Malibu was owned by one **May K. Rindge**, who hired armed guards and dynamited roads to keep travelers from crossing her land on their way to and from Santa Monica. Rindge fought for years to prevent the state from building the Pacific Coast Highway across her property, but lost her legal battle in the State Supreme Court, and her money in the Depression. Her son took over the ranch and quickly sold much of the land, establishing the **Malibu Colony** at the mouth of Malibu Canyon as a haven for movie stars. There's very little to see here except the garage doors of the rich and famous; if you must get a glimpse of the elite, visit the **Malibu Colony Plaza**, near the area's gated entrance – good for star-spotting and stocking up on food and drink before a day on the sands.

Much of **Malibu Creek State Park**, at the crest of Malibu Canyon Road along Mulholland Drive, used to belong to 20th Century Fox studios, who filmed many Tarzan pictures here and used the chaparral-covered hillsides to simulate South Korea for the TV show *M*A*S*H*. The 4000-acre park includes a large lake, some waterfalls, and nearly fifteen miles of hiking trails. Nearby **Paramount Ranch**, near Mulholland Drive on Cornell Road, is another old studio backlot, with a phony railroad crossing, cemetery, and Western movie set used for, among other things, the interminable TV drama *Dr. Quinn Medicine Woman*.

The beaches

Five miles along the coast from Malibu Pier, **Zuma Beach** is the largest of the Los Angeles County beaches, popular with San Fernando Valley high-school kids who drive over Kanan Dume Road to escape the sweltering inland summer heat. Adjacent **Point Dume State Beach**, below the bluffs, is a lot more relaxed, especially up and over the rocks at its southern tip, where **Pirate's Cove** is used by nudists. The rocks here are also a good place to look out for seals and migrating gray whales in winter, as the point juts out into the Pacific at the northern lip of Santa Monica Bay. **El Matador State Beach**, about 25 miles up the coast from Santa Monica, is about as close as an ordinary Joe can get to the private-beach seclusion enjoyed by the stars. Thanks to its northern location and an easily missable turn off PCH, its rocky-cove sands are a recluse's dream. Another five miles along PCH, where Mulholland Drive reaches the ocean, **Leo Carrillo State Beach Park** marks the northwestern border of LA County and the end of the MTA bus route (#434). The mile-long sandy beach is divided by Sequit Point, a small bluff that has underwater caves and a tunnel you can pass through at low tide. Leo Carrillo is also the nearest and most accessible **campground** for the rest of LA (see p.78). Five miles further on, at **Point Mugu State Park**, there are some very good walks through mountain canyons, and campsites right on the beach. Point Mugu is also the site of the US Navy's Pacific Missile Test Center, which takes up most of the five miles of coast south of Ventura (see p.357).

The South Bay and Harbor Area

South of Venice, Marina del Rey and the faded resort town of Playa del Rey offer little to interest visitors; beyond that, the coast is dominated by the runways of LAX, a huge Chevron Oil refinery, and LA's main sewage treatment plant. South of this industrial zone, however, is an eight-mile strip of beach towns – **Manhattan Beach**, **Hermosa Beach** and **Redondo Beach** – collectively known as the **South Bay**. These are more modest (though far from poor), quieter, more suburban and smaller than the Westside beach communities. Along their shared beach-side bike path the joggers and roller skaters are more likely to be locals than poseurs from other parts of LA, and all three can make a refreshing break if you like your beaches without pretentious packaging. Each has a beckoning strip of white sand, and Manhattan and Hermosa especially are well equipped for surfing and beach sports. They're also well connected to the rest of the city – within easy reach of LAX and connected by regular buses to Downtown LA.

Visible all along this stretch of the coast, the large vegetated peninsula of **Palos Verdes** is an upmarket residential area, while the comparatively rough-hewn little district of **San Pedro** (where you can find a good youth hostel, the area's cheapest accommodation by far; see p.79) is sited on the LA harbor, the busiest cargo port in the world and still growing. On the other side of the harbor, **Long Beach**, connected to Downtown by bus #60, is best known as the resting place of the *Queen Mary*, even though it is also the region's second largest city with nearly half a million people. Perhaps the most enticing place in the area is **Santa Catalina Island**, twenty miles offshore and easily reached by ferry. It's almost completely conserved wilderness, with many unique forms of plant and animal life and just one main center of population, **Avalon**.

Manhattan Beach, Hermosa Beach and Redondo Beach

Accessible along the bike path from Venice, or by car along PCH, **MANHATTAN BEACH** is a likeable place with a healthy well-to-do air, home mainly to white-collar workers whose middle-class stucco homes tumble towards the beach, uncluttered by high-rise hotels. There's not much to see or do away from the beach, but then that's the main reason for coming. Surfing is a major local pastime – there's a two-week international surf festival each August – and the city is a major center for beach volleyball, evidenced by the profusion of nets across the sands. If you can, call at the **historical center** in the post office building at 1601 Manhattan Beach Blvd (Sat–Sun noon–3pm; free), for its entertaining collection of photos and oddities from the city's earliest days. If these whet your appetite, you can purchase (for $1) a map that describes a history-oriented **walking tour**.

HERMOSA BEACH, across Longfellow Boulevard, is lower-income than Manhattan Beach, its houses smaller and less showy, but is in many ways more enjoyable. The center, near the foot of the pier around Hermosa and Pier avenues, is the setting for one of the South Bay's best-known nightspots, *The Lighthouse* (see p.161). While the beach is the main focus of interest, there are enough good restaurants and shops to keep you busy, such as the **Either/Or** bookshop, 124 Pier Ave (see p.170), once a haunt of writer Thomas Pynchon.

Despite some decent strips of sand, and fine views of Palos Verdes' stunning greenery, **REDONDO BEACH**, south of Hermosa, is less inviting. Condos and hotels line the beachfront, and the eateries around the yacht-lined King's Harbor are off-limits to curious visitors.

Palos Verdes

A great green hump marking LA's southwest corner, **PALOS VERDES** isn't of special interest, but it can be enjoyable to explore the bluffs and coves along the protected coastline. **Malaga Beach**, by Torrance County Beach just south of Redondo, is a popular scuba-diving spot; **Abalone Cove**, reached from the parking lot on Berkentine Road, off Palos Verdes Drive, boasts rock and tide pools and offshore kelp beds alive with rock scallops, sea urchins and, of course, abalone. A couple of miles east at the end of a path off Peppertree Drive, Smugglers Cove is a renowned **nudist beach**.

While you're in the area, don't miss **Wayfarer's Chapel**, at 5755 Palos Verdes Dr. Designed by Frank Lloyd Wright's son, Lloyd, it's a tribute to the eighteenth-century Swedish scientist and mystic Emanuel Swedenborg. The ultimate aim is for the redwood grove around the chapel to grow and entangle itself around the glass-framed structure – a fusing of human handiwork with the forces of nature of which Swedenborg would have been proud. A few miles further on, just before the end of Palos Verdes Drive, **Point Fermin Park** is a small tip of land prodding into the ocean.

In the park is a curious little wooden lighthouse dating from 1874 (no admittance), and a whale-watching station where you can read up on the winter migrations. Bottle-nosed dolphins can often be seen during their fall departure and spring return, and there's also the less seasonally dependent thrill of spotting hang-gliders swooping down off the cliffs.

From the park, it's an easy stroll along Bluff Place and down the 29th Street stairway to Cabrillo Beach and the excellent **Cabrillo Marine Museum**, at 3720 Stephen White Drive (Tues–Fri noon–5pm; Sat–Sun 10am–5pm; free, parking $6.50). A diverse collection of marine life has been imaginatively and instructively assembled: everything from predator snails and the curious "sarcastic fringehead" to larger displays on otters, seals and whales.

San Pedro and around

About three miles further on along Bluff Place, the scruffy harbor city of **SAN PEDRO** is in stark contrast to the affluence of Palos Verdes. It was a small fishing community until the late nineteenth century, when the construction of the LA harbor nearby brought a huge influx of labor, much of it drawn from the migrants who arrived on the ships, chiefly from Portugal, Greece and Yugoslavia. Many of these, and their descendants, never left the place, lending a striking racial mix to the town, manifest around the narrow sloping central streets in one of LA's densest groupings of ethnic groceries.

Some of this history is revealed in the **Maritime Museum**, on the harbor's edge at the foot of Sixth Street (Tues–Sun 10am–5pm; free), while the **Bloody Thursday Monument**, on the corner of Sixth and Beacon close to the City Hall, is another reminder of the city's gritty past. It marks the 1934 strike by local waterfront workers, commemorating the two who were killed when police and private guards opened fire. A fifteen-minute walk along the shore from the museum will bring you to the overrated **Ports O' Call Village** – a dismal batch of wooden and corrugated iron huts supposedly capturing the flavor of exotic seaports around the world.

Between San Pedro and Long Beach (connected by LADOT bus #142) soar two tall road bridges, giving aerial views of oil wells and docks, and the vast Naval Supplies Center. Just inland, the community of **WILMINGTON** is home to the Greek-style **Banning House** at 401 E Main St (guided tours hourly Tues–Thurs 12.30–2.30pm, Sat & Sun 3.30pm; $2). A mid-nineteenth-century entrepreneur, Phineas Banning, made his fortune when the value of his land increased astronomically as the harbor was developed. Through his promoting of the rail link between the harbor and central LA he also became known as "the father of Los Angeles transportation" – no mean accolade at a time when the local transportation system was one of the best in the world. While you're in the area, make sure to visit the **Drum Barracks and Civil War Museum**, 1052 Banning Blvd (hourly tours Tues & Thurs 10am–noon, Sat 12.30pm–2.30pm; $2.50), if you have the slightest interest in how Union troops used LA as a staging point for attacks against Confederates and, later, Indians.

Long Beach

With San Pedro, **LONG BEACH** is home to the world's third-largest port, and biggest outside China. Once the stomping ground of off-duty naval personnel, the city's porn shops and sleazy bars lasted until the last few decades, when a billion-dollar cash injection into the town led – in the downtown area at least – to a spate of glossy office buildings, a convention center, new hotels, a swanky shopping mall and a clean-up campaign that has restored some of the best turn-of-the-century buildings on the coast. Inland from downtown, however, it's a different story – grim, uninviting housing developments on the perimeter of the impoverished district of South Central LA (see p.92).

Downtown Long Beach is clearly the place to spend most of your time, with, especially along Pine Avenue, the best of Long Beach's rescued architecture and numerous thrift stores, antique/junk emporiums and bookstores. Nearby, on Third Street, is **"The Mural,"** whose depiction of the Long Beach population appears to be contemporary, but was in fact painted in the 1930s under Roosevelt's New Deal. From the mural, the pedestrian Promenade leads towards the sea, passing a concrete, open-air auditorium – often the site of free art and music events – and crossing the busy Ocean Beach Boulevard into **Shoreline Village**, a waterfront entertainment belt. It's a bit contrived but fine for a quick look, especially on weekends when Long Beach youth are on parade. Here you can explore the intriguing **Aquarium of the Pacific** (daily 10am–6pm; $14; *www.aquariumofpacific.org*), a recent arrival that explores the aquatic flora and fauna of three distinct climates and regions from around the world.

Ocean Boulevard leads away from Shoreline Village down to the **Breakers Hotel**: twelve stories of Spanish Revival pinkness topped by a green copper roof. A mile further on, 2300 Ocean Boulevard was once owned by Fatty Arbuckle and now houses the **Long Beach Museum of Art** (Wed–Thurs & Sat–Sun 10am–5pm, Fri 10am–8pm; $2; *www.lbma.org*), fringed by a sculpture garden and featuring a good collection of contemporary Southern Californian art and some experimental work in a video annex. Several blocks north of the ocean, another institution, **The Museum of Latin American Art**, 628 Alamitos Ave (Tues–Sat 11.30am–7.30pm, Sun noon–6pm; $5; *www.molaa.com*), is LA's only museum devoted to the increasingly broad subject of Hispanic art. Showcasing artists from Mexico through South America, the collection includes big names like Diego Rivera and José Orozco as well as lesser-known newcomers using styles that range from social criticism to magical realism.

Between November and March, more than fifteen thousand whales cruise the "Whale Freeway" past Long Beach on their annual migration to and return from winter breeding and berthing grounds in Baja California. Shoreline Village Cruises (☎310/495-5884) and Star Party Cruises (☎562/799-7000) operate good whale-watching trips for around $10–15.

The Queen Mary

Long Beach's most famous attraction is not indigenous at all. The mighty ocean liner, the **Queen Mary** (daily 10am–6pm; $15 guided tours, kids $9) was acquired by the local authorities with the specific aim of bolstering tourism, and has generally succeeded in doing so. The *Queen Mary* lies across the bay, opposite Shoreline Village, and is easily accessible either by a lengthy walk or free Long Beach Transit shuttle from downtown. Now a luxury hotel, the ship, through its exhibits, suggests that all who sailed on the vessel – the flagship of the Cunard Line from the 1930s until the 1960s – enjoyed the extravagantly furnished lounges and the luxurious cabins, all carefully restored and kept sparkling. But a glance at the spartan third-class cabins reveals something of the real story, and the tough conditions experienced by the impoverished migrants who left Europe on the ship hoping to start a new life in the USA. The red British telephone kiosks around the decks and the hammy theatrical displays in the engine room and wheelhouse – closer to *Star Trek* than anything nautical – don't help, but it's nonetheless a marvelous ship, well worth a look.

Santa Catalina Island

Though overlooked by many visitors, **SANTA CATALINA ISLAND**, a mix of uncluttered beaches and wild hills twenty miles off the coast, is favored by Californians in the know. Claimed by the Portuguese in 1542 as San Salvador, and renamed by the Spanish in 1602, it has somehow stayed firmly outside the historical mainstream. Since 1811, when the indigenous Tongva Indians were forced to resettle on the mainland, the island has been in private ownership, and has over the years grown to be something of a resort – a process hastened by businessman William Wrigley Jr (part of the Chicago chewing-gum dynasty), who financed the Art Deco Avalon Casino, the island's major landmark, in the 1920s. Occupying mostly LA county territory, the island has become a popular destination for boaters and nature lovers, and its small marina overflows with luxury yachts and cruise ships in summer. Even so, tourism has been held largely at bay: the hotels are unobtrusive among the whimsical architecture and cars are a rarity, as there's a ten-year waiting list to bring one over from the mainland. Consequently, most of the 3,000 islanders walk, ride bikes or drive electric golf carts.

Arrival and accommodation

Depending on the season, a round-trip **ferry** from San Pedro or Long Beach to Catalina Island's one town, **Avalon**, costs between $25 and $35. Catalina Cruises (☎1-800/228-2546) and Catalina Express (☎562/519-1212) run several services daily. From Newport Beach (see p.135) to Avalon, the Catalina Passenger Service (☎714/673-5245) runs a daily round-trip for about $30. If you get seasick or feel extravagant, **helicopter** services to Avalon, costing around $120 round-trip, are offered by Island Express (☎310/510-2525) from Long Beach and San Pedro.

Be warned that the price of hotel **accommodation** in Avalon hovers upwards of $85, and most beds are booked up throughout the summer and at weekends. The most interesting **hotel** is the *Zane Grey Pueblo Hotel* (☎1-800/446-0271 or 310/510-0966; ④–⑤), detailed below, but the cheapest is usually the *Atwater*, on Sumner Avenue (☎1-800/626-1496; ③). The *Bayview Hotel*, on Whittley Avenue (☎310/510-7070; ③), is also reasonable. The only budget option is **camping** ($8.50 per person). *Hermit Gulch* (☎310/510-8368) is the closest site to Avalon and thus the busiest. Three other sites – *Blackjack*, *Little Harbor* and *Two Harbors* – in Catalina's interior, all bookable at ☎310/510-8368, are usually roomier. For **eating**, *Catalina Cantina*, 313 Crescent Ave (☎310/510-0100), is the best, offering tasty and affordable Mexican staples washed down with margaritas, and live music on weekends.

Transportation and trips

Catalina Safari Shuttle Bus (☎1-800/785-8425) runs between Avalon and Two Harbors for around $30 round-trip. Catalina Island Company (☎1-800/343-4491) offers **tours** of the island, ranging from views of the Casino ($9) to a fuller four-hour affair exploring the island's natural setting ($35) – the only way to see the interior of Catalina without hiking. **Golf carts**, for which you need a driver's license, and **bikes** (both banned from the rough roads outside Avalon) can be rented for $30 a day from stands throughout the island.

The waters around Catalina are rich in yellowtail, calico bass, barracuda and sharks. Catalina Mako (☎1-800/296-MAKO or 310/510-2720) runs **charter fishing trips** for around $100 an hour (though you can fish for free from the pier), and snorkel and scuba gear is available for rent at Catalina Divers Supply (☎1-800/353-0330 or 310/510-0330).

Avalon

AVALON can be fully explored on foot in an hour, with maps issued by the **Chamber of Commerce** at the foot of the ferry pier (☎310/510-1520). The best place to begin is at the **Avalon Casino**, a 1920s structure that still shows movies, featuring mermaid murals, gold-leaf ceiling motifs, an Art Deco ballroom, and a small **museum** (daily 10.30am–4pm; $1.50) displaying Native American artifacts from Catalina's past.

On the slopes above the casino, the **Zane Grey Pueblo Hotel** (see above) is the former home of the Western author, who visited Catalina with a film crew to shoot *The*

Vanishing American and liked the place so much he never left, building for himself this pueblo-style house, complete with a beamed ceiling and thick wooden front door. Its hotel rooms are themed after his books and the pool is shaped like an arrowhead.

The interior

If possible, venture into the **interior** of Catalina. You can take a tour (see above) if time is short; if it isn't, get a free **wilderness permit**, which allows you to hike and camp, from the Chamber of Commerce or the **Parks and Recreation office** (☎310/510-0688), both in Avalon. Mountain biking requires a $50 permit from the **Catalina Island Conservancy**, 125 Calressa Ave, Avalon (☎310/510-1421) or the *Two Harbors* campsite.

The carefully conserved wilderness of the interior holds a wide variety of native flora and fauna. Look for the Catalina Shrew, so rare it's only been sighted twice, and the Catalina Mouse, bigger and healthier than its mainland counterpart thanks to abundant food and lack of natural enemies. There are also buffalo, descended from a group of fourteen left behind by a Hollywood film crew and now a sizable herd wandering freely about the island.

Anaheim: Disneyland and around

In the early 1950s, illustrator and filmmaker Walt Disney conceived a theme park where his cartoon characters – Mickey Mouse, Donald Duck, Goofy and the rest, already indelibly imprinted on the American mind – would come to life, and his fabulously successful company would rake in even more money from them.

Disneyland opened in 1955, in anticipation of the acres of orange groves thirty miles southeast of Downtown – at **ANAHEIM** and, inland, in **Orange County** – becoming the nexus of population growth in Southern California. The area around Anaheim is pure Eisenhower era: staunchly conservative suburbs made up of mile after mile of unvarying residential plots and still one of the US's fastest growing areas, with Hispanics and Asians increasingly populating areas like Anaheim, Garden Grove, Santa Ana and Westminster (the latter being a key center for Vietnamese expatriates) – to the chagrin of white Orange County dwellers, many of whom have left the center of the county in "white fright" to find more distant digs in Irvine, Dana Point and San Juan Capistrano.

Certainly, Disneyland dominates the Anaheim area and contributes to its commercial growth, and the boom doesn't look like it's slowing. If you're not coming to see Disneyland, you may as well give the place a miss: it hasn't an ounce of interest in itself. But if you do come, or are staying in one of Anaheim's many hotels, the creakier rides at **Knott's Berry Farm** go some way to restoring antique notions of what amusement parks used to be like; the **Movieland Wax Museum** is occasionally entertaining; and, on an entirely different note, the **Crystal Cathedral** is an imposing reminder of the potency of the evangelical movement. If you're a sports fan, note that baseball's Anaheim Angels play at Anaheim Stadium and hockey's Mighty Ducks play at Arrowhead Pond; the latter team is owned by the town's mouse-in-chief.

Disneyland

It's hard to think of anything that comes closer to demonstrating the wishful thinking of the modern US than **DISNEYLAND** (summer daily 8am–1am; rest of year Mon–Fri 10am–6pm, Sat 9am–midnight, Sun 9am–10pm; $38 adults, $30 kids, parking $6; ☎714/781-4565; *www.disney.go.com/Disneyland*), the most famous, carefully constructed, influential theme park anywhere. Disneyland is a cultural phenomenon, with the emphasis strongly on family fun. While it has been known for people to cruise around Disneyland on LSD, it is not a good idea; the authorities take a dim view of anything remotely antisocial, and anyone acting out of order will be thrown out. In any case the place is surreal enough without the need for mind-expanding drugs. Bear in mind, too, that Disneyland is not LA's only large-scale amusement park; the whirlwind rides at Magic Mountain, for example (see p.143), are always much better.

Practicalities

Disneyland is at 1313 Harbor Blvd, Anaheim, about 45 minutes by **car** from Downtown using the Santa Ana Freeway (I-5). By **train** from Downtown (there are seven a day), make the thirty-minute journey to Fullerton, from where OCTD buses will drop you at Disneyland or Knott's Berry Farm. By **bus**, use MTA #460 from Downtown, which takes about ninety minutes, or the quicker Greyhound service, which runs thirteen times a day, and takes 45 minutes to Anaheim, from where it's an easy walk to the park.

As for **accommodation**, most people try to visit Disneyland just for the day and spend the night somewhere else, or at home. It's not a very appealing area, and anyway most of the hotels and motels close to Disneyland cost well in excess of $70 per night; still, the park is at its least crowded first thing after opening, so staying nearby can help avoid the crowds. If you must stay, the *HI-Anaheim/Fullerton* hostel is by far the best bet (see p.78).

A massive central kitchen produces all the **food** that's eaten in the park (you're not permitted to bring your own), unloading popcorn, hot dogs, hamburgers and other all-American junk food from the many stands by the ton. For anything healthier, you'll need to leave the park and travel a fair way. The "Eating" listings on p.146 suggest some options.

The park

The admission price includes all the rides, although during peak periods you might have to wait in line for hours – lines are shortest when the park opens, so choose a few top rides and get to them very early. From the front gates, **Main Street** leads through a scaled-down, camped-up replica of a turn-of-the-century Midwestern town, filled with souvenir shops, food stands and penny arcades, to Sleeping Beauty's Castle, a pseudo-Rhineland palace at the heart of the park that isn't much more than a giant Disney prop. **New Orleans Square**, nearby, contains two of the best rides in the park: the Pirates of the Caribbean, a boat trip through underground caverns, singing along with drunken pirates, and the Haunted Mansion, a riotous "doom buggy" tour in the company of the house spooks. In **Adventureland**, you may, or may not, wish to spend time on the anti-quated Jungle Cruise listening to your "tour guides" make crude puns about the fake animatronic beasts creaking amid the trees, or in Tarzan's Treehouse, little more than a movie tie-in taking up the space once occupied by the Swiss Family Robinson Treehouse.

Over four hundred "Imagineers" worked to create the **Indiana Jones Adventure**, Disney's biggest opening in years. Two hours of queuing are built into the ride, with an interactive archeological dig and 1930s-style newsreel show leading up to the main fea-ture – a giddy journey along 2500ft of skull-encrusted corridors in which you face fire-balls, burning rubble, venomous snakes and inevitably, a rolling-boulder finale. Less fun is **Frontierland**, the smallest and most all-American of the various theme lands, taking its cues from the Wild West and the tales of Mark Twain, with the less savory and more complex elements of each carefully deleted. The main attraction, Big Thunder Mountain Railroad, is a drab, slow-moving coaster, while Splash Mountain at least has the added thrill of getting drenched by a log-flume ride. **Fantasyland**, across the drawbridge from

Main Street, shows off the cleverest but also the most sentimental aspects of the Disney imagination: Peter Pan, a fairytale flight over London, and It's a Small World, a tour of the world's continents in which animated dolls warble the same cloying song over and over again. Tots who just can't get enough saccharine can wander into **Toontown**, a cartoonish zone aimed only for the under-10 set and generally unbearable for older, thrill-seeking visitors.

Fantasyland eventually gives way to **Tomorrowland**, Disney's vision of the future, where the Space Mountain roller coaster zips through the pitch-blackness of outer space, silly scientists dabble with 3-D trickery in Honey, I Shrunk the Audience, and R2D2 pilots a runaway space cruiser through George Lucas' Star Tours galaxy. This fun zone has been updated somewhat in recent years, with new speed rides like Rocket Rods taking the place of quaint old favorites like the torpid PeopleMover.

In addition to these fixed attractions, over-the-top **firework displays** explode every summer night at 9pm, and all manner of parades and special events celebrate important occasions – such as Mickey Mouse's birthday.

Around Disneyland

It's hard to escape the clutches of Disneyland even when you leave: everything in the surrounding area seems to have been designed to service the needs of its visitors. A few places within easy reach offer a chance to forget, at least temporarily, its existence, but if Disneyland has given you a taste for distortions of reality, there's always the **Richard Nixon Library and Birthplace** to enjoy in Yorba Linda.

Knott's Berry Farm and the Movieland Wax Museum

If you're a bit fazed by the excesses of Disneyland, you might prefer the more traditional **Knott's Berry Farm**, four miles northwest off the Santa Ana Freeway at 8039 Beach Blvd (summer Sun–Thurs 9am–11pm, Fri–Sat 9am–midnight; rest of year Mon–Fri 10am–6pm, Sat 10am–10pm, Sun 10am–7pm; $36, kids $25; *www.knotts.com*). This relaxed, rough-at-the-edges park was born during the Depression when people began queuing up for the fried chicken dinners prepared by Mrs Knott, a local farmer's wife. To amuse the children while they waited for their food, Mr Knott reconstructed a Wild West ghost town and added amusements until the park had grown into the sprawling sideshow of roller coasters and carnival rides that stands today. Unlike Disneyland, this park can easily be seen in one day, as long as you concentrate on the roller coasters, which now make Knott's second only to Magic Mountain (see p.143) for number of thrill rides per acre. Although there are ostensibly six themed lands here, several of them, namely the **Ghost Town** and **Indian Lands**, consist only of mid-level carnival rides, fast-food stands, and uneven historical interpretation. **Camp Snoopy** is the Knott's equivalent of Disney's Toontown, and just as tiresome, while the so-called **Wild Water Wilderness** isn't really a theme area at all, but simply a showplace for the moderately exciting Bigfoot Rapids inner-tube ride. Simply put, you should spend most of your time in just two areas, **Fiesta Village** – home to Montezooma's Revenge, the original one-loop coaster, and Jaguar, a high-flying coaster that spins you around the park concourse – and especially the **Boardwalk**, which is all about thrill rides: the Boomerang, a forward-and-back coaster that can easily induce nausea; WindJammer, two racing coasters looping and dipping around each other; Supreme Scream, a delightfully terrifying freefall drop; and Hammerhead, featuring huge loops. Ultimately, these rides have helped Knott's slough off its antiquated reputation, making it the only worthwhile spot to visit in Orange County for high-speed action.

Across the street at 7711 Beach Blvd, the **Movieland Wax Museum** (summer daily 9am–7pm; $13; kids $7), is a Madame Tussaud's for the Hollywood set, displaying a collection of wax dummies posed in scenes from favorite films and TV shows. The Marx Brothers, Captain Kirk and the crew from the *Starship Enterprise*, and Arnold Schwarzenegger may not be essential viewing, but they're good for a laugh, provided you haven't had the same experience in Hollywood (see p.101).

South of Disneyland

To the **south of Disneyland**, the giant **Crystal Cathedral**, just off the Santa Ana Freeway on Chapman Avenue (daily 9am–4pm; free), is a Philip Johnson design of tubular space frames and plate glass walls that forms part of the vision of evangelist Robert Schuller, who, not content with owning the world's first drive-in church (next door to the cathedral), commissioned this dramatic prop to boost the ratings of his televised Sunday sermons. These shows reach their climax with the special Christmas production, using live animals in biblical roles and people disguised as angels suspended on ropes. Schuller raised $1.5 million for the construction of the building during one Sunday service alone – a statistic worth pondering as you wander the cavernous interior.

A more worthwhile attraction, perhaps, lies in the nearby, unappealing burg of Santa Ana, where the splendid **Bowers Museum of Cultural Art**, 2002 N Main St (Tues–Sun 10am–4pm; $8, kids $4; *www.bowers.org*), features a great range of anthropological treasures from early Asian, African, Native American and pre-Columbian civilizations. Showcasing artifacts as diverse as ceramic Mayan icons, hand-crafted baskets from native Californians, and highly detailed Chinese funerary sculpture, the museum is an essential stop for anyone interested in the art and history of civilizations outside the West. Same-day visitors can, for the same entry ticket, take their children to the adjacent **Kidseum** (Sat–Sun 10am–4pm), a less invigorating look at the same subject, made easily digestible for bored youngsters. Better to visit the main site and get the full version of the Bowers story.

The Richard Nixon Library and Birthplace

Mickey Mouse may be its most famous resident, but conservative Orange County's favorite son is former US president Richard Milhouse Nixon, born in 1913 in what is now the freeway-caged **YORBA LINDA**, about eight miles northeast of Disneyland. Here, the **Richard Nixon Library and Birthplace**, 18001 Yorba Linda Blvd (Mon–Sat 10am–5pm, Sun 11am–5pm; $6, kids $2), is an unrelentingly hagiographic library and museum that features oversized gifts from world leaders, amusing campaign memorabilia, and a collection of obsequious letters written by and to Nixon (including one he sent to the boss of *McDonald's* proclaiming the fast-food chain's hamburgers to be "one of the finest food buys in America"). But it's in the constantly running archive radio and TV recordings that the distinctive Nixon persona really shines through.

Although famously embarrassed in 1960s live TV debates with John F. Kennedy (refusing to wear make-up, and with a visible growth of beard, Nixon perspired freely under the TV lights and was seen as the embodiment of sleaze), Nixon had earlier used the medium to save his political life. In 1952, the discovery of undeclared income precipitated the "fund crisis," which cast doubts over Nixon's honesty, his **"Checkers speech"** convinced 58 million viewers of his integrity, with a broadcast to rival the worst soap opera; his performance climaxed with the statement that, regardless of the damage it may do to his career, he would not be returning the cocker spaniel dog (Checkers) given to him as a gift and now a family pet. Throughout the museum,

RICHARD M. NIXON: A LIFE IN POLITICS

Qualified as a lawyer and fresh from wartime (non-combat) service in the US Navy, **Richard Milhouse Nixon** entered politics as a Republican Congressman in 1946, without so much as a civilian suit to his name. A journalist of the time observed that Nixon employed "the half-truth, the misleading quotation, the loose-joined logic" to cast doubts on his rival – traits he would perfect in the years to come.

Shortly after arriving in Washington, Nixon joined the **House Un-American Activities Committee** (HUAC), a group of scaremongers led by the fanatical Joseph McCarthy. Through the now notorious anti-Communist "witch trials," McCarthy and Nixon wrecked the lives and careers of many Americans and, in the process, launched Nixon to national prominence, culminating in his becoming Eisenhower's vice president in 1953, aged just 39. Seven years later, Nixon was defeated in his own bid for the nation's top job by the even younger John F. Kennedy, a loss which led him into the **"wilderness years."** Staying out of the public spotlight, he took several highly lucrative posts and wrote *Six Crises*, a book whose deep introspection came as a surprise – and convinced many of the author's paranoia. Seeking a power base for the next presidential campaign, Nixon contested the governorship of California in 1962. His humiliating defeat at the hands of Pat Brown (father to Jerry) did nothing to suggest that six years later he would beat Ronald Reagan to the Republican nomination and be **elected president** in 1968.

Nixon had attained his dream, but the country he inherited was more divided than at any time since the Civil War. The **Vietnam conflict** was at its height, and his large-scale illegal bombing of Cambodia earned him worldwide opprobrium. Nixon was not, however, a conservative by modern standards. By breaking with his own party's right wing, he was able to re-establish diplomatic relations with China, begin arms reduction talks with the Soviet Union, create the Environmental Protection Agency, and reluctantly oversee the implementation of court-ordering busing to alleviate racial segregation. Nixon's actions surprised many and contributed to his winning re-election in 1972.

Despite his huge victory over George McGovern, Nixon's second term was ended prematurely by the cataclysmic **Watergate Affair**. In January 1973, seven men were tried for breaking into and bugging the headquarters of the Democratic Party in the Watergate building in Washington, an act that was financed with money allocated to the Committee to Re-Elect the President (CREEP). Nixon may not have sanctioned the actual bugging operation, but there was ample evidence to suggest that he participated in the cover-up. Ironically, his insistence on taping all White House conversations to ease the writing of his future memoirs was to be the major stumbling block to his surviving the crisis. Facing the threat of impeachment, President Nixon **resigned** in 1974.

The full **pardon** granted to Nixon by his successor, Gerald Ford did little to arrest a widespread disillusionment with the country's political machine, but did ensure Ford's defeat in the 1976 presidential election. Ultimately, thanks in part to Nixon, the rose-tinted faith, long held by many Americans, in the unflinching goodness of the President *per se* seemed irredeemably shattered. Remarkably, the years since his ignoble demise saw him quietly seek to establish elder-statesman credentials, opining on world and national affairs through books and newspaper columns. He died in 1994 and was buried at Yorba Linda.

Nixon's face leers down in Orwellian fashion from almost every wall, but only inside the **Presidential Auditorium** (at the end of the corridor packed with notes attesting to the president's innocence in the Watergate Affair) do you get the chance to ask him a question. Many possibilities spring to mind, but the choice is limited to those already programmed into a computer. Ten or so minutes after making your selection, Nixon's gaunt features will fill the overlarge screen and provide the stock reply – as endearingly and believably as ever.

The Orange County Coast

As Disneyland grew, so did the rest of Orange County. Besides providing tourist services, the region become a major center for light industry and home to many of the millions who poured into Southern California during the 1960s and 1970s – its population density is even greater than that of neighboring, more metropolitan, LA County. But it was expansion without style, and those who could afford to soon left the anonymous inland sprawl for the more colorful coast. As a result, the **ORANGE COUNTY COAST**, a string of towns stretching from the edge of the Harbor Area to the borders of San Diego County 35 miles south, is suburbia with a shoreline: swanky beachside houses line the sands, the general ambience is easy-going, affluent, and conservative or libertarian depending on the area.

As the names of the main towns suggest – **Huntington Beach**, **Newport Beach** and **Laguna Beach** – there's no real reason beyond sea and sand to go there. But they do provide something of a counterpart to LA's more cosmopolitan side, and, despite the destructive brushfires of 1993 and after, they do form appealing stopovers on a leisurely journey south. You might even spy a bit of countryside: unlike most of the city's other districts, the communities here don't stand shoulder-to-shoulder but are a few miles apart, in many instances divided by an ugly power station but sometimes by a piece of undeveloped coast. The one place which genuinely merits a stop is just inland at **San Juan Capistrano**, site of the best-kept of all the Californian missions. Further on, there's little to see before you reach adjoining San Diego County, but the campground at **San Clemente** provides the only cheap accommodation along the southern part of the coast.

If you're in a rush to get from LA to San Diego, you can skip the coast by passing through Orange County on the inland San Diego Freeway. The coastal cities, though, are linked by the more adventurous Pacific Coast Highway (PCH), part of Hwy-1, which you can pick up from Long Beach (or from the end of Beach Boulevard, coming from Anaheim), though it's often busy in the summer. OCTD bus #1 rumbles along PCH roughly hourly throughout the day, though Greyhound connections aren't so good: San Clemente gets nine buses a day and two early morning buses go to San Juan Capistrano, but there are none to Huntington, Laguna or Newport Beach. Amtrak is a good way to get from Downtown LA (or Disneyland) to San Juan Capistrano, but you can travel all the way along the coast from LA to San Diego using local buses for about $4 – though you should allow a full day for the journey.

Huntington Beach

HUNTINGTON BEACH is the first place of any interest on the Orange County coast, the wildest of the beach communities and one that you don't need a fortune to enjoy. It's a compact little place composed of engaging, ramshackle single-story cafés and beach stores grouped around the foot of a long pier. The beach is the sole focus: it was here that Californian **surfing** began – imported from Hawaii in 1907 to encourage curious day-trippers to visit on the Pacific Electric Railway. You can check out a great selection of boards at the **International Surf Museum**, 411 Olive Ave (Wed–Sun noon–5pm, summer open daily; $2), or see the full glory of the sport at the **Pro Surfing Championship**, a world-class event held each June. In October, the largely blonde and suntanned locals celebrate a plausible **Oktoberfest**, with German food and music. Huntington Beach is also a surprisingly good place to be based for a while, with Orange County's cheapest beds in the **youth hostel** at 421 Eighth St, three blocks from the pier (see p.79 for details).

Newport Beach and Corona Del Mar

Ten miles south of Huntington, **NEWPORT BEACH** could hardly provide a greater contrast. With ten yacht clubs and ten thousand yachts, this is upmarket even by Orange County standards, a chic image-conscious town that people visit to acquire a tan they can show off on the long stretches of sand or in the bars alongside. Needless to say, you'll need a pocketful of credit cards and a presentable physique to join them.

Newport Beach is spread around a natural bay that cuts several miles inland, but *the* place to hang out is on the thin **Balboa Peninsula**, along which runs the three-mile-long beach. The most youthful and boisterous section is about halfway along, around Newport Pier at the end of 20th Street. North of here, beachfront homes restrict access; to the south, the wide sands are occupied by a sporty crowd and, further along, around the second of Newport's two piers, the **Balboa Pier** is the most touristy part of Newport. Still, it does hold a marina from which you can escape to Catalina Island (see p.127), or take a boat ride on the *Pavilion Queen* (summer daily, hourly cruises 11am–7pm; rest of year daily 11am–3pm; $6–8) around Newport's own, much smaller, islands.

Away from the peninsula, Newport Beach is home to the recently renamed **Orange County Museum of Art** at 850 San Clemente Drive (Tues–Sun 11am–5pm; $5, free Tues; *www.ocma.net*), another of Southern California's important art museums, which stages worthwhile exhibitions of contemporary work.

Just a few miles along PCH from Newport, **CORONA DEL MAR** is a much less ostentatious place, worth a short stop for its good beach and the **Sherman Foundation Center**, devoted to the horticulture of the American Southwest and raising many vivid blooms in its **botanical gardens**. Between here and Laguna Beach lies an unspoiled three-mile-long hunk of coastline, protected as **Crystal Coves State Park**. It's perfect to explore on foot, far from the crowds.

Laguna Beach

Six miles further south, and nestled among the crags around a small sandy beach, **LAGUNA BEACH** grew up late in the nineteenth century as a community of artists, drawn by the beauty of the location. You need a few million dollars to live here

---

LAGUNA'S FESTIVALS

Laguna hosts a number of large summer **art festivals** over a six-week period during July and August. The best-known, and most bizarre, is the **Pageant of the Masters**, a kind of great paintings charade in which the participants pose in front of a painted backdrop to portray a famous work of art. It might sound ridiculous, but it's actually quite impressive, and takes a great deal of preparation – something reflected in the prices: $10–40 for shows which sell out months in advance, though you may be able to pick up cancellations on the night (call ☎1-800/487-3378 or 949/497-6582 for more information). The idea for the pageant was hatched during the Depression as a way to raise money for local artists, and the action takes place at the Irving Bowl, close to where Broadway meets Laguna Canyon Road, a walkable distance from the Laguna Beach bus station. The pageant is combined with the **Festival of the Arts** (tickets $3) held at the same venue during daylight hours.

The excitement of both festivals waned in the Sixties, when a group of hippies created the alternative **Sawdust Festival**, in which local artists and craftspeople set up makeshift studios to demonstrate their skills – now just as established but easier to get into than the other two. It takes place at 935 Laguna Canyon Rd, and admission is around $5.

nowadays, but there's a relaxed and tolerant feel among the inhabitants, who span everything from rich industrialists to leftovers from the 1960s, when Laguna became a hippie haven – even Timothy Leary was known to hang out at the *Taco Bell* on PCH. The scenery is still the great attraction, and despite the massive growth in population, Laguna remains relatively unspoiled with a still-flourishing arts scene in the many streetside galleries.

PCH passes right through the center of Laguna, a few steps from the small main **beach**. From the beach's north side, an elevated wooden walkway twists around the coastline above a conserved **ecological area**, enabling you to peer down on the ocean and, when the tide's out, scamper over the rocks to observe tidepool activity. From the end of the walkway, make your way through the legions of posh beachside homes and head down the hill back to the center. You'll pass the **Laguna Art Museum** (Tues–Sun 11am–5pm; $5), which has changing exhibitions from its stock of Southern Californian art from the 1900s to the present day. A few miles further is less-touristy **SOUTH LAGUNA**, where the wonderfully secluded Victoria and Aliso beaches are among several below the bluffs.

San Juan Capistrano

Further south, and three miles inland along the I-5 freeway, most of the small town of **SAN JUAN CAPISTRANO** is built in a Spanish Colonial style derived from the **Mission San Juan Capistrano** on Camino Capistrano in the center of town (daily 8.30am–5pm; $4), a short walk from the Amtrak stop. The seventh of California's missions, this was founded by Junipero Serra in 1776, and within three years was so well populated that it outgrew the original chapel. Soon after, the **Stone Church** was erected, the ruins of which are the first thing you see as you walk in. The enormous structure had seven domes and a bell tower but was destroyed by an earthquake soon after its 1812 completion. For an idea of how it might have looked, see the full-sized replica – now a church – just northwest of the mission.

The rest of the mission is in an above-average state of repair, due to an ongoing restoration program. The **chapel** is small and narrow, decorated with Indian drawings and Spanish artifacts, and is set off by a sixteenth-century altar from Barcelona. In a side room is the chapel of St Pereguin, a tiny room kept warm by the heat from the dozens of candles lit by miracle-seeking pilgrims who arrive here from all over the US and Mexico.

The other restored buildings reflect the mission's practical role during the Indian period: the kitchen, smelter, and workshops used for dyeing, weaving and candle-making. There's also a rather predictable **museum** (open during mission hours; free), which gives a broad historical outline of the Spanish progress through California and displays odds and ends from the mission's past. The mission is also noted for its **swallows**, popularly thought to return here from their winter migration on March 19. They sometimes do arrive on this day – along with large numbers of tourists – but the birds are much more likely to show up as soon as the weather is warm enough, and when there are enough insects on the ground to provide a decent homecoming banquet.

San Clemente

Five miles south of San Juan Capistrano down I-5, the town of **SAN CLEMENTE** is a pretty little place, its streets contoured around the hills, lending an almost Mediterranean air. Because of its proximity to one of the largest military bases in the state, **Camp Pendleton**, it's a popular weekend retreat for military personnel. It's also predominantly a retirement town which had a brief moment of fame during the 1970s, when President Nixon convened his Western White House here. The 25-acre estate and house are visible from the beach, which is clean and virtually deserted, and there's also a decent campground (see p.78).

The San Gabriel and San Fernando valleys

The northern limit of LA is defined by two long, wide valleys lying beyond the hills from the central basin, starting close to one another a few miles north of Downtown and spanning outwards in opposite directions – east to the deserts around Palm Springs, west to Ventura on the Central Coast.

The **San Gabriel Valley** was settled by farmers and cattle ranchers who set up small towns on the lands of the eighteenth-century Mission San Gabriel. The foothill communities grew into prime resort towns, luring many here around the turn of the century. **Pasadena**, the largest of the foothill communities, holds many elegant period houses, as well as the brilliant but under-publicized **Norton Simon Museum**, and has lately become an increasingly popular spot for dining, shopping and a range of cultural activities. Above Pasadena, the slopes of the San Gabriel Mountains are littered with detritus from the resort days, and make great spots for hiking and rough camping, although you'll nearly always need a car to get to the trailheads. The areas around Pasadena are generally less absorbing, although, to the south, WASP-ish **San Marino** is dominated by the **Huntington Library and Gardens**, a stash of art and literature ringed by botanical gardens that itself makes the journey into the valley worthwhile.

The **San Fernando Valley**, spreading west, is *the* valley to most Angelenos: a sprawl of tract homes, mini-malls, fast-food drive-ins and auto-parts stores. It has more of a middle-American feel than anywhere else in LA and is culturally, if not economically, similar to much of inland Orange County. There are a few isolated sights, notably **Forest Lawn**

EARTHQUAKE CITY: THE SAN FERNANDO VALLEY

The devastating 6.7 magnitude **earthquake** that shook LA on the morning of January 17, 1994 was one of the most destructive disasters in US history. Fifty-five people were killed, two hundred more suffered critical injuries, and the economic cost has been estimated at some $8 billion. One can only guess how much higher these totals would have been had the quake hit during the day, when the many collapsed stores would have been crowded with shoppers and the roads and freeways full of commuters.

As it is, the tremor toppled chimneys and shattered windows all over Southern California, with the worst damage concentrated at the epicenter in the San Fernando Valley community of **Northridge**, where a dozen people were killed when an apartment building collapsed. At the northern edge of the valley, the vital I-5/Hwy-14 interchange was destroyed, killing just one motorist but snarling traffic for at least a year, while in West LA, the Santa Monica Freeway overpass collapsed onto La Cienega Boulevard at one of LA's busiest intersections. The Northridge event just eclipsed LA's previous worst earthquake in modern times, the 6.6 magnitude tremor of February 9, 1971, which had its epicenter in Sylmar.

Small earthquakes happen all the time in LA, usually doing no more than rattling supermarket shelves and making dogs howl. In the unlikely event a sizable earthquake strikes when you're in LA, try to protect yourself under something sturdy, such as a heavy table or a door frame, and well away from windows or anything made of glass. In theory, all the city's new buildings are "quake-safe"; the extent of the crisis in January 1994, however, has forced the city to re-examine and reinforce buildings – though as the quake recedes in memory, the job seems to diminish in perceived importance. So when the inevitable "Big One," a quake in the 8+ range, arrives, no one knows exactly what will be left standing.

Cemetery – a prime example of graveyard kitsch that's hard to imagine anywhere except in LA – but otherwise, beyond a couple of minor historical sites, it's the **movies** that bring people out here. Rising land values in the 1930s pushed many studios out of Hollywood and over the hills to **Burbank**, an anodyne community now overpowered by several major film and TV companies, several of which are open to the public.

At the far west end, the ultra-conservative suburb of **Simi Valley** is known for two things: finding four police officers "not guilty" of beating Rodney King in April 1992 (see p.92), and providing a home for the **Ronald Reagan Presidential Library** (daily 10am–5pm; $4, kids free), containing all the papers pertaining to the Gipper's administration.

Pasadena

Marking the entrance to the San Gabriel Valley, **PASADENA** is as much the home of the *grandes dames* of Los Angeles society as it is to the "little old lady from Pasadena" of the Jan and Dean song. In the 1880s, wealthy East Coast tourists who came to California looking for the good life found it in this foothill resort ten miles north of Los Angeles, where luxury hotels were built and railways cut into the nearby San Gabriel mountains to lead up to taverns and astronomical observatories on the mile-high crest. Many of the early, well-to-do visitors stayed on, building the rustically sprawling houses that remain, but as LA grew so Pasadena suffered, mainly from the smog which the mountains collect. The downtown area underwent a major renovation in the 1980s, with modern shopping centers being slipped in behind 1920s facades, but the historic parts of town have not been forgotten. Maps and booklets detailing self-guided tours of Pasadena architecture and history are available from the **Pasadena Visitors Bureau** at 171 S Los Robles Ave (Mon–Fri 8am–5pm, Sat 10am–4pm; ☎626/795-9311). If you're around at the right time, watch out also for the New Year's Day **Tournament of Roses**, which began in 1890 to celebrate and publicize the mild Southern California winters, and now attracts over a million visitors every year to watch its marching bands and elaborate flower-emblazoned floats (see box on p.160).

A block north of Colorado Boulevard, a replica Chinese Imperial Palace houses the **Pacific Asia Museum** at 46 N Los Robles Ave (Wed–Sun 10am–5pm; $5, students $3), which has a wide range of objects from Japan, China and Thailand, with one particular highlight being the Courtyard Garden, with koi fish, marble statues, and trees native to the Far East.

The Norton Simon Museum

You may not have heard of the **Norton Simon Museum**, but its collections, housed in a modern building at 411 W Colorado Blvd (Wed–Sun noon–6pm, Fri open until 9pm; $6, students $4; *www.nortonsimon.org*), are at least as good as the LA County or Getty museums. Established and overseen by the eponymous industrialist until his death in 1993, the museum, perhaps because of its unfashionable location, sidesteps the hype of the LA art world to concentrate on the quality of its presentation. You could easily spend a whole afternoon, or day, wandering through the spacious galleries, which have recently undergone a multimillion-dollar facelift under the guidance of Frank Gehry; also new is a sizable sculpture garden inspired by none other than Claude Monet's own Giverny.

The core of the collection is **Western European painting** from the Renaissance to the modern period. It's a massive collection, much of it rotated, but most of the major pieces are on view constantly. You'll see Dutch paintings of the seventeenth century – notably Rembrandt's vivacious *Titus, Portrait of a Boy* and Frans Hals' quietly aggressive *Portrait of a Man* – and Italian Renaissance work from Pietro Longhi and Guido Reni. Among more modern works, there's a good sprinkling of French Impressionists and post-Impressionists: Monet's *Mouth of the Seine at Honfleur*, Manet's *Ragpicker* and a Degas capturing the extended yawn of a washerwoman in *The Ironers*, plus works by Cézanne, Gauguin, Van Gogh and Picasso. As a counterpoint to the Western art, the museum has a fine collection of **Asian sculpture** and many highly polished Buddhist and Hindu figures, a mixture of the contemplative and the erotic, some inlaid with precious stones.

Arroyo Seco

Although many outsiders may not realize it, the residential pocket northwest of the junction of the 134 and 210 freeways should be, according to architecture critic David Gebhard, "declared a national monument." The area known as **ARROYO SECO**, or "dry riverbed" in Spanish, boasts some of the region's best architecture and features some of the Valley's key attractions that visitors should by no means miss. Orange Grove Avenue leads you into the neighborhood from central Pasadena and takes you to the **Pasadena Historical Society** on Walnut and Orange Grove (Thurs–Sun 1–4pm; $4), which is decorated with its original 1905 furnishings and paintings, and has fine displays on Pasadena's history. The building was once the Finnish Consulate, and much of the folk art on display comes from Pasadena's "twin town" of Jarvenpää in Finland.

But it's the **Gamble House**, 4 Westmoreland Place (hour-long tours Thurs–Sun noon–3pm; $5), which brings people out here. Built in 1908, and one of the masterpieces of Southern California Craftsman architecture, it's a style you'll see replicated all over the state, at once relaxed and refined, freely combining elements from Swiss chalets and Japanese temples in a romantic, sprawling shingled house. Broad eaves shelter outdoor sleeping porches, which in turn shade terraces on the ground floor, leading out to the spacious lawn. The interior was crafted with the same attention to detail, and all the carpets, cabinetry and lighting fixtures, designed specifically for the house, remain in excellent condition. The area around the Gamble House is filled with at least eight other **houses** by the two brothers (the firm of "Greene & Greene") who designed it, including Charles Greene's own house at 368 Arroyo Terrace. A quarter of a mile north of the Gamble House is a private, concrete-block house by Frank Lloyd Wright, *La Miniatura*, which you can glimpse through the gate opposite 585 Rosemont Avenue. Also in the vicinity are houses by noted architects Gregory Ain, Craig Ellwood and Richard Neutra, and the area definitely rewards driving through its hilly concourses and serene setting (preferably with a copy of Gebhard's LA architecture guide). Almost incongruously, the 104,000-seat **Rose Bowl** is just to the north, out of use for most of the year but home to a very popular **flea market** on the second Sunday of each month and, in the autumn, the place where the UCLA football team plays its home games. The other kind of football was also played here in 1994, when the site hosted the World Cup Final.

Into the foothills

On the other side of the Foothill Freeway, **Descanso Gardens** (daily 9am–4.30pm; $5, students $3) in the city of La Cañada Flintridge, concentrates all the plants you might see in the mountains into 155 acres of landscaped park. The gardens are especially brilliant during the spring, when all the wildflowers are in bloom. From La Cañada, the **Angeles Crest Highway** (Hwy-2) heads up into the mountains above Pasadena. This area was once dotted with resort hotels and wilderness camps, and today you can hike up any number of nearby canyons and come across the ruins of old lodges that either burned down or were washed away towards the end of the hiking era in the 1930s, when automobiles became popular. One of the most interesting of these trails, a five-mile round trip, follows the route of the Mount Lowe Railway, once one of LA's biggest tourist attractions, from the top of Lake Avenue up to the old railway and the foundations of **"White City"** – formerly a mountaintop resort of two hotels, a zoo and an observatory. The Crest Highway passes through the **Angeles National Forest**, capped by Mount Wilson, high enough to be the major siting spot for TV broadcast antennae, and with a small **museum** (daily 10am–3pm; $1) near the 100-inch telescope of the 1904 Mount Wilson Observatory.

The Huntington Library and Gardens

South of Pasadena, **SAN MARINO** is a dull, upper-crust suburb with little of interest beyond the **Huntington Library, Art Collections and Botanical Gardens**, off Huntington Drive at 1151 Oxford Rd (Tues–Fri noon–4.30pm, Sat & Sun 10am–4.30pm; $8.50, students $5). Part of this comprises the collections of Henry Huntington, the nephew of the childless multimillionaire Collis P Huntington, who owned and operated the Southern Pacific Railroad – which in the nineteenth century had a virtual monopoly on transportation in California. Henry, groomed to take over the company from his uncle, was dethroned by the board of directors and took his sizable inheritance to Los Angeles, where he bought up the existing streetcar routes and combined them as the Pacific Electric Railway Company. It was a shrewd investment: the company's "Red Cars" soon became the largest network in the world, and Huntington the largest landowner in the state, buying up farmland and extending the streetcar system at a huge profit. He retired in 1910, moving to the manor he had built in San Marino, devoting himself full time to buying rare books and manuscripts, and marrying his uncle's widow Arabella and acquiring her collection of English portraits.

You can pick up a self-guided walking tour of each of the three main sections from the bookstore and information desk in the covered pavilion. The **Library**, right off the main entrance, is a good first stop, its two-story exhibition hall containing numerous manuscripts and rare books, among them a Gutenberg Bible, a folio edition of Shakespeare's plays, and the **Ellesmere Chaucer**, a circa-1410 illuminated manuscript of the *Canterbury Tales*. Displays around the walls trace the history of printing and of the English language from medieval manuscripts to a King James Bible, from Milton's *Paradise Lost* and Blake's *Songs of Innocence and Experience* to first editions of Swift, Dickens, Woolf and Joyce.

To decorate the **main house**, a grand mansion done out in Louis XIV carpets and later French tapestries, the Huntingtons traveled to England and returned laden with the finest art money could buy; most of it still hangs on the walls. Unless you're a real fan of eighteenth-century English portraiture, head through to the back extension, added when the gallery opened in 1934, which displays, as well as works by Turner, Van Dyck and Constable, the stars of the whole collection – Gainsborough's *Blue Boy* and Reynolds' *Mrs Siddons as the Tragic Muse*.

You'll find paintings by Edward Hopper and Mary Cassatt, and a range of Wild West drawings and sculpture, in the **Scott Gallery for American Art**. For all the art and literature, though, it's the grounds that make the Huntington really special, and the acres of beautiful themed **gardens** surrounding the buildings include a Zen Rock Garden, complete with authentically constructed Buddhist Temple and Tea House. The Desert Garden has the world's largest collection of desert plants, including twelve acres of cactuses in an artful setting. While strolling through these botanical splendors, you might also call in on the Huntingtons themselves, buried in a neo-Palladian **mausoleum** at the northwest corner of the estate, beyond the rows of an orange.

Foothill Boulevard

Parallel to the Foothill Freeway (I-210), **Foothill Boulevard** was once best known as part of **Route 66**, formerly the main route across the US: "from Chicago to LA, more than two thousand miles all the way." The freeway stole Route 66's traffic, and following Foothill Boulevard out of Pasadena nowadays leads to the adjacent town of **ARCADIA**, whose **State and County Arboretum** on Baldwin Avenue (daily 9am–5pm; $5; students $3) has forests of trees arranged according to their native continents. The site was once the 127-acre ranch home of "Lucky" Baldwin, who made his millions in the silver mines of the Comstock in the 1870s. He settled here in 1875, and built a fanciful white palace along a palm-treed lagoon (later used in the TV show *Fantasy Island*) on the site of the 1839 Rancho Santa Anita. He also bred horses, and raced them on a neighboring track that has since grown into the **Santa Anita Racetrack** (racing Oct to early Nov & late Dec to late April, Wed–Sun, post time 12.30pm or 1pm; $4), still the most glamorous racetrack in California.

The city of **SIERRA MADRE**, north of Arcadia, lies directly beneath Mount Wilson and is worth a visit if you're a hiker. A seven-mile round-trip trail up to the summit has recently been restored and is now one of the best hikes in the range. (The trailhead is 150 yards up the private Mount Wilson Road.) Southwest of Sierra Madre stands the valley's original settlement, the church and grounds of **Mission San Gabriel Arcangel** (daily 9am–4.30pm; $3). Still standing at the corner of Mission and Serra in the heart of the small town of **San Gabriel**, the mission was established here in 1771 by Junipero Serra. Although still partially covered in scaffolding after decades of damage by earthquakes and the elements, the church and grounds have recently reopened, with grapevine-filled gardens giving some sense of mission-era life.

Glendale and Forest Lawn Cemetery

GLENDALE, eight miles north of Downtown and the gateway to the San Fernando Valley, was once a fashionable suburb of LA. Now it's a nondescript bedroom community, and almost the only reason to come here is to visit the Glendale branch of **Forest Lawn Cemetery** at 1712 S Glendale Ave (daily 9am–5pm; free) – immortalized with biting satire by Evelyn Waugh in *The Loved One*, and at the vanguard of the American way of death for decades. Founded in 1917 by a Dr Hubert Eaton, this became *the* place to be seen dead, its pompous landscaping and pious artworks attracting celebrities by the dozen.

It's best to climb the hill and see the cemetery in reverse from the **Forest Lawn Museum**, whose hodgepodge of artifacts from around the world includes coins from ancient Rome, Viking relics, medieval armor, and a mysterious sculpted Easter Island figure, discovered being used as ballast in a fishing boat in the days when the statues could still be removed from the island. How it ended up here is another mystery, but it is the only one on view in the US. Next door to the museum, the grandiose **Resurrection and Crucifixion Hall** houses the biggest piece of religious art in the world, *The Crucifixion* by Jan Styka – an oil painting nearly 200ft tall and 50ft wide – though you're only allowed to see it during the ceremonial unveiling every hour on the hour. Besides this, Eaton owned a stained glass re-creation of Leonardo's *Last Supper* and, realizing that he only needed one piece to complete his set of "the three greatest moments in the life of Christ," he commissioned American artist Robert Clark to produce *The Resurrection* – an effort which is also only viewable when unveiled, though this happens on the half-hour. If you can't be bothered to stick around for the showings (with both, in any case, the size is the only aspect that's impressive), you can get a good idea of what you're missing from the scaled-down replicas just inside the entrance.

From the museum, walk down through the terrace gardens – loaded with sculptures modeled on the greats of classical European art – to the **Freedom Mausoleum**, where you'll find a handful of the cemetery's better-known graves. Just outside the mausoleum's doors, Errol Flynn lies in an unspectacular plot (unmarked until 1979), rumored to have been buried with six bottles of whiskey at his side, while a few strides away is the grave of Walt Disney, who isn't cryogenically preserved, as urban legend would have it. Inside the mausoleum itself you'll find Clara Bow, Nat King Cole, Jeanette MacDonald and Alan Ladd handily placed close to each other on the first floor. Downstairs are Chico Marx, and his brother Gummo, the Marx Brothers' agent and business manager. To the left, heading back down the hill, the **Great Mausoleum** is chiefly noted for the tombs of Clark Gable (next to Carole Lombard, who died in a plane crash just three years after marrying him), and Jean Harlow, in a marble-lined room which cost over $25,000, paid for by fiancé William Powell.

A number of other **Forest Lawn cemeteries** continue the style of the Glendale site, to a much less spectacular degree. There's a Hollywood Hills branch in Burbank (6300 Forest Hills Drive, close to Griffith Park) which has a formidable roll call of ex-stars – Buster Keaton, Stan Laurel, Liberace, Charles Laughton and Marvin Gaye – but little else to warrant a visit. The others, Covina Hills, Cypress Beach and Long Beach, also hold limited appeal.

Burbank and the studios

Although Hollywood is synonymous with the movie industry, in reality many of the big studios moved out of Tinseltown long ago, and much of the nitty-gritty business of actually making films goes on over the hills in otherwise boring **BURBANK**, the perennial butt of Johnny Carson's jokes. Hot, smoggy and in some places downright ugly, Burbank nonetheless has a media district bustling with production activity, thanks to the explosion in demand from overseas markets, cable TV and broadcast networks. Disney recently constructed a "wacky" new building to house over seven hundred animators, and **Warner Brothers** is planning an $800 million expansion to its premises over the next twenty years. The latter studio, located at Warner Blvd and Hollywood Way, offers "insider" tours of its facilities (Mon–Fri 9am–4pm; $30; ☎818/972-TOUR), as does **NBC**, at 3000 W Alameda St (Mon–Fri 9am–3pm; $7; ☎818/840-3537). With a frank and interesting ninety-minute tour of the largest production facility in the US, the TV studio offers the chance to be in the audience for the taping of a program (phone ahead for free tickets). It's worth the price of admission just to see *Tonight Show* host Jay Leno in action.

The largest of the old backlots belongs to **Universal Studios** (summer daily 7am–11pm; rest of year daily 9am–7pm; $38; ☎818/508-9600), which mainly uses the space for predictable thrill rides based on movies like *Backdraft*, *Jurassic Park*, and *Back to the Future*. The tours are also firmly tourist-oriented, four hours long and more like a trip around an amusement park than a film studio. The first half features a tram ride through a make-believe set where you can experience the fading magic of the parting of the Red Sea and a collapsing bridge; the second takes place inside the corny

---

THE LA AQUEDUCT

Just beyond the Mission San Fernando, I-5 runs past two of LA's main reservoirs, the water of which has been brought hundreds of miles through the **California Aqueduct** from the Sacramento Delta, and through the **LA Aqueduct** from the Owens Valley and Mono Lake on the eastern slopes of the Sierra Nevada mountains. However, the legality of the arrangements by which Los Angeles gained control of such a distant supply of water is still disputed. Agents of the city, masquerading as rich cattle-barons interested in establishing ranches in the Owens Valley, bought up most of the land along the Owens River before selling it on, at personal profit, to the City of Los Angeles. These cunning tactics provided the inspiration for Roman Polanski's 1974 movie *Chinatown*. For more on Mono Lake and the Owens Valley, see pp.294 and 279.

Entertainment Center, where unemployed actors and stuntmen engage in Wild West shoot-outs and stunt shows based on the latest movies. You never actually get to see any filming.

The **Universal Amphitheater**, which hosts pop concerts in summer, is also part of the complex, as is a twenty-screen movie theater complex, with a lobby reminiscent of 1920s movie palaces. **Universal CityWalk**, also on the same lot, is a few square blocks of neon-lit theme restaurants, free to all who pay the $6 parking (redeemable at the cinemas), where rock bands churn out MOR covers, street performers warble slick set pieces, and giant TV screens run ads for the latest Universal release.

The Western San Fernando Valley

At the **western end** of the San Fernando Valley, the Ventura Freeway (US-101) passes below the increasingly expensive hillside homes of **Sherman Oaks** and **Encino**, close to which the **Los Encinos State Historic Park**, on Balboa Boulevard (Wed–Sun 10am–5pm, tours 1–4pm; grounds free, tours $2), is all that remains of the original Native American settlement and later Mexican hacienda that were here. The high-ceilinged rooms of the 1849 adobe house open out onto porches, shaded by oak trees (in Spanish, "encinos") and kept cool by the two-foot-thick walls. West of Encino, Topanga Canyon Boulevard crosses the Ventura Freeway, leading south towards Malibu (p.123) or north to **Stony Point**, a bizarre outcrop of sandstone that has been used for countless Western shoot-outs, and in recent years as a popular venue for LA's contingent of lycra-clad rock climbers. The area, though crossed by both Amtrak and Metrorail coastal trains, certainly has a desolate spookiness about it, and it comes as little surprise to learn that during the late 1960s the Charles Manson "family" lived for a time at the **Spahn Ranch**, just west at 12000 Santa Susana Pass.

Mission San Fernando and Magic Mountain

At the north end of the Valley, the San Diego, Golden State and Foothill freeways join together at I-5, the quickest route north to San Francisco. Standing near the junction at 15151 San Fernando Mission Blvd, the church and many of the buildings of **Mission San Fernando Rey de España** (daily 9am–5pm; $4) had to be completely rebuilt following the 1971 earthquake. It's hard to imagine now, walking through the nicely landscaped courtyards and gardens, but eighty-odd years ago, director D.W. Griffith used the then-dilapidated mission as a film site for movies such as *Our Silent Paths*, his tale of the Gold Rush. Another twenty miles north, Hwy-14 splits off east to the Mojave desert, while I-5 continues north past Valencia and **Magic Mountain** (summer daily 10am–10pm; rest of year Sat & Sun only 10am–8pm; $39, $5 parking), a three-hundred-acre complex that has some of the wildest roller coasters and rides in the world – a hundred times more thrilling than anything at Disneyland. An appealing new waterpark, **Hurricane Harbor** (same hours; $18, or $49 for both parks), has recently been added nearby, and provides plenty of aquatic fun if you don't mind getting splashed by throngs of giddy pre-adolescents.

Eating

LA's **restaurants** cover every extreme: whatever you want to eat and however much you want to spend, you're spoiled for choice. **Budget food** is as plentiful as in any other US city, ranging from good sit-down meals in street-corner coffee shops and cafés to big franchise burgers. Almost as common, and just as cheap, is **Mexican food**, the closest thing you'll get to an indigenous LA cuisine. If you simply want to load up quickly and cheaply, the options are almost endless, and include free food available for the price of a drink at **happy hours**. However, you should also try to take at least a few meals in one of LA's **top-notch restaurants**, which serve superb food in consciously cultured surroundings. Scores of restaurants drive up their prices on the back of a good review, and get away with it because they know the place will be packed with first-timers trying to impress their cohorts by claiming that they've been eating there for years.

Catering appears to be the movie stars' sideline of choice these days, and LA is littered with **celebrity-owned** outfits – like Steven Spielberg's submarine-shaped sandwich store *Dive!* and the financially troubled *Planet Hollywood* in Beverly Hills (where displays include Forrest Gump's box of chocolates) – but the food is usually so unremarkable we haven't listed them.

Budget food: coffee shops, delis, diners and drive-ins

Budget food is everywhere in LA, at its best in the many small and stylish **coffee shops**, **delis** and **diners** that serve soups, omelets, sandwiches and so forth; it's easy to exist entirely this way and never have to spend much more than $6 for a full meal. There are of course the franchise fast-food places on every street and locally based chains of **hamburger stands**, most open 24 hours a day; *Fatburger*, originally at San Vicente and La Cienega on the border of Beverly Hills, has branches everywhere.

Sadly but surely, the best of the 1950s **drive-ins**, such as *Tiny Naylors* in Hollywood, have been torn down. So too have some of the classic googie-style **diners** met their demise; the venerable *Ships* franchise now comprises only a boarded-up ruin in Culver City and a pair of leftover boomerang signs near a gas station in West LA.

Downtown and around

Cassell's Hamburgers, 3266 W Sixth St (☎213/387-5502). No-frills, lunch-only takeout hamburger stand that some swear by.

Clifton's Cafeteria, 648 S Broadway (☎213/627-1673). Classic 1930s cafeteria, the last remaining of a chain of six, and with much bizarre decor: redwood trees, waterfall and mini-chapel. The food is traditional meat-and-potatoes American, and cheap too.

Grand Central Market, 317 S Broadway (☎213/624-2378). Although the market stalls still sell plenty of tacos, deli sandwiches and Chinese food, high rents have forced many vendors out, leaving numerous empty booths. Still, a new renovation makes this a fun, cheap place to eat.

Langer's Deli, 704 S Alvarado St (☎213/483-8050). "When in doubt, eat hot pastrami" says the sign, though you still have to choose from over twenty ways of eating what is easily LA's best pastrami sandwich. Nearby MacArthur Park Metrorail station may help you escape the dicey neighborhood.

Original Pantry, 877 S Figueroa St (☎213/972-9279). There's always a queue for the hearty portions of very meaty American cooking – chops and steaks, mostly – in this 24-hr diner owned by Mayor Riordan.

Philippe the Original French Dip, 1001 N Alameda St (☎213/628-3781). 1908 sawdust café that invented the eponymous sandwich, which is served loaded with pork, lamb or beef.

Shabazz R50K, 3405 W 43rd St, South Central (☎323/299-8688). Jazz greats waft out of the speakers, Malcolm X and Muhammed Ali grace the walls, and the chili and bean pie delights your palate.

The Yorkshire Grill, 610 W Sixth St (☎213/629-3020). New York-style deli with big sandwiches and friendly service for under $10. Lunchtime is crowded; get there early.

Hollywood

Hampton's, 1342 N Highland Ave (☎323/469-1090). Gourmet hamburgers with a choice of over fifty toppings, plus an excellent salad bar.

Johnny Rockets, 7507 Melrose Ave (☎323/651-3361). Chrome-and-glass, Fifties-derived hamburger joint, open until 2am at weekends. Three other Westside locations, with more on the way.

Maurice's Snack 'n' Chat, 5549 W Pico Blvd (☎323/931-3877). Everything here is cooked to order: spoon bread or baked chicken requires a call two hours ahead, though you could just drop in for fried chicken, pork chops, grits or salmon croquettes. Don't even think about the calorie count. Autographed pictures of celebrity diners – from Sammy Davis Jr to Ted Kennedy – line the walls.

Pink's Hot Dogs, 709 N La Brea Ave (☎323/931-4223). The quintessence of chili dogs. Depending on your taste, these monster hot dogs are life-savers or gut bombs.

Roscoe's Chicken and Waffles, 1514 N Gower St (323/466-7453). An unlikely spot for Hollywood's elite, this diner attracts all sorts for its fried chicken, greens, goopy gravy and thick waffles. Listen to the ringing pagers and cell phones as you wait in line for breakfast with movie-industry big shots.

Tommy's, 2575 Beverly Blvd (☎213/389-9060). Often called LA's best burgers: loaded with thick beef, tasty toppings, and copious grease.

Yukon Mining Company, 7328 Santa Monica Blvd (☎323/851-8833). Excellent 24-hr coffee shop with a curious clientele – don't be surprised to see a crowd of newly arrived Russians, neighborhood pensioners and glammed-up drag queens.

West LA

The Apple Pan, 10801 W Pico Blvd (☎310/475-3585). Grab a spot at the counter and enjoy freshly baked apple pie and nicely greasy hamburgers across from the *Westside Pavilion* mall.

Barney's Beanery, 8447 Santa Monica Blvd (☎323/654-2287). Two hundred bottled beers and hot dogs, hamburgers and bowls of chili served in a hip, grungy environment. Also offers karaoke and "lingerie shows" twice a week.

Canter's Deli, 419 N Fairfax Ave (☎323/651-2030). Huge sandwiches for around $7 and excellent kosher soups served by famously aggressive waitresses in pink uniforms and running shoes. Open 24-hr.

Duke's, 8909 Sunset Blvd (☎310/652-3100). A favorite haunt of visiting rock stars (the *Roxy* and *Whisky* clubs are up the street), this place attracts a motley crew of night owls and bleary-eyed locals.

Ed Debevic's, 134 N La Cienega Blvd (☎310/659-1952). The last four digits of the phone number give you a hint: a rollicking 1950s diner with brash singing waitresses, burgers 'n' fries and pricey beer.

Hard Rock Café, in the Beverly Center, Beverly Blvd at San Vicente (☎310/276-7605). Rock 'n' roll decor, loud music, and tourist duds for sale are the attractions; the bland, greasy food is an afterthought. Also at 1000 Universal Center Dr, Universal City (☎818/622-7626).

Jerry's Famous Deli, 8701 Beverly Blvd (☎310/289-1811). One of several Jerry's locations in LA, this place features a sizable deli menu and is open 24hr. Occasionally, celebrities stop in to nosh.

Johnie's, 6101 Wilshire Blvd (☎323/938-3521). Tasteless diner food and a drafty atmosphere, but this landmark café has been home to many a film shoot, including flicks by Tarantino and the Coen Bros.

John o' Groats, 10516 W Pico Blvd (☎310/204-0692). Excellent cheap breakfasts and lunches, but come at an off hour; the morning crowd can cause a headache.

Kate Mantilini, 9109 Wilshire Blvd (☎310/278-3699). Tasty versions of classic American diner food, served up in a stylish interior designed by edgy architectural firm Morphosis. Open until 2am.

Nate 'n' Al's, 414 N Beverly Drive (☎310/274-0101). The best-known deli in Beverly Hills, popular with movie people and one of the few reasonable places in the vicinity.

Swingers, *Beverly Laurel Motor Hotel*, 8018 Beverly Blvd (☎323/653-5858). Basic and cheap American food served in a strangely trendy motel environment, luring an assortment of hipsters and poseurs.

Tail o' the Pup, 329 N San Vicente Blvd (☎310/652-4517). Worth a visit for the roadside pop architecture alone, though the dogs and burgers are good too.

Santa Monica, Venice and Malibu

Bicycle Shop Café, 12217 Wilshire Blvd, Santa Monica (☎310/826-7831). Pseudo-bistro serving light meals, fish and salads that's also a good place to drink. Take note of the plethora of bike decor: chains, frames, and wheels are everywhere, delighting cycle enthusiasts.

Café 50s, 838 Lincoln Blvd, Venice (☎310/399-1955). No doubts about this place: Ritchie Valens on the jukebox, burgers on the tables.

Café Montana, 1534 Montana Ave, Santa Monica (☎310/829-3990). Good breakfasts and excellent salads and grilled fish in an upmarket section of Santa Monica.

Norm's, 1601 Lincoln Blvd, Santa Monica (☎310/450-0074). One of the last remaining classic diners, this local chain has nine other LA branches and serves $3 breakfasts and similarly cheap lunches. Great googie architecture, too.

Rae's Diner, 2901 Pico Blvd, Santa Monica (☎310/828-7937). Classic 1950s diner with heavy but tasty food. Its turquoise-blue facade and interior has been seen in many films, notably Quentin Tarantino's *True Romance*.

Reel Inn, 18661 Pacific Coast Highway, Malibu (☎310/456-8221). Seafood diner by the beach, with appealing prices and a good atmosphere. Also at 1220 W Third St, Santa Monica (☎310/395-5538).

The Sidewalk Café, 1401 Ocean Front Walk, Venice (☎310/399-5547). Somewhat grim interior and only adequate food, but a prime spot for watching the daily parade of beach people.

The South Bay and Harbor Area

East Coast Bagels, 5753 E PCH, Long Beach (☎562/985-0933). Located in a dreary mini-mall, but with an excellent wide selection of bagels, ranging from New York staples to California hybrids like the jalapeno-cheddar bagel stuffed with cream cheese.

Hof's Hut, 4828 E Second St, Long Beach (☎562/439-4775). One bite of the Hut's juicy Hofburger and you know you've found the real deal. Four other Long Beach locations, and five in Orange County.

Johnie's Broiler, 7447 Firestone Blvd, Downey (☎562/927-3383). Decent all-American food in a bleak corner of LA. On Wednesday nights, Fifties-car fanatics park in their Chevys and Fords and are waited upon by perky, roller-skating teens.

The Local Yolk, 3414 Highland Ave, Manhattan Beach (☎310/546-4407). As the name suggests, everything done with eggs, plus muffins and pancakes.

Pier Bakery, 100-M Fisherman's Wharf, Redondo Beach (☎310/376-9582). A small but satisfying menu with jalapeno cheese bread and cinnamon rolls. Probably the best food in this touristy area.

Russell's, 5656 E Second St, Long Beach (☎562/434-0226). Worth a trip to sample the great burgers and fresh pies. Also at 4306 Atlantic Ave (☎562/427-6869) and three other area locations.

Tony's Famous French Dip Sandwiches, 701 Long Beach Blvd, Long Beach (☎562/435-6238). The name says it all, but alongside the dips is a beckoning array of soups and salads.

Disneyland and around

Angelo's, 511 S State College Blvd, Anaheim (☎714/533-1401). Straight out of *Happy Days*, a drive-in complete with roller-skating car-hops, neon signs, vintage cars and, incidentally, good burgers.

Belisle's, 12001 Harbor Blvd, Garden Grove (☎714/750-6560). Open late for filling sandwiches, meat pies and a variety of things baked. Known as much for quantity as quality.

Knott's Chicken Dinner Restaurant, located just outside Knott's Berry Farm at 8039 Beach Blvd, Buena Park (☎714/220-5080). Serving cheap and tasty meals for over 65 years. People flocked here for delicious fried chicken dinners long before Disneyland was around, and they still do.

Mimi's Café, 18342 Imperial Highway, Yorba Linda (☎714/996-3650). Huge servings, low prices and a relaxing atmosphere down the street from the Nixon Library. Part of a sizable Orange County chain.

Orange County Coast

Café Zinc, 350 Ocean Ave, Laguna Beach (☎949/494-7029). A popular breakfast counter offering simple soup-and-salad meals and other light fare. Good for a day on the sands.

24-HR-EATS

These places satisfy hunger at all hours. For full restaurant reviews, see the appropriate sections.

Canter's Deli, 419 N Fairfax Ave, West LA (☎323/651-2030) – p.145.

Jerry's Famous Deli, 8701 Beverly Blvd, West LA (☎310/289-1811) – p.145.

Original Pantry, 877 S Figueroa St, Downtown (☎213/972-9279) – p.144.

Pacific Dining Car, 1310 W Sixth St, Downtown (☎213/483-6000) – p.149.

Yukon Mining Company, 7328 Santa Monica Blvd, Hollywood (☎323/851-8833) – p.145.

C'est Si Bon, 3444 E Coast Highway, Corona Del Mar (☎949/675-0994). Seaside café serving croissants, baguettes, and French cheese and paté; don't miss the savory desserts.

Ruby's, 1 Balboa Pier, Newport Beach (☎949/675-RUBY). The first and finest of the retro-streamline 1940s diners that have popped up all over LA – in a great location at the end of Newport's popular pier.

The San Gabriel and San Fernando valleys

Dr Hogly-Wogly's Tyler Texas Bar-B-Q, 8136 Sepulveda Blvd, Van Nuys (☎818/780-6701). Long lines for some of the best chicken, sausages, ribs and beans in LA, despite the depressing surroundings.

Fair Oaks Pharmacy and Soda Fountain, 1526 Mission St, South Pasadena (☎626/799-1414). A fabulous old-fashioned soda fountain with many old-time drinks like lime rickeys and egg creams.

Goldstein's Bagel Bakery, 86 W Colorado Blvd, Pasadena (☎626/792-2435). If money's tight, feast on day-old 15¢ bagels; otherwise enjoy what some call LA's best bagels, made in a New York style.

Hidden Springs Café, 23155 Angeles Forest Hwy, south of Palmdale (☎626/792-9663). The lone restaurant on this highway. Filling portions are served in open stone rooms with real fires and rustic decor as eclectic as the clientele, which includes Hell's Angels, fly-fishers, gold-miners and tourists.

Pie & Burger, 913 E California Blvd, Pasadena (☎626/795-1123). Classic coffee shop, with good burgers and excellent fresh pies.

Porto's Bakery, 315 N Brand Blvd, Glendale (☎818/956-5996). Popular and cheap café serving Cuban flaky pastries, rum-soaked cheesecakes, and muffins, danishes, croissants, torts, and cappuccino.

Rose Tree Cottage, 395 E California Blvd, Pasadena (☎626/793-3337). Scones and high tea in a country home setting so thoroughly English that it's the West Coast HQ of the British Tourist Board.

Mexican and Latin American

LA's **Mexican** restaurants are the city's best – and most plentiful – eating standby, serving tasty, healthy and filling food for as little as $5 a head. They're at their finest and most authentic in East LA, although there's a good selection of more Americanized examples all over the city. Aside from restaurants, there are far less enticing but even cheaper Mexican fast-food outlets like *Taco Bell* and *El Pollo Loco* just about everywhere. **Caribbean** food is less visible but, when sought out, can be quite rewarding.

Downtown and around

Burrito King, 2109 W Sunset Blvd, Echo Park (☎213/413-9444). Excellent burritos and tasty tostadas from this small stand; open until 2am. Also nearby at 2827 Hyperion Ave, Silver Lake (☎323/663-9378).

Ciro's Mexican Food, 705 N Evergreen Ave, East LA (☎323/267-8637). A split-level cave of a dining room, serving enormous platters of shrimp and mole specials. The *flautas* are the main draw.

El Cholo, 1121 S Western Ave (☎323/734-2773). One of LA's first big Mexican restaurants and still one of the best, despite the frequent presence of drunken frat-rats from nearby USC.

King Taco, 317 S Broadway (☎213/621-2410). One in a chain of many such restaurants around Downtown, with many varieties of tacos – most of them quite savory.

Luminarias, 3500 Ramona Blvd, Monterey Park (☎323/268-4177). Dance to salsa and merengue between bites of seafood-heavy Mexican food. The Spanish name refers to honorary candles in brown paper bags.

Hollywood

Casa Carnitas, 4067 Beverly Blvd (☎323/667-9953). Tasty Mexican food from the Yucatán: the dishes are inspired by Cuban and Caribbean cooking – lots of fine seafood, too.

Casita del Campo, 1920 Hyperion Ave, Silver Lake (☎323/662-4255). Old local favorite continues to serve fine Mexican meals for around $5–10.

Mario's Peruvian Seafood Restaurant, 5786 Melrose Ave (☎323/466-4181). Delicious and authentic Peruvian fare: supremely tender squid, and a hint of soy sauce in some dishes.

Mexico City, 2121 N Hillhurst Ave (☎323/661-7227). Spinach enchiladas and other Californian versions of Mexican standards served in a decent corner of East Hollywood.

Yuca's Hut, 2056 N Hillhurst Ave (☎323/662-1214). A small hidden jewel with good al fresco burritos.

West LA

Baja Fresh, 475 N Beverly Dr (☎310/858-6690). Cheap, predictable Mexican food served for a hungry crowd of window shoppers and movie-industry wannabes.

El Coyote, 7312 Beverly Blvd (☎323/939-2255). Labyrinthine restaurant serving heavy Mexican food, more than you can stand. But cheap and lethal margaritas are the primary draw to this gloomy setting.

El Mexicano,1601 Sawtelle Blvd (☎310/473-8056). Cozy deli and adequate restaurant; the deli is like an old-fashioned general store, selling fruit, vegetables and canned products from south of the border.

La Salsa, 11075 W Pico Blvd (☎310/479-0919). Come here for fresh, delicious soft tacos and burritos.

Versailles, 10319 Venice Blvd (☎310/558-3168). Busy and noisy Cuban restaurant with fried plantains, paella and black beans and rice. Also nearby at 1415 S La Cienega Blvd (☎310/289-0392).

Santa Monica, Venice and Malibu

La Cabana, 738 Rose Ave, Venice (☎310/392-6161). Corn tortillas as thick as pancakes, and interesting stuffed *quesadillas*. Busy on weekends. One of a citywide chain.

Mariasol, 401 Santa Monica Pier, Santa Monica (☎310/917-5050). *Cervezas* with a view, hidden away at the end of the pier. The small rooftop deck affords a sweeping panorama from Malibu to Venice.

Marix Tex-Mex Playa, 118 Entrada Drive, Pacific Palisades (☎310/459-8596). Flavorful fajitas and big margaritas in this rowdy beachfront cantina. Also at 1108 N. Flores St, Hollywood (☎323/656-8800).

The South Bay and Harbor Area

El Pollo Inka, 1100 PCH, Hermosa Beach (☎310/372-1433). Good Peruvian-style chicken to make your mouth water. For a closer visit, try the one at 11701 Wilshire Blvd, Westwood (☎310/571-3334).

Pancho's, 3615 Highland Ave, Manhattan Beach (☎310/545-6670). Big portions, cheap for the area.

The San Gabriel and San Fernando valleys

Don Cuco's, 3911 W Riverside Dr, Burbank (☎818/842-1123). Good food with a great Sunday brunch.

El Tepayac, 800 S Palm Ave, Alhambra (☎626/281-3366). Huge, luscious burritos and hot salsa. Also in East LA at 812 N Evergreen Ave (☎323/267-8668).

Merida, 20 E Colorado Blvd, Pasadena (☎626/792-7371). Unusual Mexican restaurant, featuring dishes from the Yucatán; try the spicy pork wrapped and steamed in banana leaves.

Señor Fish, 618 Mission St, South Pasadena (☎626/403-0145). Great fish tacos, with charbroiled halibut for under $10. Also at 424 E First St, Downtown (☎213/625-0566).

Wolfe Burgers, 46 N Lake Ave, Pasadena (☎626/792-7292). Knockout chili, tamales and burgers.

American, California cuisine and Cajun

Down-to-earth **American** cuisine, with its steaks, ribs, baked potatoes and salads, has a low profile in faddish LA, although it's available almost everywhere and usually won't cost more than $10 for a comparative blow-out. More prominent – and more expensive, at upwards of $20 – is **California cuisine**, based on local ingredients, more likely grilled than fried, and stylishly presented with a nod to nouvelle French cuisine. Another rage is spicy, fish-based **Cajun** cooking, still available in authentic form and often inexpensive.

Downtown and around

Bernard's, 506 S Grand Ave in the *Biltmore Hotel* (☎213/612-1580). Lushly decorated dining room in this landmark hotel, serving contemporary versions of classic American meat and fish dishes.

Café Pinot, 700 W Fifth St (☎213/239-6500). Located next to the LA Public Library, this elegant restaurant offers a mix of California and French cuisines at less exorbitant prices than you might expect.

Checkers Restaurant, 535 S Grand Ave in the *Wyndham Checkers Hotel* (☎213/624-0000). One of the most elegant Downtown restaurants, serving top-rated California cuisine all day.

Engine Co. No. 28, 644 S Figueroa St (☎213/624-6996). All-American grilled steaks and seafood, served in a renovated 1912 fire station. Great French fries and an excellent wine list.

McCormick and Schmick's, 633 W Fifth St (☎213/629-1929). Swank seafood joint for business types known for a great weekend dinner special. Also at 206 N Rodeo Drive, Beverly Hills (☎310/859-0434).

Pacific Dining Car, 1310 W Sixth St (☎213/483-6000). Would-be English supper club housed inside an old railroad carriage. Open 24hr for (very expensive) steaks. Breakfast is the best value.

Hollywood

Cha Cha Cha, 656 N Virgil Ave (☎323/664-7723). Offering paella, black-pepper shrimp, jerk chicken and other Caribbean treats. Also at 762 Pacific Ave, Long Beach (☎562/436-3900).

Hollywood Canteen, 1006 N. Seward St (☎323/465-0961). A dark club scene with fish, steak and clam chowder – just the right ambience to make you feel like a Tinseltown big shot.

Musso and Frank Grill, 6667 Hollywood Blvd (☎323/467-7788). A 1919 classic, with Hollywood atmosphere in a dark-paneled dining room. The drinks (see p.155) are better than the pricey food.

Off Vine, 6263 Leland Way (323) 962-1900. Dine on eclectic Cal cuisine – pecan chicken, duck sausage and Grand Marnier soufflé – in a renovated but still funky Craftsman bungalow.

Patina, 5955 Melrose Ave (☎323/467-1108). The height of the culinary elite, this ultra-chic place delivers exquisite California cuisine, satisfying the palate while depriving the wallet.

Pinot Hollywood, 1448 Gower St (☎323/461-8800). Upmarket American food crossed with nouvelle French, in a spacious environment with 24 types of martinis and Polish potato vodka.

West LA

Barefoot, 8722 W Third St (☎310/276-6223). Good pastas, pizzas and seafood between Beverly Hills and the Beverly Center. Considering the prime location, very affordable.

Ca' Brea, 346 S La Brea Ave (☎323/938-2863). Hip California-cuisine restaurant in a trendy part of town. Popular because of the delicious risotto and *osso buco* – be prepared to wait.

Citrus, 6703 Melrose Ave (☎323/857-0034). Trendy upmarket restaurant, at its best with Cal-cuisine stylings of fish, duck and lamb. Its competitors offer the same fine food for cheaper prices.

Georgia, 7250 Melrose Ave (☎323/933-8420). Down-home Southern cooking served in a mahogany dining room for about $15–25 a plate. Part-owned by a tag-team of celebrities including Denzel Washington.

The Gumbo Pot, 6333 W Third St in the Farmer's Market (☎323/933-0358). Delicious, dirt-cheap Cajun food in a busy setting; try the *gumbo yaya* (chicken, shrimp and sausage) or the fruit-and-potato salad.

L'Orangerie, 903 N La Cienega Blvd (☎310/652-9770). Nouvelle California-style French cuisine; if you haven't got the $150 it takes to sit down, enjoy the view from the bar.

Spago, 1114 Horn Ave (☎310/652-4025). LA's most famous restaurant, both for its chef Wolfgang Puck (inventor of "designer pizza") and its star clientele. Avoid the stuffy new Beverly Hills branch.

Santa Monica, Venice and Malibu

Gladstone's 4 Fish, 17300 PCH (☎310/454-3474). At the junction of Sunset Boulevard, this joint is known for its prime beachfront location – not for its heavily fried and breaded seafood.

Granita, 23725 W Malibu Rd (☎310/456-0488). If you can't get enough of meister-chef Puck (see *Spago* above), check out his Malibu entry – a heady mix of Cal-cuisine and Italian flavors. Delicious and pricey.

Michael's, 1147 Third St, Santa Monica (☎310/451-0843). California cuisine served amid modern art. This venerable establishment always attracts the crowds for its rich, tasty lobster, salmon and veal.

17th Street Café, 1610 Montana Ave, Santa Monica (☎310/453-2771). Seafood, pasta and burgers at moderate prices in a chic part of town. Nicely casual, unpretentious atmosphere – unusual for the area.

Italian, Spanish, Greek and pizza

After years of having nothing more exotic than the takeout pizza chains – such as *Pizza Hut* and *Shakey's* – LA has woken up to the delights of regional **Italian** cooking, and there is a growing number of specialist restaurants, especially around the Westside, serving refined and varied Italian food. Another recent phenomenon is **designer pizza**, invented at the restaurant *Spago* and topped with duck, shiitake mushrooms and other exotic ingredients. The problem with all this? It doesn't come cheap. A pasta dish in the average Italian restaurant can cost upwards of $8, and the least elaborate designer pizza will set you back $15. **Spanish** food and tapas bars have also become popular, and pricey. In contrast, if you want **Greek** food, you'll have to look hard – restaurants are good but uncommon.

Downtown

California Pizza Kitchen, 330 S Hope St (☎213/626-2616). Mid-priced designer pizza at this chain.

Cicada, 617 S Olive St (☎213/488-9488). Housed in the stunning Art Deco Oviatt Building (see p.86), this northern Italian restaurant offers fine pasta ($15) for half the price of its fish and steak entrées.

La Bella Cucina, 949 S Figueroa St (☎213/623-0014). Fabulous pizzas and homemade pastas, with the accent on northern and rural Italian cuisine.

Hollywood

Campanile, 624 S La Brea Ave (☎323/938-1447). Incredible but expensive northern Italian food; if you can't afford a dinner, try the dessert or the best bread in Los Angeles at the adjacent *La Brea Bakery*.

Louise's Trattoria, 4500 Los Feliz Blvd (☎323/667-0777). Everybody in LA knows this chain: some love it for its good mid-priced pizzas, some hate it for its overcooked, uninspired pasta. You decide.

Palermo, 1858 N Vermont Ave (☎323/663-1178). As old as Hollywood, and with as many devoted fans, who flock here for the rich southern-Italian pizzas, cheesy decor and gallons of cheapish red wine.

West LA

Cava, 8384 W Third St (☎323/658-8898). The Latin and Iberian dishes are quite good, but the real attraction is tasty tapas accompanied by shots of prime sherry – and, of course, the salsa music.
Chianti, 7383 Melrose Ave (☎323/653-8333). Old-fashioned 1930s restaurant amid Melrose chaos. Try the delicious raviolis or go with the well-crafted chicken and lamb entrées.
La Masia, 9077 Santa Monica Blvd (☎310/273-7066). Upscale Castilian dining, after which you can hit the dancefloor and enjoy a spot of salsa and merengue.
Locanda Veneta, 8638 W Third St (☎310/274-1893). Scrumptious ravioli, risotto, veal, and carpaccio – you can't go wrong at one of LA's quiet culinary joys. But be prepared to wait: the word is getting out.

Santa Monica, Venice and Malibu

Abbot's Pizza Company, 1407 Abbot Kinney Blvd, Venice (☎310/396-7334). This home of the bagel-crust pizza tops them with your choice of seeds, tangy citrus sauce or shiitake and wild mushroom sauce.
Boston Wildflour Pizza, 2206 Pier Ave, Santa Monica (☎310/452-7739). A cheese slice is $2 in the *LA Times*-nominated "Best Thin Pizza" house.
Valentino, 3115 Pico Blvd, Santa Monica (☎310/829-4313). Believe it or not, national food critics have claimed this spot as having the best Italian cuisine in the US. For a hefty sum, you can be the judge.
Wolfgang Puck Express, 1315 Third St, Santa Monica (☎310/576-4770). On the second floor of a food mall, watch Promenade tourists below while munching on great pizzas and salads. One of a growing chain.

The South Bay and Harbor Area

Alegria Cocina Latina, 115 Pine Ave, Long Beach (☎562/436-3388). Quality tapas and gazpacho served with plenty of sangria on the patio, and to the beat of live flamenco every night.
Giovanni's Salerno Beach, 195 Culver Blvd, Playa Del Rey (☎310/821-0018). Ungodly kitsch decor and cheap southern Italian food; but you can walk off the heavy meal at nearby Dockweiler beach.
Mangiamo, 128 Manhattan Beach Blvd, Manhattan Beach (☎310/318-3434). Like the name says, "Let's eat!" Fairly pricey but worth it for the specialist northern Italian seafood – and right off the beach, too.

The San Gabriel and San Fernando valleys

Café Santorini, 6470 W Union St, Pasadena (☎626/564-4200). A fine mix of Greek and Italian food – capellini, souvlaki, and risotto – with a little Armenian sausage thrown in as well.
Caioti, 4346 Tujunga Ave, Studio City (☎818/761-3588). Formerly in Hollywood, this terrific nouveau pizza spot has amazing toppings – duck sausage, oysters, cantaloupe – with a minimum of attitude.
La Scala Presto, 3821 W Riverside Dr, Burbank (☎818/846-6800). Fine antipasti, pizza and pasta.
Market City Caffé, 33 S Fair Oaks Ave, Pasadena (☎626/568-0203). Southern Italian cuisine featuring a range of Mediterranean delights, along with a supreme antipasto bar.

Chinese, Japanese, Thai and Korean

LA's most fashionable districts offer high-style **sushi** bars and **dim sum** restaurants, favored by Far East visitors and fast-lane yuppies alike, where you can easily eat your way through more than $20. Lower priced and less pretentious outlets tend, not surprisingly, to be Downtown, where you can get a fair-sized meal for around $10. **Thai** and **Korean** food – for which you can expect to pay around $15 per meal – are increasingly popular as well.

Downtown and around

Buffet Palace, 3014 Olympic Blvd (☎213/480-8949). Korean spot with good, spicy barbecued beef.

Dong Il Jang, 3455 W Eighth St (☎213/383-5757). Cozy Korean restaurant where the meat is grilled at your table. Located in the middle of bustling Koreatown.

Grand Star Restaurant, 934 Sun Mun Way, Chinatown (☎213/626-2285). Go late as there's video karaoke from 8pm–1am at this traditional Chinese place on Sun, Tues and Wed.

Horikawa, 111 S San Pedro St, Little Tokyo (☎213/680-9355). Excellent upmarket sushi restaurant.

Mandarin Deli, 727 N Broadway (☎213/623-6054). Very edible and very cheap noodles, pork and fish dumplings, and other hearty staples in the middle of Broadway's riot of activity.

Mitsuru Café, 117 Japanese Village Plaza, Little Tokyo (☎213/613-1028). Exotic snow cones made with *kintoki* (bean paste) or *milk kintoki* (sweet custard). Try the *imagawayaki* – azuki beans baked in a bun.

Mon Kee's, 679 N Spring St, Chinatown (☎213/628-6717). Long-standing favorite for fresh fish.

Ocean Seafood, 750 N Hill St (☎213/687-3088). Cavernous but often busy restaurant serving inexpensive and excellent food – abalone, crab, shrimp and duck are among many standout choices.

Hollywood

Chan Dara, 1511 N Cahuenga Blvd (☎323/464-8585). Terrific Thai food, and the locals know it. Also at other LA locations: 310 N Larchmont Blvd (☎323/467-1052) and 11940 W Pico Blvd (☎310/479-4461).

Shibucho, 3114 Beverly Blvd (☎213/387-8498). Excellent sushi bar just south of Silver Lake; go with someone who knows what to order, as the waiters don't speak English.

Tommy Tang's, 7313 Melrose Ave (☎323/937-5733). Terrific, very chic Thai restaurant and the incongruous setting for Tuesday drag nights. Also at 24 W Colorado Blvd, Pasadena (☎626/792-9700).

West LA

Chin Chin, 8618 Sunset Blvd (☎310/652-1818). Flashy but good dim sum café, open till midnight.

Chung King, 11538 W Pico Blvd (☎310/477-4917). The best neighborhood Chinese restaurant in LA, serving spicy Szechuan food: don't miss out on the *bum-bum* chicken and other house specialties.

Katsu, 8636 W Third St (☎310/273-3605). Minimalist sushi bar for the cyberpunk brigade; the only splash of color is in the artfully presented bits of fish – the teriyaki and sashimi are tops.

Mishima, 8474 W Third St (☎323/782-0181). Some of LA's best miso soup and udon and soba noodles, at very affordable prices at this chic, popular Westside eatery.

The Sushi House, 12013 W Pico Blvd (☎310/479-1507). Reggae and sushi coalesce in a small bar with limited seating. Try the "Superman," a rainbow-colored roll of salmon, yellowtail, whitefish and avocado.

Santa Monica, Venice and Malibu

Chaya, 110 Navy St, Venice (☎310/396-1179). Arty sushi bar popular with yuppies and hipsters.

Chinois on Main, 2709 Main St, Santa Monica (☎310/392-9025). Expensive Wolfgang Puck restaurant, mixing nouvelle French and Chinese cuisine for a ravenous crowd of elite diners and food critics.

Flower of Siam, 2553 Lincoln Blvd, Venice (☎310/827-0050). Some swear by this authentic Thai food guaranteed to set your tastebuds on fire and your eyes watering.

Lighthouse Buffet, 201 Arizona Ave, Santa Monica (☎310/451-2076). All-you-can-eat sushi; indulge to your heart's content for under $10 at lunchtime or $20 in the evening.

The San Gabriel and San Fernando valleys

Genmai-Sushi, 4454 Van Nuys Blvd, Sherman Oaks (☎818/986-7060). *Genmai* is Japanese for brown rice, but you can get soft shell crabs in ponzu sauce, along with sushi and macrobiotic dishes.

Saladang, 363 S Fair Oaks Ave, Pasadena (☎626/793-8123). Don't miss out on the *pad thai*, curry and salmon at this chic spot. These spicy noodles would pass muster anywhere.

Sea Star, 2000 W Main St, Alhambra (☎626/282-8833). Dim sum at its best: pork *baos*, potstickers and dumplings, and tasty sweets. Nearby, you can find other good Chinese spots in this immigrant community.

Indian/Sri Lankan and Middle Eastern

Indian restaurants are increasing in LA, as Indian food is surging in popularity – with restaurant menus embracing uniquely Californian dishes. **Middle Eastern** places in LA are few, and tend to be fairly basic. Most of the Indian and Middle Eastern restaurants in Hollywood or West LA fall into a fairly mid-range price bracket – around $10 for a full meal, less for a vegetarian Indian dish.

Hollywood
Chamika Catering, 1717 N Wilcox Ave (☎323/466-8960). Inexpensive papadums, *rotis* (garlic and coconut stuffed pancakes) and chicken, beef or lamb curries, marinated in special Sri Lankan sauces.
India Inn, 1638 N Cahuenga Blvd (☎323/461-3774). Good, low-cost Indian restaurant.
India's Oven, 6357 Wilshire Blvd (☎323/655-4596). Bring your own bottle to this friendly, award-winning Indian restaurant. Also at 7231 Beverly Blvd, West LA (☎323/936-1000).

West LA
Clay Pit, 145 S Barrington Ave (☎310/476-4700). Some of LA's best Indian food, featuring delights like lamb-stuffed *keema naan* and a fine tandoori chicken – all for around $10–15.
East India Grill, 345 N La Brea Ave (☎323/936-8844). Southern Indian cuisine given the California treatment: impressive specialties include spinach curry, ginger chicken and curried pasta.
Eat A Pita, 465 N Fairfax Ave (☎323/651-0188). Open-air stand serving cheap, cheerful and filling falafel, hummus and vegetable-juice drinks popular with locals.
Koutoubia, 2116 Westwood Blvd (☎310/475-0729). Good Moroccan lamb, couscous and seafood.
Noura Cafe, 8479 Melrose Ave (☎323/651-4581). Moderately priced Middle Eastern specialties. For beginners, the "taster's delight" plate – hummus, *baba ganoush*, tabouli, falafel, fried eggplant, zucchini and stuffed grape leaves – is a good, filling bet.
Shamshiry, 1916 Westwood Blvd (☎310/474-1410). The best of Iranian restaurant in the area, offering scrumptious kebabs, pilafs and exotic sauces.

Vegetarian and wholefood

It's small wonder that mind- and body-fixated LA has a wide variety of **wholefood** and **vegetarian** restaurants, and even less of a shock that most of them are found on the consciousness-raised Westside. Some vegetarian places can be a good value ($5 or so), but watch out for the ones that flaunt themselves as a New Age experience and include music – these can be three times as much. Otherwise for a picnic try the local *Trader Joe's* chain – which supplies imported cheeses, breads and canned foods to the Europeans who crave them most – or the area's frequent **Farmer's Markets**, heaving with organic produce, advertised in the press. (Health food stores are listed in "Shopping," p.167.)

Hollywood
Fountain of Health, 3606 W Sixth St, Mid-City (☎213/387-6621). Vegetarian chili and burgers star at this inexpensive eatery just south of Hollywood.
Inaka, 131 S La Brea Ave (☎323/936-9353). Located in the trendy La Brea district and features vegetarian and macrobiotic food with a strong Japanese theme. Live music on weekends.
Real Food Daily, 414 N La Cienega Blvd (☎310/289-9910). Avocado rolls, beet bisque and salads draw a mixed crowd of West Hollywood food poseurs and stray teens from the Beverly Center.

West LA

A Votre Sante, 242 S Beverly Dr, Beverly Hills (☎310/860-9441). Scrambled tofu and fried vegetables are on the agenda – along with veggie and turkey burgers – at this Westside mini-chain. Open for breakfast and lunch.

Erewhon, 7660 Beverly Blvd (☎323/937-0777). A good old-fashioned juice bar and deli, where you can gulp down as many wheatgrass concoctions and bee-pollen smoothies as you can stand.

Newsroom, 120 N Robertson Blvd (☎310/652-4444). A prime spot to see B-list celebrities with A-list attitudes eating veggie burgers and drinking wheatgrass "shooters." Especially popular for lunching.

Santa Monica, Venice and Malibu

Figtree's Café, 429 Ocean Front Walk, Venice (☎310/392-4937). Tasty veggie food and grilled fresh fish on a sunny patio just off the Boardwalk. Health-conscious yuppies come in droves for breakfast.

Inn of the Seventh Ray, 128 Old Topanga Rd, Topanga Canyon (☎310/455-1311). The ultimate New Age restaurant, serving vegetarian and other wholefood meals in a relatively secluded environment.

Mäni's Bakery, 2507 Main St, Santa Monica (☎310/396-7700). An array of veggie treats – from sugarless brownies to meatless sandwiches – may draw you to this coffeehouse and bakery for breakfast or lunch.

Shambala Café, 607 Colorado Ave, Santa Monica (☎310/395-2160). Apart from organic chicken, the menu is meat-free, with shrimp, pasta, tofu, eggplant and some very interesting seaweed dishes.

The South Bay and Harbor Area

Papa Jon's, 5006 E Second St, Long Beach (☎562/). Meatless Mexican entrées and garden burgers are the highlights of this quiet eatery.

The Spot, 110 Second St, Hermosa Beach (☎310/376-2355). A staggering array of veggie dishes, based on Mexican and other cuisine, and free of refined sugar or any animal products.

Drinking: bars, pubs and coffee bars

Social **drinking** in LA is far less popular than it is up the coast in San Francisco. Many bars are simply places to pose while waiting to meet friends, before heading off to pose again somewhere more exotic. However, it is possible to have a good time, provided you don't smoke, a practice now banned in most establishments under recent Californian law. You should be able to get a drink almost anywhere, and for serious, uninterrupted drinking there are bars and cocktail lounges on every other corner – just look for the neon signs.

The recommendations below are meant for an entire evening of socializing or a quick splash on the way to somewhere else. As you'd expect, they reflect their locality: a clash of beatnik artists and financial whiz kids Downtown; movie brats and leather-clad rock fans in Hollywood; the cleaner-cut trendiness of West LA; a batch of jukebox and dartboard-furnished bars in Santa Monica (evidence of the British contingent in the area); and the less fashionable, more hedonistic beachside bars of the South Bay. A few hard-bitten bars are open the legal maximum hours (from 6am until 2am daily), though you're liable to be

---

HAPPY HOURS IN LA

Many bars and restaurants have **happy hours**, usually from 5pm until 7pm, when drinks are cheap, sometimes half-price, and there'll be a selection of snacks: taco dips, chips or popcorn. A few offer piles of free food that you can attack once you've bought a drink – and thus save you the cost of dinner later on.

drinking alone if you arrive for an early liquid breakfast; busiest hours are between 9pm and midnight. If you want something of the bar atmosphere without the alcohol, present yourself at one of the fast-growing band of gregarious **coffee bars**; lately they've become the places to be seen, not least because they won't leave a hardened socialite too drunk to drive home – a crime that carries harsh penalties in California.

Downtown and around

Akbar, 4356 Sunset Blvd (☎323/665-6810). A curious blend of patrons – manual laborers and bohemians, gays and straights, old-timers and newbies – frequent this cozy, unpretentious watering hole.

Al's Bar, 305 S Hewitt St (☎213/625-9703). In the middle of a grimy industrial area; drink cans of cheap beer in post-apocalyptic-looking, smoke-filled rooms, with a pool table and frequent live acts.

Bona Vista, at the *Westin Bonaventure*, 404 S Figueroa St (☎213/624-1000). Thirty-five floors up, this rotating cocktail lounge spins faster after a few expensive drinks, offering a fine view of the sunset.

Casey's Bar, 613 S Grand Ave (☎213/629-2353). White floors, dark wood-paneled walls and nightly piano music; something of a local institution.

HMS Bounty, 3357 Wilshire Blvd (☎213/385-7275). Advertising "Food and Grog," this grungy bar is a hipster hot spot – they come for the dark ambience, elderly lounge lizard, and kitschy nautical motifs.

Hollywood

Barragan's, 1538 W Sunset Blvd (☎213/250-4256). Actually a Mexican restaurant, but reputedly producing the most alcoholic margarita in LA. So drink up, if you dare.

Boardners, 1652 N Cherokee Ave (☎323/462-9621). A likably unkempt neighborhood bar in the middle of Hollywood's prime tourist territory. Occasional guitar-poets provide the soundtrack.

Cat 'n' Fiddle Pub, 6530 Sunset Blvd (☎323/468-3800). A boisterous but comfortable pub with expensive English beers on draught and live jazz on Saturdays. See also "Live Music," p.162.

The Dresden Room, 1760 N Vermont Ave (☎323/665-4298). Wednesday night is open-mike, otherwise the husband-and-wife lounge act takes requests from the crowd of old-timers and goatee-wearing hipsters. A scene popularized, as any good Gen-Xer will tell you, in the film *Swingers*.

Formosa Café, 7156 Santa Monica Blvd (☎323/850-9050). Creaky old Hollywood institution alive with the ghosts of Bogie and Marilyn. Imbibe in the potent spirits, but stay away from the insipid food.

The Garage, 4519 Santa Monica Blvd (☎323/662-6802). With a funky lounge and a pool room, this Silver Lake bar and club offers live music after 9pm – much of it punk rock and rockabilly.

Jack's Sugar Shack, 1707 N Vine St (☎323/466-7005). Eat and drink near a famous Hollywood intersection and hear various rock and blues bands belt out tunes nightly.

Lava Lounge, 1533 N La Brea Ave (☎323/876-6612). Wallow in the cheesy retro decor and slurp down a glowing cocktail to the sounds of pounding rockabilly and freewheeling surf music. Quite an experience.

Musso and Frank Grill, 6667 Hollywood Blvd (☎323/467-7788). If you haven't had a drink in this 1940s landmark bar, you haven't been to Hollywood. It also serves pricey food. See also "Eating," p.149.

Pinot Hollywood, 1448 Gower St (☎323/461-8800). Twenty-four types of martini and Polish potato vodka, served in airy surroundings with an upscale crowd. See also "Eating," p.149.

The Powerhouse, 1714 N Highland Ave (☎323/463-9438). Enjoyable heavy rockers' watering hole just off Hollywood Boulevard; few people get here much before midnight.

Tiki Ti, 4427 W Sunset Blvd (☎323/669-9381). Tiny grass-skirted cocktail bar straight out of *Hawaii-Five-O* on the edge of Hollywood. The powerful cocktails are around $6 a slug.

West LA

Barney's Beanery, 8447 Santa Monica Blvd (☎310/654-2287). Well-worn poolroom bar, stocking over 200 beers. It also serves food, of sorts (see "Eating," p.145). Happy hour lasts eight hours (10am–6pm).

Molly Malone's Irish Pub, 575 S Fairfax Ave (☎323/935-1577). Self-consciously authentic Irish bar, from the music to the shamrocks in the foaming Guinness. See also "Live Music," p.162.

Tom Bergin's, 840 S Fairfax Ave (☎323/936-7151). Great place for Irish coffee, less rough and ready than *Molly Malone's* down the road. You can spot the regulars from the pictures on the walls.

Santa Monica, Venice and Malibu

14 Below, 1348 14th St, Santa Monica (☎310/451-5040). At this casual bar, pool tables and a fireplace compete for your attention with rock, folk and blues performers, who play nightly.

Oar House Saloon, 2941 Main St, Santa Monica (☎310/396-6658). Bar on the edge of Venice, popular with students who get suitably rowdy on a Friday night.

Red Setter Irish Pub, 2615 Wilshire Blvd, Santa Monica (☎310/828-9839). Formerly *McGinty's*, this pub features plenty of darts and beer, and an old-time crowd of locals and expats.

Ye Olde King's Head, 116 Santa Monica Blvd, Santa Monica (☎310/451-1402). Jukebox, dartboards and signed photos of all your favorite rock dinosaurs; don't miss the steak-and-kidney pie or the fish and chips.

The San Gabriel and San Fernando valleys

Blue Saloon, 4657 Lankershim Blvd, North Hollywood (☎818/766-4644). This Valley bar is enlivened by a wide range of live music, including rock, country, blues and reggae. The fairly cheap drinks are also a draw.

The Colorado, 2640 E Colorado Blvd (☎626/449-3485). A bright spot along a bleak Pasadena stretch. Salty bartenders, cheap drinks and a couple of pool tables amid a decor based around hunting.

The John Bull Pub, 958 S Fair Oaks Ave, Pasadena (☎626/441-4353). Almost too perfect expat setting: Union Jacks abound, shepherd's pie is served and warm English beers are plentiful.

Coffee bars

All-Star Theater Café, 1714 N Ivar Ave, Hollywood (☎323/962-8898). Antiques store/café/cumpool hall with a 1920s feel and overstuffed armchairs. Open 7pm–2am.

Anastasia's Asylum, 1028 Wilshire Blvd, Santa Monica (☎310/394-7113). Comfortable place with strong coffee and tea; also with nightly entertainment, of varying quality.

Bourgeois Pig, 5931 Franklin Ave, Hollywood (☎323/962-6366). Hip environment and outrageously overpriced cappuccinos – you really pay for the atmosphere of mirrors, chandeliers and loveseats.

Cobalt Café, 22047 Sherman Way, Canoga Park (☎818/348-3789). A somewhat grungy but hip coffeehouse in the Valley, with coffee, food and live music – along with poetry readings.

Highland Grounds, 742 N Highland Ave, Hollywood (☎323/466-1507). The posiest of LA's coffee bars, serving iced latte, pancakes and even beer. At night it's a club, with poetry and anonymous bands.

Hot House, 12123 Riverside Drive, North Hollywood (☎818/506-7058). Ultra-caffeinated java in a Valley joint with art, books and music on the weekend. Also sells bagels, pastries and smoothies.

Java Man, 157 Pier Ave, Hermosa Beach (☎310/379-7209). Tables lit by halogen lamps, and a rotating display of work from local artists. Not far from the beach.

King's Road Espresso House, 8361 Beverly Blvd, West Hollywood (☎323/655-9044). Sidewalk café with the usual beautiful staff. Popular with the *nuovo* beatnik crowd and, increasingly, out-of-towners.

Little Frida's, 8730 Santa Monica Blvd, West Hollywood (☎310/854-5421). Plentiful art, coffee, and pastries served to a mixed crowd of gay and straight patrons. Also with musical and comedy acts.

The Novel Café, 212 Pier Ave, Santa Monica (☎310/396-8566). Used books and high-backed wooden chairs set the tone; good coffees, teas and pastries make for relaxed browsing.

Sacred Grounds, 399 W Sixth St, San Pedro (☎310/514-0800). Combination coffeehouse and club with a sizable stage, offering open-mike night, music jams, and even some marginal comedy acts.

The World Café, 2820 Main St, Santa Monica (☎310/392-1661). Surf the Net with other technophiles, or drag yourself away and drink in the dark café/bar. Crowded and touristy.

Nightlife: clubs and discos

Like most things in LA, **nightlife** here is very style-conscious, and LA's clubs may be the wildest in the country. Ranging from absurdly faddish hangouts to industrial noise cellars, even the more image-conscious joints are like singles bars, with plenty of dressing-up, eyeing-up and picking-up (and sometimes not much else) going on, and everybody claiming to be either a rock star or in the movies. If you don't fall for the make-believe, the city's nightlife jungle can be great fun to explore, if only to eavesdrop on the vapid chat. Nowadays, many of the more interesting and unusual clubs are transient, especially those catering to the house, ambient and rave scene. As a result, the trendier side of the club scene is hard to pin down, and you should always check the *LA Weekly* before setting out.

Not surprisingly, Friday and Saturday are the busiest nights, but during the week things are often cheaper, and though less crowded, rarely any less enjoyable. Everywhere, between 11pm and midnight is the best time to turn up. There's nearly always a cover charge, usually from $6 to $10, and a minimum age of 21 (it's normal for ID to be checked, so bring your passport or other photo ID), and you should obviously dress with some sensitivity to the club's style. That said, prohibitive dress codes are a rarity, though you may be more welcome if you look completely outrageous.

Most of the top-name clubs are either in Hollywood or along a ten-block stretch of West Hollywood, in West LA. Downtown is home to a number of itinerant clubs operating above and below board, while the San Fernando Valley has its own version of a scene – usually confined to the weekends.

Downtown

Grand Avenue, 1024 S Grand Ave (☎213/747-0999). Salsa, merengue and disco on weekend nights.

Mayan, 1038 S Hill St (☎213/746-4674). Formerly a movie palace, now hosting Latin rhythms and nonstop disco and house tunes on three dance floors. Fri and Sat; $12, no sneakers.

Stock Exchange, 618 S Spring St (☎213/489-3877). An attempt to broaden the Downtown club scene, spinning enough funk and disco tunes to make the yuppie crowd gyrate with abandon.

Hollywood

Arena, 6655 Santa Monica Blvd (☎323/462-0714). Work up a sweat to funk, hip-hop and house sounds on a massive dance floor inside a former ice factory. Gay-friendly scene; $8.

Bar Sinister, 1652 N Cherokee (☎323/769-7070). A thumping grind of classic rock tunes and a grungy crowd on Friday, then spooky goth music and anemic-looking vampire types on Saturday.

Club Lingerie, 6507 Sunset Blvd (☎323/466-8557). Long-established, stylish modern dance club with intimate bar and hip-hop, dance and R&B music; $5–10. See also "Live Music," p.160.

The Conga Room, 5364 Wilshire Blvd (☎323/938-1696). A high-profile celebrity investment – Jimmy Smits, Jennifer Lopez, et al – results in a surprisingly appealing feast of Cuban food and Latin music.

The Derby, 4500 Los Feliz Blvd (☎323/663-8979). Restored supper club with gorgeous high wooden ceilings and round bar that has become the epicenter of LA's swing craze.

Dragonfly, 6510 Santa Monica Blvd (☎323/466-6111). Unusual decor, two large dance rooms, an "eye-contact" bar and house and disco club nights that are continually buzzing.

Florentine Gardens, 5951 Hollywood Blvd (☎323/464-0706). Stuck between the Salvation Army and a porno theater, but popular with the LA dance crowd, especially the under-21 set. Cover $8.

The Playroom, 836 N Highland Ave (☎323/461-8301). Get set for some head-pounding jackhammer rhythms at this new club where industrial, gothic, and electronic tunes rattle the brain.

West LA

Coconut Teaszer, 8117 Sunset Blvd (☎323/654-4773). Poseurs, rockers and voyeurs mix uneventfully on the two dance floors. The DJs play all night so you don't have to stop dancing until the sun rises.

Key Club, 9039 Sunset Blvd (☎310/274-5800). Replacing the defunct *Billboard Live*, this attracts a younger, hipper group for its hip-hop, funk, and house music spinning nightly.

Union, 8210 Sunset Blvd (☎323/654-1001). Relaxed supper club with funk, soul and R&B groove room. Frequented by the young actor crowd on Tuesdays.

The Viper Room, 8852 Sunset Blvd (☎310/358-1880). Less trendy than many clubs, though it has gained a certain notoriety since River Phoenix overdosed here in late 1993. See also "Live Music," p.162.

Santa Monica and Venice

The Pink, 2810 Main St, Santa Monica (☎310/392-1077). A weekend club with dance music on Friday and Saturday, then a weird assortment of electronic avant-garde on Sunday.

Scruffy O'Shea's, 822 Washington Blvd, Venice (☎310/821-0833). A roughneck Irish club with dance and house on some nights, and grinding hard rock on others.

The West End, 1301 Fifth St, Santa Monica (☎310/394-4647). If you love retro-tackiness, this is the place for you. DJs spin old 1970s and 1980s favorites and bartenders serve up sugary, fern-bar cocktails.

The San Gabriel and San Fernando valleys

Aftershock, 11345 Ventura Blvd, Studio City (☎818/752-9833). Disco and dance music reign supreme at this Valley club with four bars and three high-tech rooms. Wed–Sun.

The Muse, 54 E Colorado Blvd (☎626/793-0608). Old Town Pasadena is the site where dance, funk and hip-hop tunes collide in one tri-level club with no less than eleven pool tables. Thurs–Sun.

Villa Wahnsinn, 8751 Van Nuys Blvd, Panorama City (☎818/894-2876). Some devotees make the trek out here for this club's wild blend of Mexican rock music, disco and house tunes, and sick lounge decor.

Live Music

LA has a near-overwhelming choice if you're looking for **live music**. Because new bands haven't broken through until they've won over an LA crowd, there's seldom an evening without something exciting going on. Since the nihilistic punk bands of twenty years ago drew the city away from its spaced-out slacker image, LA's **rock music** scene has been second to none, to the extent that it has replaced the film industry as the quick route to riches and fame. There's a proto-rock star at every corner, and the guitar case is in some districts (notably Hollywood) almost *de rigueur*. The old punk scene has, of course, long since been overtaken, and nowadays the trend is for industrial noise, practiced with verve by the likes of Trent Reznor, and neo-punk, in the Green Day mold. The influence and popularity of South Central's **hip-hop** and **rap** music is spotty elsewhere and found mostly in dance clubs – except in dicey South Central environs.

In addition to local talent there are always plenty of British and European names in town, from major artists to independents. There's an enormous choice of **venues**, and inevitably it's a constantly changing scene. Most clubs open at 8pm or 9pm; headline bands are usually onstage between 11pm and 1am. Admission ranges from $10 to $20 and you should phone ahead to check set times and whether the gig is likely to sell out. You'll need to be 21 and will almost certainly be asked for ID. As ever, *LA Weekly* is the best source of **listings**.

In an entirely different category, **country music** is fairly prevalent, at least away from trendy Hollywood, and the Valleys are hotbeds of bluegrass and swing. There's **jazz**, too, played in a few genuinely authentic downbeat dives, though more commonly found in diluted form to improve the atmosphere of a restaurant. The lively Latin dance

WHAT'S ON AND TICKETS

Apart from the radio stations listed below, which carry details, previews and sometimes free tickets for forthcoming events, the best sources of **what's on information** are the *LA Weekly* and the "Calendar" section of the Sunday *LA Times*. You can buy seats for concerts or sports events from **Ticketmaster**, which has branches in Tower Records stores, and charge-by-phone numbers (☎213/480-3232 or 714/740-2000). A quick way through the maze of LA's **theaters** is to phone **Times Tix** (☎310/659-3678) or **Theatre LA** (☎213/614-0556) and ask for the availability of discount tickets for a given show.

RADIO STATIONS

KCBS 93.1 FM Classic rock tunes.

KCRW 89.9 FM Has interesting new music and transatlantic imports, and one of the few good sources of world news. Great evening music programs leaning toward trance, dub and eclectic tunes. NPR affiliate.

KFI 640 AM Tub-thumping talk radio, mostly from a far-right perspective.

KFWB 980 AM Frequent local news, plus talk shows.

KIIS 102.7 FM Top 40 pop hits.

KKGO 105.1 FM Classical and other orchestral.

KKTR 1650 AM Constantly updated traffic reports.

KLON 88.1 FM Blues and jazz.

KLSX 97.1 FM Talk radio, plus USC football.

KNX 1070 News with half-hourly sports reports.

KPCC 89.3 FM Jazz and blues concerts, plus arty talk radio. Another NPR affiliate.

KPFK 90.7 FM Lively opinions, news and music, from lefty political activists. Pacifica affiliate.

KROQ 106.7 FM Rock music with a touch of grunge.

KRTH 101.1 FM Nothing but oldies, advertised incessantly around town.

KSSE 97.5 FM Latino pop favorites and salsa.

KUSC 91.5 FM Classical, jazz, world music.

KXTA 1150 AM Sports and talk.

music of **salsa**, immensely popular among LA's Hispanic population, has finally started to cross over to the mainstream. It's also found in the bars of East LA, though it's worth saying that these are very male-oriented gathering places and visitors may well feel out of place – though they're rarely dangerous. Finally there's a small live **reggae** scene, occasionally featuring big names but more often sticking to the increasingly numerous local bands.

Major performance venues

Greek Theater, 2700 N Vermont Ave (☎323/665-1927). Outdoor, summer-only venue in Griffith Park, with a broad range of mainstream rock and pop acts. Parking can be a mess, so arrive early.

Hollywood Palladium, 6215 Sunset Blvd, Hollywood (☎323/962-7600). Once a big-band dance hall, with an authentic 1940s interior, now a home to all manner of hard rock, punk and rap outfits.

Staples Center, 865 S Figueroa St, Downtown (☎213/624-3100). Big new glassy sports arena with millions of municipal and corporate lucre behind it. A good showcase for Top 100 rock and pop acts.

Universal Amphitheater, 100 Universal City Plaza (☎818/622-4440). A big but acoustically excellent auditorium with regular rock shows. Located on the Universal Studios lot.

Wiltern Theater, 3790 Wilshire Blvd, Mid-Wilshire (☎323/380-5005). A striking blue Zigzag Art Deco movie palace, now converted into a top performing space for standard pop acts as well as edgy alternative groups.

LA'S FESTIVALS

January

1 Tournament of Roses in Pasadena. A parade of floral floats and marching bands along a five-mile stretch of Colorado Boulevard. Information at ☎626/795-9311.

9 Martin Luther King Parade and Celebration. The civil rights hero is honored with spirited activities at King Park and Baldwin Hills-Crenshaw Mall, among many other city-wide locations.

First full moon after 21 Chinese New Year. Three days of dragon-float street parades, tasty food, and various cultural programs, based in Chinatown and Alhambra.

February

13–14 Queen Mary Scottish Festival. All the haggis you can stand at this two-day Long Beach celebration, along with highland dancing and bagpipes.

Mid Mardi Gras. Floats, parades, costumes, and plenty of singing and dancing at this Brazilian fun fest in West Hollywood.

March

17 St Patrick's Day. Parade along Colorado Boulevard in Old Town Pasadena. No parade but freely flowing green beer in the "Irish" bars along Fairfax Avenue.

End The Academy Awards. Presented at the Shrine Auditorium or Dorothy Chandler Pavilion. Bleacher seats are available to watch the stars arrive. (Ceremony moves to Hollywood district in 2002.)

April

Early The Blessing of the Animals. A long-established ceremony, Mexican in origin. Locals arrive in Olvera Street to have their pets blessed, then watch the attendant parade.

Weekend nearest 13 Thai New Year. Focus of activity at North Hollywood's Wat Thai Temple.

Mid Long Beach Grand Prix. Scores of locals come out to watch the Indy cars race around Shoreline Drive.

May

5 Cinco de Mayo. A day-long party to commemorate the Mexican victory at the Battle of Puebla. Spirited parade in Olvera Street, and several blocks Downtown blocked off for Chicano and Hispanic music performances.

Late Old Pasadena Summer Fest. Food booths, art stands, and wafting jazz music liven up the town.

Late Valley Jewish Festival. The largest such event west of the Mississippi. Activities begin at Pierce College, in the San Fernando Valley district of Woodland Hills.

June

Early Cajun/Zydeco Festival. Heaps of Cajun and Creole food, wild parades, and plenty of high-spirited dancing at this colorful Long Beach event.

Second weekend Irish Fair and Music Festival. Fun event held at Santa Anita racetrack in Arcadia.

Late Gay Pride. Parade on Santa Monica Boulevard in West Hollywood. Carnival

Rock venues

Club Lingerie, 6507 Sunset Blvd, West LA (☎323/891-2775). Wide-ranging venue that's always at the forefront of what's new, often funk and dance sounds; $5–8. See also "Nightlife," p.157.

Doug Weston's Troubadour, 9081 Santa Monica Blvd, West Hollywood (☎310/276-6168). Used to be known for heavy riffs and shaggy manes, now for more alternative and acoustic lineups. $6–15.

Gabah, 4658 Melrose Ave, Hollywood (☎323/664-8913). Taking over the defunct punk venue *anticlub*, this eclectic spot has killed the dirt and gloom with a mix of reggae, funk, dub, rock – even flamenco. Still, the dicey neighborhood leaves much to be desired; always let the valet take charge of your car. Cover varies.

atmosphere, 250 vendors and an all-male drag football cheerleading team.

July

4 Independence Day. *Queen Mary* in Long Beach hosts particularly large fireworks display, as well as colorful entertainment. Festivities also in Santa Monica and many other LA communities.

First weekend after 4th. Lotus Festival. Echo Park celebration with dragon boats, ethnic food, pan-Pacific music, and resplendent lotus blossoms all around the lake.

Mid. Garlic festival. Visit the massive Federal Building complex for a taste of the "stinking rose," prepared in as many ways as you can stand – even ice cream. Entry fee.

August

First two weeks Culmination of the South Bay's International Surf Festival.

10–14 Nisei Week in Little Tokyo. A celebration of Japanese America, with martial arts demonstrations, karaoke, Japanese brush painting, baby shows and performance.

September

4 LA's birthday. A civic ceremony and assorted street entertainment around El Pueblo de Los Angeles to mark the founding of the original pueblo in 1781.

18–21 Koreatown Multicultural Festival. Dancing, parading and Tae Kwon Do exhibitions.

Last two weeks Los Angeles County Fair in Pomona, in the San Gabriel Valley. The biggest County Fair in the country, with livestock shows, eating contests and fairground rides.

Late Watts Jazz Festival. Two days of free music with the Watts Towers as a backdrop.

Varies. Oktoberfest. In the South Bay town of Torrance, plenty of hearty German food, beer and dancing.

October

Early Scandinavian Festival. Folk dancing with assorted food and art. Held in Santa Monica.

Early Greek Festival. Food and music celebration in a Redondo Beach Orthodox Church.

Second weekend LA Street Scene. Free rock music, theater and comedy on Downtown streets. At the same time as West Hollywood Street Festival, a display of handmade arts and crafts.

31 Halloween Parade. More West Hollywood frolicking.

November

3 Dia de Los Muertos (Day of the Dead) celebrated throughout East Los Angeles and for the tourists on Olvera Street. Mexican traditions, such as picnicking on the family burial spot, are upheld.

Saturday after Thanksgiving Doo-dah Parade. Quintessential LA event featuring absurd or bizarre characters marching through Pasadena. Surprisingly popular.

End Hollywood Christmas Parade. The first and best of the many Yuletide events, with a cavalcade of mind-boggling floats.

December

13. Christmas Boat Parade. Marina del Rey is the site for this annual display of brightly lit watercraft.

Largo, 432 N Fairfax Ave, West LA (☎323/852-1073). Cozy cabaret with some unusual live acts. $5–10.

The Lighthouse, 30 Pier Ave, Hermosa Beach (☎310/376-9833). Adjacent to the beach, this old favorite has a broad booking policy which spans rock, jazz, reggae and more; cover varies.

Lunapark, 665 N Robertson Blvd, West LA (☎310/652-0611). Eclectic musical mix – including lounge, ska, and rap – plays upstairs at this West Hollywood club; downstairs, there's a cabaret. Cover $5–20.

The Opium Den, 1605 1/2 Ivar Ave, Hollywood (☎323/466-7800). A strip club turned night club, with an array of up-and-coming rock and punk acts taking turns on the overly small stage. Cover varies.

The **Roxy**, 9009 Sunset Blvd, West LA (☎310/276-2222). The showcase of the music industry's new signings, intimate and with a great sound system; cover varies.

The **Viper Room**, 8852 Sunset Blvd, West Hollywood (☎310/358-1880). Great live acts, a famous owner and a headline-hitting past. Expect almost any musician to show up onstage. See also "Nightlife," p.158. $10-20.

Whisky-a-Go-Go, 8901 Sunset Blvd, West Hollywood (☎310/652-4202). Another critical spot for LA's rising music stars; mainly hard rock; $10-15.

Country and folk venues

The **Blue Saloon**, 4657 Lankershim Blvd, North Hollywood (☎818/766-4644). An old favorite for country and rockabilly, now with a bit more eclectic lineup. Cover varies.

Crazy Jack's, 4311 W Magnolia Blvd, Burbank (☎818/845-1121). Before the country music starts at 9pm, this place offers free dance lessons Tues & Thurs–Sat. Don't miss the Dixieland nights. Cover varies.

The **Foothill Club**, 1922 Cherry Ave, Signal Hill (☎562/984-8349). A glorious dance hall from the days when hillbilly was cool, complete with mural showing life-on-the-range. $8–10.

McCabe's, 3103 W Pico Blvd, Santa Monica (☎310/828-4497). LA's premier acoustic guitar shop; long the scene of some excellent and unusual folk and country shows; $10–20.

Molly Malone's Irish Pub, 575 S Fairfax Ave, West LA (☎323/935-1577). Traditional Irish music, American folk, rock and R&B; see also "Drinking," p.156. $5.

Jazz venues

The **Baked Potato**, 6266 1/2 Sunset Blvd, Hollywood (☎323/461-6400). A small but near-legendary contemporary jazz spot, where many reputations have been forged; $8, $5 on Thurs.

BB King's Blues Club, 1000 Universal Center Dr, Burbank (☎818/6-BBKING). A Universal CityWalk Southern diner; *Lucille's*, the club room, features acoustic blues on weekends. Low cover.

Catalina Bar & Grill, 1640 N Cahuenga Blvd, Hollywood (☎323/466-2210). Newly reopened, this Hollywood jazz institution offers plenty of style and atmosphere, for $10–20.

Cat 'n' Fiddle Pub, 6530 Sunset Blvd, Hollywood (☎323/468-3800). An English-style pub with jazz – usually a dual-sax quintet – on Sunday from 7pm until 11pm; no cover. See also "Drinking," p.155.

Harvelle's, 1432 4th St, Santa Monica (☎310/395-1676). A stellar blues joint for more than six decades offering different performers nightly and a popular band showcase on Tuesday nights. Cover varies.

House of Blues, 8430 Sunset Blvd, West Hollywood (☎323/848-5100). Over-commercialized mock sugar shack, with good but pricey live acts. Very popular with tourists. Cover $10–25.

Jazz Bakery, 3233 Helms Ave, Culver City (☎310/271-9039). More performance space than club, the brainchild of singer Ruth Price. The best local musicians play alongside big-name visitors. $10–20.

World Stage, 4344 Degnan Blvd, Crenshaw (☎323/293-2451). Bare-bones rehearsal space that attracts top-name players like drummers Billy Higgins and Max Roach. Thursday jams, Friday and Saturday gigs. Cover varies.

Salsa venues

La Bamba, 61 N Raymond Ave, Pasadena (☎818/584-9771). Terrific Latin performers nightly at this Caribbean/South American restaurant. Weekend cover $5.

El Floridita, 1253 N Vine St, Hollywood (323/871-8612). Decent Mexican food complements a fine lineup of Cuban and salsa artists, who play on weekends and jam on other nights. Reservations required. Cover varies.

Luminarias, 3500 Ramona Blvd, Monterey Park, East LA (☎323/268-4177). Hilltop restaurant (see p.148) with live salsa reckoned to be as good as its Mexican food; no cover.

Zabumba, 10717 Venice Blvd, Culver City (☎310/841-6525). In a colorful building amid drab surroundings, this venue is more bossa nova Brazilian than straight salsa, but it's still great. $3-8.

Reggae venues

Golden Sails Club Room, 6285 E Pacific Coast Highway, Long Beach (☎562/596-1631). Some of the best reggae bands from LA and beyond show up at this hotel, on Friday and Saturday nights; $8.
Kingston 12, 814 Broadway, Santa Monica (☎310/451-4423). Santa Monica's top venue for reggae music, and one of LA's best as well. Small and comfortable; $10–15.
Mobay, 1031 Abbot Kinney Blvd, Venice (☎310/450-1933). On Thursday nights and weekends, the flavors at this fine Caribbean restaurant are enlivened by free reggae music.

Classical music, opera and dance

Considering its size and stature in other arts, LA has very few outlets for **classical music**. The Los Angeles Philharmonic (☎213/850-2000), the only major name in the city, performs regularly during the year, and the Los Angeles Chamber Orchestra (☎213/622-7001) appears sporadically at different venues, while the LA Baroque Orchestra (☎310/458-0425) often performs at the lush *Biltmore* hotel Downtown. During the semester, students of the Schoenberg Institute give **free lunchtime concerts** on the USC campus. Otherwise, attractions are thin. Watch the press, especially the *LA Times*, for details, and expect to pay from $10 to $50 for most concerts, much more for really big names.

As for **opera**, the Music Center Opera (☎213/972-7211) stages productions between September and June, as does Orange County's Opera Pacific (☎949/474-4488), which performs grand opera and operettas. Prices range from $10 to $120. **Dance** in LA is not to be dismissed, either. The big event of the year is the **Dance Kaleidoscope**, held over two weeks in July at the John Anson Ford Theater and organized by the Los Angeles Area Dance Alliance (LAADA; ☎323/343-5120) – a cooperative supported by LA dance companies that provides a central source of information on events. Otherwise check for performances at the **universities**, where some of the most exciting new names in dance have residencies.

Major venues

The Dorothy Chandler Pavilion, in the Music Center, 135 N Grand Ave, Downtown (☎213/972-7211 or 7460). Home to the LA Philharmonic from October until May. Also used by the Music Center Opera and other top names. Hosts Oscars on alternate years with The Shrine Auditorium (see below).
The Hollywood Bowl, 2301 N Highland Ave, Hollywood (☎323/850-2000). The LA Philharmonic gives open-air concerts here (July–Sept Tues–Sat evenings; see p.106 for more on the Bowl).
Japan America Theater, 244 S San Pedro St, Little Tokyo (☎213/680-3700). Dance and performance works drawn from Japan and the Far East.
John Anson Ford Theater, 2850 Cahuenga Blvd, Hollywood (☎323/461-3673). Besides the summer Dance Kaleidoscope, this open-air venue also has eclectic productions by local groups.
Orange County Performing Arts Center, 600 Town Center Drive, Costa Mesa (☎714/556-ARTS or 949/740-2000). Home of the Pacific Symphony Orchestra.
The Pacific Amphitheater, 100 Fair Drive, Costa Mesa (☎949/740-2000). A big open-air venue: Orange County's answer to the Hollywood Bowl.
Pasadena Dance Theatre, 1985 Locust St, Pasadena (☎626/683-3459). One of the San Gabriel Valley's most prominent dance venues, hosting diverse groups throughout the year.
Royce Hall, on the UCLA campus (☎310/825-9261 or 2101). Classical concerts often involving big names throughout the college year.
The Shrine Auditorium, 665 W Jefferson, South Central LA (☎213/749-5123), box office at 655 S Hill St (☎213/749-5123). Hosts Oscars and regular performances by choral gospel groups.
UCLA Center for the Performing Arts, office at 10920 Wilshire Blvd, Westwood (☎310/825-4401). Coordinates a wide range of touring companies, and runs an "Art of Dance" series with an experimental emphasis between September and June.

Comedy

LA has an impressively wide range of **comedy clubs**. While rising stars and hopeless beginners can both be spotted on the "underground" open-mike scene, the vast majority of famous and soon-to-be-famous comedians, both stand-up and improvisational, appear at the more established clubs, most of them in Hollywood, West LA or the Valleys. These venues usually have a bar, charge a cover of $10–15, and put on two shows each evening, generally starting at 8pm and 10.30pm – the later one is generally more popular. The better-known places are open every night, but are often solidly booked on Friday and at weekends.

Comedy venues

Acme Comedy Theater, 135 N La Brea Ave, Hollywood (☎323/525-0202). A fancy new theater with sketch and improvised comedy, as well as variety shows.

Bang Theater, 457 N Fairfax Ave, Hollywood (☎323/653-6886). One-person shows and long-form improvisation are the specialties at this fairly recent theater/comedy club.

Comedy & Magic Club, 1018 Hermosa Ave, Hermosa Beach (☎310/372-1193). Strange couplings of magic and comedy. Jay Leno sometimes tests material here. Tickets can run $10–25.

The Comedy Store, 8433 W Sunset Blvd, West LA (☎323/656-6225). LA's comedy showcase and popular enough to be spread over three rooms – which means there's usually space, even at weekends.

Groundlings Theater, 7307 Melrose Ave, West LA (☎323/934-9700). Another pioneering improvisational venue where only the gifted survive.

Ha Ha Café, 5010 Lankershim Blvd, North Hollywood (☎818/508-4995). Amateur and even a few professional comedians face-off for your amusement on Thursday nights. $7.

HBO Workspace, 733 N Seward St, Hollywood (☎323/993-6099). If you're in the mood for free experimental comedy, this is the place. HBO runs it as a proving ground for risky acts.

The Ice House, 24 N Mentor Ave, Pasadena (☎626/577-1894). The comedy mainstay of the Valley, very established and fairly safe. Two drink minimum.

The Improvisation, 8162 Melrose Ave, West LA (☎323/651-2583). Known for hosting some of the best acts working in the area, this is one of LA's top comedy spots – so book ahead.

LA Connection, 13442 Ventura Blvd, Sherman Oaks (☎818/784-1868). An improvisation showcase for highly-rated obnoxiousness specialists. Seldom less than memorable.

The Laugh Factory, 8001 Sunset Blvd, West Hollywood (☎323/656-1336). Stand-ups of varying standards and reputations, with the odd big name. Features a variable open-mike night.

Theater

LA has a very active **theater** scene. While the bigger venues host a predictable array of tired old musicals and classics starring a crowd-pleasing line-up of movie stars, there are over a hundred "Equity waiver" theaters with fewer than a hundred seats, enabling non-Equity-cardholders to perform; and a vast network of fringe writers, actors and directors. A number of alternative theaters have sprung up in Hollywood west of Cahuenga Boulevard, revolving around **The Complex**, a group of six small theaters at 6470/6 Santa Monica Blvd. Tickets are less expensive than you might expect: a big show will cost you at least $25 (matinees are cheaper), smaller shows around $10 to $20. Always book ahead.

Fringe theaters

Cast-At-The-Circle, 800 N El Centro Ave, Hollywood (☎323/462-0265). Small Hollywood theater hosting a variety of smaller productions.

Highways, 1651 18th St, Santa Monica (☎310/453-3711). Located in an arts complex, this adventurous performance space offers a range of topical drama and one-person shows.

Lee Strasberg Theater, 7936 Santa Monica Blvd, West Hollywood (☎323/650-7777). Although method acting is plentiful here – as well as a few stars in the crowd – all types of plays and styles are performed.

Odyssey Theater Ensemble, 2055 S Sepulveda Blvd, West LA (☎310/477-2055). Well-respected Westside theater company, relocated in new home.

Powerhouse Theater, 3116 Second St, Santa Monica (☎310/396-3680). Worth seeing for the adventurous and risk-taking experimental shows.

Major theaters

Coronet Theater, 366 N La Cienega Blvd, West Hollywood (☎310/657-7377). Home of the LA Public Theater – whose productions include the odd famous name – and the Youth Academy of Dramatic Arts.

Geffen Playhouse, 10886 Le Conte Ave, Westwood (☎310/208-5454). One of the smaller of the major theaters, often with one-person shows. Solid Hollywood connections as well.

Mark Taper Forum, 135 N Grand Ave, Downtown (☎213/972-0700). Theater in the three-quarter round, frequently innovative new plays. Located in the Music Center complex.

Pantages Theater, 6233 Hollywood Blvd, Hollywood (☎323/468-1770). An exquisite, atmospheric Art Deco theater, in the heart of historic Hollywood, hosting major touring Broadway productions.

Shubert Theater, 2020 Ave of the Stars, Century City (☎1-800/447-7400). A rare reason to visit Century City is to ogle the razzmatazz Andrew Lloyd Webber musicals, among other big names.

South Coast Repertory, 655 Town Center Dr, Costa Mesa (☎714/708-5555). Orange County's major entry for institutional theater, with well-executed takes on canonical dramatic works.

Film

Many major feature **films** are released in LA months (sometimes years) before they play anywhere else in the world, and a huge number of cinemas show both the new releases and the classics – with fewer screens showing independent and foreign movies. Depending on where you go and what you see, a ticket will be around $8.

For **mainstream cinema**, Westwood still has a high concentration of movie houses, as does the Santa Monica Promenade. Of the multi-screen facilities, the eighteen-screen Cineplex Odeon, at Universal Studios (☎818/508-0588), is a plush complex that includes a pair of pseudo-Parisian cafés, and the AMC Century 14, 10250 Santa Monica Blvd (☎310/553-8900), despite being in a shopping mall, is a local favorite for its big screens and good sound. For all their screens, though, only six or seven films are typically shown in the multiple theaters. Another, more enterprisingly programmed, venue is the Goldwyn Cinemas (☎310/475-0202) in the Westside Pavilion mall in West LA, which has four small screens featuring arty independent films.

For **cheap** and **free films**, the places to hit are the Bing Theater at the County Art Museum, 5905 Wilshire Blvd (☎323/857-6010), which has afternoon screenings of many neglected Hollywood classics and charges just $2; the USC and UCLA campuses also often have interesting free screenings aimed at film students, announced on campus notice boards. Otherwise, the best places to find **art-house** and **cult films** are the New Beverly Cinema, 7165 Beverly Blvd (☎323/938-4038), especially strong on imaginative double bills, and the Nuart Theater, 11272 Santa Monica Blvd (☎310/478-6379), which runs rarely seen classics, documentaries and foreign-language films. (Be prepared to wait in a lengthy queue outside, though.) The Los Feliz Theater, 1822 N Vermont Ave (☎323/664-2169), resisted a descent into the porn movie market in the 1960s; its three small screens still show international and low-budget American independent movies. In the same area, the Vista Theatre, 4473 Sunset Blvd (☎323/660-6639), is a small, nicely remodeled gem.

If you're looking for a golden-age-of-film **atmosphere**, you'll need either to take in an action triple bill in one of the historic Downtown movie palaces (described on p.86), where the delirious furnishings may captivate your attention longer than the triple-bills, or visit one of the Hollywood landmarks. The Chinese Theatre, 6925 Hollywood Blvd (☎323/464-8186), with its large screen, six-track stereo sound and wild chinoiserie interior, shows relentlessly mainstream films, but the first-night audience's loud participation is entertainment in itself. If this doesn't appeal, you could always indulge in the Cinerama Dome's near-wraparound screen, at 6360 Sunset Blvd (☎323/466-3401), said to be the biggest in California; the amazingly renovated Egyptian, 6712 Hollywood Blvd (☎323/466-FILM; see p.101 for more); or Disney's spellbinding El Capitan, 6834 Hollywood Blvd (☎323/467-7674).

Finally, if you have even the slightest interest in films from the golden age of Charlie Chaplin and Buster Keaton, make sure to visit the Silent Movie theater, 611 N Fairfax Ave (☎323/655-2510), which has just reopened after being closed for three years because its former owner was murdered. Re-emerging after the tragedy, the theater offers an enjoyable mix of comedies and adventure flicks – Douglas Fairbanks swashbucklers and the like – along with darker fare like Fritz Lang's *Metropolis* and even the occasional talkie.

Gay and lesbian LA

Although nowhere near as big as San Francisco's, LA's **gay and lesbian scene** is far from invisible. The best known gay-friendly area is the city of **West Hollywood**, which has become synonymous with the (affluent, white) gay lifestyle, not just in LA but all over California. The section of West Hollywood on Santa Monica Boulevard east of Doheny Drive has restaurants, shops and bars primarily aimed at gay men. Another established community is **Silver Lake**, home to the bars and restaurants on Hyperion Boulevard.

Gay couples will find themselves readily accepted at just about any LA **hotel**, but there are a few that cater especially to gay travelers and can also be useful sources of information on the LA gay scene generally. We've also listed below a few restaurants that cater specifically to gay men and lesbians. For up-to-date (if ad-packed), gay-oriented publications, see "Information" on p.68.

Gay resources

AIDS Project Los Angeles, 1313 Vine St, Hollywood (☎323/993-1600). Sponsors fund-raisers throughout the year and a well-attended annual walkathon.

A Different Light, 8853 Santa Monica Blvd, West Hollywood (☎310/854-6601). The city's best-known gay and lesbian bookshop, with art shows, readings, music events and comfortable chairs for lounging.

Gay and Lesbian Community Services Center, 1625 N Schrader Blvd, Hollywood (☎323/993-7400). Counseling, health-testing and information. It publishes *The Center News*, a bimonthly magazine.

Gay Community Yellow Pages, 1604 Vista Del Mar Ave, Hollywood (☎213/469-4454). Gay businesses, publications, services and gathering places listed yearly; available all over LA.

Gay hotels

Coral Sand Hotel, 1730 N Western Ave, Hollywood (☎323/467-5141). Exclusively geared towards gay men. All rooms face the inner courtyard pool. Basically very cruisy. ④.

Holloway Motel, 8465 Santa Monica Blvd, West Hollywood (☎323/654-2454). Typical clean roadside motel, if rather dreary looking. ③.

Hollywood Metropolitan, 5825 Sunset Blvd (☎323/962-5800). Spanish-styled hotel with a mix of small, comfortable rooms and larger suites. Just off the 101 Freeway. ④.

Ramada 8585 Santa Monica Blvd, West Hollywood (☎1-800/845-8585 or 310/652-6400). Very gay-friendly, modern place with clean and comfortable rooms, in the center of the community. ⑤.

Gay and lesbian restaurants

Figs, 7929 Santa Monica Blvd, West Hollywood (☎323/654-0780). All-American down-home cooking.

French Quarter, 7985 Santa Monica Blvd, West Hollywood (☎310/654-0898). Inside the *French Market Place*, a New-Orleans theme restaurant that can be at least as much fun as Disneyland.

Gloria's Café, 3603 W Sunset Blvd (☎213/664-5732). Popular local hangout near Silver Lake that's a great spot for dinner, especially Cajun.

Mark's Restaurant, 861 N La Cienega Blvd, West Hollywood (☎310/652-5252). High-end establishment serving California cuisine.

Gay and lesbian bars and clubs

Arena, 6655 Santa Monica Blvd, Hollywood (☎323/462-0714). Many clubs under one roof, large dance floors throbbing to funk, house and hi-NRG grooves, and sometimes live bands. See also "Nightlife," p.157.

Detour, 1087 Manzanita, Silver Lake (☎323/664-1189). Friendly and cheap denim and leather bar.

Jewel's Catch One, 4067 W Pico Blvd, Mid-City (☎323/734-8849). Sweaty barn catering to a mixed crowd – gay and straight, male and female – all on two wild dance floors. Cover varies.

Le Bar, 2375 Glendale Blvd, Silver Lake (☎323/660-7595). Quiet and welcoming bar in a bland section of Silver Lake. Not as much attitude as with some WeHo spots.

The Palms, 8572 Santa Monica Blvd, West Hollywood (☎310/652-6188). Mostly house and dance nights at West Hollywood's most established lesbian bar.

The Plaza, 739 N La Brea Ave, Hollywood (☎323/939-0703). Nondescript little joint hosts funky, mind-blowing drag shows to a multi-ethnic, mostly gay crowd.

Rage, 8911 Santa Monica Blvd, West Hollywood (☎310/652-7055). Very flashy gay men's club playing the latest hi-NRG and house. Also with drag comedy. Drinks are cheap, the cover varies.

Rudolpho's, 2500 Riverside Dr, Silver Lake (☎323/669-1226). Every second Saturday of the month, it's time to "dress up, drag down" to *Dragstrip 66* night at this Mexican restaurant.

Women's LA

It's not surprising that a city as big as LA should have such an organized **women's** network, with many resource centers, bookstores, publications and clubs. Women travelers are unlikely to encounter any problems which aren't applicable to all the West Coast (for more on which see "Basics," p.46), but the resources here are much more developed.

There are many good sources of general and detailed information on the local women's movement, with some crossover with the city's sizable lesbian community – see "Gay and Lesbian LA," above. *LA Woman*, Los Angeles' largest women's magazine, profiling local personalities and providing a calendar of events, is available from most newsstands and bookstores – notably the Sisterhood Bookstore, 1351 Westwood Blvd (☎310/477-7300), a West LA landmark south of Westwood, selling books, music, cards, jewelry and literature of the women's movement. The *Women's Yellow Pages* (☎310/398-5761), another good resource, is a yearly listing of over 1400 women-owned businesses and services. Call for a copy.

Shopping

Shopping in LA is an art. The level of disposable income in the wealthy parts of the city is astronomical, and touring the more outrageous stores can be a great insight into LA life – revealing who's got the money and what they're capable of wasting it on. Whether you want to buy a new light bulb or pair of socks, lay waste to a wad or simply be a voyeur in the orgy of acquisition, there are, besides the run-of-the-mill retailers you'll find anywhere, big **department stores**, mega-sized **malls** – where most of the serious shopping goes on – and **Rodeo Drive**, two blocks of the world's most exclusive and expensive shopping. The trendiest shops line **Melrose Avenue**, between La Brea and Fairfax avenues. **Old Town Pasadena** boasts a few more upmarket chains, while the few blocks above Prospect on Vermont Avenue in **Los Feliz** are home to some of the underground's trendier boutiques.

The city also has a good assortment of specialist stores, with extensive selections of **books** and **records**. There's an equally diverse assortment of **food stores**, from corner delis and supermarkets to fancy cake stores and gourmet markets. You'll also find several stores selling perfect LA souvenirs, like the **LA County Coroner Gift Shop** at 1104 N Mission Rd (☎213/343-0760), which sells everything from skeleton-decorated beach towels and T-shirts to toe-tag key chains – all typical LA merchandise.

Department stores and malls

Each of LA's neighborhoods has a collection of ordinary **stores** and **mini-malls**. You'll find the best sources of cheap toiletries and staples at places such as K-Mart and Target. A step up from these in price and quality, though still good for general shopping, are **department stores**, which are often included within massive **malls** and resemble self-contained city suburbs, around which Angelenos do the bulk of their serious buying.

The malls

Beverly Center, 8500 Beverly Blvd, West Hollywood. Chic shopping for the masses: seven acres of boutiques, Macy's and Bloomingdale's, a multiplex cinema and a *Hard Rock Café*, all in one complex that resembles a giant brown concrete bunker – trimmed in hideous green and purple.

Century City Marketplace, 10250 Santa Monica Blvd, Century City. Outdoor mall with a hundred upscale shops, including a branch of New York's Metropolitan Museum gift shop. The place to come to see stars do their shopping, and to catch a first-run movie in the fine cineplex AMC Century 14.

Del Amo Fashion Square, Hawthorne Blvd at Carson St, Torrance. The South Bay's own supermall, one of LA's largest, with five major anchor stores and a wealth of mid-level retailers and suburban shoppers.

Seventh Street Marketplace, Seventh and Figueroa streets, Downtown. Anchored by Macy's department store, at the foot of the Citicorp office towers.

Third Street Promenade, between Broadway and Wilshire Blvd, Santa Monica. One of the most popular shopping and nightlife precincts in LA, and all the more enjoyable for being outdoors. To the south, Santa Monica Place, Broadway at Second St, is a less appealing mall with three tiers of shops.

RODEO DRIVE

The black hole for expense accounts is **Rodeo Drive** in Beverly Hills, a solid line of exclusive stores to which you might be drawn by sheer curiosity. One store worth looking into is Ralph Lauren, 444 N, which caters to well-heeled WASPS who fancy themselves as canine-fixated English gentry. Besides thousand-dollar suits and monogrammed Wellingtons, there are exquisitely carved walking sticks and mounted game heads, and a huge assortment of wooden dogs, bronze dogs and paintings of dogs. At the foot of Rodeo Drive are LA's premier department stores, including Barney's and, most famously, Neiman-Marcus, 9700 Wilshire Blvd, who sell everything from $5 Swiss truffles to his 'n' hers leopard skins. Nearby, **Two Rodeo**, the area's mock-European tourist trap, also competes for buyers' attention, though in a much cruder and less appealing fashion.

Westside Pavilion, Pico Blvd at Westwood Blvd, West LA. Giant shopping complex centered on the Nordstrom department store, which provides regular customers with a personal "shopper" (ie an employee who does all the legwork around the store and comes back with a choice of goods).

Food and drink

Since eating out in LA is so common, you may never have to shop for **food** at all. But if you're preparing a picnic, or want to indulge in a spot of home cooking, there are plenty of places to stock up. **Delis**, many open round the clock, are found on more or less every corner in LA; **supermarkets** are almost as common, some open 24 hours, or at least until 10pm – Lucky's, Pavilions, Ralphs and Trader Joe's are the names to look out for. There are also **ethnic groceries** and **markets**, and – although much more expensive – the **gourmet markets** and **stores**, not to mention a bizarre collection of one-off outlets for all kinds of food oddities, mainly clustered in fashionable West LA. To buy **drink** you need go no further than the nearest supermarket – Trader Joe's is the cheapest and best.

Pastries and cakes

Cobbler Factory, 33 N Catalina Ave, Pasadena (☎626/449-2152). An Old Pasadena bakery selling a range of scrumptious, fruity cobblers from $4–35, depending on how huge you want them.

Diamond's Bakery, 335 N Fairfax Ave, West LA (☎323/655-0534). Great old Jewish bakery with legendary pumpernickel bread and a mouth-watering array of cookies and other sweets.

La Brea Bakery, 624 S La Brea Ave, West LA (☎323/939-6813). Perhaps LA's best bakery, selling everything from cheap sourdough rolls to thick, heavy breads made with olives, cherries and cheese.

Mousse Fantasy, 2130 Sawtelle Blvd #110, West LA (☎310/479-6665). A Japanese version of a French patisserie, though in a crowded strip mall. The green tea mousse cake is a taste of heaven.

Mrs Field's Cookies, 907 Westwood Blvd, Westwood (☎310/208-0096). Chewy, sweet cookies, made to a "secret recipe" that has plenty of devoted fans – nationwide branches include eight others in LA.

Delis and groceries

Bay Cities Italian Deli, 1517 Lincoln Blvd, Santa Monica (☎310/395-8279). Basically a gigantic store, with piles of fresh pasta, spices, meats, sauces and many French and Middle Eastern imports.

The Cheese Store, 419 N Beverly Dr, Beverly Hills (☎310/278-2855). Over four hundred types of cheese from all over the world, including every kind produced in the US.

Claro's Italian Market, 1095 E Main St, Tustin (☎714/832-3081). A compact but well-stocked haven of Italian wines, chocolate, crackers and own-brand frozen meals. Located in Orange County.

Erewhon, 7660 Beverly Blvd (☎323/937-0777). Next door to the CBS studios, selling pricey health food and all the wheatgrass you can swallow. The epitome of self/health-obsessed LA.

Full o' Life, 2525 W Magnolia Blvd, Burbank (☎818/845-8343). This mother of all health food stores dates back to 1959. It offers an organic market, deli, dairy, restaurant and book department, with two nutritionists and a naturopathic doctor on the premises daily.

La Canasta in El Mercado, 1736 W Sixth St, Westlake (☎213/484-6159). A good assortment of authentic Mexican and Central American food: chilis, chayotes and tasty desserts.

Say Cheese, 2800 Hyperion Ave, Silver Lake (☎323/665-0545). A distinctive array of French and other international cheeses, priced moderately to steeply. The delicious sandwiches may be your best bet.

Standard Sweets and Snacks, 18600 Pioneer Blvd, Artesia (☎562/860-6364). A good Indian finger food joint selling vegetarian dosas (pancakes) and appealing sweets.

Wild Oats, 3474 S Centinela Ave, West LA (☎310/636-1800). An excellent organic wine store and deli that also offers flavorful fruit drinks at its smoothie bar.

Books

There are almost as many bookstores in LA as there are people. Of the ubiquitous **discount chains** in town, *Crown* offer the latest hardbacks and paperbacks at knock-down prices. On the pricier side, *Barnes and Noble* and *Borders* provide standardized branches that are also fairly sizable. The city is exceptionally well served by its **specialist bookstores** and many **secondhand bookstores**, worthy of several hours' browsing along miles of dusty shelves.

Specialist bookstores

A Different Light, 8853 Santa Monica Blvd, West Hollywood (☎310/854-6601). The city's best known gay and lesbian bookstore, with monthly art shows, readings, and musical events.

Koma Books, 1764 N Vermont Ave, Los Feliz (☎323/655-0956). Mayhem, true crime, zines and paranoid conspiracy rants: the extremes of information in print. A small shop with a large mail order base.

Bodhi Tree, 8585 Melrose Ave, West Hollywood (☎310/659-1733). New Age, occult and all things spiritually trendy. Cozy space abounds with enlightened regulars.

Book Soup, 8818 W Sunset Blvd, West Hollywood (☎310/659-3110). Great selection, right on Sunset Strip, open daily until midnight. Narrow, winding aisles stuffed pell-mell with books.

Either/Or, 950 Aviation Blvd, Hermosa Beach (☎310/374-2060). A voluminous fiction selection and a wide variety of New Age tomes, with free publications littering the floor. Open till 11pm.

Hennessey and Ingalls, 1254 Third St Promenade, Santa Monica (☎310/458-9074). An impressive range of art and architecture books makes this bookstore the best in LA in its field.

Larry Edmunds Book Shop, 6644 Hollywood Blvd, Hollywood (☎323/463-3273). Stacks of books, many of them out of print, on every aspect of film and theater, with movie stills and posters.

Midnight Special, 1318 Third St Promenade, Santa Monica (☎310/393-2923). A large general bookstore, with eccentrically filled shelves and a broad focus on lefty politics and social sciences.

Norton Simon Museum Bookstore, 411 W Colorado Blvd, Pasadena (☎626/449-6840). Prices in this museum-attached store are lower than in any other art bookstore in LA, and the stock is superb.

Samuel French Theatre & Film Bookshop, 7623 Sunset Blvd, West Hollywood (☎323/876-0570). Small store loaded with books on acting, movies, and the performing arts. Always a popular spot.

Sisterhood Bookstore, 1351 Westwood Blvd, West LA (☎310/477-7300). Westside landmark with music, cards, books and literature pertaining to the national and international women's movement.

Secondhand books

Acres of Books, 240 Long Beach Blvd, Long Beach (☎562/437-6980). Worth a trip down the Blue Line Metrorail just to wallow in LA's largest, and most disorganized, secondhand collection.

Book City, 6627 Hollywood Blvd, Hollywood (☎323/466-2525). Tightly packed from floor to ceiling with eclectic titles, many of which are physically well out of reach – so borrow a ladder.

Brand Bookshop, 231 N Brand Blvd, Glendale (☎818/507-5943). Valley used-book seller with a broad range of liberal arts titles and particular strengths in entertainment, history and politics.

Wilshire Books, 3018 Wilshire Blvd, Santa Monica (☎310/828-3115). The best used bookstore in LA for its size. Solid collection of art, politics, religion, music, science and other books, all well organized.

Music

Record stores are even more plentiful than bookstores in LA. Although the number of stores selling LPs has dropped, the plunge has stopped for the moment, thanks to the demand of die-hard vinyl fans. Most of the stores below carry used LPs, CDs and cassettes.

Aron's Records, 1150 N Highland Ave, Hollywood (☎323/469-4700). Secondhand discs – all styles, all prices, huge stock. Getting help can be a problem; the place is often busy.

Moby Disc, 28 E Colorado Blvd (☎626/449-9975) and 3731 E Colorado Blvd (☎626/793-3475), both in Pasadena. Solid secondhand and deletion stocklist.

Music and Memories, 5057 Lankershim Blvd, North Hollywood (☎818/761-9827). Three hundred Sinatra LPs, and myriad others that sound like he should be on them.

Penny Lane, 12 W Colorado Blvd, Pasadena (☎626/564-0161). New and used records at reasonable prices; this store features listening stations from which you can sample up to a hundred discs. Also in Santa Monica, 1349 Third St (☎310/319-5333), and Westwood, 1080 Gayley Ave (☎310/208-5611).

Poo-Bah Records, 1101 E Walnut Ave, Pasadena (☎626/449-3359). American and imported New Wave.

Record Surplus, 11609 W Pico Blvd, West LA (☎310/478-4217). Massive LP collection of surf music, ancient rock 'n' roll, 60s soundtracks and unintentionally hilarious spoken-word recordings.

Rhino Records, 1720 Westwood Blvd, West LA (☎310/474-8685). The biggest selection of international independent releases, not to mention the countless records put out by Rhino Records itself.

Vinyl Fetish, 7305 Melrose Ave, West Hollywood (☎323/935-1300). Besides the punk and post-punk sounds, a good place to discover what's new on the LA music scene and buy a cheesy Gen-X T-shirt or two.

Listings

Airport Information Burbank/Glendale/Pasadena ☎818/840-8847; John Wayne/Orange County ☎949/252-5006; LAX ☎310/646-5252; Long Beach ☎562/570-2600; Ontario ☎909/937-2700.

Automobile Club of Southern California, 2601 S Figueroa St, South Central LA (☎213/741-3686). For maps, guides and other motoring information.

Beach Information Weather conditions ☎310/457-9701; surfers' weather ☎310/379-8471.

Coastguard Search and Rescue ☎562/980-4444.

Consulates UK, 11766 Wilshire Blvd #400, West LA (☎310/477-3322); Canada, 550 S Hope St, 9th Floor, Downtown (☎213/346-2700); Australia, 611 N Larchmont Blvd, Hollywood (☎323/469-4300); New Zealand, 10960 Wilshire Blvd #1530, Westwood (☎310/477-8241).

Currency Exchange Outside of banking hours, daily at LAX 6am–11pm. (☎310/649-1939).

Dental Treatment The cheapest place is USC School of Dentistry, 925 W 34th St (☎1-888/USC-DENT) on the USC Campus, costing $20–200. Turn up and be prepared to wait all day. If you need emergency treatment, try the LA Dental Society for referrals 24hr a day (☎213/380-3450).

Directory Inquiries Local ☎411 (this is a free call at pay phones); Long distance 1, then area code, then 555-1212.

Emergencies ☎911. For less urgent needs: fire ☎323/890-4194 or 323/881-2411; civil defense and disaster services ☎213/974-1120; police ☎213/625-3311; poison control center ☎1-800/777-6476; food poisoning reports ☎213/240-7821; earthquake tips ☎818/787-3737.

Hospitals The following have 24-hr emergency departments: Cedars-Sinai Medical Center, 8700 Beverly Blvd, Beverly Hills (☎310/855-6517 or 5000); Good Samaritan Hospital, 1225 Wilshire Blvd, Downtown (☎213/977-2121); UCLA Medical Center, 10833 Le Conte Ave, Westwood (☎310/825-9111).

International Newspapers The USC and UCLA campuses have libraries holding overseas newspapers. Day-old English and European papers are on sale at Universal News Agency, 1645 N Las Palmas Ave (daily 7am–midnight), and World Book and News, 1652 N Cahuenga Blvd (24-hr), both in Hollywood.

Left Luggage At Greyhound stations and LAX for around $1 a day ($2 for larger lockers).

Mexican Tourist Office 10100 Santa Monica Blvd, Suite 224, Century City (☎310/203-8191). Call for general information or pick up a tourist card – necessary if you're crossing the border. Mon–Fri 9am–5pm.

Pharmacies 24-hr pharmacy at Kaiser Permanente in the LA Medical Center, 4867 Sunset Blvd, Hollywood (☎323/667-8301) and at Kaiser's West LA hospital, 6041 Cadillac Ave (☎323/857-2151). Also 24hr at Horton & Converse, 11600 Wilshire Blvd, West LA (☎310/478-0801).

Post Office The main Downtown post office is at 760 N Main St (☎1-800/275-8777), north of Union Station. Zip Code is 90012; pick up letters Mon–Fri 8am–3pm; hours run Mon–Fri 8am–7pm, Sat 8am–4pm.

Smog LA's smog is more hype than reality, yet the air quality *is* often very poor and, especially in the Valleys in late summer, can sometimes be quite dangerous. An air-quality index is published daily, and if the air is really bad, warnings are issued on TV, radio and in the press.

Sports Baseball: the LA Dodgers (☎323/224-1459) play at Dodger Stadium near Downtown, seats $6–16; Anaheim Angels (☎1-888/796-4256) at Anaheim Stadium in Orange County, seats $6–22. Basketball: the brand new Staples Center in Downtown hosts the LA Lakers (☎310/419-3182), seats $21–150, as well as the less flashy LA Clippers (☎213/745-0500), seats $10–65. Football: Los Angeles currently has no professional football teams, but Pasadena's 102,000-capacity Rose Bowl (☎626/577-3100) is used for the annual New Year's Day Rose Bowl football game and is the home field for UCLA's football team. Hockey: LA Kings are based at the Forum (☎310/419-3160), seats $10–80, while the Mighty Ducks of Orange County play at Anaheim's Arrowhead Pond (☎714/704-2500), seats $25–160.

Traffic Check AM radio news channels for updates on what freeways are suffering from congestion; if a highway section is particularly immobile, a "Sig-Alert" will be issued, meaning "avoid at all costs." One key radio station emphasizing traffic reports is KKTR 1650 AM.

travel details

Amtrak Trains

Los Angeles to: Anaheim (9 daily; 45min); Fullerton (for Disneyland) (10 daily; 35min); Las Vegas (1 daily; 9hr 30min); Oxnard (6 daily; 1hr 37min); Palm Springs (2 daily; 2hr 45min); Sacramento (1 daily; 14hr 12 min); San Bernardino (2 daily; 2hr); San Diego (10 daily; 2hr 45min); San Francisco (3 daily; 9–12hr); San Juan Capistrano (8 daily; 1hr 20min); Santa Barbara (6 daily; 2hr 45min); Tucson (1 daily; 10hr); Ventura (8 daily; 1hr 50min).

Greyhound Buses

Los Angeles to: Las Vegas (15 daily; 5–7hr); Palm Springs (17 daily; 4hr); Phoenix (5 daily; 9–11hr); Portland (5 daily; 23hr); Salt Lake City (2 daily; 17hr 15min); San Diego (30 daily; 2hr 45min); San Francisco (16 daily; 8hr); Seattle (5 daily; 27hr); Tijuana, Mexico (17 daily; 3hr 30min); Tucson (10 daily; 11hr 20min).

CHAPTER TWO

SAN DIEGO AND AROUND

R elatively free from smog, traffic jams, and shocking extremes of wealth and poverty, San Diego and much of its surrounding county represent the acceptable face of Southern California. Pipped by Los Angeles in the race to become the Southern Californian city, San Diego was for a long time considered an insignificant spot between Los Angeles and Mexico. But the second largest city in the state is now exacting revenge on its overgrown rival 125 miles to the north. Built on a gracefully curving bay, San Diego is not only scenically inviting, but also boasts a range of museums that is among the nation's most impressive, an evocative and nowadays well-tended history, several major tourist attractions, and much to discover away from the usual visitors' points of call.

Not surprisingly, the city is very much the social and commercial hub of San Diego County, and things change as you travel out from the metropolis. The **North County** divides into two quite different sections: the small and often enticing beach communities strung along the coast from the northern edge of San Diego itself to the rugged chaparral of the Camp Pendleton marine base; and, inland, the vineyards and avocado groves of a large agricultural area that reaches east towards much wilder and more mountainous land. Most settlements away from the coast are tiny and insular, and some have barely changed since the Gold Rush: a number of deep forests and several state parks are ideal for exploration by hiking and taking obscure back roads.

South from San Diego, there's little between the city and Mexico. **Tijuana**, just 25 miles from downtown, is an obvious jumping-off point for explorations of **Baja California**. While it may not be the most appealing destination in Mexico, Tijuana's an entertaining enough place to spend a few hours – as thousands of Californians do each weekend. And since most of the border formalities are waived for anyone traveling less than twenty miles or so into Mexico, day-trips to the party-time beach towns of Rosarito and Ensenada are perfectly viable.

ACCOMMODATION PRICE CODES

All accommodation prices in this book have been coded using the symbols below; prices are for the least expensive **double rooms** in each establishment. For a full explanation see p.36 in "Basics." Individual rates rather than price codes are given for **hostels** and whole **apartments**.

① up to $30	④ $60–80	⑦ $130–175
② $30–45	⑤ $80–100	⑧ $175–250
③ $45–60	⑥ $100–130	⑨ $250+

Of course, there is also heavy traffic in the other direction, as hordes of Mexicans, both legal and undocumented, flood into Southern California. Most are hotel and restaurant workers, but first- and especially second-generation migrants are gradually becoming integrated into less menial levels of the workforce. However, Mexicans in San Diego County are largely ghettoized, their presence resented by many born-and-bred Californians who can't see beyond the evident strain on the social welfare and healthcare system.

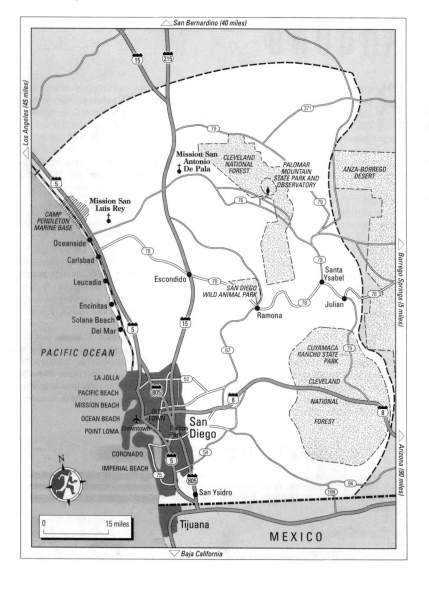

SAN DIEGO

Basking in almost constant sunshine, with its humidity tempered by the proximity of the ocean, **SAN DIEGO** is a near-perfect holiday resort. Anyone can enjoy idling on its varied beaches and viewing the obvious sights: San Diego Zoo, Sea World and the museums and sculptured greenery of Balboa Park. But at least as important as these is the recent expensive facelift given to the downtown area, restoring a sense of the city's real history and character.

The national image of San Diegans as healthy, affluent and conservative is true to a large extent – San Diego is certainly cleaner, and cleaner-cut, than Los Angeles or San Francisco. Yet it's also an extremely amiable and easy-going place. Increasing numbers of aspirant young professionals – the embodiment of the comfortable Southern Californian lifestyle – have swept away the reputation for dull smugness that San Diego acquired through the Sixties and Seventies, and given the city quite a different face. The presence of three college campuses (SDSU, UCSD, and USD) also keeps the cobwebs away – and helps sustain the image of a city that's on the up-and-up.

The first European to land on Californian soil, the Portuguese adventurer Juan Rodríguez Cabrillo (in the employ of the Spanish), put ashore at Point Loma, a spot about ten miles from the center of present-day San Diego, in 1542. White settlement didn't begin until two centuries later, however, with the building of a mission – the first in California – and a garrison, on a site overlooking San Diego Bay. Conflict between *Californios* and the fresh waves of settlers from the east led to the raising of the Stars and Stripes over San Diego in 1847, an event closely followed by the transference of the Mexican provinces to the US. But San Diego missed out on the new mail route to the west and was plagued by a series of droughts through the 1860s, causing many bankruptcies. Although the transcontinental Santa Fe railroad link was short-lived – repeated flooding led the terminus to be moved north to Los Angeles and San Bernardino, and to this day there's no direct rail service to San Diego from the east – its establishment resulted in an economic boom through the 1880s. A few decades later came the first of two international expositions in Balboa Park, which were to establish San Diego (and the park itself) nationwide.

In part because it lacks a train connection to the east, the city has long played second fiddle to Los Angeles in terms of major trade and significance, but it has used its strategic seaside location to establish an economically important military presence. During World War II, the US Navy took advantage of the numerous sheltered bays and made San Diego its Pacific Command Center – a function it retains to the present day. The military still plays a large role in the local economy, but in recent years its importance has been overshadowed by tourism.

Arrival

Drivers will find it simple to reach the city center from any of the three Interstate highways: I-5 is the main link from Los Angeles and passes through the northern parts of the central city; from the east, I-8 runs through Hotel Circle before concluding in Ocean Beach; and I-15, the main route from inland San Diego County, cuts through the city's eastern suburbs. The road system in San Diego suffers from ill-planning however, and often if you miss a turn off, you may be forced to go miles out of your way in order to get back on track. So make sure you are always armed with very specific directions. **Parking lots** are scattered around downtown, and there's plenty of metered parking – free overnight, but not allowed on evenings when the streets are being cleaned.

All forms of **public transportation** drop you in the heart of downtown San Diego: **trains** use the Santa Fe Depot, close to the western end of Broadway, while the

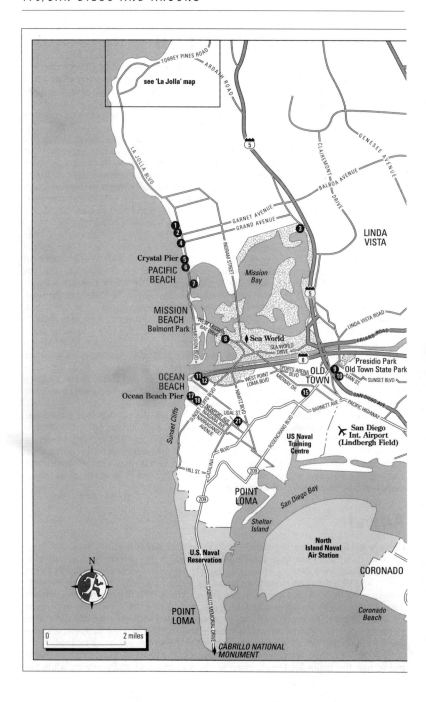

see 'La Jolla' map

TORREY PINES ROAD

ARDATH ROAD

GENESEE AVENUE

CLAIREMONT DRIVE

BALBOA AVENUE

LA JOLLA BLVD

GARNET AVENUE

GRAND AVENUE

LINDA VISTA

INGRAIM STREET

Crystal Pier

PACIFIC BEACH

Mission Bay

MISSION BEACH

Belmont Park

WEST MISSION BAY DRIVE

MISSION BLVD

Sea World

SEA WORLD DRIVE

LINDA VISTA ROAD

FRIARS ROAD

OCEAN BEACH

Ocean Beach Pier

SPORTS ARENA BLVD

WEST POINT LOMA BLVD

NIMITZ BLVD

MIDWAY DR

Presidio Park
Old Town State Park

OLD TOWN

JUAN ST

SUNSET BLVD

SAN DIEGO AVE

PACIFIC HIGHWAY

Sunset Cliffs

SUNSET CLIFFS BLVD

NEWPORT AVE

UDAL ST.

NIAGARA AVE

NARRAGANSET AVENUE

CATALINA BLVD

BARNETT AVE

ROSECRANS BLVD

US Naval
Training
Centre

San Diego
Int. Airport
(Lindbergh Field)

HILL ST.

209

POINT LOMA

San Diego Bay

Shelter Island

U.S. Naval
Reservation

North
Island Naval
Air Station

CORONADO

N

CABRILLO MEMORIAL DRIVE

POINT LOMA

Coronado
Beach

0   2 miles

CABRILLO NATIONAL
MONUMENT

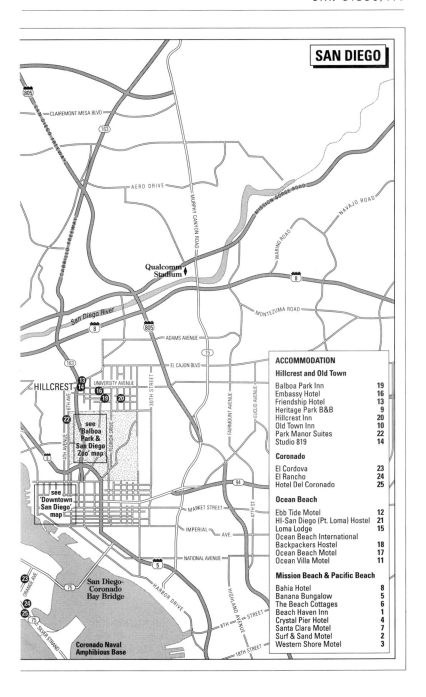

SAN DIEGO

ACCOMMODATION

Hillcrest and Old Town

Balboa Park Inn	19
Embassy Hotel	16
Friendship Hotel	13
Heritage Park B&B	9
Hillcrest Inn	20
Old Town Inn	10
Park Manor Suites	22
Studio 819	14

Coronado

El Cordova	23
El Rancho	24
Hotel Del Coronado	25

Ocean Beach

Ebb Tide Motel	12
HI-San Diego (Pt. Loma) Hostel	21
Loma Lodge	15
Ocean Beach International Backpackers Hostel	18
Ocean Beach Motel	17
Ocean Villa Motel	11

Mission Beach & Pacific Beach

Bahia Hotel	8
Banana Bungalow	5
The Beach Cottages	6
Beach Haven Inn	1
Crystal Pier Hotel	4
Santa Clara Motel	7
Surf & Sand Motel	2
Western Shore Motel	3

Greyhound terminal is even more central at Broadway and First Avenue. Lindbergh Field **airport** is only two miles from downtown, so low-flying jets are a feature of the city. There are two terminals, East and West, connected with downtown by bus #2 ($1.50), the service starting around 6am and finishing just after midnight. Obviously, given the distance, **taxis** into downtown aren't expensive, and quite a few hotels – even some of the budget ones – offer guests a free **airport limo** service. All the main **car rental** firms have desks at the airport (see "Listings" on p.204).

Information

A good first stop in the city is the **International Visitor Information Center**, 11 Horton Plaza, Downtown at F Street and First Avenue (Mon–Sat 8.30am–5pm, June–Aug also Sun 11am–5pm; ☎619/236-1212), which has maps, the useful *Official Visitors Guide*, and all kinds of information on the area including accommodation. Another useful source is the HI-AYH office inside the hostel foyer at 521 Market St (daily 7am–midnight; ☎619/525-1531, outside business hours a recorded message gives local hostel information). For eating and entertainment information, scan the free weekly *San Diego Reader* and *Metropolitan*, which can be found in many shops, bars and clubs; you could also try the tourist-oriented *In San Diego Today* and the "Night and Day" section of Thursday's *San Diego Union-Tribune*.

City transportation

Despite its size, **getting around** San Diego without a car is slow but not terribly diffi-cult, whether you use buses, the tram-like trolley or a rented bike. Traveling can be harder at night, with most routes closing down around 11pm or midnight. The trans-portation system won't break anyone's budget, but a number of cut-rate tickets and passes can reduce costs over a few days or weeks. Taxis are also an option: the average fare is $2 for the first mile and $1.40 for each mile thereafter.

Buses

Of the seven companies that operate **buses** in the San Diego area, by far the most com-mon is San Diego Transit (☎619/233-3004), which covers much of the city. There's a flat-rate fare of $1.75 (or $2 on the few express routes), transfers are free, and you should pay the exact fare when boarding (dollar bills are accepted). In general, the service is reliable and frequent, with even comparatively far-flung spots connected to downtown – known on route maps and timetables as "Center City" – at least twice an hour.

If you have any **queries** about San Diego's local buses, call into **The Transit Store**, 102 Broadway (Mon–Sat 8.30am–5.30pm; ☎619/234-1060), for detailed timetables, the

---

USEFUL SAN DIEGO BUS ROUTES

The following buses connect **downtown San Diego** with the surrounding area:

Balboa Park #7 #7a, #7b #16, #25	Imperial Beach #901
Hillcrest #1, #3, #11, #16 #25	Ocean Beach #23, #35
Mission Beach #34	East San Diego #1, #7, #7a, #7b, #15, #115
Old Town #34, #34a	La Jolla #30, #34, #34a
Coronado #19, #901, #903, #904	Pacific Beach #30, #34

CUT-RATE TICKETS AND PASSES

If you intend to use public transportation a lot, buy the **Day Tripper Transit Pass**, which lasts one, two or four consecutive days ($5, $8 and $12 respectively) and is valid on any San Diego Transit bus, as well as the trolley and the San Diego Bay ferry (which sails between Broadway Pier downtown and Coronado; $2 each way, 50¢ for bicycles – see p.193 for more details). If you're around for a few weeks and using buses regularly, get a **Monthly Pass**, giving unlimited rides throughout one calendar month for $50, or the half-price, two-week version which goes on sale midway through each month.

free *Regional Transit Guide*, and information on the Day Tripper Transit Pass and monthly passes. If you know your point of departure and destination, you can get automated bus information by phoning ☎619/685-4900.

The Trolley

Complementing bus travel around the city is the **San Diego Trolley**, often called the "Tijuana Trolley" because it runs on the sixteen miles of track from the Santa Fe Depot (departures from C Street) to the US–Mexico border at San Ysidro. Fares are $1–2.25, depending on how long you stay on. Tickets should be bought from the machines at trolley stops; occasionally an inspector may appear and demand proof of payment. Apart from being a cheap way to reach Mexico, the trolley is a link to the southern San Diego communities of National City, Chula Vista and Palm City. And from the "transfer station" at Imperial and 12th, its Euclid Avenue line makes much of southeastern San Diego easily accessible. Additionally, a new section of the network runs to Old Town San Diego, where a transit center links the trolley to ten bus lines as well as with the North County Coaster. Trolleys leave every fifteen minutes during the day; the last service back from San Ysidro leaves at 1am (and there's **one every hour on the hour** through Saturday night), so an evening of south-of-the-border revelry and a return to San Diego the same night is quite possible. The trolley service resumes its normal hours on Sunday morning at 5am, from Central Station in Old Town's Central Transit Station.

The Coaster

North County San Diego has recently been linked to downtown via a light-rail system called **The Coaster**, which starts out at Oceanside and stops at Carlsbad, Encintas, Solana Beach, Sorrento Valley and Old Town along the way. Fares range from $3.00 to $3.75 one way, $5 to $7 for a round-trip.

Cycling

San Diego has many miles of **bike paths** as well as some fine park and coastal rides, and is a good city for cycling. **Rental** shops are easy to find, especially prevalent

OLD TOWN TROLLEY TOURS

Not to be confused with the San Diego Trolley, the **Old Town Trolley Tour** is a two-hour narrated trip around San Diego's most interesting areas, including downtown, Balboa Park, the Old Town and Coronado, aboard an open-sided motor-driven carriage. A single ticket ($24) lasts all day and you can board and reboard the trolley at any of its stops. If you're short of time in San Diego, the tour is a good way to cover a lot of ground quickly, and the driver's commentary is often corny but fairly informative. Leaflets detailing the route are found in hotel lobbies and at tourist information offices; alternatively call ☎619/298-8687.

around bike-friendly areas; many such outlets also rent out rollerblades and surf-boards. Three reliable outlets are Bicycle Barn, 746 Emerald St, Pacific Beach (☎858/581-3665); Rent-a-Bike, 523 Island St, Downtown (☎619/232-4700), offering free delivery and pickup; and Hamel's Action Sport Center, 704 Ventura Place, Mission Beach (☎858/488-5050). You can carry bikes on several city bus routes; board at any bus stop displaying a bike sign and tack your machine securely (they're known to fall off) to the back of the bus. The Transit Store has copies of an explanatory leaflet enti-tled *How To Take Your Bike For a Ride*, and hands out free passes that allow you to take your bike on the trolley.

Accommodation

Accommodation is plentiful throughout San Diego, at prices to suit all pockets. Hotels and motels are abundant, and there's also a decent selection of hostels and B&Bs – only travelers with tents are likely to feel restricted, with just a couple of inconveniently located and comparatively expensive campgrounds to choose from.

The restoration of downtown – the best base if you're without a car and want to do more than idle by the ocean – has given rise to two hostels and a batch of surprisingly inexpensive hotels in renovated buildings. Sleeping is marginally more expensive at the many beach motels, though both Ocean Beach and Pacific Beach have hostels. There's another group of motels in a freeway maze called Hotel Circle close to Old Town (use-ful if you're driving or just staying for a night while seeing the immediate area), and budget motels line the approach roads to the city.

Bed and breakfast accommodation is in ever-increasing supply, especially in the Hillcrest district. Contact the downtown visitor center (see p.178), or send $3.95 for the *Bed & Breakfast Directory for San Diego*, PO Box 3292, San Diego, CA 92163 (☎1-800/619-7666, *www.sandiegobandb.com*).

Wherever you're staying, especially if you're arriving in summer, it's wise to **book in advance**. Where this is essential, we've said as much below – though again, the down-town visitor center has a large stock of accommodation leaflets (many of which carry discount vouchers) and will phone hotels, motels or hostels on your behalf for free. Bear in mind that prices increase drastically during the summer. **Gay** travelers are unlikely to encounter hostility wherever they choose to stay in San Diego, and several hotels and bed and breakfast inns are particularly noted for their friendliness to gay guests (see "Gay and lesbian San Diego," p.203).

Downtown

See the map on p.184 for locations.

Golden West Hotel, 720 Fourth Ave (☎619/233-7596). A little seedy, but with a great historic lobby and hard-to-beat location in the Gaslamp District at rock-bottom rates. Ask to see your room first. ①–②.

Horton Grand, 311 Island Ave at Third (☎1-800/542-1886 or 619/544-1886). Classy, modernized amalgam of two century-old hotels, with fireplaces in most rooms, and staff dressed in Victorian-era costumes. ⑥.

J Street Inn, 222 J St between Third and Fourth (☎619/696-6922). Located near the Gaslamp District, Greyhound terminal and the waterfront, this little gem has in-room microwaves, refrigera-tors and cable TV. ④.

La Pensione, 1700 India St, Little Italy (☎619/236-8000). Great value small hotel in a quiet area within walking distance of the city center. The rooms, around a central court, are smallish but taste-fully done out and equipped with microwave and fridge. ③.

The Maryland Hotel, 630 F St (☎619/239-9243). Amenable restored hotel, if somewhat lacking in frills, in a good downtown location. They also offer long-term rates. ③.

The U.S. Grant, 326 Broadway between Third and Fourth (☎1-800/237-5029 or 619/232-3121). Directly across the street from Horton Plaza, this has been downtown's poshest address since 1910, and has played host to presidents and celebrities. ⑦.

Century City, Los Angeles

"It's a Small World," Disneyland

Sunset Boulevard, Los Angeles

Getty Center, Los Angeles

Downtown Los Angeles

tel, 4500 Ocean Blvd, Pacific Beach (☎1-800/748-5894 or 858/483-6983). Quaint,
ituated right on the pier at Pacific Beach. All units are suites with private decks.
nettes. Very pricey, but you stay literally on the water. ⑥–⑧.
el, 839 Santa Clara Place, Mission Beach (☎858/488-1193). No-frills rooms with
sy walk from the hectic Mission Beach sands, and a good half-mile north of

el, 4666 Mission Blvd, Pacific Beach (☎858/483-7420). Cozy motel close to the

tel, 4345 Mission Bay Dr, Mission Beach (☎858/273-1121). A very standard but
mately two miles from the water. ③.

97 for locations.
n at La Jolla, 7753 Draper Ave (☎1-800/582-2466 or 858/456-2066). Cubist
gardens, great service and proximity to both the beach and the Museum of
ke this a unique stay. ⑥.
ospect St (☎1-800/832-5525 or 858/454-2181). A Twenties landmark sited in
nd a short walk from the cove; various package deals, especially in winter
s on the regular rate. ⑥–⑧.
, 1155 Coast Blvd (☎1-800/248-2683 or 858/459-2621). Kitchen-equipped
y the sea – some of the rooms have sprawling oceanfront balconies. ⑥.
Prospect St (☎1-800/451-0772 or 858/454-0771). Within these radiant pin
enjoyed themselves in the 1920s; today the place is less glamorous but r
public areas and sea views. Not just a hotel, an experience. ⑧.
10 Prospect St (☎1-800/433-1609 or 858/454-0133). Charming Europe
r the area, with views over the ocean and complimentary breakfast a
eck. Studios and a range of rooms. ⑥–⑦.

ed Ave, Pacific Beach (☎1-800/5-HOSTEL or 858/273-3060). Who ca
when you can party all night and sleep all day on the beach just outs
akfast, keg nights, barbecues, a communal kitchen and a good ri
. Six-person dorms run $18. Turn off Mission Boulevard at no.425(

Fifth Ave between F and G streets, Downtown (☎1-800/438-862
hostel on the edge of the Gaslamp District. Beds in six- to eight
ental breakfast for $18; doubles available for $40. Free bike use, (
handy shuttle to LA make this the best of the city hostels.
Hostel, 3790 Udall St, Ocean Beach (☎1-800/909-4776 or 619
minus the relentless party-time atmosphere that prevails at the
of miles back from the beach and, at six miles from downtow
about the rest of San Diego. Large kitchen, patio, and common
$14-$17, private rooms for three or more, $20 per person.
Market St at Fifth, Downtown (☎1-800/909-4776 or 619/525-
strict and Horton Plaza. $17 for HI members, $20 for others, a
fee and bagels. No curfew.
Backpackers Hostel, 4961 Newport Ave, Ocean Beac
Relatively new, predominantly fun-oriented place a block fr
ilable for rent, and videos are shown every night. Space in
, all with sheets, showers and continental breakfast.

grounds, only two accept tents. The best-placed o
on the Bay, 2211 Pacific Beach Drive (☎1-800/4B/

Malibu shores

Watts Towers, Los Angeles

Seaworld in San Diego

Coronado Bay Bridge, San Diego

Balboa Park, San Diego

New York-New York Hotel, Las Vegas

Villager Lodge, 600 G St at Seventh (☎619/238-4100
ing facilities and fridges in each room. ④.
West Park Inn, 1840 Fourth Ave (☎619/236-1600 f
erators and microwaves, in a great location two bl

Hillcrest, Balboa Park, Coronado and
See the map on pp.176–177 for locations.
Diego," p.203.

Balboa Park Inn, 3402 Park Blvd, Hillcrest
walking distance of Balboa Park and the muse
mini fridges. ⑤.

Hotel del Coronado, 1500 Orange Ave, Cor
that put Coronado on the map and still the
pering wealthy guests for over a century. ⑦.

Embassy Hotel, 3645 Park Blvd, Balboa P
close to Balboa Park and with all the amer
rates. ②.

El Cordova, 1351 Orange Ave, Corona
Coronado, but no secret so you'll need
hacienda-style buildings ranged around
rooms have kitchenettes. ⑤–⑥.

El Rancho, 370 Orange Ave, Corona
decor and one of the cheapest on thi
ovens and fridges, and there's a jacuz

Heritage Park B&B, 2470 Heritag
restored mansion with Heritage Park
and classic movies are shown nightl

Old Town Inn, 4444 Pacific Hw
strides of the Old Town's liveliest

Studio 819, 819 University Ave
dation in the heart of the Hillcre

Ocean Beach
See the map on pp.176–177
Ebb Tide Motel, 5082 W Po
the beach and has rooms wit

Loma Lodge, 3202 Rosecra
district, with a beckoning
though not close to the bea

Ocean Beach Motel, 508
the beach. A little rough a
you can't beat the locatio

Ocean Villa Motel, 514
for the sands; the ocean

Mission Beach an
See the map on pp
Bahia Hotel, 998 W
sprawling resort off
beach. ⑦.

The Beach Cotta
Banana Bungalou
ew days of quiet

Beach Haven
Comfortable, ta
of the nicest places to

Crystal Pier H
deluxe cottages
Most have kitche

Santa Clara Mo
kitchenettes an e
Belmont Park. ③.

Surf & Sand Mo
beach. ⑤–⑥.

Western Shore M
clean motel approxi

La Jolla
See the map on p.
architecture, tranquil
Contemporary Art ma

Colonial Inn, 910 Pr
the heart of La Jolla a
bring significant saving

La Jolla Cove Suite
rooms and suites right

La Valencia Hotel, 113
walls Hollywood celebs
less plush, with beautifu

Prospect Park Inn, 11
style lodge, well priced f
afternoon tea on the sun

Hostels
Banana Bungalow, 707 R
about poky, scruffy rooms
the door? A free buffet bre
board flesh out the package
take bus #34.

Grand Pacific Hostel, 720
619/232-3100). Well-placed
rooms with sheets and conti
nized tours to Tijuana and a

HI-San Diego (Pt. Loma)
4778). Well-run, friendly and
hostels. However, it's a coupl
bus #35), awkward for getting
Eight-bed (or smaller) dorms

HI-Metropolitan Hostel, 521
Convenient for the Gaslamp Di
vate doubles from $39. Free co

Ocean Beach International
800/339-7263 or 619/223-7873).
beach. Bikes and boards are ava
bed dorm $14, double rooms $18

Campgrounds
Of the city's half-dozen camp
though mall-like, is *Campland*

or 858/581-4200). A basic site costs around $20 and *Campland* boasts a number of pools and hot tubs, as well as activity rentals and a general store. It is linked to downtown by bus #30. For a more serene camping alternative, there's **San Elijo Beach State Park**, Rte. 21 south of Cardiff-by-the-Sea. Sites run from $17-$23. Call Parknet (☎800/444-7275) for reservations.

The City

You never feel under pressure in San Diego to do anything other than enjoy yourself. Though the work-hard-play-hard ethic is as prevalent here as anywhere else in Southern California, the accent is very strongly on the second part of the equation. San Diego offers the size and culture that you would expect from a large metropolis, yet the relaxed attitude and slow pace give the city a decidedly laid-back, suburban feel.

The city divides into several fairly easily defined sections. You'll probably spend at least some of your time **downtown**. Here, anonymous high-rise bank buildings stand shoulder-to-shoulder with more personable structures from San Diego's earlier boom days, in what's now the café- and bar-choked **Gaslamp District**, bestowing a mood more welcoming than is usual in American city centers. Besides being the nucleus of the public transportation network, downtown contains a fair chunk of the city's nightlife, and has much inexpensive accommodation. A few miles northeast, the well-maintained parkland of massive **Balboa Park** not only has San Diego's major museums and the highly rated San Diego Zoo, but is perfectly suited for strolls and picnics beside the walkways that cut around the many acres of carefully nurtured plant life. A similar distance northwest of downtown is where the city really got started; the first white settlement growing up beneath the hill that was site of the original San Diego mission, an area now fastidiously sanitized as **Old Town San Diego**. The sense of history here is often powerfully evoked and quite believable, despite the inevitable Mexican-themed shops and restaurants which strain credibility – though not to the extent that you should be put off visiting, especially since the trolley now stops here. A couple of other districts close to downtown don't have any points of interest as such, but can be worth a call for different reasons. You might find yourself in **East San Diego**, whose large college campus livens up what is an otherwise featureless sprawl, while **Hillcrest**'s eclectic mix of trendy young professionals, gays, bohemians and would-be artists make it one of the city's best areas for ethnic eating and intellectually slanted nightlife.

More appealing for pure relaxation are the **beach** communities, all within easy reach of downtown and good for a half-day trip – or longer, if bronzing beside the ocean is your main reason for being in San Diego (see p.192 for details).

Downtown San Diego

Always vibrant and active, **DOWNTOWN** is the urban heart of San Diego and also the best place to start a tour of the city. Improvement initiatives begun in the late 1970s have restored many of the city's older buildings, resulting in several blocks of stylishly renovated turn-of-the-century architecture, while the more recent, sleek bank buildings symbolize the city's growing economic importance on the Pacific Rim. Though downtown is largely safe by day, at night it can be an unwelcoming place, and you should confine your after-dark visits to the restaurants and clubs of the comparatively well-lit and well-policed Gaslamp District.

Along Broadway

One of the most memorable first impressions of San Diego is that received by travelers arriving by train at the **Santa Fe Railroad Depot**, whose tall Moorish archways were built to welcome visitors to the 1915 Panama-California Exposition in Balboa Park. The architecture of the depot provides a dramatic contrast to the postmodern contours of the neighboring **American Plaza**, a combination of high-rise offices and glass-roofed public areas built during San Diego's pre-eminence in international finance in the mid-1980s. The plaza throws a sheltering canopy over the main terminal of the San Diego Trolley, and over the entrance to the downtown branch of the **Museum of Contemporary Art** (Tues–Sat 10am–5pm, Sun noon–5pm; $2, free first Tues & Sun of month; *www.mcasandiego.org*), which frequently stages compelling temporary shows. (The museum also has a La Jolla location, see p.196.)

American Plaza marks the western end of **Broadway**, a busy main drag which slices through the center of downtown. The most hectic portion of Broadway is the block between Fourth and Fifth Avenues, where the pedestrian traffic is a broad mix: shoppers, sailors, yuppies, homeless people and others, some lingering around the fountains on the square outside **Horton Plaza** (Mon–Sat 8.30am–5pm; summer & holidays Mon–Sat 10am–9pm, Sun 11am–7pm, hours are seasonal). Completed in 1985 for a cool $140 million and a great contributor to the resurgence of San Diego's downtown, Horton Plaza's almost instant success caused area real estate prices to soar and condo development to surge. Additionally, the complex's whimsical, colorful style, with lots of updated Art Deco features, influenced the architecture of the surrounding area. A

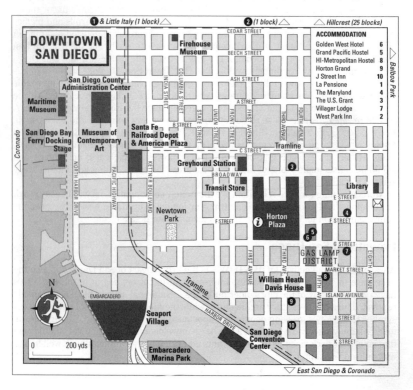

DOWNTOWN SAN DIEGO

ACCOMMODATION
Golden West Hotel 6
Grand Pacific Hostel 5
HI-Metropolitan Hostel 8
Horton Grand 9
J Street Inn 10
La Pensione 1
The Maryland 4
The U.S. Grant 3
Villager Lodge 7
West Park Inn 2

major tourist draw and a posing platform for the city's spoilt young things, the plaza has no roof, making the most of the region's sunny climate. If you don't want to join the conspicuous consumers, the top level, with its open-air eating places, is the one to make for. You'll find an array of ethnic fast-food – not especially sophisticated, but not overly expensive, either – and it's fun to sit over a coffee or snack and watch the parade go by, especially on Saturday when the suburban mall rats are out in force. All the typical American department stores and specialty shops (including the world's largest Sam Goody's record store) are represented, and don't miss the 21-foot-tall **Jessop Clock**, on level one, made for the California State Fair of 1907.

Further along Broadway things begin to get tatty and dull, but walk a couple of blocks or so for the secondhand bookstores (such as Wahrenbrock's Book House, 726 Broadway) and the **library**, 820 E St (Mon–Thurs 10am–9pm, Fri & Sat 9.30am–5.30pm, Sun 1–5pm), which has book sales on Friday and Saturday and an extensive reference section where you can pore over Californian magazines and newspapers. Tucked away on an upper floor of the library, the **Wangenheim Room** (Mon, Wed, Fri, 1.30–4.30pm or by appointment, ☎619/236-5807) holds the obsessive collection of local turn-of-the-century bigwig Julius Wangenheim, including Babylonian clay tablets, palm-leaf books from India, silk scrolls from China and many more transglobal curios documenting the history of the written word – worth a stop for its oddity value.

Less quirky, but an interesting diversion, the **Firehouse Museum**, six blocks north of Broadway at 1572 Columbia St (Thurs–Fri 10am–2pm, Sat & Sun 10am–4pm; $2), is situated in San Diego's oldest firehouse, and maintains fire-fighting paraphernalia and outfits. Photographs vividly recall some of San Diego's most horrific fires – along with the men, horses and equipment that tackled them.

The Gaslamp District

South of Broadway, the **Gaslamp District** occupies a sixteen-block area running south to K Street, bordered by Fourth and Seventh avenues. This was the heart of San Diego when it was still a frontier town, and was, according to local opinion, full of "whorehouses, opium dens and guys getting rolled." The area remained at the core of local carnality for years: street prostitution, though illegal from 1916, flourished here until the late 1970s, when a revitalization operation cleaned things up.

The few remaining adult emporia are incongruities on the smart streets lined with cafés, antique stores, art galleries – and ersatz "gaslamps," powered by electricity. This is now the heart of the city's nightlife, though its Friday and Saturday night bustle was unimaginable just over a decade ago. There's also a relatively high police profile designed to keep the area clean and safe. A tad artificial it may be, but the Gaslamp District is intriguing to explore, not least for the scores of late nineteenth-century buildings in various stages of renovation. They're best discovered – and the area's general history gleaned – during the two-hour **walking tour** (Sat 11am; $5, includes admission to the William Heath Davis House) which begins from the small cobbled square at the corner of Fourth and Island avenues.

The square is within the grounds of the **William Heath Davis House** (variable hours, call ☎619/233-4692; $2), included in the walking tour, though also visitable on your own. It was William Davis who founded "New Town" San Diego in 1850, believing that a waterfront location (the fledgling city had previously been located a few miles inland and to the north – the site of Old Town San Diego; see p.190) would stimulate growth. It didn't, at least not for some time, and Davis left the city before long, eventually dying penniless. He, and the more influential Alonzo Horton, whose later efforts to stimulate waterfront growth were ultimately successful, are remembered in the house through photographs, while the fittings and furnishings recreate something of the mood of their times.

Even without the walking tour, there's a lot to be enjoyed around this area simply by keeping your eyes open. Worth a peek is the **Horton Grand Hotel** opposite the William Davis House, created in the mid-1980s by cobbling together two historic hotels, the *Grand Hotel* and the *Kahle Saddlery*, both dating back to the 1880s; they were painstakingly dismantled and moved about four blocks from their original sites. A small, free museum with Chinese artifacts is a reminder of the once-thriving Chinatown area, where railroad laborers and their families crowded together. If you fancy staying here, see "Accommodation" on p.180.

The Embarcadero, Seaport Village and around

The once-shabby streets south of the Gaslamp District are now occupied by elegant, expensive condos – providing a fitting setting for the San Diego Convention Center, a $165-million boost to civic pride that opened in 1989 and is booked up to twenty years in advance. For non-convention-going visitors, the most interesting facet of the building is the sail-like roof imitating the yachts tethered in the marina just beyond. The marina is also the starting place of the **Embarcadero**, a pathway that continues for a mile or so along the bayside, curling around to the western end of downtown.

The path is favored by San Diegan strollers, joggers and kite-flyers, and most out-of-towners get no further along than **Seaport Village,** a mildly enjoyable collection of souvenir shops and restaurants, often with free clown and puppet shows laid on for kids. You should, however, make a point of strolling the full length of the Embarcadero, as it makes an enjoyable route to the trio of historic ships moored beside Harbor Drive (also the departure point for the ferry to Coronado; see p.193).

The three vintage sailing craft, just north of the B Street Pier, make up the **Maritime Museum** (daily 9am–8pm; $5). The most interesting of them is the *Star of India*, built in 1863 and now the world's oldest iron sailing ship still afloat. The *Berkeley*, alongside, which served for sixty years as a ferry on San Francisco Bay, is of lesser appeal, and the *Medea*, a small steam-powered yacht, has no special displays.

Landlubbers unimpressed by the Maritime Museum should explore the **San Diego County Administration Center** (Mon–Fri 8.30am–5pm; free; ☎858/694-3900), one of the most distinctive public buildings in California: a rich burst of Spanish colonial with a beaux-arts arrangement of gold and azure tiles. It's one of the unsung beauties of San Diego, and from Harbor Drive you can walk right through the foyer to the main entrance, on the way viewing the *Guardian of Water* statue (on the Harbor Drive side) and three interior murals.

Balboa Park and San Diego Zoo

The fourteen hundred sumptuous acres of **BALBOA PARK** contain one of the largest groupings of museums in the US. Yet its real charm is simply itself: a landscape full of trees, gardens, traffic-free promenades – and a great concentration of Spanish colonial-style buildings. Balboa Park was a wasteland inhabited by cactuses, rattlesnakes and lizards until 1898, when a local woman, Kate Sessions, began cultivating nurseries and planting trees there in lieu of rent. The first buildings were erected for the 1915 Panama-California International Exposition, held to celebrate the opening of the canal. The memories of its success lingered well into the Depression, and in 1935 another building program was undertaken for the California-Pacific International Exposition.

Along El Prado

Most of the major museums flank **El Prado**, the park's pedestrianized east–west axis which bulges out to form a plaza at the heart of the park. Here you'll find the **Timkin Museum of Art** (Tues–Sat 10am–4.30pm, Sun 1.30–4.30pm; Sept closed; free), repre-

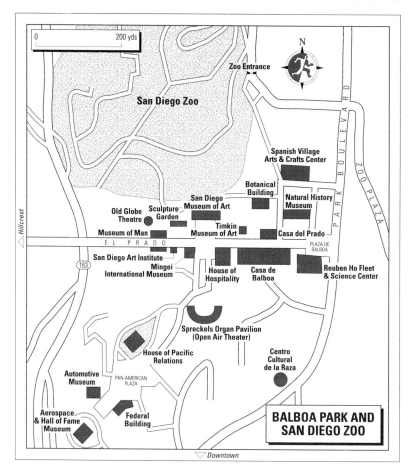

senting a sufficient number of European masters to make the stiflingly formal atmosphere and the evangelical zeal of the attendants worth enduring. Works from the early Renaissance to the nineteenth century include minor pieces by Rembrandt and El Greco, as well as a stirring collection of Russian icons.

The nearby **San Diego Museum of Art** (Tues–Sun 10am–4.30pm; $8; *www.sdmart. com*) has few individually striking items in its permanent collection, but is the main venue for any shows that come through town. There's a solid stock of European paintings from the Renaissance through to the nineteenth-century "Europe in Transition" canvases, matched by a fairly uninspiring US selection from the same century, and finally some welcome bright rooms of moderns, especially strong on California artists. The biggest surprises, perhaps, are found amid the exquisitely crafted pieces within the Asian section, mainly from China and Japan but with smaller representations from India and Korea. The Interactive Multimedia Art Gallery Explorer (IMAGE) lets you browse the collection without wearing out any shoe leather – and take home copies of your favorite pieces. It's one of the first – and finest – such interactive museum computer

THE BALBOA PARK MUSEUMS: PRACTICALITIES

Ideally, you should come to Balboa Park on the first Tuesday of the month when admission to almost all the museums is free; don't come on a Monday, when the bigger collections are closed. None of the museums are essential viewing, but at least three – the Museum of Man, the Museum of Photographic Arts and the San Diego Museum of Art – could collectively keep you engrossed for a few hours. The cheapest way to see them is to buy the $21 **Balboa Park Passport**, which allows admission to the park's twelve museums and is valid for a week, although you can visit each museum once only. The passport is available at all the museums and at the **visitor center** (daily 9am–4pm; ☎619/239-0512), located in the **House of Hospitality** on the Prado. This is the best place to find information about each individual museum, and to purchase the well-worth-it $1 Balboa Park map and guide.

The park, within easy reach of downtown on **buses** #7, #16 or #25, is large but fairly easy to get around on foot – if you tire, the free **Balboa Park tram** runs frequently between the main museum groupings and the parking lots.

systems in the US. Outside, don't miss the **Sculpture Court and Garden**, which you can walk into free at any time, with a number of important works, most notably those by Henry Moore and Alexander Calder. There's also a pleasant, if somewhat pricey, restaurant here.

Just across El Prado, the **Mingei International Museum** (Tues–Sun 10am–4pm; $5) has an appealing collection of folk art that is one of the most important in the country, featuring everything from weather vanes and carousels to furniture made from bottle caps. None of the exhibits are permanent, so you'll never know what you'll encounter. Next door, the **San Diego Art Institute** (Tues–Sat 10am–4pm, Sun noon–4pm; $3) is a venue for the works of its artist members, some more talented than others. In the David Fleet Young Artists' Gallery inside, work by students at various San Diego area schools is featured.

The contents of the **Museum of Man** (daily 10am–4.30pm; $5; *www.museumofman. org*), which straddles El Prado, veer from the banal to the excellent – and into the truly bizarre. The demonstrations of tortilla-making and Mexican loom-weaving are labored, while the large number of replicas – particularly the huge "Mayan" stones that dominate the ground level – would better be replaced by photographs of the real thing. But there's much to see and be fascinated by, not the least of which are the Native American displays. The temporary shows, too, can be absorbing.

The **Casa de Balboa**, between the House of Hospitality and the Space Theater, was built for the 1915 Expo to display the latest gadgetry and now houses four museums. Three of these are definitely worth a stop-in: the **Museum of Photographic Arts** (daily 10am–5pm; $2), with a fine permanent collection dating back to the daguerreotype and including most of the modern masters, as well as challenging temporary shows; the **Museum of San Diego History** (Tues–Sun 10am–4.30pm; $5) virtually next door, which cleverly charts the booms and busts that have turned San Diego from uninviting scrub-land into the sixth largest city in the US within 150 years; and the new **Hall of Champions Sports Museum** (daily 10am–5.30pm; $7), where mountains of sports memorabilia are on display (some of which can be handled after putting on supplied gloves) and an interactive activity center tests your sports trivia knowledge. Only the craftsmanship put into creating scaled-down versions of large portions of the US, and the tracks crossing them, make the fourth occupant of the building, the **Model Railroad Museum** (Tues–Fri 11am–4pm, Sat & Sun 11am–5pm; $3), mildly interesting.

The **Reuben H. Fleet Science Center** (Mon–Tues 9.30am–6pm, Wed–Sun 9.30am–9pm; Science Center $6, Science Center and theater or simulator $9, all three $11), close to the Park Boulevard end of El Prado, is one of the more recently added and most hyped features of Balboa Park. The Science Center has a batch of child-oriented exhibits, but more impressive sensations are induced by the **Space Theater**'s dome-shaped tilting screen and 152 loudspeakers, which take you on stomach-churning trips into volcanoes, over waterfalls and through outer space. The complex's newest addition, a high-tech motion simulator, takes you on harrowing trips through inner- and outer-space.

Across the plaza, the worthy **Natural History Museum** (daily 9.30am–5.30pm; $6; *www.sdnhm.org*) has a great collection of fossils, a comprehensive if somewhat unappetizing array of stuffed creatures, an entertaining hands-on mineral section, and an affecting section dealing with endangered wildlife called "On The Edge." A short walk behind the Natural History building, the **Spanish Village Arts and Crafts Center** (daily 11am–4pm; free) dates from the 1935 Expo and, as its name suggests, was designed in the style of a Spanish village. Some 300 craftspeople now have their work displayed here in 37 different studio/galleries, and you can watch them practice their skills, including painting, sculpture, photography, pottery and glass-working. It's fun to walk through, though you'd have to be pretty loaded to buy any of the original works.

The rest of the park

The fifteen-minute walk to the Aerospace Museum, the major collection away from El Prado, takes you past several spots of varying interest. There's a **puppet theater** (Wed–Sun shows at 11am, 1pm & 2.30; adults $2.00, children $1.50), in the Pacific Palisades building; the **Spreckels Organ Pavilion** (free Sunday concerts, 2pm) is home to the world's largest pipe organ; and the series of cottages comprising the **House of Pacific Relations** (Sun noon–5pm; free) contains extremely kitsch collections from countries all over the world – enjoy the proffered tea, coffee and cakes but don't expect any multicultural education.

An hour or so can be well spent in the **Aerospace Museum and International Aerospace Hall of Fame** (daily 10am–5.30pm; $6; *www.aerospacemuseum.org*) which not only offers an interesting history of aviation, but also presents an exhibit called *Star Station One*, a hands-on live demonstration, imparting knowledge about the International Space Station. There is a replica of *The Spirit of St Louis* (Charles Lindbergh began the journey that was to make him the first solo pilot to cross the Atlantic in San Diego), in the entrance hall. Next to the Aerospace building, the **Automotive Museum** (daily 10am–4.30pm; $6) continues the technological theme, with a host of classic cars and motorcycles, including a 1948 Tucker Torpedo – one of only fifty left.

San Diego Zoo

The **San Diego Zoo** (daily mid-June to early Sept 7am–10pm; daily early Sept to mid-June 9am–dusk; $16), immediately north of the main museums, is one of the city's biggest and best-known attractions. As zoos go, it's undoubtedly one of the world's finest, with a wide selection of animals, among them very rare Chinese pheasants, Mhorr gazelles and a freak-of-nature two-headed corn snake – as well as some pioneering techniques for keeping them in captivity: animals are restrained in "psychological cages," with moats or ridges rather than bars. It's an enormous place, and you can easily spend a full day here; take a bus tour early on to get a general idea of the layout, or survey the scene on the vertiginous Skyfari overhead tramway. Bear in mind, though, that many of the creatures get sleepy in the midday heat and retire behind bushes to take a nap. And the much-hyped pair of visiting Chinese **pandas** spend a lot of time sleeping or off being prodded by biologists who are trying to get them to breed. There's a children's zoo as well, with walk-through bird cages and an animal nursery.

The $16 **admission** only covers entry to the main zoo and the children's zoo; to add a 35-minute bus tour and a round-trip ticket on Skyfari, you'll need the $24 Deluxe

Ticket Package. A $35 ticket also admits you to the San Diego Wild Animal Park (near Escondido; see p.209) within a five-day period.

Centro Cultural de la Raza

Visiting all the museums in Balboa Park, or spending hours threading through the crowds at the zoo, could well leave you too jaded even to notice the unassuming round building on the edge of the park beside Park Boulevard. This, the **Centro Cultural de la Raza** (Thurs–Sun noon–5pm; free), mounts strong temporary exhibits on Native American and Hispanic life in an atmosphere altogether less stuffy than the showpiece museums of the park – make time for it.

Old Town

In 1769, Spanish settlers chose what's now Presidio Hill as the site of the first of California's missions. As the soldiers began to leave the mission and the *presidio* (fortress), they settled at the foot of the hill. This settlement was the birthplace of San Diego, later to be dominated by Mexican officials and afterwards the early arrivals from the eastern US. The area is now preserved as **Old Town State Historic Park** (locally referred to as "Old Town"), a state historical park that holds a number of original **adobe dwellings**, together with the inevitable souvenir shops. Although undoubtedly touristy, it's a good place to get a sense of the city's Hispanic roots, dolled up though they may be.

To get to Old Town, take bus #5 or the trolley from downtown; by car, take I-5 and exit on Old Town Avenue, following the signs. Alternatively, from I-8 turn off onto Taylor Street and head left on Juan Street; signs should prevent any confusion. Most things in the park which aren't historical – the shops and restaurants – open around 10am and close at 10pm (though a number of the restaurants do business until midnight or later), but the best time to be around is during the afternoon, when you can learn something about the general history of the area and enter the more interesting of the adobes (including several which are otherwise kept locked) with the excellent **free walking tour**, which leaves at 2pm from outside the Seeley Stable, just off the central plaza. You can get details on this, and other aspects of the park, inside the stable, which serves, for the time being, as the **visitor center** (daily 10am–5pm; ☎619/220-5422).

Exploring Old Town

Many of the old structures in the state park are thoughtfully preserved and contain a lot of their original furnishings, giving a good indication of early San Diegan life. A fine walking-tour book is available at the visitor center. Most of the houses are open daily from 10am–4pm and admission is free. Of the historic buildings, one of the more significant is the **Casa de Estudillo** on Mason Street, built by the commander of the *presidio*, José Mariá de Estudillo, in 1827. The chapel in this poshest of the original adobes served as the setting for the wedding in Helen Hunt Jackson's overblown romance about early California, *Ramona*. When the house was bought in 1910 by sugar baron J.D. Spreckels, he advertised it as "Ramona's Marriage Place." Next door, the **Casa de Bandini** was the home of the politician and writer Juan Bandini and was the social center of San Diego during the mid-nineteenth century. Following the switch of ownership of California, the house became the *Cosmopolitan Hotel*, considered among the finest in the state; some of the elegant features of that period can still be seen in the dining room. You can wander through the rest of the building freely, and reward yourself with a lavish Mexican lunch in the courtyard restaurant. Of moderate interest are the **San Diego Union Building**, where the city's newspaper began in 1868, and **Seeley Stable**, filled with Old West memorabilia.

An idealized recreation of an eighteenth-century Mexican street market, **Bazaar del Mundo**, abuts the state park. Though rife with gift shops, it's enjoyable enough on a Sunday afternoon, when there's free music and folk dancing in its tree-shaded court-yard. It's also a fair place to **eat**: stands serve fresh tortillas, *La Panadería* sells Mexican pastries for a dollar, and the two sit-down Mexican restaurants are decent enough if you can grab an outside seat.

Just beyond the park gates on San Diego Avenue, the **Thomas Whaley Museum** (daily 10am–5pm; closed Tues in winter; $4) was the first brick house in California. Once the home of Thomas Whaley, a New York entrepreneur who came to California during the Gold Rush, it displays furniture and photos from his time, as well as a recon-struction of the courtroom held here from 1869. Many people come, however, because of the house's supposed current occupants – the place has been officially stamped by the US Department of Commerce as haunted, possibly by one of the occupants of the neighboring **El Campo Santo Cemetery**. Once the site of public executions (Antonio Garra, leader of an uprising by the San Luis Rey Indians, was forced to dig his own grave here before he was killed), the inscriptions on the cemetery's tombs read like a *Who's Who* of late nineteenth-century San Diego.

Modest though it is, the cemetery makes a more interesting stop than **Heritage Park**, just north on Juan Street, where several Victorian buildings have been gathered from around the city – to be inhabited on weekends by period-attired history fanatics. They're now shops and offices and, in one case, a B&B. However, the view of the har-bor from the park is worth the climb up. Take a walk along Conde Street and peer into the atmospheric, sculpture-filled interior of the **Old Adobe Chapel**, dating from the 1850s and used as a place of worship until 1917.

Presidio Hill: the Serra Museum – and the San Diego Mission

The Spanish-style building that now sits atop Presidio Hill is only a rough approximation of the original mission – moved in 1774 – but contains the intriguing **Junípero Serra Museum** (Fri–Sun 10am–4.30pm; $5), a collection of Spanish furniture, weapons, diaries and historical documents pertaining to the man who led the Spanish colonization of California, and an acerbic commentary on the struggles of a few devoted historians to pre-serve anything of San Diego's Spanish past against the wishes of dollar-crazed developers.

Outside the museum, pause by the **Serra Cross**, a modern marker on the site of the original mission. To find the actual mission, you'll need to travel six miles north to 10818 San Diego Mission Rd, where the **Mission Basilica San Diego de Alcalá** (daily 9am–5pm; $3 donation) was relocated to be near a water source and fertile soils – and to be further from the likelihood of attack by rebellious Indians. This was wishful think-ing: Padre Luis Jayme, California's first Christian martyr, was clubbed to death here by Native Americans in 1775. The present building (take bus #43 from downtown), the fifth to be constructed on this site, is still a working parish church (Mass daily 7am & 5pm). Walk through the dark and echoey church – the fourteenth-century stalls and altar were imported from Spain – to the garden, where two small crosses mark the graves of Native American neophytes, making this California's oldest cemetery. A small **museum** holds a collection of Native American craft objects and historical articles from the mission, including the crucifix held by Junípero Serra at his death in 1834. Despite accusations that the missionary campaign was one of kidnapping, forced bap-tisms and the treatment of natives as virtual slaves, Serra was beatified in 1998 during a ceremony at the Vatican, the Pope declaring him a "shining example of Christian virtue and the missionary spirit."

The **Mormon Battalion Visitor Center**, nearby at 2510 Juan St (daily 9am–9pm; free) lets you relive, via artifacts, paintings and multimedia presentations, the 2000-mile saga of the Mormon Battalion March during the Mexican-American War – the longest U.S. military infantry march in history.

East San Diego and Hillcrest

Scruffy **EAST SAN DIEGO** is largely suburban sprawl, only really of interest if you want to venture into its western fringes as far as 1925 K St, the site of **Villa Montezuma** (Fri–Sun 10am–4.30pm; also open Thurs in Dec; $5). Ignored by the majority of visitors to San Diego, possibly due to its location, the villa is a florid show of Victoriana, with a rich variety of domes and all manner of loopy eccentricities. Local kids know the villa simply as the "haunted house," a nickname that doesn't seem unreasonable when you see the place. It was built for Jesse Shepard – English-born but noted in the US as a composer, pianist, author and all-round aesthete – and paid for by a group of culturally aspirant San Diegans in the 1880s. The glorious stock of furniture remains, as do many ornaments and oddments and the dramatic stained-glass windows. It's a house which well reflects Shepard's introspective nature and interest in spiritualism, both of which must have been entirely out of step with brash San Diego through the boom years. To get to the villa without a car, you can either make the long walk (about 45min) from downtown, take bus #3, #5 or #16, each stopping within about five blocks, or use the trolley, transferring to the Euclid Avenue line and getting off near 20th Street.

North of downtown and on the northwest edge of Balboa Park, **Hillcrest** is an increasingly lively and artsy area, thanks to the wealthy liberals who've moved into the district in recent years. It's also the center of the city's **gay community** and home to a couple of gay hotels (see "Gay and lesbian San Diego," p.203). The streets around University and Fifth, easily reached from downtown on bus #3 or #11, hold a selection of interesting cafés and restaurants (see "Eating," p.198), book and music shops, and a fine gathering of Victorian homes.

The beaches

San Diego undeniably excels with its fine array of museums and historic sites, but thousands are happy to trade time spent in Balboa Park for a few days on the city's **beaches**. In most cases, they're not strong on seclusion, but they're fine for sunbathing and swimming, and opportunities to get with the spirit of Southern California by renting rollerblades, a boogieboard or a surfboard abound.

Directly south of downtown across the bay, **Coronado** is a plush and well-manicured settlement, reflecting the wholesome nature of the large naval base to which it's home. Traditionally, Coronado's visitors have been wealthy health-seekers, here for its sea breezes, palm trees and famous (and expensive) hotel. Just beyond, and much less upscale, **Imperial Beach**'s chief draw is simply the quiet of a seldom crowded stretch of sand, and, if you are of an equestrian mind, the horse-riding trails nearby.

Across the bay to the north, the rugged **Point Loma** peninsula forms the western wall of San Diego Bay, with trees along its spine and a craggy shoreline often marked by explorable tide pools – though offering little opportunity for sunbathing. **Ocean Beach**, at the western edge of the peninsula, is extremely lively, but the exclusive and wealthy community that's developed a little way inland is tempering its reputation for all-out partying. These days much of Ocean Beach's former youthful vitality has moved to **Mission Beach**, eight miles northwest of downtown, and the adjoining, and slightly more salubrious, **Pacific Beach** – "PB" – linked by a beachside walkway which, on any weekend, is where you'll find San Diego at its most exuberant. The city is at its most chic, however, a few miles further north up the coast in stunning **La Jolla**, whose coastline of perfect caves and coves is matched on land by short, litter-free streets lined with small coffee bars, art galleries and a stylishly designed modern art museum.

Coronado

Across San Diego Bay from downtown, the bulbous isthmus of **CORONADO** is a well-scrubbed resort community with a major naval station at its western end. The many saltbox-style houses give the town an incongruous New England air, and make it pleasant to stroll around. Otherwise, Coronado is of limited interest, save for a historic hotel and the long and thin streak of sands – a natural breakwater for the bay – that runs south. The simplest way to get here is on the **San Diego Bay ferry** ($2 each way) which leaves Broadway Pier daily on the hour between 9am and 9pm (10pm Fri & Sat), returning on the half hour. From the ferry landing on First Street, shuttle bus #904 (half-hourly 9.30am–5.30pm; 50¢) runs the mile up Coronado's main street, Orange Avenue, to the *Hotel del Coronado*. Alternatively use bus #901 (or #19, though this only goes as far as the naval station) from downtown. By road, you cross the **Coronado Bridge** (southbound drivers without passengers have to pay a $1 toll), its struts decorated with enormous murals depicting daily Hispanic life, best seen from the community park beneath the bridge in the district of Barrio Logan.

The town of Coronado grew up around the **Hotel del Coronado**, a whirl of turrets and towers erected as a health resort in 1888. Using Chinese laborers who worked in round-the-clock shifts, the aim was to lure the ailing rich from all parts of the US – a plan in which it succeeds to this day, although the hotel and its elaborate architecture have lost much of their charm, dwarfed by newer high-rises, including the hotel's new tower. Nevertheless, if you're passing, the place is certainly worth dropping into, if only for its glamorous history. Through the lobby and courtyard a small basement **museum** (free) records the hotel's past. It was at the "del," as it's locally known, that Edward VIII (then Prince of Wales) met Mrs Simpson (then a Coronado housewife) in 1920 – a contact which eventually led to their marriage and his abdication from the British throne. More thrilling is the tablecloth signed by Marilyn Monroe and the rest of the cast who filmed *Some Like It Hot* at the hotel in 1958. Outside, past the tennis courts occasionally graced by world champions but more commonly by moneyed guests, are the sands and palms on and around which much of the movie's action took place. A guided, hour-long **historical tour** (Mon–Sat 11am&1pm, Sun 3pm; $15) wends its way around the hotel, beginning in the lobby.

A less grandiose place to explore Coronado's past is at the **Coronado Beach Historical Museum**, 1126 Loma Ave (Wed–Sat 10am–4pm, Sun noon–4pm; free), where photos and knick-knacks recall the community's early pioneers and some of its first naval aviators. Nearby, the **Coronado Visitor Information Center**, 1047 B Ave, just off Orange Ave (Mon–Fri 9am–5pm, Sat&Sun 11am–2pm; ☎1-800/622-8300 or 935/437-8788) carries reams of practical information on the area.

Imperial Beach

For a little isolation, follow Silver Strand Boulevard along the glistening sands south of the *Hotel del Coronado* (bus #901). Here you'll find plenty of good spots to stretch out and relax – though no food and drink facilities at all – foremost among them **Silver Strand State Beach** (daily 8am–dusk; $4 per vehicle) where you can rollerblade or bike. There are camping facilities, but for RVs only. At the end of Silver Strand Boulevard, down-at-heel **IMPERIAL BEACH** is a contrast to smart Coronado, but does have a pleasant and fairly quiet beach, disturbed only by the helicopters periodically buzzing in and out of the naval air station. In July, this beach is home to one of the nation's largest sandcastle-building competitions. Also peaceful is nearby **Border Field State Park**, a flat area noted for its horse trails, right near the Mexican border and reached by car along Tijuana Street from San Ysidro.

To return directly to San Diego from Imperial Beach, take bus #934 to the trolley and head north through dreary Chula Vista and National City.

Ocean Beach and Point Loma

Once ruled by a drug-running chapter of Hell's Angels, **OCEAN BEACH**, six miles northwest of downtown and accessible from there on bus #35, is now one of the more sought-after addresses in San Diego. Vacant plots with a sea view regularly change hands for half a million dollars, and the single-story adobe dwellings that have been home to several generations of Portuguese fishing families and characterized the area as recently as a decade ago, have virtually disappeared – the few that remain look like dinky-sized outhouses beside the opulent newer structures. The new money is less in evidence at the main beach, half a mile south by the pier; **Newport Street**, rife with the trappings of beach culture, is where most young backpackers spend their time, amid rows of cheap snack bars, T-shirt stalls, surf and skate rental shops, and some of the best second-hand music shops around. There is often good surf, and the beach itself can be good fun – especially at weekends, when you really shouldn't bother coming unless you're in the mood to party.

Further south from the pier – and the best of the beaches – rise the dramatic **Sunset Cliffs**, a great vantage point for watching the sun go down, and the grandstand of choice during the San Diego Yacht Club's defence of the America's Cup title in 1995. Be warned, though, that the cliffs are notoriously unstable and more than a few people have tumbled over the edge following an afternoon of excess on the beach.

Beyond here, you're into the hilly and very green peninsula of **POINT LOMA** – most of it owned by the navy, which has been beneficial in keeping some of the more attractive parts of the coastline unspoilt and accessible to the public. To get here from downtown, take the trolley to Old Town, where you can pick up bus #26. But, bring something to look at during the ride as there's little to see until you get past the naval base to the southern extremity, and the **Cabrillo National Monument** (daily 9am–5.15pm; seven-day pass $5 per vehicle, $2 per pedestrian or cyclist). It was here that Cabrillo and crew became the first Europeans to land in California in the sixteenth century, though that's as far as the historical interest goes, for they quickly reboarded their vessel and sailed away. The startling views from this high spot, however, across San Diego Bay to the downtown skyline and right along the coast to Mexico, easily repay the journey here. And after enjoying the view, there's ample opportunity for discovering the marine life in the numerous tide pools around the shoreline, reached on a clearly marked **nature walk** beginning close to the monument.

Also nearby, a **visitor center** informs on what creatures you might spot and when the tides are most willing to reveal them (obviously the pools are flooded at high tide). If your timing is wrong, climb the hill to the **Old Point Loma Lighthouse** and take a quick tour of the interior (usually daily 9am–5:15pm), and it's neighboring historical exhibition, a reconstruction of a World War I radio room. As it happens, the structure led an unfulfilled life: soon after it was built it was realized that the beacon would be obscured by fog, and another lighthouse was erected at a lower elevation.

Facing the Pacific, a sheltered viewing station on the southwest facing cliffs of the lighthouse makes it easy to view the November to March **whale migration**, when scores of gray whales pass by on their journey between the Arctic Ocean and their breeding grounds off Baja California. High-powered telescopes and a tape-recorded lecture on whales make the viewing station a must during the migration season.

Mission Bay and Sea World

Heading northwest from downtown towards the coast, you pass through the unredeemed area surrounding the Sports Arena – frequented by military personnel for its topless bars and by unfussy tourists for its low-priced, spartan hotels – before reaching

MISSION BAY, whose mud flats quickly become a landscaped expanse of lagoons and grassy flatlands usually crowded with watersports fanatics. From Ocean Beach, only a couple of miles away, you need to cross the San Diego River on Sunset Cliffs Boulevard.

Mission Bay is also the setting of **SEA WORLD** (daily mid-June to Labor day 9am–dusk, rest of the year 10am–dusk; $40, children $30, parking $5; *www.seaworld. com*); take Sea World Drive off I-5, or bus #9 from downtown. Although the entrance fee is a hefty one, and adding refreshments or souvenirs can cause bankruptcy, Sea World is San Diego's most popular tourist attraction for a reason: The park is a must if you're toting the kids along. But for others, experiencing the region's sea life by whale watching and snorkeling off the coast may be more rewarding (and a lot cheaper). The park's entry price dictates that you allow a whole day to make it worthwhile (better still, shell out a few more dollars for the next-day return pass). Highly regimented, Sea World has a large number of exhibits and timetabled events (get the day's schedule as you enter), ranging from the killer whale performances that make up Shamu Adventure – where you shouldn't sit in the first fourteen rows unless you're prepared to be soaked by splashes from a high-flying orca – to the new Manatee Rescue, a 215,00-gallon freshwater "river" showcasing the gentle plant-eating mammals. Other highlights include the Wild Arctic exhibit, a simulated habitat featuring walruses, beluga whales and polar bears, and the Shark Encounter, where all manner of sharks circle menacingly around visitors walking through a submerged viewing tunnel.

Mission Beach and Pacific Beach

The hands-down places to see-and-be-seen in San Diego are **MISSION BEACH** – the peninsula that separates Mission Bay from the Pacific Ocean – and its seamless northern extension, **PACIFIC BEACH**. If you aren't up for baring it all, you can always nurse a beer or a juice at one of the many beachfront bars while observing the gorgeous sand and water packed with scantily clad torsos and surfboard-clutching hunks. Or you could rollerblade or bike down Ocean Front Walk, the concrete boardwalk running the length of both beaches (and the fastest way to get about when summer traffic is bumper-to-bumper on Mission Boulevard). Although there is an undisputed surplus of *Baywatch* wannabes in attendance, that may be exactly what you've come to California for.

First impressions may suggest otherwise, but the city authorities have made major endeavours to limit the anarchic hedonism long associated with this classic example of Southern California beachlife, including approving the revitalization of the once-derelict **Belmont Park**, near the southern end of Ocean Front Walk. The park now makes a great family outing. The roller coaster, one of the few of its era still left in the US, and the pool, once the largest saltwater plunge in the world and the setting for famous celluloid swimmers Johnny Weissmuller and Esther Williams, both opened in 1925. These days the two main attractions are supplemented by a collection of swimwear stores, a pricey fitness center and lots of seaside snack stalls. The funfair has encouraged more families to use the area but, so far, has made little impact on the beach's freewheeling character.

By following Mission Boulevard north you cross from the social inferno of Mission Beach into the more sedate Pacific Beach. Here, expensive ocean-side homes with tidy lawns set a refined tone, although there's still plenty to enjoy: there's a more than serviceable beach around Crystal Pier, and Garnet Avenue, running inland from the pier, is lined by funky eating places and nightspots. Adept surfers are no strangers to Pacific Beach either – a mile north of the pier, **Tourmaline City Surf Park**, regularly pounded by promising waves, is reserved exclusively for the sport.

La Jolla and around

"A nice place – for old people and their parents," wrote Raymond Chandler of **LA JOLLA** (pronounced "La Hoya") in the 1950s, though that didn't stop him moving here (his former house is at 6005 Camino de la Costa) and setting much of his final novel *Playback* in the town, renaming it "Esmeralda." Since Philip Marlowe concluded his last case, La Jolla has been infused with new money and fresh vitality, and its opulence is now less stuffy and more welcoming. The main section, around Prospect Street and Girard Avenue, has spotless sidewalks flanked by tidy grassy verges, and numerous chic art galleries sit side-by-side with equally chic cafés.

Though it's pretty expensive, it's worth coming at least to savor the town's unique (if clearly contrived) elegance, which includes the ornate pink **La Valencia Hotel**, 1132 Prospect St, frequented by Hollywood's elite in the Thirties and Forties. On a quieter section of the same thoroughfare, the newly expanded La Jolla site of the **Museum of Contemporary Art**, 700 Prospect St (Tues & Thurs–Sat 10am–5pm, Wed 10am–8pm, Sun noon–5pm; $4, free first Tues & Sun of the month), has a huge – and regularly changing – stock of paintings and sculptures from 1955 onwards. Minimal, Pop and California schools are in evidence, bolstered by a strong range of temporary shows, and there are fabulous views of the Pacific surf crashing against the rocks immediately below the building's huge windows. The museum also has exhibition space downtown; see p.184.

The building housing the museum was once the home of Ellen Scripps, a prominent local philanthropist whose seemingly endless reserves of wealth were injected into La Jolla through the first half of the century. She commissioned architect Irving Gill (who raised several distinctive public buildings in La Jolla) to design her house, and today the Scripps name is still almost everywhere, not least in the small, neat and exquisitely tasteful **Ellen Scripps Browning Park**, on the seaward side of the museum. Where the park meets the coast is the start of **La Jolla Cove**, much of it an ecological reserve, with an underwater park whose clear waters make it perfect for snorkeling (if you can ever find a parking space nearby).

Further along the coast

North of the cove, upmarket residential neighborhoods stretch from the cliff tops to the main route, Torrey Pines Road. Following this thoroughfare and then La Jolla Shores Drive, which soon branches left, you'll find nothing of interest for several miles until you reach the **Stephen Birch Aquarium and Museum** (daily 9am–5pm; $8.50, children $5, parking $3), part of the Scripps Institute of Oceanography, which provides entertaining up-close views of captive marine life, informative displays on the earth's ecology, and exhibits detailing the marine exploration work carried out by the Institute.

On a hillside setting above the museum and also reached from Torrey Pines Road, the **University of California at San Diego (UCSD)** campus is a huge, fairly bland affair, only meriting a call if you fancy trekking around to locate the various specially commissioned works scattered about the 1200-acre grounds, which constitute the **Stuart Collection of Sculpture**. The first acquisition, in 1983, has yet to be bettered: Niki de Saint Phalle's *Sun God*, a large colorful bird whose outstretched wings welcome visitors to the parking lot opposite Peterson Hall. To find the rest, pick up a leaflet from the office in the Visual Arts Building or one of the campus's two visitor information booths.

Without the benefit of a car, you can reach the campus on bus #34 or express #30 from downtown, which end their routes a mile or two away at a spick-and-span shopping mall called University Towne Square.

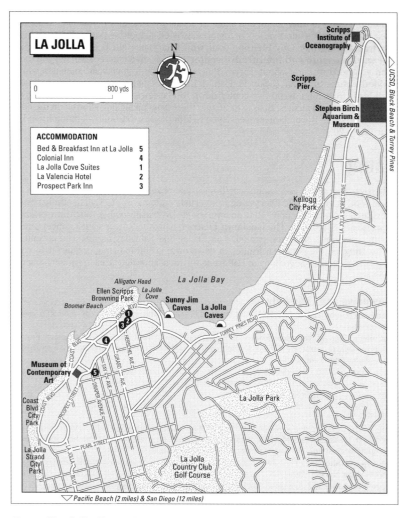

Beyond La Jolla: Torrey Pines State Preserve

As it leaves the campus area, La Jolla Shores Drive meets North Torrey Pines Road. A mile north of the junction, Torrey Pines Scenic Drive, branching left, provides the only access (via a steep path) to **Torrey Pines City Beach Park** – almost always called **Blacks Beach** – the region's premier, clothing optional, gay-friendly beach. It is also one of the best surfing beaches in Southern California, known for its huge barreling waves during big swells. The beach lies within the southern confines of the **Torrey Pines State Preserve** (daily 8am–sunset; parking $4), best entered a few miles further north, which preserves the country's rarest species of pine, the Torrey Pine – one of two surviving stands. Though scarce, the pines are not especially distinctive, although thanks to salty conditions and stiff ocean breezes, they do manage to contort their ten-foot frames into a variety of tortured, twisted shapes best viewed at close quarters from the half-mile **Guy Fleming trail**, which starts near the beachside parking lot. The small **museum and interpretive center** (daily 9am–5pm; free) will tell you more than you need to know about Torrey Pines, especially if your visit coincides with a **guided nature tour** (Sat & Sun 11.30am & 1.30pm). The less scenic and short **beach trail** leads from the interpretive center down to Flat Rock and a popular beach, great for sunbathing and picnics. Bear in mind that there is no picnicking allowed on the cliffs above the beach. Beyond the preserve you're into the North County community of Del Mar (see p.205).

Eating

Wherever you are in San Diego, you'll have few problems finding somewhere to eat **good food** at good value. Everything from crusty coffee shops to stylish ethnic restaurants are in copious supply, and, unsurprisingly, Mexican food is much in evidence, especially in **Old Town**. The **Gaslamp District**, which has the greatest concentration of hip restaurants and bars, explodes on Friday and Saturday nights. The ascendant **Little Italy**, on the northern fringes of downtown, is still too small a quarter to challenge the bohemian hegemony of **Hillcrest**, the most appealing area to simply hang out and eat.

Downtown and Little Italy

Alambres Tacos-Tacos, 756 Fifth Ave (☎619/233-2838). Well-priced Mexican food in a casual atmosphere.

Anthony's Star of the Sea Room, 1360 Harbor Drive (☎619/232-7408). Expensive Franco-California style preparations of fresh seafood, justly famed for its freshness and variety. Terrace dining available on the waterfront.

Bella Luna, 748 Fifth Ave (☎619/239-3222). This romantic, moon-adorned bistro has an artsy feel and serves up wonderful, mid-priced dishes from different regions of Italy.

Caffe Italia, 1704 India St at Date, Little Italy (☎619/234-6767). Sandwiches, salads, cakes, gelati and coffee served in a sleek modern interior or out on the sidewalk. There's a nice *frittata* bar brunch on Sunday.

Café 222, 222 Island Ave at Second (☎619/236-9902). Industrial-looking café serving some of the city's best breakfasts and lunches, with inventive twists on traditional sandwiches and burgers (including vegetarian), at reasonable prices. Open 7am–1:45pm.

The Cheese Shop, 401 G St (☎619/232-2303). A good spot for inexpensive deli sandwiches and espresso near Horton Plaza.

Croce's Restaurant & Jazz Bar, 802 Fifth Ave (☎619/233-4355). Pricey but excellent range of pastas and salads; the Sunday jazz brunch is the talk of the town. See also "Nightlife," p.201.

Dobson's, 956 Broadway Circle (☎619/231-6771). An upscale restaurant in an old two-tier building. The cuisine is continental at its best, with puff pastries adding oomph to familiar foods. Accompany the meal with a bottle from the excellent wine list.

Filippi's Pizza Grotto, 1747 India St at Date, Little Italy (☎619/232-5094). Thick, chewy pizzas and a handful of pasta dishes served in a small room at the back of an Italian grocery. A winner.

Fio's Cucina Italiana, 801 Fifth Ave at F (☎619/234-3467). Very classy, fairly expensive Italian place serving the likes of lobster ravioli and *osso buco*.

Galaxy Grill, 522 Horton Plaza (☎619/234-7211). A Fifties-style diner that's the prime location in this upscale shopping mall to munch a burger and watch the well-groomed crowds go by.

Grand Central Café, 500 Broadway (☎619/234-2233). This cozy cafe serves wholesome, inexpensive dishes from 7am-2pm. Breakfast only on Sunday.

Olé Madrid Café, 755 Fifth Ave (☎619/557-0146). Enjoyable mid-priced Spanish restaurant with an informal ambience and flamenco dancers midweek. After dinner on weekends, it turns into a popular funk and dance venue—see "Nightlife," p.202. Closed Mondays.

Sammy's, 770 Fourth Ave, outside of Horton Plaza (☎619/230-8888). Affordable California cuisine in a Mediterranean atmosphere. Pizza, pasta, salads, seafood and chicken are the staples. Messy sundaes round out dessert.

Taka, 555 Fifth Ave (☎619/338-0555). Good mid-priced sushi and hot and cold appetizers in a hip, modern atmosphere.

Hillcrest

Chilango's Mexican Grill, 142 University Ave (☎619/294-8646). Gourmet Mexican food for under $8; large veggie selection, too. Tiny storefront locale is packed to the rafters in the evenings.

City Delicatessen, 535 University Ave (☎619/295-2747). Huge New York-style deli menu with portions to match and late hours make this the stop for the seriously hungry.

Crest Café, 425 Robinson Ave (☎619/295-2510). Basic American food that's good and down-home, as are the prices. Delicious homemade desserts.

The Good Egg, 7947 Balboa Ave (☎858/565-4244). Until 9am, as much coffee as you can drink for 5¢, provided you buy a breakfast: the gigantic pancakes created from various mouthwatering ingredients are a wise choice. On the northern edge of Hillcrest.

Ichiban, 1449 University Ave (☎619/299-7203). There are few better places in which to enjoy quality Japanese cuisine than this unpretentious and simple restaurant. The combination platters are extremely well priced.

Montana's American Grill, (☎619/297-0722). Trendy California cuisine, along with an assortment of barbecue dishes and several microbrews on top, make this a popular dining spot.

Taste of Thai, 527 University Ave (☎619/291-7525). Terrific Thai for reasonable prices in the center of Hillcrest; expect a wait on weekends.

The Vegetarian Zone, 2949 Fifth Ave (☎619/298-7302). Healthy, fresh vegetarian cuisine in a non-smoking environment. Mains $8–10.

Old Town

Berta's, 3928 Twiggs St (☎619/295-2343). A far cry from the area's many touristy Mexican restaurants, offering low-priced, authentic cooking from all over Latin America. One of the best-kept secrets in town.

Cafe Pacifica, 2414 San Diego Ave (☎619/291-6666). A bit pricey but worth it for a winning California cuisine/seafood mix. Renowned wine list.

Casa de Bandini, 2754 Calhoun St (☎619/297-8211). Delicious food, combo plates and margaritas. Add those to the festive patio and it's everything you've ever wanted in a Mexican restaurant.

La Pinata, 2836 Juan St (☎619/297-1631). Affordably priced Mexican food, but not for the health conscious. Margarita pitchers are a great deal: Try the strawberry.

Old Town Mexican Café y Cantina, 2489 San Diego Ave (☎619/297-4330). Lively and informal Mexican diner; only at breakfast are you unlikely to have to wait for a table.

Old Town Thai Restaurant, 2540 Congress St (☎619/291-6720). Simply decorated place a block away from most of the restaurants and serving an extensive array of Thai dishes. Inexpensive lunches and plenty of vegetarian dishes. Closed Mon.

Coronado

Kensington Coffee Company, 1106 First St (☎935/437-8506). Aromatic coffees, imported teas and pastries that make for a tasty snack close to the landing stage.

Mexican Village Restaurant, 120 Orange Ave (☎935/435-1822). Long-standing Mexican diner of ballroom dimensions, patronized as much for its margaritas and music as for its affordable food.

Miguel's Cocina, 1351 Orange Ave (☎935/437-4237). Awesome (and cheap) fish tacos and a full range of other Mexican choices. Worth seeking out.

Stretch's, 943 Orange Ave (☎935/435-8886). Reasonably priced and extremely nutritious meals made only with fresh natural ingredients.

Ocean Beach and Point Loma

Old Venice Italian Restaurant Caffe and Bar, 2910 Canon Ave, Point Loma (☎619/222-5888). Upscale and hip atmosphere at moderate prices. Great for pizza, pasta, seafood and salads.

Point Loma Seafoods, 2805 Emerson St (☎619/223-1109). Fast, inexpensive counter where you can get San Diego's freshest fish in a basket with fries or in an oversized sandwich. This justly popular place is packed on weekends; it's not easy to find a parking spot nearby.

Ranchos Cocina 1830 Sunset Cliffs Blvd, Ocean Beach (☎619/226-7619). Come to this healthy, moderately priced Tex-Mex restaurant for tasty dishes like mahi-mahi tacos or eggplant burritos. Daily seafood and veggie specials.

The Venetian, 3663 Voltaire St, Ocean Beach (☎619/223-8197). Excellently priced pizzas and pasta, very welcome after a hard day on the beach.

Theo's, 4953 Newport Ave, Ocean Beach (☎619/225-9404). Hearty subs and pizza at cheap prices. Very popular with the locals.

Mission Beach and Pacific Beach

The Eggery, 4130 Mission Blvd, Mission Beach (☎858/274-3122). A coffee shop with imagination, serving breakfast – omelets, pancakes and so on – until 2pm. Be prepared to wait on weekends.

Kono's, 704 Garnet Ave, Pacific Beach (☎858/483-1669). The requisite place for breakfast or lunch on the boardwalk. Inexpensive, large portions of eggs, potatoes, toast, burgers and sandwiches. Beware of the long line of hungry surfers.

Luigi's Italian Restaurant, 3210 Mission Blvd, Mission Beach (☎858/488-2818). Enormous pizzas and a rowdy beachside atmosphere, bolstered by competing TV sets.

Mission Cafe, 3795 Mission Blvd, Mission Beach (☎858/488-9060). Eclectic choices, from French toast and tamales with eggs, to tortillas with exciting fillings. Beer, specialty coffees, shakes and smoothies all on tap. A good way to jump-start your day – or finish it off.

Palenque, 1653 Garnet Ave, Pacific Beach (☎858/272-7816). A family-run restaurant with fairly-priced dishes from various regions of Mexico. There is a front deck for dining on warm summer evenings.

Zanzibar Coffee Company, 976 Garnet Ave, Pacific Beach (☎858/272-4762). A great place to chill out, with good value snacks, pizzas, sandwiches, coffees and desserts.

La Jolla

Cody's The American Café, 8030 Girard Ave (☎858/459-0040). Innovative, mid-priced California cuisine with an exotic Eurasian flair. Sit on the patio and catch a glimpse of La Jolla cove.

Living Room Coffeehouse, 1010 Prospect St (☎858/458-1187). Great sandwiches, soups, quiches and pastries with fresh ingredients, in an antique-laden living room. Low prices and high quality.

Ocean Terrace at George's at the Cove, 1250 Prospect St (☎858/454-4244). If you can't afford the stuffier downstairs restaurant, head up to the roof for an only mildly overpriced lunch and an unbeatable ocean view.

Star of India, 1025 Prospect St (☎858/459-3355). Mostly northern Indian cuisine, with good vegetarian and tandoori choices. Most mains $13–15. Seek it out.

Sushi on the Rock, 1277 Prospect St (☎858/456-1138). Tempting array of inexpensive sushi combination plates served to a soundtrack of rock and reggae.

Drinking: bars, pubs and coffee bars

Most of San Diego's neighborhoods have something worthwhile to offer in terms of bars and coffeehouses. While the Gaslamp Quarter is a good place to get dressed up and have cocktails, the beach communities south of La Jolla offer a more rowdy atmosphere, with a lot of beer and loud music, as well as early evening happy hours to help ease the pain of sunburn. Pacific Beach has the best selection of coffeehouses, most of them sporting a relaxed, bohemian atmosphere.

Bars

The Daily Planet, 1200 Garnet Ave, Pacific Beach (☎858/272-6066). Sizeable sports bar with a 3–6pm happy hour, and cut-rate drinks offered through the evening. Dancing on weekends, Karaoke on Sunday and Monday night football in season.

Karl Strauss Old Columbia Brewery, 1157 Columbia St at B, downtown (☎619/234-2739). Where discerning beer hunters enjoy ales and lagers brewed on the premises.

La Jolla Brewing Company, 7536 Fay Ave, La Jolla (☎858/456-2739). Currently the liveliest evening rendezvous in La Jolla, where a youngish crowd quaffs the home-brewed beers and makes merry beneath vintage surfboards and photos of historic San Diego.

Live Wire, 2103 El Cajon Blvd, just east of Hillcrest (☎619/291-7450). The local indie rockers gather here to sample the twenty microbrews on tap. There's a loud jukebox and a pool table.

O'Hungrys, 2547 San Diego Ave, Old Town (☎619/298-0133). Tall beers and a boisterous, sing-a-long crowd. For the Irish at heart.

Red Fox Room, 2223 El Cajon Blvd, just east of Hillcrest (☎619/297-1313). Makes a popular tandem nightcrawl with *Live Wire*, one block away. An old style piano bar and good steaks draw nostalgia buffs of all ages.

Coffee bars

Café Crema, 1001 Garnet Ave, Pacific Beach (☎858/273-3558). Wake yourself up here before going to the bars, or sober up afterwards, with one of their large coffees.

Café Lulu, 419 F St, downtown (☎619/238-0114). A good selection of coffees and late food orders (2am) make this a popular scene.

Gas Haus, 640 F St, downtown (☎619/232-5866). Alcohol-free, eclectically decorated café where rollerblading teenagers, students and ageing hippies co-exist on deep couches or take each other on at pool.

Gelato Vero Caffe, 3753 India St, just at the foot of Hillcrest (☎619/295-9269). Enjoy good espresso and gelato while getting clued in to local events by staff and regulars.

Upstart Crow, Seaport Village, downtown (☎619/232-4855). Coffee bar fused with a bookstore which makes for a lively cross-section of customers – and a surfeit of reading material.

Zanzibar, 976 Garnet Ave, Pacific Beach (☎858/272-4762). Relatively serene retreat from the brash bars along this strip. Coffees, sandwiches and muffins served until 2am, or 4am at weekends.

Nightlife: live music, clubs and theater

San Diego's arch-conservatism is apparent even in the city's **nightlife**: money is lavished on pursuits such as theater and opera, but the crowds flock to the see-and-be-seen beachside discos and boozy live music venues. It may be narrow in scope, but there's plenty of it. For full listings, pick up the free *San Diego Reader*, buy the Thursday edition of the *San Diego Union-Tribune*, or seek out the youth-lifestyle-oriented *Slamm* at some of the places listed below. **Cover** charges at live music venues range from $2 to $10, unless someone big is playing.

Live music venues

Belly Up Tavern, 143 S Cedros Ave, Solana Beach (☎858/481-8140). Mid-sized concert hall that plays host to an eclectic range of live music – past acts include John Lee Hooker, the Fugees and the Cowboy Junkies.

Blind Melons, 710 Garnet Ave, Pacific Beach (☎858/483-7844). Live rock, blues, and reggae bands nightly to a crowd of beach and college hipsters in a spot right by the pier.

Brick by Brick, 1130 Buenos Ave, Mission Bay (☎619/276-3993). Tends to attract nationally known alternative, blues, and hard rock acts.

The Casbah, 2501 Kettner Blvd, downtown (☎619/232-4355). Varying roster of blues, funk, reggae, rock and indie bands.

Croce's Top Hat, 802 Fifth Ave, downtown (☎619/233-4355). Classy jazz in the back room of a pricey restaurant; has a jazz brunch on Sundays. See also "Eating," p.198.

4th and B, 345 B St, downtown (☎619/231-4343). Converted bank that now sways nightly to the sounds of rock, swing and various other forms of live music – call ahead to find out what's on.

Humphrey's by the Bay, 2241 Shelter Island Drive, Point Loma (☎619/523-1010). Live funk, soul and R&B, along with weekly disco nights and live jazz on Sundays, make this venue a local favorite.

Hurricane's Bar & Grill, 3105 Ocean Front Walk, Mission Beach (☎858/488-1780). A rowdy waterfront bar with exciting live acts performing nightly.

Island Saloon, 104 Orange Ave, Coronado (☎935/435-3456). Standard bar which rocks to local R&B groups on Friday and Saturday.

Patrick's II, 428 F St, downtown (☎619/233-3077). No-frills Irish bar with R&B, jazz and blues, New Orleans-style.

Winston's Beach Club, 1921 Bacon St, Ocean Beach (☎619/222-6822). A former bowling alley with rock bands most nights, along with reggae and an occasional 60s band. Close to the pier.

Clubs and discos

Bitter End, 770 Fifth Ave, downtown (☎619/338-9300). Two-story venue, complete with dance floor, martini bar and private lounge, for the sophisticated club-goer.

Blue Tattoo, 835 Fifth Ave, downtown (☎619/238-7191). If you want to experience foam dancing, this is the place to come. There's often a long line, as well as a strict dress code, so leave your sneakers and jeans behind.

Cafe Sevilla, 555 Fourth Ave, downtown (☎619/233-5979). Traditional Spanish cuisine upstairs, hip Latin American-flavored club downstairs. Attracts a European crowd.

Emerald City, 945 Garnet Ave, Pacific Beach (☎858/483-9920). Lively disco with drink specials at weekends, and the "Underworld" industrial and Gothic night on Sundays.

Olé Madrid Café, 755 Fifth St, downtown (☎619/557-0146). Spanish restaurant that becomes a very popular funk and dance club at night. Arrive before 11pm if you want to get in. See also "Eating," p.198.

Theater

There's a thriving **theater** scene in San Diego, with several mid-sized venues and many smaller fringe venues putting on quality shows. Tickets are over $30 for a major production, $10-$20 for a night on the fringe. The *San Diego Reader* carries full listings. The main **venues** are the **Lyceum Stage** in Horton Plaza (☎619/235-8025), the **Old Globe Theater**, part of the Simon Edison Complex for the Performing Arts in Balboa Park (☎619/239-2255), the **Civic Theater** at 202 C St, downtown (☎619/570-1100), and the **La Jolla Playhouse** at the Mandell Weiss Center on the UCSD campus (☎858/551-1010). The alternative theatrics at **Sushi Performance and Visual**

Art, 3201 11th Ave, downtown (☎619/235-8466) are sometimes pretentious but rarely boring.

Comedy
The **comedy** club scene in San Diego can barely be called a scene. If you want to catch some of the acts bound for the more glamorous venues in LA or New York, try the **Comedy Store South**, 916 Pearl St, La Jolla (☎858/454-9176).

Film
San Diego has many **cinemas**, most of them offering the latest Hollywood block-busters. Scan the newspapers for full listings; admission is usually $5–8. For more adventurous programs – foreign-language films, monochrome classics or cult favorites – look for the afternoon screenings (Mon–Sat) at the San Diego Public Library, 820 E St, downtown. After dark, **The Ken**, 4061 Adams Ave (☎619/283-5909), in the up-and-coming Kensington area, is the most popular venue for art and revival films, changing its offerings almost every evening. **The Guild**, **Park**, and **Hillcrest** cinemas, all in Hillcrest, can also be relied on to eschew popular arthouse fare.

Classical music and opera
San Diego's symphony recently fell on hard times and went under. These days, local culture vultures mostly rely on the jazz, classical, and chamber music series held at the Museum of Contemporary Art's Sherwood Auditorium at 700 Prospect St in La Jolla, (☎858/454-2594). Still thriving is the **San Diego Opera**, frequently boasting top international guest performers during its January through April season; it's based at the Civic Theater (see opposite).

Gay and lesbian San Diego

Mostly centered on the Hillcrest area, San Diego's **gay and lesbian** population makes its presence felt through a number of publications and resource centers, and a network of gay bars and clubs. Also, several hotels and bed and breakfast inns are noted for their friendliness towards gay and lesbian travelers – several being all but exclusively gay. For sun-worshippers, the place to go is **Blacks Beach** (see p.197) north of La Jolla.

Publications and resource centers
The primary source of gay and lesbian news, views and upcoming events is the free *Gay & Lesbian Times*, which appears weekly and is distributed through gay bars and clubs, many of the city's coffee bars, and most gay-run businesses. Look out, too, for the newsy *Update* with its *Etcetera* insert full of personals, classifieds and a "what's on" bulletin board. The LA-based *Edge* also makes its way down here. You can learn more by calling the **Lesbian and Gay Men's Community Center**, 3916 Normal St (☎619/692-4297).

Bars and clubs
Bourbon Street, 4612 Park Blvd, University Heights (☎619/291-0173). A smart gay crowd gathers around the piano bar at this elegant New Orleans-style club north of Hillcrest.

Brass Rail, 3796 Fifth Ave, Hillcrest (☎619/298-2233). Dancing every night, with male go-go dancers on the weekends.

Caliph, 3102 Fifth Ave, downtown (☎619/298-9495). Piano bar with live music aimed mainly at an older gay clientele.

The Flame, 3780 Park Blvd, Hillcrest (☎619/295-4163). The city's premier lesbian club, open for dancing, pool and occasional live acts from early evening to early morning. Tuesday is a no-holds-barred "Boys Night."

Flick's, 1017 University Ave, Hillcrest (☎619/297-2056). A popular bar which plays music videos on four large screens.

Number One Fifth Avenue, 3845 Fifth Ave, Hillcrest (☎619/299-1911). A fairly casual neighborhood bar with a pleasant patio. DJs play requests some nights, mainly Fifties through Seventies.

Rich's, 1051 University Ave, Hillcrest (☎619/295-2195). Popular club with heavy dance grooves on Friday and Saturday, and "Hedonism" night on Thursday when the hat-check even accepts T-shirts and jeans, so you can dance in your Calvin Kleins. Cover charge most nights.

Gay accommodation

Balboa Park Inn, 3402 Park Blvd, Hillcrest (☎1-800/938-8181 or 619/298-0823). Elegant B&B in a Spanish colonial-style building, within walking distance of Balboa Park and its museums and popular with gay, lesbian and straight guests. Some rooms have kitchenettes and there's a jacuzzi. ⑤–⑥.

Friendship Hotel, 3942 Eighth Ave, Hillcrest (☎619/298-9898). One of the least expensive hotels in the area, but still with TVs and refrigerators in rooms. Mostly gay and lesbian. ②–③.

Hillcrest Inn, 3754 Fifth Ave, Hillcrest (☎1-800/258-2280 or 619/293-7078). Predominantly gay hotel right in the heart of Hillcrest. The fairly basic, mostly non-smoking rooms all have bath, refrigerator and microwave. It's a little characterless but has a friendly atmosphere. ③.

Park Manor Suites, 525 Spruce St, near Balboa Park (☎1-800/874-2649 or 619/291-0999). The rooms – all with kitchens and nice, large sitting areas – are not quite as posh as the lobby of this residential-style inn would suggest, but then neither are the prices. Continental breakfast is included. ⑤.

Listings

American Express Main branches are downtown at 258 Broadway (☎619/234-4455) and 1020 Prospect St in La Jolla (☎858/459-4161). Both open Mon–Fri 9am–5pm.

Amtrak recorded schedule information ☎619/239-9021.

Beach and surf conditions ☎619/221-8884.

Car rental Alamo, 2942 Kettner Blvd (☎619/297-0311); Avis, 3180 N Harbor Drive (☎1-800/331-1212); Budget, 2535 Pacific Highway (☎1-800/283-4382); Hertz, 333 W Harbor Drive (☎1-800/654-3131); Rent-a-Wreck, 1904 Hotel Circle North (☎619/223-3300); Thrifty, 1120 W Laurel (☎619/702-0570); Bargain Auto, 3860 Rosecrans St (☎619/299-0009).

Disabled assistance Accessible San Diego, 1010 Second Ave, Suite 1630, San Diego 92101 (☎858/279-0704); Access Center of San Diego, 1295 University Ave, Suite 10, San Diego 92013 (☎619/293-3500, TDD 293-7757).

Flea market The huge Kobey's Swap Meet takes place at the San Diego Sports Arena, 3500 Sports Arena Blvd; Thurs–Sun 7am–3pm.

Hospitals For non-urgent treatment, the cheapest place is the Beach Area Family Health Center, 3705 Mission Blvd, Mission Beach (☎858/488-0644).

Internet: The Central Library, downtown, has free access. Or, try the *Internet Café*, also downtown at 800 Broadway (☎619/702-2233).

Left luggage At the Greyhound terminal ($2 for 6hr, $4 for 24hr) and, for ticketed travelers, at the Santa Fe Depot ($1.50 for 24hr).

Pharmacy 24-hour pharmacy at Sharp Cabrillo Hospital, 3457 Kenyon St, between downtown and Ocean Beach (☎619/221-3711).

Post offices The downtown post office is at 820 E St (Mon–Fri 8.30am–5pm, Sat 8.30am–noon), but for *poste restante* (general delivery) use the main office at 2535 Midway Drive, between downtown and Mission Beach (Mon, 7am–5pm, Tues-Fri 8am-5pm, Sat 8am–4pm; zip code 92138; ☎800/275-8777).

Rape Crisis Center/Hotline 4508 Mission Bay Drive (☎619/233-3088).

Sport Baseball: the San Diego Padres play in the same stadium as the Chargers (football), tickets from the stadium office or Ticketron (☎619/283-4494). Football: the San Diego Chargers play in the Qualcomm Stadium in Mission Valley (☎619/525-8282).

Ticketmaster Call ☎619/220-TIXS for the nearest branch, or look in the phone book.

Traveler's Aid At the airport, daily 9am–10pm (☎619/231-7361), and at Santa Fe Depot (☎619/234-5191).
Weather Recorded information ☎619/221-8884
Victims of Crime Resource Center ☎619/688-9200
Western Union ☎1-800/325-6000.

AROUND SAN DIEGO

San Diego County lies largely north of the city, and runs from small, sleepy suburban communities to completely open – and rugged – country. Passing through at least some of it is unavoidable, though how much time you actually spend in the region depends on whether you want to allow several days to camp out and follow forest and desert hikes, or simply to dash along the coast as fast as possible to Los Angeles.

To the south there's Mexico, or more accurately the Mexican border city of **Tijuana**. To be honest, the city isn't much, giving the merest hint of how Mexico really is and a much stronger taste of the comparative affluence of the US – most visitors are shoppers and it's hard to avoid the tensions that arise from that. However, it is at least a different country – very cheap and extremely easy to reach from San Diego.

Transportation around the region is straightforward. By car, I-5, skirting along the coast, and I-15, a little deeper inland, are the main links with the north, while I-8 heads east from San Diego towards the southern part of the Anza-Borrego Desert (see p.237). The area east of I-15, around the scattered rural communities, is covered by a simple network of smaller roads. Public transportation is no problem between San Diego and the North County coast, with the San Diego Coaster running from downtown San Diego up to Oceanside, along with frequent Greyhound buses and Amtrak trains between LA and San Diego. Heading south, you're as spoiled for choice with the numerous ways to get to the Mexican border. In contrast, travelers heading inland on public transportation will find only a skeletal bus service available.

The North County Coast

The towns of the **North County Coast** stretch forty miles north from San Diego in a pretty much unbroken line as far as the Camp Pendleton marine base, which divides the county from the outskirts of Los Angeles. The communities tend to get less upmarket the farther they are from San Diego and the closer they are to military bases, but generally tend to mix slick San Diego commuters, beach bums and crewcuts. The main attraction is the coast itself: miles of fine sandy beaches with great opportunities for swimming and surfing.

Del Mar

The tall bluff that marks the northern edge of the city of San Diego and holds Torrey Pines State Preserve (see p.197) forms the southern boundary of **DEL MAR**, a smart and pleasant little town whose **fairgrounds** are famous for the **racetrack** where the rich and famous gather between early July and early September for one of the most fashionable meets in California. The fairgrounds are also the address for the **Southern California State Exposition**, held for twenty days just before the racing season begins. It's largely an old-fashioned event, with barbecues and livestock shows, though it's mixed with a fair amount of contemporary arts and music events. Otherwise, Del Mar is a place to eat well and shop well – at a price. Additionally, the train station is just a pebble's throw from an inviting beach.

Solana Beach

SOLANA BEACH, the next town north from Del Mar, makes a better place for an overnight stop. Motels line the coast road, there's some decent nightlife – the *Belly Up Tavern*, 143 S Cedros Ave (☎858/481-9022), is one of the major mid-sized music venues in the area (see "Nightlife" on p.201 for details) – and striking views over the ocean from the Solana Beach County Park. If you're driving, take a quick detour inland along Hwy-8, passing the rolling Fairbanks Ranch (built by the film star, Douglas Fairbanks Jr) to **Rancho Santa Fe**, a small but extremely rich community shaded by trees, given its distinctive Spanish architectural flavor through the 1920s and 1930s. It got a great deal of unwelcome attention in 1997 as home to the Heaven's Gate cult, which committed mass suicide upon the appearance of the Hale-Bopp comet.

Encinitas and Leucadia

ENCINITAS is a major flower-growing center, its abundant blooms at their best during the spring, when soft waves of color from the flowers cast a calm and collected air over the whole place. It's no surprise that an Indian guru chose the town as the HQ of the Self-Realization Fellowship, near the Sea Cliff Roadside Park, a popular surfing beach dubbed "Swami's" by the locals. The Fellowship's serene **Meditation Gardens**, around the corner at 215 K St (Tues–Sun 9am–5pm; free), are open to all, and there's further flower power nearby at the **Quail Botanical Gardens**, 230 Quail Gardens Drive (daily 9am–5pm; $5). For more local information call at the **visitor center**, 138 Encinitas Blvd (☎760/753-6041; Mon-Fri 9am–5pm, weekends 10am–2pm). Encinitas, and the adjoining community of **LEUCADIA** three miles to the north, both offer reasonably priced **accommodation**, such as the *Moonlight Beach Motel*, 233 Second St, Encinitas (☎1-800/ 323-1259 or 760/753-0623; ②–③), nicely located for beach access with kitchenettes in all rooms. Otherwise, there's the landscaped **campground** at San Elijo Beach State Park (Parknet ☎1-800/444-7275; $17–23), near **Cardiff-by-the-Sea** just to the south, whose name – the whim of its founder's British wife, which also explains the presence of Manchester and Birmingham avenues – is its only interesting feature.

Carlsbad

Surfers constitute the major element of **South Carlsbad State Beach** (with a busy cliff-top campground (RVs only); ☎760/438-3143 or Parknet ☎1-800/444-7275; $17–25; day parking $4), marking the edge of **CARLSBAD**, one of the few coastal communities with a past worth shouting about, though it is manifested in lots of cutesy pseudo-Teutonic structures. During the early 1880s, water from a local spring was deemed to have the same invigorating qualities as the waters of Karlsbad, a European spa town in Bohemia (now part of the Czech Republic). Carlsbad thus acquired its name and a money-spinning reputation as a health resort, ably promoted by pioneer-settler turned entrepreneur John Frazier, whose bronze image overlooks the (now dry) original springs.

The most popular family attraction in Carlsbad these days is the brand new **Legoland California** (1 Lego Dr, exit Cannon Rd off of I-5; ☎760/918-5346; adults $32, kids $25). Here, kids (and adults) can climb on larger-than-life Lego structures, make their way through mazes, and operate miniature cars and boats. The park is surrounded by golf courses, resorts and a discount shopping center.

The springs and most things you'll need are close to the junction of Carlsbad Boulevard (the coast road) and Carlsbad Village Drive; along the latter, inside the train station, the **visitor center** (Mon–Fri 9am–5pm, Sat 10am–4pm, Sun 10am–3pm; ☎1-800/ 227-5722 or 760/434-6093) will give you a sense of the town's history.

Other than the campground, the best **accommodation** is at the *Ocean Palms Beach Resort*, 2950 Ocean St (☎760/729-2493; ④), overlooking the water but with its own pool and rooms with kitchenettes. Two good places to **eat** are *Pollos Maria*, 3055 Harding St (☎760/729-4858), for fast, tasty Mexican food, and, *The Armenian Café*, 3126 Carlsbad Blvd (☎760/720-2233), where the menu is a marriage of American and Middle Eastern food. Open for breakfast, lunch, and dinner.

Oceanside, Mission San Luis Rey and around

The most northerly town on the San Diego county coast, **OCEANSIDE** is dominated by the huge **Camp Pendleton marine base**, though the downtown area is charming, and the beaches are, once again, beautiful. For those without a car, it's a major transportation center (Amtrak, Greyhound, the San Diego Coaster and local bus services all pass through) and the easiest place from which to reach Mission San Luis Rey (see below).

If you find yourself **staying** here, the *Beechwood Motel*, 210 Surfrider St (☎760/722-3866; ②), is decent and cheap. For **eating**, *The Hill Street Coffee House*, 524 S Hill St (☎760/966-0985), is a real find in Oceanside's fast-food wasteland. It's an old house with bohemian leanings, with great coffee, cakes, sandwiches and salads, and live music on Saturday nights. For a surfeit of entertainment, you could take a look at the lagoon-centered **Buena Vista Audubon Nature Center**, 2202 S Hill St (Tues–Sat 10am–4pm, Sun 1–4pm; free). And, if you're a surfing enthusiast, head for the **California Surf Museum**, 233 Rt 21 (☎760/721-6876; Thurs–Mon 10am-4pm; free), which explains the history of the favorite local sport.

Four miles inland from Oceanside along Hwy-76 and accessible on local bus #313, **Mission San Luis Rey**, 4050 Mission Ave (daily, 10am–4.30pm; $4), is the largest of the Californian missions, founded in 1798 by Padre Laséun and once home to three thousand Native Americans. Franciscan monks keep the impressively restored mission's spiritual function alive and there's a **museum** and a serene candle-lit **chapel**. Even if you don't go inside, look around the foundations of the guards barracks immediately outside the main building, and, across the road, the remains of the mission's ornate **sunken gardens** (daily 9am–4.30pm; free), once *lavanderías*, where the mission's inhabitants did their washing.

The strong sense of history at the mission is fast being diluted by new property developments all around, mainly the commercial spillover from Oceanside that is creeping into the community of **San Luis Rey** itself. To escape, push on another four miles beyond San Luis Rey to the **Rancho Guajome Regional Park** (9.30am to an hour before dusk; $2 per vehicle), with its centerpiece, the ranch, a twenty-room adobe building erected in the mid-eighteenth century as home for the newly married Cave Couts and Ysidora Bandini, socialites who turned the place into a major social gathering spot. Among the many celebrities entertained at the ranch were Ulysses S. Wright and Helen Hunt Jackson, who, according to legend, based the central character of *Ramona*, her sentimental tale of Indian life during the mission era, on Ysidora's maid. After Cout's death in 1874, Ysidora fought to maintain the upkeep of the place but over the years it became dilapidated, until it was bought and restored by the county authorities. There are **guided tours** of the house (11am & 2pm Sat & Sun; $2).

Highway 76 continues inland to Mission Asistencia San Antonio de Pala, and to the Palomar Observatory, both described overleaf. Along the coast beyond Oceanside, the **military** has kept its territory in a raw state, creating a vivid impression of how stark the land was before industrialization took hold. When maneuvers aren't in progress, it's possible to pitch a tent in the lower parts of the camp area, close to the uncluttered **beach**. The northern part of the camp, around the San Onofre Nuclear Plant, is popular with surfers thanks to its slow-rolling longboard waves.

The North County inland

Inland, the North County is quite different from the coastal strip, given over to farming as far as the terrain allows and with no sizeable towns, the outlook one of thick forests, deep valleys and mile-high mountain ranges. Besides a few reminders of the ancient indigenous cultures, remnants from the mission era and a few tiny settlements – some of which can comfortably consume an hour or two of your time – it's best to make for the area's state parks and enjoy some leisurely countryside walks, or venture further east to the dramatic Anza-Borrego desert (see p.237).

Escondido

About forty miles north of San Diego on I-15, the unhurried dormitory town of **ESCONDIDO** sits in a quiet valley. The town is accessible on bus #20 from downtown San Diego; you're dropped seven miles out at the North County Fair shopping mall, but bus #382 or #384 will get you into town. The extremely well-informed **CVB**, 720 N Broadway (Mon–Fri 8.30am–5pm, Sat 10am–3pm; ☎1-800/848-3336 or 760/745-4741), provides information for the entire north San Diego County area.

In Escondido itself, the main focus of visitor attention is **Heritage Walk** in Grape Day Park, which leads into and around several restored Victorian buildings (Thurs–Sat 1–4pm; free) and to a 1925 railroad car that holds an elaborate scale model of the railroad which once linked Escondido to Oceanside. The **California Center for the Arts**, 340 N Escondido Blvd (Tues–Sat 10am–5pm, Sun 12pm–5pm; $4), features a good contemporary art museum, as well as two theaters that are the focus of a variety of high-tone music and dance performances. The **Orfila Winery**, 13455 San Pasqual Valley Rd (daily 10am–5pm), five miles south of the Escondido town center and set in stunning scenery, offers tastings of wines produced by a former Napa Valley vintner, while six miles north of town, the **Deer Park Winery and Auto Museum**, 29013 Champagne Blvd (daily 10am–5pm), also shows off a sizeable collection of vintage cars to anyone who turns up to sample the product of its vines.

To most Americans over 65, however, Escondido is best known for the **Lawrence Welk Resort**, a thousand-acre vacation complex of golf courses, guest villas and the Welk Dinner Theater, eight miles north of the town off I-15 (no public transportation) at 8860 Lawrence Welk Dr (☎760/749-3000 or 1-800/932-9355). Welk himself rose from accordion-playing obscurity to become an adored band leader, TV celebrity and inventor of an anodyne sound known as "champagne music." Even if you don't consider Welk a role model for aspiring composers, there's something to be said for taking a look at the hagiographic account of his life displayed around the lobby of the theater, and for gorging yourself on the cheap lunch buffet laid out in the nearby restaurant.

North from Escondido

Hwy-S6 leads fifteen miles north from Escondido to **Mission San Antonio de Pala** (Tues–Sun 10am–4pm; $2), close to the junction with Hwy-76 from Oceanside. Built as an outpost of Mission San Luis Rey, this lay in ruins until the Cupa Indians were ousted from their tribal home (to make room for the building of Warner Hot Springs) and moved to this area, where the mission was revived to serve as their church. The buildings here now are rarely used and are all reconstructions of the originals, but they're not without atmosphere, with a breeze whispering through the gaping windows and an eerie silence hanging over the cemetery. The gardens here are lovely, and a single-room museum contains artifacts created by the Pala Indians and dating back to the days of the original mission. There's a small basic **campground** opposite the mission.

Continuing east, Hwy-76 runs into **Cleveland National Forest** and a good sprinkling of **campgrounds** (both state and federal-run). The enormous forest stretches south from here almost to the Mexican border, although less-than-hardcore backpackers tend to prefer the **Palomar Mountain State Park** (☎760/742-3462), on Hwy-S7, for its cooler, higher altitude (some parts rise above 5000ft) and enjoyable, fairly easy hiking trails. Camping at the Doane Valley campground can be reserved through Parknet (☎1-800/444-7275) and supplies are available at the well-stocked Palomar Mountain General Store at the junction of routes S6 and S7.

Capable of seeing a billion light years into the cosmos, the two-hundred-inch telescope of the **Palomar Observatory** on Hwy-S6 (daily 9am–4pm; free) is something of a legend in astronomy circles. As a visitor, it's not possible to view the distant galaxies directly, but look in on the observatory's impressive collection of deep-space photographs taken using the powerful telescope.

East from Escondido

Ten miles east from Escondido on Hwy-78 (bus #307; Mon–Sat) and thirty miles north of San Diego (bus #878 or #879 from the Grossmont Center; Tues–Sat), the **San Diego Wild Animal Park** on San Pasqual Valley Road (opens daily at 9am, closing times vary; $19.95, combined ticket with San Diego Zoo $35; parking $3) is the major tourist target in the area: a 2100-acre enclosure that's well worth a day's visit. It's obviously a place for kids, and attractions include a sizeable aviary, noisy with the massed squawks of tropical birds; a mock African bush; a **Kilimanjaro hiking trail**; and elephant rides and various films and exhibitions. Admission includes a fifty-minute ride on the **Wgasa Bush Line Monorail**, which skirts through the outer reaches of the park, where the animals – including lions, tigers, cheetahs, deer and monkeys – roam in relative freedom, lending credence to the park's jungle theme.

In contrast to the crowded coast, the population – and the landscapes – become increasingly sparse as you press further east along Hwy-78, into a region that's a near-impossible nut to crack without personal transportation (see box above). If you're coming this way by car directly from San Diego, use Hwy-67 and join Hwy-78 at **Ramona**, eighteen miles from Escondido, and continue east for sixteen miles to **SANTA YSABEL**, a tiny crossroads community enlivened by two things. Right on Hwy-78 just before the junction with Hwy-79 you can't miss **Dudley's Bakery**, famous far and wide for its homebaked breads and pastries at giveaway prices – the date, nut and raisin loaf is justly a popular line (open Wed–Sun). A mile and a half north of town on Hwy-79, the tiny **Mission Santa Ysabel** (☎760/765-0810; daily 8am–4pm; $1), a 1924 replacement of an 1818 original, sits in moody isolation. There's a small chapel and, around the side, a one-room **museum** (same hours; $1) detailing the history of the mission. Outside is an Indian burial ground, and the church continues to serve several local Native American communities.

Julian

A different atmosphere prevails in **JULIAN**, seven miles southeast of Santa Ysabel on Hwy-78, and surrounded by pines – a sure sign that you're entering the foothills of the mountains that divide the coastal side of the county from the desert. Indeed, you're some 4000ft up, and even in summer it can get a bit brisk. Hard as it may be to believe today, the discovery of gold here in 1869 turned Julian into the second-biggest town in the San Diego area. Since then, the local population has stayed constant at around 1500, and has earned more from harvesting apples than from precious metal; the cider and apple pies produced here bring thousands of weekend visitors. You might also consider using Julian as a temperate base from which to make forays into the Anza-Borrego desert (see p.237) less than ten miles to the east.

With its little buildings and carefully nurtured down-home charms, Julian is immediately appealing, but a short stroll reveals little of consequence beyond the shops, realty stores and restaurants grouped along Main Street. The *Julian Café*, 2112 Main St (☎760/765-2712), has the best atmosphere and good-value, basic **food**, including the ubiquitous apple pie. As its name suggests, *Bailey Barbecue*, 2307 Main St (☎760/765-9957), features grilled meat, served fall-off-the-bone tender in a down-home setting. A visit to the *Julian Pie Company* on Main is a must. The **Chamber of Commerce**, 2129 Main St (daily 10am–4pm; ☎760/765-1857), has details of the town's many **B&Bs**. Among these, the *Julian Hotel*, at the junction of Main and B (☎1-800/734-5854 or 760/765-0201; ⑤), is the oldest functioning hotel in the state, opened in 1897 by a freed slave; rates include afternoon tea and a full breakfast. The *Julian Lodge*, Fourth and C streets (☎1-800/542-1420 or 760/765-1420; ③) is only a replica of a historic hotel, but has a similar country cozy atmosphere; breakfast is buffet-style continental. A less expensive option is to **camp** in the Cuyamaca Rancho State Park (see opposite).

If you find yourself with a few spare hours in Julian, take a look at the absorbing clutter inside the **Julian Pioneer Museum** on Fourth and Washington (April–Nov daily

---

HIKES IN THE CUYAMACA MOUNTAINS

Widely considered a four-season **hiking** area, the trails in the **Cuyamaca Mountains** seldom fall below 4500ft. Outside the summer months snow is always a possibility, and even in summer, nights are cool and thunderstorms common.

Cuyamaca Peak Trail (6 miles; 4hr; 1600ft ascent). Despite following the vehicle-free, paved Cuyamaca Peak Fire Road, this is the most rewarding of all the park's trails; a steep climb from either the *Paso Picacho* campsite (day-use fee) to a 6512-foot summit giving views east to the desert and west to the Pacific Ocean.

Harvey Moore Trail (12 miles; 7–8hr; 1000ft ascent). This well-signposted loop trail is relatively flat and winds through several ecological zones – prairie, oak woodland, meadowland and chaparral – all perfect territory for a cowboy such as Harvey Moore, the park's first superintendent in the 1930s. Starts a mile south of the park HQ.

Middle Peak (6 miles; 4hr; 1000ft ascent). There are several routes to Middle Peak, all easier than the Cuyamaca Peak Trail. The most direct is Sugar Pine Trail, named after the tall pines which bear the world's longest cones. The trail starts at the *Boy Scout* camp, ten miles south of Julian where the road turns sharply east at the end of the dammed Cuyamaca Lake.

10am–4pm; Dec–March Sat & Sun & holidays 10am–4pm; $1). Alternatively, wander half a mile up C Street to the **Eagle Mining Company** (daily 10am–3pm, weather permitting; $7), where hour-long tours of the old gold mine give an inkling of the subterranean perils faced by the town's early settlers. The **Volcan Mountain Wilderness Preserve** also makes for an interesting visit. Go north on Farmer Rd from Julian to get there (24 hrs, free). The short trail passes through orchards, oak groves, and manzanitas, leading to an excellent viewpoint of the area.

Cuyamaca Rancho State Park

You could spend at least a few hours among the oaks, willows, sycamores, Ponderosa and Jeffrey pines that fill the **Cuyamaca Rancho State Park** (unrestricted entry), which starts nine miles south of Julian and nine miles east of I-8 along Hwy-79. Even if you stay for days, you won't see everything: from lush sub-alpine meadows to stark mountain peaks, the park spans more than 25,000 acres, much of it designated wilderness area and only crisscrossed by a hundred miles of hiking trails (see box opposite), many of them hugging the 5000-foot contour.

Pick up information and maps, from the **park headquarters** (Mon–Fri 8am–5pm; ☎760/765-0755), sixteen miles south of Julian beside Hwy-79 in the heart of the park. At the same location, check the latest on the park's **campgrounds** strung along Hwy-79 (reservation through Parknet ☎1-800/444-7275; $12–16), chiefly *Paso Picacho*, twelve miles south of Julian, and *Green Valley*, five miles further south. These sites (where a $5 day-use fee is charged) are the only accommodation on offer unless you are prepared to hike into the $3 backcountry sites: *Arroyo Seco* is a mile and a half northwest of *Green Valley*, and *Granite Spring* is almost five miles east. There are also $30 **cabins.**

For some historical back-up to the scenery, drop into the excellent **museum** (Mon–Fri 10am–4pm, Sat & Sun 10am–2pm; free) in the park HQ, which details the formidable resistance of the local Native Americans to Spanish attempts to cut down the area's forests; this group also strongly resisted the arrival of settlers from the eastern US and was one of the last to be forced onto reservations. For more on the native peoples, take a stroll along the nature trails at Paso Picacho and at the park headquarters.

Tijuana and northern Baja California

TIJUANA has the odd distinction of being both one of the least culturally interesting places in Mexico, and one of the most visited cities in the world. Twenty million people a year cross the border here, most of them Californians and tourists on day-long shopping expeditions seeking somewhere cheap and colorful to spend money. And they find it: blankets, pottery, cigarettes, tequila, dentistry or car repair – everything is lower-priced in Tijuana than in the US (though more expensive than in the rest of Mexico), and all of it is hawked with enthusiasm.

What's most dramatic about Tijuana for first-time arrivals is the abrupt realization of the vast economic gulf separating the two countries. Crossing the *frontera*, or border, takes you past beggars crouched in corners and dirty children scuffling for change thrown by tourists. It's both a depressing and revealing experience. For regular visitors, however, it's a shock that soon fades; it's also unrepresentative of Tijuana itself which is, in fact, one of the wealthiest Mexican cities, thanks to the influx of well-heeled residents from Mexico City and the large number of international manufacturing companies who operate *maquiladoras* (factories) here to get a cheaper workforce.

Whatever its faults, Tijuana is, at least, quite unique, and you could hardly find a more intriguing day-trip out from San Diego. However, it's not typical Mexico, and if you want a proper taste of the country you'd do well to hurry on through. Things are much safer these days than was the case decades ago when Tijuana lived up to its rough border town image. Then, prostitution was rife and the streets extremely creepy after dark; these days the red-light area is limited to the easily avoided blocks around the junction of Avenida Artícula and Mutualismo. Provided you take the usual amount of care there's little danger in most parts of town.

The main streets and shopping areas are a few blocks from the border in **downtown**, where the major thoroughfare is Avenida Revolución, lined with street vendors and people trying to hustle you into the shopping emporia. Stroll up and down for a while to get the mood and then retire to one of the plentiful bars and watch the throng in the company of a sizeable margarita (in the bigger bars expect to pay $2.50 for a large one, $2 for a tequila and about $1.50 for a beer). At night, the action mostly consists of inebriated American and Mexican youths dancing themselves silly in flashy discos and rowdy rock 'n' roll bars – not hard to find around the main streets.

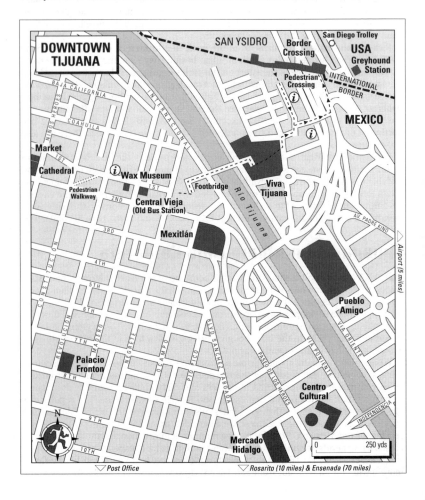

As a break from shopping or drinking, visit the **Centro Cultural**, sitting like a huge golf ball amid high-rise office towers on the corner of Paseo de los Héroes and Avenida Independencia, in the Rio Tijuana area. The museum's permanent and rotating exhibits (daily 9am–8pm; $2) give strong accounts of Mexico's history and culture; films in the Omnimax Theater ($3.50, including museum admission) focus on Mexican landscapes and cityscapes. Nearby, on Independencia at Avenida Taboada, is the **Mercado Hidalgo**, the city market, featuring everything from produce to *pinatas*.

Lesser attractions include **Mexitlán**, Avenida Ocampo between Calles 2 and 3 (Wed–Sun 9am–5pm; $2.50), a miniature Mexican theme park with models of famous Mexican buildings; a very tacky **wax museum** at Madero and First (don't waste your money); and lively *jai alai* – a Basque game similar to handball – at the Moorish-style **Palacio Fronton** on Avenida Revolucion at Calle 8 (Tues–Sat 8pm; $5).

Practicalities

Getting to Tijuana from San Diego could hardly be easier. The San Diego Trolley (see p.179) ends its route close to the elevated concrete walkway which leads over the border, as does bus #932 from the Santa Fe Depot in downtown San Diego. Mexicoach operates a bus service from the US side of the border to Avenida Revolucion in Tijuana (☎619/232-5049). Though traffic and insurance problems make public transportation a better option, if you do decide to drive, make sure you invest in auto insurance, which you can procure for a nominal fee in San Ysidro (see box overleaf).

Crossing into Mexico, **border formalities** are minimal: simply negotiate a turnstile and you're there. Customs and immigration checks are only carried out twenty miles or so inside the country, so you only need to be carrying a Mexican Tourist Card if you're continuing on from Tijuana. These are available free from any Mexican consulate in the US – see the phone book for the one nearest you – and also at the Mexican customs office just inside the Tijuana side of the border. Returning to the US, however, the formalities are as stringent as anywhere (see "Basics," p.14). Even if you've just traveled down for the day, you will need to satisfy the usual entry requirements. Dollars are accepted as readily as pesos everywhere in Tijuana, but although you can **change money** at any of the banks along Avenida Revolución or at the *casas de cambio* on both sides of the border, it's only worth doing so if you're traveling further into Mexico. That said, you'll get marginally better prices if you do pay in pesos. Bánamex and the *casas de cambio* will change travelers' checks.

Many people come to Tijuana just to experience the nightlife. *Como Que No*, Avenida Sanchez Taboada 95, (☎66/84-27-91) is a fairly sophisticated venue, where club-goers dress to impress. *Baby Rock*, Diego Rivera 1482, Zona Rio, (☎66/34-24-04) is for the younger crowd. Most discos in Tijuana enforce a no-sandals, no-jeans dress code.

If you do want to sample Tijuana's discos into the small hours and stay overnight, the **accommodation** options are fairly good, if basic. You'll spend much less here for a **hotel** room than you would north of the border, and many passable lodgings can be found close to the central streets. At the lowest end of the price scale is *Hotel Jaliscense*, Calle 1 #7925 (☎66/85-34-91; ①). Slightly more upmarket, *La Villa de Zaragoza*, Avenida Madero 1120 (☎66/85-18-37; ③), has clean rooms with air-conditioning and cable TV. Another step up is *Camino Real*, Paseo de los Heroes 10305 (☎66/33-40-01; ⑤), where the rooms are plush, and there are two restaurants and bars.

Into Mexico

As for traveling further **into Mexico**, on the whole the northwest of the country has fewer cultural attractions than the mainland, and many people head straight for Mexico City and the regions beyond. A closer option, though, is the peninsula of **Baja California**, which has miles of unspoilt coast and a few moderately sized cities. The

---

GETTING TO AND AROUND NORTHERN BAJA

Customs formalities present no problems for a quick trip to **northern Baja**: visitors to Tijuana, Rosarito and Ensenada staying for up to 72 hours need only their passports and are not required to obtain tourist cards. **Vehicle permits** are not required in Baja but most US rental agencies don't allow their vehicles into Mexico, so you'll need to approach companies such as California Baja Rent-A-Car (☎935/470-8368, 1-888/470-7368) who rent cars for use throughout Baja. With your own vehicle ensure you get **Mexican insurance**, easily obtainable from numerous companies whose fliers are all over San Ysidro: try "Instant" Mexico, 223 Via de San Ysidro (☎1-800/345-4701 or 760/428-4717). All things considered, it's probably easier to take the bus.

---

only sensible destinations within easy reach of Tijuana are **Rosarito**, *the* south-of-the-border party beach, and the sizeable town of **Ensenada**, your best introduction to more typical Mexican life. Both are briefly described below, and for full details, pick up the *Rough Guide to Mexico*, most easily available in San Diego from Le Travel Store, 745 Fourth Ave (☎760/544-0005).

Rosarito

Forty-five minutes south of Tijuana, on buses from Central Vieja bus terminal at First and Madero, the old coast road hits the sea at **ROSARITO** which boasts one of the best beaches in these parts, although the water can be polluted. It is much more restful here than in Tijuana, but at weekends it has an all-pervasive frat house atmosphere. **Surfers** are drawn here from across the boarder for the fine waves at beaches like Calafia, at Km 35.5, and Popotla, at Km 33. You can rent gear at Tony's Surf Shop, Blvd. Juarez 312. The area is also popular with **golfers**, who frequent the Real del Mar Golf Club, (☎66/31-34-01). The town's landmark is the smart and once elegant *Rosarito Beach Hotel* (☎661/2-01-44; ⑨), to which Hollywood's Prohibition refugees fled for a little of the hard stuff in the Thirties. For cheaper **accommodation**, try *Brisas del Mar* at Blvd Juarez 22 (☎661/2-25-47; ②), just across the boulevard from the ocean, with TV, air conditioning, and a pool (some rooms have hot tubs). There's no shortage of reasonable taco stands and inexpensive **restaurants**, many specializing in fish dishes: just wander along and gauge which seems currently the most popular. The weekend bonhomie is particularly frenzied at the beachside *Papas and Beer*, Blvd Juarez near the *Rosarito Beach Hotel*, a bohemia-and-beach-volleyball bar. *El Patio*, Blvd Juarez in the Festival Plaza (☎661/2-29-50), is an excellent place for a more upmarket taste of authentic Mexican food, trading in tacos for shrimp crepes in a pleasant, modern atmosphere.

Ensenada

Venturing to **ENSENADA**, two hours south from Tijuana's Central Vieja, brings a taste of the real Mexico. Cruise ships from San Diego dock here, and at weekends the bars are thronged with Americans, but otherwise Ensenada ticks by, gently milking dollars from *norteños* who have wised up to the town's superiority over Tijuana. On Avenida Mateos you'll find the majority of the bars, restaurants, souvenir shops and places organizing **fishing** trips. Drag yourself away for a little while to tour and taste the products of the Bodegas de Santo Tomás **winery** (tours Mon–Sat 11am, 1pm & 3pm, Sun 11am & 1pm; $1; ☎61/78-33-33) at Miramar 666 between Calle 6 and Calle 7. Sadly, most vintages aren't a patch on even run-of-the-mill offerings from north of the border. The restaurant in the winery is considered one of the best in Baja. *La Esquina de Bodegas*, across the street from the winery, is a pleasant café/gallery and wine-shop annex. The other famous local attraction is **La Bufadora**, a natural blowhole six miles south of Ensenada, which occasionally spouts up to eighty feet, though thirty is more common.

Buses leave roughly hourly from the Tres Cabezas park on the coast road at the bottom of Avenida Riveroll.

The pick of the **accommodation** (book at weekends) is the *San Nicolas*, Mateos at Guadalupe (☎61/76-19-01; ④); *Hotel del Valle*, Avenida Riveroll 367, (☎61/78-22-24; ①–②), is a good budget option, offering clean rooms with fans, TV, and phones. Be sure to ask for a rate discount. For **eating**, *Hussongs Cantina*, Ruiz 113 – famous throughout Southern California – has managed to maintain its rambunctious reputation and heaves at weekends. Soak up the beer with fish tacos from the **fish market** by the harbor, or the straightforward Mexican dishes at *El Charro*, Mateos 475.

travel details

Trains

San Diego to: Anaheim (10 daily; 2hr); Los Angeles downtown (11 daily; 2hr 45min to 3 hr 20min); Oceanside (11 daily; 45min to 1hr; San Juan Capistrano (11 daily; 1hr 15min to 2hr); Solana Beach (nr Del Mar; 11 daily; 30–40 min). For more information, call Amtrak (☎1-800/872-7245).

Buses

San Diego downtown to: Anaheim (10 daily; 2hr 30min); Long Beach (7 daily; 2hr 30min); Los Angeles downtown (32 daily; 2hr); Oceanside (16 daily; 55min); San Clemente (7 daily; 1hr 30min). For more information, call Greyhound (☎1-800/231-2222)

San Diego, Grossmont Center to: Cuyamaca (6 monthly; 2hr 30min); Julian (1 daily; 2hr); Ramona (1 daily; 45min); Santa Ysabel (1 daily; 1hr 30min). For more information, call the Northeast Rural Bus System (☎760-767-4287)

International buses

San Diego to: Tijuana (21 daily; 50min).

CHAPTER THREE

THE DESERTS, LAS VEGAS AND THE GRAND CANYON

The deserts of Southern California represent only a fraction of the half a million square miles of North American Desert that stretch away eastward into another four states and cross the border into Mexico in the south. Contrary to the monotonous landscape you might expect, California's deserts are a varied and ever-changing kaleidoscope, dotted with everything from harsh settlements to posh resorts. The one thing you can rely on is that, for a large part of the year, they will be uniformly hot and dry. In fact, during the hottest summer months temperatures in the deserts can reach such dangerous heights that you'd be well advised to give them a miss altogether. And don't count on rain to cool things off – desert rainfall is highly irregular and a whole year's average of three or four inches may fall in a single storm.

Most of the 25 million acres that make up the desert are protected in state and national parks, but not all are entirely unspoiled. Three million acres are used by the US Government as military bases for training and weapons testing, and when explosions aren't shaking up the desert's fragile ecosystem, the region's many fans flock here to do their own damage.

In spite of this, most of the desert remains a wilderness, and with a little foresight could be the undisputed highlight of your trip. Occupying a quarter of the state, California's desert divides into two distinct regions: the **Colorado** or **Low Desert** in the south, stretching down to the Mexican border and east into Arizona where it's an extension of the Sonoran Desert, and the **Mojave** or **High Desert**, which covers the south-central part of the state. The Low Desert is the most easily reached from LA, with the extravagantly wealthy **Palm Springs** serving as an access point – though, pulling in the likes of Donald Trump for events like the Bob Hope Chrysler Classic Golf

---

ACCOMMODATION PRICE CODES

All accommodation prices in this book have been coded using the symbols below; prices are for the least expensive **double rooms** in each establishment. For a full explanation see p.36 in "Basics." Individual rates rather than price codes are given for **hostels** and whole **apartments**.

① up to $30	④ $60–80	⑦ $130–175
② $30–45	⑤ $80–100	⑧ $175–250
③ $45–60	⑥ $100–130	⑨ $250+

Tournament, it's the kind of town where it helps to have a bankroll for optimum enjoyment. The hiking trails around **Joshua Tree** are the big attraction for serious desert people, bridging the divide between Low and High Desert in a vast silent area of craggy trees. In contrast, **Imperial Valley** to the south – agricultural land, though you could pass through without realizing anyone lived there – and the **Salton Sea** beyond, are undiluted Low Desert. There's no reason to visit them except that they lead into the vast expanse of the **Anza-Borrego Desert**, the largest state park in the country, boasting multifarious varieties of vegetation and geological quirks which can, with a little effort, be as rewarding as the better-known deserts to the north.

Interstate 10 crosses the Low Desert from east to west and carries a considerable flow of traffic. This includes packs of bikers heading out for a long weekend ride and some high jinks in the popular gambling resorts, like **Lake Havasu City**, that dot the stunning **Colorado River** region on the California/Arizona border. I-15 cuts north from I-40 at **Barstow**, often a first stop for those heading into the High Desert, where the **Mojave National Preserve** makes a worthwhile natural detour en route to the unnatural neon oasis of **Las Vegas**, just across the border in Nevada, where gambling is legal. Once you've got that far, a day's drive east (or a thirty-minute flight) takes you to the magnificent **Grand Canyon** in Arizona. Afterwards you can loop back into California by way of Death Valley, part of the desert region but covered in Chapter Four.

Desert practicalities

Public transportation in the desert is poor to nonexistent: Los Angeles connects easily with the major points – Palm Springs, Barstow, Las Vegas – and the Anza-Borrego is

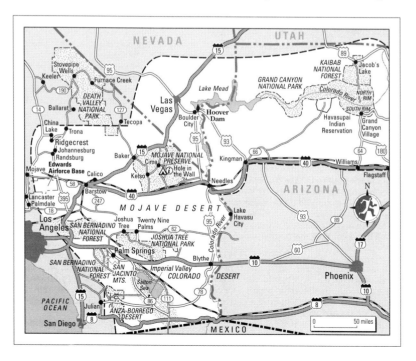

DESERT SURVIVAL

To survive the rigors of the desert, you have to be cool in more ways than one. Don't let adventure get the better of you and go charging off into the wilderness without heeding the warnings. The desert is rarely conquered by a pioneering spirit alone, and every year people die here. **Hikers** are particularly vulnerable, especially those who venture beyond the designated areas of the National Parks, but **drivers** too should not be blasé and should take considerable precautions whatever their destination. On the highways, extra water and as full a tank of gas as possible should be all the precautions you need, but anything more adventurous requires planning. Above all, think. Tell somebody where you are going, and your expected time of return. Carry an extra two days' **food** and **water** and never go anywhere without a **map**. Only the well prepared can enjoy the desert with any sense of security.

Bear in mind too that while the desert may be a danger to man, man is also a danger to the desert. These days, smog from Los Angeles drifts quickly eastward, and you may notice patches of it obscuring the panoramic view of the desert. Remember, use common sense: remove nothing from the land except your trash, and leave only footprints behind.

CLIMATE AND WATER

First and most obviously you're up against a pretty formidable **climate**. This varies from region to region, but the basic safety procedures remain the same: not only are you doing battle with incredible heat, but at high elevations at night you should be prepared for below-freezing temperatures too. Between May and September, when daytime temperatures frequently exceed 120°F, you really shouldn't come at all (although, of course, people do).

Outside of the summer months, the daytime temperatures are more manageable, ranging between the mid-sixties and low nineties. At any time of year, you'll stay cooler during the day if you wear full-length sleeves and trousers, though you'll look incongruous among the bare legs and torsos. Also, a wide-brimmed hat and a pair of good sunglasses will spare you the blinding headaches that can result from the desert light. And, of course, copious amounts of sunscreen should be used.

You can never drink enough **liquid** in the desert: the body loses up to a gallon each day and even when you're not thirsty you are continually dehydrating and should keep drinking. Before setting off on any expedition, whether on foot or in a car, two gallons of water per person should be prepared; one is an absolute minimum, and don't save it for the walk back, drink it as you need it. Waiting for thirst, dizziness, nausea or other signs of dehydration before doing anything can be dangerous. If you notice any of these symptoms, or feel weak and have stopped sweating, it's time to get to the doctor. Watch your alcohol intake too: if you must booze during the day, compensate heavily with pints of water between each drink. Any activity in this heat can be exhausting so you also need to **eat** well, packing in the carbohydrates.

Campers need to take particular heed of these warnings, especially if backpacking away from the main roads. In summer, ventures of more than one night are all but impossible as you end up having to carry more water than is comfortable. In the valleys, you may also have to contend with **flash floods**, which can appear from nowhere: an innocent-looking dark cloud can turn a dry wash into a raging river. Never camp in a dry wash and don't attempt to cross flooded areas until the water has receded.

ROADS: ON WHEELS AND ON FOOT

Roads and **highways** across much of the desert are not maintained, and in an area where it's often a challenge to make it across existing dirt roads, trailblazing your own path through the desert is insanity. Of course you'll be tempted – if you must, rent a dune buggy or four-wheel drive and tear about one of the off-road driving areas specifically designated for this purpose.

Even sticking to the main highways, you stand a good chance of getting an **overheated engine**. If your car's temperature needle rises alarmingly – most likely when negotiating steep gradients – turn the air-conditioning off and the heater on full-blast to cool the engine quickly. If this fails and the engine blows, stop with the car facing into the wind and the engine running, pour water over the radiator grille and top up the water reservoir. In an **emergency**, never leave the car: you'll be harder to find wandering around alone.

Among other things you might consider taking along, an **emergency pack** with flares, a first aid and **snakebite kit** (see below), matches and a compass, a shovel, a tire pump and extra gas are always a good idea. A few white towels to drape over the dashboard, steering wheel and back ledge will save you a lot of discomfort when you get back in your car after leaving it parked for a few hours.

When **hiking**, try and cover most of your ground in the early morning: the midday heat is too debilitating, and you shouldn't even think about it when the mercury goes over 90°F. Almost all parks will require you to register with them – this is very wise, especially for those who are hiking alone. If you get lost, find some shade and wait. So long as you've registered, the rangers will eventually come and fetch you. However, they'll have a lot of trouble if you've fallen down an old mine shaft, so watch your footing and keep your eyes peeled for unexploded artillery.

DESERT WILDLIFE

Most people's biggest fear of the desert is of encountering **poisonous creatures**. If you do, you'll be far better served by strong boots and long trousers than sport sandals and shorts. Not only do they offer some protection in case of attack, but firm footfalls send vibrations through the ground giving ample warning of your approach. Walk heavily and you're unlikely to see anything you don't want to.

Of all the **snakes** in the California desert, only the rattlesnake is poisonous. You might not be able to tell a rattler from any other kind of snake; in fact many rattlers don't rattle at all. If in doubt, assume it is one. When it's hot, snakes lurk in shaded areas under bushes, around wood debris, old mining shafts and piles of rocks. When it's cooler, they sun themselves out in the open, but they won't be expecting you and if disturbed will attack. While **black widow spiders** and **scorpions** are non-aggressive, they are extremely venomous and easily disturbed. A bite from any of the above is initially like a sharp pinprick, but within hours the pain becomes severe, usually accompanied by swelling and acute nausea. Forget any misconceptions you may harbor about sucking the poison out; it doesn't work and even tends to hasten the spread of venom. Since venom travels mainly through the lymph system just under the skin, the best way of inhibiting the diffusion is to wrap the whole limb firmly, but not in a tourniquet, then contact a ranger or doctor as soon as possible. Do all you can to keep calm – a slower pulse rate limits the spread of the venom. Keep in mind that even if a snake does bite you, about fifty percent of the time it's a dry – or non-venomous – strike. Snakes don't want to waste their venom on something too large to eat. However, it's a wise precaution to carry a **snakebite kit**, available for a couple of dollars from most sports and camping stores.

Tarantulas are not at all dangerous. A leg span of up to seven inches means they're pretty easy to spot, but if you're unlucky and get bitten don't panic – cleansing with antiseptic is usually sufficient treatment once you've gotten over the initial pain.

Nasty critters aren't the only things to avoid. Most **cactuses** present few problems, but you should keep an eye out for the eight-foot *cholla* (pronounced "choya"), or jumping *cholla* as they're called because of the way segments seem to jump off and attach themselves to you if you brush past. Don't use your hands to get them off, you'll just spear all your fingers; instead use a stick or comb to flick off the largest piece and remove the remaining spines with tweezers. The large pancake pads of prickly pear cactus are also worth avoiding: as well as the larger spines they have thousands of tiny, hair-like stickers that are almost impossible to remove. You should expect a day of painful irritation before they begin to wear away. For more on the delights of desert flora and fauna, see "Contexts," p.657.

an easy trip from San Diego, but on arrival you're stuck without your own vehicle. If you do have a car, it will need to be in very good working order – don't rely on the Thunderbird you picked up in LA for $250 to get you through the worst of the desert. Three major Interstate highways cross the desert from east to west. I-15 cuts directly through the middle of the Mojave on its way from Los Angeles to Las Vegas, joined at Barstow by I-40, which then heads eastwards to the Grand Canyon. I-10 takes you from LA through the Palm Springs and Joshua Tree area, heading into Arizona. Some fast, empty secondary roads can get you safely to all but the most remote areas of the desert, but be wary of using the lower-grade roads in between, which are likely to be unmaintained and are often only passable by four-wheel drive. Other than in the Palm Springs area, **motels** in the California deserts are low in price, and you can generally budget for under $40 per night. However, even if cost is no object, you'll get a greatly heightened sense of the desert experience by spending some time **camping** out.

THE LOW DESERT

Despite the **Low Desert**'s hundreds of miles of beauty and empty highways, most visitors to the region have no intention of getting away from it all. They're heading for where it's at, **Palm Springs**, a few square miles overrun with the famous, the starstruck, the aging and the aspirational. It is said, not completely in jest, that the average age and average temperature of Palm Springs are about the same – a steady 88. This is a town that fines homeowners who don't maintain their property to what local officials deem to be a suitable standard. But it's got a prime location, and you'll find it hard to avoid: it's the first stopping point east from LA on I-10, and hub of a resort area – the **Coachella Valley** – that stretches out for miles around, along Hwy-111. The valley's farming communities have the distinction of forming part of the most productive irrigated agricultural center in the world, growing dates, oranges, lemons and grapefruit in vast quantities, though sadly they're steadily giving way to the condos and complexes that comprise Palm Springs' ever-growing industry.

Fortunately you don't have to travel impossible distances to see the desert at its natural best. **Joshua Tree**, one of the most startling of California's National Parks, lies less than one hour's drive east of Palm Springs, three from LA. A day-trip in a fast car would give you a taste, but you really need a couple of days to get to grips with Joshua Tree's sublime landscape, taking in the sunsets and the howl of coyotes at twilight. The desert east of the park, to the Colorado River and Nevada, and south to the Mexican border, is arid and uncomfortable, with only the highly saline **Salton Sea** to break the monotony. A drive in this direction is rewarded, however, by the **Anza-Borrego desert**, southwest of Joshua Tree, whose starkly beautiful vistas are punctuated by several oases and unusual vegetation.

Palm Springs and around

With its manicured golf courses, condominium complexes and some seven hundred millionaires in residence, **PALM SPRINGS** does not conform to any typical image of the desert. Purpose-built for luxury and leisure, it tends to attract conspicuous consumers and comfort seekers rather than the scruffier desert rats and low-rent retirees of less geographically desirable areas. But though it may seem harder to find the natural attractions and reasonably priced essentials among the glitz, they do exist.

Palm Springs and its adjacent resort towns sit in the lushest agricultural area of the Colorado Desert, with the massive bulk of the San Jacintos and neighboring mountain

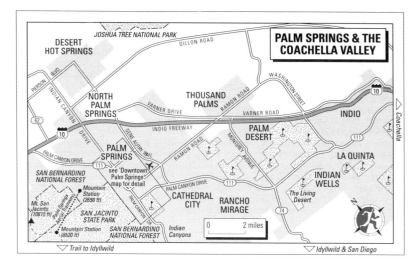

ranges looming over its low-level buildings, casting an instantaneous and welcome shadow over the area in the late afternoon. Since Hollywood stars were spotted enjoying a bit of mineral rejuvenation out here in the 1930s, it has taken on a celebrity status all its own, a symbol of good LA living away from the amorphous, smoggy city. In recent years it has also become a major **gay** resort, with many exclusively gay – and generally expensive – hotels, bars and restaurants. Every Easter weekend twenty thousand gay men flock here for the "White Party," four days of hedonism centered on the *Wyndham* and *Marquis* hotels in downtown Palm Springs. **Lesbians** get their turn a couple of weeks earlier during the Nabisco Dinah Shore women's golf tournament.

For years, high-school kids arrived in the thousands, too, for the drunken revelry of Spring Break (around the end of March and beginning of April). Local antipathy finally persuaded the city council, under the leadership of the late Sonny Bono, to ban the annual invasion in 1993, and the inebriated youth promptly decamped east to Lake Havasu City (see p.247). The alcoholically inclined still flock to Palm Springs, but not to get drunk: the **Betty Ford Center**, smack in the middle of the valley at Rancho Mirage, draws a star-studded patient list to its booze- and drug-free environment, attempting to undo a lifetime's behavioral disorders in an $11,000 month-long stay.

The town's setting is superb, surrounded by the beautiful Indian Canyons with the snowcapped mountains behind. Meteorologists have noted changes in the humidity of the desert climate around the town which they attribute to the moisture absorbed from the hundreds of swimming pools – the consummate condo accoutrement, and the only place you're likely to want to be during the day if you come in the hotter months. When scarce water supplies aren't being used to fill the pools or nourish the nearby orchards, each of Palm Springs' vast golf-course complexes receives around a million gallons daily to maintain their rolling green pastures.

Palm Springs wasn't always like this. Before the wealthy settlers moved in it was the domain of the **Cahuilla**, who lived and hunted around the San Jacinto Mountains, to escape the heat of the desert floor. They still own much of the town, and via an odd checkerboard system of land allotment, every other square mile of Palm Springs is theirs and forms part of the **Agua Caliente Indian Reservation** – a Spanish name which means "hot water," referring to the ancient mineral springs on which the city

THE WINDMILLS OF PALM SPRINGS

After trawling through the dull eastern suburbs of Los Angeles, I-10 throws you a surprise at the San Gorgonio Pass just before Palm Springs. Over four thousand **wind turbines** dot the valley, their glinting steel arms sending shimmering patterns across the desert floor. This is the largest concentration of windmills in the country, generating enough electricity to service a small city, and the conditions are perfect. The sun beating down on the desert creates a low-pressure zone that sucks air up from the cooler coastal valleys, funnelling it through the San Gorgonio Pass, the only break between two 10,000-foot-plus ranges of mountains. Strong winds often howl for days in spring and early summer, reaching an average speed of between fourteen and twenty miles per hour. You'll learn more than you ever wanted to know about these structures and about alternative energy in general if you book one of the surprisingly interesting ninety-minute **Windmill Tours** (☎760/251-1997; $20), conducted via wind-powered golf cart. Even if you don't do the tour, stop in at the **windfarm visitors center** (8:30am–4:30pm; get off I-10 at the Indian Ave exit; it's on the north frontage road, one mile west of Indian Road) to see all kinds of unusual electric vehicles, and informative films on windmills.

rests. The land was allocated to the tribe in the 1890s, but exact zoning was never settled until the 1940s, by which time the development of hotels and leisure complexes was well under way. The Cahuilla, finding their land built upon, were left with no option but to charge rent, a system that has made them the second richest of the native tribes in America – and the money continues to pour in, thanks in part to revenue from their new **spa** and **casino**.

Arrival, information and getting around

Palm Springs lies 110 miles east of Los Angeles along the Hwy-111 turn-off from I-10. Arriving by **car**, you drive into town on N Palm Canyon Drive (Hwy-111), the main thoroughfare. Coming by **bus**, you'll arrive at the Greyhound terminus at 311 N Indian Canyon Drive, linked with LA ten times daily – a three-hour journey. **Trains** from LA stop in Indio (at Jackson and Railroad Avenue) and Palm Springs (N Indian Avenue, just south of I-10) on Tuesday, Friday and Sunday, unfortunately in the middle of the night. You can also **fly**, but this can be expensive – you'll land at the Palm Springs Regional Airport, 3400 E Tahquitz-McCallum Way (☎760/323-8161), from where you take bus #21 into town.

The very helpful **visitor center**, 2781 N Palm Canyon Drive (daily 9am–5pm; ☎1-800/347-7746 or 760/778-8418), can offer accommodation deals and has an exhaustive selection of maps – including one that details the homes of the famous ($5) – and brochures, plus various "what's on" guides.

Travel to the resorts around Palm Springs – **Cathedral City, Desert Hot Springs, Rancho Mirage, Palm Desert, Indio, Indian Wells, La Quinta** – is possible with the Sun Bus (☎760/343-3451), which operates daily from 6am to 8pm (until 11pm on some routes) and charges 75¢ to get around town, plus an extra 25¢ for two transfers (good for two hours after purchase); a day pass costs $3. It's unlikely that you'll need to use the bus to get around Palm Springs itself: downtown is no more than several blocks long and wide, and except in the summer heat, walking is easy. For a **taxi**, call Yellow Cab of the Desert (☎760/345-8398).To get the absolute best out of Palm Springs and the surrounding towns though, you might think about **car rental**. Aztec Rent-A-Car, 477 S Palm Canyon Drive (☎760/325-2294), has cars for as little as $30 per day, while Foxy Wheels, 440 S El Cielo Rd (☎760/321-1234), also has good deals.

CENTRAL PALM SPRINGS

LITTLE TUSCANY

Palm Springs Aerial Tramway

Palm Springs Visitor Center

O'Donnell Golf Course

Palm Springs Desert Museum

Greyhound Station

Spa Hotel, Casino & Mineral Springs

Palm Springs Swim Center

Palm Springs Regional Airport

Moorten's Botanical Gardens

Canyon Golf Club

Oasis Water Park

14 & Cathedral City

Indian Canyons

ACCOMMODATION

Bee Charmer Inn	11
Budget Host Inn	9
Casa Cody	5
Desert Lodge	8
Hampton Inn	2
Ingleside Inn	6
Mira Loma	3
Motel 6	7
Palm Court Inn	1
Quality Inn	13
Vagabond Inn	12
The Villa Hotel	14
Villa Royale	10
The Willows	4

Streets: SAN RAFAEL, FRANCIS DRIVE, VERONA, RACQUET CLUB ROAD, NORTH PALM CANYON DRIVE, 111, INDIAN CANYON DRIVE, AVENIDA CABALLEROS, SUNRISE WAY, FARRELL DRIVE, VISTA CHINO, WEST VEREDA SUR, TACHEVAH ROAD, TAMARISK ROAD, PALM CANYON DRIVE, ALEJO ROAD, AMADO ROAD, CALLE EL SEGUNDO, CALLE ENCILIA, TAHQUITZ CANYON WAY, BARISTO ROAD, SOUTH CAHUILLA RD, RAMON RD, WARM SANDS DRIVE, GRENFALL ROAD, SUNNY DUNES ROAD, MESQUITE AVENUE, EL CIELO, SOUTH INDIAN TRAIL, SONORA ROAD, EAST PALM CANYON DRIVE, SOUTH PALM CANYON DRIVE, LAVERNE WAY, TOLEDO AVENUE, MURRAY CANYON DRIVE

0 — 1 mile

N

Accommodation

Palm Springs was designed for the rich, and big luxury **resorts** are abundant here and in most of the Coachella Valley's other towns. If you want to take a shot at seeing how the other half lives, consider visiting in summer when temperatures rise and prices drop dramatically. Many of the bigger hotels slash their prices by up to seventy percent, and even the smaller concerns give twenty to thirty percent off. The visitor center (see above) also offers special deals. If you couldn't care less about cachet, Motel 6 and other **low-priced chains** are still represented.

The north end of town along Hwy-111 holds the most affordable places, in the main perfectly acceptable and all with pools. **Bed and breakfast** inns are becoming more common, and with double room rates at around $80 per night they are a good bargain when you add up comfort, hospitality, and a nice breakfast. If you're traveling in a group, it may work out cheaper to rent an **apartment**: many of the homes in Palm Springs are used only for a brief spell and are let out for the rest of the year. Again summer is the best time to look, but there is generally a good supply throughout the year. The Coachella Valley's daily paper, the *Desert Sun*, has rental information in its classified pages, and many rental agencies operate around town – the visitor center will be able to point you to the more affordable ones. **Camping** is not really a viable option, unless you have an RV; the only campground accommodating tents is *Lake Cahuilla* (☎1-800/234-PARK or 760/564-4712; $12). In La Quinta, some six miles east of central Palm Springs, the campground also has 18 corrals where horses stay for free, a fishing lake, and 70 RV sites. Otherwise, tent-carriers will have a better time exploring Joshua Tree or Anza-Borrego.

Listed below are some of the more reasonable and/or interesting options, with summer rates quoted; in the popular October to April period, when you should also book in advance, you can expect the rates to be hiked up by a price bracket – or two or three. Also keep in mind that weekend prices are also a price bracket or two higher than weeknights. Always ask for a discount wherever you stay; the visitor center may also be helpful in this matter. Some historical quirk of snobbery on the part of the city council dictates that accommodation can't be referred to as a motel, though some of the places listed obviously are.

Palm Springs now claims to have overtaken Key West as America's largest gay resort and has around 35 exclusively **gay hotels**, most of them in the Warm Sands district, half a mile southwest of downtown. However, such is the power of the pink dollar in Palm Springs that virtually all hotels here are gay-friendly.

Hotels, motels and B&Bs

Budget Host Inn, 1277 S Palm Canyon Drive (☎1-800/829-8099 or 760/325-5574). One of the budget options in town with clean, pleasant rooms, cable and a pool. ③.

Casa Cody, 175 S Cahuilla Rd (☎1-800/231-2639 or 760/320-9346). Built in the 1920s by glamorous Hollywood pioneer Harriet Cody, this historic B&B offers tastefully furnished Southwestern-style rooms, a shady garden, great pool and wonderful breakfasts in a good location two blocks from downtown. Large kitchen suites also available. ③.

Desert Lodge, 1177 S Palm Canyon Drive (☎1-800/385-6343 or 760/325-1356). Spacious motel-style place with free continental breakfast and in-room movies. Closed July and August. ③.

Hampton Inn, 2000 N Palm Canyon Drive (☎760/320-0555). Comfortable hotel with a beautiful outdoor pool – a must in the desert – plus continental breakfast. ③.

Ingleside Inn, 200 W Ramon Rd (☎1-800/772-6655 or ☎760/325-0046). Expensive, but with real class, having attracted such guests as Garbo, Dali and Brando over the years. Built on a private estate downtown, each room has a personal steam bath and individual whirlpool. The restaurant still lures the glitterati. ⑤.

Mira Loma, 1420 N Indian Canyon Drive (☎760/320-1178). Small, welcoming hotel with well-appointed rooms around a central pool where breakfast is served at weekends. In 1949 Marilyn Monroe stayed in Room 3 while awaiting her big break. ②.

Motel 6, 660 S Palm Canyon Drive (☎760/327-4200). The most central of the budget motels, with a good pool. ②.

Palm Court Inn, 1983 N Palm Canyon Drive (☎1-800/667-7918 or 760/416-2333). On four nicely landscaped acres, so it doesn't feel like a faceless motel. There's a jacuzzi as well as two pools and a fitness center, and continental breakfast is included in the room rate. ②.

Quality Inn, 1269 E Palm Canyon Drive (☎1-800/472-4339 or 760/323-2775). Modern motel with spacious grounds and restaurant. ③.

The Willows, 412 W Tahquitz Canyon (☎760/320-0771). The former estate of a US Secretary of State whose friends – among them Clark Gable, Carole Lombard and Albert Einstein – holed up here during the 1930s. Opulently decorated rooms, gorgeous lush grounds, a stunning San Jacinto Mountain backdrop and an ideal downtown location make this worth the splurge. ⑧.

Vagabond Inn, 1699 S Palm Canyon Drive (☎1-800/522-1555 or 760/325-7211). Well-run three-story motel halfway between downtown Palm Springs and Cathedral City with its own reasonably priced coffee shop. Coffee makers in each room and refrigerators available. ④.

Villa Royale, 1620 S Indian Trail (☎1-800/245-2314 or 760/327-2314). Beautiful inn with individually designed and exquisitely furnished rooms and suites, most with jacuzzi, situated around a pool. In the winter season meals and drinks are served from the bougainvillea-draped restaurant. ⑤.

Exclusively gay accommodation

Bee Charmer Inn, 1600 E Palm Canyon Drive (☎760/778-5883). Comfortable lesbian motel a mile or so south of downtown, offering continental breakfast and pool. ④.

The Villa Hotel, 67-670 Carey Rd, Cathedral City (☎1-800/845-5265 or 760/328-7211). The area's largest gay resort, attracting an older, less party-oriented crowd. Rooms are spacious. ③.

Palm Springs

Downtown Palm Springs stretches for about half a mile along Palm Canyon Drive, a wide, bright and modern strip full of boutiques and restaurants that's engulfed the town's original Spanish-village-style structures. Shops run the gamut from Saks Fifth Avenue to schlocky T-shirt emporia and bookstores devoted exclusively to Hollywood stars. Ditto restaurants, which range from casual sports bars to overdressed Continental eateries with jacked-up prices. Should your budget not run to the conventional extravagance of a luxury stay in Palm Springs, there are a handful of things to do that won't break the bank. The concentration of wealth in Palm Springs has fostered a disproportionate number of **art galleries**, not all of them good, along and around Palm Canyon Drive. The attractive **Palm Springs Desert Museum**, 101 Museum Drive (Tues–Sat 10am–5pm, Sun noon–5pm; $7.50; *www.psmuseum.org*), is a part-art, part-natural history collection that's especially strong on Native American and Southwestern art – its holdings are so large, in fact, that despite the enormous exhibition space, only a small part can be shown at any given time. The only permanent display is the late actor William Holden's collection of Asian and African art. The natural science exhibits focus on the variety of animal and plant life in the desert, proving that it's not all sandstorms and rattlesnakes. Also inside the museum, the Annenberg Theater has a seasonal program of shows, films and classical concerts (10am–4pm; ☎760/325-4490).

Downtown's most anarchic piece of landscape gardening can be seen at **Moorten Botanical Garden**, 1701 S Palm Canyon Drive (Mon–Sat 9am–4.30pm, Sun 10am–4pm; $2), a bizarre cornucopia of every desert plant and cactus, lumped together in no particular order, but interesting for those who won't be venturing beyond town to see them in their natural habitat.

Knowing that they're in the thick of a megastar refugee camp, few can resist the opportunity to see the homes and country clubs of the international elite on a **celebrity tour**. As tacky as they are, these tours have some voyeuristic appeal, allowing you to spy on places like Bob Hope's enormous house, and the star-studded area known as **Little Tuscany** – Palm Spring's prettiest quarter, where the famous keep their weekend homes. The best part of the tour is not the houses, but the fascinating trivia about the lives of those who live in them. Several companies offer these excursions, the best of them being Palm Springs Celebrity Tours, 4751 E Palm Canyon Drive (☎760/770-2700), which conducts one-hour jaunts for $15 and longer excursions around the country clubs and the Sinatra estate (where Frank used to bring Ava Gardner) for $20. Of course if you've got a car, you can do it yourself with a $5 map of the stars' homes from the visitor center (see p.222), but you'll miss the sharp anecdotal commentary that makes it such fun.

One reason people come here is to enjoy the Californian obsession with all things physical, and get fit. The **mineral spring** that the Cahuilla discovered on the desert floor over a century ago has grown into the elaborate *Spa Hotel and Mineral Springs* complex, 100 N Indian Canyon Drive (daily 8am–7pm; ☎1-800/854-1279 or 760/325-1461, *www.spahotelandcasino.com*). The "basic spa experience" is $28.75, an all-day pass that includes use of the pool and eucalyptus room, although you're encouraged to spend a lot more at the on-site casino. Just as therapeutic is a swim in the **Olympic-sized pool** in the Palm Springs Swim Center, Sunrise Way at Ramon Road (Mon, Wed, Fri 11am–5pm, all other days 11am–3pm, open later in summer; $3; ☎760/323-8278), a good alternative to the often crowded, and generally small hotel pools. Lots more water gets used up at the 22-acre playground **Oasis Waterpark**, at 1500 Gene Autry Trail between Ramon Road and E Palm Canyon Drive (daily 11am till dusk March 5–Labor Day; 11am till dusk weekends through Oct 24; ☎1-800/247-4664 or 760/327-0499) where, for $18.95 for adults, $11.95 for children, you can surf on its one-acre wavepool and mess around on its thirteen waterslides. For a seriously relaxing experience, check out one of Palm Springs' *day spas*. *The Guest House*, 246 N Palm Canyon Drive (☎760/320-3366, *www.tropicalspa.com*) offers everything from reflexology massages ($30) to the "Twin Palms Salt Glow" ($70), where two masseuses pummel and soothe you simultaneously.

Hard-core desert enthusiasts visit Palm Springs for the **hiking** and **riding** opportunities in the **Indian Canyons** (daily year-round 8am–5pm, summer schedule varies; ☎760/325-5673; $6) on part of the Agua Caliente Indian Reservation that lies to the east of downtown. Centuries ago, ancestors of the Cahuilla tribe settled in the canyons and developed extensive communities, made possible by the good water supply and animal stock. Crops of melons, squash, beans and corn were grown, animals hunted and plants and seeds gathered for food and medicines. Evidence of this remains, and despite the near extinction of some breeds, mountain sheep and wild ponies still roam the remoter areas. To reach the best of them, follow S Palm Canyon Drive about three miles southeast to the clearly sign-posted entrance. Of the three canyons here, **Palm Canyon** and **Andreas Canyon** are very beautiful and have the easiest hiking trails. About fifteen miles long, they're surprisingly lush oases of waterfalls, rocky gorges and palm trees, easily toured by car, although to appreciate them at their best, you should get out and walk for at least a few miles. A tiny trading post at Palm Canyon sells hiking maps, refreshments and even raccoon hats. To indulge in real Wild West fantasy you should see things on **horseback**. The Smoke Tree Stables, 2500 Toledo Ave (☎760/327-1372), offer scheduled one- and two-hour riding tours of the Canyons at $30 per hour, $55 for two hours – well worth it, especially if you go early morning (tours start from 7am) to escape the midday heat. Longer rides are available by advance arrangement.

Sections of the canyons and surrounding land are set aside for the specific lunacy of **trailblazing** in jeeps and four-wheel drives. If you're a good, experienced driver with nerves of steel (or know one), you should rent your own from OffRoad Rentals, 59755 Hwy-111 (Sept–June only; ☎760/325-0376; $30 per hour, including instruction and safety equipment), about four miles north of the Palm Springs tram. For those who can't face the driving and want to learn something about the area while zooming through it, the **guided jeep adventure** is probably nearer the mark: Desert Adventures, 67-555 E Palm Canyon Drive, Cathedral City (☎760/324-JEEP), offers excellent tours of the Santa Rosa mountains for $70 for three hours in the morning, $99 for three hours in the afternoon, or $129 for four hours anytime. One of the most popular tours takes you across the desert floor and two thousand feet up through bighorn sheep preserves, spectacular cliffs and steep-walled canyons. It's a bit expensive, but brilliant fun for the fearless.

The other Coachella Valley cities

Many visitors to the area think of the Coachella Valley towns strung along Hwy-111 as a single sprawling resort named Palm Springs. The towns are initially somewhat hard to distinguish from each other – not all the boundaries between them are clearly marked, and on their main drags they tend to share faceless low-slung architecture – but differences become evident to those who have time to explore.

About twelve miles north of Palm Springs – the only one of the towns that's on the other side of I-10, separated by a fault line – the city of **DESERT HOT SPRINGS** was chosen in a national competition as having the best-tasting water in the country. The underground wells for which the town is named supply water for the multitude of swimming pools as well as for drinking. A good jumping-off point for Joshua Tree, it's somewhat more casual than the other communities. One exception to this is **Two Bunch Palms** (☎1-800/472-4334, *www.twobunchpalms.com*; ⑦–⑨), a luxury resort nestled in between trailer parks and a favorite of celebrities from Los Angeles. Normal people are also welcome if they can pay the price – spa treatments run about $80 per hour. But spending your days soaking in the hot-springs pool with a book and a cocktail, with intermittent breaks for mud baths and massages, is not a bad way to pass the time.

Adjacent to Palm Springs, about five miles east along Hwy-111, is **Cathedral City** ("Cat City"), named for soaring rock formations that are now, sadly, obscured by development. The town has recently added an **IMAX theater**, 68510 East Palm Canyon Drive (☎760/324-7333), and a large **sports park**, 33700 Date Palm Dr (☎760/324-5600), complete with three stadiums. For more information, head for the **visitor center**, 68845 Perez Rd #6 (☎760/328-1213). Alternatively, the IMAX theater lobby also has a visitor information center. Although it's fairly family-oriented during the day, it comes out at night with a **gay scene** that's second only to the one in Palm Springs itself.

Next in line, the generally more staid **RANCHO MIRAGE** tends to attract dignitaries – and high-profile substance abusers. Home to former President Gerald Ford and his wife, it's also host to the latter's upscale drunk tank, the **Betty Ford Center**.

PALM DESERT, directly east along Hwy-111, is the safest place to witness the animal life that flourishes despite the inhospitable climate. Here, the **Living Desert**, 47-900 Portola Ave (☎760/346-5694; daily Sept–June 9am–5pm, July–Aug 8am-2pm; $6.50), is home to coyotes, foxes, bighorn sheep, snakes, gazelles and eagles, on view around a series of trails that cover the 1200-acre park. There's also a **botanical garden**, but this is only worth a look in spring when the desert is in bloom. You can glimpse a different species of local creature on **El Paseo**, the Rodeo Drive of the desert, a long strip of **trendy restaurants** and **shops** looping south of Hwy-111. And come November, the non-indigenous but increasingly populous species *homo golfus* turns out en masse for the nation's only **golf cart parade**.

Adjacent **INDIAN WELLS** has the largest per capita income in the US, as well as the largest concentration of the Coachella Valley's grand **resorts**. It's known for its four-day New Year **Jazz Festival**, its high profile **tennis tournaments**, and its prestigious Desert Town Hall **lecture series**, four or five talks that run into spring. Recent speakers include Newt Gingrich, Andrea Mitchell, and Jean Michel Cousteau.

THE AERIAL TRAMWAY

When the desert heat becomes simply too much to bear, you can travel through five climatic zones from the arid desert floor to snow-covered alpine hiking trails on top of Mount San Jacinto on the **Palm Springs Aerial Tramway** on Tramway Drive, just off Hwy-111 north of Palm Springs (Mon–Fri 10am–8pm, Sat & Sun 8am–8pm; $17.65, $21.65 with dinner; ☎1-888/515-TRAM or 760/325-1391, *www.pstramway.com*). Every thirty minutes large cable cars grind and sway over nearly six thousand feet to the Mountain Station near the 10,815ft summit. Literally breathtaking, it's well worth the nerve-wracking fourteen-minute ascent for both the view, some 75 miles all the way to the Salton Sea, and the welcome change from the blistering heat to temperatures that drop an average of 30°F. Cinder trails stretch for a couple of miles around, leading into the 13,000-acre Mount San Jacinto Park, a wilderness area through which, in a few hours, you can reach Idyllwild (on the Devil's Slide; see below). From November 15 through April 15, snow conditions permitting, the **Nordic Ski Center** (same information as Tramway office) offers cross-country skiing high above the desert floor.

Next comes **LA QUINTA**, named for the Valley's first **exclusive resort**, built in 1927 and thriving during the Depression, when Hollywood's escapist popularity rose as the country's income fell. Director Frank Capra wrote the script for multiple Academy Award winner *It Happened One Night* at the resort in 1934, and considered the place so lucky he kept coming back, bringing the likes of Greta Garbo in his wake. It's still so posh that it's not marked on the main road (take Washington Street south to Eisenhower to find it). The Santa Rosa Mountain backdrop is stunning, and the rich no longer get very duded up, so you won't feel out of place if you come for a drink at the piano lounge.

In stark contrast is neighboring **INDIO**, a low-key town whose agricultural roots show in its many date and citrus outlets (take 50th Avenue east from behind La Quinta Resort to get here and you'll pass so many date groves you'll think you're in Saudi Arabia – in fact, the town of Mecca is not far away). Stop in at **Shields** on Hwy-111, built in 1924 but renovated in the 1950s, for a date shake at the original soda fountain and a look at the kitschy free film *The Romance and Sex Life of the Date*. The town's huge February **Date Festival** draws people from as far as LA to its wonderfully goofy camel and ostrich races. More serious animal lovers might want to stop in at the **Wild Bird Center**, 46-500 Van Buren St (10am–5pm daily; ☎760/347-2647; donations), where injured owls, hawks and other desert avians are cared for and, if feasible, released back into the wild.

Idyllwild

Fifty miles from Palm Springs and five thousand feet up the opposite side of Mount San Jacinto, **IDYLLWILD** is the perfect antidote to in-your-face success. Fresh, cool and snow-covered in winter, this small alpine town of about two thousand inhabitants has only a few chalet-style restaurants and hotels, but it's a great place to slow up the cash drain that inevitably occurs on a visit to Palm Springs. It is accessible by heading twenty miles west along I-10 to Banning, then taking the exit for Hwy-243 which sweeps you up the mountain on a sharply curved road.

Idyllwild attracts visitors who want to walk on magnificent trails away from the searing heat of the desert basin below. **Mount San Jacinto State Park** surrounds the town and has numerous trails, ranging from a gentle meander along beautiful **Strawberry Creek** to a more strenuous trek along **Deer Springs Trail** to the stunning Suicide Rock and San Jacinto Peak, and the moderately difficult **Devil's Slide** to the Aerial Tramway (see above).

The **Forest Service Ranger Station**, 54270 Pine Crest Ave (daily 8am–4.30pm; ☎909/659-2117), has stacks of information about hiking and camping in the area and hands out the free **permits** required for all wilderness sites. You can set up **camp** anywhere over two hundred feet away from trails and streams, or in designated Yellow Post Sites ($5 parking fee per day, $30 a year with an Adventure Pass parking permit) with fire rings but no water. There are also drive-in campgrounds run by the Forest Service (☎1-800-444-7255) and the county park (☎1-800/234-PARK) at a cost of $8–$14 per night.

Otherwise, you can stay in **chalets** and **log cabins**, most of which cost from $50–$125 and usually sleep four or more people. The cheapest rooms are the little red-and-white chalets of *Atipahato Lodge*, 25525 Hwy-243, half a mile north of the ranger station (☎909/659-2201; ③), where the rooms have been newly renovated, while *The Fireside Inn* at 54540 North Circle Drive, about half a mile east, is considerably more appealing with cozy wood-panelled rooms, kitchens and fireplaces (☎909/659-2966; ④). The *Strawberry Creek Inn*, 26370 Hwy-243 (☎1-800/262-8969 or 909/659-3202; ⑤), a few hundred yards south, is a B&B-style place for those craving real luxury.

Eating, drinking and nightlife

Palm Springs restaurants run the gamut, from super posh to fast-food, with some reasonable ethnic options in between. **Nightlife** tends to the retro side, although there are some hipper options, especially for the gay crowd and concentrated in Cathedral City. The visitor center (see p.222) has details of **what's on** around town, and stocks the seasonal *Palm Springs Visitors Guide* and the gay bi-monthly *The Bottom Line*.

Restaurants

If you come off season, the desert sun may squelch your appetite sufficiently that you go without eating most of the day and find yourself ravenous at dusk. Although most of the more famous **restaurants** in Palm Springs are ultra-expensive, more reasonable options can be found with a little effort. For the really budget-conscious, supermarket shopping is the best bet: Von's in the Palm Springs shopping mall is open from early morning until around 11pm for basics.

Daily Grill, 73-061 El Paseo (☎760/779-9911). A bustling, elegant coffee shop-style restaurant with large portions at reasonable prices. The chicken pot pie is a favorite along with excellent steaks, fish, salads and lemonade.

El Gallito, 68820 Grove St, Cathedral City (☎760/328-7794). A busy Mexican cantina that has the best food for miles and lines to prove it – get there around 6pm to avoid the crowds.

John Henry's Café, 1785 Tahquitz Canyon Way at Sunrise Way (☎760/327-7667). Large portions of eclectic American fare, from rack of lamb to imaginative fish, perfectly served and at half the price you'd expect. Dinner is around $15; reserve after 2pm. Closed Sundays and June–Sept.

Las Casuelas, 368 N Palm Canyon Drive (☎760/325-3213). Opened in 1958, the original of what has become a string of Valley Mexican restaurants, all owned by the same family. This one is still the most popular with locals, but the others are also good and reasonably priced. Misted outdoor patio cools you off on hot summer nights.

Le Peep, 73-725 El Paseo (☎760/773-1004). Casual coffeehouse serving breakfast and lunch that tastes just like home-cooking.

Le Vallauris, 385 W Tahquitz Canyon Way (☎760/325-5059, reservations only). Palm Springs' best restaurant does not exactly hide its light under a bushel, describing itself as "*the* restaurant where the Stars entertain their friends"; you are indeed likely to run into one or two once-renowned artistes. Even if star-gazing is not your style, the Californian/French/Italian cuisine is excellent, and the service impeccable. The price, however, is around $80 per head.

Mykonos, 139 E Andreas Road (☎760/322-0223). A family-run Greek place just off Palm Canyon Drive with friendly service, large portions of excellent, unpretentious food, and low prices.

Native Foods Café, 1775 E Palm Canyon Dr (☎760/416-0070). This totally vegan café puts a creative twist on traditional vegetarian fare. An eclectic menu, including tacos, pizzas, salads, and a variety of veggie burgers, and excellent prices make this a worthwhile spot. The Jamaican jerk "steak" salad is highly recommended.

The Red Tomato, 65-751 Grove St at Hwy-111, Cathedral City (☎760/328-7518). Terrific pizza, especially the garlicky "white" pies.

Shame on the Moon, 69-950 Frank Sinatra Drive at Hwy-111, Rancho Mirage (☎760/324-5515). Long-standing bistro with California cuisine and an intimate bar, attracting a loyal gay crowd.

Thai Smile, 653 N Palm Canyon Drive (☎760/320-5503). Few points for decor or ambiance but great, authentic Thai green curries and the occasional Szechuan dish for around $10.

Wheel-Inn Eat, 16 miles west on I-10 at the Cabazon exit (marked by two 50ft concrete dinosaurs). Humble, 24-hour desert truck stop with a burly clientele and enormous portions – so unpretentious you'd think they'd never heard of Palm Springs. One of the dinosaurs houses a wonderfully kitsch gift shop.

The Wild Goose, 67-938 E Palm Canyon Drive, Cathedral City (☎760/328-5775). An antique-crammed award-winning restaurant serving great food for around $40 per head.

Nightlife: bars and clubs

If you're not a member of one of the exclusive country clubs, or disco-crazy, you'll have to work a little to find good nightlife. If you're not looking for anything raucous, stop in at one of the resort **piano lounges**, where, if you shell out for an over-priced drink, you can sometimes catch surprisingly good jazz. Lots of people just sit out at one of the **coffeehouses**, like *Starbucks*, on downtown's main drag. The area is especially crowded on Thursday evenings, when the surprisingly funky Village Fest **street fair** along N Palm Canyon Drive draws equal numbers of tourists and young locals to booths selling everything from fresh baked bread to tacky souvenirs, plus there's a kid's play zone. A few venues lay on live music, and you may find a trailer hosting a live alligator, $1 for a look. Pick up the *Desert Guide*, a local publication, to find out the current nightlife situation.

If you're around in January, don't miss out on the **Palm Springs International Film Festival**, which brings more nightlife to the city than the rest of the year combined. And in late March, the **La Quinta Arts Festival** serves up fine art and entertainment.

Agua Bar & Grill, Spa Hotel & Casino, 110 N Indian Canyon Dr (☎760/778-1515). Festive, upscale piano bar that attracts an older crowd.

Peabody's Jazz Studio and Coffee Bar, 134 S Palm Canyon Dr (☎760/322-1877). An eclectic crowd patrons here to enjoy live jazz, poetry readings and extensive coffee selections.

La Taqueria, 125 E Tahquitz Way (☎760/778-5391). With the ever popular margaritas and a misted outdoor patio on which to cool off, this is a great place to people watch.

Zelda's, 169 N Indian Canyon Drive (☎760/325-2375). Pick-up joint for teeny-boppers.

Listings

Bank Bank of America, 588 S Palm Canyon Drive (☎760/340-1867).

Bookstore Super Crown Books, 332 S Palm Canyon Drive (☎760/325-1265). Travel guides, paperback fiction, maps, etc.

Cinema Courtyard 10, 777 Tahquitz Canyon Way (☎760/322-3456).

Dry cleaning American Cleaners and Laundry, 364 S Indian Ave (☎760/320-8414).

Hospital Desert Hospital, 1150 N Indian Canyon Drive (☎760/323-6511).

Internet: The Palm Springs Public Library, 300 S Sunrise Way (☎760/323-8294), offers Net access, as does *Peabody's Coffee Shop*, 134 S Palm Canyon Dr (☎760/322-1877).

Left luggage at Greyhound station, 311 N Indian Canyon Drive

Pharmacy Rite Aid Drug Store, 366 S Palm Canyon Drive.

Police ☎760/323-8116 in Palm Springs; ☎760/321-0111 in Cathedral City.

Post office 333 E Amado Rd (Mon–Fri 8.30am–5pm; ☎1-800/275-8777). Zip code 92262.

Travel agency Las Palmas Travel, 403 N Palm Canyon Drive (☎760/325-6311).

Joshua Tree National Park

In a unique transitional area where the high Mojave meets the lower Colorado desert, 800,000 acres of freaky trees, their branches ragged and gnarled, flourish in an otherwise sparsely vegetated landscape, making **JOSHUA TREE NATIONAL PARK** one of the most unusual and fascinating of California's national parks. In recognition of the uniqueness of the area, and the need for its preservation, the national park system took the land under its jurisdiction as a national monument in 1936 and has vigilantly maintained its beauty ever since. The park lost some of the original area to mining interests in the 1950s, but that was more than compensated for in 1994 when it was promoted to a national park, with the addition of 234,000 acres. If you're staying in Palm Springs, there's no excuse not to visit; if you've further to come, make the effort anyway.

The startling trees, which can reach forty feet or more in height, have to contend with extreme aridity and rocky soil and, with the exception of springtime, when creamy white blossom clusters on the tips of the branches, the strain of their struggle to survive is evident. Complementary to the trees, which can only be seen in certain parts of the park, are great rock piles, heaps of boulders pushed up from the earth by the movements of the Pinto Mountain fault, which runs directly below. Often as high as a hundred feet, their edges are rounded and smooth from thousands of years of flash floods and winds.

In all it's a mystical, even unearthly, landscape, best appreciated at sunrise or sunset when the whole desert floor is bathed in red light; at noon it can feel like an alien and threatening furnace, with temperatures often reaching 125°F in summer, though dropping to a more bearable 70°F in winter. If you're visiting between May and October you must stick to the higher elevations to enjoy Joshua Tree with any semblance of comfort. In the Low Desert part of the park, the Joshua trees thin out and the temperature rises as you descend below three thousand feet. Over eighty percent of the park is designated wilderness – get out of the car at least once or twice and absorb the silence.

Some history

"Joshua Tree" may be a familiar name nowadays, thanks to U2, but previously it was almost unknown. Unlike the vast bulk of the state, nobody, save a few Native Americans, prospectors and cowboys, has had the chance to spoil it. Despite receiving less than four inches of annual rainfall, the area is surprisingly lush, and although craggy trees and rockpiles are what define Joshua Tree today, it was grass that attracted the first significant pioneers. Early cattlemen heard rumours of good pastures from the forty-niners who hurried through on their way to the Sierra Nevada gold fields. The natural corrals made perfect sites for cattle rustlers to brand their illegitimate herds before moving them out to the coast for sale. Ambushes and gunfights were common. Seeking refuge in the mountains, rustlers, by chance, discovered small traces of gold and sparked vigorous mining operations that continued until the 1940s. To the Mormons who traveled through here in the 1850s, the area signified something entirely different; they saw the craggy branches of the trees as the arms of Joshua leading them to the Promised Land – hence the name.

Practicalities

Less than an hour's drive northeast from Palm Springs, Joshua Tree National Park (always open; $10 per vehicle for 7 days, $5 per cyclist or hiker) is best approached from Hwy-62, which branches off I-10. You can enter the park via the west entrance at the town of **Joshua Tree**, or the northern entrance at **Twentynine Palms**, where you'll also find the **Oasis Visitor Center** (daily 8am–5pm; ☎760/367-5500) and several good

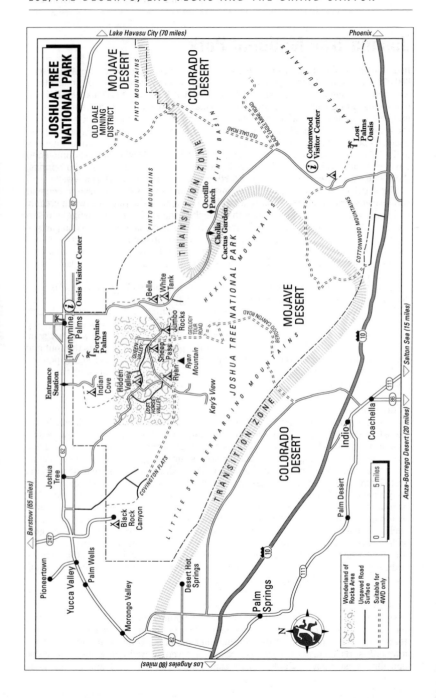

motels. Alternatively, if you're coming from the south, there is an entrance and the **Cottonwood Visitor Center** (daily 8am–4pm; hours may vary; ☎760/367-5500) seven miles north of I-10 on the Cottonwood Spring Road exit. It's worth stopping at one of the visitor centers to collect **maps** and the free *Joshua Tree Guide*.

Visiting the park using **public transportation** is not really an option. Morongo Basin Transit Authority (☎1-800/794-6282 or 760/367-7433) runs a regular bus service (2 daily; $7 one-way, $11 round-trip) between Palm Springs and the towns of Joshua Tree and Twentynine Palms, but not into the park itself. At best, you're looking at a ten-mile desert walk to get to anything very interesting. **Cyclists** are restricted to roads open to motor vehicles, so don't expect any off-road action: the nearest you'll get are the dirt surfaces of Geology Tour Road and the Covington Flats road. There is no bike rental anywhere near the park.

Twentynine Palms and Joshua Tree

The appealing desert settlement of **TWENTYNINE PALMS** is a small, serviceable place that enjoys good weather and low-key living. It is also home to the Marine Corps Air Ground Combat Center, the world's largest marine base. Apart from the boom of gunfire that can be heard for miles around, Twentynine Palms is a pleasant place to visit. Just two minutes' drive from the park, it's a fairly busy town by desert standards, stretching for about a mile along Hwy-62 with a fair selection of places to eat, drink and bed down. The climate has been considered perfect for convalescents ever since physicians sent World War I poison gas victims here for treatment of their respiratory illnesses; development of health spas and real estate offices has been considerable. The town is now billing itself as an "Oasis of Murals"; you can get a map of these interesting hyperrealistic historical artworks – there's one of the Dirty Sock Camp (named for a method used by miners to filter out gold) – as well as other **information** at the Twentynine Palms Chamber of Commerce, 6455 Mesquite Ave (☎760/367-3445).

The best place in town to **stay** is the *Twentynine Palms Inn*, 73950 Inn Ave off National Monument Drive (☎760/367-3505; ⑤), where an array of characterful adobe bungalows and wood frame cabins are set around attractively arid grounds and gardens, and a central pool area contains a restaurant and bar. Owned by the same large family since 1928, the inn was built on the Oasis of Mara, the only privately owned oasis in the High Desert, and (like the rest of the town) has several fault lines – including the Pinto Mountain fault – running beneath it.

Among the cheaper options nearby are the *Motel 6*, 71487 Twentynine Palms Hwy (☎760/367-2833; ②), and the *El Rancho Dolores Motel*, along the same road at no. 73352 (☎760/367-3528; ②). Both have perfectly acceptable pools and good rooms, but are nowhere near as much fun as the inn, which is also the best place to **eat**, with excellent $12–15 meals including soup and salad. For less pricey Mexican, check out *Ramona's*, 72115 Twentynine Palms Hwy (☎760/367-1929). **JOSHUA TREE** town is home to the Joshua Tree Rock Climbing School; if you're interested in doing mountain-goat maneuvers in the national park, call ☎1-800/890-4745 or 760/366-4745 for details.

Exploring the park

The best way to enjoy the park is to be selective. As with any desert area, you'll find the heat punishing and an ambitious schedule impossible in the hotter months. Casual observers will find a day-trip plenty, though it's a nice idea to camp out for a couple of nights, and serious rock-climbers and experienced hikers may want to take advantage of the park's excellent if strenuous trails. The rangers and staff at the visitor centers will

CAMPING IN JOSHUA TREE

Joshua Tree National Park has nine **campgrounds**, all concentrated in the northwest except for one at Cottonwood by the southern entrance. All have wooden tables, places for fires (bring your own wood) and pit toilets, but only two (*Black Rock Canyon* and *Cottonwood*) have water supplies and flush toilets. These cost $10 and $8 respectively; there's a fee for *Indian Cove* ($10), but all the rest are free. You can reserve sites at Black Rock and Indian Cove by phoning ☎1-800/365-2267; the rest are on a first-come-first-served basis with no facility for reservations, unless you're traveling with a group.

Each campground has its merits, but for relative solitude and a great, central location, the *Belle* (often closed in summer) and *White Tank* sites are perfect. The much larger *Jumbo Rocks* site is one of the highest, at 4400ft, and is therefore a little cooler, while for the winter months you may prefer the lower altitude of *Cottonwood* in the south. *Black Rock Canyon* and *Indian Cove* cannot be reached from within the park; if you've entered, you have to retrace your steps to the entrances on Hwy-62. The lack of showers, electrical and sewage hook-ups at any of the sites keeps the majority of RVers at bay, but in the popular winter months the place fills up quickly, especially at weekends. Each campsite is good for up to six people and two vehicles.

Backcountry camping is permitted provided you register before you head out. Twelve backcountry boards are dotted through the park at the start of most trails. Here you can self-register, leave your vehicle and study the regulations which include prohibition of camping within a mile of a road, five hundred feet of a trail and 440 yards of a water source.

be able to recommend the most enjoyable itineraries, tailored to your requirements and abilities.

Never venture anywhere without a **map**: either the *Topographic Trail Map* or the *Recreation Map*, both available at the visitor centers. Many of the roads are unmarked, hard to negotiate and restricted to four-wheel-drive use. If a road is marked as such, don't think about taking a normal car – you'll soon come to a grinding halt, and it could be quite a few panic-stricken hours before anybody finds you. Of course, maps are even more essential if you are planning to explore the park's **hiking trails** (see box opposite).

Starting in the north of the park, quartz boulders tower around the *Indian Cove* camping area, and a trail from the eastern branch of the campground road leads to **Rattlesnake Canyon** – its streams and waterfalls (depending on rainfall) breaking an otherwise eerie silence among the monoliths. The **Fortynine Palms Oasis** to the east can only be visited on foot.

Moving south into the main section of the park, you drive through the **Wonderland of Rocks** area comprising giant, rounded granite boulders that draw **rock climbers** from all over the world. The various clusters flank the road for about ten miles giving plenty of opportunity to stop for a little bouldering or, for those suitably equipped and skilled, to try more adventurous routes. Pick up a *Climber Ethics* leaflet from the visitor centers. Well-signposted nature trails lead to **Hidden Valley** (1 mile), where cattle rustlers used to hide out, and to the rain-fed **Barker Dam** (1 mile) to the east. The latter is Joshua Tree's crucial water supply, built around the turn of the century by cattlemen (and rustlers) to prevent the poor beasts expiring halfway across the park. The route back from the dam passes a number of petroglyphs.

If you're **driving**, you can reach **Key's View** from here. This 5185-foot-high spot was named after Bill Keys, an eccentric miner who raised his family in this inhospitable landscape until he was locked away in 1943 for shooting one of his neighbors over a right-of-way argument (the mystery writer Erle Stanley Gardner helped him get paroled). He was revered for being a tough desert rat and indefatigable miner, who dug on long after less hardy men had abandoned the arid wasteland. The best views in the whole park can be had from up here, on a good day as far as the Salton Sea and beyond to Mexico – a brilliant desert panorama of badlands and mountains.

The road then passes the start of the Ryan Mountain hike and the turn-off for Geology Tour Road, which leads down through the best of Joshua Tree's **rock formations**. A little further on, the Jumbo Rocks campground is the start of a loop (1.7 miles) through boulders and desert washes to **Skull Rock**.

Almost at the transition zone between the Colorado and Mojave deserts and on the fringes of the Pinto Basin, the **Cholla Cactus Garden** is a quarter-mile loop through an astonishing concentration of the "jumping" *cholla* cactus (see box on p.219) for which it is named, as well as creosote bushes, jojoba and several other cactus species. Come at dusk or dawn for the best chance of seeing the mainly nocturnal desert wood rat.

HIKING IN JOSHUA TREE NATIONAL PARK

To get a real feel for the majesty of the desert you'll need to leave the main roads behind and hike. But **stick to the trails**: Joshua Tree is full of abandoned gold mines and although the rangers are fencing them as quickly as possible, they don't have the funds to take care of all of them. Watch for loose gravel around openings, undercut edges, never trust ladders or timber, and bear in mind that the rangers rarely check mines for casualties. Some of the shafts contain water and poisonous fumes, and even if you survive a fall, you'll still have to contend with snakes, scorpions and spiders.

Most of the trails listed below are all in the slightly cooler and higher Mojave Desert. There's tougher stuff on the eastern side of the park around **Pinto Basin**, a notorious danger zone when the flash floods strike. To cover this area on foot, it's essential that you **register** at one of the visitor centers first and check the trail conditions with the rangers. You'll need to be well armed with maps and water supplies, and on the whole it's unwise even to attempt it unless you're a very experienced hiker or are traveling as part of a group. If you do reach here, you'll find no Joshua trees and few other signs of life. Even on the easier trails allow around an hour per mile: there's very little shade and you'll tire quickly.

SOME HIKES
These are listed northwest to southeast through the park.

Fortynine Palms Oasis (3 miles; 2hr). Moderately strenuous, this leaves the badly signposted Canyon Road six miles west of the visitor center at Twentynine Palms. A barren rocky trail leads to this densely clustered and partly fire-blackened oasis which, since it was named, seems to have flourished on the seepage down the canyon. There's not enough water to swim in, nor are you allowed to camp (the oasis is officially closed 8pm–7am), but a late afternoon or evening visit presents the best wildlife rewards.

Lost Horse Mine (4 miles; 3hr). Another moderately strenuous trail climbs 450ft to the mine which in the 1890s made an average of $20,000 a week. The hike takes you through abandoned mining sites, with building foundations and equipment still intact, to the top of Lost Horse Mountain. The trail starts a mile east of Keys View Road.

Ryan Mountain (3 miles; 2hr). Some of the best views in the park are from the top of Ryan Mountain (5461ft), seven hundred strenuous feet above the desert floor. Start at the parking area near the *Sheep Pass* campground and follow the trail past the Indian Cave, which contains bedrock mortars once used by the Cahuilla and Serrano.

Mastodon Peak (3 miles; 2hr). Another peak climb, less strenuous but with great views, especially south to the Salton Sea. Start from the *Cottonwood* campground.

Lost Palms Oasis (8 miles; 5hr). This moderate trail leads across desert washes, past palo verde, cottonwood and ironwood trees to the largest stand of palms in the park, and presents possible scrambling side-trips to Victory Palms and Munsen Canyon. There's little surface water, but often enough to lure bighorn sheep. Start from the *Cottonwood* campground.

Around Joshua Tree

Just west of Joshua Tree Town is the rather more developed **Yucca Valley**. The town's **Hi-Desert Nature Museum**, 57117 Twentynine Palms Hwy (Tues–Sun 10–5pm; free), holds a largely poor collection of paintings and tacky souvenirs, but some commendable catches of snakes and scorpions and a pinecone from the world's oldest living tree; the **Desert Christ Park**, Sunnyslope Drive at the 26000 block (dawn–dusk; free), has 37 of local sculptor Antone Martin's massive fifteen-foot concrete figures depicting tales from the Bible – a fittingly bizarre addition to the region. Finally, **Pioneertown** is an old West town created in the 1940s for the filming of movies and TV serials; today it's a residential settlement with full eating amenities – a nice bit of synthetic cowboy country when the real thing gets too much.

If you've got a good car that can handle bad roads and mountain passes, then **back road driving** on the way back from Yucca Valley to LA via the Morongo Valley is a fun way to get a sense of the Wild West. Arm yourself with a San Bernardino County map and explore the Lucerne Valley and the small towns of **Big Bear City**, **Fawnskin** or **Landers**.

The Imperial Valley and Salton Sea

The patch of the Colorado desert **south** of Joshua Tree and Palm Springs is one of the least friendly of all the Californian desert regions and its foreboding aspect discourages exploration. It's best not to come in summer, when intense heat makes journeys uncomfortable and services are greatly reduced.

Sandwiched between Hwy-111 and Hwy-86, which branch off I-10 soon after Palm Springs and the Coachella Valley, the area from the **Salton Sea** down to the furnace-like migrant-worker towns of the agricultural **Imperial Valley** lies in the two-thousand-square-mile Salton Basin: aside from a small spot in Death Valley, the largest area of dry land below sea level in the western hemisphere. Hwy-86, for what it's worth, was California's most notorious two-lane highway, with a staggering record of deaths and accidents, though it's now been widened into four lanes. There's not a lot to come here for unless you're heading into the Anza-Borrego desert or the Mexican border.

Created accidentally in 1904, when engineers tried to divert the Colorado River to get water to the Imperial Valley, the Salton Sea and its shores were once extremely toney, attracting the likes of Frank Sinatra and Dean Martin to its yacht clubs; in its 1940s heyday, the sea was a bigger tourist draw than Yosemite National Park. A series of mid-1970s storms caused the sea to rise and swallow shoreline developments, but more serious damage to tourism was due to fact that the Salton Sea, without a natural outlet (it is 235 feet below sea level), has over the years become grossly polluted – plagued by agricultural runoff and toxic wastes carried in by two rivers from Mexico – and excessively saline. Fish carry a consumption warning, and people rarely swim and waterski here these days.

In the meantime, the Salton Sea remains an important wintering area for shore birds and waterfowl. Brown pelicans come by in summer and terns and cormorants nest here. The best place to see them is the **National Wildlife Refuge** (daily dawn–dusk; free) at the sea's southern tip. By the informative **visitor center** (Nov 1–March 30 9am–4pm, rest of the year weekends and holidays only; recreation area ☎760/393-3059) there's a viewing platform, or you can take the twenty-minute Rock Hill Trail to the water's edge for a closer look. To get to the refuge, take the poorly signposted backroads off Hwy-111 south of **Niland** or off Hwy-86 at **Westmorland**; both run past fields of alfalfa, cantaloupe, tomatoes and other crops – proof that just about anything will grow in this fertile land provided it is suitably irrigated.

Although you probably wouldn't want to spend the night there, if you've come this far it's worth turning east on the main street of Niland and traveling three miles to see **Slab City**, a huge settlement of squatters that swells in size in winter when Canadian RVers come down for warmth – and free city water. At the entrance to the town, **Salvation Mountain** is a fantastic work of religious folk art, incorporating for example an abandoned motorboat, to represent Noah's Ark.

The only other reasons you might stop are to **camp** at one of several lakeside sites on the eastern side of the Salton Sea (primitive $7, equipped sites $13, hook-ups $19) or to eat some authentic **Mexican food**. Agricultural work brings thousands of Mexicans north of the border, and the restaurants generally cater to them: practice your Spanish.

The Anza-Borrego desert

Southwest of the Salton Sea, though usually approached from San Diego (see Chapter Two), the **ANZA-BORREGO DESERT** is the largest state park in the country, covering 600,000 acres and, in contrast to the Imperial Valley, offering a diverse variety of plant and animal life as well as a legend-strewn history spanning Native American tribes, the first white trailfinders and Gold Rush times. It takes its double-barrelled name from Juan Baptista de Anza, a Spanish explorer who crossed the region in 1774, and the Spanish for the native bighorn sheep, *borrego cimarron*, which eats the brittle-brush and agave found here. Some of Anza-Borrego can be covered by car (confidence on gravel roads is handy), although you'll need four-wheel drive for the more obscure – and most interesting – routes, and there are over five hundred miles of hiking trails where vehicles are not permitted at all.

During the fiercely hot summer months, the place is best left to the lizards, although most campgrounds stay open all year. The desert **blooming season**, between March and May, is popular, when scarlet octillo, orange poppies, white lilies, purple verbena and other peacock-like wildflowers are a memorable – and fragrant – sight. As well as taking the usual desert precautions (see box on p.218), you should read the comments in "Basics" on p.53 – this is mountain lion territory.

Practicalities

Anza-Borrego State Park is served by **public transportation**; from San Diego, the North East Rural Bus System (see p.209) makes daily trips to **BORREGO SPRINGS**, the park's one sizeable settlement, at the northern end of Hwy-S3. There's not much happening in Borrego Springs, but it's one of the most pleasant of all the desert towns, self-contained and remarkably uncommercialized; the lack of development is in part due to the efforts of San Diego's Copley family, conservative newspaper magnates who want to keep it a pristine escape for the rich. If you're camping out it's the place to gather (expensive) supplies – but don't expect any big supermarket chains here – or to use the **Chamber of Commerce**, 622 Palm Canyon Drive (daily 10am–4pm; ☎760/767-5555), for details of motels and restaurants. Though the Chamber of Commerce doesn't like to mention it, the town of Borrego Springs is three miles southwest of the most seismically active area in the western hemisphere, Clark's Dry Lake, where some ten thousand earthquakes a year are registered. For information on this phenomenon, as well as on desert hiking, camping, flora and fauna, head two miles west to the excellent **Visitor Information Center**, 200 Palm Canyon Drive (June–Sept weekends & holidays 9am–5pm; Oct–May daily 9am–5pm; ☎760/767-5311), where you can also pick up an informative free newspaper and a detailed map of the park. The center is landscaped into the desert floor so you barely notice it as you wander through the short **Desert Plant Trail** (it's a bit confusing; don't take the dirt Visitor Center Loop but the paved path to

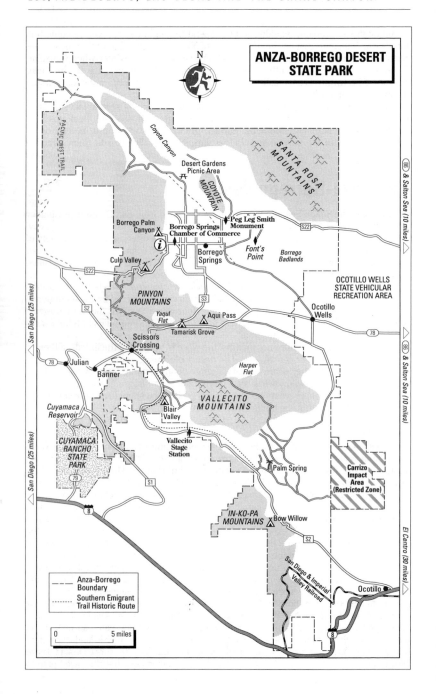

ANZA-BORREGO DESERT STATE PARK

N

PACIFIC CREST TRAIL

Coyote Canyon

SANTA ROSA MOUNTAINS

Desert Gardens Picnic Area

COYOTE MOUNTAIN

Borrego Palm Canyon

Peg Leg Smith Monument

Borrego Springs Chamber of Commerce

S22

Culp Valley

Borrego Springs

Font's Point

Borrego Badlands

S22

OCOTILLO WELLS STATE VEHICULAR RECREATION AREA

PINYON MOUNTAINS

S2

S3

Yaqui Flat

Aqui Pass

Tamarisk Grove

Ocotillo Wells

78

Scissors Crossing

78 Julian

Banner

Harper Flat

VALLECITO MOUNTAINS

Cuyamaca Reservoir

Blair Valley

CUYAMACA RANCHO STATE PARK

79

Vallecito Stage Station

S1

Palm Spring

Carrizo Impact Area (Restricted Zone)

8

IN-KO-PA MOUNTAINS Bow Willow

S2

San Diego & Imperial Valley Railroad

Ocotillo

8

- - - Anza-Borrego Boundary
······ Southern Emigrant Trail Historic Route

0   5 miles

San Diego (25 miles)

San Diego (25 miles)

86 & Salton Sea (10 miles)

86 & Salton Sea (10 miles)

El Centro (30 miles)

enter). When the center is closed, the administration office adjacent (Mon–Fri 9am–5pm) fills in.

If you're not feeling adventurous enough to camp (see below), there are a handful of **motels** in Borrego Springs, though only *Oasis*, at 366 W Palm Drive (☎760/767-5409; ③), with available kitchenettes, and *Hacienda del Sol* (☎760/767-5442; ③), near the Chamber of Commerce, are at all affordable. If you want to live it up, *La Casa del Zorro,* 3845 Yaqui Pass Rd (☎1-800/824-1884 or 760/767-5323; ④–⑨) is a beautiful hotel with a hefty pricetag. For plain but decent diner **meals**, make for *Kendall's Café* (☎760/767-3491), almost opposite the Chamber of Commerce. More upscale and far more interesting is the *Krazy Coyote Saloon & Grille*, 2220 Hoberg Road (☎760/767-7788), the local favorite with a good bar, tasty American/Continental fare and a terrific desert setting. Just outside the eastern park boundary, **OCOTILLO WELLS** has basic facilities and the attractively located *Desert Ironwoods Resort,* 4875 Hwy-78 (☎760/767-5670; ②–③).

Recreational opportunities in the park are strictly controlled to preserve the fragile ecosystem. The main exception to this rule is the **Ocotillo Wells State Vehicular Recreational Area**, a region to the east of the park mapped out for dune buggies and the like. Owners drive like demons in a maelstrom of tossed sand and engine noise; if you're tempted to join them, call Recreation Headquarters (daily 8am–4pm; ☎760/767-5391) for information or contact Desert Rat Tours (☎760/767-3755) in Borrego Springs ($39 for an hour-long accompanied spin); otherwise stay well clear. **Mountain biking** is permitted but only on paved and dirt roads; the hiking trails are off limits. Bikes can be rented from Carrizo Bikes, 648 Palm Canyon Drive (☎760/767-3872), behind the Borrego Springs Chamber of Commerce. For guided excursions into the park, contact Desert Jeep Tours (☎1-888/BY-JEEPS); rates start at $59 for a two-hour tour of the badlands and go up to $89 for half-day jaunts that cover Indian ruins and mudcaves.

The park

Coming from the San Diego area through Julian (see p.210), you'll first hit the western section of the park which contains some of the more interesting historical debris. At

---

CAMPING IN ANZA-BORREGO

Two developed and nine primitive campgrounds exist within the Anza-Borrego Desert State Park, but this is one of the few parks which allows **open camping**, giving you the freedom to pitch a tent pretty much anywhere without a permit, although it's advisable to let a park ranger know your plans. The few provisos are that you don't drive off-road, don't camp near water holes, camp away from developed campgrounds, light fires only in fire rings or metal containers, collect no firewood, and leave the place as you found it, or cleaner.

The largest site, and the only one with RV hook-ups, is the *Borrego Palm Canyon* campground a mile from the visitor center. *Tamarisk Grove*, thirteen miles south on Hwy-S3, is the only other developed site (both $15-$22, depending on the season). Each charge $5 for day use of the facilities. Both also organize **guided hikes** and have regular discussion and activity evenings led by a park ranger. Places can be reserved through Parknet on ☎1-800/444-7275 (essential for holidays and weekends, and in the March–May blooming season). The other primitive campgrounds fill on a first-come-first-served basis; those in the backcountry always have space. All are accessible by road vehicles and are free, except for *Bow Willow* which charges $7-$9 and is the only one with drinking water. Most sites are below 1500ft which is fine in winter, but in the hotter months you might try *Culp Valley*, ten miles southwest of Borrego Springs, at a blissfully cool 3400ft. There is spring water here but you're better off bringing your own.

Scissors Crossing, Hwy-78 intersects Hwy-S2 which follows the line of the old **Butterfield Stage Route**, which began service in 1857 and was the first regular line of communication between the eastern states and the newly settled West.

From Scissors Crossing, Hwy-S2 heads towards the park's southeast corner, traversing **Blair Valley**, with a primitive campground, and **Box Canyon**, where the Mormon Battalion of 1847, following what is now known as the **Southern Emigrant Trail Historic Route**, forced a passage along the desert wash. It isn't especially spectacular, but makes for some safe desert-walking, never more than a couple of hundred yards from the road. Nine miles further on, the **Vallecito Stage Station** is an old adobe stage rest stop that gives a good indication of the comforts – or lack of them – of early desert travel. To the south lies the least-visited portion of Anza-Borrego, good for isolated exploration and undisturbed views around Imperial Valley, where there's a vivid and spectacular clash as gray rock rises from the edges of the red desert floor, and a cool oasis at Palm Spring.

Northwest of Scissors Crossing, Hwy-S2 meets Hwy-S22, which descends tortuously through fields of popcorn-shaped rock formations to Borrego Springs. Six miles further east is a memorial marker to Peg Leg Smith, an infamous local spinner of yarns from the Gold Rush days who is further celebrated by a festival of tall stories – the **Peg Leg Liars Contest** – which takes place at this spot on the first Saturday in April; anybody can get up before the judges and fib their hearts out, the most outrageous tales earning a modest prize. Roughly four miles further on, a fairly tough dirt road leads to **Font's Point** and a view over the **Borrego Badlands** – a long sweeping plain devoid of vegetation whose strange, stark charms are oddly inspiring. Sunset is the best time to fully appreciate the layered alluvial banding.

In the north of the park, the campground at Borrego Palm Canyon marks the start of the **Borrego Palm Canyon Trail** (3 miles; 2hr; 350ft ascent), one of the most popular paths in the park. It follows a detailed nature trail to a dense concentration of desert palms – the only palms native to California.

THE HIGH DESERT

Desolate, lifeless and silent, the **Mojave Desert**, mythic badland of the West, has no equal when it comes to hardship. Called the High Desert because it averages a height of around two thousand feet above sea level, the Mojave is very dry and for the most part deadly flat, dotted here and there with the prickly bulbs of a Joshua tree and an occasional abandoned miner's shed. For most, it's the barrier between LA and Las Vegas, an obstacle to get over before they reach either city; and, short on attractions as it is, you may want to follow their example. But you should linger a little just to see – and smell – what a desert is really like: a vast, impersonal, extreme environment, sharp with its own peculiar fragrance, and alive in spring with acres of fiery orange poppies – the state flower of California – and other brightly coloured wildflowers.

You will have relatively little company. If LA is the home of the sports car, the Mojave is the land of huge dust-covered trucks, carrying goods across the state to Nevada. Other signs of life include the grim military subculture marooned on huge weapons-testing sites. There is also a hard-core group of desert fans: backdrop for the legion of road movies spawned by the underground film culture in the late 1960s and early 1970s, the Mojave is a favorite with bikers and hippies drawn by the barren panorama of sand dunes and mountain ranges. Members of the California Sierra Club and other savvy in-state nature lovers light out for the less barren beauties of the Mojave National Preserve. But otherwise visitors are thin on the ground, and for most of the year you can rely on being in sparse company.

I-15 cuts through the heart of the Mojave, dividing it into two distinct regions. To the north lies the desolate Western Mojave, as well as **Death Valley** (which, because of its unique character and proximity to the Owens Valley, is covered in Chapter Four), and to the south lies **Barstow** and the **Mojave National Preserve**. Barstow, the lackluster capital of the Mojave, is redeemed only by its location halfway between LA and **Las Vegas** on I-15, which makes it both a potential stopover between the two points and a good base for the surrounding attractions, explorable by dune buggy, on horseback or even on foot.

If Barstow isn't exactly alluring, the huge Mojave National Preserve, which lies just south of the road to LasVegas, is. Here you can see spectacular sand dunes, striking rock formations and a huge variety of plant life, including large concentrations of Joshua trees. Much of the preserve rises to about 4000 feet, so it also offers respite from the harshest of the area's heat. South and east of here, close to the Nevada and Arizona borders, the desert is at its most demanding, largely empty, inhospitable and potentially miserable, and the only reason you might find yourself in the region is if you're driving through on the way to the **Grand Canyon**.

The Western Mojave

The **western expanse** of the Mojave Desert spreads out on the north side of the San Gabriel Mountains, fifty miles from Los Angeles via Hwy-14. It is a barren plain that drivers have to cross in order to reach the alpine peaks of the eastern Sierra Nevada mountains or Death Valley, at the Mojave's northern edge. The few towns that have grown up in this stretch of desert over the past couple of decades are populated in the main by two sorts of people: retired couples who value the dry, clean air, and aerospace workers employed in one of the many military bases or aircraft factories. **Lancaster**, near Edwards Air Force Base, is the largest town and one of the few places to pick up supplies; **Mojave**, thirty miles north, is a main desert crossroads that caters mainly to drive-by tourists. **Tehachapi**, twenty miles west and a few thousand feet higher, offers a cool retreat. Hwy-14 joins up with US-395 another forty miles north, just west of the huge naval air base at **China Lake** and the faceless town of **Ridgecrest**, a good jumping off point for some interesting attractions.

Lancaster and the Antelope Valley

From the north end of LA's San Fernando Valley, Hwy-14 cuts off from I-5 and heads east around the foothills of the San Gabriel Mountains, passing **Placerita Canyon**, site of an early gold discovery that's been preserved as a nature reserve (daily 9am–5pm; free). Ten miles further on stands the massive sandstone outcrop of the 700-acre **Vasquez Rocks County Park** (daily 8am–sunset; $3 per vehicle) once a hiding place for frontier bandits and bank robbers, and later used by Hollywood movie studios as the backdrop for a variety of TV shows and films. Beyond here Hwy-138 cuts off east, heading up to the ski resorts and lakes along the crest of the San Gabriel Mountains, while Hwy-14 cuts north across the sparsely settled flatlands of the Mojave Desert.

The biggest places for miles are the twin towns of **LANCASTER** and **PALMDALE**, two soulless side-by-side communities of retirees and RV parks whose economy is wholly based on designing, building and testing airplanes, from B-1 bombers for the military to the record-setting *Voyager*, which flew non-stop around the globe in 1987. The free **Blackbird Airpark**, at 25th Street East in Palmdale, three miles west along Avenue P, can be recognized by the two sinister-looking black planes standing by the roadside. These are in fact the fastest and highest-flying planes ever created. The A-12 was designed in the 1950s as prototype for the SR-71 – the *Blackbird* – a reconnaissance plane which could reach 2100 miles per hour at 85,000ft. Unless you strike one of the infrequent "open cockpit" days, all you can do is circle the planes admiring the sleek lines and astonishing statistics. There are several other impressive aircraft in the park, and more are being added all the time.

If you're not a military buff, there's little else to draw you into Lancaster except a need for a bed or supplies. The **Chamber of Commerce** at 544 Lancaster Blvd (Mon–Fri 9am–5pm; ☎661/948-4518) has information on **accommodation** – at motels such as the *Tropical* (☎805/945-7831; ②) at 43145 Sierra Hwy, on the east side of town, and the *Motel 6* (☎661/948-0435; ②) at 43540 W 17th St, just off Hwy-14.

Unlikely as it may seem at first glance, there are some things to see in the surrounding area, known as the **Antelope Valley**, where the **California Poppy Reserve** (daily sunrise–sunset; $5 per vehicle, $3 in the off-season; fifteen miles west of Hwy-14 on Lancaster Road), is in full bloom in the spring with the state flower, the Golden Poppy. Depending upon the amount and timing of the winter rains, the flowers peak between March and May, when the reserve is covered in bright orange blossom; in season, the Poppy Reserve **visitor center** (seasonal, Mon–Fri 9am–5pm; ☎661/942-0662) has interpretive displays of desert flora and fauna. The building itself is proof that passive-solar underground architecture works: built into the side of a hill, it keeps cool naturally and is powered entirely by an adjacent windmill generator. The Palmdale **visitor center** (Mon–Fri 9am–5pm; ☎661/273-3232) has additional information on local attractions.

Saddleback Butte State Park, seventeen miles east of Lancaster at the junction of Avenue J and 170th St (daily dawn–dusk; ☎661/942-0662; $5 per vehicle), centers on a smallish hill whose slopes are home to a splendid collection of Joshua trees. It's also a likely spot to catch a glimpse of the desert tortoise, for whom the park provides a refuge from the motorcyclists and dune buggy enthusiasts who tear around the region. There's a **visitor center** (usually open Saturdays, call the park for hours), a half-mile nature trail, and under-used **campgrounds** ($10). The visitor center runs a campfire program on Saturday evenings and nature hikes Sunday morning. Three miles southwest, the **Antelope Valley Indian Museum** on Avenue M (mid Sept–June 1 Sat & Sun 11am–4pm; $3), housed in a mock Swiss chalet painted with Native American motifs, contains an extensive collection of ethnographic material from all over the state.

The desert and dry lake beds north of Lancaster make up **Edwards Air Force Base**, the US military testing ground for experimental, high-speed and high-altitude aircraft (such as the *Blackbird*; see above). Ninety-minute **tours** of NASA's Dryden Flight Research Facility (Mon–Fri 10.15am & 1.15pm; free; reserve at least a day in advance on ☎661/258-3446) include a short film (a jingoistic cross between *The Right Stuff* and *Top Gun*) and a look at hangars full of unique aeroplanes, including the missile-like X-15. The base is currently a backup landing spot for the space shuttle, though in the past, when it was on the regular route, thousands of people made the journey out here to welcome the astronauts home. If all of this sounds interesting, the Dryden Flight Research Facility can be reached from the north via the Rocket Site exit of Hwy-58, between Mojave and Boron.

Mojave and Tehachapi

MOJAVE, strung out along the highway thirty miles north of Lancaster, is a major junction on the interstate train network, though it's used solely by goods trains. The town itself – mostly a mile-long highway strip of gas stations, $30-a-night motels and franchised fast-food restaurants, open around the clock – is a good place to fill up on food and gas before continuing north into the Owens Valley or Death Valley.

About twenty miles west from Mojave, Hwy-58 rises to the rolling hillsides of **TEHACHAPI**, an apple-growing center which, at an elevation of around 4000 feet, offers a nice respite from the Mojave's heat. In addition to its pretty setting, the town has a couple of minor claims to fame. Some 5100 **wind generators** – both familiar three-bladed windmills and more unusual egg-beater-style Darreius turbines – make the Tehachapi Wind Resource Area, ranked along Cameron Ridge to the east, one of the world's most productive renewable energy stations. Train enthusiasts, meanwhile, cross states to see groaning Santa Fe diesels hauling their mile-long string of boxcars around the **Tehachapi Loop**, eight miles west of town. Built in the 1870s as the only means of scaling the steep slopes of the region, the tracks cleave to the rockface, doubling back on themselves to make a complete 360° loop. The sight of a train twisting around a mountain, its front end 77ft above its tail, is awesome. You can't see it properly from Hwy-58, so follow the signs three miles from the Keene exit to a roadside plaque commemorating the loop's engineers. For **information** about these and other local attractions, ranging from pick-your-own-fruit orchards and antiques shops to ostrich farms, stop in at the **Chamber of Commerce**, 209 E Tehachapi Blvd (daily 9am–5pm; ☎661/822-4180). You can also find out about **accommodation**, including the *Santa Fe Motel*, 120 W Tehachapi Blvd (☎661/822-3184; ②) and the *Best Western Mountain Inn*, 416 W Tehachapi Blvd (☎661/822-5591; ③). Eight miles southwest of town, there's **camping** ($8) at a refreshing range 5500 to 7000 feet in the Tehachapi Mountain Park. For information and reservations call ☎661/868-7000. Popular local **restaurants** include the *Apple Shed*, 333 E Tehachapi Blvd (☎661/823-8333), good for country-style breakfasts or apple-pie breaks, and *Domingo's*, 201416 Valley Blvd (☎661/822-7611), a family-owned Mexican place in the newer section of town.

Randsberg and Ridgecrest

Northeast from Mojave, along Hwy-14, the desert is virtually uninhabited, the landscape only marked by the bald ridges of the foothills of the Sierra Nevada mountains that rise to the west, though you might see the odd ghostly sign of the prospectors who once roamed the region in search of gold and less precious minerals. Twenty miles north of Mojave, Hwy-14 passes through **Red Rock Canyon**, where brilliantly colored rock formations have been eroded into a miniature version of Utah's Bryce Canyon; the highway passes right through the center of the most impressive section, though if you walk just a hundred yards from the road you're more likely to see an eagle or coyote than another visitor. There's a **state park** (day use $5 per vehicle) with a **visitor center** (☎661/942-0662; open spring & fall Fri–Sun) and a fairly primitive but beautifully sited **campground** ($10).

Continuing north of Red Rock Canyon, Hwy-14 merges into US-395 for the run into the Owens Valley. But a worthwhile detour cuts fifteen miles east to **RANDSBERG**, a near ghost town of two bars and a dozen shops, its lifeblood provided by the Rand gold deposit of the Yellow Aster and Baltic mines, the last to be worked commercially in California. The **Desert Museum**, 161 Butte Ave (Sat & Sun 10am–2pm; free), has displays on the glory days of the 1890s, when upwards of three thousand people lived in the town, mining gold, silver and tungsten out of the arid, rocky hills. The nearby **General Store**, almost always open (unlike the rest of the town which pretty much shuts down during the week), is a good source of local **information** (☎760/374-2418). In neighboring **Johannesburg**, the *HI-Death Valley Hostel* (301 Hwy 395; ☎760/374-2323) has forty beds ($12 members, $15 non-members) and one private room.

Twenty miles north of Randsberg Hwy-178 cuts east towards Death Valley to the sprawling desert community of **RIDGECREST**, dominated by the huge China Lake Naval Weapons Center. Jet fighters scream past overhead, taking target practice on land that's chock-full of ancient **petroglyphs**. Though access to the sites is strictly controlled, you can get some idea of the native culture of the Mojave Desert by visiting the **Maturango Museum**, off China Lake Boulevard at 100 E Las Flores Ave (daily 10am–5pm; $2; ☎760/375-6900), which as well as acting as regional **visitor center**, has exhibits on both the natural and cultural history of the region, including examples of the rock-cut figures. To get out and see the figures and designs in their natural surroundings, plan ahead and join one of the volunteer-led five-hour **tours** (spring and fall only; $20) by contacting the museum (Ridgecrest, CA 93555; ☎760/375-6900, fax ☎375-0479) well in advance. You can check out some more recent inhabitants of the desert at the **wild horse** and **burro corrals** run by the Bureau of Land Management three miles east of town on Hwy-178. The animals are waiting for adoption, but even if you're not prepared to take one home, you can arrange to see them (Mon–Fri 7.30am–4pm; ☎760/446-6064). To ensure an enthusiastic reception, bring along some apples or carrots.

Twenty miles east along Hwy-178 from Ridgecrest, an eight-mile dirt road (passable except after rain) leads to the **Pinnacles National Natural Landmark** (Mon–Fri 7.30am–6pm ☎831/389-4485) where five hundred tufa spires stretch up to 140ft. They were considered extra-terrestrial enough to form a backdrop for parts of *Star Trek V* and can be viewed best on the half-mile nature trail. The park's campground was washed out during an El Niño storm, but there is **camping** at a private campground next door to the park. For information, call Pinnacles Campground Inc. (☎831/389-4462).

Take Hwy-178 west to Hwy-395 north, and turn off at Cinder Rock Road to reach **Fossil Falls**, another rather unearthly formation some 27 miles northwest of Ridgecrest. Relatively recent volcanic eruptions (about 20,000 years ago) drove lava through one of this region's dry river channels, creating what looks like a petrified cataract. Some remaining petroglyphs as well as various small artifacts and polished indentations in the rocks, used for grinding grain, attest to widespread human habitation in this area. Continuing north up Hwy-395 will lead you into both the Owens Valley and Death Valley, regions covered in depth in Chapter Four.

Barstow

Just a few hours from LA along the thundering, seemingly endless I-15, **BARSTOW** looms up out of the desert, providing a welcome opportunity to get out of the car. Though capital of the Mojave and the crossroads of three major thoroughfares (I-40 and Hwy-58 also run through here), it's a small town, consisting of just one main road lined with a selection of motels and restaurants that make an overnight stop possible. This main street was once part of the famed **Route 66**, so fans of neon will enjoy some classic examples, and two nearby **outlet malls** attract area bargain hunters. There, however, the town's appeal ends. For many months of the year, the relentless sun manages to keep people in their air-conditioned homes for a good part of the day; in summer Barstow can seem more like a ghost town.

Practicalities

Located in the Tanger Outlet Mall off of I-15 at Lenwood Rd, the **California Welcome Center** (daily 9am–8pm; ☎1-888/4BARSTOW) has a good selection of maps of the surrounding area, lodging and restaurant guides and various flyers on local attractions.

If you're arriving by bus or train, you'll be dropped at the Greyhound or Amtrak station, both on First Street. A few blocks away, Main Street is the best place to look for a **motel**. All are of a similar standard and price, generally only distinguished by the condition of the neon sign outside. Cruise up and down until you find the best deal, but among those you might try are: *Days Inn*, 1590 Coolwater Lane (☎760/256-1737; ①–②) and the *Budget 8 Motel*, 1271 E Main (☎760/256-2204; ①). For a little more comfort, try the corporate-style *Holiday Inn*, 1511 E Main St (☎760/256-5673; ④). You can **camp** eight miles north of Barstow in the simple *Owl Canyon Campground* ($6) at Rainbow Basin (see below), or if you need more facilities, at **CALICO**, a re-created ghost town (detailed below) with shaded canyons where you can pitch a tent for $18 or hook-up campers for $22 per night including showers.

Food in Barstow, though far from exotic, is plentiful and cheap. Restaurants sit snugly between the many hotels on Main Street and are usually of the rib and steak variety (*Idle Spurs Steak House*, 29557 Hwy-58, is tops in that mode) although you can get good authentic Mexican food at *Rosita's*, 540 W Main St, or more American-ized Mexican at *Carlos & Toto's*, 901 W Main. Evening **entertainment** comes in the form of a few grubby bars frequented by bike gangs, the least threatening of which is *Katz*, 127 W Main Street at First, open from 6am to 2am.

Around Barstow

Most people who stop in Barstow are not here to enjoy the desert, but to visit the contrived **Calico Ghost Town** (☎760/254-2122; daily 9am–5pm; $6, admission is free with camping), ten miles east along I-15. In the late nineteenth century Calico produced millions of dollars worth of silver and borax and supported a population of almost four thousand. Attractively set in the color-streaked Calico Hills, but subject to the extreme heat of the Mojave, the town was quickly deserted when the silver ran out. It's since been rather cynically – and insensitively – restored, with souvenir shops and hot-dog stands, and a main thoroughfare lined with ersatz saloons, an old school house, a vaudeville playhouse and shops kitted out in period styles. However, should you so desire, there are miles of mining shafts and tunnels open to crawl around in – until claustrophobia forces you up for air.

Calico is brightened by its festivals, held throughout the year. The best of these is the **Spring Festival** in May, which features the World Tobacco Spitting Championships. Huge beast-like men gather to chew the wad and direct streams of saliva and tobacco juice at an iron post, cheered on by rowdy crowds who take their sport seriously and their drink in large quantities. There is also a chili cook-off, music and a he-man triathlon.

Primitive males are also featured five miles northeast of Calico along I-15. The **Calico Early Man Site** (visit by guided tour only Wed 1.30pm–3.30pm, & Thurs–Sun 9.30am–4pm; free), more popularly known as the "Calico Dig," has become one of the most important archeological sites in North America since it was excavated in 1964 by Louis Leakey. Some of the old tools and primitive shelter found here have been dated at around 20,000 years old, establishing mankind's presence far earlier than was previously thought. Pick up details of the tour from the small caravan that serves as an information office.

Of equal prehistoric importance, but far more vivid, the **Rainbow Basin** (unrestricted access), eight miles north of town along Fort Irwin Road, is a rock formation that after thirty million years of wind erosion has been exposed as a myriad of almost electric colors. You'll see plenty of fossilized animal and insect remains, but most visitors will probably be content to weave the car through the tricky four-mile loop road around the canyon and marvel at the prettiness of it all. You can camp here (see "Practicalities" opposite) at minimally-equipped sites.

Heading some eight miles east on the other main highway out of Barstow, I-40, just past Dagget, the original Department of Energy's Solar One Power Plant has been replaced by the **SEGS II Solar Power Plant**, which, marked by a hundred-acre field of mirrors, is a surreal example of how California is putting its deserts to use. Anyone who has seen the film *Bagdad Café* will remember the light reflections the mirrors give off for miles around.

Two designated **off-road recreational areas** lie south of Barstow: **Rasor** and **Stoddard Valley**. If you didn't bring your own dune buggy, you're out of luck – there's nowhere to rent them in Barstow – but you can always travel out to the dunes and get friendly with someone there. Camping is permitted in much of Stoddard Valley, a pretty area of rolling hills but one that's dotted with abandoned mineshafts. Watch where you lay down your backpack.

If you're heading out from here to Palm Springs or Joshua Tree National Park, consider the scenic Apple Valley back route via **VICTORVILLE**, some 34 miles south of Barstow on I-15. Take the Roy Rogers exit and drive down Civic Street to reach the **Roy Rogers-Dale Evans Museum**, 15650 Seneca Rd (daily 9am–5pm; $7), a repository of the Hollywood cowboy couple's memorabilia, some of it extremely bizarre – including Trigger and Buttermilk, the horses they rode in many of their films, preserved by an expert taxidermist. Also dedicated to American myth, the small **California Route 66 Museum**, on D Street between Fifth and Sixth streets (Thurs–Mon 10am–4pm; free), has displays relating to the westernmost strip of the Mother Road. Relics from an old roadside attraction called "Hulaville" are the museum's most interesting feature.

Baker and the Eastern Mojave

Once you get past Barstow and off the main roads, you'll be amazed to discover that some of the most spectacular – and undervisited – scenery in the state lies in the **Eastern Mojave**, where 1.4 million acres of land between I-15 and I-40 were set aside by the 1994 Desert Protection Act to create the **Mojave National Preserve**. Adventurous types heading for Las Vegas might enjoy a detour through the vast and undeveloped country that the Eastern Mojave has to offer. However, you are well advised to skip it in the hot months.

Driving west from Barstow, take the Afton Road turn off I-15 to get to **Afton Canyon**, outside of the preserve proper and dubbed the "Grand Canyon of the Mojave." It's not quite as impressive as the Arizona original, but it's striking nevertheless, with multicolored strata formed by erosion from an extinct lake. The lake may be gone, but Afton Canyon is one of the three places where the Mojave River flows above-ground throughout the year, making this a marshy mecca for almost two hundred types of birds and desert creatures. There's camping here on a first-come first-served basis ($10).

You'll next come to the road leading four miles south to the western edge of the preserve and the oasis of **Zzyzx**, a former health resort that's now home to the Soda Springs Desert Studies Center, run jointly by the National Park Service and the California State University system. If there are no happy-to-be-distracted researchers around, go to the unmanned visitor center to learn about the area's colorful history.

BAKER is the main supply source for the immediate region. The town's claim to fame is the world's tallest functioning thermometer, rising to 134 feet to commemorate the highest temperature ever recorded in Death Valley, which lies directly to the north via Hwy-127. You can pick up **information** on the national park and other desert recreation areas at the very helpful Mojave Desert Information Center, located at the base of the thermometer (daily 9am–5pm; ☎760/733-4040). If you're looking for **lodging**, the *Bun Boy* (☎760/733-4363; ③) and *Wills* (sic) *Fargo* (☎760/733-4477; ③) motels are owned by the same people, so the prices are exactly the same (the latter has a pool and slightly more character to its rooms). The supplies at the town's **general store** aren't cheap, but this is your last chance to stock up. If you buy a lottery ticket here, you may never have to worry about such matters again: the place has produced the most jackpot winners in the state of California. Standing out from the fast-food joints, the *Bun Boy* **restaurant** has good diner food, though it's not as interesting inside as its Twenties facade would suggest.

West of Baker, a series of roads lead south from I-15 into the main part of the **Mojave National Preserve**. Kelbaker Road, the farthest west, shoots past a series of dramatic black-red **cinder cones**, created relatively recently (a thousand years ago), before reaching the graceful Spanish-style **Kelso depot**, built in 1924 for workers on the Union Pacific Railroad. Closed in 1985, the building is in the process of being restored, perhaps to serve as a visitor center for the preserve. Visible to the south of the depot are the spectacular **Kelso Dunes**, a golden five-mile stretch of sand reaching up as high as seven hundred feet. The faint booming sound you might hear is caused by dry sand cascading down the steep upper slopes.

Turn northeast at Kelso to get to the small town of **Cima** (there's a little store here, but no gas) and the adjacent **Cima Dome**, a perfectly formed batholith rising some 1500ft above the desert floor. Cloaked in Joshua trees, parts of it can be visited on foot. To the southeast, along Black Canyon Road, you'll see a turnoff for the **Mid Hill Campground**, beautifully sited in piñon-juniper woodland; from here a moderately difficult eight-mile trail winds through Wild Horse Canyon and ends up at the park's other developed campground, **Hole-in-the-Wall** (both cost $10). Named by Bob Hollimon, a member of the Butch Cassidy gang, because it reminded him of his former hideout in Wyoming, Hole-in-the-Wall sits in at an elevation of 4500 feet among striking volcanic rock formations. If you've driven here and don't want to take a long hike, an interpreted nature trail leads from the **visitor center** (☎760/928-2572; call for hours). In the off-season, you'll still find someone at the visitor center for the 5900-acre **Providence Mountain State Recreation** area ($5 per day, free for those taking cave tours), a further ten miles south, then six miles west. Vegetation here changes from scrubby bushes at lower desert elevations to the piñon pines that grow along rocky Fountain Peak (6996 feet) and Edgar Peak (7171 feet). Some people come to camp at the small campground (six spaces only; $12), but most are here to tour **Mitchell Caverns**. (At this writing, tours were discontinued temporarily due to an earthquake. Call ☎760/928-2586 for reservations & tour times; $6.) The caverns were used by the Chemehuevi Indians for almost five hundred years. There's one brief claustrophobia-inducing part, but otherwise this ninety-minute walk through stalactites and stalagmites and rarer limestone formations is superb.

The Colorado River area

The eastern portion of the **Colorado Desert**, around the Colorado River, offers a respite from the barren environment of the desert. The strength of the river, over a thousand miles long, has by this southern stage of its course been sapped by a succession of dams (though even in the Grand Canyon there are whitewater rapids), until here it proceeds towards the Gulf of California in a stately flow, marking the border between California and Arizona as it goes.

If you're not heading east to the Grand Canyon itself – or if you're looking for an overnight stop en route – the stretch between Needles, the small border town on I-40, and Blythe a hundred miles south where I-10 meets Hwy-95, and especially **Lake Havasu City** in between the two, is marginally the most interesting area. Most of the small waterfront settlements that dot its course are dependent on watersports, though some, such as **Laughlin** in Nevada, right on the border with California and Arizona, have taken advantage of Arizona's restrictions on gambling and turned themselves into mini-Vegases, enjoying considerable popularity with packs of bikers who make a weekend of driving across the desert, spending all their money on gambling and drink and then riding back again.

Lake Havasu City

Ten miles east of the California state line on I-40, a twenty-mile detour south on Hwy-95 brings you to the most incongruous sight of the Southwestern deserts. At **LAKE**

HAVASU CITY, the old gray stones of **London Bridge** reach out across the stagnant waters of the dammed Colorado River.

Californian chainsaw manufacturer **Robert P. McCulloch** moved his factory to this unlikely spot – occupied by a disused military airstrip – in 1964, so he could try out his new sideline in outboard motors on the waters of Lake Havasu. Three years later, he heard Johnny Carson mention that London Bridge was up for sale; in the words of the nursery rhyme, it really was falling down, unable to cope with all those new-fangled automobiles. McCulloch bought it for $2,460,000, and painstakingly shipped ten thousand numbered blocks of granite across the Atlantic. Lacking anything for the bridge to span, he dug a channel that turned a riverbank promontory into the island of Pittsburg Point. Despite the jibes that McCulloch thought he was buying picturesque Tower Bridge – the turreted one that opens in the middle – instead of merely the latest in a long line of London Bridges, dating only from 1831, his investment paid off handsomely. The bridge now ranks second among Arizona's tourist attractions, after the Grand Canyon, and Lake Havasu City has become a major vacation resort and retirement center, with a population of thirty thousand.

That said, it's not often you see anything quite as boring in Arizona as London Bridge. Lake Havasu City is one of those places with an undeniable attraction for the parched urbanites of cities such as Phoenix, who flock to fish on the lake or charge up and down in motorboats and on jet-skis, but holds minimal appeal for travelers from further afield.

Only when you cross the bridge onto the island and then look back, do you appreciate how large Lake Havasu City has grown, sprawling up the gentle slope away from the river. Most of those broad hillside streets are lined with condo blocks and minor malls; the only place tourists bother to visit is the **English Village**, a mock-Tudor shopping mall, which also holds a handful of riverview restaurants, at the base of the bridge. Out on the island, if you head south from the bridge past the *Island Inn Resort*, you'll soon come to **London Bridge Beach**. The "beach" is more grit than sand, and few people swim from it. With its bizarre fringe of date palms, however, and its panorama of weird desert buttes and the Chemehuevi Mountains, it does at least linger in the memory.

The local **visitor center** is up from the river at 1930 Mesquite Ave (Mon–Fri 9am–5pm; ☎1-800/242-8278 or 520/453-3444); there's also an information kiosk at 420 English Village (daily 10am–4pm; ☎520/855-5655).

Several operators, such as Dreamcatcher (☎760/858-4593) and Dixie Belle Cruises (☎520/453-6776), offer short **river cruises** from the quayside of the English Village, charging around $12 for an hour-long trip focusing on the bridge, or $25 for a two-hour excursion to see rock formations upriver. Companies renting **jet-skis** (at around $40 per hour) and the like include Arizona Jet Ski (☎1-800/393-5558 or 520/453-5558) and Fun Time Boat Rentals (☎1-800/680-1003 or 520/680-1003).

Lake Havasu City has a good 25 or so **motels**, though relatively few of them are immediately obvious from Hwy-95. They range from the perfectly adequate *Windsor Inn Motel*, 451 London Bridge Rd (☎1-800/245-4135 or 520/855-4135; ②), by way of the fancier, all-suite *Ramada at Lake Havasu*, 271 S Lake Havasu Ave (☎1-800/528-5169 or 520/855-5169; ③), to the frankly ridiculous riverfront *London Bridge Resort*, 1477 Queen's Bay Rd (☎1-800/624-7939 or 520/855-0888; ④), where everything has a British-royalty theme.

As for **nightlife**, most of Lake Havasu City seems to be tucked up in bed by 9pm. For a night out, the districts at either end of London Bridge are your best bet. The *London Bridge Brewery* (☎520/855-8782) is a lively **microbrewery** in the English Village on the mainland, while *Shugrue's* (☎520/453-1400), across the bridge in the **Island Fashion Mall**, serves good fresh fish and even sushi, plus salads and pasta.

Las Vegas

Little emphasis is placed on the gambling clubs and divorce facilities – though they are attractions to many visitors – and much is being done to build up the cultural attractions. No cheap and easily parodied slogans have been adopted to publicize the city, no attempt has been made to introduce pseudo-romantic architectural themes or to give artificial glamor or gaiety. Las Vegas is itself – natural and therefore very appealing to people with a wide variety of interests.

WPA Guidebook to Nevada, 1940

Shimmering from the desert haze of Nevada like a latter-day El Dorado, **LAS VEGAS** is the most dynamic, spectacular city on earth. At the start of the twentieth century, it didn't even exist; now it's home to over one million people, with enough newcomers arriving all the time to need a new school every month. Boasting nine of the world's ten largest hotels, it's a monument to architectural exuberance, whose flamboyant, no-expense-spared **casinos** lure in thirty million tourists each year. Las Vegas has been stockpiling superlatives since the 1950s, but never rests on its laurels for a moment. Long before they lose their sparkle, yesterday's showpieces are blasted into rubble, to make way for ever more extravagant replacements. A few years ago, when the fashion was for fantasy, Arthurian castles and Egyptian pyramids mushroomed along the legendary Strip; now Vegas demands nothing less than entire cities, and has already acquired pocket versions of New York, Paris, Monte Carlo and Venice.

While Las Vegas has certainly cleaned up its act since the early days of Mob domination, there's little truth in the notion that it's become a family destination. In fact, for kids, it's not a patch on Orlando. Several casinos have added theme parks or fun rides to fill those odd non-gambling moments, but only five percent of visitors bring children, and the crowds that cluster around the exploding volcanoes and pirate battles along the Strip remain almost exclusively adult. Neither is Vegas as consistently cheap as it used to be. It's still possible to find good, inexpensive rooms, and the all-you-can-eat buffets offer unbeatable value, but the casino owners have finally discovered that high-rollers happy to lose hundreds of dollars per night don't mind paying premium prices to eat at top-quality restaurants, and some of the latest developments are budgeting on room rates closer to $300 than $30 per night.

Your first hours in Las Vegas are like entering another world, where the religion is luck, the language is money, and time is measured by revolutions of a roulette wheel. Once you're acclimatized, the whole spectacle can be absolutely exhilarating – assuming you haven't pinned your hopes, and your savings, on the pursuit of a fortune. Las Vegas is an unmissable destination, but one that palls for most visitors after a couple of (hectic) days.

If you've come solely to **gamble**, there's not much to say beyond the fact that all the casinos are free and open 24 hours per day, with acres of floor space packed with ways to lose money: million-dollar slots, video poker, blackjack, craps, roulette wheels and much much more. The casinos will just love it if you try to play a system; with the odds stacked against you, your best hope of a large win is to bet your entire stake on one single play, and then stop, win or lose.

Some history

The name *Las Vegas* – Spanish for "the meadows" – was originally applied to a group of natural springs that served as a way-station for travelers on the Old Spanish Trail from 1829 onwards. For the rest of the nineteenth century, the Paiute Indians shared the region with a handful of Mormon ranchers, and the valley had a population of just thirty in 1900. Things changed in 1905, with the completion of the now-defunct rail link between Salt Lake City and Los Angeles. Las Vegas itself was founded on May 15 that year, when the railroads auctioned off lots around what's now Fremont Street.

Ironically, Nevada was the first state to outlaw gambling, in 1909, but it was made legal once more in 1931, and the workers who built the nearby Hoover Dam flocked to Vegas to bet away their pay-checks. Providing abundant cheap electricity and water, the dam amounted to a massive federal subsidy for the infant city. Hotel-casinos such as the daring 65-room *El Rancho* began to appear in the early 1940s, but the Midwest Mafia were the first to appreciate the potential for profit. Mobster Bugsy Siegel raised $7 million to open the *Flamingo* on the Strip in December 1946; early losses forced him to close again in January 1947, and although he swiftly managed to re-open in March his erstwhile partners were dissatisfied enough with their returns to have him murdered in LA in June.

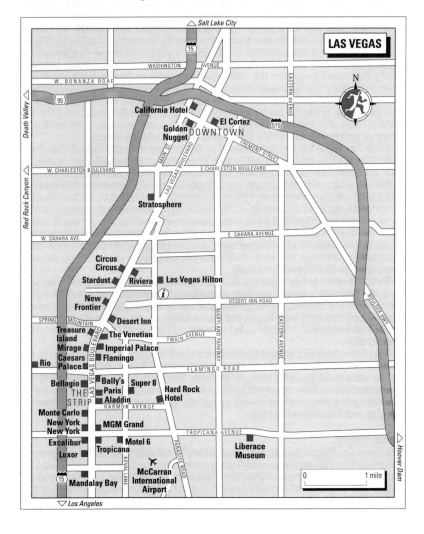

By the 1950s, Las Vegas was booming. The military had arrived – mushroom clouds from **A-bomb tests** in the deserts were visible from the city and visitors would drive out with picnics to get a better view – and so, too, had big guns like **Frank Sinatra**, who debuted at the *Desert Inn* in 1951, and **Liberace**, who received $50,000 to open the *Riviera* in 1955. As the stars gravitated towards the Vegas honeypot, nightclubs across America went out of business, and the city became the nation's undisputed live-entertainment capital.

The beginning of the end for Mob rule in Vegas came in 1966, after reclusive airline tycoon **Howard Hughes** sold TWA for $500 million and moved into the *Desert Inn*. When the owners tired of his stingy – specifically non-gambling – ways, he simply bought the hotel, and his clean-cut image encouraged other entrepreneurs to follow his example. **Elvis** arrived a little later; the young rock'n'roller had bombed at the *New Frontier* in 1956, but started a triumphant five-year stint as a karate-kicking lounge lizard at the *International* (now the *Las Vegas Hilton*) in 1969. He married Priscilla at the *Aladdin* on May 1, 1967, nine months to the day before the birth of Lisa Marie, and just eight years before Michael Jackson met Lisa Marie at a Jackson Five gig in Vegas.

Endless federal swoops and stings drove the Mob out of sight by the 1980s, in time for Vegas to re-invent itself on a surge of junk-bond megadollars. The success of Steve Wynn's *Mirage* in enticing a new generation of visitors, from 1989 onwards, spawned a host of imitators. The 1990s kicked off with a spate of casino building, including *Excalibur* and the *MGM Grand*, that has barely let up since, with *Luxor* and *New York–New York* followed as the millennium approached by the opulent quartet of *Bellagio, Mandalay Bay*, the *Venetian* and *Paris*. Beneath the glitz, however, **gambling** remains the bedrock, and Las Vegas' pre-eminence seems little dented by the spread of casinos elsewhere in the US. City boosters point out that only fifteen percent of Americans have so far seen Vegas, and they're confidently expecting the rest to turn up any day now.

Arrival, information and getting around

Las Vegas' busy **McCarran International Airport** (☎702/261-5743) is a mile south-east of the Strip, and four miles from downtown. Some hotels run free shuttle buses for guests, while Bell Trans (☎702/739-7990) run a minibus service to the Strip ($3.50) and downtown ($5). A **cab** to the Strip costs from $9 for the southern end up to $15 for casinos further north.

Another option for arriving into Las Vegas is Amtrak's new **express train** service from Los Angeles. The train, a five-and-a-half-hour journey, arrives and departs once a day; call ☎1-800-USA-RAIL for more details.

If you plan to see more of Vegas than the Strip, a **car** is invaluable. Typical **rental** rates would be $30 per day, $150 per week. All the major chains have outlets at the airport; Dollar (☎1-800/421-6868) is also represented at ten Strip casinos, Avis (☎1-800/331-1212) at *Bally's, Caesars Palace* and the *Las Vegas Hilton*, and Hertz (☎1-800/654-3131) at the *Desert Inn*. Allstate (☎1-800/634-6186) is an inexpensive local alternative, with additional locations at the *Riviera, Sahara* and *Plaza* casinos. To rent a Harley Davidson **motorcyle**, contact Drive With Passion (☎702/736-2592 or 1-800/372-1981).

Public transport does exist, however. The oak-veneered streetcars of the **Las Vegas Strip Trolley** (☎702/382-1404) ply the Strip between *Mandalay Bay* and the *Stratosphere*, for a flat fare of $1.40, while the similar **Downtown Trolley** (☎702/229-0624) loops between the *Stratosphere* and downtown for 50¢. CAT buses (☎702/228-7433) serve the whole city; #301 and #302 connect the Strip to downtown ($1.50). Greyhound's long-distance buses use a terminal at 200 S Main St downtown. Several Strip casinos are also connected by free **monorail systems**, but these don't link up with each other, and most require you to walk through the full length of the casinos in order to use them.

Any number of local freesheets and magazines provide local information. There are also **visitor centers** at 3150 Paradise Rd (Mon–Fri 8am–6pm, Sat & Sun 8am–5pm; ☎1-800/332-5333 or 702/892-0711), half a mile east of the Strip in the Convention Center, and 711 E Desert Inn Rd (Mon–Fri 8am–5pm; ☎702/735-1616). There can be no easier city in which to **change money**: the casinos gladly convert almost any currency, and their walls are festooned with every conceivable ATM machine.

Accommodation

Although Las Vegas has well over 100,000 motel and hotel **rooms** (most of them hitched to casinos), it's best to book accommodation ahead if you're on a tight budget, or arriving on Friday or Saturday; upwards of 200,000 people descend upon the city every weekend. Rooms can be very inexpensive, but be sure to get the rate confirmed for the duration of your stay – that $30 room you found on Thursday may cost $100 on Friday, and if a championship fight or other special event is on, room rates hit the roof. The CVB runs a **reservation service** on ☎1-800/332-5333.

If you're planning a trip from elsewhere in North America, check local newspaper advertisements for the latest Vegas bargains – virtually all hotels and motels offer discounts and food vouchers.

Bellagio, 3600 S Las Vegas Blvd (☎1-888/987-6667 or 702/791-7111, *www.belagiolasvegas.com*). The very top of the spectrum. Extremely luxurious rooms, with plush European furnishings and marble bathrooms; amazing pool complex; and the best restaurants in town. Sun–Thurs ⑦, Fri & Sat ⑧.

Caesar's Palace, 3570 S Las Vegas Blvd (☎1-800/634-6661 or 702/731-7222, *www.caesarspalace.com*). Right in the heart of the Strip, this epitome of 1960s luxury has recently trebled in size, and offers the last word in pseudo-Roman splendor, with top-class restaurants and shops. Sun–Thurs ⑤, Fri & Sat ⑥.

California Hotel, 12 Ogden Ave at First St (☎1-800/634-6255 or 702/385-1222). Mid-range downtown casino, with a mere 800 rooms, where the guests are mostly Hawaiian, and Hawaiian food and drink dominates the bars and restaurants. Sun–Thurs ③, Fri & Sat ④.

Circus Circus, 2880 S Las Vegas Blvd (☎1-800/444-2742 or 702/734-0410, *www.circuscircus-lasvegas.com*). Venerable Strip hotel that's a big hit with budget tour groups, and, especially, kids, with circus acts performing live above the casino floor. Sun–Thurs ③, Fri & Sat ④.

El Cortez Hotel, 600 E Fremont St (☎1-800/634-6703 or 702/385-5200). Long-standing downtown hotel, charging bargain rates for reasonable rooms; suites cost just a little extra. ①.

Excalibur, 3850 S Las Vegas Blvd (☎1-800/937-7777 or 702/597-7700, *www.excalibur-casino.com*). Arthurian legend built larger than life, with plenty to amuse the kids while the adults gamble away their college funds. Four thousand unexciting rooms – with showers not baths – plus assorted drawbridges, turrets and nightly jousting matches; staff have to call guests M'Lord and M'Lady. Sun–Thurs ④, Fri & Sat ⑤.

Hard Rock Hotel, 4455 Paradise Rd (☎1-800/693-ROCK or 702/693-5000, *www.hardrockhotel.com*). "The world's only rock'n'roll casino," over a mile east of the Strip, is a pale imitation of Las Vegas' showcase giants, but the guest rooms are above average, and there's a great pool. Sun–Thurs ⑤, Fri & Sat ⑦.

Las Vegas Backpackers Hostel, 1322 Fremont St (☎702/385-1150). Well-kept private hostel in a grim neighborhood ten blocks east of downtown, with dorms from $15 plus en-suite doubles, on-site bar and restaurant, and use of a good pool.

Las Vegas International Hostel, 1208 S Las Vegas Blvd (☎702/385-9955). Bare-bones AAIH hostel in a small, dilapidated former motel, in an insalubrious area on the fringes of downtown. Dorm beds cost for $14, rooms with shared bath under $30 – little cheaper than some Strip, and many downtown, hotels. ①.

Luxor, 3900 S Las Vegas Blvd (☎1-800/288-1000 or 702/262-4000, *www.luxor.com*). A night in this vast smoked-glass Egyptian-themed pyramid is one of the great Las Vegas experiences. All the

2000 large rooms in the pyramid itself face outwards, with tremendous views. Unlike the additional 2000 rooms in the new Tower next door, however, most have showers not baths. Sun–Thurs ③, Fri & Sat ⑥.

Mandalay Bay, 3950 S Las Vegas Blvd (☎1-877/632-7000 or 702/632-7777, *www.mandalaybay.com*). Young-adult playground that can feel a little far removed from the bustle of the central Strip. Each of its luxurious rooms has both bath and walk-in shower; the theming varies, but some have great Strip views. Guests have exclusive access to the spectacular wave pool. Sun–Thurs ⑥, Fri & Sat ⑦.

MGM Grand, 3799 S Las Vegas Blvd (☎1-800/929-1112 or 702/891-7777, *www.mgmgrand.com*). Waiting for any kind of service, especially check-in, at the world's largest hotel (it has 5005 rooms), can be horrendous, while walking from one end to the other can take half an hour. However, you get a good standard of accommodation for the price, and it holds several of Las Vegas' finest restaurants. Sun–Thurs ④, Fri & Sat ⑤.

Mirage, 3400 S Las Vegas Blvd (☎1-800/627-6667 or 702/791-7111, *www.themirage.com*). Glitzy casino, with its own volcano, rainforest and coral reef, some good restaurants and surprisingly tranquil rooms. Sun–Thurs ⑤, Fri & Sat ⑦.

Motel 6 – Tropicana, 195 E Tropicana Ave (☎702/798-0728). At 880 rooms, the largest *Motel 6* in the country; a ten-minute walk off the Strip from the *MGM Grand*. Sun–Thurs ②, Fri & Sat ③.

New York–New York, 3790 S Las Vegas Blvd (☎1-800/NYFORME or 702/740-6969, *www. nynyhotelcasino.com*). Mock Manhattan, looped by a high-speed roller-coaster and a riot of neon at night; the 2000 rooms are small, but plush by usual Strip standards. Sun–Thurs ⑤, Fri & Sat ⑦.

Paris-Las Vegas, 3645 S Las Vegas Blvd (☎1-888/BONJOUR or 702/967-4611, *www.paris-lv.com*). Flamboyant new casino, where the rooms and services are pitched slightly below those of Las Vegas' most upscale Vegas joints, but the location, views and general ambience are superb. Sun–Thurs ⑤, Fri & Sat ⑦.

Super 8, 4250 Koval Lane (☎1-800/800-8000 or 702/794-0888). The closest of Vegas' three *Super 8*s to the Strip has its own little casino and a reasonable restaurant. Sun–Thurs ②, Fri & Sat ③.

Treasure Island, 3300 S Las Vegas Blvd (☎1-800/944-7444 or 702/894-7111, *www.treasureisland. com*). Sister hotel to the neighboring *Mirage*, where an endless pirate battle plays to the passing crowds on the Strip, the restaurants within are swathed with rigging, and one TV channel shows the movie *Treasure Island* non-stop. Sun–Thurs ④, Fri & Sat ⑦.

The Venetian, 3355 S Las Vegas Blvd (☎1-888/283-6423 or 702/414-1000, *www.venetian.com*). Even the standard rooms at this upscale behemoth are split-level suites, offering antique-style canopied beds on a raised platform, plus roomy living rooms. Each also has a marble bath and walk-in shower. Sun–Thurs ⑦, Fri & Sat ⑧.

The City

Though the Las Vegas sprawl measures fifteen miles wide by fifteen miles long, most tourists stick to the six-mile stretch of Las Vegas Boulevard that includes the **Strip**, home to the major casinos, and **downtown**, slightly southeast of the intersection of I-15 and US-95. In between the two lie two somewhat seedy miles of gas stations, fast-food drive-ins and wedding chapels, while the rest of town is largely residential, and need barely concern you.

The Strip

For its razor-edge finesse in harnessing sheer, magnificent excess to the deadly serious business of making money, there's no place like the **Las Vegas Strip**. It's hard to imagine a time when Las Vegas was an ordinary city, and Las Vegas Boulevard a dusty thoroughfare scattered with the usual edge-of-town motels. After five decades of capitalism run riot, with every new casino-hotel setting out to surpass anything its neighbours ever dreamed of, the Strip seems to be locked into a hyperactive craving for thrills and glamour, forever discarding its latest toy in its frenzy for the next jackpot.

Each casino is a self-contained fantasyland of high camp and genuine excitement. Almost against your will, huge moving walkways sweep you in from the sidewalk; once inside, it can be almost impossible to find your way out. The action keeps going day and night, and in this sealed and windowless environment you rapidly lose track of which is which. Even if you do manage to get back onto the streets during the day, the scorching heat is liable to drive you straight back in again; night is the best time to venture out, when the neon's blazing at its brightest.

As the Strip pushes deeper into the desert, the newest casinos tend to rise at its southern end, not far west of the airport. The procession kicks off with the glowing gilded tower of **Mandalay Bay**, which opened in 1999. Financed through the profits from its neighbors, *Luxor* and *Excalibur*, *Mandalay Bay* is more upmarket than either, though all it has to offer the casual sightseer is the "Treasures of Mandalay Bay" museum (daily 9.30am–11pm; $7), a dull collection of old coins and banknotes. With an excellent assortment of restaurants as well as the *House of Blues* music venue, however, it's lively at night.

From the palm-fringed avenue of sphinxes guarding the entrance, to the reconstruction of Tutankhamun's tomb inside, the 36-story smoked-glass pyramid of **Luxor** next door plays endless variations upon Egyptian archeology. Three simulator rides and 3-D movies combine to reveal the *Secrets of the Luxor Pyramid*, a confusing saga of derring-do that's overpriced at $21.

Luxor's architect, Veldon Simpson, had previously designed **Excalibur**, immediately north. A less-sophisticated mock-up of a medieval castle, complete with drawbridge, crenellated towers, and a basement stuffed with fairground-style sideshows for the kids, it's usually packed out with low-budget tour groups. Its brief reign as the world's largest hotel, from 1990 to 1993, ended when the five-thousand-room **MGM Grand** – another Simpson creation – opened across the street. At that time, Las Vegas was in the midst of its misguided attempt to re-style itself as a destination for kids, and the *MGM Grand* sold itself on the strength of having its own **theme park**. Adding up to little when compared to the theme parks of Orlando or LA, however, that theme park has long since been scaled down, but the *Grand* is prospering nonetheless. As well as an excellent assortment of restaurants, it has become the most prestigious big-fight venue in town. Its latest attraction, the **Lion Habitat**, is a walk-through wooded zoo near to the front entrance where real lions lounge around a ruined temple beneath a naturally-lit dome. Admission is free (daily 11am–11pm), while for $20 you can have a degrading photo taken with a cute little lion cub (daily except Tues, 11am–5pm).

Excalibur and the *MGM Grand* are not the only giants facing off across the intersection of Las Vegas Boulevard and Tropicana Avenue, said to be the busiest traffic junction in the US. The northwest corner, diagonally opposite the veteran *Tropicana*, is occupied by the exuberantly meticulous **New York–New York**. This miniature Manhattan – created, like the original, in response to space limitations – boasts a skyline featuring twelve separate skyscrapers, and is fronted by the Statue of Liberty. Unusually, the interior is every bit as carefully realized, with a lovely rendition of Central Park at dusk. In one respect, it even surpasses New York itself; for $8 you can swoop around the whole thing at 65mph on the hair-raising *Manhattan Express* **roller coaster**.

North again, **Paris** was the 1999 handiwork of the same team of designers as *New York–New York*. With a half-size Eiffel Tower straddling the Arc de Triomphe and the Opera, it all feels a little compressed, but once again the attention to detail is a joy. Beret-wearing bread-toting bicyclists whistle Gallic tunes as they scurry along its cobbled streets, dodging the stripey-shirted accordionists and smart gendarmes, and there's a fine assortment of top-notch French restaurants. Elevators soar through the roof of the casino and up to the summit of the Eiffel Tower, for stunning views of the city, at their best after dark (daily 10am–1am; $8).

The Eiffel Tower was cheekily positioned to enjoy perfect views of **Bellagio**, opposite, *Mirage* owner Steve Wynn's 1998 attempt to build the best hotel in world history. *Bellagio* is undeniably a breathtaking achievement, but Wynn set himself a pointless and self-defeating task. While casino theming has always been playful – you're not supposed to think that being in *Luxor* is like being in ancient Egypt, just that it's fun to pretend – *Bellagio* wants to be real, and somehow more authentic than its original models. The trouble is that *Bellagio* is not in Europe, it's in Las Vegas, and it's stuffed full of slot machines. Inlaid with jewel-like precision into marble counters, perhaps, but still slot machines. *Bellagio*'s proudest boasts are the **Via Bellagio**, a covered mall of impossibly glamorous designer boutiques, and its opulent **Conservatory**, where a network of flowerbeds beneath a Belle Epoque canopy of copper-framed glass, is replanted every few weeks with ornate seasonal displays. Further back, near the pool, the thirty or so pieces on display at the **Bellagio Gallery of Fine Art** (daily 8am–11pm; $12) may form a very small, "Greatest Hits"-style collection, and the admission fee is expensive, but they're uniformly excellent, ranging from a Renoir from 1874, via canvases by Picasso, Monet and Degas, to a Liechtenstein from 1995.

Across Flamingo Road from *Bellagio*, **Caesar's Palace** still encapsulates Las Vegas at its best. Here the walkway delivers you past grand marble staircases that lead nowhere, and full-sized replicas of Michaelangelo's David, into a vast labyrinth of slots and green baize, peopled by strutting half-naked Roman centurions and Cleopatra-cropped waitresses. Above the stores, restaurants and "living statues" of the extraordinary **Forum**, the blue-domed ceiling dims and glows as it endlessly cycles from dawn to dusk and back again. The Forum is also home to **Race for Atlantis**, Las Vegas' only 3-D Imax simulator ride (Sun–Thurs 10am–11pm, Fri & Sat 10am–midnight; $9.50). What you pay is expensive for what you get – shaken to smithereens in front of a short sci-fi B-feature – but few kids leave disappointed. Caesar's itself has its own giant-screen OMNIMAX movie theater ($7), as well as the elaborate *Magical Empire*, a dinner-cum-magic-show for which tickets cost $75.

Night-time crowds jostle for space on the sidewalk outside the glittering **Mirage**, beyond *Caesar's*, to watch the somewhat half-hearted volcano that erupts every fifteen minutes, spewing water and fire into the lagoon below. Inside, a couple of Siegfried and Roy's white tigers lounge dopily in a glass-fronted enclosure near the main entrance. Next door, a pirate galleon and a British frigate, crewed by actors, do noisy battle outside **Treasure Island** (every ninety minutes, daily 4–11pm).

Across the Strip, the facade of another 1999 newcomer, the **Venetian**, includes loving facsimiles of six major Venice buildings. The main emphasis in the casino itself is on the lavish **Grand Canal Shoppes**, reached via a stairwell topped by vivid frescoes copied from yet more Venice originals. The ludicrous re-creation of the **Grand Canal** at the top, complete with gondolas and singing gondoliers ($10 a ride), is quintessential Las Vegas, and as such utterly irresistible – for God's sake, it's *upstairs*. Set on the second and third floors of the *Venetian*'s Library, the first US outpost of **Madame Tussaud's** renowned waxwork museum eschews boring old history in favor of styling itself as the **Celebrity Encounter** (daily 10am–10pm; $12.50, ages 4–12 $10). What that means is that visitors can pose with, touch, caress and mock effigies such as Siegfried and Roy, Liberace, Tom Jones and Frank Sinatra; the whole experience is seriously over-priced, its token animatronic showpieces not a patch on the free shows at *Caesar's*.

The family-oriented **Circus Circus**, another mile north, uses live circus acts to pull in the punters – a trapeze artist here, a fire-eater there – and also has an indoor theme park, **Grand Slam Canyon** (Sun–Thurs 10am–6pm, Fri & Sat 10am–midnight), where you pay separately for each roller coaster or river-ride. If you really want to cool off, you'd do better to head on to the flumes and chutes of Vegas' one purpose-built water park, **Wet'n'Wild**, 2601 S Las Vegas Blvd (summer daily 10am–8pm; $24).

Meanwhile, the **Las Vegas Hilton**, half a mile east of *Circus Circus* at 3000 Paradise Rd, is home to the very busy **Star Trek Experience** (daily 11am–11pm; $15). In a museum-like atmosphere, glossy display panels recount a wordy Star Trek chronology that takes in World War III in 2053, and the birth of Spock in 2230, while diminutive Ferengi stroll among you. The whole thing culminates when you're sent on a mildly vomitous motion-simulator ride through deep space, to emerge in a shopping area you could have reached without paying anyway, where memorabilia prices boldly go to well over $2000 for a leather jacket.

Circus Circus has traditionally marked the northern limit of the Strip, though the 1996 opening of the **Stratosphere**, half a mile towards downtown, tried to change that. At 1149 feet, the *Stratosphere* is the tallest building west of the Mississippi, and the outdoor deck and indoor viewing chamber in the sphere near the summit offer amazing panoramas across the city ($5). Two utterly demented thrill rides can take you even closer to heaven; the world's highest roller coaster swirls around the outside of the sphere, while the ludicrous Big Shot shunts you to the very top of an additional 160-foot spire, from which you free-fall back down again ($5 each).

Downtown and the Liberace Museum

As the Strip has gone from strength to strength, **downtown** Las Vegas, the city's original core, has by comparison been neglected. Long known as "Glitter Gulch," and consisting of a few compact blocks of lower-key casinos, it has recently embarked upon a revival. Between Main Street and Las Vegas Boulevard, five entire blocks of Fremont Street, its principal thoroughfare, have been roofed with an open-air mesh to create the **Fremont Street Experience**. This "Celestial Vault" is studded with over two million colored light bulbs, choreographed by computer in dazzling nightly displays (hourly, 8pm–midnight; free), but there's a long way to go before the district as a whole can compete with the Strip once again.

Almost all Las Vegas' handful of museums are eminently missable, with one unarguable exception: the **Liberace Museum**, two miles east of the Strip at 1775 E Tropicana Ave (Mon–Sat 10am–5pm, Sun 1–5pm; $7). Popularly remembered as a beaming buffoon who knocked out torpid toe-tappers, Liberace, who died in 1987, started out playing piano in the rough bars of Milwaukee during the 1940s. A decade later, he was being mobbed by screaming adolescents and ruthlessly hounded by the scandal-hungry press. All this is recalled by a yellowing collection of cuttings and family photos, along with electric candelabra, bejewelled quail eggs with inlaid pianos, rhinestone-covered fur coats, glittering cars and more. The music, piped into the scented toilets, may not have improved with age, but the museum is a satisfying attempt to answer the seminal question "how does a great performer top himself on stage?".

Red Rock Canyon

For a blast of sunlight and fresh air away from the casinos, and a sample of some classic southwestern canyon scenery, head twenty miles west of the Strip along Charleston Boulevard to the **Red Rock Canyon National Conservation Area**. This BLM-run park consists of a cactus-strewn desert basin surrounded by stark red cliffs that are pierced repeatedly by narrow canyons accessible only on foot.

Red Rock Canyon's **visitor center**, which has displays about the canyon and a viewing window overlooking its main features (daily 8am–5pm; ☎702/363-1921), stands just before the start of the **Scenic Drive** (daily 7am–dusk; $5 per vehicle). As this thirteen-mile loop road meanders around the edge of the basin, it passes trailheads like the one for the cool, slender **Ice Box Canyon** (a 2.5-mile round-trip hike), and the three-mile **Pine Creek Trail**, which follows a flower-lined creek beyond a ruined homesite towards a towering red-capped monolith.

Lake Mead and the Hoover Dam

Almost as many people as go to Las Vegas visit **LAKE MEAD**, the vast reservoir thirty miles southeast of the city that was created by the construction of the Hoover

Dam. A bizarre spectacle, its blue waters a vivid counterpoint to the surrounding desert, it gets excruciatingly crowded all year round.

Though the **Lake Mead National Recreation Area** straddles the border between Nevada and Arizona, the best views come from the Nevada side. Even if you don't need details of how to sail, scuba-dive, water-ski or fish from the marinas along the five-hundred-mile shoreline, call in at the **Alan Bible visitor center** (daily 8.30am–4.30pm; ☎702/293-8990), four miles northeast of Boulder City on US-93, to enjoy a sweeping prospect of the whole thing.

Eight miles on, beyond the rocky ridges of the Black Mountains, US-93 reaches the **Hoover Dam** itself, completed in 1935. Designed to block the Colorado River and provide low-cost electricity for the cities of the southwest, it's among the tallest dams ever built (760ft high), and used enough concrete to build a two-lane highway from the West Coast to New York. Informative thirty-minute guided tours of the dam leave from the **Hoover Dam Visitor Center** on the Nevada side of the river (daily 8.30am–5.45pm; $8; ☎702/293-1824). Five-hour, $20 **bus tours** to the dam from Las Vegas are run by Gray Line (☎702/384-1234).

Eating and drinking

Barely ten years ago, the **restaurant** scene in Las Vegas was governed by the notion that visitors were not prepared to pay for gourmet food, and the only quality restaurants

---

GETTING MARRIED IN LAS VEGAS

Second only to making your fortune as a reason to visit Las Vegas is the prospect of **getting married**. Over a hundred thousand weddings are performed here each year, many so informal that bride and groom just wind down the window of their car during the ceremony, and a Vegas wedding has become a byword for tongue-in-cheek chic.

You don't have to be a local resident or take a blood test to get wed in Las Vegas. Assuming you're both at least eighteen years old and carrying picture ID, and neither of you is already married, simply turn up at the Clark County Marriage License Bureau, downtown at 200 S Third St (Mon–Thurs 8am–midnight, and continuously from 8am on Fri to midnight on Sun; ☎702/455-4416), and buy a marriage license for $35 cash.

Wedding chapels claim to charge as little as $50 for their most basic ceremonies, but at that sort of rate even the minister is regarded as an "extra" costing an additional $40. Reckon on paying at least $100 for the bare minimum, which is liable to be as romantic a process as checking in at a hotel, and to take about as long. The full deluxe service ranges up to around $500.

Candlelight Wedding Chapel, 2855 Las Vegas Blvd S; ☎702/735-4179 or 1-800/962-1818. Busy little chapel across from *Circus Circus*, where you get a garter with the $169 wedding package, or two white T-shirts with the $499 option.

Graceland Wedding Chapel, 619 S Las Vegas Blvd; ☎702/474-6655 or 1-800/824-5732. Home of the King – an Elvis impersonator will act as best man, give the bride away or serenade you, but unfortunately he can't perform the service.

Little Church of the West, 4617 Las Vegas Blvd S; ☎702/739-7971 or 1-800/821-2452. Once part of the *Last*

Frontier casino, this fifty-year-old chapel is on the National Register of Historic Places, and has moved progressively down the Strip to its current site south of *Mandalay Bay*. Among the more peaceful and quiet places to exchange your Vegas vows – if that's really what you want.

Little White Chapel, 1301 S Las Vegas Blvd; ☎702/382-5943 or 1-800/545-8111. Where Bruce Willis and Demi Moore married each other, and Michael Jordan and Joan Collins married other people. Open all day every day, with the "The One & Only 24hr Drive-Up Wedding Window," if you're in a major hurry.

were upscale Italian places well away from the Strip. Now, however, the situation has reversed, as the major casinos compete to attract culinary superstars from all over the country to open Vegas outlets. Many tourists now come to the city in order to eat at several of the best restaurants in the United States, without having to reserve a table months in advance or pay sky-high prices.

Nonetheless, almost every casino still features an all-you-can-eat **buffet**. The better buffets tend to be in casinos that are neither on the Strip nor downtown, and depend on locals as well as tourists. By contrast, those at the largest casinos, like *Excalibur* and the *MGM Grand*, only have to be good enough to ensure that the crowds already in the building don't leave, while also coping with a daily deluge of customers.

Though there are plenty of dining places away from the Strip, only a small proportion of eccentric tourists bother to venture off in search of them. **Drinks** – beer, wine, spirits and cocktails – are freely available in all the casinos to anyone gambling, and are very cheap for anyone else.

Buffets

The Buffet, *Bellagio*, 3600 S Las Vegas Blvd (☎702/791-7111). Far and away Las Vegas' best buffet. With other buffets, you may rave about what good value they are; with this one, you'll rave about what good food it is. Breakfast is $10; lunch is $12.50, and includes sushi, sashimi and dim sum; and dinner, with choices like lobster claws, fresh oysters and venison, is $20.

Carnival World Buffet, *Rio*, 3700 W Flamingo Rd (☎702/252-7777). Excellent value, half a mile west of the Strip. The variety is immense, including Thai, Chinese, Mexican and Japanese stations as well as the usual pasta and barbecue, and even a fish'n'chip stand. $8 for breakfast, $10 for lunch and $12 for dinner.

Garden Court Buffet, *Main Street Station*, 200 N Main St (☎702/387-1896). Downtown's best-value buffet, ranging from fried chicken and corn at "South to Southwest," to tortillas at "Ole," and pork chow mein and oyster tofu at "Pacific Rim." Breakfast is $5, lunch $7 and dinner $10.

Le Village Buffet, *Paris*, S 3655 Las Vegas Blvd (☎702/967-7000). Superb French-only cuisine, with great seafood, succulent roast chicken and super-fresh vegetables. The setting is a little cramped, squeezed into a very Disney-esque French village, but the food is *magnifique*. Breakfast is $10, lunch $13 and dinner $20.

Restaurants

Binion's Horseshoe Coffee Shop, *Binion's Horseshoe*, 128 E Fremont St (☎702/382-1600). The 24-hour Las Vegas coffee shop of your dreams, in the basement of a veteran downtown casino. Between 10pm and 5am, a steak dinner costs just $3, but even at prime time, 4.45–11.45pm, a 16-oz T-bone is only $6.75. Breakfast is highly recommended; the $3 "Benny Binion's Natural," served 2am–2pm, comes with two eggs, bacon or ham and magnificent home fries.

Emeril's New Orleans Fish House, *MGM Grand*, S 3799 Las Vegas Blvd (☎702/891-7374). An authentic slice of New Orleans in the heart of the *MGM Grand*. Cajun seafood with a modern (but never low-cal) twist is the specialty, with barbecue shrimp for $18 at lunchtime and redfish in red bean sauce for $25 at dinner.

Il Fornaio, *New York–New York*, 3790 S Las Vegas Blvd (☎702/740-6403). The nicest place to enjoy the atmosphere of *New York–New York*, this rural-Italian restaurant is a real joy. Grab a pizza for around $10, or linger over a full meal of soft-shell crab ($9) or carpaccio of beef ($8) to start, followed by gnocchi with smoked salmon ($14), baked seabass with cherry tomatoes ($18.50), or rotisserie chicken ($14.50).

Mr Lucky's 24/7, *Hard Rock Hotel*, 4455 Paradise Rd (☎702/693-5000). Stylish 24-hour coffee shop, with an open kitchen, *faux*-fur booths and subdued tan-and-cream paint-job, where the food is well above average.

Olives, *Bellagio*, 3600 S Las Vegas Blvd (☎702/693-8181). *Bellagio*'s finest restaurant may call a $10 pizza an "individual oven-baked flatbread," and your food is more likely to be arranged vertically than horizontally, but the largely Mediterranean menu is uniformly fresh and superb. It's a great spot for lunch, at well under $20; dinner is pricier, but at least you get a platter of huge, delicious olives as soon as you sit down.

Wolfgang Puck Cafe, *MGM Grand*, S 3799 Las Vegas Blvd (☎702/895-9653). Designer-diner-cum-café, where they'll whisk you through your meal in the blink of an eyelid, but you won't be disappointed with the food. No reservations. Open daily for breakfast, lunch and dinner.

Nightlife and entertainment

There was a time when Las Vegas represented the pinnacle of any show-business career. In the early 1960s, when Frank Sinatra's Rat Pack were shooting hit movies like *Ocean's 11* during the day then singing the night away at the *Sands*, the city could claim to be the capital of the international entertainment industry. It was even hip. Now, however, although the money is still there, the world has moved on. As the great names of the past fade from view, few of the individual performers popular with traditional Vegas visitors are considered capable of carrying an extended-run show. The tendency instead is to rely on lavish stunts and special effects. A fair number of old-style Vegas revues are still soldiering on, but there are more stimulating contemporary productions than you might imagine. Most hold at least a few tickets back for sale on the day of performance, but for the big-name shows it's worth booking your seats as far in advance as possible.

Imagine, *Luxor*, 3900 S Las Vegas Blvd (☎702/262-4400). A stunning array of tumblers, acrobats and contortionists, some sexy traditional showgirls and showboys, and lots of magical illusions, all accompanied by a barrage of thunderous semi-orchestral rock. Mon, Wed, Fri & Sat 7.30pm & 10pm, Sun & Tues 7.30pm. $40.

Lance Burton, *Monte Carlo*, 3770 S Las Vegas Blvd (☎702/730-7160). The best family show in Las Vegas, featuring master magician Lance Burton. Most of it consists of traditional but very impressive stunts with playing cards, handkerchiefs and doves, but large-scale illusions include the disappearance of an entire airplane and a narrow escape from hanging. Tues–Sat 7.30pm & 10.30pm. $35 and $40.

Legends in Concert, *Imperial Palace*, 3535 S Las Vegas Blvd (☎702/794-3261). Enjoyable celebrity-tribute show, with a changing roster of stars that ranges from the Righteous Brothers to Shania Twain. Daily except Sun 7.30pm & 10.30pm. $34.50, ages 12 and under $19.50, including 2 drinks.

O, *Bellagio*, 3600 S Las Vegas Blvd (☎702/693-7722). Las Vegas' most expensive show is a remarkable testament to how much is possible when the budget is barely an issue. Any part of the stage at any time may be submerged to any depth. One moment a performer can walk across a particular spot, the next someone may dive headfirst into it from the high wire. From the synchronized swimmers onwards, the Cirque du Soleil display their magnificent skills to maximum advantage. Fri–Tues 7.30 & 10.30pm. $90 & $100.

Siegfried and Roy, *The Mirage*, 3400 Las Vegas Blvd S (☎702/792-7777). Austrian magicians Siegfried and Roy have appeared over four thousand times at the *Mirage*, and it shows, not just in their professionalism but in their air of going through the motions. The highest-paid entertainers in Vegas history put on an impressive display of illusions, causing elephants and even dragons to vanish, and teleporting themselves across the arena, but even if you can't tell how it's done, you know they're basically technicians operating industrial machinery. When the stage fills up with their beloved white lions and tigers, Siegfried and Roy finally perk up enough to take a cloying, self-congratulatory bow; the narcissism of the whole thing is as breathtaking as the magic. Mon, Tues & Fri–Sun 7.30pm & 11pm. $89, including drinks.

The Grand Canyon

The **GRAND CANYON OF THE COLORADO** in Arizona, three hundred long and featureless driving miles from Las Vegas, is one of those sights that you really *have* to see once in your life, and once you've ventured east of the California state line it would be a real shame to exclude it from your itinerary.

Although three million people come to see the Grand Canyon every year, it remains beyond the grasp of the human imagination. No photograph, no set of statistics, can prepare you for such vastness. At more than one mile deep, it's an inconceivable abyss; at from four to eighteen miles wide it's an endless expanse of bewildering shapes and colors, glaring desert brightness and impenetrable shadow, stark promontories and soaring never-to-be-climbed sandstone pinnacles. Somehow it's so impassive, so remote – you could never call it a disappointment, but at the same time many visitors are left feeling peculiarly flat. In a sense, none of the available activities can quite live up to that first stunning sight of the chasm. The **overlooks** along the rim all offer views that shift and change unceasingly from dawn to dusk; you can **hike** down into the depths on foot or by mule, hover above in a **helicopter** or raft through the **whitewater rapids** of the river itself; you can spend a night at **Phantom Ranch** on the canyon floor, or swim in the waterfalls of the idyllic **Havasupai Reservation**; and yet that distance always remains – the Grand Canyon stands apart.

The vast majority of visitors come to the **South Rim**, which you'll find described in full on the next few pages – it's the most accessible part of the canyon, there are far more facilities (mainly at **Grand Canyon Village**), and it's open year-round. There's another lodge and campground at the **North Rim**, which by virtue of its isolation can be a whole lot more evocative (for accommodation reservations, see p.262), but at one thousand feet higher this is usually closed by snow from mid-October until May. An even less eventful drive from Las Vegas brings you here via St George in southern Utah. Few people visit both rims; to get from one to the other demands either a two-day hike down one side of the canyon and up the other, or a 215-mile drive by road. Until the 1920s, the average visitor would stay for two or three weeks; these days it's more like two or three hours – of which forty minutes are spent actually looking at the canyon.

Finally, there's a definite risk that on the day you come the Grand Canyon will be invisible beneath a layer of **fog**; many people blame the 250 tons of sulphurous emissions pumped out every day by the Navajo Generating Station, seventy miles upriver at Page. **Admission prices** to the park, valid for seven days on either rim, are $20 per vehicle, or $10 per pedestrian or cyclist.

Practicalities

The most usual approach to the South Rim of the Grand Canyon is by **road**, turning north off I-17 at **Williams** to drive the last 56 miles on Hwy-64, or detouring further east via the larger town of **Flagstaff** and then following Hwy-180 past the San Francisco mountains. The two roads join twenty miles before the canyon, at Valle. Most of this stretch is through thick ponderosa pine forests, so the ride up from Williams on the restored **steam trains** of the Grand Canyon Railway is not especially scenic (departs Williams 9.30am: daily late March to Oct; rest of year weekends only; $50 round-trip; ☎1-800/THE-TRAIN or 520/774-5003). Passengers who arrive on Flagstaff's two daily Amtrak **trains** can reach Grand Canyon Village on connecting Nava-Hopi **buses** ($12.50; ☎520/774-5003 or 1-800/892-8687); one leaves Flagstaff at 7.30am, calls at Williams at 8.20 am, and arrives at the canyon at 9.45am, the other runs straight from Flagstaff to the canyon, departing at 2.30pm and arriving 4.30pm. Return trips leave *Maswik Lodge* at 10.30am – a direct service to Flagstaff, arriving at 12.30pm – and 5pm, reaching Williams at 6.15pm and Flagstaff at 7pm.

The small **airport** at Tusayan – six miles from the South Rim, and used primarily by "flight-seeing" tour companies (see p.265) – also welcomes scheduled services, especially from Las Vegas, with operators such as Scenic Airlines (from $60 one-way; ☎702/739-1900 or 1-800/634-6801).

Under plans due to be implemented from September 2000 onwards, private vehicles will no longer be able to drive to the edge of the canyon. All day-trippers will have to park at Tusayan, and be carried by a light railway system to the new **Canyon View Information Plaza** near Mather Point. From there, shuttle buses will ferry visitors

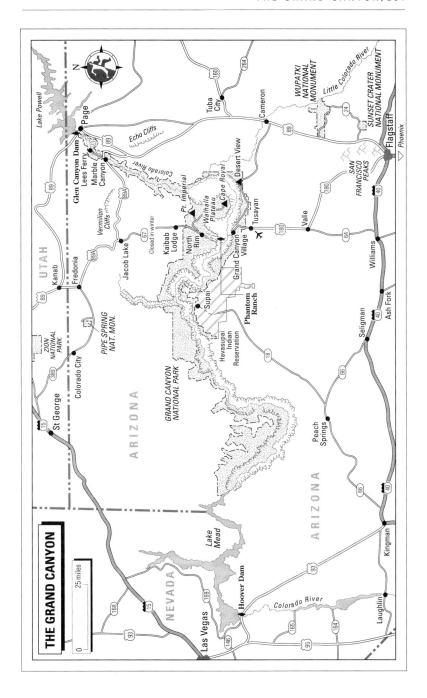

THE GRAND CANYON

> All in-park **accommodation reservations** – for the lodges on both the South and the
> North rims, as well as for Phantom Ranch and RV camping – are handled by Amfac Parks
> & Resorts, 14001 East Iliff, #600, Aurora, CO 80014 (same-day ☎520/638-2631; advance
> ☎303/297-2757; *www.amfac.com*). The best rooms are often booked as much as a year in
> advance, and your chances of turning up without a reservation and finding a place in
> summer are minimal.

along the South Rim, while it will also be possible to hike or cycle along rim-edge trails.
Grand Canyon Village will however still be accessible by car, so overnight guests with
reservations can reach their lodgings. For the moment, free **shuttle buses** run on
three separate routes, between mid-March and mid-October only; one heads west from
the village, one east, and the other circles the village itself stopping at all its hotels and
other facilities.

Grand Canyon Village

GRAND CANYON VILLAGE is not a very stimulating place to spend any time.
However, in the absence of significantly cheaper accommodation within fifty miles (for
example, in **Tusayan** at the park entrance), there's little option but to stay here. The
centerpiece is the magnificent **terrace** in front of *Bright Angel Lodge* (usually the liveliest spot in town) and the black-beamed 1905 *El Tovar Hotel*, which gives many visitors
their only look at the canyon – though the Colorado itself is too deep in the Inner
Gorge to be seen from here. Further back are more lodges and giftshops, and employee housing, while about a mile east through the woods are the informative **visitor
center** (daily 8am–6pm; ☎520/638-7888), the **post office**, the **general store** and the
campground.

Grand Canyon accommodation

All the "lodges" in the village charge similar prices, with no budget **accommodation**
alternative. To see the canyon, it makes little difference where in the village you stay.
Even in the "rim-edge" places – *El Tovar Hotel* (⑥) and the *Bright Angel* (rooms ④, rim-
side cabins ⑤), *Thunderbird* and *Kachina* lodges (both ④) – few rooms offer much of
a view, and in any case it's always dark by 8pm. Further back are *Maswik Lodge* (cabins and rooms ④), *Yavapai Lodge* near the visitor center (⑤), and *Moqui Lodge* at the
park entrance (mid-Feb to Nov; ⑤).

    Camping facilities (and a laundry) are available at the *Mather* campground and RV
park ($12) near the visitor center, at least one section of which is open year-round. If
you arrive on foot, you don't need a reservation; all vehicles should, however, check in
well in advance (you can book through *BIOSPHERICS* on ☎1-800/365-2267). The summer-only *Desert View* campground, 26 miles east, is first come, first served, costs $10,
and has no hook-ups. It's also possible to camp inside the canyon itself, if you first
obtain a $20 permit from the **Backcountry Reservations Office** near *Maswik Lodge*
(daily 8am–noon & 1–5pm; ☎520/638-7875); indeed you can camp anywhere in **Kaibab
National Forest** so long as you're more than 200 yards from a roadway.

    If all the park accommodation is full, the nearest alternative is the underwhelming
service village of **TUSAYAN**, just over a mile south of the park entrance. *Seven Mile
Lodge* (☎520/638-2291; ④) offers the least expensive rooms; the new *Grand Hotel*
(☎520/638-3333; ⑥) is more stylish. The most popular of the commercial **campgrounds** outside the park– with families, at least – is *Flintstone's Bedrock City* (mid-
March to Oct; ☎520/635-2600; $12–16), 22 miles south at the junction of Hwy-64 and
Hwy-180, which has its own prehistoric theme park.

Grand Canyon eating

Thanks to the canyon's remoteness and lack of water, **food prices** tend to be well above average; if you're on a tight budget, bring your own. However, *Yavapai* and *Maswik* lodges have reasonable basic cafeterias, open until 10pm. *Bright Angel Lodge* has its own **restaurant**, as well as the *Arizona Steakhouse*, both also open until 10pm, and both costing $15–30. At *El Tovar*, where the dining room looks right out over the canyon, the sumptuous menu is enormously expensive. Breakfast is the most afford-able meal; lunch and dinner can easily cost upwards of $40. In **Tusayan**, *We Cook Pizza & Pasta* (☎520/638-2278) is good but pricey.

Along the South Rim

It's possible to walk along the South Rim for several miles in either direction from the village, the first few of them on railed, concrete pathways. The most obvious short excursions are to see the sun rise and set. At or near the village, the giant wall that reaches out in the west overshadows much of the evening view. If, however, you walk right out to **Hopi Point** at its end, looking down as you go onto the Bright Angel Trail as it winds across the Tonto Plateau, you may well see a magical **sunset**, with the Colorado – 350ft wide at this point – visible way below.

The best place within walking distance to watch the **dawn** is **Mather Point**, a mile east of the visitor center. Nearby, if you can tear your eyes away from its panoramic bay windows, the **Yavapai Geologic Museum** (summer daily 9am–7pm; free) has illumi-nating displays on how the canyon may have been formed.

Further dramatic views are available along the **East Rim Drive** – although unless you take an excursion you'll need your own vehicle to see them. **Desert View**, 23 miles out from the village, is at 7500ft the highest point on the South Rim. Visible to the east are the vast flatlands of the **Navajo Nation**; to the northeast, **Vermillion and Echo Cliffs**, and the gray bulk of **Navajo Mountain** ninety miles away; to the west, the gigantic peaks of **Vishnu** and **Buddha temples**. Through the plains comes the nar-row gorge of the **Little Colorado**; somewhere in the depths, before it meets the Colorado itself, is the *sipapu*, the hole through which the Hopi believe that men first entered this, the Third World. The odd-looking construction on the very lip of the canyon is **Desert View Watchtower**, built by Fred Harvey in 1932 in a conglomeration of Native American styles (though a steel frame props it all up) and decorated with Hopi pictographs. It contains a gift shop, as does the general store a few yards away. Groups of tarantulas are often seen in the evenings at Desert View, scuttling back into the warmth of the canyon for the night.

Tusayan Ruin, three miles west of Desert View (and not to be confused with mod-ern Tusayan) is a genuine Anasazi pueblo, though not comparable in scale to the relics elsewhere in this region.

Into the Canyon

Hiking any of the trails that descend into the Grand Canyon offers something more than just another view of the same thing. Instead you pass through a sequence of ut-terly different landscapes, each with its own distinct climate, wildlife and topography. However, while the canyon can offer a wonderful wilderness experience, it's essential to remember that it can be a hostile and very unforgiving environment, gruelling even for expert hikers.

The South Rim is 7000 feet above sea level, an altitude which for most people is fatiguing in itself. Furthermore, all hikes start with a long, steep descent – which can

GEOLOGY AND HISTORY OF THE CANYON

Layer upon layer of different rocks, readily distinguished by color and each with its own **fossil record**, recede down into the Grand Canyon and back through time, until the strata at the riverbed are among the oldest exposed rocks on earth. And yet how the canyon was formed is a mystery. Satellite photos show that the Colorado actually runs through the heart of an enormous hill (what the Indians called the *Kaibab*, the mountain with no peak); experts cannot agree on how this could happen. Studies show that the canyon still deepens, at the slow rate of 50ft per million years. Its fantastic sandstone and limestone formations were not literally carved by the river, however; they're the result of erosion by wind and extreme cycles of heat and cold. These features were named – **Brahma Temple, Vishnu Temple**, and so on – by Clarence Dutton, a student of comparative religion who wrote the first Geological Survey report on the canyon in 1881.

It may look forbidding, but the Grand Canyon is not a dead place. All sorts of desert **wildlife** survive here – sheep and rabbits, eagles and vultures, mountain lions, and, of course, spiders, scorpions and snakes. The **human** presence has never been on any great scale, but signs have been found of habitation as early as 2000 BC, and the **Anasazi** were certainly here later on. A party of **Spaniards** passed through in 1540 – less than twenty years after Cortes conquered the Aztecs – searching for cities of gold, and one Father Garcés spent some time with the Havasupai in 1776. **John Wesley Powell's** expeditions along the fearsome and uncharted waters of the Colorado in 1869 and 1871–72 were what really brought the canyon to public attention. A few abortive attempts were made to mine different areas, but facilities for tourism were swiftly realized to be a far more lucrative investment. With the exception of the Indian reservations, the Grand Canyon is now run exclusively for the benefit of visitors; although even as recently as 1963 there were proposals to dam the Colorado and flood 150 miles of the Canyon, and the Glen Canyon dam has seriously affected the ecology downstream.

come as a shock to the knees – and unless you camp overnight you'll have to climb all the way back up again when you're hotter and wearier.

If you're day-hiking, the golden rule is to keep track of how much time you spend hiking down, and allow twice that much to get back up again. Average summer temperatures inside the canyon exceed 100°F; to hike for eight hours in that sort of heat, you have to drink an incredible thirty pints of water. Always carry at least a quart per person, and much more if there are no water sources along your chosen trail. You must have food as well, as drinking large quantities without also eating can cause water intoxication.

There's only space here to detail the most popular trail, the **Bright Angel**. Many of the others, such as the **Hermit**, date from the days prior to 1928, when the obstreperous Ralph Cameron controlled access to the Bright Angel and many other rim-edge sites by means of spurious mining claims and the Fred Harvey company had to find other ways to get its customers down to the Colorado. These other trails tend to be overgrown now, or partially blocked by landslides; check before setting out.

Bright Angel Trail

The **Bright Angel Trail**, followed on foot or mule by thousands of visitors each year, starts from the wooden shack in the village which was once the Kolb photographic studio. It takes 9.6 miles to switchback down to **Phantom Ranch** beside the river, but park rangers have a simple message for all would-be hikers: don't try to hike down and back in a single day. It might not look far on the map, but it's harder than running a marathon. The longest feasible day-hike is to go instead as far as **Plateau Point** on the edge of the arid Tonto Plateau, an overlook above the Inner Gorge from which it is not possible to descend any further – a twelve-mile round trip that will probably take you at

GRAND CANYON TOURS

The Fred Harvey Company (contact the "transportation desks" in the South Rim lodges, or call ☎520/638-2401) runs at least two short daily **coach tours** along the **rim** to the west ($13.50) and east ($24.50) of the village, **sunrise** and **sunset** trips to Yavapai Point ($10), and **mule** rides to Phantom Ranch (from $295; see below). It also operates a five-hour **Smooth Water River Raft Excursion** through Marble Canyon ($80); whitewater rafting trips in the canyon proper – such as those run by Western River Expeditions (☎801/942-6669 or 1-800/453-7450) – are booked up literally years in advance, so this is probably your only chance of a trip along the river at short notice.

Airplane tours cost from around $65 for 30min ($45 child) up to as long as you like for as much as you've got. Operators include Air Grand Canyon (☎520/638-2686 or 1-800/AIR-GRAND) and Grand Canyon Airlines (☎520/638-2463). **Helicopter tours**, from $90 for 30min, are offered by AirStar Helicopters (☎520/638-2622) and Papillon Helicopters (☎520/638-2419), who also operate $440 day-trips to the Havasupai Reservation. Unless otherwise specified, all the companies are in **Tusayan**, at or near the airport.

least eight hours. In summer, water can be obtained along the way. The first section of the trail was laid out by miners a century ago, along an old Havasupai route, and has two short tunnels in its first mile. After another mile, the **wildlife** starts to increase (deer, rodents and the ubiquitous ravens), and there are a few **pictographs** which have been all but obscured by graffiti.

At the lush **Indian Gardens** almost five miles down, where you'll find a ranger station and campground with water, the trails split, to Plateau Point or down to the river via the **Devil's Corkscrew**. The latter route leads through sand dunes scattered with cactuses and down beside **Garden Creek** to the Colorado, which you then follow for more than a mile to get to Phantom Ranch.

Phantom Ranch

It's a real thrill to spend a night at the very bottom of the canyon, at the 1922 **Phantom Ranch**. The **cabins** are reserved exclusively for the use of excursionists on Fred Harvey two-day mule trips ($295 per person for one night, $524 for the winter-only two-night trips). Beds in the four ten-bunk **dorms** ($22) are usually reserved way in advance, through Amfac (see p.262), but it's worth checking for cancellations at the Bright Angel transportation desk as soon as you reach the South Rim. Do not hike down without a reservation, and even if you do have one, reconfirm it the day before you set off. All supplies reach Phantom Ranch the same way you do (an all-day hike on foot or mule), so **meals** are expensive, a minimum of $12 for breakfast and $17 for dinner.

The **suspension bridge** here was set in place in 1928 (hanging from twin cables carried down on the shoulders of 42 Havasupai). The delta of **Bright Angel Creek**, named by Powell to contrast with the muddy **Dirty Devil** upriver in Utah, is several hundred feet wide here, and strewn with boulders. All the water used on the South Rim now comes by pipeline from the North Rim, and crosses the river on the 1960s Silver Bridge nearby.

The Havasupai Reservation

The **Havasupai Reservation** really is another world. A 1930s anthropologist called it "the only spot in the United States where native culture has remained in anything like its pristine condition"; things have changed a little since then, but the sheer magic of its turquoise waterfalls and canyon scenery make this a very special place. Traditionally, the Havasupai would spend summer on the canyon floor and winter on the plateau above. However, when the reservation was created in 1882, they were only granted land at the bottom of the canyon, and not until 1975 did the concession of another 251,000 acres up above make it possible for them to resume their ancient lifestyle.

Havasu Canyon is a side canyon of the Grand Canyon, about 35 miles west of Grand Canyon Village as the raven flies, but almost two hundred miles by road. Turn off the Interstate at Seligman or Kingman, onto AZ-66, which curves north between the two, stock up with food, water and gas, and then turn on to Arrowhead Hwy-18. Plans to build a road – or even a tramway – down into Havasu Canyon have always been rejected, in part because much of the income of the five or six hundred Havasupai comes from guiding visitors on foot, mule or horseback. Instead, the road ends at **Hualapai Hilltop**, from where an eight-mile trail zigzags down a bluff and leads through the stunning waterless Hualapai Canyon to the village of **SUPAI**. Riding down costs $50 one way, $80 for a round-trip, while hiking is free; all visitors, however, pay a $15 entry fee on arrival at Supai.

Beyond Supai the trail becomes more difficult, but leads to a succession of spectacular waterfalls, including **Havasu Falls**, one of the best for swimming, and **Mooney Falls**, which was named after an unfortunate prospector who dangled here for three days in the 1890s, at the end of a snagged rope, before falling to his death.

A **campground** (☎520/448-2141), charging $10 per night, stretches between Havasu and Mooney Falls, and Supai itself holds the motel-like *Havasupai Lodge* (☎520/448-2111; summer ⑤; winter ③), along with a café, a general store, and the only post office in the US still to receive its mail by pack train. Only visitors who have made definite advance arrangements at either the campground or lodge should set off the trailhead; note also that from time to time Supai is hit by freak floods, which can result in the temporary closure of both.

Flagstaff

As the nearest town of any size to the canyon, seventy miles northwest, **FLAGSTAFF** remains the major junction for road and rail passengers heading for the Grand Canyon. Although some of its old streets are still charmingly redolent of the Wild West – its main thoroughfare, Santa Fe Avenue, was once part of Route 66, and before that, the pioneer trail west – there's not all that much of interest in the town itself. However, the exceptional **Museum of Northern Arizona** (daily 9am–5pm; $5), three miles northwest on Hwy-180 (and not on a local bus route), provides a good introduction to Arizona's native American cultures, past and present. At all times there are pots, rugs and kachina dolls on display, but *the* time to come is for the Indian Artists Exhibitions each summer. The **Zuni** show lasts for five days around Memorial Day weekend in late May; the **Hopi** one is on the weekend closest to July 4, and the nine-day **Navajo** event is at the end of July and the start of August, with every item for sale.

Practicalities

Two Amtrak **trains** still pull in each day – the 5.52am to Albuquerque and the 8.49pm to Los Angeles – at the wooden station house right in the heart of town, adjoining the helpful **visitor center** at 101 W Santa Fe Ave (summer Mon–Sat 7am–6pm, Sun 7am–5pm; rest of year Mon–Sat 8am–6pm, Sun 8am–5pm; ☎1-800/842-7293 or 520/774-9541). Connecting buses to the Grand Canyon's South Rim, run by Nava-Hopi, 114 W Route 66 (☎1-800/892-8687 or 520/774-5003), are detailed on p.260. The least expensive **car rental**, which shared between a group should cost less than the bus, is Budget Rent-a-Car at 100 N Humphreys St (☎520/779-0307). Cosmic Cycles, 113 S San Francisco St (☎520/779-1092), rent out **mountain bikes** for $20 per day, $75 per week.

Nava-Hopi also operate a wide range of one-day **tours**, not only of the Grand Canyon ($38 by bus, $64 for a combination bus-and-train tour via Williams), but also to the nearby towns of Sedona and Jerome ($36), and northeast to stunning Monument Valley ($74). Greyhound, a few blocks south of downtown at 399 S Malpais Lane (☎1-800/231-2222 or 520/774-4573), run **buses** south to Phoenix, west to Las Vegas and LA, and east towards Albuquerque.

Several basic central **hostels** offer dorm beds for around $13 and private rooms for more like $30. Both the *DuBeau International Hostel*, 19 W Phoenix Ave (☎1-800/398-7112 or 520/773-1656; ③) and the *Grand Canyon International Hostel*, 19 S San Francisco St (☎520/779-9421; ③) run excursions up to the Grand Canyon, while the HI-AYH-approved *Hotel Weatherford*, 23 N Leroux St (☎520/774-2731; ①–②) has cheap central rooms north of the tracks. The *Monte Vista*, 100 N San Francisco St (☎520/779-6971; ③/④) is a very pleasant little **hotel** that in addition to dorm beds has some much more comfortable rooms, each named after a movie star, while budget **motels** like the *Super 8*, 3725 Kasper Ave (☎1-888/324-9131 or 520/526-0818; ④), abound just off the Interstate further east. The best **campground** is three miles south on US-89A, at *Fort Tuthill County Park* (☎520/774-5139).

For **food**, *Charly's Pub and Grill* in the *Weatherford Hotel* makes a classy if unlikely contrast with the hostel rooms upstairs, serving good cheap food accompanied by live music (cocktail piano at lunch, bands at night). The area around San Francisco Street, south of the tracks and near the university, has largely been taken over by the alternative student crowd. The *Mad Italian* at no. 101 S (☎520/779-1820) is a highly sociable **bar** with several pool tables, while *Hassib's* at no. 211 S (☎520/774-1037) does a variety of mid-Eastern and European dishes, but closes early. The *Museum Club*, 3404 E Route 66 (☎520/526-9434), is a real oddity: a 1930s log-cabin taxidermy museum that somehow transmogrified into a classic Route 66 roadhouse, saloon and country music venue, and became a second home to hordes of dancing cowboys.

travel details

Trains

LA to: Barstow (1 daily & 1 Amtrak Thruway daily; 3hr); Flagstaff (1 daily; 10hr); Las Vegas (1 daily; 5hr 20min); Palm Springs (4 weekly; 2hr 20 min).

Buses

All buses are Greyhound unless otherwise stated.

Grand Canyon to: Flagstaff (2 Nava-Hopi daily; 2hr).

Las Vegas to: Barstow (10 daily & 2 Amtrak Thruway daily; 3hr); Flagstaff (2 daily; 5hr).

LA to: Barstow (14 daily; 3hr); Las Vegas (16 daily & 2 Amtrak Thruway; 4hr/6hr); Palm Springs (12 daily; 3hr).

Palm Springs to: Bakersfield (9 daily and 1 Amtrak Thruway daily; 5hr 45min); Joshua Tree (1 Morongo Basin Transit Authority daily; 55 min).

San Diego to: Borrego Springs (1 Northeast Rural Bus System daily; 2hr 50min).

CHAPTER FOUR

DEATH VALLEY AND THE EASTERN HIGH SIERRA

T he far eastern edge of California, rising up from the Mojave and cleaving to the border with Nevada, is a long narrow strip as scenically dramatic as anywhere else in the state, veering from blistering desert to ski country, much of it in the lee of the mighty High Sierra. It's a region devoid of Interstates, scarcely populated and, but for the scant reminders of gold-hungry pioneers, developed in only the most tentative way.

At the region's base, technically forming the Mojave's northern reach but more usually visited along with the Owens Valley, is **Death Valley**. With the highest average summer temperatures on earth and so remote that it's almost a region unto itself, this vast national park is a distillation of the classic desert landscape: an arid, otherworld terrain of brilliantly colored, bizarrely eroded rocks, mountains and sand dunes, a hundred miles from the nearest town.

Heading north, the towering **eastern** peaks of the High Sierra drop abruptly to the largely desert – and deserted – landscape of the Owens Valley far below. Seen from the eastern side, the mountains are perfectly described by their Spanish name, **Sierra Nevada**, which literally translates as "snowcapped saw." Virtually the entire range is preserved as wilderness, and hikers and mountaineers can get to higher altitudes quicker here than almost anywhere else in California: well-maintained roads lead to trailheads at over eight thousand feet, providing swift access to spires, glaciers and clear mountain lakes. **Mount Whitney**, the highest point in the continental US at almost 14,500ft, marks the southernmost point of the chain, which continues north for an uninterrupted 150 miles to the backcountry of Yosemite National Park.

ACCOMMODATION PRICE CODES

All accommodation prices in this book have been coded using the symbols below; prices are for the least expensive **double rooms** in each establishment. For a full explanation see p.36 in "Basics." Individual rates rather than price codes are given for **hostels** and whole **apartments**.

① up to $30	④ $60–80	⑦ $130–175
② $30–45	⑤ $80–100	⑧ $175–250
③ $45–60	⑥ $100–130	⑨ $250+

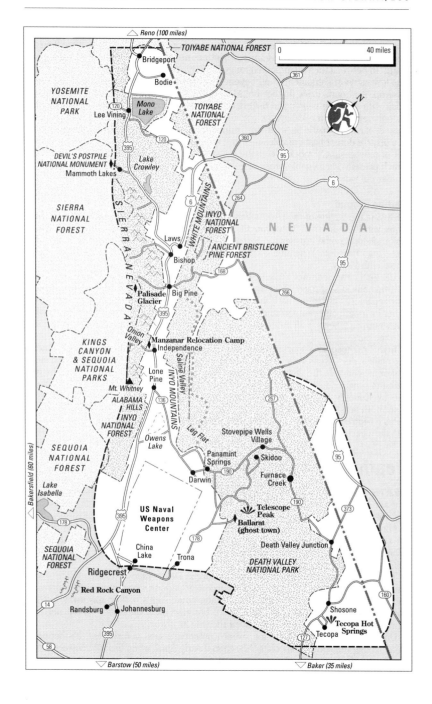

The five-mile-wide **Owens Valley** starts at the foot of Mount Whitney, hemmed in to the east by the **White Mountains**, nearly as high but drier and less hospitable than the High Sierra, and home to the gnarled **bristlecone pines**, the oldest living things on earth. In between the two mountain ranges, US-395 runs the length of the Valley, which has few signs of settlement at all beyond the sporadic roadside towns and the larger **Bishop**. An hour's drive further on, **Mammoth Lakes** is the region's busiest resort, thick with skiers in winter and fishers and mountain bikers in summer. Finally, at the far northern tip of the Valley, the placid blue waters of ancient **Mono Lake** (once the subject of a fierce battle between environmentalists and the City of Los Angeles) are set in a bizarre desert basin of volcanoes and steaming hot pools. Beyond, and far enough out of most people's way to deter the crowds, is the wonderful ghost town of **Bodie**, which preserves a palpable sense of gold-town life eight thousand feet up in a parched, windswept valley.

Getting around

US-395 is the lifeline of the Owens Valley, and pretty much the only access to the area from within California. Once north of Mojave, where Hwy-58 branches west to Bakersfield, no road crosses the Sierra Nevada until Hwy-120, a spur over the 10,000-foot Tioga Pass into Yosemite. To the east Hwy-190 cuts through the Panamint Range into Death Valley.

US-395 is traveled once daily by Greyhound between LA and Reno in Nevada (note that this bus is best used when traveling from north to south; otherwise most arrivals and departures are in the early hours of the morning) and has plenty of cheap motels along its length and campgrounds in the nearby foothills. Access to Death Valley without your own wheels is all but impossible: **no public transportation** whatsoever runs into the park.

Inyo Trailhead Transportation (☎760/876-5518) runs minivans out of Lone Pine to the main lower Owens Valley trailheads, picking up passengers from Greyhound stops and other points in the Owens Valley; make arrangements well in advance and be prepared to send a deposit. A similar service to the more northern trails and ski slopes is run by Kountry Korners (☎1-877/656-0756 or 760/872-4411, *williams@qnet.com*) in Bishop. In addition, Inyo Mono Dial-a-Ride (☎1-800/922-1930 or 760/876-5518) run a service running once a day (Mon–Fri only) from Lone Pine to Bishop in the early morning, then back again in the early afternoon.

Death Valley National Park

DEATH VALLEY is an inhuman environment: barren and monotonous, burning hot and almost entirely without shade, much less water. At first sight it seems impossible that the landscape could support any kind of life, yet it is home to a great variety of living creatures, from snakes and giant eagles to tiny fishes and bighorn sheep. But it's the rocks that you come to see: deeply shadowed, eroded crevices at the foot of sharply silhouetted hills, whose exotic mineral content turns million-year-old mud flats into rainbows of sunlit phosphorescence.

Throughout the summer, the air temperature in Death Valley averages 112°F – with a recorded high of 134°F – and there are frequent periods when it tops 120°F daily. At such times, the ground can reach near boiling point, so it's best to stay away, leaving the place to car companies who have been bringing their latest models out here for extreme testing ever since Dodge paved the way in 1913.

Unless you're a real glutton for sweaty, potentially fatal punishment, it's better to come during the spring, especially March and early April, when the wild flowers are in bloom and daytime temperatures average a manageable 83°F, dropping to the mid-fifties at night. Any time between October and May it's generally mild and dry, with occasional rainfall on the surrounding mountains causing flash floods through otherwise bone-dry gullies and washes.

The central north–south valley, after which the park is named, holds the park's two main outposts for provisions and accommodation: **Stovepipe Wells** and **Furnace Creek**. It is surrounded by many more, equally inhospitable desert valleys, punctuated with the remains of mine workings. High above stand the less visited but far cooler peaks of the Panamint Range – from where you can see both the highest (Mount Whitney) and the lowest (near Badwater) points in the continental United States.

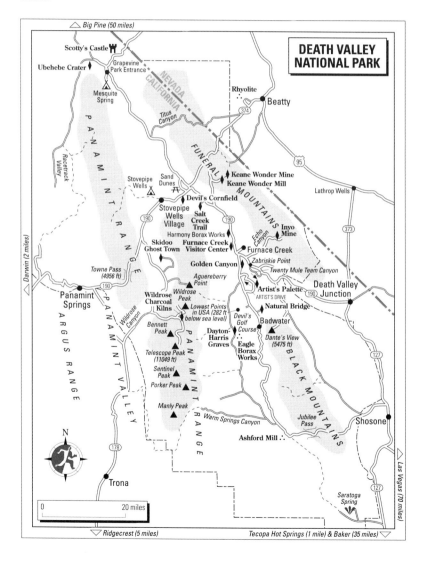

Geology and history

The sculpted rock layers exposed in Death Valley, tinted by oxidized traces of various **mineral deposits**, comprise a nearly complete record of the earth's past, from 500-million-year-old mountains to the relatively young **fossils** of marine animals left on the valley floors by the Ice Age lakes, which covered most of the park's low-lying areas. There's also dramatic evidence of volcanic activity, as at the massive **Ubehebe Crater** on the north side of the park.

Humans have lived in and around Death Valley for thousands of years, beginning about ten thousand years ago when the valley was still filled by a massive lake; the climate was then quite mild and wild game was plentiful. Later, wandering tribes of desert **Shoshone** wintered near perennial freshwater springs in the warm valley, spending the long, hot summers at cooler, higher elevations in the surrounding mountains; there is still a small, inhabited Shoshone village near the *Furnace Creek Inn*.

The first non-natives passed through in 1849, looking for a shortcut to the Gold Rush towns on the other side of the Sierra Nevada; they ran out of food and water but managed to survive, and gave Death Valley its name. For the next 75 years the only people willing to brave the hardships of the desert were miners, who searched for and found deposits of gold, silver and copper. The most successful mining endeavours were centered on **borates**, a harsh alkaline used in detergent soaps (and, eventually, in a variety of industries – everything from cosmetics to nuclear reactors). In the late nineteenth century borate miners developed twenty-mule-team wagons to haul the powders across the deserts to the railroad line at Mojave. In the 1920s the first tourist facilities were developed, and in 1927 the mining camp at Furnace Creek was converted into the *Furnace Creek Inn*. Six years later the two million acres of Death Valley and around were purchased by the US government, to be preserved as a national monument. In 1994, as part of the **California Desert Protection Act**, Congress accorded it national park status and added a further 1.3 million acres to its area, making Death Valley the largest national park in the country outside Alaska.

> For advice on **desert survival**, see the box on p.218.

Getting to Death Valley

Death Valley is a long way from anywhere, and there's **no scheduled public transportation** into the park. The nearest places served by buses are **Beatty**, just inside Nevada and 35 miles from Furnace Creek, and Lone Pine in the Owens Valley (see p.279); neither is much use unless you have a bicycle. **Las Vegas** in Nevada (see p.249), is the nearest city to Death Valley. For the most direct and interesting route from Las Vegas, take US-95 or Las Vegas Boulevard south to Blue Diamond Rte (Hwy-160 west), which leads past the scenic **Red Rock Canyon Recreation Area** to the town of **Pahrump**; the Smith's supermarket there is a good spot to load up on supplies. Just past the town, make a left at Bella Vista Road, where there's also a sign for the **Ash Meadows National Wildlife Refuge** (unrestricted access), a desert oasis worth a detour for its concentration of indigenous species – the second largest in North America. Beyond the turn-off for the refuge, at **Death Valley Junction** (see opposite), take Hwy-190 west into Death Valley. Alternatively, if you want to take advantage of the cheap (and cooler) lodging outside the park in Beatty, take US-95 past Nellis Air Force Base and the old US nuclear weapons testing range; from Beatty, you'll coast down into the park on Hwy-374, watching Death Valley unfold from above.

If driving to Death Valley from within California, you should follow one of the routes below. Fill up your vehicle before you enter the park, as gas inside is pricey.

The western approaches

From the west, there are two routes towards Death Valley, of equal length and running along either side of the China Lake Naval Weapons Base. Five miles west of Ridgecrest (see p.243), US-395 runs north along the west side of China Lake up to the dry bed of what, until the 1920s, used to be Owens Lake. The water that would naturally flow into the lake has been diverted to Los Angeles via the aqueduct that parallels US-395, leaving a pan of toxic alkali dust. Schemes are now underway to control this by planting native vegetation and reintroducing some water to the ecosystem. Just south of here, Hwy-190 cuts off due east to Hwy-136, the Lone Pine to Death Valley road – perhaps the prettiest drive into the park. Fifteen miles west of this junction a loop peels southeast to **Darwin**, and shortly after another road cuts north to **Lee Flat** and the **Saline Valley** – see p.278. At nearby **Panamint Springs** there's an expensive gas station and a motel (see opposite) with restaurant, bar and a pool.

The less-traveled route loops sixty miles around the eastern side of China Lake and allows the quickest access into the more mountainous backcountry of Death Valley, an area once home to Charles Manson and his "family." Wildrose Road, the continuation of Hwy-178 beyond Ridgecrest, curves through the chemical plants of **Trona** past the gold-mining town of **Ballarat** – whose eroded adobe ruins still stand in the foothills three miles east of the highway – before joining Hwy-190 for the final fifteen miles east to the entrance to Death Valley. What makes this route worthwhile is the possibility of following the steep Mahogany Flat Road – which cuts off Wildrose Road thirteen miles south of Hwy-190 – up the Panamint Mountains to **Telescope Peak** (see p.278), the highest and coolest part of the park. The road is well maintained, but although there is excellent free **camping** (see box on p.275), the nearest food, drinking water or gas are 25 miles away at Stovepipe Wells village. Another potential side trip is to the **Skidoo Ghost Town** (see p.278) a few miles to the north.

The southern approaches

Hwy-127 branches off I-15 at Baker (see p.246) – the last stop for supplies on the southern route into Death Valley – and cuts across fifty miles of desolate Mojave landscape before reaching any civilization. A couple of miles east of Hwy-127 two dilapidated settlements of scrappy trailer homes make unexpectedly decent places to stop off. The settlement of **TECOPA HOT SPRINGS** has become a popular winter retreat, thanks to its natural hot springs always open to the public and bequeathed in perpetuity by a local chief provided they remain free. While here, drive five miles southeast to **China Ranch Date Farm**, China Ranch Rd (☎760/852-4415, *www.chinaranch.com*) where you are free to wander among the mostly-young groves, follow a shady streamside nature trail, explore wider along the Old Spanish Trail which ran nearby, then repair to the cactus garden for a refreshing date shake and, of course, buy some dates. Many people stay across the road from the hot springs at the bleak campground ($6.50), though the hostel in nearby **Tecopa** is a better bet (see overleaf).

The hamlet of **SHOSHONE**, eight miles north of Tecopa, wouldn't really rate a mention but for a decent motel (see p.275) within striking distance of the park. **Death Valley Junction**, a further thirty miles north, offers no fuel, but its *Amargosa Hotel* houses the **Amargosa Opera House**, the creation of Marta Becket, a New York dancer and artist who settled here in the late 1960s. The inside of the theater is painted with trompe l'oeil balconies peopled by sixteenth-century Spanish nobles and revelers. Ballet-pantomimes, in which Ms Becket takes almost all the parts herself, are staged here between October and May ($10; ☎760/852-4441).

Entrance and information

Entrance to the park is $10 per vehicle, or $5 if you are walking or cycling. For that you get unrestricted entry for seven days, an excellent map and a copy of the *Death Valley National Park* newspaper with up-to-date details on campgrounds and visitor services.

Most visitor facilities are concentrated in two settlements, both comprised mostly of gas stations, motels, restaurants and grocery stores. The busiest of the two, **FUR-NACE CREEK**, is right in the center of the Valley and has an excellent **visitor center** (daily 8am–6pm; ☎760/786-2331, *www.nps.gov/deva*) with a small but interesting **museum** (same hours; free). **STOVEPIPE WELLS**, 25 miles to the northwest, is slightly smaller. More information is available from the **ranger stations** close to the park boundaries. The main ones are on the west side at *Wildrose Campground* on Hwy-178 and on the northern edge of the park at Scotty's Castle. There are **no banks** in the park but Furnace Creek and Stovepipe Wells both have ATMs.

Accommodation

To get the full impact of a desert visit you really need to **camp** out. For most of the year you don't even need a tent – it isn't going to rain – though a sleeping bag is a good idea. Camping is also much the cheapest way to stay in Death Valley: all the campgrounds are operated by the National Park Service and most cost $10 a night, while sites without a water supply are free. If camping isn't an option you are limited to fairly expensive **hotels** and **motels** inside the park, or lower-cost possibilities on the fringes. Reservations should be made as early as possible, especially during peak holiday periods. The following listings cover all the rooms in the park and the settlements nearby, but also see Lone Pine (p.280) for accommodation slightly further afield.

Hotels, motels and hostels

Amargosa Hotel, Death Valley Junction (☎760/852-4441, fax 852-4138). Pleasantly run-down adobe hotel built by the Pacific Coast Borax Company in 1924. It has no TVs or phones, but boasts an attached opera house (see above). Ask to see a few rooms before choosing as they vary enormously – there's a trompe l'oeil wardrobe in the Jezebel room and cherubs in the Baroque. ②.

Exchange Club Motel, Junction of US-95 and Hwy-374, Beatty (☎775/553-2333). Nice rooms with refrigerators, adjoining a casino (its 1906 bar dates back to the days when miners used to exchange gold nuggets for cash – thus the name) with a decent restaurant. ②.

Furnace Creek Inn, Furnace Creek (☎1-800/236-79167 or 760/786-2345, fax 786-2514, *www. furnacecreekresort.com*). A beautifully sited hotel built of local stone in the 1920s amid date palms and tended lawns and *the* place to stay if you're in the Valley with money to burn. Rooms are modern but tastefully done, many with great views across the Valley to the Panamint Mountains. Best of all you can spend the day in the pool which has bar service in the more fashionable cooler months, when prices are hiked by fifty percent. ⑦.

Furnace Creek Ranch, Furnace Creek (☎1-800/236-79167 or 760/786-2345, fax 786-2514, *www.furnacecreekresort.com*). Cheaper than the *Inn*, but redolent of a holiday camp and with no sense of being in a desert. The comfortable but ordinary motel rooms are rather overpriced. ⑤.

HI-Desertaire Hostel, Old Spanish Trail, Tecopa (☎760/852-4580). A relaxed hostel an hour south of Furnace Creek. There are only ten beds ($12), but you can sleep outside in the warm desert air in a wooden tower with commanding views of the surrounding desert. Book the first night by phone or in writing: PO Box 306, Tecopa, CA 92389.

Panamint Springs Resort, Panamint Springs (☎775/482-7680, fax 482-7682, *www.deathvalley. com*). Basic motel 35 miles west of Stovepipe Wells at a mountain pass. There's a restaurant, bar, $10 tent sites and $20 RV hook-ups, but no pool, though one is planned. ③.

Phoenix Inn, 350 First St, Beatty (☎ 1-800/845-7401 or 775/553-2250, fax 553-2260, *info@phnxinn. com*). On a quiet side street, and one of the few Beatty motels not in or attached to a casino. ②.

CAMPING IN DEATH VALLEY

Most sites cannot be reserved and stays are limited to thirty days (so that people don't move in for the winter). Take note of the **altitude** listed for each, as this gives an idea of the temperatures you might expect.

The main sites are at **Furnace Creek** ($16, $10 in summer; open all year, reservable up to five months in advance mid-Oct to mid-April, ☎1-800/365-2267; -196ft) which fills up very early each day in winter; the enormous **Sunset** ($10; Oct–April; -190ft) and the designated "quiet" **Texas Spring** ($6; Oct–April; sea level), both close to Furnace Creek; and at **Stovepipe Wells** ($10; Oct–April; sea level) – though the smaller and relatively shady site at **Mesquite Spring** ($10; all year; 1800ft), near Scotty's Castle on the north side of the park, is much more pleasant. There is one free site with water, **Emigrant** (all year; 2100ft), eight miles west of Stovepipe Wells. This is on the way to the only place with guaranteed shade, the canyons on the forested slopes of Telescope Peak, on the western edge of the park. Here there are three free sites, **Wildrose** (all year, water available April–Nov; 4100ft), **Thorndike** (open March–Nov; 7400ft) and **Mahogany Flat** (March–Nov; 8200ft), just off the mostly paved Wildrose Road. The upper two are (just) accessible in ordinary cars, but high clearance or four-wheel-drive vehicles are better. **Fires** are allowed in all sites except *Sunset* and *Emigrant*, but designated fireplaces must be used and no collecting of firewood is allowed.

Free **backcountry camping** is allowed in most areas of the park provided you keep two miles away from any roads (paved or otherwise) and two hundred yards from water sources. No permits are required, but voluntary backcountry **registration** is strongly recommended.

Shoshone Inn, Shoshone (☎760/852-4335). Reasonable motel with pool an hour south of Furnace Creek on Hwy-127 and near Tecopa Hot Springs. ③.

Stovepipe Wells Motel, Stovepipe Wells (☎760/786-2387, fax 786-2389). The best-priced option inside the park, offering comfortable rooms, a mineral-water pool, restaurant and bar. ③.

Eating

There's not a great variety of **eating places** in Death Valley – you're limited to the hotel dining rooms and restaurants at Furnace Creek and Stovepipe Wells, all of which are fairly pricey. *Furnace Creek Ranch* is the only place with any choice, housing both the *Fortyniner Cafe*, an upgraded coffee shop, and the *Wrangler Steakhouse*. Unless you're dying for a big slab of meat, you're much better off at the similarly steep but more interesting restaurant at the *Furnace Creek Inn* (for dinner reservations ☎760/786-2345; no shorts in the cooler months), where the likes of rattlesnake fritters, vichyssoise and Atlantic salmon are served up in a room almost unchanged since the 1920s. Beatty, with restaurants attached to all-night casinos, offers a number of inexpensive diners, though it's quite a long drive back to the park after dark.

To quench a **thirst** after a day in the sun, do as the few locals do and head to the *Corkscrew Saloon*, also at *Furnace Creek Ranch* and open until 1am; or stroll up to the *Furnace Creek Inn* for cocktails on the terrace. Expensive **grocery stores** with a limited supply are located at Furnace Creek and at Stovepipe Wells.

Exploring Death Valley

You can get an unforgettable feel for Death Valley just by passing through, and you could quite easily see almost everything in a day. If you have the time, though, aim to spend at least a night here, if possible camped out somewhere far from the main centers of activity. Even if you've got your own car, the best way to experience the huge, empty spaces and the unique landforms of Death Valley is to leave the roads and crowds behind and wander off – taking care to remember the way back. Sunrise and sunset are the best times to experience the color that's bleached out by the midday sun, and they're also the most likely times for seeing the **wildlife**, mostly lizards, snakes and small rodents, which hide out through the heat of the day.

Along the Badwater road

Many of the park's most unusual sights are located south of Furnace Creek along the road to Badwater, which forks off Hwy-190 by the *Furnace Creek Inn*. A good first stop, two miles along, is **Golden Canyon**. Periodic rainstorms over the centuries have washed a slot-shaped gully through the clay and silt here, revealing golden-hued walls that are particularly vibrant in the early evening. A three-quarter-mile-long interpretive trail winds into the U-shaped upper canyon, and a hike to Zabriskie Point (see box on p.279) continues from there.

Five miles further on, signs point to **Artist's Drive**, a tortuous one-way loop road, perhaps best left until the drive back, especially if this means catching the afternoon sun on the **Artist's Palette**, an evocatively eroded hillside covered in an intensely colored mosaic of reds, golds, blacks and greens.

A couple of miles further south, a dirt road heading west leads a mile to the **Devil's Golf Course**, a weird field of salt pinnacles and hummocks protruding a couple of feet from the desert floor. Capillary action draws saline solutions from below the surface where alternate layers of salt and alluvial deposits from ancient lakes have been laid down over the millennia. As the occasional rainfall evaporates, the salt accretes to form a landscape as little like a golf course as you could imagine.

It is another four miles south to **Badwater**, an unpalatable but non-poisonous thirty-foot-wide pool of water, loaded with chloride and sulphates, that's also the only home of the endangered, soft-bodied Death Valley snail and a species of tiny fish. Notice how much hotter it feels in the humid air beside the water. From the pool, two rather uninteresting hikes, both around four miles long, lead across the hot, flat valley floor to the two **lowest points in the western hemisphere**, both at 282ft below sea level.

Zabriskie Point and Dante's View

The badlands around **Zabriskie Point**, overlooking Badwater and the Artist's Palette, four miles south of Furnace Creek off Hwy-190, were the inspiration for Antonioni's eponymous 1970 movie. Even so, its sculpted spires of banded rock are less interesting than **Dante's View**, a further 21 miles south off Hwy-190 and then ten miles on a very

---

PARK ACTIVITIES

Besides hiking and sightseeing, Death Valley offers ample opportunities for **mountain biking**. Only roads open to road vehicles are accessible to cyclists (hiking trails are off limits) but this still leaves plenty to go at for those who bring their machine along: there are no rentals available. The map provided with your entry ticket shows the major four-wheel-drive routes: Echo Canyon into the Funeral Mountains and the Inyo Mine, Cottonwood Canyon from Stovepipe Wells, and the Warm Springs Canyon/Butte Valley road in the south of the park are all worthwhile. Topographical maps are available at Furnace Creek visitor center. **Horseback riding** is offered at the *Furnace Creek Ranch* for $25 an hour, $40 for two and, when the phase of the moon is right, $35 for an hour-long evening ride.

After a day in the desert, **swimming** in a tepid pool is an ideal way to enjoy a balmy evening. The pools at the *Furnace Creek Ranch* and the *Stovepipe Wells Motel* are open to the public for a $2 fee.

steep (and very hot) road. At a point almost six thousand feet above the blinding white saltpan of Badwater, the valley floor does indeed look infernal. The view is best during the early morning, when the pink and gold Panamint Mountains across the Valley are highlighted by the rising sun.

North from Furnace Creek

In the township of Furnace Creek you could spend a few minutes in the **Borax Museum** (Mon–Fri 9am–4.30pm; free), which rather ploddingly tells the story of the mineral and its excavation, but you are better advised to head two miles north to the old **Harmony Borax Works** (unrestricted entry) where a quarter-mile interpretive trail tells of the mine and processing plant.

Twelve miles to the north, the **Keane Wonder Mine** and **Keane Wonder Mill** (unrestricted entry to both) were indeed wonderful during their heyday between 1904, when the mine was discovered by Jack Keane, and 1916. Gold and silver worth $1.1 million was extracted at the mountainside mine and worked at in the valley-floor mill, where it was carried down a three-quarter-mile-long aerial tramway which is still more or less intact. From the parking lot by the remains of the mill, a very steep path climbs alongside the thirteen tramway towers to the lowest of the mineshafts. It is only a mile but seems a lot more in the noonday heat. Don't be tempted to seek shelter in the adits and shafts leading off the path; all are dangerous and most unfenced.

Near Stovepipe Wells on the western side of the park spread the most extensive of the Valley's **sand dunes**, some fifteen rippled and contoured square miles of ever changing dunes, just north of Hwy-190 to the east of the campground and ranger station. On the opposite side of Hwy-190 stands the **Devil's Cornfield**, an expanse of tufted grasses quite out of character with its surroundings.

West of the campground, at the end of a ten-mile dirt road, stand the sheer black walls of **Marble Canyon**, on which are scratched ancient and mysterious petroglyph figures.

Scotty's Castle

On the northern edge of the park (45 miles from the visitor center) and thus well out of the way of most of the rest of the tourist attractions, **Scotty's Castle** (tours daily 9am–5pm; $8) is nevertheless the most popular single stop in the park; hordes of over-heated tourists wait in long lines for the chance to wander through the surreal attraction of this unfinished but still luxurious mansion. Executed in extravagant Spanish Revival style, the castle was built during the 1920s as the desert retreat of wealthy Chicago insurance broker Albert Johnson, but was known and named after the cowboy, prospector and publicity hound, "Death Valley" Scotty, who managed the construction, and claimed the house was his own, financed by his hidden gold mine. The $2 million house features intricately carved wooden ceilings, waterfalls in the living room and, most entertaining of all, a remote-controlled player piano. In winter, you may have to wait as long as three hours for a place on one of the fifty-minute-long **tours** of the opulently furnished house, left pretty much as it was when Johnson died in 1948. Scotty himself lived here until 1954, and is buried on the hill just behind the house: a good place to wander while waiting for your tour.

Ubehebe Crater, Racetrack Valley and the Eureka Sand Dunes

Eight miles southwest of Scotty's Castle – though it might as well be five hundred miles for all the people who venture a look – gapes the half-mile wide **Ubehebe Crater**, the rust-colored result of a massive volcanic explosion; a half-mile south sits its thousand-year-old younger brother, **Little Hebe**. Beyond the craters the road (high clearance vehicles recommended) continues south for another 27 dusty miles to **Racetrack Valley**, a two-and-a-half-mile-long mud flat across which giant boulders seem slowly to be racing, leaving faint trails in their wake. Scientists believe that the boulders are pushed along the sometimes icy surface by very high winds; sit and watch (but don't hold your breath) from the rock outcrop at the northern end, known as the **Grandstand**.

The extension of Death Valley into a national park claimed several features formerly outside its boundaries. The **Eureka Sand Dunes**, forty miles northwest of Scotty's Castle, are the most exciting. Far more extensive than those around Stovepipe Wells, these stand up to seven hundred feet above the surrounding land, making them the highest dunes in California and a dramatic place to witness sunrise or sunset. While here, keep your eyes open for the Eureka Dunes grass and evening primrose, both indigenous to the area and federally protected.

Skidoo Ghost Town, Wildrose Charcoal Kilns and Telescope Peak

To escape the heat and dust of the desert floor, head up Emigrant Canyon Road, off Hwy-190 in the west, into the Panamint Mountains. Ten miles up the canyon, a nine-mile dirt track turns off to the east toward **Skidoo Ghost Town**. Only a few ruins – and a number of roaming wild burros – remain of what in 1915 was a gold-mining camp of seven hundred people watered by snowmelt from Telescope Peak, 23 miles away, and kept informed by telegraph from Rhyolite. Well above the valley floor, it is tolerably cool but otherwise there's not much going for it.

The main road leads for another, very steep, fifteen miles over Emigrant Pass and down to the Wildrose ranger station and campground. To the right the road leads to Trona and Ridgecrest (see p.243), while a left turn carries you steeply up into the Panamint range, initially on tarmac, then on gravel. Five miles beyond the ranger station the **Wildrose Charcoal Kilns** loom into view. This series of ten massive, bee-hive-shaped stone kilns some 25 feet high was used in the 1880s to make charcoal for use in the smelters of local silver mines. The road continues through juniper and pine forests past the free Thorndike campground to its end at Mahogany Flat, where there's another free campground and the trailhead for the strenuous hike up **Telescope Peak**, which at 11,049ft is the highest – and coolest – point in the park (see box opposite).

Darwin Falls, Lee Flat and Saline Valley

A mile west of Panamint Springs along Hwy-190, a dirt road leads south to the tumble-down wooden ruins of **DARWIN**, a ghost of a mining town (though forty people still live here) that was built in the 1870s by prospectors searching for seams of silver, inspired by tales of an Indian who repaired an explorer's rifle by fashioning a gunsight out of solid silver. Nearby, and more interesting, are the thirty-foot, spring-fed **Darwin Falls**, reached by following a quarter-mile creekside trail up a small canyon.

You might not expect to see Joshua trees in Death Valley, but **Lee Flat**, a dozen miles west of Panamint Springs, has a whole forest of them on its higher slopes. At this point a dirt road leads north to Saline Valley. The main forest starts eight miles along at lower Lee Flat; a side road branches left to the densest section.

In **Saline Valley** in the far northwest corner of the park, old mine workings and the remains of a dilapidated salt tramway can be seen on your way to the generally cloth-ing-free **hot springs** at Saline Warm Spring and Palm Hot Spring. It's a very rough and un-signed fifty-mile trek out here, so obtain the best map you can, ask for local advice and be prepared to camp out at the free, primitive site nearby. After a dip it is possible to continue north to meet US-395 at Big Pine.

Rhyolite

As ghost towns go, **RHYOLITE**, up a side road three miles west of Beatty, Nevada, is one of the more appealing. Rhyolite was a gold mining town whose mines were prema-

HIKES IN AND AROUND DEATH VALLEY

Anything more than a short stroll in the desert heat can become an ordeal. This is less true when hiking the Telescope Peak and Wildrose Peak trails in the Panamint Range, but you still need to carry all your **water** with you. It sounds strange, but you might also consider carrying a umbrella to use as a parasol: regular Death Valley hikers often do. Always register your intended route at the visitor center or any of the ranger stations and for anything a little more adventurous than the walks listed here, get yourself a **topographic map** from the visitor center. All listed distances and times are for the round-trip.

Golden Canyon to Zabriskie Point (5 miles; 3hr; 500ft ascent). Start at Golden Canyon and follow the interpretive trail, continuing on an unmaintained, moderately strenuous trail to Zabriskie Point. Done in reverse it is all downhill.

Mosaic Canyon (4 miles; 2hr; 300ft ascent). A rough three-mile access road just west of Stovepipe Wells leads to the trailhead for a relatively easy hike through this water-smoothed canyon. There's some scrambling at the upper end.

Telescope Peak (14 miles; 8hr; 3000ft ascent). The easy-to-follow but moderately strenuous trail climbs from the trailhead by Mahogany Flat campground, skirting a pair of 10,000-foot peaks, through bristlecone pines to the summit and its grand panorama of Death Valley and across to Mount Whitney and the eastern face of the Sierra Nevada mountains. Sign the summit register while you admire the view. There's no water en route except for snowmelt (often well into June) which should be treated. Crampons and ice axes may be required in harsh winters, and at all times you should self-register in the book a short way along the trail.

Wildrose Peak (8 miles; 5hr; 2000ft ascent). If winter conditions or your own level of fitness rule out Telescope Peak, this hike makes a perfect, easier alternative. Start by the Charcoal Kilns on Wildrose Canyon Road and wind up through piñon pines and juniper to a stunning summit panorama.

turely closed after just six boom years in 1912, due to a combination of mismanagement and lack of technological know-how (the working Bullfrog Mine just outside the town attests to the area's continuing mineral wealth). By then the town had spread over the hillside (made of the rock which gave the town its name) and had its own train station. The station is still the dominant structure, but the remains of other buildings, including a jail, schoolhouse and bank, still stand, as does Tom Kelly's **bottle house** built of some fifty thousand beer and spirit bottles in 1906. A more recent attraction is the distinctly off-beam roadside **sculpture garden** (unrestricted access), complete with structures built from car parts and an arresting series of white fibreglass figures arranged in imitation of *The Last Supper*. As you enter town you'll be greeted by the most conspicuous piece, installed not long ago: a huge metal miner accompanied by a similarly proportioned penguin. Visiting Rhyolite before Scotty's Castle (see p.277) gives you the opportunity to explore the one-way Titus Canyon road which winds past several crumbling lead mines. High-clearance or four-wheel drive vehicles are recommended.

The Owens Valley

Rising out of the northern reaches of the Mojave Desert, the Sierra Nevada Mountains announce themselves with a bang two hundred miles north of Los Angeles at **Mount Whitney**, the highest point on a silver-gray knifelike ridge of pinnacles that forms a nearly sheer eleven-thousand-foot wall of granite. It provides a wonderful backdrop to the **OWENS VALLEY**, a hot, dry and numinously thrilling stretch of desolate semi-desert landscape running from Lone Pine north beyond Bishop. Along its length, twisting mountain roads spur off to ten-thousand-foot-high trailheads perfect for access into some of the most spectacular sections of the Sierra.

The region is almost entirely unpopulated outside of the few towns along the highway, though a few solitary souls live in old sheds and caravans off the many dirt roads and tracks that cross the floor of the Valley. Years ago the area was a prime spot for growing apples and pears, but since 1913 its plentiful natural water supply, fed by the many streams which run down from the Sierra Nevada, has been drained away to fill the swimming pools of Los Angeles.

Lone Pine and Mount Whitney

Straddling the desert and the mountains, the town of **LONE PINE** has a funky, low-key appeal, though in reality it is little more than a string of motels and gas stations straggling along US-395. What really makes it special is the unparalleled access it provides to the 14,496-foot summit of **Mount Whitney** – the highest point in the US outside Alaska – whose sharply pointed peaks dominate this small roadside town. The view of the High Sierra summits from the town – captured by photographer Ansel Adams in a much-reproduced shot of the full moon suspended above stark cliffs – is fantastic.

Lone Pine makes a good base for exploring the area, particularly if you're not prepared to camp out, and acts as a final supply post for eastbound travelers approaching Death Valley. There are more immediate distractions in the **Alabama Hills** immediately west of Lone Pine, a rugged expanse of sedimentary rock that's been sculpted into bizarre shapes by 160 million years of erosive winds and rains. Some of the oddest formations are linked by the **Picture Rocks Circle**, a paved road that loops around from Whitney Portal Road, passing rocks apparently shaped like bullfrogs, walruses and baboons; it takes a degree of imagination and precise positioning to pick them all out, but it is an attractive drive nonetheless, especially at sunset. A map (free from the visitor centers) details the best spots and marks the sites used as backdrops for many early Westerns, including the epic *Gunga Din*. In celebration of its movie heritage, the town now hosts the **Lone Pine Film Festival**, usually in early October, showing only films made in the area. Contact the Chamber of Commerce (see p.282) for details.

Ten miles west of the Alabama Hills lies **Whitney Portal**, the eight-thousand-foot high trailhead for hiking up Mount Whitney. Even if a full-on slog to the summit is furthest from your mind, you might appreciate a refreshing break from the valley frazzle in the cool shade of the pines and hemlocks. What's more there's a small café and general store for when you need fortifying between strolls around the trout-stocked pond, along the cascading stream or along the Whitney trail to Lone Pine Lake (5 miles round-trip; no permit required).

SIERRA PASS CLOSURES

After coming through the Mojave or Death Valley it seems hard to imagine that many of the passes across the Sierra Nevada can remain closed well into June. Theoretically, Memorial Day (at the end of May) is the date for the **Tioga Pass** (into Yosemite) just below Mono Lake to open, but harsh winters frequently leave it closed until early July. Passes to the north of here, **Hwy-108** and **Hwy-4**, tend to open a couple of weeks earlier, in mid-May. All three close again with the first heavy snowfall, perhaps around late October or early November. **Hwy-88**, yet further north, stays open all year For information on the state of the highways call CalTrans on ☎1-800/427-7623 (see box on p.30).

CLIMBING MOUNT WHITNEY AND BACKCOUNTRY PERMITS

Climbing up to the 14,496-foot **summit** of Mount Whitney is a real challenge: it's a very strenuous, 22-mile round-trip, made especially difficult by the lack of oxygen in the rarefied air of what is the highest point in the lower 48 states (see our comments on Acute Mountain Sickness in "Basics," p.53). Vigorous hikers starting before dawn from the 8000-foot trailhead can be up and back before dark, but a couple of days spent acclimatizing up here is advisable, and the whole experience is enhanced by camping out at least one night along the route. The trail gains over a mile in elevation, cutting up past alpine lakes to boulder-strewn Trail Crest Pass – the southern end of the 220-mile John Muir Trail that heads north to Yosemite. From the pass it climbs along the clifftops, finally reaching the rounded hump of the summit itself, where a **stone cabin** serves as an emergency shelter – though not one you'd choose to be in during a lightning storm. Water is available along the first half of the route but must be filtered or treated.

Between late May and mid-October – the only time the trail is normally free of snow – you must book a permit to hike the mountain. You can – and should – book up to six months in advance of the day you'd like to come (especially for weekends and school vacations); permits are limited and get snapped up quickly. Contact the **Inyo National Forest Wilderness Reservation Service** (PO Box 430, Big Pine, CA 93513; ☎1-888/374-3773 or 760/938-1136, fax 938-1137, *www.sierrawilderness.com*). An overnight permit for Whitney costs $4.50 per person, a day-use permit $3.50. Any remaining permits are distributed on a lottery basis at the Mount Whitney Ranger Station in Lone Pine (see practicalities) at 7am the day before the permit becomes valid; line up, take a number and cross your fingers. Be warned that this system is likely to change; the latest information can be found on the Inyo National Forest Web site at *www.r5.fs.fed.us/inyo*.

Once armed with a permit, hikers should drive to Whitney Portal or catch the shuttle bus service; Inyo Trailhead Transportation (☎760/876-5518) is the current concessionaire but that frequently changes. Check with the helpful Mount Whitney Ranger Station for the latest information. Day hikers will want to **camp** at the first-come-first-served *Whitney Portal Trailhead* campground ready for an early start. Overnight hikers have more leisure and can plan to hike to one of two designated campgrounds (both first-come-first-served and free): Outpost Camp at 3.8 miles and Trail Camp at 6.2 miles.

Ambitious hikers with some experience of scrambling or technical rock climbing might like to tackle the so-called "**Mountaineers' Route**" which follows the North Fork of Lone Pine Creek, taking a more direct and much steeper (though no quicker) route to the summit past the base of the numerous rock climbs on the mountain's east face. Ropes aren't generally needed, but a head for heights is. Ask for directions and current advice at the ranger station and at the Whitney Portal store.

The **Inyo National Forest Wilderness Reservation Service** also manages permits for various other sections of the 78,000-acre wilderness area detailed in this chapter. Except for the Whitney trail, day-use permits are not required in the Inyo wilderness area, but permission is needed if you want to spend the night; inquire at the Eastern Sierra Interagency Visitor Center (see below) for the ranger station nearest the region you'd like to hike. Out of season (mid-Sept to mid-June) self-issue permits are available at the various trailheads.

Practicalities

Greyhound buses stop once a day in Lone Pine at 1452 S Main St not far from the **Mount Whitney Ranger Station** (daily 7am–4.30pm; ☎760/876-6200) where you can obtain wilderness permits. There's more information on hiking, camping, high pass conditions and the whole of eastern California – including the High Sierra, Owens Valley, White Mountains, Death Valley – at the excellent **Eastern Sierra Interagency Visitor Center** (daily: June–Aug 8am–6.50pm; Sept–May 8am–5.50pm; ☎760/876-6222), a mile south of town on US-395 at the junction of Hwy-136, the Death Valley road. Most of the region is protected within the massive **Inyo National Forest**, and if you're planning to spend any amount of time in the area, pick up the very helpful **map** ($4), which covers everything between Mount Whitney and Yosemite National Park, including all hiking routes and campgrounds. Interestingly, this is the only map that makes clear the extent of the City of Los Angeles' holdings in the Owens Valley – basically the entire Valley floor, bought in the early years of the twentieth century as it became obvious that the waters of the Owens Valley offered the best chance of satisfying the demands of the expanding city.

For more **information** on local services, contact the **Chamber of Commerce** at 126 S Main St (Mon–Fri 8am–4pm; ☎760/876-4444). If you're looking for a **motel**, try the *Dow Villa Motel/Historic Dow Hotel* (☎1-800/824-9317 or 760/876-5521, fax 876-5643, *www.dowvillamotel.com*; ②) at 310 S Main St, built in 1923 to house movie industry visitors (John Wayne always requested Room 20); the *Best Western Frontier Motel* (☎1-800/231-4071 or 760/876-5571; ③), 1008 S Main St; or the *Alabama Hills Inn* (☎1-800/800-6468 or 760/876-8700; ③), close to the Death Valley junction at 1920 S Main St, all with pools. There are also plenty of **campgrounds** nearby, all off Whitney Portal Rd, which heads west from town at the lights. The closest is the *Portage Joe* campground ($6) on Tuttle Creek Road, though you can save a few dollars by driving a couple of miles further to the *Tuttle Creek* campground (free; no water) on Horseshoe Meadow Rd. At the Mount Whitney trailhead, thirteen miles west of Lone Pine lie a couple more sites: the family-oriented *Whitney Portal* (late-May to mid-Oct; $12; ☎1-800/280-2267), and the hikers' *Whitney Portal Trailhead* (late-May to mid-Oct; $6; maximum one night stay).

Lone Pine's range of **restaurants** isn't great, but the *Mt Whitney Restaurant*, 227 S Main St (☎760/876-5751) backs up its claim to serve "the best burgers in town" with over half a dozen types of patties – bean, ostrich, venison, veggie – on which to build your creation; *Pizza Factory*, 301 S Main St (☎760/876-4707) produces passable pizza; and *Nacho's Grill*, 104b N Main St (closed Tues), serves basic but filling Mexican. In summer, the **swimming pool** at the high school opposite is open daily ($2); after a week in the mountains, you can get cleaned up at Kirk's Sierra Barber Shop, 104 N Main St, where you can take a **hot shower** for $4.

Manzanar National Historic Site and Independence

Just west of US-395, ten miles north of Lone Pine, on the former site of the most productive of the Owens Valley orchards, stand the concrete foundations of the **Manzanar Relocation Camp**, where more than ten thousand Americans of Japanese descent were corralled during World War II. Considering them a threat to national security, the US government uprooted whole families and confiscated all their property; they were released at the end of the war, though claims for compensation were only settled in 1988, when the government agreed to pay damages amounting to millions of dollars, and finally offered an official apology. The camp was once ringed by barbed wire and filled with row upon row of wooden barracks; now only a couple of guardhouses and a small cemetery remain among the sagebrush and scraggy cottonwoods. As the bronze plaque on the guardhouse says: "May the injustices and humiliation suffered here as a result of hysteria, racism and economic exploitation never emerge again." This was a sentiment shared by many at the time, and photographer **Ansel Adams** (see box, p.350) spent several weeks here in 1943 depicting the prisoners as industrious and loyal Americans.

The remains of the camp have been designated a national historic site (daytime access only; free), and funds were recently allocated to install a visitor center and restore some of the barracks and one of the guard towers. Some of the former internees return each year, on the last Saturday in April, in a kind of pilgrimage. A visit to the site is a little meaningless without some interpretation, something provided on a free two-hour **walking tour** (late June–early Sept Wed–Sat 8.30am & 11am, Sun 8.30am only; meet at the main entrance).

An evocative and affecting exhibit about Manzanar, detailing the experiences of many of the young children who were held there, is on display inside the **Eastern California Museum** at 155 N Grant St (Wed–Mon 10am–4pm; donation), three blocks west of the porticoed County Courthouse in the sleepy town of **INDEPENDENCE**, six miles further north. The cinder-block museum also has displays on the natural environment of the Owens Valley, including the bighorn sheep that live in the mountains west of town, and exhibits on the region's history, from native Paiute basketry to old mining and farming equipment. There's also a reconstructed pioneer village behind the museum, made up of old buildings from all over the Owens Valley that have been brought together and restored here.

Independence takes its heroic name not from any great libertarian tradition but from a Civil War fort that was founded north of the town on the Fourth of July, 1862; every year on that day there's a parade down Main Street (US-395) followed by a mass barbecue and fireworks show in **Dehy Park**, along tree-shaded Independence Creek on the north side of town. The park is marked by a large steam locomotive, which once ran from here to Nevada on narrow gauge tracks and is now being gussied up again.

The minor Onion Valley Road leads west past Independence's campground ($5), twisting up the mountains to **Onion Valley**, fifteen miles away. Once there, you'll find the *Onion Valley* **campground** (June to Sept; $11; ☎1-877/444-6777) and a trailhead for **hiking** across the Sierra Nevada into Kings Canyon National Park, a sixteen-mile journey over Kearsarge Pass to Cedar Grove (see p.327). This is the easiest and shortest route across the Sierra and you can get the required **wilderness permit** from the Inyo National Forest Wilderness Reservation Service (see box on p.281) or, off-season, at the trailhead.

The slopes of Mount Williamson, south of Onion Valley, and of Mount Baxter to the north are the protected home of the increasingly rare **California bighorn sheep**: nimble creatures that roam around the steep, rocky slopes and sport massive, curling horns. Far more common these days, however, are **black bears** and many of the local campgrounds require you to have bear-resistant food containers (you can buy or rent them at area sporting goods stores).

Practicalities

If you're in the anti-camping camp, Independence offers a few places to bed indoors. Try the inexpensive *Independence Courthouse Motel* at 157 N Edwards St (☎1-800/801-0703 or 760/878-2732; ②), or the much more atmospheric 1920s *Winnedumah Hotel*, 211 N Edwards St (☎760/878-2040, fax 878-2833, *winnedumah@qnet.com*; ③), once a film-star haven, now including a continental breakfast. For **food** stop by *Mair's Market*, or (before 9pm) enjoy sandwiches, salads or full meals at either the *Whistle Stop* diner or the more upmarket *Bill & Linda's*, which is open for evening meals from Friday to Sunday. All are on the US-395.

North from Independence: Big Pine and the White Mountains

Ten miles north of Independence is the actual start of the **LA Aqueduct**. Follow any of the dirt tracks that head east from US-395 and you can't fail to spot the traces of the railroads built to haul in the material needed to construct the great ditch – which Space Shuttle astronauts claim to have seen while orbiting the globe.

Twenty miles north of Independence, the **Tinnemaha Wildlife Viewpoint** warrants a brief pause to see if you can spot any of the five-hundred-strong herd of tule elk, now-protected California natives which were nearly wiped out by the end of the nineteenth century.

The town of **BIG PINE**, a further ten miles north, is slightly larger than Independence but doesn't have much more in the way of services. There are a few gas stations, Greyhound buses stop once a day in each direction, and there are a couple of serviceable **motels** along US-395 – the *Big Pine Motel*, 370 S Main St (☎760/938-2282; ②), and the *Starlight Motel*, 511 S Main St (☎760/938-2011; ②). There is also the *Glacier View* **campground** ($5) half a mile north of town at the junction of Hwy-168, several more camping spots up Glacier Lodge Road (see below), and good diner **food** at the *Country Kitchen*, 181 S Main St, almost opposite the **visitor center** at 126 S Main St (daily 8am–4.30pm; ☎760/938-2114, *www.bigpine.com*). Big Pine is, however, the gateway to three of the most unusual natural phenomena in California: the **Palisade Glacier** in the Sierra Nevada to the west of town; the ancient Bristlecone Pine Forest in the barren **White Mountains** to the east; and the northern reaches of Death Valley, in particular the Eureka Sand Dunes (see p.278) and the hot springs of the Saline Valley (see p.278).

The Palisade Glacier

The southernmost glacier in the US, the **Palisade Glacier** sits at the foot of the impressive Palisade Crest, center of one of the greatest concentrations of enjoyably climbable (though only for the experienced) peaks in the Eastern Sierra. To the south is Norman Clyde Peak, named after California's most prolific early mountaineer. To the north, Thunderbolt Peak and Mount Agassiz are highlights of the Inconsolable Range. And in the center, the immense bulk of Temple Crag offers a range of routes unparalleled outside of Yosemite Valley. Even the Palisade Glacier itself an excellent introduction to snow and ice-climbing. The trailhead for these climbs and numerous local hikes is ten miles west of Big Pine, at the end of Glacier Lodge Road; follow Crocker St in Big Pine. Here you'll find three, three-season, $11-a-night **campgrounds** – *Sage Flat, Upper Sage Flat* and *Big Pine Creek* – all above 7000ft and with water and toilets; and a free walk-in site at 8200ft, a mile beyond the trailhead. *Glacier Lodge* (☎760/938-2837; ④) right at the end of the road, is a slightly more luxurious option, with cabins and a limited general store.

The imposing glacier is nine miles from the end of the road on a well-marked trail along the north fork of Big Pine Creek, past a number of alpine lakes. Before heading off into the wilderness, get a backcountry camping **permit** (see box on p.281).

The White Mountains

Big Pine is also the gateway to the intimidating **White Mountains**, a bald, dry and little-visited range almost as high as the Sierra and forming the eastern wall of the Owens Valley. It is made up of some of the oldest, fossil-filled rock in California and geologically has more in common with the Great Basin to the east than the spiky Sierra, which came into being several hundred million years later. It looks like it too: the scrubby undulating high country appears more Scottish than Californian. The mountains are accessible only by car (or bike) via Hwy-168. Be sure to fill up on gas and **drinking water**, both of which are unavailable east of US-395.

The gnarled trees that are the prime reason for coming here stand on the lower slopes in the ancient **Bristlecone Pine Forest**, but snow renders them inaccessible for all but three or four months in the summer. **Schulman Grove** ($2 per person or $5 per car), is the most accessible collection, some 23 miles from Big Pine along a paved road that twists up from Hwy-168. The grove is split up into two self-guided nature trails. One, the mile-long Discovery Trail, passes by a number of splendid examples; the other, longer Methuselah Trail loops around past the oldest tree, the 4700-year-old Methuselah, though you'll have to guess which of the trees it is since it is unmarked due to fears of vandalism. Both trails start at the **visitor center** (daily late

May–Aug 10am–5pm or later, Sept and Oct Sat & Sun 10am–5pm; ☎760/873-2503) which explains the importance of the grove's namesake, Dr Edmund Schulman. An early practitioner of dendrochronology, he revealed the extreme age of these trees in the mid-1950s and applied the knowledge gained from core samples of the trees to correct a puzzling error in early carbon dating techniques, in turn changing our perception of history. If you want to know more, show up at one of the free ranger talks scheduled frequently through July and August, plus there is usually a ranger-led walk on Saturdays.

Patriarch Grove, twelve miles further on, along a dusty dirt road that gives spectacular views of the Sierra Nevada to the west and the Great Basin ranges of the deserts to the east, contains the Patriarch Tree, the largest of the bristlecone pines. Four miles beyond here, a research station (closed to the public) studies the physiology of high-altitude plant and animal life, which is in many ways similar to that of the arctic regions. From here you can **hike to the summit of White Mountain** (15 miles round-trip; 6–8 hr; 2500ft ascent), the highest point in the range, and at 14,246 feet the third highest in California, though local boosters like to claim that recent satellite measurements suggest it may just pip Whitney in the altitude stakes. A gate prevents unauthorized vehicles from getting to the research station, though all-terrain **mountain bikes** are permitted to continue. In fact, the canyons running down from the ridge between the bristlecone groves are tailor-made for thrill-seekers, who race down the steep washes at incredibly high speeds. **Silver Canyon**, descending from just beyond Schulman Grove, is the route taken by the **Plumline Outback**, a rigorous mountain bike race held each July; cyclists begin in Bishop, race up to the ridge and career back down again.

There is **camping** available, but no water; the only campground is 8600ft up at *Grandview* (May–Oct; free), two miles south of Schulman Grove. Backcountry camping is not permitted in the ancient Bristlecone Pine Forest, but is allowed in the surrounding forest provided you have a campfire permit for your stove. The ranger station in Bishop can provide this and tell you which springs and small creeks (if any) are flowing.

BRISTLECONE PINES

Great Basin **bristlecone pines** (*pinus longaeva*) are the oldest known living things on earth. Some of them have been alive for over 4500 years (1500 years more than any sequoia), earning them a place in the *Guinness Book of Records*. The oldest examples cling to thin alkaline soils (predominantly dolomite) between 10,000 and 11,000 feet, where the low precipitation keeps the growing season to only 45 days a year. But such conditions, which limit the trees' girth expansion to an inch every hundred years, promotes the dense resin-rich and rot-resistant wood that lasts for millennia. Battered and beaten by the harsh environment into bizarrely beautiful shapes and forms, they look like nothing so much as twenty-foot lumps of driftwood. The most photogenic examples comprise mostly **dead wood**, the live section often sustained by a thin ribbon of bark. Even when dead, the wind-scoured trunks and twisted limbs hang on without decaying for upwards of another thousand-odd years, slowly being eroded by wind-driven ice and sand.

Bristlecones thrive at lower altitudes and richer soils than those in the White Mountains, growing tall and wide. But they seldom live as long as specimens subjected to the harsher conditions and, in fact, they're hardly recognizable as bristlecone pines, only the five-needle bundles and the egg-shaped, barbed cone which lends the tree its name giving the game away.

For more information, consult the Inyo forest Web site at *www.r5.fs.fed.us/inyo* or better still the excellent *www.sonic.net/bristlecone*.

Bishop

BISHOP, to a Californian, means **outdoor pursuits**. It is the largest town in the Owens Valley with a population of 3500 and yet maintains a laid-back ambiance which makes it worth hanging around to enjoy. Its proximity to the wilderness also makes an excellent base from which to explore the surrounding mountains; if you want to try cross-country skiing, fly-fishing, and especially rock climbing, there's no better place to be, with some of the world's best mountaineers offering their services through lessons and guided trips.

For **expert instruction** or **guided trips** in the High Sierra backcountry, contact: A Taste For Adventure (☎760/873-8526, fax873-8526, *atfa@aol.com*); John Fischer Mountain Guide (☎760/873-5037, fax 873-9128, *pescador@qnet.com*); Nidever Mountain Guides (☎760/648-1122, fax 648-7221, *www.themountainguide.com*); Sierra Mountain Guides (☎760/872-3811, fax 872-3811, *www.cosleyhouston.com*); or Sierra Mountaineering International (☎760/872-4929, fax 872-2489, *wedberg@qnet.com*). All cover rock climbing, alpine climbing and ski mountaineering. Another place worth a stop is Wilson's East Side Sports, 224 N Main St (☎760/873-7520, *www.eastsidesports.com*), an excellent mountaineering and sporting goods supply shop.

While in Bishop, be sure to call in at the **Paiute Shoshone Indian Cultural Center**, 2300 W Line St (Mon–Fri 9am–5pm, Sat & Sun 9am–4pm; $2), run by local natives who mostly live on a reservation on the edge of town, similar to those found outside each of the Valley settlements. Here they put on displays of basketry and weaving, food gathering and processing, and of traditional ways of building; they also run a good bookstore. Their ancestors once roamed the area and left their mark all over the Owens Valley in the form of petroglyphs, the best examples of which are found a few miles outside town (see opposite).

Practicalities

Bishop and its surroundings is an easy place to get to, with Greyhound calling at the station at 201 S Warren St (☎760/872-2721) and Kountry Korners (☎760/872-4411) supplying rides out to the trailheads. For specific information on **hiking** and **camping** in the area, contact the White Mountain Ranger Station at 798 N Main St (July & Aug daily 8am–4.30pm; rest of year Mon–Fri 8am–5pm; ☎760/873-2500), which also issues the first-come-first-served wilderness permits. The main **visitor center** (Mon–Fri 9am–5pm, Sat & Sun 10am–4pm; ☎760/873-8405, fax 873-6999, *www.bishopvisitor.com*) is a block away at #690 and has a visitor guide listing **accommodation**. The best budget options are the *El Rancho Motel*, 274 W Lagoon St on the south side of town (☎760/872-9251; ②), and the *Thunderbird Motel*, 190 W Pine St (☎760/873-4215; ②). The more upmarket *Best Western Creekside Inn*, 725 N Main St (☎760/872-3044; ⑤) offers large rooms and complimentary breakfast though you may prefer the antique-filled Victorian-era *Chalfant House B&B*, 213 Academy St (☎760/872-1790; ④), just off the 200 block of North Main St.

With a 24-hour Vons store at 174 S Main St, and a number of cafés and diners, Bishop is a good spot to buy **food** and **supplies**. *Jack's Waffle Shop*, 437 N Main St, is open seven fluorescent-lit days a week for breakfasts and burgers. For good espresso and pastries, head along N Main St to the pseudo-Dutch *Erick Schat's Bakkery* at #736, or the hipper, more central *Kava Coffeehouse* at #206. For lunch or dinner try *Bar-B-Q Bill's* at 187 S Main St (☎760/872-5535), *Amigo's Mexican Restaurant*, 285 Main St (☎760/872-2189), or *Whiskey Creek*, 524 N Main St (☎760/873-7174), which also has a lively **bar** open till 2am.

Hikers and backcountry campers in need of a **shower** can get one seasonally at the Bishop City Pool, 688 N Main St (late May–early Sept Mon–Sat 7am–8pm; $1.50), or year-round at Sierra Bodies Gym, 192 E Pine St (Mon–Fri 6am–9pm, Sat 8am–3pm Sun 9am–3pm; $5).

Around Bishop and north towards Mammoth

US-6 heads north and east from Bishop into Nevada, passing by the **Laws Railroad Museum** (daily 10am–4pm; donation), a restoration of the old town of **Laws**, four miles off US-395, with some relocated old buildings and a slender black narrow-gauge train that used to run along the eastern edge of the Owens Valley. It's worth a quick look on your way to see the **Red Rock Canyon Petroglyphs**, four miles west of US-6; the rock carvings have been terribly vandalized, but enough remains of the spacey figures to justify a trip. Obtain a free entry permit from the Bureau of Lands Management, Suite E, 785 N Main St in Bishop (Mon–Fri 8.30am–4pm; ☎760/872-4881).

Hwy-168 runs west from Bishop past the Paiute Shoshone Indian Cultural Center and climbs through aspens and cottonwoods and past the golden granite rock climbers' paradise of the **Buttermilk Boulders**, into the Sierra Nevada. The road finishes nineteen miles away at the dammed **Lake Sabrina**. Nearby **South Lake** is also nineteen miles from Bishop. A number of **hiking routes** set off up into the High Sierra wilderness from trailheads at these lakes. The trail from South Lake over Bishop Pass heads into Dusy Basin, where you can see the effects of centuries of glaciation in the bowl-like cirques and giant "erratic" boulders left by receding glaciers. Another path follows the northern fork of Bishop Creek under the rusty cliffs of the Paiute Crags, before climbing over Paiute Pass into the Desolation Lakes area of the John Muir Wilderness. There are a number of **campgrounds** between 7500 and 9000 feet up – almost all with water and costing $11 a night. The shady *Sabrina* site, right by the lake of the same name, is perhaps the best.

North of Bishop, US-395 climbs out of the Owens Valley up Sherwin Grade onto the 6500-feet-high **Mono Basin**. Eighteen miles north of Bishop, at the foot of the climb, Gorge Road leads west into the 1000-feet deep **Owens River Gorge**, one of the best rock climbing spots on this side of the Sierra.

Much more of the money that flows into Bishop comes from the brigades of fishing enthusiasts, who spend their summer vacations angling for rainbow trout placed in the streams and lakes by the state government. The largest assembly of fisherfolk gather on the last Saturday in April around **Lake Crowley**, an artificial reservoir built to hold water diverted from Mono Lake, thirty miles north of town.

Mammoth Lakes and around

During winter, masses of weekend skiers speed through the Owens Valley from LA on their way to the slopes of Mammoth Mountain, forty miles north along US-395 from Bishop then nine miles west on Hwy-203. The pistes rise above the resort town of **MAMMOTH LAKES** which, outside the Lake Tahoe basin, is the state's premier ski mountain. It is for this and the summer fishing that Mammoth is traditionally known, although the town is now increasingly hyped for its accessible mountain biking terrain and a number of on- and off-road bike races. Mammoth is unbeatable for outdoor activities and is scenically as dramatic as just about anywhere in the Sierra, although you may find the testosterone overload oppressive and the town overpriced. That said, hikers keen to return each evening to good food, lively bars and even a couple of movie theaters, have found the right spot.

Practicalities

The daily Greyhound stops in the *McDonald's* parking lot on Hwy-203. During the ski season, get around on the four-route Mammoth Shuttle (☎760/934-3030) which goes everywhere you'll want to. During the warmer months, **rent a bike** (see "Listings," p.293), and make use of the summer **shuttle** which plies a route between

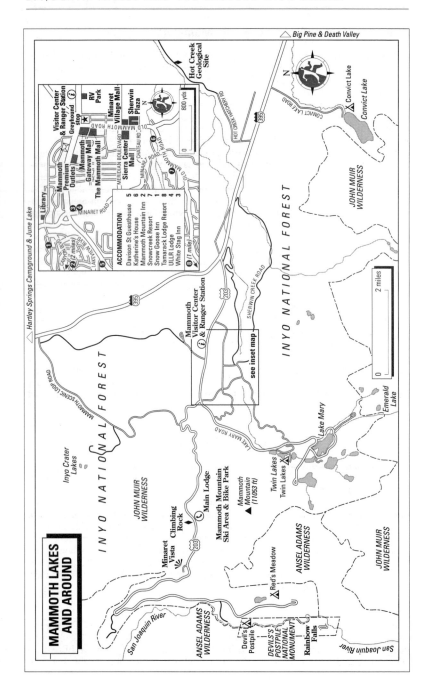

MAMMOTH LAKES AND AROUND

△ Big Pine & Death Valley

△ Hartley Springs Campground & June Lake

Hot Creek Geological Site

HOT CREEK HATCHERY RD

Convict Lake
✕ Convict Lake

CONVICT LAKE ROAD

JOHN MUIR WILDERNESS

INYO NATIONAL FOREST

ACCOMMODATION
Davison St Guesthouse   5
Katherine's House   6
Mammoth Mountain Inn   2
Snowcreek Resort   7
Snow Goose Inn   1
Tamarack Lodge Resort   8
ULLR Lodge   4
White Stag Inn   3

Visitor Center & Ranger Station
Greyhound stop
RV Park
Minaret Village Mall
Sherwin Plaza
Mammoth Gateway Mall
Sierra Center Mall
The Mammoth Mall

MERIDIAN BOULEVARD
MAMMOTH ROAD
MINARET CHATEAU RD
OLD MAMMOTH ROAD

Library
MINARET ROAD

0   800 yds

(2 miles)
CANYON BLVD
LAKEVIEW BLVD

(1 mile)

395

Mammoth Visitor Center & Ranger Station
203

SHERWIN CREEK ROAD

see inset map

INYO NATIONAL FOREST

2 miles

0

Inyo Crater Lakes

MAMMOTH SCENIC LOOP ROAD

JOHN MUIR WILDERNESS

LAKE MARY ROAD

Lake Mary

Emerald Lake

Minaret Vista

Climbing Rock

Main Lodge

203

Mammoth Mountain Ski Area & Bike Park
▲ Mammoth Mountain (11,053 ft)

Twin Lakes
Twin Lakes

ANSEL ADAMS WILDERNESS

✕ Red's Meadow

JOHN MUIR WILDERNESS

San Joaquin River

ANSEL ADAMS WILDERNESS

Devil's Postpile ✕

DEVIL'S POSTPILE NATIONAL MONUMENT

Rainbow Falls ✕

San Joaquin River

the main ski lodge and Devil's Postpile National Monument, some fifteen miles west of town.

The best source of practical information for the area is the combined US Forest Service and Mammoth Lakes **visitor center** (daily 9am–5pm; ☎1-888/466-2666 or 760/924-5500, *www.visitmammoth.com*) on the main highway half a mile east of the town center.

Accommodation

About every second building in Mammoth is a condo, but there are numerous other **accommodation** opportunities (including a couple of hostels), so beds are at a premium only during peak-season weekends. Winter prices are highest, summer rates (quoted here) come next, and in between some relative bargains can be found. There is also plenty of family camping (see box) and mile upon mile of backcountry (see "Hiking" box, p.292) in which to pitch a tent.

Davison St Guesthouse, 19 Davison St, off Main St (☎760/544-9093, fax 544-9107). Wooden A-frame chalet with mountain views. Four-bed rooms for $50 and dorm space from $18, with a kitchen available for guests' use. Call the San Diego number above or walk in between 3pm and 7pm.

Katherine's House, 201 Waterford Ave (☎1-800/934-2991 or 760/934-2991, fax 924-5903, *www.katherineshouse.com*). Attractive and comfortable B&B set among Jeffrey pines with a couple of rooms, and cottages sleeping two ($155) or four ($205). ⑤.

Mammoth Mountain Inn, Mammoth Mountain (☎1-800/228-4947 or 760/934-2581, fax 934-0701, *www.mammothlodging.com*). *The* place to stay – right where the action is at the foot of the ski tows, adjacent to the bike park and overlooking the climbing rock. It's a touch sterile but you'll be well looked after. ⑥.

Snowcreek Resort, Old Mammoth Rd, by the golf course (☎1-800/544-6007 or 760/934-3333, *www.snowcreekresort.com*). Well-appointed condos with a two-night minimum stay, spring and fall discounts (three nights for two), and use of the pool, spa and tennis club. Especially good value for groups. ⑤.

CAMPING

Campers are almost overwhelmed with choice with some twenty **campgrounds** in a ten mile radius of town; the two main concentrations being around Twin Lakes, and along the Devil's Postpile/Reds Meadow road. Almost all come with water, cost $10–13 and are let on a first-come-first-served basis. The *Inyo National Forest Mammoth Lakes Area visitor guide* (available free from the visitor center) has full details along with details of rules for free dispersed camping on national forest lands around about.

Convict Lake (late-April to Oct; $10; 7600ft). Wooded, lakeside campground just west of US-395 around four miles south of the Mammoth turn-off, with the longest opening season in the area. Showers are available at the nearby *Convict Lake Resort* (☎760/934-2368; $1 for two minutes).

Devil's Postpile (mid-June to mid-Sept; $12; 7600ft). National Park Service's campground half a mile from rocks themselves along the Devil's Postpile/Red's Meadow road, and a good base for hikes to Rainbow Falls or along the John Muir Trail.

Hartley Springs (June–Oct free; 8200ft). Primitive waterless campground located 1.5 miles west of US-395 around eleven miles north of the Mammoth turn-off.

Red's Meadow (mid-June to mid-Sept; $12; 7600ft). National forest campground along the Devil's Postpile/Red's Meadow road and within easy hiking distance of Devil's Postpile, Rainbow Falls and a nice nature trail around Sotcher Lake. It also comes with a natural hot spring bathhouse open to all (donations appreciated).

Twin Lakes (June–Oct; $13; 8600ft). The longest opening of five near-identical sites in this area of glacially-scooped lake beds, a mile southwest of Mammoth Lakes township. Lakeside setting among the pines and plenty of hiking trails nearby.

Snow Goose Inn, 57 Forest Trail (☎1-800/874-7368 or 760/934-2660). Relatively reasonable rates and generous morning and late afternoon spreads help compensate for the typical bed and breakfast cutesiness. ④.

Tamarack Lodge & Resort, Lake Mary Rd (☎1-800/237-6879 or 760/934-2442, fax 934-2281, *www.tamaracklodge.com*). Lodge rooms ($75–145) or rustic cabins ($100 and up) with fully-equipped kitchens, beautifully situated beside Twin Lake right on the edge of a cross-country ski area.

ULLR Lodge, 5920 Minaret Rd (☎760/934-2454, *ullr@cris.com*). Private rooms from $30 midweek in summer, and popular 4-bed dorms with lockers for $15. Showers are available to non-residents for $4 (it's an extra $1 if you don't have your own towel).

White Stag Inn, corner of Main and Minaret (☎1-800/376-4134 or 760/934-7507). Pleasant, centrally located motel; some rooms with kitchenettes. ③.

Mammoth Mountain: biking, hiking and other activities

Mammoth is all about getting into the outdoors. Aside from eating, drinking and mooching around the sports shops and factory clothing outlets, you'll find little to do in town. There's much more fun to be had four miles west of the center up on the slopes of the dormant volcano that is **Mammoth Mountain**. Once the ski runs have freed themselves of the winter snows (usually mid-June to Sept), the slopes transform into the 3500-acre **Mammoth Mountain Bike Park** (daily 9am–6pm) with over seventy miles of groomed singletrack trails. Chairlifts quickly give you and your bike and altitude boost, allowing you to hurtle down the twisting sandy trails, brushing pines and negotiating small jumps and tree roots. The emphasis here is definitely on going downhill, and when you're transported to the rarefied eleven-thousand-foot air at the top of the chair you very quickly appreciate the logic of this. The bike park produces a color map of the mountain showing the lifts and trails in three grades of difficulty. Beginners often take the **Downtown** run into Mammoth (from where a bike shuttle bus returns you to the bike park), while those with a little more skill or ambition might opt for the **Beach Cruiser** which carves its way down the western side of the mountain from near the summit. Experts and those with a death wish can tackle the **Kamikaze**, scene of the ultimate downhill race which forms the centerpiece of the annual World Cup racing

---

WINTER AND SPRING IN MAMMOTH

With one of the longest Californian seasons (often stretching well into June), 2200 vertical feet of skiing and more than its fair share of deep powder, **Mammoth Mountain** is understandably popular. Add to that a cat's-cradle of intersecting gondolas and chairlifts – seemingly being added to each year – bundles of snow-making equipment, and a whole resort of bars and restaurants designed with après-ski in mind, and you can hardly go wrong. Pick up **lift tickets** ($52 per day, $62 if you add in night skiing; $42 from May on) from the Main Lodge on Minaret Road, where you can also rent **equipment** ($24 for basic skis, boots and poles; $30 for snowboard and boots), and book **lessons** ($32 per half-day). For information call ☎1-888/SNOWRPT to get a recorded snow report, ☎1-888/4MAMMOTH to reach the mountain, or check out the Web site at *www.mammoth-mtn.com*.

Off the mountain there are stacks of **cross-country skiing** trails; *Tamarack Lodge Resort* (see "Accommodation," above) offers ski packages, including instruction, tours and rentals. If you prefer a motorized approach to the white stuff, you can rent gear and clothing from Center Street Snowmobiles (☎760/934-6888) and DJ's Snowmobile Adventures (☎760/935-4480) for around $43 an hour for a single, $67 for a double. Beyond that, there's **ice skating**, **bobsled riding**, and even shooting down the bobsled course on a giant inner tube.

weekend (usually around the middle of July) at which competitors hit speeds of sixty miles per hour.

The basic **park use fee** ($20) includes an all-day trail pass, and two rides either on the chairlift running halfway up the mountain or the bike shuttle bus from the village back to the bike park. An extra $5 gives you unlimited access to the lifts and bike shuttle bus, and $43 gets you the same for two full days. If you're not toting your own machine you need to rent a full-suspension bike and helmet ($25 half day, $35 full day). For an affordable sampler of all this, there's the $30 Midweek Special; a two-hour taster that includes bike rental, trail access and one chairlift ride halfway up the mountain.

If you don't fancy forking out for use of the bike park, or just fancy something a little gentler, there is plenty more riding on trails and roads around the resort, made comfortable by mid-summer temperatures reliably in the seventies. Several bike stores around town will point you in the right direction and rent bikes (see below) which can also be taken to the bike park. The same shops organize easy-going group rides every few days through the summer, and August sees the family-oriented **Adventure Week** (☎1-800/367-6572 or 760/934-3068 for information) with guided tours, night rides and special children's events.

Interwoven among the bike trails are a couple of **hiking paths** which top out at the summit. The views are stupendous but, in common with many volcanoes, the hiking isn't the best and you're better off riding the gondola to the summit ($10) and saving your legs for hikes elsewhere (see box overleaf). If you fancy something considerably more (or much less) adventurous, there are stacks of people willing to get you mobile; ballooning, horseback riding, kayaking and rock climbing, are all covered in "Listings" on p.293.

Along Minaret Road: Devil's Postpile National Monument

From the ski area, the narrow and winding **Minaret Road** climbs briefly to a nine-thousand-foot pass in the San Joaquin Ridge, then plummets into the headwaters of the Middle Fork of the San Joaquin River ending some eight miles on at the Red's Meadow pack station. When the road is free of snow (typically mid-June to Oct) this is the only road access seven miles beyond the bike park to the evocatively named **Devil's Postpile National Monument** (unrestricted access), a collection of slender, blue-gray basalt columns ranged like hundreds of pencils stood on end. Some are as tall as sixty feet, others are twisted and warped, while vulnerable sections are shorter where the brittle rock has cracked and the upper sections have fallen forward to form a talus slope of shattered rubble. It was formed as lava from Mammoth Mountain cooled and fractured into multi-sided forms, a phenomenon best appreciated by skirting round to the top of the columns. The Postpile itself is a half-mile stroll from the Devil's Postpile campground where there is a small **visitor center** (daily 10am–5pm in summer), from where rangers guide daily walks and lead evening campfire programs.

The second highlight of the National Monument is **Rainbow Falls**, where the Middle Fork of the San Joaquin River plunges 101 feet into a deep pool, the spray refracting to earn its name, especially at midday. It is two miles away through Red's Meadow, reached on a pleasant hike (see box overleaf).

In the height of the summer season, unless you're camping in the area (in which case restrictions apply), the road is closed throughout the day and you must go via the **shuttle bus** (daily 7.30am–5.30pm; $9 round-trip, valid all day) which leaves every thirty minutes from the *Mammoth Mountain Inn*, opposite the bike park. Once over the hill, rides between stops in the valley are free; and in the early morning, evening, and at the ends of the season when the shuttle has stopped but the road is still open, you can drive there along Minaret Road. During the day, the furthest you can drive without taking the shuttle bus is **Minaret Vista**, a parking lot high on the

HIKING FROM MAMMOTH

Listed below are some of the best of the **short hikes** around Mammoth. No permits are required for these, though you'll need to obtain a free **wilderness permit** if you want to spend the night in the Ansel Adams or John Muir wilderness areas to the south and west. On most heavily used trails there is a quota season from late June to mid-September when numbers of campers are limited. Call ☎1-888/374-3773 or 760/938-1136, fax 938-1137 up to six months and at least two days in advance.

Crystal Lake (6 miles; 3—4hr). From the Lake George trailhead the path skirts high above Lake George revealing increasingly dramatic views as you climb Mammoth Crest and on to Crystal Lake, hunkered below Crystal Crag.

Panorama Dome Trail (1 mile round-trip; 30min). Great views over the town and the Owens Valley reward this short sylvan trail from Twin Lakes on Lake Mary Road (see town map p.288).

Sky Meadows (4 miles; 1.5—2hr). Delightful hike along the wildflower-flanked Coldwater Creek past Emerald Lake to Sky Meadow at the foot of the striking Blue Crag. Starts at the southern end of Lake Mary.

Devil's Postpile to Rainbow Falls (5 miles; 2hr). Moderate hike that combines the two key features of the Devil's Postpile National Monument. Start from the Devil's Postpile campground and stroll to the monument itself, then continue to the top of Rainbow Falls.

San Joaquin Ridge with wonderful views of the **Minarets Peaks**, a spiky volcanic ridge just south of pointed Mount Ritter – one of the Sierra's most enticing high peaks.

Eating, drinking and nightlife

Mammoth offers by far the widest selection – and some of the best examples –of **restaurants**, **cafés** and **bars** (some with live **music**) on this side of the Sierra. That may be reason enough to stick around for a while but if you've got used to the relative austerity elsewhere in the mountains, the drain on your finances may come as something of a shock. If you're just after replenishing your cooler, pick up **groceries** at Vons, in the Minaret Village Mall, and healthy goodies at Sierra *Sundance Earth Foods* in The Mammoth Mall.

Angel's, Main St at Sierra Blvd (☎760/934-74270). The menu has a southwestern kick at this friendly place, popular with families and couples alike; good salads and fish tacos. Main courses around the $10–15 mark.

Cervino's, 3752 Viewpoint Rd (☎760/934-4734). Pricey but excellent northern Italian fare; try mushrooms stuffed with goat's cheese and pecans followed by Italian sausage linguini.

Giovanni's, Minaret Village Mall, Old Mammoth Rd (☎760/934-7563. The favorite local stop for low-cost dining; three out of ten for decor and ambiance but very good pasta and pizza, and great lunchtime deals.

Good Life Café, The Mammoth Mall (☎760/934-1734). Doesn't cater to vegetarians and vegans as well as they'd like you to believe, but probably the best around with veggie burritos, good salads and vegetable wraps as well as plenty of burgers and egg dishes at modest prices, all served inside or on the sunny deck.

Grumpy's, Old Mammoth Rd, just off Main St (☎760/934-8587). Non-smoking sports bar with pool table, video games and a good grill.

The Lakefront Restaurant, *Tamarack Lodge* (☎760/934-3534). Superb lake views to accompany dishes from a menu with French-California leanings. Expect to pay $20–25 for a grill of duck, boar and elk or Provençal vegetable Wellington.

Looney Bean Coffee Roasting Co., Main St (☎760/934-1345). Come here for the scene; the coffee's better at other places in town. Open until 11pm at weekends, later in the ski season.

Nevados, cnr Main St & Minaret Rd (☎760/934-4466). Another favorite with the foodies with an eclectic menu from crisp Nori wrapped shrimp with wasabi to hazelnut crust rack of lamb and a $30 *prix fixe* deal for an appetizer, main and dessert.

Schat's Bakery & Café, 3305 Main St (☎760/934-6055). Easily the best baked goods in town, either to take out or eat in with a coffee.

The Stove, 644 Old Mammoth Rd, opposite the Sherwin Plaza Mall (☎760/934-2821). Long-standing Mammoth favorite, serving egg, waffle and pancake breakfasts, sandwiches and full meals later on – all served in massive portions.

Whiskey Creek, Main St and Minaret Rd (☎760/934-2555). One of the town's liveliest bars and restaurants, with its own good microbrews. Bands Wed–Sun in winter; Thurs–Sat in summer.

World Cup Coffee, 588 Old Mammoth Rd, opposite the Sherwin Plaza Mall. The java you're after.

Listings

Ballooning Mammoth Ballooning (☎760/934-7188, *www.mammothweb.com*) and Mammoth Sierra Connection (☎760/934-0606) both run flights for $175–250 depending on group size, involving an hour or two airborne and a brunch to follow.

Banks Several around town (all with ATMs) including the Bank of America, corner of Main St and Old Mammoth Rd.

Bookstores Book Warehouse, 3399 Main St (☎619/924-3551) is stacked with remaindered books of all sorts at bargain prices.

Cinemas First-run Hollywood fare at the Plaza Theatre in the Sherwin Plaza Mall and Minaret Cinema in the Minaret Village Mall.

Festivals The annual Jazz Jubilee, held in the second week in July (details on ☎760/934-2478), packs the town out with trad-jazz types.

Horseback riding Mammoth is surrounded by pack stations all geared to get you out on horseback, most charging around $50 for a half-day ride, $70 for a full day, and around $200 a day for all-inclusive multi-day trips in the backcountry. The two biggies are Red's Meadow (☎1-800/292-7758 or 760/934-2345, *www.mammothweb.com/redsmeadow*) based at the end of the Devil's Postpile road; and Mammoth Lakes Pack Outfit (☎1-888/475-8748, *www.mammothpack.com*).

Internet access The library (see below) has free surfing machines, and email charged at $6 an hour.

Kayaking Caldera Kayaks (☎760/935-4942, *www.calderakayak.com*) are based ten miles south of Mammoth at Crowley Lake Marina and run guided kayak trips on Mono and Crowley lakes ($60) and rent out gear for $30–45 a day.

Laundry Mill City Laundry, cnr Main St and Old Mammoth Rd.

Library The public library is located at 960 Forest Trail (Mon–Fri 10am–7pm, Sat 9am–5.30pm) and has Internet access.

Mountain biking Footloose Sports, cnr Canyon Blvd and Minaret Rd (☎760/934-2400, *www.footloosesports.com*) rent road bikes from $18 (full suspension ATB, $33), organize weekly group rides and rent in-line skates ($20 a day); Mammoth Sporting Goods, Sierra Center Mall (☎760/934-3239, *www.mammothsportinggoods.com*) offer similar rates and also run group rides; and Mountain Bike Hall of Famer Cindy Whitehead (☎760/934-8989) gives private lessons costing $25 per-person, per-hour for 2–6 people.

Rock climbing There's a 32-foot artificial **climbing rock** (daily 10am–6pm; $13 an hour, $22 per day, shoes $3; ☎760/924-5683) in front of the *Mammoth Mountain Inn*, and an adjacent **ropes course** which costs $43 for a four-hour confidence-building session including a 500ft zip line ($10 separately). To get out on the real stuff, contact Mammoth Mountaineering School (☎1-800/549-7515 or 760/924-9100, *www.californiarock.com*) who run a "just for fun" day ($65), and rock classes at all grades ($80).

Showers In Mammoth township try *ULLR Lodge* (see "Accommodation," above; 9am–noon & 2–7.30pm; $4, $5 with towel), though it is cheaper up at the Twin Lakes Store (daily 7am–8pm; $2; ☎760/934-7295). In the Devil's Postpile area, head for the natural hot spring bathhouse at the Red's Meadow campground (donations appreciated).

Around Mammoth: Hot Creek and June Lake

Mammoth makes a good base for exploring a little of the **surrounding area**, even as far as Mono Lake and Bodie Ghost town (see p.296). Just east of US-395, three miles south of the exit for Mammoth Lakes, is one of the more pleasurable and easily accessible examples of the region's volcanic activity in the hot springs that bubble up at **Hot Creek** (daily dawn–dusk; free), on Hot Creek Hatchery Road. Hot Creek is one of the best, and best known, springs in the region. Jets of boiling water mix with the otherwise chilly, snow-melt water to form pools ranging from tepid to scalding; you have to search to find a happy medium, and it's a bit of a challenge since the flows are ever-changing. Note, too, that the US Forest Service discourages bathing, as chemicals are sometimes produced in the springs – not that anyone takes any notice. Paths and wooden steps lead down to the most likely spots, but wear shoes – as well as bathing suits, which are required – because idiots have shattered bottles under the water. If you want details on more hot springs in the area, check out George William's *Hot Springs of the Eastern Sierra*, found in the area's bookshops and visitor centers.

The crowding of Mammoth Lakes sends some skiers and summer visitors a few miles further north to the relative solitude of **June Lake** and its neighbors, Grant, Silver and Gull lakes. Reached by way of the seventeen-mile **June Lake Loop** road, which branches off US-395 fifteen miles north of the Mammoth turning, this region of high-altitude lakes is one of the most striking in these parts, and offers Mammoth's attractions on a more manageable scale. If you're camping you'll find a selection of $12 Forest Service campgrounds scattered beside the various lakes, including the relatively busy June Lake, two miles off US-395 and the more serene Grant Lake, nine miles further on, where there is boat and fishing tackle rental. The small township of **JUNE LAKE** has a broad selection of accommodation at all levels, though you may be happy just to stop in for lunch, a smoothie or a coffee at *Trout Town Joe* on the main street.

Mono Lake

The blue expanse of **Mono Lake** sits in the middle of a volcanic, desert tableland, its sixty square miles reflecting the statuesque, snowcapped mass of the eastern Sierra Nevada. At close to a million years old, it's an ancient lake (one of the oldest in North America) with two large volcanic islands, the light-colored **Pahoa** and the black **Negit**, surrounded by salty, alkaline water. It resembles nothing more than a science-fiction landscape, with great towers and spires formed by mineral deposits ringing the shores; hot springs surround the lake, and all around the basin are signs of lava flows and volcanic activity, especially in the cones of the Mono Craters, just to the south.

The lake's most distinctive feature, the strange, sandcastle-like **tufa** formations, have been increasingly exposed over the past fifty years or so since the City of Los Angeles began draining away the waters that flow into the lake (see box opposite). The towers of tufa were formed underwater, where calcium-bearing freshwater springs well up through the carbonate-rich lake water; the calcium and carbonate combine and sink to the bottom as limestone, slowly growing into the weird formations you can see today. Before striking out for a close look at the lake and its tufa, call in at the excellent **Mono Basin Scenic Area Visitor Center**, a mile north of Lee Vining beside US-395 (daily May–Sept 9am–5.30pm; Oct–April Thurs–Mon 9am–4.45pm; ☎760/647-3044, *www.r5.fs.fed.us/inyo/vvc/mono*). Exhibits and a good short film detail the lake's geology, and rangers give talks on various aspects of its ecology. The center is also the place to check the **guided walks** (July to early Sept daily 10am, 1pm & 6pm) which leave from the **South Tufa Reserve** ($2), one of the best places to look at the tufa spires, five miles east of US-395 via Hwy-120. Also here is **Navy Beach**, where you can float in

THE BATTLE FOR MONO LAKE

At around a million years old, **Mono Lake** is one of the oldest bodies of water on the continent. It has survived several ice ages and all the volcanic activity that the area can throw at it, but the lake's biggest threat has been the City of Los Angeles, which owns the riparian rights to Mono Lake's catchment. In 1941, the Los Angeles Department of Water and Power diverted four of the five streams that fed the lake into its Owens Valley Aqueduct, which drains the Mono Basin through an eleven-mile tunnel. This was an engineering marvel, dug through the volcanically active Mono Craters, but it's been overshadowed by the legal battle surrounding the depletion of the lake itself, long one of the biggest **environmental controversies** raging in California.

The **water level** in Mono Lake has dropped over forty feet since 1941, a disaster not only because of the lake's unique beauty, but also because Mono Lake is the primary nesting ground for California gulls and a prime stopover point for thousands of migratory geese, ducks and swans. The lake is now roughly half its natural size, and as the levels dropped, the islands in the middle of the lake where the gulls lay their eggs became peninsulas, and the colonies fell prey to coyotes and other mainland predators. Also, as less fresh water reached the lake, the landlocked water became increasingly saline, threatening the unique local ecosystem. Brine shrimp and alkali flies are about all that will thrive in the harsh conditions, but these are critical to the birdlife. Humans are not immune to the harmful effects: winds blowing across the salt pans left behind by the receding lake create clouds containing selenium and arsenic, both contributors to lung disease.

Seemingly oblivious to the plight of the lake, the City of Los Angeles built a second aqueduct in 1970 and the water level dropped even faster, sometimes falling eighteen inches in a single year. Prompted by scientific reports of an impending ecological disaster, a small group of activists set up the Mono Lake Committee in 1978, fighting for the preservation of this unique ecosystem partly through publicity campaigns – "Save Mono Lake" bumper stickers were once de rigueur for concerned citizens – and partly through the courts. Though the California Supreme Court declared in 1983 that Mono Lake must be saved, it wasn't until 1991 that emergency action was taken. A target water height of 6377ft above sea level (later raised to 6392ft) was grudgingly agreed to make Negit Island once again safe for nesting birds. Streams dry for decades are now flowing again, and warm springs formerly located by lakeside interpretive trail are now submerged, but target levels won't be reached for another twenty to thirty years. For more information consult the Mono Lake Committee's Web site at *www.monolake.org*.

salty water three times as buoyant as sea water. Adjacent to the south shore of the lake stands the **Panum Crater**, a 640-year-old volcano riddled with deep fissures and fifty-foot towers of lava, visited on two short and fairly easy trails, the **Plug Trail** and **Rim Trail**.

On the north shore of the lake, three miles along US-395, stands **Mono County Park**, where a guided boardwalk trail leads down to the lakefront and the best examples of mushroom-shaped tufa towers. Accessible by trail from the county park, or by a two-mile dirt road off Hwy-167, **Black Point** is the result of a massive eruption of molten lava some thirteen thousand years ago. As the lava cooled and contracted, cracks and fissures formed on the top, some only a few feet wide but as much as fifty feet deep.

Regular hour-long Mono Lake Committee-run **canoe trips** (mid-June to mid-Sept Sat & Sun 8am, 9.30am & 11am; $17; reservations recommended ☎760/647-6595) give a closer look at what the lake has to offer; or you can go by kayak with Crowley Lake-based Caldera Kayaks (☎ & fax 760/935-4942, *www.calderakayak.com*) who run natural history tours on Mono Lake ($60) and rent kayaks for $40 a day (doubles $50).

Lee Vining

Within easy walking distance of Mono Lake, the appealing small town of **LEE VINING** offers the usual range of visitor services along either side of US-395, and not a great deal more. Greyhound buses stop here daily at 11am (there's no terminal in town, so simply flag the bus down from outside the Lee Vining Supermarket). The town's **Mono Lake Committee Information Center** (daily 9am–5pm, often until 9pm in July & Aug; ☎760/647-6595, *www.leevining.com*) is partly the showcase for the committee's battle for Mono Lake featuring an excellent twenty-minute slide presentation, but also has helpful staff, many books on the Eastern Sierra, and a nice gift shop. There are several **motels** along US-395 including *El Mono Motel* (☎760/647-6310; ③) and *Murphey's* (☎1-800/334-6316 or 760/647-6316; ④). More expensive but more characterful are the recently refurbished cabins at the 1918 *Tioga Lodge* (☎1-800/647-6423 or 760/647-6423; ⑤), three miles north along US-395 and overlooking the lake. A number of **campgrounds** lie along Lee Vining Creek off Tioga Pass Road, Hwy-120 (see p.345). **Eat** breakfast at *Nicely's Restaurant* on US-395 (☎760/647-6477), a great Fifties vinyl palace that opens at 6am. For lunch and dinner, the *Mono Inn Restaurant*, (☎760/647-6581; closed Tues), almost five miles north along US-395, owned by Ansel Adams' granddaughter, serves up lovingly prepared meals ($30–40 for the works) on the patio or inside, both with a superb lake view. The *Inn* also houses a gallery presenting touring exhibits by top photographers, and an art/gift shop stocking Ansel Adams books and prints. If you're heading through Lee Vining on the way to **Yosemite**, you might consider using the town as an affordable base outside of the park (see p.336 for more details).

Bodie Ghost Town and Bridgeport

In the 1870s the gold-mining town of **BODIE** boasted three breweries, some sixty saloons and dance halls and a population of ten thousand, with a well-earned reputation as the raunchiest and most lawless mining camp in the West. Contemporary accounts describe a town that ended each day with a shootout on Main Street, and church bells, rung once for every year of a murdered man's life, that seemed never to stop sounding. The town boomed for less than ten years, from 1877, when a fairly poor existing mine collapsed, exposing an enormously rich vein. Within four years this was the second largest town in the state after San Francisco, even supporting its own Chinatown. By 1885, the population was down to three thousand, and the gold and silver – now valued at over $750 million – was all but mined out. A series of fires progressively destroyed the town, and it was evacuated and closed down in 1942. What remains has been turned into the **Bodie Ghost Town and State Park** ($2, $1 for a good tour booklet; ☎760/647-6445), thirteen miles (three of them dirt) along Hwy-270, which branches off US-395 eighteen miles north of Lee Vining. The park is open throughout the year (8am to an hour before sunset), but phone for the road conditions if you're going off season, as snow often prevents access between December and April. If you can get in during that time, bundle up: Bodie is often cited on the national weather report as having the lowest temperature in the US.

There are over 150 wooden buildings – about six percent of the original town – surviving in a state of arrested decay around the intact town center. Some buildings have been re-roofed and others supported in some way, but it is by and large a faithful preservation: even the dirty dishes are much as they were in the 1940s, little damaged by fifty years of weathering. The **Miner's Union Building** on Main Street was the center of the town's social life; founded in 1877, the union was one of the first in California, organized by workers at the Standard and Midnight mines. The building now houses a small **museum** (free), which paints a graphic picture of mining life. Various **tours** depart from here in the summer, including one of the stamp mill ($3) and one detailing the mining works ($5). Other highlights of the town include the **Methodist church** with its intact pipe organ, the **general store** with its beautiful pressed-steel ceiling, and the working **saloon**.

Its many remaining structures and freedom from theme-park-type tampering give Bodie an authentically eerie atmosphere absent from other US ghost towns. The place should keep you entertained for a few hours, especially if you join one of the ridge tours (Wed, Thurs, Sat & Sun 3.30pm; $3) which guide you to some of the best views of Bodie. Remember to bring all you need; there's no food available out here.

Bridgeport

Six miles further north is the mountain hamlet of **BRIDGEPORT** – an isolated village that provided the new start in life for fugitive Robert Mitchum in the *film noir* masterpiece *Out of the Past*. The gas station he owned in the film is long gone, though the place is otherwise little change; a pretty high-country community of ranchers and fishermen, worth stopping at for a look at the dainty white 1880 **County Courthouse** and the small local history **museum** (daily Memorial Day to Sept 10am–5pm; $1), behind the town park in a restored old schoolhouse. Bridgeport is small and time-warped enough to retain a viable main street, pleasant enough to lure you to stay for a sunset stroll. **Accommodation** ranges from a beautifully furnished B&B, *The Cain House*, 340 Main St (☎1-800/433-2246 or 760/932-7040, fax 932-7419, *www.cainhouse.com*; ⑤), through decent motels such as the *Silver Maple Inn*, 310 Main St (☎760/932-7383; ③) to the decidedly decrepit *Victoria House* across the street (☎760/932-7020; ②), a building which, like several in Bridgeport, is said to have been transported here from Bodie. All are closed October through April; the *Best Western Ruby Inn*, 333 Main St (☎760/932-7241; ④), is one of the only lodgings that stays open year round. For **eating**, *Hays Street Café*, on the southern approach to town, does the best breakfasts and lunches.

From Bridgeport, US-395 continues north into Nevada, through the capital Carson City and the gambling city of Reno, both described fully in Chapter Eight.

travel details

Buses

Los Angeles to: Bishop (1 daily; 7hr 55min); Bridgeport (1 daily; 10hr 15min); Lee Vining (1 daily; 9hr 20min); Lone Pine (1 daily; 6hr 45min); Mammoth Lakes (1 daily; 8hr 50min); Reno (1 daily; 13hr 10min). Note that this one bus leaves LA in the late afternoon and arrives at most of these destinations in the middle of the night.

Reno to: Bishop (1 daily; 6hr); Bridgeport (1 daily; 2hr 55min); Lee Vining (1 daily; 3hr 30min); Lone Pine (1 daily; 7hr 15min); Los Angeles (1 daily; 13hr 25min); Mammoth Lakes (1 daily; 4hr 15min). This bus leaves Reno in the morning and arrives at most of these destinations in late morning and early afternoon.

CHAPTER FIVE

THE CENTRAL VALLEY AND THE WESTERN HIGH SIERRA

T he vast interior of California – stretching three hundred miles from the edges of the Mojave Desert in the south right up to the Gold Country and northern California – comprises the wide floor of the agricultural Central Valley (also known as the San Joaquin Valley), flanked on the east by the massive Sierra Nevada mountains. It's a region that contains unparalleled beauty, yet the ninety per-cent of Californians who live on the coast are barely aware of the area, encountering it only while driving between LA and San Francisco on the admittedly tedious I-5, and consider it the height of hicksville.

The **Central Valley** is radically different from anywhere else in the state. During the 1940s, this arid land was made super-fertile by a massive program of aqueduct building, using water flowing from the mountains to irrigate the area. The valley, as flat as a pan-cake, now almost totally comprises farmland, periodically enlivened by scattered cities that offer a taste of ordinary Californian life away from the glitz of LA and San Francisco. More than anywhere else in the state, the abundance of low-paying agricultural jobs has encouraged decades of immigration from south of the border, and there are now towns in the Central Valley where Spanish is the first language and *taquerías* outnumber burg-er joints ten to one. Fertile land and cheap labor has brought relative wealth to large numbers of Central Valley residents who have responded by becoming increasingly mobile. This, and town planning which dictates that everyone must drive everywhere, has led to a dense photochemical haze – trapped by mountains on both flanks – that is often so thick the pristine peaks once visible throughout the year are now seldom seen.

The only reason most coastal Californians head through the Central Valley is to reach the **national parks** that cover the foothills and upper reaches of the Sierra

---

ACCOMMODATION PRICE CODES

All accommodation prices in this book have been coded using the symbols below; prices are for the least expensive **double rooms** in each establishment. For a full explanation see p.36 in "Basics." Individual rates rather than price codes are given for **hostels** and whole **apartments**.

① up to $30	④ $60–80	⑦ $130–175
② $30–45	⑤ $80–100	⑧ $175–250
③ $45–60	⑥ $100–130	⑨ $250+

Nevada Mountains. From the Valley, a gentle ascent through rolling, grassy foothills takes you into dense forests of huge pine and fir trees, interspersed with tranquil lakes and cut by deep rocky canyons. The most impressive sections are protected within three national parks. **Sequoia** is home to the last few stands of huge prehistoric trees, giant sequoias which form the centerpiece of a rich natural landscape. **Kings Canyon** shares a common border with Sequoia – together they make up one huge park – and

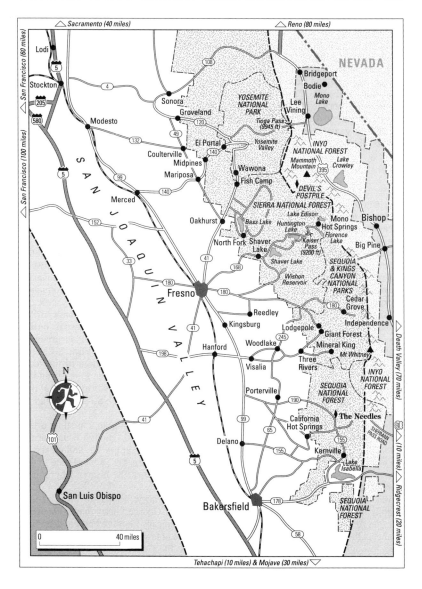

presents a similar, slightly wilder array of Sierra wonders. **Yosemite**, with its towering walls of silvery granite artfully sculpted by Ice Age glaciers, is the most famous of the parks and one of the absolute must-sees in California. While only a few narrow, twisting roads penetrate the hundred miles of wilderness in between these three parks, the entire region is crisscrossed by hiking trails leading up into the pristine alpine backcountry of the western **High Sierra**, which contains the glistening summits of some of the highest mountains in the country.

Getting around

Drivers who aren't particularly interested in exploring the wilds can simply barrel through on I-5, an arrow-straight Interstate through the western edge of the Central Valley that's the quickest route between LA and San Francisco. Four daily **trains** and frequent Greyhound **buses** run through the Valley, stopping at the larger cities and towns along Hwy-99 – two of which, Merced and Fresno, have bus connections to Yosemite. Otherwise, getting to the mountains is all but impossible without a car, though with a bit of advance planning, you might be able to join one of the many camping trips organized by the Sierra Club, the California-based environmentalist group (see p.335).

THE CENTRAL VALLEY

The **Central Valley** grows more fruit and vegetables than any other agricultural region of its size – a fact that touches the lives, in one way or another, of its every inhabitant. The area is much more conservative and midwestern in feel than the rest of California, but even if the nightlife begins and ends with the local ice-cream parlor, it can all be refreshingly small-scale and enjoyable after visiting the big cities of the coast. Admittedly, none of the towns have the energy to detain you long and, between the settlements, the drab hundred-mile vistas of almond groves and vineyards can be sheer torture; as can the weather – summers in the Central Valley are frequently scorching.

Bakersfield, the first town you come to across the rocky peaks north of Los Angeles, is hardly the most prepossessing destination, but in recent years its **country music** scene has burgeoned into the best in the state. And, surprisingly enough, there are few better places on this side of the Atlantic to sample Basque cuisine. Bakersfield also offers a museum recording the beginnings of the local population, and the chance to mess about on the nearby Kern River. Further on lies **Visalia**, a likeable community, near which are two well-restored turn-of-the-century towns, **Hanford** and **Reedley**, plus the bizarre would-be Swedish village of **Kingsburg**.

In many ways the region's linchpin, **Fresno** is the closest thing to a bustling urban center the Valley has – and it's just about impossible to avoid. Though economically thriving, it's frequently voted the least desirable place to live in the US, and on arrival it's easy to see why. Its redeeming features, such as they are, take a bit of time to discover, though you shouldn't pass up the opportunity to visit the bizarre labyrinth of Forrestiere Underground Gardens.

Beyond Fresno, in the northern reaches of the Valley, lie sedate **Merced** and slightly more boisterous **Modesto**, the inspiration for George Lucas' movie *American Graffiti*. At the top end of the Valley, **Stockton** is scenically improved by the delta that connects the city to the sea, but is otherwise a place of few pleasures, though you may pass through on your way from San Francisco to the Gold Country or the national parks.

Bakersfield and around

An unappealing vision behind a forest of oil derricks, **BAKERSFIELD**'s flat and featureless look does nothing to suggest that this is one of the nation's liveliest country music communities, with a batch of venues where locally- and nationally-rated musicians will blow your socks off. Oddly enough, it's also the place to taste Basque cuisine at its best in one of the specialist restaurants run by descendants of sheep-herders who migrated to the San Joaquin valley in the early twentieth century.

If the hills are calling out to you, it's only an hour's drive east to the **Lake Isabella**, a reservoir in the Sierra foothills that's well geared to family camping and watersports. Without your own equipment you're better making for **Kernville**, a few miles up the Kern River, which provides the venue for a full range of springtime **whitewater rafting**.

Arrival, information and accommodation

Bakersfield is an important public transportation hub and the downtown area – roughly four blocks each way from the junction of 19th and J streets – is home to both the **Amtrak station**, 1501 F St, the southern terminus of Amtrak's San Joaquin route from San Francisco (connections to LA via Thruway bus), and the bus station. Traveling by Greyhound (1820 18th St) you may need to change routes here – although overnight stops are rarely necessary. The best source of information is the **Kern County Chamber of**

ACCOMMODATION

Downtowner Inn	5
EZ-8	2
La Quinta	3
Motel 6	1
Padre Hotel	4

Commerce, 2101 Oak St (Mon–Fri 8am–5pm; ☎1-800/500-5376 or 661/861-2367, fax 861-2017, *www.kerncountyonline.com*), though the **Bakersfield Chamber of Commerce**, 1725 Eye St (Mon 9am–5pm Tues–Fri 8am–5pm; ☎661/327-4421, fax 327-8751), is handier to downtown. If you need to get online, the library, 701 Truxton Ave at Q St (Mon–Thurs 10am–9pm, Fri & Sat 10am–6pm), has public **Internet access**, though email use is discouraged.

Bakersfield is dotted with clusters of cheap **motels**, though there is little else. Two handily placed a short stagger from *Buck Owens Crystal Palace* are the *EZ-8*, 2604 Buck Owens Boulevard (☎1-800/326-6835 or 661/322-1901, fax 323-9013; ②), and the adjacent, and considerably smarter *La Quinta*, 3232 Riverside Drive (☎1-800/531-5900 or 661/325-7400, fax 324-6032; ④); both have pools. A couple of miles north around the Olive Drive exit, off Hwy-99, you get fractionally better value for money at the pool-equipped *Motel 6*, 5241 Olive Tree Court (☎661/392-9700, fax 392-0223; ②). The best bets in the center of town are the *Downtowner Inn*, 1301 Chester Ave (☎661/327-7122, fax 327-8350; ①), and the *Padre Hotel*, 1813 H St (☎805/322-1419; ①), a relic of yesteryear that's just hanging on with engagingly dingy yet comfortable rooms, many with original fittings, and ancient plumbing in the en-suite bathrooms.

The Town

Unless you're a country music fan (see box), or using Bakersfield as pit stop for the area's natural attractions, there's little reason to be here: the town owes its existence to the fertile soil around the Kern River – once the longest river in the state but now dammed to form Lake Isabella – and to the discovery of local oil and gas deposits. There is some hope, though, and in the last few years the moribund downtown area has seen something of a renaissance, with half a dozen new bars opening up.

The **Kern County Museum & Pioneer Village**, a mile north of downtown at 3801 Chester Ave (Mon–Fri 8am–5pm, Sat 10am–5pm, Sun noon–5pm; $5), documents Bakersfield's development with an impressive collection of over fifty (mostly) restored rail wagons and buildings, many of them dating from the late-nineteenth or early-twentieth century. Presumably unintentionally, the cumulative effect is to emphasize how boring the place is today. In the grounds, the hands-on science exhibits of the **Lori Brock Children's Museum** (Mon–Fri 1–5pm, Sat 10am–5pm, Sun noon–5pm; no additional fee) provide an excuse to get the kids out of the heat of the day.

Eating, drinking and nightlife

Don't pass Bakersfield without **eating** Basque food. The most authentic experience is at the turn-of-the-century *Noriega Hotel*, 525 Summer St, just east of downtown (☎661/322-8419), where louvered shutters and ceiling fans cool diners communally sat at long tables and served an all-you-can-eat set menu of soup, salad, beans, pasta, a meat dish and cheese to finish, along with jug wine to wash it all down. There are three sittings ($8 breakfast from 7–9am, $9 lunch at noon sharp, and $15 dinner at 7pm); reservations are recommended for dinner. *Pyrenees*, 601 Sumner St (☎661/323-0053), and *Wool Growers*, 620 E 19th St (☎661/327-9584), both have a similar set-up.

If Basque doesn't appeal, the *24th Street Café*, 1415 24th St, does top-rate breakfasts; *Joseph's*, hidden back off the road at 3013 F St (☎661/322-7710), serves a huge, very impressive calzone to a band of dedicated regulars; while *The Garden Spot*, 3320 Truxton Ave, makes healthy eating a pleasure with an all-you-can-eat salad bar buffet for around $7. To stay in tune with Bakersfield's country-music persona, eat at *Zingo's*, 3201 Buck Owens Boulevard, a 24-hr truck stop whose frilly-aproned waitresses deliver plates of diner staples; or try the extensive Sunday brunch at the *Buck Owens Crystal Palace* (9.30am–2pm; $16).

COUNTRY MUSIC IN BAKERSFIELD

The main reason to dally for more than a few hours in Bakersfield is to hear **country music** – on any weekend the town's numerous honky-tonks reverberate to the sounds of the best country musicians in the US, many of them local residents.

The **roots** of Bakersfield's country music scene are with the dust bowl Okies who arrived in the Central Valley during the Depression, bringing their hillbilly instruments and campfire songs with them. This rustic entertainment quickly broadened into more contemporary styles, developed in the bars and clubs that began to appear in the town, where future legends such as Merle Haggard and Buck Owens (who now owns the local country radio station, KUZZ 107.9 FM) cut their teeth. A failed attempt to turn Bakersfield into "Nashville West" during the 1960s, and bring the major country music record labels here from their traditional base, has left the town eager to promote the distinctive **"Bakersfield Sound"**: a far less slick and commercial affair than its Tennessee counterpart. You can gain an inkling of the Bakersfield Sound from the 1988 hit *Streets of Bakersfield*, a duet by Buck Owens and Dwight Yoakam, but you really need to get out and listen to some live music.

VENUES

To find out **what's on**, read the Friday edition of the *Bakersfield Californian*, check the flyers at the tourist offices mentioned above, or phone one of the venues we've listed. Fridays and Saturdays are the liveliest nights, although there's often something to enjoy during the week, even if it's only the free **country dancing lessons** offered at many of the town's bars. There's never a cover charge for someone spinning platters, and seldom one for live sets, usually entailing one band playing for four or five hours from around 8pm and taking a fifteen-minute break every hour – though big names might demand $3–5 a head. Stetson hats and flouncy skirts are the sartorial order of the day, and audiences span generations.

Most **venues** are hotel lounges or restaurant backrooms, though there are a couple which don't fit the mold: one not to be missed is *Trouts*, 805 N Chester Ave (☎661/399-6700), a country music bar a couple of miles north of downtown that's been in business for over forty years. Closer to town, the ersatz-Western *Buck Owens Crystal Palace*, 2800 Buck Owens Boulevard (☎661/328-7560; $6 cover), represents the latest addition to the master's ever-expanding empire: a cabaret-style set-up with a burgers and grills available while local bands perform midweek (Tues–Thurs) and Buck does a turn on Friday and Saturday nights (7pm & 9pm), playing audience requests from his own back catalogue, classic country tunes and beyond. If you can't make Buck's set, it is broadcast live on KCWR 107.1 FM. Cases around the walls make up a small museum of knickknacks ($6 during the day, included in the price of a show) Buck has picked up over the years – promo photos, Buck Rogers bolo tie clasps, platinum records, red-white-and-blue guitars and a glittering display of rhinestone jackets. The other hotspot to add to your itinerary is the younger and more clubby *Rockin' Rodeo*, 3745 Rosedale Hwy (☎661/323-6617), with a New Country/Rock DJ every night and a Texas-style oval dancefloor.

Nightlife now extends beyond slide-guitar and torch songs with a number of places downtown offering local rock bands several nights a week, usually with no cover charge. Stroll 19th Street and see what turns up, but you could kick off at the cocktail bar in the *Hotel Padre* and move across the road to *Guthrie's Alley Cat*, 1525 Wall St, tucked down an alley parallel to 18th and 19th streets.

Lake Isabella, Kernville and the Kern River

After a night spent in Bakersfield's smoky honky-tonks, you might like to clear your head by driving forty-five miles east to the mile-wide **Lake Isabella**, typically alive with windsurfers, jet skiers and anglers. Mountain-biking and rock-climbing are also popular activities here, and the place is heaving in the summer. Information on activities and rental outlets are available from the lakeside **visitor center** (mid-May to Oct daily 8am–5pm, Nov to mid-May Mon–Fri 8am–4.30pm; ☎760/379-5646, fax 379-8597, *www.kernvalley.com*) half a mile north of Hwy-178 along Hwy-155. Developed though barely shaded **campsites** ring the dry, sagebrush lakeside, almost all costing $14 a pitch: there are always first-come-first-served sites or you can reserve at least a week in advance with ReserveUSA on ☎1-877/444-6777. If the frenetic lake activity doesn't suit, you might want to backtrack to *Hobo* campground ($12) on Old Fern Canyon Rd, parallel to Hwy-178, where a short path leads to the mineral-rich **Miracle Hot Springs** ($5) which now fills a rock tub.

Lake Isabella is fed by the **Kern River** which churns down from the slopes of Mount Whitney and spills into the lake at the small, appealing town of **KERNVILLE** on its northern shore. Come on a summer weekend, or anytime in July and August and it is full of folk toting aquatic paraphernalia. Most people come to ride the Kern which ranks as one of the steepest runnable rivers in the United States, dropping over 12,000ft along 150 miles, and producing some of the world's most exhilarating whitewater opportunities. The tougher stuff is generally left to the experts, but during the season, which usually runs from May until mid-August (longer if there has been a heavy winter), commercial rafting operators vie for custom (see box). If you've got time to kill while friends raft, delve into the Native, gold mining and lumbering history in the **Kern Valley Museum**, 49 Big Blue Rd (Thurs–Sun 10am–4pm; free), or take a look at their video library of movies filmed in the area.

Kernville is big enough to have a bank, ATM, post office, and supermarket, but only campers will find cheap **accommodation**. Central motels start at around $60, the best

---

KERN RIVER ADVENTURES

Three main sections of the Kern River are regularly rafted: the **Lower Kern**, downstream of Lake Isabella (generally June–Aug); the **Upper Kern**, immediately upstream of Kernville (early May–June); and **The Forks**, fifteen miles upstream of Kernville (early May–June).

By far the most popular section is the Upper Kern, the site for the **Lickety-Split** rafting trip – one for families and first-timers, with some long, bouncy rapids. This one-hour excursion (including the bus ride to the put-in) costs $15–18, and with over half a dozen operators running trips throughout the day there is little need to book ahead. Other trips are run less frequently and you should reserve in advance, though you've got a better chance mid-week when crowds are thinner and prices a few dollars lower. The pick of these are the day trips on the Upper Kern which run close to the $100 mark ($120 at weekends), the two-day Lower Kern trip ($250, weekends $300) and the three-day backcountry trips on The Forks which range around $500–600. Wetsuits (essential early in the season and for the longer trips) are extra. Within this basic framework there are any number of permutations: check with Chuck Richards' Whitewater, 11200 Kernville Rd (☎1-800/624-5950 or 760/379-4444, *www.chuckrichards.com*).

As you'd expect, kayaking is also big here, and Sierra South, 11300 Kernville Rd (☎760/376-3745 & 1-800/457-2082, *www.sierrasouth.com*), supplement their rafting operation with one of southern California's top **kayaking** schools, offering Eskimo rolling sessions, instruction at all levels and guided multi-day river trips, all generally costing around $130 a day. They also offer beginner **rock climbing** lessons ($50 half-day, $90 full day) on the nearby Kernville Slab, as do Mountain & River Adventures, 11113 Kernville Rd (☎1-800/861-6553 or 760/376-6553, fax 376-1267, *www.mtnriver.com*), who stretch up to intermediate grades and have their own outdoor climbing wall a couple of miles north along Sierra Way.

If you have the equipment for private rafting or kayaking expeditions, you'll still need to grab a free **permit** from any of the area's Forest Service offices.

value being *The Kernville Inn*, 11042 Kernville Rd (☎1-877/393-7900 or 760/376-2206, fax 376-3735; ③), right in the center and with a pool and comfortable rooms, some with kitchens. Up the scale, there's the *Kern River Inn B&B*, 119 Kern River Drive (☎1-800/986-4382 or 760/376-6750, fax 376-6643; ⑤) and the luxurious *Whispering Pines Lodge*, 13745 Sierra Way (☎760/376-3733, fax 376-3735; ⑥), a mile north of town, with a nice pool and balconies overlooking the river. The cheapest rooms lie over two miles north at *Falling Waters*, 15729 Sierra Way (☎1-888/376-2242 or 760/376 2242, fax 376-2243; studios ②, rooms ④), a rambling array of motel-style studios and larger rooms with self-catering facilities and barbecue areas out front. There are several RV parks around town, but tent campers are better off in the string of riverside campgrounds to the north (see below).

There are several **restaurants** around town including two by the central park: the reliable *That's Italian*, and the inexpensive, diner-style *Hardwick Café*. Espresso coffee can also be had in the same area at the *Big Blue Bear* gift shop, but almost all the other eating places are on Sierra Way.

If you can't find all this yourself, consult the central **Chamber of Commerce**, 11447 Kernville Rd (Mon–Sat 10am–3pm; ☎1-800/350-7393 or 760/376-2629, fax 376-4371), and for information on the wooded country to the north call in at the **Sequoia Forest Ranger Station**, 105 Whitney Rd (mid-May to Oct daily 8am–5pm, Nov to mid-May Mon–Fri 8am–4.30pm; ☎760/376 3781, fax 376 3795) tucked away behind the park.

The Sequoia National Forest

Wedged between Lake Isabella and its national park namesake, the **Sequoia National Forest** is a vast canopy of pine trees punctuated by massive, glacier-polished domes and gleaming granite spires. Much of it is untouched wilderness that's barely less stunning than the national parks to the north (and boasts just as many sequoias), but it is less rigidly controlled and far less visited, making it perfect if you're seeking total solitude; hiking trails run virtually everywhere. Backcountry camping only requires a free permit for your stove or fire, available from the Sequoia Forest Ranger Stations which are dotted around the perimeter of the forest and which also have details of the scores of drive-in campsites which stud the forest – some free, others up to $12 a pitch.

There's **no public transportation** through here; the roads are in good shape though, if subject to **snow-closure** in winter. The best access is along Sierra Way from Lake Isabella, which passes through Kernville and follows the Upper Kern River past numerous shaded, waterside, $12 campsites to Johnsondale Bridge, fifteen miles north of Kernville. From the bridge, a riverside **trail** heads upstream giving access to the numerous rapids of The Forks section of the Kern, great for spotting rafters and kayakers on weekend afternoons and even for camping at one of several free walk-in sites along the river.

The road splits at Johnsondale Bridge. The eastern branch follows the Sherman Pass Road which cuts through the Golden Trout Wilderness to Hwy-395 and the Owens Valley, passing numerous free "dispersed" **campgrounds**; essentially just designated sites with no toilets or piped water. Sticking with Sierra Way, you turn west and start climbing to tiny Johnsondale where a trail access road cuts 23 miles north to the Jerkey Meadow trailhead. Along with great views of The Needles there is abundant dispersed **camping**, best at *Camping Area 4*, four miles along, where the stream has sculpted a lovely series of **bathing pools** and smooth rocks for sunning yourself. The *Lower Peppermint* campground ($12), a few miles further along, has toilets and water.

Continuing along Sierra Way, you soon reach a junction signed straight ahead to **California Hot Springs**, 42177 Hot Springs Drive (Mon–Fri 9am–4pm Sat & Sun 9am–5pm; ☎661/548-6582; $8), a small resort down in the foothills with indoor and outdoor pools. The popular *Leavis Flat* campground ($10 pitch) is just across the road.

North from the road junction you're on the twisting and narrow **Western Divide Highway** (Hwy-190) which, after a couple of miles, passes the **Trail of a Hundred Giants**, an easy, shaded interpretive trail around the second most southerly stand of giant trees. Among more sequoias across the road is the *Redwood Meadow* campground ($12).

Continuing north, you catch glimpses of magnificent sierra vistas as the road climbs above the 7000-foot mark, but for the best views it is worth pressing on five miles to the 7200-foot exfoliated scalp of **Dome Rock**, just half a mile off the highway, or **The Needles**, a further three miles on. This series of tall pinnacles – the magician, the wizard, the warlock and more – present some of America's most demanding crack climbs, and can be visited on the moderate, undulating hiking and biking **Needles Lookout Trail** (5 miles round-trip; 2hrs) which starts three miles off the highway up a dirt road. The final switchback leads to a fire lookout station (open May–Oct Wed–Sun 9am–6pm), precariously perched atop a rock pinnacle with supreme views over the Kern Valley and across to Mount Whitney. Nearby **accommodation** extends to the *Quaking Aspen* campsite (mid-May to mid-Nov; $12) half a mile to the north of the Needles, the rustic *Mountain Top B&B*, half a mile to the south (☎1-888/867-4784 or 559/542-2639, fax 542-1318, *rainwaterpad.com/mountaintop*; ⑤), and the adjacent *Ponderosa Lodge* (☎559/542-2579; ④) with pleasant motel rooms, a restaurant, bar, grocery store and expensive gas. The Western Divide Highway then executes endless twists and turns forty miles down to the valley town of Porterville.

Visalia and Tulare County

As you leave Bakersfield heading north on Hwy-99, the oil wells fade into full-blown agricultural territory. You can turn east onto Hwy-190 at Tipton for the Sequoia National Forest (see above). Otherwise, nowhere merits a stop until you reach Tulare County, some seventy miles north of Bakersfield, where several small communities repay quick visits and make viable bases for day-trips into the Sequoia and Kings Canyon National Parks.

Visalia

The first and largest of the towns north of Bakersfield is **VISALIA**, just east of Hwy-99 on Hwy-198. Due to a large oak forest that offered both shade and timber for home-building, Visalia was the first place in the Central Valley to be settled. Although the forest is gone, large numbers of oaks and eucalyptus are still planted around the city and local people put an extraordinary amount of care into the upkeep of parks and gardens. In short, it's a pretty place, with a calm and restful air – if you're seeking anything more active you'll be disappointed.

Visalia is best seen on foot: self-guided walking tours of its older parts can be obtained free from the **Chamber of Commerce** (see below); or you could visit the **Tulare County Museum**, Mooney Grove Park, about two miles from the city center at the end of South Mooney Boulevard. The museum (mid-May to mid-Sept daily except Tues 10am–4pm; $2) has a hotchpotch of local historical curios, and in the park you'll find the *End of the Trail* statue, originally made for the 1915 Panama Pacific Exhibition in San Francisco, which portrays the defeat of Native Americans at the hands of advancing white settlers. Intentionally gloomy, the statue became well known throughout the West, and still inspires a host of copies and numerous snap-happy tourists.

Practicalities

Greyhound buses, and Orange Belt Stages from Hanford, arrive at the **bus station** at 1927 E Mineral King Ave, inconveniently distant from either downtown or the **Chamber** of Commerce at 720 W Mineral King Ave (Mon–Fri 8.30am–5pm; ☎559/734-5876, fax 734-7478, *www.visaliachamber.org*).

As the closest substantial town to the southern entrance of the Sequoia National Park – less than an hour's drive away along Hwy-198 – Visalia makes a comfortable base for exploring this raw wilderness. The most sumptuous **accommodation** is at the pool- and spa-equipped *Ben Maddox House B&B*, 601 N Encina St (☎1-800/401-9800 or 559/739-0721, fax 625-0420; ⑤), a large redwood house built in 1876 for Ben Maddox, the man who brought hydroelectricity to the Central Valley. South Mooney Boulevard has the densest concentration of **motels**: *Mooney Motel* at no. 2120 (☎559/733-2666; ②) has a pool but marginal rooms, so for a few dollars more you are better off at *Econolodge*, no. 1400 (☎559/732-6641; ③), or *Lamp Liter Inn*, 3300 W Mineral King Ave (☎1-800/662-6692 or 559/732-4511, fax 732-1840; ④), which has a very nice pool and a sports bar and grill restaurant on site.

Visalia also has some of the best places to **eat** for miles around: try *Merle's* Fifties-style drive-in diner down the street at 604 South Mooney Boulevard, or stop in at *Little Italy*, 303 W Main St, for excellent wood-fired pizzas and a strong line in veal and chicken mains for around $12. Downtown, *Java Jungle*, 208 W Main St, is the place for good coffee and occasional acoustic bands, and *Brewbakers*, 219 E Main St, serves its own microbrews with bar meals. Upscale diners are catered for at the *Vintage Press*, 216 N Willis St (☎559/733-3033), where you might ease down wild mushrooms sautéed in cognac followed by red snapper with toasted almonds and capers, a dessert and coffee for around $40 a head, much more if you explore the vast and wonderful wine list.

Hanford

HANFORD, twenty miles west of Visalia on Hwy-198, was named after James Hanford, a paymaster on the Southern Pacific Railroad who became popular with his employees when he took to paying them in gold. The town formed part of a spur on the railroad and remains a major stopover on the route between Los Angeles and San Francisco.

Hanford's visitor center (see overleaf) can give you a map of the center of town detailing the now spotless and spruced-up buildings around Courthouse Square, once the core of local life at the beginning of the twentieth-century. The honey-colored **Courthouse** (Mon–Sat 10am–6pm, Sun 10am–5pm; free) retains many of its Neoclassical features – not least a magnificent staircase – and has, more recently, been occupied by shops and galleries. As you'd expect, the old Hanford **jail**, rather pretentiously modelled on the Paris Bastille, is only a ball-and-chain's throw away. It was used until 1968 and is now restored as a restaurant (*The Bastille*, see overleaf), although you can wander through to see the old cells – now and again used for secluded dining.

Much less ostentatiously, rows of two-storey porched dwellings, four blocks east of the square, mark the district that was home to most of the eight hundred or so Chinese families who came to Hanford to work on the railroad. At the center of the community was the **Taoist Temple** on China Alley (open for groups of 6–20 only and by appointment; more details from the visitor center or call ☎559/582-4508). Built in 1893, the temple served a social as well as a spiritual function, providing free lodging to work-seeking Chinese travelers, and was used as a Chinese school during the early 1920s. Everything inside is original, from the teak burl figurines to the marble chairs, and it's a shame that entry is so restricted. You can, however, take a look at another institution of Hanford's Chinese community: the **Imperial Dynasty Restaurant**, two doors along from the temple, still run by the family who opened it fifty years ago. The interior is simple and modest, but the fame of the cooking – oddly French, not Chinese – has spread far and wide and prices have risen as a result.

Mildly absorbing oddments from Hanford's past are gathered at the **Carnegie Museum**, 109 E Eighth St (Tues–Fri noon–3pm, Sat noon–4pm; $1), filling part of the interior of the town's elegant 1905 library – one of many small-town libraries financed by altruistic millionaire industrialist Andrew Carnegie. The only other item of possible interest is the **Kings Art Center**, 605 N Douty St (Tues–Sun noon–3pm; free), with its temporary displays of contemporary painting, sculpture and photography.

Practicalities

Orange Belt Stages (☎1-800/266-7433) provide twice-daily **bus** links to Visalia and the Greyhound station at Goshen Junction, near Visalia (for connections to Los Angeles and San Francisco), and also run a service across to San Luis Obispo on the coast. The town's **visitor center** (Mon–Fri 9am–5pm; ☎559/582-5024, fax 582-0960) is conveniently located inside the handsomely restored Amtrak depot at 200 Santa Fe Ave. If you decide to **stay** in Hanford your choice is limited to the *Irwin St Inn*, 522 N Irwin (☎559/583-8000; ⑤) and a couple of motels, the cheapest and most central being the *Downtown Motel*, 101 N Redington (☎559/582-9036; ②). For **eating**, the most atmospheric place is *The Bastille*, 113 Court St. which does fine deep dish pizzas, mountainous lean burgers and sandwiches until late, followed by *Wired Angels*, 700 N Irwin St, a good café (with Internet access) in a Victorian house a couple of blocks north of the center. During the day, don't miss the rich creaminess of the made-on-the-premises ice cream at *Superior Dairy*, 325 N Douty St just across from *The Bastille*.

Kingsburg and Reedley

Over half the inhabitants of **KINGSBURG**, twenty miles north of Visalia on Hwy-99, are of Swedish descent, but it's only in the last thirty years that they've sought to exploit their roots, converting the town's buildings to Swedish-style architecture and plastering their windows and walls with tributes to the Swedish royal family and the Dala Horse (an object traditionally carved by woodcutters from the Dalarna district of Sweden). Save for such peculiarities, it hardly warrants a call, except perhaps on the third Saturday in May when it stages – predictably – a Swedish festival. Compared to Kingsburg, **REEDLEY**, five miles northeast, is a metropolis, though beyond its main thoroughfare – G Street – it's just as quiet, and the only attraction is the **Mennonite Quilting Center**, 1012 G St (Mon–Fri 9.30am–4.30pm, Sat 10am–2pm; free), essentially a shop selling Amish quilts ($500–900) from Pennsylvania. Quilters can be seen working away on local versions on Mondays until 3pm.

Fresno

Almost classic in its ugliness, **FRESNO** is very much the hub of business in the Central Valley. Caught between being a farming town and a fully blown commercial city, Fresno seems to have missed out on the restoration programs that have improved similar communities elsewhere in California. It seems significant, too, that the indoor shopping mall was first seen here. Fresno's residents once looked down their noses at Bakersfield, but that city's rise, and Fresno's status as one of the US's crime hot spots has reversed the snobbery. For all that, Fresno does have its good points (not least a daily bus service to Yosemite). You might even want to spend a night or two here to take in the fascinating Forestiere Underground Gardens in the northern suburbs and something of the nightlife in the vibrant Tower district.

Arrival, information and accommodation

The **bus** and **train** terminals are downtown – Greyhound at 1033 H St and Amtrak at Tulare and Q – both an easy walk from the **CVB**, on the corner of Fresno and O streets

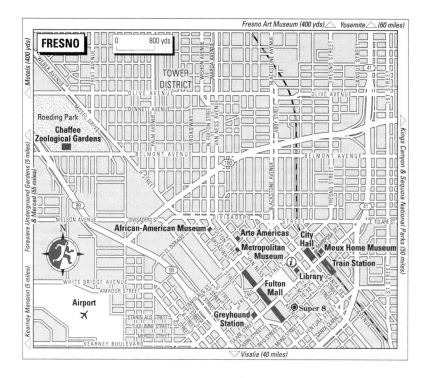

Map labels:
Fresno Art Museum (400 yds) — Yosemite (60 miles)
FRESNO
0 — 800 yds
TOWER DISTRICT
Motels (400 yds)
WEBER AVENUE
FRUIT AVENUE
WISHON AVENUE
MARQA AVENUE
BLACKSTONE AVENUE
FRESNO STREET
ANGUS STREET
41
OLIVE AVENUE
MOTEL DRIVE
DENNETT AVENUE
BROADWAY
PALM AVENUE
FULTON STREET
VAN NESS AVENUE
ABBY STREET
OLIVE AVENUE
Roeding Park
Chaffee Zoological Gardens
BELMONT AVENUE
H STREET
BELMONT AVENUE
180
FRESNO STREET
41
99
NIELSON AVENUE
DIVISADERO ST.
DIVISADERO STREET
E. TULARE ST.
N
African-American Museum
Arte Américas
City Hall
Meux Home Museum
EL DORADO
Metropolitan Museum
Train Station
Library
99
WHITE BRIDGE AVENUE
AMADOR STREET
Airport
Fulton Mall
Super 8
Greyhound Station
STANISLAUS STREET
TUOLUMNE STREET
MERCED STREET
KEARNEY BOULEVARD
Foresiere Underground Gardens (5 miles) & Merced (55 miles)
Kearney Mansion (5 miles)
Kings Canyon & Sequoia National Parks (50 miles)
Visalia (40 miles)

(Mon–Fri 8am–5pm; ☎1-800/788-0836 or 559/233-0836, fax 445-0122) recently relocated to a distinctive, conical-roofed water tower that dates back to the 1890s. Here you can check details on everything in and around the city including the Fresno County Library, 2420 Mariposa St (☎559/488-3195), where there is free **Internet access**.

Buses to Yosemite National Park (see p.333) are available with VIA Yosemite Connection service (May–Oct, ☎1-888/727-5287, $25 each way, $48 round-trip; 4hr) which picks up at the Amtrak station and major local hotels by reservation; tickets include park entry. Downtown is just about small enough to walk around if you don't mind the heat, but non-drivers will want to make use of the *Fresno Area Express* (☎559/498-1122; 75¢ per ride, exact change), if only to reach the Forestiere Underground Gardens. Route #20, picked up downtown on Van Ness (Mon–Sat every 30min) comes within a mile, and you can transfer to the #9 for the last stretch. Route #28 travels between Van Ness and the Tower district.

If you decide to **stay**, you'll appreciate the low prices at numerous **motels**, all with pools, clustered together near the junction of Olive Avenue (the Tower district's main drag) and Hwy-99. Some charge rock-bottom rates for rooms that are well below par, so the best deals here are the *Welcome Inn*, 777 N Parkway Drive (☎559/237-2175; ②), and *Motel 6*, 1240 N Crystal (☎559/237-0855, fax 497-5869; ②). For smarter rooms, a better pool and an exercise room, splash out on the Best Western *Parkside Inn*, 1415 W Olive Ave (☎559/237-2086; ④). The cheapest place **downtown** is *Super 8*, 2127 Inyo St at L St (☎559/268-0621, fax 233-9300; ③) which also has a pool.

The Town and around

To get the best of Fresno you'll have to leave the center, and if time is short, the place to start is **Forestiere Underground Gardens**, a fascinating warren of rooms hewn out of the hardpan to protect one man and his crops from the heat. The **Kearney Mansion** also warrants an hour of your time before you return to the lesser attractions of downtown.

Forestiere Underground Gardens and Kearny Mansion

The one place which turns Fresno into a destination in its own right is **Forestiere Underground Gardens**, 5021 W Shaw Ave (late May–early Sept Wed–Sun tours at 10am, noon, 2pm & 4pm; late March–late May & early Sept–mid-Nov Sat & Sun tours at 10am, noon & 2pm; ☎209 271-0734; $6), seven miles northwest of the center, a block east of the Shaw Ave exit off Hwy-99. A subterranean labyrinth of over fifty rooms, the gardens were constructed by Sicilian emigré and former Boston and New York subway tunneler Baldasare Forestiere, who came to Fresno in 1905. In a fanatical attempt to stay cool and protect his crops, Forestiere put his digging know-how to work, building underground living quarters and skylit orchards with just a shovel and wheelbarrow. He gradually improved techniques for maximizing his yield but wasn't above playful twists like a glass-bottomed underground aquarium and a subterranean bathtub fed by water heated in the midday sun. He died in 1946, his forty years of work producing a vast earth honeycomb, part of which was destroyed by the construction of Hwy-99 next door, while another section awaits restoration. Wandering around the remainder of what he achieved is a fascinating way to pass an hour out of the heat of the day, enlivened by the tour guide's homespun anecdotes.

With more time to spare, head seven miles west from downtown along Kearney Boulevard, a long, straight, palm-lined avenue that was once the private driveway through the huge Kearney Park ($3 per car; free with Mansion entry) to the **Kearney Mansion** (Fri–Sun tours at 1pm, 2pm & 3pm; $4). It was built for M. Theo Kearney, an English-born turn-of-the-century agricultural pioneer and raisin mogul, who maintained it in the opulent French Renaissance style to which he seemed addicted. He had even grander plans to grace Fresno with a French chateau, the mind-boggling designs for which are displayed here. Regarded locally as something of a mystery man, Kearney apparently led a busy social life on both sides of the Atlantic, which may explain why he died following a heart attack during an ocean crossing.

Downtown Fresno

Once you've seen the Forestiere Underground Gardens and the Kearney Mansion, you've really seen the best of the town. **Downtown Fresno** is the business heart, an odd mix of urban decay and civic pride exhibited in stridently modern buildings like the delta-winged steel-and-glass form of the **Fresno City Hall** close to the Amtrak station. Sights are limited to a quintet of minor museums all worthy of half an hour of your time, if only to get out of the searing heat. The City Hall stands in marked contrast opposite the **Meux Home Museum**, corner of Tulare and R streets (guided tours Fri–Sun noon–3.30pm; $4), Fresno's only surviving late nineteenth-century house, built for what was then the staggering sum of $12,000. This was the home of a doctor who arrived from the Deep South, bringing with him the novelty of a two-storey house and a plethora of trendy Victorian features. What isn't original is a convincing reconstruction, and the turrets, arches, and octagonal master bedroom help make the place stylish and absorbing – quite out of synch with the Fresno that has sprawled up around it.

Each of the three museums clustered a dozen blocks to the west helps illustrate the historic and continuing importance of immigration to Fresno – now a predominantly

Hispanic city. The **Metropolitan Museum**, 1555 Van Ness Ave (daily 11am–5pm, $5; free from 5–8pm on Thurs, *www.fresnomet.org*), mainly hosts temporary exhibitions but has a small collection of jigsaw puzzles dating back a century and a half, and a delightful display of over two hundred mostly nineteenth-century Chinese snuff boxes arranged thematically – flowers, deities, mythological creatures, etc. Fresno's most famous son, the novelist and scriptwriter **William Saroyan**, gets hagiographic treatment in the museum despite his early desire to leave Fresno and never come back. He did keep coming back, creating a fictional identity for Fresno in his writing, and died here in 1981 at the age of 72. He is best known for his Pulitzer prize-winning *The Time of your Life*, and as the writer of the screenplay for Louis B. Mayer's *The Human Comedy*, for which he was awarded an Academy Award. He refused to pick up his award after a tiff with Mayer, but the Oscar is on display along with his Underwood typewriter and panels with telling quotes from throughout his life. Along the street, **Arte Américas**, 1630 Van Ness (Tues–Sun noon–5pm, $2; free from 5–8pm on Thurs) has several galleries exploring mostly Hispanic American visual and performing arts along with Mexican and Central and South American contributions. Fresno's black history is told at the **African American Historical and Cultural Museum**, 1857 Fulton St (Mon–Fri 9am–4pm; $4), though the hundreds of portraits and assorted newspaper clippings are unlikely to divert you long from the often impressive temporary exhibits and the African statuary for sale in the museum store. The **Fresno Art Museum**, 2233 N First St at Clinton, in Radio Park (Tues–Fri 10am–5pm, Sat & Sun noon–5pm; $2, Tues free), has a worthy but slightly desperate selection of paintings, sculpture and lithographs.

The Tower District

In a town with a tradition of almond-growing and cattle-rustling, Fresno's **Tower District**, three miles north of downtown, comes as a pleasant surprise. Proximity to the City College campus made the area something of a hippy hangout during the Sixties; today it has a well-scrubbed liberal feel, plus several blocks of antique shops and bookstores, ethnic restaurants and coffee bars to fill a few hours of idle browsing.

On the Tower District's western edge at the end of Olive Avenue, the tree-filled **Roeding Park** (Feb–Oct $1 per car, Nov–Jan free) boasts the **Chaffee Zoological Gardens** (daily 9am–5pm; $5), a couple of amusement parks and a lake. This is where Fresnoites come to convince themselves that the city is a nice place to live, and when strolling here on a day that's not totally baking you could almost believe them.

Eating and drinking

To pick up fresh, good **food**, head for the **outdoor produce market**, at Merced and N (Tues, Thurs & Sat 7am–3pm), and downtown check out the *Kern St Coffee Company*, 2134 Kern St, for good java. Otherwise, the Tower District, centered on the Tower Theatre at the junction of Olive and Wishon avenues, is very much the place to eat and drink. You'll get good-value lunches and dinners, and excellent home-brewed beers, at the *Butterfield Brewing Company Bar & Grill*, 777 E Olive Ave (☎559/264-5521); the relaxed *Java Café*, 805 E Olive Ave, excels with its shady backyard and presents soups and salads, healthful sandwiches and mugs of very fine coffee; and the *Daily Planet*, 1211 N Wishon Ave (☎559/266-4259), serves a fixed-price four-course dinner (usually under $20) in Art Deco surroundings. For seafood that's surprisingly good this far from the coast, head to the moderately priced *Tower Bay Fish Co*, 737 E Olive Ave (☎559/442-3474); then step along the street to *Devotion*, 1145 N Fulton Ave (Wed–Sun; $2–10; information line ☎559/264-7646), for regular DJs and live bands. For less fraught entertainment try the *Java Café*, which puts on comedy, jazz, folk and blues from Thursday to Saturday evenings.

The free monthly *Talk of the Tower District* (*www.tower2000.com*) **lists** upcoming events, gigs and the Tuesday night outdoor movies shown on the back wall of the Tower Theatre (June–Aug only).

Continuing north: Merced and Modesto

The best thing about sluggish **MERCED**, fifty miles north of Fresno, is its courthouse, a gem of a building in the main square that's maintained as the **County Courthouse Museum** (Wed–Sun 1–4pm; free). The striking Italian Renaissance-style structure, with columns, elaborately sculptured window frames and a cupola topped by a statue of the Goddess of Justice (minus her customary blindfold), was raised in 1875, dominating the town then as it does now. Impressively restored in period style, the courtroom retained a legal function until 1951, while the equally sumptuous offices were vacated in the 1970s, leaving the place to serve as storage space for local memorabilia – most exotic among which is a Taoist shrine, found by chance in the back room of a Chinese restaurant.

Six miles out of Merced, close to the dormitory community of **ATWATER** – and signposted off Hwy-99 – lies the **Castle Air Museum** (daily 9am–5pm; $5). Forty-odd military aircraft – mostly bulky bombers with a few fighters thrown in, including the world's fastest plane, the SR-71 – are scattered outdoors, while inside there's a static B52 simulator, assorted military paraphernalia and a collection of some 120 model planes crafted by one enthusiast from redwood. Route #8 of Merced's transit system, "The Bus" (Mon–Fri only; ☎1-800/384-3111), runs out here every hour or so for $1 each way.

Practicalities

Neither of the sights are much of a reason to visit Merced, though the convenient **bus links to Yosemite** are. Greyhounds from Bakersfield, Sacramento and San Francisco stop downtown at the **bus station** on W 16th St at N St where you'll find the **Chamber of Commerce**, 690 W 16th St (Mon–Fri 8.30am–5pm; ☎ 1-800/446-5353 or 209/384-3333, fax 384-8472, *www.yosemite-gateway.org*). The **Amtrak station** ($26 from San Francisco, $31 from LA) is somewhat isolated at 24th and K streets, about ten blocks away on the opposite side of the town center. Both stations are stops for the VIA Yosemite Connection ($38 round trip, $20 one-way, free for Amtrak pass holders; 2hr 30min; ☎1-888/727-5287), which makes the trip to Yosemite Village, via Mariposa, three or four times daily – currently departing 6.45am, (8.45am June to early Sept only), 10.15am & 3.15pm – and includes the park entry fee.

If you are relying on public transportation, by far the best **place to stay** is the reservations-only *HI–Merced Home Hostel* (☎209/725-0407, *merced-hostel@juno.com*; $14). You can only check in between 5.30pm and 9am, and must be out of the house by 7.30am but this is a small price to pay for a ride to and from the stations, an enthusiastic welcome, as much information as you can handle and a free dessert every evening. It is a great place to hook up with Yosemite-bound travelers, and they'll put you in touch with a local rental agency who let you have a car for the day for $35, great value for two or more people traveling together. Drivers in need of a motel should take the Mariposa/Yosemite exit from Hwy-99 which leaves you right by two good places to stay: the *Holiday Inn Express*, 730 Motel Drive (☎209/383-0333; ⑤), and the bargain *Happy Inn*, 740 Motel Drive (☎722-6291; ②), both with pool and continental breakfast.

For **something to eat**, you'll find authentic Mexican at *La Nina's*, 1327 18th St at T (closed Mon) some ten blocks from the bus station, and a broad range of ethnic and

American dishes at very reasonable prices at *Paul's Place*, 2991 G St at Alexander; try the Portuguese *linguisa* sausage omelette.

Modesto

Forty miles further along Hwy-99, **MODESTO**, the childhood home of movie director George Lucas, became the inspiration (though not the location) for his movie *American Graffiti*, the classic portrayal of growing up in small-town America during the late 1950s. The movie contains a number of references to local people, particularly the teachers who rubbed Lucas the wrong way in his formative years. Sadly, local ordinances (enacted in 1992 after several years of bad behavior) have put an end to both the fine art of **cruising** and the annual festival which saw dozens of classic cars from all over the state and beyond dusted off and cruised through the city. One of the only reminders of those heady days is a rather token duck-tail, bobby-sox and '57 Chevy statue at the corner of J St and McHenry Avenue. A more evocative celebration of the era is the **A&W Root Beer Drive-In**, 1404 G St, which has roller-skating waitresses serving root beer floats ordered from illuminated car-side menus. Despite the ban you'll still see the better-kept cruising rigs parked here on Friday and Saturday nights until 10pm.

It may seem hard to believe, but as a fairly typical Valley town, Modesto does have a history stretching back beyond the Fifties. Its (comparatively) distant past is encapsulated by the shabbily grand **Modesto Arch** – erected in 1912 over Ninth and I to attract attention to the city's expanding economy – and, more imposingly, the Victorian **McHenry Mansion** at 906 15th St (Sun–Thurs 1–4pm Fri noon–3pm; free), which is jam-packed with fixtures, fittings and the personal features of a family whose fate was linked with Modesto's for years. Robert McHenry was a successful wheat-rancher who did much to bring about a general uplift in the agricultural well-being of the area. Surprisingly, his luxurious dwelling was still being rented out as apartments, at quite low rates, as recently as the early 1970s.

A block from the mansion, the **McHenry Museum**, 1402 I St (Tues–Sun noon–4pm; free), originally financed by the McHenry family, sports mock-ups of a doctor's office, blacksmith's shop, dentist's surgery and gathering of cattle brands, revealing something of bygone days, although lacking the period atmosphere of the mansion. Adjoining the museum, the **Central California Art League Gallery** (Mon–Sat 10am–4pm; free) displays a show of regional painting and sculpture that should consume no more than a few minutes.

Practicalities

There's not much reason to stop and spend the night in Modesto – if you're looking for a place to stop before diving into Yosemite for a day-trip, Merced is the better bet. But, if you decide to stay, you can find out more about the town and pick up maps and general information about the various food factory tours that draw in the tour groups – including the massive Hershey's chocolate factory in nearby Oakdale – at Modesto's **CVB**, 1114 J St (Mon–Fri 8.30am–5pm; ☎1-800/266-4282, fax 209/571-6486).

The Greyhound **bus** station is at J St and Ninth, and if you're looking **something to eat**, there is a range of restaurants within walking distance. *DeVa*, at J St and Ninth, is an affordable café and coffeehouse that serves meals throughout the day. If you would like something a bit stronger than coffee, stop by *St Stan's Brewery*, 821 L Street, and wash down a burger with one of their home-brewed beers. **Accommodation** in town ranges from the affordable *Chalet Motel*, 115 Downey Street (☎209/529-4370; ②), to the more upscale *Doubletree Hotel*, 1150 Ninth Street (☎209/526-6000; ⑥), which includes a pool, sauna and exercise room.

Stockton and around

Perched at the far northern limit of the Central Valley, the immediately striking thing about **STOCKTON** is the sight of ocean-going freighters so far inland. The San Joaquin and Sacramento rivers converge here, creating a vast delta with thousands of inlets and bays, and a man-made deep-water channel enables vessels to carry the produce of the Valley's farms past San Francisco and directly out to sea. But the geography that aided commerce also saddled Stockton with the image of being a grim place to live and a tough city to work in. During the Gold Rush it was a supply stop on the route to the gold mines, and it became a gigantic flophouse for broken and dispirited ex-miners who gave up their dreams of fortune and returned here to toil on the waterfront. Though valiant efforts have been made to shed this reputation and beautify the less attractive quarters, it's still primarily a hard-working, sleeves-rolled-up city.

A scattering of buildings downtown evoke the early decades of the twentieth century, thanks to which Stockton is often in demand as a film set. John Huston's downbeat boxing picture, *Fat City*, for example, was shot here.

Marginally more appealing are the blocks bordered by Harding Way and Park Street, and El Dorado and California, a short way north of the center. This area has been preserved as the **Magnolia Historical District**, with sixteen intriguing specimens of domestic architecture spanning seven decades from the 1860s. To find them all, pick up the free leaflet from the **San Joaquin CVB**, downtown at 46 W Fremont St (Mon–Fri 8am–5pm; ☎1-800/350-1987, fax 209/943-6235, *www.ssjcvb.org*).

Roughly a mile west of the Magnolia district, in Victory Park alongside Pershing Avenue, Stockton gathers totems of its past in the varied and large stock of the **Haggin Museum**, 1201 N Pershing Ave (Tues–Sun 9am–5pm; donation requested). Not surprisingly, much is given over to agriculture, including the city's finest moment: the invention by local farmers of a caterpillar tread to enable tractors to travel over muddy ground, adapted by the British for use on tanks and standard use since for the military everywhere. In tremendous contrast, the museum also contains a batch of nineteenth-century French paintings, including works by Renoir and Gauguin, as well as Bouguereau's monumental *Nymphs Bathing*.

With kids in tow, pop along to the **Children's Museum of Stockton**, 402 W Weber Ave (Mon–Sat 9am–4pm; $4), which aims to be both educational and fun; and with a few more minutes to spare, continue along the same street and under the freeway to the **World Wildlife Museum**, 1245 W Weber Ave (Wed–Sun 9am–5pm; $4), basically two vast rooms stacked to the rafters with stuffed beasts. Forget context and interpretation, we're talking quantity – elephants, giraffes, zebras, eland, bears, moose, tigers and a whole artificial mountain of goats, and assorted nimble hillside creatures.

Practicalities

Stockton's **Greyhound station** is at 121 S Center St; **Amtrak** at 735 S San Joaquin St. Even traveling by public transportation doesn't mean you have to stay overnight in Stockton; connections both onwards to San Francisco and south down the valley are plentiful – but it can be worth stopping here to **eat**, ethnic restaurants being in good supply. For Chinese there's *On Lock Sam*, 333 S Sutter St (☎209/466-4561), in town for over a century, or *Dave Wong's*, 5602 N Pershing Ave. Downtown try the stuffed sandwiches at the *Fox Café*, in the foyer of the newly restored Fox Theater at 220 Main St, and *Yasoo Yani*, 326 E Main St (☎209/464-3108) where Nick's Greek salad is more than a meal. There's more choice along the so-called **Miracle Mile**, a stretch of Pacific Avenue starting around a mile north of downtown – follow Madison from the CVB. Here, among the bookshops, espresso bars and restaurants, you'll find *Fernando's Santa Fe Café*, 2311 Pacific Ave, which turns out tasty fajitas for $11.

Afterwards, stroll across the road for a microbrew to the *Valley Brewing Company*, 157 West Adams St. For **entertainment**, you may catch stars of yesteryear at the Fox Theater, downtown.

If you're forced to stay over, there's a **campground** eight miles south of Stockton – *Dos Reis Park* (☎209/953-8800), just off I-5 – or you can stay in the city in one of the plentiful mid-range chain **hotels** and budget **motels**, mostly near the Waterloo Road exit off Hwy-99. Downtown try the *Stockton Travelers Motel*, 631 N Center St (☎209/466-8554; ②), or if this seems a little unsavory go for the *Days Inn*, 33 N Center St (☎948-6151, fax 948-1220; ④), close to the Greyhound station.

Micke Grove Park and Lodi

If Stockton begins to pall, or it's simply too nice a day to spend in a city, venture five miles north to the Armstrong Road exit off Hwy-99 for the pastoral relief – at least outside weekends and holidays – of the **Micke Grove Park** (daily 8am–dusk; parking $4 at weekends, $2 midweek), an oak grove which holds a Rose Garden, a Japanese Garden and a zoo. It also features the **San Joaquin Historical Museum** (Wed–Sun 1–4.45pm; $1), recording the evolution of the local agricultural industry and, more revealingly, the social history that accompanied it. Don't miss the Stockton clamshell dredge bucket, a tool used in the reclamation of the delta and restored and displayed like a major work of art.

Some seven miles beyond the park, on the way north to Sacramento, the state capital (see p.543), sits **LODI**, a small country town immortalized in song by Creedence Clearwater Revival ("Oh Lord, stuck in Lodi again"), though these days it's best known for its mass-market **wineries**, several of which offer daily tours and tastings. You can get a full list from the **Chamber of Commerce**, 215 W Oak St (Mon–Fri 8.30am–4.30pm; ☎334-4773), or the San Joaquin CVB Visitors' Bureau in Stockton.

SEQUOIA AND KINGS CANYON NATIONAL PARKS

Separate parks but jointly run and with a long common border, the **SEQUOIA AND KINGS CANYON NATIONAL PARKS** contain an immense variety of geology, flora and fauna. **Sequoia National Park**, as you might expect from its name, contains the thickest concentration – and the biggest individual specimens – of giant sequoia trees to be found anywhere. These ancient trees tend to outshine (and certainly outgrow) the other features of the park – an assortment of meadows, peaks, canyons and caves. Notwithstanding a few notable exceptions, **Kings Canyon National Park** doesn't have the big trees but compensates with a gaping canyon gored out of the rock by the Kings River, which cascades in torrents down from the High Sierra during the snow-melt period. There's less of a packaged tourism feel here than in Yosemite: the few established sights (like the drive-on Auto Log) of both parks are near the main roads and concentrate the crowds, leaving the vast majority of the landscape untrammeled and unspoiled, but well within reach for willing hikers.

To the north of the parks lies the even more vast and almost equally spectacular **Sierra National Forest**, which is bound by fewer of the national-park-style restrictions on hunting and the use of motorized playthings. Consequently there is a greater potential for disturbance, though this is counteracted by the sheer immensity of the region.

The **best time to come** is in late summer and fall, when the days are still warm, the nights are getting chilly at altitude, the roads remain free of snow and most visitors have left. Bear in mind that although most roads are kept open through the winter, snow blocks Hwy-180 into Kings Canyon and the road into Mineral King (see "Winter in the parks" box on p.318). May and June can also be good, especially in Kings Canyon where snowmelt swells the Kings River dramatically.

Some history

The land now encompassed by the Sequoia and Kings Canyon National Parks was once the domain of **Yokut sub-tribes** – the Monache, Potwisha and Kaweah peoples – who made summer forays into the high country from their permanent settlements in the lowlands, especially along the Marble Fork of the Kaweah River. The first real European contact came with the 1849 California **gold rush** when prospectors penetrated the area in search of pasture and a direct route through the mountains. Word of abundant lumber soon got out and loggers came to stake their claim in the lowlands. The high country was widely ignored until, in 1858, local natives led Hale Tharp, a cattleman from Three Rivers, up to the sequoias around Moro Rock. Tharp spent the next thirty summers up there in his log home where he was occasionally visited by John Muir who wrote about the area and brought it to the attention of the general public and the loggers. Before long narrow gauge railways and log flumes littered the area, mainly for clearing fir and pine rather than the sequoias which tended to shatter when felled. Nonetheless, Visalia conservationist George Stewart campaigned in Washington for some degree of **preservation** for the big trees and, in 1890, four square miles around Grant Grove became the country's second national park after Yellowstone. In 1940 this was incorporated into the newly formed Kings Canyon National Park.

Arrival and information

Although easy to reach by **car** – a fifty-mile drive along the tortuous Hwy-198 from Visalia or a slightly longer but faster journey from Fresno on Hwy-180 – Sequoia and Kings Canyon are not served by public transportation. RVs longer than 22 feet and anything with a trailer shouldn't consider tackling Hwy-198. Once in Sequoia, reduce traffic congestion and your own parking problems by using the **free shuttle bus** (late June–early Sept daily 9am–6pm; every 30min) which runs between Wuksachi, Lodgepole, the Sherman Tree, Giant Forest, Moro Rock and Crescent Meadow. Visitors should prepare by stocking up with **cash** and **gas** before entering the parks, though some of both is available (see "Listings," p.327).

The parks are always open: **park entry** costs $10 per car, or $5 per hiker or biker and is valid for seven days. This will be collected at the entrance stations, where you'll be given an excellent map and a copy of the free newspaper, *The Sequoia Bark*, which has details and timetables for the numerous **guided hikes** and other interpretive activities, as well as general information on the parks.

There are currently four **visitor centers** in the two parks: the Park Headquarters at Foothills, a mile north of the southern (Hwy-198) entrance to the park (daily 8am–5pm); and others at Lodgepole, Grant Grove Village and Cedar Grove Village (see the relevant accounts for details). There is also a useful **ranger station** at Mineral King. For details of hikes and campsites in the surrounding Sequoia National Forest, visit the **Hume Lake Ranger District Office**, 35860 Hwy-180, at Clingan's Junction, 17 miles west of the Big Stump entrance (Mon–Sat 8am–4.30pm; ☎559/338-2251, *www.r5.fs.fed.us/sequoia*).

In addition there is a comprehensive 24-hour recorded information line (☎559/565-3341), with details on camping, lodging, road conditions, and the facility to order information by mail; check out a stack more of stuff on the parks' **Web site**: *www.nps.gov/seki*.

Accommodation

Inside the parks, all facilities, including accommodation, are managed by one of two concessionaires: Kings Canyon Park Services (KCPS ☎559/335-5500, fax 335-2498)

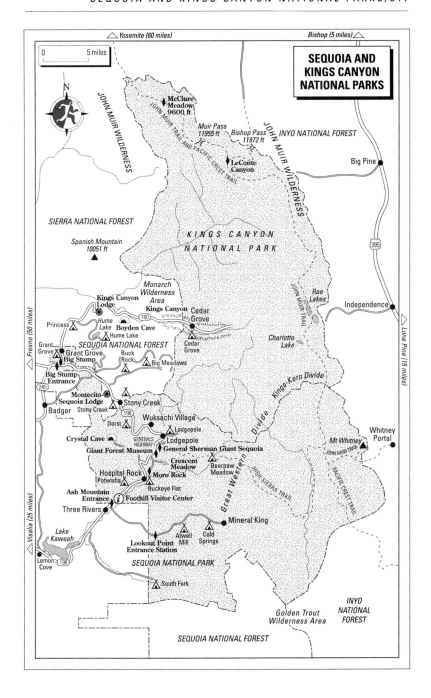

WINTER IN THE PARKS

The high country of both parks is covered in a blanket of **snow**, usually from November until April or May, and while this limits a great deal of sightseeing and walking, it also opens up opportunities for some superb cross-country skiing. With chains, **access** is seldom much of a problem. Both main roads into the parks – Hwy-198 to Giant Forest and Hwy-180 to Grant Grove – are kept open all year, except for exceptional circumstances when they are still cleared quickly. The General's Highway is usually open as far north as Lodgepole and as far south as the *Montecito-Sequoia Lodge*, but the stretch in between is often cleared only when no further snowfalls are expected: it's best then to choose one section of the parks as a base. The Cedar Grove section of Kings Canyon is off limits to cars from late September to early May, but Grant Grove stays open all year. Facilities are restricted and camping is only available at snow-free lowland sites.

The big winter activities up here are **cross-country skiing** and **snowshoeing**. The northern highway gives access to two places at the hub of miles of marked trails: the Grant Grove Ski Touring Center at Grant Grove (Nov–April; call KCPS on ☎559/335-5500) where there's ski and snowshoe rental, guided naturalist snowshoe walks at weekends, restaurants and accommodation; and the *Montecito-Sequoia Lodge* (see "Accommodation," below), a resort with their own groomed trails, also open to visitors for around $10 a day. Nearby, the mile-long Big Meadows Nordic Ski Trail is perfect beginner's terrain. To the south, the Sequoia Ski Touring Center at Wolverton, just over two miles south of Lodgepole (Nov–April; call DPNS on ☎559/565-3301), has excellent day-use facilities along with rentals, lessons and a retail shop. Unless you're a super-hardy camper, you'll need to return to Three Rivers for somewhere to stay.

who operate in Cedar Grove and Grant Grove; and Delaware North Parks Services (DPNS ☎1-888/252-5757 or 559/565-3301, fax 456-0542) who cover Lodgepole and Wuksachi. With the recent opening of two new lodges to replace those removed from Giant Forest (see below), the standard of **accommodation** has shifted away from rustic towards greater luxury, though simple cabins are still available. You can occasionally pick up cancellations on the day, but in the main space is at a premium during the summer when booking a couple of months in advance is advisable. This, and the relatively high price of accommodation, forces many to stay in the surrounding area.

Outside the parks, the most reasonably priced accommodation is in the motels lining the approach roads, a few miles from the entrances. The best selection is in the south at Three Rivers where booking ahead is advised at weekends through the summer and holidays

Under the first two headings below, all available roofed accommodation has been included, with just a selection of the best places to stay listed under the final two headings. For **camping** see the box on p.320.

In the parks

Bearpaw Meadow Camp (mid-June to mid-Sept; call DPNS). Soft beds, fluffy towels, hot showers and hearty meals served up in magnificent wilderness are the trump cards for this cluster of wooden-floored permanent tents (sleeping a total of twelve) on the High Sierra Trail, 11 miles walk east of Giant Forest Village: just follow the High Sierra Trail from Crescent Meadow. There's no electricity, everything is helicoptered in for the season and all meals are included in the price tag. Bookings are accepted from January 2 when most weekends and holidays are taken, though you've a reasonable chance of an on-spec place on weeknights in June and September. ⑥.

Cedar Grove (May–Sept; call KCPS). Cozy lodge with private bathroom and air conditioning, right by the Kings River and in the same block as the restaurant and shops. ⑤.

Grant Grove and John Muir Lodge (all year; call KCPS). The widest selection of ways of sleeping under a roof, most options accommodating up to four people. The most basic are the kerosene lamp-lit tent cabins (②) which are too cold for winter use, rising through the more solid rustic cabins (③)

with cooking stove, to comfortable standard cabins (⑤) with baths and the swanky new *John Muir Lodge* (⑥) with very comfortable hotel rooms.

Wuksachi Lodge (all year; call DPNS). Directly competing with the *John Muir Lodge* for the best rooms in the park, the Wuksachi consists of several blocks of rooms (ask for mountain views on the upper floor) widely scattered in the woods around an elegant central lounge and restaurant area. Rooms ⑥, suites ⑦.

In Sequoia National Forest

Kings Canyon Lodge (mid-April to mid-Nov; ☎559/335-2405). Small lodge with bar and restaurant located midway between Grant Grove and Cedar Grove, offering woodsy cabins with private bathroom (④) along with pleasant rooms (④), one sleeping four with private bathroom (⑤).

Montecito-Sequoia Lodge (☎1-800/227-9900 or 650/967-8612, fax 967-0540, *www.montecitosequoia. com*), on the Generals Highway (Hwy-198) between Grant Grove Village and Giant Forest Village. A large but low-key and informal resort with the emphasis on fun for all the family; a communal atmosphere prevails especially around the huge fireplaces. It is tastefully set next to an artificial lake and has all manner of activity programs: canoeing, tennis, swimming, volleyball in summer; and snowshoeing, skating and cross-country skiing in winter (see box, opposite). Several all-inclusive packages invite multi-day stays but outside peak times you can stay for just a night or two in rustic cabins (③) or lodge rooms with private bath (④), with breakfast and dinner included.

Stony Creek (May–Oct; ☎559/565-3909, fax 565-3912). Plain, comfortable motel-style rooms with showers in a block with a good restaurant and a grocery store. ⑤.

Along Hwy-198: Lemon Cove and Three Rivers

Buckeye Tree Lodge, 46000 Hwy-198, Three Rivers (☎559/561-5900, *www.buckeyetree.com*). Small but comfortable modern rooms with TV, video and private bathrooms, and a five-berth cottage (⑥), all located right by the park entrance and equipped with a pool. ④.

Gateway Lodge, 45978 Hwy-198, Three Rivers (☎559/561-4133, fax 561-3656). Spartan but perfectly functional motel-style rooms and a large house sleeping six with self-catering facilities ($150). It is located right by the park entrance and beside the Kaweah River. ④.

Mesa Verde Plantation B&B, 33038 Hwy-198, Lemon Cove (☎1-800/240-1466 or 559/597-2555, fax 597-2551, *www.plantationbnb.com*). Luxurious B&B with heated pool and spa, and gourmet breakfasts, located on a citrus orchard 17 miles from the park entrance. Rooms follow a *Gone with the Wind* theme to the extent that the Belle Watling room comes bordello-hued with a mirrored bedstead. ⑤.

Sierra Lodge, 43175 Hwy-198, Three Rivers (☎559/561-3681, fax 561-3264). Spacious lodge with large, modern rooms with bathrooms and many with decks plus the use of a pool. Rooms ④, suites ⑥

Three Rivers Trailer Park, 43365 Hwy-198 (☎559/561-4413). RV-only site with a few aging and very basic cabins at the lowest prices for miles around. ③.

Along Hwy-180

Sierra Inn Motel, 37692 Hwy-180, Dunlap (☎559/338-2144, fax 338-0789). Small and functional motel rooms with TV and air-conditioning, located 14 miles west of the Big Stump entrance and next to a sandwiches-and-steaks restaurant and bar. ③.

Snowline Lodge, 44138 Hwy-180, Dunlap (call KCPS). Woodsy collection of spartan but appealing rooms, some with a veranda that catches the morning sun, located 7 miles west of the Big Stump entrance. ⑤.

Eating

There are **food** markets and fairly basic cafeterias at Lodgepole (the most extensive), Stony Creek and Cedar Grove Village, though none of them are spectacular and prices will be higher than places outside the park, such as Three Rivers. Much the same applies to restaurants, with Three Rivers offering the best local selection at reasonable prices. In the restaurants in the parks, diner fare prevails with the exception of the restaurant at Wuksachi.

CAMPING IN KINGS CANYON

Except during public holidays, there is always plenty of **camping space** in the parks and the surrounding National Forest. All sites operate on a first-come-first-served basis except for *Lodgepole* and *Dorst* which can be reserved through the National Park Reservation System (☎1-800/365-2267, fax 301/722-1174, *www.reservations.nps.gov*). RV drivers won't find any hook-ups but there are dump stations at Potwisha, Lodgepole, Dorst, Grant Grove and Cedar Grove. Collecting "dead and down" firewood is permitted in both the national park and national forest, but for cooking you really want to bring along a portable stove. For **backcountry** camping see the "Hiking" box on p.324. There are public **showers** at several locations (see "Listings," p.327).

Campsites are listed south to north, and the night-time temperatures you can expect are indicated by the site's altitude. **Fees** are sometimes reduced or waived outside the main summer season and when piped water is disconnected, especially in winter.

South Fork (all year; $8; 3600ft). Trailer-free site a twisting thirteen miles east of Lake Kaweah on the very southwestern tip of the park. River water available.

Cold Springs, Mineral King (late-May–Oct; $8; 7500ft). Excellent shaded riverside site 25 miles west of Hwy-198, with some very quiet walk-in sites. Water available.

Atwell Mill, Mineral King (late-May–Oct; $8; 6650ft). Slightly less appealing than *Cold Springs*, but still quiet and pleasant, and five miles closer to the highway. Some tent-only sites. Water available.

Potwisha (all year; $14; 2100ft). Smallish, RV-dominated site close to Hwy-198 three miles northeast of the park's southern entrance and beside the Marble Fork of the Kaweah River. Water available.

In the parks and surrounding national forest

Grant Grove Restaurant, Grant Grove. Basic diner fare – burgers, sandwiches and breakfasts – at tolerable prices.

The Lodge at Wuksachi (reserve for dinner with DNPS). The finest dining in the twin parks, with the likes of *chorizo con huevos* ($6.50), Baja chicken sandwiches ($6), snow crab cakes on sautéed spinach ($9) and Cajun cuttlefish ($13), all served in a modern baronial-style room. The bar is open daily until 11pm.

Lodgepole Deli, Lodgepole. The best of the parks' budget eating places with respectable low-cost breakfasts, sandwiches and pizza.

Montecito-Sequoia Lodge. Resort which also serves nutritious buffet meals to non-residents. Hearty breakfasts (8–9.30am; $7), lunches (noon–1.30pm; $8) and dinners (6–7.30pm; $15) are all served communally at large tables, and there's a bar operating until 9pm.

Three Rivers

The Bakery, 43368 Hwy-198. A good and friendly stop for breakfast, especially for the freshly baked cakes and pastries.

Gateway Restaurant, 45978 Hwy-198. Superbly set restaurant with a sunny deck overlooking the Kaweah River. Burgers, sandwiches and pasta dishes go for $8–10, meat and fish mains for around $15. Closed Monday.

Noisy Water Café, 41775 Hwy-198. Cozy, friendly and locally-popular family restaurant with an extensive menu of American and Mexican staples.

Sequoia National Park

The two main centers in **SEQUOIA NATIONAL PARK** are **Giant Forest** and **Lodgepole** – the starting points for most of the hiking trails. To the south there's also the more isolated Mineral King area. While trees are seldom scarce – patches where

Buckeye Flat (late-May to mid-Oct; $14; 2800ft). Peaceful, trailer-free site six miles east of Hwy-198, close to the park's southern entrance and beside the Middle Fork of the Kaweah River. Water available.

Lodgepole (all year; $16; 6700ft). Largest and busiest of the sites, four miles north of Giant Forest Village and close to the highway. Reserve through Destinet in the high season, when there are pay showers, a camp store, water and flush toilets.

Dorst (late May to Sept; $16; 6800ft). Another large site, eight miles north of Lodgepole, with flush toilets and water during the season. In summer, reserve through the National Park Reservation System.

Buck Rock (all year; free; 6300ft). Excellent and under-utilized National Forest site three miles west of the highway, midway between Lodgepole and Grant Grove Village. No water.

Big Meadows (all year; free; 6500ft). Similar site to *Buck Rock*, a mile further west among exfoliated granite domes. No water.

Princess (late May–Sept; $12; 6000ft). National Forest campground with water and toilets, handily sited on the way into Kings Canyon.

Hume Lake (all year; $14; 5200ft; ☎1-888/833-6777 or 518/885-3639). Reservable National Forest site with water, toilets and lake swimming for the brave.

Sunset, Azalea and **Crystal Spring**, Grant Grove Village. (*Azalea* year round, others as needed; $14; 6500ft). Comparable large sites all within a few hundred yards of the Grant Grove visitor center.

Sheep Creek, Sentinel, Canyon View and **Moraine**, Cedar Grove Village (early May to Oct; $14; 4600ft). A series of all-but contiguous forest sites around the Cedar Grove visitor center. *Canyon View* is tents-only.

the giant sequoias can't grow are thickly swathed with pine and fir – the scenery varies throughout the park: sometimes subtly, sometimes abruptly. Everywhere paths lead through deep forests and around meadows; longer treks rise above the tree line to reveal the barren peaks and superb sights of the High Sierra.

The history of the park is laced with political intrigue. In the 1880s the Giant Forest area was bought by the Co-operative Land Purchase and Colonization Association, a group of individuals known as the **Kaweah Colony** that had the idea of forming a workers' colony here. They began what became the four-year task of building a road from the Central Valley up to Giant Forest, intending to start commercial logging of the huge trees there. Due to legal technicalities, however, their rights to the area were disputed, and in 1890 a bill (probably instigated by a combination of agricultural and railroad interests) was passed by the Senate which effected the preservation of all sequoia groves. The colony lost everything, and received no compensation for the road, which remained in use for thirty years – although decades later the ex-leader of the colony acknowledged that the eventual outcome was of far greater benefit to society as a whole than his own scheme would have been.

Three Rivers, Kaweah and Mineral King

Approaching the park from the south, you pass through **THREE RIVERS**, a lowland community strung out for seven miles along Hwy-198 and providing the greatest concentration of accommodation and places to eat anywhere near the park. As you approach the center of town a sign directs you three miles west to what remains of the Kaweah Colony, essentially just the **Kaweah Post Office**, which must be one of the smallest still operating in the country. What is little more than a shed still has the original brass-and-glass private boxes and, even outside normal opening times, the tiny lobby acts as the local secondhand book exchange.

A couple of miles north of Three Rivers, the century-old, twisting Mineral King Road branches 25 miles east into the southern section of the park to **Mineral King**, sitting in a scalloped bowl at 7800ft surrounded by snowy peaks and glacial lakes. This is the only part of the high country accessible by car and makes a superb hiking base when you can reach it; essentially late-May to mid-October, or a little longer if the snows hold off. Eager prospectors built the thoroughfare hoping the area would yield silver. It didn't, the mines were abandoned and the region was left in peace until the mid-1960s when Disney threatened to build a huge ski resort here, only to be defeated by the conservation lobby which campaigned for the region's inclusion in the Sequoia National Park, something finally achieved in 1978. Now there's just a couple of basic campgrounds and near-complete tranquillity. Having negotiated the seven-hundred-odd twists and turns from the highway, you can relax by the river before hiking up over steep Sawtooth Pass and into the alpine bowls of the glaciated basins beyond. There's also a gentler introduction to the flora and fauna of Mineral King by way of a short **nature trail** from the *Cold Springs* campground.

Pick up practical information and wilderness permits from the **ranger station** (late May to Sept daily 7am–3.30pm; ☎559/565-3768) opposite the *Cold Springs* campground. Permits are required until late September and are in great demand, especially in July and August. Reservations can be made in advance from March 1 and some permits are offered on a first-come-first-served basis. The *Silver City Resort* (☎559/561-3223, fax 805/528-8039, *www.silvercityresort.com*; rustic cabins ④, deluxe chalets ⑧) is near the *Atwell* campsite and is the only place you'll find food; it has limited provisions and a café/restaurant.

Giant Forest

Entering the park on **Hwy-180 from Visalia**, you pass **Hospital Rock**, easily spotted by the side of the road and decorated with rock drawings and grain-grinding holes from an ancient Monache settlement. The rock got its name from a trapper who accidentally shot himself in the leg and was treated by the local tribe – who are further remembered by a small outdoor exhibition telling something of their evolution and culture. The road opposite leads to the small and appealing *Buckeye Flat* campground.

From Hospital Rock, the road soon becomes the **Generals Highway** and twists rapidly uphill into the densely forested section of the park, the aptly labeled **Giant Forest**. A major tourist draw, with the greatest accessible concentration of giant sequoias, Giant Forest contained a small village until 1998. But, over the years, it was recognized that the huge numbers of visitors ambling around the hotel and restaurant buildings were damaging the area's ecosystem. Concerns over the health of the sequoias prompted the park service to raze the settlement. Certain areas are currently off limits while roads are being torn up and re-seeding takes place. One of the more historic of the old buildings is being retained and converted into an interpretive center, possibly by the summer of 2001.

Along Crescent Meadow Road

A spur off the main highway, **Crescent Meadow Road**, provides easy access to a host of photo opportunities. The first attraction is the **Auto Log**, a fallen trunk chiseled flat enough to enable motorists to nose up onto it. Beyond here, a side loop leads to the dramatic **Moro Rock**, a granite monolith streaking wildly upward from the green hillside. Views from its remarkably level top can stretch 150 miles across the Central Valley and, in the other direction, to the towering Sierra (incidentally, the top is also reputed to make a good platform for feeling vibrations of distant earthquakes). Thanks to a concrete staircase, it's a comparatively easy climb up the rock, although at nearly 7000ft the altitude can be a strain.

Back on the road, you pass under the **Tunnel Log**: a tree that fell across the road in 1937 and has since had a vehicle-sized hole cut through its lower half. Further on, **Crescent Meadow** is, like other grassy fields in the area, more accurately a marsh, and too wet for the sequoias that form an impressive boundary around. Looking across the meadow gives the best opportunity to appreciate the changing shape of the aging sequoia. The trail circling its perimeter (1.5 miles; 1hr; mainly flat) leads to **Log Meadow**, to which a farmer, Hale Tharp, searching for a summer grazing ground for his sheep, was led by local Native Americans in 1856. He became one of the first white men to see the giant sequoias, and the first to actually live in one – a hollowed-out specimen which still exists, remembered as **Tharp's Log**. Peer inside to appreciate the hewn-out shelves. From here the loop presses on to the still living **Chimney Tree**, its center completely burnt out so that the sky is visible from its hollow base. Hardy backpackers can pick up the John Muir Trail here and hike the 74 miles to Mount Whitney (the tallest mountain in the continental US; see p.280).

The big trees and Crystal Cave

North of Crescent Meadow Road, the Generals Highway enters the thickest section of Giant Forest and the biggest sequoia of them all (reachable on foot by various connecting trails). The three-thousand-year-old **General Sherman Tree** is 275ft high, with a base diameter of 36ft (and was, for a time, renamed the Karl Marx Tree by the Kaweah Colony). While it's certainly a thrill to be face-to-bark with what is widely held to be the largest living thing on earth, its extraordinary dimensions are hard to grasp alongside the almost equally monstrous sequoias around – and the other tremendous batch that can be seen on the **Congress Trail** (2 miles; 1–2hr; negligible ascent), which starts from here.

When you've had your fill of the magnificent trees, consider a trip nine miles from Giant Forest along a minor road to **Crystal Cave** (50min guided tours mid-May to mid-June and Sept Fri–Mon 11am–4pm, mid-June to Aug daily 11am–4pm; $6) which has a mildly diverting batch of stalagmites and stalactites. Tickets can only be purchased at the Lodgepole and Foothill visitor centers at least a couple of hours beforehand. The early morning tours are not usually full, and whatever time you go, remember to take a jacket. More adventurous, reasonably athletic and non-claustrophobic spelunkers might like to try getting on the four-hour **Wild Cave Tour** (early June to late Sept Fri–Sun 4.30pm; $60). This can be a difficult tour to join, as numbers are limited: call ☎559/565-3759 or write to SNHA, HCR 89 Box 10, Three Rivers, CA 93278, before May to enter the tour lottery, or just front up and hope for cancellations.

North of Giant Forest, the Generals Highway passes the short spur road to **Wolverton**, site of a pack station (see "Listings," p.327) and an important trailhead for some serious hikes (see box, overleaf).

Lodgepole and around

Whatever your plans, you should stop at **LODGEPOLE VILLAGE** – a couple of miles north of Wolverton – for the geological displays, film shows and general information at the **visitor center** (mid-May to Aug daily 8am–6pm, rest of year daily 8am–5pm). With its grocery store, burger bar, showers, laundromat and campground, Lodgepole is very much at the center of Sequoia's visitor activities, and its situation at one end of the Tokopah Valley, a glacially formed canyon (not unlike the much larger Yosemite Valley), makes it an ideal starting point to explore a number of hiking trails (see box overleaf). Foremost among them is the **Tokopah Valley Trail** – leading from Lodgepole through the valley to the base of Tokopah Falls, beneath **The Watchtower**, a 1600-foot cliff. The top of The Watchtower, and its great view of the valley, are accessible by way of the **Lakes Trail**, or try the sharpest ascent of all the Lodgepole hikes, the **Alta Peak and Alta Meadows Trail**, which rises four thousand feet over seven miles.

HIKING IN SEQUOIA AND KINGS CANYON

The **trails** in Kings Canyon and Sequoia see far less traffic than those in Yosemite, but can still get busy in high summer. There are no restrictions on day-walks, but a quota system (operational late May–Sept) applies if you are planning to camp in the backcountry. Numbers are severely limited, but around a third of the places are offered on a first-come-first-served basis and provided you are fairly flexible you should be able to land something by turning up at the ranger station nearest your proposed trailhead early in the afternoon on the day before you wish to start. **Wilderness permits** are free, but reservations cost $10 (per group per entry into the wilderness) and can be obtained in advance by contacting Wilderness Permit Reservations, Sequoia & Kings Canyon National Park, HCR 89 Box 60,Three Rivers, CA 93271 (☎559/565-3708, fax 565-4239) stating entry and exit dates, desired route with an alternative, number of people and estimated camping spots. Reservations are accepted after March 1 and at least three weeks before your start date, and outside the quota period, permits can be self-issued at trailheads. More details are available in the free *Backcountry Basics* newspaper available in the park and from the above address. The visitor centers also sell localized hiking maps ($2 each) and more detailed topographical maps.

Remember that this is **bear country**: read the box on p.338. Bear canisters can be rented ($3 a day and $75 deposit) from the ranger station in Mineral King and camp stores at Foothills, Lodgepole, Grant Grove and Cedar Grove; and bought ($65) at the Lodgepole store.

FROM MINERAL KING, SEQUOIA

Eagle Lake Trail (7 miles; 4–6hr; 2200ft ascent). Starting from the parking area a mile beyond the ranger station, this trail starts gently but gets tougher towards Eagle Lake. Highlights include the Eagle Sink Hole (where the river vanishes) and some fantastic views.

Groundhog Meadow Trail (2 miles; 1–2hr; 900ft ascent). A short but demanding trail which switchbacks up to Groundhog Meadow, from where there's a great view of Sawtooth Ridge. Starts a quarter of a mile back from the road beyond the ranger station.

Mosquito Lakes No. 1 Trail (7 miles; 4–5hr; 1150ft ascent).

Follows the first half of the Eagle Lake Trail, then branches left to the lowest of the Mosquito Lakes at 9000ft.

Mosquito Lakes No. 5 Trail (10 miles; 6–8hr; 2300ft ascent). As above plus a bit, bringing you to the uppermost lake at over 10,000ft. Stupendous views.

Paradise Peak via Paradise Ridge Trail (9 miles; 9hr; 2800ft ascent). Superb walk starting opposite the *Atwell Mill* campground and climbing steeply to Paradise Ridge, which affords views of Moro Rock. From there it is a fairly flat stroll to the 9300-foot Paradise Peak.

Beyond Lodgepole the Generals Highway turns west and runs four miles to **WUKSACHI**, a new creation, with a fancy lodge and restaurant, partly designed to replace Giant Forest Village. The road soon swings north again and passes into the Sequoia National Forest – where there is accommodation and food to be had at both **Stony Creek** and the *Montecito-Sequoia Lodge*, and free camping at a couple of primitive sites – before striking into the Kings Canyon National Park.

Kings Canyon National Park

KINGS CANYON NATIONAL PARK is wilder and less visited than Sequoia, with just two small settlements containing the park's main visitor facilities: Grant Grove lies

FROM GIANT FOREST, WOLVERTON AND LODGEPOLE, SEQUOIA

Alta Peak and Alta Meadows Trail (14 miles; 8–10hr; 4000ft ascent). Strenuous but rewarding trail rising four thousand feet over seven miles. The trail starts at the Wolverton trailhead and splits after three miles: there's an easy, level walk to Alta Meadow and its fine views of the surrounding peaks (and a four-mile trail to the desolate Moose Lake), or the daunting near-vertical hike to the stunning Alta Peak.

Little Baldy Trail (3 miles; 2–3hr; 700ft ascent). Starting from Little Baldy Saddle, six miles north of Lodgepole, this loop trail leads to the rocky summit of Little Baldy.

Tokopah Trail (3 miles; 2–3hr; 200ft ascent). Easy valley walk beside the Marble Fork of the Kaweah River and leading to impressive granite cliffs and the Tokopah Falls, which cascades into a cool pool, perfect for a bracing dip. Starts at the eastern end of the Lodgepole campground.

The Watchtower and Lakes Trail (13 miles; 6–8hr; 2300ft ascent). A popular if fatiguing trail leading up from the Wolverton trailhead to The Watchtower (3–5hr round-trip), an exposed tower of granite overlooking Tokapah Falls far below. From there the path leads past three lakes in increasingly gorgeous and stark glacial cirques. The two furthest lakes, Emerald Lake (9200ft) and Pear Lake (9500ft), have campgrounds which, for the really adventurous (and experienced), make good starting points for self-guided trekking into the mountains.

FROM KINGS CANYON

Cedar Grove Overlook Trail (5 miles; 3–4hr; 1200ft ascent). Starting half a mile north of Cedar Grove Village on Pack Station Road, this switchback trail rises through forest and chaparral to a viewpoint overlooking Kings Canyon.

Don Cecil Trail to Lookout Peak (13 miles; 7–9hr; 4000ft ascent). Starting 400 yards east of Cedar Grove Village, a strenuous trail which largely follows the pre-highway road route. After two miles you reach the shady glen of Sheep Creek Cascade before pressing on up the canyon to the wonderfully panoramic summit.

Hotel Creek–Lewis Creek Loop Trail (8 miles; 5hr; 1200ft ascent). Follows the first two miles of the Cedar Grove Overlook trail, before branching downhill and returning to Cedar Grove through some extensively fire-damaged forest.

Mist Falls Trail (8 miles; 3–5hr; 600ft ascent). An easy sandy trail starts from Road's End, eventually climbing steeply past numerous thundering cataracts to Mist Falls, one of the largest waterfalls in the twin parks.

Rae Lakes Loop (4–5 days). One of the best of the multi-day hikes in these parts following the Kings River up past Mist Falls and beyond through Paradise Valley and Castle Domes Meadow to Woods Creek Crossing, where it meets the John Muir Trail. It follows this for eight miles, passing Rae Lakes before returning to Kings Canyon along Bubbs Creek and the South Fork of the Kings River. Trail maps ($3.50) are available from the Lodgepole visitor center.

close to the Big Stump entrance, and Cedar Grove huddles in the bottom of the canyon some 25 miles to the east at the start of most of the marked hikes. The one real road (closed in winter; usually Oct–May) links the two, spectacularly skirting the colossal canyon. Away from these two places, you're on your own. The vast untamed park has a maze of canyons and a sprinkling of isolated lakes – the perfect environment for careful self-guided exploration.

Grant Grove, the Big Stump Area and Hume Lake

Confusingly, **Grant Grove** is an enclave of Kings Canyon National Park within the Sequoia National Forest, but unless you're planning a major backcountry hike across the parks' boundaries you'll have to pass through here before reaching Kings Canyon proper. Grant Grove has the largest concentration of visitor facilities in the Kings Canyon National Park, with accommodation, post office, restaurant, small supermarket, showers and a useful **visitor center** (daily: mid-May to Aug 8am–6pm, rest of year 8am–5pm) with all the background information you'll need.

This concentrated stand of sequoias, sugar pines, incense cedar, black oak and mountain dogwood is named after the **General Grant Tree**, which along with the **Robert E. Lee Tree** (also here), rivals the General Sherman for bulk. A half-mile trail (guides $1) wends its way among these and other giants, calling in at the **Fallen Monarch**, which you can walk through, and the **Gamlin Cabin**, where Israel and Thomas Gamlin lived while exploiting their timber claim until 1878. The massive stump of one of their scalps remains after a slice was shipped to the 1876 Centennial Exhibition in Philadelphia – an attempt to convince cynical easterners that such enormous trees really existed.

Two miles south of Grant Grove, the **Big Stump Area** unsurprisingly gets its name from the gargantuan stumps that litter the place – remnants from early logging of sequoias carried out during the 1880s. A mile-long trail (almost meaningless without the leaflet from the Grant Grove visitor center; 75¢) leads through this scene of devastation to the **Mark Twain Stump**, the headstone of another monster killed to impress: a sliver of this one resides in the American Museum of Natural History and another was sent to London's British Museum. Look too for the meager foundations of the sawmill and pine boughs laid on the ground to break the fall of their larger kin.

Hume Lake and around

About eight miles north of Grant Grove, a minor road spurs off three miles to **HUME LAKE**, actually a reservoir built in 1908 to provide water for logging flumes, and now forming the heart of an underpopulated area of the Sequoia National Forest. It's a delightful spot to swim or launch your canoe, is handily placed for the local hiking trails and makes a good place to **spend a night** beside the lake at the comparatively large *Hume Lake* campground (see p.321). At the head of the lake, the facilities of the *Hume Lake Christian Camp* provide expensive gas, groceries, a post office and a coffee shop.

Kings Canyon Highway

For most, Hume Lake doesn't even warrant a diversion from the northern park's main attraction, Kings Canyon, which some measurements make the deepest canyon in the US, at some 7900ft. Whatever the facts, its wall sections of granite and gleaming blue marble and the yellow pockmarks of yucca plants are visually outstanding: this is especially true from Junction View as Hwy-180 winds its way down to the riverside. A vast area of the wilderness beyond is drained by the South Fork of the Kings River, a raging torrent during the springtime snowmelt spate, and perilous for wading at any time: people have been swept away even when paddling close to the bank in a seemingly placid section.

You approach the canyon through a section of the Sequoia National Forest with two rewarding excursions. The first is a short drive to the **Chicago Stump**, yet another epitaph to a felled giant, this one carted in numbered sections to Chicago in 1895 where it was reassembled for the World's Colombian Exposition. A more alluring diversion leads to a trailhead for the **Boole Tree**, the world's fattest sequoia and one seldom visited despite the fine examples of fire scarring. It is only about ten minutes walk to the tree, but the whole 2.5 mile loop trail helps put this behemoth in context.

Near the foot of the canyon, the road passes the less diverting of the region's two show caves, the **Boyden Cave** (daily: June–Aug 10am–5pm, late April–May & Sept–early Nov 11am–4pm, 45min tours on the hour; $7), whose interior has a number of bizarre formations grown out of the forty-thousand-year-old rock, their impact intensified by the stillness and cool inside. The cave stays at a constant 55°F, causing the numerous small animals who tumble in through the hole in the roof to enter instant hibernation.

Cedar Grove

Once properly into the national park, the canyon sheds its V-shape and gains a floor, where the settlement of **Cedar Grove** sprawls among incense cedars. With a lodge, a food store and snack bar, several campgrounds and, across the river, a **ranger station** (June–Aug daily 9am–5pm, May, Sept & Oct hours reduced), this is as close to a built-up area as the park gets.

Three miles east are the **Roaring River Falls** which, when in spate, undoubtedly merit their name. Apart from the obvious appeal of the scenery, the main things to see around here are the **flowers** – leopard lilies, shooting stars, violets, Indian paintbrush, lupines and others – and a variety of bird life. The longer hikes through the creeks, many of them seven or eight miles long (see box on p.324), are fairly stiff challenges and you should carry drinking water. An easy alternative is to potter along the **nature trail** (1.5 miles; 1–2hr; flat) around the edge of **Zumwalt Meadow**, a beckoning green carpet a mile beyond the falls and a short walk from the road, beneath the forbidding gray walls of Grand Sentinel and North Dome mountains. The meadow boasts a collection of big-leaf maple, cat's-tails and creek dogwood, and there's often a chance of an eyeful of animal life.

Just a mile further, Kings Canyon Road comes to an end at **Copper Creek**. Thirty years ago it was sensibly decided not to allow vehicles to penetrate further. Instead the multitude of canyons and peaks that constitute the Kings River Sierra are networked by **hiking paths**, all accessible from here and almost all best enjoyed armed with a tent and some provisions. To obtain **wilderness permits** in this area, call at the Road's End Wilderness Permit Station (June to mid-Sept daily 7am–2pm, rest of Sept Fri & Sat 7am–2pm) at the end of Hwy-180. The less ambitious only need to venture a hundred yards riverward to **Muir Rock**, to see where John Muir (see box on p.335) conducted early meetings of the Sierra Club. On the way back down the valley, cut right and follow the **Motor Nature Trail** (westbound only) along the north side of the river back to Cedar Grove.

Listings

Banks There are no banks in either park, but credit cards and travelers' checks are widely accepted, and Grant Grove and Lodgepole have ATMs, though they are frequently out of cash.

Cycling Bikes are not permitted off trails, limiting you to park roads, many of which are very steep and with limited space for passing. A better bet is the network of trails in the surrounding national forest.

Gas There is currently no gas in the parks, so drivers should fill up with cheap gas in Visalia or Fresno, or slightly pricier stuff at Three Rivers. In desperation, you can get expensive gas at the *Hume Lake Christian Camp* (see opposite) or at *Kings Canyon Lodge* on Hwy-180, which claims to have the oldest gravity-fed pumps in the country, dating back to the 1920s.

Horse riding Stables and pack stations exist in five locations through the national parks and surrounding forest: Mineral King (☎561-3039), Wolverton (☎565-3039), Grant Grove (☎565-3464), Big Meadows (☎565-3404) and Cedar Grove (☎565-3464). All offer anything from an hour or two in the saddle (roughly $30 for two hours) to multi-day backcountry excursions.

Laundry Lodgepole (daily 9am–5pm) and Cedar Grove Village (daily 8am–8pm) both have coin-operated laundries.

Post offices Both post offices accept general delivery mail: at Lodgepole (Mon–Fri 8.30am–4pm) write to c/o General Delivery, Sequoia National Park, CA 93262; and at Grant Grove (Mon 9.30am–3pm, Tues–Thurs 9.30am–1pm Fri 9.30am–4.30pm Sat 9am–3pm) write to Kings Canyon National Park, CA 93633.

Rafting From late April to the end of June Kaweah Whitewater Adventures, 41891 Sierra Drive, Three Rivers (☎559/561-1000) run a series of rafting trip on the Kaweah River between Three Rivers and Lake Kaweah. Trips range from a relatively gentle two hours ($45) to serious Class IV and V full-day trip for $120.

Roads For road conditions call ☎559/565-3341.

Showers There are $3 showers at Lodgepole (summer daily 8am–1pm & 3–8pm), Stony Creek (daily 8am–8pm), Grant Grove Village (summer daily 1am–4pm) and Cedar Grove Village (summer daily 8am–1pm & 3–8pm).

The Sierra National Forest

Consuming the entire gaping tract of land between Kings Canyon and Yosemite, the **SIERRA NATIONAL FOREST** boasts some of the Californian interior's most beautiful mountain scenery, though it is less well known – and less visited – than either of its national park neighbors. A federally run area that lacks the environmental protection given to the parks, many of the rivers here have been dammed and much of the forest developed into resort areas that are better for fishing and boating than hiking. Central Valley residents stream up here at weekends through the summer. That said, there are far fewer people and any number of remote corners to explore, not least the rugged, unspoilt terrain of the vast **John Muir Wilderness**, and the neighboring **Ansel Adams Wilderness** which contain some of the starkest peaks and lushest alpine meadows of the High Sierra. If you want to discover complete solitude and hike and camp in isolation, this is the place to do it – the sheer challenge of the environment can make the national parks look like holiday camps. But don't try any lone exploration without thorough planning aided by accurate maps, and don't expect buses to pick you up if you're tired. Public transportation is virtually nonexistent. We haven't highlighted any walks in this area; there are hundreds of them and any of the **ranger stations** can suggest suitable hikes, supply free permits (necessary for any overnight hikes into most of the forest) and sell you the detailed *Sierra National Forest Map* ($4.30), useful even if you are driving.

The paltry network of roads effectively divides the forest into three main areas: the more southerly **Pineridge** district, accessible by way of Hwy-168; the **Bass Lake** and Mariposa districts, just off Hwy-41 between Fresno and Yosemite; and the Minarets Loop, which reaches out into the Sierra to the southeast of Yosemite. Call ☎559/855-5360 for road information.

The Pineridge District and the John Muir Wilderness

A forty-mile drive from Fresno along Hwy-168 through a parched and knobbly landscape dotted with blue, live and scrub oak soon brings you to the best place for adventurous hiking, the **Pineridge** district. Around **Kaiser Pass**, which scrapes 9200ft, you'll find isolated alpine landscapes, served by decent campgrounds, a couple of minor resorts and even some hot springs. The western section of the district is dominated by the weekend boating and fishing playgrounds of Huntington and Shaver lakes, while the east, up and over Kaiser Pass and around three hours drive from Fresno, is bigtime hiking territory.

The region is swamped by **reservoirs** – Edison, Florence, Mammoth Pool, Redinger and others – built as part of the "Big Creek" project, which more than anything else made the San Joaquin the agricultural heart of California. With only modest hyperbole, the Sierra meltwater in these parts is touted as "the hardest working water in the world."

Hwy-168 – aka **The Sierra Heritage National Scenic Byway** – penetrates seventy miles into the forest among the snow-capped peaks of the **John Muir Wilderness**. It's a drive of at least four hours, even in good weather – and this is an area prone to bad weather and road closure, although you can always get to the lakes. The best-placed source of information is the **Pineridge Ranger Station** (daily 8am–4.30pm; ☎559/855-5360), located along Hwy-168 at Prather, five miles west of the forest entrance.

Shaver and Huntington lakes

From the ranger station, the good and fast Hwy-168 climbs rapidly over eighteen miles from undulating foothills studded with oaks to **SHAVER LAKE**, a mile-high community scattered among the pines, where Dinkey Creek Road (see below) cuts deep into the forests to the south. If you fancy an afternoon dodging the jetskiers out on the lake, drop in at Shaver Lake Watersports, on the highway in Shaver (☎559/841-8222), to rent windsurfers, canoes and double kayaks (all $45 a day). Otherwise, there's little reason to stop

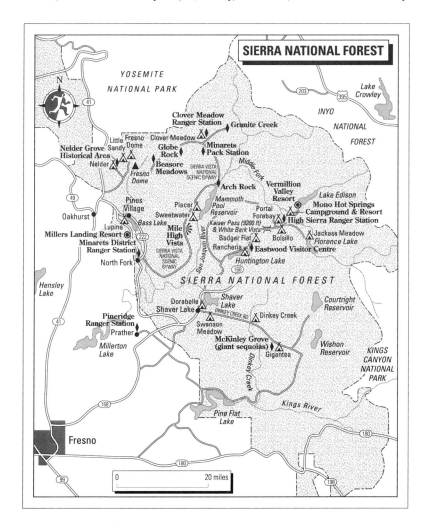

except for groceries, gas, meals at one of the half-dozen restaurants, and perhaps to stay at *Knotty Pine Vacation Cabins* (☎559/298-6314; ④-⑥), which has fully-self-contained cabins: one sleeping up to four, the other six. There are more rustic cabins three miles east at *Shaver Lake Lodge* (☎559/811-3326; ③-⑤), where the cheaper units come without bedding, though the plush ones have queen-sized beds and a kitchenette. The *Lodge* serves burgers-and-fries type meals in the bar or on the sunny deck overlooking Shaver Lake. There are a couple of decent **campsites** hereabouts: *Dorabelle*, near the lake on Dorabelle Road (June to mid-Sept; book with ReserveUSA ☎1-877/444-6777, *www.ReserveUSA.com*; $14), which has water; and *Swanson Meadow*, two miles east on Dinkey Creek Road ($10) beside some gorgeous meadows.

Beyond Shaver Lake, Hwy-168 heads twenty miles east to **Huntington Lake**, climbing the 7500-foot Tamarack Ridge that effectively separates the lake from the Central Valley. This lake is more isolated than its neighbor over the hill, but is almost equally popular; again watersports and angling are the pastimes of choice.

Just before the lake, the *Rancheria* campground (open all year; $14; reserve with ReserveUSA June–Sept) marks the turn-off to **Rancheria Falls**. A sideroad, east off Hwy-168, leads a mile to a trailhead from where the mile-long **Rancheria Falls Trail** (350ft ascent) heads off through broadleaf woods to the 150-foot falls. A mile beyond the turn-off, Hwy-168 reaches the lake by the **Eastwood Visitor Center** (late May–early Sept daily 8am–5pm), where the Kaiser Pass Road splits east over Kaiser Pass (see below). Continuing west around Huntington Lake you soon hit the 1920s *Lakeshore Resort* (☎559/893-3193, fax 893-2193, *www.lakeshoreresort.com*; ④), with rustic knotty pine cabins sleeping four. There's a great restaurant, a lively bar, a gas station, post office and general store all a few yards from the lake. From here on, the lakeshore is almost entirely taken up by $14 campsites. If you crave solitude, head to the lake's western end, where a winding forty-mile, partly-gravel road skirts the whole of the Kaiser Wilderness, passing a couple of free, primitive campgrounds, before rejoining Kaiser Pass Road on the east side. It's a trek, but once you're here you'll feel a million miles from anywhere.

Beyond Kaiser Pass: Mono Hot Springs and around

Beyond the Eastwood Visitor Center (see above), you're into the wild country climbing Kaiser Pass on a rapidly deteriorating road up to 9200 feet, passing the *Badger Flat* campground (free; no water) along the way. Eight miles from Eastwood, a mile-long side road (passable in a high clearance vehicle) leads to **White Bark Vista**, one of the best mountain views in these parts. Over the pass is a vast basin, draining the south fork of the San Joaquin River. The lumpy single-lane road drops past the beautifully-sited *Portal Forebay* campground ($8; lake water), and the free but drab *Bolsillo* campground (no water). The **High Sierra Ranger Station** (late May–early Sept Thurs–Mon 8am–4.30pm; ☎559/877-3138) heralds a fork from where two very narrow and winding seven-mile roads split: north to Lake Edison, its approach marred by a huge earth dam, and west to Florence Lake.

Mono Hot Springs, two miles north of the junction on the road to Lake Edison, is the best thing about the region and a great place to relax and clean up after hikes. For the full hot springs experience, head for the *Mono Hot Springs Resort* (mid-May to mid-Oct; ☎559/325-1710, *www.monohotsprings.com*; ②). Located on the banks of the San Joaquin River, the resort is a modest affair with individual mineral baths ($4) and showers ($3), and massages for $35 per half hour. Outside there's a chlorinated spa filled with spring water, costing $4 for an all-day pass. Accommodation at the resort ranges from simple cabins with communal ablutions and no linen, to much more commodious affairs with toilets and kitchen. Rates are thirty percent higher at weekends, when reservations are essential. The resort also has a small restaurant, a limited general store, the *Mono Hot Springs* campground (book through ReserveUSA; $12), and a post office used for mail and food pick-ups by hikers on the nearby Pacific Crest Trail. Better still, across the river there's a five-foot-deep concrete **bathing tank** (unrestricted access) that's perfect for soaking your bones while stargazing. This is just one of many pools on this side of the river; ask around.

Beyond Mono Hot Springs, the road continues past several more campgrounds amid wonderful scenery to **Lake Edison** and the *Vermillion Valley Resort* (☎559/855-6558, *www.edisonlake.com*; ③), mainly geared towards boaters and anglers but also useful for folk heading out into the John Muir Wilderness. Save yourself a dull seven-mile hike by taking the small **ferry** (mid-May–late Oct twice daily; $8 one way) across the lake.

Florence Lake is more immediately appealing than Lake Edison: there's a greater sense of being hemmed in by mountains, and it is reached through an unearthly landscape of wrinkled granite shattered over the centuries by contorted junipers. There's a small store, the *Jackass Meadow* campground ($12) (unnervingly located below the dam), and another **ferry** across the lake (late-May to mid-Sept; $8 one way). This opens up multi-day hikes along the John Muir and Pacific Crest trails, and to the northern end of Kings Canyon National Park. If you can't face being totally self-sufficient, you can sometimes stay at the *Muir Trail Ranch* (☎209/966-3195 from Oct to mid-June, *www.muirtrailranch.com*), a cabin and tent retreat with hot pools and horses located in magical scenery four miles beyond the far end of Florence Lake. When not taken over by groups, it is open for short stays (usually the first three weeks in June, the last week in Sept and the first two in Oct) at $95 a night for room, breakfast, sack lunch and dinner, but not including horses, charged at $50 a day. Access is by the cross-lake ferry, and then you either hike or arrange to be met with a horse.

Dinkey Creek Road and the Kings River District

The region to the southeast of Shaver Lake is accessible along Dinkey Creek Road which threads its way through thirty miles of thick forests and around lush meadows to the Wishon reservoir. It is altogether less alpine than the regions farther east, but no less impressive and a good deal warmer. Deep in the forest thirteen miles southeast of Shaver Lake lie *Dinkey Creek Chalets* (☎559/841-3435; camping cabins ②, chalets ⑤), adjacent to a $14 campground and store which serves breakfast and lunch. Six miles further on is **McKinley Grove**, a stand of giant sequoias that is somewhat less impressive than others in the Sierra, though it is always an honor to be among these giants. The adjacent *Gigantea* campground ($8) is free outside the main summer season. Beyond lies Wishon reservoir from where tracks penetrate the Woodchuck and Red River Basin portions of the John Muir Wilderness.

Bass Lake

The northern reaches of the Sierra National Forest are most easily reached from **Oakhurst** (see "Approaching Yosemite" on p.336), the center of the Mariposa district and just seven miles west of much the biggest tourist attraction in the area – the pine-fringed **BASS LAKE**. A stamping ground of Hell's Angels in the 1960s – the leather and licentiousness memorably described in Hunter S. Thompson's book *Hell's Angels* – Bass Lake is nowadays a family resort, crowded with boaters and anglers in summer, but a good spot to rest for a day or two. For detailed campground and hiking information, consult the Minarets District Ranger Station (see below).

Road 222 runs right around the lake, though not always within sight of it. At the main settlement, **Pines Village**, you can buy groceries, eat moderately well and **spend the night** at *The Pines* (☎1-800/350-7463 or 209/642-3121; ⑦) in luxurious two-story chalets with kitchens or even more palatial lakeside suites. By the southwestern tip of the lake, *Miller's Landing Resort*, 37976 Road 222 (☎559/642-3633, ②-⑦), offers cabins without bathrooms right up to fancy chalets and suites. *Miller's Landing* is also the best place to rent aquatic equipment – **canoes** and **fishing boats** are $25 and $60 a day respectively, while **jetskis** are $55 an hour – and they have public showers and laundry.

The western side of Bass Lake is slung with $16-a-night family **campgrounds**, most oriented towards long stays beside your camper. In summer, book well in advance (call ReserveUSA on ☎1-877/444-6777), though no-shows are sometimes available at the California Land Management Office, 39900 Road 222, on the southwest side of the lake (late May to early Sept Mon–Fri 8am–8pm Sat & Sun 8am–9pm; ☎209/642-3212). For tent campers, the best site is *Lupine* ($16), just north of *Miller's Landing*.

The Minarets Loop

If Bass Lake is too commercial and overcrowded for you, the antidote starts immediately to the north. The Sierra Vista National Scenic Byway, more succinctly known as the **Minarets Loop**, makes a ninety-mile circuit east of Hwy-41, topping out at the Clover Meadow Station (7000ft), trailhead for much of the magnificent **Ansel Adams Wilderness**. Apart from a lot of trailheads and campgrounds, there's not a great deal to it, though the views are fantastic and people are scarce. A straight circuit (snow-free July–Oct at best) takes five hours, and is especially slow going on the rough dirt roads of the north side. Stock up on supplies before you start: there are a couple of stores and gas stations dotted along its length but they're not cheap and the range is limited. Accommodation on the circuit is largely limited to campgrounds, all (except two free sites) costing $11–13.

The best source of information on the circuit is the **Minarets District Ranger Station** (daily 8am–4.30pm; ☎559/877-2218) in the hamlet of North Fork at the southern end of Bass Lake, where you can pick up a map – important as there are numerous confusing forestry roads and few signposts.

The south side

Before setting out from North Fork, check out the **Sierra Mono Indian Museum**, (Tues–Sat 9.30am–3.30pm; $2), with some good examples of local Native American basketry and beadwork, as well as a lot of stuffed animals in glass cases. Once on your way, there's little to stop for on the first 25 miles until **Mile High Vista**, which reveals endless views of muscle-bound mountain ranges and bursting granite domes stretching back to Mammoth Mountain (see p.290). A little further on, an eight-mile side road cuts south to the dammed **Mammoth Pool**, where anglers boat on the lake and smoke their catch at one of the four campgrounds. The quietest of them are *Sweetwater* ($11; 3800ft) and *Placer* ($11; 4100ft), away from the pool but by streams. Back on the Minarets Loop you'll pass the rather disappointing **Arch Rock**, where the earth under a slab of granite has been undermined to leave a kind of bridge, and continue climbing to a small ranger outpost (late June–Sept daily 8am–noon & 1–5pm; ☎559/877-2218), and the *Minarets Pack Station* (June–Oct; ☎559/868-3405; ①). Apart from a general store and reasonable meals, the station offers simple lodging and horseback trips from $55 a day. It's a great base for wilderness trips, many of which start by the **Clover Meadow Ranger Station**, a couple of miles up a spur road (June–Oct daily 9am–5pm; permits available). Nearby are two free and wonderfully sited campgrounds, *Clover Meadow* and *Granite Creek*, both at 7000 feet, the former with potable water.

The north side

The *Minarets Pack Station* marks the start of the descent from the backcountry and the end of the asphalt; for the next few miles you're on rough dirt, generally passable in ordinary passenger vehicles when clear of snow. The hulking form of **Globe Rock** heralds the return to asphalt, which runs down to **Beasore Meadow**, where the summer-only Jones Store has supplied groceries, gas and meals for the best part of a century, and offers showers to hikers. A short distance further on you reach Cold Springs Meadow, the junction with Sky Ranch Road (follow it left to continue the loop) and a spur to the wonderful *Fresno Dome* campground ($11; no water; 6400ft), a great base for a moderately strenuous walk to the top of the exfoliated granite namesake. *Little Sandy* (6100ft), just up the road from *Fresno Dome*, is free.

The Minarets Loop then passes several $11 campsites, most without running water, en route to the **Nelder Grove Historical Area** (unrestricted entry), a couple of miles north along a dirt road. Over a hundred giant sequoias are scattered through the forest here, though the overall impression is of devastation evidenced by the number of enormous stumps among the second-growth sugar pine, white fir and cedar. The mile-long "Shadow of the Giants" interpretive walk explains the logging activities which took place here in the 1880s and early 1890s and, with its low visitor count, offers a more serene communion with these majestic trees than in any of the national parks. A second interpretive trail leads from the attractive but often mosquito-ridden *Nelder Campsite* (free; 5500ft; stream water) to **Bull Buck Tree**, once a serious contender for the world's largest tree. From here it is only seven twisting miles back to Hwy-41, reached at a point around four miles north of Oakhurst.

YOSEMITE NATIONAL PARK

No temple made with hands can compare with the Yosemite. Every rock in its walls seems to glow with life. Some lean back in majestic repose; others, absolutely sheer or nearly so for thousands of feet, advance beyond their companions in thoughtful attitudes, giving welcome to storms and calms alike, seemingly aware, yet heedless, of everything going on about them.

John Muir, *The Yosemite*

More gushing adjectives have been thrown at **YOSEMITE NATIONAL PARK** than at any other part of California. But however excessive the hyperbole may seem, once you enter the park and turn the corner which reveals Yosemite Valley – only a small part of the park but the one at which most of the verbiage is aimed – you realize it's actually an understatement. For many, **Yosemite Valley** is, very simply, the single most dramatic piece of geology to be found anywhere in the world. Just seven miles long and one mile across at its widest point, it's walled by near-vertical, mile-high cliffs whose sides are streaked by cascading waterfalls and whose tops, a variety of domes and pinnacles, form a jagged silhouette against the sky. At ground level, too, the sights can be staggeringly impressive. Grassy meadows are framed by oak, cedar, maple and fir trees, with a variety of wild flowers and wildlife – deer, coyotes and even black bears are not uncommon. As if that wasn't enough, in the southern reaches of the park near Wawona, sequoias grow almost as densely and to as vast dimensions as those in the Sequoia National Park.

Perhaps understandably, tourists are even more common. Each year Yosemite has to cope with four million visitors, and if you're looking for a little peace it's advisable to avoid the Valley and Wawona on weekends and holidays. That said, the whole park is diverse and massive enough to endure the crowds: you can visit at any time of year, even in winter when the waterfalls turn to ice and the trails are blocked by snow, and out of high summer even the valley itself resists getting crammed. Further-flung reaches of the park, especially around the crisp alpine Tuolumne Meadows (pronounced Too-ol-uh-me), and the completely wild backcountry accessible beyond them, are much less busy all year round – nature in just about the most peaceful and elemental setting you could imagine. Everywhere you go, it is, of course, essential to be careful not to cause ecological damage or upset the wildlife population (see pp.51–54 for advice).

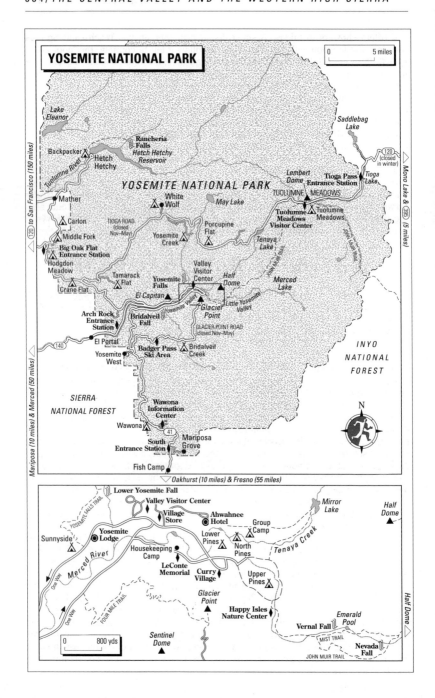

Yosemite has had more than its fair share of negative press in the past few years. In the spring of 1997, flooding wiped out one of the valley's campgrounds and prompted the park service to reassess their management of the region, a process which may lead to the re-siting of accommodation and the introduction of a more extensive bus service, and perhaps even the banning of cars from the valley. More recently, five BASE jumpers – parachutists who dive off of buildings, bridges, towers and cliffs – launched themselves off El Capitan to illustrate how safe the sport is to the national park authorities who don't allow it in their parks. One died. But, perhaps the greatest notoriety was gained by the gruesome activities of Cary Stayner, who confessed to four brutal murders which took place close to Yosemite Valley in 1999. For all that, Yosemite remains a very safe place to visit; *Outside* magazine recently claimed that the chances of being killed in an American national park are around two million to one, about the same as drowning in your own bath.

Some history

Yosemite Valley was created over thousands of years by glaciers gouging through and enlarging the canyon of the Merced River; the ice scraped away much of the softer portions of granite but only scarred the harder sections, which became the present cliffs. As the glaciers melted a lake formed, filling the valley, and eventually silting up to create the present valley floor.

The Awahneechee people occupied the area quite peaceably for some 4000 years until the mid-nineteenth century, when the increasingly threatening presence of white Gold Rush settlers in the Central Valley led the tribes here to launch raiding parties against the nearest encampments. In 1851 Major James Savage led a force, the Mariposa Battalion, in pursuit of the Native Americans, trailing them into the foothills and beyond, and becoming the first white men to set foot in Yosemite Valley. It wasn't long before the two groups clashed properly, and the original population was moved out to white settlements to make way for farmers, foresters and, soon after, tourists (the

JOHN MUIR AND THE SIERRA CLUB

Scottish immigrant **John Muir** worked as a mechanical inventor in Wisconsin until he nearly lost an eye in an accident. Discouraged, he set off in search of adventure and walked, via the Gulf of Mexico, to San Francisco. Arriving in 1868, he immediately asked directions for "anywhere that's wild" and began months of camping and exploration, reputedly carrying no more than a notebook, a tin cup and a supply of tea. His diary wasn't published until forty years later as *My First Summer in the Sierra* but was an instant hit, becoming a classic of American geographical writing.

Muir was so taken by the Sierra – which he dubbed "The Range of Light" – and Yosemite in particular, that he made it his home. Over the years, appalled by the destruction he saw taking place around him, he campaigned for the preservation of the Sierra Nevada range, and is credited with having prompted Congress to create Yosemite National Park in 1890. In 1892, he set up the **Sierra Club**, an organization whose motto "take only photographs; leave only footprints" has become a model for like-minded groups around the world.

In 1913, the construction of the Hetch Hetchy dam (see p.351) in the northern reaches of Yosemite to provide water for San Francisco was a setback in the struggle to keep Yosemite free of development and many think the struggle to prevent it led to John Muir's death the following year. But the publicity actually aided the formation of the present National Park Service in 1916, which promised – and has since provided – greater protection. Muir's name crops up throughout California as a memorial to this inspirational figure, not least in the 212-mile John Muir Trail which twists through his favorite scenery from Yosemite Valley south to Mount Whitney.

first group of sightseers arriving in 1855). Moves were quickly afoot to conserve the natural beauty of the area: in 1864 Yosemite Valley and Mariposa Grove were preserved as the Yosemite Land Grant, the nation's first region specifically set aside to protect the wilderness. In 1890 it became America's third national park, thanks in great part to the campaigning work of Scottish naturalist John Muir (see box overleaf).

Approaching Yosemite

Getting to Yosemite by car is straightforward. Three roads enter the park from the west: Hwy-41 from Fresno, Hwy-140 from Merced and Hwy-120 from Stockton and the San Francisco Bay area. All are generally kept open throughout the year as far as the Valley, though in extreme circumstances Hwy-140 is the first to close. The only road into the eastern side of the park is Hwy-120, the 10,000-foot Tioga Pass Road, which branches off US-395 close to Lee Vining – though this is usually closed from late October to early June and in bad weather. **Gas** (see "Listings") is not available in the Valley, and though Crane Flat, some fifteen miles away has 24-hour pumps, it is expensive; fill up before heading into the mountains.

Public transportation into the park is less easy, but possible from two Central Valley towns, both connected to San Francisco by Amtrak. VIA Yosemite Connection (☎1-888/727-5287) has a once-daily service (April–Sept only; $25 one way, $48 for the one-day round-trip) from Fresno (see p.309) through Oakhurst and Wawona, and runs three or four times a day (year round; $20 one way and $38 round-trip) from **Merced** (see p.312) through Mariposa and El Portal. Both services terminate in Yosemite Village and fares include park entrance fees. There is no public transportation over the Tioga Pass from Lee Vining and Hwy-395, but buses do connect the Valley with Tuolumne Meadows (see below).

Generally speaking, anything called a **sightseeing tour** which begins outside the park will involve you in an unsatisfying race through the Valley. You might, however, want to consider Green Tortoise's three-day packages (including camping near Tuolumne Meadows; see p.349) from San Francisco, costing $129 per person, plus around $30 for the food fund; or their two-day weekend trip at $110 including food and park entry.

The hinterland towns

The heavy demand for accommodation within the Park drives many to consider staying in one of the small, mostly former gold-mining towns along the main access roads. These are increasingly gearing themselves to park-bound tourists and do a reasonable job offering both lodging and food (for both of which see the following pages), though they are a poor substitute for actually staying in the park.

APPROACHING FROM THE EAST: LEE VINING

If approaching from the east and US-395 you could stop at **LEE VINING** (see p.296) or the *Tioga Pass Resort*, PO Box 7, Lee Vining, CA 93541 (no phone reservations), two miles east of the Tioga Pass entrance. This resort is mostly geared towards fishermen and offers self-contained cabins rented by the week only ($665–825), and motel units let with a two-night minimum ($70). There is a grocery store and diner on site and the site is handy for visits to Tuolumne Meadows, less than ten miles away, but you're a long way from the Yosemite Valley heartland.

APPROACHING FROM THE WEST: GROVELAND, COULTERVILLE, MARIPOSA

Better bets for bases outside of the park are the western towns, particularly tiny **GROVELAND**, forty miles from the Valley on Hwy-120, which retains verandahed wooden sidewalks and exudes a liberal air. South of here, and slightly off the main routes into the park, lies ancient **COULTERVILLE**, the entirety of its diminutive heart listed as a State Historical Site. Most of the buildings and covered boardwalks date back to the mid-nineteenth-century when this was on the main stage route into Yosemite. Travelers often stayed at the George Coulter's Hotel, now transformed into a small local **museum** (Feb–April Sat & Sun 10am–4pm, May–Dec Wed–Sun 10am–4pm; donations welcome), while others – John Muir and Theodore Roosevelt among them – stayed across the road at *Hotel Jeffrey* (see "Accommodation" on p.342). Built in 1854, it remains the centerpiece of the town, and after a few minutes following the self-guided tour around the old town you should definitely repair to the long wooden bar of the hotel's Magnolia Saloon. Horse tack and mining paraphernalia hang from the ceiling, old aquatints and prints cover the walls, and there might even be someone bashing away at the honky-tonk piano in the corner.

Further south, Hwy-140 runs through the bustling Gold Rush town of **MARIPOSA**, 45 miles from the Valley, which, in the **Mariposa Country Courthouse**, corner of Jones and 10th streets (June–Aug Fri 6–8pm, Sat & Sun 10am–5pm; free), boasts the oldest law enforcement establishment west of the Mississippi still in continuous use. Built without nails, the lumber was rough-cut from a nearby stand of white pine, and you can still see the saw marks on the hand-planed spectator benches. The town's heritage is further celebrated at the **Museum and History Center**, corner of Jesse and 12th streets (March–Oct daily 10am–4.30pm; Feb, Nov & Dec daily 10am–4pm, Jan closed; donations welcome), mildly diverting for its mock-up of a gold-era store and the large-scale mining paraphernalia scattered outside. In truth, you're better off at the **California State Mining and Mineral Museum**, 2 miles south on Hwy-49 (May–Sept daily except Tues 10am–6pm, Oct–April Wed–Sun 10am–4pm; $3.50), which revels in the glory days of the mid-nineteenth century with realistic reconstructions of a mine and stamp mill plus a vault where, among the assorted treasures, lies the largest single nugget ever uncovered in California, a thirteen-pound chunk valued at over $1 million. There's a very helpful **visitor center** in Mariposa at 5158 Hwy-140 (mid-May to mid-Sept Mon–Sat 8am–9pm Sun 10am–6pm, mid-Sept to mid-May Mon–Sat 8am–5pm Sun closed; ☎966-2456 & 1-800/208-2434, fax 966-4193, *www.yosemite.net/mariposa*) with all you need to know about Yosemite and around.

Further east along Hwy-140, on the way to Yosemite, the small towns of **MIDPINES** and **EL PORTAL** also offer affordable lodging outside of the park (see "Accommodation" on p.342).

APPROACHING FROM THE SOUTH: OAKHURST AND FISH CAMP

Yosemite visitors arriving from the south will come through **OAKHURST**, fifteen miles south of the southern park entrance and fifty miles south of the Valley proper, a growing huddle of malls and sky-high signs for chain hotels and fast-food joints. Nonetheless, it makes a handy base for the southern section of the park and, with your own transport, day trips into the Valley are by no means out of the question. The relocated buildings of the **Fresno Flats Historical Park** (unrestricted access) won't detain you for long, though you should make use of the **Yosemite Sierra Visitors Bureau**, 41729 Hwy-41, 2 miles north of Oakhurst (Mon–Sat 9am–5pm, Sun 9am–4pm; ☎559/683-4636, fax 683-5697, *www.yosemite-sierra.org*), which stocks armloads of information on Yosemite.

The tiny huddle of hotels which makes up **FISH CAMP** lies ten miles north of Oakhurst, handy for Wawona, the Mariposa Grove and something to keep the kids quiet – *The Logger*, 56001 Hwy-41 (March–Oct daily; ☎559/683-7273; $11), an oil-burning train which plies a two-mile track into the forest from where hewn timber was once carted. In the height of summer several trains run each day giving you the option of spending some time at the picnic area in the woods at the far end.

SMARTER THAN THE AVERAGE BEAR

You may never see a **bear** anywhere else in California, but spend a couple of days in Yosemite Valley and you're bound to see one, probably breaking into a car or roaming the campgrounds looking for free food. Banging pans and yelling – from a safe distance, of course – will probably drive them off, but their dependence on human food leads to several bears being shot each year. Do them and yourself a favor by keeping all food and smelly items – deodorant, sun screen, toothpaste etc – either inside your room or the metal lockers in campgrounds; tents do not deter bears, nor do cars. Despite poor eyesight, Yosemite bears have learnt to recognize coolers, bags of groceries and even trash inside vehicles, and once on the trail all the bear needs to do is pop a window by leaning on it or peel back a door with one paw.

Arrival and information

Yosemite is always open: **park entry** costs $20 per vehicle including passengers, $10 for each cyclist, hiker or bus passenger and is valid for seven days. Pay at the ranger stations when you enter, or if they're closed, at the visitor center in the Valley, or when you leave. If you're just passing through and over the Tioga Pass, there's a $5 transit ticket allowing a two-hour passage (three hours from the South Entrance).

On arrival at any of the park entrances you'll be given an excellent map of the park and the pertinent, quarterly *Yosemite Guide* which covers pretty much everything you need to know. If you have more specific inquiries, try the park's most useful **visitor center** at Yosemite Village (daily mid-June to mid-Sept 8am–7pm, mid-Sept to mid-June 8.30am–5pm; ☎209/372-0265), where you can pick up information and maps, including a topographic map ($6) essential for any adventurous walks. There are other visitor centers at **Tuolumne Meadows** (daily July to mid-Oct 9am–7pm; ☎209/372-

---

WINTER IN YOSEMITE

From December to April, those prepared to cope with blocked roads – the Tioga Pass is always closed in winter – and below-freezing temperatures are amply rewarded at Yosemite; thick snow, frozen waterfalls and far fewer people make for almost unimaginable beauty and silence. **Accommodation** is cheaper at these times too, and much easier to obtain, though weekends can still get pretty full. Many low-country **campgrounds** are open, and restrictions on backcountry camping are eased – you'll want a good sleeping bag and tent.

Much of Yosemite is fabulous **skiing** country. Lessons, equipment rental and 45 miles of groomed trails are available at the **Badger Pass Ski Area**, on the road to Glacier Point, accessible via a shuttle from the Valley. All-day lift tickets cost $28 at weekends and $22 midweek. Daily equipment rental will set you back $18 for downhill, $15 for cross-country and $30 for snowboards. Lessons start from $40. There are also various special deals offered from Sunday through Thursday between January and March when guests at *Yosemite Lodge, The Ahwahnee* and the *Wawona Hotel* get a **free ski pass** for the following day. This deal also gives you free entry to the open-air Curry Village **ice skating** rink (normally $5, plus $2 skate rental). If you want someone to take you out on Badger Pass' groomed trails, contact the *Yosemite Cross Country Ski School* (☎209/372-8444), who run all manner of beginners, improvers and Telemark and skating lessons, and lead overnight ski tours.

Be aware if driving into the park that **tire chains** are recommended from November to April and can be rented in towns approaching the Park. Inside the Park, they are only available for sale.

USEFUL CONTACTS	
Campground reservations (from North America) ☎1-800/436-7275	Recorded general park information ☎209/372-0200
Campground reservations (international) ☎301/722-1257	Recorded road information ☎209/372-0200
Lodging reservations ☎559/252-4848	

WEB SITES

Park Service Web site: *www.nps.gov/yose*	Yosemite Fund Web site with details of current conservation projects in the park: *www.yosemitefund.org*
Camping reservations: *reservations.nps.org*	
Yosemite Association Web site with visitor information, a bookstore, weather forecast and video valley tour: *yosemite.org*	YATI, Yosemite Area Traveller Information for lodging and road conditions in the park's vicinity: *www.yosemite.com*
Yosemite Concession Services for park lodging, dining and activities and off-season lodging reservations: *www.yosemitepark.com*	Ansel Adams Gallery: *www.anseladams.com*

0263), at the **Big Oak Flat** entrance (daily July–Sept 8am–6pm; ☎209/379-1899), and **Wawona** (daily mid-May to mid-Sept 8.30am–4.30pm; ☎209/375-9501). For **free** hiking permits, the *Keep it Wild* guide to wilderness trips and all the route planning help you could ask for, pop next door to the **Wilderness Center** (mid-June to early Sept daily 7am–7pm, early Sept to Oct daily 8am–5pm): wilderness permits are self-issued once the Wilderness Center closes.

Useful **phone numbers** and **Web sites** are covered in the box above, and all manner of other services are included in the "Listings" section (see p.352).

Getting around

The three roads from the Central Valley end up at **Yosemite Valley**, roughly in the center of the park's 1200 square miles, and home to its most dramatic scenery. At the southern edge of the park, Hwy-41 passes the **Mariposa Grove** and **Wawona**; from here it's 27 miles further to the Valley. **Tuolumne Meadows** is in the high country, sixty-odd miles northeast of the Valley, close to the Tioga Pass entrance (Hwy-120) on the eastern side of the park.

Free and frequent **shuttle buses** operate on the Valley floor, running anticlockwise on a loop that passes through, or close to, all the main points of interest, trailheads and accommodation areas. In high season they run roughly every ten minutes between 7am and 10pm to most sections of the Valley, with slightly reduced hours at other times. The summer-only **Tuolumne Bus** makes the two-and-a-half hour run to Tuolumne Meadows ($13 one way), leaving hotels around Yosemite Valley around 8.20am and departing Tuolumne at 2.35pm. There's also a **hikers' bus** running up to Glacier Point three times daily through the summer ($10.50 one way), and as far as the Badger Point ski area in winter.

Cars spoil everybody's fun on the valley floor; if you're driving in just for the day, leave your vehicle in the day-use parking lot at Curry Village. In any case, **cycling** is the best way to get around: a number of good bicycle paths cross the valley floor, but bike rental is limited to the outlets at *Yosemite Lodge* and *Curry Village* (April–Nov only) which charge $5 per hour or $20 per day. Bikes are basic machines, but since cycling is only allowed on asphalt surfaces, that's all you need: leave your mountain bike at home.

ROCK CLIMBING

Rock climbers the world over flock to Yosemite, drawn by the challenge of inching up three-thousand-foot walls of sheer granite which soar skyward under the California sun. Quite simply, the Valley is seen as the pinnacle of climbing aspiration with acres of superb, clean rock, easily accessible world-class routes and reliable summer weather drawing a vibrant climbing community bubbling over with campfire tales.

The best place to marvel at climbers' antics is **El Cap Meadows**, always dotted with tourists craning their necks and training binoculars on the biggest slab of granite of them all, El Capitan. The apparently featureless face hides hairline crack systems a thousand feet long, seemingly insurmountable overhangs and gargantuan towers topped off with narrow ledges only given any sense of scale by the flea-like figures of climbers. If you can't spot them, look for their haul sacks; or come out here after dark and when the light from head torches and the faint, distant chatter give the game away.

The routes are highly convoluted, but the most famous, **The Nose** route of El Capitan, lies straight ahead, tracing a line up the prow of the cliff and passing the relative luxury of El Cap Towers. This twenty-foot by six-foot patio, over 1500 feet above the valley floor, is used as a bivvy spot by climbers who typically spend three to five nights on the route. "In-a-day" attempts usually involve 24 hours of continuous climbing, though the current record stands at an astounding four hours and twenty minutes. The famous **North American Wall** route lies to the right passing directly through a massive stain on the rock which looks remarkably like a map of North America.

BATHOOKS AND BUGABOOS

Many of the most celebrated routes in Yosemite are what's known as "Big Wall" routes, tackled by **aid climbing**, where bits of metal are hammered into cracks and hauled on to achieve upward movement. The demands of ever harder climbs have pushed the development of an extensive armory that's totally baffling to the uninitiated: bathooks, birdbeaks, bongs, bugaboos, circleheads, fifi hooks, a funkness device, lost arrows and RURPs are all employed either to grapple a ledge or wedge into cracks of different sizes. The scale of Yosemite's walls is such that few cracks can be followed from bottom to top and to get from one crack to another, climbers employ death-defying **pendulums**, and repeatedly sweep across the face gaining momentum until they can lunge out at a tiny flake or fingertip hold. All this "nailing" and swinging takes time and most Big Wallers are forced to spend nights slung in a kind of lightweight camp bed known as a **portaledge**. Food, gallons of water, sleeping bags, warm clothing and wet weather gear must all be lugged up in haul sacks, along with a boombox and a rack of cassettes deviously strapped and arranged so they can't be dropped – after all it can get a bit tedious hammering away up there for hours on end. As Yosemite veteran John Long writes: "Climbing a wall can be a monumental pain in the ass. No one could pay you enough to do it. A thousand dollars would be too little by far. But you wouldn't sell the least of the memories for ten times than sum."

SOME HISTORY

Yosemite has long captured the imagination of climbers but technical rock climbing didn't kick off here until 1933, when four Bay Area climbers reached what is now known as the Lunch Ledge, 1000 feet up Washington Column – the tower opposite Half Dome – using hemp ropes to afford meager protection in case of a fall. With the aid of heavy steel **pitons** for driving into cracks, and equally weighty **carabiners** for attaching the ropes to the pitons, climbers began to knock off climbs such as the fifteen-pitch **Royal Arches** route which weaves its way up the ledges and slabs behind the *Ahwahnee Hotel*.

After WWII, demobbed climbers employed newly developed, tough nylon ropes and lightweight safety equipment to push standards to new levels, and pipe dreams became realistic propositions. An early conquest, in 1947, was **Lost Arrow Spire**, which rises to the right of Yosemite Falls and is easy to spot in the early morning and late afternoon light when the spire casts a shadow on the wall nearby. This was the first route intentionally approached as a multi-day ascent, much of the groundwork being laid by Swiss-born blacksmith **John Salathé**. He was at the cutting edge of climbing, putting up technically demanding aid routes through the late 1940s and early 1950s, and even fashioning his own tougher carbon-steel pitons from the axles of a Model A Ford.

For the next twenty years Salathé's mantle was assumed by classical purist **Royal Robbins** and **Warren Harding**, who was prepared to bang in a piton just about anywhere if it would help him get up something new. Little love was lost between them but, in 1957, they formed the backbone of a team which scaled the face of **Half Dome**, a magnificent effort which ranked as the hardest climb in North America at the time. Yosemite became an international forcing ground for aid climbing, and Americans were suddenly matching, and even surpassing, the achievements of previously dominant Europeans.

Now even the mighty El Cap seemed possible. **The Nose** was the most obvious line but refused to submit for seventeen months, even after Warren Harding fashioned four massive pitons from stove legs scavenged from the Berkeley city dump and drove them into what are still known as the Stoveleg Cracks. Harding and two colleagues finally topped out in 1958 after a single thirteen-day push, the culmination of 47 days work on the route.

With these critical ascents completed, climbers' aspirations broadened and the 1960s became the **Golden Age** of climbing in the Yosemite Valley, when it drew a motley collection of dropouts and misfits, many ranking among the world's finest climbers. Almost all the major walls and hundreds of minor routes were completed at this time. Purists at the top of their sport became disenchanted with the artificiality of aid ascents and began to "free" pitches; not hauling up on the all the hardware, but using it only for protection in case of a fall. The culmination of years of cutting-edge climbing, and months of route-specific training was Lynn Hill's ground-breaking free ascent of The Nose in 1993, praised and admired by all, if ruefully by some in Yosemite's traditionally macho climbing community.

PRACTICALITIES

The **best months** for climbing in the Yosemite Valley are April, May, September and October. In summer, the climbs on the domes around Tuolumne Meadows are cooler and usually considered a better bet. Some areas, notably the southeast face of El Capitan, are occasionally off limits to protect the nesting sites of peregrine falcons. Whatever type of climbing you do, follow the guidelines for "**minimum impact climbing**" – never chip holds or add bolts to existing routes, and remove all litter, including human waste.

Everyone stays at the bohemian **Camp 4** (aka *Sunnyside Walk-In* campground), near *Yosemite Lodge*, a trampled, dusty and noisy site often entirely taken over by climbers. It is relatively cheap, with a great sense of camaraderie, and an excellent **bulletin board** for teaming up with climbing partners, selling gear, organizing a ride or just meeting friends. Normally you can only stay for seven nights at a stretch, but after the middle of September you're allowed to settle in for a month.

For a more organized introduction to the climber's craft or to brush up on a few skills, engage the services of the Yosemite Mountaineering School which is based a Tuolumne Meadows in summer (June–Aug, ☎209/372-8435) and in Yosemite Valley in spring and autumn (☎209/372-8344). Experts run daily courses ranging from the one-day beginners' classes ($70–85) through various intermediate classes to private full-day guided climbs (one person $220, two people $155 each).

Rock-climbing **gear** is available from the Mountain Shop in Tuolumne Meadows (summer only), and the well-stocked and competitively-priced Mountain Shop in *Curry Village* (daily 8am–6pm).

The essential **guidebooks** to local climbs are Don Reid's *Yosemite: Free Climbs* and *Yosemite: Big Walls*, published by Falcon Guides. To catch something of the spirit of the scene, read *Camp 4: Recollections of a Yosemite Rockclimber* (The Mountaineers) by Yosemite veteran Steve Roper, and *The Vertical World of Yosemite* (Wilderness Press), a collection of inspiring stories on the Valley, both available in the Ansel Adams Gallery. You can also glean something of what it is all about by checking out the interesting rock-climbing **exhibition** in the *Ahwahnee Hotel* Cocktail Bar and the additional displays in the Winter Club Room and the Indian Room, both off the Great Hall.

Failing that, there are always **guided tours** (☎209/372-1240), which range from the rather dull two-hour valley floor spin, costing $17.50, to the all-day Mariposa and Glacier Point Grand Tour (June–Nov) at $45; all bookable through accommodation reception areas.

Accommodation

Once in the park, **accommodation** can be a problem; it's almost essential to book well in advance and anything other than camping can be surprisingly expensive. Even canvas tents cost what you would pay for a reasonable motel elsewhere. All accommodation in the national park – the majority of it right in the Valley – is operated by **Yosemite Concession Services** (YCS; 5410 East Home, Fresno, CA 93727; ☎209/252-4848, *www.yosemitepark.com*) and can be reserved up to a year and a day in advance, though a few weeks is adequate at most times. Places generally reduce their charges in winter, though weekend prices remain close to high season levels. One solution to the problem is to stay just outside the park (see "Approaching Yosemite" on p.336) and commute into it daily.

If you are really well organized you might also want to consider the High Sierra Camp Vacations (see "Listings," p.353).

In the Valley

Ahwahnee Hotel, a short distance from Yosemite Village at shuttle stop 4 (call YCS). Unless you strike lucky, you'll need to book months in advance to stay in this wonderfully grand but surprisingly low-key hotel (see p.347), though it is well worth popping in for a look around, a coffee or a meal. ⑨.

Curry Village, a mile from Yosemite Village at shuttle stops 1 and 14 (call YCS). A large area dotted mostly with canvas tent cabins each fitted with four beds on a wooden plinth. There are also cramped solid-walled cabins and spacious motel-style rooms. Tents ② cabins ④ rooms ⑤.

Housekeeping Camp, half a mile from Yosemite Village at shuttle stop 12 (call YCS). Ranks of simple canvas tent cabins with beds on sleeping platforms and the use of a fire grate and picnic table. Mid-March to late Oct only. ②.

Yosemite Lodge, half a mile west of Yosemite Village (call YCS). Sprawling site popular with tour groups, its proximity to half-decent restaurants and grocery shops making it perhaps the most convenient accommodation in the Valley. It has reasonable wooden huts with and without bath, and much nicer regular rooms, though all need to be booked well in advance for most of the year. ⑤.

The rest of the park

Tuolumne Meadows Lodge, Tuolumne Meadows (call YCS). A large cluster of canvas tent cabins each with four beds and a stove, but no electricity, located at nearly 9000ft and perfect for the first or last night of a long hiking trip. Only available late April to Oct. Meals served. ③.

Wawona Hotel, Wawona (call YCS; front desk ☎209/375-6556). An elegant hotel, parts of which date from 1879. Rooms are comfortable though smallish and over-modernized, but the marvelous public areas and distinctive wooden veranda with white wicker chairs make it all worthwhile. There's also a pool, tennis courts and a nine-hole golf course in the grounds. ⑤.

White Wolf Lodge, about halfway from the Valley to Tuolumne Meadows (call YCS). Primitive tent cabins perfectly sited for day hikes to Lukens and Harden Lakes, and the Grand Canyon of the Tuolumne River. May–Sept only. ③.

Yosemite Falls B&B, 7210 Yosemite Park Way, Yosemite West (☎209/375-1414, *www.yosemitefalls.com*). Extravagant B&B where rooms all have private bath, satellite TV, VCR and a complimentary bottle of bubbly. Spend the evening around the bar's pool table then fortify yourself for another day's sightseeing with a huge breakfast. Located in a small enclave fourteen miles from the Valley, just outside the national park but only accessible from Wawona Road. ⑦.

Yosemite Peregrine, 7509 Henness Circle, Yosemite West (1-800/396-3639 or 209/372-8517, fax 372-4241, *www.yosemitewest.com/falcons*). Well-appointed B&B a few blocks from the Yosemite Falls B&B, tastefully decorated in Southwestern or woodsy themes, and with a hot tub. Home cooked breakfast is served on the deck if the weather cooperates. The adjacent *Falcon's Nest* (same contact details) has a couple of more budget-oriented rooms and a two night minimum (④). ⑦.

Hwy-120: Groveland and Coulterville

Hotel Charlotte, 18959 Hwy-120, Groveland (☎209/962-6455). Old-fashioned hotel, dating back to 1921, that's in good condition with small rooms, some with private bath. ④.

Hotel Jeffery, jcn Hwy-49 & Hwy-132, Coulterville (☎1-800/464-3471 & 209/878-3471, fax 878-3473). Classic gold-era hotel used by original Yosemite sightseers as well as John Muir and Theodore Roosevelt. Accommodation is in smallish, old-fashioned but well-kept rooms, some with private bath, others with just a basin in the room, but all with access to a communal lounge and sunny deck. ④.

Groveland Hotel, 18767 Hwy-120, Groveland (☎1-800/273-3314 & 209/962-4000, fax 962-6674, *www.groveland.com*). Gorgeous mining-era hotel with luxurious individually-styled antique-filled rooms mostly with deep baths. Suites (⑧) feature spa tubs and real fires. ⑥.

Groveland Motel, 18933 Hwy-120, Groveland (☎209/962-7865, fax 962-0664). Woodsy air-conditioned cabins with TV at what for these parts are bargain rates (④), plus an assortment of mobile homes (⑥), a three-bedroom house that sleeps six (⑦) and even some teepees fitted out with beds (②).

Yosemite Lakes Inn, 31191 Hwy-120, eighteen miles east of Groveland (☎1-800/533-1001 or 209/962-0121, fax 962-5534). Combined hostel (with limited self-catering facilities), campground and RV site in the middle of nowhere. Simple double rooms (②), cabins (②) and four-berth tent-cabins equipped with satellite TV (④) are scattered around among the $12 tent sites. Not especially appealing but close to the park.

Hwy-140: Mariposa, Midpines and El Portal

Comfort Inn, 4994 Bullion Street (☎1-800/321-5261 or 209/966-4344). Comfortable motel with helpful staff and outdoor pool; part of a national chain. ④.

5th Street Inn, cnr 5th and Bullion streets, Mariposa (☎1-800/867-8584 or 209/966-6048). Luxurious B&B with a nice sunny veranda and a/c rooms all equipped with cable TV, and some with a kitchenette. ④.

Mariposa Lodge, 5052 Hwy-140, Mariposa (☎1-800/341-8000 or 209/966-3607, fax 742-7038). Good value motel right on Mariposa's main street with outdoor pool, spa and spacious rooms equipped with coffee filters, HBO and VCRs. ④.

Sierra View Motel, 4993 Seventh St, Mariposa (☎1-800/627-8439 or 209/966-5793, fax 742-5669). Peaceful, welcoming and good value motel just off Mariposa's main drag offering continental breakfast with smallish a/c rooms and larger suites. ④.

Yosemite Bug Hostel, 6979 Hwy-140, Midpines,10 miles east of Mariposa (☎209/966-6666, fax 966-6667, *www.yosemitebug.com*). Numerous buildings scattered through the woods operate as a HI-AYH hostel without the usual limitations. Individually-decorated rooms come with kitsch artwork, dorms ($15 each) are clean and comfortable, and there are double rooms (②, ③ with private bath), and on-site tents ($17 for two). As well as self-catering facilities, there's the licensed *Recovery Café* (see "Eating" on p.345) with low-cost Internet access. Its location, 35 miles west of the Valley and well placed on the *VIA Yosemite Connection* bus route from Merced, makes it the handiest budget lodgings near Yosemite. Mountain bike rental ($12 a day).

Yosemite View Lodge, 11136 Hwy-140, one mile east of El Portal (☎1-800/321-5261, fax 742-7189, *www.yosemite-motels.com*). Vast, luxurious and slightly soulless complex beside the Merced River featuring rooms with kitchenettes, and some with riverside balconies and whirlpool baths. This is about as close to the park as you can get without being in it. ⑥.

Hwy-41: Oakhurst and Fish Camp

Hounds Tooth Inn, 42071 Hwy-41, almost three miles north of Oakhurst (☎1-888/642-6610 or 559/642-6600, fax 658-2946; *www.houndstoothinn.com*). New and luxurious bed and breakfast with a dozen individually-decorated rooms, most with either a fireplace or a spa bath and all air-conditioned. Complimentary wine served each evening and there are delicious buffet breakfasts. ⑥.

Narrow Gauge Inn, 48571 Hwy-41, Fish Camp (☎1-888/644-9050 or 559/683-7720, *www.narrowgaugeinn.com*). Cozy rooms, most with balconies and forest views, and an easy stroll to the establishment's fine restaurant and bar. ⑤.

Owl's Nest B&B, 1235 Hwy-41, Fish Camp (☎559/683-3484, fax 683-2486, *owlsnest@sierratel.com*). About the best deal on the southern side of the park, with large guest rooms for two (④) and self-contained chalets (⑥) each with deck and barbecue, which will sleep up to six ($15 per extra person). Nicely decorated, friendly and right by a stream.

Ramada, 48800 Royal Oaks Drive, Oakhurst (☎1-800/658-2888 or 559/658 5500, fax 658-5505). Brand new and slightly soulless chain hotel, but with large airy rooms, cable TV, outdoor pool and spa, and a complimentary breakfast. ⑤.

Snowline Lodge, 42150 Hwy-41, 3 miles north of Oakhurst (☎ & fax 559/683-5854). Small, cozy cabins with bathrooms and TV, plus an outdoor pool. Great value. ③.

Tenaya Lodge, 1122 Hwy-41, Fish Camp (☎1-800/635-5807 or 559/683-6555, fax 683-0249). Extensive establishment that's a cross between a conference hotel and a holiday camp with over 200 modern comfortable rooms, three on-site restaurants open to all-comers, including a good deli and coffee shop, indoor and outdoor pools, free sauna, hot tubs and gym, and all sorts of outdoor activities like mountain biking, horseback riding and guided hiking. Midweek winter rates can drop as low as $80, but in summer it pays to reserve well in advance to get anything. In shoulder seasons rates can drop to $130. ⑧.

White Chief Mountain Lodge, 7776 White Chief Mountain Rd, Fish Camp (☎559/683-5444, fax 683-2615). Basic and functional but clean motel units for two (④)and nicer cabins for up to four (⑥). Just 300yd off Hwy-41 and with a very good on-site restaurant. Closed Nov–March.

Yosemite Fish Camp B&B, Hwy-41, Fish Camp (☎ & fax 559/683-7426, *bazhowley@sierratel.com*). Attractive and homey B&B with a highly entertaining host, a couple of bargain rooms sharing a bathroom (③) and one bathroom-equipped room. A full breakfast is served. ④.

Camping

As with any national park, **camping** is the best way to really feel part of your surroundings, though this is perhaps less true in Yosemite Valley where the campgrounds are large and crowded. You can, and should, book beforehand (☎1-800/436-7275; from outside the US or Canada ☎301/722-1257; *reservations.nps.gov*): reservations open in one month chunks, four months in advance, so to book for the month beginning July 15 you can, and should, call from March 15 (7am–7pm Pacific time). Otherwise you'll need to show up at the Curry Village Reservations Office very early in the morning and hope for cancellations. Other than the *Camp 4*, all sites cost $15 and none have **showers** or **laundry** facilities (see "Listings," p.352). Camping in the Valley is restricted to a month in any calendar year but between May and mid-September a week is the maximum stay.

In addition to the main campgrounds there are **backpacker campgrounds** in Yosemite Valley, Tuolumne Meadows and Hetch Hetchy, designed for hikers about to start (or just finishing) a wilderness trip and costing $3 per night. People with vehicles who are heading into the backcountry can stay at these sites for one night at the beginning and end of the trip. Camping outside recognized sites in the Valley is strictly forbidden.

Finally, with enough time you really should get out to one of the many **primitive campgrounds** in the backcountry. Designed specifically for hikers, these have fire rings and some form of water source, which must be treated. To use them, or to camp elsewhere in the backcountry, you must get a **free wilderness permit** (see "Hiking" box, p.352) – as ever, you must camp a mile from any road, four miles from a populated area, and at least a hundred yards from water sources and trails. Remember to carry a stove and fuel as indiscriminate use of trees could jeopardize future freedom to camp in the backcountry. Camping on the summit of Half Dome is not permitted.

IN THE VALLEY

Camp 4 (all year; $3 per person; 4000ft). West of and away from the other valley sites, and very popular with rock climbers who recently succeeded in getting the park service to recognize their name and ditch the previous title of *Sunnyside Walk-in*. Each plot is just a few yards from the inadequate parking spaces. The campground is non-reservable and often full by 9am, especially in spring and fall when climbers are here in numbers; join the line early.

North Pines, Upper Pines, Lower Pines (March–Oct; $15; 4000ft). Largely indistinguishable, pine-shrouded sites, all with toilets, water and fire rings. Popular with RV users. Reservations essential.

OUTSIDE THE VALLEY

Bridalveil Creek (July–early Sept; $10; 7200ft). High country first-come-first-served site off Glacier Point Road with good access to wilderness trails.

Carlon (April–Nov; free; 4400ft). Just outside the park in the surrounding Stanislaus National Forest. Spacious sites with vault toilets but no water. Take Evergreen Road north for a mile and a half.

Crane Flat (June–Sept; $15; 6200ft). Northwest of the Valley, at the start of Hwy-120 and close to a stand of sequoias. Reservations required.

Hodgdon Meadow (all year; $15; 4900ft). Relatively quiet site right on the park's western boundary just off Hwy-120. Take Old Big Oak Flat Road for half a mile. Reservations required May–Sept, first-come-first-served at other times.

Middle Fork (all year; free; 4300ft). Half a mile south of and similar to the *Carlon* site.

Porcupine Flat (July–early Sept; $6; 8100ft). Attractive and small site near the road to Tuolumne Meadows, nearly forty miles from the valley. Stream water.

Tamarack Flat (June–early Sept; $6; 6300ft). Small site two miles off the Hwy-120 Tioga road, 23 miles from the Valley and with only limited RV access. Stream water.

Tuolumne Meadows (July–Sept; $15; 8600ft). A streamside site in a sub-alpine meadow. It's popular with backpackers and car-campers alike, but you'll probably find a place. Several walk-in sites are reserved for hikers who wish to camp away from vehicles. Showers ($2) are available nearby. When this campground is full, or closed, campers head to either *Porcupine Flat, White Wolf,* or a cluster of campgrounds in the Inyo National Forest around ten miles east over the Tioga Pass. Here you'll find the RV-dominated sites, *Tioga Lake* ($11), the less appealing *Junction* ($6), and *Saddlebag Lake* ($11), located two miles north of Hwy-120. Close to Saddlebag Lake is the *Sawmill Walk-in* ($6), around four hundred yards from its parking lot amid jagged peaks that feel a world away from the glaciated domes around Tuolumne. There are yet more campgrounds – *Boulder, Aspen, Big Bend, Moraine* and *Lower Lee Vining* ($7–11), all streamside on Poole Power Plant Road around seven miles closer to Lee Vining.

Wawona (all year; $15; 4000ft). The only site in the southern sector of the park, approximately a mile north of the *Wawona Hotel*. Some walk-in sites are reserved for car-free campers. Reservations required May–Sept.

White Wolf (July–early Sept; $10; 8000ft). First-come-first-served tent and RV site a mile north of Hwy-120 midway between the Valley and Tuolumne Meadows.

Yosemite Creek (July to early Sept; $6; 7600ft). First-come-first-served tent-only site ideal for escaping the crowds, though it can fill up very quickly in the summer. Inconveniently sited five miles off Hwy-120, but almost equidistant between the Valley and Tuolumne Meadows. Stream water.

Eating, drinking and entertainment

With the notable exception of the *Ahwahnee Dining Room* (see below), **eating** in Yosemite is a function rather than a pleasure. Food, whether in restaurants or in the grocery stores around Yosemite Village (where there's a well-stocked supermarket), *Curry Village*, Wawona and Tuolumne Meadows, is much more expensive inside the park than out. **Outside the valley**, the choice is considerably better with plenty of good restaurants and a smattering of bars in the gateway towns of Groveland, Mariposa and Oakhurst.

Yosemite Village is the center of the park's **evening entertainment**, in the form of talks, photographic shows and even theatrical productions. The *Yosemite Guide* has the full program (and see "Listings" on p.352). *Yosemite Lodge* and the *Ahwahnee Hotel* have the valley's liveliest **bars**.

In the Valley

Ahwahnee Cocktail Lounge, *Ahwahnee Hotel* (noon–10.30pm). Inappropriately-named but a real find, this admirable café and bar serves good coffee, beer and the likes of chicken *quesedilla* and chocolate espresso torte in dark wood and stone surroundings at much the same prices you pay elsewhere in the park for inferior goods.

Ahwahnee Dining Room, *Ahwahnee Hotel* (☎209/372-1489; reserve well in advance). Quite simply one of the most beautiful restaurants in the US, in baronial style and serving by far the best food in Yosemite – especially in winter when it brings in top chefs for weekend gourmandizing. À la carte dining on, say, crab and avocado cocktail followed by roast duckling costs around $50 for three courses with wine. Jacket and tie preferred though not essential; breakfast and lunch are more casual and appreciably cheaper, and there is a stupendous Sunday brunch ($20).

Curry Village. The home of assorted food outlets – cafeteria, ice cream shop, burger bar – but mostly notable for the terrace where you fight for a table while you wait for a fairly good pizza and a pitcher of daiquiris or margaritas.

Degnan's Deli, Yosemite Village (daily 7am–10pm). Some of the best snacking in the Valley with massive sandwiches, burritos and salads at under $5; or go upstairs to the Pasta Place, where you can fill up with salad, pasta and a drink for around $10.

Yosemite Lodge, Yosemite Village. Casual dining in the *Garden Terrace*, where an $8 pasta and salad bar operates from noon to 8.30pm, with meat from the carvery an extra $4. There's also the fairly pricey, evening-only à la carte *Mountain Room Restaurant*, which serves grilled trout and rack of lamb for around $16, a downbeat cafeteria and the lively *Mountain Room Bar*.

The rest of the park

Tuolumne Meadows Grill, Tuolumne Meadows. Basically a burger joint, also serving cheap breakfasts and sandwich lunches.

Tuolumne Meadows Lodge, (☎209/372-1313). Family-style breakfasts and dinners at moderate prices served in tents beside the Tuolumne River.

Wawona Hotel Dining Room at the *Wawona Hotel* (☎209/375-6556). Relatively formal dining in a grand room with white linen tablecloths. Expect to fork out $40 for an evening meal of smoked trout or roast corn chowder followed by rib eye steak. Lunch goes for $10.

White Wolf Lodge, Just off Hwy-120 on the way to Tuolumne (☎209/252-4848). Large portions of good value American food in rustic surroundings.

Hwy-120: Groveland

Cocina Michoacana, 13955 Hwy-120. Excellent, authentic and low-priced Mexican specializing in dishes from immediately west of Mexico City.

Coffee Express, 18961 Main St. The place to be for standard American breakfasts and well-cooked diner fare; espresso too.

Groveland Hotel, 18767 Hwy-120, (☎1-800/273-3314). Lovely restaurant (in keeping with the rest of the hotel) serving the likes of crab cakes with cilantro and caper sauce, and poached salmon. Expect to pay $40–50 for three courses including a glass or two from their award-winning wine list.

PJ's Café, 18986 Hwy-120. Good-value diner serving burgers and sandwiches all day and pizza from 4pm.

Hwy-140: Mariposa, Midpines and El Portal

Castillo's, 4995 5th Street, Mariposa. Small Mexican restaurant offering a cozy atmosphere with good portions of decent home-cooked meals at around $10, fajitas for around $12 and juicy steaks for a little more.

Happy Burger, Hwy-140 at 12th St, Mariposa. Good cheap diner food eaten in booths fitted with jukebox consoles and decorated with Seventies album covers. Take-out available.

Meadows Ranch Café, 5027 Hwy-140, Mariposa. Excellent all-day combination of family restaurant – with delectable sandwiches, burgers and grills – juice bar, café and bar.

Recovery Café, at Yosemite Bug Hostel, Midpines. Superb value licensed café serving wholesome breakfasts ($4–5), packed lunches ($5.50) and dinners ($7–11) to all-comers, not just hostel guests.

Sal's, 5081 Hwy-140, Mariposa. Fine Mexican fare in a fun atmosphere at great prices.

Hwy-41: Oakhurst and Fish Camp

Castillo's, 49271 Golden Oak Loop, behind the *Talking Bear* in Oakhurst. Larger sister restaurant to the Mariposa establishment and equally good.

El Cid, 41939 Hwy-41. Reasonable Tex-Mex belly-filler with a strong line in frosty margaritas.

Firefall Café, cnr Hwy-41 & Hwy-49 (☎559/641-7373). Cavernous, moderately priced restaurant doing a good line in gourmet pizza – caramelized onion, roasted vegetables, etc – Chinese barbecue ribs, or tarragon chicken followed by espresso and dessert.

The Narrow Gauge Inn, 48571 Hwy-41, Fish Camp (☎559/683-6446). Fine dining in an old world setting where you can start by dipping sourdough into a rich fondue and continue with charbroiled swordfish or filet mignon. Expect to pay $40 each, more with wine.

Yosemite Coffee Roasting Company, 40879 Hwy-41, a mile north of Oakhurst. Local java joint with savory muffins, sandwiches and cakes.

White Chief Mountain Lodge, Hwy-41, just outside the park at Fish Camp (☎559/683-5444). Simple surroundings, but great value for steaks, fish and sandwiches.

Yosemite Valley

Even the most evocative photography can only hint at the pleasure to be found in simply gazing at **Yosemite Valley**. From massive hunks of granite rising five thousand feet up from the four-thousand-foot valley floor to the subtle colorings of wild flowers, the variations in the valley can be both enormous and discreet. Aside from just looking, there are many easy walks around the lush fields to waterfalls and lakes, and much tougher treks up the enormous cliffs (see box, p.352). Whichever way you decide to see it, the valley's concentration of natural grandeur is quite memorable. If there is any drawback, it's that this part of Yosemite is the busiest, and you're rarely far from other visitors or the park's commercial trappings: a couple of days exploring the Valley leaves you more than ready to press on to the park's less populated regions.

Yosemite Village

Very much the heart of things in the Valley, **YOSEMITE VILLAGE** has shops, restaurants, banking facilities, a post office (see "Listings" on p.352 for the last two) and one of the park's **visitor centers** (see p.338). Beside the visitor center, the small but interesting **Yosemite Museum and Indian Village of Ahwahnee** (daily: June–Aug 8am–5.30pm, Sept–May 8am–4.30pm; free), comprises a roomful of artifacts from the local Native Americans (including some very fine basketwork) and, outside, a self-guided trail around a reconstructed group of their buildings. There's something of the more recent past to be found in the nearby **cemetery**, which holds the unkempt graves of some of the early white settlers who attempted to farm the valley, and often perished in its isolation. By contrast, and worth a quick look even if you don't intend to stay or eat there, is the **Ahwahnee Hotel**, a short signposted walk or shuttle bus ride from Yosemite Village. It was built in grand style in 1927 from local rock, and is decorated with Native American motifs and some wonderful rugs and carpets. It was intended to blend into its surroundings and attract the richer type of tourist and still does both fairly effortlessly – pop in for a few minutes to sink into the deep sofas, view the collection of paintings of Yosemite's early days, or browse the rock climbing and skiing exhibitions in the Cocktail Lounge and the Winter Club Room off the Great Hall.

The Valley floor

There's little around the village to divert attention from Yosemite's beckoning **natural features** for long. It's true that you'll never be alone on the Valley floor, but most of the crowds can be easily left behind by taking any path which contains much of a slope. The more strenuous hikes are detailed below.

One of the more popular easy strolls is to **Lower Yosemite Falls** (shuttle bus stop 7) just a few minutes' walk from *Yosemite Lodge*, at the western end of the Valley. Come towards the end of summer and the falls disappear altogether, but in spring ice-cold melt-water thunders down three hundred feet, drenching onlookers in spray. If this inspires you, consider the walk to the far more impressive **Upper Yosemite Falls**, which crash down almost 1500ft in a single cascade. Together with the cataracts in between, the two drop the Yosemite River 2500ft, constituting the highest fall in North America.

Three other waterfalls can be easily reached from the Valley. One of the more sensual is the 600-foot **Bridalveil Falls**, a slender ribbon at the Valley's western end which in Ahwahneechee goes by the name of *Pohono*, "spirit of the puffing wind." The base of the falls is at the end of a quarter-mile trail from a parking lot four miles west of the village and is not on the shuttle route. More rugged routes head up Little Yosemite Valley to the 300-foot **Vernal Falls** and the 600-foot **Nevada Falls** beyond – the only two cascades guaranteed to be still active in September and October.

Perhaps one of the most rewarding of the easy trails leads from shuttle stop 17 around the edge of the valley floor to **Mirror Lake** (2 miles; 1hr; 100ft ascent). This compellingly calm lake lies beneath the great bulk of Half Dome (see below), the rising cliff reflected on the lake's surface, and is best seen in the early morning, before too many others arrive. The lake is a microcosm of the whole Yosemite Valley, its meditative stillness due in part to the fact that it's slowly silting up as the valley floor has done since the last Ice Age: already the lake dries up by summer's end but re-emerges each spring. From Mirror Lake, trails continue around the lake (1 mile), to Tenaya Lake (11 miles) and to Tuolumne Meadows (21 miles). Most visitors to Mirror Lake follow the traffic-free paved road from the shuttle stop, but several easily found diversions steer you clear of the asphalt and the crowds.

Fans of John Muir and Ansel Adams (see boxes on pp.335 and 350) might like to pop along to the **LeConte Memorial Lodge** (April–Sept Wed–Sun 10am–4pm; free; shuttle stop 12), built by the Sierra Club to commemorate one of its original members, Joseph LeConte, an eminent scholar who died in Yosemite but whose wishes to be buried here were ignored. The granite block structure was formerly the Sierra Club's headquarters and Adams managed it for a couple of summers in the early 1920s. It now contains a library and displays on the Sierra Club and offers a free program of nature walks (Thurs–Sun 10am–noon) and educational lectures and slide shows (Fri–Sun 8pm).

The big cliffs: El Capitan and Half Dome

Of the two major peaks that you can see from the Valley, **El Capitan**, rising some 3600ft above the floor, is the biggest piece of exposed granite in the world. Though undoubtedly a domineering presence, its enormous size isn't really apparent until you join the slack-jawed tourists craning their necks and pointing binoculars and cameras at rock climbers on the face. Eventually you'll pick out flea-sized specks inching up what is the holy grail of rock-climbing worldwide (see box on p.340).

Much the same applies to **Half Dome**, the sheerest cliff in North America, only seven degrees off the vertical and topping out at 8842 feet, almost 5000 feet above the valley floor. A true sense of its bulk, and the amazingly sheer face, is best appreciated from Glacier Point (see below), but better still, you can hike to its top from the far end of Little Yosemite Valley. The final 400 feet of ascent is by way of a steep staircase hooked on to its curving whale back which leaves you at the nearly-flat summit, where the brave or foolish can inch out along a finger of rock projecting out from the lip. The steps and cable supports stay in place throughout the summer (May to mid-Oct) and the cables remain all year making a winter ascent difficult but possible.

Views of the Valley: Glacier Point, Taft Point and Sentinel Dome

The most spectacular views of Yosemite Valley are from **Glacier Point**, the top of a 3200-foot almost sheer cliff, 32 miles by road (usually open mid-May to late Oct) from the Valley. It's possible to get there on foot using the very steep four-mile track (see the box on p.352) which begins at the western end of the Valley, beside Hwy-41, though you can use the bus (see p.339) to take you up on a longer road route and then hike the trail down. The valley floor lies directly beneath the viewing point, and there are tremendous views across to Half Dome (easy from here to see how it got its name) and to the distant snowcapped summits of the High Sierra. In winter, one of the best **cross-country ski** trips is the eight miles here from the Badger Pass ski area.

The road to Glacier Point passes a number of signposted trailheads for easy and longer hikes. One of the best is to the 8122-foot summit of **Sentinel Dome** (2 miles round-trip), a gleaming granite scalp topped by a gnarled and much photographed skeleton of a Jeffrey pine which still bore cones until a few years ago when a drought finally killed it off. From the Sentinel Dome parking lot, a second dusty, undulating trail leads west to **Taft Point** (2 miles round-trip), which trades Glacier Point's Half Dome vista for a view across the Valley to the of the top of El Capitan and Yosemite Falls. Far fewer people follow this trail, perhaps because of the vertiginous drops all around, only protected by the flimsiest of barriers in one spot. Here, the granite edges have been deeply incised to form the **Taft Point Fissures**.

Outside the Valley

However crowded the Valley might be, the rest of the park sees very few tourists. Even places you can get to by car, like **Wawona** and **Mariposa Grove** on the park's southern edge, remain peaceful most of the time, and if you're willing to hike a few miles and camp out overnight, you've got the 99 percent of Yosemite that's untouched by road; acres of pristine scenery, especially around **Tuolumne Meadows** on the park's eastern border.

East to Tuolumne Meadows

From the Valley, **Tioga Road** (Hwy-120) climbs rapidly passing a mile-long walking trail to the **Tuolumne Grove** of giant sequoias, which is nowhere near as spectacular as the Mariposa Grove (see below), but more convenient. The road continues through deep pine forests past the White Wolf and Porcupine campgrounds to **Olmsted Point**, which is up there with Glacier Point as one of the finest views on Yosemite's roads, looking down Tenaya Creek to Half Dome. In the late 1950s when the Tioga Road was being upgraded, Ansel Adams fruitlessly fought against its re-routing past here and along the gorgeous shores of **Tenaya Lake** to Tuolumne.

The alpine **Tuolumne Meadows** have an atmosphere quite different from the Valley. Here, at 8500ft, it is much more open; you almost seem to be level with the tops of the surrounding snow-covered mountains and the air always has a fresh, crisp bite. That said, there can still be good-sized blasts of carbon monoxide at peak times in the vicinity of the campground and lodge – the only accommodation base in the area and within easy reach of the park's eastern entrance at Tioga Pass (Hwy-120). But it's a better starting point than the Valley for backcountry hiking into the High Sierra, where seven hundred-odd miles of trails, both long and short, crisscross their way along the Sierra Nevada ridge. Also, because the growing season is short so high up, early summer in Tuolumne reveals a plethora of colorful wild blossoms. If you haven't the time for a long hike from here, at least stroll the half-mile trail from the foot of the distinctive smooth granite of Lembert Dome to the naturally carbonated **Soda Springs**,

ANSEL ADAMS

Few photographers have stamped their vision as unforgettably as **Ansel Adams** has done with Yosemite Valley. While he worked all over the American West, Yosemite was Adams' home and the site of his most celebrated works: icons of American landscape photography such as 1944's *Clearing Winter Storm, Jeffrey Pine, Sentinel Dome* from the following year, and *Moon and Half Dome* from 1960.

Born in 1902 into a moderately wealthy San Francisco family, Adams was given his first camera – a Box Brownie – when he was fourteen, on his first trip to Yosemite. Though classically trained as a concert pianist, he claimed that he knew his "destiny" on that first visit to Yosemite, and soon turned his attentions to the mountains, returning every year and taking up a job as custodian of the Sierra Club headquarters there.

He first made a mark in 1927 with *Monolith, The Face of Half Dome*, his first successful **visualization**: Adams believed that, before pressing the shutter, the photographer should have a clear idea of the final image and think through the entire photographic process, considering how lenses, filters, exposure, development and printing need to be used to achieve that visualization. This approach may seem obvious today, but compared to the hit-and-miss methods of the time, it was little short of revolutionary. Visualization was made easier by applying the **zone system** of exposure calculation, which, though not new, was codified and promoted by Adams as the basis for his teaching. This blend of art and science divides the range of possible tones into ten zones from velvet black (I) through middle gray (V) to pure white (X), and allows precise tone control, something Adams felt was the key to full expression through photography.

As Adams fine-tuned his artistic theories through the 1930s, the idea of photography as fine art was still considered novel, and Adams spent much of his time lobbying for

described in 1863 as "pungent and delightful to the taste." And so it is, though the park service discourage drinking it. From the Lembert Dome parking lot a second trail leads to its namesake's summit (3 miles round-trip; 2–3hr; 850ft ascent), which commands a superb view of the meadows and the surrounding assortment of jagged spires and smooth domes.

Between July and mid-August, a bus links Tuolumne and Yosemite Valley ($10 each way; ☎209/372-1240), and a free shuttle service also links Tuolumne to Olmsted Point, just west of Tenaya Lake (July to early Sept 7am–6pm). Alternatively, it's possible to hike between here and Yosemite Valley using part of the **John Muir Trail**, a distance of roughly twenty miles from the Happy Isles trailhead. The Pacific Crest Trail, stretching from Mexico right up to Canada, also passes through Tuolumne, and there are innumerable other paths into the canyons and valleys in the area. One of the best hikes leads north and west through the Grand Canyon of the Tuolumne River; get the full details for the **visitor center** at the Tuolumne campground.

Note that vehicles are not allowed to stay overnight at Tioga Pass Road trailheads (including Tuolumne Meadows) after mid-October, even if the road is open, effectively ruling out overnight hikes in this region at that time.

Wawona and the Mariposa Grove

Driving to Yosemite from Fresno, you'll probably pass through **WAWONA**, 27 miles south of the Valley on Hwy-41, whose landmark is the *Wawona Hotel* (see p.342), surrounded by a nine-hole golf course where $22 will get you a full eighteen-hole round (plus $9 for club rental, if needed), and tennis courts ($2.50 per hour). Close by, the **Pioneer Yosemite History Center** (mid-June to early Sept daily 9am–5pm; free) is a collection of buildings culled from the early times of white habitation. The jail, homesteads, covered bridge and the like are good for a scoot around, and, once you're away from the main road, the area makes a quiet spot for a picnic.

more respect for his craft. Adams was therefore delighted when, in 1940, he was made vice chairman of the newly established **Department of Photography** at the Museum of Modern Art (MoMA) in New York City. Even so, there was still very little money in photography, and Adams continued to take commercial assignments, including shooting menu photos for Yosemite's *Ahwahnee Hotel*. Commercial and personal work through the 1940s and 1950s earned Adams a wider audience. While still demanding the highest standard of reproduction, the artist had tempered his perfectionism, and allowed his work to appear on postcards, calendars and posters. By now, he was virtually a household name, and for the first time in his life he began making money to match his status as the grand old man of Western photography. His final triumph came in 1979, when the MoMA put on the huge "Yosemite and the Range of Light" exhibition. That same year, he was asked to make an official portrait of president Jimmy Carter – the first time a photographer had been assigned an official portrait – and was subsequently awarded the nation's highest civilian honor, the Medal of Freedom.

Throughout his life, Adams had another great passion, one that he pursued with the same fervor as photography: **conservation**. Back in 1932, the artist had a direct hand in creating Kings Canyon National Park. Two years later, he became a director of the **Sierra Club**, a position he held until 1971, overseeing several successful environmental campaigns. He never quit campaigning for the cause of conservation, and, after an interview in which he suggested he'd like to drown Ronald Reagan in his own martini, agreed to meet the president to promote the environmental cause.

Adams died on April 22, 1984 aged 82, and has become even more honored. The mountain that had been widely known as Mount Ansel Adams since 1933 now bears that name officially, and a huge chunk of the High Sierra south of Yosemite National Park is known as the Ansel Adams Wilderness.

Mariposa Grove, three miles east of Hwy-41 on a small road which cuts off just past the park's southern entrance, is the biggest and best of Yosemite's groves of giant sequoia trees. To get to the towering growths, walk the two-and-a-half mile loop trail from the parking lot at the end of the road, or take the narrated shuttle tour from the park entrance (9am–5.30pm; $8.50), which follows a paved road to the major sights. There is also a free shuttle to the parking area from Wawona.

Trails around the sequoia groves call first at the **Fallen Monarch**, familiar from the 1899 photo, widely reproduced on postcards, in which cavalry officers and their horses stand atop the prostrate tree. The most renowned of the grouping, well marked along the route, is the **Grizzly Giant**, thought to be 2700 years old and with a lower branch thicker than the trunk of any non-sequoia in the grove. Other highlights include the now-fallen **Wawona Tunnel Tree** through which people drove their cars until it fell in 1969, the similarly bored **California Tunnel Tree**, which you can walk through, and all manner of trees which have grown together, split apart, been struck by lightning, or are simply staggeringly large. It's also worth dropping into the **Mariposa Grove Museum** (daily 9am–4pm; free), towards the top end of the trail, which has modest displays and photos of the mighty trees. For more on the life of the sequoia, see p.660 of "Contexts."

Hetch Hetchy

John Muir's passion for Yosemite Valley was matched, if not exceeded, by his desire to preserve the beauty of **Hetch Hetchy**, eighteen miles north of the valley, five miles west of the Oak Flat Entrance. When it came under threat from power and water supply interests in San Francisco, he battled for 25 years, instigating the first environmental letter-writing campaign to Congress. Eventually, in 1913, the cause was lost to a federal bill which paved the way for the Tuolumne River to be blocked by the **O'Shaughnessey Dam**, thereby creating the slender Hetch Hetchy reservoir. This

HIKING IN YOSEMITE NATIONAL PARK

To **camp out overnight** in most of Yosemite's designated wilderness you need a free **wilderness permit**. Popular trails – Merced River Trail up to Little Yosemite or Tuolumne Meadows to Lyle Fort – fill up quickly, but with flexibility you should be able to get something, even in high summer. Don't despair if you have trouble landing the trail you want: paths are so numerous that you may start at a less popular trailhead but end up doing largely the same hike. Between May and October a quota system is in operation, half of which can be reserved up to 24 weeks and at least two days in advance ($3 per person reservation fee) through Wilderness Permits, PO Box 545, Yosemite, CA 95389 (☎209/372-0740), stating your requirements, the size of your party and your desired itinerary with alternatives. The other half are offered on a first-come-first-served basis and are available the day before you plan to start: line up at one of the park's ranger stations – at Yosemite Village, Wawona, Big Oak Flat, Hetch Hetchy and Tuolumne – early in the day. From November to April when demand is lowest, permits are self-issued at trailheads.

Camping gear can be rented quite reasonably from Yosemite Mountaineering School (see p.341), as can bear-resistant canisters ($3 per trip plus $75 deposit), which you'll also find in Yosemite's stores, the Wilderness Center, and numerous other spots. Canisters can be returned to any rental location.

Unless otherwise noted, the following distances and times are for a round trip.

Glacier Point Four-mile Trail (10 miles; 5–6hr; 3200ft ascent). The steep asphalt path from the Valley floor to Glacier Point doesn't give much of a sense of being in the wilderness, but the magnificent views make this one of the

drowned a valley which some claim rivaled Yosemite Valley for scenic splendor. It is certainly no match now, but the view of granite domes and waterfalls from the path with crosses the dam gives some sense of what it must have been like. It is barely worth the trip though, unless you plan on using the backpacker campground (wilderness permit required) as a base for trekking through the little-visited northern reaches of the park. A short and mostly flat alternative crosses the dam, passes through a short tunnel and follows the north bank of the reservoir to Wapama Falls (five miles round-trip) and on to Rancheria Falls (a further four miles each way).

Listings

Activity Programs The park service operates an extensive and worthwhile range of mostly free walks, talks, films and slide shows, for both adults and kids, mostly in the Valley but also at Glacier Point, Tuolumne Meadows and at the Tuolumne Grove. Consult the *Yosemite Guide* for details and look out especially for the Yosemite Theater program which presents the admirable *Conversations with a Tramp* ($5) evoking the spirit of John Muir.

Banks The Bank of America in Yosemite Village is open daily from 8am to 4pm and operates a 24hr ATM. There are more ATMs at Yosemite Village and *Curry Village* (all charge a transaction fee of at least $1.50), but there is no provision for foreign currency exchange.

Bike rental Bikes are only allowed on the Valley's flat, paved roads and bikeways so the basic single-speed bikes ($20 per day) available at *Yosemite Lodge* (all year) and *Curry Village* (summer only) are quite adequate.

Books The Yosemite Village Visitor Center has a good selection of Yosemite-related books and maps; the Ansel Adams Gallery specializes in photography and nature publications; and the Mountain Shop at *Curry Village* stocks climbing guides.

Campfires Summertime air quality restrictions exist limiting campfires to 5pm to 10pm from May to mid-October. For ecological reasons, firewood must not be gathered in the valley or above 9600 feet, but is available for sale at the Yosemite Store.

Valley's more popular day walks. Closed in winter.

Half Dome (17 miles; 10–12hr; 4800ft ascent). Probably the Valley's finest, if most arduous, walk. The route starts by following the Vernal and Nevada Falls Trail (below) and continues around the back of Half Dome. The final 400ft ascent is over the huge, smooth, humped back aided by a pair of steel cables and wooden steps which are partly removed in winter (Nov–May) to discourage ascent: gloves to grip the cables are a good idea at any time. Even with a head for heights, the near vertical 5000-foot drop from the top can induce vertigo. If you plan a one-day assault, you'll need to start at the crack of dawn.

Tuolumne Meadows to Yosemite Valley (20 miles one way; 2 days; strenuous in parts; 10,000ft ascent). Several routes, all quite popular, leave from Yosemite to Tuolumne. All can be done fairly easily in two days if you're in rea-

sonably good shape, less if done in reverse using the Tuolumne Shuttle. One of the best routes (reserve your permits early) follows the **John Muir Trail** up Little Yosemite Valley past Vernal and Nevada Falls and the base of the final climb up Half Dome.

Upper Yosemite Falls (7 miles; 4hr; 2700ft ascent). A fairly strenuous walk, the almost continuous ascent sapping on the leg muscles, but with fine views and, during the meltwater period at least, a chance to appreciate the power and volume of the water at the end. Start just by the *Camp 4* campground (shuttle stop 7).

Vernal and Nevada Falls (7 miles; 6hr; 1900ft ascent). The trail begins at the southeastern side of the valley (shuttle bus stop 16).The route is steep and can be wet and slippery – it's not referred to as the "mist trail" for nothing – but otherwise is not especially tough, and the visual rewards of reaching either or both falls are tremendous.

Camping equipment Camping gear can be rented from the Yosemite Mountaineering School at Curry Village – expect to pay $10 for a sleeping bag and $8 for a pack and comparable rates for tents, bear canisters, snowshoes etc – and bought from the Village Sport Shop in Yosemite Village, or better from the Mountain Shop in Curry Village. The store in Tuolumne Meadows also stocks camping equipment, climbing gear and lightweight food.

Gas Available at good prices in Oakhurst, moderate prices in Mariposa and Groveland and expensively in the park, year-round at Wawona and seasonally at Tuolumne Meadows and Crane Flat. The Valley has no gas.

Guided trips Southern Yosemite Mountain Guides, PO Box 301, Bass Lake CA 93604 (☎1-800/231-4575 or 559/658-8735, fax 658-8734) run High Sierra backpacking trips (4-day $265, 10-day $985), 7-day horseback trips ($1345), weekend and week-long mountain biking trips ($225/$945), 5-day rock-climbing camps ($395) and more, all based in the south of Yosemite.

Horseback riding Saddle trips accommodating riders of all standards are run from stables in Yosemite Valley (☎209/372-8348), Tuolumne Meadows (☎209/372-8427) and Wawona stables (☎209/375-6502): scenic rides cost $35 for two hours, $70 for the day. There are also multi-day High Sierra Saddle Trips starting at $560 for four days.

High Sierra camp vacations Visitors organized enough to enter a lottery (mid-Oct to Nov) can apply for July to September stays in a series of five dormitory-style tent cabin complexes – complete with proper beds, hot showers and meals cooked for you – dotted around the Yosemite high country. Most combine them in a circuit, either the seven-day guided hike with one rest day, the six-day mule-back saddle trip or the four-day saddle trip. Prices are around $100 a night per person and include a delicious breakfast and dinner. *Merced Lake*, the largest of the camps, sometimes has spare short-notice spaces for those willing to hike the thirteen miles from Yosemite Valley or the fifteen miles from Tuolumne Meadows, and all camps will serve meals to passing hikers if you reserve in advance. Write for an application form to *Yosemite Reservations*, 5410 East Home Avenue, Fresno, CA 93727 (☎559/253-5674, *www.yosemitepark.com/activities/sierra*)

Internet access Limited facilities at the Yosemite Village public library (see below) and at the libraries and copy centers in the hinterland towns.

Laundry There's a coin-op affair at *Housekeeping Camp* (7am–10pm).

Library A public research library (usually Tues–Fri 8am–5pm) is situated upstairs from the museum entrance in Yosemite Village and contains all manner of Yosemite, backcountry and climbing information, including recent magazines and daily papers. There is also a public library which opens for three or four hours a day (usually Mon–Thurs only) and is located close to the Yosemite Village visitor center in a building signed "Girls Club."

Lost property ☎209/372-4357 for items lost at hotels and restaurants; ☎209/379-1001 (Mon–Fri 8am–4pm) for stuff lost elsewhere.

Medical assistance Yosemite Medical Clinic, between Yosemite Village and the *Ahwahnee Hotel* (☎209/372-4637) has 24-hour emergency care and accepts appointments (Mon–Thurs 8am–5pm). Dental treatment (☎209/372-4200) is also available.

Photography The Ansel Adams Studio in Yosemite Village stocks slide, professional and ordinary print film at reasonable prices. They also run free two-hour guided photography walks at noon on weekends. The *Ahwahnee Hotel* also runs free photography walks, open to all-comers each Monday and Wednesday morning at 7.30am.

Post office Located in Yosemite Village (Mon–Fri 8.30am–5pm, Sat 10am–noon) and accepting general delivery (aka poste restante). Also year-round services at *Yosemite Lodge* and Wawona and summer-only service at *Curry Village* and Tuolumne Meadows.

Rafting Inside the park itself, *Curry Village* rent guideless six-berth rafts ($12.50 per person; min 2; June and July only) allowing you to float gently along the placid and ride a relatively gentle section of the Merced River – the cost includes a return bus ride. Outside the park, from April to June, far more rugged (Class III–IV) one-day stretches are run in the traditional guided fashion by Mariah Wilderness Expeditions (☎1-800/462-7424), Ahwahnee Whitewater (☎1-800/359-9790, *www.ahwahnee.com*), Whitewater Voyages (☎1-800/488-RAFT) and others, all charging around $100 midweek and $130 at weekends.

Recycling Glass, aluminum, newspapers and plastic are recycled at Yosemite Village, and beverage containers may be returned for deposits at all retail outlets.

RVs Campers can use all the main campgrounds, but there are no hook-ups in Yosemite. Dump stations are in Yosemite Valley, Wawona and Tuolumne Meadows (summer only).

Showers In the Valley the best showers are at *Curry Village* (24 hours; $2), though there are also showers at *Housekeeping Camp* (7am–10pm; $2); both include use of a towel.

Swimming There are pools at *Yosemite Lodge*, *Curry Village* and *Wawona Hotel* (all free to hotel guests and $2 for others) and numerous small beaches throughout the Valley along the Merced River.

travel details

Trains

The **San Joaquin** service runs four times daily between Bakersfield and Emeryville, near Oakland, from where Amtrak Thruway buses run into San Francisco. Amtrak Thruway bus connections from San Diego, Orange County, Banta Barbara, Palm Springs and Los Angeles link with the train at Bakersfield.

Bakersfield to: Fresno (1hr 45min); Hanford (1hr 15min); Merced (2hr 45min); Emeryville (6hr); Stockton (4hr).

Buses

Buses are either Greyhound, Amtrak Thruway or Orange Belt Stages (☎1-800/266-7433), which often use Amtrak stations as hubs for their network.

Bakersfield to: Merced (12 daily; 4–5hr).

Fresno to: Merced (15 daily; 1hr 10min); Modesto (17 daily; 2hr 10min); Stockton (9 daily; 3hr); Yosemite (1 daily; 3hr 30min).

Hanford to: San Luis Obispo (1 daily; 3hr).

Los Angeles to: Bakersfield (18 daily; 1hr 25min); Fresno (16 daily; 6hr 45min); Merced (9 daily; 6–8hr); Modesto (12 daily; 8hr 25min); Stockton (11 daily; 6hr 45min); Visalia (6 daily; 6hr 15min).

Merced to: Los Angeles (13 daily; 6–8hr); Modesto (6 daily; 1hr); Sacramento (8 daily; 3hr); San Francisco (6–7 daily; 4–5hr); Yosemite (3–5 daily; 2hr 45min).

San Francisco to: Bakersfield (7 daily; 7hr 20min); Fresno (9 daily; 4hr 40min); Merced (8 daily; 3hr 30min–5hr); Modesto (8 daily; 2hr 10min); Stockton (3 daily; 1hr 30min); Visalia (2 daily; 5hr).

Stockton to: Lodi (5 daily; 30min); Merced (6–7 daily; 2hr); Sacramento (11 daily; 1hr).

Visalia to: Hanford (2 daily; 1hr 30min); Reedley (1 daily; 40min).

CHAPTER SIX

THE CENTRAL COAST

The four hundred miles of coastline in between LA and San Francisco is arguably one of the most beautiful ocean-side stretches of land anywhere in the world. From sandy beaches to rocky cliffs and from rural charm to upscale sophistication, the allure of the Central Coast is wide in range. Sparsely populated outside a few medium-sized towns, much of the area is barely disturbed by modern life. Indeed, first-time visitors may be surprised to find just how much of the region survives in its natural state, nestled snugly between two of America's largest and richest cities. The mountain ranges that separate the shore from the farmlands of the inland valleys are for the most part pristine wilderness, sometimes covered in thick forests of tall and slender redwood trees, while, in winter especially, fast-flowing rivers and streams course down valleys to the sea. All along the shore, sea otters and seals play in the waves, and endangered gray whales pass close by on their annual migration from Alaska to Mexico.

Big Sur, where the brooding Santa Lucia mountains rise steeply out of the thundering Pacific surf, is the heart of the region, and **Point Lobos**, at its northern tip, is the best place to experience this untouched environment at its most dramatic. Nature aside, though, the Central Coast also marks the gradual transition from Southern to Northern California. The two largest towns here, **Santa Barbara** and **Santa Cruz**, are poles apart: Santa Barbara, a hundred miles north of Los Angeles, is a conservative, wealthy resort; in Santa Cruz, 75 miles south of San Francisco, long hair and tie-dye are very much the order of the day. What they have in common is miles of broad clean **beaches**, with chilly waters but excellent surf, and a branch of the University of California energizing the local nightlife. In between, the small town of **San Luis Obispo** provides a languorous contrast to them both, and is a feasible base for the Central Coast's biggest tourist attraction, **Hearst Castle**, the opulent hilltop palace of publishing magnate William Randolph "Citizen Kane" Hearst.

The Central Coast also contains the bulk and the best of the late-eighteenth-century Spanish colonial **missions** – the first European settlements on the West Coast, set up to convert the natives to Christianity while co-opting their labor. Almost all of the towns that exist here today grew up around the adobe walls and red-tiled roofs of these Catholic colonies, strung out along the Pacific, each deliberately situated a long day's walk from the next and typically composed of a church and a cloistered monastery,

---

ACCOMMODATION PRICE CODES

All accommodation prices in this book have been coded using the symbols below; prices are for the least expensive **double rooms** in each establishment. For a full explanation see p.36 in "Basics." Individual rates rather than price codes are given for **hostels** and whole **apartments**.

① up to $30	④ $60–80	⑦ $130–175
② $30–45	⑤ $80–100	⑧ $175–250
③ $45–60	⑥ $100–130	⑨ $250+

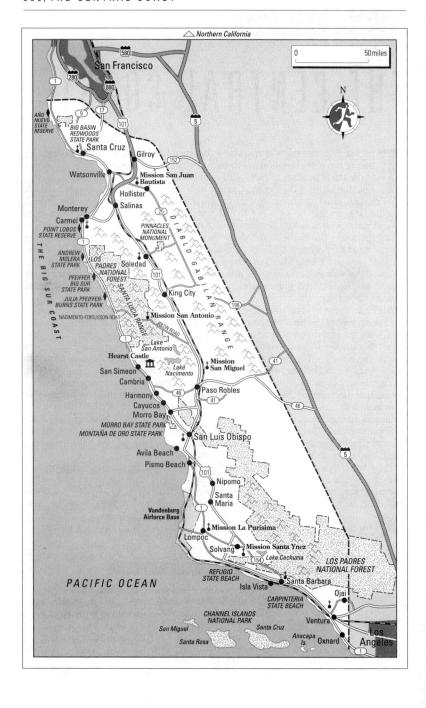

enclosed within thick walls to prevent attacks by native tribes. **Monterey**, a hundred miles south of San Francisco, was the capital of California under Spain, and later, Mexico, and today retains more of its early nineteenth-century architecture than any other city in the state; it's also a good base for one of the most beautiful of the missions, which stands three miles south in the uppercrust seaside resort of **Carmel**.

Practicalities

Getting around is easy by Californian standards: some of the best views in the state can be had from Amtrak's *Coast Starlight* train, which runs right along the coast up to San Luis Obispo before cutting inland north to San Francisco. Greyhound buses stop at most of the towns, particularly those along the main highway, US-101 – though the best route, if you've got a car, is the smaller Hwy-1, which follows the coast all the way but takes twice as long. **Places to stay** are relatively easy to find, at least outside summer weekends when otherwise quiet towns and beaches are packed solid with vacationing families. Opportunities for **camping** are plentiful, too, in a string of state parks, beaches and forests.

Ventura and Ojai

The valleys of suburban Los Angeles meet the Pacific coast at **VENTURA**, a long-standing farming and fishing community that's slowly being submerged beneath fast-food restaurants and mini-malls, many spilling over from the larger industrial city of **OXNARD** to the south. The only real reason to stop, besides buying fresh strawberries or other seasonal produce from the many roadside stalls, is to catch a boat out to the offshore Channel Islands (see below) from the harbor four miles southwest of town. But if you've got time to spare, look in on the seemingly time-warped town center, just north of the US-101 and Hwy-1 intersection, around the restored church of **San Buena Ventura Mission** at 211 E Main St (daily 10am–5pm; $1). This mission, raised in 1782, was the ninth of the 21 California missions and the last to be founded by Father Junipero Serra. Also on Main Street are two small but reasonably engaging museums: the **Albinger Archaeological Museum**, at no. 113 (summer Wed–Sun 10am–4pm; winter Wed–Fri 10am–2pm, Sat–Sun 10am–4pm; free), has exhibits explaining 3500 years of local history, from ancient Native American cultures to the mission era; while across the street the **Ventura County Museum of History and Art** (Tues–Sun 10am–5pm; $4) takes up where the former leaves off, with exhibits on local pioneer families and their farming equipment.

Amtrak trains pull in near Harbor Boulevard and Figueroa Street, three blocks from the Greyhound stop at Thomson Boulevard and Palm Street. The **CVB** at 89 California St (Mon–Fri 8.30am–5pm, Sat 9am–4pm, Sun 10am–4pm; ☎1-800/333-2989 or 805/648-2075) can help with accommodation and has local bus maps. As Ventura is a springboard for visiting the Channel Islands there is a **Channel Islands National Park visitor center** (daily 8am–5pm; ☎805/658-5730; *www.nps.gov/chis*), next to the ferry landing in Ventura Harbor, which has well-presented displays on the geology and the native plant and animal life of the islands, including seals, sea lions, pelican rookeries and giant kelp forests. It also has up-to-date information on arranging trips, and a tower from which, on fine days, you can view the islands.

Nestled in the hills above Ventura, the small town of **OJAI** (pronounced "O-hi") is a wealthy resort community, and center for the exclusive health spas and tennis clubs that dot the surrounding countryside. It's also headquarters of the Krishnamurti Society, which spreads the word of the theosophist who lived and lectured here during the 1920s, considering the Ojai Valley "a vessel of comprehension, intelligence and truth." The **Krishnamurti Library**, several miles northeast of town at 1130 McAndrew Rd (Wed 1–9pm, Thurs–Sun 1–5pm; ☎805/646-4948), has details on his teachings. In town, the **Ojai Valley Museum**, 130 W Ojai Ave (Wed–Fri 1pm–4pm; Sat–Sun 10am–4pm; ☎805-640-1390; donation), housed in a former Mission Revival style church built in 1919, has ambitious exhibits on history, agriculture, art, indigenous life and other matters of local interest. The **Chamber of Commerce**, next door (Mon-Fri 9am–4.30pm, Sat & Sun 10am–4pm; ☎805/646-8126), is the place for information on the town's numerous B&B **inns**. The friendly *Farm Hostel*, on a country farm ten minutes from downtown (☎805/646-0311), offers free pick-up from the Greyhound and Amtrak stations in Ventura and dorm beds for $12, but you must be an international traveler to stay. The cushy **Ojai Valley Inn & Spa**, Country Club Road (☎800/422-6524 or 805/646-5511; ⑦), which all but swallows up the sleepy little town, has justifiably been voted one of the state's best spa and hotel complexes in California in several publications' readers polls. Near Ojai is the massive **Los Padres National Forest** with some good hiking and several **campgrounds** (reservations: ☎1-800/280-2267). The **Ranger Station** (☎805/646-4348) at 1190 E. Ojai Ave has information and maps.

The Channel Islands National Park

Stretching north from Catalina Island off the coast of Los Angeles, a chain of little-known desert islands has been protected in its natural state as the **CHANNEL ISLANDS NATIONAL PARK**, offering excellent hiking and close-up views of sea lions, as well as fishing and scuba/skin diving through the many caves, coves and shipwrecks in the crystal-clear Pacific waters. All five of the main islands are accessible, though it is the closest, Anacapa, some fourteen miles south of Ventura, which sees the most traffic.

Tiny **Anacapa** is actually two islets. West Anacapa is mostly a refuge for nesting brown pelicans and is closed to the public with the exception of Frenchy's Cove, a great beach and base for scuba or snorkeling expeditions. More happens on East Anacapa, where there's a small **visitor center** and a mile-and-a-half-long nature trail. There are no beaches, but swimming in the cove where the boats dock is allowed. West of Anacapa, **Santa Cruz** is the largest and highest of the islands. The Nature Conservancy acquired ninety percent of the island in 1988 as part of its effort to protect environmentally significant lands and has made them accessible to the public on **day-trip tours** (see operators below). **Santa Rosa**, with its grasslands, is less rugged but still has its share of steep ravines. Hiking inland requires a permit and divers can explore the two exposed **wrecks** on either side of the island. The most distant island – windswept **San Miguel**, fifty miles offshore – is thought to be the burial place of sixteenth-century Spanish explorer Juan Cabrillo. No grave has been found but a monument has been erected at Cuyler Harbor on the eastern end. Seasoned hikers may wish to make the rugged cross-island trip to Point Bennett to spy on the plentiful wildlife.

South of the main group lies **Santa Barbara** Island, named by Sebastian Vizcaíno who dropped by on Saint Barbara's Day (December 4) in 1602. The island's appeal these days is largely ornithological, as kestrels, larks and meadowlarks can all be seen on land gradually recovering its native flora after years of destruction by now extinct rabbits. The small **museum** at the landing cove has detailed information on the island's unique geography, flora and fauna.

Practicalities

The only way to visit the Channel Islands National Park by boat is through the operators that run from Ventura Harbor. Anacapa Island is served by several **tours** run by Island Packers, 1867 Spinnaker Drive, three miles west of US-101 and a mile south of town (☎805/642-7688 for 24hr recorded information; ☎805/642-1393 for reservations

9am–5pm; *www.islandpackers.com*). Trips range from half-day cruises without landings ($22), through two-day excursions for campers ($48), with several other itinerary options in-between. The fifteen-mile trip takes ninety minutes each way, and there's a free, very basic **campground** a half-mile walk from the landing cove on East Anacapa. Bring plenty of **food** and especially **water**, as none is available on the boat or on the island. Permits are required for camping. Boats don't run every day and often fill up, so call at least a couple of days ahead.

The **other islands** are more difficult to visit, though Island Packers run boats, less frequently, to them all. **Day-trips** to the western end of Santa Cruz (3hr each way) are $42, overnight excursions to the eastern end are $54. Visits to Santa Rosa (5hr one way; $62 for the day, $80 including camping) are often combined with a stop (or camp) on San Miguel for the same price. Santa Barbara trips are a fraction cheaper. Truth Aquatics, 301 W Cabrillo Blvd (☎805/962-1127 or 805/963-3564), has alternative itineraries to all the islands on smaller vessels at higher prices.

An alternative way to reach Santa Rosa island is to **fly** with Channel Islands Aviation (☎805/987-1301), which runs day-trips and weekend excursions ($98 & $150 respectively) from Camarillo Airport off Hwy-101, twenty miles south of Ventura. Santa Cruz is also the venue for **kayak** trips from Ventura and Santa Barbara (see p.363).

Perhaps the best time of all to visit the islands is between February and April when there's the opportunity for **whale-watching**. During these months, Island Packers and Harbor Village Sportfishing, 1449 Spinnaker Drive (☎805/658-1060), organize whale-watching excursions which last about three hours and start at $22.

The **Channel Islands National Park visitor center** in Ventura (see above) can help with trips, and has lots of information on the islands' flora and fauna.

Santa Barbara

The six-lane freeway that races past the oil wells and offshore drilling platforms along the coast beyond Ventura slows to a more leisurely pace a hundred miles north of Los Angeles at **SANTA BARBARA**, a moneyed seaside resort that for years has been known as the "home of the newly wed and the nearly dead" – not entirely inaccurate summary. Despite the vast modern El Paseo Nuevo shopping mall in the center of town and a growing selection of budget hotels and fast-food joints on the outskirts, Santa Barbara has managed to preserve the homogeneity of its architecture. Beautifully situated on the gently sloping hills above the Pacific, the insistent red-tiled roofs and white stucco walls of the low-rise buildings form a background to some fine Spanish Revival buildings. The golden beaches below are wide, clean and lined with palm trees along a gently curving bay.

Once home to Ronald Reagan, and a weekend escape for much of the old money of Los Angeles, Santa Barbara is a highly conservative town, with locals doing everything money can buy to look tanned, healthy and well-dressed. The town, too, is as well-groomed as you might expect, and many areas feel like a break-away block of Beverly Hills. Still, it's a fairly provincial place; local culture is confined predominantly to playing volleyball, surfing, cycling, sipping coffee or cruising in expensive convertibles along the shore. After an essential visit to the mission, a quiet lunch and a leisurely walk along the pier, it shouldn't take much longer than half a day to grow tired of the place.

Arrival, information and transportation

Getting to Santa Barbara is easy. Greyhound **buses** arrive from LA and San Francisco every couple of hours, stopping downtown at 34 W Carrillo St; Amtrak **trains** stop at the old Southern Pacific station at 209 State St, a block west of US-101. Santa Barbara

airport (☎805/683-4011), eight miles from the town center (near the University of California at Santa Barbara) at 515 Marxmiller Drive in Goleta, has a limited and very expensive scheduled service to other Californian cities. Carriers include American Eagle (☎1-800/433-7300) and United Express (☎1-800/241-6522).

For more **information** on Santa Barbara, or for help with finding a place to stay, contact the **Visitor Information Office** on East Beach at 1 Santa Barbara St (Mon–Sat 9am–5pm, Sun 10am–5pm; ☎805/965-3021). The **US Forest Service** office in Goleta, near UCSB at 6144 Calle Real (☎805/683-6711), has information on **hiking** in the vicinity of Santa Barbara, and the many good trails easily accessible from downtown.

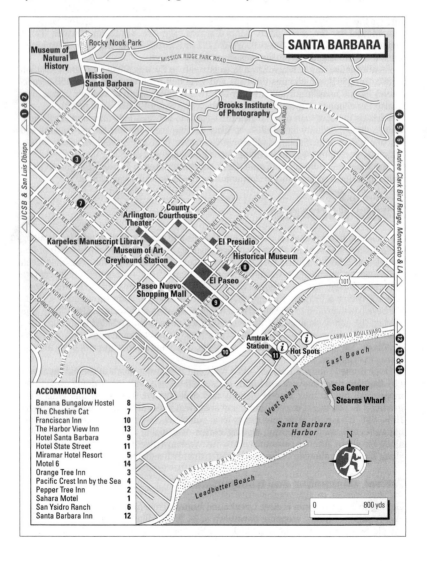

ACCOMMODATION

Banana Bungalow Hostel	8
The Cheshire Cat	7
Franciscan Inn	10
The Harbor View Inn	13
Hotel Santa Barbara	9
Hotel State Street	11
Miramar Hotel Resort	5
Motel 6	14
Orange Tree Inn	3
Pacific Crest Inn by the Sea	4
Pepper Tree Inn	2
Sahara Motel	1
San Ysidro Ranch	6
Santa Barbara Inn	12

Getting around Santa Barbara is simple: your feet can take you most places and there's a quarter-a-ride shuttle bus which loops between downtown and the beach on a ten- to fifteen-minute schedule, and along the waterfront to Montecito every thirty minutes until 5.30pm, and 8pm on Friday and Saturday. The outlying areas are covered by Santa Barbara Metropolitan Transit District buses (☎805/683-3702). If you want to **rent a car**, the best value is U-Save Auto Rental, 510 Anacapa St (☎805/963-3499), which rents late-model cars for as little as $24 a day including one hundred free miles. Two of the chain offices available are Budget (☎805/963-6651) and Hertz (☎805/967-0411), both at the airport.

Accommodation

Home to some of the West Coast's most deluxe resorts – the sort of places movie stars use for romantic hideaways – Santa Barbara is among the most expensive places to **stay**, with rooms averaging over $110 a night. However, there is a hostel, and with a bit of advance planning, finding somewhere good shouldn't take too big a bite out of your budget – especially if you are willing to stay in one of the junkier chain motels along the western stretch of State St. The least expensive as well as most of the more moderate places are usually booked throughout the summer, but if you get stuck, enlist the assistance of *Hot Spots*, a 24-hour hotel reservation center and espresso bar at 36 State St (☎1-800/793-7666 or 805/5641637) or the Passport Reservation Service (☎1-800/289-6255). Also, while there's no **camping** in Santa Barbara proper, there are several grounds along the coast to the north, including *El Capitan State Beach* and *Refugio State Beach* (☎1-800/444-7275 or 805/968-1033; $15-17) and to the south, including the *Carpinteria State Beach* (☎1-800/444-7275 or 805/684-2811; $17). In the mountains of the Santa Ynez Valley, there are a number of other options, including sites around *Lake Cachuma* (☎805/688-4658; $15-21).

Banana Bungalow Hostel, 210 E Ortega St (☎800/3HOSTEL or 805/9630154). Converted from commercial premises and catering to raucous backpackers. A party atmosphere prevails, engendered as much by the 2.30am curfew as the occasional keg parties, $17–22 per night.

The Cheshire Cat, 36 W Valerio St (☎805/569-1610). Tastefully decorated B&B with hot tub and bikes for guests' use. Complimentary wine on arrival and breakfast under a palm tree. Ten minutes' walk from the restaurant zone. ⑥.

Franciscan Inn, 109 Bath St (☎805/963-8845). Comfortable, quiet and very clean motel just a block from the beach, with a pool, spa and complimentary breakfast. ⑤.

The Harbor View Inn, 28 W Cabrillo Blvd (☎1-800/7550222 or 805/9630780) Oceanfront elegance, or at least Santa Barbara's casual shorts and short-sleeves interpretation of the same. ⑦.

Hotel Santa Barbara, 533 State Street (☎1-888/259-7700 or 805/957-9300) Surprisingly good rates for comfortable rooms in a prime downtown location. ⑤.

Hotel State Street, 121 State St (☎805/966-6586). Near the wharf and beach in a characterful old mission-style building, though with some noise from the nearby railway. Reasonable rates include breakfast. Communal bathrooms. ②.

Miramar Hotel Resort, 1555 S Jameson Lane (☎1-800/537-8483 or 805/969-2203). Slightly faded, once elegant beach resort with (higher priced) sea-view rooms; the only place in town with a private strand. ⑤.

Motel 6, 443 Corona del Mar (☎1-800/466-8356 or 805/564-1392). Inexpensive but extremely popular beachfront lodging in no-frills chain motel. There's another north of the town center at 3505 State St (☎805/687-5400). Both ③.

Orange Tree Inn, 1920 State St (☎1-800/536-6764 or 805/569-1521). Basic hotel close to the center of town with a pool and complimentary pastries in the morning. ⑤.

Pacific Crest Inn by the Sea, 433 Corona Del Mar (☎805/966-3103) A good alternative to the more pricey neighbors along the beach. ④.

Pepper Tree Inn, 3850 State Street (☎1-800/338-0030 or 805/687-5511) A bit set back from the main center, this comfortable Best Western property offers slightly better rates than accommodation of the same standard along the beach. ⑥.

Sahara Motel, 2800 State St (☎805/687-2500). As basic as they get, but also as cheap as they get in Santa Barbara. ②.

San Ysidro Ranch, 900 San Ysidro Lane (☎1-800/368-6788 or 805/969-5046). Gorgeous, ultra-posh resort with private cottages in lovely gardens (Jackie and JFK spent their honeymoon here), in the hills ten minutes' drive south of town. ⑨.

Santa Barbara Inn, 901 E Cabrillo Blvd (☎1-800/231-0431 or 805/966-2285). Upscale oceanfront motel with large pool, lovely views, and renovated rooms. ⑥.

The Town

The mission-era feel of Santa Barbara is no accident. Following a devastating earth-quake in 1925, the city authorities decided to rebuild virtually the entire town in the image of an apocryphal Spanish Colonial past – even the massive "historic" El Paseo shopping mall is covered in pseudo-whitewashed adobe plaster – with numerous arcades linking shops, offices, and restaurants. It's surprisingly successful, and the square-mile town center, squeezing between the south-facing beaches and the foothills of the Santa Ynez mountains, attracts one of the region's liveliest pedestrian scenes. **State Street** is the main drag, home to a friendly assortment of diners, bookstores, cof-fee bars and nightclubs catering as much to the needs of locals – among them twenty thousand students at the nearby UCSB – as to visitors.

The town's few remaining genuine mission-era structures are preserved as **El Presidio** (daily 10.30am–4.30pm; donation), in the center of which are the two-hundred-year-old barracks of the old fortress, **El Cuartel**, standing two blocks east of State Street on Canon Perdido Street. The second-oldest building in California, the old barracks now house historical exhibits and a scale model of the small Spanish colony. The more recent past is recounted in the **Santa Barbara Historical Museum** (Tues–Sat 10am–5pm, Sun noon–5pm; donation), a block away at 136 E de la Guerra St.

On the corner of State and Anapamu streets, the **Museum of Art** (Tues–Thu & Sat 11am–5pm, Fri 11am–9pm, Sun noon–5pm; $5; *www.sbmuseart.org*) is of more interest, a refreshingly accessible small museum with some fine classical Greek and Egyptian statuary and a fairly comprehensive collection of American painting, as well as some French Impressionists. Just east of here, on Anacapa Street, the **County Courthouse** is the one first-rate piece of Spanish Revival architecture in Santa Barbara, an idiosyn-cratic variation on the mission theme that has been widely praised as one of the finest public buildings in the US. Take a break in the sunken gardens, explore the quirky stair-cases, or climb the seventy-foot-high **clocktower** (Mon–Fri 8am–4:45pm, Sat & Sun 10am–4:45pm; free) for a view out over the town. Two blocks up State Street at 1317, the landmark **Arlington Theater** (☎805/963-4408) is an intact and still-functioning 1930s movie palace and performance venue, whose trompe l'oeil interior simulates a Mexican village plaza. And nearby at 21 Anapamu St, the beautifully deco-rated **Karpeles Manuscript Library** (daily 10am–4pm; ☎805/962-5322; free) is the surprising home to a diverse array of original documents such as the Constitution of the Confederate States of America as well as the original manuscripts of many famous writers, scientists and politicians. Falling slightly out of the town's center, not far from Highway 101, the **Santa Barbara Winery**, at 202 Anacapa St at Yanonali St (10am–5pm; ☎805/963-3646), is worth a detour as it's one of the oldest commercial wineries in the county.

The beaches and around

Half a mile down State Street from the town center, Cabrillo Boulevard runs along the south-facing shore, a long, clean strand stretching from the yacht and fishing harbor beyond palm-lined **West Beach** to the volleyball courts and golden sands of **East Beach**, which hosts an outdoor arts and crafts market every Sunday. At the foot of State

Street, take a stroll among the pelicans on **Stearns Wharf**, the oldest wooden pier in the state, built in 1872. It was nearly destroyed in November 1998, when a third of the structure was engulfed in flames. There is still a local dispute on as to the cause of the fire, but restoration efforts have brought the structure back to its former glory. Still, postcards of the flaming pier remain popular at the tourist shops which line the wharf along with seafood restaurants, ice-cream stands and the **Sea Center** (summer 10am–5pm; winter 12pm–5pm; $3), an annex of the natural history museum. Just west of the pier, athletes keep in shape in the Los Baños open-air fifty-meter swimming pool (☎805/966-6110; $2.25), while **windsurfers** can be rented from beach-front stalls. **Kayaks** are available from Paddle Sports, 100 State St (☎805/899-4925), and Aqua Sports, 111 Verona Ave (☎805/968-7231), starting at $20 for two hours and $40 for a full day. These are just two of several companies that conduct lessons and run all-inclusive paddling and snorkeling trips out to Santa Cruz Island (about $150). Beach Rentals, 22 State St (☎805/966-6733), and Cycles 4 Rent Inc., 101 State Street (☎805/652-0462), offer **bicycles** for around $30 a day, and provide a map of Santa Barbara's extensive system of bike paths; the longest and most satisfying leads west along the bluffs all the way to Isla Vista and UCSB, and passes a mile or so back from the rarely crowded, creekside **Arroyo Burro Beach** (locally known as "Hendry's"), four miles west of the wharf at the end of Las Positas Road. Alternatively head along the beachfront bike path two miles east past the Santa Barbara **zoo** (daily 10am–5pm; ☎805/962-5339; $6), and cycle around the **Andree Clark Bird Refuge** (unrestricted access) just beyond, an enclosed saltwater marsh where you can see a variety of seabirds, including egrets, herons and cormorants.

The Mission and around

The one city sight that does even more than the beaches to put Santa Barbara on the map is the mission from which it takes its name. In the hills above the town on the upper end of Laguna Street, the **Mission Santa Barbara** (daily 9am–5pm; $3) is known as the "Queen of the Missions." Its colorful twin-towered facade – facing out over a perfectly manicured garden towards the sea – combines Roman and Spanish mission styles, giving it an immediate, imposing force lacking in some of the more overall impressive missions in the chain. The present structure was finished and dedicated in 1820, built to replace a series of three adobe churches that had been destroyed by earthquakes. In 1925, another earthquake damaged the mission, and restoration costs totalled nearly $400,000. Today, a small **museum** displays historical artifacts from the mission archives, and in the cemetery lie the remains of some 4,000 Native Americans, many of whom helped build the original structure. The inside, much like the rest of Santa Barbara, is something of a disappointment as there's nothing particularly grand about the trimmings. To get to the mission, take the SBMTD bus, or walk or ride the half-mile from State Street up Mission Street and Mission Canyon.

Just beyond the mission at 2559 Puesta del Sol Rd, the **Museum of Natural History** (Mon–Sat 9am–5pm, Sun 10am–5pm; $5; *www.sbnature.org*) has intriguing and informative displays on the plants and animals of Southern California, viewed after walking through an entrance constructed out of the skeleton of a Blue Whale. Across the road, **Rocky Nook Park** is a great place to picnic or wander among the trees.

Eating

Because of its status as a prime resort area, Santa Barbara has a number of very good and very expensive **restaurants**, but it also has numerous more affordable options that offer a range of good food. Since it's right on the Pacific, you'll find a lot of seafood (and sushi); Mexican places are also numerous and of a very high standard. Smoothies – blended fruit and yogurt milkshakes – are everywhere, a welcome snack on a hot summer day.

Andria's Harborside Restaurant, Oyster Bar and Piano Bar 336 W. Cabrillo (☎805/966-3000). Enjoy good, mid-range meals throughout the day, along with a happy hour, in a lively atmosphere across from the yacht harbor.

Chad's, 625 Chapala St (☎805/5681876). Serving modern American cuisine in the intimate atmosphere of an historic Victorian home at relatively modest prices considering the quality.

Citronelle, 901 E Cabrillo Blvd in the Santa Barbara Inn (☎805/963-4717). Michel Richard's restaurant has been written up just about everywhere, and the high prices on the menus attest to this fame. Sweeping coastal views.

El Paseo, 10 El Paseo (☎805/962–6050). An upscale Mexican restaurant with a festive fountain courtyard.

Esau's Coffee Shop, 403 State St (☎805/965-4416). Ancient-looking café serving Santa Barbara's most popular greasy-spoon breakfasts. Open until 1pm daily; additional hours for the drinking crowd from 9pm–3am on Fri and Sat only.

Greek Café, 1150 Coast Village Road, Montecito (☎805/969-3717). The moderately priced Mediterranean and Southern Italian dishes like eggplant parmigiano are popular with locals, and the patio is a great place to watch those who aren't dining pass by.

Jag's India Restaurant, 14 E. Cota Street (☎805/884-1988). Simple yet elegant Indian food favored by locals and critics; slightly upscale. Dinner only.

Joe's Café, 536 State St (☎805/966-4638). Long-established bar and grill. A great place to stop off for a burger and a beer, more or less midway between the beach and the downtown museums.

La Tolteca Tortilla Chip Factory and Restaurant, 600 N Milpas St (☎805/963-5957). Fine Mexican food in a casual atmosphere.

Mousse Odile, 18 E. Cota St (805/9625393). The locals' latest favorite for French cuisine with a California flair; slightly pricey but intimate.

Natural Café, 508 State St (☎805/9629494). Scrumptious, cheap veggie meals in a prime spot for people watching.

Palazzio Trattoria Italiana, 1151 Coast Village Rd, Montecito (☎805/969-8565). Trattoria of choice for the region's smart set, though by no means intimidating. The portions are huge, the prices moderate, and the tiramisu divine. Ten minutes' drive south of town.

Paradise Café, 702 Anacapa St (☎805/962-4416). Stylish, slightly upmarket 1940s era indoor/outdoor grill, with good steaks and ultra-fresh seafood.

Pascucci, 729 State St (☎805/963-8123). Cheap and delicious pastas, gourmet pizzas, and panini served in a small, chic dining room or outside among the beautiful shoppers.

Pierre Lafond, 516 State St (☎805/962–6050). The best place in town for a homebaked continental breakfast, café-style.

Your Place, 22 N. Milpas St (☎805/966-5151). Voted best Thai food in town for 15 consecutive years by *Santa Barbara Independent* readers.

Waterfront Grill and the Endless Summer Bar/Café, 113 Harbor Way (☎805/564-1200). Specializing in seafood and views. Downstairs is casual fine dining. Escape the higher prices by heading upstairs and enjoy the surfing-inspired decor.

Drinking and nightlife

There are quite a few **cafés**, **bars** and **clubs** along the entire length of State Street, especially in the downtown strip; for the most up-to-date nightlife listings, check out a copy of the free weekly *Santa Barbara Independent*, available at area bookstores, record stores and convenience stores.

Coffee Bean & Tea Leaf at 811-A State Street (☎805/9662442). A great place to watch the mostly student locals parade back and forth on the strip.

Fathom, at 423 (☎805/730022). Bills itself as a gay disco, making it all the more popular with trendy college students of all persuasions.

Madhouse Martini Lounge, 434 State St (☎805/962-5516). Drink classic martinis and exotic cocktails in a swanky, slightly contrived bar full of Santa Barbara's hipsters.

Santa Barbara Brewing Company, 501 State St (☎805/730-1040). Popular microbrewery and restaurant with live music on weekends.

Sojourner Coffee House, 134 E Cañon Perdido (☎805/965-7922). Coffee, beer, wine, and a range of vegetarian food in a friendly, hippyish setting, with live music some nights.

Zelo, 630 State St (☎805/966-5792). One of Santa Barbara's more fashionable bars and restaurants, which evolves into a dance club as the night wears on, offering alternative dance, Latin, retro and such throughout the week. Closed Mon.

On from Santa Barbara

Continuing north from Santa Barbara you can either cut inland through the wine region of the Santa Ynez Valley (see below) or continue along the coast where you'll pass **Goleta Beach** – popular with families – as well as the characterless town of **ISLA VISTA**, which borders the forty-year-old campus of the **University of California at Santa Barbara** (UCSB). **Isla Vista Beach** has some good tidepools and, at the west end, a popular surfing area at **Coal Oil Point** ("Devereux" to locals); the estuary nearby has been preserved as a botanical study center and nature refuge where birdwatchers will find much of interest.

All along this part of the coast the **beaches** face almost due south, so the surf is very lively, and in winter the sun both rises and sets over the Pacific. About twenty miles out from Santa Barbara, **El Capitan State Beach** is a popular surfing beach, while **Refugio State Beach**, another three miles along, is one of the prettiest in California, with palm trees dotting the sands at the mouth of a small creek, giving the area a tropical feel. Inland on Refugio Road, up the canyon high in the hills, stands Rancho El Cielo, the one-time Western White House of retired President **Ronald Reagan**. Ten miles west, **Gaviota State Beach** is not as pretty, but there's a fishing pier and a large wooden railway viaduct that bridges the mouth of the canyon. All the state beaches have **campgrounds** (☎805/968-3294 or Parknet ☎1-800/444-7275; $18), and parking is $5.

Just beyond Gaviota the highways split, US-101 heading inland and the more spectacular Hwy-1 branching off nearer the coast. Half a mile off the highway, but a world away from the speeding traffic, is the small **Las Cruces hot spring** (daylight hours; parking $2), a pool of 95°F mineral water set in a shady, peaceful ravine. Take the turn-off for Hwy-1, but stay on the east side of the freeway and double back onto a small road a quarter of a mile to the parking lot at the end. Walk half a mile or so up the trail until you smell the sulfur.

The Santa Ynez Valley

An alternative to the coastal route out of Santa Barbara is to take Hwy-154 up and over the very steep **San Marcos Pass** through the **Santa Ynez Valley**, a pleasant route through a prime wine-growing region that's popular with leather-clad bikers and masochistic cyclists.

Three miles out of Santa Barbara, the walls of the **Chumash Painted Cave**, on the narrow Painted Caves Road, are daubed with pre-conquest Native American art. You can't actually enter the sandstone cave as it has been closed off to protect against vandalism. But peering through the bars will give you a good look at the colorful paintings inside.

Several miles further, beyond the San Marcos Pass, Paradise Road follows the Santa Ynez River up to **Red Rocks**, an excellent swimming area amidst the stony outcrops. **Lake Cachuma**, six miles further along Hwy-154, is a popular recreation area with a large **campground** (☎805/686-5054 or 805/686-5075; $15); it's not actually a lake but a massive reservoir that holds the over-stretched water supply for Santa Barbara.

Beyond the lake, Hwy-246 cuts off to Solvang, while Hwy-154 continues on through the vineyards around **LOS OLIVOS**, where wineries like Fess Parker, Firestone, and

Bridlewood are clustered. The **Santa Barbara County Vintners' Association** publishes a handy map to the area (☎800/218-0881) which includes each winery's address, hours and varietals.

Solvang and around

It is difficult to imagine anyone falling for the sham windmills and plastic storks that fill the saccharine sweet town of **SOLVANG**, but people come by the busloads to see the community, which was established in 1911 by Danes looking for a place to found a Danish folk school. Nowadays, the town, three miles off US-101 on Hwy-246, lives on tourism, and locals dress in "traditional" costume to entertain visitors. There are **visitors information** stands around the little town run by the local CVB (☎1-800/GO-SOLVANG or 805/688-6144), but the only things that make the town worth a stop are the fresh coffee and pastries sold in one of the many Danish bakeries in town.

While Solvang may mean "Sunny Fields" in Danish, life wasn't so bright for the thousands of Native Americans buried in the cemetery at the **Mission Santa Ínes** (June–Sept daily 9am–7pm; Oct–May daily 9.30am–4.30pm; $2), hidden away behind the rows of gingerbread buildings on the eastern edge of town. A century before the Danes tried to make the place look like home, the Spanish were here doing the same, and in 1804 they erected the nineteenth Spanish mission in their chain. Though the structure has undergone numerous restorations, the buildings are original, and the trompe l'oeil green marble trim on the church's interior walls is one of the best surviving examples of mission-era decorative art. There is also one of the better mission museums, displaying period furnishings and church documents, including a set of plaques thanking the Franciscan fathers for improving the lives of the native Chumash.

If you'd like to see for yourself how the natives fared, head over to **Santa Ynez**, three miles east of Solvang, where the **Chumash Casino** (Tue–Wed 10am–2am; Thu-Mon 24 hours; ☎800/728-9997) has been trying its best to suck in whatever money tourists haven't blown on Danish pastries. Recent initiatives put before California voters have tried to make slot machines, even on Native American lands, illegal. Things seem to be at a standstill, and in the meantime you can shake hands with the one-arm bandit all you like. Passing through the town proper, it's hard to imagine a town that serves as a sharper contrast to prosperous Solvang, or what another blow to the local economy would do.

If the whole spectacle makes you weary of humanity, you can always escape to the **Nojoqui Falls County Park** (☎805/688-4217) six miles from Solvang off US-101, where a gentle ten-minute walk brings you to a 75-foot waterfall. The route to the park is gorgeous, winding along Alisal Road under thick garlands of Spanish moss that dangle from a canopy of oak trees.

Lompoc

Hwy-1 splits off US-101 near Gaviota on a marvelous route through the inland valleys of the Santa Ynez mountains. **LOMPOC** (pronounced Lom-*poke*), the only town for miles, calls itself the "flower seed-growing capital of the world," and claims to produce as much as three-quarters of the flower seeds sold on earth, the products of which during summer form a thick carpet of color over the gently rolling landscape of the surrounding countryside. For a leaflet detailing where particular species have been planted this season, contact the **Lompoc Valley Chamber of Commerce**, 111 South I St (Mon–Fri 9am–5pm; ☎1-800/240-0999 or 805/736-4567), where you can also find out about the **murals** which, in recent years, have sprung up to beautify an otherwise faceless downtown.

Lompoc Museum, 200 South H St (Tues–Fri 1–5pm, Sat & Sun 1–4pm; $2 donation), is strong on Chumash and other Native American artifacts, and also has material on the town's **original mission site**, the scant remains of which can be found three blocks to the south on F Street off Locust Avenue.

Lompoc is also the home of **Vandenburg Air Force Base** sprawled along the western side of town, where various new missiles and guidance systems get put through their paces over the Pacific Ocean. Their vapor trails are visible for miles, particularly at sunset, though the only way to see any of it up close is by the Amtrak *Coast Starlight* **train**, which runs along the coast. The route was writer **Jack Kerouac**'s favorite rail journey: he worked for a while as a brakeman on the train and subsequently used the "*Midnight Ghost*" for a free ride between LA and the Bay area. Aerospace enthusiasts who plan at least a week ahead can visit the air base on four-hour **tours** (Wed 10am–2pm; reservations required ☎805/734-8232 extension 63595; free) that visit launch pads and a missile silo.

The **beaches** along this section of coast are secluded and undeveloped, and nearly inaccessible much of the year, either because of bad weather or impending missile launches. **Jalama Beach** (☎805/736-6316 or 805/736-3504; $5) at the end of Jalama Road, twisting fourteen miles off Hwy-1, spreads beneath coastal bluffs where you can camp overnight ($15); the large sand dunes of **Ocean Beach**, a broad strand at the mouth of the Santa Ynez River ten miles west of Lompoc, are the nesting grounds of many seabirds.

La Purisima Mission

Four miles east of Lompoc and signposted off Hwy-246, **La Purisima Mission State Park** (June–Aug daily 8am–6pm; Sept–May daily 9am–5pm; ☎805/733-3713; $5 per car) is the most complete and authentic reconstruction of any of the 21 Spanish missions in California, and one of the best places to get an idea of what life might have been like in these early colonial settlements. La Mission la Purisima Concepcion de Maria Santisima, as it's called, was founded in 1787 on a site three miles north of here, and by 1804 had converted around 1500 Chumash, five hundred of whom died in a smallpox epidemic over the next two years. In 1812 an earthquake destroyed all the buildings, and the fathers decided to move to the present site. With the threat of the native population reduced through illness, and also the continued threat of earthquakes, this was the only mission in the chain to have been built in a linear fashion rather than in the defensive quadrangle style – used both to confine Native Americans and to keep them out. The complex did not last long, however, after the missions were secularized in 1834; like all the rest, it was soon abandoned and gradually fell into disrepair.

The buildings that stand here today were rebuilt on the ruins of the mission as part of a Depression-era project for the unemployed. From 1933 to 1940 over two hundred men lived and worked on the site, studying the remaining ruins and rebuilding the church and outbuildings using period tools and methods. Workers made adobe bricks from straw and mud, shaped roof timbers with handtools, and even took the colors of their paints from native plants.

The focus of the mission is a narrow church, furnished as it would have been in the 1820s; nearby, at the entrance, small but engaging displays of documents and artifacts from the mission era and photographs of the reconstruction are housed in the old wagon house that serves as a **museum** and gift shop. On summer weekends you might catch a "living history day," when volunteers dress up as padres and natives and hold a traditional Mass, along with craft demonstrations. Call ☎805/733-1303 for information on special events and tours.

Pismo Beach and Avila Beach

Most of the land along the Santa Maria River, 75 miles north of Santa Barbara, is given over to farming, and both Hwy-1 and US-101 pass through a number of agriculture-based towns and villages. SANTA MARIA is the largest and most developed, though it's hardly worth stopping except to refuel or for a peek at the historic planes on display at the **Museum of Flight**, 3015 Airpark Drive (call for hours ☎805/922-8758; free). Other towns seem hardly to have changed since the 1930s, when thousands of Okies, as they were known, fled to the region from the dust bowl of the Midwest – an era portrayed in John Steinbeck's novel and John Ford's movie, *The Grapes of Wrath* (see p.380 for information on the Steinbeck Center in Salinas). Twenty-five miles north of Lompoc, Hwy-1 passes through the center of **GUADALUPE**, a small farming village where Spanish signs and advertisements far outnumber those in English, and ramshackle saloons, cafés and vegetable stalls line the dusty streets. Along the coast, just several miles west, lies the **Guadalupe/Nipomo Dunes Preserve** (☎805/545-9925), where you can look for whales out at sea or climb the 500ft sand dunes, the highest on the California coast, which surround wetlands that are an essential habitat for endangered seabirds.

Pismo Beach

The dunes stretch ten miles up the coast, reaching as far as two miles inland and ending just south of boisterous town of **PISMO BEACH**, where the two highways merge. The southern portion of the dunes, three miles south of the town, is open to off-road vehicle enthusiasts, who excite themselves flying up and over the sandpiles of the **Pismo Dunes State Vehicle Recreation Area** in dune buggies and four-wheel drives, motoring along the beach to reach them. Recently, the State Coastal Commission voted to allow even greater vehicle access to California's only drive-on beach, bringing some four million dollars in tourist venue to the area. Stranger still, scenes from *The Ten Commandments* were once filmed in this very same area. Thankfully, inland, the northern portion of the dunes is protected as a **nature reserve**.

North from the nature reserve, between the town and the dune buggy area, a number of beach-front **campgrounds** line Hwy-1; mostly RV-packed, they all charge around $20 a site. The **Pismo Beach State Park** has hot showers and beach camping for $18, and is a good place to see the black and orange Monarch butterflies that winter in the eucalyptus trees here (Nov-March) and leave before the summer crowds. However, the once-plentiful **Pismo clams** that gave the town its name (from the local Indian word *pismu*, or "blobs of tar" that the shells resemble), have been so depleted that any you might dig up nowadays are probably under the four-and-a-half inch legal minimum size.

Most of the town's commercial activity happens at the junction where Pomeroy Avenue crosses Hwy-1. If you have no interest in dunes or watersports, you're in the wrong place as the dozens of surf shops around you will attest to. You can, however, walk out on the gigantic pier for views back to town over the heads of surfers riding the waves. The **Chamber of Commerce**, 581 Dolliver St (Mon–Sat 9am–5pm, Sun 10am–4pm; ☎ 1-800/773-7778 or 805/773-4382), will help with accommodation. There are a number of affordable **motels** including the *Sea Gypsy*, 1020 Cypress (☎1-800/592-5923 or 805/7731801; ③), and the *Ocean Palms*, 390 Ocean View Ave (☎1-805/773-4669; ③). For something right on the beach try the *Edgewater*, 280 Wadsworth Ave (☎1-800/634-5858 or 805/773-4811; ④), which has a heated pool, hot tubs and some rooms with kitchens. With a little more to spend, *The Best Western Shorecliff Lodge*, 2555 Price St (☎805/7734671; ⑥), is dramatically situated, with a cliff-hugging swimming pool and gazebo and excellent views.

People have been known to drive to Pismo Beach just to sample the Clam Chowder at *Splash Café*, 197 Pomeroy Avenue (☎805/773-4653), and *Brad's* across the street at 209 (☎805/773-6165) also has chowder, along with all the American diner staples. For something a little fancier, *Old Vienna*, 1527 Shell Beach Road (☎805/773-4521), will transport you to a place you never thought you'd find on the beach, an Old World *Gasthaus*. The only **public transportation** is Greyhound, which stops downtown five times a day in each direction.

Avila Beach

North of Pismo Beach the coastline becomes more rugged, with caves and tidepools below ever-eroding bluffs, and sea lions in the many coves. The three-mile-long strand in front of the summer resort town of **AVILA BEACH**, the last outpost of Southern California beach life, was recently damaged by a spill from the nearby Unical Refinery. The entire beach was wiped out, reminding everyone just how fragile the coastal environment really is. An ambitious clean up and reconstruction project began soon after the spill, and much of the beach and boardwalk has now been restored to its pre-disaster status.

The area has a high concentration of burger stands and one good budget **motel**, the *Inn at Avila Beach*, 256 Front St (☎805/595-2300; ③). On the road into town, *Sycamore Mineral Springs*, at 1215 Avila Rd (☎1-800/234-5831 or 805/595-7302; ⑥), boasts rooms with their own private mineral baths. *The Olde Port Inn*, dramatically situated out on Port San Luis (☎805/595-2515) is *the* spot to dine in Avila and has magnificent views.

On the beach, you'll find teenagers on the loose from their families cruising the boardwalk, while anyone old enough takes refuge in the loud, local **bars**. The party atmosphere continues all summer long, and no one seems to mind the presence of the **Diablo Canyon Nuclear Plant**, which straddles an earthquake fault six miles up the coast (for what it's worth, three long bursts of a loud siren indicate catastrophe). The scenic route north from here to San Luis Obispo, **See Canyon Road**, cuts off north a mile from US-101, climbing gradually up the narrow, overgrown canyon between sharply profiled volcanic cones, with great views out over the Pacific.

San Luis Obispo

SAN LUIS OBISPO is almost exactly halfway between LA and San Francisco and a main stop-off for both Amtrak and Greyhound. It's primarily an agricultural town with a Middle American feel, though the 16,000 students at the adjacent Cal Poly campus help keep things reasonably active. On the whole it's an appealing enough place to pass an afternoon, with a town center boasting some interesting architecture, from turreted Victorian residences along **Buchon Street** south of the town center to some fine commercial buildings. There are a number of good places to eat, a couple of pubs and nightclubs, and – outside summer holiday weekends – affordable accommodation.

Arrival and information

The Greyhound terminal is at 150 South St, half a mile down Higuera Street from the center of town near US-101, and there are regular **bus connections** with both LA and San Francisco. Amtrak trains and Thruway buses stop several times each day in each direction at the end of Santa Rosa Street, half a mile south of the business district. You can pick up a free walking-tour map highlighting much of the town's best architecture from the **Chamber of Commerce** at 1039 Chorro St (Sun & Mon 10am–5pm, Tues &

Wed 8am–5pm, Thurs & Fri 8am–8pm, Sat 10am–8pm; ☎805/781-2777), which will also help with finding **accommodation**. The **Visitors and Conference Bureau** at 1037 Mill Street (☎1-800/634-1414 and 805/541-8000) may also come in handy. To find out **what's on** and where, check out the free weekly *New Times*.

Accommodation

Monterey Street was the site of the world's first (long gone) **motel** – the *Motel Inn*. Rates in its modern counterparts are generally low. The best **camping** nearby is south of town beyond Pismo Beach, or north off Hwy-1 in Morro Bay.

Campus Motel, 404 Santa Rosa St (☎805/544-0881) Clean, standard rooms, free continental breakfasts and a heated pool. ③.

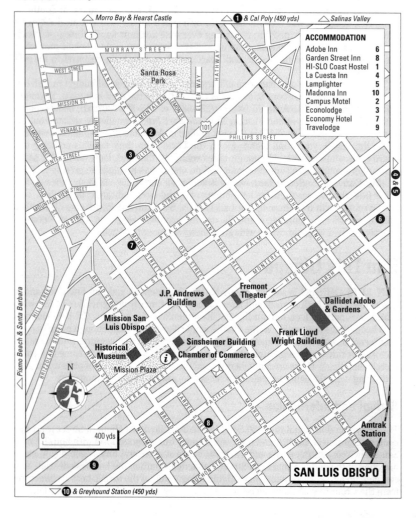

ACCOMMODATION

Adobe Inn	6
Garden Street Inn	8
HI-SLO Coast Hostel	1
La Cuesta Inn	4
Lamplighter	5
Madonna Inn	10
Campus Motel	2
Econolodge	3
Economy Hotel	7
Travelodge	9

SAN LUIS OBISPO

Econolodge, 950 Olive St (☎805/544-8886) Part of a national chain and offers a good standard of accommodation at a great price. ②.

Economy Motel, 652 Morro Street (☎805/5437024) A particularly good value among the budget choices. ②.

Garden Street Inn, 1212 Garden St (☎805/545-9802). Very central B&B in a restored 1880s house with comfortable rooms, complimentary wine on arrival and tasty breakfasts. ⑥.

HI-San Luis Obispo Coast Hostel, 1292 Foothill Blvd (☎805/544-4678). A 20min walk from the center following Santa Rosa Street north, this comfortable hostel has dorm beds at $14 for members, $17 for others.

La Cuesta Inn, 2074 Monterey St (☎1-800/543-2777 or 805/543-2777). As popular with business-people as vacationers, with spacious modern rooms and a good-sized swimming pool and spa. ④.

Lamplighter Inn, 1604 Monterey St (☎1-800/547-7787 or 805/547-7777). Older but comfortable motel with a pool. Popular with families. ③.

Madonna Inn, 100 Madonna Rd (☎1-800/543-9666 or 805/543-3000). Local landmark (see below) set in over 2000 acres, but the very standard "theme" rooms in this shocking kitsch monstrosity are a big disappointment at such inflated rates, especially after touring the imposingly pink, chalet-style lobby. ⑤.

Travelodge Downtown, 345 Marsh St (☎1-800/578-7878 or 805/543-6443). Simple motel but excellent value and location. There is another chain location at 1825 Monterey St (☎805/5435110). both ③.

The Town

San Luis is eminently walkable, with a compact core centered around the late eighteenth-century **Mission San Luis Obispo de Tolosa** (daily June–Dec 9am–5pm; Jan–May 9am–4pm; donation). A fairly dark and unremarkable church, it was the fifth structure in the mission trail and the prototype for the now ubiquitous red-tiled roof – developed as a replacement for the original, flammable thatch, which caught fire here in 1776 upon attack by Native Americans. Between the mission and the tourist office, **Mission Plaza**'s terraces step down along San Luis Creek, along which footpaths meander, crisscrossed by bridges every hundred feet and over-looked by a number of stores and outdoor restaurants on the south bank. Downstream, across a small park, the San Luis Obispo County **Historical Museum** (Wed–Sun 10am–4pm; free) holds a low-key collection of local artifacts tending toward the domestic, housed in the richly detailed 1904 Carnegie Library building. The main drag, **Higuera Street** (pronounced "Hi-Geara"), a block south of Mission Plaza, springs to life every Thursday afternoon and evening for the **Farmer's Market**, when the street is closed to cars and filled with vegetable stalls, mobile bar-becues and street-corner musicians. All of San Luis comes out to sample the foods and entertainment of this weekly county fair.

Though a number of commercial buildings of minor architectural note are detailed on the Chamber of Commerce's **self-guided walking tour**, the only one that should not be missed is the doctor's surgery designed by Frank Lloyd Wright at Santa Rosa and Pacific streets – where you'll also find the **Dallidet Adobe and Gardens**, 1185 Pacific St (☎805/543-6762), one of the county's oldest buildings set among manicured grounds with 125-year-old redwoods.

If you have neither the time nor the inclination to sample the small-town charms of San Luis, at least stop to look at the now famous **Madonna Inn** (see "Accommodation" above). Featured in the cult classic film *Aria*, the inn contains rooms decorated in a variety of themes from fairy-tale princesses to Stone Age cavemen. A very different sort of place is the **Shakespeare Press Museum** on the Cal Poly campus (Mon–Fri by appointment; ☎805/756-1108) – nothing to do with the Bard, but a great collection of old printing presses and lead typefaces, collected mainly from the frontier newspapers of California's Gold Rush towns.

Eating and drinking

Higuera Street is the place to head to **eat**, especially during the Thursday afternoon Farmer's Market, when barbecues and food stalls set up amidst the jostling crowds. You'll also find a couple of popular **bars** and **cafés** on and just off Higuera, around the Mission Plaza area.

Apple Farm Restaurant, 2015 Monterey St (☎805/544-6100). In the four star *Apple Farm Inn*, this casual, family-style restaurant is a surprisingly good value.

Benvenuti Ristorante, 450 Marsh St (☎805/541-5393). Slightly upscale Italian food in an almost painfully cute restored home. Good wine list and lots of patio seating.

Big Sky Café, 1121 Broad St (☎805/545-5401). An airy, modern place with an emphasis on Cajun and Creole food. $7 dishes and an assortment of coffees.

Buona Tavola, 1037 Monterey St (☎805/545-8000). Small and stylish bistro with good range of moderately priced northern Italian food and wine.

Café Roma, 1819 Osos St (☎805/541-6800). Extremely popular family-owned Italian restaurant with excellent pasta dishes served in a romantic setting for around $10.

Linnea's Café, 1110 Garden St (☎805/541-5888). A very successful, small café, serving up good espresso and top-notch breakfasts, sandwiches, pastries, pies and cakes. There's occasionally live music at night, too.

Linn's Restaurant, 1141 Chorro St at Marsh (☎805/546-8444) Casual restaurant featuring a large variety of salads, soups and sandwiches.

Royal Thai, 777 Foothill Blvd (☎805/5449777) Extensive Thai menu. Cheap and fresh.

SLO Brewing Company, 1119 Garden St, (☎805/5431943) A loud, sports-bar like restaurant offering tasty homemade brews, grilled meats and fish.

Taj Palace, 795 Foothill Blvd (☎805/5430722). The city's one Indian choice is slightly pricier than what you might find in a city with more competition, but good.

This Ole House, 740 W/ Foothill Road (☎805/543-2690) Informal Wild West atmosphere with open-pit barbecue meats and cocktail lounge.

Tortilla Flats, 1051 Nipomo St at Higuera (☎805/544-7575). Raucous, neon-lit Mexican restaurant, better known for copious margaritas than great food, but with free happy hour nachos and dancing from 9pm.

Morro Bay and the coast to Cambria

North of San Luis Obispo the highways diverge again, US-101 – the route favored by trains and buses – speeds up through the Salinas Valley (see p.377), while Hwy-1 takes the more scenic route along the coast. The first dozen miles of Hwy-1 follow the line of a ridgeback string of hills, a series of plugs from extinct volcanoes the most prominent of which have been dubbed the **Seven Sisters**. Two more continue the chain; the last is invisible under the sea, while the eighth is the coastal **Morro Rock** which, according to local lore, was named by the sixteenth-century explorer Juan Cabrillo, who thought it looked like the Moorish turbans in southern Spain. Nowadays it's off limits to the public in order to protect the nesting areas of the endangered peregrine falcons; in any case it's most impressive from a distance, dominating the fine harbor at **MORRO BAY**, where the local fishing boats unload their catches to sell in the many fish markets along the waterfront.

This easy-paced resort town is accessible from San Luis Obispo via CCAT **bus** #7 (6 times daily; ☎805/541-CCAT), though apart from the many seafood restaurants the only places worth coming here for are spread out around the bay, miles from public transportation. You get one of the best views of the rock and surrounding coastline from the top of **Cerro Alto**, eight miles east of Morro Bay off Hwy-41, a 2620-foot volcanic cone with good hiking and camping.

Closer in, on a point above the bay a mile south of town at the end of Main Street but providing a good view of Morro Rock, there's a small **Museum of Natural History**

Joshua Tree National Monument

Carmel

Grand Canyon

The ghost town of Bodie

Death Valley

Sequoia National Forest

Yosemite Valley

Blue Jay, Yosemite National Park

Sequoia trunks

Neptune Pool, Hearst Castle

Cannery Row, Monterey

Big Sur

(daily 10am–5pm; $2) best saved for a foggy day; otherwise, the **campground** across the street in **Morro Bay State Park** (reserve through Parknet ☎1-800/444-7275) costs $18 a night and has hot showers. Across the bay, the thin sandy peninsula that protects the harbor is hard to reach except by boat – it's entirely undeveloped and about the only place where you stand a chance of finding any Pismo clams. You can rent **kayaks**, which cost about $8 per hour, from the likes of Kayak Horizons, 551 Embarcadero (☎805/772-6444), or hike the two miles out there from Los Osos Valley Road.

 Montaña de Oro State Park (☎805/528-0513; free), four miles south at the end of Los Osos Valley Road, is much more primitive than the Morro Bay park, and has some

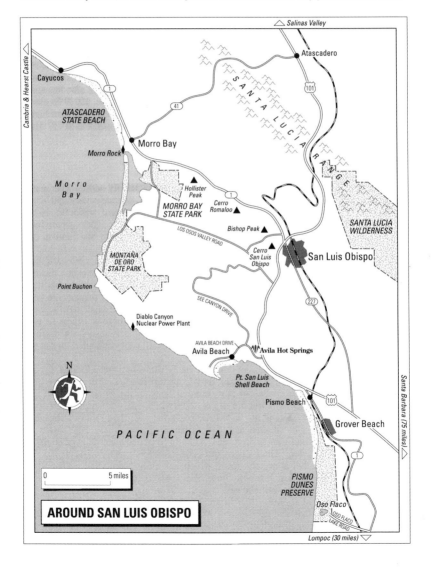

AROUND SAN LUIS OBISPO

excellent tidepools as well as a good beach at Spooner's Cove. The windswept promontory stands solidly against the crashing sea, offering excellent hiking along the shore and through the sagebrush and eucalyptus trees of the upland hillsides, which in spring are covered in golden poppies.

There are $10 **campgrounds** in the park, and numerous reasonably priced **motels** in town, including a *Motel 6*, 298 Atascadero Rd (☎805/772-5641; ②), close to the beach, and the cozier *El Morro Lodge*, 1206 Main St (☎805/772-5633; ④). For **eating** try *Hofbrau Der Albatross*, 571 Embarcadero (☎805/772-2411), a deluxe burger joint with bratwurst on the menu; *Lolo's*, 2848 Main St (☎805/772-5686), for Mexican; and *The Coffee Pot Restaurant*, 1001 Front St (☎805/772-3176), for hearty breakfasts and lunches. The **Chamber of Commerce** is at 880 Main St (Mon–Fri 8:30am–5pm, Sat 10am–3pm; ☎1-800/231-0592 or 805/772-4467).

The next town north is **CAYUCOS**, four miles along Hwy-1, originally a small port built by Englishman James Cass in the 1870s, and now a sleepy place ranged along sandy beaches with a nice pier. The *Cypress Tree Inn*, 125 S. Ocean Ave (☎805/995-3917; ②), is just one block from the beach. For coffee, muffins and pastries, you can't beat *Kelley's*, 155 N Ocean Ave (☎805/995-2980). Surprisingly, the town also has some of the area's best **nightlife** in *Ye Olde Cayucos Tavern and Card Room*, 130 N Ocean St (☎805/995-3209), in the heart of the two-block-long ramshackle center, with live bands on weekends and late-night poker games. The **Chamber of Commerce** is at 767 Main St (daily 9am–4pm; ☎805/927-3624).

Harmony and Cambria

About six miles to the north, you could drive right past **HARMONY** without even noticing it. This tiny hamlet has a population of 18, yet manages to operate several gift shops and offer wine tastings at *Harmony Cellars* (daily 10am–5pm; ☎805/927-1625). **CAMBRIA**, a few miles further, is a touch pricey and more than a little pretentious, partly due to everything it has done to cash in on its proximity to San Simeon and Hearst Castle, another seven miles further on. Hidden away in a wooded valley half a mile off Hwy-1, Cambria was an established town serving the local ranchers and fishermen long before Hearst Castle became the region's prime tourist attraction. Scenes from the shocker *Arachnophobia* were shot here, though with all the hotels that have sprung up, the only thing invading this town today is tourism. Still, it manages to keep its growing pains to a minimum, perhaps because its residents have enacted ordinances that make view-blocking development illegal. The older section of town is a half a mile east of Hwy-1 on Main Street, and though there's not a lot to see here, it's a comfortable enough place to stretch your legs or kill some time till your scheduled tour at the castle begins.

The **Chamber of Commerce**, 767 Main St (daily 9am–5pm; ☎805/927-3624), can help with accommodation. Back across Hwy-1, picturesque, seafront **Moonstone Beach Drive** has plenty of **places to stay**, but you'll pay for the views. The most reasonable rates are at *Cambria Shores Inn*, at no. 6276 (☎1-800/433-9179 or 805/927-8644; ④) and *Castle Inn by the Sea*, at no. 6620 (☎805/927-8605; ④). Even more affordable, though less dramatically situated are the *Cambria Palms Motel*, 2662 Main St (☎805/927-4485; ②), the *Bluebird Motel* at 1880 Main St (☎1-800/552-5434 or 805/927-4634; ③), or the *Cambria Pines Lodge* (☎1-800/445-6868 or 805/927-4200; ④), on Burton Drive on the hill above the town, which has large rooms and a rustic bar. **Camping** is available at **San Simeon State Park** (☎805/927-2035), two miles north along the coast, where sites with showers cost $14, $7 without.

You'll find good **food** at *Linn's*, 2277 Main St (☎805/927-0371), which serves a good selection of soups, salads and sandwiches; *Robin's*, 4095 Burton Dr (☎805/927-5007), which serves internationally-influenced California meals at reasonable prices; and the

Sow's Ear, 2248 Main St (☎805/927-4865), which attracts locals and visitors alike with giant American dinners heavy on seafood and meat. The *West End Bar & Grille*, 774 Main St (☎805/927-5525), is a friendly neighborhood pub with a large selection of beers, good meals and live music.

Hearst Castle and San Simeon

Forty-five miles northwest of San Luis Obispo, **HEARST CASTLE** sits on a hilltop overlooking rolling ranchlands and the Pacific Ocean. Far and away the biggest single attraction for miles, the former holiday home of publishing magnate **William Randolph Hearst** is one of the most opulent and extravagant houses in the world. Its interior combines walls, floors and ceilings torn from European churches and castles with Gothic fireplaces and Moorish tiles. Nearly every room is bursting with Greek vases and medieval tapestries, and even the many pools are lined with works of art. Ironically, the same financial power and lust for collecting that allowed Hearst to hoard these artifacts to himself have made them viewable to more people than ever would have seen them had they stayed in their respective lands. The castle, once only a weekend retreat for the most famous politicians and movie stars of the 1920s and 1930s – guests invited via invitation only included Winston Churchill, Charlie Chaplin and Charles Lindbergh – now brings in more than a million visitors a year.

The Castle

Hearst Castle, which Hearst himself referred to as "the ranch" (the official name is now "Hearst San Simeon State Historic Monument"), is the extravagant palace one would expect from the man whose domination of the national media inspired Orson Welles' classic film *Citizen Kane*. The structure is actually more of a complex of buildings than a "castle." Three guesthouses circle the hundred-room main *Casa Grande*, in which Hearst himself held court. What may come as a surprise is the harmony with which the many diverse art treasures that Hearst collected were brought together by architect Julia Morgan, who designed each room and building in the spirit of the masterpieces destined to be housed inside. Construction began after the death of Hearst's mother in 1919, on the southern edge of the inherited 250,000-acre ranch that became Hearst's own private free-roaming zoo with lions, tigers, zebras and bears. The work was never truly completed: rooms would often be torn out as soon as they were finished in order to accommodate more acquired treasure. The main facade, a twin-towered copy of a Mudejar cathedral, stands at the top of steps that curve up from an expansive swimming pool (the most photographed in the world), which is filled with pure spring water and lined by a Greek colonnade and marble statues. Indoors there is another pool, lined with blue Venetian glass and gold tiles with soft lights reflecting in the water's steamy surface.

Highlights inside the castle include the Refectory, lined with choir stalls from Spanish and Italian churches and the Gothic Suite, where Hearst conducted his daily business in Middle Age splendor. The private cinema should not be missed either – inside, Hearst saw first cuts of leading Hollywood films of the day before they were released to the general public. Outside the Castle proper there are several other major buildings, including the seventeen Neptune Pool Dressing Rooms, still hung with period swimwear and sports equipment; the Casa del Mar, an elaborate guest house with a largely Eastern theme; and the Casa del Monte, a smaller guesthouse with fully-furnished rooms overlooking the Santa Lucia mountains. The estate's extensive Italian and Spanish influenced gardens, terraces and walkways, require a full tour in themselves as they are extensive and feature hundreds of species of rare and imported flowers, bushes and trees.

Practicalities

To see Hearst Castle, you must take one of the guided **tours** (summer daily 8am–4pm; rest of year daily 8am–3pm; $14; ☎1800/444-4445; *www.hearstcastle.org*). Tour One, comprising of a short film, an introductory spin around the guesthouse and the main rooms of the *Casa Grande*, is best for the first visit – to guarantee a spot on the tour, make a **reservation**. If you're coming back, or are simply fascinated enough to stay for the whole day, there are three other tours: Tour Two takes in the upper floors of the main house, including Hearst's library and bedroom suite, which occupies an entire floor; Tour Three concentrates primarily on the Casa del Monte guesthouse; Tour Four (summer only) is of the grounds, gardens and wine cellar. During the spring and fall, docents in period dress take visitors on evening tours through the castle, speaking of Hearst in the present tense. These romantic tours end at the lamplit Neptune Pool, where guides tell stories of the legends who frolicked with each other there after dark. For more information on the tours, or to arrange for a wheelchair, phone ☎805/927-2020.

All tours take about two hours, and leave from the parking lot and visitor center on Hwy-1, where you also buy tickets. While waiting for the tour bus, find out more about Hearst and his castle from the excellent **museum** (daily 9am–5pm; free) in the rear half of the visitor center, beyond the point where you board the buses.

Finally, try and visit the castle first thing in the morning, when coastal fogs often hide the castle from the world below. After a long bus ride from the visitor's center to the top of the steep hill on which the mansion rests, you poke through the clouds into sunlight, as if entering Heaven. The cherubic white statues seem to lift off the icy blue pool along with the last misty vapors of the morning.

W.R. HEARST – CITIZEN KANE

It would be quite easy to portray **William Randolph Hearst** (or "W.R.") as a power-mad monster, but in retrospect he seems more like a very rich, over-indulged little boy. Born in 1863, the only son of a multi-millionaire mining engineer, he was avidly devoted to his mother, Phoebe Apperson Hearst, one of California's most sincere and generous philanthropists, a founder of the University of California and the Traveler's Aid society.

Hearst learned his trade in New York City working for the inventor of inflammatory **"Yellow Journalism,"** Joseph Pulitzer, who had four rules for how to sell newspapers: one – emphasize the sensational; two – elaborate on the facts; three – manufacture the news; four – use games and contests. When he published his own newspaper, Hearst took this advice to heart, his *Morning Journal* fanning the flames of American imperialism to ignite the Spanish-American War of 1898. As he told his correspondents in Cuba: "You provide the pictures, and I'll provide the war." Hearst eventually controlled an empire that at its peak during the 1930s sold 25 percent of the newspapers in the entire country, including two other New York papers, the *Washington Times*, and the *Detroit News* – as well as *Cosmopolitan* and *Good Housekeeping* magazines. In California Hearst's power was even more pronounced, with his San Francisco and Los Angeles papers controlling over sixty percent of the total market.

Somewhat surprisingly, considering his warmongering and extreme nationalism, Hearst was fairly middle-of-the-road politically, a lifelong Democrat who served two terms in the House of Representatives but failed in bids to be elected Mayor of New York and President of the US. Besides his many newspapers, Hearst owned eleven radio stations and two movie studios, in which he made his mistress Marion Davies a star. He was forced to sell off most of his holdings by the end of the Depression, but continued to exert power and influence until his death in 1951 aged 88.

San Simeon and north

The boarded-up pier of **SAN SIMEON**, an all-but-abandoned harbor town along the coast just north of Hearst Castle, is where all of Hearst's treasures were unloaded, as were the many tons of concrete and steel that went into the building of the house. Before the Hearsts bought up the land, San Simeon was a whaling and shipping port, of which all that remains is a one-room schoolhouse and the 1852 *Sebastian's Store*, a combination post office, café and souvenir shop. The beach south of the pier is protected by San Simeon Point, which hooks out into the Pacific, making it safe for swimming. Along the highway three miles south there's a concentrated blot of gas stations, fast-food restaurants and **motels**, mostly overpriced with the exception of a few along Castillo Rd such as the *Motel 6 Premiere*, no. 9070 (☎805/927-8691; ②) and the *Sands Motel*, no. 9280 (☎805927-3243; ②), both with heated pools and rates that tend to double on weekends in summer. There's **camping** four miles south along the beach at San Simeon State Park (see p.374).

North of Hearst Castle the **coastline** is mostly rolling grasslands and cattle ranches, still owned and run by the Hearst family, with few buildings on the distant hills. About three miles past San Simeon, a small strip of sand provides a resting point for a large colony of seals in the fall and early winter; trails – officially off-limits to the public, though easily negotiated by the brave and healthy – lead past a gate near the car park down to the beach, where you can watch the huge piles of blubber cuddle one another and frolic in the waves. Beyond here the highway seems to drop off in mid-air, marking the southern edge of Big Sur (see p.381), one of the most dramatic stretches of coastline in America.

The Salinas Valley and Steinbeck Country

If you're in a hurry, US-101 through the **Salinas Valley** takes four hours to cover the 220 miles between San Luis Obispo and San Francisco, compared to the full day it takes to drive the more scenic coast along Hwy-1 through Big Sur. In any case, as both Greyhound and Amtrak take the inland route, you may not have the choice; Amtrak's Thruways service barrels through the area, while Greyhound's local buses stop at all the small rural towns. The four-lane freeway closely follows the path of El Camino Real, the trail that linked the 21 Spanish **missions** – each a day's travel from its neighbor – through the miles of farmland along the Salinas River that are some of the most fertile in the nation.

This region is also popularly known as **Steinbeck Country** for having nurtured the imagination of Nobel-Prize-winning writer John Steinbeck, whose naturalistic stories and novels, including the epic *East of Eden*, were set in and around the valley.

The Salinas Valley

North of San Luis Obispo over the steep Cuesta Pass, US-101 drops down into the **Salinas Valley**, and, before long, **ATASCADERO**: a small town laid out to a curiously grand plan in 1914 that centers on its Palladian **City Hall**, a huge red-brick edifice whose domed rotunda now houses a small **museum** (Mon–Sat 1–4pm; free) describing the area's history. A few miles north, **TEMPLETON** has a strip of historic buildings along Main Street, among them the town's **museum** and **information** center in the Albert Horstman House (call for hours ☎805/434-0807). Down the block at no. 424, chocolate is a science at Herrmann's Chocolate Lab (☎805/434-3007), which sells chocolate-dipped everything and can custom shape chocolate with some advance notice.

PASO ROBLES, a few more miles north, is a thriving little town surrounded by horse ranches, nut farms and a number of **wineries** that are among the finest in the state. The Paso Robles Vintners and Growers (☎805/239-8463) publish a free map to their wine country which can also be picked up at the town's **Chamber of Commerce**, 1225 Park St (Mon–Fri 8:30am–5pm, Sat 10am–4pm; ☎1-800/406-4040 or 805/238-0506). Eberle, just east of town on Hwy-46 (daily 10am–5pm; ☎805/238-9607) and Wild Horse, on a scenic detour along Templeton Road back near the town of the same name (daily 11am–5pm; ☎805/434-2541) are among the finest. In town, there are a number of **accommodations** of much better value than anything you'll find closer to Hearst's former abode. Both the *Melody Ranch Motel* at 939 Spring St (☎805/238-3911; ②) and the brand new *Holiday Inn Express Hotel* at 2525 Riverside Ave (☎805/237-6500; ③) have pools. In the center of town, just off the **town square**, excellent **restaurants** include *Villa Creek*, 1144 Pine St (☎805/238-3000) with a full range of Mexican influenced American lunches and dinners, and the *Park Grill* at 1510 Park St (☎805/239-3721), with everything from burgers and pizza to pastas and salads. Ten miles east of town, past the junction of Hwy-41 near Cholame, pay your respects at the stainless steel monument near the site where **James Dean** crashed in a silver Porsche Speedster on September 30, 1955.

Even if you're racing up US-101, it's only a thirty-minute break from your journey for an essential peek at one of the least visited yet the most intact and authentic of California's Spanish missions, **Mission San Miguel Arcangel** (daily 9.30am–4.30pm; donation), just off the freeway in the small town of **SAN MIGUEL**. Built in 1816, it's the only mission in the chain not to have suffered the revisionist tendencies of a restoration. It was actually used for a while as a saloon and dance hall, though the chapel has been left pretty much unscathed, with colorful painted decoration and a marvelous sunburst reredos, complete with a striking Eye of God. The other buildings are interesting too, in their rough imprecision, with irregularly arched openings and unplastered walls forming a courtyard around a cactus garden. The *Western States Inn*, right off Hwy 101 on Tenth St (☎805/467-3674; ②), is the only hotel in town and has surprisingly comfortable rooms.

There's a second mission, accessible only by car, twenty miles west of US-101 along the Jolon Road (G-18), which splits off the highway twelve miles north of San Miguel. The **Mission San Antonio de Padua** (daily 8am–6pm; ☎831/385-4478; donation) is a rarely visited restoration of the 1771 settlement, less sanitized than some of the other California missions and giving a very good idea of what life might have been like for the missionaries and their converts. This mission was among the most prosperous of the entire chain, and around the extensive grounds, in a wide valley of oak trees and tall grasses, a number of scattered exhibits describe the work that went on in the long-abandoned vineyard, tannery and gristmill. There's a monastic peace to Mission San Antonio these days, and the brown-robed Franciscan friars who live here are rarely disturbed, despite being eerily situated in the middle of the Hunter Liggett Army Base; indeed the only sign of the military is at the gates of the base, five miles east of the mission, where you'll have to show your passport or some other form of ID. The large house across the valley from the mission used to belong to W.R. Hearst, who sold it and most of the land between here and Hearst Castle to the government in 1940 to help clear a $120 million debt. Today, the *Hacienda Inn* (☎831-386-2900; ②), as it's now called, offers basic **accommodation** at terribly reasonable rates. If the thought of sleeping in the midst of an Army base gives you the chills, you might just stay for **lunch or dinner** (☎831/386-2446) then be off again.

Nearby **JOLON** has a market and gas station, and the washed-out **ruins** of an 1840s stagecoach stop at the Old Dutton Hotel. **Lake San Antonio** (☎1-888/588-2267 or 805/472-2311), five miles southeast, has swimming, **camping** ($18-22) and showers along the west shore, as does the Nacimiento Reservoir further south. There are normally more campsites along the **Nacimiento-Fergusson Road**, which leads west from Jolon on a tortuous but picturesque journey over the mountains to Big Sur (see p.381); recently, 80,000 acres of the **Ventana Wilderness** burned in a tragic fire – started by a particularly violent lightning storm – taking months to be contained. Though things are nearly back to normal, it's not uncommon for natural disasters to befall this area and visitors should call ahead for the latest updates before planning any excursions in the area. The **US Forest Service** office, off the freeway at 406 S Mildred Ave (Mon–Fri 8am–4.30pm; ☎831/385-5434), handles questions about the area and issues backpacking permits for the **Santa Lucia Mountains**, which divide the Salinas Valley from the Big Sur coast.

The Jolon Road loops back to US-101 at **KING CITY**: "the most metropolitan cow town in the West," as it likes to be known. On the town's western edge, just off US-101, San Lorenzo Park is the site of the **Agricultural and Rural Life Museum** (daily 9am–5pm; ☎831/385-5964; parking $5), a collection of old barns, farmhouses and a one-room schoolhouse, all gathered here from various sites in Monterey county. The park also has a **campground** along the Salinas River.

The Pinnacles National Monument and around

From King City, you have a choice of approaches to the bizarre rock formations of the **Pinnacles National Monument** ($5 per vehicle, good for seven days); either follow G-13 and Hwy-25 to the eastern entrance and the **visitor center** (daily 8am–5pm; ☎831/389-4485; *www.nps.gov/pinn*), or continue up Hwy-101 to Soledad (see below) and turn onto Hwy-146 to the more spectacular western side. Contrary to what appears on some maps, no road goes right through the monument, but the place is small and it is quite possible to hike from one side to the other and back in a day.

This region of startling volcanic spires, brilliant reds and golds against the blue sky, is best visited in the spring, when the air is still cool and the chaparral hillsides are sprinkled with wildflowers, in particular the orange California poppy and deep-lilac Owl's Clover. Its many **trails** include a popular two-mile loop around the high peaks on the **Juniper Canyon Trail**, and the two-mile **Balconies Trail** to the multicolored, 600-foot face of the **Balconies** outcrop – good for **rock-climbing** (register at the visitor center and use only brown chalk when climbing) – and a nearby series of talus **caves** (take a flashlight), formed by huge boulders that have become wedged between the walls of the narrow canyons. These dark caves were popular with bandits who would hide out here after robbing stagecoaches. Rangers at both the east and west entrances can set you up with information and permits if you're interested in trying out some of the more advanced trails or if you'd like to do **climbing**, **top-roping** or **bouldering**. The trails are exposed so avoid hiking in the middle of the day in summer, and remember to carry plenty of **water**. There are several private and state-run **campgrounds** on either side of the park, the largest of which is the swimming pool-equipped *Pinnacles Campground Inc* (☎831/389-4462; $7 per person). All are first-come-first-served.

Soledad, Mission Soledad and Paraiso hot springs

The nearest town to the Pinnacles is **SOLEDAD**, a quiet farming community twelve miles west of the western entrance, best known as the site of the **Soledad State Penitentiary** – a grim building looming alongside US-101 two miles north of town where black militant "Soledad Brother" George Jackson was imprisoned for many years. The town itself has a definite Mexican flavor, its *panaderias* selling cakes and fresh tortillas – a good place to stock up on food and drink for a trip to the monument. But the main reason to stop is for a visit to **Mission Nuestra Señora de la Soledad** (daily except Tues 10am–4pm; donation), three miles west of US-101 on the south side of town. The thirteenth mission in the chain lay neglected for over a hundred years until it was little more than a pile of mud. The mission was never a great success (perhaps because of its full name, which translates as the "most sorrowful mystery of the solitude"), suffering through a history of epidemics, floods and crop failures. Parts have been dutifully restored and now contain a museum on mission life, but the **ruins** adjacent to the rebuilt church are the most evocative section.

More hedonistically you could head out to **Paraiso Hot Springs** (daily 8am–5pm; ☎831/678-2882), seven miles further west, high above Soledad in the foothills of the Santa Lucia Mountains: a palm-treed oasis looking out across the Salinas Valley to the Gabilan Mountains and the Pinnacles National Monument. The natural hot springs were popular with the local Native Americans for their healing properties, and have been operated as a commercial venture since 1895. The series of pools costs $25 a day to enter, and you can **camp** here overnight for an additional $5.

Salinas and around

The second-largest city between LA and San Francisco and the seat of Monterey County, **SALINAS**, twenty miles north, is a sprawling agricultural town of 120,000 people. It's best known as the birthplace of **John Steinbeck**, and for the **California Rodeo** (info and reservations: ☎1-800/549-4989, tickets: $10-18), held during the third week in July and the biggest in the state,. These attractions aside, you may well find yourself here anyway: Salinas is a main stop for Greyhound buses and the *Coast Starlight* train, and makes an inexpensive base for exploring the perhaps more obvious attractions of the **Monterey Peninsula**, twenty miles away over the Santa Lucia mountains, with the MST bus #21 making the 55-minute trip every hour from the Transit Center on Salinas Street.

Salinas and the agricultural valley to the south are often bracketed together as Steinbeck Country. The writer John Steinbeck was born and raised in Salinas, but left the town in his mid-twenties to live in Monterey and later in New York City. His childhood home at 132 Central Ave (☎831/424-2735) has been turned into an English-style tearoom. The gigantic new **National Steinbeck Center**, 1 Main St (daily 10am–5pm; ☎831/831/775-4720; *www.steinbeck.org*), takes you on an interactive journey through his life work. An informative biographical film shown in a constant loop at the museum's entrance is an excellent introduction to Steinbeck, and sets the tone for the rest of the museum. If you know very little of the author, then you will find the exhibits throughout engaging enough and might even be inspired to purchase a novel or two from the center's large supply. However, if you're already well versed in Steinbeck's life and work, your time will be better spent using the center's informative **map** to cruise by all the actual places in the surrounding area that were influential in the writer's life.

Today, as much as in Steinbeck's day, Salinas is a hotbed of labor disputes, with the gap between the low-paid manual laborers who pick the produce and the wealthy owners of agribusiness empires who run the giant farms still unbridged. In the 1960s and early 1970s, the United Farm Workers union, under the leadership of Cesar Chavez and Dolores Huerta, had great success in organizing and demanding better pay and conditions for the almost exclusively Latino workforce, most notably masterminding a very effective boycott of the valley's main product, lettuce. But workers are once again under siege, with wages less than half of what they were fifteen years ago amidst increasing worries about the dangers of exposure to pesticides and agricultural chemicals.

At the end of West Laurel Drive, a mile west of US-101, the **Boronda Adobe** is worth a visit only if you have an afternoon to spare. Located in the middle of beautiful drive through rich farmland, the building has been virtually unaltered since its construction in 1848, and rests alongside other historic structures that have been brought to the site as part of an expanding regional history center.

THE NOVELS OF JOHN STEINBECK

John Steinbeck's novels and stories are as valuable and interesting for their historical content as for their narratives. **The Grapes of Wrath**, his best-known work, was made into a film starring Henry Fonda while still at the top of the bestseller lists, having captured the popular imagination for its portrayal of the miseries of the Joad family on their migration to California from the dust bowl. *Cannery Row* followed in 1945, a nostalgic portrait of the Monterey fisheries, which ironically went into steep decline the year the book was published. Steinbeck spent the next four years writing *East of Eden*, an allegorical retelling of the biblical story of Cain and Abel against the landscape of the Salinas Valley, in which he expresses many of the values that underlie the rest of his work. Much of Steinbeck's writing is concerned with the dignity of labor, and with the inequalities of an economic system that "allows children to go hungry in the midst of rotting plenty." Although he was circumspect about his own political stance, when *The Grapes of Wrath* became a bestseller in 1939 there was a violent backlash against Steinbeck in Salinas for what were seen as his Communist sympathies. He died in New York City in 1968; today his ashes are buried in Salinas in the **Garden of Memories Cemetery**, 768 Abbott St.

Between Salinas and the Monterey Peninsula, twenty miles distant via Hwy-68, are a couple of other places of divergent interest. **SPRECKELS**, five miles southwest, is a small factory town built in 1898 for employees of the Spreckels sugar factory, at the time the largest in the world: the small torchlike wooden objects on the gable ends of the many workers' cottages are supposed to represent sugar beets. Parts of the movie *East of Eden* were filmed here, including the famous scene when James Dean – playing Cal – hurls blocks of ice down a chute to get his father's attention.

Practicalities

Hourly Greyhound buses between LA and San Francisco stop in the center of town at 19 W Gabilan St near Salinas Street, while Amtrak trains leave once a day in each direction, two blocks away at 40 Railroad Ave. For a handy **place to stay** try the *Traveler's Hotel* at 16 E Gabilan St (☎831/758-1198; ②), which is convenient, if seedy; if you're driving, choose from the many $45-a-night **motels** along Main Street on either side of US-101. For help with finding a place to stay, and for a free **map** and guide to the places that Steinbeck wrote about, contact the **Chamber of Commerce** at 119 E Alisal St (Mon 9am–5pm, Tues–Fri 8.30am–5pm, Sat 9am–3pm; ☎831/424-7611). There are quite a few good **Mexican restaurants** around the city, the best, oldest and most central being *Rosita's Armory Café*, 231 Salinas St (☎831/424-7039), open daily from 9am until midnight for fine food and stiff margaritas.

The Big Sur Coast

...a region where one is always conscious of eloquent silence...the face of the earth as the Creator intended it to look

Henry Miller on Big Sur

The California coastline is spectacular along the ninety miles of rocky cliffs and crashing sea known as **BIG SUR**. This is not the lazy beachfront of Southern California, but a rugged landscape at the edge of a continent, where redwood groves line river canyons and the Santa Lucia mountains rise straight out of the blue Pacific. Named by the Spanish *El Pais Grande del Sur*, the "big country to the south" (of their colony at

Monterey), it's still a wild and undeveloped region except for occasional outposts along the narrow **Hwy-1**, the dramatic coast road that follows a tortuous, exhilarating route carved out of bedrock cliffs five hundred feet above the Pacific Ocean, passing by mile after mile of rocky coves and steep, narrow canyons. Whether coming from San Francisco to the north or San Luis Obispo to the south, it's always a good idea to stop by the local tourism offices at either end of the long coastal road to check on the current weather and driving conditions before braving the drive.

Before the highway was completed in 1937, the few inhabitants of Big Sur had to be almost entirely self-sufficient: farming, raising cattle and trapping sea otters for their furs. The only connections with the rest of the world were by infrequent steamship to Monterey, or by a nearly impassable trail over the mountains to the Salinas Valley. Perhaps surprisingly, even fewer people live in the area today than a hundred years ago, and most of the land is still owned by a handful of families, many of whom are descendants of Big Sur's original pioneers. Locals have banded together to fight US government plans to allow offshore oil-drilling, and to protect the land from obtrusive development. If you'd like to know more about Big Sur's history and the contentious present, an excellent free **guide** to the area, *El Sur Grande*, is available at **ranger stations** and the Big Sur **post office**.

The coast is also the protected habitat of the **sea otter**, and **gray whales** pass by close to the shore on their annual winter migration. Visit in April or May to see the vibrant **wildflowers** and lilac-colored ceanothus bushes, though the sun shines longest, without the morning coastal fog, in early autumn through until November. Hardly anyone braves the turbulent winters, when violent storms drop most of the eighty inches of rain that fall each year, often taking sections of the highway with it into the sea. Summer weekends, however, see the roads and campgrounds packed to overflowing – though even in peak season, if you're willing to walk a mile or two, it's still easy to get away from it all.

The best way to see Big Sur is slowly, leaving the car behind to wander through the many parks and wilderness preserves, where a ten-minute walk takes you from any sign of the rest of the world. The only **public transportation** is by the summer-only MST bus #22 from Monterey (see p.388) running as far south as Nepenthe, four times a day in each direction, though the narrow Hwy-1 is a perennial favorite with cyclists.

Much the most interesting, and most developed, stretch of Big Sur is the northern end, ranged along the wide and clear Big Sur River, 25 miles south of Monterey (on Hwy-1) and focusing on **Pfeiffer Big Sur State Park**, where you can swim among giant boulders, hike up redwood canyons to a waterfall or sunbathe on a fine sandy beach. The **Ventana Wilderness** and **Santa Lucia Mountains** inland also supply outdoor adventures, although lately both have suffered great damage due to wild fires.

There is no Big Sur village as such, just a ten-mile string of grocery stores, gas stations and places to eat and drink dotted at roughly one-mile intervals on either side of the park. The main concentrations are by the post office two miles south of the Pfeiffer Big Sur State Park, at Fernwood, a mile north of the park entrance and, confusingly, at The Village, a further mile and a half north. Almost everything you may need to know is in the free *El Sur Grande* newspaper, but you could also call the **Chamber of Commerce** (☎831/667-2100) or the **park headquarters** (☎831/667-2315).

We've gathered all our **accommodation**, **camping** and **eating** recommendations for the Big Sur area into comprehensive listings starting on p.384.

Southern Big Sur

The southern coastline of Big Sur is the region at its most gentle – not unlike Portugal's Algarve, with sandy beaches hidden away below eroding yellow-ochre cliffs. The landscape grows more extreme the further north you go. Twenty miles north of Hearst Castle, a steep trail leads down along Salmon Creek to a coastal waterfall, while the chaparral-covered hills above were booming during the 1880s with the gold mines of the **Los Burros Mining District**.

Another ten miles north, the cliffs get steeper and the road more perilous around the vista point at **Willow Creek**, where you can watch the surfers and the sea otters playing in the waves. **Jade Cove**, a mile north, takes its name from the translucent California jade stones that are sometimes found here, mainly by scuba divers offshore. The rocky cove is a ten-minute walk from the highway, along a trail marked by a wooden stile in the cattle fence.

Just beyond the Plaskett Creek **campground**, half a mile to the north, **Sand Dollar Beach** is a good place to enjoy the surf or watch for **hang gliders**, launched from sites in the mountains off the one-lane Plaskett Ridge Road. This steep road is good fun on a mountain bike, and passes by a number of free basic campgrounds along the ridge, ending at the paved Nacimiento-Fergusson Road. Check at the **Pacific Valley ranger station** (irregular hours ☎805/927-4211) for up-to-date information on backcountry camping, since some areas may be closed in summer during the peak of the fire season. The station also handles the 25 permits a day allowed to people wanting to hang-glide, ten of which are given out on a first-come-first-served basis on the day. **Pacific Valley Center**, a mile north, has an expensive gas station, a grocery store and a good coffee shop, open from 8am until dark.

Kirk Creek to Julia Pfeiffer Burns State Park

The coastal **campground** at **Kirk Creek** (see p.385) sits at the foot of the **Nacimiento-Fergusson Road** which twists over the Santa Lucia mountains to the Salinas Valley. The road passes the excellent Mission San Antonio de Padua (see p.378), but it would be a shame to break the continuity of the drive up the coast, and in any case the views are better coming over the hills in the other direction. Two miles north of here, **Limekiln Creek** is named after the hundred-year-old kilns that survive in good condition along the creek behind the privately owned **campground**. In the 1880s local limestone was burned in these kilns to extract lime powder for use as cement, then carried on a complex aerial tramway to be loaded onto ships at Rockland Landing. The ships that carried the lime to Monterey brought in most of the supplies to this isolated area.

ESALEN, ten miles further north, is named after the local Native Americans, the first tribe in California to be made culturally extinct. Before they were wiped out, they frequented the healing waters of the natural **hot spring** here, at the top of a cliff two hundred feet above the raging Pacific surf – now owned and operated by the Esalen Institute (☎831/667-3000 or 831/667-3005). Since the 1960s, when all sorts of people came to Big Sur to smoke dope and get back to nature, Esalen has been at the forefront of the "New Age" human potential movement. Today's devotees tend to arrive in BMWs on Friday nights for the expensive, reservation-only massage treatments, yoga workshops and seminars on "potentialities and values of human existence."

Julia Pfeiffer Burns State Park (daily dawn–dusk; ☎831/667-2315; $6 parking), three miles north of Esalen along McWay Creek, has some of the best day hikes in the Big Sur area: a ten-minute walk from the parking area leads under the highway along the edge of the cliff to an overlook of McWay Falls, which crash onto a beach below Saddle Rock. A less-traveled path leads down from Hwy-1 two miles north of the waterfall (at milepost 37.85) through a two-hundred-foot-long tunnel to the wave-washed remains of a small wharf at **Partington Cove**, one of the few places in Big Sur where you can get to the sea.

Nepenthe and Pfeiffer Beach

Big Sur's commercial development starts in earnest with **NEPENTHE**, a complex of restaurants and stores named after the mythical drug that induces forgetfulness of grief. It stands atop the hilltop site where star-crossed lovers Orson Welles and Rita Hayworth once shared a cabin. The terribly overpriced restaurant here has been emptying the pockets of reflective visitors in search of upscale romance since the 1960s, though *Café Kevah* (see "Eating and drinking" below), on a slightly lower terrace in the same building, is more affordable and has better views. Downstairs there's an outdoor sculpture gallery and a decent bookstore, including works by Henry Miller, who lived in the area on and off until the 1960s. The **Henry Miller Library** across Hwy-1 (daily hours vary, ☎831/667-2574; donation) displays an informal collection of first-edition books and a few scant mementos of the writer's life in the house of Miller's old friend Emil White.

Two miles north along Hwy-1, the unmarked Sycamore Canyon Road leads a mile west to Big Sur's best beach, **Pfeiffer Beach** (open until dusk), a sometimes windy, white-sand stretch dominated by a charismatic hump of rock whose color varies from brown to red to orange in the changing light. Park where you can at the end of the road, and walk through an archway of cypress trees along the lagoon to the sands.

The Big Sur River Valley

Two miles north of Pfeiffer Beach, Hwy-1 drops down behind a coastal ridge into the valley of the Big Sur River, where most of the accommodation and eating options are located. The first stop should be the US Forest Service **ranger station** (daily 8am–6pm; ☎831/6672315), which handles the camping permits for the Ventana Wilderness in the mountains above and is the center for information on all the other parks in the area. A popular hike, requiring a permit, leads steeply up from the Pine Ridge trailhead behind the station, six miles into the mountains to **Sykes Hot Springs** (unrestricted entry), just downstream from the free **campground** at Sykes Camp along the Big Sur River.

Plumb in the middle of the valley, the **Pfeiffer Big Sur State Park** ($6 per vehicle) is one of the most beautiful and enjoyable parks in California, with miles of hiking trails and excellent swimming along the Big Sur River – which in late spring and summer has deep swimming holes among the large boulders in the bottom of the narrow steep-walled gorge. The water is clean and clear, nude sunbathing is tolerated (except on National Holidays, when the park tends to be overrun with swarms of screaming children) and, since it's sheltered a mile or so inland, the weather is warmer and sunnier than elsewhere along the coast. This is also the main **campground** ($22-24) in the Big Sur region.

The most popular hiking trail in the park leads to the sixty-foot **Pfeiffer Falls**, half a mile up a narrow canyon shaded by redwood trees, from a trailhead opposite the entrance. The thoroughly functional bridges over the river have an understated grace, as does the nearby amphitheater – built by the Civilian Conservation Corps during the Depression – where rangers give excellent campfire talks and slide shows about Big Sur.

Accommodation

In keeping with Big Sur's backwoodsy qualities, most of the available **accommodation** is in rustic (but rarely inexpensive) mountain lodges, and the very few rooms on offer are full most nights throughout the summer, especially on weekends. Mid-range accommodation is limited to a few cabins and motels, usually adjoining a privately operated campground or right along the highway, and not really ideal for getting the total Big Sur experience.

Lodges and cabins

Big Sur Campgrounds and Cabins, a mile north of Pfeiffer Big Sur State Park (☎831/667-2322). Campground with the best of the cabins: wooden tent affairs sleeping up to three for $40 and fancier places from $65. ②.

Big Sur Lodge, in Pfeiffer Big Sur State Park (☎1-800/424-4787 or 831/667-3100). Good-sized modern cabins arranged around a large swimming pool; popular with families. ④.

Big Sur River Inn Resort, two and a half miles north of Pfeiffer Big Sur State Park (☎1-800/548-3610 or 831/667-2700). Woodsy lodge with a handful of very nice (if pricey) rooms overlooking the river, and more basic motel-style rooms across Hwy-1. ④.

Deetjen's Big Sur Inn, on Hwy-1 seven miles north of Julia Pfeiffer Burns State Park (☎831/667-2377). The southernmost, oldest and perhaps nicest of the Big Sur lodges, with twenty very different rooms hand-crafted from thick redwood planks, all with fireplaces. ⑤.

Glen Oaks Motel, just over a mile north of Pfeiffer Big Sur State Park (☎831/667-2105). Tidy simple rooms with baths, close to the highway. ④.

Eating and drinking

Most of the places to **eat and drink** in Big Sur are attached to the inns and resorts listed above. Many of these are fairly basic burger-and-beer bars right along the highway,

CAMPING IN BIG SUR

Public campgrounds are dotted all along the **Big Sur coast**, in addition to a few less developed ones in the **Santa Lucia mountains** above, where you can also see deer, bobcats and (rarely) mountain lions. Sites along the coast are popular year-round, and all, unless otherwise stated, are available for around $15 a night (a rare few with $3 per person hiker/biker sites) on a first-come-first-served basis, so get there early in the day to ensure a space. Reservations are, however, taken at **Pfeiffer Big Sur State Park**, through Parknet ☎1-800/444-7275. For further **information** on camping in Big Sur, phone the park directly (☎831/667-2315). The following campgrounds are listed south to north.

Plaskett Creek (☎877/444-6677 or 805/995-1976). Thirty miles north of Hearst Castle and a mile south of Pacific Valley. Across the highway from the ocean with some hiker/biker sites.

Kirk Creek (☎805/995-1976). Three miles north of Pacific Valley and more exposed, but right on the ocean and with hiker/biker sites.

Limekiln State Park (☎831/667-2403). Two miles south of Lucia, with hot showers, general store, and developed trail to the limekilns. $22.

Julia Pfeiffer Burns State Park. Has two campgrounds, beautifully situated

overlooking the Pacific at the end of the Overlook Trail. There's no water, the toilets are primitive, and the area is often windy and chilly even in summer.

Pfeiffer Big Sur State Park. This is the main campground in the area, with spacious and well-shaded sites, many among the redwoods. Hot showers, a well-stocked store, a laundrette and some (officially) biker-only sites.

Andrew Molera State Park. The only walk-in site around. A vast meadow, half a mile from the beach, with water and latrines. First-come-first-served basis, so show up early. Camping payment waives day-use fee. $3.

There are also four commercially operated **campgrounds** in the Big Sur Valley: *Ventana* (☎831/667-2331 or 831/6244812), *Fernwood* (☎831/667-2422), *Riverside* (☎831/667-2414), and *Big Sur* (☎831/667-2322). All charge about $24 a night for two people, offer deluxe facilities, and accept reservations; they also rent out **cabins** (see "Accommodation" opposite). By Californian standards, all are fairly crowded, and all but *Riverside* mix tents with RVs.

but there are a few special ones worth searching out, some for their good food and others for their views of the Pacific. Because of its isolation, prices anywhere in Big Sur are around 25 percent higher than you'd pay in town.

Big Sur River Inn Resort, at the north end of The Village (☎1-800/548-3610 or 831/667-2700). The slightly upscale restaurant features a creative range of sautéed and grilled seafood starters and hearty main dishes served in a spacious, redwood-log dining room. In summer, you can linger over lunch and cocktails on the sunny terrace or in the riverside garden; in winter, the fireplace attracts locals and visitors alike. Live entertainment on the weekend.

Café Kevah, Nepenthe (☎831/667-2344). Tasty, if slightly overpriced, organic concoctions served up café-style on a sunny, outdoor terrace where hippies turned techies surf the web from their laptops while sipping cappuccino. March–Dec 9am–4pm.

Deetjen's Big Sur Inn, on Hwy-1 seven miles north of Julia Pfeiffer Burns State Park (☎831/667-2378). Excellent, unhurried breakfasts ($8) and a variety of top-quality fish and vegetarian dinners ($13–25) in a snug, redwood-paneled room.

Fernwood, Hwy-1 a mile north of Pfeiffer Big Sur State Park (☎831/667-2422). For burgers or fish-and-chips, this budget diner is the place. There's a small grocery store/deli in the same building if you want to pick up supplies for a picnic.

Glen Oaks Restaurant, Hwy-1 in The Village (☎831/667-2264). Gourmet California cuisine – mostly fresh fish and pasta dishes, with some vegetarian options – in a cozy, flower-filled cottage. $12–16.

Nepenthe, Nepenthe (☎831/667-2345). Next to the *Café Kevah*, this overpriced steak-and-seafood place has raging fires, an amazing view, and a James Bond-ish après-ski atmosphere.

North to Monterey

Though it's rarely visited, **Andrew Molera State Park** (daily dawn–dusk; ☎831/667-2315; parking $4), five miles north of Pfeiffer Big Sur State Park is the largest park in Big Sur with two and a half miles of rocky oceanfront reached by a mile-long trail. It occupies the site of what was the El Sur Ranch, one of the earliest and most successful Big Sur cattle ranches, initially run by Juan Bautista Alvarado, who later became California governor, and later by English sea captain Roger Cooper, whose cabin is preserved here. You can reach the cabin on some of the fifteen miles of hiking trails also used for guided two-hour **horseback rides** from the stables (weather permitting; ☎ 1-800/942-5486 or 831/625-5486; $25–55). There is also walk-in **camping** (see box above).

From the north end of the park the Old Coast Road takes off inland from Hwy-1 up over the steep hills, affording panoramic views out over miles of coastline. The part-paved, roughly ten-mile road winds over wide-open ranch lands and through deep, slender canyons until it rejoins the main highway at **Bixby Creek Bridge**, fifteen miles south of Carmel. When constructed in 1932 this was the longest single-span concrete bridge in the world, and is the most impressive (and photogenic) engineering feat of the Coast Road project.

A mile and a half north, beyond the **Point Sur Light Station** (weather permitting tours Sat 10am & 2pm, Sun 10am $5; ☎831/625-4419), a paved road turns off up **Palo Colorado Canyon**, past a number of houses and the remains of an old lumber mill obscured behind the redwood trees, finishing up eventually at Bottcher's Gap campground on the edge of the Ventana Wilderness. On the coast at the foot of the road, the derelict buildings at **Notley's Landing** were once part of a bustling port community. The northernmost stop on the wild Big Sur coast is at **Garrapata State Park** (daily dawn–dusk ☎831/624-4909), three miles south of Point Lobos and the Monterey Peninsula. A mile-long trail leads from Hwy-1 out to the tip of **Soberanes Point**, about ten miles south of Carmel – a good place to watch for sea otters and gray whales.

The Monterey Peninsula

*Waves which lap quietly about the jetties of Monterey grow louder and larger in the distance
... and from all around, even in quiet weather, the low, distant, thrilling roar of the Pacific
hangs over the coast and the adjacent country like smoke from a battle.*

Robert Louis Stevenson, *The Old Pacific Capital.*

The dramatic headlands of the **Monterey Peninsula** mark the northern edge of the
spectacular Big Sur coast, a rocky promontory where gnarled cypress trees amplify the
collision between the cliffs and the thundering sea. The towns here thrive on the tourist
trade, though each has a character very much its own. **Monterey**, the largest of the
three and a lively harbor town, was the capital of California under the Spanish and
Mexicans, and retains many old adobe houses and places of genuine historic appeal
alongside some overstated attractions. **Carmel-by-the-Sea**, on the other hand, three
miles to the south, is a quaint village of million-dollar holiday homes, best known for
the many golf courses that line the coast nearby. Smallest of the trio, **Pacific Grove**, at
the very tip of the peninsula amid its most arresting scenery, is far enough off the beat-
en track to preserve its Victorian seaside character reasonably intact.

Arrival, information and getting around

The Monterey Peninsula juts out into the Pacific to form the Monterey Bay, a hundred
miles south of San Francisco; coastal Hwy-1 cuts across its neck, and Hwy-68 links up
with US-101 at Salinas, twenty miles east. Greyhound **buses** (three daily in each direction between LA and San Francisco) stop at the Exxon station, 1042 Del Monte Ave,
along the Monterey waterfront. Amtrak **trains** stop in Salinas, connecting with local
bus #21 for the 55-minute trip (every hour) to Monterey.

Monterey's **visitor center**, 401 Camino El Estero at Franklin St (April–Oct Mon–Sat
9am–6pm, Sun 9am–5pm; Nov–March Mon–Sat 9am–5pm, Sun 10am–4pm; ☎831/649-
1770) has free parking and lots of advertiser-based brochures. Both it and the less busy
Chamber of Commerce **tourist office** at 380 Alvarado St (Mon–Fri 8.30am–5pm) can
help with accommodation. The **Monterey County Visitors Center**, 137 Crossroads
Blvd, in Carmel (daily 9.30am–6pm; ☎831/626-1424) has extensive information on the
entire peninsula and will help with hotel reservations. The Pacific Grove **Chamber of
Commerce** (Mon–Fri 9am–5pm, Sat 11am–3pm; ☎1-800/656-6650 or 831/373-3304),
across from the Natural History Museum at Forest and Central, has walking tour maps
of Pacific Grove's historic buildings and can help find a room in the many local bed and
breakfast inns. The best guides to **what's on** in the area are the widely available free-
bies *Go!*, *The Coast Weekly* and *Peninsula*, all with listings of movies, music and art galleries.

Getting around is surprisingly easy: Monterey–Salinas Transit (MST) buses
(☎831/899-2555) run between 7am and 6pm (11pm on some routes), radiating out
from Transit Plaza in the historic core of Monterey, and covering the entire region
from Nepenthe on the Big Sur coast north to Watsonville near Santa Cruz and inland
to the agricultural heartland of the Salinas Valley. The region is divided into four
zones: the peninsula, Salinas, Big Sur and the north coast; fares are $1.50 per zone, $3
for an all-day, single zone pass, and $6 for an all routes, all zones day pass. The most
useful routes are buses #4 and #5, which link Monterey with Carmel; #21, which runs
between Monterey and Salinas; and #1, which runs along Lighthouse Avenue out to
Pacific Grove; there's also the WAVE shuttle bus which runs every ten minutes from

downtown to the Monterey Bay Aquarium on Cannery Row, and from Cannery Row to Pacific Grove, costing $1.25 but free if you can present an MST receipt for that day. The only way to get to the Big Sur coast on public transportation is on bus #22, which leaves four times a day, in summer only.

Another option is to **rent a bike** for $24 a day: in Monterey, try Adventures by the Sea, 201 Alvarado Mall (☎831/372-1807) outside the Maritime Museum, or Bay Bikes, 640 Wave St on Cannery Row (☎831/659-5824). For more leisurely riding, Monterey Mopeds (☎831/373-2696) at 1250 Del Monte north of the Wharf rents mopeds for $20 per hour and $50 per day.

Accommodation

What Santa Barbara is to southern California, the Monterey Peninsula is to the north, meaning the area is among the most exclusive and expensive resort areas in California, with **hotel** and **bed and breakfast** room rates averaging $120 a night. This may tempt you to stay elsewhere – in Santa Cruz, or in agricultural Salinas – and come here on day-

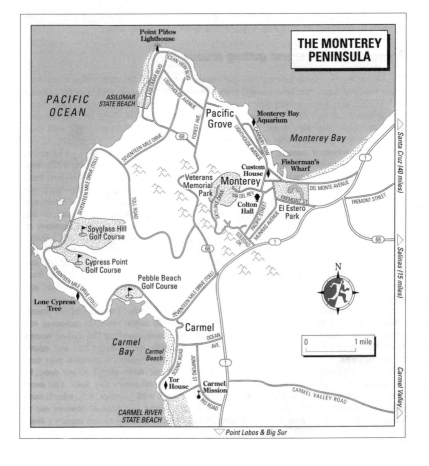

trips; the other budget option is to avail yourself of one of the many **motels** along Fremont Street and along Munras Ave, about one mile from the center.

The only **camping** within walking distance is in Veteran's Memorial Park, site of Steinbeck's fictional Tortilla Flat, at the top of Jefferson Street in the hills above town; it's only $3 a night if you're on foot or bike, or $15 per car, and is operated on a first-come-first-served basis.

Motels

Bide-a-Wee Motel, 221 Asilomar Blvd, Pacific Grove (☎831/372-2330). Excellent value, no-frills rooms, including a few with kitchenettes. A two-minute walk to the ocean. ③.

Borg's Ocean Front Motel, 635 Ocean View Blvd, Pacific Grove (☎831-375-2406). Good value for basic rooms, some with great views from Lovers' Point. ④.

Carmel River Inn, Rio Road at Hwy-1, Carmel (☎831/624-1575). Clean, pleasant and functional motel that was the model for Brian Moore's novel *The Great Victorian Collection*. Right on the banks of the Carmel River, near the beach and Carmel Mission. ③.

Econolodge, 2042 Fremont St, Monterey (☎831/372-5851). Comfortable, standard rooms with free local calls and continental breakfast. ③.

El Dorado Inn, 900 Munras Ave, Monterey (☎1-800/722-1836 or 831/373-2921). Cheap, basic accommodation at budget rates. ③.

Montero Lodge, 1240 Munras Ave, Monterey (☎831/375-6002). More basic accommodation at budget rates, though prices can double on popular weekends. ③.

Pacific Grove Motel, Lighthouse Avenue at Grove Acre, Pacific Grove (☎1-800/858-8997 or 831/372-3218). Simple, small motel in marvelous setting, 100 yards from the sea. Rates rise in summer and at weekends. ③.

Hotels and inns

Carmel Resort Inn, Carpenter and 2nd Ave, Carmel (☎1-800/454-3700 or 831/624-3113). One of the least expensive properties in Carmel; cottage rooms with fireplaces. ④.

Del Monte Beach, 1110 Del Monte Ave, Monterey (☎831/649-4410). A bargain B&B close to the center of Monterey. All the usual trappings for half the normal cost. ③.

Green Gables Inn, 104 Fifth St, Pacific Grove (☎1-800/722-1774 or 831/375-2095). Plush doubles in one of the prettiest houses in a town of fine homes, on the waterfront just a few blocks from the Monterey Bay Aquarium. ⑥.

Homestead, Eighth and Lincoln, Carmel (☎831/624-4119). The least expensive B&B in Carmel. Centrally placed, with rooms and cottages in attractive gardens. ④.

Horizon Inn, Third and Junipero, Carmel (☎1-800/350-7723 or 831/624-5327). Comfy bed and breakfast place with a pool. ⑥.

Mariposa Inn, 1386 Munras Ave, Monterey (☎831/6491414 or 800/2835663). The best deal in town. Cozy rooms with fireplaces and full amenities at reasonable rates. ③.

Monterey Marriott, 350 Calle Principal, Monterey (☎831/649-4234). Luxurious modern hotel right at the heart of historic Monterey, with views out over the bay and peninsula. Pricey, but in winter and spring the good-value "Aquarium Package" includes two tickets to the Monterey Bay Aquarium. ⑥.

Pacific Grove Inn, 581 Pine Ave at Forest, Pacific Grove (☎831/375-2825). Thoughtfully modernized 1904 mansion with spacious rooms, five blocks from the shore. ⑤.

Seven Gables Inn, 555 Ocean View Blvd, Pacific Grove (☎831/372-4341). Great views out over the beautiful coast from this immaculately restored, antique-filled Victorian mansion. Rates include full breakfast and afternoon tea and scones. ⑥.

Monterey

The town of **MONTEREY** rests in a quiet niche along the bay formed by the forested Monterey Peninsula, proudly proclaiming itself the most historic city in California, a boast which, for once, may be true. Its compact town center features some of the best vernacular **buildings** of California's Spanish and Mexican colonial past, most of which stand unassumingly within a few blocks of the tourist-thronged waterfront. The single best stop, though, not to be missed if you've got an afternoon to spare, is the **Monterey Bay Aquarium**, a mile west of town at the end of Cannery Row.

Monterey was named by the Spanish merchant and explorer Vizcaíno, who landed in 1602 to find an abundant supply of fresh water and wild game after a seven-month voyage from Mexico. Despite Vizcaíno's enthusiasm for the site, the area was not colonized until 1770, when the second mission in the chain – the headquarters of the whole operation – was built in Monterey before being moved to its permanent site in Carmel. Under the Spanish, the *Presidio de Monterey* was also the military headquarters for the whole of Alta California, and thereafter Monterey continued to be the leading administrative and commercial center of a territory that extended east to the Rocky Mountains and north to Canada, but had a total population, excluding Native Americans, of less than seven thousand.

American interest in Monterey was purely commercial until 1842, when an American naval commodore received a false report that the US and Mexico were at war, and that the English were poised to take California. Commodore Catesby Jones anchored at Monterey and demanded the peaceful surrender of the port. Two days later the American flag was raised, though the armed but cordial US occupation lasted only until Jones examined the official documents closely, and realized he'd got it all wrong. When the Mexican-American War began in earnest in 1846 the United States took possession of Monterey without resistance. The discovery of gold in the Sierra Nevada foothills soon focused attention upon San Francisco, and Monterey became something of a backwater, hardly affected by the waves of immigration which followed.

The Waterfront and Old Monterey

More than half a century ago, when Monterey first tried to pass itself off to wealthy visitors from San Francisco and beyond as an upscale resort, there was a great deal of doubt whether or not the demand would ever match the supply. Today, those worries have been put neatly to bed along with the visiting mass that stays here nightly, and tourism is now Monterey's main livelihood. A good deal of the trade is concentrated along the waterfront, around the tacky **Fisherman's Wharf**, where the catch-of-the-day is more likely to be families from San Jose than the formerly abundant sardines. Most of the commercial fishermen moved out long ago, leaving the old wharves and canneries as relics of a once-prosperous industry; fat sea lions float by under the piers.

The most prominent building near the wharf, at the foot of Pacific Street, is the modern **Maritime Museum of Monterey** (daily 9am–5pm; $5) with well-displayed but essentially mundane collections of ships in glass cases enlivened by interesting background on the town's defunct sardine industry. If none of this appeals, you should still pop in for the free, fourteen-minute film on Monterey history in preparation for a stroll on the **Path of History**. This loosely organized, roughly mile-and-a-half-long trail connects 37 sites in the **Monterey State Historic Park** scattered throughout the quarter-mile square of the modern city. Many of Monterey's historic buildings have survived in pristine condition and can be found along the way, though some can only be entered if you're part of the ninety-minute guided historic **walking tour** (daily 10am, 11am, 2pm; ☎831/649-7118; $5), leaving from the Maritime Museum.

Among the essential buildings to visit, the **Pacific House** (daily 10am–5pm; free), is just across the plaza; since its construction in 1847, it has been a courthouse, a rooming house and a dance hall. It is now the best of the local **museums**, with displays on Monterey history and a fair collection of Native American artifacts. While in the area, wander by the **Customs House** (daily 10am–5pm; free). This is the oldest governmental building on the West Coast, portions of which were built by Spain in 1814, Mexico in 1827 and the US in 1846. The balconied building has been restored and now displays 150-year-old crates of confiscated coffee and liquor in a small museum inside. A block west, look out for the unusual whalebone vertebrae sidewalk in front of the period-furnished **Old Whaling Station** (now a residence and office – if you're curious enough, knock and they might let you take a peek) and, next door, Monterey's **First Brick House** (daily 10am–5pm; free), which was built in 1847 and has a small display on the area's history.

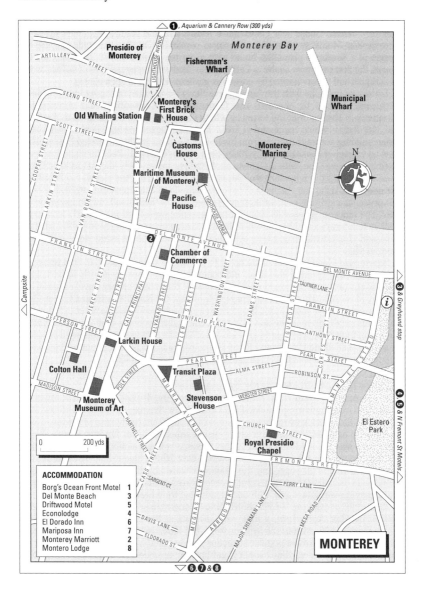

But the best place to get a feel for life in old Monterey is at the **Larkin House** (daily 45min-tours 11am, 2pm & 3pm or as part of Path of History tour; $5), on Jefferson Street a block south of Alvarado, home of the first and only American Consul to California and successful entrepreneur, Thomas Larkin. New England-born Larkin, the wealthy owner of a general store and redwood lumber business, was one of the most important and influential figures in early California. He was actively involved in efforts to attract American settlers to California, and lobbied the Californians to turn towards the United States and away from the erratic government of Mexico. Through his designs for his own house, and the Customs House near Fisherman's Wharf, Larkin is credited with developing the now-familiar Monterey style of architecture, combining local adobe walls and the balconies of a Southern plantation home with a puritan Yankee's taste in ornament. The house, the first two-story adobe in California, is filled with many millions of dollars' worth of antiques and is surrounded by gorgeous gardens which are open all day.

Larkin, as unhappy with the American military government as he had been with the Mexicans, helped to organize the Constitutional Convention that convened in Monterey in 1849 to draft the terms by which California could be admitted to the US as the 31st state – which happened in 1850. The meetings were held in the grand white stone building across the street from his house, the then newly completed **Colton Hall**, now an engaging **museum** (daily 10am–5pm; ☎831/646-3851; free) furnished as it was during the convention, with quill pens on the tables and an early map of the West Coast, used to draw up the boundaries of the nascent state. Across the street, the **Monterey Museum of Art** at 559 Pacific St (Wed–Sat 11am–5pm; Sun 1pm–4pm; ☎831/372-5477; $3) presents a striking case for its much-touted title of "best small town museum in the US." The museum's four galleries – featuring a rotating collection of mostly local art as well as temporary exhibits – are housed in a two-room adobe surrounded by splendid rose and rhododendron gardens and surrounded in turn by stone walls inlaid with painted tiles.

Stevenson House, at 530 Houston St (daily 45min-tours 10am, 2pm, 4pm or as part of Path of History tour; $5), is an old rooming house now filled with Robert Louis Stevenson memorabilia, much of it collected by the writer on his travels around the South Sea Islands. The oldest building in Monterey, the **Royal Presidio Chapel** (daily 8.30am–6pm; free), stands on Church Street at the top of Figueroa Street, half a mile east. This small and much-restored Spanish colonial church was built in 1795 as part of a mission founded here by Junipero Serra in 1770, the rest of which was soon removed to a better site along the Carmel River. In the rear garden is a fragment of the ancient oak tree under which explorer Vizcaíno said Mass back in 1602.

Cannery Row and the Monterey Bay Aquarium

A waterfront **bike path** runs from the wharf along the disused railroad two miles out to Pacific Grove, following the one-time Ocean View Avenue, renamed **Cannery Row** after John Steinbeck's evocative portrait of the rough-and-ready men and women who worked in and around the thirty-odd fish canneries here. During World War II Monterey was the sardine capital of the Western world, catching and canning some 200,000 tons of the fish each year. However, overfishing meant that by 1945 the fish were more or less all gone, and the canneries were abandoned, falling into disrepair until the 1970s, when they were rebuilt, redecorated and converted into shopping malls and flashy restaurants, many with names adopted from Steinbeck's tales.

Ride, walk or take the WAVE shuttle from Fisherman's Wharf to visit the engaging **Monterey Bay Aquarium**, a mile west of town at the end of Cannery Row (daily 10am–6pm; $15.95; ☎1800/756-3737 or ☎831/6484888, *www.mbayaq.org*). Reservations at Monterey's single most popular attraction are essential in any season. Built upon the foundations of an old sardine cannery and housed in modernist buildings that blend a sense of adventure with pleasant promenades along the Bay, the aquarium is one of the

---

ROBERT LOUIS STEVENSON AND MONTEREY

The Gold Rush of 1849 bypassed Monterey for San Francisco, leaving the community little more than a somnolent Mexican fishing village – which was pretty much how the town looked when a 29-year-old, feverishly ill Scotsman arrived by stagecoach, flat broke and desperately in love with a married woman. **Robert Louis Stevenson** came to Monterey in the fall of 1879 looking for Fanny Osbourne, whom he had met while traveling in France two years before. He stayed here for three months, writing occasional articles for the local newspaper and telling stories in exchange for his meals at Jules Simoneau's restaurant behind what is now the **Stevenson House**, halfway between the Larkin House and the Royal Presidio Chapel (see above).

Stevenson witnessed Monterey (no longer politically important but not yet a tourist attraction) in transition, something he wrote about in his essay *The Old and New Pacific Capitals*. He foresaw that the lifestyle that had endured since the Mexican era was no match for the "Yankee craft" of the "millionaire vulgarians of the Big Bonanza," such as Charles Crocker, whose lavish *Hotel Del Monte* which opened a year later (the site is now the Naval Postgraduate School, east of downtown), turned the sleepy town into a seaside resort of international renown almost overnight.

---

largest, most stunning displays of underwater life in the world. Comprising over 100 exhibits of over 300,000 creatures from the Bay – which happens to be the largest marine sanctuary in the United States – in innovative replicas of their natural habitats, the Aquarium requires at least half a day for a proper visit. Even those tourists who swear they'll be able to tear themselves away in half the time tend to linger. Museum highlights include a 335,000 gallon Kelp Forest tank, a touch pool where you can pet your favorite bat rays, a pool of sea otters, and a stunning jellyfish exhibit which uses the latest lighting technology to bring out the creatures' myriad colors. The recently installed Mysteries of the Deep exhibit is the largest living deep-sea display in the world Try also to catch the sea otters at feeding time (usually 11am, 2pm & 4.30pm); the playful critters were hunted nearly to extinction for their fur – said, with some one million hairs per square inch, to be the softest in the world.

Pacific Grove

PACIFIC GROVE – or "Butterfly Town USA," as it likes to call itself – stands curiously apart from the rest of the peninsula, less known but more impressively situated than its two famous neighbors. The town began as a campground and Methodist retreat in 1875, a summertime tent city for revivalist Christians in which strong drink, naked flesh and reading the Sunday papers were firmly prohibited. The Methodists have long since gone, but otherwise the town is little changed. Its quiet streets, lined by pine trees and grand old Victorian wooden houses, are enlivened each year by hundreds of thousands of golden **monarch butterflies**, which come here each winter from all over the western US and Canada to escape the cold and have become the town's main tourist attraction. In fact these little orange-and-black butterflies are so important to the local economy that they're protected by local law; there's a $1000 fine for molesting a monarch.

Downtown Pacific Grove centers upon the intersection of Forest Street and Lighthouse Avenue, two miles northwest of central Monterey. Two blocks north at 667 Lighthouse Ave, the **Bookworks** bookstore and café (Sun–Thurs 9am–10pm, Fri & Sat 9am–11pm; ☎831/372-2242), is the place to pick up more detailed guides to the local area, or just stop for a cup of coffee and a pastry. A block down Forest Street, on the corner of Central Avenue, the **Pacific Grove Museum of Natural History** (Tues–Sun

10am–5pm; ☎831/648-3116; free) has an interesting collection of local wildlife, including lots of butterflies, over four hundred stuffed birds, a relief model of the undersea topography and exhibits on the ways of life of the native Costanoan and Salinan peoples. Across the park, the **Chautauqua Hall** was for a time in the 1880s the focus of town life as the West Coast headquarters of the instructional and populist Chautauqua Movement, a left-leaning, traveling university which reached thousands of Americans long before there was any accessible form of higher education. Nowadays the plain white building is used as a dance hall, with a three-piece band playing favorites from the Thirties and Forties every Saturday night, and square dancing on Thursday.

About the only reminder of the fundamentalist camp meetings are the intricately detailed, tiny wooden **cottages**, along 16th and 17th streets, which date from the revival days; in some cases wooden boards were simply nailed over the frames of canvas tents to make them habitable year-round. Down Central Avenue at 12th, at the top of a small wooded park overlooking the ocean, stands the deep-red Gothic wooden church of **Saint Mary's By-The-Sea**, Pacific Grove's first substantial church, built in 1887, with a simple interior of redwood beams polished to a shimmering glow, and an authentic signed Tiffany stained-glass window, nearest the altar on the left.

Ocean View Boulevard, which runs between the church and the ocean, circles along the coast around the town, passing the headland of **Lovers Point** – originally called Lovers of Jesus Point – where preachers used to hold sunrise services. Surrounded in early summer by the colorful red and purple blankets of blooming ice plants, it's one of the peninsula's best **beaches**, where you can lounge around and swim from the intimate, protected strand – if you're lucky enough to have arrived on one of the rare fog-free days in summer – or rent a glass-bottomed boat and explore the sheltered cove. Ocean View Boulevard runs another mile along the coast out to the tip of the peninsula, where the 150-year-old **Point Piños Lighthouse** (Thurs–Sun 1–4pm; free), is the oldest continuously operating lighthouse on the California coast.

Around the point, the name of the coastal road changes to Sunset Drive and leads on to **Asilomar State Beach**, a wilder stretch with more dramatic surf, too dangerous for swimming, though the rocky shore provides homes for all sorts of tidepool life. The **Butterfly Trees**, where the monarchs discretely congregate from November through early March in giant brown clusters way up in the treetops, are on Ridge Road, a quarter of a mile inland along Lighthouse Avenue. Hwy-68 from the end of Sunset Drive takes the inland route over the hills, joining Hwy-1 just north of Carmel, while the **Seventeen Mile Drive** ($7.25 per car), a privately owned, scenic toll road, loops from Pacific Grove along the coast south to Carmel and back again, passing by the golf courses and country clubs of Pebble Beach. Halfway along stands the trussed-up figure of the **Lone Cypress**, subject of many a postcard, and there are enough beautiful vistas of the rugged coastline to make it almost worth braving the hordes who pack the roads on holiday weekends.

Carmel

Set on gently rising headlands above a sculpted rocky shore, **Carmel** is confined to a few neat rows of quaint shops and miniature homes running along either side of Ocean Avenue towards the largely untouched coastline. Besides all the rampant cuteness, Carmel's only real crime is its ridiculously inflated price scale.

The town's reputation as a rich resort belies its origins; there was nothing much here until the San Francisco earthquake and fire of 1906 led a number of artists and writers from the city to take refuge in the area, forming a bohemian colony on the wild and uninhabited slopes that soon became notorious throughout the state. Figurehead of the group was the poet George Sterling, and part-time members included Jack London, Mary Austin and the young Sinclair Lewis. But it was a short-lived alliance, and by the

1920s the group had broken up, and an influx of wealthy San Franciscans had put Carmel well on its way to becoming the exclusive corner it is today.

Today, Carmel seems the epitome of parochial snobbishness. Local laws, enacted to preserve the gingerbread charm of the town, prohibit parking meters, street addresses and postal deliveries (all mail is picked up in person from the post office) and franchise businesses are banned outright within the city limits.

Carmel's center, fifteen minutes south of Monterey on MST bus #4 or #5, doesn't have much to recommend it – it's largely designer-shopping territory, in which Armani and Ralph Lauren rub shoulders with mock-Tudor tearooms and a number of tacky **art galleries** along Dolores Street. The Weston Gallery on Sixth Street between Dolores and Lincoln (✆831/624-4453) is worth a look, however, hosting regular shows of the best contemporary photographers and with a permanent display of works by Fox Talbot, Ansel Adams and Edward Weston – who lived in Carmel for most of his life. To get the lowdown on the other galleries, check out the free, widely available *Carmel Gallery Guide*.

The town's best feature, however, is the largely untouched nearby coastline, among the most beautiful in California. **Carmel Beach** is a tranquil cove of emerald blue water bordered by soft white sand and cypress-covered cliffs; the tides are deceptively strong and dangerous, so be careful if you chance a swim. A mile south from Carmel Beach along Carmel Bay, **Tor House** was, when built in 1919, the only building on a then treeless headland. The poet Robinson Jeffers (whose very long, starkly tragic narrative poems were far more popular in his time than they are today) built the small cottage and adjacent tower by hand, out of granite boulders he carried up from the cove below. Hourly guided **tours** of the house and gardens (Fri & Sat 10am–4pm; $7; reservations essential on ✆831/624-1840 or 831/624-1813) include a rather obsequious account of the writer's life and work.

Another quarter of a mile along Scenic Road, around the tip of Carmel Point, the mile-long **Carmel River State Beach** (✆831/624-4909) is less visited than the city beach, and includes a bird sanctuary on a freshwater lagoon that offers safe and sometimes warm swimming. Again, if you brave the waves, beware of the strong tides and currents, especially at the south end of the beach, where the sand falls away at a very steep angle, causing big and potentially hazardous surf.

Carmel Mission

Half a mile or so up the Carmel River from the beach, also reachable by following Junipero Avenue from downtown, **Carmel Mission Basilica** (daily 9am–5pm; $3) – San Carlos Borromeo de Carmelo – was founded in 1770 by Junipero Serra as the second of the California missions and the headquarters of the chain. Father Serra never got to see the finished church – he died before its completion and is buried under the floor in front of the altar. Finally completed by Father Lasuén in 1797, the sandstone church has undergone one of the most painstakingly authentic restorations in the entire mission chain, a process well-detailed in one of the three excellent **museums** in the mission compound. At the time of reconstruction, the building was little more than a pile of rubble, but today the whimsically ornate structure stands firmly as the most romantic mission in the chain. The dainty building has a dark side too: three thousand local Native Americans are buried in the adjacent **cemetery**.

Point Lobos State Reserve

Two miles south of the mission along Hwy-1, accessible in summer on MST bus #22, the **Point Lobos State Reserve** (daily: summer 9am–7pm; winter 9am–5pm; ✆831/624-4909; $7 parking) has plenty of natural justifications to support its title of "the greatest meeting of land and water in the world." There are over 250 bird and animal species along the **hiking trails** in the area, and the sea here is one of the richest underwater habitats in California. Because the point juts so far out into the ocean, there are some of the earth's best undisturbed views of the ocean: craggy granite pinnacles, land-forms which inspired Robert Louis Stevenson's *Treasure Island*, reach out of jagged blue coves. Sea lions and otters frolic in the crashing surf, just below the many vantage points along the park's coastal trail. Gray whales are often seen offshore – sometimes as close as a hundred yards away – migrating south in January and returning with young calves in April and early May. The park, named after the *lobos marinos* – the noisy, barking sea lions that group on the rocks off the reserve's tip – protects some of the few remaining Monterey cypress trees on its knife-edged headland, despite being buffeted by relentless winds.

Except for a small parking lot, the reserve is closed to cars, so lines sometimes form along the highway to wait for a parking space. A worthwhile **guide** and **map** is included in the admission fee.

Carmel Valley

About 15 miles inland, east along route G16, lies **CARMEL VALLEY VILLAGE**, a coun-try hamlet that bills itself as the epicenter of the Monterey County's wine country, a clus-ter of vineyards encompassing an area as far afield as King City to the south on Hwy–101. In the **Carmel Valley** that surrounds the village, you'll find a number of vine-yards such as Durney, Bernardus and River Ranch in a quiet pastoral setting – a big breath of relief after crowded, coastal Carmel. The Monterey County Vintners and Growers Association (☎831/375-9400) publishes a map to the area, and the **Chamber of Commerce** (☎1-888/659-4228 or 831/659-4000) lures visitors from Carmel with a new local map – available from most any visitors' center in Monterey County – crammed with shopping and dining possibilities.

Eating

There are many excellent **eating places** all over the peninsula, and though prices tend to float near resort prices, the competition for tourist dollars insure quality. For a full list of the hundreds of eating options in the area, check out a copy of the free, weekly and widely available *Go!* or *Coast Weekly*. If you're on anything like a tight budget, the best eats are on the north side of Monterey along Fremont Street, on and around Lighthouse Avenue (just south of Cannery Row), and in the shopping malls along Hwy-1 south of Carmel.

La Boheme, Dolores Street between Ocean and Seventh, Carmel (☎831/624-7500). Fine dining the Carmel way – in a scaled-down replica of a French country hotel courtyard, complete with white-washed walls and hanging laundry. Multi-course, *prix-fixe* meals for about $20 plus wine and service.

Bytes, 403 Calle Principal, Monterey (☎831/372-2987). There's no reason to wait till after lunch to check your email here. Full computer services and a full espresso bar as well as a selection of rela-tively affordable sandwiches.

Café Fina, middle of Fisherman's Wharf, Monterey (☎831/372-5200). Pricey pastas, wood-oven piz-zas, and, of course, grilled fresh fish in the Wharf's most style-conscious setting.

Fishwife at Asilomar Beach, 1996 Sunset Drive at Asilomar, Pacific Grove (☎831/375-7107). Long-standing local favorite, serving great food at reasonable prices – king prawns sautéed in red peppers and lime juice with rice and steamed vegetables for $10 – in cozy, unpretentious surroundings.

India's Clay Oven, 150 Del Monte Ave., 2nd Floor, Monterey (☎831/373-2529). If you're overcome by the sudden desire for *papadums* and *saag paneer*, you now know where to go for slightly upscale versions of the same.

Little Napoli, Dolores St b/w Ocean & 7th, Carmel (☎831/626-6335). One of the town's many excellent mid-range Italian restaurants, serving oversized portions of fresh pasta with original sauces in an atmosphere with all the romantic charm you'd expect from a Carmel address.

Old Monterey Café, 489 Alvarado St, Monterey (☎831/646-1021). Reasonable more-than-you-can-eat breakfasts, with great omelets and buckwheat pancakes, plus tasty sandwiches; daily except Tues 7am–2.30pm.

Monterey Wine Company, 251 Alvarado, Monterey (☎831/648-9463). This gourmet market is a great place to get together all the fixings for a coastal picnic.

Paolina's, San Carlos b/w Ocean & 7th, Carmel (☎831/624-5599). Fresh homemade pastas in a casual courtyard setting at half the price of other Carmel dining.

Papa Chano's Taqueria, 462 Alvarado St, Monterey (☎831/646-9587). Delicious and cheap Mexican food, featuring great burritos. The chicken rotisserie of the same name, two doors down at 470 Alvarado, serves roasted chicken, also cheap.

Pasta Mia Trattoria, 481 Lighthouse, Pacific Grove (☎831/375-7709). Tasty homemade pastas, grilled seafood, and veal in a rustic, homey setting. Pasta entrées for about $11.

Pâtisserie Boissière, Mission St b/w Ocean & 7th, Carmel (☎831/624-5008). With savory quiches, salads, and even Coquille Saint Jacques on the menu, this mid-range restaurant also serves the pastries you'd expect from the name and prepares picnic lunches with advance notice.

Pepper's Mexicali Café, 170 Forest Ave, Pacific Grove (☎831/373-6892). Gourmet Mexican seafood Californified into healthy, high-style dishes at reasonable prices.

Rosine's, 434 Alvarado St, Monterey (☎831/375-1400). The huge menu at this popular high-ceilinged establishment right in the center of town features basic sandwiches, pastas, salads, and burgers at reasonable prices. Also serves breakfast.

Sardine Factory, 701 Wave St, Monterey (☎831/373-3775). California seafood cuisine served in French château splendor at less-than-expected prices.

Schooners, in the Monterey Plaza Hotel, 400 Cannery Row, Monterey (☎831/372-2628). Colorful upscale California bistro in an historic hotel with views over the bay.

Stokes Adobe, 500 Hartnell St, Monterey (☎831/373-1110). Built in 1833, the historic former home is now an elegant restaurant serving Mediterranean cuisine with a Californian flare.

Triples, 220 Oliver St, Monterey (☎831/372-4744). Light and healthy upscale California cuisine, fresh fish and great salads, on a sunny outdoor patio or inside historic Duarte's Store. Behind the Pacific House in the Monterey State Historic Park.

Tuck Box Tearoom, Dolores Street between Ocean and Seventh, Carmel (☎831/624-6365). Breakfast, lunch and afternoon tea in half-timbered mock-Tudor Old England setting; costly and kitsch but fun.

Bars and nightlife

Monterey has always been better known as a sleepy, romantic getaway than as a hub of hip nightlife, but the **Monterey Jazz Festival** in mid-September (☎800/3073378) is the oldest continuous jazz festival in the world and draws crowds from afar. Check out the widely available *Go!* or *Coast Weekly* for the most current listings.

Bay Books, 316 Alvarado St, Monterey (☎831/375-1855). Sip coffee until 10pm (11pm at weekends) while browsing in one of Monterey's better book shops.

Bookworks, 667 Lighthouse Ave, Monterey (☎831/3722242). Café frequented by locals, featuring live music and light lunch fare at reasonable prices.

Franco's Norma Jean Club, 10639 Merritt St, Castroville (☎831/6332090). Heading towards Santa Cruz, this disco serves up Latin, house and techno to local trendsters.

Lighthouse Bar & Grill, 281 Lighthouse Ave, Monterey (☎831/3734488). Friendly gay pub where the locals hang.

The Mucky Duck, 479 Alvarado St, Monterey (☎831/655-3031). The menu at this friendly and popular Tudor-style bar/restaurant features British food with a California flair. Occasional live music; DJ dancing on back patio.

Planet Gemini, 625 Cannery Row, Monterey (☎831/373-1449). Mixed music and comedy venue usually with a $6-8 cover. Closed Mon.

North from Monterey

The landscape around the **Monterey Bay**, between the peninsula and the beach town of Santa Cruz, 45 miles north, is almost entirely given over to agriculture. **CASTROVILLE**, ten miles north along Hwy-1, is surrounded by farmland which grows more than 85 percent of the nation's artichokes (try them deep-fried in one of the local cafés), while the wide **Pajaro Valley**, five miles further north, is covered with apple orchards, blossoming white in the spring. The marshlands that ring the bay at the mouths of the Salinas and Pajaro rivers are habitats for many of California's endangered species of coastal wildlife and migratory birds. **MOSS LANDING** is an excellent place to stop for seafood. Try dramatically situated *Phil's Fish House* (☎831/633-2152), where you can pick from the catch of the day then fish a bottle of white wine for yourself from the cooler. At the nearby **Elkhorn Slough Estuarine Sanctuary** (Wed–Sun 9am–5pm; ☎831/384-7695; $2.50; free guided tours Sat & Sun 10am & 1pm) you may spot a falcon or an eagle among the 250 species of birds that call it home. Guided nature **boat tours** can be booked through Elkhorn Slough Safari on the harbor (☎831/633-5555). The **beaches** along the bay to Santa Cruz are often windy and not very exciting, though they're lined by sand dunes into which you can disappear for hours on end.

Sunset State Beach, fifteen miles south of Santa Cruz, has **campgrounds** (book through Parknet ☎1-800/444-7275; information only ☎831/763-7062; $15-18) along a seven-mile strand. Four miles inland, east of Hwy-1, the earthquake-devastated town of **Watsonville** was more or less the epicenter of the October 1989 Loma Prieta tremor that rattled San Francisco. Its once-quaint downtown of ornate Victorian houses and 1930s brick structures was virtually flattened, and more recently the area economy has been hard-hit by closure of its Green Giant vegetable-packing plant, once one of the largest in the country. Like many American cities, the place is saturated with fast-food restaurants and outlet malls and there isn't a lot of interest for travelers, but Watsonville is still the main transfer point between the Monterey and Santa Cruz **bus** systems, so you may well have to pass through.

San Juan Bautista and Gilroy

Inland from the Monterey Bay area, on US-101 between Salinas and San Francisco, **SAN JUAN BAUTISTA** is an old Mexican town that, but for a modest scattering of craft shops, has hardly changed since it was bypassed by the railroad in 1876. The early nineteenth-century **Mission San Juan Bautista** (daily 9.30am–5pm; donation), largest of the Californian mission churches – and still the parish church of San Juan Bautista – stands on the north side of the town's central plaza, its original bells still ringing out from the bell tower; the arcaded monastery wing that stretches out to the left of the church contains relics and historical exhibits. If it all looks a bit familiar, you may have seen it before – the climactic stairway chase scene in Alfred Hitchcock's *Vertigo* was filmed here. In front of the church are explanatory panels on the **San Andreas Fault** which runs just a few yards away.

The town that grew up around the mission was once the largest in central California and has been preserved as a **state park** (daily 10am–4.30pm; ☎831/623-4881; $2) with exhibits around the evocative central square interpreting the restored buildings. On the west side of the plaza, the two-story, balconied adobe **Plaza Hotel** was a popular stopping place on the stagecoach route between San Francisco and Los Angeles; next door, the 1840 **Castro-Breen Adobe**, administrative headquarters of Mexican California, later belonged to the Breen family – survivors of the ill-fated Donner Party (see p.579) – who made a small fortune in the Gold Rush.

Across from the mission, the large **Plaza Hall** was built to serve as the seat of the emergent county government, but when the county seat was awarded instead to Hollister (a small farming community eight miles east, and scene of a motorcycle gang's rampage that inspired the movie *The Wild One*), the building was turned into a dance hall and saloon. The adjacent stables display a range of old stagecoaches and wagons, and explain how to decipher an array of cattle brands, from "lazy H" to "rockin double B." The commercial center of San Juan Bautista, a block south of the plaza, lines Third Street in a row of evocatively decaying facades. If you're hungry, the best of the half-dozen **places to eat** is the *Mission Café*, on the corner of Mariposa Street: for more information contact the **Chamber of Commerce**, 402a Third St (☎831/623-2454)

A bit further north, you'll know you've come to **GILROY** by the smell, for this farming community is best known for its garlic. For information on the annual summer Garlic Festival, which features everything from vampire-chasing garlands to garlic ice cream (not nearly as bad as it sounds), contact the Gilroy Visitors Bureau, (Mon-Fri 9am-5pm; Sat 10am-3pm; ☎408/842-6436).

Santa Cruz

Santa Cruz is part of the post-orgy world, the world left behind after the great social and sexual convulsions. The refugees from the orgy – the orgy of sex, political violence, the Vietnam War, the Woodstock crusade – are all there, jogging along in their tribalism.

Jean Baudrillard, *America*

Seventy-five miles south of San Francisco, the unassuming – if somewhat seedy – community of **SANTA CRUZ** is a hard place to pin down. In many ways it's the quintessential Californian coastal town with miles of beaches for sunning and surfing, thousands of acres of mountaintop forests for hiking, and a lively historic boardwalk amusement park – complete with a wild wooden roller coaster – for strolling. But there's another side to Santa Cruz: the town has grown unwieldy over the last couple of decades, fueled largely by its role as a dormitory suburb for San Jose and Silicon Valley. It's also home to a great number of homeless people who've spilled over from San Francisco and neighboring communities to benefit from the town's numerous liberal resources. And some of the town's suburbs have a redneck feel more akin to the Central Valley than the laidback languid coast. Only rarely do you get the impression of a resort totally at ease with itself, and the underlying conflicts are one of the many reasons why the town is so slow to change.

The town's enduring reputation as a holdout from the 1960s is only fitting since this is where it all began. Ken Kesey and his Merry Pranksters turned the local youth on to the wonders of LSD years before it defined a generation, a mission recorded by Tom Wolfe in *The Electric Koolaid Acid Test*, and the area is still considered among the most politically and socially progressive in California. One upshot of this is that Santa Cruz has, in recent years, become something of a lesbian Mecca, although the scene is still small. The town is also surprisingly untouristy: no hotels spoil the miles of wave-beaten coastline – in fact, most of the surrounding land is used for growing fruit and vegetables, and roadside stalls are more likely to be selling apples or sprouts than postcards and souvenirs. Places to stay are for once good value and easy to find, and the town sports a range of bookstores and coffeehouses, as well as some lively bars and nightclubs where the music varies from hard-core surf-punk to longtime local Neil Young and friends.

Arrival, information and city transportation

By **car**, Santa Cruz is on Hwy-1, 45 miles north of Monterey; Hwy-17 runs over the mountains, 33 miles from San Jose and US-101. **Greyhound buses** (☎831/423-1800) stop five times a day in each direction at 425 Front St in the center of town, with connecting services to all the major cities in the state. Amtrak Thruway buses connect the town with San Jose four times daily; there's also a weekly Green Tortoise. Coming from the Monterey peninsula, local MST and SCMTD buses link up in Watsonville.

The **Santa Cruz Conference and Visitors Center** at 1211 Ocean St (Mon–Sat 9am–5pm, Sun 10am–4pm; ☎ 1-800/833-3494 or 831/425-1234) has lots of handy

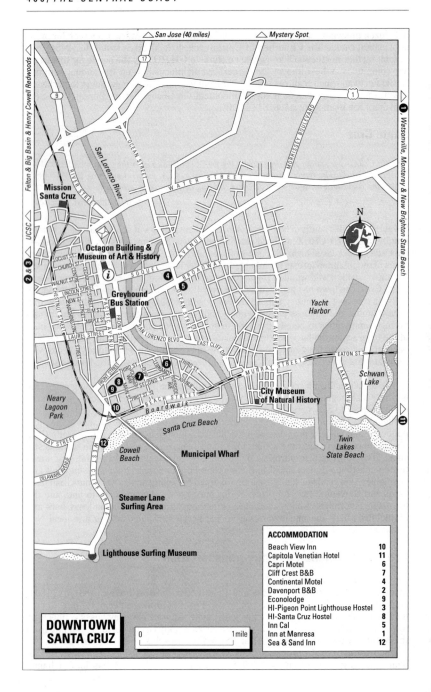

DOWNTOWN
SANTA CRUZ

0   1mile

ACCOMMODATION

Beach View Inn	10
Capitola Venetian Hotel	11
Capri Motel	6
Cliff Crest B&B	7
Continental Motel	4
Davenport B&B	2
Econolodge	9
HI-Pigeon Point Lighthouse Hostel	3
HI-Santa Cruz Hostel	8
Inn Cal	5
Inn at Manresa	1
Sea & Sand Inn	12

information on places to stay, and sells a detailed map of the entire county for $1.50. To find out what's on in the area, check out the free magazine rack at the **Bookshop Santa Cruz**, 1520 Pacific Ave (☎831/423-0900), where you'll find generally useful weeklies like *Good Times* and the *Santa Cruz Metro*.

Santa Cruz has an excellent **public transportation** system, based around the Metro Center wedged between Front Street and Pacific Ave, and operated by the Santa Cruz Metropolitan Transit District or SCMTD (information Mon–Fri 8am–5pm; ☎831/425-8600), which publishes *Headways*, a free bilingual guide to getting around the area. The basic fare is $1 and an all-day pass costs $3. Some of the most useful routes are: #1, which runs up the hill to UCSC; #71 to Watsonville; #67 along the eastern beaches; and #3 to the western beaches. Route #35, which runs up Hwy-9 into the mountains to Big Basin Redwoods State Park, is equipped with bike racks.

Though there are buses to most of the beaches, you might find it easier to get around by **bicycle**: Bicycle Rental Center, 131 Center St (☎831/4268687), rents **bikes** from $25 a day, while the waterfront Go-Skate, 601 Beach St (☎831/425-8578) also rents out roller skates and surfboards. You can get ocean-going **kayaks** for $15 an hour or $30 a day from Venture Quest on the wharf and at 125 Beach St (Mon–Fri 10am–5:30pm; Sat–Sun 8am–5:30pm; ☎831/427-2267) and Santa Cruz Boat Rentals, 15 Municipal Wharf (☎831/426-4690) rent skiffs and **fishing** equipment along with bait and tackle.

Accommodation

Compared to most California beach resorts, **accommodation** in Santa Cruz is inexpensive and easy to come by, especially during the week or outside of summer. Most of the establishments we've listed offer good-value weekly rates. **Camping** opportunities in and around Santa Cruz are abundant and varied, from beaches to forests and points in between; **reservations** for all state park campgrounds are handled through Parknet (☎1-800/444-7275).

Hotels, motels and B&Bs

Beach View Inn, 50 Front St (☎831/426-3575). Clean budget motel near the boardwalk. ③.

Capitola Venetian Hotel, 1500 Wharf Rd, Capitola (☎1-800/332-2780 or 831/476-6471). Quirky, aging beachfront hotel just across the bridge from Capitola's lively esplanade. All rooms have kitchens, some are two-bedroom suites; rates increase at weekends when there's a two-night minimum. Weekly rental begins at $325. ⑦.

Capri Motel, 337 Riverside Ave (☎831/426-4611). The cheapest of a dozen or so budget motels near the beach and the boardwalk. ②.

Cliff Crest B&B Inn, 407 Cliff St (☎1-800/427-2609 or 831/427-2609). Nicely furnished 1887 Queen Anne-style Victorian home set in lovely gardens at the top of Beach Hill. Rates include a full breakfast and afternoon sherry. ⑤.

Continental Motel, 414 Ocean St (☎1-888/685-5759 or 831/429-1221). Top value for an off-the-bottom-rung motel. Comfortable, tastefully decorated rooms an easy walk to everything. ③.

Davenport Bed and Breakfast Inn, 31 Davenport Ave, Davenport (☎1-800/870-1817 or 831/423-1160). At a comfortable distance from the more boisterous coastal towns with a good restaurant and great views. ⑤.

Econolodge, 550 Second St (☎1-800/553-2666 or 831/426-3626). The most salubrious of the beachfront motels, with a heated pool and continental breakfast. On Beach Hill: take Front Street from the boardwalk and then first right. ②.

Inn at Manresa Beach, 1258 San Andreas Road, Aptos/La Selva Beach (☎1-888/523-2244 or 831/728-1000). Curious-looking farmhouse modeled after Abraham Lincoln's original home in Springfield, Illinois and renovated as a B&B. ⑦.

Inn Cal, 370 Ocean St (☎1-800/550-0055 or 831/458-9220). Across the river from the center of town, with clean, no-frills double rooms. A winter bargain and very popular in summer. ③.

Sea and Sand Inn, 201 West Cliff Drive (☎831/427-3400). Small and well-placed hotel with great views over the bay, beaches and Steamer Lane surfers. Complimentary breakfast. ⑤.

Hostels

HI–Pigeon Point Lighthouse Hostel, Pescadero (☎650/879-0633). Located some 25 miles north of town, near Año Nuevo State Park, but well worth the effort for a chance to bunk down in the old lighthouse keeper's quarters right on the point. Dorm beds $13–15 per person, plus $3 for non-HI members; more expensive private doubles, and there's an excellent hot tub ($6 per half-hour) hanging out over the thundering surf.

HI–Santa Cruz Hostel, 321 Main St (☎831/423-8304). Well-situated hostel in a set of cottages just a couple of blocks from the beach. The atmosphere is informal but the place is closed during the day and is often booked up in advance. Members $13–15.

Campgrounds

Big Basin Redwoods State Park, Hwy-236, Boulder Creek (☎831/338-8860). High-up in the hills; sites with showers for $18, and numerous backcountry sites for hikers and mountain bikers.

Henry Cowell Redwoods State Park, Graham Hill Rd (☎831/335-4598). In the hills above town and UC Santa Cruz, in a redwood grove along the San Lorenzo River. Bus # 35 serves the park, and sites cost $18 a night.

New Brighton State Beach, 1500 Park Avenue, Capitola (☎831/464-6330). Three miles south of Santa Cruz on the edge of the beachfront village of Capitola, set on bluffs above a lengthy strand. Sites cost $16 a night, including hot showers.

The Town

Santa Cruz provides a sharp contrast with the upscale resort sophistication of Monterey Peninsula across the bay. This sleepy community of 45,000 residents, along with 10,000 students, is spread out at the foot of thickly wooded mountains along a clean, sandy shore. There's not a lot to see in the town, almost all of which is within a ten-minute walk of the beach, apart from the many blocks of Victorian wooden houses.

The sluggish San Lorenzo river wraps around the town center, two blocks east of **Pacific Garden Mall,** a landscaped, prettified and pedestrianized stretch of Pacific Avenue that is Santa Cruz's main street, lined with bookstores, record stores, beachwear shops and cafés. Disheveled hippies, trapped forever in their favorite decade, wander ceaselessly along the mall's length, brushing shoulders with wealthy shoppers who dodge occasionally into clothing and furniture stores. The homeless and the practically homeless cluster around park benches in the area, playing instruments, distributing literature, or simply dozing off.

One place that survived the massive 1989 earthquake which damaged a large portion of the town is the ornate brick-and-stone **Octagon Building,** 118 Cooper St, at the north end of Pacific Avenue. Completed in 1882 as the Santa Cruz Hall of Records, it now houses the store along with an exhibit or two from the **Museum of Art and History** next door at 705 Front St (Tue–Sun 12pm–5pm, Fri 12pm–7pm; $3; ☎831/429-1964; *www.santacruzmah.org*) with history and modern art of the region on display. Several blocks away, past the clocktower fountain on Pacific and up the hill at 126 High St, fragments dating from the region's earlier Spanish colonial days are shown off in a restored army barracks, next to a scaled-down copy of **Mission Santa Cruz** (daily 9am–5pm; donation). The original adobe church, the sixteenth in the mission chain, was destroyed by an earthquake in the mid-nineteenth century; the replica that stands on its site today is one third the size of the original, dwarfed by a large Gothic Revival church next door.

Between the town center and the beach, **Beach Hill** rises at the foot of Pacific Avenue, its slopes lined with some of Santa Cruz's finest turn-of-the-century homes, such as the striking Queen Anne-style house at 417 Cliff St, and the slightly odd structure around the corner at 912 Third St, constructed out of the remains of a shipwreck.

The boardwalk and around

Standing out at the foot of the low-rise town, the **Santa Cruz Boardwalk** (May–Sept daily 11am–10pm; rest of year hours vary; $1.50–3 per ride, unlimited rides $19.95; ☎831/423-5590). stretches half a mile along the sands, one of the last surviving beachfront amusement parks on the West Coast. Packed solid on weekends with teenagers on the prowl, most of the time it's a friendly funfair where barefoot hippies mix with mushroom farmers and their families. First opened in 1907 as a gambling casino, the elegant Coconut Grove at the west end has recently undergone a $10 million restoration, and the grand ballroom now hosts 1940s swing bands and salsa and R&B combos, offering a change of pace from the raucous string of bumper cars, shooting galleries, log flume rides and ferris wheels that line up beside the wide beach, filled in with every sort of arcade game and test of skill. The star attraction is the 75-year-old **Giant Dipper**, a wild wooden roller coaster that's been ridden by more than 45 million people and is listed on the National Register of Historic Places; it often doubles for a Coney Island attraction in the movies.

Half a mile west of the boardwalk, the hundred-year-old wooden **Municipal Pier** juts out into the bay, crammed with fresh fish shops, burger joints and seafood restaurants, at the end of which people fish for crabs – you don't need a license, and can rent tackle from one of the many bait shops. Just east of the boardwalk, across the river, the small **Santa Cruz City Museum of Natural History**, 1305 East Cliff Drive (Tues–Sun 10am–5pm; ☎831/420-6115; $2), marked by a concrete whale, has concise displays describing local animals and sea creatures, and a brief description of the local Native American culture.

The beaches

The **beach** closest to town, along the boardwalk, is wide and sandy, with lots of volleyball courts and water that is warm enough for swimming in summer. Not surprisingly, it can get crowded, rowdy and dirty, so for a bit more peace and quiet, or to catch the largest waves, simply follow the coastline east or west of town to one of the smaller beaches hidden away at the foot of the cliffs: most are undeveloped and easily accessible.

From the City Museum, **East Cliff Drive** winds along the top of the bluffs, past many coves and estuaries. The nearest of the two coastal lagoons that border the volleyball courts of **Twin Lakes State Beach** half a mile east (☎831/429-2850), was dredged and converted into a marina in the 1960s; the other, **Schwan Lake** is still intact, its marshy wetlands serving as a refuge for sea birds and migrating waterfowl. Beyond Twin Lakes there's **Lincoln Beach** and good tidepools at **Corcoran Lagoon**, a half mile on.

East Cliff Drive continues past popular surfing spots off rocky **Pleasure Point**, to the small beach-front resort of **CAPITOLA**. The town, three miles east of central Santa Cruz, began as a fishing village, living off the many giant tuna that populated the Monterey Bay, but soon became popular as a holiday spot, with its own railway line. The large wooden trestle of the now-disused railroad still dominates what is now a money-eyed town, rising over the soft and peaceful sands of **Hooper Beach**, west of the small fishing pier. Capitola is especially attractive in late summer, when the hundreds of begonias – the town's main produce – are in bloom; at any time of year, the town is a relaxing escape from the rowdier Santa Cruz crowd. The **Chamber of Commerce**, 621B Capitola Ave (☎831/475-6522), has all the usual information for the asking.

A bit further east you'll come upon **APTOS** – originally named Awatos by Native Americans, meaning "where the waters meet" – a quirky coastal community featuring the shortest parade on earth every Fourth of July and the remains of the *Palo Alto*, an experimental concrete ship which dropped anchor in 1919 to become a long-defunct restaurant and dancehall. The **Chamber of Commerce** at 7605A Old Dominion Court (☎1-800-278-6722 or 831/688-1467) has plenty of information and can help with accommodation reservations.

The beaches west of the Santa Cruz Boardwalk, along **West Cliff Drive**, see some of the biggest waves in California, not least at **Steamer Lane**, off the tip of Lighthouse Point beyond the Municipal Pier. Cowell Beach, just north of the municipal pier, is the best place to give surfing a try; Club Ed (☎831/459-9283) in the parking lot, will rent boards and assist with lessons. The ghosts of surfers past are animated at the **Surfing Museum** (daily except Tues noon–4pm; donation; ☎831/420-6289), housed in the old lighthouse on the point, which holds surfboards ranging from twelve-foot redwood planks used by the early pioneers to modern, high-tech, multi-finned cutters. A cliff-top bicycle path runs two miles out from here to **Natural Bridges State Park** (8am–dusk; ☎831/423-4609; $6 per car), where waves have cut holes through the coastal cliffs, forming delicate arches in the remaining stone; three of the four bridges after which the park was named have since collapsed, leaving large stacks of stone sticking out of the surf. The park is also famous – like Pacific Grove further south – for its annual gathering of **monarch butterflies**, thousands of whom return each winter.

Above Santa Cruz: UCSC and the mountains

The **University of California Santa Cruz**, on the hills above the town (served by SCMTD bus #1), is very much a product of the 1960s: students don't take exams or get grades, and the academic program stresses individual exploration of topics rather than rote learning. Architecturally, too, it's deliberately different, its 2000-acre park-like campus divided into small, autonomous colleges, where deer stroll among the redwood trees overlooking Monterey Bay – a decentralized plan, drawn up under the then-Governor Ronald Reagan, that cynics claim was intended as much to diffuse protests as to provide a peaceful backdrop for study. You can judge for yourself by taking one of the guided tours that start from the **visitor center** at the foot of campus (☎831/459-0111). If you don't have time to visit the entire campus, at least stop by the **UCSC Arboretum** (daily 9am–5pm; ☎831/427-2998; free) world-famous for its experimental cultivation techniques and its collections of plants from New Zealand, South Africa, Australia and South America.

On the south side of the San Lorenzo River, three miles up Branciforte Drive from the center of town, there's a point within the woods where normal laws of gravity no longer apply: trees grow at odd angles, balls roll uphill and bright yellow stickers appear on the bumpers of cars that pass too close to the **Mystery Spot** (frequent 40-min tours; daily summer 9am–8pm; winter 9am–5pm; ☎831/423-8897; $4). Many explanations are offered – including extraterrestrial interference – but most of the disorientation is caused by perspective tricks used in the exhibits spread out around the forest to magically attract tourist dollars.

High up in the mountains that separate Santa Cruz from Silicon Valley and the San Francisco Bay Area, SCMTD bus #35 runs to the village of **FELTON**, six miles north of Santa Cruz on Hwy-9, where the hundred-year-old **Roaring Camp and Big Trees Narrow Gauge Railroad** (summer daily 11am–3pm; rest of year most weekdays 11am, Sat & Sun noon–3pm, departing approximately every 90min; $14; ☎831/335-4484), steams on a six-mile loop amongst the massive trees that cover the slopes of the **Henry Cowell Redwoods State Park** (9am–dusk; $6 per car; ☎831/335-4598) along the San Lorenzo River gorge. From the same station the 1920s-era **Santa Cruz Big Trees and Pacific Railway Company** (early June to early Sept daily; late May to early June & early Sept to Oct Sat & Sun; $15 round trip; ☎831/335-4484) powers down to the boardwalk and back (or you can board there and ride up) in around two and a half hours. **Felton Covered Bridge** out on the same road a mile east of town is also worth a look, if you've got a car; it spans the river between heavily wooded slopes.

Buses continue further up the mountains to the **Big Basin Redwoods State Park** ($5 per vehicle; ☎831/338-8860), an hour's ride from Santa Cruz, where acres of three-hundred-foot-tall redwood trees cover some 25 square miles of untouched wilderness, with excellent hiking and camping. A popular "Skyline-to-the-Sea" backpacking **trail** steps down through cool, moist canyons ten miles to the coast – fifteen miles north of Santa Cruz and less than ten from the former whaling town of **DAVENPORT** – at **Waddell Creek Beach**, a favorite spot for watching world-class windsurfers negotiate the waves. From here, SCMTD bus #40 (twice daily) can take you back to town.

Eating

Restaurants in Santa Cruz run are surprisingly diverse: from vegetarian cafés and all-American burger-and-beer bars to elegant dining options including a number of good seafood establishments on the wharf. The Wednesday afternoon **Farmer's Market** downtown, popular with local hippies, is a good place to pick up fresh produce.

The Bagelry, 320a Cedar St (☎831/429-8049). Spacious, but usually packed, bakery selling coffees and cakes and an infinite range of filled bagels. Open 6.30am–5.30pm.

Bittersweet Bistro, 787 Rio Del Mar Blvd, Rio Del Mar (☎831/662-9799). Delicately prepared gourmet fish and pasta dishes for $15–20. Don't miss the beautifully presented desserts. A few miles east of Santa Cruz along Hwy-1 but worth the trip.

Clouds Downtown, 110 Church St (☎831/429-2000). Well-seasoned meats and Cal-Italian dishes in a pleasantly upbeat environment. The stuffed portobello mushrooms are especially good. Entrées go for $10–20.

Costa Brava, 1222 Pacific Ave (☎831/425-7871). Innovative Latin-American food with Italian and Californian influences. Exceptional atmosphere and portions for the price. There's another location at 505 Seabright Ave (☎831/423-8190).

Davenport Restaurant and Cash Store in the Davenport Inn, 31 Davenport Ave, Davenport (☎831/425-1818). Rustic atmosphere in a peaceful coastal inn with undisturbed views of the coast and notoriously decadent cinnamon rolls.

Dharma's Natural Foods, 4250 Capitola (☎831/462-1717). A little way south of central Santa Cruz. Low-priced, healthy fast food; used to be called *McDharma's* before they got sued (guess who by?) for breach of trademark. Claims to be the oldest completely vegetarian restaurant in the country.

Gabriella Café, 910 Cedar St (☎831/457-1677). Elegant without being snooty, this place is gaining quite a reputation for its California cuisine.

Margaritaville, 221 Esplanade, Capitola (☎831/476-2263). One of many good restaurants lined up along the beach, offering sunset cocktails and huge plates of Mexican food.

Miramar Fish Grotto, 45 Municipal Wharf (☎831/423-4441). Long-established, family-owned seafood restaurant, with gorgeous views – especially at sunset – of the Pacific and seafront homes. Modern menu and reasonable prices.

El Paisano, 609 Beach St at Riverside (☎831/426-2382). Very good and inexpensive Mexican place with great *tamales* a specialty. Two blocks from the boardwalk and beach.

El Palomar, 1336 Pacific Ave (☎831/425-7575). On the ground floor of an historic building that was once a resort hotel and now houses government-subsidized apartments (thought you'd never know it from looking), this restaurant is as popular for its full mid-range Mexican dinners in the elegant, mission-style dining room as it is for a casual margarita at the sky-lit bar out back.

Shadowbrook, 1750 Wharf Rd, Capitola (☎831/475-1511). Very romantic, slightly upscale steak and seafood place, stepping down along the banks of a creek.

Taqueria Vallarta, 608 Soquel Ave at Ocean (☎831/457-8226). Don't be put off by the fast-food ambiance, the food is authentically Mexican and abundant, and can be washed down with rice or tamarind drinks.

Zoccoli's Deli, 1534 Pacific Ave at Water St (☎831/423-1711). Great old Italian deli serving up great food, including a minestrone that's a meal in itself.

Zoccoli's Pasta House, 431 Front Ave (☎831/423-1717). Same owners as the deli of the same name, this restaurant serves giant mid-range pasta dinners in a casual setting.

Bars and nightlife

Santa Cruz has the central coast's rowdiest **nightlife**, ranging from coffeehouses to bars and nightclubs where the music varies from surf-thrash to reggae to the rowdy rock of local resident Neil Young – sometimes all on the same dancefloor. Residents may wear tie-dye, but that doesn't mean they're not capable of breaking into fist fights. For hanging out and watching the local traffic, your best bet is the range of **espresso bars** and **coffeehouses** lining Pacific Ave.

Blue Lagoon, 923 Pacific Ave (☎831/423-7117). Bills itself as gay bar – meaning about five percent of the aggressive scene-seeking young clientele is gay, while the other 95% is emphatically heterosexual. Good deejays spin techno and hip-hop on weekends.

The Catalyst, 1011 Pacific Ave (☎831/423-1336). The main venue for big-name touring artists and up-and-coming locals, this medium-sized club has something happening nearly every night. Usually 21 and over only; cover varies.

Club Dakota 1209 Pacific Ave (☎831/454-9030). New gay bar that's about 50 percent lesbian and 20 percent gay, with the remainder still deciding.

Espresso Royale Caffe 1545 Pacific Ave (☎831/429-9804). Stylish yet cozy café near the clocktower.

Herland, 902 Center St (☎831/429-6636). Café with light food and an attached feminist and lesbian bookstore.

Kuumbwa Jazz Center, 320 Cedar St (☎831/427-2227). The Santa Cruz showcase for traditional and modern jazz, friendly and intimate with cover ranging from $1–15.

Palookaville, 1133 Pacific Ave (☎831/454-0600). Touring bands and local talent play here. Cover varies widely.

Caffe Pergolesi, 418a Cedar St (☎831/426-1775). Great coffeehouse in an old wooden house with a garden. Open until around midnight.

Mr Toots Coffee House, 221a Esplanade (upstairs), Capitola (☎831/475-3679). Bustling tea-and-coffee café overlooking the beach and wharf, with live music most nights; open 8am until midnight (at least) every day.

Red Room, 1003 Cedar St (☎831/426-2994). Hip spot for cocktails and conversation.

Santa Cruz Coffee Roasting Co, 1330 Pacific Ave (☎831/459-0100). Just the place to start the day, with an excellent range of coffees, by the bean or by the cup.

Zachary's, 819 Pacific (☎831/427-0646). Another good café along the main drag of Pacific Ave for watching locals parade past.

The coast north to San Francisco

The **Año Nuevo State Reserve** (☎1-800/444-4445 or 650/879-0227; 8am–sunset; parking $5), twenty-five miles north of Santa Cruz, was named by the explorer Vizcaíno, who sailed past on New Year's Day 1603. It's a beautiful spot to visit at any time of year, and in winter you shouldn't miss the chance to see one of nature's most bizarre spectacles – the mating rituals of the Northern Elephant Seal. These massive, ungainly creatures, fifteen feet long and weighing up to three tons, gather on the rocks and sand dunes to fight for a mate. The male's distinctive, pendulous nostrils aid him in his noisy honking, which is how he attracts the females; their blubbery forms are capable of diving deeper than any other mammal, to depths of over 4500ft. Obligatory three-hour **tours** (☎650/879-0227 for information; $4; reserve through Parknet ☎1-800/444-7275) are organized during the breeding season; throughout the year you're likely to see at least a few, dozing in the sands. See "Contexts," p.659 for more on the elephant seal's mating habits, and on other coastal creatures.

Five miles north of Año Nuevo, Gazos Creek Road heads inland three miles to **Butano State Park** ($5 per car; ☎650/879-2040), which has five square miles of redwood trees, views out over the Pacific and **camping** amongst the redwoods for $16 ($3 for hiker/biker sites). Another two miles north along Hwy-1, and fifty miles south of the Golden Gate Bridge, the beginning of the San Francisco Peninsula is marked by the **Pigeon Point Lighthouse** and the adjacent **hostel** (see p.402), where you can spend the night in the old lighthouse keeper's quarters and relax in a hot tub, cantilevered out over the rocks. Pigeon Point took its name from the clipper ship, *Carrier Pigeon*, that broke up on the rocks off the point, one of many shipwrecks that led to the construction of the lighthouse in the late nineteenth century.

The cargo of one of these wrecked ships inspired residents of the nearby fishing village of **PESCADERO**, a mile inland on Pescadero Road, literally to "paint the town," using the hundreds of pots of white paint that were washed up on the shore. The two streets of the small village are still lined with white wooden buildings, and the descendants of the Portuguese whalers who founded the town keep up another tradition, celebrating the **Festival of the Holy Ghost** every year, six weeks after Easter, with a lively and highly ritualized parade. Pescadero is also well known as one of the better places to **eat** on the entire coast, with the excellent *Duarte's* restaurant, 202 Stage Rd (☎650/879-0464), and, at the other end of the price scale, *Los Amigos*, a celebrated fastfood Mexican restaurant in the gas station on the corner.

Half Moon Bay is the next place of note north along the coast, and is covered in the San Francisco and the Bay Area chapter on p.521.

travel details

Trains

LA to: Amtrak's *Coast Starlight* leaves at 9.30am for Oakland (1 daily; 10hr 45min; a shuttle bus connects to San Francisco); Salinas (1 daily; 8hr 15min); San Jose (1 daily; 9hr 50min); San Luis Obispo (3 daily; 5hr 20min); Santa Barbara (1 daily; 2hr 30min); and continues on through Sacramento, Chico, Redding, through Oregon to Seattle.

One train a day leaves **Oakland** at 9.30am on the return route.

Long-distance buses

All buses are Greyhound unless otherwise stated.

LA to: Salinas (8 daily; 8hr); San Francisco (19 daily; 8–12hr; also one Green Tortoise per week in each direction along the coast); San Luis Obispo (7 daily; 4hr 45min); Santa Barbara (11 daily; 3hr 10min); Santa Cruz (6 daily; 10hr 30min).

Oakland to: Santa Cruz (4 daily; 2 hr).

San Francisco to: LA (19 daily; 8–12hr); Monterey (6 daily; 4hr); Sacramento (21 daily; 2hr 20min); Salinas (10 daily; 2hr 45min); San Luis Obispo (6 daily; 6hr); Santa Barbara (6 daily; 7hr); Santa Cruz (4 daily; 2hr 40min); San Jose (16 daily; 1hr 30min).

San Jose to: Santa Cruz (4 daily; 1hr).

CHAPTER SEVEN

SAN FRANCISCO AND THE BAY AREA

A merica's favorite city sits at the edge of the Western world, a position which lends even greater romantic currency to its legend. Arguably the most beautiful, certainly the most liberal city in the US, and one which has had more platitudes heaped upon it than any other, **SAN FRANCISCO** is in serious danger of being clichéd to death. But in the last twenty-five years the city has undergone a steady transition away from – or maybe out of – the iconoclasm which made it famous, to become a swanky, high-end town with a palpable air of widespread affluence. One by one the central neighborhoods have been smartened up, with poorer families edged out into the suburbs, leaving only a couple of areas that could still be considered transitional. Interestingly, this gentrification is a by-product of the city's willingness to embrace all comers – the now wealthy and influential gay and singles communities, and the peculiarly eccentric entrepreneurism that has flourished here, are at the root of the city's steady growth.

For all the change, though, San Francisco remains a funky, individualistic, surprisingly small city whose people pride themselves on being the cultured counterparts to their cousins in LA – the last bastion of civilization on the lunatic fringe of America. A steadfast rivalry exists between the two cities. San Franciscans like to think of themselves as less obsessed with money, less riddled with status than those in the south – a rare kind of inverted snobbery that you'll come across almost immediately. But San Francisco has its own element of narcissism, rooted in the sheer physical aspect of the place. Downtown streets lean upwards on impossible gradients to reveal stunning views of the city, the bay and beyond. It has a romantic weather pattern, blanket fogs roll in unexpectedly to envelop the city in mist, adding a surreal quality to an already unique appearance. It's a compact and approachable place, one of the few US centers in which you can comfortably survive without a car. (In fact, finding parking is so time-consuming and expensive that it's *easier* to survive without one.) This is not, however, the California of monotonous blue skies and slothful warmth – the temperatures rarely exceed the seventies, and even during summer can drop much lower, when consistent

---

ACCOMMODATION PRICE CODES

All accommodation prices in this book have been coded using the symbols below; prices are for the least expensive **double rooms** in each establishment. For a full explanation see p.36 in "Basics." Individual rates rather than price codes are given for **hostels** and whole **apartments**.

① up to $30	④ $60–80	⑦ $130–175
② $30–45	⑤ $80–100	⑧ $175–250
③ $45–60	⑥ $100–130	⑨ $250+

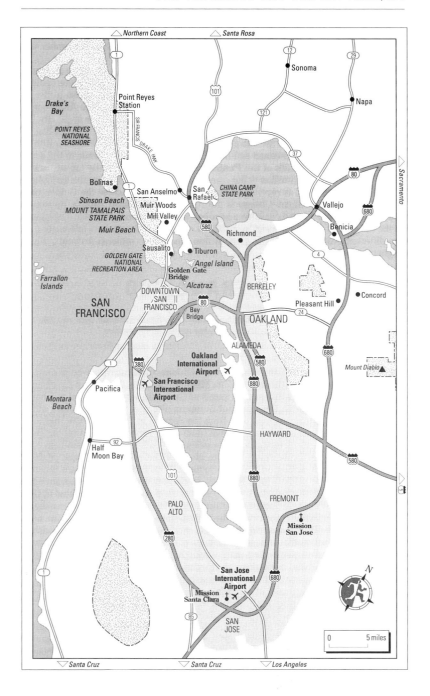

and heavy fogs muscle in on the city and the area as a whole. Autumn is the best time to visit, as warm temperatures and cloudless skies fill the days of September and October.

San Francisco proper occupies just 48 hilly square miles at the tip of a slender peninsula, almost perfectly centered along the California coast. But its metropolitan area sprawls out far beyond these narrow confines, east and north across to the far sides of the bay, and south back down the coastal strip. This is the **Bay Area**, one of the most rapidly growing regions in the US: less than 750,000 people live in the city, but there are seven million in the Bay Area as a whole. It's something of a mixed bag. In the **East Bay**, across one of the two great bridges that connect San Francisco with its hinterland, are industrial Oakland and the radical locus of Berkeley while to the south lies the gloating new wealth of the **Peninsula**, which has earned the tag of "Silicon Valley" thanks to its multi-billion dollar computer industries, wiping out the agriculture which was predominant as recently as twenty-five years ago. Across the Golden Gate Bridge to the north, **Marin County** is the Bay Area's wealthiest suburb, its woody, leafy landscape and rugged coastline a bucolic – though in places *very* chic – harbinger of the delights of California's earthy northern coast. Specific practical information on the different Bay Area locales is given within the various regional accounts, which begin on p.487.

SAN FRANCISCO

One day, if I do go to heaven, I'm going to do what every San Franciscan does who goes to heaven. I'll look around and say, "It ain't bad, but it ain't San Francisco."

Herb Caen, San Francisco journalist

The original inhabitants of San Francisco were **Ohlone Indians**, who lived in some 35 villages spread out around the bay. In 1776, **Mission Dolores**, the sixth in the chain of Spanish Catholic missions that ran the length of California, was established and harsh mission life, combined with the spread of European diseases, killed the natives within a few generations. Mexicans took over from the Spanish in the early 1820s, but their hold was a tenuous one and the area finally came under American rule after the **Bear Flag Revolt** of 1846, which took place a few miles north in Sonoma. The bloodless coup – supported by local land-owning *alcaldes* who saw the potential of huge profits – brought US Marines, sailing on the *USS Portsmouth*, into the San Francisco Bay that year, prompting one soldier, John Fremont, to christen its spectacular entrance the "**Golden Gate**." The Marines docked their boat at the tiny town plaza founded in 1835 by British sailor William Richardson and renamed it **Portsmouth Square**, raising an American flag and claiming the city for the United States. The following year, the hamlet known as Yerba Buena was rechristened San Francisco, honoring the dying wish of Father Junipero Serra, the Franciscan founder of Mission Dolores. In 1848, pioneer Sam Brannan bounded across the square waving bottles of gold dust he claimed came from the Sierra foothills, beginning the rip-roaring **Gold Rush**. Within a year, fifty thousand pioneers had traveled west, and east from China, turning San Francisco from a muddy village and wasteland of dunes into a thriving supply center and transit town. By the time the **transcontinental railroad** was completed in 1869, San Francisco was a lawless, rowdy boomtown of bordellos and drinking dens, something the monied elite – who hit it big on the much more dependable silver Comstock Lode – worked hard to mend, constructing wide boulevards, parks, a cable car system and elaborate Victorian redwood mansions, the latter replacing the whores as San Francisco's famed "Painted Ladies."

In 1906, however, a massive **earthquake**, followed by three days of fire, wiped out most of the town. Rebuilding began immediately, resulting in a city more magnificent than before, drawing anew writers, artists, and free spirits. In the decades that followed, writers like Dashiell Hammett and Jack London lived and worked here, as did Diego Rivera and other WPA-sponsored artists. During the Great Depression of the 1930s, San Francisco's position as the nexus of trade with Asia, coupled with its engineering projects – including both the Golden Gate and Bay bridges – made the Depression seem a slight recession for its residents. While the strict anti-immigration laws against Chinese and the deportation of its Japanese citizens in the Forties remains in memory, people here prefer to canonize the exploits of the Beat Generation in North Beach and Cow Hollow during the Fifties and the message of the Hippies during 1967's "Summer of Love" in the Haight-Ashbury district.

The city also prides itself in being a liberal oasis, a model of tolerance and the **gay capital** of the world. San Francisco remains a haven for Democrats, with the 1999 race for mayor a campaign between left-leaning incumbent, and eventual winner, Willie Brown facing off against even-lefter Supervisor Tom Ammiano, who won a place on the ballot despite not campaigning thanks to 25 percent of the city's voter writing his name in on the ballot. The fact that one candidate is African-American and one is openly gay never became a campaign issue, as it would in any other American city. As one local columnist wrote, "We got over that stuff decades ago."

Coupled with its "live and let live" attitude, San Francisco has always meant business and wealth, evinced today by a walk through the skyscraper-filled Financial District. Exquisite restaurants, new art museums, "shopping-entertainment" in designer malls and the further gentrification of neighborhoods point to a **second Gold Rush**. San Francisco is at the heart of the information revolution, making many locals worried that one day they'll live in "SanFrancisco.com," a bedroom community of bistros for Silicon Valley. The once shabby South of Market area is now crowded with Internet start-ups, tenancy rates throughout the city hover at 99 percent full and housing prices are sky high, forcing out not only the city's poor, but middle class as well. This in turn has led to a growing homeless population who have yet to benefit from the economic boom and are unable to afford the increasing cost of living. Rudyard Kipling once said, "San Francisco has only one drawback. 'Tis hard to leave." And nowadays, it's hard to get into as well.

Arrival

All international and most domestic flights arrive at **San Francisco International Airport** (SFO), located about fifteen miles south of the city. There are several ways of getting into town from here, each of which is clearly signed from the baggage reclaim areas. The least expensive is to take a **San Mateo County Transit** (SamTrans) **bus,** which leave every half-hour from the upper level of the airport; the #KX express ($3) takes around 25 minutes to reach the Transbay Terminal downtown, while the slower #292 ($1.10) stops frequently and takes nearly an hour. On the #KX, you're allowed only one carry-on bag; on the #292, you can bring as much as you want provided you can carry it onto the bus yourself. The **SFO Airporter** bus ($10) makes pick-ups outside each baggage claim area every fifteen minutes and travels to both Union Square and the Financial District. The **Supershuttle, American Airporter Shuttle** and **Yellow Airport Shuttle** minibuses depart every five minutes from the upper level of the circular road and take passengers to any city-center destination for around $12 a head. Be ruthless – competition for these and the several other companies running shuttle services is fierce and queues non-existent. **Taxis** from the airport cost $25–30 (plus tip) for any downtown location, more for East Bay and Marin County – definitely worth it if

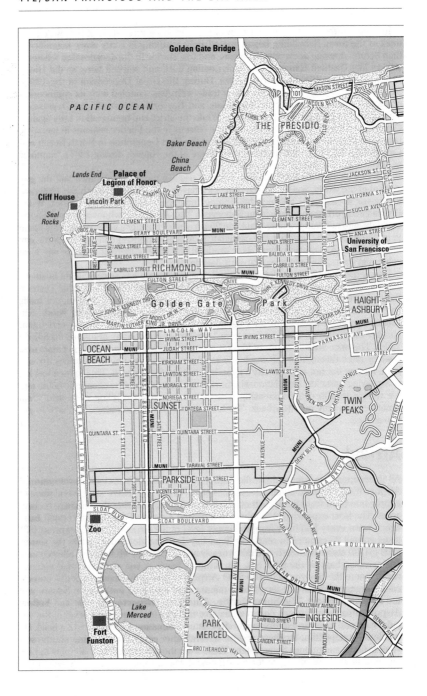

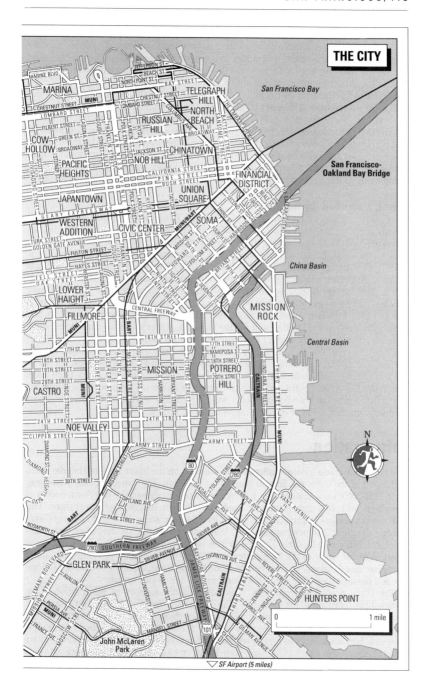

THE CITY

San Francisco Bay

MARINA

TELEGRAPH HILL

NORTH BEACH

RUSSIAN HILL

COW HOLLOW

CHINATOWN

San Francisco-Oakland Bay Bridge

PACIFIC HEIGHTS

NOB HILL

FINANCIAL DISTRICT

JAPANTOWN

UNION SQUARE

WESTERN ADDITION

SOMA

CIVIC CENTER

China Basin

LOWER HAIGHT

MISSION ROCK

FILLMORE

Central Basin

MISSION

POTRERO HILL

CASTRO

NOE VALLEY

N

HUNTERS POINT

GLEN PARK

0   1 mile

John McLaren Park

▽ SF Airport (5 miles)

you're in a group or too tired to care. If you're planning to drive, the usual **car rental** agencies operate free shuttle buses to their depots, leaving every 15 minutes from the upper level. A shuttle train, now under construction, will speed up the process once completed. **Driving** from SFO, head north on gritty US-101 or northwest on prettier I-280 for the 20–30-minute drive downtown.

Several domestic airlines (including America West, Southwest and United) fly into **Oakland International Airport** (OAK; see p.489 for details), across the bay. As close to downtown San Francisco as SFO, OAK is efficiently connected with the city by the $2 **AirBART** shuttle bus, which drops you at the Coliseum BART station. Get on BART and San Francisco's downtown stops are fifteen minutes away ($2.75). The third regional airport, **San Jose International** (SJO), also serves the Bay Area, but should only be considered if you plan to begin your stay in Silicon Valley. Fares in and out of SJO are comparable to the airports north and public transportation to the city is inconvenient.

Buses, trains and driving

All of San Francisco's **Greyhound** services use the **Transbay Terminal** at 425 Mission Street, near the Embarcadero BART station in the South of Market (SoMa) district. Plans are underway to improve the drafty terminal into a regional transit hub from which buses and trains will stop, along with underground access for transferring to BART. **Green Tortoise** buses stop behind the Transbay Terminal on First and Natoma. **Amtrak** trains stop across the bay in **Oakland**, from where free shuttle buses run across the Bay Bridge to the Transbay Terminal, or you can take BART. A more efficient route is to get off the train at **Richmond**, where a transfer to the nearby BART can get you into San Francisco more quickly. Although technically closer to San Francisco, don't get off at the stop before Oakland, **Emeryville**, as consistent public transportation to the city doesn't exist, though you can hail a cab here.

From the east, the main route **by car** into San Francisco is I-80, which runs via Sacramento all the way from Chicago. I-5, fifty miles east of San Francisco, serves as the main north-south route, connecting Los Angeles with Seattle. From I-5, I-580 takes you to the Bay Area. US-101 also runs the length of California from north to south, but if you have time and a tolerance of a winding road take Hwy-1, the Pacific Coast Highway, which traces the edge of California.

Information

The **San Francisco Visitor Information Center**, on the lower level of Hallidie Plaza at the end of the cable car line on Market Street (Mon–Sat 9am–5pm, Sun 9am–3pm; ☎415/391-2000; *www.sfvisitor.org*), has free maps of the city and the Bay Area, oodles of pamphlets on hotels and restaurants, and can help with lodging and travel plans. The staff speaks several languages, as well. Its free *San Francisco Book* and *Lodging Guide* provide detailed, if somewhat selective, information about accommodation, entertainment, exhibitions and stores. The center also sells the **City Pass** ($27.75), a half-price ticket valid for entry to the Exploratorium, Palace of the Legion of Honor, Steinhart Aquarium and Academy of Sciences, M.H. de Young Museum, the Museum of Modern Art and passage on a Blue and Gold Fleet San Francisco Bay cruise.

The city's several **newspapers** are indispensable sources of information. Two dailies have competed for decades: The morning *Chronicle* (50¢) and afternoon *Examiner* (25¢), although economic necessity saw them reach a joint-operating agreement in 1965 to produce the Sunday edition ($1.50) in tandem. Late in 1999, the *Chronicle* began attempts to merge with its competition – a sale still under review and being challenged in court. Both papers are heavy on local news, with extensive arts and food reporting, and Sunday edition's *Datebook* (also known as the "Pink Pages") contains previews and reviews for the coming week. The city's alternative press picks up the slack the more conservative dailies leave behind, resulting in two fine free weekly papers, *The Bay Guardian* (*www.sfbg.com*) and *SF Weekly* (*www.sfweekly.com*), available from racks around town. Both offer more in-depth features on local life and better music and club listings than the dailies. More detailed information on the East Bay can be found in its daily, the *Oakland Tribune*, and alternative free weekly, the *East Bay Express*, as well as in UC-Berkeley's two free daily student newspapers. Down south, look to the *San Jose Mercury News*, the thick daily that focuses on the Peninsula. **Online**, check out *www.sfstation.com* for the best of the many Web sites that cover the Bay Area.

City transportation

San Francisco is a rare American city where you don't need a car to see everything. In fact, given the chronic shortage of parking downtown, horrible traffic and zealous meter maids, going without one makes more sense. The **public transportation** system, **MUNI**, though much maligned by locals for its unpredictable schedule, covers every neighborhood inexpensively via a system of cable cars, buses and trolleys. **Cycling** is a good option, though you'll need stout legs to tackle those hills. **Walking** the compact metropolis is still the best bet, with each turn revealing surprises.

MUNI

The city's public transportation is run by the **San Francisco Municipal Railway**, or MUNI (☎415/673-6864; *www.transitinfo.org*). A comprehensive network of **buses**, **trolley buses** and **cable cars** run up and over the city's hills, while the underground **trains** become **streetcars** when they emerge from the downtown metro system to split off and serve the suburbs. On buses and trains the flat **fare** (correct change only) is $1; with each ticket you buy, ask for a **free transfer** – good for another two rides on a train or bus in any direction within ninety minutes to two hours of purchase. Cable cars cost $2 one-way, and do not accept transfers. Using **single-ride tokens**, passport passes or a **fast pass** are all great ways to save money when using MUNI, but can only be purchased at select groceries, hotels and ticket booths; call MUNI or visit their Web site for a list of vendors. Single-ride tokens (80¢) are cheaper than the flat fare and take care of the annoyance of not having correct change (a token plus $1 is valid fare for cable cars). MUNI passport passes are available in one-day, three-day, and seven-day denominations ($6, $10, $15) and are valid for unlimited travel on the MUNI system and BART stations (see below) within the city limits. A fast pass costs $35 for a full calendar month and also offers unlimited travel within the city limits. MUNI trains run **throughout the night** on a limited service, except those on the M-Ocean View line, which stop around 1am. Most buses run all night, but services are greatly reduced after midnight. For **more information**, pick up the handy MUNI map ($2) from the Visitor Information Center or bookstores.

BART and other transportation services

Along Market Street downtown, MUNI shares station concourses with **BART** (Bay Area Rapid Transit), which is the fastest way to get to the East Bay – including downtown Oakland and Berkeley – and outer suburbs east and south of San Francisco. Tickets aren't cheap ($2.65 one way across the bay), but the trains feature four routes that follow a fixed schedule, usually arriving every ten minutes. Trains run from early morning to midnight, and tickets can be purchased on the station concourse; save your ticket after entering the station as it is also needed when exiting the train. Free schedules are available at BART stations, or visit *www.bart.org* for complete information. The **CalTrain** commuter railway (depot at Fourth and Townsend, South of Market) links

MAIN MUNI ROUTES

USEFUL BUS ROUTES

#5 From the Transbay Terminal, west alongside Haight-Ashbury and Golden Gate Park to the ocean.

#7 From the Ferry Terminal (Market St) to the end of Haight St and to Golden Gate Park.

#15 From Third St (SoMa) to Pier 39, Fisherman's Wharf, via the Financial District and North Beach.

#20 (Golden Gate Transit) From Civic Center to the Golden Gate Bridge ($1.75).

#22 From the Marina up Pacific Heights and north on Fillmore.

#28 and **#29** From the Marina through the Presidio, north through Golden Gate Park, the Richmond and Sunset.

#30 From the CalTrain depot on Third Street, north to Ghirardelli Square, via Chinatown and North Beach, and out to Chestnut Street in the Marina district.

#38 From Geary St via Civic Center, west to the ocean along Geary Blvd through Japantown and the Richmond, ending at Cliff House.

MUNI TRAIN LINES

Muni F-Market Line Restored vintage trolleys from around the world run downtown from the Transbay Terminal up Market Street and into the heart of the Castro. The new extension along the refurbished Embarcadero to Fisherman's Wharf is one of MUNI's most popular routes.

Muni J-Church Line From downtown to Mission and the edge of the Castro.

Muni K-Ingleside Line From downtown through the Castro to Balboa Park.

Muni L-Taraval Line From downtown west through the Sunset to the zoo and Ocean Beach.

Muni M-Ocean View From downtown west by the Stonestown Galleria shopping center and San Francisco State University.

Muni N-Judah Line From the Caltrain station, past the new baseball stadium, along South Beach to downtown west through the Inner Sunset to Ocean Beach.

CABLE CAR ROUTES

Powell–Hyde From Powell Street/Market along Hyde through Russian Hill to Fisherman's Wharf.

Powell–Mason From Powell Street/Market along Mason via Chinatown and North Beach to Fisherman's Wharf.

California Street From the foot of California Street at Robert Frost Plaza in the Financial District through Nob Hill to Polk Street.

San Francisco south to San Jose; call ☎1-800-660-4287 or 650/817-1717, or check out *www.caltrain.com*, for schedules and fares. **Golden Gate Ferry** boats (☎415/923-2000) leave from the Ferry Building at the Embarcadero, crossing the bay past Alcatraz to Sausalito and Larkspur in Marin County. **Blue & Gold Fleet** (☎415/773-1188) sails to Sausalito and Tiburon (Marin County) from Pier 41 at Fisherman's Wharf. And the **Alameda-Oakland ferry** (☎510/522-3300) sails between Oakland's Jack London Square, the Ferry Building and Fisherman's Wharf ($4.50 one-way) and, in summer, to Angel Island (daily May–Oct; $13 round-trip).

Driving: taxis and cars

Taxis ply the streets, and while you can flag them down (especially downtown), finding one can be difficult. The granting of more taxi licenses is a contentious issue in San

Francisco, with many arguing that the streets are clogged enough. Phoning around, try Veterans (☎415/552-1300) or Yellow Cab (☎415/626-2345). Fares (within the city) are roughly $2.00 to start the meter and $1.80 per mile thereafter, plus the customary fifteen percent tip.

The only reason to rent a **car** in San Francisco is if you want to explore the Bay Area, the Wine Country or the landscape north or south along the coast. **Driving** in town, pay attention to San Francisco's attempts to control downtown traffic: the posted speed limit is 30mph, speeding through a yellow light is illegal, and pedestrians waiting in a crosswalk have the right-of-way. In addition, it's almost impossible to make a left turn anywhere in town, meaning you'll have to get used to looping the block, making three rights instead of one left. Cheap, available **parking** is even rarer than a left-turn signal, but it's worth playing by the rules: police issue multiple tickets for illegally-parked vehicles and won't hesitate to tow your car if it's violating any posted laws. Downtown, plenty of garages exist, most advertising rates beginning at $2.50 per fifteen minutes. New public garages under Union Square downtown, Portsmouth Square in Chinatown or Ghirardelli Square near Fisherman's Wharf are cheaper than the private garages. Metered spots on the street usually fill up fast, but a good bet is to prowl the residential areas for a spot, where you can leave the car for up to two hours. Take care to observe the San Francisco law of **curbing wheels** – turn wheels into the curb if the car points downhill and away from the curb if it points up. Violators are subject to a $20 ticket. **Bridge tolls** are collected only when entering San Francisco by car; the Golden Gate Bridge toll costs $3, while the Bay Bridge runs $2.

Cycling, scootering, and skating

Cycling is a great way to experience San Francisco. Golden Gate Park, the Marina and Presidio, and Ocean Beach all have great, paved trails and some off-road routes. And throughout the city, marked bike routes – with lanes – direct riders to all major points of interest, but note that officials picked the routes for their lack of car traffic, not for the easiest ride. If you get tired, bikes can be carried on most trains and an increasing number of buses. Park Cyclery, 1749 Waller Street (☎415/751-7368), in the Haight near Golden Gate Park, rents mountain bikes, as do American Bicycle Rental (☎415/931-0234), 2715 Hyde Street near Fisherman's Wharf, and Blazing Saddles (☎415/202-8888), 1095 Columbus in North Beach. All three rent bikes for $5 per hour, $25 per day. In addition to renting bikes at rates comparable to the above, Adventure Bicycle Company, 968 Columbus Ave (☎415/771-TREK), also rents tandem bikes ($45/day) and jogging strollers ($15/day). For a tranquil trek through undeveloped nature, head north over the Golden Gate Bridge (the western side is reserved solely for bikes) to either Angel Island (see p.534) or into the Marin Headlands for a series of off-road trails along cliffs, ocean and into valleys (see p.530).

American Bicycle Rental also rents **scooters** and **motorcycles**, with liability insurance and helmets included in the price. A scooter for one starts at $50/day, while a two-seater begins at $65/day. Motorcycles begin at $150/day; weekly rentals bring discounted rates.

San Francisco's roads and pathways aren't skate-friendly, but there's enough smooth trail around the Marina and, to a lesser extent, in Golden Gate Park to make **in-line skating** mildly popular. On Sunday, most of Golden Gate Park's roads are closed to autos, bringing out hordes of bladers. Skaters also use the flat sidewalk along Ocean Beach, and the good trails around Lake Merced, although both are away from the action of downtown. San Francisco's many plazas are more welcoming to **skateboarding**, even if local law conspires to ban thrashers from city limits. Skates on Haight, 1818 Haight Street (☎415/752-8375), rents both boards and blades for $6/hr.

Organized tours

One way to orient yourself is an **organized tour**. Gray Line Tours (☎415/558-9400), for example, take three-and-a-half fairly tedious hours to tour the city for around $28 a head. Likewise, Tower Tours (☎415/434-TOUR) can zip you around to all the major must-sees in the city for $30, with deals that combine city stops with Muir Woods, Alcatraz or even Monterey, the Wine Country or Yosemite in a day. Considerably more exciting is the El Volado Mexican Bus Tour (☎415/546-3747; *www.mexicanbus.com*) through the Mission District, which takes in local Mexican restaurants and salsa clubs for drinking and dancing for $35.

For breathtaking views of the bay, take a chilly 75-minute **bay cruise** with the Red & White Fleet (☎414/447-0597) or the Blue & Gold Fleet (☎415/705-5555) from pier 39 and pier 41 – though be warned that everything may be shrouded in fog, making the $16 ticket less than worth it. If you want to take a loop out under the Golden Gate Bridge and back, several independent boat operators troll for your business along Fisherman's Wharf ($10/person). Expensive **aerial tours** of the city and Bay Area in

---

WALKING TOURS

A great way to get to know the quieter, historical side of San Francisco is to take a walking tour. The better ones keep group size small and are run by natives who truly love their subject matter and jobs. Some, like those sponsored by the library, are free. Reservations are recommended for all walks. The Visitor Information Center can give you a full list of available walks – every neighborhood has at least one – but among those you should consider are:

All About Chinatown (☎415/982-8839). Led by Chinatown native and director of the Chinese Historical Society of America, Linda Lee, who takes you through the heart and history of the neighborhood. There's a $25 two-hour walk or a $35 three-hour walk that includes a dim sum lunch.

City Guides (☎415/557-4266; *www.wenet.net/users/jhum*). A terrific series sponsored by the library covering every San Francisco neighborhood, as well as themed walks on topics ranging from the Gold Rush to the Beat Generation.

Cruisin' the Castro (☎415/550-8110; *www.webcastro.com/castrotour*). The Grand Dame of San Francisco walks, Ms. Trevor Hailey, leads you through her beloved neighborhood and explains how and why San Francisco became the gay capital of the world. Tour includes the story of the rise and murder of Harvey Milk, the city's first openly gay politician, as well as other tales from this beautiful neighborhood continually under threat from developers. $40 per person, including brunch.

Footnotes Literary Walk (☎800/820/2220; *www.tactileheart.com*). San Francisco has harbored dozens of famous writers, including Mark Twain, Dashiell Hammett and Jack Kerouac. Guide Shelley Campbell leads a three-and-a-half hour walk around North Beach detailing their exploits. $20 per person.

Haight-Ashbury Flower Power Walking Tour (☎415/863-1621; *sixties.astrid.net*). Learn about the Human Be-in, Grateful Dead, Summer of Love and also the Haight's distant past as a Victorian resort destination. $15 per person.

Mission Mural Walk (☎415/285-2287). Two-hour presentation by mural artists leads around the Mission District's outdoor paintings. Includes a slide presentation on the history and process of mural art. $7 per person.

Victorian Home Walk (☎415/252-9485). Leisurely tour through Pacific Heights and Cow Hollow where you'll learn to tell the difference between a Queen Anne, Italianate and Stick-Style Vic and appreciate the quieter, tourist-free side of San Francisco. $20 per person for a 2-hour tour.

light aircraft are available from several operators, such as San Francisco Helicopter Tours (☎800/400-2404), which offers a variety of spectacular flights over the Bay Area beginning at $79 per passenger for a twenty-minute flight.

Accommodation

Annual visitors far outnumber San Francisco's 750,000 people, and the city isn't short on lodging. But finding a comfortable room in the neighborhood you want and at a price you can afford is another matter. There isn't really an "off-season" in San Francisco, so booking a room in advance is always recommended. Accommodation prices run the gamut from $15 dormitory-style beds to a whopping $575 for a suite at the *Ritz*. **Hotels and motels** in the developing South of Market and the very seedy Tenderloin can be found at around $30 per night, or $120 a week, though they tend to be of the welfare variety and you shouldn't expect a private bath or even a toilet. These come and go with the same regularity of the fog, so check with the **Visitor Information Center** (☎1-888/782-9673; *www.sfvisitor.org*) for the latest – and safest – options in this and all parts of town if you're concerned. In the well-groomed areas around Union Square and Nob Hill, it's hard to find a place for under $125 a night. Wherever you end up staying, keep in mind that during the winter months prices can drop considerably, and special deals are often available year-round for guests who stay for longer periods. Always ask about reductions and promotional rates. If you're having problems finding a room, San Francisco Reservations (22 Second Street, Fourth Floor, San Francisco, CA 94105; ☎1-800/677-1500 or 415/227-1500; *www.hotelres.com*) can help find accommodation from around $80 a double. If all else fails and you've got a car, **motels** are legion along the highways and bigger roads throughout the Bay Area, at a standard rate of $35–45 a night. In all cases, bear in mind that all quoted room rates are subject to a **fourteen percent room tax**.

For **B&Bs** – the city's fastest-growing source of accommodation – consult our choices below, or contact a specialist agency such as *Bed and Breakfast California* (12711 McCartysville, Saratoga, CA 95070; ☎800/872-4500 or ☎408/867-9662; *www.bbintl.com*) or *Bed and Breakfast San Francisco* (PO Box 420009, San Francisco, CA 94142; ☎415/931-3083). Visitors can also reserve rooms through **Colby International** (see p.39). **Camping** isn't an option as there are no sites within a short drive of the city, and while throwing down a bag in Golden Gate Park or the Presidio may seem tempting, it's both illegal and dangerous.

Hotels and B&Bs are listed below by neighborhood, with hostels listed separately. In case you're arriving on a late flight, or leaving on an early one, we've also listed a few places to stay near the **airport**. Specifically **gay** and **women-only** accommodation options listed in special sections on pp.476 and 479.

Downtown

See the map on p.426 for hotel locations.

Allison Hotel, 417 Stockton St (☎800/628-6456 or 415/986-8737). Located at the lip of the Stockton tunnel, two blocks off Union Square and Chinatown. Slightly aged, but clean and one of the best all-around hotel values in San Francisco. Ask about their five-person "family suite" for $109. ④.

Amsterdam Hotel, 749 Taylor St (☎1-800/637-3444 or 415/673-3277). On Nob Hill, but actually closer to the Tenderloin, with good-value clean and pleasant rooms. ⑤.

Baldwin Hotel, 321 Grant Ave (☎1-800/6-Baldwin or 415/781-2220). Beautiful hotel two blocks off Union Square, at the foot of Chinatown and cable cars; adjacent to a parking garage. ⑤.

Beresford Arms Hotel, 701 Post St (☎415/673-2600). Luxury B&B in the heart of town. The suites are the better value, as they come with jacuzzi bathtubs, kitchen and wet bar for $30 more than the nondescript double rooms. Chandeliers, raised ceilings and crushed velvet give the inn a museum quality. ⑤.

Campton Place, 340 Stockton St (☎415/781-5555). Smallish Union Square hotel that draws in a quietly moneyed crowd. Luxurious, but not showy, with a first class restaurant. ⑨.

Cartwright, 524 Sutter St (☎1-800/227-3844 or 415/421-2865). Distinguishes itself from its rivals with little touches such as fresh flowers, afternoon tea and bend-over-backwards courtesy. Good location one block north of Union Square. ⑥.

Clarion-Bedford Hotel, 761 Post St (☎415/673-6040). Charming mid-sized hotel offering tremendous value in the traditionally pricey Theater District. ⑥.

Clift Hotel, 495 Geary St (☎1-800/658-5492 or 415/775-4700). One of the city's oldest and most reliable hotels, a block off Union Square and often offering special rates. ⑧.

Commodore International, 825 Sutter St (☎415/923-6800). Classic Art Deco structure a couple of blocks from Union Square, with spacious, affordable rooms and a great atmosphere. ⑥.

David, 480 Geary St (☎1-800/524-1888 or 415/771-1600). By no means the least expensive place in town, but a great Theater District location above San Francisco's largest and best Jewish deli. You get an all-you-can-eat breakfast, and free transportation from the airport if you stay two nights or more. ⑨.

Fairmont Hotel, 950 Mason St (☎415/772-5000). Most famous of the city's top-notch hotels, an over-ornate palace with four restaurants and lounges, and fantastic views from the rooms. Site of US TV series *Hotel*. Don't miss the terrace garden overlooking Powell, or the splendor of the basement Tonga Room. ⑧.

Foley's Inn, 235 O'Farrell St (☎415/397-7800). Surprisingly affordable, clean rooms over famed Irish pub of the same name, between Market St and Union Square in the heart of downtown. ③.

Grant Plaza Hotel, 465 Grant Ave (☎415/434-3883). Clean, comfortable Chinatown hotel. One of the best values in San Francisco. ③.

Harbor Court, 165 Steuart St (☎1-800/346-0555 or 415/882-1300). Plush rooms, some of which offer the best bay views of any hotel in the city, and guests have free use of the excellent YMCA health club next door. ⑦.

Huntington Hotel, 1075 California St (☎415/474-5400). Understated and quietly elegant compared to its Nob Hill counterparts, this is *the* hotel for the wealthy who don't need to flash it about. ⑨.

Mandarin Oriental, 222 Sansome St (☎1-800/622-0404 or 415/276-9888). You'll need silly amounts of money – rooms *start* at $395 – if you want to stay in one of the city's most luxurious hotel, but the views from its rooms, which start on the 38th floor of this impressive building, across the Financial District, are memorable. Amenities include valet, concierge and 24hr-room service. ⑨.

Monaco, 501 Geary St (☎1-800/214-4220 or 415/292-0100). Best of the new wave of San Francisco hotels, offering great style and decor – though prices have gone up in recent years. Next door to the sumptuous but reasonable *Grand Café*. ⑧.

Nob Hill Hotel, 835 Hyde St (☎877-NOBHILL or 415/885-2987. Inexpensive accommodation in the lower Nob Hill area. Small, clean and comfortable rooms with shared bath; private bath available. ⑥.

Petite Auberge, 863 Bush St (☎1-800/365-3004 or 415/928-6000). One of two opulent B&Bs, next to one another on Bush Street. This one offers complimentary afternoon tea, wine and hors d'oeuvres as well as full breakfast. ⑥.

Prescott, 545 Post St (☎1-800/283-7322 or 415/563-0303). The flagship of hotelier Bill Kimpton's San Francisco properties, this small Union Square hotel offers understated luxury, four-star comfort – and preferred seating at one of the city's most popular restaurants, *Postrio*, with which it shares space. ⑨.

Ritz-Carlton, 600 Stockton St (☎1-800/241-3333 or 415/296-7465). Arguably the most luxurious hotel in San Francisco, perched on the stylish slope of Nob Hill with gorgeously appointed rooms, a swimming pool, multi-million-dollar art collection and one of the city's best hotel restaurants, the *Dining Room*. ⑨.

Sir Francis Drake, 450 Powell St (☎415/392-7755 or 1-800/227-5480). Don't be put off by the Beefeaters outside, this is a colonial California hotel whose greatest attraction is the 21st-floor *Harry Denton's Starlight Room*, offering jazz, smart drinks and great views to a good-time crowd. ⑦.

Triton, 342 Grant Ave (☎1-888/364-2622 or 415/394-0500). Very stylish, very comfortable and very central hotel, catering to design professionals and weekend shoppers. Across the street from the Chinatown gate and two blocks from Union Square. ⑧.

Westin St Francis, 335 Powell St (☎1-800/WESTIN or 415/397-7000). This completely renovated landmark hotel has a sumptuous lobby, five restaurants, two bars and a disco on the 32nd floor, but disappointingly plain rooms. ⑦.

White Swan Inn, 845 Bush St (☎415/775-1755). The other Bush Street B&B, this one with a convincing English manor-house theme: raging fires, oak-paneled rooms and afternoon tea. ⑦.

York Hotel, 940 Sutter St (☎415/885-6800 or 1-800/808-9675). Quiet, older hotel on the western edge of downtown; the location for the dramatic stairway scenes in *Vertigo*. ⑦.

North Beach and the northern waterfront

See the map on p.426 for hotel locations.

Art Center Bed and Breakfast, 1902 Filbert St (☎415/567-1526). Quirky little inn that's a real home away from home. ⑦.

Bed and Breakfast Inn, 4 Charlton Court (☎415/921-9784). One of the first B&Bs to be established in the city, this lovely, sun-drenched Victorian house, tucked away down a quiet side street, offers some of San Francisco's most pleasant accommodation. ⑤.

Bel Aire Travelodge, 3201 Steiner St (☎1-800/280-3242 or 415/921-5162). Good-value motel, one block from Lombard Street. ③.

Edward II, 3155 Scott St (☎1-800/473-2846 or 415/922-3000). Large and comfortable inn-style accommodation in the Marina district with free breakfast and afternoon sherry. ④.

Holiday Lodge, 1901 Van Ness Ave (☎415/776-4469). Comfortable motel with free parking and outdoor pool, near Fisherman's Wharf. ④.

Hotel Boheme, 444 Columbus Ave (☎415/433-9111). Fifteen-room, cozy hotel in the heart of North Beach featuring sumptuous decor and canopied, queen-size beds. ⑦.

Hotel Del Sol, 3100 Webster St (☎415/921-5520). Bright, sunny refurbished Fifties motor lodge in the heart of the Marina, near Union and Fillmore St shopping. A delight to the eye. ⑥.

San Remo Hotel, 2237 Mason St (☎1-800/352-7366 or 415/776-8688). Pleasant, old-fashioned rooms (shared bath) in nice North Beach Victorian house a block off Columbus Ave. Friendly staff, good bar and restaurant. ④.

Tuscan Inn, 425 North Point (☎1-800/648-4626 or 415/561-1100). The most upmarket hotel on the waterfront, with afternoon wine reception and free limo downtown in the mornings. ⑦.

Washington Square Inn, 1660 Stockton St (☎415/981-4220). Cozy B&B right on North Beach's lovely main square. Non-smokers only. ⑥.

Civic Center, South of Market and the Mission

See the map on p.447 for hotel locations.

Abigail Hotel, 246 McAllister St (☎415/861-1560). Comfortable, stylish and affordable, this Civic Center hotel caters to travelers performing at the nearby arts centers. ⑤.

Albion House Inn, 135 Gough St (☎415/621-0896). Small and comfortable B&B above a fine restaurant. ⑤.

Andora Inn, 2438 Mission (☎1-800/967-9219 or 415/282-0337). Fully restored twelve room Victorian manor located in the heart of the Mission with a great staff. ⑤.

Atherton, 685 Ellis St (☎1-800/474-5720 or 415/474-5720). Cozy, clean, good-value hotel four blocks from Civic Center. ④.

Bay Bridge Inn, 966 Harrison St (☎415/397-0657). Basic and somewhat noisy, but perfectly sited for late nights in SoMa's clubland. ②.

Golden City Inn, 1554 Howard St (☎415/255-1110). Best of the inexpensive SoMa hotels, smack in the middle of the district's nightlife scene. Due to a contract with the city, the hotel rents overnight rooms May–Sept starting at $29, and Oct–April only on a weekly basis, beginning at $137. ②.

Inn at the Opera, 333 Fulton St (☎415/863-8400). Very fancy, small hotel with a classical music theme. Across the street from the Opera House. ⑥.

Pension San Francisco, 1668 Market St (☎415/864-1271). A good, clean and basic base near the Civic Center, within walking distance of SoMa and the Castro. ③.

The Phoenix Hotel, 601 Eddy St (☎415/776-1380). Converted Fifties-style motel in a slightly dodgy neighborhood on the edge of the Tenderloin, but the music-biz crowd who lounge around the pool drinking cocktails don't seem to mind. Next to the hip *Backflip* bar (see p.465). ⑤.

Renoir Hotel 45 McAllister St (☎415/626-5200). Good location just opposite the Civic Center. Glitzy lobby and large, comfy rooms close enough to the sites to make this somewhat of a bargain. ⑥.

Sherman House, 2160 Green St (☎415/563-3600). This small Pacific Heights hotel is one of the city's lesser-known jewels, complete with canopied feather-beds and in-house French cuisine, but carries a whopper of a tariff; rooms start at $325. ⑨.

The central neighborhoods

See the map on p.447 for hotel locations.

Alamo Square Inn, 719 Scott St (☎415/922-2055). A beautifully restored Victorian building. The rates are par for the course for a B&B, and guests get the use of a handsome dwelling, some rooms complete with fireplace and one with hot tub. ⑤.

Archbishop's Mansion, 1000 Fulton St (☎415/563-7872). Grandly camp Alamo Square mansion that was once a school for wayward Catholic boys and is now a really interesting, gay-friendly B&B. Attentive personalized service, a variety of "theme" rooms, the ballroom chandelier from *Gone With the Wind*, and everything from fitness training to image consultancy. A riot. ⑦.

Baby Bear's House, 1424 Page St (☎1-888/9BEAR4U or 415/255-9777). Lovely B&B in a restored Haight Victorian. ⑤.

Best Western Miyako, 1800 Sutter St (☎1-800/528-1234 or 415/921-4000). Immaculate Japan Center hotel, with quiet rooms. ⑤.

Chateau Tivoli, 1057 Steiner St (☎1-800/228-1647 or 415/776-5462). Unbelievable Victorian B&B built by William H. Armitage for a lumber baron and decorated with furnishings from the estates of Charles de Gaulle and J. Paul Getty. Just off Alamo Square. A favorite of Mark Twain. ⑥.

Grove Inn, 890 Grove St (☎1-800/829-0780 or 415/929-0780). Nothing fancy (some shared baths), but good value and a fine location on Alamo Square. ⑤.

The Herb'N Inn, 525 Ashbury St (☎415/553-8542). Four-room B&B in the Haight run by the guides of the Flower Power walking tour (see box on p.418). ④.

Jackson Court, 2198 Jackson St (☎415/929-7670). Lovely converted Pacific Heights mansion, now a B&B. ⑦.

Laurel Motor Inn, 444 Presidio Ave (☎1-800/552-8735 or 415/567-8467). Just-renovated hotel in Laurel Heights, steps from Sacramento Street's antique shops and near the bustling Fillmore strip of cafes and stores. All rooms come with a VCR. Pets allowed. ⑦.

The Red Victorian Bed, Breakfast and Art, 1665 Haight St (☎415/864-1978). Bang in the middle of Haight-Ashbury, a lively New Agey B&B, which also calls itself the *Peace Center*, with a hippie art gallery. A real Sixties relic. ⑤.

Golden Gate Park, the beaches and outlying areas

Carl Hotel, 198 Carl St (☎1-888/661-5679 or 415/661-5679). Hidden jewel in Cole Valley, near Golden Gate Park, Haight-Ashbury and restaurants of the Inner Sunset. ④.

Ocean Park Motel, 2690 46th Ave (☎415/566-7020). A fair way from downtown (25min by MUNI), this is nonetheless a great Art Deco motel (San Francisco's first), opposite the zoo and the beach. Includes an outdoor hot tub and a play area for children. ③.

Oceanview Motel, 4340 Judah (☎415/661-2300). No-frills lodging out in the Sunset District. ③.

Stanyan Park Hotel, 750 Stanyan St (☎415/751-1000). Gorgeous small Victorian hotel in a great setting across from Golden Gate Park, with friendly staff and free continental breakfast. ⑥.

Sunset Motel, 821 Taraval St (☎415/681-3306). One of the finest little motels in San Francisco – clean, friendly and safe. ④.

Hostels

See the maps on pp.426 and 447 for hostel locations.

Green Tortoise Hostel, 494 Broadway (☎1-800/867-8647 or ☎415/834-1000). Funky North Beach hostel amongst strip clubs. Dorm beds $16–$19 per night, double rooms $42–$48; both options include complimentary breakfast, use of sauna, and Internet access. They also run a daily bus to Seattle, departing at 8pm (24hrs; $59).

HI-San Francisco Union Square, 312 Mason St (☎415/788-5604). Large, newish downtown hostel with dorm beds from $14–$16 and twins $28–$32. Members only; day membership costs $3. The cleanest and most central of the bunch.

AIRPORT HOTELS

Best Western Grosvenor Hotel, 380 South Airport Blvd (☎1-800/722-7141 or 650/873-3200). Large comfortable hotel with pool and free shuttle service to the airport. ⑥.

Days Inn, 1113 Airport Blvd (☎1-800/329-7466 or 650/873-9300). Basic rooms and a free shuttle to the airport. ⑤.

Goose & Turrets Bed and Breakfast, 835 George Street, Montara (☎650/728-5451). Twenty minutes west of the airport, in the seaside hamlet of Montara, this is a more restful and intimate alternative to the other airport accommodation. Close to the beaches and hiking trails, this is a perfect place to unwind either before or after a long trip. ⑥.

Hyatt Regency San Francisco Airport, 1333 Bayshore Hwy (☎1-800/223-1234 or 650/347-1234). Gigantic hotel south of the airport with all the amenities (pool, hot tub, bars) and a free shuttle to the airport. ⑥.

La Quinta Inn, 20 Airport Blvd (☎650/583-2223). Overnight laundry service and a pool make this a comfortable stopover near the airport. Free shuttle service to the airport. ④.

Motel 6, 1101 Shoreway Road, Belmont (☎650/591-1471). A no-frills motel which is good preparation for a long and uncomfortable journey. ④.

Park Plaza Hotel San Francisco, 1177 Airport Blvd (☎1-800/411-775 or 650/373-7061). Great facilities include restaurant, pool, hot tub, live music and a free shuttle to the airport. ⑦.

Interclub/Globe Hostel, 10 Hallam Place (☎415/431-0540). Lively South of Market hostel with young clientele and no curfew. $15 per person; doubles $36.

Pacific Tradewinds Guesthouse, 680 Sacramento St (☎415/433-7970). Great location in Chinatown, and no curfew. Laundry and a host of other services. $14–16 per person.

San Francisco International Guest House, 2976 23rd St (☎415/641-1411). Popular with European travelers, this Mission District Victorian house has dorms and a few private rooms. $15 per person – 5-day minimum stay ($13 a day if you stay a month). There are two kitchens and no curfew; reservations not accepted.

San Francisco International Youth Hostel, Building 240, Fort Mason (☎415/771-7277). On the waterfront between the Golden Gate Bridge and Fisherman's Wharf. One of the most comfortable and convenient hostels around. Open 24hr, 150 beds, free parking. From $16 per person, $32 for a twin. Includes breakfast, and because it is on federal land, no membership fee.

YMCA Central Branch, 220 Golden Gate Ave (☎415/885-0460). Good central single and double rooms, two blocks from Civic Center. Rates include breakfast and use of gym, pool and sauna. $30 single, $40 double.

The City

There are no end of ways of enduring time in San Francisco, pleasantly, beautifully, and with the romance of living in everything . . . If you are alive, you can't be bored in San Francisco. If you're not alive, San Francisco will bring you to life. You may be a fool for a week or two, but nobody will notice that because everybody else has been a fool, too, and is likely to be a fool again.

William Saroyan

The first and most obvious thing that strikes visitors is that San Francisco is a city of hills and distinct neighborhoods. As a general rule, geographical elevation is a stout indicator of wealth – the higher you live, the better off you are. Commercial square-footage is surprisingly small and mostly confined to the downtown area, and the rest of the city is made up of primarily residential neighborhoods with street-level shopping districts, easily explored on foot. Armed with a good map and strong legs, you could plough through much of the city in a couple of days, but frankly the best way to get to know San Francisco is to dawdle, unbound by itineraries: the most interesting districts merit, at the very least, a half a day each of just hanging out.

The forty odd hills that rise above the town usually serve as geographic barriers between neighborhoods. The flattest stretch of land, created by landfill and bulldozing, at the top right-hand corner of the Peninsula, bordered by I-80 to the south, US-101 to the west, and the water, comprises **downtown**. The city center is bisected by the wide, diagonal thoroughfare **Market Street**, the main reference point for your wanderings. Lined with stores and office buildings, Market Street begins at the **Ferry Building** at the water's edge of the **Embarcadero**, and runs southwest alongside the corporate high-rises of the **Financial District**, the cable car and shopping quarter of **Union Square**, past City Hall and **Civic Center**, beside the gritty **Tenderloin** district and on to the primarily gay district of the **Castro** before spiraling around **Twin Peaks**, the most prominent of San Francisco's heights.

North of Market Street, the land rises dramatically, and with it, property values, as evinced by the stunning mansions atop the province of robber barons: **Nob Hill**. Beside the posh residential quarter, a short cable car ride or walk, rests clustered **Chinatown**, a thriving neighborhood of apartments, restaurants, temples and stores built around **Portsmouth Square**, the spiritual heart of San Francisco.

The land east of the square, towards the bay, used to be entirely water before hundreds of sailors heading for the Gold Rush abandoned their ships, resulting in an unnatural extension of the waterfront. The beached boats rapidly piled up along the shore of Portsmouth Square, until merchants began using the dry docked vessels as hotels, bars and shops. Now it's filled by the towering **Transamerica Pyramid**, which shadows the **Jackson Square** historical neighborhood of restored red-brick businesses. The diagonal artery **Columbus Avenue** separates Portsmouth from Jackson Square, forming the Italian enclave of **North Beach**, much loved by Beat writers and espresso drinkers. North Beach extends to the northernmost tip of the city, the tourist-trap waterfront known as **Fisherman's Wharf**, but not before passing the peaks of **Russian Hill**, home to the famously curvy **Lombard Street**, and **Telegraph Hill**, perch of the famous **Coit Tower**.

New paved trails along the northern water's edge lead west towards the **Golden Gate Bridge**, but not before passing the expansive green parkland of **Fort Mason** and through the ritzy **Marina** district, home to the **Palace of Fine Arts** and some of the city's best shopping. High above, the mansions and Victorians of **Pacific Heights** snuggle up against neighborhood cafés and designer boutiques, along with spectacular views of the bridges and bay. The Heights slope down to the south to workaday **Japantown** and suburban **Western Addition** districts.

The western and southern sides of San Francisco is where most of the city's residents live, and much to their dismay, the area is experiencing skyrocketing rents. **Geary Street**, the main east-west passage, begins in the Financial District and ends at the Pacific Ocean in the **Richmond** district. Geary's lined with some of the city's best Asian and Russian restaurants, and the **Clement Street** area is known as "New Chinatown" for its collection of Chinese groceries, hot-pot restaurants and dumpling cafeterias. The Richmond is hugged by nature on three of its sides: the beaches, Golden Gate Bridge and **Presidio** to the north, **Land's End** and **Ocean Beach** to the west, and expansive **Golden Gate Park** to the south. On the other side of Golden Gate Park, the **Sunset** district stretches on in suburban sameness south to San Francisco State University, though the district's 9th Avenue and Irving Street strip of restaurants is the city's most famous collection of boutique eateries.

East of the Sunset, up against Golden Gate Park and the long sliver of grass known as the **Panhandle**, the **Haight-Ashbury** district was once San Francisco's Victorian resort quarter before hippies and flower children took over. Today it's a rag-tag collection of used-clothing stores and Ben & Jerry ice cream shops.

Further east, **South of Market** (or **SoMa**) used to be one of the city center's few industrial enclaves, until the arty, nightclubbing crowd discovered it. Now it finds itself in the heart of the information revolution, as Internet start-ups pay exceedingly higher rents to stake their claim in SoMa's warehouses and lofts. Commercial development has poured in, too, marked by the opening of Sony's futuristic **Metreon** shopping mall and the waterfalls at the **Yerba Buena Gardens**, home to the new **San Francisco Museum of Modern Art**. SoMa's waterfront, long-neglected **South Beach**, has been re-zoned for housing and businesses, and is anchored by **PacBell Ballpark**, the new waterfront stadium built for baseball's San Francisco Giants.

South of SoMa sits San Francisco's largest, and one of its most interesting, neighborhoods, the **Mission**. Built around Mission Dolores and, thanks to fog-blocking hills, almost always sunny, the largely Hispanic Mission District offers enough food, cinema, nightclubs and shops to fill a separate vacation, or at least a day off the well-trodden tourist path around downtown.

Union Square

The best place to start a visit to San Francisco is under the palm trees of its de facto center, **UNION SQUARE**. Located north of Market Street and bordered by Powell and Stockton streets, the area always bustles with activity. Cable cars clank past crowds of shoppers and theater-goers who gravitate to the district's many upscale hotels, department stores and boutiques; by contrast, bums and winos sprawl across the green lawns of the square, underneath the statue commemorating Admiral Dewey's success in the Spanish-American War. The square itself takes its name from being a gathering place for stumping Northern speechmakers demonstrating their loyalty to the Union during the US Civil War, but these days it's remembered more for the attempted assassination of President Gerald Ford outside the bordering **Westin St. Francis Hotel** in 1975. It was also the location of Francis Ford Coppola's film *The Conversation*, where Gene Hackman spied on strolling lovers. The opulent hotel played a similar role in many of **Dashiell Hammett's** detective stories, including *The Maltese Falcon*, as well as in his own life – in the 1920s he worked there as a Pinkerton detective, investigating the notorious rape and murder case against silent film star Fatty Arbuckle. Hammett fans should check out *John's Grill*, around the corner at 63 Ellis Street, for Sam Spade's favorite eating spot. A parking garage has been recently added under Union Square, and given the dearth of spots downtown, may be the best place to leave your car.

From the corner of Post and Powell, marked by the towering Border's bookstore, take a stroll west on Post or Sutter Streets to see some of downtown's least visible landmarks: some fourteen private clubs hidden behind discreet facades. Money isn't the only criteria for membership to these highly esteemed institutions, though being *somebody* usually is. Most notorious is the **Bohemian Club** at Post and Taylor. Better known for its *Bohemian Grove* retreat at the Russian River (see p.608), where ex-presidents and corporate giants get together for masonic rituals and schoolboy larks, the San Francisco chapter is housed in a Lewis Hobart Moderne-style building. Organized in the 1872 as a breakfast club for newspapermen, it evolved into a businessmen's club with an arty slant, including Ambrose Bierce, Jack London, Bret Harte and Frank Norris among its members. A plaque on the Taylor Street corner bears the group's logo, an owl, and the motto, "Weaving Spiders Come Not Here."

Also west of Union Square, at 415 Geary Street, is the American Conservatory Theater's restored **Geary Theater**. The ACT has become a world-renown company, and there's hope that the steam it's generating will help transform the two blocks west of their playhouse. While dubbed the **Theater District**, it can so far only boast the

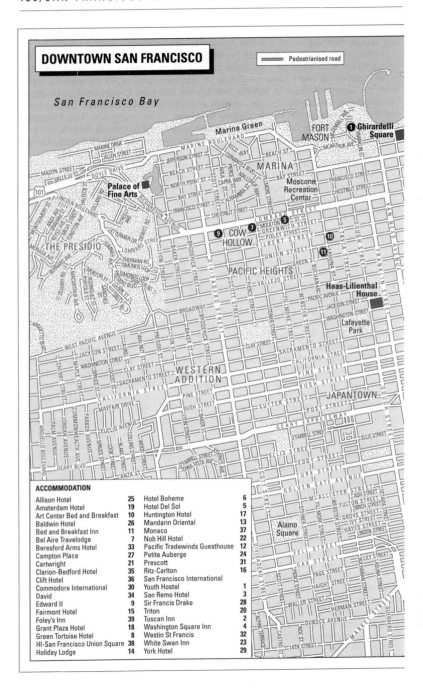

DOWNTOWN SAN FRANCISCO

===== Pedestrianised road

San Francisco Bay

Marina Green

FORT MASON

❶ Ghirardelli Square

MARINA

Moscone Recreation Center

Palace of Fine Arts

❾ COW ❼ HOLLOW ❺

❿ ⓫

THE PRESIDIO

PACIFIC HEIGHTS

Haas-Lilienthal House

Lafayette Park

WESTERN ADDITION

JAPANTOWN

Alamo Square

ACCOMMODATION

Allison Hotel	25	Hotel Boheme	6
Amsterdam Hotel	19	Hotel Del Sol	5
Art Center Bed and Breakfast	10	Huntington Hotel	17
Baldwin Hotel	26	Mandarin Oriental	13
Bed and Breakfast Inn	11	Monaco	37
Bel Aire Travelodge	7	Nob Hill Hotel	22
Beresford Arms Hotel	33	Pacific Tradewinds Guesthouse	12
Campton Place	27	Petite Auberge	24
Cartwright	21	Prescott	31
Clarion-Bedford Hotel	35	Ritz-Carlton	16
Clift Hotel	36	San Francisco International	1
Commodore International	30	Youth Hostel	
David	34	San Remo Hotel	3
Edward II	9	Sir Francis Drake	28
Fairmont Hotel	15	Triton	20
Foley's Inn	39	Tuscan Inn	2
Grant Plaza Hotel	18	Washington Square Inn	4
Green Tortoise Hotel	8	Westin St Francis	32
HI-San Francisco Union Square	38	White Swan Inn	23
Holiday Lodge	14	York Hotel	29

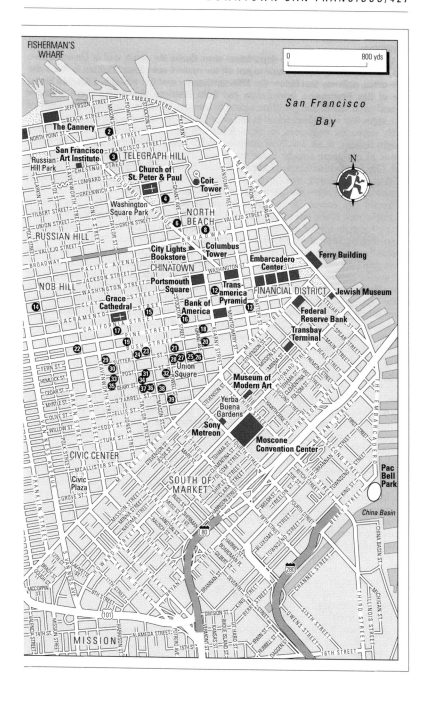

Geary Theatre and a handful of other venues that rub elbows with adult entertainment emporiums.

A huge, renovated Macy's department store flanks the south end of Union Square, and more shopping can be found to just off the eastern side down **Maiden Lane**, a chic little urban walkway that before the 1906 earthquake and fire was called Morton Street, one of San Francisco's lowest-class red light districts. Homicides there averaged around ten a month and prostitutes used to lean out low-hung windows of "cribs" that bore signs that read "Men taken in and done for." Nowadays, aside from some prohibitively expensive boutiques, its main feature is San Francisco's only **Frank Lloyd Wright** building at no. 140. Now occupied by the *Xanadu* ethnic art gallery, the structure is an intriguing circular space which was a try-out for the Guggenheim in New York City. Just behind Maiden Lane, at 135 Post Street, is **Gump's**, one of the city's oldest department stores, and certainly its most unique. Browsing its odd collection of housewares feels more like perusing a museum than a shop.

Around the corner, at the intersection of Kearney and Market, lies **Lotta's Fountain**, one of the city's most beloved landmarks. Restored and repainted in 1999, Lotta's Fountain served as the legendary message center after the 1906 earthquake, where distraught locals gathered to hear the latest damage reports. Named in honor of actress Lotta Crabtree, the fountain enjoyed its greatest moment when world-renown opera diva Luisa Tetrazinni sang a free Christmas Eve performance atop it in 1910.

If you're heading back up to the waterfront, **cable cars** run beside Union Square along Powell Street but are usually too packed to board at their **Hallidie Plaza** origin at the intersection of Powell and Market Streets. Head a few blocks up where there a fewer people trying to get on, and while walking admire the grand **Flood Building**, at 870 Market Street, overlooking the plaza. This flat-iron building, constructed in 1904 by the silver-mining Flood family, is one of the few structures that remained standing after the 1906 earthquake and fire.

The Financial District

From Hallidie Plaza to the waterfront, Market Street marks the southern edge of the **FINANCIAL DISTRICT**, San Francisco's patch of boxy steel skyscrapers where large banks and other trade-related businesses hold court. The Financial District comprises a veritable hodgepodge of architectural styles and periods, from Palladian piles to postmodern redoubts. Scattered between the banks and bars are the copy centers and computer boutiques that serve the offices above, with an occasional restaurant of note, usually set up in alleyways, like those tucked off the corner of Kearney and Pine Streets. There's not a lot reasons to come here, and after 6pm and on weekends it's nearly deserted – although on Friday evenings the bars buzz with relieved workers.

Once cut off from the rest of San Francisco by the double-decker Embarcadero Freeway – damaged in the 1989 earthquake and torn down in 1991 – the **Ferry Building**, at the foot of Market Street, was modeled on the cathedral tower in Seville, Spain. Before the bridges were built in the 1930s, it was the arrival point for fifty thousand cross-bay commuters daily. A few ferries still dock here, but the characterless office units inside do little to suggest its former importance. The area in front of the Ferry Building is the site of the much-loved **Ferry Plaza Farmers' Market** (year-round Sat 8:30am–1.30pm, April–Thanksgiving Tues 10.30am–2.30pm), a good place to buy local produce.

Since the freeway was pulled down, the area around it, known as the **Embarcadero**, has experienced a dramatic renaissance – from an area of charmless office blocks it has developed into a swanky waterfront district with fashionable restaurants and hotels springing up beside palm trees and views of the bay. The **Vaillancourt Fountain** in **Justin Herman Plaza**, at the foot of Market Street, usually triggers a strong emotional reaction; people either love or hate its tangled mass of concrete tubing. During an impromptu free U2 concert here in 1988, Bono left his mark on the structure by spray-painting "Rock and Roll Stops the Traffic." He then angrily stopped the concert when someone hung a banner from a window reading "SF loves U2," erroneously thinking the "SF" stood for Sinn Fein. Today, skateboarders and trick-bike riders share the open concrete square with seagulls and pigeons. On the last Friday of every month, cyclists gather here to promote the bike as an environmentally-sound alternative to driving. **Critical Mass**, as the event is known, makes this point by clogging city streets with two-wheelers, aggravating commuters already entangled in thick downtown traffic. Nearby, the **Embarcadero Center** contains four buildings' worth of chain stores, crowned by the **Sky Deck** (daily 9.30am–9pm; $7), from which you can observe the cityscape from the 41st floor.

The district's other sights are themed around money. The imposing building at the corner of Pine and Sansome Streets is the former site of the **Stock Exchange**. In a sign of the times, it closed its doors in 2000, opting to begin an electronic exchange system instead of face-to-face trading. From here, it's a few blocks down to **Montgomery Street**, where the grand pillared entrances and banking halls of the post-1906 earthquake buildings era jostle for attention with a mixed bag of modern towers. For a hands-on grasp of modern finance, the **World of Economics Gallery** in the **Federal Reserve Bank**, 101 Market Street (Mon–Fri 9am–6pm; free), is unbeatable: computer games allow you to engineer your own inflationary disasters, while exhibits detail recent scandals and triumphs. The **Wells Fargo History Museum**, 420 Montgomery Street (Mon–Fri 9am–5pm; free), traces the far-from-slick origins of San Francisco's big money, right from the days of the Gold Rush, with mining equipment, gold nuggets, photographs, and a genuine retired stagecoach.

Two interesting museums hide amidst the caverns of commerce. The **Pacific Heritage Museum**, 608 Commercial Street (Tues–Sat, 10am–4pm; free), exhibits Asian art in the former US Subtreasury Building, now beautifully sky-lit and fronting the bench-lined avenue that used to be San Francisco's longest pier. Tucked discreetly in a nondescript building at 121 Steuart Street is the little-known **Jewish Museum San Francisco** (Mon–Wed & Sun noon–5pm, Thurs noon–8pm; $5, free first Mon of month), which far from being the somber trudge through history its name suggests, has an impressive collection of contemporary work by Jewish artists.

The Barbary Coast and Jackson Square

A century or so ago, the eastern flank of the Financial District formed part of the **BARBARY COAST**, an area of land that grew due to the hundreds of ships that lay abandoned by sailors heading for the Gold Rush. Enterprising San Franciscans used the dry ships as hotels, bars and stores, and soon after land reclamation began in earnest with the dumping of landfill around the beached ships. Today, construction crews still strike ship hulls while digging. From the 1860s to 1900s, San Francisco grew to be the busiest port on the West, and sailors who docked here clambered for entertainment. This then rough-and-tumble waterfront district gave the city an unsavory reputation as **Baghdad by the Bay**, packed as it was with saloons and brothels around Murderer's Corner and Deadman's Alley, where hapless young males were given "Mickey Finns" and "shanghaied" into involuntary servitude on merchant ships. William Randolph Hearst's *Examiner* lobbied frantically to shut down the quarter, resulting in a 1917 California law prohibiting prostitution. Remains of the cradle of San Francisco can be seen today in the restored red-brick buildings of the **Jackson Square Historic District**, not an actual square but an area bordered by Washington, Columbus, Sansome and Pacific streets.

The **Transamerica Pyramid**, at the foot of diagonal Columbus Avenue and Washington Street, is San Francisco's most unmistakable (some would say unfortunate) landmark. There was a rumpus when this went up, and it earned the name "Pereira's Prick" after its LA-based architect William Pereira, but since then it's been institution-alized as a symbol of San Francisco. Rudyard Kipling, Robert Louis Stevenson, Mark Twain and William Randolph Hearst all rented office space in the Montgomery block that originally stood on this site, and regularly hung around the notorious *Bank Exchange* bar within. Legend also has it that Dr Sun Yat-Sen – whose statue is in Chinatown, three blocks away – wrote the Chinese constitution and orchestrated the successful overthrow of the Manchu dynasty from his second-floor office here. Next door is a pleasant **redwood tree park**, with fountains perfect for an outdoor lunch. Across the street from the park, **Hotaling Place**'s winding brickwork, hitching posts and antique lamps recall the neighbourhood's past. On Jackson Street, at numbers 451-455, the **Hotaling Building** was miraculously spared in the 1906 fire, much to the delight of a city craving its storehouse of alcohol. A piece of doggerel from the time runs, "If as they say God spanked the town for being over frisky, why did he burn the churches down and spare Hotaling's whiskey?"

Heading west on Jackson or Pacific Streets from the area leads you back to Columbus and the distinctive green-copper siding of the **Columbus Tower**, 906 Kearny, the beginning of North Beach. Director and San Francisco native Francis Ford Coppola owns the building, and his *Neibaum-Coppola Café* on the ground floor serves sandwiches, pasta, and wine from his Napa Valley winery (see p.597).

Portsmouth Square

One block south of Columbus Tower, **PORTSMOUTH SQUARE** was San Francisco's original city center and the first port of entry. It's hard to imagine the city springing up from this once-dusty patch of land nestled between Nob, Telegraph and Rincon Hills, but it was here that Englishman William Richardson received permission from Mexican rulers to begin a trading post on the coast of the bay. John Montgomery came ashore in 1846 to claim the hamlet for the United States, raising a flag whose location is marked by the Stars and Stripes that flies in the square today. A small settlement was built on the edges of the square, but it was Sam Brannan's 1848 cry of "Gold!" here that sent property prices and development skyrocketing to levels from which they still haven't returned.

Portsmouth Square is a sunny spot for a picnic and poking around. Five monuments mark its space. Aside from the American flag, a monument to writer **Robert Louis Stevenson** recalls the man who loved to lounge here and people-watch. Another plaque honors California's first public school, built here in 1848, and another pays tribute to Andrew Hallidie, whose first cable car line ran on Clay Street, down the steps from the stairs. But it's the presence of Thomas Marsh's bronze *Goddess of Democracy*, erected in memory of the 1989 Tiananmen Square protests, that signals Portsmouth Square is more than just another park. All around the square, dozens of elderly Chinese practice *tai chi*, play Chinese chess, and watch grandchildren climb the new playground equip-ment. Portsmouth Square marks the beginning of Chinatown.

Chinatown

CHINATOWN's twenty-four square blocks smack in the middle of San Francisco make up the second-largest (after New York City) Chinese community outside Asia. Its roots lie in the migration of Chinese laborers to the city after the completion of the transcon-tinental railroad, and the arrival of Chinese sailors keen to benefit from the Gold Rush. San Francisco is still known in China as "Old Gold Mountain," its storied moniker from the nineteenth century. The city didn't extend much of a welcome to Chinese immi-grants: they were met by a tide of vicious racial attacks and the 1882 Chinese Exclusion Act that banned new immigration, a law that resulted in thousands of single Chinese men being forbidden from both dating local women and bringing wives from China. A rip-roaring prostitution and gambling quarter developed, controlled by gangs known as *tongs*. With the loosening of immigration rules due to China's partnership with the US during World War II, and decades of hard work by its residents, Chinatown has grown into a self-made success.

Many visitors assume that the neighborhood remains autonomous – cut-off from San Francisco by language and cultural barriers. But Chinatown's residents are as American as the rest of the city's citizens, and the district has one of the highest voter turn-outs come election day. Nowadays the population of Chinatown, descendants of Cantonese and Fujianese-speaking southern mainlanders, as well as Taiwanese, have been joined by Mandarin-speaking northerners, Vietnamese, Koreans, Thais and Laotians, making the area a sort of Asiatown. By day the area bustles with activity, by night it's a blaze of neon. Overcrowding is compounded by a brisk tourist trade – sadly, however, Chinatown boasts some of the tackiest stores and facades in the city, making it more similar to shopping in a bad part of Hong Kong than in Beijing. Indeed, Chinese tourists are often disappointed in the neighborhood's disorder and pandering to tourists. The new, some say true, Chinese neighborhood is in the Richmond along Clement Street.

One major improvement to Chinatown, an attempt to keep tourists coming, is the new **nightmarket** which happens under the stars every Saturday night from 6pm to 11pm in Portsmouth Square, spring through autumn. Free performances of classical opera and traditional music are surrounded by stalls pitching everything from fresh honey to leather jackets.

You can approach Chinatown from many directions: as well as from Portsmouth Square, North Beach blends into its northern edges, and if you're coming from the south, Union Square is just a few blocks away. Walking north from Union Square on **Grant Avenue**, you'll pass under the large dragon-clad archway whose four-character inscription reads, "*Xia tian wei gong*," loosely, "The reason to exist is to serve the public good." Grant is the neighborhood's main north-south artery, lined with gold-ornamented portals, brightly painted balconies and kitsch shops. The sidewalks are paved with plastic Buddhas, cloisonné "health balls," noisemakers and chirping mechanical crickets that assault the ear and eye from every doorway, making the Kite Store, at no.717 a tranquil respite of artistic flying contraptions. Grant was once named Dupont Street, a wicked ensemble of opium dens, bordellos and gambling huts policed, if not terrorized, by *tong* hatchet men. Note the two pagoda-topped buildings on the corner of Grant and California Streets, the **Sing Fat** and **Sing Chong**, important because they were the first to be constructed after the 1906 fire, signaling Chinese resolve to remain on the much-coveted land.

Old St Mary's Church, also on this corner, has been around since the days of the neighborhood's criminal past. Made from granite brought from China and red brick imported from Africa, the church survived the 1906 fire and there's a good photo display of the damage done to the city and the church in its entranceway. Across California Street in St Mary's Square, a Benjamin Bufano **statue** of Dr Sun Yat-Sen, founder of China's first democratic revolution, glistens in the sun.

Parallel to Grant Avenue, **Stockton Street** is crammed with exotic fish and produce markets, bakeries and herbalists. Inside the **Ellison Herb Shop** (no. 805 Stockton), Chinatown's best-stocked herbal pharmacy, you'll find clerks filling orders the ancient Chinese way — with hand-held scales and abacuses – from drug cases filled with dried bark, roots, sharks' fins, cicadas, ginseng and other staples. Nearby, on **Waverly Place**, three opulent but skillfully hidden **temples** (nos. 109, 125 and 146), their interiors a riot of black, gold and vermilion, are still in use and open to visitors. Chinatown's oldest, **Tian Hou**, no. 125, is a Daoist temple nestled on the fourth floor of a nondescript building paying homage to the Goddess of Heaven. The temples do not charge admission, but ask for a donation and the absence of cameras and camcorders.

CHINESE NEW YEAR

If you're visiting at the end of January or in February, make an effort to catch the city-wide celebration of **Lunar New Year**, known as **Chinese New Year**, when downtown streets from Market to Columbus almost self-combust with energy and noise. Floats and papier-mâché dragons trundle up Kearney Street alongside a cavalcade of local politicians, movie stars and writers. Carnival booths are set up on Portsmouth Square, and the sound of firecrackers fill the air.

North of Waverly Place, between Jackson and Washington streets, **Ross Alley** features the *Golden Gate Fortune Cookie Company*, where you can watch the cookies – a San Francisco invention – being made on two ancient-looking iron presses, then folded by hand. The bakers will insert your own custom-written fortunes, or sell you a bag of cookies complete with "sexy" fortunes inside. Nearby, the best of Chinatown's very few **bars** is *Li Po's* at 916 Grant Ave, unique for its caverned entranceway and dimly lit interior. Some of the hundred-plus restaurants (see p.459 for recommendations) are historical landmarks in themselves. **Sam Woh**, at 813 Washington, is a cheap and churlish ex-haunt of the Beats where Gary Snyder taught Jack Kerouac to eat with chopsticks and had them both thrown out with his loud and passionate interpretation of Zen poetry.

Chinatown's history is well documented in the **Chinese Historical Society of America**, 650 Commercial Street (Tues–Fri 10am–4pm; donations), which traces the beginnings of the Chinese community in the US and has a small but worthy collection of photographs, paintings and artifacts from the pioneering days of the last century. Visitors interested in Buddhism should head to **Buddha's Universal Church**, 720 Washington, where America's largest Zen sect gives free tours on the second and fourth Sunday of each month, the only time it's open to the public. This five-story building was painstakingly built by the sect's members from an exotic collection of polished woods, adorned everywhere by the mosaic images of Buddha. Not as rich with history, the **Chinese Cultural Center**, inside the *Holiday Inn* at 750 Kearny (Tues–Sun 10am–4pm), does nonetheless host a sporadic program of art shows, mostly contemporary, that go some way to dispelling the popular myth that Chinese art is all pastel colors and oblique images.

North Beach

Bordering Chinatown at the junction of Grant and Broadway Avenues, with Fisherman's Wharf to the north, **NORTH BEACH** has always been a gateway for immigrants. Though known principally as an Italian neighborhood, the district has played host to Chinese, Chileans and Irish before taking on its present face of espresso shops, wine bars and salami grocers in the 1900s. Drawn to its free-wheeling European flavor, sleazy Broadway nightclubs, and the otherworldliness of Chinatown, writers like Allen Ginsberg and Jack Kerouac made North Beach the nexus of the Beat Generation in the 1950s. Bohemians weren't the only ones drawn to North Beach. Grey Line tours cashed in on the much-misunderstood nationwide craze by offering "Beatnik tours" to busloads of tourists expecting sidewalks clogged with black-bereted artists banging bongos. These days, locals are more likely to be found banging on expensive laptop computers, as the booming local economy has made North Beach one of the city's most exclusive addresses. Still, North Beach's sunny location, nestled as it is in the hollow between Russian and Telegraph hills, and diagonal promenade Broadway Avenue, remains one of San Francisco's more happening districts, good for its bars, Italian restaurants, coffee shops and hanging out amongst the smells of olive oil and sourdough bread.

A good place to begin a tour of North Beach is **City Lights Bookstore**, 261 Broadway, opened by Beat poet Lawrence Ferlinghetti in 1953 as America's first paperback book store. City Lights also published poetry, and quickly found itself in the national spotlight as a defendant in the obscenity trial over Ginsberg's *Howl*. The poem, beginning, "I saw the best minds of my generation destroyed by madness, starving hysterical naked," coupled with the phenomenal success of Kerouac's *On the Road*, helped make North Beach the beacon for beatniks from all over the world. City Lights, though, is much more than just a place to get a *Howl* T-shirt; it's actually one of San Francisco's best bookstores, with an upstairs section of poetry that includes $1 poems from contemporary writers, as well as poster-size poems by Ferlinghetti and Ginsberg. The basement contains an excellent selection of Asian texts in translation and lingering over books is encouraged. Next to the bookstore, across Jack Kerouac Lane, you'll find **Vesuvio's**, an old North Beach bar where the likes of Dylan Thomas and Kerouac

THE BEATS IN NORTH BEACH

North Beach has always been something of a literary hangout: it was home to Mark Twain and Jack London for a while, among other boomtown writers. But it was the **Beat generation** in the late 1950s that really put the place on the map, focusing media attention on the area – and the **City Lights Bookstore** – as literary capital of California. The first Beat writings had emerged a decade earlier in New York's Lower East Side from Jack Kerouac, Allen Ginsberg and William Burroughs, who, like many writers of the time, were frustrated by the conservative political climate, and whose lifestyle and values emphasized libertarian beliefs that America wasn't perhaps ready for. Nothing really ly crystallized, however, until a number of the writers moved out West, most of them settling in North Beach and forming an esoteric cluster of writers, poets, musicians and inevitable hangers-on around the City Lights. It wasn't long before the Beats were making news. In 1957 a storm of controversy rose up when police moved in to prevent the sale of Ginsberg's poem **Howl** under charges of obscenity – an episode the press latched onto immediately, inadvertently hyping the Beats to national notoriety, as much for their hedonistic antics as for the literary merits of their work. (The Supreme Court heard the case, acquitting Ginsberg and ruling that so long as a work has "redeeming social value," it cannot be considered pornographic.) Within six months, Jack Kerouac's **On the Road**, inspired by his friend Neal Cassady's benzedrine monologues and several cross-country drives, and recorded in a marathon two-week typing session in New York six years earlier – previously rejected by all the publishers he had taken it to – shot to the top of the bestseller lists. As well as developing a new, more personal style of fiction and poetry, the Beats eschewed most social conventions of the time, and North Beach soon became almost a symbol across the nation of a wild and subversive lifestyle. The road trips and riotous partying, the drug-taking and embrace of Eastern spiritualism were revered and emulated nationwide. Whether the Beat message was an important one is a moot point; in any case, the Beats became more of an industry than a literary movement, and tourists poured into North Beach for "**Beatnik Tours**" and the like. The more enterprising fringes of bohemia responded in kind with "The Squaresville Tour" of the Financial District, dressed in Bermuda shorts and carrying plaques that read "Hi, Squares."

The legend has yet to die, not least in North Beach itself, where Ferlinghetti has had his wish granted by City Hall and many of the city's streets have been renamed as a tribute to the famous figures who have graced the neighborhood; indeed the small alley which runs down the side of the City Lights store has been called "Jack Kerouac Lane." Enamored of the way Paris honors its writers with street names, Ferlinghetti also campaigned for the inclusion of local non-Beat writers and artists. Due to his efforts, San Francisco now has streets bearing the names of many authors, including Mark Twain, Jack London and Dashiell Hammett.

would get loaded, that remains a haven for the lesser-knowns to pontificate on the state of the arts.

From Vesuvio's, a short walk south on the other side of Columbus leads to William Saroyan Place and **Spec's Adler Museum Café**, next to **Tosca Café**, both North Beach standbys for decades. The small wooden bar at *Spec's* is packed with mementos left by the thousands of sailors who have drank inside its exposed-brick walls. Heading north, at the crossroads of **Columbus and Broadway**, poetry meets porn in a raucous assembly of strip joints, coffeehouses and drag queens. Most famous, the *Condor Club* was where Carol Doda's revealing of her silicone-implanted breasts started the topless waitress phenomenon. Now reincarnated as the (fully-clothed) *Condor Sports Bar*, the landmark site still preserves her nipples, once immortalized in neon above the door, in its museum, along with photos and clippings from the *Condor Club*'s heyday. Nearby, *The Lusty Lady*, 1033 Kearney Street, distinguishes itself for probably being the only female owned-and-operated strip club in the world, or at least the only unionized one. One of San Francisco's unique traditions happens here in December, when the strippers lead patrons on a backstage tour to raise money for their Christmas party. Given the gentrification of San Francisco, the clubs of Broadway are one of the few anti-establishment districts in town. Beat tourists will want to walk a few blocks down to 1010 Montgomery Street, at the corner of Broadway, where Ginsberg lived when he wrote *Howl*.

At the intersection of Columbus, Grant and Broadway, notice the **large history mural** on the left side of the intersection, which represents the area's Chinese, Italian and maritime past. Lyle Tuttle's **Tattoo Museum**, 841 Columbus Avenue (Sun–Thurs noon–9pm, Fri–Sat noon–10pm), exhibits art of a different sort, etched onto flesh canvases. The museum is also a working tattoo parlor, should you want a permanent souvenir from North Beach. Continuing north on Columbus Avenue, you enter the heart of the old **Italian neighborhood**, an enclave of narrow streets and leafy enclosures. Explorations lead to small landmarks like the **Café Trieste**, where the jukebox blasts out opera classics to a heavy-duty art crowd, toying with cappuccinos and browsing slim volumes of poetry. Despite its founder's death in 1999, the café still hosts free Saturday afternoon opera performances. Photos of its star patrons line the walls, and legend has it that Francis Ford Coppola wrote the screenplay for *The Godfather* at the table under his picture. North along quiet Grant Avenue lies the neighborhood's **shopping street** lined with a variety of clothing and knick-knack stores.

Nearby, **Washington Square Park**, isn't, with five sides, much of a square; neither, due to urban overcrowding, is it much of a park. However, it's big and green enough for the Chinese practicing *tai chi* and young people tossing frisbees. On the Columbus Avenue side of the park is one of San Francisco pioneer Lillie Coit's many tributes to her fascination with firefighters; a big, bronze macho monument with men holding hoses. On the north side of the park, the lacy spires of the **Church of St Peter and Paul** rise beneath the shadow of Coit Tower. In 1954, local baseball phenom Joe DiMaggio and Marilyn Monroe had their wedding blessed here (the ceremony took place at City Hall). Inside is *La Madre del Lume*, a wonderful painting of a Madonna, child on hip, reaching into the inferno to pull out a sinner by his arm.

Telegraph Hill

Rising above North Beach to the east is **TELEGRAPH HILL**, named after an old communications station that once stood here, and home to some of the best views in San Francisco. From Washington Square, the most direct path up is to take Filbert Street, a very steep climb past clapboard houses and flowery gardens up to Telegraph Hill Boulevard. Once atop the hill, it's easy to see why it was once used as a signal tower for ships entering the Golden Gate. A watchman atop the hill would identify the boat's origin and name via the flags flying on the mast, and relay the information via telegraph to the docks along Fisherman's Wharf. A plaque in **Pioneer Park**, in front of the statue honoring Christopher Columbus, marks the watchman's spot.

Nearby stands the neighborhood's dominant feature, **Coit Tower** (daily 10am–6pm; free). Built with money bequeathed by Lillie Coit in 1929 as a tribute to the city's firemen, the tower is an attractive component of the city's skyline, and rewards those who trudge uphill with sweeping views from its observation deck. Legend has it that as a young girl, Lillie Coit answered the cries of "Help!" and helped the Knickerbocker Engine Company No. 5 of the Volunteer Fire Department tow their engine up Telegraph Hill. Grateful firefighters made Coit their mascot, and even after she married wealthy Easterner Howard Coit in 1868, Lillie continued attending firemen's balls and playing poker over cigars with "her" men of Company No. 5. Local stories abound of her character and exploits, including scenes of dashing away from society balls and chasing after clanging fire engines. Upon her death, she left behind $125,000 "to be expended in an appropriate manner for the purpose of adding to the beauty of the city which I have always loved." The result is a 212-foot pillar that looks alarmingly like a firehose nozzle. Coit's rumored liaisons with firemen add fuel to the speculation that the tower was actually her parting memorial to another part of a fireman's equipment.

The tower's interior base was chosen for the site of a public works project during the Great Depression, an effort which employed artists to decorate public and government buildings. Students of famed Mexican muralist **Diego Rivera** – known for his links with Russian Communists – were selected to adorn the tower's entranceway with frescoes. Though the paintings are thematically linked, the styles vary greatly. One section depicts muscle-bound Californians working on the land, while another shows a man reading Marx in front of a wall of books written by left-leaning authors like Upton Sinclair and Jack London. You can take a **free tour** of the murals Tuesdays and Thursdays at 10.15am and Saturday at 11am.

The best way down Telegraph Hill is on the eastern side, where the **Greenwich Steps** cling to the hill at a 45-degree angle. The narrow sidewalk passes glitzy homes and gardens before leveling out at Montgomery Street. At 1360 Montgomery Street stands the fine Art Moderne apartment building in which Lauren Bacall lived in the classic film *Dark Passage*. Next you'll encounter the landscaped **Filbert Steps**, which drop down even more steeply, looking out over the Bay Bridge and giving access to narrow footpaths like **Darell Place** and **Napier Lane** – one of the last boardwalk streets in the city — that cut off to either side. The steps spill onto **Levi Strauss Plaza**, headquarters of Levi Strauss & Co., inventors of blue jeans (hence the "SF" on the pocket rivets). There's an exhibit on blue jean history and the company's less successful products inside the buildings, but the allure of the plaza for locals lies in its lovely pond and park, across Battery Street and a wonderful place to rest after tackling Telegraph Hill.

Russian Hill

To the west of North Beach, **RUSSIAN HILL** is an elegant neighborhood named after the Russian sailors who died on an expedition here in the early 1800s. Today the neighborhood draws a steady stream of visitors, most who queue up to drive down **Lombard Street**: a narrow, tightly curving street with a 5mph speed limit and some very rich, but very annoyed, homeowners at its sides. Residents have proposed, numerous times, that the road be closed, to no avail. Surrounded by palatial dwellings and herbaceous borders, Lombard is featured as often as the Golden Gate Bridge in San Francisco publicity shots, and at night when the tourists leave and the city lights twinkle below, it makes for a thrilling drive. At the top of the street is the tiny but immaculate **Alice Marble Park**, good for taking a breather or stretching out in the sun.

SAN FRANCISCO'S STEEPEST STREETS

A San Francisco thrill that'll test the brakes of your rental car is a white-knuckle ride down some of the city's steepest streets. Don't worry about traffic on these routes; most people prefer not to brave them, even when forced to make an elaborate detour. Though no street can match Lombard for its fabled curves, the wait to go down it may force you to consider another itinerary if pressed for time or seeking release from tourist throngs. The City's second-twistiest street lies coiled in the Potrero Hill neighborhood, on Vermont Street between McKinley and 22nd Street. It has five full and two half-turns, compared to Lombard's eight.

1) Filbert between Leavenworth and Hyde, Russian Hill	31.5 percent grade
2) 22nd Street between Church and Vicksburg, Castro/Noe Valley	31.5 percent grade
3) Jones between Union and Filbert, Russian Hill	29.0 percent grade
4) Duboce between Buena Vista and Alpine, Lower Haight	27.9 percent grade
5) Jones between Green and Union, Russian Hill	26.0 percent grade
6) Webster between Vallejo and Broadway, Pacific Heights	26.0 percent grade
7) Duboce between Alpine and Divisadero, Lower Haight	25.0 percent grade
8) Jones between Pine and California, Nob Hill	24.8 percent grade
9) Fillmore between Vallejo and Broadway, Pacific Heights	24.0 percent grade

It's easy to get your bearings in the neighborhood, as the cable car tracks along Hyde Street neatly divide the district in two. Most tourists only pass through on the Powell-Hyde cable car line, but Russian Hill's worth a visit for quiet neighborhoods, awesome views of the bay, and the **San Francisco Art Institute**, 800 Chestnut Street (Tues–Sat 10am–5pm; free). The oldest art school in the West, the Institute has been central in the development of the arts in the Bay Area, and has four excellent galleries, three dedicated to painting and one to surrealist photography. But the highlight of the institute is unquestionably the **Diego Rivera Gallery**, which has an outstanding mural executed by the painter in 1931 at the height of his fame. A small **cafeteria** at the back of the building's annex offers cheap refreshments and a fantastic vista of North Beach, Telegraph Hill and the bay.

Nob Hill

From Nob Hill, looking down upon the business wards of the city, we can decry a building with a little belfry, and that is the stock exchange, the heart of San Francisco; a great pump we might call it, continually pumping up the savings of the lower quarter to the pockets of the millionaires on the hill.

Robert Louis Stevenson

Bordering Russian Hill to the south is the most famous of San Francisco's provinces of wealth. If Telegraph and Russian Hills are representative of new money in the city, the posh hotels and masonic institutions of **NOB HILL**, exemplify San Francisco's old wealth; it is, as Joan Didion wrote, "the symbolic nexus of all old California money and power." Once you've made the stiff climb up (or taken the California cable car), there are very few real sights as such, but nosing around is pleasant enough, taking in the aura of luxury and enjoying the views over the city and beyond.

Originally called the California Street Hill, the 376-foot-high hill used to be scrubland occupied by sheep. The invention of the cable car made it an accessible haven for Gold Rush millionaires to show off their riches. The area became known as Nob Hill (either from "nabob," a Moghul prince, or from "snob" or "knob," as in rounded hill) after **The**

Big Four – Leland Stanford, Collis P. Huntington, Mark Hopkins and Charles Crocker – came to the area to construct the Central Pacific Railroad, and built their mansions here. Only one of these ostentatious piles survived the 1906 earthquake and fire – the brownstone mansion of James C. Flood, which cost a cool $1 million in 1886 and is now the **Pacific Union Club**, a private retreat for the rich. Across the street, at 950 Mason, the **Fairmont Hotel** is another survivor of the 1906 fire that has been restored to its former opulence. It has a great rooftop garden behind the lobby from which you can watch the cable cars clank up Powell Street directly below, as well as the city's most unique locale for a cocktail in the *Tonga Room* downstairs. Ride the elevators to the top for an inspiring view of San Francisco. Another jaw-dropping drink (for both its price and the view) can be found inside the **Mark Hopkins Hotel**, 1 Nob Hill, across California Street from the Fairmont. San Francisco's most famous vista-bar, *The Top of the Mark*, is allegedly where Tony Bennett found inspiration for one of the city's theme songs, *I Left My Heart in San Francisco*.

One block west on California stands one of the biggest hunks of sham-Gothic architecture in the US, the Episcopal **Grace Cathedral** (Sun–Fri 7am–6pm, Sat 8am–6pm; free tours Mon–Fri 1–3pm, Sat 11.30am–1.30pm, Sun 12.30–2pm). Construction began soon after the 1906 earthquake, though most of it was built of faintly disguised reinforced concrete in the early 1960s. Areas worth a look include the entrance, adorned with faithful replicas of the fifteenth-century Ghiberti doors of the Florence Baptistery, and the labyrinth floor tapestry inside that duplicates the sacred design at Chartres Cathedral. Outside, the Cathedral's **Cloister Maze** – annually elected the city's "Best Place to Calm Down" by locals – is modeled after the mazes cloistered monks once walked in contemplative prayer. Just to the right of the main entrance is the AIDS Interfaith Chapel, with an altarpiece by the late artist **Keith Haring**. The best time to visit is on Sunday at 11am, when the choral service fills the chapel with sound powerful enough to move the ungodly.

Across from Grace Cathedral, quaint **Huntington Park** is more a place to have a wine picnic than toss a football, and its prim grounds and fountains are always a peaceful rest stop before picking up the California cable car west to the shops and movie theaters of Polk Street, one of San Francisco's first gay neighborhoods (since eclipsed by the Castro), now a rag-tag mix of the seedy and upscale.

Fisherman's Wharf

San Francisco doesn't go dramatically out of its way to court and fleece the tourist, but with **FISHERMAN'S WHARF**, it makes a rare exception. An inventive use of statistics allows the area to proclaim itself the most visited tourist attraction in the entire country; in fact this crowded and hideous ensemble of waterfront kitsch and fast-food stands make for a sad and rather misleading introduction to the city. Unless you have kids in need of a cotton-candy fix, the best thing you can do with Fisherman's Wharf is skip it all together, and head for the parkland around Fort Mason and the Marina, a far more San Franciscan segment of waterfront.

Hard to believe now, but Fisherman's Wharf was originally a serious fishing port, trawling in real crabs and not the frozen sort now masquerading as fresh on the stalls; the few fishermen that can afford the exorbitant mooring charges are usually finished by early morning and get out before the tourists arrive. Snacking on a fresh (you'll have to ask for it, and wait for it to cook) crab and chunk of sourdough bread from **Boudin** (pronounced "bo-deen") **Bakery**, 156 Jefferson Street, with a glass of California wine is a wonderful San Francisco experience, though you'll have to have patience and resourcefulness in gathering the three foods.

The most charming sight here is the large colony of boisterous sea lions (no feeding allowed) that have taken over a number of floating platforms between piers 39 and 41.

These wild animals have made the wharf their home for over eight years and, protected by the Marine Mammal Act, live undisturbed and are free to come and go as they please. To see more aquatic life, you could check out **Underwater World**, at Pier 39 (daily 9am–9pm; $12.95 adults, $6.50 kids, reservations available ☎415/623-5300), which puts you on a moving walkway and scoots you through a viewing tunnel under an aquarium. If you have time, head for the aquarium down the coast in Monterey (see p.392) before wasting money here.

The big thing to do at Fisherman's Wharf is eat crab and shop for souvenirs with the words "San Francisco" on them. One of the more tasteful malls – all things being relative — the **Cannery**, on Leavenworth Street, is a one-time fruit-packing factory that has experienced similar refurbishment. And at the far eastern end of the wharf, about half a mile away, **Pier 39** is another shopping complex, contrived to look like San Francisco of old, but failing rather miserably and charging heavily for the privilege. In between the two a cluster of exorbitantly priced museums and exhibitions are designed to relieve you of more money; not one is worth expending time on, unless you're with restless children. Further east, **Ghirardelli Square** at 900 North Point is perhaps a fitting conclusion to this part of the waterfront, a former chocolate factory whose major parts have been transformed into pricey stores, galleries and restaurants – although some small-scale production does continue here.

Walking east from the wharf, you'll pass a collection of street performance artists spray painted as tin men or spray-painting your name on T-shirts. As you walk the piers, note the refurbished, palm-tree lined **Embarcadero**, just completed following the razing of the old freeway. Massive plans are afoot to turn this still-working stretch of piers into restaurants, shops and clubs – just what the city needed.

Bay cruises depart from piers 39 and 41 several times a day. Provided the fogs aren't too heavy, they give good city views (see p.418 for details).

Alcatraz

The rocky little islet of **Alcatraz**, rising out of San Francisco Bay north of Fisherman's Wharf, was originally home to nothing more than the odd pelican. In the late nineteenth century, the island became a military fortress, and in 1934 it was converted into America's most dreaded **high-security prison**. Surrounded by freezing, impassable water, it was an ideal place for a jail, and safely kept some of America's most wanted criminals behind bars – Al Capone and Machine Gun Kelly were two of the villains imprisoned here. The conditions were grim, but perhaps no more so than any other prison at the time. Prisoners ate communally and were supplied with basics such as soap, tobacco and a broom for sweeping out their cells. Unlike most other jails, though, inmates didn't share a room, living alone in their own cramped cell, which was no larger than five by nine feet, and about seven feet high. And escape really was impossible. In all, nine men managed to get off "The Rock," but there is no evidence that they made it to the mainland.

For all its usefulness as a jail, the island turned out to be a fiscal disaster. After years of generating massive running costs, not to mention whipping up a storm of public protest for its role as a prison for petty criminals, it closed in 1963. The remaining prisoners were distributed among decidedly less horrific detention centers, and the island remained abandoned until 1969, when a group of Native Americans staged an occupation as part of a peaceful attempt to claim the island for their people – citing treaties which designated all federal land not in use as automatically reverting to their ownership. What began as an inspired revolution soon fell victim to infighting among Indian leaders and the 1970 arrival of occupiers influenced by hippie culture and bringing with them drugs and alcohol, up until then forbidden on the land. Using all the bureaucratic trickery it could muster, the government finally ousted the floundering movement in

1971, claiming the operative lighthouse qualified it as active. The occupation may have seemed a failure, but in marking the 25th anniversary of the event, participant Fortunate Eagle noted that it acted as a huge bargaining chip for American Indians, citing President Nixon's return of contested lands back to Native American tribes as a victory made possible by the precedent action.

At least 750,000 tourists each year take the excellent hour-long, self-guided audio **tours** ($4) of the abandoned prison, which include some sharp anecdotal commentary and even the chance to spend a minute (it feels like forever) in a darkened cell. Blue and Gold fleet (☎415/705-5555) runs **boats** to Alcatraz, leaving from Pier 41 (frequent departures from 9:30am, last boat back at 4:30pm; $12.25 including audio tour, $8.75 without). Advance reservations are strongly recommended, especially in peak tourist season. Allow two weeks to book a ticket, which can be purchased via Blue and Gold's Web site (*www.blueandgoldfleet.com*). In summertime, the company also has a day tour than combines a visit to Alcatraz with a stop at Angel Island ($33.25). Check in at the National Park Service's Web site (*www.nps.gov/alcatraz*) for updated hours and restrictions for visiting the rock.

Fort Mason, the Marina, Cow Hollow and Pacific Heights

A little way west of the wharf, beyond Ghirardelli Square, the **Golden Gate National Recreation Area** was established in 1972 to protect much-needed central park space for the city, and now encompasses almost seventy square miles of waterfront property, from the beaches to the south right up to the cliffs of Marin County across the Golden Gate Bridge. Closest to the wharf, the **Aquatic Park** complex of buildings groups around the foot of Hyde Street, at its center the "bathhouse" – a bold, Art Deco piece of architecture that is now home to the **Maritime Museum** (daily 10am–5pm; free). It's worth dropping by just to see Hilaire Hiler's mural, symbolizing the lost continent of Atlantis in 37 hallucinogenic panels that dominate the main room. The rest of the complex includes a maritime library, and a forgettable collection of ocean-going memorabilia. At the adjacent **Hyde Street Pier** (daily 9.30am–5.30pm; $5, free first Tues each month), the museum has restored a number of old wooden ships that are worth clamoring around on to get a sense of the boats that voyagers like Richard Henry Dana entrusted with their lives. The best is the square-rigger *Balclutha*, built in 1886 and the sole survivor of the great sailing ships that journeyed around Cape Horn in the 1800s. Of course, being that it's now in California, the boat also had a second career in the movies, playing bit parts in 1930s films like *Mutiny on the Bounty*.

Fort Mason

Fort Mason, half a mile west along the waterfront, sits behind a lovely open park giving great views of the Golden Gate Bridge. The area can be reached by walking along the Golden Gate Promenade, a stretch of pavement popular with joggers and in-line skaters. Originally a Civil War defense installation, now turned over to public use, the old buildings of Fort Mason are occupied by around fifty non-profit groups and include four theaters and four museums, two galleries and a **youth hostel** (see p.423). The acclaimed **Magic Theater** (see p.474) presents first-run plays while the Bay Area Theater Sports puts on improvisational shows in the Bayfront Theater. The centerpiece of the museums, all of which are free and open until 7pm the first Wednesday of the month, is the expanding **Museum of Craft and Folk Art** (Tues–Fri & Sun 11am–5pm, Sat 10am–5pm; $3). With an array of materials from around the world, the museum offers a wide-range of exhibits, from sculptures made out of newspapers to native artifacts from Papua New Guinea. Displays at the **Museo Italo-Americano** (Wed–Sun noon–5pm; $3) relate to the culture and history of the Italian community in the US; the rather better **Mexican Museum** (Wed–Fri noon–5pm, Sat & Sun 11am–5pm; $4), while awaiting the construction of a new building South of Market, still exhibits its large collection of funky folk art and representational works. Finally, there's the San Francisco **African-American Historical and Cultural Society** (Wed–Sun noon–5pm; $2), a museum commemorating local black leaders.For an updated roster of events and exhibits, log on to *www.fortmason.org*.

San Francisco's most theatrical piece of architecture lies at Marina Boulevard and Baker Street. The **Palace of Fine Arts** is not the museum its name suggests, but a huge, freely interpreted classical ruin originally built of wood and plaster for the Pan Pacific International Exhibition in 1915 – held to celebrate the rebirth of the city after the 1906 catastrophe. Sentimental San Franciscans saved it from immediate demolition after the exhibition, and it crumbled with dignity until a wealthy resident put up the money for its reconstruction in 1958, making it the sole survivor of the Pan Pacific pageant, surrounded by a swan-filled lagoon and other touches of urban civility. Next door, in what has to be the coolest museum in San Francisco – the **Exploratorium** (summer daily 10am–6pm, Wed until 9.30pm; winter Tues–Sun 10am–5pm, Wed until 9.30pm; $9 adults, free first Wed of the month; ☎415/561-0362) – over 650 hands-on exhibits demonstrate scientific principles of electricity, sound waves, lasers and more. From real traveling flea circuses to a giant, completely dark labyrinth called the "Tactile Dome" (you explore it on hands and knees; reservations required), this place will boggle your mind and keep any kid enthralled for hours. From here the waterfront stretches west through the **Presidio National Park** and the intriguing Presidio **pet cemetery** on Crissy Field Avenue, to Fort Point, the Golden Gate Bridge and beach area close to the Golden Gate Park (see p.452).

The Marina

The area around the Palace of Fine Arts has been tagged the **MARINA** district by the young, image-conscious, money-no-object sort of professionals who live there. One of the city's greenest districts, the Marina enjoys a prime waterfront location, open spaces and lots of trees. Ironically, though it was built specifically to celebrate the rebirth of the city after the massive earthquake of 1906, the Marina was the worst casualty of the earthquake in 1989 – tremors tore through fragile landfill and a good number of homes collapsed into smoldering heaps. The neighborhood's commercial center runs along **Chestnut Street** between Broderick and Fillmore. As a neighborhood, it has a reputation for being something of a haven for swinging singles; the local watering holes are known as "high intensity breeder bars" and even the local Safeway has been dubbed "The Body Shop" because of the inordinate amount of cruising that goes on in the aisles.

Cow Hollow

Originally a small valley of pastures and dairies in the post-Gold Rush years, **COW HOLLOW** languished until the 1950s when enterprising merchants decided its old clapboard dwellings had possibilities. Gorgeous old Victorian houses received face-lifts, and now the stretch of Union between Van Ness and Divisadero holds some very cutesy boutiques and cafés. Best seen on foot because of all the little alleyways and tucked-away basements, Cow Hollow's an excellent place to use up any excess dollars and loll over a cup of coffee in the sight of upscale shoppers in search of the perfect dress or cabinet handle along Union Street's designer fashion and hardware shops.

Insofar as sights, Cow Hollow's assortment of homes makes for a pleasant walk around Filbert and Green Streets on either side of Union Street. If you're in town when it's open, don't miss the **Octagon House Museum** at the corner of Union and Gough Streets (☎415/441-7512; donations). Tours of the home's Colonial and Federal period furniture, porcelain and portraits are given on the second Sundays and second and fourth Thursdays of the month, from 12pm to 3pm (closed January). Built in 1861, when it was believed increased exposure to sunlight benefited one's health, the house remains in excellent, and sunny, condition. Next door, leafy **Allyne Park** feels more like someone's backyard than a public space, but its redwood trees and comfy benches are a nice place to rest. The western border of the neighborhood is **Fillmore Street**. Allen Ginsberg first read *Howl* at no. 3119 Fillmore, then the location of the Six Gallery.

Pacific Heights

Looming above Cow Hollow on one side and Japantown on the other, wealthy **PACIFIC HEIGHTS** is home to some of the city's most monumental Victorian and stone mansions. Framed by the trendy **shopping quarter** of Upper Fillmore Street on the west and Franklin Street to the east, the neighborhood's amazing homes spread out from the tall, wind-swept **Lafayette Park**.

Take in the florists, pet stores and home furnishing shops of Fillmore Street before turning east on Washington Street, which leads to Lafayette Park. Facing the park to the north are several mansions, among them no. 2150 Washington, the **Mary Phelan Mansion**, built for her by her brother, turn-of-the-nineteenth-century San Francisco mayor and later US Senator James Phelan, whose cries of "The Chinese must go!" make him an example of the protectionists who controlled the city for decades. Phelan's neighbor, at **2080 Washington Street**, was the Spreckels family, whose white-stoned palace is now the home of romance writer Danielle Steele.

If you can't get enough of the city's Victorian-style abodes, pass by the 2000 block of Gough Street, a block from the Spreckels Mansion. The Queen Anne Victorians at no. 2000-2010 are some of the city's oldest, dating from 1889. To see the inside of a Victorian, go to the wooden turrets of the **Haas-Lilienthal House** at 2007 Franklin (Wed & Sun noon–3pm; $5; ☎415/441-3000), a grand symbol of Old California wealth with its Tiffany art glass and stenciled leather paneling. The stretch of California Street from Franklin west to Fillmore is another treasure trove of Victorians worth seeing.

West of Fillmore Street, lower Pacific Heights is centered on the quiet and restful **Alta Plaza Park**, at Clay and Steiner Streets. A lovely piece of urban landscaping, this is where local dog-walkers earn their keep, exercising pretty pooches, and you can enjoy good views of St. Mary's Cathedral and Civic Center from its crest, as well as play a game of tennis on the upper courts.

VICTORIANS

Constructed from redwood culled from the Marin Headlands across the Golden Gate, San Francisco's **Victorians** enjoyed their greatest popularity in the late nineteenth century, preferred by homeowners who could use "signature details" in crafting the facade to differentiate their house from every other. This ostentatiousness came at a price: unlike many of the stone-built homes, the earthquake and fire of 1906 easily destroyed most of the city's grandest Victorians on Nob Hill, and the axe-stripped hillsides of Marin Country made replacing them difficult. Also, a post-1906 trend made embellishment embarrassing, ushering in an era of muted stone or stucco designs still seen around town today.

Nostalgia coupled with tourism and a thriving economy, plus thousands of new homebuyers, resurrected the Victorian style in San Francisco. A 1976 survey by the National Endowment for the Arts found 13,487 Victorians in the city, and restoration efforts were undertaken to save the crumbling edifices in the Haight-Ashbury, Western Addition, Bernal Heights, Noe Valley and other southern neighborhoods. Today, Victorian restoration is a lucrative – and grueling – profession for city engineering firms, and a "saved" home rarely sells for less than $500,000, no matter how seedy the neighborhood.

The Tenderloin, Civic Center and South of Market

While parts of San Francisco can almost seem to be an urban utopia, the adjoining districts of the **Tenderloin** and **Civic Center** reveal harsher realities and are a gritty reminder that not everybody has it so easy. Particularly in the Tenderloin, the homeless and disaffected are very much in evidence – the flipside of California's low-tax prosperity is alive and unwell – and their constant presence in front of City Hall is an ironic reminder of governmental failures. Thus far, sporadic attempts to improve the areas have been at best well-meaning hit-and-misses or, at worst, patently cosmetic gestures bound to fail. On the other hand, **South of Market** (SoMa) has, like the Embarcadero, taken a previously unimaginable upswing. A new entertainment complex surrounding Yerba Buena Gardens – anchored by the high and low culture appeals of the San Francisco Museum of Modern Art and Sony's Metreon mall – has transformed it from a bleak post-industrial wasteland into a thriving extension of the crowded downtown area.

The Tenderloin

Wrapped in a thick layer of fog, most of San Francisco feels as safe and snug as an old blanket. The **TENDERLOIN**, sandwiched between Civic Center and Union Square on the north side of Market, provides a sharp contrast, a small, uninviting area – no more than four blocks by five – that remains a blight on the heart of the city. According to popular myth, the neighborhood gained its rather odd moniker in the nineteenth century because police were rewarded with choice cuts of steak for serving a particularly perilous tour of duty here. Still, as the section of the city with the greatest concentration of theaters and cheap hotels, you may find yourself staying in one of the numerous budget accommodations. You'll be safe as long as you keep your wits about you and don't mind vagrants asking you for money. Exercise extra caution at night, and the vicinity of **Taylor Street**, particularly around **Turk** and **Eddy**, is best avoided altogether.

Recent waves of Pakistani and South Asian immigrants have begun transforming the neighborhood, establishing numerous spots for a cheap bowl of curry or Vietnamese *pho* soup. If you're not too busy hurrying to your destination, there are a few sights worth seeing tucked into the neighborhood's dark corners. Along the neighborhood's northwestern frontier, **Polk Street** has largely been abandoned by all but the most downtrodden. Several historically famous gay bars line the streets, harking back to the days before the community moved to the Castro district, and young hustlers and prostitutes still lounge on every corner. There's also a bit of history for heterosexually inclined gutter fetishists – the intersection of O'Farrell and Polk is home to the **Mitchell Brothers' O'Farrell Theater** (11:30am–2am), whose former owners achieved considerable notoriety in the 1970s when they persuaded a young Ivory Soap model named Marilyn Chambers to star in their porno film *Behind the Green Door*, which they debuted at the Cannes film festival. While the pair slowly slipped back into obscurity over the ensuing decade, they made a tragic return to tabloid fame when Jim Mitchell shot and killed his brother Artie.

Civic Center

Built in the years following the 1906 earthquake and fire to demonstrate the city's return to glory, the monumental complex of buildings in the **CIVIC CENTER** manages to be impressive without being particularly appealing. Its grand Beaux Arts structures, flags and fountains are at odds with the quirky wooden architecture that characterizes the rest of the city. It's the city's center for the performing arts, and by night can look quite impressive – beautifully lit, and swarming with dinner suits heading in and out of the ballet, opera and symphony hall. But by day it's much less tempting, populated either by office workers from the various local governmental departments situated here, or by the homeless who loiter on the grass verges of the elegant quadrangle.

Emerging from the BART/MUNI station, the first thing you see is the **United Nations Plaza**, a memorial to the founding of the UN here in 1949 – though the only current sign of life appears on Wednesdays and Sundays, when from 8am until 5pm it's the site of San Francisco's largest and cheapest **farmers' market**. Along the south side of the Plaza is the **Main Library** (Mon 10am–6pm, Tues–Thu 9am–8pm, Fri 11am–5pm, Sat 9am–5pm, Sun 12pm–5pm; ☎415-557-4700), which moved into its current location at the corner of Grove and Larkin in 1996, amidst both fanfare and criticism. The controversy was caused by the building's sleek new design, which included a large, light-filled central atrium, but not much room for storing books: portions of the library's expanding holdings have repeatedly been sold off in order to squeeze everything into the new stacks. Besides gawking at the massive skylight inside, a trip up the stairway will reward you with an elongated sculpture listing the names of prominent local authors. On the top floor is the **San Francisco History Room**, used primarily for research, but with an interesting collection of old prints, maps and photographs.

Opposite the library on the far side of a repeatedly refurbished, yet unrelentingly dismal public park is **City Hall** (Mon–Fri 8am–8pm, Sat and Sun 8am–4pm; call ☎415-554-6075 for tour information). Modelled on St Peter's in Rome, this huge, green-domed Baroque building of granite and marble is the city's most grandiose structure and forms the nucleus of the Civic Center. After extensive work to repair the effects of time, weather and earthquakes, the building's gleaming dome has recently reopened for public viewing. Designed by architect Arthur Brown Jr with all the stylistic pomp he could muster, the building features an appropriately ostentatious amount of gold inlay – a tribute to the city's Gold Rush-era lucre. It was here in 1978 that conservative ex-supervisor Dan White got past security and assassinated Mayor George Moscone and gay supervisor Harvey Milk; later, when White was found guilty of manslaughter (not murder), it was the scene of violent demonstrations as protesters set fire to police vehicles and stormed the doors of the building (see box on p.449).

Directly behind City Hall are San Francisco's cultural mainstays. The ritzy **War Memorial Opera House**, on Van Ness at Grove, is the pride and joy of the city's performing arts institutions. Also designed by Brown, who used a fairly severe monumental facade to hide an opulent (and borderline garish) interior. Brown again used gold liberally, and the sculpturally inlaid surfaces surrounding the stage threaten to outshine anything but a stellar performance. The stage is home to the San Francisco Opera during fall and the San Francisco Ballet during spring. In thoroughly modern contrast, the giant aquarium-like **Louise M. Davies Symphony Hall** across the street is home to the highly-rated San Francisco Symphony, led by the adventurous and relentlessly self-promoting Michael Tilson Thomas, and whose season runs from September to May (see p.472).

To get a handle on the area's cultural venues, the **San Francisco Performing Arts Library and Museum**, 399 Grove Street (Wed 1–7pm, Thurs & Fri 10am–4pm, Sat noon–4pm; free), is not really a museum but a research library, though it does contain a one-room gallery showing exhibits related to performing arts not just in Civic Center, but the Bay Area as a whole. In addition, a number of galleries and smart shops are beginning to group themselves around the district: the **Vorpal Gallery**, 393 Grove Street (Tue–Sat 11am–6pm), has earned a reputation for consistently high-class contemporary paintings and has a room dedicated to surrealist sketch artist M.C. Escher, while the **Arts Commission Gallery**, 401 Van Ness (Wed–Sat noon–5:30pm), has both indoor and outdoor exhibitions by emerging Bay Area artists. Continuing west from here will lead you to the small boutique shopping district of **HAYES VALLEY**. Long hidden under the shadow of the Central Freeway, the neighborhood bloomed to life when the Loma Prieta earthquake forced the city to knock down the looming structure. Proximity to the Civic Center makes this an appealing spot to grab lunch, though if you're not looking to buy a pair of $200 shoes, chances are you'll be moving on quickly.

South of Market

Though you wouldn't know it from looking at it today, parts of **SOUTH OF MARKET** were once San Francisco's most desirable residential real estate. Rincon Hill and the streets around South Park were home to wealthy business leaders working in the Financial District, but with the invention of the cable car, the city's wealthier half quickly fled to mansions on the hills (a trend that continues to this day). The large working class community that remained was largely erased by the fires that followed the 1906 earthquake, and Rincon Hill was eventually cleared in the 1930s to make way for the new Bay Bridge. Still, some odd pockets of the old glory still exist, and the latest wave of development and regeneration makes it an interesting, if not universally attractive, activity-filled destination.

Confusingly, the neighborhood stretches diagonally from the Mission in the southwest until the Embarcadero in the northeast. The northern end, near downtown, is essentially an extension of the business district and is home to numerous office buildings. Along the bay, an array of new upscale condominium complexes have sprung up in the nascent **SOUTH BEACH** district, aided by public works aimed at improving transportation and beautifying a waterfront long hidden in the shadows of the thankfully-departed freeway. A block inland from the waterfront and the Ferry Building (see p.428), at the corner of Mission and Steuart, is the **Rincon Center**, an office and residential court highlighted by its impressive landmark **Post Office**. Built in 1939, the building's interior boasts the largest work ever commissioned by the WPA: a series of murals by ex-patriot Russian painter Anton Refreiger depicting a populist take on California's history. More recently, the ground floor of the building has become home to a procession of upscale supper clubs.

A new wave of ambitious public buildings, just down Mission Street, is the complex surrounding the sculpted greens of **Yerba Buena Center**. Designed by the Swiss architect Mario Botta, the **San Francisco Museum of Modern Art**, 151 Third Street (Fri–Tues 11am–6pm, Thurs 11am–9pm, closed Wed; $8, $3.50 Thurs 6–9pm, free the first Tues of the month; *www.sfmoma.org*), was an immediate bright spot when it opened here in 1995, heralding the resurgence of an artistic community that had become increasingly moribund and provincial. Competing to be the West Coast's premier exhibition space, the SFMOMA plays host to touring shows from New York and Europe while struggling to rapidly assemble a collection worthy of its name. As it stands, the building itself is still the most dramatic attraction: a huge central skylight floods the space with light, while the upper galleries are connected by a vertigo-inducing metal catwalk. The permanent collection focuses on painters in the California school, such as Richard Diebenkorn, and the works of Mexican painters Frida Kahlo and Diego Rivera. There are also notable Abstract Expressionist works by Jackson Pollock, Clyfford Still and Philip Guston, along with an odd over-representation of the German Expressionist Sigmar Polke. What has thus far distinguished the SFMOMA from its contemporaries is a strong interest in architecture, design and new media works.

Across the street from the SFMOMA is the **Yerba Buena Center for Art** (Tues–Sun 11am–6pm; $5, $3 for students, free the first Thurs of the month; *www.yerbabuenaarts.org*), which is less a competitor than a smaller, funkier companion. Spread out along the periphery of the Yerba Buena Gardens, the Center for Art is a loosely connected complex of low-lying buildings, including a gallery space, screening room and large theater. Like the museum, the gallery frequently hosts touring exhibitions from other cities, but its smaller confines are also home to exhibitions of local artists. Stretching up a slope away from downtown's tall buildings is the Yerba Buena Gardens' postage-stamp-sized patch of green. Covered with lunching office workers around midday, free musical concerts, ranging from traditional Chinese music to jazz, are routinely given.

If it's your brain you're looking to rest, wander across the garden to the **Metreon**, Fourth Street and Mission (hours vary, though most stores remain open Sun–Thurs

10am–10pm, Fri–Sat 10am–12pm), Sony's new urban mall. Aesthetically, it's a baffling jumble, with objects protruding from virtually every surface, desperate to grab your attention. The space is also chock-a-block with big-name commercial entertainments, such as the first-ever Microsoft store (providing a thrilling opportunity to test drive the next version of Word for Windows, or better yet, check your email for free). For the kids there is a "Where the Wild Things Are" play area and a massive IMAX theater. Diagonally across the street is the **Ansel Adams Center for Photography**, 4th Street and Folsom (Tues–Sun 11am–5pm; $5, $3 for students and $2 for seniors), named after the landscape photographer and pioneering environmentalist (see box p.350). In addition to a solid sampling of Adams' work, the Center puts on regular exhibitions by a wide range of contemporary photographers. And around the corner on Folsom is the imposing **Moscone Convention Center,** named after the Mayor who was assassinated along with Harvey Milk. Unless you have a trade-show to attend, skip it. Shyly hidden on the second floor of another building in the vicinity is the **Cartoon Art Museum,** 814 Mission (Wed–Fri 11am–5pm, Sat 10am–5pm, Sun 1–5pm; $4), a tiny space that houses touring exhibitions by such twentieth century masters as Charles Schulz (Peanuts) and French illustrator Moebius. Admission to the small space is a little dear, but it's worth the elevator ride for a visit to the bookshop.

A walk down the entirely unscenic Third Street might not seem to promise much, but hidden down a short alley next to a gas station is the surprising sanctuary of **South Park**, a picturesque European-style common. Ringed by trendy shops and cafés occupying the first floors of the last remaining nineteenth century houses in the neighborhood, South Park has become a haven for young multimedia professionals. Its shops and cafés are pricey, but it's still an extremely pleasant place to get a meal or just lounge with the young workers taking sunny refuge from the glow of their computer screens. Along with Jackson Square, it's also one of the only spots in the city that truly feels like a window into another time – it's not hard to imagine horse drawn carriages leisurely passing the park's slender oval. Just down the street, a plaque at Third and Brannan marks *Call of the Wild* author **Jack London's birthplace,** though he soon escaped to the then-safer confines of Oakland.

The name may not be pretty, but **Pac Bell Park,** the San Francisco Giants' new stadium south of South Park, is undoubtedly a major improvement over their much-maligned old home at Candlestick Park. Prone to gusts of brutally cold wind, the "Stick" (as it was semi-affectionately known) was everything you didn't want in a baseball stadium, making an afternoon at the ballgame feel like leisure time in a meat locker. The new stadium, in one of the sunniest parts of town, has an outfield that opens onto the Bay and a short right-field fence specifically designed to allow team star Barry Bonds to hit home runs more easily.

Farther southeast, the strip of **Folsom Street** centered on Eleventh Street isn't much to look at during the day, but comes alive at night. Longtime home to the city's leather community, the area now hosts a range of bars, clubs and restaurants serving every subculture under the stars. Eleventh Street is the kernel of activity and an obvious destination for a night out, provided you don't mind waiting in a line or two. If you happen to be in the vicinity during daytime hours, wander over to Sixth and Mission to look at **Defenestration**, a Quixotic piece of public art involving furniture that has been bolted to the outside of an abandoned building. Just don't linger too long: it's one of the nastier corners in town.

The Mission

San Franciscans often speak of the **MISSION** today as a "neighborhood in transition." But the same phrase could just as easily be applied to much of the district's 200-year history. After California's annexation, the area became home to succeeding waves of immigrants, first Scandinavians, followed more notably by a significant Irish influx and then the currently predominant Latin American community. The blocks around Valencia Street bear witnesses to the latest wave: young gentrifiers who have made the area a prime evening-time destination. According to a recent poll, it's now the second hippest neighborhood in the US (after New Orleans' Lower Garden District) and rising rents have engendered a certain amount of ill-will toward newcomers. Still, at various points in its history the Mission has been one of the city's richest neighborhoods and one of its poorest, making this latest transformation but one in a long line of face-lifts. What doesn't change is the Mission's gloriously sunny skies: the mass of Twin Peaks acts as a giant windbreak and even when the rest of the city is cold and foggy, the Mission is bright and (relatively) warm.

The neighborhood gets its name from **Mission San Francisco de Asis**, 16th Street and Dolores (open daily 9am–4pm, $2 suggested donation), more commonly known as Mission Dolores, which was consecrated by Spanish missionaries in 1776 and is the oldest building in San Francisco. The first mass celebrated at Mission Dolores on June 29 of that year marks the official founding of the city, though the community was then known as Yerba Buena. The evolution of San Francisco is reflected in the mission's architecture: the original building, dating from 1782, is squat and relatively spare, while the more prominent basilica next door, built in 1913, is a riot of ornate designs. Aside from periodic tour bus herds, the building can be quite serene, with a stained-glass-lit interior offering a pleasant opportunity to gaze into the city's long-erased past. The backyard cemetery (made famous in Hitchcock's *Vertigo*) holds the graves of the mission's founders, as well hundreds of "converted" Native Americans. Far removed from the plastic gimmickry of Fisherman's Warf, this is one of the city's best historical icons, and is well worth a visit.

A short walk from the mission down the stately, palm-tree-lined boulevard Dolores Street, arguably the most attractive stretch of asphalt in the city, brings you to the sunbather-covered slope of **Dolores Park**. Though during the week much of the park is little more than a glorified dog run, on weekends the southwest corner transforms into "Dolores Beach," where members of the Castro gay community come to bronze their gym-toned muscles. A further climb uphill is rewarded by **Liberty Street**, where the Victorian architecture rivals Alamo Square's more touristed "Painted Ladies" (see p.452). Retreating downhill, make your way to **Valencia Street** and the main drag of the Mission's youthful population. Once the stomping grounds of a sizeable lesbian community, the street now caters to weekend shoppers looking for funky household items on the cheap, and in the evenings is a prime dining destination. Looking completely out-of-place, on an exceedingly urban stretch of real estate two blocks north of Valencia Street's main shopping district, is the original **Levi Strauss factory building** at 250 Valencia near 14th Street (free tours Tues and Wed 9am, 11am & 1:30pm; call ☎415-565-9155 for reservations). The company's denim jeans began their existence during the Gold Rush, as the distinctly unfashionable apparel of miners looking for something sturdy to wear while slogging through mountain rivers. Nowadays, most Levis are made in factories outside the US, and the somewhat perfunctory tour is minimally informative. For a more interactive experience, try the company's new Union Square shop, which lets shoppers shrink fit new pants by sitting in a giant tub of hot water.

Just one block east of Valencia is **Mission Street**, the commercial hub of the city's Latino community. Noticeably low rent, the street is lined with five-and-dime shops selling a virtually identical stock of cheaply made goods. If you're a fan of Christian kitsch, every shop is a gold mine, filled to the bursting point with Virgin Mary candles, papal key chains and car air fresheners graced by the image of Jesus. It's also the best area to grab a burrito, San Francisco's trademark meal-in-a-tortilla – a gut-buster filled to the bursting-point with meat, beans, rice, cheese and tongue-numbing hot salsa. Attracted by relatively low real estate prices, a crop of trendy new bars has sprung up along the

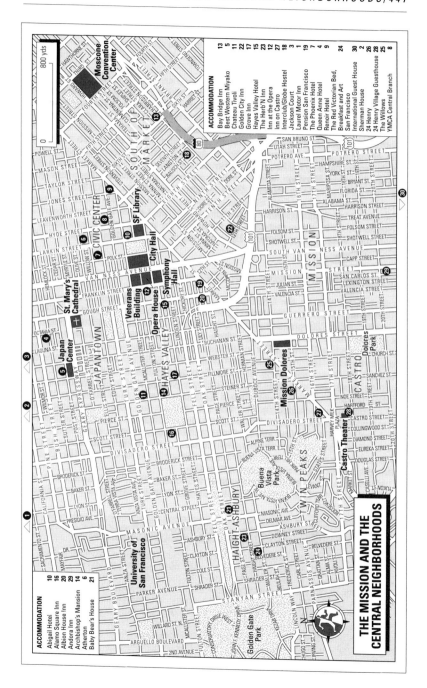

Moscone Convention Center

SF Library

St. Mary's Cathedral

CIVIC CENTER

City Hall

Veterans Building

Opera House

Symphony Hall

Japan Center

JAPANTOWN

HAYES VALLEY

University of San Francisco

Mission Dolores

CASTRO

Dolores Park

Castro Theater

Buena Vista Park

TWIN PEAKS

HAIGHT-ASHBURY

Golden Gate Park

800 yds

SOUTH OF MARKET

THE MISSION AND THE CENTRAL NEIGHBORHOODS

street, their snazzy new signs often glowing incongruously beside long-shuttered grocery and clothing stores. But be aware that, though this is arguably now the city's hottest nightlife district, you should still exercise significant caution at night, as the area remains rife with gang activity.

Even after an intensive cross-cultural immersion on Mission Street, turning down 24th Street west of Mission can feel like a trip into another country. Once the exclusive domain of low riders, the street remains the heart of the Mission's Latino community. Visual evidence of the community's pride is provided by dozens of brightly-painted **murals**, fanning out down side streets like a peacock's feathers to celebrate the shared identity of *La Raza*, a name meant to signify the mestizo (of mixed Spanish and indigenous ethnicity) peoples throughout South America. The greatest concentration of murals can be found by ducking off 24th Street down Balmy, an unassuming back alley between Treat and Harrison, where the walls are completely covered. For a little guidance and history, call the **Precita Eyes Mural Arts Center**, 2981 24th Street at Harrison (Mon–Fri 10am–5pm, Sat–Sun 11am–4pm; ☎415-285-2287) which has sponsored most of the paintings since its founding in 1971 and offers a variety of tours on weekends for $5-10. If you just can't get enough of the neighborhood, turn south on Folsom for a steep hike up **Bernal Hill**, which offers an unusual vantagepoint on the city.

The Castro, Twin Peaks and Noe Valley

Formerly a wild frontier, the **CASTRO** has settled down considerably in recent years, mellowing into middle age. Gentrified by the city's gay community during the 1970s as a primarily residential community, the Castro was part of the bacchanalian atmosphere that prevailed in San Francisco's gay culture during that decade. The assassination of gay city supervisor **Harvey Milk** in 1978 (see box), which sparked the most intense rioting in the city's history, and the onset of the AIDS epidemic motivated many in the community to focus their energy on political organizing instead of the wild life. As a result the community now finds itself increasingly wealthy and politically influential – adopting the self-consciously enlightened demeanor of what is probably the world's most prominent gay community. But with this comfort has come a certain conservatism, and while activists argue that residents must still lead the fight on human rights issues such as AIDS funding and legal recognition of gay couples, many in the area seem increasingly concerned about more immediate quality of life issues such as chain stores and rising rents. For an insider's view, Trevor Hailey's "Cruisin' The Castro" **walking tour** (see p.418) is just about unbeatable.

Oddly enough, for a neighborhood bursting with energy, there's not an awful lot to do in the Castro and the best way to while away an afternoon or evening here is to simply

---

CAROUSING IN THE CASTRO

Popular radio personality Howard Stern once described **Halloween** as being "the Gay Christmas." While it is a big celebration, it's really more like Mardi Gras or Carnival, with the entire town dressing up and dancing in the streets. Originally an informal Castro event, the partying eventually became too rowdy for the city's liking, with shop owners complaining of destruction to their property and many neighborhood locals complaining about the noise and mess. Though City Hall responded by creating an official party in the Civic Center, the revelry continues all over town. Slightly more subdued and politically enlightened festivities abound during **Pride month**, with events spread over the month of June and culminating in the Pride Parade the last weekend of the month.

THE ASSASSINATION OF HARVEY MILK

In 1977, eight years after New York's Stonewall riots brought gay political activism into the spotlight, Castro camera shop owner **Harvey Milk** won election as the city's first openly gay supervisor (or councilor), and quickly became one of the most prominent gay officials in the country. Milk was a celebrated figure for the city's gay community, nicknamed the "Mayor of Castro Street," so it came as a horrifying shock when, in 1978, Milk's former fellow supervisor, Dan White walked into City Hall and shot both Milk and Mayor George Moscone dead. White was an ex-cop who had resigned from the board, claiming he couldn't live on the small salary. In fact, he was angered that the liberal policies of Moscone and Milk didn't accord with his conservative views: a staunch Catholic, White was a spokesman for San Francisco's many blue-collar Irish families and, as an ex-policeman, saw himself as the defender of the family values he believed gay rights were damaging. At his trial, White claimed that harmful additives in his fast food-laden diet had driven him temporarily insane – a plea which came to be known as the **"Twinkie defense"** (Twinkies being synthetic-cream cakes) – and was sentenced to five years' imprisonment for manslaughter. The gay community exploded when the news of White's light sentence was announced and the "White Night" **riots** that followed were among the most violent San Francisco has ever witnessed, as protesters stormed City Hall, turning over and burning police cars as they went. White was released from prison in 1985 and moved to Los Angeles, where he committed suicide shortly after. In a happier coda, current city supervisor **Tom Ammiano**, a former stand-up comedian who has said that he found the courage to come out publicly as gay through Milk's activism, is now one of the most powerful political figures in the city.

wander around people-watching. The neighborhood sprawls up and down several hillsides between the Lower Haight, Mission and Noe Valley, rising to the west toward the impressive summits of Twin Peaks. A good place to start is the MUNI stop at **Harvey Milk Plaza**, on the corner of Castro Street and Market, where a massive rainbow flag flaps in the breeze. Walking downhill on either street you will encounter the heaviest foot traffic, while the neighborhood's various side streets offer some pretty, brightly painted architecture. With its lovely Art Deco neon sign rising high above the street, the **Castro Theater**, 429 Castro Street, is a landmark that shines brightly in a neighborhood where people, not places, are the star attractions. Screening a well-curated schedule of classic film revivals and unusual premieres, the unofficial "Castro Cathedral" manages to find quality cinema that's more than a match for the theater's ambiance. The ornate balconies, wall-mounted busts of heroic figures and massive ceiling ornament would provide ample visual stimulation, even without a film showing on the gigantic screen. Come early for an extra treat: before each evening screening a Wurlitzer organ rises from the stage for a pre-showtime serenade. The musical medley always draws to a close with "San Francisco," as the crowd merrily claps along.

After leaving the Castro, make an effort to go to **TWIN PEAKS**, about a mile and a half along Market from the Harvey Milk Plaza. (Travel west until you hit Twin Peaks Boulevard; the #37 Corbett bus will take you to Park Ridge.) The highest point in the city, Twin Peaks gives a **360-degree view** of the Peninsula. Real estate prices in the city are gauged in part by the quality of the views, so it's no surprise that the curving streets that wind around the slopes of Twin Peaks hold some of the city's most outrageously unaffordable homes. During the day, busloads of tourists arrive to point their cameras, and during the summer crowds often build up waiting for the fog to lift. It's better to go at night, picking out landmarks from either side of the shimmering artery of Market Street. If you want to avoid the crowds, **Tank Hill**, a small promontory just beneath Twin Peaks – where you'll need a map to find your way through the maze of small streets – is a nice option, though sometimes sketchy after dusk.

You might also consider a quick visit to **NOE VALLEY**. Despite being just a couple of blocks from both the Castro and Mission, the quiet bedroom community feels worlds apart, thanks to some very steep hills that help keep the area isolated. The neighborhood's heart is 24th Street, where baby strollers often seem to outnumber cars. Frankly, there's not much to do once here besides sipping cappucinos or shopping for cardigans.

Haight-Ashbury, the Western Addition and Japantown

Two miles west of downtown San Francisco, **HAIGHT-ASHBURY** is a neighborhood that lent its name to an era, giving it a fame that far outstrips its size. A small area centered around the intersection of Haight and Ashbury and bordered by Golden Gate Park at its western edge, the "Haight," as it's known, was a respectable Victorian neighborhood-turned-slum that emerged in the 1960s as the epicenter of the counterculture. Much to the chagrin of locals – including many increasingly comfortable ex-hippies – young people continue to flock here in droves, looking to recapture the 1960s spirit, or at the very least to find a decent bootleg copy of the Grateful Dead's last concert. The constant influx of latter-day hippies and gawkers has helped transform the neighborhood into something of an alternative culture shopping mall and it's now one of the best areas in town to burn money, complete with numerous coffee shops, record stores and places to get pierced or buy a bong. Consequently, the district has one of the highest concentration of oddball characters per square foot of any neighborhood in the country. On a darker note, the street's long association with **drugs** has kept the number of people seeking, selling and using them here alarmingly high, and during a typical tour of the eight-block commercial stretch of the Upper Haight, it's not uncommon to step over at least one passed-out junkie on your way into an overpriced rag-and-bead shop.

Roughly divided into half by Divisadero Street, the Haight consists of the Upper and Lower Haight districts, with the **Upper Haight** stretching west to the park and the **Lower Haight** running east up to Buchanan Street. Though less famous, the Lower Haight is currently the more vibrant neighborhood, though it makes for less interesting people-watching. Long an African-American neighborhood, the Lower Haight has been transformed over the past decade by youthful immigrants from the British Isles into the center of the city's rave culture. DJ shops line Haight Street between Webster and Divisadero, while bars blatantly capitalize on Old World nostalgia (even for the food). Still, the African-American community remains very much a presence and it's not uncommon to see older men dressed in suits and fedoras whiling away a weekend afternoon playing dominoes in an open garage or just sitting on a stoop chatting with the neighbors. Though the Mission has stolen much of the Lower Haight's trend-hopping spotlight, the neighborhood remains very much torn between its older and newer identities – a conflicted identity that has lead to some tensions. It's best to exercise caution at night, particularly in the vicinity of Webster Street.

In much the same way that the Lower Haight tends to be overshadowed by its flashier neighbor up the hill, longtime resident **Kenneth Rexroth** (1905-1982) has largely been overshadowed by the writers he inspired. As a poet, novelist and translator of Chinese literature, Rexroth lived a wildly adventurous life that was an inspiration for Kerouac and crew. While not open to the public, you can take a walk past Rexroth's old apartment at 250 Scott Street, a place where several of the early beats crashed upon first arriving in San Francisco.

Continuing uphill toward the heart of the Haight will bring you to **Buena Vista Park**, a mountainous forest of Monterey pines and California redwoods. Used by dog walkers in the daylight hours, come nightfall the park plays host to much sex-in-the-shrubbery; walk here accompanied by day and not at all at night, unless you're male and looking for some action. Things get livelier as you move west, with the street crowded by an increasing number of musicians, panhandlers and hard-core hippie burnouts. Two blocks west, the **Grateful Dead House**, 710 Ashbury at Haight, was once ground zero for the counter culture. A 1967 drug bust only added to the band's myth, which survived countless tours and a rotating cast of keyboard players. Even the 1995 death of guitarist Jerry Garcia has done little to quell fans' devotion. The **Haight-Ashbury Free Clinic**, at 558 Clayton Street, is a venerable Sixties hangover: an unusual institution, certainly by American standards, which first began providing free health care when drugs-related illnesses became a big problem in the Haight. It now survives – barely – on contributions, continuing to treat local drug casualties and the indigent, both disproportionately large groups in this area of the city. Particularly in the Haight-Ashbury, the contrast between the city's new-found wealth and seemingly intractable homeless problem can be shockingly stark – with the rapid rise in rents only exacerbating an unhappy situation.

To the north of Haight Street, the **Panhandle** is a rivulet of greenery that runs like a tributary into Golden Gate Park. Though the grass is noticeably scraggly these days, it was once a ritzy thoroughfare catering to horse-drawn carriages and the lovely houses speak of wealthier times. For a better sense of the lay of the land, head across the Panhandle to the **University of San Francisco**'s scenic campus.

HIPPIES

The first **hippies** were an offshoot of the **Beats**, many of whom had moved out of their increasingly expensive North Beach homes to take advantage of the low rents and large spaces in the Victorian houses of the Haight. The post-Beat bohemia that subsequently began to develop here in the early 1960s was initially a small affair, involving drug use and the embrace of Eastern religion and philosophy, together with a marked anti-American political stance and a desire for world peace. Where Beat philosophy had emphasized self-indulgence, the hippies, on the face of it at least, attempted to be more embracing, focusing on self-coined concepts such as "universal truth" and "cosmic awareness." Naturally it took a few big names to get the ball rolling, and characters like **Ken Kesey and his Merry Pranksters** soon set a precedent of wild living, challenging authority and dropping (as they saw it) out of the established norms of society. Drugs were particularly important, and seen as an integral – and positive – part of the movement. **LSD** especially, the effects of which were just being discovered and which at the time was not actually illegal, was claimed as an avant-garde art form, pumped out in private laboratories and distributed by Timothy Leary and his network of supporters with a prescription ("Turn on, tune in, drop out") that galvanized a generation into inactivity. An important group in the Haight at the time was **The Diggers**, who, famed for their parties and antics, truly believed LSD could be used to increase creativity. Before long life in the Haight began to take on a theatrical quality: Pop Art found mass appeal, light shows became legion, dress flamboyant, and the Grateful Dead, Jefferson Airplane and Janis Joplin made names for themselves. Backed by the business weight of promoter Bill Graham, **the psychedelic music** scene became a genuine force nationwide, and it wasn't long before kids from all over America started turning up in Haight-Ashbury for the free food, free drugs and free love. Money became a dirty word, the hip became "heads," and the rest of the world were "straights."

Other illustrious tenants of the Haight at this time include Kenneth Rexroth, who hosted a popular radio show and wrote for the *San Francisco Examiner*. Hunter S. Thompson, too, spent time here researching and writing his book *Hell's Angels*, and was notorious for inviting Angels round to his apartment on Parnassus Street for noisy, long and occasionally dangerous drinking and drug-taking sessions.

Things inevitably turned sour towards the end of the decade, but during the heady days of the massive "be-in" in Golden Gate Park in 1966 and the so-called **Summer of Love** the following year, this busy little intersection became home to no less than 75,000 transitory pilgrims who saw it as the Mecca of alternative culture.

Spreading north and east of here, the **WESTERN ADDITION** is one of the central city's few predominantly black neighborhoods and almost relentlessly poor – dangerous in parts and certainly not tourist territory. The exception that proves the rule is a small area surrounding **Alamo Square park**, at Hayes and Scott – just uphill from the Lower Haight. A staple of every tour bus company in town, the park's southeast slope is home to small flocks of amateur photographers eager to snap a picture of "**the Painted Ladies.**" These six Victorian houses, originally built in 1894, and colorfully and attractively restored, have been a postcard staple for years. If that isn't enough of a Kodak moment, the view beyond the houses is more brilliant still – on a clear day you can see over the city and across the bay all the way to the hills of North Berkeley. The determinedly thorough can continue north on a dismal strip of Fillmore Street to reach **JAPANTOWN**, something of a misnomer for what is basically a shopping mall with an eastern flavor – the Japan Center – around which only a small percentage of San Francisco's Japanese Americans actually live. Visit only to check out the **Kabuki Hot Springs**, 1750 Geary Blvd (Mon–Fri 10am–10pm, Sat & Sun 9am–10pm; ☎415/922-6000): community baths with shiatsu massage, steam baths and other luxuriating facilities for around $12 per visit, $37 and up for massage. If you're in the area, jump over a few blocks to where Geary Boulevard meets Gough and look at the elaborately modern **St Mary's Cathedral**, affectionately mocked by locals for its bizarre resemblance to a washing machine agitator (earning it the nickname "Our Lady of the Maytag"). Inside, it's a surprisingly pleasant and open space, where the pulpit seems more like an afterthought than the seat of holy authority.

Golden Gate Park

Unlike most American cities, San Francisco is not short on green space, and **GOLDEN GATE PARK** is its largest, simultaneously full of the bustle of urban living and hidden natural environments offering welcome respite to city residents. The park was designed in 1871 by park commissioner William Hall in the style of Frederick Law Olmsted (who created Central Park in New York). Spreading three miles or so west from the Haight as far as the Pacific shore, it was constructed – on what was then an area of wild sand dunes buffeted by the spray of the nearby ocean – with the help of a dyke to protect the western side from the sea. Even so, the landscape still undergoes a natural transition as it approaches the ocean and, in contrast to the relatively placid Bay, the strong winds blowing through the Park and gusting up streets in the surrounding neighborhoods are a constant reminder of the sea's more turbulent temperament. It's generally best to visit in late morning or early afternoon – even on seemingly sunny days, a chilly fog often rolls in before dusk.

Exploration of the whole place could take days of footwork. Among its more evident attractions, there's a **Japanese Tea Garden**, a **horticultural museum** (modeled on the Palm House at Kew Gardens), a **Shakespeare Garden** with every flower or plant mentioned in the writer's plays, not to mention the usual contingent of serious joggers, cyclists and in-line skaters. If you're feeling energetic, activities are many and quite cheap: **boat rental** is available on Stow Lake (parallel with 19th Avenue) for $10–14 per hour, and **horse-riding** for around $25 per hour from the Golden Gate Park Stables at John F. Kennedy Drive and 36th Avenue. **Admission** to all park museums and the tea garden is discounted with the $14 Explorer Pass, available from the museums and the TIX Bay Area booth at Union Square (see "Theater," p.473).

Of the park's numerous museums, the **M.H. de Young Museum** (Wed–Sun 9.30am–5pm; $7, $2 off with MUNI transfer and free first Wed of each month) is the largest, with San Francisco's most diverse range of painting and sculpture, ranging from the ancient art of Greece and Rome to an outstanding twentieth-century collection in the American Wing – a hundred or so paintings bequeathed by John D. Rockefeller

III. Rubens, Rembrandt and seventeenth-century European painters are also well represented; you can get an exhaustive commentary on all with a free "Directors' Tour," actually a personal headset that you wear for about an hour. Next door, in the West Wing, the **Asian Art Museum** (same hours) has a thorough collection of ten thousand paintings, sculptures, ceramics and textiles from all over Asia. Donated by Avery Brundage in 1966, the collection receives much attention for its sheer vastness, but it's only worth seeing if you're an enthusiast.

You'll find another group of museums opposite, in the **California Academy of Sciences** (summer daily 9am–6pm; winter daily 10am–5pm; $8.50, $1 off with MUNI transfer and free first Wed of each month) – the perfect place to amuse restless children. There's a natural history museum with a thirty-foot skeleton of a 130 million-year-old dinosaur, and life-size replicas of elephant seals and other California wildlife, and a colony of twenty black-footed penguins. The Academy's "educational" earthquake ride – simulating a range of tremors – provides morbid enjoyment. But the show-stealer is the collection of 14,500 specimens of aquatic life in the **Steinhart Aquarium** (daily 10am–5pm; included with Academy admission), the best of which are the alligators and other reptiles lurking in a simulated swamp. Also, if you catch it at the right time, the **Morrison Planetarium** (☎415/750-7141; $2.50) can be a great experience. Daily skyshows, laser light shows and rock music draw often acid-crazed crowds for evening performances.

Slightly west of the museums is the usually crowded **Japanese Tea Garden** (daily 9am–5.30pm; $2.50). Built in 1894 for the California Midwinter Exposition, the garden was beautifully landscaped by the Japanese Hagiwara family, who were also responsible for the invention of the fortune cookie (despite the prevalent belief that fortune cookies are Chinese). The Hagiwaras looked after the garden until World War II, when along with other Japanese Americans they were sent to internment camps. A massive bronze Buddha dominates the garden, and bridges, footpaths, pools filled with shiny oversized carp, plus bonsai and cherry trees lend the place a peaceful feel – as long as you can ignore the busloads of tourists that pour in regularly throughout the day. The best way to enjoy the garden is to get there around 9am when it first opens and have a breakfast of tea and fortune cookies in the teahouse.

To enjoy the quieter corners of the park, head west through the many flower gardens and eucalyptus groves towards the ocean. Perhaps the most unusual thing about Golden Gate Park is its small herd of **bison**, roaming around the Buffalo Paddock off JFK Drive near 38th Avenue; you can get closest to these noble giants in their feeding area at the far west end. Moving towards the edge of the park at Ocean Beach, passing a **tulip garden** and two crumbling **windmills** donated by the Queen of Holland, you'll come to the **Beach Chalet** (daily 8am–midnight, free). This two-story, white-pillared structure, designed by Willis Polk, is home to some of San Francisco's lesser-known public art. A series of frescoes painted in the 1930s depicts the growth of San Francisco as a city and the creation of Golden Gate Park, while upstairs is a lively brewery-restaurant.

Sunset, Richmond and the Beaches

Golden Gate Park is hugged by the large, residential neighborhoods of **RICHMOND** to the north and **SUNSET** to the south. As late as the 1940s, much of what comprises these two districts was still mile after mile of sand dunes, stretching to the ocean. And while residents of the city's more intensely urban eastern half might turn up their noses and say that, in terms of liveliness, not much has changed in the half century since, the truth is that both neighborhoods – the multi-ethnic Richmond in particular – offer some rewarding oases of activity. More than the tourist-saturated downtown neighborhoods, this area is a window into the less seen side of San Francisco: a comfortable, though occasionally lethargic, blend of cultures. Numerous good, cheap restaurants, serving food from around the world, and the Palace of the Legion of Honor's remote cultural outpost will reward those who stop here en route to the breathtaking (but often fogbound) coastline at the city's edge.

Partly due to the weather and partly due to the coldness of the ocean water, beach culture doesn't exist in San Francisco the way it does in Southern California, and people here tend to watch the surf rather than ride it. Powerful currents and crashing waves dissuade all but the most fearless swimmers, and as a result the city's beaches remain blissfully uncrowded. Stretching south a mile from the Golden Gate Bridge, **Baker Beach** is San Francisco's prettiest and most popular, drawing a mixed crowd of fishermen and nude sunbathers, and giving some great views of the soaring red bridge. It's also easy to reach: stairways drop down from Lincoln Avenue, and MUNI bus #29 stops at the main parking lot every thirty minutes. A half-mile further southwest at the foot of the ritzy Sea Cliff district, China Beach is more protected and better for swimming, and also offers free showers and changing rooms.

Rising to the west from the beaches, paths curl south around the Peninsula to **Land's End**: it takes about thirty minutes to get round the cliffs, tricky to negotiate but worth it for the brilliant views of the ocean. A small beach in a rocky cove beneath the cliffside walk is a favorite spot for gay sunbathers. Inland lies **Lincoln Park**, primarily a golf course, but as part of the Point Lobos Headlands it has some striking trails.

Sitting in stately isolation at the park's summit, the **California Palace of the Legion of Honor** (Tues–Sun 9.30am–5pm; $7, $2 off with MUNI transfer and surcharge for special exhibitions) – most easily reached by taking the #38 bus from Geary Boulevard and transferring to the #18 at the Lincoln Park Golf Course – is arguably San Francisco's best art museum, housing a remarkable collection of fine art. The building itself is no less impressive than its holdings: built in 1920, its parade of white columns is a copy of Paris' Legion de Honneur. Adding to the monumentality is a cast of Rodin's *The Thinker*, set in the center of the museum's front courtyard. The museum was reopened in 1995 after several years of extensive seismic engineering and a grand facelift, and it now displays the permanent collection to even greater advantage. The Renaissance is represented with the works of Titian, El Greco and sculpture from Giambologna, while some great canvases by Rembrandt and Hals, as well as Rubens' magnificent *Tribute Money*, are highlights of the seventeenth-century Dutch and Flemish collection. Among the Impressionist and post-Impressionist paintings are works by Courbet, Manet, Monet, Renoir, Degas and Cézanne, but the room dedicated to one of the world's finest collection of Rodin's work steals the show.

Rounding the peninsula, a rather bigger stop for the tour buses is the **Cliff House**, precipitously balanced on the western tip of the Peninsula above the head of Ocean Beach. There's a visitor center here (daily 10am–5pm), with information on the surrounding area and an exhibit on the original Cliff House built by Prussian immigrant Adolph Sutro in the late-nineteenth-century as an exclusive resort for the leisured classes, which burned down long ago. There's also the quirky **Musée Mécanique** (Mon–Fri 11am–7pm, Sat & Sun & holidays 10am–8pm; free), home to 145 antique but functional coin-operated penny arcade machines, dating from the nineteenth century, such as a mechanical opium den and can-can dancer. Across a landing from the Musée is a rare **Camera Obscura**, open 11am until sunset. Using a rotating mirror – and a trick of light – the camera allows entrants to see a panoramic view of the surrounding area. Unfortunately, the camera is mostly surrounded by water, making the view less interesting than the presentation. The Cliff House **restaurant** (see p.457) is where most visitors end up, enjoying the view and a drink from the bar.

Down by the water you'll find the remains of other bygone amusements – the **Sutro Baths**. This collection of opulent recreational pools, gardens and elegant sculptures, all covered with 100,000 feet of stained glass, was sadly destroyed by fire in the 1960s.

From here you can explore the ramparts and tunnels of the fortified coastline – a bit frightening at night, when the surf really starts crashing, but there's a certain romance too, and on a rare warm evening it becomes one of the city's favorite snogging spots.

Stretching to the city's southern border, buffeted by sea breezes and fog, the thin strip of **Ocean Beach** seems to constantly be on the brink of either being washed out to shore or blown into locals' backyards. Aside from a small community of particularly hearty surfers (most notably country-rock crooner Chris Isaak), the beach is the almost exclusive territory of joggers and dog walkers. Along the beach's southward trajectory sits the small, rather forlorn **San Francisco Zoo**, Sloat Blvd at 45th Street (☎415-753-7061; $9 for adults, $6 for youths aged 11–18, $3 for children), open daily from 10am to 5pm. While parts of the zoo have been modernized, much of it is depressingly archaic, rewarding only those with steely nerve or morbid curiosity. While a recently renovated Primate exhibit offers a promising glimpse into the future, most animals languish in undersized concrete boxes while the zoo's trustees dicker over redevelopment plans. At the city's southern corner the beach rises up to the windswept bluffs of **Fort Funston**. Haunting and remote, the small park's bunker-strewn cliffs serve as a quiet launching pad for hang-gliders, bobbing and swooping majestically off the edge of the western hemisphere.

The Golden Gate Bridge

The orange towers of the **Golden Gate Bridge** – probably the most photographed bridge in the world – are visible from almost every point of elevation in San Francisco. As much an architectural as an engineering feat, the bridge took only 52 months to design and build and was opened in 1937. Designed by Joseph Strauss, it was the first really massive suspension bridge with a span of 4200ft, and until 1959 ranked as the world's longest. Over 5000 gallons of paint are used annually to keep the structure's colors bright. Connecting the Peninsula's northwesterly point to Marin County and Northern California, the bridge rendered the hitherto essential ferry crossing redundant, and was designed to stand winds of up to a hundred miles an hour. Handsome on a clear day, the bridge takes on an eerie quality when the thick white fogs pour in and hide it almost completely. Perhaps the best-loved symbol of San Francisco, in 1987 the Golden Gate proved an auspicious place for a sunrise party when crowds gathered to celebrate its fiftieth anniversary. Some quarter of a million people turned up (a third of the city's population); the winds were strong and the huge numbers caused the bridge to buckle, but fortunately not to break.

You can either drive or walk across the bridge. Barring traffic (a constant on weekends) the drive is probably the more thrilling of the two options, as you race under the bridge's towers, but the windy, thirty-minute walk across gives you time to take in its enormity and absorb the striking views of the city behind you and the headlands of Marin County straight ahead. Pause at the midway point and consider the seven or so suicides a month who choose this spot, 220ft up, for jumping off – apparently always facing the city as they do so. In 1995, when the suicide toll had reached almost one thousand, police kept the figures quiet to avoid a rush of would-be-suicides going for the dubious distinction of being the thousandth person to leap.

Standing beneath the bridge is almost as memorable as traveling over it. The **Fort Point National Historic Site**, a brick fortress built to guard the bay in the 1850s on the initial landing place of the city's first Spanish settlers, gives a good sense of the place as the westernmost outpost of the nation. Formerly part of the Presidio Army Base (now a National Park), it was to have been demolished to make way for the bridge above, but the redesign of the southern approach – note the additional arch which spans overhead – left it intact. It's a dramatic site, the surf pounding away beneath the great span of the bridge high above – a view made famous by Kim Novak's suicide attempt in Alfred

Hitchcock's *Vertigo*. It is alleged by some that the water here makes for one of the best (and certainly most foolhardy) surfing spots in the area. A small **museum** (Wed–Sun 9am–4pm; free) inside the fort shows some rusty old cannons and artillery, although a far superior military collection can be seen in the **Presidio Army Museum** (Tues–Sun 10am–4pm; free) at Lincoln Blvd and Funston Ave in the Presidio proper, with uniforms, photographs and some detailed documentation of San Francisco's military history.

Eating

With well over three thousand restaurants of every possible ethnicity and style crammed onto the small peninsula, and scores of bars and cafés that are open all day (and some all night), **eating** is the culture in this town. San Franciscans gourmandize expertly around the city and most people will have at least four restaurant recommendations up their sleeves. It doesn't have to be expensive either, with **budget options** ranging from the usual array of pizza and burger joints to the **Chinese** restaurants in Chinatown and the **Mexican** places of the Mission – indeed, these are the two cuisines that San Francisco does best, or at least most widely. A little more expensively, **Italian** restaurants are common in North Beach and around much of the rest of downtown; **French** food is a perennial favorite, at least with the power-broking crowd, although nouvelle cuisine is finally beginning to loosen its grip on San Franciscan menus. **California cuisine** nowadays has grown away from its minimalist roots, but still features the freshest food, beautifully presented. **Japanese** food, notably sushi, is also still massively popular though not always affordable. **Thai**, **Korean** and **Indonesian** food is similarly in vogue, and is usually cheaper. Not surprisingly, health-conscious San Francisco also has a wide range of **vegetarian** and **wholefood** restaurants, and it's rare to find anywhere that doesn't have at least one meat-free item on the menu. With the vineyards of Napa and Sonoma Valley on the city's doorstep, quality **wines** are a high-profile feature in most San Francisco restaurants. It's also very worthwhile to plan on one splurge meal while in town – the high price you'll pay for a world-class meal here is still far below the big-city average. Be warned: San Francisco closes up early and you'll be struggling to find places that will serve you much after 10 or 11pm, unless they're of the 24-hour diner variety. And thanks to recent statewide legislation you now cannot **smoke** in any restaurant in the city.

In the listings that follow, the **restaurants** are arranged by cuisine, together with a roundup of where to eat around the clock. However, San Francisco chefs being the innovators that they are, the enduring craze is for combining styles – Chinese/French for example – and it can be difficult to categorize restaurants. So don't take the breakdowns below as set in stone: there's no such thing as a straight anything in this town.

Budget food: breakfasts, burgers and diners

Bagdad Café, 2295 Market St at 16th St, Castro. Good, hearty breakfasts and burgers served 24 hours per day.

Brain Wash Laundromat/Café, 1122 Folsom St at Seventh, SoMa. If you don't mind watching people pile their dirties into the machines, this is a surprisingly good venue for well-prepared, simple sandwiches, pizzas and salad. A boisterous hangout, providing a good opportunity to check out the locals. See also "Drinking: bars and cafés," p.464.

The Grubstake, 1525 Pine St at Polk, Tenderloin. Converted 1920s railroad dining car, with some of the city's best late-night burgers.

Hamburger Mary's, 1582 Folsom St at 12th, SoMa. Raucous burger bar, with punky waiting staff and good range of vegetarian options. Inexpensive, and open late for the club-going crowds.

Mel's Drive-In, 3355 Geary Blvd at Beaumont, Richmond, and 2165 Lombard St at Fillmore, Marina. Straight out of *American Graffiti*, with burgers, fries, milkshakes and a lot of rock'n'roll on the jukebox. No longer a drive-in, but open late – after midnight every night, till 3am at weekends.

SAN FRANCISCO RESTAURANTS

Orphan Andy's, 3991 17th St at Castro. Favorite Castro hangout, serving burgers, omelets and breakfast 24 hours a day.

The Pine Crest, 401 Geary St at Mason, Union Square. Every inch the greasy diner, but ideal for getting rid of your spare change and hunger at the same time.

Spaghetti Western, 576 Haight St at Fillmore, Lower Haight. Best breakfasts for miles and a lively crowd to look at while you chow down.

Sparky's, 240 Church St at Market. 24hr Castro diner cooking up burgers, pastas and pizzas plus breakfasts, including a very good eggs florentine on weekends. Beer and wine too.

American and California cuisine

Aqua, 253 California St at Battery, Financial District (☎415/956-9662). Gorgeously decorated, mainly seafood restaurant that pulls in a discerning crowd.

Asia SF, 201 9th St at Howard, SoMa (☎415/255-2742). More of an "experience" than a restaurant, this only-in-San Francisco spot features an all-drag-queen staff who put on a nightly revue. Though it can't compete with the show, the moderately pricey food's not half bad, either.

Chow, 215 Church at Market (☎415/552-2469). Neighborhood eatery near the Castro serving absolutely wonderful, lovingly-made dishes for cheap. Perpetually popular, so expect a wait on weekend evenings.

Cliff House, 1090 Point Lobos Ave, Richmond (☎415/386-3330). Much maligned by some as a tourist trap (complete with a gift shop), the *Cliff House*'s unmatched views make it a San Francisco institution. Eat dinner elsewhere; come instead for a drink at sunset, or to sample some of their excellent desserts.

Cypress Club, 500 Jackson St near Columbus (☎415/296-8555). Jackson Square hot spot famed for its delicately presented, inventive California cuisine, served up in one of the most stylish dining rooms to be found in San Francisco – a cross between the *Ritz Carlton* and a Bedouin tent.

Farallon, 450 Post between Mason and Powell, Union Square (☎415/956-6969). Sumptuously styled as an undersea grotto, serving small portions of creative seafood dishes. Definitely worth a splurge if you're into elegant dining experiences; if you can't afford it, go for a drink in the fanciful bar that looks like the Octopus's Garden.

Firefly, 4288 24th St at Douglass, Noe Valley (☎415/821-7652). Noe Valley restaurant with wideranging, innovative menu and a knowing crowd. Very much a neighborhood joint for a casually wealthy neighborhood, prices are still far below the downtown competition.

Flying Saucer, 1000 Guerrero St at 22nd, Mission (☎415/641-9955). Popular hot spot offering exquisitely assembled, dramatically presented, adventurous cuisine that mixes fruit with meat and every wacky combination you can think of. Reserve in advance and bring your credit card, though cheap compared to the competition, prices are still stiff.

42 Degrees, 235 16th St at Third (☎415/777-5558). Fashionable jazz supper club, in an appealingly remote location down on the old dockyards with a stark modern interior and expensive, wellmade simple California cuisine.

Hard Rock Café, 1699 Van Ness Ave at Sacramento, Civic Center (☎415/885-1699). Standard Hard Rock clone. Loud music, rock'n'roll decor and the sort of crowd who don't mind waiting in line for hours for the above-average burgers.

Hayes Street Grill, 320 Hayes between Gough and Franklin, Hayes Valley (☎415/863-5545). Fresh ingredients perfectly prepared and not overwrought. Excellent grilled fish and standard American fare, drawing a well-heeled conservative crowd at lunch and opera – and theatergoers at dinner.

Indigo, 687 McAllister St at Gough, Hayes Valley (☎415/673-9369). Stylish without being pretentious, this little sibling among the splashier Cal-cuisine spots delivers generous portions of inventive, seasonally-inspired entrées at moderately expensive prices, accompanied by top-notch service.

John's Grill, 63 Ellis St at Powell, Union Square (☎415/986-0669). Dashiell Hammett was such as regular at this meat and potatoes joint that he gave it a free plug in *The Maltese Falcon*, and noir fans have been flocking ever since.

Julie's Supper Club, 1123 Folsom St at Seventh, SoMa (☎415/861-0707). The affordable cuisine, both at the bar and in the backroom restaurant, can only be described as eclectic. The decor however, is straight out of a B-52's/Jetsons dream. Worth a look, especially if you can get there before 9pm and escape the $5 cover for the live jazz, R&B, and Seventies retro bands in the evenings. See also "Drinking: bars and cafés," p.464.

Liberty Café, 410 Cortland Ave (☎415/695-8777). Excellent food, beautifully prepared in this remote Bernal Heights favorite. Best of all, you get dinner for under $20.

LuLu, 816 Folsom St between Fourth and Fifth, SoMa (☎415/495-5775). Gone downhill in recent years, from stellar to merely satisfying. The loud, high-ceilinged dining room is packed regularly with those who know no nostalgia, chowing down on expensive Cal-cuisine served family-style in large portions.

Maye's Original Oyster House, 1233 Polk St at Sutter, Nob Hill (☎415/474-7674). In business since the 1860s, this is one of the city's oldest restaurants, turning out reasonably priced, well-cooked fish dishes in plush surroundings.

Moose's, 1652 Stockton St at Filbert, North Beach (☎415/987-7800). Run by the former proprietors of the *Washington Square Bar and Grill*, who have taken many of their old clients and become the latest word in power-lunching for the media-politico crowd. The moderate-to-expensive California cuisine satisfies.

Original Joe's, 144 Taylor St at Eddy, Union Square (☎415/775-4877). Inexpensive to moderate American/Italian restaurant, good for steaks, ribs, salads and the like.

Patio Café, 531 Castro St at 18th, Castro (☎415/621-4640). Casual terrace restaurant serving wholesome grills and pastas, and good-value weekend brunches where you can sling back inexpensive cocktails.

Postrio, 545 Post St at Mason, Union Square (☎415/776-7825). A top-notch San Francisco restaurant that's slightly over-rated due to the high-style ambiance and five-star reputation of chef Wolfgang Puck who serves up Californian dishes with Asian and Mediterranean influences. Hang out at the bar if you can't score a dinner reservation.

Slow Club, 2501 Mariposa St at Hampshire, Portero Hill (☎415/241-9390). Venerable SoMa hangout, serving good, reasonably-priced imaginative cooking and populated by *San Francisco Bay Guardian* writers and other arty types.

Stars, 555 Golden Gate Ave at Van Ness, Civic Center (☎415/861-7827). "See and be seen" home of the rich and powerful, the food is indisputably good but not within the price range of most mortals. Best to sit at the bar with a martini and some oysters, watching San Francisco society glide by.

Swan's Oyster Depot, 1517 Polk St at California, Nob Hill (☎415/673-1101). You wouldn't know it by the simple decor, but this is one of the city's best and oldest seafood places – take a seat at the bar (there are no tables) for half a dozen fresh-shucked oysters, washed down with a glass of ice-cold Anchor Steam beer. Open 8am–5pm.

Tadich Grill, 240 California St between Front and Battery, Financial District (☎415/391-2373). The oldest restaurant in California, this place is wood-paneled and very much an old money San Francisco institution. Grilled fresh seafood and excellent desserts.

2223 2223 Market at Sanchez, Castro (☎415/431-0692). Rather less daunting than *Mecca*, the Castro's other prime-dining destination, the top-notch food here should have you glowing – try the wonderful roast chicken with garlic mash potatoes.

Washington Square Bar and Grill, 1707 Powell St at Union, North Beach (☎415/982-8123). It may have lost a little of its cachet since the owners sold it and opened *Moose's* across the square (see above), but this is still the place to sip smart cocktails at the bar and sample the heartily-priced food, cooked to rich and heavy perfection. See also "Drinking: bars and cafés," p.464.

Zuni Café, 1658 Market St at Gough, Civic Center (☎415/552-2522). Despite the unprepossessing location on Market Street, *Zuni* has remained a chic place to be seen for the last five years, simply because the food is so damned good. Despite the Southwestern name, you get French/Italian-inspired cuisine for around $30 a head with a glass of wine.

Chinese, Thai and Southeast Asian

Borobudur, 700 Post St at Jones (☎415/775-1512). A fairly inexpensive little pocket of authentic Indonesia just a couple of blocks from Union Square. Eat early if you want to avoid the karaoke.

Burma Superstar, 309 Clement at 5th, Richmond (☎415/387-2147). If you've never had the chance to sample traditional Burmese dishes such as green tea salad, *poodhi* or the enigmatically named "Ants Climb Tree," this small, plain restaurant is a terrific place to start.

Eliza's, 205 Oak near Gough, Hayes Valley (☎415/621-4819). Not your average Chinese dive, this place is all stained glass and fresh flowers, serving excellent, mid-range Chinese food to a knowing crowd.

Empress of China, 838 Grant Ave at Washington, Chinatown (☎415/434-1345). Without doubt, the poshest place in town to get to grips with Chinese cooking, with an incredible selection of dishes and amazing views over neighboring North Beach. You'll be paying $13–20 for a main course, but if you're in the mood for a blowout it's quite the place to be decadent.

The Golden Turtle, 2211 Van Ness at Broadway, Marina (☎415/441-4419). Upscale Vietnamese restaurant serving delicious, well-priced dishes.

Harbor Village, 4 Embarcadero Center, lobby level, between Clay and Drumm (☎415/781-8833). Downtown's best dim sum, especially popular for Sunday lunch, with standard Cantonese dishes for dinner.

House of Nanking, 919 Kearny St between Jackson and Columbus, North Beach (☎415/421-1429). Always packed, this hole-in-the-wall serves up some of the best, fastest and cheapest Chinese food downtown. You have to endure lining up outside, tiny tables, bumping elbows with yuppies, and being hurried out, but it's all part of the *Nanking* cult experience. Not to be missed.

Manora's Thai Cuisine, 1600 Folsom St at 12th (☎415/861-6224). Massively popular SoMa hangout, you may have to wait, but it's worth it for the light, spicy and fragrant dishes at around $7–11 each.

New Asia, 722 Pacific Ave between Stockton and Grant (☎415/391-6666). Considering Chinatown is so pressed for space, it's amazing that a place this big survives. It serves some of the most authentic dim sum in town – every day from 8.30am to 3.30pm – with waitresses pushing carts down the aisles, shouting out their wares as they pass. Per-item prices are moderate, though it's easy to quickly build a long tab.

Oriental Pearl, 760/778 Clay St between Grant and Kearny, Chinatown (☎415/433-1817). Dependably delicious with exemplary service and decent prices. Don't miss the house-made *yee min* noodles with *enoki* mushrooms.

The Pot Sticker, 150 Waverly Place, off Clay St between Stockton and Grant (☎415/397-9985). Extensive menu offering your average Szechuan and Hunan dishes in this inexpensive and touristy Chinatown joint.

Sam Woh, 813 Washington St at Grant, North Beach (☎415/982-0596). Basic late-night (until 3am) restaurant that attracts the crowds when the bars turn out. You have to climb dodgy old steps through the kitchen to reach the eating area.

Slanted Door, 584 Valencia St at 16th (☎415/861-8032). The ever-wary locals knew the Mission was officially becoming gentrified when this high-end Vietnamese place showed up. Everyone else was too busy proclaiming the delicately crafted dishes to be among the best in the city to worry too much about any sociopolitical meaning behind it all.

Thai Stick, 698 Post St at Jones (☎415/928-7730). Popular downtown Thai hangout that offers a wide selection of reasonably-priced vegetarian dishes and promises that everything is made without MSG.

Thep-Phanom Restaurant, 400 Waller St at Fillmore, Lower Haight (☎415/431-2526). Simple, delicate decor and beautifully prepared Thai dishes make this restaurant seem more expensive than it really is. You'll pay no more than $8 for main course dishes, but you'll have to wait in line.

Tu Lan, 8 Sixth St at Market, SoMa (☎415/626-0927). If you can brave the seedy neighborhood, you can stuff your face with fresh Vietnamese food for $4.

Yank Sing, 427 Battery St at Clay, Financial District (☎415-781-1111). A cavernous spot that regularly tops locals' list for the best dim sum in the city. Despite being routinely packed during lunch hours, the waitstaff can almost always find a spot for you in the seemingly endless warren of dining rooms. You might need their help to get out, as well.

Yuet Lee, 1300 Stockton St at Broadway, Chinatown (☎415/982-6020). Cheap and cheerful Chinese restaurant with a good seafood menu and enthusiastic crowds of diners. Beer only, but you can bring your own wine. Surprisingly good food can be had here as late as 3am.

French

Boulevard, 1 Mission St at Steuart, Embarcadero (☎415/543-6084). When you want great French food without the attitude, look no further than this beautiful brasserie-style restaurant. Not cheap, but worth every cent; book in advance.

Café Claude, 7 Claude Lane, between Grant and Kearny, Financial District (☎415/392-3505). More than any of the other imitations in town, this one feels like Paris with its great old furnishings. Go in the evening to find a young, loose crowd listening to jazz. Dinner costs around $20.

Fleur de Lys, 777 Sutter St at Taylor, Union Square (☎415 673-7779). Old-fashioned French that's routinely voted as the best place to impress a date. If you're in town near Valentine's Day, forget about it, but during the rest of the year all you have to do it book far in advance and check that there's plenty of room on your credit card.

Julius' Castle, 1541 Montgomery St at Telegraph Hill (☎415/392-2222). A San Francisco institution for lovers, or just lovers of the romantic, this Telegraph Hill restaurant serves pretty pricey, if delicious food, but hopefully the incredible view of the San Francisco Bay will keep your eyes off the bill – easily $100 for two.

Le Charm, 315 Fifth St between Folsom and Harrison, SoMa (☎415/546-6128). Good, unpretentious French food in this SoMa bistro ideally placed for the new museums and arts centers. You can park, too.

Masa's, 648 Bush St at Stockton, Union Square (☎415/989-7154). The state-of-the-art cuisine has it consistently rated one of the best French restaurants in the country. It also has some of the highest prices in the city.

Pastis, 1015 Battery St at Green (☎415/391-2555). Well-executed dishes served in a stylish but relaxed atmosphere, as good as you'll find in the downtown venues but thankfully not as pricey. The out-of-the-way location is just off Levi's Plaza near Embarcadero.

South Park Café, 108 South Park, SoMa (☎415/495-7275). Chic gathering place for aficionados of all things French, especially pastries and good brandy. See also "Drinking: bars and cafés" on p.464.

German

Suppenküche, 601 Hayes at Laguna, Hayes Valley (☎415/252-9289). Satisfying and delicious German cooking served at a reasonable price in this loud, lively bar/restaurant decked out like a traditional Bavarian pub. Don't miss the potato pancakes appetizer – it's enough alone for a light supper. See also "Drinking: bars and cafés," p.464.

Greek and Middle Eastern

Helmand, 430 Broadway between Kearny and Montgomery, North Beach (☎415/362-0641). Excellent, inexpensive Afghani food. Exotic, unique and very popular.

Pasha's, 1516 Broadway at Polk, Russian Hill (☎415/885-4477). An extraordinary dining experience. Expensive, delicious Moroccan and Middle Eastern dishes served while you sit on the floor watching belly dancers gyrate past your table, proffering their cleavage for you to insert dollar bills. Go with a group of rowdy drunks, or not at all.

Socca Restaurant, 5800 Geary Blvd at 22nd Avenue, Richmond (☎415/379-6720). Inspired Mediterranean and Middle-Eastern cooking in this smart, affordable restaurant that has comfortable booths and fine bar.

Truly Mediterranean, 1724 Haight St at Cole, Haight-Ashbury (☎415/751-7482), and 3109 16th St at Valencia, Mission (☎415/252-7482). Threatening to overtake the beloved burrito as the locals' favorite portable dinner item, *Truly Mediterranean*'s version of the falafel comes wrapped in thin, crispy lavash bread. Neither location gets points for atmosphere, but for a cheap lunch they can't be beat.

Yaya Cuisine, 1220 Ninth Ave at Lincoln, Sunset (☎415/566-6966). Romantic, candle-lit Middle-Eastern restaurant near Golden Gate Park, with a Californian twist. Good vegetarian selection and overall excellent value.

La Mediterranee, 2210 Fillmore St at Sacramento, Pacific Heights (☎415/921-2956). You won't find belly dancers or hookahs in this slender space, just some of the best Middle Eastern food in town, served up cheap.

Indian

Appam, 1261 Folsom St at Ninth, SoMa (☎415/626-2798). Moderately-priced Indian food with a mild, modern slant. Great atmosphere, and the old Indian method of *dum pukht* cooking is employed.

Dishes are prepared in large clay pots in an open kitchen where you can watch as nan breads and kulchas bake in the tandoori oven.

Gaylord, Ghirardelli Square, 900 North Point at Larkin, Ghirardelli Square (☎415/771-8822). One of the very few Indian restaurants in San Francisco and probably the best, though you should expect to pay around $25 a head for dinner. Still, it's worth it if you're dying for a curry.

Maharani, 1122 Post St at Polk, Tenderloin (☎415/775-1988). Voted one of the top ten restaurants in the US by the Academy of Restaurant Sciences (whoever they are), this is indeed an intimate place to eat delicious food from traditional low-seated alcoves. For the romantic curry lover unwilling (or unable) to pay first-class prices.

Scenic India, 532 Valencia St at 16th, Mission (☎415/621-7226). Spartan restaurant that serves inexpensive Indian food. Part of the host of Valencia Corridor restaurants that is changing the face of the area.

Shalimar, 532 Jones St at Geary (☎415/928-0333). A happy find in the otherwise downtrodden Tenderloin. This divey spot serves delicious, cheap Indian food, all of it made to order before your eyes, so you know it's fresh. Can get packed during dinner hours.

Zante's, 3489 Mission between 30th St and Cortland, Bernal Heights (☎415/821-3949) and 3083 16th St at Valencia, Mission (☎415/621-4189). This is a weird one, an Indian restaurant that serves pizza, Indian-style. If you've been craving cauliflower as a topping, your prayers have been answered.

Italian

Café Delle Stelle, 395 Hayes St at Gough, Hayes Valley (☎415/989-2589). Serving strong renditions of the hearty cooking of northern Italy, with an emphasis on rich flavors and roasted meats. Not cheap, but still a bargain.

Capp's Corner, 1600 Powell St at Union, North Beach (☎415/989-2589). Funky, family-style restaurant, where fashionable clients line up for the big, cheap portions.

Enrico's, 504 Broadway at Kearny, North Beach (☎415/982-6223). Though its days as a nightclub breaking in such comic talents as Woody Allen, Whoopee Goldberg and Robin Williams are probably gone for good, this intrepid North Beach bastion retains a spirited atmosphere, plus above-average cooking at average prices.

Fior d'Italia, 601 Union St at Stockton, North Beach (☎415/986-1886). This is the place to go when you're fed up with fancy new-age Italian cooking and posturing and you just want the real thing: very traditional Northern Italian cooking at a hearty price. Great old-timer scene going on at the bar.

Frascati, 1901 Hyde St at Green (☎415/928-1406). Attractive Russian Hill venue for delicious pastas and seafood, with a fusion twist. Moderately-priced entrées for $12–16.

Gold Spike, 527 Columbus Ave between Green and Union, North Beach (☎415/986-9747). More like a museum than a restaurant, with enough photographs, mooseheads and war souvenirs to keep you occupied during what can be a long wait for the excellent-value six-course dinner.

Golden Boy, 542 Green St at Columbus, North Beach (☎415/982-9738). Good venue to sample exotic pizza by the slice. Seven different kinds at $2–3 a slice.

Il Pollaio, 555 Columbus Ave at Green, North Beach (☎415/362-7727). You'd be hard pushed to spend more than $15 for a blow-out meal in this cubby hole restaurant, where sheer value for money more than makes up for the lack of elbow room.

Kuleto's, 221 Powell St between Geary and O'Farrell, Union Square (☎415/397-7720). Action-packed downtown hangout with modern Italian cuisine and a very inviting bar. Featuring the ornate bar from the historic *Palace Hotel* and prices that are reasonable for the address.

Little Joe's, 523 Broadway at Columbus (☎415/433-4343). There's always a line, but the inexpensive, enormous portions of well-cooked food in this North Beach institution are well worth waiting for.

North Beach Pizza, 1499 Grant Ave at Union (☎415/433-2444). Good location in one of the best bar-hopping areas in the city. Their low-priced pizza used to be some of the best; sadly it's become inconsistent of late. Adequate for a drink-induced munchie.

Ristorante Ecco, 101 South Park, between Second and Third, Bryant and Brannan (☎415/495-3291). Robust, imaginative cuisine served in this modern SoMa trattoria. Very nice.

Rose Pistola, 532 Columbus near Stockton and Green (☎415/399-0499). The latest addition to North Beach's Cal-Ital dining scene, headed by one of SF's hottest chefs. Appealing for the wide range of eclectic tapas and thin-crust pizzas that won't break the bank, and serving until 1am. Highly creative entrées – don't miss the gnocchi in calamari bolognese sauce.

Vicolo Pizza, 20 Ivy off Franklin at Market, Hayes Valley (☎415/863-2382). Exotic, very California pizzas made with only the finest ingredients, and costing their weight in gold.

Zinzino, 2355 Chestnut St between Divisadero and Scott (☎415/346-6623). Lively Marina-district bistro decked out like a Roman piazza and serving Italian favorites tinged with San Francisco creativity, at reasonable prices. The wild mushroom lasagne is very good.

Japanese and Korean

Brother's, 4128 Geary Blvd at 6th, Richmond (☎415/387-7991). The oldest among a burgeoning row of Korean barbecue houses along Geary Street, and one of the few with the name written in English outside (which makes it the easiest to find), *Brother's* specializes in family-sized feasts of grilled marinated meats.

Ebisu, 1283 Ninth Ave between Irving and Lincoln, Sunset (☎415/566-1770). Rated as one of the top sushi bars in town, the fish is fresh and the queue for a seat at the 18-seat sushi bar can be long. Around $40 for two, including sake and service.

Hamano Sushi, 1332 Castro St at 24th, Noe Valley (☎415/826-0825). Another excellent and popular sushi bar; dinner for two will set you back around $45 but it's worth it.

Ma Tante Sumi, 4243 18th St at Diamond, Castro (☎415/552-6663). Interesting one this: Japanese with a French twist, producing innovative combinations of dishes ranging from the very light to the incredibly rich. A popular dining spot with slightly high prices.

Mifune, 1737 Post St at Webster, Japantown (☎415/922-0337). Fast, inexpensive Japanese place, specializing in house-made noodles to eat in or take out.

Sushi Bune Restaurant, 181 O'Farrell between Stockton and Grant, Union Square (☎415/781-5111). Perfect for those who can't resist a gimmick, this place will make your sushi and then float it over to you on a little boat. Hours of fun for the kids, if you can find any that'll eat sushi.

We Be Sushi, 1071 Valencia at 22nd, Mission (☎415/522-0129), 538 Valencia at 16th, Mission (☎415/565-0749), 3226 Geary Blvd at Parker, Richmond (☎415/221-9960), and 94 Judah Ave at 6th, Sunset (☎415/681-4010). Originally called "McSushi," this plucky upstart was forced to adopt its current egalitarian name when a certain worldwide restaurant chain decided to sue. The sushi's not the best around, but it may just be the cheapest.

Yoshida Ya, 2909 Webster St at Union, Japantown (☎415/346-3431). San Francisco has countless sushi bars, but few where you can actually kick off your shoes and eat at low tables on futoned floors (three or more people only). This is just such a place; expect to pay around $25 per head for a good selection of sushi and a few drinks.

Mexican and South American

Café do Brasil, 104 Seventh St at Mission St, Mission (☎415/626-6432) and 1106 Market St at 7th, SoMa (☎415/626-6450). Good Brazilian tapas and reasonably-priced dinners.

Cadillac Bar, 1 Minna St between Fourth and Fifth, SoMa (☎415/543-8226). By the standards of most Mexican restaurants, this one is fairly upmarket, and offers live guitar music to help your burritos go down.

Cha Cha Cha, 1801 Haight St at Shrader, Haight-Ashbury (☎415/386-5758). First-rate and well-priced Caribbean/Cuban cuisine served in loud, brightly painted surroundings. Great place for swilling oversized margaritas. Open late and always packed.

Chava's Mexican Restaurant, 3245 18th St at Shotwell, Mission (☎415/552-9387). Packed-out Mission favorite that serves good, honest grub. Their *huevos rancheros* (served all day) are the perfect hangover cure for Sunday brunch.

El Balazo, 1654 Haight St at Clayton (☎415/864-8608). Mexican food, healthy style. Have your burrito filled with prawns, vegetables, tofu and any other unlikely ingredients, for not-much more than a Mission special. Very popular with the Haight-Ashbury crowd who come to listen to the Spanish guitar music and slug back beers.

El Farolito, 2777 Mission St at 24th, Mission (☎415/826-4870). Huge, tasty burritos which will last you all day, served in a cafeteria atmosphere.

La Taqueria, 2889 Mission St at 25th, Mission (☎415/285-7117). Always busy with locals, which is as good a recommendation as any for its fairly standard Mexican menu. Service is slow, but the food is fresh and delicious.

LATE NIGHT EATING

For that midnight snack or 3am binge, here are a few last resorts.

Downtown:

Grubstake, 1525 Pine St at Polk (☎415/673-8268). Burgers and breakfasts until 4am.

Lori's Diner, 336 Mason St at Geary and O'Farrell (☎415/392-8646). Long-standing 24hr diner two blocks from Union Square, selling breakfast, omelets, burgers and sandwiches.

Pine Crest, 401 Geary Blvd at Mason (☎415/885-6407). 24hr diner.

North Beach and Waterfront:

Globe, 290 Pacific at Battery (☎415/391-4132). This posh new spot is the place where chefs go after work to get their dinner. It's hard to imagine a better recommendation.

Rose Pistola, 532 Columbus near Stockton and Green (☎415/399-0499). Tapas and thin-crusted pizzas. Open until 1am Fri & Sat; until midnight Sun–Thurs.

Yuet Lee, 1300 Stockton St at Broadway (☎415/982-6020). Terrific Chinese seafood until 3am; daily except Tues.

The Marina:

Mel's Diner, 2165 Lombard St at Fillmore (☎415/921-3039). Your basic 24hr donut shop popular with pretty Marina people who get the munchies after the bars and clubs close.

International House of Pancakes, 2299 Lombard St at Pierce (☎415/921-4004). 24hr diner specializing in pancakes, waffles and breakfasts, but serving burgers, shrimp and steaks as well.

The Castro:

Bagdad Café, 2295 Market St at 16th Street (☎415/621-4434). 24hr diner.

Orphan Andy's, 3991 17th St at Market and Castro (☎415/864-9795). 24hr diner.

Sparky's, 242 Church St (☎415/621-6001). 24hr diner.

Mom Is Cooking, 1166 Geneva Ave between Edinburgh and Naples, Excelsior (☎415/585-7000). Small and crowded place out in the foggy Excelsior district. You may have to wait for a table, but it's well worth it for the super-inexpensive fresh Mexican food.

Pancho Villa, 3071 16th St at Valencia, Mission (☎415/864-8840). Though locals tend to scoff at the largely out-of-neighborhood clientele frequenting this oversized taqueria, the cynics would be well advised to find out what all the fuss is about. In contrast to some of the neighborhood's grungier establishments, the food here is consistently fresh and flavorful.

Roosevelt Tamale Parlor, 2817 24th St, Mission (☎415/550-9213). For a couple of dollars you couldn't find a better meal in town. Tamales, rice and a beer should set you up for around $6.

Tommy's, 5929 Geary Blvd at 23rd, Richmond (☎415/387-4747). A perennially festive restaurant and bar, serving what may just be the best margaritas in town. The hearty mid-range food helps you keep your balance walking out the door.

Vegetarian

The Ganges 775 Frederick at Lincoln, Sunset (☎415/661-7290). An original and inventive restaurant where the completely vegetarian creations range from the delicious to the plain weird.

Greens, Building A, Fort Mason Center (☎415/771-6222). A converted army supply warehouse that's now San Francisco's only Zen Buddhist restaurant, serving unusual and delicious macrobiotic and vegetarian food to an eager clientele. Stunning views mean it's always busy, despite average cost of $40 per head.

Herbivore, 983 Valencia at 21st, Mission (☎415/826-5657). Midway between a cafe and a full-fledged restaurant, serving passable vegan food to healthy types about to head out to the neighborhood bars.

Kowloon, 909 Grant Ave at Washington, Chinatown (☎415/362-9888). This small dim sum house also offers cheap sit-down meals and specializes in delicious vegetarian dishes made with seitan and wheat gluten that will satisfy even the most determined carnivore.

Millennium, Abigail Hotel, 246 McAllister St, Civic Center (☎415/487-9800). You'd swear it couldn't be done, but this upscale restaurant has managed to make delicious meals for vegans – egg-, dairy- and flesh-free, and predominantly organic to boot. Stylish decor complements the subterranean setting.

Organica, 1224 Ninth Ave at Lincoln across from Golden Gate Park (☎415/665-6519). Only in San Francisco will you find a restaurant where everything served is a hundred percent organic, totally vegan and completely raw (actually, some of it's dehydrated). Much talked about, but you'll have to decide for yourself whether it's palatable.

Valentine's, 1793 Church St at 30th (☎415/285-2257). Way out in Noe Valley – and with suitably restrained prices and presentation – this is one of the best vegetarian restaurants in town.

Drinking: bars and cafés

San Francisco, while famous for its restaurants, has a huge number of **drinking** establishments, ranging from comfortably scruffy jukebox joints to the chic watering holes of social climbers. Though spread fairly evenly over the city, happening bars are particularly numerous in North Beach and the Mission, where they line up one after the other. Some of the more colorful (and seedy) are to be found in the Tenderloin and the Haight, yuppie cruising zones populate the Marina, slick lounges speckle downtown and have begun to spread into SoMa, and of course, gay bars fill the Castro. According to new California law, there is **no smoking** allowed in any bar unless its sole employees are the owners, though the debate still rages and enforcement has been spotty.

The city is also dotted with excellent **cafés** serving first-rate coffees, teas and soft drinks in addition to beer and wine. More social than utilitarian, people hang out in these generally lively venues to pass time as much as refresh themselves. Other non-drinkers looking for social alternatives to bars are opting for the old English tradition of **afternoon tea** (see p.467). So far it has only taken root in the big hotels, but neighborhood cafés are catching on fast.

Unsurprisingly, the city has many specifically **gay bars** (see p.477), most plentifully in the Castro, Polk Street and the Mission – although few bars are at all threatening for either gay men or lesbians, or women on their own.

Downtown

The Big Four, *Huntington Hotel*, 1075 California St at Taylor. Classy hotel bar, aimed squarely at the sedate set who want a well-made drink in civilized surroundings.

ROOFTOP BARS

Carnelian Room, 555 California St at Kearny. The best of the rooftop cocktail lounges, 52 floors up in the Bank of America Building. A truly elegant spot for some smart cocktails; bring smart money.

Equinox, *Hyatt Regency*, 5 Embarcadero Center. Good for the novelty value only, this rooftop cocktail lounge attracts crowds of tourists who ascend its dizzy spires just to look at the views. The whole thing revolves, so you get a 360° view of the city without ever leaving your seat. Serious drinkers wouldn't be caught dead in here – have a drink, revolve and leave.

Harry Denton's Starlight Room, *Sir Francis Drake Hotel*, 450 Powell St at Sutter. Dress up and drink martinis. This is a sophisticated grown-up scene with a moneyed crowd who come for the live jazz.

Top of the Mark, *Mark Hopkins Hotel*, California St at Mason. The most famous of the rooftop bars, its reputation surpasses the actual experience of drinking up here, and generally it only attracts tourists and hotel guests who can't be bothered to find anywhere else.

The London Wine Bar, 415 Sansome St at Sacramento. Dubiously tagged as "America's first wine bar," this place is a suitably pretentious and expensive locale for the Financial District clones that flock here after work. Open Mon–Fri until 9pm.

Occidental Grill, 453 Pine St at Kearny. This Barbary Coast-style den is supposedly the birthplace of the martini, and while that's open to more than some debate, they certainly do make a mean one.

Royal Exchange, 301 Sacramento St at Front St. Where the young suits come after a long day getting rich. At lunch you can feel penny wise with moderately priced lunches.

Tonga Room, *Fairmont Hotel*, Powell and Mason streets. Outrageously lavish Polynesian theme bar with waitresses in grass skirts, a native-laden raft floating around the room, an indoor rainstorm, and expensive cocktails. Fun if you like the joke and are in the mood for camp hilarity. They also feature music nightly.

North Beach and the northern waterfront

Balboa Café, 3199 Fillmore St at Greenwich. A favorite with the young upmarket singles of the Marina. Very good food, too.

Gino and Carlo, 548 Green St at Grant. Transforming gracefully with age from a dive into a landmark, this is the classic drunken pressman's bar.

Li Po's Bar, 916 Grant Ave at Jackson. Named after the Chinese poet, Li Po's is something of a literary hangout among the Chinatown regulars. Enter through the false cavern front and sit at the very dimly lit bar where Wayne Wang filmed *Chan is Missing*.

Lost & Found Saloon, 1353 Grant Ave. North Beach's most enticing dive, where your outfit doesn't matter. Live music usually means the place starts rocking around midnight.

Paragon, 3251 Scott St at Francisco. Slick Marina supper club that's more about the music and drinking than eating, though that too is tasty and inexpensive. A smooth crowd jam-packs it on weekends. Recommended.

Perry's, 1944 Union St at Buchanan. Sophisticated meat market, featured in Armistead Maupin's *Tales of the City* as the quintessential breeder bar.

The Saloon, 1232 Grant Ave at Vallejo. This bar has stood for over a hundred years and seen use as a whorehouse and Prohibition speakeasy. Today the old structure creaks nightly as blues bands and crowds of enthusiastic dancers do their thing.

San Francisco Brewing Co, 155 Columbus Ave at Pacific. A must for beer fans who tire quickly of the insipid corporate variety, this North Beach hangout makes its own full-flavored brews on the premises.

Savoy Tivoli, 1434 Grant Ave at Green. Without a doubt, this place is North Beach's most attractively decorated and populated bar, also serving good, reasonably priced food – although the emphasis is definitely on liquid enjoyment.

Spec's, 12 Saroyan Pl at Columbus. Proclaiming itself a museum (though definitely not of ophthamology); if so, this must be the only museum where you can get cross-eyed on cocktails.

Tosca Café, 242 Columbus Ave at Broadway. The theme here is opera, in timeworn but still stylish surroundings. Mingle with media people at the bar or slump into a comfy red leather booth and try to talk above the sound-level of the arias.

Vesuvio's, 255 Columbus Ave at Broadway. Legendary North Beach Beat haunt in the 1950s, and still catering to an arty but friendly crowd who prop up the bar into the small hours. Next to City Lights Bookstore, it's a good place to peruse your new purchases over a drink.

Civic Center, SoMa and the Mission

Backflip, *Phoenix Hotel* 601 Eddy St (formerly *Miss Pearl's Jam House*). The latest cool place to sip cocktails and munch unusual appetizers, this fantastically retro bar overlooks the hotel's pool patio. You'll be amused by the black vinyl-clad waitstaff, the entirely blue, clubby decor and the menagerie of lively patrons.

Blondie's Bar and No Grill, 540 Valencia St between 16th and 17th. Packed nightly with Marina yuppies who love the singles vibe, the garrulous, khaki-clad crowd routinely spills onto the street.

Brain Wash Laundromat/Café, 1122 Folsom St at Seventh. Great idea – a café/bar and laundrette where you can have breakfast or a beer while you do your washing. Needless to say it's popular with the young and novelty-conscious. See also "Eating," p.456.

Café du Nord, 2170 Market St near Church. One of the first to revive the old tradition of supper clubs, this popular bar is quite the place to experience hot jazz combos over good food, though it's OK just to have a beer at the bar and shoot some pool. See also "Live music," p.472.

Casanova, 527 Valencia St at 16th. Laid-back neighborhood lounge redecorated to resemble an apartment frozen in time – circa 1974. The crowd is local, mellow twenty-to-thirty-somethings who come to converse, down a microbrew and take in tunes on the jukebox.

Edinburgh Castle, 950 Geary at Polk. Just your average Scottish bar, except that it's run by Koreans. Be sure to order some fish and chips from the co-owned restaurant. With occasional bands and plays (including the local premiere of *Trainspotting*) upstairs.

El Rio, 3158 Mission St near Cesar Chavez. Mixed crowds gather for changing nightly entertainment. All music styles and some great give-aways, like oysters on the half-shell on a Friday. Most popular though, live salsa on a Sunday afternoon that draws a predominantly female crowd. See also "Clubbing," p.469.

Gordon Biersch Brewery, 2 Harrison St at Embarcadero. Bayfront microbrewery housed in converted Hills Brothers coffee warehouse. Good bar food and some of the best beers in San Francisco bring out downtown's overpaid twenty-somethings.

Harry Denton's, 161 Steuart St at Howard. For the after-work Financial District crowd, this is San Francisco's prime place to cruise and be cruised. Fortunately, the fully stocked bar has enough rare bourbons and West Coast microbrews to make whiling away an evening very pleasant indeed, even if you're not on the prowl. Great interior.

Julie's Supper Club, 1123 Folsom St at Seventh. A popular restaurant, but best for sitting at the bar munching good-value Cajun snacks and listening to the free live jazz – if you get in before 9pm, after that it's $5 on weekends. Dancing happens later.

La Rondalla, 901 Valencia at 20th. It's always Christmas and New Year at this festive Mexican restaurant. Sit at the bar if you don't want food with your margaritas, and prepare to duck: they manage to squeeze a full mariachi band – including string section - into the narrow space.

The Make-Out Room, 3225 22nd at Mission. Primarily a bar, this ultra-hip Mission spot hosts live acts early in the week for performances that tend to be jovial and homey.

Paradise Lounge, 1501 Folsom St at 8th. Cleverly constructed on two floors, you can suit your mood with a game of pool and a quiet drink upstairs or dance to live music downstairs. See also "Live music," p.471.

The Red Room, 827 Sutter St at Jones. Like the name says, everything – including the walls, the furniture, the glasses and many of the drinks – is red in this popular *faux*-dive.

The Ramp, 855 China Basin. Way out on the old docks, this is well worth the half-mile trek from downtown (you'll need a car unless you're a seasoned walker) to sit out on the patio and sip beers overlooking the abandoned piers and new boatyards.

Timo's, 842 Valencia between 19th and 20th streets. Intimate neighborhood bar where you can get some of the best tapas in the city to go with your Pernod.

Central neighborhoods

Club Deluxe, 1511 Haight St at Ashbury. An unusually-situated bastion of the wing-tipped swinger crowd in a stretch of Upper Haight dominated by shaggy hippies.

Harry's, 2020 Fillmore St at California. A bona fide saloon, this elegantly decorated hangout serves a mixed, unpretentious crowd and makes for a great night's drinking.

Hayes & Vine, 377 Hayes St. Cozy, well-designed spot in trendy Hayes Valley with a truly excellent selection of local and international wines.

Johnny Love's, 1500 Broadway at Polk. Straight pick-up scene on an industrial scale. Hormone-driven Young Republicans line up around the block nightly to get a piece of the action.

The Mad Dog in the Fog, 530 Haight St at Steiner. Aptly named by the two lads from Birmingham, England, who own the joint, this is one of the Lower Haight's most loyally patronized bars, with darts, English beer, copies of the *Sun* newspaper and a typical pub menu that includes bangers and mash, hearty ploughman's and the like. Amazingly, it is not the ex-pat English, but the trend-conscious young blades of the Lower Haight who find it so groovy.

Noc Noc, 557 Haight St at Steiner. Decorated like an Egyptian tomb. Draws a fashionable but informal young crowd for new wave music and flasks of hot sake.

Persian Aub Zam Zam Room, 1663 Haight at Clayton. Don't distract yourself by trying to figure out the name, because you'll need your wits about you once you walk in the door. Getting kicked out by Bruno, the owner/bartender is a local tradition, as are his famous gin martinis. Also, the bar keeps absolutely arbitrary and random hours.

Golden Gate Park, the beaches and outlying areas

Pig & Whistle Pub, 2801 Geary Blvd at Wood. Good range of English and California microbrews, and still the cheapest happy hour in SF – $2 pints of beer served 4–6pm daily. Pool table and dartboards, plus very good pub food.

The Plough and Stars, 116 Clement St at Second Avenue. Irish ex-pat bar with live music seven nights a week starting at 9.15pm. Cover charge Fri & Sat $3–4.

Trad'r Sam's, 6150 Geary Blvd at 26th. Just keep repeating to yourself, "that's not fog, it's steamy tropical mist," and you'll get yourself in the right mood for this classic tiki bar, complete with flaming bowls.

Yancy's Saloon, 734 Irving St at Eighth Avenue. Mellow, plant-festooned collegiate bar with free darts and cheap drinks. Across the street from a great oyster house, which will call you over from Yancy's when your table is ready.

Cafés

Buena Vista Café, 2765 Hyde St at Beach, Fisherman's Wharf. If you like your coffee with a kick, this is the place for you. Claims to be the home of the world's first Irish coffee, which isn't hard to believe – it's certainly the best in town and the crowds who pack the place are testimony to the generously laced coffee. Good, inexpensive food too, making it a decent stop-off for a sightseeing lunch.

Café Flore, 2298 Market St at Noe, Castro. Lively, mostly gay café near the Castro serving great food until 10pm. A popular cruising spot for the locals who come to string a coffee out for hours and be seen reading the latest in hip gay literature. Drown in a sea of newspapers and pretty faces. See also "Gay and lesbian bars," p.477.

Café La Boheme, 3138 24th St at Mission. As the name suggests, a badly dressed crowd, but a staggering range of coffees keeps the Mission's caffeine addicts coming from sunrise until late at night.

AFTERNOON TEA

One of the nicest ways to finish an afternoon of intense consuming in the downtown stores is to partake of afternoon tea in one of the plush Union Square hotels. In true California style, the food is exquisite, and you'll be offered the gamut from cucumber and watercress sandwiches to fresh fruit sorbets and scones with cream.

Garden Court, *Sheraton Palace*, 2 New Montgomery St at Market (☎415/392-8600). The best thing about the recent renovation of this landmark hotel was the restoration of its exquisite lobby, where you can sip fine teas while enjoying the soothing live harp music. Make reservations, it fills up. Wed–Sat 2–4.30pm & Sun 2–3.30pm.

Imperial Tea Court, 1411 Powell St at Broadway (☎415/788-6080). A traditional Chinese tea house, with decor evocative of old Shanghai. Open daily 11am–6.30pm.

King George Hotel, 334 Mason St between Geary and O'Farrell (☎415/781-5050). A Laura Ashley nightmare, where customers nibble at finger sandwiches in mock-British cottage surroundings. Only for Anglophiles and homesick Brits. Tues–Sun 3–6.30pm.

Mark Hopkins, 999 California St (☎415/392-3434). Standard high teas served on lovely Wedgwood china. Mon–Fri 3–5pm.

Neiman Marcus, 150 Stockton St (☎415/362-3900). Tea is served in the glorious *Rotunda* restaurant at the top of the store. Watch the social x-rays nibble fearfully at the calorie-laden food. Daily 2.30–5pm.

Ritz-Carlton, 600 Stockton St (☎415/296-7465). The fanciest of them all, this is the place to slurp tea to the accompaniment of a tinkling harp. Mon–Fri 2.30–4.30pm, Sat & Sun 1–4.30pm.

Café Macondo, 3159 Sixteenth at Guerrero, Mission. Named after Gabriel Garcia Marquez's fictional town, this scruffy, somewhat self-consciously bohemian café entertains a steady stream of notepad poets and coffee-cup philosophers.

Caffè Greco, 423 Columbus Ave between Green and Vallejo. One of North Beach's best cafés for people watching with its big windows and outdoor tables. Excellent espresso.

Caffè Trieste, 601 Vallejo St at Grant. Noisy North Beach Italian café, popular with a serious literary crowd who hang out and listen to the opera classics that boom from the jukebox. Saturday lunchtimes are a treat – the family who run it get up and sing. Get there by noon to get a seat.

Mario's Bohemian Cigar Store, 566 Columbus Ave at Union. Small informal North Beach hangout for sipping coffee or slinging beers.

Momi Toby's Revolution Cafe, 528 Laguna at Linden, Hayes Valley. Nothing more radical in the air than the scent of herbal tea and the sounds of locals playing Scrabble.

Red Dora's Bearded Lady, 485 14th St at Guerrero, Mission. A small coffee shop catering primarily to the local lesbian community, with frequent spoken word nights and performances by local artists.

South Park Café, 108 South Park. Chic SoMa rendezvous, where architects and other creative professionals meet their peers to drink in tasteful surroundings. See also "Eating," p.460.

Specialty's Café & Bakery, 101 New Montgomery St at Mission, plus other downtown locations. Not a hangout; just a good place to grab a takeout sandwich on your way to the SFMOMA or Center for the Arts. Huge selection of luscious baked goods, vegetarian and meat sandwiches on housebaked bread, excellent soups, and the usual range of coffees.

Steps of Rome, 348 Columbus at Vallejo. Venerable North Beach late-night café where the taxi drivers congregate. If you're looking for caffeine action after midnight, this is your place.

Nightlife

Compared to Los Angeles, where you need money and attitude in equal amounts, San Francisco's **nightlife** demands little of either. This is no 24-hour city, and the approach to socializing is often surprisingly low-key, with little of the pandering to fads and fashions that goes on elsewhere. The casualness is contagious, and manifest in a **club scene** that, far as it is from the cutting edge of hip, is encouragingly inexpensive compared to other cities. Thirty to forty dollars can buy you a decent night out, including cover charges and a few drinks, and maybe even a taxi home. The **live music scene** is similarly economical – and, frankly, what the city does best. San Franciscans may be relatively unconcerned with fashion, but there are some excellent rock, jazz and folk venues all over town, many entertaining you for no more than the price of a drink. Be sure to always bring a **picture ID** with you to get past the bouncers.

San Francisco has a great reputation for **opera and classical music**; its orchestra and opera company are among the most highly regarded in the country. **Theater** is accessible and much less costly than elsewhere, with discount tickets available, but most of the mainstream downtown venues – barring a couple of exceptions – are mediocre, forever staging Broadway reruns, and you'd do better to take some time to explore the infinitely more interesting fringe circuit.

Cabaret and **comedy** are also lively, and **film**, too, is almost as big an obsession as eating in San Francisco; you may well be surprised by the sheer number of movie theaters – repertory and current release – that flourish in this city.

Clubbing

Still trading on a reputation for hedonism earned decades ago, San Francisco's **nightclubs** in fact trail light years behind those of other large American cities. That said, the compensations are manifold – it is rare to encounter high cover charges, ridiculously priced drinks, feverish posing or long lines, though a few of the cavernous dance clubs in SoMa do have lines on weekends. Instead you'll find a diverse range of small to medium-

---

LISTINGS AND TICKET INFORMATION

Apart from the flyers posted up around town, the *Sunday Chronicle*'s "Pink Pages" supplement is about the best source of **listings** and **what's on** information; you might also check the free weeklies *San Francisco Bay Guardian, SF Weekly,* and a host of other more specific publications listed below under the relevant sections.

For **tickets,** the Bay Area Seating Service (BASS, ☎510/762-BASS) is the major Bay Area booking agency. You can either reserve with a credit card on these numbers, or in person at one of their many branches in record stores such as Tower Records or Wherehouse. **Theater tickets** are also on sale at the TIX Bay Area ticket booth on Union Square; see "Theater" on p.473 for details.

---

sized, affordable clubs in which leather-clad goths rub shoulders with the bearded and beaded, alongside a number of gay hangouts (listed on p.478) still rocking to the sounds of high-energy funk and Motown. You'll find the occasional place which is up to the minute, playing techno, drum 'n' bass and the like, but what San Francisco does best is all the old favorites – songs you know the words to; clubbing is more of a party than a pose in this city and much the better for it. The greatest concentration of clubs is in **SoMa**, especially the area around Eleventh St and Folsom, though the **Mission** is similarly well provided with bars and small live music venues – not to mention a couple of outrageous drag bars – of almost exclusively Latino origin. There are a few places in **North Beach** too, so just pick a neighborhood and explore.

Unlike most other cities, where the action never gets going until after midnight, many San Francisco clubs have to **close at 2am** during the week, so you can usually be sure of finding things well under way by 11.30pm. At weekends, most places stay open until 3 or 4am. Very few venues operate any kind of dress code or restrictive admission policy, and only on very busy nights are you likely to have to wait. Unfortunately, most live music and dancing opportunities are restricted to those 21-and-over, forcing underage revellers to be more creative when it comes to late night entertainment.

Clubs

Cat's Alley Club, 1190 Folsom St at Eighth (☎415/431-3332). Perfect for the mature clubber, the Cat's Alley Club puts on varied entertainment. Live bands and DJs play nightly, everything from drum 'n' bass to goth-industrial, hip-hop and acid-jazz, with several women-oriented nights a week (including standup comedy). Call for the lineup.

Club Townsend, 177 Townsend St at 3rd 974-6020 (☎415/974-6020). A massive barn, generally packed to the gills with sweaty dancers getting down to the latest in house and techno.

Covered Wagon Saloon, 917 Folsom St (☎415/974-1585). Scruffy SoMa spot serves up a very varied menu of one-nighters, offering everything from rockabilly to drag shows. Cover most nights.

DNA Lounge, 375 11th St at Harrison (☎415/626-1409). Club which changes its music style nightly but draws the same young hipsters. Large dance floor downstairs, and when the dancing gets too much you can lounge around in comfy sofas on the mezzanine. Cover charge.

El Rio, 3158 Mission St at Army (☎415/282-3325). When it isn't staging one of its specials (live salsa and BBQ on Sunday, DJ dancing Wed, Fri & Sat), this is a great place for a quiet drink and a game on one of San Francisco's most handsome pool tables. See also "Drinking: bars and cafés," p.466.

The End Up, 401 Sixth St at Harrison (☎415/357-0827). A mostly gay crowd ("Girl Spot Saturdays" and "Fag Fridays" dance parties) but recently discovered by the weekend clubbers, and a good place for the hardcore party animal. Famous continuous T-dance starts at 5am Saturday and goes until 9pm Sunday. See also "Gay and lesbian San Francisco," p.475.

Holy Cow, 1531 Folsom St at 12th (☎415/621-6087). Young college kids try hard to be cool, but a good rave once it warms up. A huge plastic cow hangs outside, so you can't miss it. Never a cover. Tues–Sun.

THREE BABES AND A BUS

One excellent way to get the flavor of **San Francisco's clubs** when you first arrive is to experience the Three Babes and a Bus **tour** (☎415/552-2582) of various hot spots around town. For $35, the three women who organize the tours will drag you around on their bus on a Friday or Saturday night, visiting clubs, which you get into for free, and throwing in the odd drink. In between visits there is much carousing and game-playing on board.

Justice League, 628 Divisadero at Hayes (☎415/289-2038). A former rock club somewhat awkwardly converted into a danceclub. Also hosts live salsa and hip-hop. Cover charge.

Nickie's, 460 Haight St at Fillmore (☎415/621-6508). This place rocks every night. Whether it's "Grateful Dead Night," African, Latino or Seventies funk, *Nickie's* is for the very lively. Cover some nights.

The Palladium, 1031 Kearny St at Columbus (☎415/434-1308). Three dance floors, MTV screens and a teenybopper crowd that can't be persuaded to quit before 6am (Fri & Sat). Good old disco-fun. $10 and up cover.

Sound Factory, 525 Harrison (☎415/979-8686). Huge multilevel place with three rooms for simultaneous house, hip-hop and Latin dance parties. Saturday nights 9.30pm–4am; cover charge.

Ten15, 1015 Folsom (☎415/431-0700). Another huge club for serious sweating: six rooms with different music in each, especially deep jungle, house, and cool laser light shows. Very popular – you may have to wait in a long line. Thurs–Sat. Cover charge.

The Top, 424 Haight at Webster (☎415/864-7386). Tiny but the best place in the city to hear up-and-coming DJs and catch up on the latest styles you haven't heard of yet. Cover charge.

330 Ritch, 330 Ritch St, South of Market (☎415/541-9574). Low-ceilinged and crowded with slender SoMa types. Serves food until 10pm, then DJs spin funk, soul, disco and British pop music on different nights. Cover charge.

Live music: rock, jazz, blues, and folk

San Francisco's **music scene** reflects the character of the city as a whole: laid back and not a little nostalgic. The options for catching live music are wide and the scene is consistently progressive, characterized by the frequent emergence of good young bands. San Francisco has never recaptured its crucial Sixties role, though in recent years the city has helped launch acid jazz (a simplified style that makes for pleasant background music, if not much more), a classic swing revival and the East Bay pop-punk sound.

Bands are extremely easy to catch. Many restaurants offer live music, so you can eat, drink and dance all at once and often with no cover charge; ordinary neighborhood bars regularly host groups, often for free, and there are any number of good and inexpensive small venues spread out across the city. Few fall into any particular camp, with most varying their bill throughout the week, and it can be hard to specify which of them cater to a certain music style.

What follows is a pretty comprehensive list of established venues, but be sure to check the weeklies or the local Web sites *www.sfstation.com* or *www.sanfrancisco.citysearch.com*. Between the lot you should be able to find exhaustive listings of events in the city and Bay Area as a whole.

The large performance venues

Although San Francisco has a couple of major-league concert halls, bear in mind that some of the Bay Area's best **large-scale venues**, where the big names tend to play, are actually across the bay in Oakland and Berkeley. See the relevant listings later in this chapter.

Bimbo's, 365 Club, 1025 Columbus Ave at Chestnut (☎415/474-0365). Though Frank Sinatra would have felt right at home crooning the night away in *Bimbo's* plush setting, the current line-up features an eclectic array of first-class rock and world music acts.

The Fillmore Auditorium, 1805 Geary St at Fillmore (☎415/346-6000). A landmark. Famed focal point for the Sixties counter culture, established by promoter Bill Graham. While Graham's "bigger is better" philosophy brought us the bland arena rock of the Seventies, this shrine to the local icon still has heart – they give you apples after every show.

Great American Music Hall, 859 O'Farrell St at Polk (☎415/885-0750). Civic Center venue, too small for major names but too large for local yokels, and hosting a range of musical styles from balladeers to thrash bands. The lovely interior – it used to be a burlesque house and upscale bordello – makes for a great night out.

The Warfield, 982 Market St at Sixth (☎415/775-7722). The *Warfield* can usually be relied upon to stage major rock crowd-pullers. Chart bands, big-name indie groups and popular old-timers keep the place packed.

Rock, blues, folk and country

Albion, 3139 16th St at Albion (☎415/552-8558). Primarily just a simple Mission neighborhood bar, which hosts local bands on its tiny stage on Sundays. Small, inexpensive and intimate, it's ideal for a night out on the cheap. No cover.

Biscuits and Blues, 401 Mason St at Geary (☎415/292-2583). Primarily a supper club, though the emphasis is on music. Sounds too good to be true, but you can eat great Southern food for around $10 a head and listen to live blues. Call for ticket prices, which range from $3–20.

Bottom of the Hill, 1233 17th St at Missouri (☎415/621-4455).The best place in town to catch up-and-coming or determinedly obscure rock acts. Frequently packed for shows, there's a small patio out back to catch a breath of fresh air or, on Sundays, have a bite of barbecue.

Cocodrie, 1024 Kearny St at Broadway (☎415/986-6678). Old North Beach club, has changed hands a lot, and now probably books more bands than any other: four a night, seven nights a week. Crowd and quality change daily, from 18-and-over punk shows to world music. Cover charge $3–8.

Hotel Utah, 500 Fourth St at Bryant (☎415/421-8308). Good selection of mainly country bands which you can usually see for free or a very small cover.

Last Day Saloon, 406 Clement St at Fourth (☎415/387-6343). Very lively bar in the Richmond with regular live music including rock, surfer rock, blues and soul. Cover $5.

Lost and Found Saloon, 1353 Grant Ave at Columbus (☎415/397-3751). Informal North Beach hangout with a catch-all selection of music styles.

Lou's, 300 Jefferson St at Taylor (☎415/771-0377). Country/rock and blues bar on Fisherman's Wharf that hosts good local bands. Weekend lunchtimes are a good time to check out the lesser-knowns in relative peace – come nightfall it's madness. No cover before 9pm.

Mick's Lounge, 2513 Van Ness Ave at Lombard (☎415/928-0404). Books local San Francisco bands ranging from rock and funk to Seventies retro and alternative. Cover $4–8.

Paradise Lounge, 308 11th St at Folsom (☎415/861-6906). Good SoMa venue to see up-and-coming rock bands (usually three per night), or take a break for a game of pool upstairs. See also "Drinking: bars and cafés," p.466.

Plough and Stars, 116 Clement St (☎415/751-1122). In Richmond, this is quite a way from downtown but worth the trip if you're into Irish folk music. Very much the haunt of the Irish ex-pat community. Fri & Sat $3–4 cover.

Purple Onion, 140 Columbus Ave at Broadway (☎415/398-8415). Established North Beach venue for hearing a good selection of rock and country.

Saloon, 1232 Grant St at Columbus (☎415/397-3751). Always packed to the gills, this is undeniably North Beach's best spot for some rowdy R&B.

Slim's, 333 11th St at Folsom (☎415/522-0333). Owned by local yokel Bozz Skaggs, what was once a blues bar is now a prime venue to catch an array of punk, alternative, world music and country bands.

The Up & Down Club, 1151 Folsom St at Eighth (☎415/626-2388). One of the city's best jazz venues, this small club split across two floors serves great drinks and draws a lively attractive crowd out for a good time.

Jazz and Latin American

Bahia Cabana, 1600 Market St at Franklin (☎415/861-4202). Lively bar and supper club with good Brazilian and salsa bands – attracts a skilled dancing crowd who can shake it with a vengeance. 21 and over only. Live music and DJ dancing seven nights a week. Cover charge $7–10.

Bruno's, 2389 Mission St at 20th (☎415/550-7455). Swank new jazz bar and restaurant drawing the kind of attractive young crowd who find it titillating to be in the seedy section of town. Cover charge about $5.

Café du Nord, 2170 Market St at Church (☎415/861-5016). Excellent, friendly and affordable venue to catch nightly live music while you sample the food on offer or just drink at the bar. Mostly jazz with some mambo and salsa thrown in. Recommended. See also "Drinking: bars and cafés," p.466.

Elbo Room, 647 Valencia St at 17th (☎415/552-7788). The birthplace of acid jazz, a popular local variant that emphasizes a danceable groove over complex improvisation. Also hosts world music performers.

John Lee Hooker's Boom Boom Room, 1601 Fillmore St at Geary (☎415/673-8000). Recently opened, this small, intimate bar delivers straight-ahead jazz or classic blues acts nightly; no cover Sun & Tues, otherwise $3 cover weekdays and $7 weekends.

Paragon, 3251 Scott St at Francisco (☎415/922-2456). Smart, cool Marina venue for a fashion-conscious crowd who come to enjoy the nightly jazz, jazz fusion, funk and soul. Recommended.

The Plush Room, *York Hotel*, 940 Sutter St at Hyde (☎415/885-2800). A San Francisco institution, which has successfully revived jazz cabaret in the city and on a good night attracts a very glamorous crowd. Tickets around $20.

The Tonga Room, *Fairmont Hotel*, 950 Mason St at Powell (☎415/772-5000). An absolute must for fans of the ludicrous, or just the very drunk. The whole place is decked out as a Polynesian village, complete with pond and simulated rainstorms, and a grass-skirted band play terrible jazz and pop covers on a raft in the middle of the water. See also "Drinking: bars and cafés," p.465.

Classical music, opera and dance

Though the San Francisco arts scene has to fight against a reputation for provincialism, this is the only city on the West Coast to boast its own professional symphony **orchestra**, **ballet** and **opera** companies, each of which has a thriving upper-crust social support scene, wining and dining its way through fundraisers and the like. During the summer months, look out for the **free concerts** in Stern Grove (at 19th Avenue and Sloat Boulevard) where the symphony orchestra, opera and ballet give open-air performances for ten successive Sundays (starting in June).

Concert halls

Louise M. Davies Symphony Hall, 201 Van Ness Ave at Hayes (☎415/431-5400). The permanent home of the San Francisco Symphony Orchestra, which offers a year-round season of classical music and sometimes performances by other, often offbeat musical and touring groups. Established in 1909 as a small musical group, the orchestra rose to international prominence in the 1950s when it started touring and recording. Although not quite on par with the New York Philharmonic or Chicago Symphony, with the arrival of conductor Michael Tilson Thomas they've catapulted into the top half-dozen US orchestras. Though Thomas' relentless self-promotion can be off-putting (he frequently bills himself above a piece's composer), he has undoubtedly added vibrancy and flexibility to the Symphony's programming, bringing a significant emphasis on twentieth century composers to the program. Prices obviously depend on the performance, but are marginally lower than either the opera or ballet, with the least expensive seats going for around $20 and bargain standby tickets available 2 hours before performances.

The San Francisco Ballet, in the War Memorial Opera House, 301 Van Ness Ave at Grove (☎415/865-2000). The city's ballet company, the oldest and third largest in the US, puts on an ambitious annual program (Feb–May) of both classical and contemporary dance, and a Christmas production of *Nutcracker*. Founded in 1933, the ballet was the first American company to stage full-length productions of *Swan Lake* and *Nutcracker*. They've won Emmys, broadcast, toured and generally earned themselves a reputation for ambition, which drove them toward bankruptcy in the

1970s. They seemed to be sliding until 1985, when the Icelandic Helgi Tomasson, *premier danseur* of the New York City Ballet, stepped in as artistic director. Since his appointment, the company can seem to do no wrong and some proud San Franciscans consider it "America's premier ballet company." Tickets range upward from $30.

War Memorial Opera House, 301 Van Ness Ave at Grove (ticket and schedule information ☎415/864-3330). A night at the opera in San Francisco is no small-time affair. The Opera House, designed by architect Arthur Brown Jr, the creator of City Hall and Coit Tower, makes a very opulent venue for the San Francisco Opera Association which has been performing here since the building opened in 1932. Still probably the strongest of San Francisco's cultural trio, the Opera Association has won critical acclaim for its performances of the classics, lesser known Russian works that other companies prefer not to tackle, plus some very daring original commissions. The SF Opera carries considerable international weight and pulls in big names like Placido Domingo and Kiri Te Kanawa on a regular basis. Its main season runs from the beginning of September through the end of January, and its opening night is one of the principal social events on the West Coast. In addition, there is also a summer season during June and July. Tickets cost upwards of $20 – for which you do at least get supertitles. Standing room begins at a bargain $15, and 250 tickets are available (one per person) at 10.30am on the day of performance.

Theater

The majority of the city's **theaters** congregate downtown around the Theater District. Most aren't especially innovative (although a handful of more inventive fringe places are scattered in other parts of town, notably SoMa), but tickets are reasonably cheap – up to $30 a seat – and there's usually good availability. Check out the *Sunday Chronicle*'s "Pink Pages" to read up on the latest productions around town.

Tickets can be bought direct from the theater box offices, or, using a credit card, through BASS (☎510/762-2277). The TIX Bay Area ticket booth on the Stockton Street side of Union Square regularly has day-of-performance tickets for half price as well as full-price advance sales. (Tues–Thurs 11am–6pm, Fri–Sat 11am–7pm; ☎415/433-7827).

Downtown

American Conservatory Theater, 415 Geary St (☎415/749-2ACT). San Francisco's flagship theater company, the Tony-award-winning ACT puts on eight major plays each season. The city's best serious theater venue often has rush tickets available ninety minutes before the show.
Golden Gate Theater, 1 Taylor St at Market (☎415/551-2000). Originally constructed during the 1920s and recently restored to its former splendor, the Golden Gate's marble flooring, rococo ceilings and gilt trimmings make it one of San Francisco's most elegant theaters. It's a pity that the programs don't live up to the surroundings – generally a mainstream diet of Broadway musicals on their latest.
Lorraine Hansberry Theater, 620 Sutter St at Mason (☎415/474-8800). The mainstay of African-American theater in San Francisco. Traditional theater as well as contemporary political pieces and jazz/blues musical revues. Impressive.
The Orpheum, 1192 Market St at Eighth (☎415/474-3800). Arguably the top local space, in terms of seating capacity and glitz, hosting big-name Broadway productions.
Stage Door Theater, 420 Mason St at Post (☎415/749-2228). Attractive, medium-sized turn-of-the-century theater, run by the American Conservatory Theater group.
Theater On The Square, 450 Post St at Mason (☎415/433-9500). Converted Gothic theater with drama, musicals, comedy and mainstream theater pieces.

Elsewhere

Beach Blanket Babylon, Club Fugazi, 678 Green St at Powell (☎415/421-4222). One of the few musts for theatergoers in the city, its formality smacks of a Royal Command Performance, but the shows themselves are zany and fast-paced cabarets of jazz singers, dance routines and current political comedy, very slickly put together. Recommended.
Intersection for the Arts, 446 Valencia St at 16th (☎415/626-3311). Well-meaning, community-based group that tackles interesting productions in inadequate facilities.

The Magic Theater, Fort Mason Center, Building D (☎415/441-8822). The busiest and largest company after the ACT, and probably the most exciting, the Magic Theater specializes in the works of contemporary playwrights and emerging new talent; Sam Shepard traditionally premieres his work here.

Mission Cultural Center, 2868 Mission St at 24th (☎415/821-1155). An organization dedicated to preserving and developing Latino culture, staging small but worthy productions using the wealth of talented but underrated performers in San Francisco's Latino community.

Theater Artaud, 450 Florida St (☎415/621-7797). Very modern theater in a converted warehouse that tackles the obscure and abstract; visiting performers, both dance and theatrical. Always something interesting.

Theater Rhinoceros, 2926 16th St (☎415/861-5079). San Francisco's only uniquely gay theater group, this company (not surprisingly) tackles productions that confront gay issues, as well as lighter, humorous productions.

Comedy

Comedians have always found a welcoming audience in San Francisco (local stand-up performer Tom Ammiano is Mayor Willie Brown's prime rival), with venues catering to tastes beyond the usual one-liners. Few of the comedians are likely to be familiar: as with any cabaret you take your chances, and whether you consider a particular club to be good will depend on who happens to be playing the week you go. You can expect to pay roughly the same kind of cover in most of the clubs ($7–15), and two-drink minimums are common. There are usually two shows per night, the first kicking off around 8pm and a late show starting at around 11pm. For bargains, check the press for "Open Mike" nights when unknowns and members of the audience get up and have a go; there's rarely a cover charge for these evenings and, even if the acts are diabolical, it can be a fun night out.

Comedy venues

Cobb's Comedy Club, The Cannery, 2801 Leavenworth St at Beach (☎415/928-4320). Pricey and usually full of tourists, but the standard of the acts is fairly consistent. Worth a look if everything else is booked up.

Josie's Cabaret and Juice Joint, 3583 16th St at Noe (☎415/861-7933). A good all-rounder offering a mixed menu of cabaret and comedy during the week, and live music and dancing weekends. The bill changes weekly.

The Marsh, 1062 Valencia at 21st (☎415/641-0235). Successful alternative space hosting solo shows, many with a political bent.

The Punch Line, 444 Battery St at Washington (☎415/397-7573). Frontrunner of the city's "polished" cabaret venues, this place has an intimate, smoky feel that's ideal for downing expensive cocktails and laughing your head off. The club usually hosts the bigger names in the world of stand-up and is always packed.

Film

After eating, watching **films** is the next favorite San Francisco pastime. For one thing it's inexpensive (rarely more than $8, sometimes as little as $4 for a matinee), and secondly there's a staggering assortment of current-release and repertory film houses, with programs that range from the latest general-release films to Hollywood classics, iconoclastic Sixties pieces, and a selection of foreign and art films. Film-going in San Francisco is a pleasure: there are rarely lines, and the cinemas are often beautiful Spanish Revival and Art Deco buildings that are in themselves a delight to behold. For screening times and locations of current run films, call ☎415/777-FILM.

Cinemas

ATA-Artists Television Access, 992 Valencia St at 21st (☎415/824-3890). Nonprofit media center that puts on the city's most challenging barrage of film, video and performance art, often with a

FILM FESTIVALS

The San Francisco Film Festival, specializing in political and short films you wouldn't normally see, is held at the Kabuki eight-screen cinema, the Castro Theater, and the Pacific Film Archive in Berkeley (see p.501), at the end of April and first week or so of May. Tickets sell extremely fast and you'll need to book well in advance for all but the most obscure movies. If you know you're going to be in town, call ☎415/931-FILM or buy tickets on the Web at *www.sfiff.org*. Just as popular is the Lesbian, Gay and Transgender Film Festival, held in June at the Castro and other theaters. Call ☎415/703-8663 for program and ticket information.

political or psychosexual bent; or sometimes just trashy entertainment. Screenings Thurs–Sat.

The Castro Theater, 429 Castro St at Market (☎415/621-6120). San Francisco's most beautiful movie house, offering a steady stream of reruns, art films, Hollywood classics and (best of all) a Wurlitzer organ played between films by a man who rises up from below the stage.

AMC Kabuki 8, 1881 Post St and Fillmore (☎415/931-9800). Attractive, modern building in the Japan Center complex, where eight screens show mainly current-release movies.

Embarcadero Center Cinemas, One Embarcadero Center, Promenade level (☎415/352-0810). A good choice for American, international and some art films. Five screens, two with digital sound; free parking on weekends and evenings with validation, or just take the BART.

Four Star, 2300 Clement at 23rd Avenue. (☎415/666-3488) Way out in the fog belt, but worth a visit for the interesting mix of Asian, international and American culture films; two screens.

The Lumiere, 1572 California St at Polk (☎415/352-0810). Another opulent Spanish Revival art house, a bit run-down but often with an interesting program of obscure art films as well as a select choice of current-release films. Beware – nighttime parking is nearly impossible so take a cab or MUNI bus.

The Red Vic, 1727 Haight St at Cole (☎415/668-3994). Friendly collective, housed in a room full of ancient couches where you can put your feet up and munch on organic popcorn.

The Roxie, 3117 16th at Valencia (☎415/863-1087). An adventurous rep house and film distributor, the Roxie is one of the few theaters in the country willing to take a risk on documentaries and little-known foreign directors. Usually the risk pays off.

Gay and lesbian San Francisco

San Francisco's reputation as a city of **gay celebration** is not new – in fact it may be a bit outdated. Though still considered by many to be the gay capital of the world, the gay community here has made a definite move from the outrageous to the mainstream, a measure of its political success. The exuberant energy that went into the posturing and parading of the 1970s has taken on a much more sober, down-to-business attitude, and these days you'll find more political activists organizing conferences than drag queens throwing parties. Nowadays San Franciscans appreciate and recognize the huge economic and cultural impact of gays on the city, and to be an openly gay politician or businessperson is not as much of an issue to locals as it would be anywhere else in the United States, making it easy to forget things were not always this way.

Socially, San Francisco's gay scene has also mellowed, though in what is an increasingly conservative climate in the city generally, gay parties, parades and street fairs still swing better than most. Like any well-organized section of society, the gay scene definitely has its social season, and if you're here in June, you'll coincide with the Gay and Lesbian Film Festival, Gay Pride Week, the Gay Freedom Day Parade and numbers of conferences. September brings Folsom Street Fair, a chance for S&M'ers to strut their leather and chains in public. Come October, the street fairs are in full swing and Halloween still sees some of the most outrageous carryings-on (see box on p.448).

Lesbian culture flowered in the 1980s, but today, though women's club nights do exist, the scene is more in evidence in bookstores than bars. Many dykes have claimed Oakland for their own, though some areas of the Mission continue to be girl-friendly.

Details of gay accommodation, bars and clubs appear below; mention of gay bookstores and theater and film ventures are under the relevant headings throughout this chapter.

Gay accommodation

Not surprisingly, San Francisco has many **accommodation** options that cater specifically to gay travelers. Most are geared towards men, although it's unlikely that lesbians would be turned away; see "Women's San Francisco" on p.479, for women-only alternatives. All of the places we've listed below are in San Francisco, but throughout the entire Bay Area, gay travelers (including couples) rarely raise eyebrows, and your sexual orientation shouldn't be an issue in any hotel.

Andora Inn 2434 Mission St at 21st (☎415/282-0337). Lovingly-restored Victorian manor in the lively Mission district, catering to gays but straight-friendly. Free continental breakfast, plus wine and cheese in the evenings. Recommended. ⑤.

CONTACTS AND RESOURCES

AIDS Hotline (☎415/863-2437). 24hr information and counseling.

Bisexual Resources Line (☎415/703-7977). Contacts and voicemail boxes of various bisexual groups.

Dignity, 1329 Seventh Ave (☎415/681-2491). Catholic worship and services.

Gay Health Care 45 Castro (☎415/861-2400). Health services for a fee.

Gay/Lesbian Band Info Line 1519 Mission (☎415/255-1355). Information on performances and how to join the San Francisco Gay and Lesbian Freedom Band.

Gay/Lesbian Lawyers, 235 Montgomery (☎415/956-5764). Inquiries regarding legal problems and legal representation.

Gay Therapy Center, 3393 Market St

(☎415/558-8828). Counseling and help with coming out.

Lesbian/Gay Switchboard, Pacific Center, 2712 Telegraph Ave, Berkeley 94705 (☎510/841-6224). 24hr counseling and advice. Contacts and activities referral service.

Lyric (☎415/863-3636). For gay and lesbian youth aged 23 and younger, discussion groups, movie nights, camping and sporting events, women's issues.

New Leaf, 1853 Market St at Guerrero (☎415/626-7000). Outpatient mental health on a sliding fee scale.

San Francisco Sex Information, PO Box 881254 (☎415/989-7374). Free, anonymous and accurate information.

SF AIDS Foundation, 25 Van Ness Ave (☎415/864-4376). Referral service providing advice, testing, support groups.

PUBLICATIONS

New clubs and groups spring up all the time, and you should keep an ear to the ground as well as referring to the many free **gay publications**: *Frontiers*, *Creampuff*, *Odyssey*, *The Bay Area Reporter* and *Bay Times* all give listings of events, services, clubs and bars in the city and Bay Area. Women should also keep an eye out in bookstores for *On Our Backs* and *Bad Attitude*, two magazines that often have pointers to lesbian organizations in town. Also useful for men and women is the **Lavender Pages**, a telephone-cum-resource book available in gay bookstores. Alternatively, if you don't mind forking out $11, a must-have for every visiting gay man and woman with a sense of humor is *Betty & Pansy's Severe Queer Review* by Betty Pearl, listing everything from the best place to eat upscale food to the best cruising alleys – in unashamedly explicit detail.

Archbishop's Mansion, 1000 Fulton St (☎415/563-7872). Grandly camp Alamo Square mansion that was once a school for wayward Catholic boys and is now a really interesting, gay-friendly B&B. Attentive personalized service, a variety of "theme" rooms, the ballroom chandelier from *Gone With the Wind*, and everything from fitness training to image consultancy. ⑦.

Hayes Valley Hotel, 417 Gough St (☎415/431-9131). Bit of a flop-house, but popular with a rowdy crowd. ④.

Inn on Castro, 321 Castro St (☎415/861-0321). Luxury B&B; well worth the price for the large rooms and good breakfasts. Smack in the middle of the Castro. ⑤.

Queen Anne Hotel, 1590 Sutter St (☎415/441-2828). B&B with antique-laden rooms and complimentary afternoon tea and sherry. ⑥.

24 Henry, 24 Henry St (☎415/864-5686). Quiet, intimate guesthouse near the heart of the Castro. ④.

24 Henry Village Guesthouse, 4080 18th St (☎415/864-0994). Branch of the above. Right in the heart of the Castro. ⑥.

Twin Peaks Hotel, 2160 Market St at Dolores (☎415/621-9467). Set in the hills above, this is a quieter and prettier location not far from the Castro, even if the rooms are small and short on luxury. ②.

The Willows, 710 14th St (☎415/431-4770). Affordable, well furnished and near the Castro. ⑤.

Bars

San Francisco's **gay bars** are many and varied, ranging from cozy cocktail bars to no-holds-barred leather-and-chain hangouts. In the last few years, nearly every single lesbian bar has disappeared, with the notable exception of *Lexington Club* (see below). Otherwise, if you want exclusively female company you'll have to check out clubs that have lesbian nights. Bear in mind, too, that the increasingly integrated nature of the gay scene means that formerly exclusively male bars now have a sizeable lesbian contingent; indeed, most are perfectly welcoming for straights. Take note that places we've listed as bars may switch on some music later on and turn into a club; we've listed the better ones that do this under "Clubs," see below.

The Café, 2367 Market St at Castro. A Castro institution, this place has gone from being a gay bar to a lesbian bar and is now fifty-fifty. One of the busiest bars in the Castro, there's DJ dancing every night of the week and it's especially packed on weekends.

Café Flore, 2298 Market St at Noe. Very much the in-spot before dark. Attractive café, with matching clientele and leafy outdoor area, and no shortage of people eyeing each other up. Very mixed, lots of women. See also "Drinking: bars and cafés" on p.467.

The Castro Station, 456 Castro St at 18th. Noisy disco bar that manages to pack 'em in even in the middle of the day. Very much the die-hard scene of the Seventies, with a fair number in their leather trousers.

Detour, 2348 Market at Castro. Brutally loud techno bar catering to the young and fit.

El Rio, 3158 Mission St near Army. Mixed crowds gather for changing nightly entertainment.

Harvey's 500 Castro St at 18th. Formerly the Elephant Walk, this newly reincarnated hangout is a lively place drawing a friendly, community-oriented mixed gay and lesbian crowd for socializing. Serves food, too.

Hole in the Wall Saloon, 289 Eighth St at Folsom. A biker and rock club that's quite popular and generally all in good spirit, but occasionally a little rough.

Kimo's, 1351 Polk at Bush. Polk Gulch drag bar that is home to the weekly rock night "Alcoholocaust." Raunchy fun for the jaded.

Lexington Club 3464 19th St at Lexington. Perhaps San Francisco's only lesbian bar: laid-back, no frills and packed with the pretty as well as the butch. Friendly folks and a good jukebox.

Midnight Sun, 4067 18th St between Castro and Hartford. Young white boys dressed to the nines and cruising like maniacs in this noisy Castro video bar.

The Mint, 1942 Market St at Guerrero. Gay karaoke bar where a mixed crowd goes to live out its fantasies of being Diana Ross, or at least a Supreme.

Moby Dick, 4049 18th St at Hartford. Civilized-looking neighborhood bar by day, gets rowdier by night. Pool tables and TV screens for the shy.

Pilsner Inn, 225 Church at Market. A relaxed, mixed crowd hanging out with old friends and playing pinball and pool.

SF Eagle, 12th and Harrison St. Easily the best-known leather bar in San Francisco. Large outdoor area with stage. Best time for a visit is for the $8 Sunday brunch when they have a "beer bust" 3–6pm to raise money for AIDS.

The Stud, 399 Ninth St at Harrison. A favorite dancing spot with a mixed but mostly gay crowd. Variable cover charge depending on the night, and some raucous times and shameless freaking out on the dance floor. A San Francisco institution, highly recommended.

The Swallow, 1750 Polk St between Clay and Washington. This sophisticated piano bar pulls in a well-behaved middle-aged crowd who just want a good drink and some conversation. Not for randy party animals.

Twin Peaks, 401 Castro at Market and 17th. The Castro's first blatantly gay bar, with large windows to make the point. Draws a low-key older crowd who gather for quiet drinks and conversation.

Uncle Bert's Place, 4086 18th St at Castro. Lives up to its name – a cozy neighborhood bar.

Clubs

Many **gay clubs** are simply bars that host various club nights at least once a week. Pleasingly unpretentious, they rank among the city's best, and although a number are purely male affairs, with a few women-only dance parties gaining a solid following in recent years, the majority, particularly those listed below under the heading "Mixed," welcome gay people of both sexes. The nature of these club nights mean that they change all the time – numbers are listed in the free magazines distributed at bars in the Castro.

Mixed

The Box, at 715 Harrison St at Third. Very popular, split-level dance club that plays a good selection of funk and house music. Still the hot favorite for dance-serious men and women. Thurs $6.

The Café, 2367 Market St at Castro, upstairs (☎415/861-3846). Always one of the busiest bars in the Castro, there's DJ dancing every night of the week. You may find long lines on weekends. No cover.

Club Townsend, 177 Townsend St (☎415/974-6020). Site of long-running gay and lesbian dance parties (Club Q for women, Club Universe and Pleasuredome for men) on Friday, Saturday and Sunday respectively. Call their information line for the latest events.

The End Up, Sixth St at Harrison (☎415/495-9550). Changes its bill weekly, but Fridays are gay and Saturdays lesbian – always a safe bet when you're stuck for a place to go. See also "Nightlife," p.469.

The Stud, 399 Ninth St at Harrison (☎415/252-STUD). An oldie but a goodie. Has been popular for years for its energetic, uninhibited dancing and good times.

Mainly for men

Club Universe at *Club Townsend*, 177 Townsend at Third (☎415/985-5241). Easily San Francisco's hottest gay dance club, on Saturday nights this large, cavernous space draws mainly a twenty- to thirtysomething crowd (21 and up; ID required) for dancing to progressive house music until 7am. $10.

Esta Noche, 3079 16th St at Valencia (☎415/861-5757). Discomania Latin-style. Young men and their pursuers dance to a hi-NRG disco beat reminiscent of the Seventies.

Fag at *The End Up*, Sixth at Harrison (☎415/495-9550). House music going strong until 6am. Hang out by the waterfall, dance on the patio, or shoot some pool. $5

Mainly for women

Co-Co Club, 139 Eighth St at Minna between Mission and Howard (☎415/626-2337). Lesbian-owned, with a new restaurant upstairs, this dyke clearinghouse hosts different events each night of the week, from dance parties to open mike.

Club Q at *Club Townsend*, 177 Townsend St (☎415/974-6020). Lesbian dance party held the first Friday of the month and patronized by a young, ethnically mixed group of women. Always packed.

Girl Spot and Club Skirts at *The End Up*, 401 Sixth St at Harrison (☎415/337-4962). The city's most friendly women-only evening where everyone from the toughest dyke to the most fey femme just wants to have a good time. No politics, no posturing, just fun.

Junk at *The Stud*, 399 Ninth St at Harrison (☎415/252-STUD). The fourth Saturday of the month attracts spunky, leather and flannel girls ready for anything.

Women's San Francisco

The flip side of San Francisco's gay revolution has in some **women**'s circles led to a separatist culture, and women's resources and services are sometimes lumped together under the lesbian category. While this may be no bad thing, it can be hard to tell which organizations exist irrespective of sexuality. Don't let this stop you from checking out anything that sounds interesting; nobody is going to refuse you either entry or help if you're not a lesbian – support is given to anybody who needs it. Similarly women's health care is very well provided for in San Francisco and there are numerous clinics you can go to for routine gynecological and contraceptive services: payment is on a sliding scale according to income, but even if you're flat broke, you won't be refused treatment.

Women's accommodation

Campton Place, 340 Stockton St at Post (☎415/781-5555). Not specifically a women's hotel, but favored by female executives who like the discreet profile and safe, quiet floors. ⑨.

Mary Elizabeth Inn, 1040 Bush St (☎415/673-6768). Run by the United Methodist Church; a safe but unexciting place for women. Weekly rates available, breakfast and dinner included. ③.

Women's Hotel, 642 Jones St (☎415/775-1711). Comfortable, secure, women-only building, unfortunately situated in the shabby Tenderloin district. Weekly rates only: singles $185 per week, doubles $235.

CONTACTS AND RESOURCES FOR WOMEN

Bay Area Women and Children's Resource Center, 318 Leavenworth St (☎415/474-2400). Services, information and clothing.

Lyon Martin Women's Health Services, 1748 Market, Suite 201 (☎415/565-7667). Targets lesbian-bisexual-transgender community, but encourages all women to come for anonymous AIDS testing, gynecological care, pregnancy tests, counseling and legal help. Non-profit, and operating since 1979.

Radical Women/Freedom Socialist Party, New Valencia Hall, 1908 Mission St (☎415/864-1278). Socialist feminist organization dedicated to building women's leadership and achieving full equality. Meetings, discussion groups and poetry readings held on various issues: call for details.

Rape Crisis Center and Hotline, 1841 Market St (☎415/647-7273). 24hr switchboard.

Rape Treatment Center San Francisco General Hospital, 1001 Potrero (☎415/821-3222). Staffed Mon-Fri 8am-4pm, but also has 24hr treatment and switchboard.

Shelley's Body Therapy, 1041 Guerrero (☎415/282-1779). Specializes in massages for pregnant women and infants, but popular with all women for her healing touch after a hard day of walking.

Women's Building, 3543 18th St (☎415/431-1180). Central stop in the Mission for women's art and political events. A very good place to get information also – the women who staff the building are happy to deal with the most obscure of inquiries.

Women's Needs Center, 1825 Haight St (☎415/487-5632). Low-cost health care and referral service.

Shopping

San Francisco is a fabulous place for **shopping**; all the international names are displayed in downtown storefronts, but where the city really excels is in its wealth of smaller-scale outlets, great for picking up odd and unusual things you wouldn't find at home. Most are clustered along several-block-long streets alongside coffee shops, cafés and movie theatres, making browsing and buying a regular full day out for the natives.

If you want to run the gauntlet of designer labels, or just watch the style brigades in all their consumer fury, **Union Square** is the place to aim for. Heart of the city's shopping territory, it has a good selection of big-name and chic stores, but good for browsing and a laugh watching teens jump into the steel washbasins at Levi's on Post Street to shrink-fit their new jeans. In 1999, Macy's opened its newly renovated palace, across the square on Geary Street and the area around 4th Street in **SoMa** has of late become a booming area for commerce, celebrating itself with a massive Old Navy shop on the corner of Market that feels more like a disco than a low-cost clothing store. Nearby, at 4th and Mission, Sony's **Metreon mall** aims to redesign "the shopping experience" with a futuristic center in which it's easy to play with the merchandise, but difficult to find a cash register at which to buy it.

For things that you can actually afford, you'll have a less disheartening and more interesting time in the surrounding neighborhoods, which specialize in everthing from

---

SHOPPING STREETS

San Francisco has always been a coalition of independent neigborhoods, each centered around a version of "Main Street," and the city's residents pride themselves on the dearth of chain stores in town, a trend that is beginning to change in recent years with the encroachment of Starbucks and Rite Aids into several sections of town. Still, San Francisco is truly a city of communities, evinced by spending some time strolling through these shopping streets, listed by district and the types of items they generally sell:

Castro and Market Streets: Castro, between 17th and 19th Streets, and from Castro to Church. Gay-oriented bars and boutiques, clubwear, unusual designer clothes and shoes.

Chestnut Street: The Marina, between Broderick and Fillmore. Health foods, some chain stores (Gap) and wine shops.

Clement Street: Richmond, between 2nd and 10th Avenues. The "new Chinatown," supported by grocers, dim sum and coffee shops, and book stores. Hugged by Irish pubs and Thai restaurants.

Fillmore Street: Pacific Heights to Western Addition, between Jackson and Geary. Home furnishings, antiques, designer clothes, popular cafés and bars.

Irving Street: Sunset, between 7th and 23rd Avenues. Wealth of excellent Chinese restaurants around 9th, along with an eclectic grouping of knick-knack shops.

Haight Street: Haight-Ashbury, between Stanyan and Masonic. Tons of used clothing, retro fashions, head shops, book and music stores, and bars to relax in afterwards.

Polk Street: Polk Gulch, between Clay and Geary. Mixed-bag of used book stores, shoe stores, restaurants and porn outlets. At the terminus of the California cable car line.

Sacramento Street: Laurel Heights, between Arguello and Divisadero. Antique capital of San Francisco, and lots of used designer clothes for women.

Union Street: Cow Hollow, between Octavia and Fillmore. Expensive boutiques and shoes stores; mainly for women.

Valencia Street: Mission, between 14th and 21st Streets. Used furniture and clothing, bars and Mexican eateries.

used book stores and record shops to housewares and designer fashions (see box opposite).

Department stores and shopping malls

If you want to pick up a variety of things in a hurry, without having to roam all over town, it's hard to beat the one-stop convenience of **department stores** or, increasingly, **shopping malls**. These have gotten classier and pricier but they're still useful, and can be quite lively.

Macy's Union Square, Stockton and O'Farrell (☎415/397-3333). Probably the city's best-stocked store, and as such a good place for general shopping. A dangerous place to go with a full wallet as beautifully presented merchandise beckons from all sides. There's also a new men's store across Stockton Street.

Nieman Marcus, 150 Stockton St at O'Farrell (☎415/362-3900). The sheer cheek of the pricing department has earned this store the nickname "Needless Mark-up." Undoubtedly Union Square's most beautiful department store, however, with its classic rotunda, and good for browsing.

Nordstrom, 865 Market St at Powell (☎415/243-8500). Shoppers flock here for the high-quality (and expensive) fashions, as well as a chance to ride on the spiral escalators that climb the four-story atrium.

Sak's Fifth Avenue, 384 Post St at Powell (☎415/986-4300). A scaled-down version of its New York sister store, geared largely to the middle-aged shopaholic, Saks is *the* high-end specialty shopping store.

Shopping malls

Crocker Galleria, 50 Post St at Kearny (☎415/393-1505). A modern, Italianate atrium, this Financial District mall features some very pricey showcase boutiques. It's all very nice for a wander, but expensive.

Embarcadero Center, at Embarcadero BART/Muni station at the foot of California Street (☎415/772-0500). Ugly, six-block shopping complex with 125 stores and a few unremarkable restaurants, distinguished from other anodyne shopping malls only by the occasional work of art and a quite carefully planned layout. Good stores, though they tend to cater to rich yuppies.

Ghirardelli Square, 900 North Point at Larkin (☎415/775-5500). This attractive turn-of-the-century building used to be a chocolate factory, but is now home to more than forty stores and five restaurants – the nicest way to drop dollars at the wharf.

Japan Center, Post St at Buchanan (☎415/922-6776). Surprisingly characterless five-acre complex of stores, movie theaters and restaurants with a Japanese theme. A few redeemable antique and art shops and a great stationery store, Kinokuniya, on the second floor.

San Francisco Shopping Center, Fifth and Market streets (☎415/495-5656). A good-looking mall; glass, Italian marble, polished green granite and spiral escalators up and down its eight stories all add to the seductive appeal of spending money with California-style panache. Sumptuous Parisian cakes at *La Nouvelle Patisserie* vie for your attention with Bugs Bunny paraphernalia at the Warner Bros store.

Sony Metreon, 4th St and Mission (☎415/369-6000). Anchored on the ground floor by a Discovery Channel shop and on top by a state-of-the-art movie theater, this latest San Francisco mall embodies "shoppertainment." The Microsoft Store is a fun place to play free video games or check your email, and the views of the Modern Art Museum and Yerba Buena Gardens make the patio a great place to have a drink.

Food and drink

Food faddists will have a field day in San Francisco's many **gourmet stores**, which are on a par with the city's restaurants for culinary quality and diversity. The simplest neighborhood deli will get your taste buds jumping, while the most sophisticated places are enough to make you swoon. Be sure to try such **local specialties** as Boudin's sourdough bread, Gallo salami and Anchor Steam beer. Bear in mind, too, that however overwhelming the food on offer in San Francisco itself may seem, some of the very best places are to be found across the bay in Berkeley. For more basic stocking up there are, of course, **supermarkets** all over the city (Safeway is probably the most widespread name), some of them open 24 hours per day.

Andronico's Market, 1200 Irving St between Funston and 14th Ave (☎415/753-0403); also four locations in Berkeley. The California gourmet's answer to Safeway. Pricey but gorgeous produce: microbrews, good wine, craft breads, fancy cheeses, an olive bar and a pretty good deli. Not the cheapest, but way better quality than your average supermarket.

Boudin, 156 Jefferson St, Fisherman's Wharf (☎415/928-1849). They only make one thing – sourdough bread – but it's the best around. Cafés pushing their dough are scattered all over the city.

California Wine Merchant, 3237 Pierce St at Chestnut (☎415/567-0646). Before you set off for the Wine Country (see p.589), pick up a sample selection at this Marina wine emporium so you know what to look out for.

Casa Lucas, 2934 24th St at Guerrero (☎415/826-4334). Mission store with an astonishing array of exotic fruits and vegetables.

David's, 474 Geary St at Taylor (☎415/771-1600). The consummate Jewish deli, open until 12am. A downtown haven for the after-theater crowd and night owls.

Heart of the City Farmer's Market, United Nations Plaza at Market Street near Civic Center (☎415/558-9455). Huge, friendly certified farmer's market (which means everything is sold by the growers themselves), distinguished from others by catering to the multiethnic inner city clientele at low prices. Mouthwateringly fresh local produce. Wed & Sun 7am–5pm.

Ferry Plaza Farmer's Market, on the Embarcadero in front of the Ferry Building at Market Street. Higher prices accompany the mostly organic produce in this very popular downtown market. Beautiful produce and fine foodstuffs. Sat 8.30am–2pm.

Graffeo Coffee, 733 Columbus Ave at Filbert (☎415/986-2420). Huge sacks of coffee are piled up all around this North Beach store – you can smell the place from half a block away.

Haig's Delicacies, 642 Clement St (☎415/752-6283). Curries, teas, pickle and spices from around the world.

Harvest Ranch Market, 2285 Market St at Church (☎415/626-0805). Health-nut heaven. Organic everything.

Liguria Bakery, 1700 Stockton St at Filbert, North Beach (☎415/421-3786). Marvelous old-world Italian bakery, with deliciously fresh *focaccia*.

Molinari's, 373 Columbus Ave (☎415/421-2337). Bustling North Beach Italian deli, jammed to the rafters with goodies.

Pasta Gina, 741 Diamond at 24th in Noe Valley (☎415/921-7576). Fresh pasta and sauces to heat and eat. Everything you need, including wine, for an Italian dinner when you don't want to cook.

Rainbow Grocery, 1745 Folsom St (☎415/863-0620). Progressive politics and organic food in this huge SoMa wholefood store.

Sunrise Deli and Café, 2115 Irving St at 22nd (☎415/664-8210). Specialty Middle Eastern foodstuffs – stuffed vine leaves, *baba ghanoush* and hummus.

Urban Cellars, 3821 24th St at Church (☎415/824-2300). The dipsomaniac's dream – hundreds of wines and exotic spirits taking booze shopping to its zenith.

Bookstores

San Francisco boasts some truly excellent **bookstores**, not surprising for a city with such a literary reputation. The established focus for literature has long been in North Beach, in the area around the legendary City Lights Bookstore, but increasingly the best spots, particularly for contemporary creative writing, are to be found in the lower-rent Mission district, which is home to some of the city's more energized – and politicized – bookstores. There are a few **secondhand booksellers** in the city itself, but these can't compare with the diverse bunch across the bay in Oakland and Berkeley. Most bookstores tend to open every day, roughly 10am–8pm, though City Lights is open daily until midnight.

General bookstores

Barnes & Noble, 2550 Taylor Street near Bay (☎415- 292-6762). Large bookstore with a huge selection of mainstream books and a busy café to read them in; best sellers often discounted up to thirty percent.

The Booksmith, 1644 Haight St near Cole (☎415/863-8688). Good general bookstore with an excellent stock of counter-cultural titles. Very Haight-Ashbury.

Borders Books and Music, 400 Post St at Powell (☎415/399-1633). Massive, emporium-style bookstore with over 160,000 books to chose from as well as CDs, videos and software. They've thoughtfully included a café, popular with cruising singles.

City Lights Bookstore, 261 Columbus Ave at Broadway (☎415/362-8193). America's first paperback bookstore, and still the city's best, with a range of titles including City Lights' own publications. Check out the basement's "Evidence" section, an Eden for *X-Files* fans.

Green Apple, 506 Clement St (☎415/387-2272). A close runner-up to City Lights for the "Best of San Francisco" distinction. A funky, cluttered shop sprawling over three storefronts in the Richmond, with great staff selections, a good kid's section, and a large used book and music annex next door

Tillman Place Bookstore, 8 Tillman Place, off Grant Ave, near Union Square (☎415/392-4668). Downtown's premier general bookstore and certainly one of the oldest, with a beautifully elegant feel.

Specialist and secondhand bookstores

Aardvark Books, 227 Church St (☎415/552-6733). A haven of lesbian fiction and mysteries. Buys used books every day, so the stock is always changing.

A Different Light, 489 Castro St at 18th (☎415/431-0891). Well-stocked gay bookshop, diverse and popular.

Acorn Books, 1436 Polk St (☎415/563-1736). Specializes in first and rare editions. Smells and looks – ladders abound – the way an old book store should.

Around the World, 1346 Polk St at Pine (☎415/474-5568). Musty, dusty and a bit of a mess, this is a great place to spend hours poring over first editions, rare books and records.

Books Etc, 538 Castro St at 18th (☎415/621-8631). Stocks the gamut of gay publishing, from psychology to soft-core porn.

Bound Together Anarchist Collective Bookstore, 1369 Haight St (☎415/431-8355). Haight-Ashbury store specializing in radical and progressive publications.

China Books, 2929 24th St (☎415/282-2994). Mission bookstore with books and periodicals from China, and a good number of publications on the history and politics of the Third World.

Columbus Books, 540 Broadway at Union (☎415/986-3872). North Beach store with a good selection of new and used books, and a large guide and travel books section.

Get Lost, 1825 Market St (☎415/437-0529). Travel books, travel books, travel books. Plus some maps and gear. Best travel bookshop in town.

Good Vibrations, 1210 Valencia St at 23rd (☎415/974-8980) and 2504 San Pablo, Berkeley (☎510/841-8987). A comfortable, decidedly un-sleazy place to buy how-to sex books and erotica. So keen is this outfit to promote women's sexuality they even publish their own titles under the Down There Press imprint. Also sells a bewildering diversity of sex toys, condoms and intimate apparel.

Great Expectations, 1512 Haight St at Ashbury (☎415/863-5515). Radical liberal bookstore with hundreds of T-shirts bearing political slogans, some funnier than others.

Modern Times, 888 Valencia St at 20th (☎415/282-9246). Good selection of gay and lesbian literature, many radical feminist publications, and a hefty stock of Latin American literature and progressive political publications. Stages regular readings of authors' works.

Rand McNally Map & Travel Store, 595 Market St at Second (☎415/777-3131). Large store selling travel guides, maps and paraphernalia for the person on the move.

Sierra Club Bookstore, 85 Second St at Mission (☎415/977-5600). Indispensable for the camper or hiker, check in here before you wander off to explore the great wide yonder.

William Stout Architectural Books, 804 Montgomery St at Jackson (☎415/391-6757). One of San Francisco's world-class booksellers, with an excellent range of books on architecture, building, and urban studies.

Record stores

San Francisco's **record stores** are of two types: massive, anodyne warehouses pushing all the latest releases, and impossibly small specialist stores crammed to the rafters with obscure discs. The big places like Tower Records are more or less identical to those throughout the world, though foreign visitors tend to find the prices marginally cheaper than back home. More exciting is the large number of **independent** retailers and **secondhand and collectors' stores**, where you can track down anything you've ever wanted, especially in West Coast jazz or psychedelic rock.

Amoeba Records, 1855 Haight St (☎415/831-1200). This big sister to Berkeley's renowned emporium of new and used records is quite possibly the largest retailer in America specializing in used music. A giant trading post, it's stocked to the gills with hard-to-find releases on vinyl and rarities of every stripe. Over 100,000 used CDs too.

Aquarius Records, 3961 24th St at Noe (☎415/647-2272). Small neighborhood store with friendly, knowledgeable staff. Emphasis on indie rock, jazz and blues.

CD & Record Rack, 3987 18th St at Castro (☎415/552-4990). Castro emporium with a brilliant selection of dance music including a few Seventies twelve-inch singles. The accent is definitely on stuff you can dance to.

Discolandia, 2964 24th St at Mission (☎415/826-9446). Join the snake-hipped groovers looking for the latest in salsa and Central American sounds in this Mission outlet.

Flat Plastic Sound, 24 Clement St (☎415/386-5095). Shop in the Richmond received props in local press for having a hard-to-find Mr. T album in stock. Actually specializes in classical music, but DJs come here for their wide array of loops as well.

Groove Merchant Records, 687 Haight St (☎415/252-5766). Very groovy Lower Haight soul and jazz shop.

Hear Music, 1314 Howard (☎415/487-1822). Amazing selection of world and independently-released music, with dozens of listening stations. Very cool.

Jack's Record Cellar, 254 Scott St at Page (☎415/431-3047). The city's best source for American secondhand records – R&B, jazz, country and rock'n'roll. They'll track down rare discs and offer you the chance to listen before you buy.

Musica Latina/American Music Store, 2653 Mission St between 22nd and 23rd streets (☎415/664-5554). Mission store selling music from all over the continent, especially South America.

Rasputin's, 2401 Telegraph Ave. Open until 11pm, and good for jazz, rock and ethnic.

Reckless Records, 1401 Haight St at Masonic (☎415/431-3434). Specializes in independent music, buys and sells new and used.

Record Finder, 258 Noe St at Market (☎415/431-4443). One of the best independents, with a range as broad as it's absorbing. Take a wad and keep spending.

Recycled Records, 1377 Haight St at Masonic (☎415/626-4075). Good all-round store, with a decent selection of music publications, American and imported.

Rooky Ricardo's, 448 Haight St at Fillmore (☎415/864-7526). Albums and singles specializing in Fifties to Seventies soul, funk and jazz. Vinyl only.

Streetlight Records, 3979 24th St (☎415/282-3550). Also at 2350 Market St (☎415/282-8000). A great selection of used records, tapes and CDs. The perfect opportunity to beef up your collection on the cheap.

Tower Records Columbus Avenue and Bay Street, near Fisherman's Wharf (☎415/885-0500). Main San Francisco location of the multinational empire.

Virgin Megastore, 2 Stockton at the corner of Market Street (☎415/397-4525). As the name implies, it's a big shop, claiming to be "the largest music, media and book store in America."

Drugs, beauty products and toiletries

Body Time, 2072 Union St (☎415/922-4076), with outlets at 1932 Fillmore and in the Haight. Though this Bay Area-born company sold the original name to the UK-based Body Shop, they still put out a full range of aromatic natural bath oils, shampoos and skin creams, and will custom-scent anything.

Common Scents, 3920 24th St (☎415/826-1019). Essential oils, bath salts as well as hair and skin-care products, stocked in bulk and sold by the ounce. They'll refill your empties.

Embarcadero Center Pharmacy, 1 Embarcadero Center (☎415/788-4511). Prescription drugs and general medical and toiletry supplies. Not open late.

Fairmont Pharmacy, 801 Powell St (☎415/362-3000). Huge pharmacy, perfumery and toiletry supply store that also has a good selection of maps and books on San Francisco.

Mandarin Pharmacy, 895 Washington St (☎415/989-9292). This amiable, well-stocked drugstore is a sanctuary in the bustle of Chinatown.

Skin Zone, 575 Castro St (☎415/626-7933). Every unguent imaginable at very reasonable prices. Look for Skin Zone's own brand for real bargains.

Walgreens, various locations around the city. 24hr pharmacies at 498 Castro St (☎415/861-6276), 3201 Divisadero (☎415/931-6415) and 25 Point Lobos between 42nd and 43rd Ave near Geary (☎415/386-0706). The largest chain pharmacy, selling prescription drugs and general medical supplies, as well as cosmetics and toiletries.

Miscellaneous

In among the **designer clothes** stores and **art galleries** of the Union Square area, a handful of stores sell treasureable objects; though prohibitively expensive, many repay a look-in at least. Check out also the countless **secondhand clothes** stores specializing in period costume, from Twenties gear to leftover hippie garb. Better still, explore the myriad of charitable **thrift stores**, where you can pick up high-quality cast-offs for next to nothing. In trendier shopping areas, such as Fillmore Street, these shops tend to have higher prices, along with niftier goods. We've also pulled together in this section some of the city's **miscellaneous** shops specializing in things you often need desperately but never know where to find.

American Rag Co, 1305 Van Ness Ave at Bush (☎415/474-5214). As secondhand clothing stores go, this one is expensive, but it's probably also superior to most others in San Francisco. Also a good collection of stylish new clothing.

Brooks Cameras, 125 Kearny St at Post (☎415/362-4708). High-quality camera store with full repair department.

Community Thrift, 625 Valencia St at 18th (☎415/861-4910). Gay thrift store in the Mission with clothing, furniture and general junk. All proceeds are ploughed back into local charities and AIDS organizations.

FAO Schwarz, 48 Stockton St at O'Farrell (☎415/394-8700). Mega-toystore on three floors designed to turn children into monsters.

Good Vibrations, 1210 Valencia St at 23rd (☎415/974-8980) and 2504 San Pablo, Berkeley (☎510/841-8987). Dildo store, sex toy emporium and a great selection of adult books. Owned and operated by women who have created a safe and friendly atmosphere for women, men, and giddy couples to probe the depths of their sexuality (see also "Bookstores," p.483).

Gump's, 135 Post St at Kearny (☎415/982-1616). Famous for its jade, oriental rugs and objects cast in crystal, silver and china. Fuel for fantasies rather than genuine consumption.

Headlines, 838 Market St (☎415/989-8240) and 557 Castro St (☎415/626-8061). Good, cheap clothes and huge range of novelty gift items. Fun to browse, even if you don't want to spend any money.

Lost Weekend Video, 1034 Valencia St (☎415/643-3373). Video shop perfect for homesick Brits or Anglophiles, with a huge BBC section giving a needed dose of Vic Reeves.

Mom's Bodyshop, 1408 Haight (☎415/864-MOMS). Along with Lyle Tuttle's ink palace in North Beach (see p.434), Mom's Bodyshop is the most raved about tattoo parlor in town.

San Francisco Symphony Thrift Store, 2223 Fillmore St (☎415/563-3123). Top-rate vintage clothing store in Pacific Heights, with flamboyant and original pieces going for top dollar.

Wasteland, 1660 Haight (☎415/863-3150). Huge granddaddy of Haight-Ashbury vintage clothing stores.

Worn Out West, 1850 Castro St at 19th (☎415/431-6020). Gay secondhand cowboy gear – a trip for browsing, and if you're serious about getting some Wild West kit, this is the least expensive place in town to pick out a good pair of boots, stylish Western shirts and chaps.

Listings

American Express 560 California St between Kearny and Montgomery (Mon–Fri 9am–5pm; ☎415/536-2600). Park at the garage at 635 Sacramento, as they validate. Travel Service Office, 455 Market St at First Street (Mon-Fri 8.30am–5.30pm, Sat 9am–2pm). Also at 333 Jefferson at Jones in Fisherman's Wharf (Mon-Thurs 10am–6pm, Fri-Sat 10am–9pm, Sun 11am-6pm).

Baby-sitting Bay Area Child Care (☎650/991-7474).

Car rental All the major firms have branches in the airport. Here we've listed their offices in town: Alamo, 687 Folsom St (☎415/882-9440) and 750 Bush (☎415/693-0191); Avis, 675 Post St (☎415/885-5011); Dollar, 364 O'Farrell St (☎415/771-5300); Enterprise, 1133 Van Ness Ave (☎415/441-3369); Hertz, 433 Mason St (☎415/771-2200); Reliable, 349 Mason St (☎415/928-4414).

Children San Francisco is very much a place for adults – more so than, say, LA, where Disneyland and Universal Studios are major attractions – and there aren't many things to occupy young ones. Of the few places that exist (they tend to be more learning-oriented than commercial), the Exploratorium in the Marina District is excellent, as is the Steinhart Aquarium in Golden Gate Park, and the Lawrence Hall of Science in Berkeley will captivate any young mind. For more organized distractions, try the Great America amusement park in Santa Clara, or the animal-themed Marine World/Africa USA in Vallejo, accessible by transbay ferry and chock-full of rollercoasters and kiddie rides.

Churches and synagogue Grace Cathedral on Nob Hill at 1051 Taylor St caters to an Episcopalian (Anglican) congregation, and Catholics can worship at St Mary's Cathedral, 600 California St. The grandest synagogue is Congregation Emanu-El, 2 Lake St, at the eastern edge of the Richmond district by the Presidio.

Consulates UK, 1 Sansome St (☎415/981-3030); Ireland, 44 Montgomery St (☎415/392-4214); Australia (for New Zealand as well), 1 Bush St (☎415/362-6160); Netherlands, 1 Maritime Plaza (☎415/981-6454).

Dental treatment San Francisco Dental Office, 131 Steuart (☎415/777-5115). 24hr emergency service and comprehensive dental care.

Disabled visitors Steep hills aside, the Bay Area is generally considered to be one of the most barrier-free cities around, and physically challenged travelers are well catered for. Most public buildings have been modified for disabled access, all BART stations are wheelchair-accessible, and most buses have lowering platforms for wheelchairs – and, usually, understanding drivers. The Center for Independent Living, 2539 Telegraph Ave in Berkeley (☎510/841-4776), has long been one of the most effective disabled people's organizations in the world; they have a variety of counseling services and are generally a useful resource.

Ferries Golden Gate Ferry, commute-hours to Sausalito and Larkspur in Marin County, leaves from the Ferry Building, east end of Market Street (☎415/923-2000); Red and White Fleet has bay cruises from Pier 431/2, Fisherman's Wharf (☎415/447-0597); Blue and Gold Fleet bay ferries to Sausalito, Tiburon, Vallejo, and the Alcatraz island tour, from Pier 41 and 39, Fisherman's Wharf (☎415/705-5555).

Hospitals The San Francisco General Hospital, 1001 Potrero Ave (☎415/206-8000 or 206-8111 emergency), has a 24hr emergency walk-in service and rape treatment center (☎415/821-3222). Castro-Mission Health Center, 3850 17th St (☎415/487-7500), offers a drop-in medical service with charges on a sliding scale depending on income, and free contraception and pregnancy testing. California Pacific (formerly Davies) Medical Center, Castro and Duboce streets (☎415/600-6000) has 24-hr emergency care and a doctors' referral service. The Haight-Ashbury Free Clinic, 558 Clayton St (Mon–Thurs 9am–9pm, Fri 9am–5pm; ☎415/487-5632), provides a general health care service with special services for women and detoxification, by appointment only. Lyon Martin Women's Health Services, 1748 Market, Suite 201 (☎415/565-7667). See listing under "Women's" section above.

Internet Free Internet access can be found downtown at Computown, 710 Market, and in the Microsoft store on the second floor of the Sony Metreon mall in SoMa. There's also access at the hostels listed in the "Accommodations" section, but there's often a wait to get on a machine. If you don't mind paying to surf, or want a cup of coffee while trolling, head to *Coffee Net*, at 744 Harrison in SoMa (☎415/495-7447; $2.50/hour before 10am, $5/hour after 10am). Also in SoMa, the *CyberWorld Café* at 528 Folsom (☎415/278-9669) charges $10/hour, $8 if you're a member (membership costs $2). Finally, if you have your own laptop, you can plug into a phone line at the chic

Circadia, a plush café in the Mission at 2727 Mariposa Street (☎415/552-2649). Access here is $2.95 to $3.95/hour, and looking at the decor, you'd never guess that Microsoft started the joint.

Left luggage Greyhound, First and Mission St (☎415/495-1555); open daily 6am–8pm.

Legal advice Lawyer Referral Service, 465 California (☎415/989-1616).

Passport and visa office US Dept of Immigration, 630 Sansome St (☎1-800/375-5283).

Post office You can collect general delivery mail (bring your ID) from the main post office, 101 Hyde St, in the Civic Center (Mon–Fri 8.30am–5.30pm, Sat 10am–2pm; ☎1-800/275-8777), but letters will only be held for thirty days before being returned to sender, so make sure there's a return address on the envelope. If you're receiving mail at someone else's address, it should include "c/o" and the regular occupant's name; otherwise it too is likely to be returned. San Francisco's two main post offices, with telephone and general delivery facilities, are at Sutter Street Station, 150 Sutter St (Mon–Fri 8.30am–5pm), and Rincon Finance Station, 180 Steuart St (Mon–Fri 7am–6pm, Sat 9am–2pm).

Main public library Civic Center, at 100 Larkin Street at Grove (☎415/557-4400). Mon 10am–6pm, Tues–Thurs 9am–8pm, Fri 11am–5pm, Sat 9am–5pm, Sun noon–5pm. Free Internet use for members.

Sports Advance tickets for all Bay Area sports events are available through the BASS charge-by-phone ticket service (☎510/762-BASS), as well as from the teams themselves. Baseball: The San Francisco Giants play in the new PacBell Ballpark where homeruns over the right-field fence will splash into the bay (☎1-800/544-2687). The Giants' East Bay counterparts, the Oakland's A's, play at the usually sunny Oakland Coliseum (☎510/638-0500). Ticket prices range from $4 for bleacher seats to $125 for a field-side box, but promotions, like Wednesday Dollar Days, make seeing a baseball game the cheapest major sports event in town. Basketball: the Golden State Warriors play at the Oakland Arena (☎510/762-BASS). Football: the San Francisco 49ers appear at blustery 3COM Park on Candlestick Point, south of town (☎415/468-2249). All tickets are priced at $50 and are almost impossible to come by. The boisterous Oakland fans don silver and black to root on their Raiders, who knock helmets at the Coliseum. Tickets are also around $50, but are almost always available; call BASS for information. Ice hockey: the Bay Area's newest sports team is the San Jose Sharks (☎408/287-7070), based at their own arena in the South Bay.

Tax In San Francisco and the Bay Area the sales tax is 7.5 percent, plus a 0.5 percent "earthquake" tax. Hotel tax will add fourteen percent onto your bill.

Telegrams Western Union, citywide locations. Call ☎1-800/325-6000 to find the nearest.

Travel agents Council Travel, 530 Bush St (☎415/421-3473); STA Travel, 51 Grant Ave (☎415/391-8407); Ticket Planet, 59 Grant St (☎1-800/799-8888).

Volunteer work Bay Area Volunteer Information Center (*www.meer.net/users/taylor*); San Francisco Volunteer Center, 425 Jackson (☎415/982-8999, *www.vcsf.org*).

Whale-watching The nonprofit Oceanic Society, Building E, Fort Mason Center(☎415/441-1104), runs seven-hour boat trips from the Marina to observe the gray whales on their migration from Alaska to Baja. Incredible, but even the strongest constitutions will need travel sickness pills to survive the choppy seas in the small boat. Trips cost $50 and should be booked in advance. For the same price in July–Sept, the society also runs bird-watching trips out to the Farallones Islands.

THE BAY AREA

Of the six million people who make their home in the San Francisco **Bay Area**, only a lucky one in eight lives in the actual city of San Francisco. Everyone else is spread around one of the many smaller cities and suburbs that ring the bay, either down the Peninsula or across one of the two impressively engineered bridges that span the chilly waters of the world's most exquisite natural harbor. There's no doubt about the supporting role these places play in relation to San Francisco – always "the city" – but each has a distinctive character, and contributes to the range of people and landscapes that makes the Bay Area one of the most desirable places in the US to live or to visit.

Across the steel **Bay Bridge**, eight miles from downtown San Francisco, the **East Bay** is home to the lively, left-leaning cities of **Oakland** and **Berkeley**, which together have some of the best bookstores and restaurants, and most of the live music venues in the greater Bay Area. The weather's generally much sunnier and warmer here too, and it's easy to reach by way of the BART trains that race under the bay. The remainder of the East Bay is contained in Contra Costa County, which includes the short-lived early state capital of California, **Benicia**, as well as the former homes of writers John Muir and Eugene O'Neill.

South of the city, the Peninsula holds some of San Francisco's oldest and most upscale suburbs, spreading down through the computer-rich **Silicon Valley** and into **San Jose** – California's fastest-growing city, and now a larger one in both square milage and population than San Francisco – though apart from a few excellent museums there's not a lot to see. To the west, however, the **beaches** are excellent – sandy, clean and uncrowded – and there's a couple of youth hostels in old lighthouses perched on the edge of the Pacific.

For some of the most beautiful land and seascapes in California, cross the Golden Gate Bridge or ride a ferry boat across the bay to **Marin County**, a mountainous peninsula that's one-half wealthy suburbia and one-half unspoiled hiking country, with **redwood forests** rising sheer out of the thundering Pacific Ocean. A range of 2500-foot peaks divides the county down the middle, separating the yacht clubs and plush bayview houses of **Sausalito** and **Tiburon** from the nearly untouched wilderness that runs along the Pacific coast, through Muir Woods and the Point Reyes National Seashore. North of Marin County, at the top of the bay, and still within an hour's drive of San Francisco, the Wine Country regions of the Sonoma and Napa Valleys make an excellent day-trip; they're detailed in "Northern California," beginning on p.589.

The East Bay

The largest and most-traveled bridge in California, the **Bay Bridge** heads east from downtown San Francisco, part graceful suspension bridge and part heavy-duty steel truss. Built in 1933 as an economic booster during the Depression, the bridge is made from enough steel cable to wrap around the earth three times. Completed just seven months before the more famous (and better-loved) Golden Gate, it works a lot harder for a lot less respect: a hundred million vehicles cross the bridge each year, though you'd have to search hard to find a postcard of it. Local scribe Herb Caen dubbed it, "the car-strangled spanner," a reflection of its often-clogged lanes. Indeed, the bridge's only claim to fame – apart from the much-broadcast videotape of its partial collapse during the 1989 earthquake – is that **Treasure Island**, where the two halves of the bridge meet, hosted the 1939 World's Fair. During World War II the island became a Navy base, which, pending post-Cold War closures, it remains; just inside the gates there's a small **museum** (daily 10am–3pm; free) with pictures of the Fair amid maritime memorabilia. The island also offers great views of San Francisco and the Golden Gate.

The Bay Bridge empties into **Oakland**, a hard-working, blue-collar city that is at the heart of the East Bay. The city traditionally earned its livelihood from shipping and transportation services, as evidenced by the enormous cranes in the massive Port of Oakland, but is in the beginning stages of a renaissance as it lobbies to attract businesses and workers from the information technology industry. Oakland spreads north along wooded foothills to **Berkeley**, an image-conscious university town that looks out across to the Golden Gate and collects a mixed bag of pinstriped Young Republicans, much-pierced dropouts, ageing 1960s radicals, and Nobel prize-winning nuclear physicists in its cafés and bookstores.

Berkeley and Oakland blend together so much as to be virtually the same city, and the hills above them are topped by a twenty-mile string of **regional parks**, providing much needed fresh air and quick relief from the concrete grids below. The rest of the East Bay is filled out by Contra Costa County, a huge area that contains some intriguing, historically important waterfront towns – well worth a detour if you're passing through on the way to the Wine Country region of the Napa and Sonoma valleys – as well as some of the Bay Area's most inward-looking suburban sprawl. Curving around the **North Bay** from the oil-refinery landscape of Richmond, and facing each other across the narrow **Carquinez Strait**, both Benicia and Port Costa were vitally important during California's first twenty years of existence after the 1849 Gold Rush; they're now strikingly sited but little-visited ghost towns. In contrast, standing out from the soulless dormitory communities that fill up the often baking hot **inland valleys,** are the preserved homes of an unlikely pair of influential writers: the naturalist John Muir, who, when not out hiking around Yosemite and the High Sierra, lived most of his life near **Martinez,** and playwright Eugene O'Neill, who wrote many of his angst-ridden works at the foot of **Mount Diablo,** the Bay Area's most impressive peak.

Arrival

You're most likely to be staying in San Francisco when you visit the East Bay, though it is as convenient and sometimes better value to fly direct to **Oakland Airport** (OAK; ☎510/577-4000), particularly if you're coming from elsewhere in the US. All major domestic airlines serve the facility, which is less-crowded and more desirable than its San Francisco counterpart. It's an easy trip from the airport into town. The **AirBART Shuttle** van (every 15min; $2; ☎510/562-7700) runs to the Coliseum BART station, from where you can hop on BART to Berkeley, Oakland or San Francisco. There are several door-to-door shuttle buses that run from the airport to East Bay stops, such as Bayporter ($15; ☎510/467-1800). The shuttles also make runs into San Francisco; expect to pay around $30.

The **Greyhound** station is in a dodgy part of northern Oakland alongside the I-980 freeway on San Pablo Avenue at 21st Street. **Amtrak** terminates at Second Street near Jack London Square in West Oakland, where a free shuttle bus heads across the Bay Bridge to the Transbay Terminal. A better option for heading into San Francisco is to get off at Richmond and change onto the nearby BART trains. The most enjoyable way to arrive in the East Bay is aboard a Blue and Gold Fleet **ferry** ($4.50 each way; ☎510/522-3300), which sails every hour from San Francisco's Ferry Building and Pier 39 to Oakland's Jack London Square. The fleet also runs a service to Angel Island, departing from Oakland (Sat–Sun 10.50am and 12.30pm May 1–Oct 31; $13 roundtrip).

Getting around

The East Bay is linked to San Francisco via the underground BART transbay **subway** (Mon–Sat 6am–midnight, Sun 9am–midnight). Three lines run from Daly City through San Francisco and on to downtown Oakland, before diverging to service East Oakland out to Fremont, Berkeley, north to Richmond, and east into Contra Costa County as far as Concord. Fares range from $1.10 to $4.45, and the cost of each ride is deducted from the total value of the ticket, purchased from machines on the station concourse. If you're relying on BART to get around a lot, buy a **high-value ticket** ($5, $10 or $20) to avoid having to stand in line to buy a new ticket each time you ride. For $3.80, you can tour the entire system and get off at any of the 39 stations for up to three hours, so long as you enter and exit at the same station. To phone BART from San Francisco dial ☎415/989-BART; from the East Bay ☎510/465-BART, or check *www.bart.org*. Bikes are allowed on most trains.

From East Bay BART stations, pick up a **free transfer**, saving you 35¢ on the $1.35 fares of the revamped AC Transit (☎510/839-2882), which provides a good **bus service** around the entire East Bay area, especially Oakland and Berkeley. AC Transit also runs buses on a number of routes to Oakland and Berkeley from the Transbay Terminal in San Francisco. These operate all night, and are the only way of getting across the bay by public transit once BART has shut down. You can pick up excellent free maps of both BART and the bus system from any station. A smaller-scale bus company that can also prove useful, the Contra Costa County Connection (☎925/676-7500), runs buses to most of the inland areas, including the John Muir and Eugene O'Neill historic houses.

One of the best ways to get around is by bike; a fine **cycle route** follows Skyline and Grizzly Peak Boulevards along the wooded crest of the hills between Berkeley and Lake Chabot. If you haven't got one, rent touring bikes or mountain bikes for $25 a day from Around World, 2416 Telegraph Ave in Oakland (☎510/835-8763), or from Cal Adventures, 2301 Bancroft Way on the UC Berkeley campus (☎510/642-4000). For those interested in **walking tours**, the city of Oakland sponsors free "discovery tours" (☎510/238-3050) of various neighborhoods. A popular excursion is the Oakland Historical Landmark Tour (Sun 1–3.30pm; free; ☎510/835-1306), beginning in front of the Oakland Museum at 10th and Fallon, and covering areas like Chinatown, Lake Merritt, Preservation Park and Jack London Square.

If you're **driving**, allow yourself plenty of time to get there: the East Bay has some of California's worst traffic, with the Bay Bridge and I-80 in particular jam-packed sixteen hours a day.

Information

The **Oakland Visitor Information Booth**, on Broadway between Water Street and Embarcadero Street in Jack London Square (daily 11am–5pm; ☎1-800/262-5526), offers free maps and information, as does its counterpart at 550 Tenth Street near the 12th Street BART station in downtown Oakland (Mon–Fri 8.30am–5pm; ☎510/839-9000). In Berkeley, check in at the **Berkeley CVB**, 2015 Center Street (Mon–Fri 9am–5pm; ☎510/549-7040). The **Berkeley TRiP Commute Store** (Mon–Wed & Fri 8.30am–5.30pm, Thurs 9am–6pm; ☎510/644-7665), right beside the visitor center, sells passes to all Bay Area transit systems and can help you figure out how to get just about anywhere in the area on public transportation. Before leaving, pick up a copy of the free pamphlet, *UC Berkeley Student Guide to East Bay Hot Spots*, which lists all major points of interest and the bus routes that'll lead you there. The **University of California's Visitor Services**, 101 University Hall, at the corner of Oxford and University, gives ninety-minute tours of campus (Mon–Sat 10am, Sun 1pm; free; ☎510/642-5215). The tours are led by Cal students trained in talking about the campus' history, architecture and flavor. Be sure to take one if you want a fuller picture of Berkeley beyond looking at facades and faces of passing students. If you're spending any time at all in the Berkeley area, pick up a copy of *Berkeley Inside/Out* by Don Pitcher (Heyday Books, $12.95), an informative guide that'll tell you everything you ever wanted to know about the town and its inhabitants. For information on hiking or horseriding in the many parks that top the Oakland and Berkeley hills, contact the **East Bay Regional Parks District**, 11500 Skyline Blvd (☎510/562-7275). The widely available (and free) *East Bay Express* has the most comprehensive listings of what's on in the vibrant East Bay music and arts scene. The daily *Oakland Tribune* (50¢) is also worth a look for its coverage of local politics and sporting events.

East Bay accommodation

The East Bay's **motels** and **hotels** are barely a better value for money than their San Francisco equivalents. However, they give visitors the chance to stay just outside of the city's hubbub whilst affording easy access to it. **Bed and breakfasts** often give the best value, tucked as they are in Berkeley's leafy hills. Check with the *Berkeley &*

Oakland Bed and Breakfast Network (☎510/547-6380) for a complete list, or get their brochure from the Berkeley CVB or UC's Visitor Services office. A few **campgrounds** and **dorm beds** are available in summertime.

Hotels, motels and B&Bs

Bancroft Hotel, 2680 Bancroft Way, Berkeley (☎1-800/549-1002 or 510/549-1000). Small hotel with 22 rooms, a good location and fine service. Breakfast included. ⑥.

Berkeley City Club, 2315 Durant Ave, Berkeley (☎510/848-7800). Two blocks from the UC campus, this B&B was designed by Hearst Castle architect Julia Morgan, with indoor swimming pool and exercise room. Each of the spacious rooms has a private bath. ⑤.

The Claremont Resort & Spa, 41 Tunnel Road, Berkeley (☎1-800/551-7266 or 510/843-3000) Built in 1915, the Claremont is the lap of luxury among Berkeley hotels. Luxurious rooms come with coffeemakers, data ports for your laptop, hairdryers, cable TV, and big windows, some overlooking the large outdoor pool; spa sessions begin at $95/hour for facials or massages. ⑧.

Dean's Bed and Breakfast, 480 Pedestrian Way, Rockridge (☎510/652-5024). A hidden gem with heated swimming pool (May-October) and Japanese garden, near a trendy shopping strip and the Rockridge BART stop. Tidy but simple rooms come with private bath, cable TV and private phone line with answering machine. Highly recommended. ⑤.

Hotel Durant, 2600 Durant Ave, Berkeley (☎1-800/238-7268 or 510/845-8981). Upscale hotel at the heart of UC-Berkeley, featuring large, airy rooms with refrigerators. Best location to stay if you can afford it. ⑦.

East Brother Light Station, 117 Park Place, San Pablo Bay (☎510/233-2385). A handful of rooms in a converted lighthouse, on an island in the middle of the bay. Not a handy base for seeing the sights, this is a retreat and adventure for an evening. Prices include highly rated gourmet dinners as well as breakfast. ⑨.

Elmwood House, 2609 College Ave, Berkeley (☎510/540-5123). Attractive, turn-of-the-century house with small and sunny B&B rooms, not far from UC Berkeley. ④.

French, 1538 Shattuck Ave, North Berkeley (☎510/548-9930). Small and comfortable hotel with 18 standard rooms in the heart of Berkeley's Gourmet Ghetto. ⑤.

Golden Bear Motel, 1620 San Pablo Ave, West Berkeley (☎1-800/525-6770 or 510/525-6770). The most pleasant of the many motels in the "flatlands" of West Berkeley, though somewhat out of the way. ④.

Gramma's Rose Garden Inn, 2740 Telegraph Ave, Berkeley (☎510/549-2145). Pleasant, if slightly dull, rooms with fireplaces in a pretty mock-Tudor mansion half a mile south of UC Berkeley. ⑥.

Holiday Inn Bay Bridge, 1800 Powell St, Emeryville (☎510/658-9300). Not outrageously pricey considering the great views to be had from the upper floors. Free parking. ⑦.

Jack London Inn, 444 Embarcadero West (☎510/444-2032). Kitschy motorlodge with a 1950s feel; located next to Jack London Square. ⑤.

Mac, 10 Cottage Ave, Point Richmond (☎510/235-0010). Built in 1907, the recently refurbished *Hotel Mac* boasts luxurious rooms with unbeatable prices. This was supposedly John Rockefeller's favorite place to stay when visiting his Standard Oil enterprise. ⑤.

Shattuck, 2086 Allston Way, Berkeley (☎510/845-7300). Comfortable rooms in a central and well-restored older hotel. ⑥.

Travelodge, 423 Seventh St, downtown Oakland (☎1-800/255-3050 or 510/451-6316). Spacious rooms, some of which have kitchens, make this a good option for families or groups; also at 1820 University Ave, Berkeley (☎510/843-4262). ⑤.

Union Hotel and Gardens, 401 First St, Benicia (☎707/746-0100). A bordello from 1882 until 1950, since converted into a comfortable bed and breakfast with twelve rooms. ⑥.

Waterfront Plaza Hotel, 10 Washington St, Oakland (☎510/836-3800 or 1-800/729-3638). Plush, modern hotel moored on the best stretch of the Oakland waterfront. ⑧.

Hostels

Berkeley YMCA, 2001 Allston Way at Milvia St, a block from Berkeley BART (☎510/848-6800). Berkeley's best bargain accommodation; rates include use of gym and pool. $38.

Haste-Channing Summer Visitor Housing, 2424 Channing Ave, Berkeley (☎510/642-4444). Summer-only dorm rooms for $50.

Campgrounds

Chabot Family Campground, off I-580 in East Oakland (☎510/562-2267). Walk-in, tent-only places, with hot showers and lots of good hiking nearby; reserve through ParkNet ☎1-800/444-7275 in summer; $20.

Mount Diablo State Park, 20 miles east of Oakland off I-680 in Contra Costa County (☎510/837-2525). RV and tent places; book through Parknet ☎1-800/444-7275 in summer; $16.

Oakland

> *What was the use of me having come from Oakland, it was not natural for me to have come from there yes write about it if I like or anything if I like but not there, there is no there there.*
>
> Gertrude Stein, *Everybody's Autobiography*

As the workhorse of the Bay Area, **OAKLAND** is commonly known as a place of little or no play. One of the busiest ports on the West Coast and the western terminal of the rail network, it's also the spawning ground of some of America's most unabashedly revolutionary **political movements**, such as the militant **Black Panthers**, who gave a voice to the African-American population, and the **Symbionese Liberation Army**, who demanded a ransom for kidnapped heiress Patty Hearst in the form of free food distribution to the poor.

The city is also the birthplace of literary legends **Gertrude Stein** and **Jack London**, who grew up here at approximately the same time, though in entirely different circumstances – Stein was a stockbroker's daughter, while London was an orphaned delinquent. Most of the waterfront where London used to steal oysters and lobsters in now named in his memory, while Stein, who was actually born in East Oakland, is all but ignored here, not surprising given her unflattering quote. Still, until very recently, locals found it hard to come up with anything better: Oakland businesses have a long history of deserting the place once the going gets good, and even the city's football team, the Raiders, defected to Los Angeles for thirteen years.

But residents who've stuck by the city through its duller and darker days recently elected a new mayor, former California governor and one-time presidential candidate **Jerry "Moonbeam" Brown**, who has promised to revitalize (some residents say gentrify) the town and slash its infamous crime rate. Advertising his city's lower rents and always-sunny climate – consistently rated the best in the US – Brown is well on his way to meeting his promise of bringing 10,000 new residents downtown, an area being rapidly transformed by the prosperity of the information age boom, along with increasingly popular **Rockridge** and **Lake Merrit**, whose rents are already approaching San Francisco prices. The city has also attracted a significant number of lesbians, who've left San Francisco's Castro and Mission, as well as a great number of artists pushed from their SoMa lofts by sky-high rents for the warehouses of West Oakland.

Still, "Oaktown" (the local name for Oakland) is a better place in which to live than to visit. Locals call San Francisco "the city" and will point visitors to its myriad attractions before recommending those in the East Bay. But given it's a short hop on BART or quick drive across the Bay Bridge, a day-trip to Oakland is worth it to get a feel for the East Bay's diversity and changing times.

Downtown Oakland

Coming by BART from San Francisco, get off at the 12th Street–Civic Center station and you're at the new, open-air shopping and office space of **City Center** in the heart of **DOWNTOWN OAKLAND**. Downtown's compact district of spruced-up Victorian storefronts overlooked by modern hotels and office buildings has been in the midst of an ambitious program of restoration and redevelopment for over a decade. Fraught with allegations of illegal dealings and incompetent planning, so far the program has been less than a complete success. To make way for the moat-like I-980 freeway – the main route through Oakland since the collapse of the Cypress Freeway in the 1989 earthquake – entire blocks were cleared of houses, some of which were saved and moved to **Preservation Park** at 12th Street and Martin Luther King Jr Way. The late nineteenth-century commercial center along Ninth Street west of Broadway, now tagged **Old Oakland**, underwent a major restoration some years ago, and while some of the buildings are still waiting for tenants, others are occupied by architect and design firms, much like San Francisco's Jackson Square. By way of contrast to the subdued Old Oakland area, stroll a block east of Broadway, between Seventh and Ninth, to Oakland's **Chinatown**, whose bakeries and restaurants are as lively and bustling – if not as picturesque – as those of its more famous cousin across the Bay.

Luckily, not all of downtown Oakland has the look of a permanent building site. The city experienced its greatest period of growth in the early twentieth century, and many of the grand buildings of this era survive a few blocks north along Broadway, centered

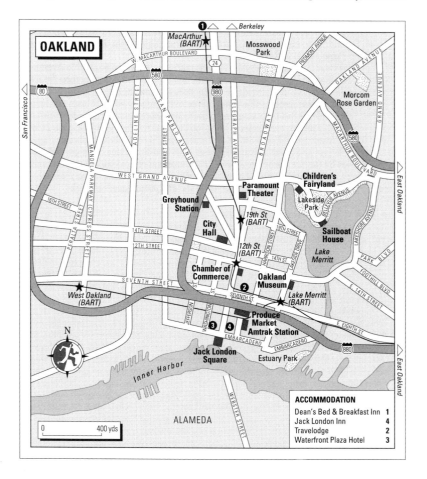

OAKLAND

ACCOMMODATION

Dean's Bed & Breakfast Inn	1
Jack London Inn	4
Travelodge	2
Waterfront Plaza Hotel	3

around the gigantic grass knoll of **Frank Ogawa Plaza** and the awkwardly imposing 1914 **City Hall** on 14th Street. Two blocks away at 13th and Franklin stands Oakland's most unmistakable landmark, the chateauesque lantern of the **Tribune Tower**, the 1920s-era former home of the *Oakland Tribune* newspaper. Further north, around the 19th Street BART station, are some of the Bay Area's finest early twentieth-century buildings, highlighted by the outstanding Art Deco interior of the 1931 **Paramount Theater** at 2025 Broadway (tours 10am first and third Sat of the month; $1; ☎510/465-6400). The West Coast's answer to Radio City Music Hall, the Paramount shows Hollywood classics, and hosts occasional concerts by the likes of Tom Waits and Neil Young and performances by ballet troupes and the Oakland Symphony. Nearby buildings are equally flamboyant, ranging from the wafer-thin Gothic "flatiron" office tower of the **Cathedral Building** at Broadway and Telegraph, to the Hindu-temple-like facade of the magnificent 3500-seat **Fox Oakland** (now closed) on Telegraph at 19th – the largest movie house west of Chicago at the time it was built in 1928 – and, across the street, the 1931 **Floral Depot**, a group of small modern storefronts faced in black-and-blue terracotta tiles with shiny silver highlights. If you're tired of walking, lace up skates at the nearby **Oakland Ice Center**, 519 18th Street (☎510/268-9000). The facility is the finest in the Bay Area, evinced by the Olympians, such as Kristi Yamaguchi and Brian Boitano, who often practice here (Mon–Thur 12pm–5pm, Fri–Sat 7pm–10pm, Sun 12–5; $8 skate rental and all-day use).

West of Broadway, the area around the Greyhound bus station on San Pablo Avenue is fairly seedy. San Pablo used to be the main route in and out of Oakland before the freeways were built, but many of the roadside businesses are now derelict, especially around the industrial districts of **Emeryville**. Some of the old warehouses have been converted into artists' lofts and studios in an ongoing real-life workshop by architects to transform the area into a glitzy design centerpiece. Most intriguing is the new city hall, called **Civic Center**, at Park Avenue and Hollis Street, for which the 1902 town hall has been wrapped in a sheer glass box of 15,000 additional square feet of office space. Any gentrification here is diffused by the scenes on the street. Prostitutes and drug-dealers hang out under the neon signs of the dingy bars and gambling halls such as the *Oaks Card Club*, where Oaktown rapper M.C. Hammer, who once made the city proud, used to work.

Lake Merritt and the Oakland Museum

Five blocks east of Broadway, the eastern third of downtown Oakland comprises **Lake Merritt**, a three-mile-circumference tidal lagoon that was bridged and dammed in the 1860s to become the centerpiece of Oakland's most desirable neighborhood. All that remains of the many fine houses that once circled the lake is the elegant **Camron-Stanford House**, on the southwest shore at 1418 Lakeside Drive, a graceful Italianate mansion whose sumptuous interior is open for visits (Wed 11am–4pm, Sun 1–5pm; $4). The lake is also the nation's oldest wildlife refuge, and migrating flocks of ducks, geese, and herons break their journeys here. **Lakeside Park** lines the north shore, where you can rent canoes and row-boats ($4 per hour), and a range of sailing boats and catamarans ($4–10 per hour) from the **Sailboat House** (summer daily 10am–5pm; winter Fri–Sun 10am–4.30pm; ☎510/238-2196) – provided you can convince the staff you know how to sail. A miniature Mississippi riverboat makes thirty-minute lake **cruises** ($1) on weekend afternoons, and kids will like the puppet shows and pony rides at the **Children's Fairyland** (summer daily 10am–5.30pm; winter Fri–Sun 10am–5.30pm; $3.25), along Grand Avenue on the northwest edge of the park. Every year, on the first weekend in June, the park comes to life during the **Festival at the Lake**, when all of Oakland gets together to enjoy nonstop music and performances from local bands and entertainers. At night, the lake's lit up by the "Necklace of Lights," an elegant source of local pride.

Two blocks south of the lake, or a block up Oak Street from the Lake Merritt BART station, the **Oakland Museum** (Wed–Sat 10am–5pm, Sun noon–5pm; $5, free Sun after

4pm) is perhaps Oakland's most worthwhile stop, not only for the exhibits but also for the superb modern building in which it's housed, topped by a terraced rooftop sculpture garden that gives great views out over the water and the city. The museum covers many diverse areas: displays on the **ecology** of California, including a simulated walk from the seaside through various natural habitats up to the 14,000-foot summits of the Sierra Nevada mountains; state history, ranging from old mining equipment to the guitar that Berkeley-born Country Joe MacDonald played at the Woodstock festival in 1969; and a broad survey of works by California artists and craftspeople, some highlights of which are pieces of turn-of-the-century **arts and crafts furniture**. You'll also see excellent **photography** by Edward Muybridge, Dorothea Lange, Imogen Cunningham and many others. The museum also has a collector's gallery that rents and sells works by California artists.

The waterfront, Alameda, and West Oakland

Half a mile down from Downtown Oakland on AC Transit bus #51, at the foot of Broadway on the waterfront, **Jack London Square** is Oakland's sole concession to the tourist trade. Also accessible by direct ferry from San Francisco (see "Arrival," p.489), this somewhat anesthetic complex of harborfront boutiques and restaurants, anchored by a huge Barnes and Noble bookstore, was named after the self-taught writer who grew up pirating shellfish around here, but is about as distant from the spirit of the man as it's possible to get. Jack London's best story, *The Call of the Wild*, was written about his adventures in the Alaskan Yukon, where he carved his initials in a small cabin that has been reconstructed here. The one sight worth stopping at is **Heinold's First and Last Chance Saloon**, a slanting tiny bar at the eastern end of the promenade. Built in 1883 from the hull of a whaling ship, Jack London really did drink here, and the collection of yellowed portraits of him on the wall are the only genuine thing about the writer you'll find on the square. Massive redevelopment plans, to the tune of $200 million, are afoot to revamp the square into a top-notch entertainment venue by 2005.

If you're not a keen fan of London (and if you are, you'd be better off visiting his Sonoma Valley ranch – see p.600), there are still a few worthwhile things to do here. **The Ebony Museum of Arts** at 30 Alice Street on the second floor (Tues–Sun noon–6pm; donation) is worth a visit for its African art and pop American counterculture collectibles. Otherwise, walk a few short blocks inland to the **Produce Market**, along Third and Fourth streets, where a couple of good places to eat and drink lurk among the rail tracks (see "Eating" on p.507). This bustling warehouse district has fruit and vegetables by the forklift load, and is at its most lively early in the morning, from about 5am. On the Embarcadero between Clay and Washington, **Yoshi's World Class Jazz House** is the Bay Area's, if not West Coast's, premier jazz club (see "Nightlife," p.513).

AC Transit bus #51 continues from Broadway under the inner harbor to **Alameda**, a quiet and conservative island of middle America dominated by a large, empty naval air station, one of the first to be closed by President Bill Clinton in 1995 – although massive nuclear-powered aircraft carriers still dock here occasionally. Alameda, which has been hit very hard by post-Cold War military cutbacks, was severed from the Oakland mainland as part of a harbor improvement program in 1902. The fine houses along the original shoreline on Clinton Street were part of the summer resort colony that flocked here to the *contra costa* or "opposite shore" from San Francisco, near the now demolished Neptune Beach amusement park. The island has since been much enlarged by dredging and landfill, and 1960s apartment buildings now line the long, narrow shore of **Robert Crown Memorial Beach** along the bay – a quiet, attractive spot.

West Oakland – an industrial district of warehouses, rail tracks, 1960s housing projects and decaying Victorian houses – may be the nearest East Bay BART stop to San Francisco, but it's light years away from that city's prosperity. Despite the obvious poverty, it's quite a safe and settled place, but the only time anyone pays any attention to it is when something dramatic happens; in the double-whammy year of 1989, for example, when former Black Panther Huey Newton was gunned down here in a drugs-related revenge attack, and the double-decker I-880 freeway that divided the neighborhood from the rest of the city collapsed in on itself during the earthquake, killing dozens of commuters. Now the neighborhood is a magnet for artists and skate punks from across the bay, who revel in its dirt-cheap rents and open spaces.

Local African-American leaders successfully resisted government plans to rebuild I-880, the old concrete eyesore which they asserted created an unsightly barrier within their community; the broad and potentially very attractive **Nelson Mandela Parkway** has replaced it. Otherwise, this remains one of the Bay Area's poorest and most neglected neighborhoods, and apart from a marvelous stock of turn-of-the-century houses there's little here to tempt tourists. But locals – and Mayor Brown – say take a long look and buy now; given the district's proximity to San Francisco, West Oakland is bound to smarten up unrecognizably within five years.

East Oakland

The bulk of Oakland spreads along foothills and flatlands to the east of downtown, in neighborhoods obviously stratified along the main thoroughfares of Foothill and MacArthur Boulevards. Gertrude Stein grew up here, though when she returned years later in search of her childhood home it had been torn down and replaced by a dozen Craftsman-style bungalows – the simple 1920s wooden houses that cover most of **EAST OAKLAND**, each fronted by a patch of lawn and divided from its neighbor by a narrow concrete driveway.

A quick way out from the gridded streets and sidewalks of the city is to take AC Transit bus #64 from downtown east up into the hills to **Joaquin Miller Park**, the most easily accessible of Oakland's hilltop parks. It stands on the former grounds of "The Hights," the misspelled home of the "Poet of the Sierras," Joaquin Miller, who made his name playing the eccentric frontier American in the literary salons of 1870s London. His poems weren't exactly acclaimed (his greatest poetic achievement was rhyming "teeth" with "Goethe"), although his prose account, *Life Amongst the Modocs*, documenting time spent with the Modoc people near Mount Shasta, does stand the test of time. It was more for his outrageous behavior that he became famous, wearing bizarre clothes and biting debutantes on the ankle. For years, Japanese poet Yone Noguchi also lived here, working the sprinkler as Miller impressed lady visitors with a rain dance he claimed to have learned from American Indians.

Perched in the hills at the foot of the park, the pointed towers of the **Mormon Temple**, 4766 Lincoln Ave, look like missile-launchers designed by the Wizard of Oz – unmissable by day or floodlit night. In December, speakers hidden in the landscaping make it seem as if the plants are singing Christmas carols. Though you can't go inside (unless you're a confirmed Mormon), there are great views out over the entire Bay Area, and a small museum explains the tenets of the faith (daily 9am–9pm; free).

Some twenty miles of tract house suburbs stretch along the bay south to San Jose, and the only vaguely interesting area is around the end of the BART line in **FREMONT**, where the short-lived Essanay movie studios were based. Essanay, the first studios on the West Coast, made over 700 films in three years, including Charlie Chaplin's *The Tramp* in 1914. Not much remains from these pre-Hollywood days, however, and the only real sight is the **Mission San Jose de Guadalupe** on Mission Boulevard south of the I-680 freeway (daily 10am–5pm; donation), which in the best traditions of Hollywood set design was completely rebuilt in Mission style only a few years ago.

North Oakland and Rockridge

The horrific October 1991 **Oakland fire**, which destroyed 3000 homes and killed 26 people, did most of its damage in the high-priced hills of **NORTH OAKLAND**. It took the better part of two years, but most of the half-million dollar houses have been rebuilt, and though the lush vegetation that made the area so attractive will never be allowed to grow back in order to prevent any more fires, things are pretty much back to normal. Which is to say that segregation is still in place; these bay-view homes, some of the Bay Area's most valuable real estate, look out across some of its poorest – the neglected flat-lands below that in the 1960s were the proving grounds of Black Panthers Bobby Seale and Huey Newton.

Broadway is the dividing line between the two halves of North Oakland, and also gives access (via the handy AC Transit #51 bus) to most of what there is to see and do. One of Oakland's most neighborly streets, **Piedmont Avenue**, is lined by a number of small bookstores and cafés, and it makes for a nice stroll or day of hanging out. At the north end of Piedmont Avenue, the **Mountain View Cemetery** was laid out in 1863 by Frederick Law Olmsted (designer of New York's Central Park) and holds the elaborate dynastic tombs of San Francisco's most powerful families – the Crockers, the Bechtels and the Ghirardellis. You can jog or ride a bike around the well-tended grounds, or just wonder at the enormous turtles in the pond. Next door, the columbarium, known as the **Chapel of the Chimes**, 4499 Piedmont Ave (daily 9am–5pm; free; ☎510/654-0123), was designed by Julia Morgan of Hearst Castle fame during her decade-long involvement with the structure beginning in 1921. The structure is remarkable for its seemingly end-less series of urn-filled rooms, grouped together around sky-lit courtyards, bubbling fountains and intimate chapels – all connected by ornate staircases of every conceivable length. Morgan wanted the space to sing of life, not death, and she's succeeded. There's no better place in Oakland to wander about in peace, or even plop down with a book. Try and visit during one of the regular concerts held here for a completely unique – and dis-tinctly Californian – experience.

Back on Broadway, just past College Avenue, Broadway Terrace climbs up along the edge of the fire area to **Lake Temescal** – where you can swim in summer – and contin-ues on up to the forested ridge at the **Robert Sibley Regional Preserve**. This includes the 1761-foot volcanic cone of Round Top Peak and offers panoramas of the entire Bay Area. The Peak has been dubbed the **Volcanic Witch Project** by the local media due to the five mysterious mazes, carved into the dirt and lined with stones, located in the canyons around the crater. Nobody knows where they came from, but navigating the designs leads to their center, where visitors add to the pile of diverse offerings ranging from trinkets to cigarettes to poetry. Skyline Boulevard runs through the park and is popular with cyclists, who ride the twelve miles south to Lake Chabot or follow Grizzly Peak Boulevard five miles north to Tilden Park through the Berkeley Hills.

Most of the Broadway traffic, and the AC Transit #51 bus, cuts off onto College Avenue through Oakland's most upscale shopping district, **ROCKRIDGE**. Spreading for half a mile on either side of the Rockridge BART station, the quirky stores and restaurants here, despite their undeniable yuppie overtones, are better than Piedmont's in variety and volume, and make for a pleasant afternoon's wander.

Berkeley

This Berkeley was like no somnolent Siwash out of her own past at all, but more akin to those Far Eastern or Latin American universities you read about, those autonomous culture media where the most beloved of folklores may be brought into doubt, cataclysmic of dissents voiced, suicidal of commitments chosen – the sort that bring governments down.

Thomas Pynchon, *The Crying of Lot 49*

More than any other American city, **BERKELEY** conjures up an image of 1960s student dissent. When college campuses across the nation were protesting against the Vietnam

War, it was the students of the University of California, Berkeley, who led the charge – gaining a name as the vanguard of what was increasingly seen as a challenge to the authority of the state. Full-scale battles were fought almost daily here at one point, on the campus and on its surrounding streets, and there were times when Berkeley looked almost on the brink of revolution itself: students (and others) throwing stones and gas bombs were met with tear-gas volleys and truncheons by National Guard troops under the nominal command of Governor Ronald Reagan.

Such action was inspired by the mood of the time, and in an increasingly conservative America, Berkeley politics are nowadays far more middle-of-the-road. But despite an influx of conformist students, a surge in the number of exclusive restaurants, and the dismantling of the city's rent control program, something of the progressive legacy manages to linger in the city's independent bookstores and at sporadic political demonstrations. In recent years, perhaps the biggest nationwide cause célèbre on campus was the plight of Naked Man, an undergrad who refused to wear clothing while attending class. While locals were pretty blasé about that tabloid news tale, they were enraged in 1999 by the attempt to change the format of their progressive radio station, KPFA, 94.1 FM. This leftist media outlet has been community staple since 1949, running talk programs like *Democracy Now!* and *Herbal Highway*. Station parent company Pacifica decided to update 94.1's delivery by switching to less subversive themes in an attempt to raise donations from area businesses. KPFA staffers wouldn't play along, however, and Pacifica fired them en masse, sending in armed security guards to remove DJ Dennis Bernstein off the air. The standoff – Bernstein holding out in his locked booth until the guards burst in – was broadcast live to a shocked Berkeley community. Within weeks, 10,000 supporters organized marches in support of the staffers, with one event ending in a riot at the station headquarters. For now, KPFA remains on the air, as unrepentant as ever, though relationships with management stay strained.

The **University of California**, right in the center of town, completely dominates Berkeley and makes a logical starting point for a visit. Its many grand buildings and 30,000 students give off a definite energy that spills down the raucous stretch of Telegraph Avenue which runs south from the campus and holds most of the student hangouts, including a dozen or so lively cafés, as well as a number of fine bookstores. Older students, and a good percentage of the faculty, congregate in the **Northside** area, popping down from their woodsy hillside homes to partake of goodies from the "Gourmet Ghetto," a stretch of Shattuck Avenue crammed with restaurants, delis, and bakeries. Of quite distinct character are the flatlands that spread through **West Berkeley** down to the bay, a poorer but increasingly gentrified district that mixes old Victorian houses with builder's yards and light industrial premises. Along the bay itself is the **Berkeley Marina**, where you can rent sailboards and sailboats or just watch the sun set behind the Golden Gate.

The University of California

Caught up in the frantic crush of students who pack the **UNIVERSITY OF CALIFORNIA** campus during the semesters, it's nearly impossible to imagine the bucolic learning environment envisaged by its high-minded founders. When the Reverend Henry Durant and other East Coast academics decided to set up shop here in the 1860s, these rolling foothills were still largely given over to dairy herds and wheatfields, the last remnants of the Peralta family's Spanish land-grant rancho which once stretched over most of the East Bay. In 1866, while surveying the land, a trustee recited "Westward the course of the empire takes its way," from a poem by George Berkeley. Moved by the moment, all assembled agreed to name their school after the bishop. Construction work on the two campus buildings – imaginatively named North Hall and South Hall – was still going on when the first 200 students, including 22 women, moved here from Oakland in 1873. Since then an increasing number of buildings have been squeezed into the half-mile-square main campus, and the state-funded university has become one of America's most prestigious, with so many Nobel laureates on the faculty that it's said you have to win one just to get a parking permit. University physicists built the first cyclotron, and plutonium was discovered here in 1941, along with 13 other synthetic elements (including berkelium and californium). As such, sketches for the first atomic bomb began here. Nuclear weaponry and overcrowding aside, the beautifully landscaped campus, stepping down from the eucalyptus-covered Berkeley Hills toward the Golden Gate, is eminently strollable. With maps posted everywhere, you'd have to try hard to get lost – though enthusiastic students will show you around on a free ninety-minute **tour** (Mon–Sat 10am, Sun 1pm; ☎510/642-5215).

A number of footpaths climb the hill from the Berkeley BART station on Shattuck Avenue, but the best way to get a feel for the place is to follow Strawberry Creek from the top of Center Street across the southeast corner of the campus, emerging from the

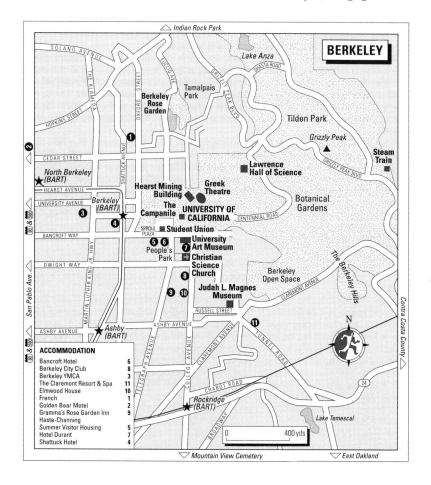

groves of redwood and eucalyptus trees at **Sproul Plaza**. It's the newest and largest public space on campus, enlivened by street musicians playing for quarters on the steps of the **Student Union** building and conga drummers pounding away in the echoing courtyard below. **Sather Gate**, which bridges Strawberry Creek at the north end of Sproul Plaza, marks the entrance to the older part of the campus. Up the hill, past the imposing facade of Wheeler Hall, the 1914 landmark **Campanile** (Mon–Fri 10am–4pm, Sat–Sun 10am–5pm; $1) is modeled after the one in the Piazza San Marco in Venice; take an elevator to the top for a great view of the campus and the entire Bay Area. At the foot of the tower stands the red-brick **South Hall**, the sole survivor of the original pair of buildings.

Inside the plain white building next door, the **Bancroft Library** (Mon–Fri 9am–5pm, Sat 1–5pm) displays odds and ends from its exhaustive accumulation of artifacts and documents tracing the history of California, including a faked brass plaque supposedly left by Sir Francis Drake when he claimed all of the West Coast for Queen Elizabeth I. It also contains an internationally important collection of manuscripts and rare books, from Mark Twain to James Joyce – though to see any of these you have to show some academic credentials. Around the corner and down the hill, just inside the arched main entrance to Doe Library, you'll find the **Morrison Reading Room**, a great place to sit for a while and read foreign magazines and newspapers.

Also worth a look if you've got time to kill is the **Museum of Paleontology** (Mon–Thurs 8am–10pm, Fri 8am–5pm, Sat 10am–5pm, Sun 1–10pm; free) in the nearby Valley Life Sciences Building, which details evolutionary concepts with hundreds of fossils, skeletons, and geological maps displayed along the corridors on the lower floors. From here it's a quick walk to the collection of cafés and restaurants lining Euclid Avenue and Hearst Avenue, and the beginning of Berkeley's Northside (see below).

The Hearst family name appears with disturbing regularity around the Berkeley campus, though in most instances this is due not to the notorious newspaper baron William Randolph but to his altruistic mother, Phoebe Apperson Hearst. Besides inviting the entire senior class to her home every spring for a giant picnic, she sponsored the architectural competition that came up with the original campus plan, and donated a good number of the campus buildings, including many that have since been destroyed. One of the finest survivors, the 1907 **Hearst Mining Building** (daily 8am–5pm), on the northeast edge of the campus, conceals a delicate metalwork lobby topped by three glass domes, above aging exhibits on geology and mining – which is how the Hearst family fortune was originally made, long before scion W.R. took up publishing. Another Hearst legacy is the **Greek Theatre**, modeled after the amphitheater at Epidauros, Greece, which hosts a summer season of rock concerts.

Higher up in the hills, above the 80,000-seat Memorial Stadium, the lushly landscaped **Botanical Garden** (daily 9am–5pm; free) defeats on-campus claustrophobia with its thirty acres of plants and cactuses. Near the crest, with great views out over the bay, a full-size fiberglass sculpture of a whale stretches out in front of the space-age **Lawrence Hall of Science** (daily 10am–5pm; $6), an excellent museum and learning center that features earthquake simulations, model dinosaurs and a planetarium, plus hands-on exhibits for kids in the Wizard's Lab. Both the gardens and the Lawrence Hall of Science are accessible on weekdays via the free UC Berkeley Shuttle bus from the campus or the Berkeley BART station.

In the southeast corner of the campus, the **Hearst Museum of Anthropology** in Kroeber Hall (Wed–Sun 10am–4.30pm, Thurs until 9pm; $3, free Thurs) holds a variety of changing exhibits as well as an intriguing display of artifacts made by Ishi, the last surviving Yahi Indian who was found near Mount Lassen in Northern California in 1911. Anthropologist (and father of writer Ursula Le Guin) Alfred Kroeber brought Ishi to the museum (then located on the UC San Francisco campus), where he lived under the scrutiny of scientists and journalists – in effect, in a state of captivity – until his death from tuberculosis a few years later.

The brutally modern, angular concrete of the **University Art Museum** across Bancroft Way (Wed–Sun 11am–5pm, Thurs until 9pm; $6, free Thur 11am-noon and 5pm to 9pm) is in stark contrast to the campus' older buildings. Its skylit, open-plan galleries hold works by Picasso, Cézanne, Rubens and other notables, but the star of the show is the collection of Fifties American painter Hans Hofmann's energetic and colorful abstract paintings on the top floor. The museum is renowned for its cutting-edge, changing exhibitions: the main space hosts a range of major shows – such as Robert Mapplethorpe's controversial photographs – while the Matrix Gallery focuses on lesser known, generally local artists. The new quarters of the **Pacific Film Archive**, 2575 Bancroft at Bowditch, features nightly showings of classics, Third World and experimental films. Call for listings (☎510/642-5249) or pick up a free monthly calendar around campus. The other rep house on campus is **UC Theatre**, 2036 University Avenue (☎510/843-FILM), featuring funky theme-weeks of noir, melodrama and other genres. Other artistic fare runs at **Zellerbach Hall** (☎510/642-9988), which showcases classical music, dance and performances by modernists like Laurie Anderson and Phillip Glass.

BERKELEY'S BOOKSTORES

Berkeley's **bookstores** are as exhaustive as they are exhausting – not surprising for a university town. Perfect for browsing and taking your time, you won't be made to feel guilty or obliged to buy a book you've been poring over for ages.

Black Oak Books, 1491 Shattuck Ave (☎510/486-0698). Huge selection of secondhand and new books for every interest; also holds regular evening readings by internationally acclaimed authors.

Cody's Books, 2454 Telegraph Ave (☎510/845-7852). The flagship of Berkeley booksellers, with an excellent selection of fiction, poetry and literary criticism.

Comics and Comix, 2502 Telegraph Ave (☎510/845-4091). Great selection of comic books, both current and classic.

Comic Relief, 2138 University (☎510/843-5002). All the mainstream stuff, plus self-published mini-comics by locals.

Easy Going, 1385 Shattuck Ave (☎510/843-3533). The essential bookstore for every traveler. Packed with printed travel paraphernalia, it offers a wide selection of guidebooks and maps for local, countrywide and worldwide exploration. Talks and slide shows by travel writers are also held on a regular basis.

Moe's Books, 2476 Telegraph Ave (☎510/849-2087). An enormous selection of new and used books on four floors with esoteric surprises in every field of study; for academics, book-collectors and browsers. There's also an excellent art section on the top floor.

Serendipity Books, 1201 University Ave (☎510/841-7455). This vast garage-like bookstore is off the loop of Berkeley bookstores but an absolute must for collectors of first edition and/or obscure fiction and poetry, and black American writers. The prices are fair, and the owner – incredibly, given the towers of unshelved books – knows exactly where everything is to be found.

Shakespeare and Company, 2499 Telegraph Ave (☎510/841-8916). Crammed with quality secondhand books at reasonable prices. The best place to linger and scour the shelves for finds.

Shambala Booksellers, 2482 Telegraph Ave (☎510/848-8443). Have a transcendental out-of-body experience where eastern and western religious traditions meet in this cozy store near campus.

Telegraph Avenue

Downtown Berkeley – basically two department stores, a few banks, a post office, and the City Hall building – lies west of the university campus around the Berkeley BART station on Shattuck Avenue, but the real activity centers on **Telegraph Avenue**, which runs south of the university from Sproul Plaza. This thoroughfare saw some of the worst of the Sixties riots and is still a frenetic bustle, especially the four short blocks closest to the university, which are packed with cafés and secondhand bookstores. Sidewalk vendors hawk handmade jewelry and brilliantly colored T-shirts, while down-and-outs hustle for spare change and spout psychotic poetry.

People's Park, now a seedy and overgrown plot of land half a block up from Telegraph between Haste Street and Dwight Way, was another battleground in the late Sixties, when organized and spirited resistance to the university's plans to develop the site into dormitories brought out the troops, who shot dead an onlooker by mistake. To many, the fact that the park is still a community-controlled open space (and outdoor flophouse for Berkeley's legions of pushers and homeless) symbolizes a small victory in the battle against the Establishment, though it's not a pleasant or even very safe place to hang about, especially after dark. A mural along Haste Street recalls some of the reasons why the battles were fought, in the words of student leader Mario Savio: "There's a time when the operation of the machine becomes so odious, makes you so sick at heart, that you can't take part, you can't even tacitly take part. And you've got to put your bodies upon the gears and upon the wheels, upon the levers, upon all the apparatus, and you've got to make it stop" – ideals that can't help but be undermined by the state of the place these days. Efforts by the university to reclaim the space with volleyball and basketball courts in 1991 were met with short-lived but violent protests: rioters trashed Telegraph Avenue storefronts, and a nineteen-year-old woman enraged at the university's plans for the park was shot dead by the police while trying to assassinate the Chancellor with a knife in his home.

Directly across Bowditch Street from People's Park stands one of the finest buildings in the Bay Area, Bernard Maybeck's **Christian Science Church**. Built in 1910, it's an eclectic but thoroughly modern structure, laid out in a simple Greek Cross floor plan and spanned by a massive redwood truss with carved Gothic tracery and Byzantine painted decoration. The interior is only open on Sundays for worship and for tours at 11am, but the outside is worth lingering over, its cascade of gently pitched roofs and porticoes carrying the eye from one handcrafted detail to another. It's a clever building in many ways: while the overall image is one of tradition and craftsmanship, Maybeck also succeeded in inconspicuously incorporating such materials as industrial metal windows, concrete walls and asbestos tiles into the structure – thereby cutting costs.

North Berkeley

NORTH BERKELEY, also called "Northside," is a subdued neighborhood of professors and postgraduate students, its steep, twisting streets climbing up the lushly overgrown hills north of the campus. At the foot of the hills, some of the Bay Area's finest restaurants and delis – most famously *Chez Panisse*, started and run by Alice Waters, the acclaimed inventor of California cuisine – have sprung up along Shattuck Avenue to form the so-called "Gourmet Ghetto," a great place to pick up the makings of a tasty al fresco lunch.

Euclid Avenue, off Hearst and next to the north gate of the university, is a sort of antidote to Telegraph Avenue, a quiet grove of coffee joints and pizza parlors frequented by grad students. Above Euclid (if you want to avoid the fairly steep walk, take the daily #65 bus or the weedays only #8), there are few more pleasant places for a picnic than the **Berkeley Rose Garden** (daily dawn–dusk; free), a terraced amphitheater filled with some three thousand varietal roses and looking out across the bay to San

Francisco. Built as part of a WPA job-creation scheme during the Depression, a wooden pergola rings the top, stepping down to a small spring.

Along the crest of the Berkeley Hills, a number of enticing parks give great views over the bay. The largest and highest of them, **Tilden Park**, spreads along the crest of the hills, encompassing some 2065 acres of near wilderness. Kids can enjoy a ride on the carved wooden horses of the carousel or the 1950s mini-steam train through the redwood trees. In the warmer months, don't miss a swim in Lake Anza (lifeguard on duty May–Oct daily 11am–6pm; $3).

Nearer to town at the north end of Shattuck Avenue and close by the shops and cafés along Solano Avenue, the gray basalt knob of **Indian Rock** stands out from the foot of the hills, challenging rock-climbers who hone their skills on its forty-foot vertical faces. (Those who just want to appreciate the extraordinary view can take the steps around its back.) Carved into similarly hard volcanic stone across the street are the mortar holes used by the Ohlone to grind acorns into flour. In between, and in stark contrast, stands the rusting hulk of a Cold War-era air-raid siren.

West Berkeley and the waterfront

From downtown Berkeley and the UC campus, **University Avenue** runs downhill toward the bay, lined by increasingly shabby frontages of motels and massage parlors. The liveliest part of this **West Berkeley** area is around the intersection of University and San Pablo Avenues – the pre-freeway main highway north – where a community of recent immigrants from India and Pakistan have set up stores and restaurants that serve some of the best of the Bay Area's rare curries.

The area between San Pablo Avenue and the bay is the oldest part of Berkeley, and a handful of hundred-year-old houses and churches – such as the two white-spired Gothic Revival structures on Hearst Avenue – survive from the time when this district was a separate city, known as Ocean View. The neighborhood also holds remnants of Berkeley's industrial past, and many of the old warehouses and factory premises have been converted into living and working spaces for artists, craftspeople and computer software companies. The newly polished and yuppified stretch of **Fourth Street** between Gilman and University features upscale furniture outlets and quaint gourmet delis, as well as some outstanding restaurants. A safe bet is a stop at **Takara Sake USA Inc**, 708 Addison St. Open daily from noon–6pm, they provide free tastings and sell bottles of their famed rice wine.

The I-80 freeway, and the still-used rail tracks that run alongside it, pretty well manage to cut Berkeley off from its waterfront. The best way to get there is to take AC Transit bus #51, which runs regularly down University Avenue. Once a major hub for the transbay ferry services – to shorten journey times a three-mile-long pier was constructed, much of which still sticks out into the bay – the **Berkeley Marina** is now one of the prime spots on the bay for leisure activities, especially windsurfing and kayaking.

The North Bay and inland valleys

Compared to the urbanized bayfront cities of Oakland and Berkeley, the rest of the East Bay is sparsely populated, and places of interest are few and far between. The **North Bay** is home to some of the Bay Area's heaviest industry – oil refineries and chemical plants dominate the landscape – but also holds a few remarkably unchanged waterfront towns that merit a side trip if you're passing by. Away from the bay, the **inland valleys** are a whole other world of dry rolling hills dominated by the towering peak of **Mount Diablo**. Dozens of tract house developments have made commuter suburbs out of what were once cattle ranches and farms, but so far the region has been able to absorb the numbers and still feels rural, despite having doubled in population in the past twenty years.

The North Bay

North of Berkeley there's not a whole lot to see or do. Off the Eastshore Freeway in **ALBANY**, Golden Gate Fields has **horse-racing** from October to June, and San Pablo Avenue's strip of **bars** and **clubs**, including *Club Mallard* (no. 752), *The Ivy Room* (no. 858) and *The Hotsy-Totsy* (no. 601), are some of the best in the East Bay. That is, if you're looking for authentic, gritty saloons featuring live rock n' roll on weekends, well-stocked jukeboxes and pool tables reminiscent of San Francisco's Mission district. **EL CERRITO**'s main contribution to world culture was the band Creedence Clearwater Revival, who staged most of their *Born on the Bayou* publicity photographs in the wilds of Tilden Park in the hills above; El Cerrito is still home to one of the best record stores in California, Down Home Music, at 10341 San Pablo Ave, which stocks an amazing array of blues, gospel, Cajun, Tex-Mex, old time, jazz, world and rock. **RICHMOND**, at the top of the bay, was once a boomtown, building ships during World War II at the Kaiser Shipyards, which employed 100,000 workers between 1940 and its closure in 1945. Now it's the proud home of the gigantic Standard Oil refinery, the center of which you drive through before crossing the **Richmond–San Rafael Bridge** ($2) to Marin County. About the only reason to stop in Richmond is that it marks the north end of the BART line, and the adjacent Amtrak station is a better terminal for journeys to and from San Francisco than the end of the line in West Oakland.

Though not really worth a trip in itself, if you're heading from the East Bay to Marin County, **Point Richmond** merits a look. A cozy little town tucked away at the foot of the bridge between the refinery and the bay, its many Victorian houses are rapidly becoming commuter territory for upwardly mobile professionals from San Francisco. Through the narrow tunnel that cuts under the hill stands the most obvious sign of this potential gentrification: "Brickyard Landing," an East Bay docklands development with modern bay-view condos, a private yacht harbor, and a token gesture to the area's industrial past – disused brick kilns, hulking next to the tennis courts on the front lawn. The rest of the waterfront is taken up by the broad and usually deserted strand of **Keller Beach**, which stretches for half a mile along the sometimes windy shoreline.

The Carquinez Straits

At the top of the bay some 25 miles north of Oakland, the land along the Carquinez Straits is a bit off the beaten track, but it's an area of some natural beauty and much historic interest. The still-small towns along the waterfront seem worlds away from the bustle of the rest of the Bay Area, but how long they'll be able to resist the pressure of the expanding commuter belt is anybody's guess. AC Transit #74 runs every hour from Richmond BART north to **CROCKETT** at the west end of the narrow straits – a tiny town cut into the steep hillsides above the water that seems entirely dependent upon the massive C&H Sugar factory at its foot, whose giant neon sign lights up the town and the adjacent Carquinez Bridge.

From Crockett, the narrow Carquinez Straits Scenic Drive, an excellent cycling route, heads east along the Sacramento river. A turn two miles along drops down to **PORT COSTA**, a small town that was dependent upon ferry traffic across the straits to Benicia until it lost its livelihood when the bridge was built at Crockett. It's still a nice enough place to watch the huge ships pass by on their way to and from the inland ports of Sacramento and Stockton. If you don't have a bike (or a car), you can enjoy the view while riding on one of the Amtrak trains which run alongside the water from Oakland and Richmond, not stopping until Martinez at the eastern end of the straits, two miles north of the John Muir house (see p.506).

Benicia

On the north side of the Straits, and hard to get to without a car, **BENICIA** is the most substantial of the historic waterfront towns, but one that has definitely seen better days.

Founded in 1847, it initially rivaled San Francisco as the major Bay Area port and was even the state capital for a time; but despite Benicia's better weather and fine deep-water harbor, San Francisco eventually became the main transportation point for the fortunes of the Gold Rush, and the town very nearly faded away altogether. Examples of Benicia's efforts to become a major city stand poignantly around the very compact downtown area, most conspicuously the 1852 Greek Revival structure that was used as the **first State Capitol** for just thirteen months. The building has been restored as a museum (daily 10am–5pm; $2), furnished in the legislative style of the time, complete with top hats on the tables and shining spittoons every few feet.

A walking-tour map of Benicia's many intact Victorian houses and churches is available from the **tourist office**, on 601 First Street (Mon–Fri 8am–5pm, Sat–Sun 11am–3pm; ☎707/745-2120), including on its itinerary the steeply pitched roofs and gingerbread eaves of the **Frisbie-Walsh house** at 235 East L Street – a prefabricated Gothic Revival building that was shipped here in pieces from Boston in 1849. Across the City Hall park, the arched ceiling beams of **St Paul's Episcopal Church** look like an upturned ship's hull; it was built by shipwrights from the Pacific Mail Steamship Company, one of Benicia's many successful nineteenth-century shipyards. Half a dozen former brothels and saloons stand in various stages of decay and restoration along First Street down near the waterfront, from where the world's largest train ferries used to ply the waters between Benicia and Port Costa until 1930.

In recent years Benicia has attracted a number of artists and craftspeople, and you can watch glass-blowers and furniture-makers at work in the **Yuba Complex** at 675 and 701 East H Street (Mon–Fri 10am–5pm, Sat 10am–4pm). Ceramic artist Judy Chicago and sculptor Robert Arneson are among those who have worked in the converted studios and modern light industrial parks around the sprawling fortifications of the old **Benicia Arsenal** east of the downtown area, whose thickly walled sandstone buildings formed the main Army storage facility for weapons and ammunition from 1851 up to and including the Korean War. One of the oddest parts of the complex is the **Camel Barn** in the **Benicia Historical Museum** (Wed–Sun 1–4pm; free; ☎707/745-5869). The structure used to house camels that the Army imported in 1856 to transport supplies across the deserts of the Southwestern US. The experiment failed, and the camels were kept here until they were sold off in 1864.

Vallejo and Six Flags Marine World

Across the Carquinez Bridge from Crockett, the biggest and dullest of the North Bay towns – **VALLEJO** – was, like Benicia, an early capital of California, though it now lacks any sign of its historical significance. In contrast to most of the other Gold Rush-era towns that line the Straits, Vallejo remained economically vital, largely because of the massive military presence here at the **Mare Island Naval Shipyard**, a sprawling, relentlessly gray complex that covers an area twice the size of Golden Gate Park. Closed in late 1997, Mare Island was once Vallejo's largest employer, and its less than glamorous history – the yard built and maintained supply ships and submarines, not carriers or battleships – is recounted in a small **museum** in the old city hall building at 734 Marin Street (Tues–Sat 10am–4.30pm; $1.50), where the highlight is a working periscope that looks out across the bay. Though no great thrill, it's worth a quick stop, sited in the center of town right on Hwy-29, the main route from the East Bay to the Wine Country.

The best reason to come to Vallejo, however, is the newly renovated **Six Flags Marine World** (daily 10am–10pm; $34; ☎707/643-ORCA), five miles north of Vallejo off I-80 at the Marine World Parkway (Hwy-37) exit. Billing itself as the nation's only wildlife park, oceanarium and theme park, it offers a well above average range of performing sea lions, dolphins, and killer whales kept in approximations of their natural habitats, as well as water-ski stunt shows and several newly constructed roller coasters, including the floorless Medusa, on which your legs dangle as you zoom through inversions at 65mph. The animals in the park seem very well cared for, their quarters are clean and spacious, and the shows are fun for all but the most jaded. The shark exhibit lets you walk through a transparent tunnel alongside twenty-foot Great Whites, and the tropical butterfly aviary is truly amazing. The most enjoyable way to get here from San Francisco is on the Blue and Gold Fleet **ferry** from Fisherman's Wharf, which takes an hour each way and costs $15 round trip (☎415/773-1188 for details). You can also take BART, getting off at the El Cerrito Del Norte stop where you catch the Vallejo BARTLink bus (☎707/648-4666) to the park.

The inland valleys

BART tunnels from Oakland through the Berkeley Hills to the leafy-green stockbroker settlement of **ORINDA**, continuing east through the increasingly hot and dry landscape to **CONCORD**, site of a controversial nuclear weapons depot. A few years ago, a civilly disobedient blockade here ended in protester Brian Wilson losing his legs under the wheels of a slow-moving munitions train. The event raised public awareness – before it happened few people knew of the depot's existence, and earned Wilson a place in a Lawrence Ferlinghetti poem, "A Buddha in the Woodpile" – but otherwise it's business as usual.

From the Pleasant Hill BART station, one stop before the end of the line, Contra Costa County Connection buses leave every thirty minutes for **MARTINEZ**, the seat of county government, passing the preserved home of naturalist **John Muir** (Wed–Sun 10am–4.30pm; $2), just off Hwy-4 two miles south of Martinez. Muir, an articulate, persuasive Scot whose writings and political activism were of vital importance in the preservation of America's wilderness, spent much of his life exploring and writing about the majestic Sierra Nevada mountains, particularly Yosemite. He was also one of the founders of the **Sierra Club** – a wilderness lobby and education organization still active today (see p.335 for more). Anyone familiar with the image of this thin, bearded man wandering the mountains with his knapsack, notebook and packet of tea might be surprised to see his very conventional, upper-class Victorian home, now restored to its appearance when Muir died in 1914. Built by Muir's father-in-law, only those parts of the house Muir added himself reflect much of the personality of the man, not least the massive, rustic fireplace he had built in the East Parlor so he could have a "real mountain campfire." The bulk of Muir's personal belongings and artifacts are displayed in his study on the upper floor, and in the adjacent room an exhibition documents the history of the Sierra Club and Muir's battles to protect America's wilderness.

Behind the bell-towered main house is a large, still productive orchard where Muir cultivated grapes, pears and cherries to earn the money to finance his explorations (you can sample the fruits free of charge, pre-picked by staff gardeners). Beyond the orchard is the 1849 **Martinez Adobe**, homestead of the original Spanish land-grant settlers and now a small **museum** of Mexican colonial culture. The contrast between Mexican and American cultures in early California is fascinating and, as a bonus, the building's two-foot-thick walls keep it refreshingly cool on a typically hot summer day.

At the foot of Mount Diablo, fifteen miles south, playwright **Eugene O'Neill** used the money he got for winning the Nobel Prize for Literature in 1936 to build a home and sanctuary for himself, which he named **Tao House**. It was here, before 1944 when he was struck down with Parkinson's Disease, that he wrote many of his best-known plays: *The Iceman Cometh*, *A Moon for the Misbegotten* and *Long Day's Journey into Night*. Readings and performances of his works are sometimes given in the house, which is open to visitors, though you must reserve a place on one of the free guided **tours** (Wed–Sun 10am & 12.30pm; ☎925/838-0249). There's no parking on site, so the tours pick you up in the tony town of **DANVILLE**. Danville's richest neighborhood,

Blackhawk, is the home of the **Blackhawk Automotive Museum,** 3700 Blackhawk Plaza Circle (Wed–Sun 10am–5pm; $8; ☎925/736-2277), an impressive collection of classic cars from Britain, Germany, Italy and the US, along with artwork inspired by them.

As for **Mount Diablo** itself, it rises up from the rolling ranchlands at its foot to a height of nearly four thousand feet, its summit and flanks preserved within **Mount Diablo State Park** (daily 8am–sunset; parking $5). North Gate, the main road through the park, reaches within three hundred feet of the top, so it's a popular place for an outing and you're unlikely to be alone to enjoy the marvelous view: on a clear day you can see over two hundred miles in every direction. There's no public transportation, though the Sierra Club sometimes organizes day-trips: see "Basics," p.54.

Two main entrances lead into the park, both well marked off I-680. The one from the southwest by way of Danville passes by the **ranger station**, where you can pick up a trail map ($1) which lists the best day-hikes. The other runs from the northwest by way of Walnut Creek, and the routes join together five miles from the summit. March and April, when the wildflowers are out, are the best times to come, and since mornings are ideal for getting the clearest view, you should drive to the top first and then head back down to a trailhead for a hike, or to one of the many picnic spots for a leisurely lunch. In summer it can get desperately hot and dry, and parts of the park are closed because of fire danger.

Livermore and Altamont

Fifteen miles southeast of Mount Diablo on the main road out of the Bay Area (I-580) or via WHEELS #12X from the Dublin/Pleasanton BART, the rolling hills around sleepy **LIVERMORE** are covered with thousands of shining, spinning, high-tech **windmills**, placed here by a private power company to take advantage of the nearly constant winds. The largest wind farm in the world, you'll probably have seen it used in a number of TV ads as a space-age backdrop to hype flashy new cars or sexy perfumes. Though the federal government provides no funding for this non-polluting, renewable source of energy, it spends billions of dollars every year designing and building nuclear weapons and other sinister applications of modern technology at the nearby **Lawrence Livermore Laboratories**, where most of the research and development of the nuclear arsenal takes place. A small **visitor center** (Mon–Fri 9am–4.30pm, Sat & Sun noon–5pm; free) two miles south of I-580 on Greenville Road, holds hands-on exhibits showing off various scientific phenomena and devices.

Up and over the hills to the east, where I-580 joins I-5 for the four-hundred-mile route south through the Central Valley to Los Angeles, stand the remains of **Altamont Speedway**, site of the nightmarish Rolling Stones concert in December 1969. The free concert, which was captured in the film *Gimme Shelter*, was intended to be a sort of second Woodstock, staged in order to counter allegations that the Stones had ripped off their fans during a long US tour. The event was a complete disaster: three people died, one of whom was kicked and stabbed to death by the Hell's Angels "security guards" – in full view of the cameras – after pointing a gun at Mick Jagger while he sang *Sympathy for the Devil*. Needless to say, no historical plaque marks the site.

East Bay eating

Official home of **California cuisine** and with some of the best restaurants in the state, Berkeley is an upmarket diner's paradise. But it's also a college town, and you can eat cheaply and well, especially around the southern end of the campus, along and around Telegraph Avenue. The rest of the East Bay is less remarkable, except for when it comes to **plain American** food such as barbecued ribs, grilled steaks or deli sandwiches, for which it's unbeatable.

Budget food: diners and delis

Barney's, 4162 Piedmont Ave, Oakland (☎510/655-7180), 5819 College Ave, Rockridge (☎510/601-0444) and 1591 Solano Ave, Berkeley (☎510/526-8185). The East Bay's most popular burgers – including meatless ones – smothered in dozens of different toppings.

Bette's Ocean View Diner, 1807 Fourth St, Berkeley (☎510/548-9494). Named after the neighborhood, not after the vista, but serving up some of the Bay Area's best breakfasts and lunches. Very popular on weekends, when you may have to wait an hour for a table, so come during the week if possible.

Flint's Barbecue, 3314 San Pablo Ave, Oakland (☎510/653-0593). Open until the early hours of the morning for some of the best ribs and link sausages west of Chicago, served at moderate prices.

Genova Delicatessen, 5095 Telegraph Ave, Oakland (☎510/652-7401). Friendly deli complete with hanging sausages that serves up superb sandwiches for around $5.

Holy Land Kosher Food, 677 Rand Ave, Oakland (☎510/272-0535). Casual diner-style restaurant near the lake serving moderately-priced Israeli food, including excellent falafel, to those who can find it.

Homemade Café, 2454 Sacramento St, Berkeley (☎510/845-1940). Non-traditional California-style Mexican and Jewish food served for breakfast and lunch at shared tables when crowded. Expect to pay $10-$20 per person.

Lois the Pie Queen, 851 60th St at Adeline, Oakland (☎510/658-5616). Famous around the bay for its Southern-style sweet potato and fresh fruit pies, this cozy diner also serves massive, down-home breakfasts and Sunday dinners, all for under $10.

Rick & Ann's, 2922 Domingo Ave, Berkeley (☎510/649-8538). Every weekend the crowds line up outside this neighborhood diner. Hey, even in Berkeley sometimes folks want meatloaf and mashed potatoes instead of arugula.

Saul's Deli, 1475 Shattuck Ave, Berkeley (☎510/848-DELI). For pastrami, corned beef, kreplach or knishes, this is the place. Great sandwiches and picnic fixings to take away, plus a full range of sit-down evening meals.

Top Dog, 2534 Durant Ave, Berkeley (☎510/843-7450). OK, so the competition isn't exactly stiff, but when locals and starving college kids get a craving for the all-American treat, this dog always has its day.

Your Black Muslim Bakery, 5836 San Pablo Ave, Oakland (☎510/658-7080), 365 Seventeenth St (☎510/839-1313). Pastries and pamphlets bringing together Oakland's diverse masses over some awesome sweet rolls.

American/California

Bay Wolf, 3853 Piedmont Ave, Oakland (☎510/655-6004). Comfortable restaurant serving grilled meat and fish dishes on an ever-changing, moderately expensive menu.

Café Fanny, 1603 San Pablo, Berkeley (☎510/524-5447). Delicious and relatively cheap breakfasts and lunches in a small and unlikely space with a sparse industrial decor. Owned by Alice Waters, of *Chez Panisse* fame (see below).

Cafe Rouge, 1782 Fourth St, Berkeley (☎510/525-1440). Specializing in delicately prepared organic meats; they have their own butcher shop.

Chez Panisse, 1517 Shattuck Ave, North Berkekey (☎510/548-5525). The California restaurant to which all others are compared. Chef Alice Waters is widely given credit for first inventing California cuisine. She hasn't lost a step on the years since, though it is pricey – expect to pay about $100 for a meal for two with wine.

Citron, 5484 College Ave, Rockridge (☎510/653-5484). Neighborhood gem that rivals San Francisco's best restaurants. Warm, unpretentious service and exquisite food, but expensive.

Fatapple's, 1346 Martin Luther King Jr Way, Berkeley (☎510/526-2260). Crowded but pleasant family-oriented restaurant with excellent cheap American breakfasts and an assortment of sandwiches and burgers for lunch or dinner.

Gulf Coast Oyster Bar & Specialty Co, 736 Washington St, Oakland (☎510/836-3663). Popular and reasonably priced Cajun-flavored seafood restaurant.

Lalime's, 1329 Gilman St, North Berkeley (☎510/527-9838). A culinary dissertation on irony, as rich leftist Berkeley professors chow down on rich veal, pate fois gras and other distinctly un-PC fare, in a casual setting.

Rivoli, 1539 Solano Ave, Berkeley (☎510/526-2542). Delivering all that is wonderful about Berkeley dining: first-rate fresh food, courteous service and a casual, friendly atmosphere. All followed by a steep bill.

Spenger's, 1919 Fourth St, West Berkeley (☎510/845-7771). About as far as you can get from the subtle charms of Berkeley's high-style restaurants, this is nonetheless a local institution. As one of the largest chains in the Bay Area, *Spenger's* serves up literally tons of seafood to thousands of customers daily.

Asian, African and Indian

Blue Nile, 2525 Telegraph Ave, Berkeley (☎510/540-6777). Offering Ethiopian comfort food at the end of the teeming Telegraph Avenue strip, and just the place to flee the endless parade of bead merchants and incense burners.

Breads of India, 2448 Sacramento, Berkeley (☎510/848-7648). This gourmet curry house turns out delicious fresh specials daily for under $10.

Cha Am, 1543 Shattuck, Berkeley (☎510/848-9664). Climb the stairs up to this unlikely, always crowded small restaurant for deliciously spicy Thai food at bargain prices.

Jade Villa, 800 Broadway, downtown Oakland (☎510/839-1688). For endless dim sum lunches or traditional Cantonese meals, this is one of the best places in Oakland's thriving Chinatown.

Kirala, 2100 Ward St, Berkeley (☎510/549-3486). Many argue that *Kirala* serves the best sushi in the Bay Area. Others argue that it's the best in the world. Moderate pricing, too – expect to pay $10-$20 to get your fill.

Le Cheval, 1007 Clay St, Oakland (☎510/763-8495). Serving simple Vietnamese the way it was meant to be, the spacious surroundings and affordable prices here won't let you down.

Long Life Vegi House, 2129 University Ave, Berkeley (☎510/845-6072). Vegetarian cooking (as the name suggests) that's perpetually popular with Cal students.

Nan Yang, 6048 College Ave, Oakland (☎510/655-3298). Burmese food served in colorful, large, palate-exciting portions. The political refugee owner/chef is willing to discuss all his esoteric delicacies.

O Chame, 1830 Fourth St, West Berkeley (☎510/841-8783). One of the very best Japanese restaurants in the US, with beautifully prepared sashimi and sushi as well as a full range of authentic Japanese specialties. A treat and not too expensive, either, in the $10-$20 range.

Sala Thai, 807 First St, Benicia (☎707/745-4331). Small-town, moderately priced Thai food can be just as delicious here as in any big city. Check out the enormous fish tank as your feet dangle in foot caves under the tables.

Steve's Barbeque, in the Durant Center, 2521 Durant Ave, Berkeley (☎510/848-6166). Excellent, low- priced Korean food (*kim chee* to die for); other cafés in the center sell Mexican food, healthy sandwiches, deep-fried doughnuts and slices of pizza – not to mention bargain pitchers of beer.

Vik's Chaat Corner, 726 Allston Way at Fourth (☎510/644-4412). A terrific lunchtime destination offering wide array of Indian snacks. The ambiance is minimal, leaving nothing to distract you from the large selection of delicious morsels. The small portions and low prices only open more possibilities for experimentation.

Yoshi's, 510 Embarcadero West, Oakland (☎510/238-9200). Classy sushi restaurant attached to the equally classy jazz club. The cornerstone of the redeveloped Jack London Square district, so it gets pretty packed on weekends.

Italian and pizza

Blondie's Pizza, 2340 Telegraph Ave, Berkeley (☎510/548-1129). Delicious takeout New York-style pizza by the slice ($2.25, plus topping) or by the pie; stays open until 2am, and is always crowded.

Café Rustica, 5422 College Ave, Oakland (☎510/654-1601). Intimate adobe-style, upscale eatery for designer pizza with a pesto and sun-dried tomatoes motif. If it's too expensive, try the tapas bar upstairs.

Cheese Board Pizza, 1512 Shattuck Ave, Berkeley (☎510/549-3055). Tiny storefront selling some of the world's best "designer pizza" at very reasonable prices: $2.50 a slice, with a different topping every day. Worth searching out, but keeps irregular hours; usually Tues–Sat 11.30am–2pm & 4.30–7pm.

LaVal's Pizza, 1834 Euclid Ave, Berkeley (☎510/843-5617). Great graduate student hangout near the North Gate of campus. Pool table, widescreen TV broadcasting sports, good selection of beers, and great pizza. Lunch special of a big slice and soda for $2.25.

Locanda Olmo, 2985 College Ave, Berkeley (☎510/848-5544). Simple but discriminating menu at this tiny, intimate trattoria in the charming Elmwood neighborhood with moderate prices.

Oliveto, 5655 College Ave, Rockridge (☎510/547-5356). With his back-to-basics recipes and dependence on home-grown ingredients, chef Paul Bertolli creates appetizing gourmet Italian cuisine. Expensive, but worth it.

Zachary's, 5801 College Ave, Rockridge (☎510/655-6385) and 1853 Solano Ave, North Berkeley (☎510/525-5950). Zealously defended as the best pizza in the Bay Area. It's also one of the only places offering the rich, deep-dish Chicago style of pizza.

Mexican and South American

Cesar, 1515 Shattuck Ave, Berkeley (☎510/883-0222). Eternally crowded tapas bar serving small dishes overflowing with taste; Loosely affiliated with *Chez Panisse*, the combination of quality and a relaxed atmosphere has made it a cultish destination for locals.

Cancun Taqueria, 2134 Allston Way, Berkeley (☎510549-0964). Popular cheap neighborhood burrito joint with live music some nights of the week.

Juan's Place, 941 Carleton St, West Berkeley (☎510/845-6904). The original Berkeley Mexican restaurant, with cheap, great food (tons of it) and an interesting mix of people.

Mario's La Fiesta, 2444 Telegraph Ave, Berkeley (☎510/540-9123). Always crowded with students and other budget-minded souls who flock here for the heaped portions of good, inexpensive Mexican food.

Picante, 1328 Sixth St, West Berkeley (☎510/525-3121). Good, inexpensive tacos with fresh salsa, plus live jazz on weekends.

Taqueria Morelia, 4481 E 14th St, East Oakland (☎510/535-6030). Excellent burritos and the more unusual but authentic *tortas*.

Tijuana Restaurant, 1308 E. Fourteenth St, East Oakland (☎510/532-5575). Excellent and authentic Mexican food; famed for its *mariscada* – a plate piled high with garlicky seafood and fresh vegetables.

Tropix, 3814 Piedmont Ave, Oakland (☎510/653-2444). Large portions of fruity Caribbean delicacies at reasonable prices, with authentic jerk sauce and thirst-quenching mango juice.

French

Britt-Marie's Cafe and Wine Bar, 1369 Solano Ave, Albany (☎510/527-1314). Along with a fine selection of mostly Californian wines by the glass, well-priced eclectic home cooking, plus outstanding chocolate cake, is also served.

La Note, 2337 Shattuck Ave, Berkeley (☎510/843-1535). The appropriately sunny, light cuisine of Provence isn't the only flavor you'll find in this petite dining room: students and teachers from the Jazzschool (sic) next door routinely stop in for casual jam sessions.

Ice cream and desserts

Dreyers Grand Ice Cream Parlor, 5925 College Ave, Oakland (☎510/658-0502). Oakland's own rich ice cream, which is distributed through California, is served at this small, slightly dull Rockridge café.

Fenton's Creamery, 4226 Piedmont Ave, N Oakland (☎510/658-7000). A brightly lit 1950s ice cream and sandwich shop, open until 11pm on weeknights, midnight on weekends.

Yogurt Park, 2433a Durant Ave, Berkeley (☎510/549-0570). Frozen yogurt a specialty; open until midnight for the student throngs.

Specialty shops and markets

Acme Bread, 1601 San Pablo Ave, West Berkeley (☎510/524-1327). Small bakery that supplies most of Berkeley's better restaurants; the house specialty is delicious sourdough baguettes.

Berkeley Bowl, 2777 Shattuck Ave, Berkeley (☎510/841-6346). A converted bowling alley which is now an enormous produce, bulk and healthfood market. The least expensive grocery in town, with the largest selection of fresh food.

Cheese Board, 1504 Shattuck Ave, North Berkeley (☎510/549-3183). Collectively owned and operated since 1967, this was one of the first outposts in Berkeley's gourmet ghetto and is still going strong, offering over 200 varieties of cheese and a range of delicious breads. Great pizzas a few doors down, too; see above.

La Farine, 6323 College Ave, Rockridge (☎510/654-0338). Small but highly rated French-style bakery, with excellent pain au chocolat.

Monterey Foods, 1550 Hopkins St, North Berkeley (☎510/526-6042). The main supplier of exotic produce to Berkeley's gourmet restaurants, this boisterous market also has the highest quality fresh fruit and vegetables available.

East Bay drinking: cafés and bars

One of the best things about visiting the East Bay is the opportunity to enjoy its many **cafés**. Concentrated most densely around the UC Berkeley campus, they're on a par with the best of San Francisco's North Beach for bohemian atmosphere – heady with the smell of coffee, and from dawn to near midnight full of earnest characters wearing their intellects on their sleeves. If you're not after a caffeine fix, you can generally also get a glass of beer, wine, or fresh fruit juice, though for serious drinking you'll be better off in one of the many **bars**, particularly in rough-hewn Oakland. Grittier versions of what you'd find in San Francisco, they're mostly blue-collar, convivial, and almost always cheaper. Not surprisingly, Berkeley's bars are brimming with students and academics.

Cafés

Anna's, 1801 University Ave at Grant (☎510/849-2662). A local institution, thanks to owner Anna de Leon's prominent involvement with city politics, not to mention her regular singing gig.

Brewed Awakenings,1807 Euclid Ave, Berkeley (☎510/540-8865). Spacious coffee and tea house near the North Gate of campus frequented by professors and grad students. Friendly staff, plenty of seating, and lovely artwork on the red-brick walls. Annually confirmed as "Best Café to Study In" by the student press.

Cafe Intermezzo, 2442 Telegraph Avenue at Dwight, Berkeley (☎510/849-4592). Huge sandwiches on homemade sliced bread, even bigger salads, and great coffee – all very fresh and cheap.

Café Mediterraneum, 2475 Telegraph Ave, Berkeley (☎510/841-5634). Berkeley's oldest café featuring sidewalk seating. Straight out of the Beat archives: beards and berets optional, battered paperbacks de rigueur.

Café Milano, 2522 Bancroft Way, Berkeley (☎510/644-3100). Airy, arty café across from UC Berkeley.

Café Strada, 2300 College Ave (☎510/843-5282). Upmarket, open-air café where art and architecture students cross paths with would-be lawyers and chess wizards.

Coffee Mill, 3363 Grand Ave, Oakland (☎510/465-4224). Spacious room that doubles as an art gallery, and often hosts poetry readings.

Mama Bear's, 6536 Telegraph Ave, N Oakland (☎510/428-9684). Mainly a women's bookstore, it doubles as a café and meeting place and has regular readings, often for women only, by lesbian and feminist writers.

Royal Ground, 6255 College Ave, Oakland (☎510/653-5458). Bright, modern and relaxing spot in the Rockridge area, with outdoor seating. Perfect for a leisurely afternoon with the newspaper.

Bars

Albatross Pub, 1822 San Pablo Ave, Berkeley (☎510/THE-BIRD). Popular student super-bar, replete with darts, pool, board games and fireplace. Serves a large selection of ales from around the world, including a pretty good pint of Guinness. Live jazz, flamenco and blues music on weekends (free-$2).

Bison Brewing Company, 2598 Telegraph Ave, Berkeley (☎510/841-7734). Eat and drink on the terrace, at great prices, where some of the best Bay Area beers are brewed. Honey Basil ale is highly recommended. Noisy bands on the weekend.

Brennan's, Fourth Street and University, Berkeley (☎510/841-0960). Solidly blue-collar hangout that's a great place for drinking inexpensive beers and watching a game on TV.

Cato's Alehouse, 3891 Piedmont, Oakland (☎510/655-3349). Very local and casual with a good beer selection. Relax with a couple of beers and a pizza or sandwich.

Heinhold's First and Last Chance Saloon, 56 Jack London Square, Oakland (☎510/839-6761). Authentic waterfront bar that's hardly changed since the turn of the century, when Jack London was a regular. They still haven't bothered to fix the slanted floor caused by the 1906 earthquake.

Jupiter, 2181 Shattuck Ave, Berkeley (☎510/THE-ROCK). Many types of beer to select from at this local favorite. Live jazz on weekends, an excellent atmosphere, wood-fired pizza, and an outdoor beer garden.

The Kingfish, 5227 Claremont Ave, Oakland (☎510/655-7373). More like a tumbledown shed than a bar, selling low-priced pitchers of cold beer to UC Berkeley rugby players and other headbangers.

Pyramid Brewery, 901 Gilman St, Berkeley (☎510/528-9880). Huge post-industrial space makes a surprisingly casual spot to sip the suds. Outdoor film screenings on weekend nights during summer.

Rickey's Sports Lounge, 15028 Hesperian Blvd, San Leandro, near Bayfair BART (☎510/352-0200). With seven giant-screen TVs and 35 others spread around the cavernous room, this bar-cum-restaurant is the place to go to watch sports.

Triple Rock Brewery, 1920 Shattuck Ave, Berkeley (☎510/843-2739). Buzzing, all-American beer bar: the decor is Edward Hopper-era retro, and the beers (brewed on the premises) are highly carbonated to suit the soda-pop palates of the studenty crowd, but it's still fun.

The White Horse, 6560 Telegraph Ave at 66th St, Oakland (☎510/652-3820). Oakland's oldest gay bar – a smallish, friendly place, with mixed nightly dancing for men and women.

Nightlife

Nightlife is where the East Bay really comes into its own. Even more than in San Francisco, dancing to canned music and paying high prices for flashy decor is not the thing to do, which means that discos are virtually non-existent. Instead there are dozens of **live music** venues, covering a range of musical tastes and styles – from small, unpretentious jazz clubs to buzzing R&B venues – of which Oakland's hot spots are unsurpassed. Berkeley's clubs tend more towards folk and world music, with occasional bouts of hard-core thrash, and the university itself holds two of the best medium-sized venues in the entire Bay Area, both of which attract touring big-name stars. **Tickets** for most venues are available at their box office or, for a $3 service charge, through BASS (☎510/762-2277).

Though not bad by US standards, the East Bay theater scene isn't exactly thriving, and shows tend to be politically worthy rather than dramatically innovative. By contrast, the range of **films** is first class, with a dozen movie theaters showing new releases and Berkeley's revamped Pacific Film Archive, one of the world's finest film libraries, filling its screens with obscure but brilliant art flicks. Check the free *East Bay Express* or the *SF Weekly* for details of who and **what's on**.

The large performance venues

Berkeley Community Theater, 1930 Allston Way, Berkeley (☎510/845-2308). Jimi Hendrix played here, and the 3500-seat theater still hosts major rock concerts (Oasis to Tracy Chapman) and community events.

Center for Contemporary Music, Mills College, 5000 MacArthur Blvd, Oakland (☎510/430-2191). One of the prime centers in the world for experimental music.

Oakland Coliseum Complex, Coliseum BART, near the airport (☎510/639-7700). Mostly stadium shows, inside the 18,000-seat arena or outdoors in the adjacent 55,000-seat coliseum.

Paramount Theater, 2025 Broadway, downtown Oakland (☎510/465-6400). Beautifully restored Art Deco masterpiece, hosting classical concerts, big-name crooners, ballets, operas and a growing roster of rap and rock shows. Tickets $6–50. Some nights they play old Hollywood classics for $7.

Zellerbach Hall and the outdoor **Greek Theater** on the UC Berkeley campus (☎510/642-9988). Two of the prime spots for catching touring big names in the Bay Area. Zellberbach usually showcases classical music and dance, while the Greek welcomes popular acts like the Indigo Girls or Ben Harper. Tickets $20–50.

Live music venues

Ashkenaz, 1317 San Pablo Ave, Berkeley (☎510/525-5054). World music and dance café. Acts range from modern Afro-beat to the best of the Balkans. Kids and under-21s welcome. Cover $4–10.

Blakes on Telegraph, 2367 Telegraph Ave, Berkeley (☎510/848-0886). Student-patroned saloon with a funky roster of live music most nights of the week. Latin, funk, soul, hip-hop, roots, rock, reggae, blues and more. $3-5.

Eli's Mile High Club, 3629 Martin Luther King Jr Way, N Oakland (☎510/655-6661). The best of the Bay Area blues clubs. Waitresses balance pitchers of beer on their heads to facilitate a safer passage through the rocking crowds. Cover $6–15.

Freight and Salvage, 1111 Addison St, W Berkeley (☎510/548-1761). Singer-songwriters in a coffeehouse setting. Cover averages $15.

Gilman Street Project, 924 Gilman St, W Berkeley (☎510/525-9926). On the outer edge of the hard-core punk scene. Cover $5–10.

Jimmie's, 1731 San Pablo Ave, Oakland (☎510/268-8445). Live blues, disco, ballads and the occasional comedy act and fashion show at this lively bar. $5-30.

Kimball's East, 4800 Shellmound St, Emeryville (☎510/658-2555). Fairly slick, high-style jazz and dancing venue. Cover $10–25.

La Peña Cultural Center, 3105 Shattuck Ave, Berkeley near Ashby BART (☎510/849-2568). More folk than rock, often politically charged. Cover averages $15.

Maiko Dance Club, 1629 San Pablo Ave, Berkeley (☎510/527-8226). Salsa and ballroom dance set to a live band. Very chic. Lessons available. $10-20.

Mr. E's, 2286 Shattuck Ave, Berkeley (☎510/848-2009). Owned by salsa performer Pete Escovedo (the father of Prince percussionist Sheila E) and with a salsa-centric schedule to match. Free to $20.

Starry Plough, 3101 Shattuck Ave, Berkeley (☎510/841-2082). Music ranges from noisy punk to alternative pop to country to traditional Irish folk, and the crowd is just as varied. Doubles as a friendly saloon and restaurant in the afternoon and early evening. Free to $5.

Yoshi's World Class Jazz House, 510 Embarcadero West, Oakland (☎510/238-9200). If you only have time or money to visit one music venue, let it be this one. The West Coast's premier jazz club near Jack London Square regularly attracts a world-class roster of performers nightly. The place is almost always full. $5-40.

Cinemas

Act One and Act Two, 2128 Center St, Berkeley (☎510/548-7200). Foreign films and non-mainstream American ones.

Grand Lake Theater, 3200 Grand Ave, Oakland (☎510/452-3556). The grand dame of East Bay picture palaces, right on Lake Merritt, showing the best of the current major releases.

Pacific Film Archive, 2575 Bancroft at Bowditch, Berkeley (☎510/642-5249). The archive's splendid new digs plays the West Coast's best selection of cinema. It features nightly showings of classics, third world and experimental films world, plus revivals of otherwise forgotten favorites. Call for listings or pick up a free monthly calendar around campus. Two films a night; tickets $7.

UC Theater, 2036 University Ave, Berkeley, just below Shattuck Ave (☎510/843-FILM). Popular revival house, with a huge auditorium and a daily double feature featuring funky theme-weeks of noir, melodrama and other genres. Tickets $5 matinee, $7 thereafter.

Theater

Berkeley Repertory Theater, 2025 Addison St, Berkeley (☎510/845-4700). One of the West Coast's most highly respected theater companies, presenting updated classics and contemporary plays in an intimate modern theater. Tickets $10-30.

Black Repertory Group, 3201 Adeline St, Berkeley near Ashby BART (☎510/652-2120). After years of struggling, this politically conscious company moved into its own specially built home in 1987, since when they've encouraged new talent with great success. Tickets $10–25.

California Shakespeare Festival, Siesta Valley, Orinda (☎510/548-3422). After fifteen seasons in a North Berkeley park, this summer-long outdoor festival was forced to move to a larger home in the East Bay Hills. Tickets $12–50.

Julia Morgan Center for the Arts, 2640 College Ave, Berkeley (☎510/883-7024). A variety of touring shows stop off in this cunningly converted old church. Tickets $12-30.

The Peninsula

The city of San Francisco sits at the tip of a five-mile-wide neck of land commonly referred to as the **Peninsula**. Home of old money and new technology, the Peninsula stretches for fifty miles of relentless suburbia south from San Francisco along the bay, past the wealthy enclaves of Hillsborough and Atherton, winding up in the futuristic roadside landscape of the **"Silicon Valley"** near **San Jose**, the fastest growing city in California.

There was a time when the region was largely agricultural, but the continuing computer boom – spurred by Stanford University in **Palo Alto** – has replaced orange groves and fig trees with office complexes and parking lots. Surprisingly, however, most of the land along the **coast** – separated from the bayfront sprawl by a ridge of redwood-covered peaks – remains rural and undeveloped; it also contains some excellent **beaches** and a couple of affably down-to-earth communities, all well served by public transportation.

Getting around

BART only travels down the Peninsula as far as Daly City, from where you can catch SamTrans (☎1-800/660-4287) buses south to Palo Alto or along the coast to Half Moon Bay. For longer distances, **Caltrain** (☎1-800-660-4287 or 650/817-1717; *www.caltrain. com*) offers an hourly rail service from its terminal at Fourth and Townsend streets in downtown San Francisco, stopping at most bayside towns between the city and San Jose ($1–5); Greyhound (☎1-800/231-2222) runs regular **buses** along US-101 to and from their San Jose terminal at 70 S Almaden, on the corner of Santa Clara Street. Santa Clara Valley Transit Authority (VTA) (☎408/321-2300) runs buses and modern trolleys around metropolitan San Jose. If you're going to be spending most of your time there, it's possible to fly direct into **San Jose International Airport** (SJO), very close to downtown San Jose.

Information

The **Palo Alto Chamber of Commerce**, 325 Forest Ave (Mon–Fri 9am–noon & 1–5pm; ☎650/324-3121), has lists of local restaurants and cycle routes; for information on Stanford University, call its visitor center (☎650/723-2560) in the Memorial Hall library under Hoover Tower, or get a copy of the free *Stanford Daily*, published weekdays. To find out what's on in the area and where, pick up a free copy of the *Palo Alto Weekly*, available at most local shops. Or log onto *www.paloaltoonline.com*, a well-organized, rich databank of everything from local bike shops and restaurants to history and movie times. At the southern end of the bay, the **San Jose's Visitor Center** is at 333 W San Carlos St (Mon–Fri 8am–5.30pm, Sat & Sun 11am–5pm; ☎1-800/SAN-JOSE or 408/295-9600; *www.sanjose.org*), and also has a branch in the convention center across the street. It's the best bet for tourist information; for local news and events pick up a copy of the excellent *San Jose Mercury* newspaper (*www.mercurycenter.com*) or the free weekly *Metro* (*www.metroactive.com*), although the latter usually lists as many events for San Francisco as it does for Silicon Valley. The Web site *www.sanjose.citysearch.com* also holds a treasure of reviews and features on the area. Along the coast, the **Half**

Moon Bay Chamber of Commerce, at 520 Kelly Ave (Mon–Fri 9am–4pm, Sat 10am–3pm; ☎650/726-5202), gives out walking tour maps and information on accommodation.

Peninsula accommodation

Many visitors to San Francisco choose to stay on the Peninsula rather than in the city. Dozens of $60-a-night motels line Hwy-82 – "El Camino Real," the old main highway – and, with a bit of advanced planning (and a car), sleeping here can save a lot of money. Also, if you're **arriving late** or departing on an early flight from SFO you might want to avail yourself of one of the many airport hotels listed in the box on p.423. Perhaps the best reasons to spend the night down on the Peninsula are its low-priced, pleasant **hostels**, two of which are housed in old lighthouses right along the Pacific coast. San Jose's hotels are grossly overpriced, as they cater more to the conventioning corporate world than the tourist or traveler, though it's possible to find a decent deal.

Motels and hotels

Best Western Inn, 455 S Second St, San Jose (☎408/298-3500). Right in downtown San Jose, with pool and sauna. ④.

Best Western Stanford Park Hotel, 100 El Camino Real, Menlo Park (☎650/322-1234). Very pleasant first-class hotel near Stanford University. ⑤.

Cardinal Hotel, 235 Hamilton Ave, Palo Alto (☎650/323-5101). Affordable rates and comfortable rooms in the heart of downtown Palo Alto. Some rooms with shared bath. ④.

Craig Hotel, 164 Hamilton Ave, Palo Alto (☎650/853-1133). Dumpy and threadbare, but right downtown and dirt cheap. ②.

Days Inn Palo Alto, 4238 El Camino Real, Palo Alto (☎1-800/325-2525 or 650/493-4222). A mile from anywhere, but the rooms are particularly clean and well kept. ④.

Executive Inn, 1215 S First St, San Jose (☎408/280-5300). Basic rooms downtown near the few cafés in the city. ⑤.

Executive Inn, 3930 Monterey Rd, San Jose (☎408/281-8700). Basic rooms without frills fifteen minutes south of downtown. ⑤.

Fairmont Hotel, 170 S. Market St, San Joe (☎408/998-1900 or ☎1-800/527-4727). San Jose's finest hotel and part of the luxury chain which began in San Francisco is located in the heart of downtown San Jose, on the Plaza. All the expected amenities, such as room service, swimming pool, lounge and sparkling rooms. ⑥.

Pacifica Motor Inn, 200 Rockaway Beach Ave, Pacifica (☎650/359-7700). Large rooms just a block off the beach in hamlet alongside Hwy-1. ⑥.

Sea Breeze Motel, 100 Rockaway Beach Ave, Pacifica (☎650/359-3903). Beachfront hotel with attached restaurant, *Nick's*. Rooms are well-kept, but standard motel-style. ④.

Valley Inn, 2155 The Alameda, San Jose (☎408/241-8500). Standard motel not far from the Rosicrucian Museum. ⑤.

Bed and breakfast

Cowper Inn, 705 Cowper St, Palo Alto (☎650/327-4475). Restored Victorian with pleasant parlor and attractive rooms close to University Avenue. ④.

Old Thyme Inn, 779 Main St, Half Moon Bay (☎650/726-1616). Half a dozen incredibly quaint rooms, each with private bath, in lovely Victorian house surrounded by luxuriant herb and flower gardens. ⑦.

San Benito House, 356 Main St, Half Moon Bay (☎650/726-3425). Twelve restful B&B rooms in a hundred-year-old building, just a mile from the beach. Excellent restaurant downstairs. ⑦.

Hostels

HI-Hidden Villa, 26807 Moody Rd, Los Altos Hills (☎650/949-8648). Located on an 1800-acre ranch in the foothills above Silicon Valley; closed June–Sept. $15 a night.

HI-Pigeon Point Lighthouse, Hwy-1, just south of Pescadero (☎650/879-0633). Worth planning a trip around, this beautifully sited hostel, fifty miles south of San Francisco, is ideally placed for exploring the redwood forests in the hills above or for watching the wildlife in nearby Año Nuevo State Reserve. Outdoor hot tub. Office hours 7.30–9.30am & 4.30–9.30pm; doors locked at 11pm. Members $13 per night, non-members $16; reservations essential in summer. Private rooms $30 a night, minimum two people.

HI-Point Montara Lighthouse, 16th Street/Hwy-1, Montara (☎650/728-7177). Dorm rooms in a converted 1875 lighthouse, 25 miles south of San Francisco and accessible by bike or SamTrans bus #1L or #1C (Mon–Fri until 5.50pm, Sat until 6.15pm). Outdoor hot tub. Office hours 7.30–9.30am & 4.30–9.30pm; doors locked 11pm. Members $13 per night, non-members $16; reservations essential in summer.

Sanborn Park Hostel, 15808 Sanborn Rd, Saratoga (☎408/741-0166). Comfortable rooms in a beautiful wooded area fifteen minutes outside San Jose. Call from downtown Saratoga and they will arrange to pick you up. $8.50 members; $10.50 non-members.

Campgrounds

Butano State Park, Pescadero (☎650/879-2040). RV and tent spaces in a beautiful redwood forest; $16.

Half Moon Bay State Beach, Half Moon Bay (☎650/726-8820). Sleep out (illegally but safely) along the beach for free, or in the campground for $16.

South along the Bay

US-101 runs **south** from San Francisco along the bay through over fifty miles of unmitigated sprawl lined by light industrial estates and shopping malls to San Jose. One place along the freeway worth a visit is the **Coyote Point Museum** (Tues–Sat 10am–5pm, Sun noon–5pm; $3), four miles south of the airport off Poplar Avenue in a large bayfront park, where examples of the natural life of the San Francisco Bay – from tidal insects to birds of prey – are exhibited in engaging and informative displays, enhanced by interactive computers and documentary films.

Six-lane freeways don't usually qualify as a scenic route, but an exception is **I-280**, one of the newest and most expensive freeways in California, which runs parallel to US-101 but avoids the worst of the bayside mess by cutting through wooded valleys down the center of the Peninsula. Just beyond the San Francisco city limits the road passes through **COLMA**, a unique place filled with cemeteries, which, other than the military burial grounds in the *presidio*, are prohibited within San Francisco. Besides the expected roll call of deceased San Francisco luminaries like Levi Strauss and William Hearst, are a few surprises, such as Wild West gunman Wyatt Earp. If you're interested, contact the Colma Historical Association (☎650/757-1676) for graveyard tour information.

Beyond Colma, the scenery improves quickly as I-280 continues past the **Crystal Springs Reservoir**, an artificial lake which holds the water supply for San Francisco – pumped here all the way from Yosemite. Surrounded by twenty square miles of parkland, hiking trails lead up to the ridge from which San Francisco Bay was first spotted by eighteenth-century Spanish explorers; it now overlooks the airport to the east, but there are good views out over the Pacific coast, two miles distant.

At the south end of the reservoir, just off I-280 on Canada Road in the well-heeled town of **WOODSIDE**, luscious gardens surround the palatial **Filoli Estate** (tours Tues–Thurs 9.30am, 11.30am & 1.30pm; $10; advance reservations required ☎650/364-2880). The 45-room mansion, designed in 1915 in neo-Palladian style by architect Willis Polk, may look familiar – it was used in the TV series *Dynasty* as the Denver home of the Carrington clan. It's the only one of the many huge houses around here that you can visit, although the gardens are what make it worth coming, especially in the spring when everything's in bloom.

Seals near San Simeon

Alamo Square, San Francisco

Golden Gate Bridge

San Francisco

Cable car, with Alcatraz beyond

Sacramento

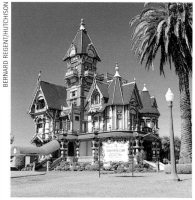

Carson Mansion, Eureka

Houseboat in Sausalito

Muir Woods, Bay Area

Lassen Volcanic National Park

Ripening grapes, Sonoma Valley

Emerald Bay, Lake Tahoe

Palo Alto and Stanford University

PALO ALTO, just south and three miles east of Woodside between I-280 and US-101, is a small, leafy community, and despite its proximity to Stanford, retains little of the college town vigor of its northern rival, Berkeley. In recent years, Palo Alto has become somewhat of a social center for Silicon Valley's nouveau riche, as evidenced by the trendy cafés and chic new restaurants that have popped up along its main drag, **University Avenue**. The booming computer industry job market has made more than a few people rich, and this is where many of them come to spend their cash; small houses in the quaint neighborhoods surrounding the downtown area can cost close to a million dollars.

The town doesn't have a lot to offer in terms of sights other than Spanish colonial homes, but it's a great place for a lazy stroll and a gourmet meal. Monthly historic tours of Palo Alto's neighborhoods take place during summer (☎650/299-8878). Otherwise, the best of the city's designs can be seen along **Ramona Street**. If you're feeling particularly energetic, or are tired of browsing in overpriced designer furniture stores, try cycling around the town's many well-marked bike routes; bikes are available for $10–20 a day from Action Sports Limited at 401 High St (☎650/328-3180), near the Caltrain station a block west of University Avenue. Be aware, however, that **East Palo Alto**, on the bay side of US-101, has a well-deserved reputation for gang- and drug-related violence, with one of the highest per capita murder rates of any US city. Founded in the 1920s as the utopian Runnymeade colony, an agricultural, poultry-raising co-operative, the local historical society (☎650/329-0294) can point out the surviving sites. East Palo Alto, where Grateful Dead guitarist Jerry Garcia grew up, is about as far as you can get off the San Francisco tourist trail.

Stanford University, spreading out from the west end of University Avenue, is by contrast one of the tamest places you could hope for. The university is among the top – and most expensive – in the United States, though when it opened in 1891, founded by railroad magnate Leland Stanford in memory of his dead son, it offered free tuition. Ridiculed by East Coast academics, who felt that there was as much need for a second West Coast university (after UC-Berkeley) as there was for "an asylum for decayed sea captains in Switzerland," Stanford was defiantly built anyway, in a hybrid of Mission and Romanesque buildings on a huge arid campus that covers an area larger than the whole of downtown San Francisco.

Stanford, whose reputation as an arch-conservative think-tank was enhanced by Ronald Reagan's offer to donate his video library to the school (Stanford politely declined), hasn't always been an entirely boring place, though you wouldn't know it to walk among the preppy future-lawyers-of-America that seem to comprise the majority of the student body. Ken Kesey came here from Oregon in 1958 on a writing fellowship, working nights as an orderly on the psychiatric ward of one local hospital, and getting paid $75 a day to test experimental drugs (LSD among them) in another. Drawing on both experiences, Kesey wrote *One Flew over the Cuckoo's Nest* in 1960 and quickly became a counter-culture hero.

Approaching from the Palo Alto Caltrain and SamTrans bus station, which acts as a buffer between the town and the university, you enter the campus via a half-mile-long, palm-tree-lined boulevard which deposits you at its heart, the **Quadrangle**, bordered by the phallic **Hoover Tower** and the colorful gold-leaf mosaics of the **Memorial Church**. Free hour-long walking tours of the campus leave from here daily at 11am and 3.15pm, though it's fairly big and best seen by car or bike.

While Stanford isn't really on the tourist trail, visitors should seek out the area if only to experience one of the finest museums in the Bay Area. **The Iris and B. Gerald Cantor Center for Visual Arts** comprises 27 galleries (spread over 120,000 square feet) of treasures from six continents, dating from 500 BC to the present (Wed–Sun

11am–5pm, Thurs 11–8; free). Housed in the old Stanford Museum of Art at the intersection of Lomita Drive and Museum Way, the Cantor Center is the result of a decade-long refurbishing effort undertaken to repair damage caused by the Loma Prieta earthquake in 1989. The enchanting result incorporates the former structure with a new wing, including a bookshop and café. Visiting exhibitions have featured the work of such artists as Duchamp, Oldenburg and Lucien Freud. One of the finest pieces in the permanent collection is the stunning *Plum Garden, Kameido*, by Japanese artist Hiroshige. Another reason to come to the museum is to have a look at its distinguished collection of over 200 **Rodin sculptures**, including a *Gates of Hell* flanked by a shamed *Adam and Eve*, displayed in an attractive outdoor setting on the museum's south side. There's a version of *The Thinker* here, as well, forming a sort of bookend with the rendition that fronts the Palace of the Legion of Honor museum in San Francisco.

Also, if you keep up on the latest trends in subatomic behavior, you won't want to miss the **Stanford Linear Accelerator** (Mon–Fri by appointment only; ☎650/926-3300), a mile west of the central campus on Sand Hill Road, where infinitesimally small particles are crashed into one another at very high speeds to see what happens. For a bird's eye view of the campus (and the rest of the Bay Area) head up one of the **hiking trails** that leads from the gate along Junipero Serra Boulevard at Stanford Avenue to Stanford's giant communications dish atop the foothills to the west of the campus.

San Jose

Burt Bacharach could easily find the way to **SAN JOSE** today – heading south from San Francisco, it's about an hour's drive (on those rare occasions when traffic is actually fluid) into the heart of the heat and smog that collects below the bay. Sitting at the southern end of the peninsula, San Jose has in the past 25 years emerged as the civic heart of Silicon Valley, spurred by the growth of local behemoths Apple, Intel and Hewlett-Packard. It's now the fastest growing city in California and close to twice the size of San Francisco in terms of population. San Jose's current priority is the development of a culture outside the computer labs that surround the city, and new museums, shopping centers, restaurants, clubs and performing arts companies have mushroomed throughout the compact downtown area. While the nightlife and cultural scene here still can't compete with San Francisco, there are enough attractions around the city's clean and sunny streets to warrant a day-trip.

Downtown San Jose

Though now a city of the future, San Jose's 1777 founding makes it one of the oldest settlements – and the oldest city – in California. The only sign of that downtown is the 1797 **Peralta Adobe**, at 184 W. St. John St (Tue–Sun noon–5pm; $6), notable more for its having survived the encroaching suburbia than anything on display in its sparse, white-washed interior. Admission includes a tour of the **Fallon House**, a Victorian mansion across the street. Built by the city's seventh mayor in 1855, a one-time frontiersman in the Fremont expedition, the guided tours through the 15 rooms furnished from the period also include a comprehensive video presentation on the home and adobe's relationship to the development of the cityscape.

The two blocks of San Pedro Street which run south of the adobe form a restaurant row known as **San Pedro Square**. There's no central plaza as such, just a collection of some of San Jose's best eateries (see "Peninsula eating," p.523). Further south, down Market Stree, lies the pleasant and palm-dotted **Plaza de Cesar Chavez**. The Plaza is San Jose's town square and there is no better place to catch some rays on the grass, read while sitting on one of the many wooden benches, or play in the unique **fountain** whose shooting spumes are a favorite hang out for kids in the summer.

A block north of the plaza lies the **Cathedral Basilica of St. Joseph**, which stands on the site of the first Catholic parish in California, circa 1803. The present building was dedicated in 1997, and it's worth entering to see its painted cupola, stained glass windows and stations of the cross. Masses are held daily, often in Spanish. Next door to the church at 110 Market is the fantastic **San Jose Museum of Art** (Tues–Wed 10am–5pm, Thurs 10am–8pm and Fri–Sun 10am–5pm; $7, free the first Thursday of the month; *www.sjmusart.org*). Set in the old post office building built in 1892 (along with a new wing added in 1991), the museum contains more than one thousand twentieth-century works, with the spotlight falling on post-1980 Bay Area artists. A relationship with New York's Whitney Museum of American Art has recently been formed, allowing the museum to exhibit works from the Whitney's vast permanent collection. The sweeping, open galleries are flooded with light, as is the attached café, including its outdoor patio facing the Plaza.

Facing the southwest corner of the Plaza, downtown's biggest draw is the **Tech Museum of Innovation**, at 201 South Market Street (summer daily 10am–6pm, Thurs 10am–8pm, fall Tues–Sun 10am–5pm; $8; *www.thetech.org*), with its hands-on displays of high-tech engineering. There are three floors of exhibits, as well as the inevitable IMAX theater. Highlights include a program that allows you to design a virtual roller coaster, regular demonstrations of high tech surgical instruments, and the chance to communicate with interactive robots. Unfortunately, the queues to access many of the best exhibits can seem like a virtual hell, and, unless you're a computer junkie, you may leave the museum feeling more like you've attempted to read an impervious software manual than visited a popular museum.

Aside from the attractions around the Plaza, San Jose's other area worth walking through is the up-and-coming "**SoFA**" entertainment district, short for South First Street. To get here from the southern tip of the Plaza, turn east on San Carlos Street and walk one block to First Street. SoFA forms the heart of San Jose's nightlife, with a half-a-dozen clubs and discos along with a popular wine bar (see "Peninsula nightlife," p.524). There's plenty to see during the day as well, including the **Institute of Contemporary Art** (Tues–Sat noon–5pm; free), at no. 451 South First Street. The ICA's large sunny room exhibits modern art, mainly Bay Area artists but also work by international painters and sculptors. On the same street is downtown San Jose's **art cinema** house, the Camera 1, no. 366 (☎408/998-3300), and at no. 490, one of its performing arts companies, **The Stage** (☎408/283-7142). Performances of contemporary work, like Steve Martin's *Picasso at the Lapin Agile*, regularly run Wednesday–Saturday, with tickets available for $20-$25.

Walking north on First Avenue leads past the **Pavilion** shopping center, which is currently in the midst of a major renovation, preparing it to be the anchor of commercial San Jose. The area could use it, having laid stagnant for decades as locals shopped at suburban malls. To combat this flight, city planners have zoned all of First and Second Streets for redevelopment.

Around San Jose

Head four miles northwest of downtown and you'll come across two of San Jose's more intriguing, and relaxing, places to hang out. The first is the **Rosicrucian Museum**, 1342 Naglee Ave (daily 10am–5pm; $7; ☎408/947-3636), a grand structure that contains a brilliant collection of Assyrian and Babylonian artifacts, with displays of mummies, amulets, a replica of a tomb and ancient jewellery. The museum is a dark and musty room, befitting its contents. Don't miss the mummies of baboons, birds and fish on the left-hand side of the tomb wing. Aside from the corpses and models within, the best part about the Rosicrucian is its garden grounds, featuring a replica of the Akhenaten Temple from Luxor. Across the street and two blocks west of the museum is the second relaxing locale, San Jose's **rose garden** (daily dawn–dusk). The beautiful expanse of green and rows of rose bushes is perfect for a picnic, and the fountain in the garden's center is a popular wading pool for local kids. Roll up your pants, soak your feet, and take in a nice view of the Santa Cruz mountains to the west amidst the sweet scents.

North of San Jose, the small community of **SANTA CLARA** holds a few tourist bargains of its own. The late eighteenth-century **Mission Santa Clara de Asis**, just south of The Alameda (Route 82), is one of the least impressive structures in the mission chain that runs along the California coast on the traces of the El Camino Reál. Hidden on the grounds of the Jesuit-run **University of Santa Clara**, there's not a lot to see of the original mission era buildings here, though it can be interesting to note how their remnants have been subtly preserved, integrated into the overall campus design. The **de Saisset Museum** (Tues–Sun 11am–4pm; $1 donation suggested) on the grounds traces the history of the mission through a permanent display of objects recovered from its ruins – the mission burned in a 1926 fire – along with changing shows of contemporary art. The bell in the belfry is original, a gift from King Carlos IV of Spain in 1798. Overall, the university is a green, quiet place to stroll around and pass an afternoon.

A few miles south of here is a true American tourist trap, unmissable if you're into a good yarn. The **Winchester Mystery House**, 525 S Winchester Blvd, just off I-280 near Hwy-17 (daily 9.30am–4.30pm; $12.95), belonged to Sarah Winchester, heiress to the Winchester rifle fortune, who was convinced upon her husband's death in 1884 that he had been taken by the spirits of men killed with his weapons. The ghosts told her that unless a room was built for each of them, the same fate would befall her. She took them so literally that the sound of hammers never ceased – 24 hours a day for the next thirty years. Now, unfinished, the house is a hodgepodge of extensions and styles: extravagant staircases lead nowhere and windows open onto solid brick walls. Today, the ghosts can't be much happier seeing that construction has stopped and the place has been converted into a shameless money maker, where visitors have to run a gauntlet of ghastly gift stores and soda stands to get in or out.

One other Peninsula place might exercise a certain attraction, particularly to those fond of roller coasters, log rides and all-American family fun; **Paramount's Great America** (summer daily 10am–10pm; winter Sat & Sun 10am–10pm; $34). This hundred-acre amusement park on the edge of San Francisco Bay, just off US-101 north of San Jose, may not be in the same league as Disneyland, but the range of high-speed thrills and chills available – from the looping Top Gun Jetcoaster to Stealth, which zooms over the rails at 65mph – should satisfy even the most hard-core adrenaline junkies.

The coast

The **coastline** of the peninsula south from San Francisco is worlds away from the inland valleys: mostly undeveloped, a few small towns, and countless beaches and sea lions trace the way 75 miles south to the mellow summer fun of Santa Cruz and **Capitola**. Bluffs protect the many nudist beaches from prying eyes and make a popular launching pad for hang-glider pilots, particularly at **Fort Funston**, a mile south of the San Francisco Zoo – also the point where the earthquake-causing San Andreas Fault enters the sea, not to surface again until Point Reyes. **Skyline Boulevard** follows the coast from here past the repetitious tracts of proverbial ticky-tacky houses that make up Daly City, before heading inland toward Woodside at its intersection with Hwy-1, which continues south along the coast. Driving Hwy-1 can be a relaxing jaunt providing jaw-dropping views of the ocean, provided you miss the masses. Summer and weekend afternoons find the route clogged with campers creeping along at 30mph and little opportunities to pass. Try hitting the road early in the morning (as in at sunrise) and, provided the fog isn't obscuring everything, expect a magical ride.

Pacifica and around

San Pedro Point, a popular surfing beach fifteen miles south of the city proper, and the town of **PACIFICA**, mark the southern extent of San Francisco's suburban sprawl. Pacifica is a pleasant stop-off for lunch and wave-gazing around Rockaway Beach. Stop in at the ultra-friendly **Chamber of Commerce**, 225 Rockaway Beach Ave (Mon-Fri 9am-12pm, 1pm-5pm; Sat-Sun 10am-4.30pm; ☎650/355-4122) for free maps of the area, including trail guides for **Sweeney Ridge**, from where Spanish explorer Gaspar de Portola discovered the San Francisco Bay in 1769. Pacifica's old **Ocean Shore Railroad Depot** here, now a private residence, is one of the few surviving remnants of an ill-advised train line between San Francisco and Santa Cruz. Wiped out during the 1906 earthquake, the line was in any case never more than a third complete. Its few patrons had to transfer back and forth by ferry to connect the stretches of track that were built, the traces of which you can still see scarring the face of the bluffs. The continually eroding cliffs make construction of any route along the coast difficult, as evidenced a mile south by the **Devil's Slide**, where the highway is washed away with some regularity in winter storms. The slide area was also a popular dumping spot for corpses of those who fell foul of rum-runners during Prohibition, and is featured under various names in many of Dashiell Hammett's detective stories.

Just south of the Devil's Slide, the sands of **Gray Whale Cove State Beach** (daily dawn–dusk; $5 parking) are clothing-optional. Despite the name it's not an especially great place to look for migrating gray whales, but the stairway at the bus stop does lead down to a fine strand of sand. Two miles south, the red-roofed buildings of the 1875 **Montara Lighthouse**, set among the windswept Monterey pine trees at the top of a steep cliff, have been converted into a youth hostel (see p.516). Just south of the hostel, on California Street, the **Fitzgerald Marine Reserve** (☎650/728-3584; free) has three miles of diverse oceanic habitat, peaceful trails, and, at low tide, the best tidal pools in the Bay Area. The ranger often gives guided interpretive walks through the reserve at low tide, the best time to explore, so call ahead for low tide times. At the south end of the reserve, **Pillar Point** juts out into the Pacific; just to the east, along Hwy-1, fishing boats dock at **Pillar Point Harbor**. Mavericks Beach, just off Pillar Point beyond the enormous communications dish, with the largest waves in North America, attracts some of the world's best (and craziest) surfers when conditions are right – just watching them can be an exhilarating way to spend an hour or so, and hundreds of people do every day. There's a long breakwater you can walk out on, too, but remember to never turn your back to the ocean; rogue waves have crashed in and swept unsuspecting tourists to their deaths. The surrounding villages of **Princeton-By-The-Sea** and El Grenada have good roadside lunch stops serving freshly caught fish and hamburgers. Further along, the best of the local surfing is just offshore from **Miramar Beach**; after a day in the water or on the beach, the place to head for is the beachfront *Douglass Beach House* (☎650/726-4143), an informal jazz club and beer bar that faces the sands.

Half Moon Bay

HALF MOON BAY, twenty miles south of the city and the only town of any size along the coast between San Francisco and Santa Cruz, takes its name from the crescent-shaped bay formed by Pillar Point. Lined by miles of sandy beaches, the town is surprisingly rural considering its proximity to San Francisco and Silicon Valley, and sports a number of ornate Victorian wooden houses around its center. The oldest of these, at north end of Main Street, was built in 1849 just across a little stone bridge over Pillarcitos Creek. The **Chamber of Commerce** (see p.515 for details) on Hwy-1 has free walking tour maps of the town and information on the two annual festivals for which the place is well known. These are the **Holy Ghost and Pentecost Festival**, a parade and barbecue held on the sixth Sunday after Easter, and the **Pumpkin Festival**, celebrating the harvest of the area's many pumpkin farms, just in time for Halloween when the fields around town are full of families searching for the perfect jack-o'-lantern to greet the hordes of trick-or-treaters. Free, basic campgrounds line the coast in **Half Moon Bay State Park**, half a mile west of the town. Stop here if you're low on gas, as the fifty-mile stretch of Hwy-1 to Santa Cruz doesn't offer many places to fill up.

SamTrans bus #294 route ends in Half Moon Bay; to continue south, transfer here to route #15, which runs every three hours to Waddell Creek, twenty miles south. **San Gregorio State Beach**, ten miles south of Half Moon Bay, is at its best in the spring, after the winter storms, when flotsam architects construct a range of driftwood shelters along the wide beach south of the parking area. On hot summer days, the beach is packed with well-oiled bodies, but the sands around the bluffs to the north are quieter. You can bathe nude at San Gregorio Private Beach, though you pay to park and enter; follow Hwy-1 one mile north of San Gregorio Road and watch for the white gate that marks the turning. Just north of Half Moon Bay, Dunes Beach and Venice Beach are also beautiful expanses of sand and ocean. You can ride a horse along the beaches from the Sea Horse Ranch, Hwy-1 one mile north of Hwy-92 (☎650/726-2362; $20 per hour).

The Butano redwoods and the Año Nuevo State Reserve

If you've got a car and it's not a great day for the beach, head up into the hills above, where the thousands of acres of the **Butano redwood forest** feel at their most ancient and primeval in the greyest, gloomiest weather. About half the land between San Jose and the coast is protected from development in a variety of state and county parks, all of which are virtually deserted despite being within a thirty-minute drive of the Silicon Valley sprawl. Any one of a dozen roads heads through endless stands of untouched forest, and even the briefest of walks will take you seemingly miles from any sign of civilization. Hwy-84 climbs up from San Gregorio through the Sam McDonald County Park to the hamlet of **LA HONDA**, from where you can continue on to Palo Alto, or, better, loop back to the coast via Pescadero Road. A mile before you reach the quaint town of **PESCADERO**, Cloverdale Road heads south to **Butano State Park**, where you can hike and camp overlooking the Pacific. Tiny Pescadero itself has one of the best places to eat on the Peninsula – *Duarte's* (see below).

Back on Hwy-1, five miles south of Pescadero, you can stay the night in the old lighthouse keeper's quarters and soak your bones in a marvelous hot tub at the **HI-Pigeon Point Lighthouse Hostel** (see p.516). The calmest, most pleasant beach in which to wade is at **Bean Hollow State Beach**, a mile north of the hostel. If you're here during December through March, continue south another five miles to the **Año Nuevo State Reserve** for a chance to see one of nature's most bizarre spectacles – the mating rituals of the northern elephant seal. These massive, ungainly creatures, fifteen feet long and weighing up to three tons, were once found all along the coast, though they were nearly hunted to extinction by whalers in the last century. During the mating season the beach is literally a seething mass of blubbery bodies, with the trunk-nosed males fighting it out for the right to sire as many as fifty pups in a season. At any time of the year you're likely to see a half dozen or so dozing in the sands. The reserve is also good for bird watching, and in March you might even catch sight of migrating gray whales.

The slowly resurgent Año Nuevo seal population is still carefully protected, and during the breeding season the obligatory guided tours – designed to protect spectators as much as to give the seals some privacy – begin booking in September (hourly 8am–4pm; ☎650/879-0227). Otherwise tickets are usually made available to people staying at the *Pigeon Point Hostel*, and SamTrans (☎1-800/660-4287) sometimes runs charter bus tours from the town of **San Mateo** on the bay side of the Peninsula. (See "The Central Coast" chapter for an account of the area from Año Nuevo south to Santa Cruz and Monterey.)

Peninsula eating

The **restaurants** on the Peninsula, particularly in pseudo-ritzy Palo Alto and newly yup-pified Burlingame, are increasingly on par with their San Franciscan counterparts, and many, filled with wealthy young computer executives, require dinner reservations every night of the week. In San Jose, consider dining around San Pedro Square for a good choice of cuisine. The following list concentrates primarily on establishments cen-trally located in the downtown areas of the various Peninsula cities, with a few others that are worth almost any effort to get to.

Restaurants

AP Stump's, 163 W. Santa Clara St., San Jose (☎408/292-9928). Best place to go if you have an unlimited expense account. Pricey ($20 a plate) California cuisine, but one of *the* places to be seen in Silicon Valley. Great wine list.

Alpine Inn, 3915 Alpine Rd, Woodside (☎650/854-4004). Stagecoach stop turned greasy burger joint in the hills with outdoor picnic tables and an interesting mix of locals and computer guys.

Barbara's Fish Trap, 281 Capistrano Rd, off Hwy-1, Princeton-by-the-Sea (☎650/728-7049). Oceanfront seafood restaurant with good-value fish dinners and an unbeatable view.

Bistro Elan, 448 S. California Ave, Palo Alto (☎650/327-0284). Serving spiffy Cal cuisine to the cyber-elite. Prices are rather steep, so consider a lunchtime visit.

Bistro Vida, 641 Santa Cruz Ave, Menlo Park (☎408/462-1686). Giving Silicon Valley a much-need-ed style infusion by serving delicious Left Bank Parisian bistro fare.

Blake's Steakhouse and Bar, 17 N. San Pedro St, San Jose (☎408/298-9221). Craving a New York strip, or a steamed lobster, washed down with a fine martini? *Blake's* is the place. Entrées begin at $20.

Casa Castillo, 206 S. First St, San Jose (☎408/971-8132). Moderately-priced Mexican food and a full bar serving monster margaritas made with Cuervo 1800.

Chateau des Fleurs, 523 Church St, Half Moon Bay (☎650/712-8837). The exquisite flower gar-den in front welcomes you to this small, reasonably priced French restaurant.

Duarte's, 202 Stage Rd, Pescadero (☎650/879-0464). Platefuls of traditional American food, (espe-cially fish) for around $10 are served in this down-home find connected to a bar full of locals in cow-boy hats. Famous for their artichoke soup.

E&O Trading Company, 96 S. First St, San Jose (☎408/938-4100). Upscale Southeast Asian grill featuring curried fish and other Vietnamese/Indonesian fare.

Eulipia, 374 S First St, San Jose (☎408/280-6161). Stylish dinner spot featuring well-prepared ver-sions of California cuisine staples like grilled fish and fresh pastas. Entrées from $15-$25. Closed Mondays.

Evvia, 420 Emerson St, Palo Alto (☎650/326-0983). California/Greek lamb and fish dishes with names like *paidakia arnisia* and *arni kapama* served in a cozy, yet elegant dining room. Full bar.

Fresco, 3398 El Camino Real, Palo Alto (☎650/493-3470). Wide selection of pastas, pizzas and sal-ads with palpably fresh ingredients in unusual combinations.

Il Forniao, 327 Lorton Ave, Burlingame ☎650/375-8000. Part of an upscale chain serving reliably well-prepared Italian staple entrées and baked goods.

Joanie's Cafe, 447 California Ave, Palo Alto (☎650/326-6505). Homestyle breakfasts and lunches in a comfortable neighborhood restaurant.

John's Market, Town and Country Village, Embarcadero at El Camino, Palo Alto (☎650/321-8438). Steer past the high school kids on lunch break to get one of the best (and biggest) deli sandwiches around. Located across the street from Stanford Stadium.

L'Amie Donia, 530 Bryant St, Palo Alto (☎650/323-7614). How do you simultaneously splurge and keep your budget? A $30 three course prix-fixe menu from this classy French bistro serves you well.

Little Garden, 4127 El Camino Real, Palo Alto (☎650/494-1230). Simple, spicy, well-prepared Vietnamese food – fried chicken on a bed of cabbage, shrimp and hot peppers in peanut sauce – in unpretentious surroundings.

Los Gallos Taqueria, 3726 Florence St, Redwood City (☎650/369-1864). Simply put, they make the best burritos on the Peninsula. Take the Marsh Road exit from Hwy-101 and look for the Marsh Manor shopping center.

Mike's Cafe, Etc., 2680 Middlefield Rd, Palo Alto (☎650/473-6453). Unpretentious neighborhood restaurant hidden behind a hardware store. Excellent fresh salads, pastas, and simple meat dishes are sometimes brought to your table by Mike himself.

Mongo's, 83 S. Second St, San Jose (☎408/280-1738). San Jose's most unique eatery. You pile the veggies and meats onto your plate, and then watch as the cook stir-fries it for you. $9.95 dinner, $7.95 lunch.

Original Joe's, 301 S First St, San Jose (☎408/292-7030). Grab a stool at the counter or settle into one of the comfy vinyl booths and enjoy a burger and fries or a plate of pasta at this San Jose institution, where $10 goes a long way. Open 11am-1am.

Peggy Sue's, 29 N. San Pedro St., San Jose (☎408/298-6750). Inexpensive milkshakes, burgers and fries served in a 1950s setting. Also has a vegetarian and kids' menu.

Peninsula Creamery, 566 Emerson St, Palo Alto (☎650/323-3175). Nearly authentic 1950s American diner, serving the staples and shakes.

71 Saint Peter, 71 N. San Pedro St, San Jose (☎408/971-8523). Patio dining and oyster bar centered around a menu of filet mignon, pork loin, chicken and salads. Extremely hot with the in-crowd. Lunch Mon-Fri, dinner nightly.

Spiedo, 151 W. Santa Clara St, San Jose (☎408/971-6096). Handmade pasta, pizza, calamari, salmon and more delight the tastebuds at lunch and dinner daily. Entrées begin at $10.

St Michael's Alley, 806 Emerson St, Palo Alto (☎650/326-2530). This former student café hangout has transformed itself into one of Palo Alto's hottest bistros and the "casual California" cuisine served at lunch and dinner couldn't be farther from the old fare of bagels and coffee. A fine wine list and weekend brunch ($10) keeps guests coming back for seconds.

Peninsula nightlife

For a serious night out on the town, you're better off heading up to San Francisco, though many San Jose residents may try to convince you otherwise. Nevertheless, there are several good **bars and clubs** on the Peninsula – particularly in San Jose's SoFA district, but also in the studenty environs of Palo Alto. If you're in the mood for quiet conversation rather than wild beer drinking, check out one of the **cafés** listed, many of which feature fresh sandwiches and salads along with the requisite microbrewed beers (Gordon Biersch originated in San Jose) and gourmet coffees.

Bars and clubs

Agenda, 399 S First St, San Jose (☎408/287-4087). A bar/restaurant/lounge in SoFA which heralded the arrival of night life in San Jose. DJ dancing and live jazz nightly.

B-Hive, 372 S. First St, San Jose (☎408/298-2529). Upstairs dance club spinning hip-hop, R&B and reggae. Rhythm Records, below, keeps them supplied with loops.

Blue Chalk Café, 630 Ramona St, Palo Alto (☎650/326-1020). Yuppies and other young Siliconites have been flocking to this wildly successful bar/pool-hall/restaurant ever since it opened in 1993.

Cactus Club, 417 S First St, San Jose (☎408/491-9300). One of two very good clubs near each other in downtown San Jose, hosting some of the better up-and-coming bands with music ranging from roots reggae to hard-core thrash. Cover $5–10.

Douglass Beach House, Miramar Beach, two and a half miles north of Half Moon Bay on Hwy-1, go west down Medio Avenue (☎650/726-4143). Two-story country beach house with fireplace and outside deck hosting West Coast jazz performers.

Emma's Club Miami, 177 W. Santa Clara St, San Jose (☎408/279-3670). Huge San Pedro Square bar/Mexican restaurant with Latin music and dancing on weekends. Great patio.

Gordon Biersch Brewery, 640 Emerson St, Palo Alto (☎650/323-7723). Among the first and still the best of the Bay Area's microbrewery-cum-restaurants. Also in San Francisco (see p.466) and in downtown San Jose at 33 E San Fernando St (☎408/294-6785).

Katie Bloom's, 150 S. First St, San Jose (☎408/294-4408). Irish pub in the Pavilion that also serves Irish pub fare and occasionally has live Irish acts.

Kleidon's Cocktails, 152 Post St, San Jose (☎408/293-2461). Old downtown San Jose dive bar that's perfect for if you get tired of drinking amongst the beautiful people.

Moss Beach Distillery, Beach and Ocean, Moss Beach (☎650/728-0220). If you don't feel like paying out $20 per entrée at the popular restaurant, snuggle up under a wool blanket, order a drink and an appetizer, and watch the sunset from the patio overlooking the ocean.

Polly Esther's Culture Club, 394 S. First St, San Jose (☎408/280-1977). Retro Seventies and Eighties dance club, replete with divas and dancers trying to win John Travolta look-alike contests. The choice spot to sport your vintage fashions.

Tied House, 65 N. San Pedro St, San Jose (☎408/295-2739). San Pedro Square sports bar and brewery which also serves burgers and the like inside its gigantic space.

Toon's, S. Second St at Santa Clara, San Jose (☎408/292-7464). Downtown San Jose's hip-hop dance club. Sister club the *Voodoo Lounge*, next door, is for 21 and over only and enforces a strict dress code of no hats, baggies or tennis shoes.

Trials Pub, 265 N. First St, San Jose (☎408/947-0497). Only authentic British pub in town, with all the expected stouts, ales and dartboards.

The Usual, 400 S. First St, San Jose (☎408/535-0330). Live music venue in SoFA featuring retro Eighties acts and current artists of all stripes.

Waves Smokehouse and Saloon, 65 Post St, San Jose (☎408/885-WAVE). Live country music in a genuine country and western bar.

Wine Galleria, 377 S. First St, San Jose (☎408/298-1386). Large wine bar with plush sofas next to *Café Matisse*. Runs specials, like three wine tastings for $9. Huge array of vintages for sale by the glass.

Cafés

Café Matisse, 371 First St, San Jose (☎408/298-7788). Modern art hangs on the walls of this funky artist studio space, which serves fresh coffee and pastries.

Café at Printer's Inc, 320 California Ave, Palo Alto (☎650/323-3347). Good food and coffees served adjacent to Palo Alto's best bookstore.

Caffé Verona, 236 Hamilton Ave, Palo Alto (☎650/326-9942). Relaxing hangout for Palo Alto's intellectual crowd.

Global Village Café, 172 N. Main St, Sebastopol (☎650/829-4765). A popular breakfast gathering spot for techie types – when they make time for breakfast, that is.

M Coffee, 522 Main St, Half Moon Bay (☎650/726-6241). Coffees, teas, sandwiches and ice cream in a small, homely eatery.

Marin County

Across the Golden Gate from San Francisco, **Marin County** (pronounced "Ma-RINN") is an unabashed introduction to Californian self-indulgence: an elitist pleasure zone of conspicuous luxury and abundant natural beauty, with sunshine, sandy beaches, high mountains, and thick redwood forests. Often ranked as the wealthiest county in the US, Marin has attracted a sizeable contingent of northern California's wealthiest young professionals, many of whom grew up during the Flower Power years of the 1960s and lend the place its New Age feel and reputation. Though many of the cocaine-and-hot-tub devotees who seemed to populate the swanky waterside towns in the 1970s have traded in their drug habits for mountain bikes – which were invented here – life in Marin still centers around personal pleasure, and the throngs you see hiking and cycling at weekends, not to mention the hundreds of esoteric self-help practitioners – rolfing, rebirthing, and soul-travel therapists fill up the classified ads of the local papers – prove that Marinites work hard to maintain their easy air of physical and mental well-being.

Flashy modern ferry boats, appointed with fully stocked bars, sail across the bay from San Francisco and give a good initial view of the county. As you head past desolate Alcatraz Island, curvaceous **Mount Tamalpais** looms larger until you land at its foot in one of the chic bayside settlements of **Sausalito** or **Tiburon**. **Angel Island**, in the middle of the bay but accessible most easily from Tiburon, provides relief from the excessive style-consciousness of both towns, retaining a wild untouched feeling among the eerie ruins of derelict military fortifications.

Sausalito and Tiburon (and the lifestyles that go with them) are only a small part of Marin. The bulk of the county rests on the slopes of the ridge of peaks that divides the Peninsula down the middle, separating the sophisticated harborside towns in the east from the untrammeled wilderness of the Pacific coast to the west. The **Marin Headlands**, just across the Golden Gate Bridge, hold time-warped old battlements and gun emplacements that once protected San Francisco's harbor from would-be invaders, and now overlook hikers and cyclists enjoying the acres of open space and wildlife. Along the coastline that stretches north, the broad shore of **Stinson Beach** is the Bay Area's finest and widest stretch of sand, beyond which Hwy-1 clings to the coast past the rural village of **Bolinas** to seascapes around **Point Reyes**, where it is thought Sir Francis Drake may have landed in 1579 and claimed all of California for England. Whale- and seal-watchers congregate here year-round for glimpses of migrations and matings.

Inland, the heights of Mount Tamalpais, and specifically **Muir Woods**, are a magnet to sightseers and nature-lovers, who come to wander through one of the few surviving stands of the native coastal redwood trees. Such trees covered most of Marin before they were chopped down to build and rebuild the wooden houses of San Francisco. The long-vanished lumber mills of the rustic town of **Mill Valley**, overlooking the bay from the slopes of Mount Tam, as it's locally known, bear the guilt for much of this destruction; the oldest town in Marin County is now home to an eclectic bunch of art galleries and cafés. Further north, Marin's largest town, **San Rafael**, is best left alone, though its outskirts contain two of the most unusual attractions in the county: **Frank Lloyd Wright**'s peculiar Civic Center complex and the preserved remnants of an old Chinese fishing village in **China Camp State Park**. The northern reaches of Marin County border the bountiful wine-growing regions of the Sonoma and Napa valleys, detailed in Chapter 9, "Northern California."

Arrival and getting around

Just getting to Marin County can be a great start to a day out from San Francisco. Golden Gate Transit **ferries** (☎415/923-2000) leave from the Ferry Building on the

MARIN COUNTY BUS SERVICES ON GOLDEN GATE TRANSIT	
#2: San Francisco–Marin City–Marin Headlands; weekdays.	**#30**: San Francisco–Larkspur Ferry–San Rafael; weekdays.
#4: San Francisco–Mill Valley; weekdays.	**#50**: San Francisco–Sausalito–San Rafael–Novato–San Marin.
#8: San Francisco–Tiburon; weekdays.	
#10: San Francisco–Sausalito–Marin City–Mill Valley–Tiburon.	**#60**: San Francisco–San Rafael.
	#63: Marin City–Stinson Beach; weekends only
#18: San Francisco–Corte Madera–College of Marin–San Anselmo; weekdays.	**#65**: San Rafael–Point Reyes National Seashore–Inverness; weekends only.
#20: San Francisco–Corte Madera–San Anselmo–Canal.	
#24: San Francisco–Greenbrea–San Anselmo–Manor–Lagunitas.	**#90**: San Francisco–San Rafael–Sonoma Valley; weekdays.
#26: San Francisco–San Rafael–Sleepy Hollow; weekdays.	**#93**: San Francisco Civic Center–Golden Gate Bridge; weekdays.

SAN FRANCISCO–MARIN COUNTY FERRIES

Because ferry schedules change slightly four times a year, you should use the following timetable as an estimate of arrival and departure times. Current schedules are always available from the terminals.

GOLDEN GATE TRANSIT FERRIES (☎415/923-3000)

San Francisco–Larkspur: Mon–Fri depart 6.35am, 7.20am, 7.50am, 8.20am, 8.55am, 10.45am, 11.25am, 12.45pm, 1.35pm, 3.05pm, 3.25pm, 3.45pm, 4.30pm, 4.50pm, 5.20pm, 6.15pm, 6.30pm, 7.35pm & 8.45pm; Sat, Sun & holidays 10.45am, 12.45pm, 2.45pm, 4.45pm & 6.45pm.

Larkspur–San Francisco: Mon–Fri depart 5.50am, 6.50am, 7.05am, 7.35am, 8.15am, 8.45am, 9.45am, 10.35am, 11.45am, 12.35pm, 2.20pm, 2.35pm, 3.45pm, 4.15pm, 4.50pm, 5.10pm, 5.40pm, 6.50pm & 7.50pm; Sat, Sun & holidays 9.45am,

11.45am, 1.45pm, 3.45pm & 5.45pm.

San Francisco–Sausalito: Mon–Fri depart 7.40am, 9.15am, 10.25am, 11.45am, 1.10pm, 2.35pm, 4.10pm, 5.30pm, 6.40pm & 8pm; Sat, Sun & holidays 11.30am, 1pm, 2.30pm, 4pm, 5.30pm & 6.55pm; also May–Sept 8.05pm.

Sausalito–San Francisco: Sat, Sun & holidays depart 7.05am, 8.15am, 11.05am, 12.25pm, 1.55pm, 3.20pm, 4.45pm, 6.05pm & 7.20pm; Sat, Sun & holidays 10.50am, 12.15pm, 1.45pm, 3.15pm, 4.45pm & 6.10pm; also May–Sept 7.30pm.

BLUE AND GOLD FLEET FERRIES (☎415/773-1188).

San Francisco–Sausalito: Mon–Fri depart 11am, 12.15pm, 1.50pm, 3pm & 4.50pm; Sat, Sun & holidays 10.40am, 12.25pm, 1.50pm, 3.15pm, 4.45pm & 6.30pm; also May–Sept Fri & Sat 8.25pm.

Sausalito–San Francisco: Mon–Fri depart 11.50am, 1.05pm, 2.25pm, 3.35pm, 5.45pm & 8pm; also May–Sept Fri 8.50pm; Sat, Sun & holidays 11.20am, 1.05pm, 2.30pm, 3.55pm, 5.25pm & 7.10pm; also May–Sept Sat 9pm.

San Francisco–Tiburon: Mon–Fri depart 11am, 12.15pm, 1.35pm, 2.45pm, 4.05pm & 4.50pm; Sat, Sun & holidays 9.30am, 11.30am, 2pm, 4pm, 4.45pm & 6.30pm; also May–Sept Fri & Sat 8.25pm.

Tiburon–San Francisco: Mon–Fri depart 11.25am, 12.40pm, 1.55pm, 3.10pm, 5.25pm & 7.45pm; also May–Sept Fri 9.10pm; Sat, Sun & holidays 10.35am, 12.25pm, 2.35pm, 5.05pm, 5.50pm & 7.30pm; also May–Sept Sat 9.20pm.

Embarcadero, crossing the bay past Alcatraz Island to **Sausalito** and **Larkspur**; they run from 5.30am until 8.30pm, approximately every thirty minutes during the rush hour, less often the rest of the day, and every two hours on weekends and holidays. Tickets cost $4.80 one-way to Sausalito, $2.85 to Larkspur Monday to Friday ($4.80 weekends); refreshments are served on board. The more expensive Blue and Gold Fleet ($12 round trip; ☎415/773-1188) sail from Pier 41 at Fisherman's Wharf to **Sausalito** and **Tiburon** – from where the Angel Island Ferry ($6 round trip, plus $1 per bicycle; ☎415/435-2131) nips back and forth to **Angel Island State Park** daily in summer, weekends only in the winter. Blue and Gold Fleet provides additional service to Angel Island ($10) and Tiburon from the Ferry Building downtown during commute hours ($6 one way).

Golden Gate Transit also runs a comprehensive **bus service** around Marin County and across the Golden Gate Bridge from the Transbay Terminal in San Francisco (in Marin County, call ☎415/455-2000; in San Francisco ☎415/923-3000), and publishes a helpful and free system map and timetable, including all ferry services. Bus fares range from $1.25 to $4.50 with routes run every thirty minutes throughout the day, and once an hour late at night. But, some area can only be reached by GGT commuter services, which run only during the morning and evening rush hours. Call ahead to check schedule. Also, San Francisco's MUNI bus #76 runs hourly from San Francisco direct to the

Marin Headlands on Sundays only. Golden Gate Transit bus route #40, the only service available between Marin County and the East Bay, runs from the San Rafael Transit Center to the Del Norte BART station in El Cerrito ($2 each way).

If you'd rather avoid the hassle of bus connections, Gray Line ($30; ☎415/558-9400) offers four-hour guided bus tours from the Transbay Terminal in San Francisco, taking in Sausalito and Muir Woods (daily 9am, 10am, 11am, 1.30pm & 2.30pm); the Blue and Gold Fleet ferry also has a boat-and-bus trip to Muir Woods, via Tiburon ($32).

One of the best ways to get around Marin is by bike, particularly using a mountain bike to cruise the many trails that crisscross the county, especially in the Marin Headlands. If you want to ride on the road, Sir Francis Drake Highway – from Larkspur to Point Reyes – makes a good route, though it's best to avoid weekends, when the roads can get clogged up with cars. All ferry services (except Alcatraz) allow bicycles.

Information

Three main on-the-spot sources can provide further information on Marin County: the Marin County Visitors Bureau, 1013 Larkspur Landing Circle, Larkspur (Mon–Fri 9am–5pm; ☎415/499-5000; *www.visitmarin.org*), the Sausalito Chamber of Commerce, Fourth Floor, 777 Bridgeway (Tues–Sun 11.30am–4pm; ☎415/332-0505), and the Mill Valley Chamber of Commerce, 85 Throckmorton (Mon, Tues, Thurs & Fri 11am–4pm; ☎415/388-9700), in the center of the town.

For information on hiking and camping in the wilderness and beach areas, depending on where you're heading, contact the Golden Gate National Recreation Area, Building 201, Fort Mason Center, San Francisco (Mon–Fri 9.30am–4.30pm; ☎415/556-0560) or in Sausalito at Fort Cronkhite (daily 9.30am–4.30pm; ☎415/331-1540); Mount Tamalpais State Park, 801 Panoramic Highway, Mill Valley (daily 8.30am–10.30pm; ☎415/388-2070); or the Point Reyes National Seashore, Bear Valley Visitors Center, Point Reyes (Mon–Fri 9am–5pm, Sat & Sun 8am–5pm; ☎415/663-1092). Information on what's on in Marin can be found in the widely available local freesheets, such as the down-to-earth *Coastal Post* or the New-Agey *Pacific Sun*.

Accommodation

You might prefer simply to dip into Marin County using San Francisco as a base, and if you've got a car or manage to time the bus connections right it's certainly possible, at least for the southernmost parts of the county. However, it can be nicer to take a more leisurely look at Marin, staying over for a couple of nights in some well-chosen spots. Sadly there are few hotels, and those that there are often charge in excess of $100 a night; motels tend to be the same as anywhere, though there are a couple of attractively faded ones along the coast. If you want to stay in a B&B, contact the Bed and Breakfast Exchange, 45 Entrata Drive, San Anselmo (☎415/485-1971), which can fix you up with rooms in comfortable private homes all over Marin County from $50 a night for two, ranging from courtyard hideaways on the beach in Tiburon to houseboats in Sausalito. The best bet for budget accommodation is a dorm bed in one of the beautifully situated hostels along the western beaches.

Motels and hotels

Acqua Hotel, 555 Redwood Hwy, Mill Valley (☎415/380-0400) Newly-opened sumptuous hotel on Richardson Bay run by the owners of the *Mill Valley Inn*. ⑦.

Casa Madrona, 801 Bridgeway, Sausalito (☎1-800/567-9524 or 415/332-0502). Deluxe hideaway tucked into the hills above the bay. ⑦.

Colonial Motel, 1735 Lincoln Ave, San Rafael (☎415/453-9188). Quiet, cheap and friendly motel in a residential neighborhood. ③.

Grand Hotel, 15 Brighton Ave, Bolinas (☎415/868-1757). Budget rooms in a funky, run-down old hotel. ②.

Mill Valley Inn, 165 Throckmorton Ave, Mill Valley (☎1-800/595-2100 or 415/389-6608). By far the best hotel in Marin County. Gorgeous European-style inn with elegant rooms and two private cottages. ⑦.

Ocean Court Motel, 18 Arenal St, Stinson Beach (☎415/868-0212). Just a block from the beach, west of Hwy-1. Large simple rooms with kitchens. ⑤.

Stinson Beach Motel, 3416 Shoreline Hwy, Stinson Beach (☎415/868-1712). Basic roadside motel right on Hwy-1, with tiny rooms. Five minutes' walk to the beach. ④.

Bed and breakfast

Blue Heron Inn, 11 Wharf Rd, Bolinas (☎415/868-1102). Lovely double rooms in an unbeatable locale. Breakfast is served at the owner's cozy restaurant, *The Shop Café* at 46 Wharf Rd, which also serves lunch and dinner. ⑤.

Lindisfarne Guest House, Green Gulch Zen Center, Muir Beach (☎415/383-3134). Restful rooms in a meditation retreat set in a secluded valley above Muir Beach. Price includes excellent vegetarian meals. ⑤.

Mountain Home Inn, 810 Panoramic Highway, Mill Valley (☎415/381-9000). Romantically located on Mount Tamalpais' crest, this bed and breakfast offers great views and endless hiking. Some rooms with hot tubs. ⑦.

Olema Inn, 10000 Sir Francis Drake Blvd, Olema (☎1-800/532-9252 or 415/663-9559). Wonderful little B&B near the entrance to Point Reyes National Seashore, on a site that's been a hotel since 1876. Features a gourmet restaurant serving seafood and a full bar with heady wine list. Comfy rooms and absolutely no nightlife or traffic-noise to speak of; perfect if you want to really take a break from the city. ⑥.

Pelican Inn, 10 Pacific Way, Muir Beach (☎415/383-6000). Very comfortable rooms in a romantic pseudo-English country inn, with good bar and restaurant downstairs, ten minutes' walk from beautiful Muir Beach. ⑦.

Ten Inverness Way, 10 Inverness Way, Inverness (☎415/669-1648). Quiet and restful, with a hot tub, in small village of good restaurants and bakeries on the fringes of Point Reyes. ⑦.

Hostels

HI-Marin Headlands, Building 941, Fort Barry, Marin Headlands (closed 9.30am–4.30pm; ☎415/331-2777). Hard to get to unless you're driving – it's near Rodeo Lagoon just off Bunker Road, five miles west of Sausalito – but worth the effort for its setting, in cozy old army barracks just across the Golden Gate Bridge. On Sundays and holidays only, MUNI bus #76 from San Francisco stops right outside. Dorm beds $12-$14 a night, plus $1 linen rental.

HI-Point Reyes, in the Point Reyes National Seashore (closed 9.30am–4.30pm; ☎415/663-8811). Also hard to reach without your own transportation: just off Limantour Road six miles west of the visitor center and two miles from the beach, it's located in an old ranch house and surrounded by meadows and forests. Dorm beds $12–14 a night.

Campgrounds

China Camp State Park, off N San Pedro Rd, north of San Rafael (☎415/456-0766). Walk-in plots (just 600 ft from the parking lot) overlooking a lovely meadow. First-come-first-camped for $16 a night. Reserve through ParkNet April-Oct (☎1-800/444-7275).

Marin Headlands, just across the Golden Gate Bridge (☎415/331-1540). Five campgrounds, the best of which is *Kirby Cove* (open April-Oct only, and very popular), at the northern foot of the Golden Gate Bridge (reservations Tues-Thur 10am-2pm; $20; ☎415/561-4304). Of the remaining sites, one is a group camp ($20), and the other three are free.

Mount Tamalpais State Park, above Mill Valley (☎415/388-2070). Sixteen plots for backpackers on the slopes of the mountain ($16), and a few rustic cabins ($30 a night), along the coast at Steep Ravine. Reserve cabins via ParkNet (☎1-800/444-7275).

Point Reyes National Seashore, forty miles northwest of San Francisco (☎415/663-1092). A wide range of hike-in sites for backpackers, near the beach or in the forest. Reserve sites up to two months in advance (weekdays 9am-2pm; ☎415/663-8054; $10).

Samuel Taylor State Park, on Sir Francis Drake Blvd, fifteen miles west of San Rafael (☎415/488-9897). Deluxe, car-accessible plots with hot showers, spread along a river for $16 a night. Don't miss the swimming hole or bat caves. In summer, reserve a place through ParkNet, ☎1-800/444-7275.

Across the Golden Gate: Marin Headlands and Sausalito

The largely undeveloped **Marin Headlands** of the Golden Gate National Recreation Area, across the Golden Gate Bridge from San Francisco, afford some of the most impressive views of the bridge and the city behind. Take the first turn as you exit the bridge (Alexander Avenue) and follow the sign back to San Francisco – the one-way circle trip back to the bridge heads first to the west along Conzelman Road and up a steep hill. You'll pass through a largely undeveloped land, dotted by the concrete remains of old forts and gun emplacements standing guard over the entrance to the bay, dating from as far back as the Civil War and as recent as World War II. The coastline here is much more rugged than it is on the San Francisco side, making it a great place for an aimless cliff-top hike or a stroll along one of the beaches dramatically situated near the crashing waves at the bottom of treacherous footpaths.

The first installation as you climb the steep hill up the headlands, is **Battery Wallace,** the largest and most impressive of artillery sites along the rugged coast here, cut through a hillside above the southwestern tip of the peninsula. The clean-cut military geometry survives, framing views of the Pacific Ocean and the Golden Gate Bridge. If you're interested in such things, come along on the first Sunday of the month and take a guided tour of an abandoned 1950s ballistic missile launchpad, complete with disarmed nuclear missiles. Otherwise, continue along Conzelman for incredible views of the city from any of the many turnouts. Following the road to it brings you to a parking area. For birdwatching, walk from here through tunnels that lead 500m to the opposite bluff, overlooking **Rodeo Beach** and **Point Bonita lighthouse** far below. From the parking lot, drive down the one-way lane that Conzelman becomes and keep winding down to the Point Bonita Lighthouse. It stands sentry at the very end of the headlands and is often open for tours (Sat–Mon 12.30-3.30pm; free). Conzelman comes to a "T" in the road at the YMCA camp bunkhouse; turn left and park your car on the side of the road or at the parking lot 300 yards west, at the end of the drive. To reach the lighthouse, you have to walk the half-mile pathway down, a beautiful stroll that takes you through a tunnel cut into the cliff, and across a precarious suspension bridge.

Looping back around, you'll be heading northeast on Bunker Road. Stop off at the **Marin Headlands Information Center** (daily 9.30am–4.30pm; ☎415/331-1540), alongside Rodeo Lagoon, for free maps of popular hiking trails in the area. Across the road and a bit further along, the largest of the **Fort Barry**'s old buildings has been converted into the spacious but homey *HI-Marin Headlands* **hostel,** an excellent base for more extended explorations of the inland ridges and valleys.

Turn off to the left where Bunker Road snakes down to wide, sandy **Rodeo Beach** (#76 MUNI bus from San Francisco: Sun & holidays only). The beach separates the chilly ocean from the marshy warm water of **Rodeo Lagoon,** where swimming is prohibited to protect nesting seabirds. North of the lagoon, the **Marine Mammal Center** rescues and rehabilitates injured and orphaned sea creatures, which you can visit while they recover; there's also a series of displays on the marine ecosystem and a bookstore that sells T-shirts and posters.

Sausalito
SAUSALITO, along the bay below US-101, is a pretty, smug little town of exclusive restaurants and pricey boutiques along a picturesque waterfront promenade. Expensive, quirkily designed houses climb the overgrown cliffs above **Bridgeway Avenue,** the main road and bus route through town. Sausalito used to be a fairly gritty

community of fishermen and sea-traders, full of bars and bordellos, and despite its upscale modern face it still makes a fun day out from San Francisco by ferry, the boats arriving next to the Sausalito Yacht Club in the center of town. Hang out in one of the waterfront bars and watch the crowds strolling along the esplanade, or climb the stairways above Bridgeway and amble around the leafy hills. If you have sailing experience, split the $130 daily rental fee of a four- to six-person sailboat at Cass's Marine, 1702 Bridgeway (☎415/332-6789). The other main diversion is sea kayaking. Sea Trek (☎415/332-4465) rents single or double sea kayaks beginning at $20 for two hours' worth of paddling the bay. They offer sit-on-top kayaks, lessons and safe routes for first-timers or closed kayaks and directions around Angel Island for more experienced paddlers.

The old working wharves and warehouses that made Sausalito a haven for smugglers and Prohibition-era rum-runners are long gone; most have been taken over by dull steakhouses. However, some stretches of it have, for the moment at least, survived the tourist onslaught. Half a mile north of the town center along Bridgeway Avenue, an ad hoc community of exotic barges and houseboats, some of which have been moored here since the 1950s, is being threatened with eviction to make room for yet another luxury marina. In the meantime, many of the boats – one looks like a South Pacific island, another like the Taj Mahal – can be viewed from the marina behind the large brown shed at 2100 Bridgeway that houses the **Bay Model Visitor Center**, 2100 Bridgeway (Tues–Sat 9am–4pm; donation). Inside the huge building, elevated walkways lead you around a scale model of the bay, surrounding deltas and its aquatic inhabitants, offering insight on the enormity and diversity of this area.

The Marin County Coast to Bolinas

The **Shoreline Highway**, Hwy-1, cuts off west from US-101 just north of Sausalito, following the old main highway towards Mill Valley (see p.533). The first turn on the left, Tennessee Valley Road, leads up to the less-visited northern expanses of the Golden Gate National Recreation Area. You can take a beautiful three-mile hike from the parking lot at the end of the road, heading down along the secluded and lushly green **Tennessee Valley** to a small beach along a rocky cove, or you can take a guided tour on horseback from Miwok Livery at 701 Tennessee Valley Rd (☎415/383-8048; $40 per hr).

Hwy-1 twists up the canyon to a crest, where **Panoramic Highway** spears off to the right, following the ridge north to Muir Woods and Mount Tamalpais (see overleaf); Golden Gate Transit bus #63 to Stinson Beach follows this route every hour on weekends and holidays only. Be warned, however, that the hillsides are usually choked with fog until 11am, making the approach from San Francisco to Stinson Beach/Bolinas via Hwy-1 both dangerous and uninteresting. Two miles down from the crest, a small unpaved road cuts off to the left, dropping down to the bottom of the broad canyon to the **Green Gulch Farm and Zen Center** (☎415/383-3134), an organic farm and Buddhist retreat, with an authentic Japanese tea house and a simple but refined prayer hall. On Sunday mornings the center is opened for a public meditation period and an informal discussion of Zen Buddhism, after which you can stroll down to Muir Beach. If you already have some experience of Zen, inquire about the center's Guest Student Program, which enables initiates to stay from three days to several weeks at a time (it costs about $10 a night). If you just want a weekend's retreat, you can also stay overnight in the attached *Lindisfarne Guest House* (see "Listings"). Residents rise well before dawn for meditation and prayer, then work much of the day in the gardens, tending the vegetables that are eventually served in many of the Bay Area's finest restaurants (notably *Greens* in San Francisco – see p.463).

Beyond the Zen Center, the road down from Muir Woods rejoins Hwy-1 at **Muir Beach**, usually uncrowded and beautifully secluded in a semicircular cove. Three miles north, **Steep Ravine** drops sharply down the cliffs to a small beach, past very rustic $30-a-night cabins and a $10-a-night campground, bookable through Mount Tamalpais State Park (see "Listings"). A mile on is the small and lovely **Red Rocks** nudist beach, down a steep trail from a parking area along the highway. **Stinson Beach**, which is bigger, and more popular despite the rather cold water (it's packed on weekends in summer, when the traffic can be nightmarish), is a mile further. You can rent boogie boards for $8 and wet suits for $10 a day from the Livewater Surf Shop (☎415/868-0333), 3448 Shoreline Hwy, or kayaks for $35–60 per day a bit further down the road at the Stinson Beach Health Club, 3605 Shoreline Hwy (☎415/868-2739).

Bolinas and southern Point Reyes

At the tip of the headland, due west from Stinson Beach, is the village of **BOLINAS**, though you may have a hard time finding it – road signs marking the turn-off from Hwy-1 are removed as soon as they're put up, by locals hoping to keep the place to themselves. The campaign may have backfired, though, since press coverage of the "sign war" has done more to publicize the town than any road sign ever did; to get there, take the first left beyond the estuary and follow the road to the end. Bolinas is completely surrounded by federal property: the Golden Gate National Recreation Area and Point Reyes National Seashore. Even the lagoon was recently declared a National Bird Sanctuary. Known for its leftist hippy culture, the village itself is a small colony of artists, bearded handymen, stray dogs and writers (the late trout-fishing author Richard Brautigan and basketball diarist Jim Carroll among them), and there's not a lot to see – though you can get a feel for the place (and pick up tasty sandwiches and bags of fresh fruit and vegetables) at the *Bolinas People's Store* in the block-long village center.

Beyond Bolinas there's a rocky beach at the end of Wharf Road west of the village, and **Duxbury Reef Nature Reserve**, half a mile west at the end of Elm Road, is well worth a look for its tidal pools, full of starfish, crabs and sea anemones. Otherwise, Mesa Road heads north from Bolinas past the **Point Reyes Bird Observatory** (☎415/868-0655) – open for informal tours all day, though best visited in the morning. The first bird observatory in the US, this is still an important research and study center. If you time it right you may be able to watch, or even help, the staff as they put colored bands on the birds to keep track of them. Beyond here, the unpaved road leads onto the **Palomarin Trailhead**, the southern access into the Point Reyes National Seashore (see p.536). The best of the many beautiful hikes around the area leads past a number of small lakes and meadows for three miles to **Alamere Falls**, which throughout the winter and spring cascade down the cliffs onto Wildcat Beach. **Bass Lake**, the first along the trail, is a great spot for a swim and is best entered from one of the two rope-swings that hang above its shore. At the junction of Bolinas Road and Hwy-1, cross the highway and head due east. If there's no sign warning the road is closed (landslides and washouts are common), continue up this route, the **Bolinas-Fairfax Road**, for a superb, winding drive through redwoods and grassy hillsides. When you reach the "T" in the road, turn left to get to Fairfax, or right to scale Mount Tamalpais.

Mount Tamalpais and Muir Woods

Mount Tamalpais dominates the skyline of the Marin peninsula, hulking over the cool canyons of the rest of the county and dividing it into two distinct parts: the wild western slopes above the Pacific coast and the increasingly suburban communities along the calmer bay frontage. Panoramic Highway branches off from Hwy-1 along the crest through the center of **Mount Tamalpais State Park** (☎415/338-2070; *www.mtia.net*), which has some thirty miles of hiking trails and many campgrounds, though most of the redwood trees which once covered its slopes have long since been chopped down to form the posts and beams of San Francisco's Victorian houses. One grove of these towering trees does remain, however, protected as the **Muir Woods National Monument** (daily 8am–sunset; $2), a mile down Muir Woods Road from Panoramic Highway. It's a tranquil and majestic spot, with sunlight filtering through the 300ft trees down to the laurel- and fern-covered canyon below. The canyon's steep sides are what saved it from Mill Valley's lumbermen, and today it's one of the few first-growth redwood groves between San Francisco and the fantastic forests of Redwood National Park, up the coast near the Oregon border (see p.619).

Its proximity to San Francisco makes Muir Woods a popular target, and the paved trails nearest the parking lot are often packed with bus-tour hordes. However, if you visit during the week, or outside midsummer, it's easy enough to leave the crowds behind, especially if you're willing to head off up the steep trails that climb the canyon sides. Winter is a particularly good time to come, as the streams are gurgling – the main creek flows down to Muir Beach, and salmon have been known to spawn in it – and the forest creatures, including the colonies of ladybugs that spend their winter huddling in the rich undergrowth, are more likely to be seen going about their business. Keep an eye out for the various species of salamanders and newts that thrive in this damp environment; be warned, though, that some are poisonous and will bite if harassed.

One way to avoid the crowds, and the only way to get here on public transportation, is to enter the woods from the top by way of a two-mile hike from the **Pan Toll Ranger Station** (☎415/388-2070) on Panoramic Highway – which is a stop on the Golden Gate Transit #63 bus route. As the state park headquarters, the station has maps and information on hiking and camping, and rangers can suggest hikes to suit your mood and interests. From here the **Pan Toll Road** turns off to the right along the ridge to within a hundred yards of the 2571-foot summit of Mount Tamalpais, where there are breathtaking views of the distant Sierra Nevada, and red-necked turkey vultures listlessly circle.

Mill Valley

From the East Peak of Mount Tamalpais, a quick two-mile hike downhill follows the **Temelpa Trail** through velvety shrubs of chaparral to **MILL VALLEY**, the oldest and most enticing of Marin County's inland towns – also accessible every thirty minutes by Golden Gate Transit bus #10 from San Francisco and Sausalito. Originally a logging center, it was from here that the destruction of the surrounding redwoods was organized, though for many years the town has made a healthy living out of tourism. The **Mill Valley and Mount Tamalpais Scenic Railroad** – according to the blurb, "the crookedest railroad in the world" – was cut into the slopes above the town in 1896, twisting up through nearly three hundred tight curves in under eight miles. The trip proved so popular with tourists that the line was extended down into Muir Woods in 1907, though road-building and fire combined to put an end to the railroad by 1930. You can, however, follow its old route from the end of Summit Avenue in Mill Valley, a popular trip with daredevils on all-terrain bikes, which were, incidentally, invented here.

Though much of Mill Valley's attraction lies in its easy access to hiking and mountain-bike trails up Mount Tam, its compact yet relaxed center has a number of cafés and some good shops and galleries. The *Depot Bookstore and Café* (Mon–Sat 7am–10pm, Sun 8am–10pm; ☎415/383-2665) is a popular bookstore, café and meeting place at 87 Throckmorton Ave; there's a small **visitor center** next door (Mon–Tues, Thurs–Sat 10am–4pm; ☎415/388-9700), which has free maps of Mount Tam and area hiking trails. Across the street, the **Pleasure Principle** is a reminder of the Northern California eclecticism hidden beneath a posh surface – the store, the self-declared UFO headquarters of Mill Valley, is also the proud purveyor of a large vintage porn collection. If in the area in early October, don't miss the **Mill Valley Film Festival**, a world-class event that draws a host of up-and-coming directors, as well as Bay Area stars like Robin Williams and Sharon Stone; for program information, call ☎415/383-5346, or check *www.finc.org*.

Tiburon

TIBURON, at the tip of a narrow peninsula three miles east of US-101, is, like Sausalito, a ritzy harbourside village to which hundreds of people come each weekend, many of them via direct Blue and Gold Fleet **ferries** from Pier 41 in San Francisco's Fisherman's Wharf. It's a relaxed place, less touristy than Sausalito, and if you're in the mood to take it easy and watch the boats sail across the bay, sitting out on the sunny deck of one of the many cafés and bars can be idyllic. There are few specific sights to look out for, but it's pleasant enough to simply wander around, browsing the galleries and antique shops. The best of these are grouped together in **Ark Row**, at the west end of Main Street, where the quirky buildings are actually old houseboats that were beached here early in the century. On a hill above the town stands **Old St Hilary's Church** (April–Oct, Wed–Sun 1–4pm; ☎415/789-0066), a Carpenter Gothic beauty that is best seen in the spring, when the surrounding fields are covered with multicolored buckwheat, flax, and paintbrush.

Cyclists can cruise around the many plush houses of **Belvedere Island**, just across the Beach Road Bridge from the west end of Main Street, enjoying the fine views of the bay and Golden Gate Bridge. More ambitious bikers can continue along the waterfront bike path, which winds from the bijou shops and galleries three miles west along undeveloped Richardson Bay frontage to a bird sanctuary at **Greenwood Cove**. The pristine Victorian house here is now the western headquarters of the National Audubon Society and open for tours on Sundays (10am–4pm); a small interpretive center has displays on local and migratory birds and wildlife.

Angel Island

However appealing, the pleasures of Tiburon are soon exhausted, and you'd be well advised to take the hourly Angel Island Ferry (hourly 10am-4pm; $7 round trip, plus $1 per bicycle; ☎415/435-2131) a mile offshore to the largest island in the San Francisco Bay, ten times the size of Alcatraz. **Angel Island** is now officially a state park, but over the years it's served a variety of purposes, everything from a home for Miwok Native Americans to a World War II prisoner-of-war camp. It's full of ghostly ruins of old military installations, and with oak and eucalyptus trees and sagebrush covering the hills above rocky coves and sandy beaches, feels quite apart from the mainland. The island offers some pleasant biking opportunities: a five-mile road rings the island, and an unpaved track (and a number of hiking trails) leads up to the 800ft hump of **Mount Livermore**, with panoramic views of the Bay Area.

The ferry arrives at **Ayala Cove**, where a small snack bar selling hot dogs and cold drinks provides the only sustenance available on the island – bring a picnic if you plan to spend the day here. The nearby **visitor center** (daily 9am–4pm; ☎415/435-1915), in an old building that was built as a quarantine facility for soldiers returning from the Philippines after the Spanish–American War, has displays on the island's history. Around the point on the northwest corner of the island the **North Garrison**, built in 1905, was the site of a prisoner-of-war camp during World War II, while the larger **East Garrison**, on the bay a half mile beyond, was the major transfer point for soldiers bound for the South Pacific.

Quarry Beach around the point is the best on the island, a clean sandy shore that's protected from the winds blowing in through the Golden Gate; it's also a popular landing spot for kayakers and canoeists who paddle across the bay from Berkeley. **Camping** on Angel Island (☎1-800/444-7275) costs $10 per night ($11 Fri & Sat), well worth the view of San Francisco and the East Bay at night. The nine sites fill up fast, so make reservations well-ahead. For **tours** of Angel Island, contact Angel Island TramTours (☎415/897-0715; *www.angelisland.com*) which rents mountain bikes ($25/day), gives tram tours ($10), and leads all-day kayak trips around the island (May-Oct weekends; $100).

Sir Francis Drake Boulevard and Central Marin County

The quickest route to the wilds of the Point Reyes National Seashore, and the only way to get there on public transportation, is by way of **Sir Francis Drake Boulevard**, which cuts across central Marin County through the inland towns of **San Anselmo** and **Fairfax**, reaching the coast thirty miles west at a crescent-shaped bay where, in 1579, Drake supposedly landed and claimed all of what he called Nova Albion for England. The route makes an excellent day-long cycling tour, with the reward of good beaches, a youth hostel, and some tasty restaurants at the end of the road.

The Larkspur Golden Gate Transit **ferry**, which leaves from the Ferry Building in San Francisco, is the longest and, surprisingly, least expensive of the bay crossings. Primarily a commuter route, it docks at the modern space-frame terminal at Larkspur Landing. The monolithic, red-tile-roofed complex you see on the bayfront a mile east is the maximum-security **San Quentin State Prison**, which houses the state's most violent and notorious criminals, and of which Johnny Cash sang so resonantly "I hate every stone of you." If you arrive by car over the Richmond–San Rafael Bridge, follow road signs off Hwy-101 for the San Quentin Prison **Museum**, Building 106, Dolores Way (Tues–Fri & Sun 11am–3pm, Sat 11.45am–3.15pm; $2).

San Anselmo, Fairfax and Point Reyes Station

SAN ANSELMO, set in a broad valley two miles north of Mount Tam, calls itself "the antiques capital of Northern California" and sports a tiny center of specialty shops, furniture stores and cafés that draws out many San Francisco shoppers on weekends. The ivy-covered **San Francisco Theological Seminary** off Bolinas Avenue, which dominates the town from the hill above, is worth a quick visit for the view and architecture. At serene **Robson-Harrington Park** on Crescent Avenue you can picnic among well-tended gardens, and the very green and leafy **Creek Park** follows the creek that winds through the town center, but otherwise there's not a lot to do but eat and drink – or browse through fine bookstores, such as Oliver's Books, at 645 San Anselmo Ave (☎415/454-4421).

Center Boulevard follows the tree-lined creek west for a mile to **FAIRFAX**, a much less ostentatiously hedonistic community than the harborside towns, though in many ways it still typifies Marin lifestyles, with an array of wholefood stores and bookstores geared to a thoughtfully mellow crowd. From Fairfax, the narrow Bolinas Road twists up and over the mountains to the coast at Stinson Beach, while Sir Francis Drake Boulevard winds through a pastoral landscape of ranch houses hidden away up oak-covered valleys.

Ten miles west of Fairfax along Sir Francis Drake Boulevard, **Samuel Taylor State Park** has excellent camping (see p.530 for details); five miles more brings you to the coastal Hwy-1 and the hamlet of **OLEMA**, at the entrance to the park, which has good food and lodging. A mile north of Olema sits the tourist town of **POINT REYES STATION**, another good place to stop off for a bite to eat or to pick up picnic supplies before heading off to enjoy the wide open spaces of the Point Reyes National Seashore just beyond.

The Point Reyes National Seashore

From Point Reyes Station, Sir Francis Drake Boulevard heads out to the westernmost tip of Marin County at Point Reyes through the **Point Reyes National Seashore**, a near-island of wilderness surrounded on three sides by more than fifty miles of isolated coastline – pine forests and sunny meadows bordered by rocky cliffs and sandy, windswept beaches. This wing-shaped landmass, something of an aberration along the generally straight coastline north of San Francisco, is in fact a rogue piece of the earth's crust that has been drifting slowly and steadily northward along the San Andreas Fault, having started some six million years ago as a suburb of Los Angeles. When the great earthquake of 1906 shattered San Francisco, the land here – the epicenter – shifted over sixteen feet in an instant, though damage was confined to a few skewed cattle fences.

The park's **visitor center** (Mon–Fri 9am–5pm, Sat, Sun & holidays 8am–5pm; ☎415/663-1092) two miles southwest of Point Reyes Station near Olema, just off Hwy-1 on Bear Valley Road, holds engaging displays on the geology and natural history of the region. Rangers dish out excellent hiking and cycling itineraries, and have up-to-date information on the weather, which can change quickly and be cold and windy along the coast even when it's hot and sunny here, three miles inland. They also handle permits and reservations for the various hike-in **campgrounds** within the park. Nearby, a replica of a native Miwok village has an authentic religious **roundhouse**, and a popular hike follows the Bear Valley Trail along Coast Creek four miles to **Arch Rock**, a large tunnel in the seaside cliffs that you can walk through at low tide.

North of the visitor center, Limantour Road heads west six miles to the **HI-Point Reyes Hostel** (see p.529), continuing on another two miles to the coast at **Limantour Beach**, one of the best swimming beaches and a good place to watch the seabirds in the adjacent estuary. Bear Valley Road rejoins Sir Francis Drake Boulevard just past Limantour Road, leading north along Tomales Bay through the village of **Inverness**, so-named because the landscape reminded an early settler of his home in the Scottish Highlands. Eight miles west of Inverness, a turn leads down past **Johnson's Oyster Farm** (Tues–Sun 8am–4pm; ☎415/669-1149) – which sells bivalves for around $8 a dozen, less than half the price you'd pay San Francisco – to **Drake's Beach**, the presumed landing spot of Sir Francis in 1579 (his voyage journal makes the exact location unclear). Appropriately, the coastline here resembles the southern coast of England, often cold, wet and windy, with chalk-white cliffs rising above the wide sandy beach. The road continues southwest another four miles to the very tip of Point Reyes. A precarious-looking **lighthouse** (Thurs–Sun 10am–5pm) stands firm against the crashing surf, and the bluffs are excellent for watching sea lions and, from mid-March to April and late December to early February, migrating gray whales. Keep in mind the distance and slow speeds it takes to reach these spots, which is hard to judge on a map. From the visitor center, it's 15 miles to Drakes Beach and 23 miles to the lighthouse. Check with the rangers on weather conditions before setting out.

The northern tip of the Point Reyes seashore, **Tomales Point**, is accessible via Pierce Point Road, which turns off Sir Francis Drake Boulevard two miles north of Inverness. Jutting out into Tomales Bay, it's the least-visited section of the park and a refuge for hefty **tule elk**; it's also a great place to admire the lupines, poppies and other wildflowers that appear in the spring. The best swimming (at least the warmest water) is at **Heart's Desire Beach**, just before the end of the road. Down the bluffs from where the road comes to a dead end, there are excellent tidal pools at rocky **McClure's Beach**. North of Point Reyes Station, Hwy-1 continues past the famed oyster beds of Tomales Bay north along the crashing surf and up the Northern California coast.

San Rafael and Northern Marin County

You may pass through **SAN RAFAEL** on your way north from San Francisco, but there's little worth stopping for. The county seat and the only big city in Marin County, it has none of the woodsy qualities that make the other towns special, though you'll come across a couple of good restaurants and bars along Fourth Street, the main drag. Its one attraction is the old **Mission San Rafael Arcangel** (daily 11am–4pm; free), in fact a 1949 replica that was built near the site of the 1817 original on Fifth Ave at A Street. The real points of interest, however, are well on the outskirts: the Marin County Civic Center to the north and the little-known China Camp State Park along the bay to the east.

The **Marin County Civic Center** (Mon–Fri 9am–5pm; tours Wed 10.30am; free; ☎415/499-6646), spanning the hills just east of US-101 a mile north of central San Rafael, is a strange, otherworldly complex of administrative offices, plus an excellent performance space that resembles a giant viaduct capped by a bright blue-tiled roof. These buildings were architect **Frank Lloyd Wright**'s one and only government project, and although the huge circus tents and amusement park at the core of the designer's conception were never built, it does have some interesting touches, such as the atrium lobbies that open directly to the outdoors.

From the Civic Center, North San Pedro Road loops around the headlands through **China Camp State Park** (☎415/456-0766), an expansive area of pastures and open spaces that's hard to reach without your own transportation. It takes its name from the intact but long-abandoned Chinese shrimp-fishing village at the far eastern tip of the park, the sole survivor of the many small Chinese communities that once dotted the California coast. The ramshackle buildings, small wooden pier and old boats lying on the sand are pure John Steinbeck; the only recent addition a chain-link fence to protect the site from vandals. On the weekend you can get beer and sandwiches from the old shack at the foot of the pier, but the atmosphere is best during the week at sunset, when there's often no one around at all. There's a hike-in **campground** ($16) with thirty primitive sites at the northern end of the park, about two miles from the end of the Golden Gate Transit bus #23 route.

Six miles north of San Rafael, the **Lucas Valley Road** turns off west, twisting across Marin to Point Reyes. Although he lives and works here, it was not named after *Star Wars* filmmaker George Lucas, whose sprawling **Skywalker Ranch** studios are well hidden off the road. Hwy-37 cuts off east, eight miles north of San Rafael, heading around the top of the bay into the Wine Country of the Sonoma and Napa valleys (see p.589).

Eating

Marin's restaurants are as varied in personality as the people who inhabit the county – homey neighborhood cafés dish out nutritious portions to healthy mountain-bikers, well-appointed waterside restaurants cater to tourists, and gourmet establishments serve delicate concoctions to affluent executives. We have listed the best of the options below.

Restaurants

Bubba's Diner, 566 San Anselmo Ave, San Anselmo (☎415/459-6862). Hip little old-fashioned diner with a friendly and casual atmosphere. Try a delicious biscuit with your meal.

Cactus Café, 393 Miller Ave, Mill Valley (☎415/388-8226). Reasonably priced, small and friendly restaurant serving fun Cal-Mex food flavored with homemade hot sauce.

Dipsea Café, 200 Shoreline Hwy, Mill Valley (☎415/381-0298). Hearty pancakes, omelets, sandwiches and salads, especially good before a day out hiking on Mount Tamalpais. Breakfast and lunch only.

Gatsby's, 39 Caledonia St, Sausalito (☎415/332-4500). Slick pizza parlor a block from the waterfront on the north side of town. Bright new interior comes with an expanded (and more expensive) menu.

Guaymas, 5 Main St, Tiburon (☎415/435-6300). Some of the most unique, inventive Cal-Mex cuisine in the Bay Area (and priced accordingly), paired with a spectacular view of the city.

Hilda's, 639 San Anselmo Ave, San Anselmo (☎415/457-9266). Great breakfasts and lunches in this down-home, cozy café.

The Lark Creek Inn, 234 Magnolia Ave, Larkspur (☎415/924-7766). The place to go in Marin for fine dining. The contemporary American food at this classy restored Victorian is expensive, but not without reason: the food is exquisite, the service first rate, and the atmosphere charming.

Mikayla, 801 Bridgeway, Sausalito (☎415/331-5888). Mediterranean staples meet California cuisine in this expensive, but highly rated restaurant in the *Casa Madrona* hotel. Romantic views of the harbor and excellent seafood. Huge Sunday brunch buffet.

Mill Valley Market, 12 Corte Madera Ave, Mill Valley (☎415/388-8466). Deliciously large sandwiches and mouth-watering pasta salads that can be enjoyed at the picnic tables in the main plaza across the street.

Mountain Home Inn, 810 Panoramic Hwy, above Mill Valley (☎415/381-9000). A place that's as good for the view as for the food, with broiled meat and fish dishes served up in a rustic lodge on the slopes of Mount Tamalpais.

New Morning Café, 1696 Tiburon Blvd, Tiburon (☎415/435-4315). Lots of healthy wholegrain sandwiches, plus salads and omelets.

Olema Inn, 10000 Sir Francis Drake Blvd, Olema (☎1-800/532-9252 or 415/663-9559). Cozy nook of an eatery serving fresh fish and oysters at around $10 per person, on a patio looking into the woods. Quiet atmosphere and excellent service.

Piazza D'Angelo, 22 Miller Ave, Mill Valley (☎415/388-2000). Good salads, tasty pasta and affordable pizzas, served up in a lively but comfortable room right off the downtown plaza.

Rice Table, 1617 Fourth St, San Rafael (☎415/456-1808). From the shrimp chips through the crab pancakes and noodles onto the fried plantain desserts, these fragrant and spicy Indonesian dishes are an excellent value and worth planning a day around. Dinners only.

Sam's Anchor Café, 27 Main St, Tiburon (☎415/435-4527). This rough-hewn, amiable waterfront café and bar has been around for more than 75 years. Good burgers, sandwiches and very popular Sunday brunches are best enjoyed on the outdoor deck.

Station House Café, 11180 Hwy-1 (Main Street), Point Reyes Station (☎415/663-1515). Serving three meals daily, this friendly local favorite entices diners from miles around to sample their grilled seafood and great steaks.

Stinson Beach Grill, 3465 Shoreline Hwy, Stinson Beach (☎415/868-2002). Somewhat pricey, but relaxed, with outdoor dining – look out for the bright-blue building right in the heart of town.

Cafés, drinking and nightlife

While the Marin County nightlife is never as charged as it gets in San Francisco, almost every town has at least a couple of **cafés** that are open long hours for a jolt of caffeine, and any number of saloon-like **bars** where you'll feel at home immediately. In addition, since most of the honchos of the Bay Area music scene and dozens of lesser-known but no less brilliant session musicians and songwriters live here, Marin's nightclubs are unsurpassed for catching big names in intimate locales.

Cafés

Café Trieste, 1000 Bridgeway, Sausalito (☎415/332-7770). This distant relative of San Francisco's North Beach institution serves good coffee, a wide menu of pastas and salads, and great gelati.

Caledonia Kitchen, 400 Caledonia St, Sausalito (☎415/331-0220). Relaxing, cheery café serving simple sandwiches, fresh pastries, and a variety of salads across from a small park.

Depot Bookstore and Café, 87 Throckmorton Ave, Mill Valley ☎415/383-2665. Lively café in an old train station, sharing space with a bookstore and newsstand. Weekly readings from local and nationally recognized authors.

Fairfax Café, 33 Broadway, Fairfax (☎415/459-6404). Excellent Mediterranean food with occasional evening poetry readings.

Java Rama, 546 San Anselmo Ave, San Anselmo (☎415/453-5282). Specialty coffees and pastries along with modern rock on the stereo attracts a young crowd.

Sweden House, 35 Main St, Tiburon (☎415/435-9767). Great coffee and marvelous pastries on a jetty overlooking the yacht harbor, all for surprisingly reasonable prices.

Bars

Café Amsterdam, 23 Broadway, Fairfax (☎415/256-8020). Live alternative folk rock nightly with an outdoor patio, microbrews, espresso drinks and an extensive menu.

Fourth Street Tavern, 711 Fourth St, San Rafael (☎415/454-4044). Gutsy, no-frills beer bar with free, bluesy music most nights.

Marin Brewing Company, 1809 Larkspur Landing, Larkspur (☎415/461-4677). Lively pub opposite the Larkspur ferry terminal, with half a dozen tasty ales – try the malty Albion Amber or the Marin Hefe Weiss – all brewed on the premises.

No Name Bar, 757 Bridgeway, Sausalito (☎415/332-1392). A smoky ex-haunt of the Beats which hosts live jazz several times per week beginning at 8pm and on Sundays at 3-7pm.

Pelican Inn, Hwy-1, Muir Beach (☎415/383-6000). Fair selection of traditional English and modern Californian ales, plus fish and chips (and rooms to rent in case you overdo it).

Smiley's Schooner Saloon, 41 Wharf Rd, Bolinas (☎415/868-1311). The bartender calls the customers by name at one of the oldest continually operating bars in the state. Basic hotel rooms are available in back for $75.90 weekdays–$86.90 weekends.

Sweetwater, 153 Throckmorton Ave, Mill Valley (☎415/388-3820). Large, open room full of beer-drinking locals that after dark evolves into Marin's prime live music venue, bringing in some of the biggest names in music, from jazz and blues all-stars to Jefferson Airplane survivors.

travel details

Trains

A daily **Amtrak** shuttle bus departs from San Francisco from the San Francisco Shopping Center, 835 Market St (8am and 8.25pm); Pier 39 at Fisherman's Wharf (8.15am and 8.35pm); and the Ferry Building (8.40am 8.55pm) to the Emeryville depot, from where the *Coast Starlight* train runs mornings northeast to Sacramento, Portland and Seattle and evenings south to Los Angeles and San Diego. Amtrak's *Capitol Corridor* route links Oakland with San Jose (four daily, 1hr). San Francisco-San Jose commuters rely on **Caltrain** (☎1-800/660-4287). Thirty-three trains make the trip each way daily, with express ones clocking in at 45min, and regulars taking 1hr30min ($4-$5.25 each way). The San Francisco station is at Fourth and King Streets.

Buses

Greyhound unless specified otherwise.

San Francisco to: Los Angeles (19 daily; 8–12hr; or 1 Green Tortoise weekly; 12hr); Redding (5 daily; 6hr); Reno (7 daily; 6hr); San Diego (8 daily; 12hr); Sacramento (17 daily; 2hr 20min); San Jose (13 daily; 1hr 30min); San Rafael (2 daily; 1hr).

CHAPTER EIGHT

THE GOLD COUNTRY AND LAKE TAHOE

The gold of California is a touchstone which has betrayed the rottenness, the baseness, of mankind. Satan, from one of his elevations, showed mankind the kingdom of California, and they entered into a compact with him at once.

Henry David Thoreau, *Journal*, 1 February 1852

About 150 years before techies from all over the world rushed to California in search of Silicon Valley gold, the rough and ready 49ers invaded the Gold Country of the Sierra Nevada in search of the real thing. The first prospectors on the scene – about 150 miles east of San Francisco – sometimes found large nuggets of solid gold sitting along the river banks. Most, however, worked long hours in the hot sun, wading through fast-flowing, ice-cold rivers to recover trace amounts of the precious metal that had been eroded out of the hard-rock veins of the Mother Lode, the name given by miners to the rich source of gold which underlies the heart of the mining district.

The region ranges from the foothills near Yosemite National Park to the deep gorge of the Yuba River two hundred miles north. In many parts throughout this area, little seems to have changed since the argonauts began their digging, and even in the air-conditioned comfort of your rental car – without one it's nearly impossible to navigate the area – distances from one town to the next may seem exponentially greater than they appear on the map: count on plenty of switch-backs and steep climbs. The heart of the **Mother Lode**, where gold was first discovered in 1848, is Sutter's Mill in **Coloma**, forty miles east of **Sacramento**. The largest city in the Gold Country, and the state capital, Sacramento was once a tiny military outpost and farming community that boomed as a supply town for miners. The mining areas spread to the north and south of Sacramento and preserve distinct identities. The **northern mines**, around the twin towns of **Grass Valley** and **Nevada City**, were the richest fields, and today retain most of their Gold Rush buildings in an unspoiled, near-alpine setting halfway up the towering peaks of the Sierra Nevada mountains. The hot and dusty **southern mines**, on the other hand, became depopulated faster than their northern neighbors. These towns were the rowdiest and wildest of all, and it's not too hard to imagine that many of the abandoned towns sprinkled over the area once supported upwards of fifty saloons and gambling parlors, each with its own cast of card sharks and thieves, as immortalized by writers like Bret Harte and Mark Twain.

Most of the mountainous forest along the Sierra crest is preserved as near-pristine wilderness, with excellent hiking, camping and backpacking. There's great skiing in winter around the mountainous rim of **Lake Tahoe** – "Lake of the Sky" to the native Washoe – on the border between California and Nevada, aglow under the bright lights of the casinos that line its southeastern shore. East of the mountains, in the dry Nevada desert, sit the highway towns of **Reno**, famed for low-budget weddings and speedy

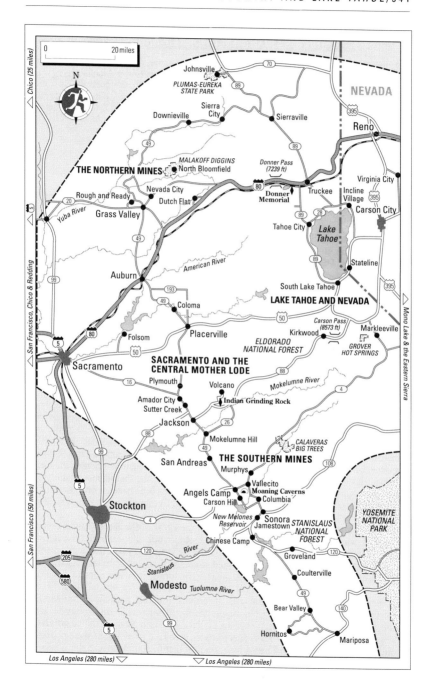

RIVER RAFTING IN THE GOLD COUNTRY

Although plenty of people come through the area to see the Gold Rush sights, at least as many come to enjoy the thrills and spills of **whitewater rafting** and **kayaking** on the various forks of the American, Stanislaus, Tuolumne and Merced rivers, which wind down through the region from the Sierra crest towards Sacramento. Whether you just want to float in a leisurely manner downstream, or fancy careening through five-foot walls of water, contact one of the many river trip operators, among them American River Recreation (☎1-800/333-7238), CBOC Whitewater Raft Adventures (☎1-800/356-2262), O.A.R.S., Inc. (☎1-800/346-6277), Tributary Whitewater Tours (☎1-800/672-3846) and Whitewater Adventures (☎1-800/977-4837). Trips run from late spring through early fall and start at about $70 per person.

---

divorces, and **Carson City**, the Nevada state capital and one-time boomtown of the Comstock silver mines.

Getting around

Hwy-49 runs north to south, linking most of the sights of the Gold Country; two main highways, US-50 and I-80, along with the transcontinental **railroad**, cross the Sierra Nevada through the heart of the region, and there are frequent Greyhound **bus** services to most of the major towns. To get a real feel for the Gold Country, however, and to reach the most evocative ghost towns, you'll need a **car**. Also, though it's all very scenic, **cycling** throughout the region is not a viable option: the distances between the sights are long, and the roads are far too hilly and narrow for comfort.

SACRAMENTO AND THE CENTRAL MOTHER LODE

Before gold was discovered in 1848, the **area around Sacramento** belonged entirely to one man, John Sutter. He came here from Switzerland in 1839 to farm the flat, marshy lands at the foot of the Sierra Nevada mountains, which were then within Mexican California. The prosperous community he founded became a main stopping place for the few trappers and travelers who made their way inland or across the range of peaks. But it was after the discovery of flakes of gold in the foothills forty miles east that things really took off. Although Sutter tried to keep it a secret, word got out and thousands soon flocked here from all over the world to mine the rich deposits of the Mother Lode.

Roughly midway between San Francisco and the crest of the Sierra Nevada mountains, and well connected by Greyhound, Amtrak and the arterial I-5 highway, **Sacramento** is likely to be your first stop in the Gold Country. It's the quintessential American state capital, with sleepy tree-lined streets fanning out from the elegant State Capitol building. The city's waterfront quarter, restored from the days of the Pony Express, contains the region's largest collection of Gold Rush era buildings. From Sacramento, two main routes climb east through the gentle foothills of the Mother Lode: US-50 passes through the old supply town of **Placerville** on its way to Lake Tahoe, and I-80 zooms by **Auburn** over the Donner Pass into Nevada. Both towns have retained enough of their Gold Rush past to merit at least a brief look if you're passing through, and both make good bases for the more picturesque towns of the northern mines.

Sacramento

Until recently, **SACRAMENTO** had the reputation of being decidedly dull, a suburban enclave of politicians and bureaucrats surrounded by miles of marshes and farmland. However, in the last decade, office towers and hotel complexes, catering to political lobbyists, have sprung up out of the faceless streetscape, and residential neighborhoods have come to life with trendy cafés and restaurants, enlivening the grid of leafy, tree-lined blocks. A revival of Gold Rush era nostalgia has also led to important historic preservation and restoration projects, injecting a hefty dose of tourist dollars into the local economy.

Set at the confluence of the Sacramento and American rivers in the flatlands of the northern Central Valley, Sacramento was founded in 1839 by a Swiss immigrant, **John Sutter**, on fifty thousand acres granted to him by the Mexican government. Sutter was a determined settler, and for ten years worked hard to build the colony into a busy trading center and cattle ranch, only to be thwarted by the discovery of gold at a nearby sawmill. Instead of making his fortune, the gold left Sutter a broken man. His workers quit their jobs to go prospecting, and many thousands more flocked to the goldfields without any respect for Sutter's claims to the land. The small colony was soon overrun: since the ships of the day could sail upriver from the San Francisco Bay, Sacramento quickly became the main supply point for miners bound for the isolated camps in the foothills above. The city prospered, and in 1854 Sacramento was chosen to be the sixth capital of the young state of California, equidistant to the gold mines, the rich farmlands of the Central Valley and the financial center of San Francisco. As the Gold Rush faded, Sacramento remained important as a transportation center, first as the western terminus of the Pony Express and later as the western headquarters of the transcontinental railroad.

Arrival, information and city transportation

At the intersection of the I-5, I-80, US-50 and Hwy-99 freeways, Sacramento is the hub for many long-distance transportation networks. Sacramento Metro **airport** (☎916/874-0700), twelve miles northwest of downtown, is served by most major domestic airlines, including America West, American, Delta, Southwest and USAir. SuperShuttle Sacramento vans (☎1-800-BLUEVAN; $12) can take you directly to any downtown destination. **Trains** from Los Angeles, San Francisco and Chicago stop at the Amtrak station at Fifth and I streets, near Old Sacramento, with good Thruway bus links to the main Gold Country towns and the Lake Tahoe area. An almost continuous stream of Greyhound **buses** pull into the bus depot at Seventh and L streets, a block from the K Street Mall.

Sacramento's most accessible **visitor information center** is at 1101 Second Street in Old Sacramento (daily 10am–5pm; ☎916/442-7644), but the handy *Sacramento Visitors' Guide* (with maps and listings of accommodation and places to eat and drink in the city) is available almost everywhere tourists congregate. For the latest on **events**

ACCOMMODATION PRICE CODES

All accommodation prices in this book have been coded using the symbols below; prices are for the least expensive **double rooms** in each establishment. For a full explanation see p.36 in "Basics." Individual rates rather than price codes are given for **hostels** and whole **apartments**.

① up to $30	④ $60–80	⑦ $130–175
② $30–45	⑤ $80–100	⑧ $175–250
③ $45–60	⑥ $100–130	⑨ $250+

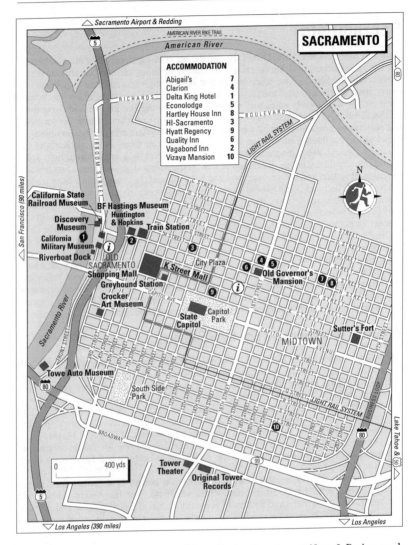

and entertainment in Sacramento, pick up the free *Sacramento News & Review*, read "Ticket," the weekend supplement of the *Sacramento Bee* newspaper, or check the free music listings publication *Alive and Kicking*. KVMR (99.3FM), a non-commercial community radio station, is also useful (and entertaining). *MGW* and *Outword* are the city's two gay and lesbian periodicals and also contain general restaurant and events listings.

The city is compact, flat and somewhat **walkable**, though many locals get around (especially along the 25-mile cycle path along the American River to Folsom Lake) by **bike** – rentals are available at The Bike Depot, 1028 2nd Street (☎916/427-5844) or Bike Sacramento, 1050 Front Street, Suite 110 (☎916/444-0200), both renting bikes for about $5 an hour. You're unlikely to need it, but there is also a combined **bus and light-**

rail system; pick up timetables and route maps from the transportation office at 1400 29th St (Mon–Fri 8am–5pm; ☎916/321-2877). One of the best ways to see the town is on a **river-boat tour**: the paddle-wheel steamboats *Matthew McKinley* and *Spirit of Sacramento* both depart from the L Street landing in Old Sacramento for varied trips along the Sacramento River ($10–27.50; ☎1-800/433-0263 or 916/552-2933). **Car rental agencies** include Budget, 6420 McNair Circle (☎916/9227317), Enterprise, 4515 Auburn Blvd (☎1-800/7368222) and Thrifty, 2409 Arden Way (☎916/9228387).

Accommodation

Sacramento has plenty of reasonably priced places to stay, all within easy walking distance of the center. A number of **motels** cluster around the old Governor's Mansion on the north side of town around 16th and H streets, a convenient walk to the trendy **Midtown** area where much of the city's nightlife is centered. Dozens of other accommodation options line the highways on the outskirts, particularly Richards Boulevard, just off I-5. **Downtown**, there are a few rather down-at-heel 1930s hotels and flashy new ones springing up every year. There's no good **camping** anywhere within easy reach of Sacramento, though KOA runs the RV-heavy *Sacramento Metro* site, 3951 Lake Rd (☎1-800/562-2747 or 916/371-6771; $24), four miles west of the center.

Abigail's, 2120 G St (☎1-800/858 1568 or 916/441-5007). Luxurious bed and breakfast in a quiet and appealingly furnished 1912 home. There's a hot tub out in the secluded gardens. ⑥.

Clarion, 700 16th St at H (☎1-800/443-0880 or 916/444-8000). Better than you might expect for a large chain motel, centrally located with excellent facilities and lower weekend rates if you book ahead. ⑤.

Delta King Hotel, 1000 Front St (☎1-800/825-5464 or 916/444-5464). A 1926 paddle-wheel river boat now permanently moored on the water beside Old Sacramento. The rooms fail to justify their "stateroom" description, but nonetheless the vessel makes an enjoyably unusual place to stay. The price rises on weekends. ⑤.

Econo Lodge, 711 16th St (☎1-800/553-2666 or 916/443-6631). Best deal in town. Basic but comfortable rooms and complimentary continental breakfast. ②.

Hartley House Inn, 700 22nd St (☎1-800/831-5806 or 916/447-7829), B&B offering turn-of-the-century elegance in the heart of Sacramento's liveliest local neighborhood. ⑥.

HI-Sacramento, 900 H St (☎916/443-1691). Hostel in a superb and rambling 1885 mansion right in the center of town. All the usual facilities, plus free bike rental, but there's a daytime lockout and 11pm curfew. $13 for members, $16 for others.

Hyatt Regency, 12th and L streets (☎1-800/233-1234 or 916/443-1234). Very flashy and perfect for an expense account stay. Lower prices on weekends. ⑦.

Quality Inn, 818 15th St (☎1-800/228-5151 or 916/444-3980). Refurbished rooms near the old Governor's Mansion, equipped with a pool. ③.

Vagabond Inn, 909 Third St (☎1-800/522-1555 or 916/446-1481). Modern place near the river and Old Sacramento, with a swimming pool and continental breakfast. ④.

Vizcaya Mansion, 2019 21st Street (☎1-800/456-2019 or 916/455-5243). A lavish, historic property with elegantly furnished rooms and marble tiled bathrooms. ⑦.

The Town

Everything you'd want to see in Sacramento is right around downtown, divided by the I-5 highway into touristy **Old Sacramento** along the river, and the commercial city center along the **K Street Mall**.

The riverfront: Old Sacramento

Sacramento grew up along the riverfront, where the wharves, warehouses, saloons and stores of the city's historic core have been restored and converted into the novelty shops and theme restaurants of **Old Sacramento**. As the largest collection of authentic Gold

Rush era architecture, it's the perfect place to take your first step back to 1849. Most of the buildings are original, though some were moved here from nearby in the Sixties, to make way for the massive I-5 highway that cuts between the river and the rest of Sacramento. Unfortunately, with Gold Rush era nostalgia at a fever pitch, the constant stampede of tourists in search of taffy and souvenirs can make you forget this is the real thing and not a Hollywood set.

At 113 I Street, between First and Second, is the Huntington & Hopkins hardware store where the **Big Four** – Leland Stanford, Mark Hopkins, Collis P. Huntington and Charles Crocker – first got together to mastermind the Central Pacific and later Southern Pacific railroads (see box opposite). It's now a **museum** (daily 10am–5pm; free), highlighting the humble beginnings of the men who became some of the richest in the country, with a collection of old woodworking and blacksmith's tools; upstairs there's a low-key homage to the men, with a re-creation of their boardroom and an archive of rail history.

The **Discovery Museum of History, Science and Technology**, 101 I St (Tues-Sun 10am–5pm; $4), a few steps away, neatly fills in the gaps in California's development before and after the Big Four, though it fails to be as stimulating as the adjacent **California State Railroad Museum** (daily 10am–5pm; $6), which brings together a range of lavishly restored 1860s locomotives with "cow-catcher" front grilles and huge bulbous smokestacks. A number of opulently decked-out passenger cars are also on display, including the 1929 *St Hyacinthe Pullman* sleeper car, which simulates movement with flashing lights, clanging bells and a gentle rhythmic swaying. The old passenger station and freight depot a block south have also been restored as part of the museum; on summer weekends a refurbished **steam train** (10am–5pm; $6) makes a seven-mile, 45-minute round-trip beside the river.

Two smaller museums are really only worth a look if you're desperate to escape the souvenir shops. The **California Military Museum**, 1119 Second St (Tues–Sun 10am–4pm; $3), provides an uninspiring chronicle – with documents, weaponry and uniforms – of California's involvement in armed struggles from pre-statehood days to the present day. The **B.F. Hastings Building**, at Second and J streets (daily 10am–4pm; free), is an even less compelling stock of early communications equipment used by companies such as Pony Express and Wells Fargo. Most people only pass through to use the ATMs located inside this 1853 bank building, which also held the first State Supreme Court, the unassuming old chambers of which are sometimes open for public view on the top floor.

The **Crocker Art Museum**, two blocks south at 216 O St between Second and Third (Tues–Sun 10am–5pm, Thurs until 9pm; $4.50; *www.crockerartmuseum.org*), exhibits European paintings collected by Supreme Court judge Edwin Crocker, brother of railroad baron Charles, in an odd complex of Renaissance Revival and modern buildings. More appropriate to its Sacramento setting, however, in the shadow of the massive I-5 and I-80 interchange and two blocks south at 2200 Front St, is the **Towe Auto Museum** (daily 10am–6pm; $6), with an impressive collection of antique cars and trucks, from Model Ts and As to classic '57 T-birds and "woody" station wagons.

K Street: the modern center

Running east from the riverfront and the Old Sacramento development, past the Greyhound and Amtrak stations, the **K Street Mall** is the commercial heart of Sacramento, with the downtown end of the modern suburban tramway running through the center of a pedestrianized shopping precinct. K Street dead-ends into the massive new **Downtown Plaza** shopping complex, and a walking tunnel at the west end of the mall leads under Hwy-99 and into Old Sacramento.

Northeast of the mall, at 16th and H, the old **Governor's Mansion** (tours on the hour 10am–4pm; $3) was the elaborate Victorian home of all California governors up to

THE BIG FOUR AND CALIFORNIA'S EARLY RAILROADS

Starting in 1861, the **Central Pacific and Southern Pacific Railroads** monopolized transportation and dominated the economy and politics of California and the western US for over twenty years. These companies were the creation of just four men – Leland Stanford, Mark Hopkins, Collis P. Huntington and Charles Crocker – known collectively as the **Big Four**.

For an initial investment of $15,000, the four financiers, along with the railroad designer and engineer Theodore Judah who died before its completion, received federal subsidies of $50,000 per mile of track laid – twice what it actually cost. On top of this, they were granted half the land in a forty-mile strip bordering the railroad: as the network expanded, the Southern Pacific became the largest landowner in the state, owning over twenty percent of California. An unregulated monopoly – caricatured in the liberal press as a grasping **octopus** – the railroad had the power to make or break farmers and manufacturers dependent upon it for the transportation of goods. In the cities, particularly Oakland and Los Angeles, it was able to demand massive concessions from local government as an inducement for rail connections, and by the end of the nineteenth century, the Big Four had extracted and extorted a fortune worth over $200 million each.

Ronald Reagan; when the white, 1874 structure was condemned as a firetrap, the future president abandoned its high ceilings and narrow staircases in favor of a ranch-style house on the outskirts of town. Today, the old mansion has been restored to its former glory, and is a perfect place to begin a self-guided **walking tour** of Sacramento's historic architecture with one of the detailed free brochures published by the Sacramento CVB.

The noble dome of the **State Capitol**, built in the Classical Revival Style in the 1860s, stands proudly in the middle of a spacious green park two blocks south of the mall, at the geographical center of Sacramento. Restored in 1976 to its original elegance (in what was then the largest restoration project in U.S. history), the luxurious building is still the seat of state government and brims over with finely crafted details. Although you're free to walk around, you'll see a lot more if you take one of the free **tours** (daily 9am–5pm; ☎916/324-0333) that leave hourly from room B-27 on the lower ground floor, passing through the old legislative chambers decked out in turn-of-the-century furnishings and fixtures.

Sutter's Fort State Historic Park (daily 10am–5pm; $3), on the east side of town at 27th and L, is a re-creation of Sacramento's original settlement, striking for its presence in the midst of an otherwise relatively modern residential area. An adobe house displays relics from the Gold Rush, and on summer weekends local volunteers dress up and pretend they're living in the 1850s. The adjacent **Indian Museum**, 2618 K St (daily 10am–5pm; $3), displays tools, handicrafts and ceremonial objects of the Native Americans of the Central Valley and the Sierra Nevada mountains.

Eating, drinking and nightlife

Dozens of fast-food stands, ice cream shops, and pricey Western-themed **restaurants** fill Old Sacramento, but you'd do better to steer clear of these and search out the places we've listed below. Some of them are clustered near the trendy **Midtown** area, around 20th and Capitol, where you'll also find the odd good **bar**. The best venues for slightly off-beat **live music** are *Old Ironsides*, 1901 10th St (☎916/443-9751), and *Capitol Garage*, 1427 L Street (☎916/444-3633). Major touring bands usually play at the newly refurbished Crest Theater, 1013 K St (☎916/442-7378). One of the city's most popular **gay and lesbian bars** is *Faces*, on the corner of K and 20th Streets (☎916/448-7798).

And if you're not in a bar or live music mood, arthouse **movies** are shown at the Tower Theater on Broadway and 16th (☎916/442-4700).

Café Bernardo, 28th Street and Capitol Avenue (☎916/443-1180). Order huge portions of healthy, cheap food from the walk-up counter and eat in the casual yet stylish dining room. The eclectic menu includes stir-fry, pastas, grilled polenta, salads and sandwiches. The adjoining *Monkey Bar* serves cocktails till 2am every night.

Café Paris, 2326 K St (☎916/442-2001). Small, down-to-earth beer joint where Sacramento's hipsters congregate to hear local indie bands.

Centro Cocina Mexicana, 28th St near J (☎916/442-2552). Innovative upscale regional Mexican cuisine and a full bar with over 50 aged tequilas.

La Bou, 901 K Street (☎916/444-8902). Part of a chain, but justifiably popular. Coffee drinks, baked goods, soups, salads and sandwiches are available at reasonable prices, along with French style pastries.

Maharani, 1728 Broadway (☎916/441-2172). Slightly pricey Californian-style Indian that's light on oil, but still heavy on all the traditional spices.

Megami, 1010 10th at J Street (☎916/448-4512). A functional, bargain Japanese restaurant with lunch and combination sushi plates for under $5. Try the sesame chicken. Mon–Fri only.

New Helvetia Roasters & Bakers, 1215 19th St at Capitol Avenue (☎916/441-1106). An old firehouse that's one of the best cafés in town, boasting home-roasted coffee, good cakes and pastries, and communal tables inside and out. Open until 11pm most nights and popular with locals.

Paesano's, 1806 Capitol Ave at 18th Street (☎916/447-8646). Reasonably priced pastas, great ovenbaked sandwiches, and delicious pizzas in a comfortable brick-walled dining room.

Paragary's, 1401 28th St at N Street (☎916/457-5737). A broad range of tastes catered for with good, giant-size portions of pasta, and tasty, brick-oven pizzas with unusual toppings. Moderate prices.

Ras Teferi, 1009 9th Street (☎916/443-8031). A mid-range Ethiopian restaurant with an extensive selection of dishes, all served on traditional *mesob* basket tables.

River City Brewing Company, 545 Downtown Plaza (☎916/447-2745). Slick modern brew pub at the west end of the shopping mall, usually packed with both diners and drinkers. A good place to unwind with a couple of pints after braving the tourist-heavy Old Sacramento.

Tapa the World, 2115 J Street (☎916/442-4353). Choose from twenty different tapas, or have a full meal of paella, lamb or fresh fish, all while being serenaded by flamenco guitar. Trendy spot to people watch in Midtown when the sidewalk tables are out.

Virga's, at 1501 14th St near O (☎916/442-8516). Scrumptious, well-priced Italian fare that was understandably selected best restaurant in a local poll.

Weatherstone Coffee & Trading Co, 812 21st St at H (☎916/443-6340). Sacramento's oldest coffeehouse with garden seating and cool brick interior. A favorite with locals both for its bulging sandwiches and many coffee concoctions. Open until 11pm or later.

The Central Mother Lode

From Sacramento, US-50 and I-80 head east through the heart of the Gold Country, up and over the mountains past Lake Tahoe and into the state of Nevada. The roads closely follow the old stagecoach routes over the Donner Pass, and in the mid-1860s local citizens, seeking to improve dwindling fortunes after the Gold Rush subsided, joined forces with railroad engineer Theodore Judah to finance and build the first railroad crossing of the Sierra Nevada over much the same route – even along much of the same track – that Amtrak uses today. While the area holds much historic interest, its towns aren't nearly as postcard perfect as those elsewhere in the region, meaning you'll have a better chance of finding affordable accommodation here during busy periods than in the Northern or Southern part of the Gold Country. Both **Placerville** and **Auburn** are worth at least a quick look; **Coloma** and **Folsom**, in between the two highways on the American River, have more to offer.

Folsom

In 1995, just as the **FOLSOM** powerhouse was gearing up for the centennial celebration of its pioneering efforts in long-distance electricity transmission, one of the sluice gates on the Folsom Dam gave way, sending millions of gallons of water down the American River towards Sacramento, twenty miles downstream. The levees held, but Folsom Lake had to be almost completely drained before repairs could be undertaken. The event sent shockwaves through California's extensive hydroelectric industry and brought a fame to Folsom unknown since Johnny Cash sang of being "stuck in Folsom Prison" after having "shot a man in Reno, just to watch him die." The stone-faced **Folsom State Prison**, two miles north of town on Green Valley Road, has an arts-and-crafts gallery (daily 10am–4pm) selling works by prisoners, who get the proceeds when released. Across the road, a small **museum** (daily 10am–4pm; $1) is filled with grisly photographs, the medical records of murderers and thieves who were hanged for their crimes, and a whole armory of handmade escape tools recovered from prisoners over the years.

Folsom itself is attractive enough, with a single main street of restored homes and buildings that date from the days of the Pony Express. A reconstruction of the 1860 Wells Fargo office makes an imposing setting for the **Folsom History Museum**, 823

EL DORADO WINE COUNTRY

Back in the 1860s, when the now-famous Napa and Sonoma valleys were growing potatoes, **vineyards** flourished in El Dorado county. However, the fields were neglected after the Gold Rush and killed off by phylloxera, only being re-established in 1972. Since then, however, the **wineries** in El Dorado county, around Placerville, have rapidly gained a reputation which belies their diminutive size. Most are low-key affairs where no charge is made for tasting or tours, and you're encouraged to enjoy a bottle out on the verandah. At quiet times, you may even be shown around by the winemaker, a far cry from the organized tours and rampant commercialism of Napa and Sonoma.

The differences in altitude and soil types throughout the region lend themselves to a broad range of grape varieties, and the producers here are often criticized as being unfocused. Nonetheless, the wines have notched up a string of gold medals in recent years. Zinfandel and Sauvignon Blanc are big, but it is the Syrah/Merlot blends which attract the attention, and the Barbera (from a Piedmontese grape) is said to be the best in the world.

If you're out for a relaxed day's tasting, avoid the **Passport Weekend**, usually the last weekend in March or the first in April and booked out months in advance (☎1-800/306-3956), when the purchase of said passport entitles you to all manner of foodie extravagances to complement the tastings. Better to pick up the **El Dorado Wine Country Tour** leaflet from the El Dorado Chamber of Commerce (see Placerville "Practicalities" on p.550) and make your way to the Boeger vineyard, 1790 Carson Rd (daily 10am–5pm; ☎530/622-8094), less than a mile from the Greyhound stop (see p.550), where you can sit in an arbor of apples and pears, or the Lava Cap vineyard, 2221 Fruitridge Rd (daily 11am–5pm; ☎530/621-0175), which in recent years has produced some excellent Chardonnay and Muscat Canelli.

The quality of the local produce – not only grapes, but also apples, pears, peaches, cherries and more – is widely celebrated around the district, especially so during the **Apple Hill Festival** in October, when a shuttle bus runs from Placerville to the majority of the orchards and wineries situated in the Apple Hill region (info ☎530/644-7692), along the winding country roads just north of I-50 and east of town. At other times, you'll have to make your own way. The Chamber of Commerce can also supply you with a *Cider Press Guide to Apple Hill* and a *Farm Trails Harvest & Recreation Guide*, which has detailed information and maps leading to farms, ranches, wineries and historic country inns in the most remote areas of the county.

Sutter St (Wed–Sun 11am–4pm; free), whose prized possessions include a working scale model of a steam-powered gold dredge, artifacts from the Chinese community that settled here in the 1850s, and a huge mural depicting the area's main Native American people, the Maidu.

In town, the Folsom **Chamber of Commerce**, 200 Wool Street (Mon–Fri 9am–5pm; Sat-Sun 11am–4pm; ☎916/985-5555), has plenty of the usual brochures. If you're looking for a lunch spot, try either *Patsy's Soda Parlour*, 717 Sutter Street (☎916/985-4250), a popular old-fashioned soda fountain with homemade pies, or *The Balcony Restaurant*, 801 Sutter (☎916/985-2605), where you can have a hearty meal while enjoying the view of the historic downtown. For **accommodation**, you'd do better heading back to Sacramento, though if you're particularly tired and on a roomy budget, you might try the *Lake Natoma Inn* (☎1-800/637-7200 or 916/351-1500; ⑥) with full amenities, restaurant and spa.

Placerville

PLACERVILLE, forty miles east of Sacramento, takes a perverse delight in having been known originally as Hangtown for its habit of lynching alleged criminals in pairs and stringing them up from a tree in the center of town. Despite these gruesome beginnings, Placerville has always been more of a market than a mining town, and is now a major crossroads, halfway between Sacramento and Lake Tahoe at the junction of US-50 and Hwy-49. For a time, it was the third-largest city in California, and many of the men who went on to become the most powerful in the state got their start here: railroad magnates Mark Hopkins and Collis P. Huntington were local merchants, while car mogul John Studebaker made wheelbarrows for the miners.

The modern town spreads out along the highways in a string of fast-food restaurants, gas stations and motels. The old Main Street, running parallel to US-50, retains some of the Gold Rush architecture, with an effigy dangling by the neck in front of the *Hangman's Tree* bar, which is built over the site where the town's infamous tree once grew. You'll also see many fine old houses scattered among the pine trees in the steep valleys to the north and south of the center. Nearby, one of the best of the Gold Country museums is located in the sprawling El Dorado County Fairgrounds, just north of US-50. This, the **El Dorado County Historical Museum** (Wed–Sat 10am–4pm; free), gives a broad historical overview of the county from the Miwok to the modern day, including logging trains and a mock-up of a general store. For more on the days of the argonauts, head across US-50 to the **Gold Bug Mine Park** on Bedford Avenue (daily May–Oct 10am–4pm; weekends only Nov & March–April noon–4pm, weather permitting; closed Dec–Feb; $3) for a self-guided tour of a typical Mother Lode mine.

Practicalities

Amtrak Thruway **buses** pull up twice daily outside the *Buttercup Pantry*, 222 Main St; while Greyhound buses on their way to South Lake Tahoe stop twice a day at 1750 Broadway, a mile and a half east of town. El Dorado Transit buses provide local transit service. Near the Greyhound stop are a number of **motels**, such as the *Mother Lode Motel*, 1940 Broadway (☎530/622-00895; ②), and the nicer but slightly pricier *National 9 Inn*, 1500 Broadway (☎530/622-3884; ②). With more money, you're far better off at the *Chichester-McKee House*, 800 Spring St (☎1-800/831-4008 or 530/626-1882; ⑤), an historic B&B and a landmark in its own right, offering guest-rooms with period furnishings and homemade baked breakfasts and reached by turning north off US-50 onto Hwy-49 at the traffic lights in town.

The El Dorado County **Chamber of Commerce** office, 542 Main St (Mon–Fri 9am–5pm; ☎ 1-800/457-6279 or 530/621-5885), has local information and can help set up **river rafting** trips in Coloma (see below).

For **eating**, try the local concoction, "Hangtown Fry," an omelet-like mix-up of bacon, eggs and breaded oysters that you can taste at *Chuck's Pancake House*, 1318 Broadway St (☎530/622-2858). *Sweetie Pies*, at 577 Main St (☎530/642-0128), serves great breakfasts and what could be the best cinnamon rolls on the planet. You can sip coffee, play chess, and listen to local folk and bluegrass inside the musty remnants of an actual gold mine at the bizarre *Placerville Coffee House*, 594 Main St (☎530/295-1481). Not to be missed if you've got a car is *Poor Red's Barbeque* (☎530/622-2901), housed in the old Adams and Co stagecoach office on Hwy-49 three miles south of Placerville, which serves the Gold Country's best barbecued dinners for under $6, with $1 beers and two-fisted margaritas. If none of these appeal, *Lil' Mama D Carlos*, 482 Main St (☎530/626-1612), serves up fine, affordable Italian food.

Coloma

Sights along Hwy-49 north of Placerville are few and far between, but it was here that gold fever began, when on January 24, 1848 James Marshall discovered flakes of gold, in the tailrace of a mill he was building for John Sutter, along the south fork of the American River at **COLOMA**. By the summer of that year, thousands had flocked to the area, and by the following year Coloma was a town of ten thousand – though most left quickly following news of richer strikes elsewhere in the region, and the town all but disappeared within a few years. The few surviving buildings, including the cabin where Marshall lived and two Chinese stores, have been preserved as the **Marshall Gold Discovery State Historic Park** (daily 8am–dusk; $5 per car).

A reconstruction of **Sutter's Mill** stands along the river, and working demonstrations are often held on weekends at 10am and 1pm. There's a small historical museum across the road, and on a hill overlooking the town a statue marks the spot where Marshall is buried. Marshall never profited from his discovery, and in fact it came to haunt him. At first, he tried to charge miners for access to what he said was his land along the river (it wasn't), and he spent most of his later years in poverty, claiming supernatural powers had helped him to find gold.

Other supernatural forces are at work in the *Coloma Country Inn* (Tues–Sun; ☎530/622-6919; ⑨), adjacent to the state park on Cold Springs Road, where the ghost of a man tormented by his wife is said to haunt the cellar – now a **bar**, featuring music on weekend nights.

If ghosts of miners past don't phase you, there's one adventure that is sure to turn your knuckles white. Coloma is the best place to begin your **whitewater rafting** journey on the American River. Tours can be booked with Mariah Wilderness Expeditions (☎1-800/462-7424) or Rapid Descent Adventures (☎530/642-2370).

Auburn and Dutch Flat

Heading north, the town of **AUBURN**, built into a hillside on three levels, manages to preserve its Gold Rush era charm, even though it's right at the crossroads of Hwy-49 and I-80. Greyhound **buses** heading from Sacramento to Reno stop at 246 Palm Ave, and Amtrak **trains** depart from Nevada and Fulleiler Streets. The outskirts are sprawling and modern, but the Old Town, on Auburn's lowest level just off Hwy-49, is one of the best-preserved and most picturesque of the Gold Rush sights, with antique stores and saloons clustered around a Spanish-style plaza. You'll also find California's oldest post office and the unmissable red-and-white tower of the 1891 **firehouse**. There are also a number of excellent and undervisited museums, including the **Gold Country Museum**, 1273 High Street (Tue–Fri 10am–3:30pm; weekends 11am–4pm), and the **Bernhard Museum Complex** at 291 Auburn-Folsom Road (Tue–Fri 10:30am–3pm;

weekends noon–4pm), which offers guided tours of an amateur viticulturist's 1851 home, as well as his carriage barn and modest winery.

For a free map and information on places to stay, stop by the **Placer County Visitor Center,** north of town at 13464 Lincoln Way (Mon–Fri 9am–5pm, Sat 9am–3pm; ☎ 1-800/427-6463 or 530/887-2111). If you're looking for a good **meal**, try either *Bootlegger's Old Town Tavern and Grill*, 210 Washington Street (☎530/889-2229), where hearty meals are served in a stately brick building, or *Latitudes*, 130 Maple Street (☎530/885-9535), for Californian interpretations of multi-cultural cuisines. Affordable **accommodation** is available at the *Super 8 Motel* at 140 E Hillcrest Drive in Auburn, which offers comfort without the frills (☎1-800/800-8000 or 530/888-8808; ③).

The twenty or so miles of Hwy-49 north of Auburn are a dull but fast stretch of freeway to one of the best parts of the Gold Country – the twin cities of Grass Valley and Nevada City. For an interesting side trip on the way there, or if you're heading for Lake Tahoe, take I-80 from Auburn 27 miles east to the small town of **DUTCH FLAT**, where old tin-roofed cottages are sprinkled among the pine- and aspen-covered slopes. Miners here used the profitable, but very destructive, method of hydraulic mining (see p.558) to get at the gold buried under the surface – with highly visible consequences.

THE NORTHERN MINES

The **northern section** of the Gold Country includes some of the most spectacularly beautiful scenery in California. Fast-flowing rivers cascade along the bottom of steeply walled canyons, whose slopes are covered in fall with the flaming reds and golds of poplars and sugar maples, highlighted against an evergreen background of pine and fir trees. Unlike the freelance placer mines of the south, where wandering prospectors picked nuggets of gold out of the streams and rivers, the gold here was (and is) buried deep underground, and had to be pounded out of hard-rock ore. In spite of that, the northern mines were the most profitable of the Mother Lode – more than half the gold that came out of California came from the mines of **Nevada County**, and most of that from **Grass Valley**'s Empire Mine, now preserved as one of the region's many excellent museums. Just north, the quaint Victorian houses of **Nevada City** make it the most alluring Gold Rush town.

A few miles away, at the end of a steep and twisting back road, the scarred yet curiously beautiful landforms of the **Malakoff Diggins** stand as an exotic reminder of the destruction wrought by overzealous miners, who, as gold became harder to find, washed away entire hillsides to get at the precious metal. Hwy-49 winds up further into the mountains from Nevada City, along the Yuba River to the High Sierra hamlet of **Downieville**, at the foot of the towering Sierra Buttes. From here you're within striking distance of the northernmost Gold Rush ghost town of **Johnsville**, which stands in an evocative state of arrested decay in the middle of the forests of **Plumas-Eureka State Park**, on the crest of the Sierra Nevada.

You'll need a **car** to get to any of the outlying sights, but there is limited public transportation to Grass Valley and Nevada City in the form of four daily Amtrak Thruway buses. Though there are no youth hostels, you'll find a few inexpensive motels and a handful of B&Bs; **camping** is an option too, often in unspoiled sites in gorgeous mountain scenery.

Grass Valley and Nevada City

Twenty-five miles north of Auburn and I-80, the neighboring towns of **GRASS VALLEY** and **NEVADA CITY** were the most prosperous and substantial of the gold-mining towns and are still thriving communities, four miles apart in beautiful surroundings high up in the Sierra Nevada mountains. Together they make one of the better Gold Country destinations, with museums and many balconied, elaborately detailed buildings, staggering up hills and hanging out over steep gorges.

Gold was the lifeblood of the area as recently as the mid-1950s, and both towns look largely unchanged since the Gold Rush days. The locals have retained a bit of the fiery determination of their rough-and-ready ancestors, as evidenced by the booming downtown businesses that combine old Western charm with big city sophistication. Since the 1960s, a number of artists and craftspeople have also settled in the old houses in the hills around the area, tempering the rugged regional culture with a vaguely alternative feel that's reflected in the *Community Endeavor* newspaper, the non-commercial community radio station KMVR (89.5FM), and in the friendly throngs that turn out for the annual Bluegrass Festival in the middle of June.

Getting around is relatively easy: both towns are very compact, and connected every thirty minutes by the Gold Country Stage **minibus** (Mon–Fri 8am–5pm, Sat 9.15am–5.30pm; $1 a trip, $2 for a day pass; ☎530/477-0103), which follows the same stretch of road that burro trains and stage coaches frequented in the twin towns' heyday, when it was the busiest four-mile route in California. Several daily Amtrak thruway **buses** from Sacramento and Auburn stop on Sacramento Street in Nevada City and on West Main Street in Grass Valley.

Accommodation

Places to stay don't come cheap, but if you can afford to splurge on a **bed and breakfast**, Nevada City in particular has some excellent options. Otherwise there are a couple of revamped old Gold Rush **hotels**, and a scattering of motels, though be warned that these may be booked up weeks in advance.

Airway Motel, 575 E Broad St, Nevada City (☎530/265-2233). Quiet, 1940s motel with swimming pool, a 10min walk from the center of town. Credit cards are not accepted. ②.

Coach N' Four Motel, 628 South Auburn Street, Grass Valley (☎530/273-8009). Clean and comfortable motel with the best rates around. ②.

Downey House, 517 W Broad St, Nevada City (☎530/265-2815). Pretty 1870s Victorian home at the top of Broad Street, looking out over the town and surrounding forest. Simple decor and original artwork makes a welcome change from the over-fancy B&B norm. Rates include wine on arrival and full breakfast. ④.

Flume's End, 317 S Pine St, Nevada City (☎530/265-9665). Across the Pine Creek bridge from the center of town, this small inn overlooks a pretty waterfall and features lovely gardens ranged along Deer Creek. ⑤.

Holbrooke Hotel, 212 W Main St, Grass Valley (☎1-800/933-7077 or 530/273-1353). Recently renovated and right in the center of town, this historic hotel, where Mark Twain once stayed, has great rooms and an opulent bar. ④.

Holiday Lodge, 1221 E. Main St., Grass Valley (☎530/2734406). Comfortable, no frills accommodation with a swimming pool, free breakfast and free local calls. ②.

Murphy's Inn, 318 Neal St, Grass Valley (☎1-800/875-2488 or 530/273-6873). Cozy rooms – some with fireplaces – in an old Victorian place close to downtown. Great breakfasts. ⑥.

National Hotel, 211 Broad Street, Nevada City (☎530-265-4551). The oldest continuously-operated hotel in the West and a state historic landmark. ④.

Northern Queen Inn, 400 Railroad Ave, Nevada City (☎530/265-5824). Good-value hotel with a heated pool. Attractive woodland cottages and chalets, along with simpler rooms in another building. ③.

Piety Hill Inn, 523 Sacramento Street, Nevada City (☎1-800/443-2245 or 530/265-2245). Cottages decorated in period furnishings with kitchenettes in a garden setting. ⑤.

Shady Rest Motel, 10845 Rough and Ready Hwy, Grass Valley (☎530/273-4232). A little way out of town, but a pleasant walk; good-value weekly rates available. ②.

Stagecoach Motel, 405 S. Auburn Street, Grass Valley (☎530/272-3701). Great rates and all the basic amenities. ③.

Swan-Levine House, 328 S Church St, Grass Valley (☎530/272-1873). Accommodation with the artist in mind; the friendly owners also give instruction in printmaking. Attractively decorated, sunny en-suite rooms in an old Victorian hospital. ④.

Grass Valley

There's nothing Gold Country folk love better than telling a long tale about their town's toughest days, making it virtually impossible to pass through **GRASS VALLEY** without getting at least one rendition of the **Lola Montez** story. This Irish dancer and entertainer – the former mistress of Ludwig of Bavaria, and friend of Victor Hugo and Franz Liszt – embarked on a highly successful tour of America, playing to packed houses from New York to San Francisco. Her provocative "Spider Dance," in which she wriggled about the stage shaking cork spiders out of her dress, didn't much impress the miners, but she liked the wild lifestyle of the town, gave up dancing and retired to Grass Valley with her pet grizzly bear, which she kept tied up in the front yard. Max Ophüls' 1955 *Lola Montès*, which had the largest budget of any film in the history of French cinema at the time of its release, tells a surreal fictionalized version of her life story.

A few mementos of Lola's life are displayed in the **Grass Valley Museum**, in the Old St Mary's Academy at the corner of Church and Chapel streets (June–Oct Tues–Sun; Nov–May Tues–Fri 12.30–3.30pm; ☎530/273-5509; donation). The town's **tourist office** (Mon–Fri 9.30am–4.30pm, Sat 10am–3pm; ☎1-800/655-4667 or 530/273-4667) is housed in a replica of her home, on the south side of town at 248 Mill St. It also has reams of historical information, lists of accommodation, and a walking tour **map** of the town, pointing out the oldest hardware store in California (which, sadly, closed in 1990 and has been converted into a tacky art gallery) among the wooden awnings and storefronts of the gas-lighted business district.

The North Star Mining Museum

Two intriguing museums illustrate the days when Grass Valley was the richest and most important of all the California mining towns. The **North Star Mining Museum**, at the south end of Mill Street (May–Oct daily 10am–5pm; donation), is one of the best of all the Gold Country museums, with enthusiastic guides and interesting exhibits. Housed in what used to be the power station for the North Star Mine, the centerpiece is the giant **Pelton wheel**. Resembling nothing so much as a thirty-foot-diameter bicycle wheel, this was patented in 1878 and became one of the most important inventions to come out of the Gold Country. Many Pelton wheels were used to generate electricity, though the one here drove an air compressor to power the drills and hoists of the mine.

A series of dioramas in the museum describe the day-to-day working life of the miners, three-quarters of whom had emigrated here from the depressed tin mines of Cornwall in England. Besides their expertise at working deep underground, the "Cousin

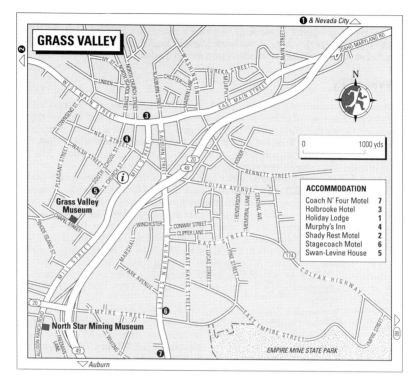

GRASS VALLEY

& Nevada City

IDAHO-MARYLAND RD

N

0   1000 yds

ACCOMMODATION

Coach N' Four Motel	7
Holbrooke Hotel	3
Holiday Lodge	1
Murphy's Inn	4
Shady Rest Motel	2
Stagecoach Motel	6
Swan-Levine House	5

Grass Valley Museum

North Star Mining Museum

EMPIRE MINE STATE PARK

COLFAX HIGHWAY

Auburn

Jacks," as they were called by the non-Cornish miners, introduced the **Cornish pump** (not to mention the Cornish pastie, a traditional pastry pie) to the mines. You can see a mock-up of one of these mammoth beasts here, as well as a replica of the old surface mechanism.

The great machines are now at peace, but when they were in action the racket could be heard for miles around. The noisiest offenders were the thundering **stamp mills**, a scaled-down version of which is operated upon request, which once mashed and pulverized the gold-bearing quartz ore.

The Empire Mine State Park

The largest and richest gold mine in the state was the **Empire Mine**, now preserved as a state park a mile southeast of Grass Valley, just off Hwy-174 at the top of Empire Street. The 800-acre park (daily 10am–5pm; June-Aug 9am–6pm; $3) is surrounded by pines, amongst which are vast quantities of mining equipment and machinery, much of it only recently re-instated here after having been sold off for scrap after the mine closed in 1956. When standing among the machines, it is easy to imagine the din that shook the ground 24 hours a day, or the cages of fifty men descending the now-desolate shaft into the 350 miles of underground tunnels. After more than six million ounces of gold had been recovered, the cost of getting the gold out of the ground exceeded $35 an ounce – the government-controlled price at the time – and production ceased. Most of the mine has been dismantled, but there's a small, very informative **museum** at the entrance with a superb model of the whole underground system, built secretly to help predict the location of lucrative veins of gold. You can get some sense of the mine's prosperity by visiting the owner's house, the **Empire Cottage** at the north end of the park – a stone and brick, vaguely English manor house with a glowing, redwood-paneled interior overlooking a formal garden.

Nevada City

Towns don't get much quainter than **NEVADA CITY**, four miles north of Grass Valley, with its crooked rows of elaborate Victorian homes set on the winding, narrow, maple tree-lined streets that rise up from Hwy-49. It gets away with all the quaintness, however, as it is one of the least changed of all the Gold Country towns with a cluster of excellent shops and restaurants in the town center – all in all, a good, if pricey, base for following the many steep streets up into the surrounding forest.

A good first stop is at the **tourist office** (Mon–Fri 9am–5pm, Sat 11am–4pm; ☎ 1-800/655-6569 or 530/265-2692) at 132 Main St, a block north of Hwy-49, where you can pick up a free walking-tour **map** of the town. It's hard to select specific highlights, but one place to start is the newly restored, lacy-balconied and bell-towered **Old Firehouse**, 214 Main St, next to the tourist office, which houses a small **museum** (May–Oct daily 11am–4pm; Nov–April Thurs–Sun 11am–4pm; donation) describing the social history of the region. The heart of town is Broad Street, which climbs up from the highway past the 1854 *National Hotel* (see "Accommodation") and a number of antique shops and restaurants, all decked out in Gold Country balconies and wooden awnings. Almost the only exception to the rule of picturesque nostalgia is the Art Deco 1937 **City Hall**, near the top of Broad Street.

The **Miner's Foundry Cultural Center** (daily 9am–5pm; free), perched precariously above the Deer Creek canyon at 325 Spring St, is an old tool foundry converted into a multi-use cultural center, art gallery, performance space and KVMR radio studios. Immediately next door stands the **Nevada City Winery**, 321 Spring St (noon–5pm; ☎530/265-9463), where you can taste the produce of one of the state's oldest vineyards. If you'd like to sample a different glass, stop by the **Indian Springs Winery**, which has its tasting room right at 303 Broad Street (11am-5pm; ☎800/273-2550 or ☎530/478-1068).

Above the town at the top of Pine Street, a small plaque marks **Indian Medicine Rock**, a granite boulder with sunbeds worn into the hollows of the rock by Native Americans who valued the healing power of sunshine. Broad Street intersects Hwy-49 a block further on, and continues up into the mountains as the North Bloomfield Road, which twists up the hills to the Malakoff Diggins (below).

Eating and drinking

Both Grass Valley and Nevada City have some surprisingly sophisticated places to **eat and drink**, including a few excellent **cafés**. Look out for pasties, brought to the Gold Country by Cornish miners, and crisp-tasting Nevada City beer, brewed locally and available at better establishments.

Cafés, restaurants, bars

Apple Fare, 121 Neal Street, Grass Valley (☎530/272-2555). Casual restaurant with an old hometown diner feel, serving up generous portions at good prices.

Broad Street Books, 426 Broad St, Nevada City (☎530/265-4204). Pastries, light fare, and espresso with wonderful tree-shaded outdoor seating.

Café Mekka, 237 Commercial St, Nevada City (☎530/478-1517). Relaxed, fabulously decorated coffee shop – from exposed piping to trompe l'oeil wallpaper – popular with teenagers, trendies and ex-hippies. Open 8am–11pm weekdays, and until 1.30am on weekends.

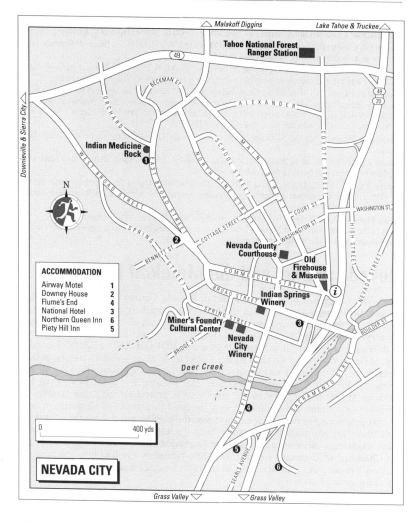

Malakoff Diggins   Lake Tahoe & Truckee

Tahoe National Forest
Ranger Station

Downieville & Sierra City

Indian Medicine
Rock **1**

Nevada County
Courthouse

Old
Firehouse
& Museum

ACCOMMODATION

Airway Motel	1
Downey House	2
Flume's End	4
National Hotel	3
Northern Queen Inn	6
Piety Hill Inn	5

Indian Springs
Winery

Miner's Foundry
Cultural Center

Nevada
City
Winery

Deer Creek

0   400 yds

NEVADA CITY

Grass Valley ▽   ▽ Grass Valley

Cirino's, 309 Broad St, Nevada City (☎530/265-2246). Good deli sandwiches for lunch and modestly priced Italian specialties at dinner, plus a full bar.

Citronée Bistro and Wine Bar, 320 Broad Street, Nevada City (☎530/265-5697). Upscale American-Mediterranean fusion cuisine in an elegant, yet unpretentious atmosphere.

Earth Song, 135a Argall Way, about a mile southwest of Nevada City, following S Pine St (☎530/265-8025). Excellent gourmet vegetarian café and wholefood supermarket. The café closes for an hour or two in the afternoon.

Friar Tuck's Restaurant and Wine Bar, 111 N Pine St, Nevada City (☎530/265-9093). A somewhat kitsch establishment, with occasional live folk and jazz music, serving fairly expensive meals – try the fondue dinner for around $15.

Heavenly Espresso, 154 Mill Street, Grass Valley (☎530/274-2600). Centrally located café with a pleasant atmosphere and plenty of pastries, coffee drinks and smoothies to choose from.

Jack's Internet Café, 115 South Church St, Grass Valley (☎530/477-7873). Light meals, decadent desserts, and a pleasant atmosphere that help make checking your email less of a chore.

La Cucina Cirino, 491 East Main Street, Grass Valley (☎530/274-1337). An Italian delicatessen that doubles as a cooking school. Italian wines served.

Mad Dogs and Englishmen, 211 Spring St, Nevada City (☎530/265-8173). Pub-like bar with darts, good beer and regular live, danceable blues and rock music. Open until 2am on weekends.

Main Street Café, 213 W Main St, Grass Valley (☎530/477-6000). The best bet for a really good meal, this casual but refined restaurant has an eclectic range of dishes – from pastas to Cajun specialties – as well as good grilled meats and fresh fish, all at moderate prices. Also has a full wine and cocktail bar next door with live local entertainment Wed-Sat.

Marshall's Pasties, 203 Mill St, Grass Valley (☎530/272-2844). Mind-boggling array of fresh filled pasties.

Moore's Café, 216 Broad St, Nevada City (☎530/265-9440). Plain-looking, all-American diner with eggs for breakfast and burgers for lunch. Closed Mon.

Railroad Café, 111 W Main St, Grass Valley (☎530/274-2233). Decent diner food accompanied by the clatter of a model railroad continuously operating overhead. Breakfast & lunch only Sun–Thurs, all three meals Fri & Sat.

Swiss House, 535 Mill Street, Grass Valley (☎530/273-8272). The Central European decor in the heart of the Sierra foothills warrants at least a grin, and you might even be tempted to stay for one of the hearty mid-range Swiss-German meals.

Nevada County and the Malakoff Diggins

Grass Valley, Nevada City and the foothills of **Nevada County** yielded more than half the gold that came out of California. But before the deep, hard-rock mines were established in the late 1860s, there were mining camps spread all over the northern Gold Country, with evocative names like "Red Dog" and "You Bet," that disappeared as soon as the easily recovered surface deposits gave out. **ROUGH AND READY**, five miles west of Grass Valley, now survives on the tourist trade alone – visitors coming to take a look at the only mining town ever to secede from the United States, which Rough and Ready did in 1850. The band of veterans who founded the town, fresh from the Mexican–American War, opted to quit the Union in protest against unfair taxation by the federal government, and although they declared their renewed allegiance in time for that summer's Fourth of July celebrations, the conflict was not officially resolved until 1948. Now the place isn't worth visiting; it's little more than a handful of ramshackle buildings, including a gas station and a general store. If you must pass through, the **Chamber of Commerce** (☎530/272-4320) publishes a well-written brochure on the town's history that's about as long as the town's entire length; you can usually find one at the general store.

Six miles northwest of Rough and Ready, off the winding Bitney Springs Road in the **South Yuba River State Park**, is the **Bridgeport covered bridge**, the longest single-span, wood-truss covered bridge in world, spanning the Yuba River. The swimming spot underneath offers some relief from a hot summer's day, and the nearby visitor's center (☎530/432-2546) has plenty of information on the area's hiking trails, as well as guided wildflower, history and bird watching tours, and the inevitable gold-panning demonstrations.

Malakoff Diggins State Park

The waters of the Yuba River are now crisp and clear, but when the bridge was completed in 1862 they were being choked with mud and residue from the many hydraulic mining or **hydraulicking** operations upstream. Hydraulic mining was used here in the late 1850s to get at the trace deposits of gold which were not worth recovering by orthodox methods. It was an unsophisticated way of retrieving the precious metal: giant nozzles or monitors sprayed powerful jets of water against the gold-bearing hillsides, washing away tons of gravel, mud and trees just to recover a few ounces of gold. It also required an elaborate system of flumes and canals to collect the water, which was sprayed at a rate of over thirty thousand gallons a minute. Some of these canals are still used to supply water to local communities. Worst of all, apart from the obvious destruction of the landscape, was the waste it caused, silting up rivers, causing floods, impairing navigation and eventually turning the San Francisco Bay muddy brown.

The worst offender, whose excesses caused hydraulic mining to be outlawed in 1884, was the **Malakoff Diggins**, sixteen miles up steep and winding North Bloomfield Road from Nevada City (or reachable via the sixteen-mile Tyler Foote Crossing Road, which turns off Hwy-49 twelve miles northwest of Nevada City). Here, a canyon more than a mile long, half a mile wide and over six hundred feet deep was carved out of the red and gold earthen slopes. Natural erosion has softened the scars somewhat, sculpting pinnacles and towers into a miniature Grand Canyon, now preserved as a 3000-acre **state park** (daily dawn–dusk; ☎530/265-2740; $5 per car). While the park may seem just a short detour from Hwy-49 on your map, its interminable unmarked gravel roads and snaking bends may give you the feeling you've landed in a sunny sequel to the *Blair Witch Project*. Inside the park, old buildings from ghost towns around the Gold Country are being moved to the restored town of **NORTH BLOOMFIELD**, where a small **museum** (June–Aug daily 10am–4pm; Sept–May Sat & Sun only, call ☎530/265-2740 for winter hours) shows a twenty-minute film on hydraulicking, and there's a **campground** (☎1-800/444-7275) near the eerie cliffs.

Downieville and the High Sierra towns

From Nevada City, Hwy-49 climbs up along the Yuba River gorge into some of the highest and most marvelous scenery in the Gold Country, where waterfalls tumble over sharp, black rocks bordered by tall pines and maple trees. In the middle of this wilderness, an hour's drive from Nevada City, **DOWNIEVILLE**, the most evocatively sited of the Gold Rush towns, spreads out along both banks of the river, crisscrossed by an assortment of narrow bridges. Hwy-49 runs right through the center of town, slowing to a near-stop to negotiate tight curves that have not been widened since the stagecoaches passed through. Thick stone buildings, some enhanced with delicate wooden balconies and porches, others with heavy iron doors and shutters, face on to raised wooden sidewalks, as their backs dangling precipitously over the steep banks of the river.

For what is now a peaceful and quiet little hamlet of three hundred people, Downieville seems strangely proud of its fairly nasty history. It has the distinction of being the only mining camp ever to have hanged a woman, Juanita, "a fiery Mexican dancehall girl," who stabbed a miner in self-defense. A restored wooden gallows, last used in 1885, still stands next to the County Jail on the south bank of the river, to mark the ghastly heritage. Across the river and two blocks north, at the end of a row of 1850s storefronts, the **Downieville Museum** (May–Oct daily 10am–5pm; ☎530/289-3423; donation) is packed full of odd bits and historical artifacts, including a set of snowshoes for horses and a scaled-down model of a stamp mill, "made by the boys of the shop classes 1947–8." Pick up a walking tour map of the town from the **tourist office** kiosk (☎1-800/720-7782 or 530/289-3507), next to the firebell tower in the center of town. The mini-office can also help out with **accommodation**, which includes the *Riverside Inn* (☎1-800/696-0310 or 530/289-1000; ④) and *Robinson's Motel* (☎530/289-3573; ③), both centrally located on Hwy-49 alongside the Yuba River, and the wonderfully sited *Sierra Shangri-La* (☎530/289-3455; ④) four miles further east, which has B&B rooms and fully-fixtured cottages, the latter available weekly in summer. **Eat and drink** on Main Street at the family-style *Downieville Diner* (☎530/289-3616) or the *Riverview Pizzeria* (☎530/289-3540), and have your favorite café drink at the *Koffee Klub*.

The full-size original of the county museum stamp mill is maintained in working order at the **Kentucky Mine Museum** (summer Wed–Sun 10am–5pm; ☎530/862-1310; $1), a mile east of **SIERRA CITY** further up Hwy-49, where a guided tour (11am, 1pm & 3pm; $4) takes you inside a reconstructed miner's cabin, down a mine shaft, and gives you a look at various pieces of equipment used for retrieving the gold-bearing ore. Until the mine was shut down during World War II, the ore was dug out from tunnels under the massive **Sierra Buttes**, the craggy granite peaks that dominate the surrounding landscape.

Sierra City is full of rustic charm, and can be a useful base for visiting the surrounding area. **Accommodation** is available on Main Street at the *Busch & Heringlake Inn* B&B (☎530/862-1501; ④), the cozy and historic *Holy House* (☎530/862-1123; ⑤); *Herrington's Sierra Pines* (☎530/862-1151; ③) or *Sierra Buttes Inn* (☎530/862-1300; ④), an historic hotel with a bar and dining room. In the area you will also find some of the most remote and attractive campgrounds in the Gold Country, including the *Sierra Campground*, seven miles beyond Sierra City, and *Chapman Creek*, another mile upstream on the Yuba River. All sites are $10 and can be reserved by calling **High Sierra Campgrounds** (☎530/993-1410).

Hwy-49 continues east, passing **SIERRAVILLE** after twenty miles, where you'll find basic facilities, and **Bassetts Junction** where Hwy-89 heads north to Johnsville and south to Truckee and the Lake Tahoe area.

Henness Pass Road Driving Tour

If all the twists and bends in Sierra County's stretch of Route 49 still aren't rugged enough for you, then consider a bumpy historical detour on the **HENNESS PASS**, Picked up just south of Sierraville or at Camptonville (southeast of Downieville near Grass Valley), the pass takes you along the route used by miners, freighters, immigrants and highwaymen in their search for fame and riches. Today, the road is still largely unpaved and unvisited, though it includes breathtaking scenery and a number of historic sites. The only town along the way is the all but abandoned **Forest City** – now home to a few Gold Rush era buildings and a tiny museum (call ranger stations below for hours). The road can take as little as an hour or up to half-a-day, depending on how much time you spend lingering at historic sights along the way. The **Mountain House**, the **Cornish House** and the **Davis Station** were all of importance to miners negotiating the treacherous pass on horseback and in stagecoaches, while the **Kyburz Interpretive Area**, near Hwy-89, has Indian rock art and a reconstructed Basque bread oven. Four wheel drives are recommended for negotiating the pass today, though not necessary; a detailed brochure with a good map is available from the **ranger stations** in Sierraville (☎530/994-3401) or Camptonville (☎530/478-6253).

Johnsville

Founded in 1870, **JOHNSVILLE**, is, after Bodie (see p.296), the best-preserved and most isolated old mining town in California. Located 25 miles north of Bassett Junction, the ghost town is surrounded by over seven thousand acres of pine forest and magnificent scenery and lies at the center of the **Plumas-Eureka State Park** – which has $16 **camping** (reserve through Parknet ☎1-800/444-7275) and miles of **hiking** trails. Johnsville's huge stamp mill and mine buildings are being restored, and in the meantime a small **museum** (daily 9am–5pm; $2) describes the difficult task of digging for gold in the High Sierra winters.

THE SOUTHERN MINES

Though never as rich or successful as the diggings further north, the camps of the **southern mines** had a reputation for being the liveliest and most uproarious of all the Gold Rush settlements, and inspired most of the popular images of the era: Wild West towns full of gambling halls, saloons and gunfights in the streets. The mining methods here were quite different from those used further north. Instead of digging out gold-bearing ore from deep underground, claims here were more often worked by itinerant, roving prospectors searching for bits of gold washed out of rocks by rivers and streams, known as **placer** gold (from the Spanish word meaning both "sand bar," where much of the gold was found, and, appropriately, "pleasure"). Nuggets were sometimes found sitting on the river banks, though most of the gold had to be laboriously separated from mud and gravel using hand-held pans or larger sluices. It wasn't a particularly lucrative existence: freelance miners roamed the countryside until they found a likely spot, and if and when they struck it rich quickly spent most of the earnings, either in celebration or buying the expensive supplies needed to carry on digging.

The boom towns that sprung up around the richest deposits were abandoned as soon as the gold ran out, but a few slowly decaying ghost towns have managed to survive more or less intact to the present day, hidden among the forests and rolling ranchland. Other sites were buried under the many **reservoirs** – built in the 1960s to provide a stable source of water for the agricultural Central Valley – that cover much of the lower elevations.

During spring, the hillsides are covered in fresh green grasses and brightly colored wildflowers, though by the end of summer the hot sun has baked everything a dusty golden brown. Higher up, the free-flowing rivers rush through steep canyons lined by oak trees and cottonwoods, and the ten-thousand-foot granite peaks in the Sierra Nevada mountains above offer excellent skiing in winter, and hiking and camping in the pine and redwood forests all year round. South from Placerville, Hwy-49 passes through **Jackson**, which makes a convenient, if unattractive, base for exploring the many dainty villages scattered around the wine-growing countryside of **Amador County**, continuing on through the mining towns of **Calaveras County**. The center of the southern mining district, then as now, is **Sonora**, a small, prosperous town of ornate Victorian houses set on ridges above steep gorges. Once an arch rival but now a ghost town, neighboring **Columbia** has a carefully restored Gold Rush era Main Street. The gold-mining district actually extended as far south as **Mariposa**, but the mines here were comparatively worthless and little remains to make it worth the trip, except perhaps as a quick stop on the way to Yosemite National Park (see p.333).

You'll need your own **transportation** to see much of the southern Gold Country. Trains steer well clear of the hilly terrain and buses only pass through Mariposa on their way from Fresno and Merced to Yosemite. Drivers be warned, however: speed traps are rampant around the Southern Mines, particularly in Amador County and on any roads leading to Yosemite, where the speed limits tend to be a bit unrealistic and regional traffic police eagerly await to rake in some of that speedy tourist revenue.

Amador County

South from Placerville and US-50, the old mining landscape of **Amador County** has been given over to the vineyards of one of California's up-and-coming **wine-growing** regions, best known for its robust Zinfandel, a full-flavored vintage that thrives in the sun-baked soil. Most of the wineries are located above Hwy-49 in the Shenandoah Valley, near Plymouth on the north edge of the county. For a detailed map to all the local establishments, contact Amador Vintners (☎209/245-4309) or pick one up anywhere tourists congregate.

Amador City and Sutter Creek

About thirty miles east of Sacramento, Hwy-16 joins Hwy-49 at **AMADOR CITY**, whose short strip of false-fronted antique shops give it a distinctive, Old West look. The landmark *Imperial Hotel* at the northern edge dominates the town, its four-foot-thick brick walls standing at a sharp bend in Hwy-49. The hotel has recently been renovated, with sunny double **rooms** (☎209/267-9172; ⑤), and a **restaurant** on the ground floor. Another option is the *Mine House Inn* B&B, on the way to Sutter Creek (☎1-800/646-3473 or 209/267-5900; ⑤), and the secluded *Rancho Cicada* B&B, near Plymouth (☎209/245-4841), which offers clothing-optional weekend retreats.

SUTTER CREEK, two miles south, is much larger than Amador City, but still little more than a row of tidy antique shops and restaurants catering to tourists along Hwy-49. Though there are a number of surprisingly large Victorian wooden houses – many styled after Puritan New England farmhouses – the town lacks the disheveled spontaneity that animates many of the other Gold Rush towns, perhaps because its livelihood was never based on independent prospectors panning for placer gold, but on hired hands working underground in the more organized and capital-intensive hardrock mines. It was a lucrative business for the mine-owners: the **Eureka Mine**, owned by Hetty Green, at one time the richest woman in the world, operated until 1958, while the **Lincoln Mine** made enough money for owner Leland Stanford to become a railroad magnate and Governor of California.

Sutter Creek holds the bulk of Amador County's **accommodation** and **eating** places, with two central and very comfortable B&Bs: *The Foxes*, 77 Main St (☎209/267-5711; ⑥), with well-appointed rooms and claw-foot baths; and the larger, more communally minded *Sutter Creek Inn*, 75 Main St (☎209/267-5606; ④), with no TVs, no phones and no fake Victoriana, but a nice garden with hammocks and a welcoming atmosphere. The *Bellotti Inn*, 53 Main St (☎209/267-5211; ②), has the cheapest accommodation in town and a decent restaurant serving full meals for $15 and pasta dishes for $7. *Susan's Place*, in the Eureka Street Courtyard, a half-block east of Hwy-49 (Wed–Sun; ☎209/267-0945), serves sandwiches, soups, and salads under a shaded gazebo and, across the street, the *Sutter Creek Coffee Roasting Co.* (☎209/267-5550) serves the best coffee in town. For dessert, don't miss the *Sutter Creek Ice Cream Emporium*, 51 Main St (☎209/267-0543), where the friendly owner will play Scott Joplin tunes on the piano while you sip on a milkshake.

Jackson

After Sutter Creek, the town of **JACKSON**, four miles south, can seem distinctly blue-collar, mainly because of the huge Georgia Pacific lumber mill that serves as its northern gateway. Nevertheless, it's a more affordable base for exploring the surrounding countryside. Most of the well-preserved buildings in the small historic downtown area were erected after a large fire in1862, and today are a bit drowned out by the encroaching modern businesses that surround it. There is a lovely, if architecturally inappropriate, 1939 Art Deco front on the **County Courthouse** at the top of the hill. Further along the crest, the **Amador County Museum**, 225 Church St (Wed–Sun 10am–4pm; donation), has displays of all the usual Gold Rush artifacts, but is worth a look most of all for its detailed models of the local hard-rock mines – with shafts over a mile deep – that were in use up until World War II. The headframes and some of the mining machinery are still standing a mile north of the museum on Jackson Gate Road, where two sixty-foot diameter **tailing wheels** (8am–dusk; free), which carried away the waste from the Kennedy Mine, are accessible by way of short trails that lead up from a well-signposted parking area. The headframe of the six-thousand-foot shaft, the deepest in North America, stands out at the top of the slope, along Hwy-49. The other major mine in Jackson, the **Argonaut Mine** (of which nothing remains), was the scene of a tragedy in 1922, when 47 men were killed in an underground fire.

The **Amador County Chamber of Commerce** (daily 9am–5pm; ☎ 1-800/649-4988 or 209/223-0350), is rather awkwardly situated at the junction of Hwy-49 and Hwy-88, but offers a *Visitors Guide to Amador County*, full of the usual maps and historical information. The best **place to stay** is the friendly, if slightly run-down, *National Hotel*, 77 Main St (☎1-800/894-3446 or 209/223-0500; ④), an 1860s hotel with individually decorated rooms, such as the "Bordello Room" with flock wallpaper, a four-poster bed and a claw-foot bath. If the *National* is full, try the *Amador Motel* (☎209/223-0970; ②) on Hwy-49 north of town, or the nearby *Jackson Gold Lodge* (☎1-888/777-0380 or 209/223-0486; ③). *Mel and Faye's Diner* (☎209/223-0835) on Hwy-49 near the town center, is open all day for **breakfasts and burgers**, while *Café Max Swiss Bakery*, 140 Main St (☎209/223-0174), serves pastries and a mean cup of coffee. For **drinking**, the *Pioneer Rex Saloon*, 28 Main St (☎209/223-3859), is the modern equivalent of a Wild West saloon, with cheap beers and all-night poker games behind swinging louvre doors.

Indian Grinding Rock and Volcano

Hwy-88 heads east from Jackson up the Sierra Crest, through hills that contain one of the most fitting memorials to the Native Americans who lived here for thousands of years before the Gold Rush all but wiped them out. Nine miles from Jackson, off Hwy-88, a side road passes by the **Indian Grinding Rock State Historic Park** (daily dawn–dusk; ☎209/296-7488, $5 per car), where eleven hundred small cups – *Chaw'Se* in Miwok – were carved into the marbleized limestone outcropping to be used as mortars for grinding acorns into flour. It's the largest collection of bedrock mortar in North America, and if you arrive near dawn or dusk and look closely from the small elevated platform next to the biggest of the flat rocks, you can just detect the faint outline of some of the 360 **petroglyphs**. The state has developed the site into an interpretive center and has constructed replicas of Miwok dwellings and religious buildings with the close participation of Miwok elders and community leaders. Descendants of the Miwok gather here during the weekend following the fourth Friday in September for "Big Time," a celebration of the survival of their culture with traditional arts, crafts and games. At the entrance to the site, the **Chaw'Se Regional Indian Museum** (Mon–Fri 11am–3pm, Sat & Sun 10am–4pm; free) explores the past and present state of the ten Sierra Nevada Native groups in a building said to simulate a Miwok roundhouse. The full process of producing acorn flour is covered, but the scant regard given to modern Miwok life is a sad testament to the extent of the devastation done to Miwok culture. If you'd like to spend the night, a **campground** in the surrounding woods costs $14 a pitch and can be booked through Parknet (☎1-800/444-7275).

Named after the crater-like bowl in which it sits, **VOLCANO**, a tiny village a mile and a half north, once boasted over thirty saloons and dance halls. Today it claims nearly as many historic sites as Jackson, but has been mercifully bypassed by all the latter town's development and traffic. The densely forested countryside around the village makes it well worth a visit, especially during spring (particularly mid-March to mid-April) when **Daffodil Hill**, three miles north of Volcano, is carpeted with more than 300,000 of the bobbing heads. Signs directing you there are only displayed when the flowers are in bloom. The sole **accommodation** in the immediate area is the friendly *St George Hotel* on Main Street (☎209/296-4458; ④), offering bed and breakfast without the comforts of televisions, phones or private bathrooms. Guests congregate in the restaurant and bar, whose walls are decked with every office poster and wisecrack bumper sticker imaginable.

Highway 88

Hwy-88 heads east beyond the Volcano turn-off to Pioneer, where it meets Hwy-26 from Mokelumne Hill (see below). Three miles east, the **Amador Eldorado Forest Ranger Station** (Mon–Fri 8am–4.30pm; ☎209/295-4251) supplies wilderness permits for overnighting in the **Mokelumne Wilderness**, a segment of the Stanislaus and Toiabe National Forests south of Hwy-88 which closely follows the route of many early settlers. The ranger station also has details of camping and hiking in the **Eldorado National Forest**, beautiful in the fall, just before the winter snows turn the Sierra Nevada mountains around the 8500-foot Carson Pass into one of California's best cross-country ski resorts (see "Kirkwood," p.574). For more off-the-beaten-path recreation, try the **Bear River Lake** (information: ☎209/295-4868), just South of Hwy-88 on the way to Kirkwood and Tahoe, which offers camping, hiking, fishing, swimming and boating, without all the hype of the better known resorts.

Calaveras County

Calaveras County lies across the Mokelumne River, eight miles south of Jackson, and is best known for being the setting of **Mark Twain**'s first published story, the *Celebrated Jumping Frog of Calaveras County*. Today, precious few sights of historic interest remain, though there are plenty of options in the country for rugged outdoor recreation. The most northerly town in the county, **MOKELUMNE HILL**, or "Moke Hill," as it's called, was as action-packed in its time as any of the southern Gold Rush towns, but tourism has been slower to take hold here, and today the town is an all-but-abandoned cluster of ruined and half-restored buildings, not without a certain melancholy appeal. **The Mokelumne Hill History Society**, 8367 East Center (Sat-Sun, summers, 11am–3pm; ☎209/286-1770; donation), has a modest exhibit on the history of the immediate area, once home to almost 10,000 people. The range of names and languages on the headstones of the **Protestant Cemetery**, on a hill a hundred yards west of town, gives a good idea of the mix of people who came from all over the world to the California mines.

San Andreas

Eight miles south, **SAN ANDREAS** hardly seems to warrant a second look: the biggest town for miles, it's now the Calaveras County seat, and has sacrificed historic character for commercial sprawl. The **Chamber of Commerce**, 3 North Main Street (☎209/754-4009), publishes a handy map to the county that includes recreational activities in the area. What remains of old San Andreas survives along narrow Main Street, on a steep hill just east of the highway, where the 1893 granite and brick County Courthouse has been restored and now houses an interesting collection of Gold Rush memorabilia in the **Calaveras County Museum**, 30 N Main St (daily 10am–4pm; ☎209/754-6513; free). Local **nightlife** revolves around the *Black Bart Inn*, 35 Main St (☎209/754-3808; ③) across the street, which hosts bands on weekends. It is named after the gentleman stagecoach robber, **Black Bart**, who was captured and convicted here. Black Bart led a double life: in San Francisco he was a prominent citizen named Charles Bolton, who claimed to be a wealthy mining engineer; in the mining camps, he made his name by committing thirty robberies between 1877 and 1883, always addressing his victims as "Sir" and "Madam" and sometimes reciting bits of poetry before escaping with the loot. He was finally discovered after dropping a handkerchief at the scene of a hold-up; police got him by tracing the laundry mark. He spent four years of a six-year sentence in San Quentin, and after his release disappeared without trace.

Angels Camp and Carson Hill

The mining camps of southern Calaveras County were some of the richest in the Gold Country, both for the size of their nuggets and for the imaginations of their residents. The author Bret Harte spent an unhappy few years teaching in and around the mines in the mid-1850s and based his short story, *The Luck of the Roaring Camp*, on his stay in **ANGELS CAMP**, thirty miles south of Jackson. There isn't much to see here these days, though the downtown feels mildly authentic. The **Visitors Center** at 1211 South Main Street (☎1-800/225-3764 or 209/736-0049) has all the information you would expect. The saloon in the *Angels Hotel* on Main Street, where the 29-year-old **Mark Twain** was told a tale that inspired him to write his famous story about a frog jumping competition, has been converted into a discount tire store. The unfortunate legacy of the story is the **Jumping Frog Jubilee** held on the third weekend in May each year and attended by thousands of people. On the north side of town, the **Angels Camp Museum**, 753 Main St (daily 10am–3pm; ☎209/736-2963; $1), presents a cornucopia of gold excavating equipment and memorabilia, as well as a carriage barn filled with historic horse-drawn vehicles.

CARSON HILL, now a ghost town along Hwy-49 four miles south of Angels Camp, boasted the largest single nugget ever unearthed in California: 195 pounds of solid gold fifteen inches long and six inches thick, worth $43,000 then and well over a million dollars today. Nearby, **New Melones Reservoir** is the third largest reservoir in California and has all the camping ($14), swimming, hiking, boating and other recreational possibilities you could hope for, yet it's seldom visited by the tourist throngs who fly through the Gold Country on their way to pricier recreational areas. The **Visitor Center** (daily 10am–4pm; ☎209/536-9094) is located just past Carson Hill on Hwy-49.

LIMESTONE CAVERNS IN THE GOLD COUNRTY

Limestone caverns abound in the southern Gold Country. Three have been developed for the public, and any one of them can provide, at the very least, a cool and constant 55°F relief from the sometimes baking-hot summer days. At Vallecito, just south of Hwy-4 and five miles east of Angels Camp on Parrot's Ferry Road, the **Moaning Cavern** (May–Oct: 9am–6pm; Nov–Apr: 10am–5pm; ☎209/736-2708 $7.75) is the largest in California, filled with strange rock formations, 150ft below ground; the human remains on display here – the oldest to be found in North America – greeted gold-seekers who found the cave in 1851. The natural acoustics of the cavern, which caused the low moaning sounds after which it is named, were destroyed by the insertion of the spiral staircase that takes visitors down into its depths (although for $35 you can rappel the 180 feet). **Mercer Caverns** (May–Oct Sun–Thu 9am–6pm, Fri–Sat 9am–8pm; Nov–April Sun–Thu 10am–4:30pm, Fri–Sat 10am–6pm; ☎209/728-2101; $7), a mile north of Murphys on Sheep Ranch Road, focus on an 800-foot-long gallery of sculpted limestone, which takes the shape of angel's wings and giant flowers. The third cave system, **California Caverns** (daily 10am–5pm; closed in winter or whenever it rains often; ☎209/736-2708; $8), six miles east of San Andreas then two miles south from Mountain Ranch, is the most extensive and impressive of public caverns, and offers a day-long Wild Cave Expedition ($75) on which you wear coveralls and a lighted helmet as you follow a professional guide through miles of craggy recesses.

Murphys

Nine miles east of Angels Camp, up the fairly steep Hwy-4, **MURPHYS'** one and only street is shaded by locust trees and graced by rows of decaying monumental buildings. One of the Gold Country's few surviving wooden water flumes still stands on Murphys' northern edge, while the oldest structure in town now houses the **Oldtimer's Museum** (Fri–Sun 11am–4pm; ☎209/728-1160; donation), a small gathering of documents and a wall-full of rifles. If you want to **stay**, head across the street to the old *Murphys Hotel*, 457 Main St (☎1-800/532-7684 or 209/728-3444; ④), which hosted some of the leading lights of the boom days in its rustic double rooms. The **Calaveras Big Trees State Park** (☎209/795-3840; $5 per car) fifteen miles east, covers six thousand acres of gigantic sequoia trees, threaded with trails. It makes for fine ski touring in winter, with **hiking** and **camping** (reserve mid-summer through Parknet ☎1-800/444-7275; $16) the rest of the year.

Sonora, Columbia, Jamestown and Chinese Camp

SONORA, fifteen miles southeast of Angels Camp, is the center of the southern mining district. Now a logging town, set on steep ravines, the town makes a good base for exploring the southern region, and has a thriving commercial center that manages to avoid tourist overkill. There's little to see beyond the false-fronted buildings and Victorian houses on the main **Washington Street** and the Gothic **St James Episcopal Church** at its far end, but it's a friendly, animated place, which warrants an afternoon's amble. You can pick up architectural and historical walking-tour **maps** (25¢) from the **Tuolumne County Visitors Bureau**, 542 W Stockton St (daily 10am–5pm, slightly longer in summer; ☎ 1-800/446-1333 or 209/533-4420). The small **Tuolumne County Museum**, in the old County Jail at 158 W Bradford Ave (Mon–Fri 10am–4pm, Sat 10am–3.30pm; free), is worth a look for the restored cell block, if not for the collection of old clothes and photographs.

The best **place to stay** in Sonora is the *Ryan House*, 153 S Shepherd St (☎1-800/831-4897 or 209/533-3445; ⑤), a comfortable and welcoming old home set in lovely rose gardens two blocks east of the town center. Other options include the old adobe *Gunn House* at 286 S Washington St (☎209/532-3421; ③), or the good-value *Miner's Motel* (☎1-800/451-4176 or 209/532-7850; ③) on Hwy-108, half way to Jamestown. For **lunch** on Washington St, try the gourmet sandwiches at *Good Heavens* at no. 49 (☎209/532-3663); after dark, make for *Alfredo's*, at no. 123 (☎209/532-8332), widely regarded as the best reasonably priced Mexican restaurant in these parts, the *Sonora Inn Restaurant and Steakhouse* at no. 160, for an old-fashioned, artery-clogging meat fest, and *Carmela's*, at no. 301 (☎209/532-8858), for homemade pastas and sauces. Of several **bars** on Washington, *The Brass Rail* at no. 131, and the *Horseshoe Club* at no. 97, are the best places to find a hint of the Wild West.

Columbia

Sonora's one-time arch-rival, tourist-loving **COLUMBIA**, three miles north on Parrots Ferry Road, now passes itself off as a ghost town with a carefully restored Main Street that gives an excellent – if slightly contrived – idea of what Gold Rush life might have been like. The town experienced a brief burst of riches after a Dr Thaddeus Hildreth and his party picked up thirty pounds of gold in just two days in March 1850. Within a month, over five thousand miners were working claims limited by local law to ten square feet, and by 1854 Columbia was California's second largest city, with fifteen thousand inhabitants supporting some forty saloons, eight hotels and one school. The town missed becoming the state capital by two votes – just as well, since by 1870 the gold had run out and the town was abandoned, but only after over two and a half million ounces of gold (worth nearly a billion dollars at today's prices) had been taken out of the surrounding area.

Columbia is preserved as a **State Historic Park** (daily 10am–5pm, longer in summer; ☎209/532-4301), though it is also a genuine town with an active main street and year-round residents. The **Columbia Museum and Visitors Center** at Main and State Streets (daily 10am–5pm; ☎209/536-1672) is the best place to pick up detailed information. Most of the buildings that survive date from the late 1850s, built in brick after fire destroyed the town for a second time. Roughly half of them house historical exhibits – including a dramatized visit to the frontier dentist's office, complete with a two-hundred-proof anesthetic and tape-recorded screams. The rest have been converted into shops, restaurants and saloons, where you can sip a sarsaparilla or munch on a hot dog. There's even a **stagecoach ride** ($5) along the old mining trails around the town, which leaves from the Wells Fargo Building. As you might imagine, the park/town can be nightmarishly crowded, especially on **Living History Days**, when volunteers dress up and act out scenes from the old days. If you want to **stay**, the *City Hotel* on Main Street (☎1-800/532-1479 or 209/532-1479; ⑤) is luxurious and central, as is the historic *Harlan House B&B*, 22890 School House (☎209/533-4862; ⑤); a mile south of town, the *Columbia Gem Motel*, 22131 Parrots Ferry Rd (☎209/532-4508; ③), offers basic accommodation in rustic cabins. Even cheaper is the *Sonora Hostel*, 11800 Columbia College Drive (☎209/533-2339), where dorm beds on the college campus cost $15.

When you've tired of the town, you might try touring the surrounding trails on **horseback**. The Columbia Stageline and Riding Stable, inside the park (☎209/532-0663), offers rides of varying duration and difficulty for about $24 per hour.

Jamestown

Three miles south of Sonora on Hwy-49, **JAMESTOWN** serves as the southern gateway to the Gold Country for drivers entering on Hwy-120 from the San Francisco Bay Area. Before 1966, when much of Jamestown burned down in a fire, it was used as location for many well-known Westerns – most famously for the filming of *High Noon*. The train from that movie can be found among many other steam giants in the **Railtown 1897 State Historic Park**, Jamestown's biggest attraction, four blocks east of Main Street (daily 9:30am–4:30pm; $6). In summer, you can ride one every hour on the hour for an additional fee ($5). Along with its train collection, Jamestown is one of the few Gold Country towns that still has a **working mine** – the huge open-pit Sonora Mining Corporation west of town on Hwy-49 – and a number of outfits take visitors on gold-mining expeditions. Among them, Gold Prospecting Expeditions ($30 for 2hr; ☎1-800/596-0009 or 209/984-4653) gives brief instruction in the arts of panning, sluicing and sniping, and allows you two hours to pan what you can from its local stream. Main Street is the town's main drag and has a few **accommodation** choices such as the *National Hotel* (☎1-800/252-8299 or 209/984-3446; ④), with a casually elegant restaurant bar and Gold Rush era ambiance. Nearby is the plush and historic *Palm Hotel B&B* at 10382 Willow Street (☎209/984-3429; ⑤). For **food** on Main Street, try the popular *Mother Lode Coffee Shop* (☎209/984-3386) or the more touristy *Smoke Café* (☎209/984-3733), which serves Southwestern-style Mexican food and huge margaritas.

China Camp

Hwy-49 winds south from Sonora through some sixty miles of the sparsely populated, rolling foothills of **Mariposa County**, but first it passes the scant remains of the town of **CHINESE CAMP**. It was here that the worst of the Tong Wars between rival factions

THE GOLD COUNTRY ROBIN HOOD

Very little is actually known of the truth behind the stories of **Joaquin Murieta**, yet virtually every southern Gold Rush town has some tale to tell of him. A romantic hero, rather than a real one, Murieta was probably a composite of many characters, mostly dispossessed Mexican miners driven to banditry by violent racist abuse at the hands of newly arrived white Americans.

In May 1853, the State Legislature hired a man named Harry Love to capture any one of five men named "Joaquin" wanted for cattle theft. Love soon returned with the head of a man pickled in a glass jar, and collected the reward. A year later, J.R. Ridge wrote a story called *The Life and Times of Joaquin Murieta, the Celebrated California Bandit*, mixing together flights of fancy with a few well-placed facts – including the pickled head – and the legend was born.

If Joaquin was indeed a living bandit and not just a legend, he would have most likely lived in the town of **Hornitos**, twenty winding miles west of Bear Valley on the isolated southern edge of the Gold Country. Hornitos was once a quiet little Mexican pueblo, but the population swelled to over fifteen thousand when Mexican miners were exiled from nearby mining camps by white miners who didn't feel like sharing the wealth. The town became notorious for its saloons, opium dens and gambling halls, and was a favorite haunt of many an outlaw like Murieta – who, it's claimed, had his own secret escape route out of town via an underground tunnel. Today, Hornitos is a heap of eerie **ruins** grouped around a central plaza.

of Chinese miners took place in 1856, after the Chinese had been excluded from other mining camps in the area by white miners. Racism was rampant in the southern Gold Rush camps, something which also accounts for its most enduring legend, the story of the so-called Robin Hood of the Mother Lode, **Joaquin Murieta** (see box).

Further south on Hwy-49 lie the southern Gold Rush towns of **Groveland**, **Coulterville** and **Mariposa**. Due to their proximity to Yosemite National Park, all three are covered in detail in Chapter Five (see pp.336–337).

LAKE TAHOE, TRUCKEE, RENO AND CARSON CITY

High above the Gold Country, just east of the Sierra ridge, **Lake Tahoe** sits placidly in a dramatic alpine bowl, surrounded by high granite peaks and miles of thickly wooded forest. It's a big tourist area; the sandy beaches and surrounding pine-tree wilderness are overrun with thousands of fun-lovers (predominantly families) throughout the summer, and in winter the snow-covered slopes of the nearby peaks are packed with skiers. The eastern third of the lake lies in Nevada and glows with light from the neon signs of the inevitable **Stateline casinos**.

Truckee, 25 miles north of Lake Tahoe, ranges along the Truckee River, which flows out of Lake Tahoe down into the desert of Nevada's Great Basin. It's a main stop on Greyhound and Amtrak cross-country routes, though, apart from an influx of skiers in winter, is little-visited. **Donner Pass**, just west of town, was named in memory of the pioneer Donner family, many of whom lost their lives when trapped here by heavy winter snows.

Across the border in Nevada, **Reno**, at the eastern foot of the Sierra Nevada, is a downmarket version of Las Vegas, popular with slot-machine junkies and elderly gamblers; others come to take advantage of Nevada's lax marriage and divorce laws. Though far smaller than Reno, **Carson City**, thirty miles south, is the Nevada state capital, with a couple of engaging museums that recount the town's frontier history. Heading deeper into Nevada, and up into the arid mountains to the east, the silver mines of the **Comstock Lode**, whose wealth paid for the building of much of San Francisco, are buried deep below the evocative, if touristy, **Virginia City**.

The two main trans-Sierra highways, **I-80** and **US-50**, head east from Sacramento and are kept open all year round, regardless of snowfall, passing by Truckee and Lake Tahoe respectively. Both places are served by Greyhound, and there are also services from the Nevada cities to the Tahoe casinos, though there's no public transportation between Truckee and the lake.

Lake Tahoe

Fault-formed **LAKE TAHOE** is one of the highest, deepest, cleanest, coldest and most beautiful lakes in the world. More than sixteen hundred feet deep, it is so cold – or so the story goes – that at its depths cowboys who drowned over a century ago have been recovered in perfectly preserved condition, gun holsters and all. The lake's position, straddling the border between California and Nevada, lends the lake a schizophrenic air, the dichotomy most evident at **South Lake Tahoe**, the lakeside's largest community, where ranks of restaurants, modest motels and pine-bound cottages stand cheek by jowl with the high-rise gambling dens of **Stateline**, just across the border. **Tahoe City**, the hub of the lake's northwestern shore, does not escape the tourists, but manages to retain a more relaxed – if somewhat exclusive – attitude. Expensive vacation homes and shabby family-oriented mini-resorts line much of the remainder of the lake. Tahoe is never truly off season, luring weekenders from the Bay Area and beyond with clear, cool waters in the summer, snow-covered slopes in the winter, and slot machines year round. On holiday weekends, expect traffic in the area to reach maddening levels; packs of cars and trucks spilling over with ski equipment and mountain bikes will serve as your convoy throughout the area. To take advantage of the natural resources and still avoid at least some of the crowds, you might consider staying south of Tahoe near **Kirkwood**, though as the California economy booms and space-loving weekenders look for getaways from the getaways, even the most remote locations around Tahoe are experiencing their own tourism explosions.

Arrival and information

One hundred miles east of Sacramento on both US-50 and US-80, Lake Tahoe is served by Greyhound **buses** and a number of coach **tours**, mainly catering to weekend gamblers. Several daily Greyhound buses from San Francisco and Sacramento use *Harrah's* casinos in South Lake Tahoe as a terminus: Amtrak Thruway buses arrive several times daily from Sacramento on their way to Carson City, but they must be booked in conjunction with long distance train routes. Tahoe Casino Express buses ($17 one-way; ☎1-800/446-6128 or 775/785-2424) run half-hourly from 9am to 5pm between Reno airport and the Stateline casinos, and Gray Line (☎775/331-1147) has daily tours from Reno around the lake, stopping off at Virginia City; their "gambler's special" coach tours leave from San Francisco. If you're **driving**, expect to get here in a little over three hours from San Francisco, unless you join the Friday night exodus in which case you can add an hour or two, more in winter when you'll need to carry **chains**; call the Caltrans road phone (☎1-800/427-7623) to check on road conditions before you depart.

There are booths claiming to be visitor centers all over South Lake Tahoe, but most are just advertising outlets for the casinos or fronts for timeshare agents. For slightly more useful **information**, you can obtain maps and brochures (all of them chock-full of advertisements), as well as limited help with finding a place to stay (if you haven't

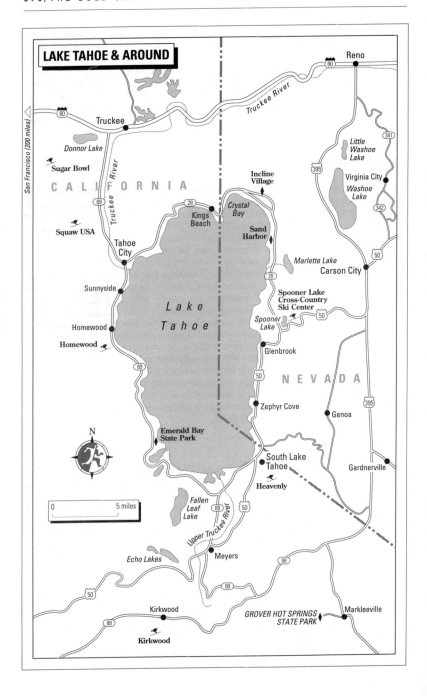

booked ahead, it won't be easy), at one of the official visitors centers. The **South Lake Tahoe Chamber of Commerce**, 13066 US-50 (Mon–Sat 8.30am–4.30pm; ☎530/541-5255) is just west of El Dorado beach. Just north of Stateline in Nevada, the **Tahoe-Douglas Visitor Center**, 195 Hwy-50 (Mon–Sat 9am–5pm; ☎775/588-4591) will help with room reservations. The **North Lake Tahoe Chamber of Commerce**, 245 North Lake Blvd in Tahoe City (Mon–Sat 9am–5pm; ☎530/581-6900 or 530/583-3494) is the best bet for information on the North Lake region. And lastly, the **Incline Village/Crystal Bay Chamber of Commerce**, 969 Tahoe Blvd (☎775/831-4440 or 775/832-1606) is another option on the Nevada side of the Lake.

Getting around

STAGE **buses** (☎530/541-6328) run 24 hours a day all over the South Lake Tahoe area, and will take you anywhere within a ten-mile radius for a flat $1.25 fare ($2 buys you an all-day pass). Tahoe Casino Express (☎1-800/446-6128) runs northeast from South Lake Tahoe to Glenbrook, then east to Carson City. In the north, TART buses (roughly 6am to 6pm; $1 flat fare, $2.50 for an all-day pass; ☎1-800/736-6365 or 530/581-6365) runs between Truckee, Tahoe City, Sugar Pine Point State Park and Incline Village. Alternatively, the Tahoe Trolley (daily 10am–11pm; ☎530/581-6365; day pass $3) runs continuous service between Emerald Bay, Squaw Valley and Sand Harbor. **Car rental**, starting at about $30 a day, is available through the South Lake Tahoe outlets of all the national chains – Alamo (☎1-800/327-9633), Avis (☎1-800/831-2847), Enterprise (☎1-800/325-8007) and Hertz (☎1-800/654-3131) – as well as slightly cheaper local firms such as Tahoe Rent-a-car (☎530/544-4500). You could also **rent a bicycle** for around $20 a day from any of over a dozen lakeside shops in South Lake Tahoe – some of them offering a full range of **sports equipment rentals** – such as the Mountain Sports Center, Hwy 89 near the "Y" junction (☎530/542-6584), and Lakeview Sports, 3131 Hwy-50 (☎530/544-0183). In Tahoe City on North Lake Blvd, try Olympic Bike Shop, no. 620 (☎530/581-2500), or Back Country, no. 255 (☎530/581-5861).

Accommodation

Most of the hundred or so **motels** that circle the lake are collected together along US-50 in South Lake Tahoe. During the week, except in summer, many have bargain rates, from around $40 for a double; however, these rates can easily double on weekends, so be sure to confirm all prices. Don't expect great deals at the **casinos**; there are fewer than in Las Vegas or Reno, and the casino hotels charge whatever the busy market will bear. If you're having trouble finding a room, the **South Lake Tahoe Visitors' Authority**, 1156 Ski Run Boulevard (☎1-800/288-2463 or 530/583-3494), runs a free **reservation service**.

Tahoe City lacks the range and competition of its southerly neighbor, so you can expect to pay slightly more for a room there, although the reprieve from the Stateline bustle may just make the extra cost worth it if you're looking for peace and quiet. **Camping** (see box on p.576) is only an option during summer (Tahoe gets upwards of 20ft of snow every winter).

South shore

Camp Richardson Resort, Hwy-89 between Emerald Bay and Stateline (☎1-800/544-1801 or 530/541-1801). Comfortable cabins with full kitchens on a 150-acre resort that also has campsites for $17. Cabins available for both nightly and weekly rentals. ④.

Caesars Tahoe Resort/Casino, US-50, Stateline, Nevada (☎1-800/648-3353 or 775/588-3515). Deluxe resort and upmarket casino; the best rooms overlook the lake. ⑥.

Doug's Mellow Mountain Retreat, 3787 Forest Ave, S Lake Tahoe (☎530/544-8065). Essentially Doug's home, operating as a relaxed, if cramped, hostel with cooking facilities, cheap bike rental and occasional barbecues. Beds are $15 a night and double rooms are available. A mile from the Greyhound stop, but Doug will pick you up. ①.

Driftwood Lodge, 4115 Laurel Ave at Poplar, S Lake Tahoe (☎530/541-7400). The heated pool and private beach access makes this otherwise basic accommodation particularly appealing in summer. ③.

Inn by the Lake, 3300 Lake Tahoe Blvd, S Lake Tahoe (☎1-800/877-1466 or 530/542-0330). Nicely furnished rooms, a heated swimming pool and jacuzzi, free breakfast and use of bicycles make this relaxing spot good value for money. Free shuttle bus to the casinos. ⑤.

Lamplighter Motel, 4143 Cedar Ave, S Lake Tahoe (☎1-888/544-4055 or 530/544-2936). Just off US-50, near the casinos and the lakeshore. It has a hot tub with views of the ski field behind. ④.

Red Carpet Inn, 4100 Lake Tahoe Blvd (Hwy-50), S Lake Tahoe (☎1-800/336-5553 or 530/544-2261). This tacky hotel is about as close as you can get to the casinos without staying in Nevada. Rooms are surprisingly comfortable. ③.

Royal Valhalla, 4104 Lakeshore Blvd (☎1-800/999-4104 or 530/2233). Balconied suites with kitchenettes overlooking the lake. Private beach. ⑤.

Seven Seas, 4145 Manzanita Ave, S Lake Tahoe (☎530/544-7031). One of the south shore's countless small motels, offering clean, simple rooms and a hot tub. ③.

Super 8, 3600 Lake Tahoe Blvd (☎530/544-3311). Basic and cheap, this property is part of a national chain. ③.

North shore

Falcon Motor Lodge, Hwy-28, Kings Beach (☎530/546-2583). Ordinary but dependable budget accommodation. ③.

Inn at Incline, 1003 Tahoe Blvd, Incline Village (☎775/832-1234). Nestled in a secluded forest setting, with private beach access, indoor pool, spa and sauna. ⑤.

Lake of the Sky Motor Inn, 955 N Lake Blvd, Tahoe City (☎530/583-3305). Justifiably a little more expensive than the *Tahoe City Inn*. ④.

Pepper Tree Inn, 645 N. Lake Blvd, Tahoe City (☎530/583-3711). Heated pool and basic, affordable accommodation. ③.

River Ranch, Hwy 89 & Alpine Meadows Road, Tahoe City (☎530/5834264 or 800/5359900). Historic and casual lodge on the Truckee River with one of the lake's best restaurants. ⑥.

Sunnyside, 1850 W Lake Blvd, Tahoe City (☎530/583-7200). Large, comfortable mountain lodge right on the lakeshore. Unbeatable views of the lake from many rooms, and a popular restaurant on the ground floor. ⑥.

Tahoe City Inn, 790 N Lake Blvd, Tahoe City (☎1-800/800-8246 or 530/581-3333). These basic facilities are centrally located and one of the better deals in the area. ③.

Tamarack Lodge, 2311 N Lake Blvd, Tahoe City (☎1-888/824-6323 or 530/583-3350). Comfortable and clean lodging that is the best deal anywhere on the lake. ③.

Travelodge, 455 N Lake Blvd, Tahoe City (☎530/583-3766). The location is unbeatable, right across from the lake in the center of town, but mid-winter and mid-summer, you'll pay for it. At other times, these well-appointed rooms can be a good deal. Lake-view spa and sauna. ④.

Further out

Sierrawood Guest House, 12 miles from South shore, Tahoe Paradise (☎800/7003802 or 530/5776073). For that romantic getaway, a secluded chalet in the woods within a few minutes' drive of the casinos' glitter. Jacuzzi, exercise room, fireplace and free snowmobiling on premises. Popular with gay and lesbian couples. ⑥.

Sorensen's, 14255 Hwy-88, Hope Valley (☎1-800/423-9949 or 530/694-2203) Nestled in the aspens of Hope Valley about a half hour drive away from South Shore on the west fork of the Carson River, kitsch and cozy cabins with a Bavarian ski lodge theme. ⑤.

South Lake Tahoe and Stateline

Almost all of Tahoe's lakeshore is developed in some way or another, but nowhere is it as concentrated and overbearing as at the contiguous settlements of **SOUTH LAKE TAHOE** and **STATELINE**. The latter is compact, a clutch of gambling houses huddled, as you might expect, along the Nevada–California border. The dozen-or-so casinos compete for the attentions of the punters who almost all base themselves in the much larger South Lake Tahoe on the Californian side. This is the best place to organize one of the many **outdoor activities** the lake has to offer. Power boating, water skiing, skurfing, parasailing, scuba diving, canoeing and mountain biking are just a few of the proposed activities on the menu of local sporting equipment rental offices (see p.571). If you happen to lose your vacation allowance at the tables and slot machines, you can always explore the beautiful hiking trails, parks, and beaches that populate the surrounding area.

Though many stretches of the route around Lake Tahoe are stunning, the 75-mile **drive** is perhaps not the most beautiful in America as at least one locally produced brochure touts. A better way to see the lake is to take a **paddlewheel boat cruise** on either the *Tahoe Queen* from South Lake Tahoe (three departures daily, call for times; ☎1800/2382463; $18-45;), or the *MS Dixie II* from Zephyr Cove (three departures daily, call for times; ☎775/5883508; $17-42), reached on a free shuttle from South Lake Tahoe. Perhaps most impressive is the view of the lake from above. For those with no athletic ambition, the lazy way to ascend is in one of the neighboring **ski resort's aerial trams**.

West around the lake

In summer, many enjoyable music and arts events take place at the **Tallac Historic Site** (April–Oct daily 10am–6pm; free), beside Hwy-89 on the western side of the lake just northwest of the "Y" (where Hwy-89 and Hwy-50 separate to the west and east of the lake). Even when there's nothing special going on, the historic site's sumptuous wood-built homes – constructed by wealthy San Franciscans as lakeside vacation retreats in the late 1800s – are well worth a look. You can also see the remains of the lavish casino-hotel erected by Elias "Lucky" Baldwin, which brought the rich and famous to Lake Tahoe's shores until it was destroyed by fire in 1914. Inside the former Baldwin house, the **Tallac Museum** (daily 11am–3pm; free) records the family's impact on the region.

The prettiest part of the lake, however, is along the southwest shore, where **Emerald Bay State Park**, ten miles from South Lake Tahoe (daily dawn–dusk; $5 per vehicle), surrounds a narrow, rock-strewn inlet and the lake's one island, Fanette Island, topped by a small and unused teahouse. In the park, at the end of a steep, mile-long trail from the parking lot, is **Vikingsholm**, an authentic reproduction of a Viking castle, believe it or not, built as a summer home in 1929. It is open for half-hourly **tours** (summer daily 10am–4pm; $2). From Vikingsholm, the **Rubicon Trail** runs two miles north along the lakeside to **Rubicon Bay**, flanked by other grand old mansions, dating from the days when Lake Tahoe was accessible only to the most well-heeled of travelers. You can also drive here on Hwy-89 and enter through the **D.L. Bliss State Park** (extremely limited parking $5). The 15,000-square-foot **Ehrman Mansion** here (guided tours daily 10am–4pm on the hour; free), decorated in a happy blend of 1930s opulence and backcountry rustic, is surrounded by extensive lakefront grounds which were used as a location for the movie *Godfather II*.

Kirkwood and Markleeville

About two dozen miles southwest of Tahoe, about a dozen miles west of where Hwy-89 joins Hwy-88, **LAKE KIRKWOOD**, is home to a popular ski resort (see box overleaf), and a destination in its own right, with plenty of **outdoor recreation** possibilities without all the Tahoe hype. Stop by the **adventure center** in Kirkwood Village (Mon–Fri 9am–5pm; Sat–Sun 9am–6pm; ☎209/258-6000 or 209/258-7357) for information on accommodation, equipment rentals and hiking in the surrounding area, which includes

TAHOE SKIING AND SNOWBOARDING

Lake Tahoe has some of the best **downhill skiing** in North America, and its larger resorts rival their Rocky Mountain counterparts. More than a few Bay Area residents head for the mountains at the first sign of snow and, in a good year, many lifts continue to operate through the end of April. Although skiing is certainly not cheap – the largest ski areas charge over $50 for the privilege of using their mountain for a single day – many resorts offer decent-value rental/lift ticket/lesson packages or multi-day discounts. **Snowboarding** has, of course, caught on in a big way, and the same resorts that once scoffed at the sport have now installed massive snow parks with radical half-pipes and jumps. **Cross-country skiing** is also a popular activity. The following list of ski resorts is not exhaustive, but highlights the best options for skiers of varying ability and financial standing. Skis can be rented at the resorts for about $25, and snowboards go for $35, but better deals for both can be found in the rental stores dotted around town. Pick up the *Reno-Tahoe Winter Vacation Guide for Skiers and Boarders* at any of the tourism information offices for a complete listing of resorts, along with prices and amenities.

DOWNHILL SKIING

Heavenly, reachable by shuttle from Southshore, two miles from the casinos, (☎775/5867000 or 800/2432836; *www.ski-heavenly.com*). Prime location and sheer scale (82 runs, 27 lifts, 3500 vertical feet) makes this one of the lake's most frequented resorts. Non-skiers can take the aerial tram for the view from the 8200 foot summit ($12.50). Lift tickets are $54.

Homewood, 6 miles north of Tahoe City on Hwy-89, (☎1-800/8246348 or 530/5252992; *www.skihomewood.com*). Smaller and more relaxed than its massive neighbors, Homewood boasts some surprisingly good skiing with unbeatable views of the lake and reasonable prices. Lift tickets go for $36. Beginner package costing $39 includes equipment, lesson, and beginner lift ticket.

Kirkwood Ski Resort, South of Lake Tahoe on Hwy-88 (☎1-800/967-7500 or 209/2586000; *www.skikirkwood.com*).

Kirkwood manages to escape the over-developed feel of many of the Tahoe resorts while still providing some amazing skiing. Lift tickets are $45.

Squaw Valley USA, Squaw Valley Rd, halfway between Truckee and Tahoe City (☎1-800/766-9321 or 530/583-6955; *www.squaw.com*). Thirty lifts service over 4000 acres of unbeatable terrain at the site of the 1960 Winter Olympics. Non-skiers can take the aerial tram ($14) and use the ice-skating/swimming pool complex for the day ($19 including tram ride). Lift tickets are $49.

Sugar Bowl, ten miles west of Truckee at the Soda Springs Norden exit (☎530/426-9000; *www.sugarbowl.com*). The closest ski area to San Francisco has twelve lifts and newly expanded terrain. Inexplicably, this excellent mountain is often less crowded than others in the area. Lift tickets cost $42.

CROSS-COUNTRY SKIING

Kirkwood Cross Country Center, South of Lake Tahoe on Hwy-88 (☎209/2587248). More than 50 miles of groomed track and skating lanes for cross-country enthusiasts. Trail fee is $16.

Royal Gorge, in Soda Springs, ten miles west of Truckee (☎1-800/500-3871 or 530/426-3871; *www.royalgorge.com*). The largest and best of Tahoe's cross-country

resorts has 204 miles of groomed trails. $19.50 trail fee, $16.50 rental fee, and $18 for lessons.

Spooner Lake, in Nevada at the intersection of Hwy-50 and Hwy-28 (☎775/7495349). The closest cross-country resort to South Lake Tahoe has lake views and 63 miles of groomed trails. Trail fees are $15, rentals $15, and lessons $34.

nearly a dozen lakes, such as Winnemucca and Woods Lakes. For accommodation, try the *Lodge at Kirkwood* in the Village which must be booked through Kirkwood Central Reservations (☎1-800/9677500; ⑤).

If you head a dozen miles southeast from the junction of Hwy-89 and Hwy-88, you'll come to **MARKLEEVILLE**, a town of two hundred people on the Sierra Crest. The major attraction here is the **Grover Hot Springs State Park**, four miles west (May to mid-Sept daily 9am–9pm; closed last two weeks in Sept, reduced hours through winter; $4; ☎530/694-2248), with two concrete, spring-filled tubs – one hot, one tepid – in which the water appears yellow-green due to mineral deposits on the pool bottom. There's a $12-a-night **campground** (reserve through Parknet ☎1-800/444-7275) on site.

Tahoe City and around

TAHOE CITY is less developed and more compact than South Lake Tahoe, and a close-knit population of permanent residents coupled with a family-oriented atmosphere give it a more relaxed, peaceful disposition. Still, you're never far from the maddening tourist crowds who flock here all year long.

At the western end of town, Hwy-89 meets Hwy-28 at Fanny Bridge, named for the body part that greets drivers as people lean over the edge to view the giant trout in the **Truckee River**. Flow-regulating sluice gates at the mouth of the river are remotely controlled from Reno, but were once operated by a gatekeeper who lived in what is now the **Gatekeeper's Museum** (mid-June to early Sept daily 11am–5pm; May to mid-June & early to late Sept Wed–Sun 11am–5pm; $2), containing a well-presented hodgepodge of artifacts from the last century, and a good collection of native basketware. Nearby, the **Truckee River Bike Trail** begins its three-mile waterside meander west to the River Ranch, which is also the end of a popular river rafting route. **Rafting** down the Truckee is the thing to do on warm summer days, though it's really more of a relaxing social affair than a serious or challenging adventure. Several well-advertised boat rental stands congregate along the river across from the Chevron Station, or call Tahoe Whitewater Tours (☎1-800442-7238 or 530/581-2441) for advance reservations.

A couple of miles south along Hwy-89, 500 yards past the Kaspian picnic grounds, you'd be well advised to **hike** ten minutes up the unmarked trail to the top of **Eagle Rock** (see box below for more ambitious hiking suggestions). The amazing panoramic views that surround you as you look down on the expansive royal-blue lake make this one of the world's greatest picnic spots. Several miles further south along Hwy-89 is **Chamber's Beach**, which, in summer, is as popular for sunning and **swimming** as it is for socializing.

You could also visit **Squaw Valley**, the site of the 1960 Winter Olympics, situated five miles west of Tahoe City off Hwy-89, although the original facilities (except the flame and the Olympic rings) are now swamped by the rampant development that has made this California's largest ski resort (see box). In the valley below, **hiking, horseback riding** and mountain **biking** are all popular summertime activities.

East from Tahoe City are unremarkable settlements, among them **Incline Village**, a short distance from **Ponderosa Ranch** (April–Oct daily 9.30am–5pm; $8.50) where *Bonanza* was filmed. If you loved the show as a kid, you'll probably find the museum fascinating for its behind-the-scenes glimpse at the filming of your favorite episodes; otherwise, give it a miss. If you're staying in Tahoe City and have the urge to **gamble** without making the hour drive to Stateline, a couple of appealingly small-scale casinos, including the *Crystal Bay* and the aptly named *Cal-Neva*, huddle on the north side of the lake just across the Nevada border. One of the best destinations on the northern side of the lake is the **Lake Tahoe Nevada State Park** at Sand Harbor, which has a great beach – though the water is always prohibitively cold – and trails winding up through the backcountry to the Tahoe Rim Trail. Just south, **Secret Harbor** is an appropriate location for an idyllic nudist beach where gawkers are not tolerated.

Eating and drinking

Lake Tahoe has few exceptional **restaurants**; average burger and steak places, rustic in decor, with raging fireplaces are commonplace. Far better are the **buffets** at the Nevada **casinos**: *Harrah's*, for example, serves a wonderful spread, with good all-you-can-eat food for low rates. The casinos are also good places to **drink** and hold most of the region's entertainment options as well: low budget Vegas-style revues, for the most part. For its size, Tahoe City has a good range of moderately priced places to eat as well, as a couple of happening **bars**, all within a few minutes of each other.

HIKING, BIKING AND CAMPING AROUND LAKE TAHOE

Of the many wonderful hikes in the Lake Tahoe area, only one – the 150-mile **Tahoe Rim Trail** – makes the circuit of the lake, some of it on the **Pacific Crest National Scenic Trail** which follows the Sierra ridge from Canada to the Mexican border. Most people tackle only a tiny section of it, such as **Kingsbury Grade to Big Meadows** (22 miles), starting off Hwy-207 northwest of South Lake Tahoe and finishing on Hwy-50, south of Lake Tahoe.

There are also many **mountain biking** trails around the lake: **Meiss Country**, between Hwy-89 and Hwy-88 twenty miles south of South Lake Tahoe is a favored area, where several beautiful lakes that escape most tourist itineraries are located. **Fallen Leaf Lake**, **Echo Lakes** and **Angora Lake** are all pleasant, somewhat remote alternatives to the big T. Biking trails near the south shore include the three-mile loop of the **Pope-Baldwin Trail**, and you can pick up the popular **Marlett Lake/Flume Trail** in the Nevada State Park.

Ask at the **US Forest Service Visitor Center**, 870 Emerald Bay Rd (summer Mon–Thurs & Sat–Sun 8am–5.30pm, Fri 8am–7pm; ☎530/573-2674), three miles northwest of the junction where Hwy-89 and Hwy-50 separate to the west and east of the lake, for recommendations, free maps and brochures on the entire area.

CAMPING

Lake Tahoe's best **campground** is *Campground by the Lake*, on the lakeshore three miles west of Stateline (☎530/542-6096; reserve through Parknet ☎1-800/444-7275; $18). Other south shore sites include *Fallen Leaf* (☎530/544-0426 reserve through NRRS 1-877/444-6777; $16) and *Eagle Point* (☎530/525-7277; reservations ☎1-800/444-7275; $16). The **north** has several sites within striking distance of Tahoe City, including *Tahoe State Recreation Area* (☎530/583-3074; reserve through Parknet ☎1-800/444-7275; $16) right in the center, and as crowded as you would expect. A mile and a half east, *Lake Forest* (☎530/583-3796, xt. 29; $12) is cheaper though far from the beach, and two miles southwest along Hwy-89, there's the large *William Kent* site (☎530/583-3642; reserve through NRRS; 1-877/444-6777; $15).

Along the western side of the lake, the Tahoe Rim Trail follows the Pacific Crest Trail through the glaciated valleys and granite peaks of the **Desolation Wilderness**. Here, **wilderness permits** ($5) are required by all users, though for day users these are self-issued. For overnighters, a quota system operates in summer: fifty percent of these are first-come-first-served on the day of entry from the Forest Service visitor center, the remainder are reservable up to ninety days in advance (☎530/644-6048). Among the most strenuous trails here is the five-mile Bayview Trail to Fontanillis Lake. The other wilderness areas around Tahoe – Granite Chief to the northwest and Mount Rose to the northeast – are used much less and consequently no wilderness permits are needed, though campfire permits are.

South shore

Café Fiore, 1169 Ski Run Blvd (☎530/541-2908). Small and intimate, serving innovative upscale Italian meals accompanied by an award-winning wine list.

Faces at 270 Kingsbury Grade, Stateline (☎775/588-2333) The lake's main gay and lesbian bar – a bit frozen in time but friendly.

Heidi's, 3485 Lake Tahoe Blvd (☎530544-8113). One in a local chain offering solid family-style meals at affordable prices.

Mackinaw's, 901 Ski Run Blvd (☎530/542-0900). Unusual, hearty mid-range combinations, such as walnut-crusted gorgonzola chicken, make this spot worth sampling.

Monument Peak Restaurant, at the top of the Heavenly Tram, (☎530/544-6263). Maybe a bit overpriced, but at 2000 feet above Lake Tahoe, it's more about the views than the food anyway.

Nephele's, 1169 Ski Run Blvd, S Lake Tahoe (☎530/544-8130). Long-standing restaurant at the foot of Heavenly ski resort, with a great selection of moderate to expensive California cuisine: grilled meat, fish and pasta dishes.

Red Hut Waffle Shop, 2723 Lake Tahoe Blvd, S Lake Tahoe (☎530/541-9024). Ever-popular coffee shop, justifiably crowded early winter mornings with carbo-loading skiers.

Sprouts, 3123 US-50 near Alameda Ave, S Lake Tahoe (☎530/541-6969). Almost, but not completely vegetarian, with good organic sandwiches, burritos and smoothies.

Taj Mahal, 3838 Lake Tahoe Blvd, S Lake Tahoe (☎530/5416495). Basic Indian fare with a daily eleven-course lunch buffet.

Tep's Villa Roma, 3450 Hwy-50, S Lake Tahoe (☎530/541-8227). Long-standing south shore institution that serves large portions of hearty Italian food, including several simple yet tasty vegetarian pasta dishes for about $10.

North shore

Coyote's Mexican Grill, 521 N Lake Blvd, Tahoe City (☎530/583-6653). Great-value burritos and enchiladas in a lively atmosphere.

Lakehouse Pizza, 120 Grove St, Tahoe City (☎530/583-2222). Tahoe's best place for pizza is also a popular spot for cocktails on the lake at sundown. Be prepared to wait in winter.

Pete and Peter's, N Lake Blvd, Tahoe City (☎530/583-2400). Play pool with the locals at this friendly bar.

Pierce Street Annex, in the back of the Lighthouse Center, Tahoe City (☎530/583-5800). The place for drinking and dancing on the north shore. Packed with sunburned skiers or drunk beachgoers, depending on the season.

River Ranch, Hwy 89 and Alpine Meadows Road, Tahoe City (☎530/5834264). A trendy place to watch whitewater rafters return from their adventure on the Truckee River as you kick back on the deck nibbling mid-range Californian cuisine.

Soule Domaine, near casinos at the northern stateline, Tahoe City (☎530/546-7529). Typical Tahoe "elegance": upscale cuisine in the cozy comfort of a real log cabin. Locals voted it "best place to take a date" six years in a row.

Sunnyside, 1850 W Lake Blvd, Tahoe City (☎530/583-7200). One of the most popular places to have cocktails at sunset, on the deck overlooking the lake.

Tahoe Restaurant & Bäckerei, Hwy 89, half a mile south of 28, Tahoe City (☎530/5831377). Family-style bakery and restaurant. Popular with locals.

Yama Sushi and Robata Grill, 950 North Lake Blvd, Tahoe City (☎530/583-9262). Voted the best Sushi bar on the north shore with prices to match.

Za's, 395 North Lake Blvd (behind *Pete & Peter's*), Tahoe City. Pizzeria with large selection of pastas featuring a wide variety of sauces.

Truckee and Donner Lake

Just off I-80, along the main transcontinental Amtrak train route, **TRUCKEE**, 25 miles north of Lake Tahoe, makes a refreshing change from the tourist-dependent towns around the lake. A small town lined up along the north bank of the Truckee River, it retains a fair amount of its late nineteenth-century wooden architecture along the main street, Commercial Row – some of which appeared in Charlie Chaplin's *The Gold Rush*. The town is more of a stop-off than a destination in its own right, with a livelihood dependent on the forestry industry and the railroad. However, the town's rough, lively edge makes it as good a base as any from which to see the Lake Tahoe area, a fact which hasn't escaped the businesses beginning to exploit the commercial opportunities. There's even public transportation between the two (see below).

Practicalities

Greyhound **buses** from San Francisco stop in Truckee five times a day and are met by TART buses to Tahoe City (daily 6.30am–6.30pm; $1.25; ☎1-800/736-6365 or 530/581-6365). Amtrak Thruway buses stop in each direction at the station on Commercial Row in the middle of town. The **Chamber of Commerce**, 100065 Donner Pass Road (Mon–Sat 9am–6pm; 530/587-2757), has a few flimsy pamphlets and lots of advertisements. Where Hwy-89 branches north off I-80, an easy to miss **Forest Service Ranger Station** (Mon–Thurs & Sat 8am–5pm, Fri 8am–6pm; ☎530/587-3558) has details of camping and hiking in the surrounding countryside. To get around, rent a **mountain bike** from Truckee Bike Works, 11400 Donner Pass Rd ($25 a day; ☎530/587-3933), or a **car** from Truckee Rent-a-Car at the Truckee Airport (☎530/587-2841); they'll deliver a car directly to you

Truckee's cheapest **place to stay** is the *Cottage Hotel*, 10178 Donner Pass Rd (☎530/587-3108; ③), central but a bit shabby. Much nicer is the *Truckee Hotel*, 10007 Bridge St almost opposite the train station (☎1-800/659-6921 or 530/587-4444; ⑤), once decorated in the grand old railroad tradition, now decked out in Victorian B&B style, as is the *Richardson House* on High Street (☎1-888-229-0365 or 530/587-5388; ⑥). A number of low-priced **campgrounds** line the Truckee River between the town and Lake Tahoe, off Hwy-89, with sites starting at $10: the closest and largest is *Granite Flat*, a mile and a half from Truckee; others are *Goose Meadows* and *Silver Creek*, four and six miles south respectively (all three campgrounds can be contacted on ☎530/587-3558). Commercial Row has several good **eating places**, especially the diner-style *Coffee And...* at no. 10106 (☎530/587-3123) and *El Toro Bravo* at 10186 (☎530/587-3557), a standard taqueria. The more expensive *Passage Restaurant* in the Truckee Hotel (☎530/587-7619) serves Pacific-Rim-influenced American cuisine and *Café Meridian* at no. 10118 (☎530587-0557) is a refreshingly modern place with a rooftop terrace, good light food, coffee and drinks. Omelets are the specialty at the *Squeez Inn*, 10060 Donner Pass Rd (☎530/587-9814), which serves breakfast daily from 7am to 2pm. Though the old Bucket of Blood saloons of frontier-lore are long gone, there are a few good places to stop for a **drink**, including the *Bar of America*, downtown at the corner of Hwy-26 and Donner Pass Road (☎530/587-3110), featuring free **live music** most nights. For chocolate so good that you might consider hibernating here through a brutal Truckee winter, try the award-winning cappuccino truffles at *Sweets* on 10118 Donner Pass Road (☎1-888/248-8840 or 530/587-6556).

Donner Lake

Two miles west of Truckee, surrounded by alpine cliffs of silver-gray granite, **Donner Lake** was the site of one of the most gruesome and notorious tragedies of early California, when pioneers trapped by winter snows were forced to eat the bodies of their dead companions (see box).

The horrific tale of the Donner party is recounted in some detail in the small **Emigrant Trail Museum** (summer daily 10am–5pm; rest of year daily 10am–4pm; ☎530/582-7892; $2) – just off Donner Pass Road, three miles west of Truckee in

---

THE DONNER PARTY

The **Donner Party**, named after two of the pioneer families among the group of 91 travelers, set off for California in April 1846 from Illinois across the Great Plains, following a short cut recommended by the first traveler's guide to the West Coast (the 1845 *Emigrant's Guide to California and Oregon*) that actually took three weeks longer than the established route. By October, they had reached what is now Reno, and decided to rest a week to regain their strength for the arduous crossing of the Sierra Nevada mountains – a delay that proved fatal. When at last they set off, early snowfall blocked their route beyond Donner Lake, and the group were forced to stop and build crude shelters, hoping that the snow would melt and allow them to complete their crossing; it didn't, and they were stuck.

   Within a month, the pioneers were running out of provisions, and a party of fifteen set out across the mountains to try and reach Sutter's Fort in Sacramento. They struggled through yet another storm and, a month later, two men and five women stumbled into the fort, having survived by eating the bodies of the men who had died. A rescue party set off from Sutter's Fort immediately, only to find more of the same: thirty or so half-crazed survivors, living off the meat of their fellow travelers.

Donner Memorial State Park – which shows a re-enactment of the events that's so over-the-top most viewers will have a hard time choking back their chuckles. Outside, the **Pioneer Monument** stands on a plinth as high as the snow was deep that fateful winter – 22 feet. From the museum, an easy nature trail winds through the forest past a memorial plaque marking the site where the majority of the Donner Party built their simple cabins. Nearby, on the southeast shore of the lake, there's a $14-a-night summer-only **campground** (reserve through Parknet ☎1-800/444-7275).

   Above Donner Lake, the Southern Pacific railroad tracks climb west over the **Donner Pass** through tunnels built by Chinese laborers during the nineteenth century – still one of the main rail routes across the Sierra Nevada. For much of the way, the tracks are protected from the usually heavy winter snow by a series of wooden sheds, which you can see from across the valley, where Donner Pass Road snakes up the steep cliffs. On Hwy-40, there's a scenic overlook where you can get that prize-winning photo of Donner Lake and possibly a glimpse beyond to Tahoe. Further on, rock-climbers from the nearby Alpine Skills Institute (☎530/426-9108) can often be seen honing their talents on the 200-foot granite faces; the institute offers a variety of climbing and mountaineering courses and trips. At the crest, the road passes the Soda Springs, Sugar Bowl and Royal Gorge **ski areas** before rejoining I-80, which runs east from Donner Pass to Reno, Nevada, and west to Sacramento.

Into Nevada: Reno and around

On I-80 at the foot of the Sierra Nevada, thirty miles east of Truckee, **RENO, Nevada** has plenty of affordable places to stay and eat, making it a good stop-off, especially if you enjoy gambling as many neighboring Californians do each weekend. The town itself, apart from the stream of blazing casino neon, may not be much to look at, having sprung up out of nowhere in the middle of the desert on the hopes that the gambling industry alone could sustain its existence. Nevertheless, its setting – with the snow-capped Sierra peaks as a distant backdrop and the Truckee River winding through – is nice enough, and unlike Las Vegas, to which it is most often compared, Reno maintains a smalltown feel that residents are proud of; As the locals love to say – over and over again – Reno is the biggest little town in the world. Even if you don't like to gamble, you can still pass a pleasant afternoon here ambling in the dry desert heat or visiting one of the mildly diverting museums. Reno is also another good place from which to visit Lake Tahoe, and a good base for exploring the evocative mining towns of **Carson City** and **Virginia City** (see below).

Arrival and information

Reno's Cannon International **airport** is served by most major domestic carriers – including American, Delta, United, Southwestern and RenoAir. Local bus #24 makes the twenty-minute journey from the terminals to the casinos in Reno's town center. Greyhound **buses** from San Francisco, via Sacramento and Truckee, and from LA, via the Owens Valley, use the terminal at 155 Stevenson St also used by KT Services (☎775/945-2282), which operate a daily bus to Las Vegas and Phoenix. The Amtrak *California Zephyr* **train** from Chicago stops in the center of town at 135 Commercial

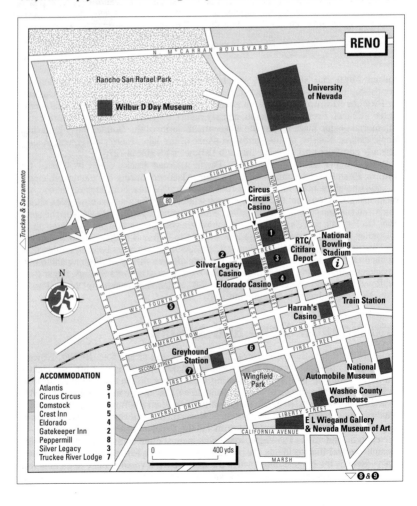

Row, as do Thruway buses from Sacramento. To **rent a car**, try Alamo (☎1-800/327-9633 or 775/323-8306), Avis (☎1-800/831-2837 or 775/785-2727) or Thrifty (☎1-800/367-2277 or 775/329-0096), all three at the airport.

The **visitor center** (daily 9am–5pm; ☎1-800/FOR-RENO) is inside the National Bowling Center at 300 N Center St near the main casinos, identified by its silver geodesic dome. This structure was built in the hope that bowling tournaments would give a permanent boost to the local economy. The visitor center has maps of the fairly extensive **local bus** services, run by RTC/Citifare, whose main depot is across the road.

Accommodation

Inexpensive **accommodation** is plentiful, but if you arrive on a weekend you should book ahead and be prepared for rates to all but double. Usually, a two nights' stay applies on weekends, especially at the **casinos**. You can also call the **Reno-Sparks Visitor and Convention Association**'s toll free information and reservation line (☎1-800-FOR-RENO) for help with finding a place to stay. **Camping** is an RV experience in Reno; for tent sites, head west to the numerous campgrounds around Lake Tahoe (see p.576).

Atlantis, 3800 S. Virginia St (☎1-800/723-6500 or 775/825-4700; *www.atlantiscasino.com*). Relatively new on the scene, this hotel's buffet, coffee shop and restaurant have all been voted best by locals in recent surveys. Great rates and plush amenities for slightly less than casinos of the same class in the center of town. ③.

Circus Circus, 500 N Sierra St (☎1-800/648-5010 or 775/329-0711; *www.circusreno.com*). One of the largest and tackiest casinos, with over 1600 popular rooms. ④.

Comstock, 200 W Second St (☎1-800/COMSTOCK or 775/329-0808; *www.thecomstock.com*). Centrally located casino that has passed its prime and consequently offers lower rates than some of the newer competitors. ③.

Crest Inn, 525 W Fourth St (☎775/329-0808). Simple motel with few trimmings and low prices. ②.

Eldorado, 345 N Virginia St (☎1-800/777-5325 or 775/786-5700). The nicer rooms are on the upper floors, those lower down are cheaper. ③.

Gatekeeper Inn, 221 W Fifth St (☎1-800/822-3504 or 775/786-3500). Mainstream motel with cable TV and clean rooms. ③.

Peppermill, 2707 S. Virginia St (☎1-800/648-6992 or 775/826-2121). Another large new casino, slightly outside of the center of town with special rates offered frequently. ③.

Silver Legacy, 407 N. Virginia St (☎1-800/687-7733 or 775/329-4777; *www.silverlegacy.com*). The flashiest of all the Reno casinos, and worth a tour even if you're not staying for its well-developed silver mining theme, which brings the gold and silver rush of yesterday right up to the present day with plenty of technological wizardry. With the constant stampede of gawkers and gamblers, actually staying here can get crowded. ④.

Truckee River Lodge, 501 W First St (☎1-800/635-8950 or 775/786-8888). Non-smoking hotel with an emphasis on recreation. It has a fitness center and rents bikes from $20 a day. ②.

The Town

It may lack the glitz and the glamour that help make Vegas a global draw, but Reno is northern Nevada's number one **gambling** spot, offering a 24-hour diet of slot machines, blackjack, craps, keno, roulette and many more ways to win and lose a fortune. Gaming was only legalized in Nevada in 1931, but silver miners in Virginia City and Gold Hill regularly tried their hands at fortune's wheel back in the mid-nineteenth century when a deck of cards was an almost mandatory part of a miner's kit.

While nowhere near as grand as the Vegas institutions to the south, most of Reno's **casinos** still warrant a quick tour. If you can only handle visiting a few, the best of the lot are: *Circus Circus*, 500 N Sierra St, where a small circus performs every half-hour, giving patrons a reason to look up from their dwindling savings; *Silver Legacy*, around

GETTING MARRIED (AND DIVORCED) IN RENO

If you've come to Reno to get **married**, you and your intended must: be at least eighteen years old and able to prove it; swear that you're not already married; and appear before a judge at the **Washoe County Court**, south of the main casino district at S Virginia and Court streets (daily 8am–midnight; ☎775/328-3275), to obtain a **marriage license** ($35). There is no waiting period or blood test required. Civil services are performed for an additional $35 at the **Commissioner for Civil Marriages**, behind the Courthouse at 195 S Sierra St (☎775/328-3461). If you want something a bit more special, however, wedding chapels all around the city will help you tie the knot: across the street from the courthouse, the Starlight Chapel, 62 Court St (☎775/786-6882) does the job quickly – "No Waiting, Just Drive In" – for around $80, providing a pink chintz parlor full of plastic flowers. Fork out more cash and you get the tux and frock, and can invite a few guests. Other chapels include the Park Wedding Chapel, 136 S Virginia St (☎775/323-1770), and Silver Bells Wedding Chapel, 628 N Virginia St (☎1-800/221-9336 or 775/322-0420). If it doesn't work out, you'll have to stay in Nevada for another six weeks before you can get a **divorce**.

the corner at 407 N Virginia St, which reveals a planetarium-style dome with a makeshift 120-foot mining derrick underneath, appearing to draw silver ore out of the ground and spilling cascades of coins in the process; and *Harrahs*, a few blocks south at 219 N Center St, the classiest casino in town with row-upon-row of high-stakes slot machines and the occasional famous entertainer. If touring the casinos solo doesn't teach you everything you want to know, contact the Reno–Tahoe Gaming Academy, 300 E. First St (☎775/329-5665), for an overview of some of rules of the major games followed by a behind-the-scenes **tour** of Reno's major gambling dens (hours vary; $10).

Once you're ready to cash in all the casino clatter for some peace and quiet, take refuge in one of Reno's many **museums**. The largest and most significant among them is the **National Automobile Museum (The Harrah Collection)**, at Mill and Lake streets (Mon–Sat 9.30am–5.30pm; Sun 10am–4pm; ☎775/333-9300; $7.50; *www. automuseum.org*), which holds the most comprehensive public display of automobiles in the western hemisphere, with more than 200 vintage and classic cars, some of them artfully arranged along re-created city streets of bygone decades. The sheer scale of the collection can't help but impress, even if you think you'd rather be pulling on the arm of a slot machine than admiring the shine on an 1892 Philion. Art buffs should take a look at the inventive contemporary exhibitions at the **E.L. Weigand Gallery and Nevada Museum of Art**, 160 W Liberty St (Tues–Sat 10am–4pm, Sun noon–4pm; ☎775/329-3333; $3). You'll find Reno's most curious trove, however, at the **Wilbur D. May Museum** (summer Tues–Sun 10am–5pm; rest of year Wed–Sun 10am–5pm; ☎775/785-5961; around $2 depending on temporary exhibits), which sits on the edge of Rancho San Rafael Park, a mile north of downtown Reno off North Sierra Street. The collection outlines the eventful life of Wilbur May – a traveler, hunter, military aviator, cattle-breeder and heir to the May department store fortunes – with several rooms of furnishings, mounted animal heads and plunder from his trips to Africa and South America.

On the other side of US-395, the University of Nevada campus hosts the **Nevada Historical Society Museum**, 1650 N Virginia St (Mon–Sat 10am–5pm; ☎775/688-1190; $2), full of items of local interest, especially Native American artifacts, and, next door, the **Fleischmann Planetarium** (Mon–Fri 8am–10pm Sat & Sun 11am–10pm; $5) where, amongst the telescopes and solar system galleries, OMNIMAX style films (2–4 shows daily; ☎775/784-4811) are projected onto a huge dome.

Eating and nightlife

All-you-can-eat-buffets are the order of the day for tourists in Reno and seemingly everyone goes out and stuffs themselves to bursting. The buffets can be fun, if a little bland, and we list the best of them below along with the alternatives most favored by locals. Tourists tend to stick to the shows in the casinos for **nightlife**, but occasionally the city holds an art and/or music festival, and there are some popular venues downtown including *Reno Live*, at Sierra and Second (☎775/329-1952), which claims to be the largest nightclub complex in Nevada. Check Reno's free independent weekly *Reno News and Review* for listings. There are a number of **gay and lesbian bars** in town, including the popular *Patio Bar* at 600 W. 5th St (☎775/323-6565).

Aloha Sushi, 3338 Kietzke Lane (☎775/828-9611). A bit of a jump southeast from casino central, but reasonable and good, and if you're staying for any length of time, you'll need to escape from the buffets eventually. Try their specialty mountain roll.

Atlantis, 3800 S. Virginia St (☎775/825-4700). Consistently voted best buffet in town by locals. The casino's moderately priced *Café Alfresco* has wood-fired pizzas, and the decor of the more upscale *Seafood Steakhouse* may have all the class of the dining room on a tacky cruise ship, but the food and service are exceptional, as is the wine list.

Circus Circus, 500 Sierra St. The place to go for a buffet meal if your budget is of greater concern than your stomach, with all-you-can-eat lunches for under $6.

Einstein's Quantum Café, 6135 Lakeside Drive (near Virginia Lake Park, ☎775/825-6611). An inexpensive new vegetarian café that's already a hit among locals.

Eldorado Casino, Fourth and Virginia. Another good Reno buffet, serving breakfast, lunch and dinner for a dollar or two more than *Circus Circus*.

La Piñata, 1575 Vassar St. (☎775/323-3210). The best Mexican buffet in town, on a street running perpendicular to Virginia South, just south of casino central.

La Vecchia Varese, 130 West St. (☎775/322-7486). Unfussy decor and an excellent, moderately priced selection of gourmet Italian dishes, with several vegetarian choices.

Rickshaw Paddy, 4944 S. Virginia St. (☎775/828-2335). Mid-range Asian food combining influences from eight different countries, eaten, if you can believe it, to the accompaniment of Celtic background music.

S.S. Super Indian Restaurant, 1030 S. Virginia St (☎775/322-5577). Fresh Indian specialties and a daily $4.95 lunch buffet.

Around Reno: Carson City

US-395 heads south from Reno along the jagged spires of the High Sierra past Mono Lake, Mount Whitney and Death Valley. Just thirty miles south of Reno it briefly becomes Carson Street as it passes through **CARSON CITY**, the state capital of Nevada. It is small compared to Reno, but despite the sprawling mess of fast-food joints, strip malls, and car dealerships that surround the town center, it is well worth a visit, especially if you are interested in the history of mining. The city has a number of elegant buildings, excellent historical museums and a few world-weary casinos, populated mainly by old ladies armed with buckets of nickels.

Named, somewhat indirectly, after frontier explorer Kit Carson in 1858, Carson City is still redolent with Wild West history: you'll get a good introduction at the **Nevada State Museum** at 600 N Carson St (daily 8.30am–4.30pm; ☎775/687-4810; $3). Housed in a sandstone structure built during the Civil War as the Carson Mint, the museum's exhibits deal with the geology and natural history of the Great Basin desert region, from prehistoric days up through the heyday of the 1860s, when the silver mines of the nearby Comstock Lode were at their peak. Amid the many guns and artifacts, the two best features of the museum are the reconstructed **Ghost Town**, from which a tunnel allows entry down into a full-scale model of an **underground mine**, giving some sense of the cramped and constricted conditions in which miners worked.

Four blocks from the museum, on the other side of Carson Street, the impressively restored **State Capitol**, 101 N. Carson St. (daily 9am–5pm; free), dating from 1871, merits a look for its stylish architecture and the commendable stock of artifacts relating to Nevada's past housed in an upper floor room.

The **Nevada State Railway Museum**, 2180 S Carson St (daily 8.30am–4.30pm; ☎775/687-6953; $2), just a stone's throw away from the visitor center (see below), displays carefully restored locomotives and carriages, several of them from the long since defunct but fondly remembered Virginia & Truckee Railroad, founded in the nineteenth century.

Further south from Carson City's diminutive center, the **Stewart Indian Culture Center**, 5366 Snyder Ave (daily 9am–4pm; ☎775/882-1808; donation), occupies one of the eye-catching stone buildings which, until 1980, formed the campus of a Native American boarding school. The first intake of 37 students was enrolled in 1890, part of a federal plan to provide Nevada's Native Americans with a basic education and work skills. The museum, established in 1982 by former staff, students and other supporters after the closure of the school by the US Bureau of Indian Affairs, actually reveals comparatively little about the school, but has many fine examples of basketry and other crafts.

Practicalities

Greyhound **buses** stop outside the *Frontier Motel* on N Carson Street. Amtrak Thruway services from Sacramento and South Lake Tahoe stop outside the *Nugget* casino at the junction of Robinson and Carson streets. The *No Stress Express* (☎800/426-5644) can be reserved in advance for transportation to Carson City from the Reno Airport. The **visitor center**, on the south side of town at 1900 S Carson St (Mon–Sat 9am–5pm; ☎1-800/NEVADA-1 or 775/687-7410), can help with practical details, and sells the *Kit Carson Trail Map* ($2.50), a leaflet detailing a **walking tour** of the town, taking in the main museums, the state capitol and many of the fine 1870s Victorian wooden houses and churches on the west side.

There are a number of reasonably priced **motels** in town, among them the *Westerner* at 555 N Stewart St (☎775/883-7711; ③) behind the *Nugget* casino, and the more colorful *Plaza Hotel*, 801 S Carson St (☎775/883-9500; ③), not far from the Capitol, while a little further out is the *Pinon Plaza Resort Hotel and Casino* at 2171 Hwy-50 (☎775/885-9000; ④). If exploring Carson City gives you an appetite, you could try the generous **breakfasts** and **lunches** served at *Heidi's Dutch Mill*, 1020 N Carson St (☎775/882-0486), *Corina's Mexican Kitchen*, 1701 N. Carson St. (☎775/885-2248) or the *Whiskey Creek Saloon and Restaurant* in the Pinon Plaza Hotel (☎775/885-9000).

Virginia City, Gold Hill and Genoa

Much of the wealth on which Carson City – and indeed San Francisco – was built came from the silver mines of the Comstock Lode, a solid seam of pure silver discovered in 1859 underneath Mount Hamilton, fourteen miles east of Carson City off US-50. Raucous **VIRGINIA CITY** grew up on the steep slopes above the mines, and a young writer named Samuel Clemens made his way west with his older brother, who'd been appointed acting Secretary to the Governor of the Nevada Territory, to see what all the fuss was about. His descriptions of the wild life of the mining camp, and of the desperately hard work men put in to get at the valuable ore, were published years later under his adopted pseudonym, **Mark Twain**. Though Twain also spent some time in the Gold Rush towns of California's Mother Lode on the other side of the Sierra – which by then were all but abandoned – his accounts of Virginia City life, collected in *Roughing It*, give a hilarious, eyewitness account of the hard-drinking life of the frontier miners.

The miners left, but Virginia City still exploits a rich vein, one which runs through the pocketbooks of tour parties bussed up here from Reno. But despite the camera-clicking throngs, there's a sense of authenticity to Virginia City missing from even the most evocative of the California mining towns. Perhaps it's the town's location, encircled by the barren Nevada desert that so sharply contrasts with the diverse countryside of California's Gold Country, or perhaps it's the colorful advertisements that lure tourists into the many quirky museums. Then again, it could simply be the raucous spirit that seems to infect almost every sarsaparilla-sippin' tourist who sets foot here. Whatever the reason, it's hard not to get caught up in the infectious Wild West atmosphere and stay longer than you'd intended. Still, not everyone who floods into town is here for the Gold Rush nostalgia – many visitors are here to frequent the legal **brothels**, another reminder of the town's frontier days.

At the **visitors center** on C St (☎775/847-0311), you can pick up pamphlets and a self-guided walking tour map, or you can just as easily wander around the town until you've bumped into all the sights in your own time. Historic highlights include the **Mackay, Chollar** and **Castle Mansions**, each with its own colorful Victorian trimmings, the **Nevada Gambling Museum**, with its historic roulette wheel and other period game room accessories, and the **Bucket of Blood Saloon**, which is delightfully crowded with period fixtures and crooked old furnishings. If you'd like to **stay in town**, there are a few decent options, but no Reno-style buffets. On C Street, the *Silver Queen* at no. 28 (☎775/847-0440; ③) and *Comstock Lodge* at 875 (☎775/847-0233; ③) are two reasonable, if basic, options for spending the night on the main drag of an old boomtown. A 35-minute train ride from the town center on the **Virginia & Truckee Railroad** will take you to the all-but-extinct town of **GOLD HILL** which consists primarily of a **hotel, restaurant** and **tavern** of the same name (☎775/847-0111, ③), Nevada's oldest, with great rates and atmosphere.

South of Carson City in the Carson Valley lies another evocative Wild West scene, **GENOA**, the oldest town in Nevada. Slightly less stampeded by tourists than Virginia City, the main draw here is the curious **Mormon Station State Park**, a replica of the original trading post and fort built on the site in 1851. For information on walking tours in town, stop by the information counter in the **Genoa Courthouse Museum** at 2304 Main St (☎775/782-4325).

travel details

Trains

Oakland/Emeryville (for San Francisco Thruway service) to: Reno (5 daily; 6hr); Sacramento (7 daily; 2hr).

Reno to: Oakland/Emeryville (for San Francisco Thruway service) (5 daily; 7hr 30min); Sacramento (5 daily; 5hr); Truckee (5 daily; 55min).

Sacramento to: Reno (5 daily; 5hr); Truckee (5 daily; 3hr).

Buses

All buses are Greyhound unless otherwise stated.

Reno to: Las Vegas (5 daily; 9hr); Los Angeles (10 daily; 12hr 30min); Sacramento (15 daily; 3hr 30min); San Francisco (15 daily; 5hr).

Reno airport to: Stateline (14 daily Tahoe Casino Express; 1hr).

Sacramento to: Auburn (4 daily; 1hr); Truckee (4 daily; 3hr); Placerville (2 daily; 1hr 30min); Reno (15 daily; 3hr 30min); South Lake Tahoe (2 daily; 3hr).

San Francisco to: Auburn (4 daily; 3hr 30min); Reno (17 daily; 5hr); Sacramento (21 daily; 2hr 20min); South Lake Tahoe (2 daily; 6hr); Truckee (4 daily; 5hr).

South Lake Tahoe to: Placerville (2 daily; 1hr 30min); Sacramento (2 daily; 2hr 10min).

CHAPTER NINE

NORTHERN CALIFORNIA

T he northern coast and interior of California covers about a third of the state, a gigantic area over 400 miles long and 300 miles wide, with a rugged rural landscape and ethic far removed from portions of the urbanized daydreams of the south. It's a schizophrenic region of a schizophrenic state, coupling volcanoes with vineyards, fog-shrouded redwoods with scorched olive trees, loggers with environmentalists and legends of Bigfoot with movies of Ewoks. Northern Californians are tied to the land, and agriculture dominates the economy as well as the vistas. Deep-rooted logging, fishing and cattle industries are also ever-present, along with the wild, crashing Pacific Coast and steady rain that supports a marijuana farming region called the Emerald Triangle. Add only two major highways and the lack of a metropolis in favor of small, Main Street towns, and you have a region that has more in common with Oregon and Washington than Los Angeles or San Francisco. In that regard, Northern Californians have long rumbled about forming a state of their own. Indeed, in 1941 there was a proposal to form a state called Jefferson near Mount Shasta, an event that could have gained steam were it not for Japan's bombing of Pearl Harbor two days later, channeling collective energies into the war.

As with elsewhere in California, the first inhabitants of the north were Native Americans, whose past has all but been erased, leaving only the odd desolate reservation or crafts museum. Much later, the Russians figured briefly in the region's history when they had a modest nineteenth-century settlement at Fort Ross on the coast, ostensibly to protect their interests in otter hunting and fur trading, though more likely to promote territorial claims. Mexican explorers and maintenance costs that exceeded revenues prevented them from extending their hunting activities further south, and in the 1840s they sold the fort to the Americans. It was the discovery of gold in 1848 that really put the north on the map, and much of the countryside bears the marks of this time, dotted with abandoned mining towns, deserted since the gold ran out. Not a lot has happened since, although in the 1980s New Ageism triggered a kind of future for the region, with low land prices drawing more and more devotees up here to sam-

---

ACCOMMODATION PRICE CODES

All accommodation prices in this book have been coded using the symbols below; prices are for the least expensive **double rooms** in each establishment. For a full explanation see p.36 in "Basics." Individual rates rather than price codes are given for **hostels** and whole **apartments**.

① up to $30	④ $60–80	⑦ $130–175
② $30–45	⑤ $80–100	⑧ $175–250
③ $45–60	⑥ $100–130	⑨ $250+

ple the delights of a landscape they see as rich in rural symbolism. Hollywood has also been drawn to the region, using the north as a cost-effective way to travel to another place and time. *Robin Hood, Gone with the Wind, The Birds, The Return of the Jedi* and *Jurassic Park: The Lost World* are just a few examples of movies filmed amongst the frozen-in-time beauty. Recently, a potent California economy has many die-hard locals fearful of an influx of new homes and lifestyles up the coast, though the Coastal Commission tightly controls development, and farmers, so far, have resisted selling out.

Immediately north of the Bay Area, the **Wine Country** might be your first – indeed your only – taste of Northern California, though it's by no means typical. The two valleys

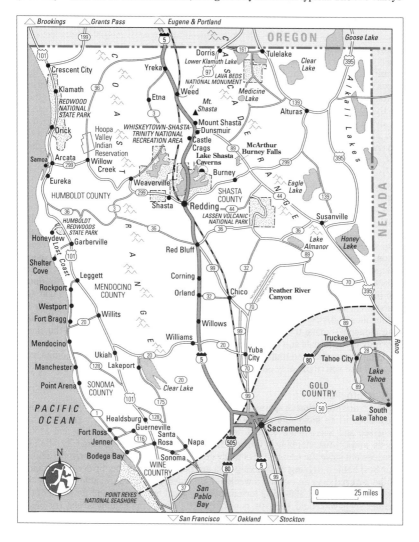

of Napa and Sonoma unfold in around thirty miles of rolling hills and premium real estate, home to the Californian wine barons and San Franciscan weekenders wanting to rough it in comfort. Napa is the reigning king of indulgence and high-caliber vintages, while Sonoma caters to a funkier set, with its interesting history and outdoor tours. The northwest corner of Sonoma County is Wine Country's other "grape escape," an area of six appellations and resorts clustered around the **Russian River** and its tributaries. Most people see the Wine Country on a day-trip from San Francisco; it is also feasible to take the area in before encountering the grittier territory further north, hooking up to the coast by bus from Santa Rosa.

It's the **coast** which provides the most appealing, and slowest, route through the region, beginning just north of Marin County and continuing for four hundred miles on Hwy-1 and US-101 along rugged bluffs and through forests as far as the Oregon border. The landscape varies little at first, but given time reveals tangible shifts from the flat oyster beds of **Sonoma County** to the seal and surfer breeding grounds around the coastal elegance of **Mendocino** and the big logging country further north in **Humboldt**. Trees are the big attraction up here: some thousands of years old and hundreds of feet high, dominating a very sparsely populated landscape swathed in swirling mists. In summer, areas like the **Redwood National Park**, stretching into the most northerly **Del Norte** county, teem with campers and hikers, but out of season it can be an idyllic experience, co-existing with the area's woodland creatures, including, some say, Bigfoot. Although the nightlife is rarely swinging, the college town **Arcata**, at the top end of the northern coast, makes a lively refuge when the great outdoors begins to pall.

The **interior** is more remote still, an enchanting land whose mystery and sheer physical enormity can't help but leave a lasting impression. I-5 neatly divides the region, cutting through the forgettable Sacramento Valley north to the **Shasta Cascade**, a mountainous area of isolated towns, massive lakes and a forbidding climate. In winter, much of this corner of the state is completely impassable, and the region's commercial activities are centered around the lower, warmer climes of the largest town and transportation hub of **Redding**. Redding, while a bore itself, is a crossroads serving **Whiskeytown-Shasta-Trinity National Recreation Area**, **Lassen Volcanic National Park**, **McArthur Burney Falls State Park** and, northward, the railroad towns in the shadows of towering **Mount Shasta**. Unlike the Wine Country and the coast, locals here are actually glad to see tourists, and visitor centers take the time to explain the many outdoors options. Food and lodging costs are cheap by California standards, and the efficient network of highways – by-products of the logging industry – make travel easy. The region fills up in summer, but given the sheer enormity of the forests and the plethora of lakes, waterfalls, parks and bird sanctuaries, escaping the masses and finding peace isn't much of a task. In the winter months, you may feel like you're the only one here at all.

Getting around

Public transportation is sparse all over Northern California, and to enjoy the region you'll need to be independently mobile. Infrequent Greyhound buses run from San Francisco and Sacramento up and down I-5, stopping in Chico, Redding and Mount Shasta, and US-101, stopping in Garberville, Eureka, Arcata and Crescent City – though this does not solve the problem of actually getting around once you've arrived. Frankly, your best bet is a **driving tour**, fixing on a few points. Each of the three regions below can be covered over an extended weekend, provided you have a reliable car. Only the largest of Northern California's towns have any local bus service and for some of the remoter spots you could, perhaps, consider an organized trip, notably Green Tortoise's one-week tours – see p.34 of "Basics" for details.

THE WINE COUNTRY

"The coldest winter I ever spent was summer in San Francisco," quipped Mark Twain. Like Twain, many visitors to San Francisco can't get over the daily fog and winds that chill even the hottest August day. So heading into the golden, arid **Napa** and **Sonoma valleys** can feel like entering another country. Less than an hour's drive north of San Francisco sit 29,000 acres of vineyards feeding hundreds of wineries and their upscale patrons, making the area the heart of the American wine industry in reputation, if not in volume. In truth, less than five percent of California's wine comes from the region, but what it does produce is America's best.

Predictably, the region is also one of America's wealthiest and most provincial, a fact that draws – and repels – a steady stream of tourists. For every grape on the vine there seems to exist a bed-and-breakfast or spa, and tourism is gaining on wine production as the Wine Country's leading industry. Expect clogged highways and full hotels during peak season (March–Oct), as well as packed tastings. The main road through Napa, Hwy 29, can begin to feel like a monotonous chain of connecting towns anchored by rustic red-brick facade antique stores.

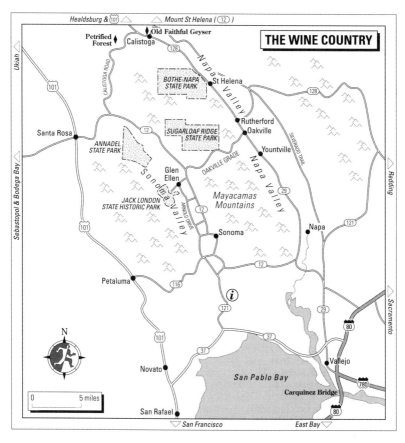

But there's two sides to the Napa and Sonoma valleys. There is, of course, its promi-nence for serious, quality **wine** experiences. Almost all of the region's many wineries offer free tours and tastings. When a fee is charged, it's usually small (under $5), and includes the wine glass or a credit towards the purchase of a bottle. But aside from the type and flavor of the drink, wineries all differ in what they offer visitors. Some delight enologists by explaining the process of growing grapes, some excite kids with tractor rides through the vineyard, and some please thirsty patrons with generous samples. A trip after the October crushing gives the added benefit of lower hotel rates and fewer tourists, allowing more time at tastings. The other reason to come to Wine Country is the **natural landscape**. Separated by the Mayacamas mountains, the Napa and Sonoma Valleys feature some of the most beautiful geography in the state, from the Valley of the Moon to Mount St Helena. Once you've tired of sipping, check out bal-looning, biking, horse riding, hiking and myriad historical sights, including Spanish missions and Jack London's homestead.

Around **Napa**, nothing is cheap, and the town can be quickly done with unless you want to board the over-hyped wine train. But many small towns further up the valley, particularly **St Helena**, have retained enough of their turn-of-the-century-homestead character to be a welcome relief. **Calistoga**, at the top of the valley, is famous for its hot springs, massages and spas. On the western side of the dividing Mayacamas Mountains, the smaller back-road wineries of the **Sonoma Valley** reflect the more down-to-earth nature of the place, which is both more beautiful and less crowded than its neighbor to the east. The town of **Sonoma** itself is by far the most attractive of the Wine Country communities, retaining a number of fine Mission-era structures around its gracious central plaza. **Santa Rosa**, at the north end of the valley, is the region's sole urban center, handy for budget lodgings but otherwise unremarkable.

Arrival and getting around

The Wine Country region spreads north from the top of the San Francisco Bay in two parallel, thirty-mile-long valleys, **Napa** and **Sonoma**. As long as you avoid the rush-hour traffic, it's about an hour's drive from San Francisco along either of the two main routes: through Marin County via the Golden Gate Bridge and US-101, or through the East Bay via the Bay Bridge and I-80. Good highways ring the region, and a loop of the two valleys is conceivable in a day or so. Consider working against the flow of traffic by taking in Sonoma, Glen Ellen and Santa Rosa first before crossing the Mayacamas and dropping into Calistoga, St Helena and Napa.

As the Wine Country's attractions are spread over a fairly broad area, a **car** is pretty much essential. There are other options however: Golden Gate Transit (☎415/923-2000) runs commuter buses every hour for the two-hour, $5.45 ride between San Francisco, Sonoma and Santa Rosa; Greyhound (☎1-800/231-2222) has one bus daily to both Napa and Sonoma, but they leaves San Francisco's Transbay Terminal, First and Mission streets, at an inconvenient 3pm for Napa ($24 roundtrip) or 3.30pm for Sonama ($21 roundtrip); and from Santa Rosa, Sonoma County Transit (☎707/576-RIDE) buses serve the entire Sonoma Valley on a comprehensive, if less than frequent, schedule. From Santa Rosa, Mendocino Transit Authority (☎1-800/696-4MTA) runs one bus daily up the Russian River Valley as far north as Fort Bragg and Mendocino ($26.50 roundtrip). Another option for the car-less is to sign up for a Gray Line **guided bus tour** (☎415/558-9400) from San Francisco. These cost $46, and leave from the Transbay Terminal at 9am. The tour covers both valleys, and visits three wineries, including favorites Sebastiani in downtown Sonoma and Sutter Home in St Helena, with a stop for lunch in pleasant Calistoga. The tour returns to San Francisco around 6.30pm. To bypass San Francisco altogether, take the Sonoma Airporter (6 daily; 1hr 30min; $20; ☎1-800/611-4246 or 707/938-4246, reservations required) from the San

Francisco airport directly to Sonoma City Hall. The bus also stops at the corner of Geary Blvd and Park Presidio in San Francisco's Richmond District, and makes 6 return trips to the city daily.

Blue and Gold Fleet **ferries** travel from the Ferry Building (12 daily; $10 roundtrip; ☎415/773-1188) in San Francisco to Vallejo, and are met by hourly Napa Valley Transit buses (Mon–Sat; ☎1-800/696-6443) which continue on to the city of Napa and beyond. Blue and Gold also runs a Wine Country tour leaving daily from Pier 41 (weekdays 11am, weekends 9.30am; $52).

The **Wine Train** (1 daily; 3hr; full meal and ticket, $27.50–$99; ☎1-800/427-4124 or 707/253-2111) runs from Napa's station at 1275 McKinstry St, east of downtown. The ten-car train of restored 1950s Pullman cars chugs up the valley to St Helena, with a stop at Grgich Hills Cellar winery. The scenery en route is pleasant, but the ride is more of a wining-and-dining experience for older travelers than a means of transportation.

Cycling in the Wine Country

If you don't want to drive all day, **cycling** is a great way to get around. You can bring your own bike on Greyhound (though it costs $10, and the bike must be in a box), or rent one locally for around $25/day and $120/week. If renting, try: Napa Valley Bike Tours, 4080 Byway East, Napa (☎707/255-3377); Yountville Bike Rentals, Vintage 1870, Yountville (☎707/944-9080); St Helena Cyclery, 1156 Main St, St Helena (☎707/963-7736); Getaway Bike Shop, 1117 Lincoln Ave, Calistoga (☎1-800/859-BIKE); or the Sonoma Cyclery, 20093 Broadway, Sonoma (☎707/935-3377).

Both valleys are generally flat, although the peaks in between are steep enough to challenge the hardiest of hill-climbers. If the main roads through the valleys are full of cars, as they are most summer weekends, try the smaller parallel routes: the **Silverado Trail** in Napa Valley and pretty **Arnold Drive** in Sonoma Valley. For the more athletically inclined, the **Oakville Grade** between Oakville in the Napa Valley and Glen Ellen in the Sonoma Valley has challenged the world's finest riders. Check with the Santa Rosa Cycling Club for itineraries, PO Box 11761, Santa Rosa, 95406 (☎707/544-4803). Alternatively, plot your own route with the *Bicycle Rider Directory* (see "Contexts," p.679).

Most local firms organize **tours**, providing bikes, helmets, food and sag wagons in case you get worn out. In Calistoga, Getaway Adventures (☎1-800/499-2453) offers trips of varying lengths, and Napa Valley Bike Tours (☎707/255-3377; *www.napavalleybiketours.com*) sets up more leisurely tours – highlighted by gourmet lunches – all over the Napa area. More ambitious (and quite expensive) overnight tours are run most weekends by Backroads Bicycle Tours, 1516 Fifth St, Berkeley (Mon-Fri 8am-5p; ☎510/527-1555; *www.backroads.com*).

The Wine Country by air

The most exciting way to see the region is on one of the widely touted **hot-air balloon rides** over the Napa Valley. These usually lift off at dawn (hot air rises more strongly in the cold morning air) and last sixty to ninety magical minutes, winding up with a champagne brunch. The first, and still the best, of the operators is Napa Valley Balloons (☎707/253-2224), who fly out of Yountville. Others include Balloons Above the Valley (☎707/253-2222) in Napa and Sonoma County's Air Flambuoyant (☎800/456-4711). The crunch comes when you realize the price – around $175 a head – but it really is worth every cent. Make reservations a week in advance, especially in summer, though with the increasing amount of balloon companies, same-day drop-bys are a possibility.

If it's thrills you're looking for, consider taking to the air in a WWII-era propeller **biplane**. Vintage Aircraft Company, 23982 Arnold Dr, Sonoma (☎707/938-2444), operates one- or two-person flights that take in the Sonoma Valley between loops and rolls.

Choose from four stomach-churning flight patterns: Scenic, Aerobatic, Kamikaze and Dawn Patrol. Flights take 15 to 40 minutes and cost $89–199.

Information

Not surprisingly for such a tourist-dependent area, the Wine Country has a well-developed network of **tourist information** outlets, though the rivalry between the two valleys makes it next to impossible to find out anything about Sonoma when you're in Napa, and vice versa. Both the **Napa Valley Visitors Bureau**, 1310 Napa Town Center off First Street in downtown Napa (daily 9am–5pm; ☎707/226-7459; *www.napavalley. com*), and the **Sonoma Valley Visitors Bureau**, 453 First St E at the center of the plaza in Sonoma (daily 9am-5pm, ☎707/996-1090; *www.sonomavalley.com*), should be able to tell you all you need to know about their respective areas. When traveling the road from San Francisco to Sonoma, there's a friendly branch office of the Sonoma Valley Visitors Bureau in the Vianza Winery, 25200 Hwy 121. If you're keen on touring the wineries, both the above places sell handy **maps** ($1.50–3) giving the lowdown on the hundreds of producers.

Accommodation

Most people are content to visit the Wine Country as a day-trip from San Francisco, visiting a few of the wineries and maybe having a picnic or a meal before heading back to the city. But if you really want to absorb properly what the region has to offer, plan to spend at least one night here, pampering yourself in one of the many (generally pricey) **hotels** and **bed and breakfast inns** that provide the bulk of the area's accommodation options. In summer, the Sonoma Valley Visitors Bureau posts a daily list of available rooms in front of their downtown office. During summer weekends, prices can rise as much as fifty percent, so call ahead. And from November to February, lodging prices drop considerably, often up to half-off. At peak times, rooms of all descriptions get snapped up, so if you have a hard time finding a place, make use of one of the many **accommodation services**: Bed and Breakfast Inns of Napa Valley (☎707/944-4444); Inns of Sonoma Valley (☎707/996-INNS); Reservations Unlimited (☎707/252-1985); or the Napa Valley Visitors Bureau (☎707/226-7459).

    Campers can find a pitch eight miles north of Sonoma at the *Sugar Loaf Ridge State Park*, 2605 Adobe Canyon Rd (Fri-Sat $16, Sun-Thur $15; ☎707/833-5712); or outside Santa Rosa at the *Spring Lake Regional Park*, Newanga Avenue (May–Sept daily; Oct–April Sat & Sun; $15; ☎707/539-8092).

Hotels and motels

Astro Motel, 323 Santa Rosa Ave, Santa Rosa (☎707/545-8555). No frills, but some of the cheapest Wine Country rooms available. ②.

Calistoga Inn, 1250 Lincoln Ave, Calistoga (☎707/942-4101). Comfortable rooms with one bed, most with private bath, in a landmark building with its own restaurant and microbrewery. ④.

Comfort Inn, 1865 Lincoln Ave, Calistoga (☎707/942-9400). Quiet, modern motel on the edge of town with heated mineral pool, steam room and sauna. ⑤.

Dr Wilkinson's Hot Springs, 1507 Lincoln Ave, Calistoga (☎707/942-4102). Legendary health spa and hotel downtown. Choose from a variety of spacious, well-lit rooms with sparse furnishings, facing the courtyard or pool patio. Air conditioning and TV standard. ⑤.

El Bonita Motel, 195 Main St, St Helena (☎1-800/541-3284 or 707/963-3216). Old roadside motel recently done up in Art Deco style, with a pool and hot tub. Surrounded by a 2.5-acre garden, the rooms here contain microwaves, refrigerator and coffee makers. ⑥.

El Pueblo Inn, 896 W Napa St, Sonoma (☎707/996-3651). Basic highway motel with a pool. ④.

Harvest Inn, 1 Main St, St Helena (☎1-800/950-8466 or 707/963-9463). English Tudor cottages at the edge of a vineyard. The place to stay if you can afford it, as the rooms are huge and loaded with perks like a down feather bed, fireplace and private terrace overlooking the garden or 14-acre vineyard. Two outdoor heated pools, whirlpool spas and jogging/biking trails on-site make the just-completed $2 million renovation seem like money well-spent. ⑨.

Hotel St Helena, 1309 Main St, St Helena (☎1-888/478-4355 or 707/963-4388). Slightly claustrophobic (or cozy, depending on your mood) country-style hotel right downtown. European breakfast included each morning. ⑥.

Hotel La Rose, 308 Wilson St, Santa Rosa (☎800-LAROSE-8). Restored lodging on Railroad Square. Clean new rooms with two phone jacks in each room for Internet use. ④.

Jack London Lodge, 13740 Arnold Drive, Glen Ellen (☎707/938-8510). Modern motel near the Jack London State Park, with a good restaurant and pool. A good place to try if Napa and Sonoma hotels are booked, or if you want a truly rural setting and fine star-gazing. ④.

Motel 6, 2760 Cleveland Ave, Santa Rosa (☎707/546-1500). A little distant from the main wine areas, but good and cheap. There's another branch down the street at 3145 Cleveland Ave. ③.

Mount View Hotel and Spa, 1457 Lincoln Ave, Calistoga (☎1-800/816-6877 or 707/942-6877). Lively Art Deco-style hotel with nightly jazz and an excellent Cajun restaurant, *Catahoula*, on the ground floor. ⑦, cottage with patio and hot tub. ⑨.

Swiss Hotel, 18 W Spain St, Sonoma (☎707/938-2884). A ninety-year-old landmark building situated right on the plaza with a fine restaurant. The five cramped rooms each have a view of either the garden patio or Sonoma's plaza, and come with a four-poster queen size bed. ⑥.

Triple-S Ranch 4600 Mount Home Ranch Road, Calistoga (☎707/942-6730). Up the hill from Calistoga, in the middle of the wilderness, these unpublicized cabins are decidedly no-frills, but clean and cheap. There's also a rustic steakhouse/bar on the premises. Take Hwy-128 north for one mile, turn left on Petrified Forest Road, follow it for five miles to Mount Home Road, turn right and continue one mile. ③.

Vintage Inn, 6541 Washington St, Yountville (☎1-800/351-1133 or 707/944-1112). Huge luxury rooms in a modern hotel complex – all with fireplaces – plus swimming pool and free bike rental. Handy for Yountville's many fine restaurants, and great for romantic getaways. ⑧.

White Sulphur Springs, 3100 White Sulphur Springs Rd, west of St Helena (☎707/963-8588). A relaxing retreat from the tourism of the Napa Valley – simple rooms in a rustic, newly remodeled 300-acre hillside resort, surrounded by hiking trails, with an outdoor sulphur pool and hot tub and swimming pool. ⑥.

Wine Country Inn, 1152 Lodi Ln, St Helena (☎707/963-7077). Patios, strolling gardens and vineyard-side swimming pool highlight this inn. The rooms are tasteful, open and uncluttered with antiques. A fireplace comes with most rooms. ⑦.

Bed and breakfast

Calistoga Wine Way Inn, 1019 Foothill Blvd, Calistoga (☎1-800/572-0679 or 707/942-0680). Small and friendly B&B with lovely garden and antique-filled rooms, a short walk from the center of town. ⑤.

The Cottage, 302 First St E, Sonoma (☎707/996-0719). A calm, downtown B&B owned by two interior designers, with hot tub and a relaxing courtyard. ⑦.

Churchill Manor 485 Brown St, Napa (☎707/253-7733). Regal nineteenth-century mansion hidden on an unlikely suburban street. Antique furnishings, delicious breakfasts, and free tandem bikes. ⑥.

Cinnamon Bear 1407 Kearney St, St Helena (☎1-888/963-4600 or 707/963-4653). Quirky, sumptuously furnished inn that has been a favorite. ⑥.

Gaige House Inn, 13540 Arnold Drive, Glen Ellen (☎1-800/935-0237 or 707/935-0237). Beautifully restored Queen Anne Victorian farmhouse in a quiet and contemporary country setting. No children under twelve permitted. ⑧.

Kenwood Inn & Spa, 10400 Sonoma Hwy, Kenwood (☎1-800/353-6966 or 707/833-1293). Deluxe, beautiful, and secluded Italian-villa-style bed and breakfast. ⑧.

Ramekins Bed and Breakfast Inn, 450 W Spain St, Sonoma (☎707/933-4052). Italian-villa-style lodging above a famous cooking school. ⑦.

Sunny Acres Bed&Breakfast, 397 Main St, St Helena (☎707/963-2826. Restored Victorian home of Valley pioneer Dr George Belden Crane, who decided in 1862 that "there was more money to be made in grapes than in medicine," and then planted zinfandel grapes at this estate. Today the quaint inn is surrounded by 26 acres of grapes which supply the Robert Biale label. ⑦.

Thistle Dew Inn, 171 W Spain St, Sonoma (☎1-800/382-7895 or 707/938-2909). Sonoma's most-raved-about B&B. The inn, near Sonoma plaza, features elegantly restored rooms, an amazing full breakfast and free bike rental. Some rooms come with private hot tub and patio. ⑥.

The Napa Valley

A thirty-mile strip of gently landscaped corridors and lush hillsides, the **Napa Valley** looks more like southern France than a near-neighbor of the Pacific Ocean. In spring, the valley floor is covered with brilliant wildflowers that mellow into autumnal shades by grape-harvest time. Local Native Americans named the fish-rich river which flows through the valley "Napa," meaning "plenty"; the name was adopted by Spanish missionaries in the early nineteenth century, but the natives themselves were soon wiped out. The few ranches the Spanish and Mexicans managed to establish were in turn taken over by Yankee traders, and by the 1850s, with California part of the US, the town of Napa had become part of the Gold Rush. Its location also made it a thriving river port, sending agricultural goods to San Francisco and serving as a supply point for farmers and ranchers. The opening of White Sulphur Springs in 1852, California's first mineral springs resort, made Napa the vacation choice for San Francisco's elite. Settlers came, too, including Jacob Beringer in 1870. The rocky, well-drained soil he saw resembled that of his hometown, Mainz, Germany, and by 1875 he and his brother had established Beringer Vineyards, today America's oldest continually operating winery. Before long, Napa was bypassed by the railroads and unable to compete with other, deep-water Bay Area ports, but the area's fine climate saved it from oblivion.

Napa, Yountville and Oakville

Ironically, the town of **NAPA** itself, at the southern end of the valley, is the anomaly of the region. The highway sprawl that greets travelers is fair warning to what the rest of this 60,000-person city has to offer. But for a proud courthouse and some intriguingly decrepit old warehouses along the Napa River, there's not much to see. That said, Napa is worth a quick stop to visit the **Napa Visitors Bureau**, 1310 Napa Town Center off First Street in downtown Napa (daily 9am–5pm; ☎707/226-7459). It's the most helpful in the whole valley and a good place to load up on free maps and brochures. Across the street, the *Napa County Historical Society* (☎707/224-1739) has free, informative materials on the region's pre-wine era.

YOUNTVILLE, nine miles north on Hwy-29, is anchored by **Vintage 1870**, 6525 Washington St (daily 10.30am–5.30pm), a shopping complex in a converted winery that rents bikes, helmets and a map of the Wine Country for $20/day. Aside from antique shops and a few restaurants, nothing in town exerts enough pull to merit a long stop, so push on three miles to tiny **OAKVILLE**, further north along Hwy-29. Dominated by the massive Robert Mondavi Winery (see box on p.596), Oakville features a dozen top-rated wineries, and almost all of them require an appointment and charge a tasting fee, ranging from $5 for a famous Silver Oak cabernet sauvignon to a whopping $25 for Opus One. Besides its high-caliber wines, Oakville is known for its wonderful **Oakville Grocery**, an unmissable deli packed with the finest local and imported foods.

St Helena

The next town worth a stop is **ST HELENA**, 18 miles from Napa, and the first of many antique-shop-filled villages you'll encounter heading north. Its main street, Hwy-29, is lined by some of the Wine Country's finest old buildings, many in pristine condition, and the town itself boasts some unlikely literary attractions. St Helena is also at the heart of a large concentration of wineries, and this combination of history and location make it the de facto tourism capital of Napa Valley, home to a large concentration of luxurious lodgings and restaurants. and with a chic appeal that you'll either love or hate.

If driving through, at least stop off to see the quaint Craftsman-style homes that line residential **Oak Avenue**, and also to see remnants of two unlikely past residents: Robert Louis Stevenson and Ambrose Bierce, both of whom lived in St Helena back in its days as a resort. The **Silverado Museum** (Tues–Sun noon–4pm; free), just off Main Street in the center of town, has a collection of over eight thousand articles relating to Stevenson, who spent just under a year in the area, honeymooning and recovering from an illness (see p.669). It's claimed to be the second most extensive collection of Stevenson artifacts in the US, though the only thing of interest to any but the most obsessed fan is a scribbled-on manuscript of *Dr Jekyll and Mr Hyde*. The other half of the building is taken up by the **Napa Valley Wine Library** (same hours), a briefly entertaining barrage of photos and clippings relating to the development of local viticulture. On the north side of town, at 1515 Main St, Bierce's former residence has been converted into the **Ambrose Bierce House** bed-and-breakfast inn (☎707/963-3003; $169-$195). The inn houses a very small collection of memorabilia relating to the misanthropic ghost-story writer, who lived here for some fifteen years, before heading off to fight for Pancho Villa in the Mexican Revolution and mysteriously vanishing.

Calistoga

Beyond St Helena, towards the far northern end of the valley, the wineries become prettier and the traffic a little thinner. At the very tip of the valley, nestling at the foot of Mount St Helena, **CALISTOGA** is an enjoyable Napa town, featuring nearly twenty wineries and some fancy bistros. The town, though, is better known for its mud baths and hot springs – and the mineral water that adorns every Californian supermarket shelf. Sam Brannan, a young Mormon entrepreneur who made a mint out of the Gold Rush, established a resort community here in 1860. In his groundbreaking speech he attempted to assert his desire to create the "Saratoga of California," modeled upon the Adirondack gem, but in the event got tongue-tied and coined the town's unique name.

Calistoga's main attraction, then as now, is the opportunity to soak in the soothing hot water that bubbles up here from deep in the earth. A multitude of spas and volcanic mud baths, together with a homey and health-conscious atmosphere, beckon city dwellers and tourists alike. The extravagant might enjoy *Dr. Wilkinson's Hot Springs*, 1507 Lincoln Ave (treatments from $50, rooms $89-$149 per night; ☎707/942-4102; *www.drwilkinson.com*), a legendary health spa and hotel whose heated mineral water and volcanic ash tension-relieving treatments have been overseen by the same family for almost fifty years. Down the street, *The Mount View Spa*, 1457 Lincoln Avenue (☎800/772-8838), can wax your chin for $25 and detoxify, exfoliate and nourish your body with an enzymatic sea mud wrap for $75. If swaddled luxury isn't what you're after, a number of more down-to-earth establishments are spread along and off the mile-long main drag, Lincoln Avenue. *Golden Haven Hot Springs*, 1713 Lake St (☎707/942-6793), for example, offers a one-hour mud bath, hot mineral jacuzzi and blanket wrap for $49. If that's still too expensive, ask a local resident to spray you down with their garden hose – although even that might cost a few bucks given Calistoga water's restorative reputation.

Heading northwest out of town on Hwy-128 takes you up the ridge of the **Mayacamas**, a picturesque and steep drive that winds to the summit and spirals southwest, depositing you in Santa Rosa. More evidence of Calistoga's lively underground activity can be seen on this route at the **Old Faithful Geyser** (daily 9am–6pm; $6), two

NAPA VALLEY WINERIES

Almost all of the Napa Valley's **wineries** offer tastings, though comparatively few have tours. There are more than three hundred wineries in all, producing wines of a very high standard, so your taste should ultimately determine the ones you visit. The following selections, listed from south to north, are some long-standing favorites, plus a few lesser-known hopefuls. Keep in mind that the intention is for you to get a sense of a winery's product, and perhaps buy some, rather than get drunk on the stuff, so don't expect more than a sip or two of any one sort – though some wineries do sell wines by the glass. If you want to buy a bottle, particularly from the larger producers, you can in fact usually get it cheaper in supermarkets than at the wineries themselves.

The Hess Collection, 4411 Redwood Rd, Napa (☎707/255-1144). A bit off the beaten track, this secluded winery features, in addition to its superior wines, a surprisingly good collection of modern art and nice view of the valley. Self-guided tour. Tasting daily 10am–4pm; $2.50.

Domaine Chandon, 1 California Drive, Yountville (☎707/944-2280). Sparkling wines from this progeny of France's Moët & Chandon are known to challenge the authentic champagnes from France. Enormous and modern, this winery and gallery is a standard to be toured by all visiting connoisseurs. Highly regarded but expensive restaurant. Tasting daily 10am–8pm; tours daily 11am–5pm.

Stag's Leap, 5766 Silverado Trail, east of Yountville (☎707/944-2020). The winery that put Napa Valley on the international map by beating a bottle of Chateau Lafitte-Rothschild at a Paris tasting way back in 1976. Still quite highly rated. From Hwy-29, turn right on Yountville, then right on Silverado Trail. Tasting daily 10am–4.30pm; tours by appointment.

Napa Wine Company, 7830-40 St Helena Hwy, Oakville (☎707/944-1710) Modeled after the co-operative wineries of France, the Napa Wine Company offers small-vineyard owners access to state-of-the-art crushing and fermentation machinery, and sells vintages of 50 small boutique wineries in the area. The result? Five of *Wine Spectator*'s recent "Top 10 wines." Their tasting room is one of the best – and certainly the broadest – in Wine Country. Appointments recommended.

Silver Oak Cellars, 915 Oakville Cross Rd, Oakville (☎1-800/273-8809). Lovers of cabernet sauvignon mustn't miss a stop at Silver Oak, the crème de la crème of the heady red. At over $100/bottle in the finest San Francisco restaurants, a tasting here in the fire-warmed stone-and-wood room is a bargain for $5. Plus, you get to keep the glass. Bottle sales are limited to one per person ($50), but you can also buy a bottle of Meyer family port ($25). Tasting daily 10am-4.30pm; tours by appointment.

Robert Mondavi, 7801 St Helena Highway, Oakville (☎707/963-9611). Long the standard-bearer for Napa Valley wines ("Bob Red" and "Bob White" are house wines at many California restaurants), they have the most informative and least hard-sell tours. Tours and tasting daily 10am-4.30pm, with reservation. Tasting free with tour, $2–5 without.

miles north of town on Tubbs Lane, which spurts boiling water sixty feet into the air at forty-minute intervals. The water source was discovered during oil-drilling here in the 1920s, when search equipment struck a force estimated to be up to a thousand pounds per square foot; the equipment was blown away and, despite heroic efforts to control it, the geyser has continued to go off like clockwork ever since. Landowners finally realized that they'd never tame it and turned it into a high-yield tourist attraction, using the same name as the famous spouter at Yellowstone National Park.

The **Petrified Forest** (daily 10am–5pm; $4; ☎707/942-6667), located five miles west of Calistoga, is another local tourist trap, and there's little worth stopping here for unless you're a geologist or really into hardened wood After an entire redwood grove

Niebaum-Coppola Estate Winery & Vineyards, 1991 St Helena Hwy, Rutherford (☎707/968-1100). Hollywood film director Francis Ford Coppola purchased this Inglenook estate in 1975, which was originally established by Gustav Niebaum in 1879. Memorabilia from Coppola's movie career is on display in the entryway to the massive new wine-tasting room, featuring their signature Rubicon wine. Tours and tasting daily 10am–5pm; $7.50, includes glass.

V. Sattui, 1111 White Lane, St Helena (☎707/963-7774). Small family-owned winery right off Hwy 29 with award winning wines – the riesling and gamay rouge are particularly good. Sattui wines are only sold at the winery or through the mail. The adjoining gourmet deli has a large selection of cheeses and breads that can be enjoyed with a bottle of wine in the popular tree-shaded picnic grove. Lauded locally as the best small winery and decidedly not snobbish. Tasting daily 9am–6pm.

Berringer Vineyards, 2000 Main St, St Helena (☎707/963-4812). Napa Valley's most famous piece of architecture, the gothic "Rhine House," modeled on the ancestral Rhine Valley home of Jacob Beringer graces the cover of many a wine magazine. Expansive lawns and a grand tasting room, heavy on dark wood, make for a regal experience. 45-minute tours and tasting daily 9.30am–5pm.

Charles Krug Winery, 2800 St Helena Hwy, St Helena (☎707/967-2200). Founded in 1861 by a Prussian immigrant, this winery was purchased by Cesare Mondavi in 1943 and is now owned by son Peter and family. Worth visiting to sample its array of wines, as Krug is renowned in Napa for its huge roster, including chardonnay, pinot noir, zinfandel, merlot and cabernet. The Sangiovese Reserve is its best-rated. Tours by appointment and tastings ($3–6) daily, 10.30am–5.30pm.

Mumm Napa Valley, 8445 Silverado Trail, Rutherford (☎707/942-3434). Opened in 1986 by G.H. Mumm, France's renowned Champagne house, and Joseph E. Seagram & Sons, the sparkling wines from this beautifully situated winery are good, but the sweeping views of the surrounding valleys are the real reason to visit. The tours are particularly engaging and witty, and the informative guides never lose sight of the primary purpose: fun. Tasting daily 10.30am–6pm, $3.50–6; hourly tours 11am–4pm.

Clos Pégase, 1060 Dunaweal Lane, Calistoga (☎707/942-4981). A flamboyant upstart at the north end of the valley, this high-profile winery emphasizes the links between fine wine and fine art, with a sculpture garden around buildings designed by postmodern architect Michael Graves. Tours daily at 11am and 2pm; tasting daily 10.30am–5pm, $2.50.

Sterling Vineyards, 1111 Dunweal Lane, Calistoga (☎707/942-3359). Famous for the aerial tram ride that brings visitors up the 300-foot knoll to the tasting room, the view of Napa Valley from Sterling Vineyards is gorgeous. The extravagant white mansion, modelled after a monastery on the Greek island of Mykonos, is Napa's most-recognizable. Tastings of their wide selection of reds and whites on the View Terrace, overlooking the spectacular scenery, is a memorable experience. Tasting 10.30am–4.30pm, self-guided tour.

was toppled during an eruption of Mount St Helena some three million years ago, the forest here was petrified by the action of the silica-laden volcanic ash as it gradually seeped into the decomposing fibers of the uprooted trees.

Mount St Helena

The clearest sign of the local volcanic unrest is the massive conical mountain that marks the north end of the Napa Valley, **Mount St Helena**, some eight miles north of Calistoga. The 4343-foot summit is worth a climb for its great views – on a very clear day you can see Point Reyes and the Pacific coast to the west, San Francisco to the south, the towering Sierra Nevada to the east and impressive Mount Shasta to the north. It is, however, a long steep climb (ten miles round-trip) and you need to set off early in the morning to enjoy it – take plenty of water (and maybe a bottle of wine).

The mountain and most of the surrounding land is protected and preserved as the **Robert Louis Stevenson Park** (daily 8am–sunset; free), though the connection is fairly weak: Stevenson spent his honeymoon here in 1880 in a bunkhouse with Fanny Osborne, recuperating from tuberculosis and exploring the valley – a plaque marks the spot where his bunkhouse once stood. Little else about the park's winding roads and dense shrub growth evokes its former notoriety, though it's a pretty enough place to take a break from the wineries and have a picnic. In Stevenson's novel, *Silverado Squatters*, he describes the highlight of the honeymoon as the day he managed to taste eighteen of local wine baron Jacob Schram's champagnes in one sitting. Quite an extravagance, especially considering that Schramsberg champagne is held in such high esteem that Richard Nixon took a few bottles with him when he went to visit Chairman Mao.

The Sonoma Valley

On looks alone the crescent-shaped Sonoma Valley beats Napa Valley hands down. This smaller, altogether more rustic valley curves between oak-covered mountain ranges from the small town of **Sonoma** a few miles north along Hwy-12 to the hamlet of **Glen Ellen** and **Jack London State Park**, and ends at the booming bedroom community of **Santa Rosa**. The area is known as the "Valley of the Moon," a label that's mined by tour operators for its connection to long-time resident Jack London, whose book of the same name retold a Native American legend about how, as you move through the valley, the moon seems to rise several times from behind the various

SONOMA WINERIES

Nearly forty fine **wineries** are scattered all over the Sonoma Valley, but there's a good concentration in a well-signposted group a mile east of Sonoma Plaza, down East Napa Street. Some are within walking distance, but often along quirky back-roads, so take a winery map from the tourist office and follow the signs closely. If you're tired of driving around, visit the handy Wine Exchange of Sonoma, 452 First St E (☎707/938-1794), a commercial tasting room where for a small fee, you can sample the best wines from all over California. Local winemakers congregate here after 5pm for a change in beverage, enjoying the bar's selection of 300 beers.

Bartholomew Park, 1000 Vineyard Lane (☎707/935-9511). A lavish Spanish colonial building, with some great topiary in the gardens and extensive vineyards. The wines are relatively inexpensive vintages that appeal to the pocket and palate alike; if you're looking to buy a case, this one's a safe bet. There's a good little museum, too, of regional history that also provides an introduction to local viticulture. The winery is set 100 yards from a replica of Haraszthy's Palladian villa (the original burned down) dating from 1862. Inside, the furnishings and fixtures give a sense of what being a wine-maker in Napa used to entail. The villa is open Wednesday, Saturday and Sunday from 10am-4pm (☎707/938-2444). Self-guided tours of the winery and free tastings daily 10am–4.30pm.

Benziger Family Winery, 1883 London Ranch Road, Glen Ellen (☎707/935-4046). Beautiful vineyard perched on the side of an extinct volcano next to Jack London State Park. Free tram tours through the fields six times daily, self-guided tour introducing trellis techniques, and free tastings. Daily 10am–5pm.

peaks. The area has long been a favorite with visitors: Spain, England, Russia and Mexico have all raised their flag in Sonoma, proclaiming it their own. The US took over in 1846 during the Bear Flag Revolt against Mexico in Sonoma's central plaza and annexed all of California.

Sonoma Valley's **wineries** are generally smaller and more casual than their Napa counterparts, even though the Sonoma Valley fathered the wine industry from which Napa derives its fame. Colonel Agostin Haraszthy first started planting grapes here in the 1850s, and his Buena Vista winery in Sonoma still operates today.

Sonoma

Behind a layer of somewhat touristy stores and restaurants, **SONOMA** retains a good deal of its Spanish and Mexican architecture. The town's charm emanates from the grassy square centering downtown, where wild chickens – escapees from an attempt to turn the bordering **Sonoma State Historic Park** into a living nineteenth-century exhibit – patrol the grounds. These feathered fugitives are indicative of the town's welcoming and relaxed feel, although as a popular retirement spot with a median age of about fifty, it's not exactly bubbling with action.

The central **Plaza** was the sight of the Bear Flag Revolt, the 1846 action that propelled California into independence from Mexico, and then statehood. In this much-romanticized episode, American settlers in the region, who had long lived in uneasy peace under the Spanish and, later, Mexican rulers, were threatened with expulsion from California along with all other non-Mexican immigrants. In response, a band of thirty armed settlers – including the infamous John Fremont and Kit Carson – descended upon the disused and unguarded *presidio* at Sonoma, taking the retired and much-respected commander, Colonel Mariano Guadalupe Vallejo, as their prisoner. Ironically, Vallejo had long advocated the American annexation of California and supported the

Buena Vista Winery, 18000 Old Winery Rd (☎707/252-7117). Oldest and grandest of the wineries, established in 1857, although the wine itself has a reputation for being pretty mediocre. The tasting room, a restored state historical landmark, features a small art gallery. Tasting daily 10.30am–5pm; tours daily at 11am and 2pm.

Chateau St Jean, 8555 Sonoma Hwy, Kenwood (☎707/833-4134). Attractive estate with an overwhelming aroma of wine throughout the buildings. Quirky tower to climb from where you can admire the view. Self-guided tours. Tasting daily 10am–4.30pm.

Gundlach-Bundschu, 2000 Denmark St, Sonoma (☎707/938-5277). Set back about a mile away from the main cluster, Gun-Bun, as it's known to locals, is highly regarded, having stealthily crept up from the lower ranks of the wine league to the point where it now regularly steals from the big names. The plain, functional

building is deceptive – this is premium stuff and definitely not to be overlooked. The winery also hosts the Sonoma Valley Shakespeare Festival, a summer-long celebration of the Bard. Three plays are staged annually, running July-September, Friday through Sunday. Tickets are $20 each, and $48 gets you a season-long pass to all performances. Daily 11am–4.30pm; tours Sat & Sun only.

Ravenswood, 18701 Gehricke Rd, Sonoma (☎707/938-1960). Noted for their "gutsy, unapologetic" zinfandel, the staff at this unpretentious winery is particularly friendly and easygoing. The tasting room is well-known to locals for its summer barbecues. Tastings daily 10am–4.30pm; tours by appointment.

Sebastiani Vineyards, 389 Fourth St E, Sonoma (☎1-800/888-5532 or 707/938-5532). One of California's oldest family wineries, only four blocks from central Sonoma. Free tasting and tours via tram every half-hour. Daily 10am–5pm.

aims of his rebel captors, but he was nonetheless bundled off to Sutter's Fort in Sacramento and held there while the militant settlers declared California an independent republic. The Bear Flag, which served as the model for the current state flag, was fashioned from a "feminine undergarment and muslin petticoat" and painted with a grizzly bear and single star. Raised on Sonoma Plaza, where a small plaque marks the spot today, the Bear Flag flew over the Republic of California for a short time. Three weeks later, the US declared war on Mexico and, without firing a shot took possession of the entire Pacific coast. While far from a frontier town now, the town once had a much wilder side and in fact gave the English language a slang word for prostitutes. Not long after the Bear Flag revolt, General Lee Hooker arrived, bringing along a group of ladies employed to cheer up the troops. The ladies soon became known as "Hooker's girls," and then simply, "hookers."

Today, a number of historic buildings and relics preserve history in the sprawling Sonoma State Historic Park ($3 combined entry to all sites; all daily 10am–5pm). The restored **Mission San Francisco Solano de Sonoma** was the last and northernmost of the California missions, and the only one established in northern California by nervous Mexican rulers fearful of expansionist Russian fur traders. Half a mile west stands the **General Vallejo Home**, the leader's ornate former residence, dominated by decorated filigree eaves and slender Gothic-revival arched windows. The chalet-style storehouse next door has been turned into a **museum** of artifacts from the general's reign.

There's more to Sonoma than historic buildings, though, and relaxing coffee shops, great restaurants, rare book stores and a 1930s-era movie house ring the plaza, making Sonoma a nice town to come back to after a day in the vineyards. To see Sonoma at its unspoiled best, get out of the car and ride across the Valley of the Moon on **horseback**. The Sonoma Cattle Co (☎707/996-8566) offers daily tours, weather permitting, starting at $25.

Glen Ellen and Jack London State Park

Continuing north on Hwy-12, beautiful winding roads lead to the cozy hamlet of **GLEN ELLEN**, and more interestingly, **Jack London State Park** (daily 9.30am-6pm; $6/car). A half-mile up London Ranch Road past the Benziger Family winery, the state park sits on the 140 acres of ranchland the famed author of *The Call of the Wild* owned with his wife Charmian. A mile walk through the woods leads to the ruins of the **Wolf House**, which was to be the London ancestral home: "My house will be standing, act of God permitting, for a thousand years," wrote the author. But in 1913, a month before they were to move in, the house burned to the ground, sparing only the boulder frame. Mounted blueprints point out the splendor that was to-be; the mansion contained a manuscript room, sleeping tower, gun room, and indoor reflecting pool. Nearby lies the final resting place of London – a red boulder from the house's ruins under which his wife sprinkled his ashes. Just off the parking lot, the **House of Happy Walls** (daily 10am-5pm; free) is a jewel of a London museum, housing an interesting collection of souvenirs he picked up traveling the globe. Manuscripts, rejection letters (over 600 before he was published the first time), and the note explaining his and Charmian's resignation from the Socialist Party fill the exhibits, along with reproductions of the Londons' rooms and plenty of photographs. A nearby trail leads past a picnic ground to London's cottage (daily, 10am-4pm; free) where he died. A video display gives background to his life, his wife, and the era. West from the cottage, a trail leads one mile toward the mountains and into the woods, ending at the lake London had built so he and Charmian could fish and swim. Bring a bottle of wine and soak in the sunny charm. Given the hoopla of the Wine Country, the usually uncrowded museum and lovely parkgrounds feel like an oasis of tranquility.

Santa Rosa

Sixty miles due north of San Francisco on US-101, and about twenty miles from Sonoma on Hwy-12, **SANTA ROSA**, the largest town in Sonoma County, sits at the top end of the Sonoma Valley and is more or less the hub of this part of the Wine Country. It's a very different world from the indulgence of other Wine Country towns, however; much of it is given over to shopping centers and roadside malls. In an attempt to form a central pedestrian-only hub, **Historic Railroad Square** – a strip of red-brick-facade boutiques – has been developed, but it will never be mistaken for St Helena's Main Street or Sonoma's Plaza. With the real estate prices higher than ever in the Bay Area, Santa Rosa is exploding with growth, making it both a bedroom community for San Francisco and site of the Wine Country's cheapest lodging, with major hotel and motel chains located around town.

Probably the most interesting thing about Santa Rosa is that it was the home town of Raymond Chandler's fictional private eye Philip Marlowe. You can kill an hour or two at the **Luther Burbank Home and Gardens**, at the junction of Santa Rosa and Sonoma avenues (Tues–Sun 10am–3.30pm; free). California's best-known horticulturist is remembered here in the house where he lived and in the splendid gardens where he created some of his most unusual hybrids. **The Redwood Empire Ice Arena**, 1667 West Steele Lane (☎707/546-7147), was built by Peanuts creator Charles Schulz as a gift for the community. The arena actually comprises two buildings: the ice skating rink and Snoopy's Gallery, a museum/gift shop of all things Peanuts (daily, 10am-6pm; free; ☎707/546-3385) and a lasting tribute to the much-loved Schulz, who died recently. If you still have time to spare, visit the Santa Rosa **Visitors Center**, 9 Fourth St (Mon-Fri 8.30am–5pm, Sat–Sun 10am–3pm; ☎707/577-8674), for more information on the town's happenings.

Santa Rosa does have a great selection of **restaurants**, along with the only *McDonald's* you'll find in Wine Country. Downtown, off the central plaza, *The Cantina*, 500 Forth St (☎707/523-3663), has a lovely garden setting and solid Mexican fare. *Arrigoni's Deli*, 701 Fourth St (☎707/545-1297), is the place to go for picnic supplies, and if you're craving Chinese cuisine, check out *Gary Chu's*, 611 Fifth St (☎707/526-5840). Hearty American grub like burgers and pizza, coupled with microbrewed beer, is served at *Third Street Aleworks*, 610 Third St (☎707/523-3060).

Wine Country eating and drinking

Culinary satisfaction looms around every corner in the Wine Country. **California cuisine** is almost standard in both valleys, and freshness and innovative presentation are very much the order of the day. **Yountville**, in particular, is little more than a string of high-style restaurants, any of which is up there with the best San Francisco has to offer, with prices to match. **Calistoga**, though more low-key, is a gourmet paradise. **Sonoma**, too, has its share and is strong on Italian food. **Bars** are locals' hangouts, and nightlife nearly non-existent, perhaps a result of the free booze on offer from the wineries.

Budget food: cafés and takeouts

Bosko's Ristorante, 1364 Lincoln Ave, Calistoga (☎707/942-9088). Standard Italian restaurant preparing good-value, fresh pasta dishes. Cheap and cheerful, and popular with families.

Café Citti, 9049 Sonoma Hwy, Kenwood (☎707/833-2690). Small, inexpensive trattoria with great Italian food and an intimate, yet casual atmosphere.

Café Sarafornia, 1413 Lincoln Ave, Calistoga (☎707/942-0555). Famous for delicious and enormous breakfasts and lunches with lines around the block on weekends. Let the owner talk your ear off.

La Casa, 121 E Spain St, Sonoma (☎707/996-3406). Friendly, festive and inexpensive Mexican restaurant just across from Sonoma Mission. Enjoy an enchilada on the sunny outdoor patio.

Checkers Pizza, 1414 Lincoln Ave, Calistoga (☎707/942-9300). Soups, salads, and sandwiches, plus adventurous pizzas and good pasta dishes. Open daily until 10pm.

The Coffee Garden, 421 First St W, Sonoma (☎707/996-6645). 150-year-old adobe converted into a café with small gift shop. Fresh sandwiches served on the back patio.

The Diner, 6476 Washington St, Yountville (☎707/944-2626). Start the day's wine-touring off right, with good strong coffee and brilliant breakfasts where locals and day-trippers mix. Open 8am–3pm for breakfast and lunch, and 5.30–9.30pm for flavorful Mexican dinners. Closed Mon.

Ford's Café, 22900 Broadway, Sonoma (☎707/938-9811). Hearty, working-class American food served to locals in this out-of-the-way diner. The generous breakfasts are worth the trip.

Lo Spuntino, 400 First St E, Sonoma (☎707/935-5656). Spacious café and deli on the plaza; good for picnic supplies.

The Model Bakery, 1357 Main St., St Helena (☎707/963-8192). Local hangout serving the best bread in Napa Valley, sandwiches and pizza.

PJ's Café, 1001 Second St, Napa (☎707/224-0607). A Napa institution, open 8am to 10pm every day for pancakes, pasta, pizzas and sandwiches.

The Spot, One mile south of St Helena on Hwy-29 (☎707/963-2844). This tacky roadside diner is conveniently located for lunchtime on the cheap.

Restaurants

Brannan's Grill, 1374 Lincoln Ave, Calistoga (☎707/942-2233). Pecan-stuffed quail, fresh steamed oysters and a wonderful wooden interior make this rather expensive, high-profile eatery worth a visit.

La Boucane, 1778 Second St, Napa (☎707/253-1177). Mouth-watering chunks of tender meat with imaginative takes on traditional sauces, plus perfect fish (especially shellfish) and vegetables. Very expensive, dinner only.

Café LaHaye, 140 E Napa St., Sonoma (☎707/935-5994). Only 11 tables, and always packed for its lovely, lively interior and tasty Italian food.

Calistoga Inn & Brewery, 1250 Lincoln Ave, Calistoga (☎707/942-4101). Very good seafood appetizers – spicy Cajun prawns, or crispy crab cakes – plus a wide range of wines, microbrewed beers, excellent desserts and occasional live music. See also "Accommodation," p.592.

Downtown Joe's, 902 Main St at Second, Napa (☎707/258-2337). One of Napa's most popular and lively spots for sandwiches, ribs and pasta, with beer brewed on the premises. Open until midnight with outdoor dining by the river and popular with singles.

The General's Daughter, 400 W Spain St, Sonoma (☎707/938-4004). Moderately-priced California/Mediterranean hybrid dishes like wild mushroom ravioli, salmon and asparagus and pork tenderloin in a Victorian building formally owned by General Vallejo's daughter.

the girl & the fig, 13690 Arnold Dr, Glen Ellen (☎707/938-3634). French dinners and weekend brunch from a menu as eclectic as its name.

Glen Ellen Inn, 13670 Arnold Drive, Glen Ellen (☎707/996-6409). Husband-and-wife team cook and serve slightly pricey gourmet dishes in an intimate, romantic dining room with half a dozen tables. Daily 5.30–9.30pm.

Mustards Grill, 7399 St Helena Highway (Hwy-29), Yountville (☎707/944-2424). Credited with starting the late-1980s trend toward "grazing" food, emphasizing tapas-like tidbits rather than main meals. Reckon on spending $15–20 a head, and waiting for a table if you come on a weekend.

Pairs Parkside Cafe, 1420 Main St, St Helena (☎707/963-7566). Tasty Cal-Asian cuisine in a funky and cozy café setting in the heart of St Helena. The chefs suggest a specific Napa Valley wine to go with every dish. Closed Tues.

Pinot Blanc, 641 Main St, St Helena (☎707/963-6191). California fusion cuisine prepared by the famous chef Sean Knight, and a nearly California-exclusive wine list. Founded by Joachim Splichal, a noteworthy Los Angeles chef. Five-course tasting menu $49.

Rutherford Grill, 1180 Rutherford Rd, Rutherford (☎707/963-1920). Large portions of basic contemporary American food – the mash potatoes should not be missed – served in a handsome new dining room. Locals recently voted restaurant both the home of the best martini and best place to meet a member of the opposite sex. A coincidence?

Tra Vigne, 1050 Charter Oak Ave, St Helena (☎707/963-4444). Just north of town, but it feels as if you've been transported to Tuscany. Excellent food and fine wines, served up in a lovely vine-covered courtyard or elegant dining room. They also have a small deli, where you can pick up picnic goodies.

Wappo Bar Bistro, 1226 Washington St, Calistoga (☎707/942-4712). Creative cuisine featuring unheard-of combinations like *chile rellenos* with walnut pomegranate sauce and roasted rabbit with potato gnocchi make this restaurant a culinary adventure.

Wine Specator Greystone Restaurant at the Culinary Institute of America, 2555 Main St, St Helena (☎707/967-1010). California/Mediterranean cuisine served in an elegant ivy-walled mansion just outside of town, with a tastefully wacky Art Deco interior. Reasonably priced considering the delicious, large portions of chicken, duck, fish and venison.

Bars

Ana's Cantina, 1205 Main St, St Helena (☎707/963-4921). Long-standing, down-to-earth saloon and Mexican restaurant with billiards and darts tournaments.

Amigos Grill and Cantina, 19315 Sonoma Hwy, Sonoma (☎707/944-2406). Award-winning margaritas using your choice of one of 20 tequilas and a homemade mix.

Compadres Bar and Grill, 6539 Washington St, Yountville (☎707/944-2406). Outdoor patio seating and amazing martinis and margaritas, with free salsa and chips.

Murphy's Irish Pub, 464 First St E, Sonoma (☎707/935-0660). Small bar with an eclectic interior and a few outdoor tables serving basic pub grub and European beers.

Pancha's, 6764 Washington St, Yountville (☎707/944-2125). If wine-tasting becomes boring, try this western-saloon style dive bar.

Sears Point Raceway, Hwys 37 &121, Sonoma (☎800/870-RACE). Not an actual bar, per se, but a cool place to sip some brew while watching America's most popular spectator sport: NASCAR motor-racing. Start your engines! And watch the draught beers flow.

Steiner's Bar, 487 W First St, Sonoma (☎707/996-3812). Local hangout for serious drinkers.

THE NORTHERN COAST

The fog-bound towns and windswept, craggy beaches of the **Northern Coast** couldn't be farther removed from Southern California's sandy, sunny strip of ocean. Stretching north of San Francisco to the Oregon border, the Northern Coast is better suited for hiking than sunbathing, with a climate of cool temperatures year-round and a huge network of national, state and regional **parks** preserving magnificent redwood trees. **Wildlife** thrives here and is always in view, from seals lounging on rocks around Goat Rock Beach in the south, to elk chomping on berry bushes in the north, all against a backdrop of spectacular scenery. Far rarer fauna has been spotted up here as well: the legendary Bigfoot supposedly leaves footprints through the forest, and Ewoks once battled the Galactic Empire under the direction of Star Wars creator George Lucas, who used areas north of Orick as the set for *The Return of the Jedi*.

The only way to see the coast properly is on the painfully slow but visually magnificent Hwy-1, which hugs the coast for two hundred miles through the wild counties of **Sonoma** and **Mendocino**, before turning sharply inland at Legget to join US-101 and **Humboldt County**. In summertime, expect legions of slow-moving campers trying to negotiate the two-lane road's hairpin curves. The hundred miles of wild coastline Hwy-1 never reaches has become known, appropriately, as the **Lost Coast**, a virgin territory of campsites and trails. North of here, the redwoods take over, blanketing the landscape all the way to Oregon, doubling as raw material for the huge logging industries (the prime source of employment in the area) and the region's prime tourist attraction, most notably in the **Redwood National Park**. **Eureka**, the coast's largest – and most boring – city, is neighbored by lively **Arcata**, home to **Humboldt State University** and thousands of Birkenstock sandals.

You'll need to be fairly independent to **get around** this region: one Amtrak Thruway and two Greyhound buses a day travel the length of US-101, which parallels the coastal highway, but they don't link up with the coast until Eureka, far to the north.

The Sonoma Coast and Russian River Valley

Hwy-1 twists and winds along the edge of the **Sonoma Coast** through persistent fog that, once burned off by the sun, reveals oyster beds, seal breeding grounds and twenty-foot-high rhododendrons. A spectacular introduction to the Northern Coast, Sonoma County's western rim is never short on visitors due to its proximity to San Francisco. But tourist activity is confined to a few narrow corridors at the height of summer, leaving behind a network of north coast villages and backwater wineries that for most of the year are all but asleep. The coast is colder and lonelier than the villages along the valley, and at some point most people head inland for a change of scene and a break from the pervasive fog. What both areas have in common, though, is a reluctance to change. As wealthy San Franciscans cast their eyes towards the north for potential second home sites, the California Coastal Commission's policy of beach access for all keeps the architects at bay, making the Sonoma Coast one of the few remaining undeveloped coastal areas in California; the southern third of the coast is almost entirely state beach. At the tiny town of Jenner, Hwy-116 heads inland along the Russian River, leading to the **Russian River Valley**, an affluent summer resort area popular for its canoeing, swimming, wineries and gay resorts.

The Sonoma Coast

BODEGA BAY, about sixty-five miles north of San Francisco, is the first Sonoma County village you reach on Hwy-1. Pomo and Miwok Indians populated the area peacefully for centuries, until Captain Lt Juan Francisco de la Bodega y Quadra Mollineda anchored his ship in the bay and "discovered" it in 1775. Hitchcock filmed the waterside scenes for *The Birds* here; an unsettling number of them are still squawking down by the harbor. Not so long ago, a depleted fishing industry, a couple of restaurants and some isolated seaside cottages were all there was to Bodega Bay, but in recent years San Franciscans have got wind of its appeal and holiday homes and modern retail developments now crowd the waterside.

If you're traveling the whole coast, Bodega Bay makes a tolerable first stop (although better beaches, weather and services exist in Jenner, fourteen miles north – see below). Of several **places to stay**, the *Bodega Harbor Inn*, 1345 Bodega Ave (☎707/875-3594; ④), is the best value in town, while the extremely comfortable *Bodega Coast Inn*, 521 Hwy-1 (☎1-800/346-6999 or 707/875-2217; ⑦), has lovely rooms with fireplaces. Reservations are pretty much essential in summer and on weekends throughout the year. If you don't have a reservation, the **Sonoma Coast Visitor Center** (☎877/789-1212), 850 Hwy-1, has information on room availability throughout the area. **Campsites** are available at the *Bodega Dunes Campground* (☎707/875-3483, reserve through ParkNet, ☎800/444-7275; $16), two miles north of the village on Hwy-1 at the base of a windy peninsula known as **Bodega Head**; laid out across sand dunes that end in coastal cliffs behind the beach. There are **hiking and horseriding** trails around the dunes behind the beach – though in summer these tend to be packed with picnicking families, and for less crowded routes you should head up the coast. *Breakers Café*, 1400 Hwy-1 (☎707/875-2513), serves nouvelle Californian **seafood** plates for around $15. *Lucas Wharf*, 595 Hwy-1 (☎707/875-3522), specializes in crab (mid-Nov–June) and salmon (mid-May–Sept) dishes around $20, and has a good menu of area wines. As part of the upscale *Inn at the Tides*, the *Tides Wharf and Restaurant*, 835 Hwy-1 (☎707/875-3652), gives a good viewpoint for watching fishing boats unload their catch. Breakfasts and lunches from $6 can be enjoyed at the *Sandpiper Restaurant*, 1410 Bay Flat Rd (☎707/875-2278). Nearby, at 1580 Eastshore Rd, *The Sea Gull Café* (☎707/875-8871) offers a more limited menu of eggs and hot sandwiches. For a **tour** of the bay, head over to Will's Fishing Adventures, 1580 Eastshore Rd (☎707/875-2323;$12), where boats leave daily at 6pm, and tour the locations where *The Birds* was filmed, the area where Drake supposedly really landed, and Bodega Rock, home to sea lions and oceanic birds.

North of Bodega Bay

North of Bodega Bay, along the **Sonoma Coast State Beach** (actually a series of beaches separated by rocky bluffs), the coastline coarsens and the trails become more dramatic. It's a wonderful stretch to hike – quite possible in a day for an experienced hiker – although the shale formations are often unstable and you must stick to the trails, which are actually quite demanding. Of Sonoma's thirteen miles of beaches, the finest are surfer-friendly **Salmon Creek Beach**, a couple of miles north of Bodega Bay and site of the park headquarters, and **Goat Rock Beach**, at the top of the coast. The latter offers the chance to get close to harbor seals. For **horseback riding**, *Chanslor Stables*, 2660 Hwy-1 (☎707/875-3333), requires a two-person minimum for their selection of rides, which range from a thirty-minute wetlands jaunt ($25/person) to ninety-minute rides along Salmon Creek ($40/person) and on the beach of Sand Dune State Park ($50/person). Located on the same property, but run under separate management, is a guest ranch/B&B (☎707/875-2721; ④). Staying here takes ten percent off the price of a ride, and is worth it only if you plan on doing a lot of riding.

Campgrounds are dotted along the coast (call ☎707/875-3483 for information), but the best **places to stay or play** are in the tiny seaside village of **JENNER**, which marks the turn-off for the Russian River Valley – a small, friendly place where you can stay in the salubrious cabins and cottages of *The Jenner Inn*, 10400 Hwy-1 (☎1-800/732-2377 or 707/865-2377; rooms ⑤, cottages and homes ⑧) or the comfortable *River's End Resort* (☎707/865-2484; ⑥). Two relatively inexpensive options exist north of town in Salt Point State Park near Fort Ross. *Salt Point Lodge*, seventeen miles north of town, past Fort Ross at 23255 Hwy-1 (☎1-800/956-3437 or 707/847-3234; ④), also houses an excellent restaurant featuring seafood and steak dinners for $12–20. *Fort Ross Lodge*, 20705 Hwy-1 (☎707/847-3333), has rooms that include a VCR, microwave, coffeemaker, small refrigerator, patio and barbecue from $70 with a queen bed to $165 including a hot tub.

The **Russian River** joins the ocean in Jenner, and a massive sand spit at its mouth provides a breeding ground for harbor seals from March to June. Seal sighting information is available at the **visitor center** (10am-4pm), next to the *Seagull Deli*, 10439 Hwy-1, which provides wonderful clam chowder on a deck along the river.

Fort Ross

North of Jenner, the population evaporates and Hwy-1 turns into a slalom course of hairpin bends and steep inclines for twelve miles as far as **Fort Ross State Historic Park** (daily 10am–4.30pm; $6). At the start of the nineteenth century, San Francisco was still the northernmost limit of Spanish occupation in Alta California, and from 1812 to 1841 Russian fur traders quietly settled this part of the coast, clubbing the Californian sea otter almost to extinction, building a fort to use as a trading outpost, and growing crops for the Russian stations in Alaska. Officially they posed no territorial claims, but by the time the Spanish had gauged the extent of the settlement, the fort was heavily armed and vigilantly manned with a view to continued eastward expansion. The Russians traded here for thirty years until over-hunting and the failure of their shipbuilding efforts led them to pull out of the region. They sold the fort and chattels to one John Sutter in 1841, who moved them to his holdings in the Sacramento Valley, so all you see is an accomplished reconstruction built using the original techniques. Among the empty bunkers and storage halls, the most interesting buildings are the Russian Orthodox Chapel and the Commandant's house, with its fine library and wine cellar. At the entrance, a potting shed, which labors under the delusion that it is a

museum, provides cursory details on the history of the fort, with a few maps and diagrams.

Fort Ross has a small beach and picnicking facilities. You can **camp** here (☎707/847-3286; $12) or in **Salt Point State Park** (☎707/847-3221, reserve through ParkNet, ☎800-444-7275; $16), six miles north on Hwy-1. One of Sonoma County's most accessible and beautiful beaches is at **Gerstle Cove**, which includes a paved, wheelchair-accessible path from the cove to Salt Point, past kelp beds, wave-battered rocks and lounging harbor seals. Gerstle Cove is also a popular place for **mushroom-gatherers** to park their cars ($5) and begin foraging. Salt Point State Park's rainfall and habitat make mushrooms thrive, and permits collecting. Ask the ranger for the sheet of guidelines when you enter the lot. Just north of Salt Point, the **Kruse Rhododendron State Reserve** (☎707/847-3221) is a sanctuary for twenty-foot-high rhododendrons, indigenous to this part of the coast and in bloom from April to June. You can drive through, or walk along a short trail. The beaches on this last stretch of the Sonoma coastline are usually deserted, save a few abalone fishermen, driftwood and the seal pups who rest here. Again, they're good for hiking and beachcombing, but stick to the trails.

The Russian River Valley

Hwy-116 begins at Jenner (see above) and turns sharply inland, leaving behind the cool fogs of the coast and marking the western entrance to a relatively warm and pastoral area known as the **Russian River Valley**. The tree-lined highway follows the river's course through twenty miles of what appear to be lazy, backwater resorts but in fact are the major stomping grounds for partying weekenders from San Francisco. The valley's seat, **Guerneville**, has the most nightlife and lodging, while **Healdsburg** serves as the gatekeeper for the **wine area**, bordering US-101 and the Dry Creek and Alexander Valleys.

The fortunes of the Russian River Valley have come full circle; back in the Twenties and Thirties it was a recreational resort for well-to-do city folk who abandoned the area when newly constructed roads took them elsewhere. Drawn by low rents, city-saturated hippies started arriving in the late Sixties, and the Russian River took on a non-conformist flavor that lingers today. More recently, an injection of affluent Bay Area property seekers, many of them gay, has sustained the region's economy, and the funky mix of loggers, sheep farmers and wealthy weekenders gives it an offbeat cachet that has restored its former popularity.

The road that snakes through the valley is dotted with campgrounds every few miles, most with sites for the asking, although during the first weekend after Labor Day when the region hosts the **Russian River Jazz Festival** (☎707/869-3940; $40), things can get a bit tight. The jazz festival is something of a wild weekend around here and a good time to come: bands set up on Johnson's Beach by the river and in the woods for impromptu jamming sessions as well as regular scheduled events. The new mid-June **Russian River Blues Festival** has proven equally popular (call ☎707/869-3940 for details).

Sonoma County Transit (☎707/576-7433) runs a fairly good weekday bus service (though patchy on weekends) between the Russian River resorts and Santa Rosa in the Wine Country, although to see much of the valley, you really need a **car**, or hire a **bike** or **kayak** from Russian River Kayak and Bicycle, in Monte Rio, ☎707/865-2141.

Guerneville

The main town of the Russian River valley, **GUERNEVILLE**, has finally come out. No longer disguised by the tourist office as a place where "a mixture of people respect each other's lifestyles," it's quite clearly a **gay resort** and has been for the last fifteen years: a lively retreat popular with tired city-dwellers who come here to unwind. Gay men predominate during the summer, except during two **Women's Weekends** (☎707/869-2971) – in early May and late September – when many of the hotels take only women.

If you don't fancy venturing along the valley, there's plenty to keep you busy without leaving town. Weekend visitors flock here for the canoeing, swimming and sunbathing that comprise the bulk of local activities: **Johnson's Beach**, on a placid reach of the river in the center of town, is the prime spot, with canoes ($12 a day), pedal boats ($5 an hour) and tubes ($3 a day). But Guerneville's biggest natural asset is the magnificent **Armstrong Redwoods State Reserve** (☎707/869-2015), two miles north at the top of Armstrong Woods Road ($6 parking) – 700 acres of massive redwood trees, hiking and riding trails and primitive camping sites. Take food and water and don't stray off the trails: the densely forested central grove is quite forbidding and very easy to get lost in. One of the best ways to see it is on horseback; the Armstrong Woods Pack Station (☎707/887-2939) offers guided horseback tours that range from a half-day trail ride ($40) to a three-day pack trip ($450). A natural amphitheater provides the setting for the **Redwood Forest Theater** which stages dramatic and musical productions during the summer.

The **Chamber of Commerce**, 16200 First St (Mon–Fri 9am–5pm; 24-hr info line ☎707/869-3533), has good free maps of the area, and **accommodation** listings. The

---

RUSSIAN RIVER VALLEY WINERIES

The Guerneville Chamber of Commerce (see above) issues an excellent *Russian River Wine Road* map, which lists all the **wineries** that spread along the entire course of the Russian River. Unlike their counterparts in Napa and Sonoma, the wineries here are neither organize guided tours nor charge for wine-tasting. You can wander around at ease, guzzling as many and as much of the wines as you please. Some of the wines are of remarkably good quality, if not as well known as their Wine Country rivals. By car, you could easily travel up from the Sonoma Coast and check out a couple of Russian River wineries in a day, although the infectiously slow pace may well detain you longer.

Chateau Souverain, 400 Souverain Rd, Geyserville (☎707/433-8281). A large selection of wines and a café. Tasting Wed-Sun 10am–5pm.

Dry Creek Vineyard, four miles northwest of Healdsburg at Dry Creek and Lambert Bridge Road (☎707/433-1000). Family-owned operation well known for its consistently top-notch wines – particularly the cabernet sauvignon and chardonnay. Picnic facilities. Tastings daily 10.30am–4.30pm.

Hop Kiln, 6050 Westside Rd, Healdsburg (☎707/433-6491). Recently established rustic winery with a traditional atmosphere but not a snobbish attitude. Tastings daily 10am–5pm.

Korbel Champagne Cellars, 13250 River Rd, two miles east of Guerneville (☎707/887-2294). Even if you're not "doing" the wineries, you shouldn't miss this place. The bubbly itself – America's

best-selling premium champagne – isn't anything you couldn't find in any supermarket, but the wine and brandy are sold only from the cellars, and are of such notable quality that you'd be crazy not to swing by for a glass or two. The estate where they are produced is lovely, surrounded by hillside gardens covered in blossoming violets, coral bells and hundreds of varieties of roses – perfect for quiet picnics. A microbrewery and upscale deli are also on the premises.

Topolos at Russian River Vineyards, 5700 Gravenstein Hwy, Forestville, five miles from Guerneville along Hwy-116 (daily 11am–5.30pm; ☎707/887-1575). One of the Russian River Valley's most accessible wineries, specializing in zinfandels. The popular on-site restaurant serves Greek-inspired California dishes – dine on the patio and feast your eyes on the wildflower gardens. Winery tours by appointment.

friendly **Russian River Region Visitors Bureau**, across the street at 14034 Armstrong Woods Rd (☎1-800/253-8800 or 707/869-9212), can recommend places to stay all over the area. As with most of the valley, B&Bs are the staple; two luxurious choices are the comfortable *Creekside Inn and Resort*, 16180 Neely Rd (☎1-800/776-6586 or 707/869-3623; ⑤), and *Applewood Inn & Restaurant*, 13555 Hwy-116 (☎707/869-9093; ⑦), which also features a highly acclaimed gourmet restaurant. *Fife's*, 16467 River Rd (☎1-800/7-FIFES-1 or 707/869-0656; ④), is the original gay resort right by the river, while *The Willows*, 15905 River Rd (☎707/869-2824; ④) is a bit more modest. *Brookside Lodge*, 14100 Brookside Lane (☎707/869-2470; ⑤), has basic rooms. A dearth of cheap motels (unless you head east to US-101) makes **camping** the economical answer: the *Austin Creek State Recreation Area*, Armstrong Woods Road ($14; ☎707/865-2391), is guaranteed RV-free, while *Johnson's Beach and Resort*, 16241 First St, also has cabins and rooms available ($10 camping; ☎707/869-2022; ②). There are a couple of free primitive sites, and $7 walk-in backcountry sites in the state reserve.

Guerneville has a good selection of reasonably priced, reliable **restaurants**, among them *Brew Moon*, 16248 Main St (☎707/869-0201), which serves tasty barbecued meats on paper plates in addition to cheap breakfasts and good coffees. *Burdon's Restaurant*, 15405 River Rd (☎707/869/2615), is slightly more upscale, with excellent gourmet meat and pasta dishes for around $12. Really, though, it's the **nightlife** that makes Guerneville a worthwhile stop. The *Bullpen*, 16246 First St (☎707/869-3377), is a happening bar with an occasional live act, while the *Russian River Resort* ("Triple R"), 16390 4th St (☎707/869-0691), and *River Business, Inc*, 16225 Main St (☎707/869-3400), both serve alcohol and food and are popular with the gay crowd – though you'd be hard pressed to find a place that isn't in Guerneville.

Monte Rio

The small town of **MONTE RIO**, three miles west along the river from Guerneville, is definitely worth a look: a lovely, crumbling old resort town with big Victorian houses in stages of graceful dilapidation. For years it has been the entrance to the 2500-acre **Bohemian Grove**, a private park that plays host to the San Francisco-based Bohemian Club. A grown-up summer camp, its membership includes a very rich and very powerful male elite – ex-presidents, financiers, politicians and the like. Every year in July they descend for "Bohemian Week" – the greatest men's party on earth, noted for its high jinks and high-priced hookers, away from prying cameras in the seclusion of the woods.

The best of Monte Rio's pricey **places to stay** are the lovely *Rio Villa Beach Resort*, 20292 Hwy-116 (☎707/865-1143; ④), in a beautiful spot on the banks of the Russian River, and the restored *Highland Dell Inn*, 21050 River Blvd (☎1-800/767-1759 or 707/865-1759; ⑤). *Huckleberry Springs Country Inn* (☎1-800/822-2683 or 707/865-2683; ⑥) is a deluxe women's retreat with massages and a spa, just outside of town on Old Beedle Road.

If you're touring the area by car, the lonely, narrow **Cazadero Highway** just to the west makes a nice drive from here, curving north through the wooded valley and leading back to Fort Ross on the coast. At the north end of the bridge over the Russian River in Monte Rio, **cyclists** can begin the world-renowned King Ridge-Meyers Grade ride. The 55-mile loop (and 4500 feet of climb) heads along the Cazadero Highway and into the hills, finally descending to the coast and Hwy-1. Contact the Santa Rosa Cycling Club (☎707/544-4803) for a complete itinerary.

Healdsburg

The peaceful town of **HEALDSBURG** straddles the invisible border between the Wine Country and the Russian River Valley, and as a result, in a quiet way manages to get the best of both worlds. While **Veterans Memorial Beach**, a mile south of the plaza along the banks of the Russian River, is a popular spot for swimming, picnicking, and canoeing in the summertime, there are also some twenty wineries, most of them family owned, within a few miles of the center of town. Romantic bed and breakfasts have sprung up all over the area, including the neighboring village of **GEYSERVILLE**, and although the town's economic well-being is almost exclusively dependent on tourism, it still manages to maintain a relaxed, backcountry feel. The Healdsburg Area **Chamber of Commerce**, 217 Healdsburg Ave (☎1-800/648-9922 or 707/433-6935), provides winery and lodging information.

As might be expected, cheap places to stay are virtually nonexistent in Healdsburg, but if you have the money to spend, the *Madrona Manor*, 1001 Westside Rd (☎1-800/258-4003 or 707/433-4231; ⑨), a luxurious Victorian-style bed and breakfast hidden on a hilltop, with meticulously maintained gardens and a gourmet restaurant, is hard to beat. The best value is the *Best Western Dry Creek Inn*, 198 Dry Creek Rd (☎707/433-0300, ☎800/222-5784; ④).

Of several gourmet restaurants that circle the plaza, *Bistro Ralph*, 109 Plaza St (☎707/433-1380), with sparse modern decor and well crafted dishes ($15–20 per main course), is your best bet. *Flying Goat Coffee Roastery and Cafe*, just off the main plaza at 324 Center St (☎707/433-9081), is a great place to unwind with a newspaper and good cup of coffee.

The Mendocino coast

The coast of **Mendocino County**, 150 miles north of San Francisco, is a dramatic extension of the Sonoma coastline – the headlands a bit sharper, the surf a bit rougher, but otherwise more of the same. Sea stacks form a dotted-line off the coast, and there's an abundance of tidal pools, making the area a prime spot for diving and exploring on foot the secrets of the ocean. Surfers love it, too, for the waves and sandy beaches at **Gualala** and **Point Arena**, and March brings out droves of people to watch migrating whales. Tourists tend to mass in charming **Mendocino** and gritty **Fort Bragg**, leaving the other small former logging towns along Hwy-1 preserved in the salt air and welcoming to visitors. The county also thrives as a location spot for the movie industry, having featured in such illustrious titles as *East of Eden*, *Frenchman's Creek*, and more recently, *The Fog*.

This is the place for a quiet getaway weekend – join all the other couples avoiding the crowds in the pricey bed and breakfasts. Inland, there's little to see beyond the small contingent of wineries – stick to the coast, which you can hug via Hwy-1 as far north as Rockport, when it turns east to join US-101. The thirty miles north, accessible by a narrow, dirt logging road that contains the only true wilderness left on California's rim. Only Willits, forty miles inland, is served by Greyhound and Amtrak Thruway. From here, the Skunk Trains (see p.612) provide the sole **public transportation** to the main towns of Mendocino and Fort Bragg, linked to each other by Mendocino Stage and Transit Authority buses (☎800/696-4MTA or 707/964-0167), which continue south to Gualala and Santa Rosa.

Mendocino

Once you leave Sonoma County, Hwy-1 winds for fifty miles along the wrinkled coast, past the communities of Gualala and Point Arena and the kelp forests of VanDamme State Park before you reach the coast's most lauded stop, the decidedly touristy village of **MENDOCINO**. The quaint town sits on a broad-shouldered bluff with waves crashing on three sides; it's hard to find a spot here where you *can't* see the ocean sparkling in the distance. New England-style architecture is abundant, lending Mendo, as the locals call it, a down-home, almost cutesy air. Its appearance on the National Register of Historic Places and reputation as something of an artists' colony draw the curious up the coastal highway, and a fairly extensive network of bed and breakfasts, restaurants, and bars are more than happy to cater to their every need.

The Town

Like other small settlements along the coast, Mendocino was originally a mill site and shipping port, established in 1852 by merchants from Maine who thought the proximity to the redwoods and exposed location made it a good site for sawmill operations. The industry has now vanished, but the large community of artists has spawned craftsy commerce in the form of art galleries, gift shops and boutique delicatessens. This preservation didn't come about by accident. The state of California traded a block of old-growth forest with the Boise-Cascade logging company in exchange for the headlands surrounding the town. The headlands became a state park, and Mendocino in turn became a living museum, with strict local ordinances mandating architectural design and upkeep.

The **visitor center**, 735 Main St (daily 11am–4pm; ☎707/937-5397), is housed in **Ford House**, one of many mansions built by the Maine lumbermen in the style of their home state. The **Kelley House Museum**, 45007 Albion St (daily 1–4pm; ☎707/937-5791), has exhibits detailing the town's role as a center for shipping redwood lumber to the miners during the Gold Rush, and conducts **walking tours** of the town on Saturday mornings at 11am – though you could do it yourself in under an hour, collecting souvenirs from the galleries as you go. Among them, the **Mendocino Art Center**, 45200 Little Lake St (daily 10am–5pm; ☎707/937-5818. ☎800/653-3328; free), gives classes and has a gallery showing some good works (if a little heavy on the seascapes) by mainly Mendocino-based artists.

Otherwise there's plenty to occupy you around the town, with a long stroll along the **headlands** top on the list. **Hiking** and **cycling** are popular, with bikes available for around $25 a day from Catch a Canoe & Bicycles, Too (☎1-800/320-2453 or 707/937-0273), just south of Mendocino at the corner of Hwy-1 and Compche-Ukiah Road. They also rent outriggers and kayaks. At the west end of Main Street, hiking trails lead out into the **Mendocino Headlands**, where you can explore the grassy cliffs and make your way down to the tidepools, next to the breaking waves. The **Russian Gulch State Park** (☎707/937-5804; $6), two miles north of town, has bike trails, beautiful fern glens and waterfalls. Just south of town, hiking and cycling trails weave through the unusual **Van Damme State Park** (☎707/937-5804; $6), which has a **Pygmy Forest** of ancient trees, stunted to waist-height because of poor drainage and soil chemicals. The coast of the park is punctuated with sea stacks and caves, carved by the pounding surf. Two-hour **sea cave tours** are available through *Lost Coast Kayaking* (three times daily, $45; 707/937-2434). After a day of hiking and shopping, you may want to pamper yourself with a **massage** and a **hot tub** at one of the town's spas..

Abalone diving is extremely popular along the coast here, particularly just south of town in the small cove beside Van Damme State Park. In an attempt to thwart poaching, the practice is strictly regulated – the tasty gastropods are not available commercially and you can only have four in your possession at any given time. In early October, four-hundred hungry judges pay a substantial fee for the opportunity to help choose the best abalone chef in the annual Abalone Cookoff. The Sub-Surface Progression Dive Center, 18600 Hwy-1 (☎707/964-3793) in Fort Bragg, leads all-inclusive half-day diving expeditions for $50.

Accommodation

Room rates in Mendocino are generally high, but provided you stay away from the chintzy hotels on the waterfront, it is possible to find adequate, reasonably priced hotels on the streets behind. The *Sea Gull Inn*, 44960 Albion St (☎1-888/937-5204 or 707/937-5204; ③), is the best of the affordable options right in the center, though the antique-filled rooms at *The Mendocino Hotel*, 45080 Main St (☎1-800/548-0513 or 707/937-0511; ④), are more luxurious. The *Blackberry Inn*, east of Hwy-1, at 44951 Larkin Rd (☎1-800/950-7806 or 707/937-5281; ⑤), is a bit far from the center of town, but is nonetheless a relatively good value. The *Agate Cove Inn*, 11201 N Lansing St (☎707/937-0551; ⑥), gets you closest to the ocean, and the biggest of the many B&Bs is the *MacCallum House Inn*, 45020 Albion St (☎707/937-0289, ☎800/609-0492; ⑥). The most romantic place to stay in the whole region is a tie. In Mendo, *Reed Manor*, on Palette Drive (☎707/937-5446; ⑧), is a five-bedroom mansion with canopied soaking tubs and in-room telescopes for whale watching. The other romantic choice is at **ALBION**, a small fishing village ten miles south of Mendocino; the *Albion River Inn*, 3790 N Hwy-1 (☎1-800/479-7944 or 707/937-1919; ⑦), just beyond the junction with Hwy-128, perches on the edge of a cliff, and all the rooms except one have ocean views. The inn also has a first-class restaurant, serving pricey, wonderful food with a spectacular wine list and top service. A few miles east on Hwy-128 sit several Anderson Valley wineries. *Mendocino Coast Accommodations* (☎707/937-1913) book rooms at B&Bs, hotels, cottages and vacation homes for free. There's $16 **camping** at Russian Gulch State Park (reserve through ParkNet ☎1-800/444-7275), and Van Damme State Park.

Eating, drinking and nightlife

Of Mendocino's **restaurants**, the best and most famous is *Café Beaujolais*, 961 Ukiah St (☎707/937-5614), which specializes in organic California cuisine and serves dinner from 5:45pm to 9pm. *955 Ukiah Street* (☎707/937-1955) serves $15-$20 entrées that are making it the best-kept secret in town (Wed-Sun from 6pm). For slightly cheaper fair, try the *Mendocino Café*, 10485 Lansing St (☎707/937-0836), serving an eclectic mix of salads, pastas, and sandwiches daily until 9pm. *Tote Féte Bakery*, behind the deli of the same name at 10450 Lansing St (☎707/937-3383; daily until 7pm), produces delicious breads, pastries and muffins, which you can eat outside on the tree-shaded deck. *Fetzer Vineyards Tasting Cellar* (☎707/937-6191), on Main Street next to the Mendoncino Hotel, sells its vintages and gives free tastings (daily 10am-6pm).

The first weekend in March brings the **Mendocino Whale Festival** (☎800/726-2780), a celebration of food and headland views of whales returning back to the Arctic. They can also be spotted in November, on the trip to the warmer waters of the California Baja. In mid-July the town hosts the two-week **Mendocino Music Festival** (☎800/937-2044), bringing in blues and jazz bands from all over the state, although the emphasis is largely on classical music and opera. For an earthier experience (and cheaper beer), *Dick's Place*, 45070 Main St, is Mendocino's oldest **bar**, with all the robust conviviality you'd expect from a spit-and-sawdust saloon.

Fort Bragg, Willits and Leggett

FORT BRAGG is very much the blue-collar flipside to its comfortable neighbor. Where Mendocino exists on wholefood, art and peaceful ocean walks, Fort Bragg brings you the rib-shack and tattoo parlor, and sits beneath a perpetual cloud of steam choked out from the lumbermills of the massive Georgia Pacific Corporation, which monopolizes California's logging industry and to which Fort Bragg owes its existence. There was once a fort here, but it was only used for ten years until the 1860s when it was abandoned and the land sold off cheaply. The otherwise attractive **Noyo Harbor** (south of town on Hwy-1) has been crammed full of commercial fishing craft, and the billowing smog does little to add to the charm. Nevertheless, its proximity to the more isolated reaches of the Mendocino Coast, an abundance of budget accommodation and bevy of inexpensive restaurants make it a good alternative to Mendocino.

As for things to do, or even just a convenient way of getting to or from the coast, you can amuse yourself on the **Skunk Trains** operated by the Californian Western Railroad ($27 one-way, $35 round-trip; ☎1-800/77-SKUNK or ☎707/964-6371 Fort Bragg depot; ☎707/459-5248 Willits depot), which run twice daily from the terminus on Laurel Street forty miles inland to US-101 and the town of Willits. Taking their name from the days when, piled up with timber from the redwood forests, they were powered by gas engines and could be smelt before they were seen, the trains now operate almost exclusively for the benefit of tourists – it's good fun to ride in the open observation car as it tunnels forty miles through mountains and rumbles across the thirty-odd high bridges on its route through the towering redwoods. Choose between a full eight-hour journey to Willits and back, or a four-hour ride that turns around half-way. **WILLITS**, where the trains end up, is the official county seat thanks only to its location in the center of Mendocino, and is no different from other strip-development, mid-sized American towns – disembark only to get a drink, if at all.

A short drive or bus ride south of Fort Bragg will take you to the **Mendocino Coast Botanical Gardens**, 18220 North Hwy-1 (summer daily 9am–5pm, winter daily 9am–4pm; $6; ☎707/964-4352), where you can see more or less every wildflower under the sun spread across 47 acres of prime coastal territory. The next stretch of Hwy-1 is the slowest, continuing north for another twenty miles of road and windswept beach before leaving Mendocino County and the coastline to turn inland and head over the mountains to meet US-101 at **LEGGETT**. Redwood country begins in earnest here: there's even a tree you can drive through for $3, though you'd do better to stay on course for the best forests further north.

Practicalities

Fort Bragg's **Chamber of Commerce** (Mon-Fri 9am-5pm, Sat 9am-3pm; ☎800/726-2780 or 707/961-6300) is almost directly across the street from the **train station** at 332 N Main St. Most of the **motels** cluster along Hwy-1 in the center of town, the lowest priced of which is the rather dingy-looking *Fort Bragg Motel*, 763 N Main St (☎1-800/253-9972 or 707/964-4787; ③). Other good options include the basic but clean *Tradewinds Lodge*, 400 S Main St (☎800/524-2244 or ☎707/964-4761; ④), the *Surf Motel*, 1220 S Main St (☎800/339-5361 or ☎707/964-5361; ③), approaching town from the south, or the more upscale *Grey Whale Inn B&B*, 615 N Main St (☎800/382-7244 or 707/964-9800; ⑤), which has great views from its rooms. The newly renovated *Old Coast Hotel*, 101 N Franklin (☎888/468-3550 or ☎707/961-4488; ⑤) has comfortable rooms in an 1892 building with a steak-and-seafood restaurant attached. Finally, there's **camping** among six miles of sandy beach and coastal pines at **MacKerricher State Park** ($14; reserve through ParkNet ☎1-800/444-7275), three miles north of Fort Bragg.

Restaurants in Fort Bragg (of which there are plenty) tend to cater for the ravenous carnivore. Both *Jenny's Giant Burger*, 940 N Main St (☎707/964-2235), and the *Redwood Cookhouse*, 118 E Redwood Ave (☎707/964-1517), serve huge tree-felling dinners of steaks, ribs and burgers, and are usually full of men from the mills. Otherwise, *The Restaurant*, at 418 Main St (☎707/964-9800), has great Cajun and Creole fish dishes for around $6, and *Café Prima*, 124 E Laurel St (☎707/964-5814), does elegant Swahili dishes from the chef's native Kenya. Vegetarians can take refuge in the hearty Italian offerings at *Headlands Coffee*, 120 East Laurel St (☎707/964-1987), which also serves wine, along with a full menu of espressos. For big breakfasts, try *Egghead's Restaurant*, at 326 N Main St (daily 7am–2pm), which lists 41 different omelets on their menu. If you're feeling thirsty, stop in for one of the "handmade ales" at the *North Coast Brewing Company*, 444 N Main St (☎707/964-3400), voted one of the ten best breweries in the world by the Beverage Testing Institute of Chicago as part of their year-long World Beer Championships. Try the Acme California Brown Ale and the Old Rasputin Russian Imperial Stout.

The Humboldt Coast

Of the northern coastal counties, **Humboldt** is by far the most beautiful, and also the one most at odds with development. The biggest news story of 1999 concerned **Eureka**'s decision to bar chainstore-behemoth WalMart from erecting an outlet, despite the company's offer to clean up and build on a now-deserted, and very polluted, stretch of waterfront. This is logging land, and the drive up US-101 gives a tour of giant sawmills fenced in by stacks of felled trees. Yet Humboldt County also contains the largest preserves of giant redwoods in the world in **Humboldt Redwoods State Park** and, north, **Redwood National Park**. Both are peaceful, surreal experiences not to be missed, though the absence of sunlight within the groves and mossy surface can be eerie.

Indeed, many locals hope that the forests are too creepy for visitors. Tourism, while good for business, encroaches on a lifestyle far removed from the glitz of Mendocino and Sonoma counties. Locals are worried that as more people discover the area, the rugged serve-yourself economy here could quickly turn into a service economy. Weekend visitors won't encounter any outright hostility, provided they tread lightly. Camping and communing with nature is cool, while expecting salad forks with dinner and a throbbing nightlife is not. The coastal highway's inability to trace Humboldt's southern coast, formerly guaranteed isolation and earned the region the name of the **Lost Coast**. The area, while still isolated, is not quite as "lost" anymore thanks to the construction of an airstrip in Shelter Cove and an infusion of hotels, restaurants and new homes.

Humboldt is perhaps most renowned for its "Emerald Triangle," as it's known, which produces the majority of California's largest cash crop, **marijuana**. As the Humboldt Coast's fishing and logging industries slide, more and more people have been turning to growing the stuff to make ends meet. In the 1980s, the Bush administration took steps to crack down on the business with CAMP (Campaign against Marijuana Planting), sporadically sending out spotter planes to pinpoint the main growing areas. Aggressive law enforcement and a steady stream of crop-poaching has been met with a defiant, booby-trapped and frequently armed protection of crops, and production goes on – the camouflage netting and irrigation pipes you find on sale in most stores clearly do their job. Thomas Pynchon's novel *Vineland* follows the escapades of hippie Zoyd Wheeler as he becomes enmeshed in CAMP's wheels and sketches the modern history of the area, when droves of city folk chose Humboldt as the place to permanently tune in, turn on and drop out.

Apart from considerable areas of clandestine agriculture, the county is almost entirely forestland. The highway rejoins the coast at **Eureka** and **Arcata**, Humboldt's two major towns and both jumping-off points for the **redwoods**. These "ambassadors from another time," as John Steinbeck dubbed them, are at their 300-foot best in the Redwood National Park, which contains three state parks and covers some 106,000 acres of skyscraping forest. Again, **getting around** is going to be your biggest problem. Although Greyhound and Amtrak Thruway buses run the length of the county along US-101, they're hardly a satisfactory way to see the trees, and you'll need a car to make the trip worthwhile. **Hitchhiking** still goes on up here, and you'll see gaggles of locals gathered at the gas stations and freeway entrances begging for rides. This is part necessity, as public transportation is scarce, and part lifestyle, as the region is a throwback to the kinder decades when hitching was a normal practice on American roads. Still, remember that stopping on the highways is illegal, and that no matter the kind appearance of a hitcher or driver, hitchhiking can be dangerous in the US. For information on **what's on** in Humboldt, two excellent, free county newspapers, *The Activist* and *North Coast View*, detail the local scene and people, and where to go and what to do in the area. Look out, too, for the campaigning Arcata-based *Econews*, which highlights the ecological plight of northern California's wild country.

Southern Humboldt: Garberville and the Lost Coast

The inaccessibility of the Humboldt Coast in the south is ensured by the **Kings Range**, an area of impassable cliffs that shoots up several thousand feet from the ocean, so that even a road as sinuous as Hwy-1 can't negotiate a passage through. To get there you have to travel US-101 through deep redwood territory as far as **GARBERVILLE**, a one-street town with a few good bars and hotels that is the center of the cannabis industry and a lively break from the freeway. Each week, the local paper runs a "bust-barometer" which charts the week's pot raids, and every August, the town hosts the massive two-day **Reggae on the River** festival. Tickets cost around $75; call ☎707/923-3368 by early May to reserve them.

Practicalities

Amtrak Thruway **buses** stop twice daily outside the *Waterwheel Restaurant* on Redwood Drive, Garberville's main street, while the two daily Greyhound services connecting north to Eureka and south to San Francisco pull in around the corner on Church Street. The town's **Chamber of Commerce** (☎1-800/923-2613 or 707/923-2613) is located at 773 Redwood Drive. For what you get, much of the town's **accommodation** is a bit overpriced. Of a couple you might try, the *Benbow Inn*, 445 Lake Benbow Drive (☎1-800/355-3301 or 707/923-2124; ⑥), is a flash place for such a rural location (former guests include Eleanor Roosevelt and Herbert Hoover); the *Humboldt House Inn*, 701 Redwood Drive (☎707/923-2771; ④); and the *Motel Garberville*, 948 Redwood Drive (☎707/923-2422; ③), round out the better options. The closest **campground** is seven miles south at **Benbow Lake State Recreation Area** (☎707/923-3238; reserve through Parknet ☎1-800/444-7275; $14). If you're independently mobile you can head five miles further south on US-101 to the **Richardson Grove State Park** in Piercy (☎707/247-3318; reserve through Parknet ☎1-800/444-7275; $16), a 1400-acre park along the Eel River.

Even if you don't intend to stay in Garberville, at least stop off to sample some of the town's **restaurants** and **bars**, which turn out some of the best live bluegrass you're likely to hear in the state. Redwood Drive is lined with bars, cafés and restaurants: the *Eel River Café* at no. 801 (☎707/923-3783) is a good bet for breakfast, while the *Woodrose Café* at no. 911 (☎707/923-3191) serves organic lunches, and the *Mateel Café* at no. 478 (☎707/923-2030) serves gourmet dishes and coffee on the terrace. For casual dining or cheap take-out, try *Calico's Deli and Pasta*, 808 Redwood Drive (☎707/923-2253). All the town bars tend to whoop it up in the evening; the noisiest of the lot is probably the *Branding Iron Saloon*, at 744 Redwood Drive, with a small cover for its nightly live music. The *Riverwood Inn* (☎707/943-3333), in nearby **Phillipsville** is especially renowned for its live bluegrass.

Shelter Cove and the Humboldt Redwoods State Park

From Garberville, via the adjoining village of **REDWAY**, the Briceland and Shelter Cove roads wind 23 miles through territory populated by old hippies and New Agers beetling around in battered vehicles, to the **Lost Coast** at **SHELTER COVE**, set in a tiny bay neatly folded between sea cliffs and headlands. First settled in the 1850s when gold was struck inland, its isolated position at the far end of the Kings Range kept the village small until recent years. Now, thanks to a new airstrip, weekenders arrive in their hordes and modern houses are indiscriminately dotted across the headland. Unfortunately, it's the closest real settlement to the **hiking** and **wildlife** explorations of the surrounding wilderness, which remains inhabited only by deer, river otter, mink, black bear, bald eagles and falcons, so you might find yourself using the *Marina Motel*, 461 Machi Rd (☎707/986-7595; ④), as a base. The **Cape Mendocino Lighthouse**, on Upper Pacific Drive (☎800/262-2683), recently opened to the public after being relocated from 25 miles south. Contact the new Shelter Cove **Information Bureau**, 21 Sea Crest Rd (☎707/986-7069), for the latest developments in this growing town. The 24-mile **Lost Coast Trail** runs along clifftops dotted with four primitive **campgrounds** ($9), all near streams and with access to black-sand beaches. Bring a tidebook, as some points of the trail are impassable at high tide. Another trail takes you to the top of **Kings Peak**, which at 4086ft, is the highest point on the continental United States shoreline.

The heart of redwood country begins in earnest a few miles north of Garberville, along US-101, when you enter the **Humboldt Redwoods State Park** (unrestricted entry; ☎707/946-2409): over 53,000 acres of predominantly virgin timber, protected from lumber companies, make this the largest of the redwood parks – though it is the least used. Thanks to the Save-the-Redwoods League, who have been acquiring land privately for the park, it continues to slowly expand year after year. At the Phillipsville exit, the serpentine **Avenue of the Giants** follows an old stagecoach road, weaving for 32 miles through trees which block all but a few strands of sunlight. This is the habitat of *sequoia sempervirens*, the coast redwood with ancestors dating back to the days of the dinosaur. The avenue parallels US-101, adding at least thirty minutes to your travel time, but several exits to the freeway mean you won't get trapped here if traffic is intolerable. Pick up a free **Auto Tour** guide at the southern or northern entrances. To explore the deepest and quietest **backcountry** areas of the park, which most visitors neglect to do, head west off the Avenue of the Giants at Mattole Road. Back along the main road, small stalls selling lumber products and refreshments dot the course of the highway, chief among them the **Chimney Tree** (daily 9am–5pm; free), a wonderfully corny gift shop built into the burnt-out base of a still-living redwood. There are three **campgrounds** ($16; reserve through Parknet; ☎1-800/444-7275 or call ☎707/946-2409 for information) within the park.

The Avenue follows the south fork of the Eel River, eventually rejoining US-101 at **Pepperwood**. Ten miles before this junction, the turn-off to **HONEYDEW** provides a possible respite from the trees in a region thin on even small settlements. A good base from which to explore the northerly Lost Coast, Honeydew is a postage-stamp town popular with marijuana growers who appreciate its remote location – and the two hundred inches of annual rain that sustains the crops, making the city the wettest in California.

Any visitors awed by the majesty of the redwood forests can soon be brought back down to earth a few miles north at **SCOTIA**, a one-industry town if ever there was one. In this case it is timber, and the stacks and stacks of logs that line the freeway are actually quite a sight. The Pacific Lumber Company has been here since 1869, but with the decline in the industry and the rise in environmental objections to clear-felling of native forests, the company is throwing itself at the tourist market. Boasting of being "The World's Largest Redwood Mill," it attempts to win you over to the loggers' cause on self-guided **sawmill tours** (Mon–Fri 7.30am–2pm; ☎707/764-2222; free), starting at the **Scotia Museum** on Main Street.

Eureka

Eureka may mean "I have found it!," but once you pull into the largest coastal settlement north of San Francisco you may wonder what it was the first settlers were seeking. Near the top of the north coast of California between the Arcata and Humboldt Bays, **EUREKA** feels – despite some rather attractive Victorian mansions – like an industrial, gritty and often foggy lumbermill town, though its fishing industry carries the most economic weight, providing ninety percent of the state's catch of Pacific

Ocean shrimp and Dungeness crab. There's not much by way of sights here, but the city has an abundance of cheap motels along Broadway, a mall-lined strip ubiquitous across America.

Downtown Eureka is fairly short on charm, lit by the neon of motels and generic chain restaurants, and surrounded by rail and shipyards, but the pretty, compact **Old Town**, bounded by C, G, First and Third Streets, at the edge of the bay, does its best to support a fledgling tourist economy. The peeling Victorian buildings and poky bars of the old sailors' district are pretty much rundown – though they do have a certain seedy appeal, along with a handful of lively, mostly Italian restaurants. What few sights there are include the **Carson Mansion**, 143 M St at Second, an opulent Gothic pile built in the 1880s by William Carson, who made and lost fortunes in both timber and oil. Carson designed the project to keep his millworkers busy during a slow period in the industry. It now operates as a private gentleman's club behind its gingerbread facade, and can only be enjoyed from the street. Nearby, at 1410 Second St, the one-room **Maritime Museum** (daily 11am–4pm; donation; ☎707/440-9440) is chock-full of photos, maps and relics from the days when Eureka was a whaling port. **Fort Humboldt State Historic Park**, 3437 Fort Ave at Highland Ave (daily 9am-5pm; free; ☎707/445-6567), gives a look at a restored army fort and not much else, disappointing given that the army general and future president Ulysses S. Grant used it for a head-quarters in 1853.

The collection of Native American applied art at the **Clarke Memorial Museum**, Third and E (Tues–Sat noon–4pm; donation; ☎707/443-1947), can't hold a candle to the stuff at the **Indian Art Gallery**, 241 F St (Mon–Sat 10am–4.30pm; free), a rare opportunity for Native American artists to show and market their works in a gallery setting, and an even rarer opportunity to get your hands on some incredibly good, inexpensive silver jewelry. If dragging yourself around town for these low-key sights doesn't appeal, you might prefer the **Eureka Health and Spa**, 601 Fifth St (☎707/445-2992), with its salt-rubs, tranquility tanks and saunas.

A few minutes by car from Eureka across the Samoa bridge, squashed against the Louisiana-Pacific plywood mill, the tiny community of **SAMOA** is a company town that is the site of the last remaining cookhouse in the West. **The Samoa Cookhouse** (daily 6am–3.30pm & 5–9pm; ☎707/442-1659) was where the lumbermen would come to eat gargantuan meals after a day of felling redwoods, and although the oilskin tablecloths and burly workers have gone, the lumbercamp style remains, making the cookhouse somewhat of an institution. Eating massive portions of red meat at its long tables makes for an entertaining meal.

Practicalities

The collection of **motels** around the Broadway area at the southern (and noisy) end of town make Eureka bearable for a night, but nearby Arcata provides a much better environment and nightlife. Try the *Town House Motel* at 933 Fourth St, which has clean rooms (☎707/443-4536; ②), or the *Downtowner*, 424 Eighth St at E (☎707/443-5061; ②). The *Eagle House Victorian Inn*, at 139 Second St (☎707/444-3344; ④), is a strangely deserted cavernous Victorian relic with surprisingly clean rooms. The dependable *Motel 6*, 1934 Broadway (☎707/445-9631; ③), has an extra phone jack in each room for Internet access. *EconoLodge's Vagabond Inn*, 1630 Fourth St (☎707/443-8041; ③), offers the same, only closer to Old Town. If you want more than just a bed and a shower, head for *An Elegant Victorian Mansion B&B*, 1406 C St at 14th St (☎707/443-6512; ⑥), which, as the name suggests, recalls the opulence and splendor of a bygone era and even offers an architectural tour of the town in a Model "A" Ford. **Campgrounds** line US-101 between Eureka and Arcata; the best is the *KOA* (☎1-800/462-5267 or 707/822-4243; $18 per two-person tent, RV hook-ups $22-$24), a large site with copious amenities five miles north of town at 4050 N US-101.

Transportation links are good: Greyhound, 1603 Fourth St, connects Eureka to San Francisco in the south and Portland in the north twice daily, while Amtrak Thruway buses head out from outside *Stanton's Restaurant* on Fifth and L streets. For getting around town and up the coast as far as Trinidad, Humboldt Transit, 133 V St (☎707/443-0826), has a weekday service. The Eureka **Chamber of Commerce** is at 2112 Broadway (June–Sept Mon–Fri 9am–7pm, Sat & Sun 10am–4pm; Oct–May Mon–Fri 9am–5pm, Sat & Sun 10am–4pm; ☎1-800/356-6381 or 707/442-3738).

In addition to the *Samoa Cookhouse* (see above), **eating** possibilities include the Italian restaurants in the Old Town, notably *Roy's*, 218 D St (☎707/442-4574), where complete meals cost under $15. The *Lost Coast Brewery and Café*, 617 Fourth St at F St (☎707/445-4480), serves large, hearty dishes to a rambunctious crowd of microbrew drinkers and sports fans, while *Adel's*, outside downtown at 1724 Broadway, has basic meat-and-potato meals and salads for under $10, making it a local hangout. The *Humboldt Bay Coffee Company*, 211 F St (☎707/444-3969), ranks as the coast's best coffee shop with its beautiful red-brick interior and sock-it-to-me roasts. It's open until around 8pm and often features live music. For delicious seafood and burgers, you might try *Cafe Waterfront*, 102 F St (☎707/443-9190), where entrées cost around $11. Eureka goes to bed early, giving the city little nightlife to speak of.

Arcata

ARCATA, twelve miles up the coast from Eureka, is by far the more appealing of the two places, focusing on a grassy central plaza that flies an Earth flag under those of the US and California. Beards and Birkenstocks are the norm in this small college town, with a large community of rat-race refugees and Sixties throwbacks, whose presence is manifest in some raunchy bars and an earthy, mellow pace. The beaches north of town are some of the best on the north coast, white-sanded and windswept, and known for their easy hikeability and random parties. But don't dive headlong into the surf without a wetsuit, as the ocean in these parts remains frigid throughout the year.

Arcata itself is centered on a main square of shops and bars, with everything you're likely to want to see and do within easy walking distance. In the middle of the square rests a statue of President McKinley. Originally intended for nearby McKinleyville, it fell off the train on the way and stayed put in Arcata. Just east of the town center, **Humboldt State University** with its nationally known environmental education and natural resource management programs, attracts a decidedly liberal student body, which contributes considerably to Arcata's leftist feel. If you're interested in the college's history and programs, take a free student-led tour, which will give you much more insight than just wandering the campus' unflattering architecture. Tours begin at the Plaza Avenue entrance on weekdays at 10am and 2pm and on Saturday at noon. Call ☎707/826-3011 for information or admissions.

At the foot of I Street, the **Arcata Marsh and Wildlife Sanctuary**, a restored former dump on 150 acres of wetland, is a peaceful place where you can lie on the boardwalk in the sun and listen to the birds. The **Interpretive Center** at the foot of South G Street (Mon–Fri 1–5pm; ☎707/826-2359) runs **guided wildlife walks** (Sat 2pm), as does the Audubon Society, which meets at the very end of I St at 8.30am every Saturday morning. For those who don't have time to explore the Redwood National Park, Arcata's own second-growth **community forest**, accessible east on 14th to Redwood Park Drive, makes a good alternative – a 575-acre, beautiful spot with manageable trails and ideal picnic areas.

If you're around over Memorial Day weekend, don't miss the three-day **Kinetic Sculpture Race**, a spectacular event in which competitors use human-powered contraptions of their own devising to propel themselves over land, water, dunes and marsh from Arcata to Ferndale; call ☎707/786-9259 for information.

Practicalities

Greyhound and Amtrak Thruway **buses** pull into the station at 925 E St between Ninth and Tenth, connecting with the Eureka services going north and south; there's also a weekday Humboldt Transit link with Eureka. The small but helpful **Chamber of Commerce**, 1062 G St (Mon–Fri 10am–4pm, Sat 9am–3pm; ☎707/822-3619), has free maps and lists of **accommodation**.

Motels just out of town on US-101 are lower-priced than the increasingly popular bed and breakfasts, if a little less inviting, and can usually be found for under $55 per night. Three blocks from the bus station, the *Arcata Youth Hostel*, 1390 I St (June 22–Aug 22 only; ☎707/822-9995), is easily the best deal in town with beds for $15 a night. *Motel 6*, at 4755 Valley West Blvd (☎707/822-7061; ③), fills up with parents visiting for gradua-tion in May, but otherwise usually has space. You can get reasonable rooms at the *Fairwinds Motel*, 1674 G St (☎707/822-4824; ②), though if you've a bit more money the *Hotel Arcata*, 708 Ninth St (☎1-800/344-1221 or 707/826-0217; ④), on the town's main square, is a very stylish way to get rid of it. Of the B&Bs, try *The Lady Anne*, an Arcata favorite for years, located between the plaza and the college at 902 14th St (☎707/822-2797; ④). There are several **campgrounds** north of Arcata along the coast, but none within easy reach of town unless you've got a car. *Big Lagoon County Park* (☎707/445-7651), fifteen miles north on Hwy-1, has spaces for $12, as does the nearby *Clam Beach County Park* (☎707/445-7651), four miles north of town on US-101.

Dotted around the plaza and tangential streets, Arcata's **bars** set the town apart. The best of the bunch, *Jambalaya* at 915 H St, draws a long-haired crowd for its nightly diet of R&B, jazz and rock bands. *The Humboldt Brewery*, 856 Tenth St (☎707/826-1734), is a working beer factory with its own bar and low-priced restaurant, where you can sam-ple the preferred stronger, darker brews of Northern California. There's also the café at the Finnish County Sauna and Tubs (☎707/822-2228), on the corner of Fifth and J streets, with live acoustic sets at the weekend, chess on Tuesdays, and tubs in the gar-den for $12 an hour. Good **restaurants** are in shorter supply, though *Wildflower Café and Bakery*, 1604 G St (☎707/822-0360), turns out good, cheap organic meals with great breakfasts, and *Abruzzi*, 780 Eighth St (☎707/826-2345), serves top-quality Italian dinners at moderate prices. Facing US-101 on 1603 G St, **Muddy Waters Coffee Company** (☎707/826-2233) supports local music with weekly free concerts and is a pleasant place to relax and mingle with students.

Around Arcata

If you've got a car, take time to explore the coastline just north of Arcata along US-101. **Moonstone Beach**, about ten miles north of town, is a vast, sandy strip that, save for the odd beachcomber, remains empty during the day, and by night heats up with gui-tar-strumming student parties that rage for as long as the bracing climate allows. **Trinidad Harbor**, a few miles further on, is a good stop for a drink, to nose around the small shops or just sit down by the sea wall and watch the fishing boats being tossed about beyond the harbor. Locals rave about the harbor's **Seascape Pier Restaurant** (summer 7am-10pm; winter 7am-8.30pm; ☎707/677-3762), whose menu of fresh fish, steaks and pasta tastes all the more delicious given its waterfront location. **Patrick's Point State Park**, five miles further north, sports an agate beach atop rocky coastal bluffs and gives tours of a recreated Yurok village by appointment (☎707/677-3570). The park also offers reasonably secluded **camping** for $16 (reserve through Parknet ☎1-800/444-7275).

A more adventurous – some would say insane – destination is **Hoopa Valley Indian Reservation**, sixty miles inland. In past years the site of often violent confrontation between Native Americans and whites over fishing territory, Hoopa is now seen by some as the badlands of Humboldt and few take the time to check out the valley. There's a dead, lawless feel about the place, the locals hanging around listlessly outside their caravans or roaring up and down the dirt tracks on their Harley-Davidsons. Even the bar and bingo hall, once the lifeblood of the community, have been closed down as a result of alcohol-induced violence. The nervous will want to move on quickly, but if you're here in the last week in July you should make an effort to catch the All Indian Rodeo, which is held southwest of the village. Otherwise it is enough to visit the **Hoopa Tribal Museum** (Mon–Fri 8am–5pm, Sat 10am–4pm; donation; ☎530/ 493-2900) – full of crafts, baskets and jewelry of the Natinixwe (aka Hupa) and Yurok tribes.

To get to the reservation, take Hwy-299 west out of Arcata for forty miles until you hit **WILLOW CREEK** – self-proclaimed gateway to "**Bigfoot Country** – then take Hwy-96, the "Bigfoot Scenic Byway," north. Reports of giant 350- to 800-pound humanoids wandering the forests of northwestern California have circulated since the late nineteenth century, fueled by long-established Indian legends, though they weren't taken seriously until 1958, when a road maintenance crew found giant footprints in a remote area near Willow Creek. Photos were taken and the Bigfoot story went worldwide, and there have been more than fifty separate sightings of Bigfoot prints since then. At the crossroads in Willow Creek stands a huge wooden replica of the prehistoric-looking apeman, who in recent years has added kidnapping to his list of alleged activities. Beside the statue, a small **Chamber of Commerce** (summer daily 9am–4pm; irregular hours rest of year; ☎530/629-2693) has details of Bigfoot's escapades, and information on the **whitewater rafting** that is done on the Smith, Klamath and Trinity rivers near here. Among the numerous rafting companies in the area, two are based in Willow Creek – Aurora River Adventures (☎1-800/562-8475 or 530/629-3843) and Bigfoot Rafting Company (☎1-800/722-2223 or ☎530/629-2263), both offering trips from $40. Otherwise, the town comprises a handful of grocery stores, diners and cheap motels such as the *Willow Creek Motel*, Hwy-96 (☎530/629- 2115; ②). Just north of town, the **Lower Trinity Ranger Station** (summer Mon–Sat 8am–4.30pm; rest of year Mon–Fri 8am–4.30pm; ☎530/629-2118) handles camping and wilderness permits for the immediate surroundings. Continue east on Hwy-299 and you'll arrive in the Weaverville/Shasta area (see p.634), as well as the super-speedy Interstate-5.

The Redwood National and State parks

Way up in the top left-hand corner of California the landscape is almost too spectacular for words, and the long drive up here is rewarded with a couple of tiny towns and thick, dense redwood forests perfect for hiking and camping. Some thirty miles north of Arcata, **Orick** marks the southernmost end of this landscape, a contiguous strip of forest jointly managed as the **REDWOOD NATIONAL AND STATE PARKS** (unrestricted access; free), a massive area that stretches up into Del Norte County at the very northernmost point of California, ending at the dull town of **Crescent City**. The fragmented Redwoods National Park and the three state parks which plug the gaps – Prairie Creek Redwoods, Del Norte Coast Redwoods and Jedediah Smith Redwoods – together contain some of the tallest trees in the world; the pride of California's forestland, especially between June and September when every school in the state seems to organize its summer camp here. Increasingly, and despite being designated a World Heritage Site and International Biosphere Reserve, it's becoming a controversial area where campers wake to the sound of chainsaws and huge lumber trucks roaring up and down the highway. Even the private grove where *Return of the Jedi* was filmed has been chopped. Despite this and other sustained cutting, local loggers are still dissatisfied, claiming that they've lost much of the prime timber they relied on to make their living before the days of the parks.

One word of warning: **bears** and **mountain lions** inhabit this area, and you should heed the warnings in "Basics" on p.52.

Practicalities

The parks' 58,000 acres divide into distinct areas: **Redwood National Park**, southwest of the **Orick Area**; the **Prairie Creek Redwoods State Park**, south of the riverside town of **Klamath**; and the area in the far north around the **Del Norte** and **Jedediah Smith State Parks**, in the environs of Crescent City in Del Norte County. The **park headquarters** are in Crescent City, at 1111 Second St (daily 8am–5pm; ☎ 1-800/423-6101 or ☎707/464-6101), but the **visitor centers** and **ranger stations** throughout the parks are far better for maps and information, including up-to-date hiking conditions and the weather forecast. Most useful is the **Redwood National Park Information Center** (daily 9am–6pm; ☎707/488-3461), right by the southern entrance before you get to Orick.

The two daily Greyhound **buses** that run along US-101 to Crescent City will, if asked, stop (and if you're lucky can be flagged down) along forested stretches of the highway, and there's a twice-daily Redwood Coast Transit service looping out from Crescent City and back. Still, unless you want to single out a specific area and stay there (not the best way to see the parks), you'll be stuck without a **car**.

As for accommodation, **camping** is your best bet. You can stay at the many primitive and free campgrounds all over the parks; for more comfort, head for the sites we've mentioned in the text below (all $16), along with a hostel and a couple of motel recommendations. If you're really desperate, get onto US-101 and look for **motels** around Crescent City.

Orick and Tall Trees Grove

As the southernmost, and therefore most used, entrance to the Redwood National Park, the **Orick** area is always busy. Its major attraction is **Tall Trees Grove**, home of one of the world's tallest trees – a mightily impressive specimen that stands at some 367 feet. (The tallest tree in the world, only a bit less than a foot taller, was recently discovered in an inaccessible grove in Mendocino County). The easiest way to get to the Tall Trees Grove, avoiding too much picking amongst the lush undergrowth, is to drive yourself, although you will need to get a free access permit at the visitor center, which also has a free trail guide that explains why some redwood cutting is being done to balance the damages inflicted on old growth in the past. Some people prefer to hike the 8.5-mile **Redwood Creek Trail** (permit needed if staying overnight in the backcountry) from near Orick: take a right off US-101 onto Bald Hills Road, then, 600 yards along, fork off to the picnic area where the trail starts. The bridge, 1.5 miles away, is passable in summer only. If you can make it from here, a bit further east another trail turns north off Bald Hills Road and winds for half a mile to **Lady Bird Johnson Grove** – a collection of trees dedicated to former US President LBJ's wife, Lady "Bird" Johnson, a big lover of flora and fauna. A mile-long self-guided trail winds through the grove of these giant patriarchs. On the western side of US-101, across from the entrance to the Redwood Creek Trail, begins the **Coastal Trail**, which follows the coastline and takes backpackers up the entire length of all three state parks. An unpaved road leads in for a few hundred yards before petering out into the hikers only path.

In **ORICK** itself (actually two miles north of the entrance and ranger station), a couple of **stores** and **cafés**, along with a **motel**, string alongside US-101. Of several places, the *Palm Cafe*, (☎707/488-3381) serves cheap burgers and sandwiches. It also has a motel with rooms from $30. You might also stop just up the road at the *Lumberjack* for a game of pool and an ice-cold beer. Three miles north of Orick, the narrow gravel

Davison Road turns coastwards for a bumpy eight miles to **Gold Bluffs Beach** (dawn–dusk) where you can camp. The $5 per vehicle fee also covers **Fern Canyon**, visited on an easy three-quarter-mile trail, its 45-foot walls slippery with mosses, fern and lichen.

Prairie Creek State Park and Klamath

Of the three state parks within the Redwood National Park area, **PRAIRIE CREEK** is the most varied and popular. Bear and elk often roam in plain sight, and you can take a ranger-led **tour** of the wild, solidly populated redwood forest. Check with the **ranger station** (summer daily 8am–6pm; rest of year daily 8am–5pm; ☎707/488-2171) for details. Whether you choose to go independently, or opt for a tour, main features of the park include the meadows of **Elk Prairie** in front of the ranger station, where herds of Roosevelt elk, massive beasts weighing up to four hundred pounds, roam freely, protected from poachers. (Remember that elk, like all wildlife, are unpredictable and should not be approached.) Day use is $5 per vehicle but you can park beside the road and wander at will. There's a **campground** ($16) on the edge of Elk Prairie, at the hub of a network of hiking trails. If you're pressed for time, there are some car-accessible routes through the woods. Just south of the ranger station, on the east side of US-101, is the entrance to Lost Man Creek, an unpaved 1.5-mile round-trip drive into a grove that passes by a cascade. To enter Prairie Creek Redwoods State Park, take the **Newton B. Drury Scenic Byway** off US-101 north of Lost Man Creek. Even if you're just passing through, the eight-mile byway is a worthwhile trip deep into the trees. A mile north of the ranger station the magnificent **Big Tree Wayside** redwood, more than three hundred feet tall and, at over 21ft in diameter, one of the fattest of the coastal redwoods, overlooks the road. North of the Big Tree Wayside and before the byway rejoins US-101, the rough gravel Coastal Drive branches off to the west following the Coastal Trail for 7.5 miles, leading to High Bluff Overlook and camping at Flint Ridge.

Prairie Creek also has a couple of **restaurants** on the southern approach on US-101. All do a good line in wild boar roasts, elk steaks and the like, as well as a more traditional menu of burgers and breakfasts. *Rolf's Park Café* (☎707/488-3841), on US-101 by the Fern Canyon turn-off, is one of the best, with outdoor seating and German entrées.

Klamath Area

KLAMATH, in Del Norte county, isn't technically part of the Redwood area nor, by most definitions, does it qualify as a town as most of the buildings were washed away when the nearby Klamath River flooded in 1964. Nonetheless, there are spectacular coastal views from trails where the Klamath River meets the ocean, famed salmon and steelhead fishing to be had in the river itself, a few decent accommodation options and, for a bit of fun, the **Trees of Mystery** (daily 8am–6pm; $6.50; ☎707/638-3389) on US-101, where you'll notice two huge wooden sculptures of Paul Bunyan and Babe, his blue ox. You can climb through, jump over and scoot under the trees – with the exception of the most impressive specimen of all, the **Cathedral Tree**, where nine trees have grown from one root structure to form a spooky circle. Enterprising Californians hold wedding services here throughout the year. Still, the most spectacular scenery in Klamath is not the trees, but the ocean: take Requa Road about three quarters of a mile down to the estuary, to a point known as the **Klamath Overlook**, from where, once the fog has burnt off, there is an awe-inspiring view of the sea and coast. From here, you can pick up the Coastal Trail on foot, which leads north for ten miles along some of California's most remote beach, ending at Endert's Beach in Crescent City.

The *Klamath Inn*, 451 Requa Rd (☎707/482-8205; ④), offers some of the best **accommodation** around. There are the simple cabins at *Woodland Villa*, a mile and a half north of Requa (☎707/482-2081; ②), and small cottages with kitchenettes at *Camp Marigold* (☎1-800/621-8513 or ☎707/482-3585; ①), one mile south of the Trees of Mystery. *The Rhode's End*, 115 Trobitz Rd (☎707/482-1654; ⑤), offers B&B accommodation along the Klamath River, and the beautifully situated *HI-Redwood National Park Hostel* three miles further along US-101(☎707/482-8265) has dorm beds for $12–14, whether you are a member or not. A couple of miles yet further north is the free, primitive *DeMartin* **campground**.

Crescent City and around

The northernmost outposts of the Redwood National Park, the Del Norte and Jedediah Smith State Parks, sit either side of **CRESCENT CITY**, a woebegone place wiped out by a typhoon thirty years ago with little to recommend it other than its proximity to the parks. That said, the city is the half-way point on US-101 between San Francisco (349 miles south) and Portland, Oregon (355 miles north), and is often used as a rest stop.

Greyhound **buses** stop at 1125 Northcrest Drive, and the **visitor center** is at 1001 Front St (Mon–Fri 9am–6pm; also June–Oct Sat & Sun 9am–5.30pm; ☎1-800/343-8300 or ☎707/464-3174). Of several passable **motels** on US-101, try the *Super 8 Motel*, 685 US-101 S (☎707/464-4111; ②), the *Crescent Beach Motel*, on the beach two miles south of town at 1455 US-101 S (☎707/464-5436; ①), or the Pacific Motor Hotel, 440 US-101 N (☎1-800/323-7917 or ☎707/464-4141; ②). For **eating**, try the moderately priced pasta and vegetarian dishes at *Bistro Gardens and Salad Gallery*, 938 K St (☎707/464-5627), or the seafood and steaks at the *Harbor View Grotto*, 150 Starfish Way (☎707/464-3815). Considerably cheaper is *Los Compadres*, a Mexican diner on US-101 opposite the marina.

While here, take an hour to visit the **Battery Point Lighthouse** (June–Sept Wed–Sun 10am–4pm; tours sporadically during low tide; $2), reached by a causeway from the western end of town. The oldest working lighthouse on the West Coast, it houses a collection of artifacts from the *Brother Jonathan*, wrecked off Point St George in the 1870s. Because of this loss, the **St George Lighthouse**, the tallest and most expensive in the US, was built six miles north of Crescent City.

Del Norte and Jedediah Smith State Parks

Del Norte State Park, seven miles south of Crescent City, is worth visiting less for its redwood forests (you've probably had enough of them by now anyway), than its fantastic beach area and hiking trails, most of which are an easy two miles or so along the coastal ridge where the redwoods meet the sea. From May to July, wild rhododendrons and azaleas shoot up everywhere, laying a floral blanket across the park's floor. **Jedediah Smith State Park**, nine miles east of Crescent City, is named after the European explorer who was the first white man to trek overland from the Mississippi to the Pacific in 1828, before being killed by Comanche tribes in Kansas in 1831. Not surprisingly, his name is everywhere: no less than eighteen separate redwood groves are dedicated to his memory. Sitting squatly on the south fork of the Smith River, the park attracts many people to canoe downstream or, more quietly, sit on the riverbank and fish. Of the hiking trails, the **Stout Grove Trail** is the most popular, a one-hour flat walk leading down to a most imposing Goliath – a 345-foot tall, twenty-foot diameter redwood.

If you're heading further east and can't face more highway, you could opt for the painfully slow, but scenic six-mile route that follows Howland Hill Road from Crescent City through the forest to the **Hiouchi Information Center** (May–Oct 9am–5pm) on Hwy-199, about five miles away. Branching off this are several blissfully short and easy trails (roughly half a mile) that are quieter than the routes through the major parts of the park. You can also access the **Little Bald Hills Trail** east of Hiouchi, which traces a strenuous ten-mile hike that should take about eight hours. You'll also find the Jedediah Smith Redwoods **campground** (reserve through Parknet (☎1-800/444-7275; $14), and **picnicking** facilities at the end of the Howland Hill Road.

THE NORTHERN INTERIOR

As big as Ohio, yet with a population of only 250,000, the **northern interior** of California is about as remote as the state gets. Cut off from the coast by the **Shasta Cascade** range, it's a region dominated by forests, lakes, some fair-sized mountains – and two thirds of the state's precipitation. It's largely uninhabited, and, for the most part, infrequently visited, which makes a spin up here all the more worthwhile. Locals take the time to chat and point out areas to explore, and the region's efficient network of hiking trails and roads usually remains empty of traffic jams.

I-5 leads through the very middle of this near wilderness, forging straight up the **Sacramento Valley** through acres of olive and nut trees, and past the college towns of **Chico** to **Redding**: the latter makes a useful base, with cheap lodging, from where you can venture out on loop trips a day or so at a time. Most accessible, immediately west and north of Redding, the **Whiskeytown-Shasta-Trinity National Recreation Area** is a series of three lakes and forests set aside for what can be heavily subscribed public use, especially in summer when it's hard to avoid the camper vans, windsurfers, jet-skiers and packs of happy holidaymakers. A better bet lies east at **Lassen Volcanic National Park**, a stunning alpine landscape of sulphur springs and peaks. Traveling on state highways north of here through national forests reveals numerous roadside surprises, including towering **Burney Falls** and access points to the **Pacific Crest Trail**, the 1200-mile path from Canada to Mexico.

Further north, the crowds swell a bit in the shadows of **Mount Shasta**, a 14,000-foot volcano whose reputation as both spiritual convergence point and climbing challenge brings together an interesting cast of characters in the small town of the same name. Train buffs should stop in the historical railroad town of **Dunsmuir**, just south of Shasta, and anglers will find trout streams filled to the gills all around the area. North of Shasta, the mountains and pines give way to cattle and caves, the latter part of the stunning lava fields of **Lava Beds National Monument**, the site of one of the saddest Indian wars in US history. Trails and monuments mark the battle's history, while all around the desolate plain, migrating birds rest up in a gigantic sanctuary before resuming their journeys on the **Pacific Flyway**.

It's the usual story with **public transportation**: reasonably frequent Greyhound and Amtrak Thruway buses connect San Francisco and Sacramento to Portland via I-5, stopping off at the Sacramento Valley towns and Redding on the way, and trains from Oakland stop in Redding and Chico. But neither route provides anything close to comprehensive access to the area, and if you're going to come here at all it should be in a **car**. Anything worth seeing lies at least five miles from the nearest bus stop. The area is too big and the towns too far apart to make traveling by bus even faintly enjoyable.

The Sacramento Valley

The **Sacramento Valley** lays fair claim to being California's most uninteresting region; a flat, largely agricultural corridor of small, sleepy towns and endless vistas of wheat fields and fruit trees. By far the best thing to do is pass straight through on I-5 – the half-empty, straight and speedy freeway cuts an almost two-hundred-mile-long swathe through the region, and you could forge right ahead to the more enticing far north quite painlessly in half a day. If you're coming from San Francisco, save time by taking the I-505 byway around Sacramento.

Chico

Charming little **CHICO**, about midway between Sacramento and Redding and some twenty miles east of I-5 from the Orland exit, is a good stop-off if you don't want to attempt to cover the whole valley from top to bottom in one day, or if you're here to visit Lassen Volcanic National Park (see p.627) and need somewhere to stay. Home to **Chico State University**, a grassy sandal-wearing institution named "Best Party School in the Country" by *Playboy* magazine a few years ago, Chico was once the grounds surrounding the mansion of General John Bidwell, one of the first men to cash in on the Gold Rush. As such, the city's traditional layout around a plaza, numerous college eateries and surrounding expanse of parkland make it something of an oasis compared to the dusty fields and sleepy towns beyond.

Arrival, information and getting around

Chico is right on Hwy-99. **Trains** (and Amtrak Thruway buses) stop at the unattended station at Fifth and Orange, as do Greyhound **buses**. The *Coast Starlight* train, from Los Angeles to Seattle, stops here once a day, though in the middle of the night. Greyhounds serving cities north and south along I-5 stop more frequently, about five times a day. See schedules posted at the station.

Chico's **Chamber of Commerce**, 300 Salem St (Mon–Fri 9am–5pm; Sat 10am-3pm; ☎ 1-800/852-8570 or 530/891-5556), has a terrific supply of information, from pamphlets

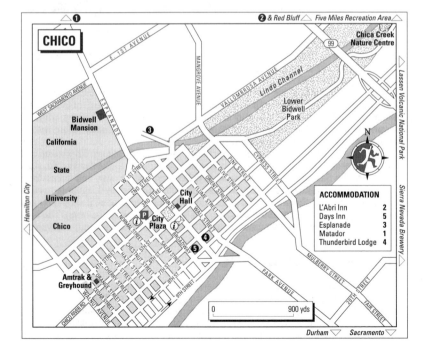

CHICO

Chica Creek Nature Centre

Lassen Volcanic National Park

Bidwell Mansion

California

State

University

Chico

Hamilton City

Lower Bidwell Park

Lindo Channel

Sierra Nevada Brewery

City Hall

City Plaza

Amtrak & Greyhound

ACCOMMODATION

L'Abri Inn	2
Days Inn	5
Esplanade	3
Matador	1
Thunderbird Lodge	4

0   900 yds

Durham ▽   Sacramento ▽

outlining a historical walking tour through downtown to mountain bike trails and swimming hole locations nearby. They also publish updated lists of lodging options, with prices. To find out **what's on**, consult the free Chico *News & Review*, published every Thursday and available all over town, or tune in to KZFR (90.1 FM) or KCHO (91.7 FM), both broadcasting eclectic local community radio.

Parking is only $0.25 an hour downtown in the new lot between Salem and Broadway, near the Chamber of Commerce. The majority of places you are likely to want to visit are within walking distance of the town center, but the trails in Bidwell Park need to be biked to be appreciated. You can **rent** one for $20 per day from Campus Bicycles right off the plaza at 330 Main St (☎530/345-2081). The shop also provides free maps for cyclists.

Accommodation

Chico has much more in the way of **accommodation** than it does in sights, though for **camping** you'll need to head to the Plumas National Forest to the east or Lassen Volcanic National Park. Motels are everywhere in town, particularly in the Main Street and Broadway area, and there are a couple of good B&Bs.

Days Inn, 740 Broadway (☎530/343-3286). About the cheapest downtown motel, just two blocks south of the Plaza, with refrigerators in rooms and a pool. ②.

Esplanade, 620 The Esplanade (☎530/345-8084). A particularly good value B&B right across from the Bidwell Mansion. The beds are so high you almost need to pole-vault onto them, and tasty breakfasts are served on the back veranda. ④.

L'Abri Inn, 4350 Hwy-99 (☎1-800/489-3319 or 530/893-0824). Five miles north of town, this place comprises three rooms in a ranch-style home with a serene country atmosphere. Enjoy a sumptuous breakfast, then go out and pet the barnyard animals. ④.

Matador, 1934 The Esplanade (☎530/342-7543). A pretty Spanish Revival building ten blocks north of the Plaza; the tasteful rooms have individual tiling. Set around a courtyard, with palms shading one of Chico's largest pools, this is one of the town's best deals. ②.

Thunderbird Lodge, 715 Main St (☎530/343-7911). Decent and low-cost motel two blocks from the Plaza. Some rooms have refrigerators and coffee-makers. ②.

The Town

Chico doesn't have much by way of sights, but strolling the leafy streets, college campus and shady riverside feels great after the monotonous drive up I-5. You might try the three-story **Bidwell Mansion** at 525 The Esplanade, the continuation of Main Street (Mon-Fri 12pm-5pm, Sat-Sun 10am-5pm; tours on the hour until 4pm; $3). Built in 1868 by the town's founder, General Bidwell, it's an attractive enough Italian country villa, filled with family paraphernalia visited on 45-minute anecdotal tours. It's reasonably interesting, but **Bidwell Park** (most sections open daylight hours; free) is a more pleasurable place to spend your time. Extending from the center of the town for ten miles to the northeast, this is a tongue of semi-wilderness and oak parkland where, incidentally, the first *Robin Hood* film, starring Errol Flynn, was made. No road runs right through the park, and it is too large to cover on foot, so cycling (see bike rental above) is by far the best way to explore. The most heavily used areas are around the recreation areas at One-Mile Dam and Five-Mile Dam, both reached off Vallombrosa Avenue, and Cedar Grove, reached off E Eighth Street, but a half-hour stroll into Upper Park will leave most of the regulars behind. Students frequent the **swimming holes** on Big Chico Creek in the Upper Park, including Bear Hole, Salmon Hole and Brown's Hole, which has a small rope swing. For the holes, take Vallombrosa Avenue all the way east until it dead ends into Manzanita Avenue. Turn left on Manzanita, and then right on Wildwood Avenue. Follow the road past the golf course, where it turns into gravel, and then on to the creek. Driving is the preferred method of getting out here, though biking the three miles from the center of town is rewarded with a cooling plunge into the creek.

Back in town, vintage American car fans will enjoy **Cruces Classic Auto Sales**, downtown on 720 Main St, a commercial showroom with a walk-through museum showing some of the really rare models that are brought here to be restored. Or visit the remodeled **Sierra Nevada Brewing Company**, 1075 E 20th St (☎530/893-3520), which gives free and fairly cursory twenty-minute tours of the plant (Tues–Fri & Sun 2.30pm, Saturday noon–3pm) and the chance to sample each of the ten or so brews on tap for under $5.

From May-September, the **Chico Heat** amateur **baseball** team play on the Chico State campus, a fun event that brings out hundreds of locals. Check with the Chamber of Commerce for schedules, or call ☎530/343-4328 (*www.chicoheat.com*) for tickets, which average $6 each. The **Farmers' Market** closes off downtown every summer Thursday at 5.30pm for three hours of produce sales. Come for the almonds and other fresh nuts grown nearby. The **Gold Cup Races** at the Silver Dollar Speedway Speedway (☎916/969-7484) brings Chico's biggest weekend. The stock car extravaganza, which takes place on the third weekend of September, fills all area hotels.

Ten miles outside Chico, south on Hwy-99 then east on Skyway to Humburg/Honey Run Road, the **Honey Run Covered Bridge** is one of the few remaining covered bridges in California. You can't drive on it, but its position in Butte Creek Canyon over a riffling river leads to peaceful walking and swimming opportunities. Further east, the apple orchards in Paradise were used as a location for *Gone With the Wind*.

Eating and nightlife

Chico also does itself proud when it comes to **food**. Being a California State University town, there are many excellent places aimed at the younger (and poorer) customer, as well as a handful of lively **bars,** that feature live music by national acts. It's noticeably quieter when school's out, but on summer Friday evenings, **free concerts** by talented locals draw the crowds to the Downtown Park Plaza, beginning at 7pm.

The Brickworks, Second and Wall (☎530/895-7700). Chico's live music spot, hosting national touring acts and local bands. On nights without live music, sample the dance club with DJ music playing either country, progressive or alternative music.

Café Sandino, 817 Main St (☎530/894-6515). Small vegetarian café with plenty of low-fat and vegan dishes, and good *tamales* for under $5. Open until 9pm, closed Sun.

Cory's, 230 W Third St (☎530/345-2955). Excellent breakfasts and lunches, featuring sandwiches served on freshly baked bread.

Gashouse Pizza, 1444 Park Ave (☎530/345-6602). Old auto repair shop turned hole-in-the-wall pizza joint that serves far and away the best pizza in town. Open 4.30pm.

Jack's Restaurant, 540 Main St (☎530/343-8383). 24-hr diner, a bit on the greasy side, but good for breakfasts and late-night munchies.

Jasco's California Cafe, 300 Broadway (☎530/899-8075). Salads, sandwiches, and gourmet pizza are all top notch and reasonable. The vegetarian sandwiches are especially delicious. Lunch and dinner only.

La Hacienda Inn, 2635 Esplanade (☎530/893-8270). *Bon Appetit* and *Gourmet* magazines have done features on this Mexican restaurant's special pink sauce, known to locals as "Heroin Sauce" for its addictive sweet flavor. Try it on a tostada, but be warned, you may not be able to stop.

LaSalle's, 229 Broadway (☎530/893-1891). The place to consume large quantities of beer, play pool, and listen to live rock bands.

Madison Bear Garden, 316 W Second St (☎530/891-1639). A place for swigging beer with students from the nearby campus. Burgers, buffalo wings and the like are also served.

Riley's, Fifth and Ivy (☎530/343-7459). Catch the ballgame on one of the many TV screens and hang out with the excited students at the most popular bar in Chico.

Sierra Nevada Brewing Company, 1075 E 20th St (☎530/893-3520). The bar food is unexceptional, but the pale ale, porter, stout and seasonal brews are a strong draw. There's usually jazz on Mondays and good local bands some weekends.

Thai Chada, downstairs at 117b W Second St (☎530/342-7121). Authentic, and predominantly vegetarian, Thai cuisine at very reasonable prices, especially at lunchtime. Closed Sun.

Tres Hombres Taco Bar, 100 Broadway (☎530/342-0425). Large restaurant popular with students for the wide selection of margaritas. Reasonably priced burritos, quesadillas, tostadas, and tacos in a fun environment. Dinner until 10pm every night, drinks until 2am on weekends. Live jazz Sunday afternoons.

Red Bluff and Corning

RED BLUFF, 45 miles north of Chico on Hwy-99, holds little of interest to travelers save for its proximity to Lassen Volcanic National Park. The Greyhound **bus** stops in front of the *Salt Creek Deli*, at the junction of Hwy-36 and Antelope Road (Hwy-99), but then heads into town for the junction with I-5, leaving no reliable form of public transportation into Lassen itself. Despite its favorable location on the Sacramento River, Red Bluff today is known more as a gas-and-lodging stop before the 50-mile drive into Lassen along Hwy-36 or the push north to Redding and Mount Shasta on I-5. If you find yourself staying over, there's a reasonable selection of $30-a-night motels along Main Street – among them the *Crystal Motel*, 333 S Main St (☎530/527-1021; ②), and the *Travelodge*, overlooking the river at 38 Antelope Rd (☎530/527-6020; ③) – and a handful of diners and burger joints in town. You may consider visiting the **Kelly-Grigs House Museum**, 311 Washington St (Thurs–Sun 1–4pm; donation), where there's an exhibit on Ishi, "the last wild Indian," who appeared out of what is now the Ishi Wilderness in 1911 and was feted until his death in 1916. Pick up more information from the **Chamber of Commerce**, 100 Main St (Mon 8.30am–4pm, Tues– Thurs 8.30am–5pm, Fri 8.30am–4.30pm; ☎530/527-6220).

If you bypass Chico and enter Red Bluff from the south on I-5, a better stop for gas and provisions is **CORNING**, home of the world-renowned **Olive Pit**, 2156 Solano St, just east off the Interstate (☎530/824-4667). This only-in-America store and restaurant sells jars of olives, olive oil, garlic, almonds, and has a good grill and ice cream bar as well. Martini lovers can get bottles of olive juice mixer, and a free tasting bar allows a trip around the world via olives – from Brine Greek wholes to Napa Valley Wine queens to French pitted and Sicilian cracked. The almond-stuffed greens are a must, and pint jars average $2.50.

Lassen Volcanic National Park

About fifty miles over gently sloping plains east from Red Bluff on Hwy-36, the 106,000 acres that make up the pine forests, crystal-green lakes and boiling thermal pools of the **LASSEN VOLCANIC NATIONAL PARK** are one of the most unearthly parts of California. A forbidding climate, which brings up to fifty feet of snowfall each year, keeps the area pretty much uninhabited, with the roads all blocked by snow and (apart from a brief June to October season) completely deserted. It lies at the southerly limit of the Cascades, a low, broad range which stretches six hundred miles north to Mount Garibaldi in British Colombia and is characterized by high volcanoes forming part of the Pacific Circle of Fire. Dominating the park at over 10,000ft is a fine example, **Mount Lassen** itself, which – although quiet in recent years – erupted in 1914, beginning a cycle of outbursts which climaxed in 1915 when the peak blew an enormous mushroom cloud some seven miles skyward, tearing the summit into chunks that landed as far away as Reno. Although eighty years of geothermal inactivity have since made the mountain a safe and fascinating place, scientists predict that of all the Californian volcanoes, Lassen is the likeliest to blow again.

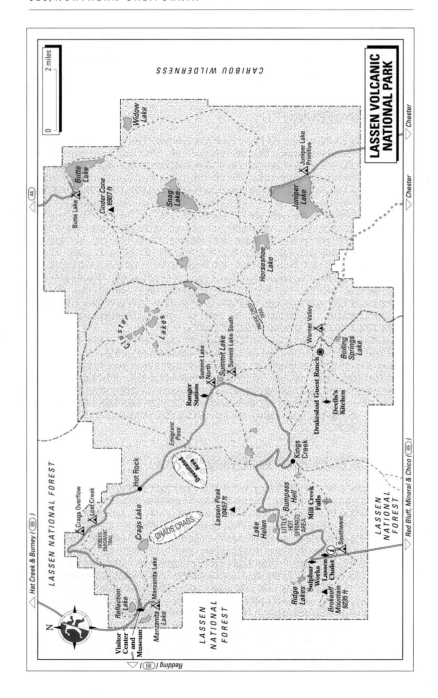

LASSEN VOLCANIC NATIONAL PARK

CARIBOU WILDERNESS

2 miles

0

N

Redding (89)

Hat Creek & Burney (89)

Red Bluff, Mineral & Chico (89)

Chester

Chester

44

LASSEN NATIONAL FOREST

LASSEN NATIONAL FOREST

LASSEN NATIONAL FOREST

Visitor Center and Museum

Reflection Lake

Manzanita Lake

Manzanita Lake

Crags Overflow

Lost Creek

Crags Lake

CHAOS CRAGS

Hot Rock

Emigrant Pass

Devastated Area

NOBLES EMIGRANT TRAIL

Lassen Peak 10457 ft

Lake Helen

LITTLE HOT SPRINGS AREA

Bumpass Hell

Mill Creek Falls

Kings Creek

Sulphur Works

Ridge Lakes

Lassen Chalet

Southwest

Brokeoff Mountain 9235 ft

Ranger Station

Summit Lake North

Summit Lake South

Cluster Lakes

Widow Lake

Butte Lake

Butte Lake

Cinder Cone 6907 ft

Snag Lake

Horseshoe Lake

Juniper Lake

Juniper Lake Primitive

PACIFIC CREST TRAIL

Warner Valley

Drakesbad Guest Ranch

Devil's Kitchen

Boiling Springs Lake

Arrival and information

Lassen is always open ($10 per vehicle for seven days, $5 per hiker or biker), but you'll have a big job ahead of you if planning to get in or around without a car. During the winter, when the roads in the park are almost always shut down due to snow, a car won't do you much good either – snowshoes and cross-country skis are popular modes of transportation. Public transportation really isn't an option, seeing as the "mail truck" of Mount Lassen Motor Transit (Mon–Sat from 8am; ☎530/529-2722) from Red Bluff only reaches **MINERAL**, some eight miles short of the park's southwestern entrance. From Mineral, Hwy-89 leads through Lassen to the northern entrance at the junction of Hwy-44 and Hwy-89 near Manzanita Lake.

The Park Service has its **headquarters** in Mineral (daily 8am–4.30pm; PO Box 100, Mineral, CA 96063; ☎530/595-4444), where you can get free maps and information (there's a box outside when it's closed, and they'll leave your backcountry permits here if you arrive late), including the *Lassen Park Guide*. The main **visitor center** (summer daily 9am–5pm; ☎530/595-4444 ext. 5180) is at Manzanita Lake, just inside the northern entrance, and occupies the same building as the Loomis Museum (see p.631).

CAMPING IN AND AROUND LASSEN

During the few months of the year when conditions are suitable for camping, this is by far the best accommodation option. All **developed campgrounds** in the park are listed below and operate on a first-come-first-served basis; not a problem except on midsummer weekends. Most remain open July-September. Remember that Lassen is Bear Country; follow the posted precautions for food and waste storage, and make your presence known when hiking.

Primitive camping requires a free **wilderness permit** obtainable in advance from the park headquarters in Mineral (see above), or in person from the visitor centers and entrance stations. There is no self-registration and chosen sites must be a mile from developed campgrounds and a quarter of a mile from most specific sites of interest. In the surrounding **Lassen National Forest**, camping is permitted anywhere, though you'll need a free permit to operate a cooking stove or to light a fire; these are sometimes refused in the dry summer months. In addition, there are a couple of dozen developed sites strung along the highways within thirty miles of Lassen, most charging between $5 and $11.

Juniper Lake ($10; 6800ft). In the far southeastern corner of the park, with good hiking trails nearby and swimming in the lake. Drinking water must be boiled or treated.

Manzanita Lake ($14; 5900ft). By far the largest of the Lassen campgrounds and the only one with a camp store (8am–8pm), firewood for sale ($6), 24-hour showers (bring quarters), and a laundry. Rangers run interpretive programs from here. Open May 28 to September 27.

Southwest ($12; 6700ft). Small tent-only campground by the southwest entrance on Hwy-89 with walk-in sites, water and fire rings.

Summit Lake ($12–14; 6700ft). The pick of the Hwy-89 campgrounds, right in the center of the park and at the hub of numerous hiking trails. It's divided into two sections, the northern half equipped with flush toilets, the southern half only vaults. There's swimming in the lake for the brave.

Warner Valley ($12; 5700ft). Off Hwy-89 in the south of the park, this is a beautiful site, but its distance from the road makes it only worth heading for if you're planning extended hiking in the region.

Accommodation and eating

The only way to **stay** inside the Lassen park is to camp (see box), but even in August night temperatures can hover around freezing, and many people prefer to stay in one of the resorts and lodges that pepper the surrounding forest. To be sure of a room in the popular summer months, it pays to book well ahead. For **food**, you don't have an awful lot to choose from. There's a reasonable general store at Manzanita Lake campground (see overleaf), and *Lassen Chalet* has a surprisingly good café (daily 9am–6pm), but beyond that you'll have to go outside the park.

Hat Creek Resort, Hwy-89, Old Station, 27 miles northwest of the northern entrance (☎530/335-7121). A complex of motel units and fancier cabins with kitchens (two-day minimum stay). ③.

Lassen Mineral Lodge, Hwy-36, Mineral, nine miles west of the southwest entrance on Hwy-36 (☎530/595-4422). Unspectacular base-rate rooms and considerably more comfortable family ones for just $5 extra. There's a pool, general store, restaurant and bar on site. ③.

Mill Creek Park, Mill Creek Road, off Hwy-44, fourteen miles east of the northern entrance (☎530/474-5384). Set amid pines and cedars, simple cabins with cold-water kitchenettes cost $30, those with hot water and bath are $10 more, and space at the campground is $9. ②.

Padilla's Rim Rock Ranch Resort, 13275 Hwy-89, Old Station, fourteen miles north of Manzanita Lake (☎530/335-7114). A collection of cabins of varying standards, the best sleeping up to six ($40–60), dotted around a meadow. Closed Nov–March. ②.

Weston House, Red Rock Road, Shingletown, a few miles east of Mineral (☎530/474-3738). One of the nicest B&Bs in all of California, with four elegant rooms beautifully sited on a volcanic ridge with pool and deck, overlooking the Ishi National Wilderness Area. ⑤.

The park

Unlike most other wilderness areas, you don't actually need to get out of the car to appreciate Lassen, as some of the best features are visible from the paved Hwy-89 that traverses the park. A thorough tour should take no more than a few hours. Pick up a copy of the *Road Guide: Lassen Volcanic National Park* ($5) in the visitor center.

Starting from the southwest entrance, you'll pass the trailhead to **Brokeoff Mountain**, a six-mile round-trip hike through wildflowers. Next is the **Lassen Chalet**, the only place to get food and, in winter, limited skiing facilities in the park. The first self-guiding trail is just up ahead – follow your nose and the **Sulphur Works** can be reached via a 200-foot boardwalk around its steaming fumaroles and burbling mud pots. The winding road climbs along the side of Diamond Peak before edging **Emerald Lake** and Lassen's show-stealer, **Bumpass Hell**, named after a man who lost a leg trying to cross it. This steaming valley of active pools and vents that bubbles away at a low rumble can be traversed on a flat, well-tended trail that loops three miles to boardwalks that put you right in the middle of the stinky action. Recall the fate of Mr Bumpass, however, and stay on the trails; the crusts over the thermal features are brittle and easy to break through, leaving you, literally, in hot water. Across the road from Bumpass Hell's parking lot, the trails around the icy-green glassy surface of Emerald Lake are also spectacular, though in much quieter fashion; the lake itself resembles a sheet of icy green, perfectly still and clear but for the snow-covered rock mound which rises from its center. Only during summer does the lake approach swimmable temperatures.

Just north of here, the road reaches its highest point (8512 feet) at the trailhead for **Lassen Peak**. The road then winds down to the flat meadows around **King's Creek**, whose trails along the winding water are popular for picnics. From roadmarker 32, a three-mile round-trip walk leads to the seventy-feet-tall **Kings Creek Falls**. At the halfway point you'll come to **Summit Lake**, a busy camping area set around a beautiful icy lake, from where you can start on the park's most manageable hiking trails.

HIKING IN LASSEN PARK

For a volcanic landscape, a surprisingly large proportion of the walking trails in the park are predominantly flat, and the heavily glaciated terrain to the east of the main volcanic massif is pleasingly gentle. Rangers will point you toward the **hiking routes** best suited to your ability – the park's generally high elevations will leave all but the most experienced walker short of breath, and you should stick to the shorter trails at least until you're acclimatized. For anything but the most tentative explorations, you should pick up a copy of *Lassen Trails* ($2.50) or the better, color *Hiking Trails of Lassen* ($12.95), which describe the most popular hikes.

Chaos Crags Lake (3.5 miles round trip; 2–3hr; 800ft ascent). From the *Manzanita Lake* campground access road, the path leads gently up through pine and fir forest to the peaceful lake. An adventurous extension climbs a ridge of loose rock to the top of Chaos Crags, affording a view of the whole park.

Cinder Cone (13 miles round trip; 1 day; flat). Check with the rangers for the best seasonal starting point for this, Lassen's most spectacular hike, through the Painted Dunes and Fantastic Lava Beds before reaching Snag Lake.

Lassen Peak (5 miles round trip; 4hr; 2000ft ascent). A fairly strenuous hike from road marker 22 to the highest point in the park. Be prepared with water and warm clothing.

Manzanita Lake (1.5 miles; 1hr; flat). Easy trails on level ground make this one of the most popular short walks in the park.

Nobles Emigrant Trail (2.5 miles; 1–2hr; 200ft ascent). The most accessible and one of the more interesting sections of a trail forged in 1850 starts opposite the Manzanita Lake entrance station and meets Hwy-89 at marker 60. It isn't maintained, but is heavily compacted and easy going.

Paradise Meadows (3 miles round trip; 3hr; 800ft ascent). Starting either at the Hat Creek parking area (marker 42) or marker 27, and passing Terrace Lake on the way, this hike winds up at Paradise Meadows, ablaze with wildflowers in the summer and a marvelous spot to pass an afternoon.

Press on further to the **Devastated Area**, where, in 1914, molten lava from Lassen poured down the valley, denuding the landscape as it went, ripping out every tree and patch of grass. Slowly the earth is recovering its green mantle, but the most vivid impression is still one of complete destruction. From here it's a gauntlet of pines to the northern entrance, site of **Manzanita Lake** and the **Loomis museum** (summer daily 9am–5pm; free), a memorial to Benjamin Loomis whose documentary photos of the 1914 eruption form the centerpiece of an exhibition strong on local geology – plug domes, composite cones and cinder cones – and flora. An easy trail circles the lake, but so do many of the campers from the nearby campground: an early start is needed for any serious wildlife spotting.

Leaving Lassen, Hwy-44 heads forty miles west to Redding, but if short on time, bypass the mundane town and continue north on Hwy-89 one hundred miles to Mount Shasta, stopping halfway at the breathtaking **McArthur-Burney Falls State Park** (☎530/335-2777; $5). The park's centerpiece is a 129-foot waterfall, unique for the way the water spills over the rim from two different levels. A paved trail leads to the misty base and pool, and a 1.5-mile steep loop takes you downstream and then back up the other side of the pool to a bridge over the falls' headwater. The Pacific Crest Trail passes alongside nearby **Lake Briton**, and paddleboat, canoes and rowboats can be rented at the park entrance. Plentiful **camping** amongst the black oaks is available for $16 a night.

Redding and around

A sprawling expanse of chain stores with a shopping mall in its heart and a poured-concrete convention center at its gate, **REDDING** is a bit of an anomaly amidst the natural splendor of the northern interior. The region's largest city, with 70,000 people, it's acted as a northern nexus since the late nineteenth century, when the Central Pacific railroad came through. Today it remains, essentially, a crossroads, bulging with cookie-cutter motels and diners that service traffic heading east to Lassen, west to Whiskeytown-Shasta-Trinity National Recreation Area, north to Mount Shasta, and south to San Francisco.

If conditions don't suit hiking, there's not a lot to do here, other than visit the town of **Shasta** on the outskirts (see opposite), a thirty-minute experience at best. You could kill an hour or two around **Turtle Bay** (daily 9am-7pm; $4 admission good for all exhibits; ☎530/243-8850), a museum and arboretum complex along the Sacramento River off of Arboretum Drive. It includes the **Redding Museum of Art & History** in Caldwell Park on the riverbank, which has a permanent display of Native American arti-

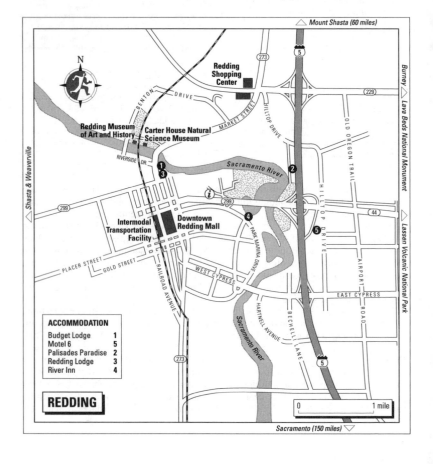

facts, and rotating contemporary and historical art exhibits. The neighboring **Carter House Natural Science Museum** is aimed at kids, with hands-on exhibits and a self-guided nature walk through an arboretum. The river bank here forms part of the **Sacramento River Trail**, a pleasant, six-mile loop designed for walkers and cyclists.

Practicalities

Considering its position at the crossroads of northern California, **public transportation** in Redding is woefully inadequate, though the new **Intermodal Transportation Facility**, the terminus for Greyhound, Amtrak, Amtrak Thruway and the local RABA bus system (☎530/241-2877), at least provides a central focus for what there is. As usual, you're not going to get to see much without a car. If you are driving, call Caltrans to check ahead for weather and road conditions (☎1-800/427-7623) and, if necessary, make extra provisions (de-icer, tire chains and so on) in case of snowstorms. Though fiercely hot in summer (100 degrees Fahrenheit even in late September), the temperature drops forbiddingly in some of the surrounding areas in winter, and what looks like a mild day in Redding could turn out to be blizzard conditions a few miles up the road (and several thousand feet up a mountainside).

The **Redding CVB**, 777 Auditorium Drive (Mon–Fri 8am–5pm, Sat-Sun 9am-5pm; ☎1-800/874-7562 or ☎530/225-4100), can give advice on accommodation in Redding, information on camping in the outlying areas and details on where to rent camping equipment. For information more specifically on the surrounding area, the **Shasta Cascade Wonderland Association** on Wonderland Boulevard, six miles north of town off I-5 (Mon–Sat 9am–6pm, Sun 10am–4pm; ☎ 1-800/474-2782 or 530/365-7500), has a more detailed collection of maps and information, and is staffed by helpful outdoor experts. As a general rule, Lassen National Volcanic Park is for hardier and more experienced hikers, and novices are pointed in the direction of the Whiskeytown-Shasta-Trinity National Recreation Area, where there are warmer climes and easier trails.

Motels are concentrated along Redding's main strip, Market Street (Hwy-273), and Pine Street. *Budget Lodge*, 1055 Market St (☎530/243-4231; ②), is a good budget option, while the *Redding Lodge*, 1135 Market St (☎530/243-5141; ③), is slightly more luxurious. *Motel 6* has three locations in Redding, including 1640 Hilltop Drive (☎530/221-1800; ②). For something grander still, try either *River Inn*, close to the river at 1835 Park Marina Drive (☎1-800/995-4341 or 530/241-9500; ④), or *Palisades Paradise*, 1200 Palisades Ave (☎530/223-5305; ④), an upscale B&B with a fabulous view of the Trinity mountains to the west.

Restaurants are as ubiquitous as motels, many of them 24-hour, most of them unappealing. Exceptions include *Jack's Grill*, 1743 California St (☎530/241-9705; closed Sun), with fine grilled steak and shrimp and chicken dishes for $10–15. You'll probably have to wait for a table, but you can always go across the road to *Downtown Espresso*, 1545 Placer St at California (☎530/243-4548), attached to the Redding Bookstore and the only place in town where you can get a decent coffee in the evening. *The Hatch Cover*, 202 Hemsted Drive (☎530/223-5606), serves tasty steak and seafood from its riverside terrace. There have been attempts at beautifying downtown along Market Street, anchored by the bakery/café *Chocolat de Nannette*, at 1777 Market, and the upscale Italian eatery *Guido's*, at 1790 Market.

Shasta

Huddling four miles west of Redding, the ghost town of **SHASTA** – not to be confused with Mount Shasta (see p.636) – is about the only option for historic entertainment, and it's a slim option at that. A booming gold-mining town when Redding was an insignificant dot on the map, Shasta's fortunes changed when the railroad tracks were laid to Redding. Abandoned since then, it remains today a row of half-ruined brick buildings that were once part of a runaway prosperity, and literally the end of the road for prospectors. All roads from San Francisco, Sacramento and other southerly points terminated at Shasta; beyond, rough and poorly marked trails made it almost impossible to find gold diggings along the Trinity, Salmon and Upper Sacramento Rivers, and diggers contented themselves with the rich pickings in the surrounding area, pushing out the local Native Americans in a brutal territorial quest for good mining land. The **Courthouse**, on the east side of Main Street, has been turned into a museum (Wed–Sun 10am–5pm; $2; closed until April 2000 for structural repairs), full of mining paraphernalia and paintings of past heroes, though best are the gallows at the back and the prison cells below – a grim reminder of the daily executions that went on here. The miners were largely an unruly lot, and in the main room of the Courthouse a charter lays down some basic rules of conduct:

> *IV Thou shalt neither remember what thy friends do at home on the Sabbath day, lest the remembrance may not compare favorably with what thou doest here.*
> *VII Thou shalt not kill the body by working in the rain, even though thou shalt make enough money to buy psychic attendance. Neither shalt thou destroy thyself by "tight" nor "slewed" nor "high" nor "corned" nor "three sheets to the wind," by drinking smoothly down brandy slings, gin cocktails, whiskey punches, rum toddies and egg nogs.*
>
> From the *Miners' Ten Commandments*

The **Shasta State Historic Park** (☎530/243-8194; unrestricted entry) straddles two blocks of Main Street, and is less grand than it sounds. Indistinguishable ruins of brick buildings are identified by plaques as stores and hotels, and the central area, not much bigger than the average garden really, features miscellaneous mining machinery and a picnic area, along with a trail that loops around the back. On the whole, the park is a place to stretch your legs before moving further west.

Whiskeytown-Shasta-Trinity National Recreation Area

Traveling west from Redding through the ghost town of Shasta (see p.633), Hwy-299 is a deserted, often precipitous but enjoyable road that leads after ten miles into the western portion of the **Whiskeytown-Shasta-Trinity National Recreation Area**. Assuming the road's open – it's often blocked off due to bad weather – this huge chunk of land is open for public use daily, year-round. Its series of three impounded lakes – Trinity, Whiskeytown and Shasta – have artificial beaches, forests and camping facilities designed to meet the needs of anyone who has ever fancied themselves as a water-skier, sailor or wilderness hiker. Sadly, during summer it's completely congested, as windsurfers, motorboats, jet skis and recreational vehicles block the narrow routes which serve the lakes. But in the winter when the California weekenders have all gone, it can be supremely untouched, at least on the surface. In fact, there's an extensive system of tunnels, dams and aqueducts directing the plentiful waters of the Sacramento River to California's Central Valley to irrigate cash crops for the huge agribusinesses. The lakes are pretty enough, but residents complain they're not a patch on the wild waters that used to flow from the mountains before the Central Valley Project came along in the 1960s.

Of the three lakes, **Whiskeytown**, just beyond Shasta, is the smallest, easiest to get to, and inevitably the most popular. Ideal for watersports, it hums with the sound of jet skis and powerboats ripping across the still waters. Those who don't spend their holiday in a wet suit can usually be found four-wheel driving and pulling action-man stunts on the primitive roads all around. The best place for **camping** and **hiking** is in the **Brandy Creek** area – a hairy five-mile drive along the narrow J.F. Kennedy Memorial Drive from the main entrance and **Whiskeytown Visitor Information Center** on Hwy-299 (daily 9am–6pm; ☎530/246-1225). There's a small store at the water's edge in Brandy Creek and three campgrounds (mostly $12–16 sites) about a mile behind in the woods.

Northeast on Hwy-3 (off Hwy-299 forty miles west of Whiskeytown), **Trinity Lake** (officially called Clair Engle Lake, but not locally referred to as such) is much quieter, rarely used in summer and in winter primarily a picturesque stop-off for skiers on their way to the **Salmon-Trinity Alps** area beyond, part of the extensive **Salmon Mountains** range. It's very remote around here, and most people only venture this far west to visit the small Gold Rush town of **WEAVERVILLE**, a few miles west along Hwy-299, 43 miles from Redding. The distinctive brick buildings, fitted with exterior spiral staircases, were built to withstand fires – indeed, the fire station itself is particularly noteworthy. The main draw, though, is the **Joss House** on Main Street (Thurs–Mon 10am–5pm; $2; ☎530/623-5284), a small Taoist temple built in 1874 by indentured Chinese mineworkers. A beautiful shrine, still in use today, it features a three-thousand-year-old altar and can be visited on a poor guided tour. Next door, the J.J. Jake Jackson Museum (☎530/623-5211; free) exhibits artifacts from the Gold Rush.

You can **stay** at the *Weaverville Hotel*, 205 Main St (☎530/623-3121; ②), a century-old, gracefully dilapidated place with large characterful rooms and no phones – register in Brady's sports store next door. Alternatives include the well-lit *49er Motel*, 718 Main St (☎530/623-49ER; ②). The friendly *Motel Trinity* (☎530/623-2129) on Main Street just south of Hwy-3, has rooms for $75 with hot tubs, or $40 without. You can **eat** well-prepared chicken, steaks, and pasta for around $11 at the cozy *La Grange Café*, 315 N Main St (☎530/623-5325), or knock back local microbrews over a hearty meal at the eclectically decorated *Pacific Brewery Restaurant & Bar*, 401 S Main St (☎530/623-3000). Also on Main Street, across from the Joss House, the *New York Saloon* is a great place to mingle with the friendly locals over a glass of beer. For more information, consult the **Chamber of Commerce**, 211 Trinity Lakes Blvd, off Hwy-299 in Weaverville (summer daily 9am–5pm; rest of year Mon–Fri 9am–5pm; ☎ 1-800/421-7259 or 530/623-3298). Continuing west on Hwy-299, 145 miles from Redding, leads you to Eureka (p.615) and the coast.

East of the other two, eight miles north of Redding, is **Shasta Lake**. The biggest of the three lakes – larger than the San Francisco Bay – it's marred by the unsightly and enormous **Shasta Dam**, 465ft high and over half a mile long, bang in the middle. Built between 1938 and 1945 as part of the enormous Central Valley irrigation project, the dam backs up the Sacramento, McCloud and Pit rivers to form the lake, the project's northern outpost. The best views are from marked vista points along the approach road (US-151, off I-5), but a more vivid way to experience the sheer enormity of the thing is to drive down to the powerhouse (daily 9am–4pm) and take the **free tour** of the dam and ancillary structures, feeling the power of millions of gallons of water gushing beneath you.

On the north side of the lake, the massive limestone formations of the **Shasta Caverns** (daily tours summer every hour 9am–4pm; April, May, Sept hourly 9am–3pm; winter 10am, noon & 2pm; $14) are the largest in California, jutting above ground and clearly visible from the freeway. The interior, however, is something of a letdown: a fairly standard series of caves and tunnels in which stalactite and stalagmite formations are studded with crystals, flow-stone deposits and miniature waterfalls. The admission price covers the short ferry journey from the ticket booth across an arm of Shasta Lake. From Lake Shasta, I-5 crosses the world's highest double-deck bridge and races up towards Mount Shasta, an impressive drive against a staggering backdrop of mountains and lakes.

Mount Shasta . . . and Mount Shasta

Lonely as God and as white as a winter moon.

Joaquin Miller, about Mount Shasta

The lone peak of the 14,162-foot **Mount Shasta** dominates the landscape for a hundred miles all around, almost permanently snow-covered, hypnotically beautiful but menacing in its potential for destruction: it last erupted over two hundred years ago, but is still considered an active volcano. Local lore is rich with tales of Lemurians – tall, barefoot men dressed in white robes – living inside the mountain, alongside their legendary neighbors the Yaktavians, who are said to be excellent bell-makers. Such tales have lent the mountain a bit of a Twilight Zone reputation. Numerous UFO sightings and otherworldly experiences make Mount Shasta a center of the American spiritualism movement, a fact heightened in 1987 when 5,000 people arrived to take part in the good vibes of the Harmonic Convergence, an attempt to channel the energies of sacred power spots into peace and harmony. Not all is peaceful on the mountain, however, as hundreds of climbers annually attempt to ascend its icy heights, an activity that has resulted in deaths, usually caused from falls or from the ever-changing weather.

In the shadow of the behemoth sits the historic railroad town of **Dunsmuir** and, right up against the mountain, tiny, pleasant **Mount Shasta City**, a one-street town of shops, outfitters, spiritual bookstores and fantastic restaurants. On the northern flank of the peak rests even smaller **Weed**, a village that offers better views of Mount Shasta in summertime and access to **Lava Beds National Monument**.

Arrival and information

Merely getting to Mount Shasta City is a rewarding journey, easily accomplished on Greyhound **buses** which connect the town with Redding to the south and stop on N Mt Shasta Blvd, downtown across from Vet's Club, a couple of blocks from the sub-standard **Visitors' Bureau**, 300 Pine St (Mon–Sat 9am–5pm, Sun 10am–4pm; ☎ 1-800/926-4865 or 530/926-4865). However, the Greyhound ticketing office is seven miles north in Weed, 628 S Weed Blvd (Mon-Fri 8.30am-4pm, Sat 8.30am-1pm; ☎800/231-2222, ☎530/938-4454). Amtrak trains stop in Dunsmuir, six miles south, in the middle of the night; from there, six daily STAGE buses (☎1-800/24-STAGE or 530/842-8295) stop at the Mount Shasta Shopping Center, next to the *Black Bear Diner*.

Accommodation

Mount Shasta City has no shortage of **accommodation**, and reservations should only be necessary on weekends in the height of summer. **Campgrounds** abound in the surrounding area, but few have full amenities (hot showers are vital when the mercury drops).

Hotels, motels and B&Bs

Alpenrose Cottage Hostel, 204 E Hinckley St (☎530/926-6724). A top-quality independent hostel with a relaxed atmosphere and a great deck for watching the sunset over Mount Shasta immediately behind. There's a fully equipped kitchen, a small double room ($30) for those who don't fancy the small dorms, and showers which are available to non-guests for $3. Rates are $15 a night, less by the week, and you may even be able to work for your board. Follow N Mount Shasta Boulevard north for a mile and follow the KOA signs.

Best Western Tree House Motor Inn, 111 Morgan Way, (☎800/545-7164 or ☎530/926-3101). Right off the freeway, a largely characterless hotel with indoor pool, spa and views of the mountain. ④.

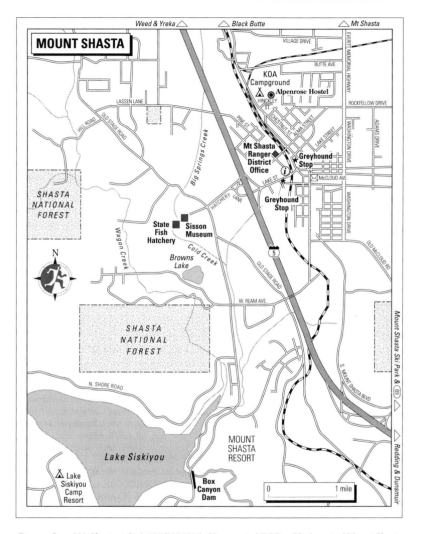

Dream Inn, 326 Chestnut St (☎530/926-1536). Very central B&B, a block east of Mount Shasta Boulevard, in a Victorian house with all the usual trappings. ⑤.

McCloud Hotel, 408 Main St, McCloud (☎800/964-2823 or ☎530-964-2822). Across the street from the *Shasta Sunset Dinner Train* and near the ski park. Clean, comfortable rooms in a restored historic building. ⑤ summer, ④ winter, room with hot tub ⑦.

Mount Shasta Cabins & Cottages, 500 S Mount Shasta Blvd (☎530/926-5396). This organization acts as an agency for a wide range of cabins and houses in and around Mount Shasta, rented by the night but particularly suited for longer stays. Most have kitchenettes, TVs and wood stoves, and drop their rates substantially outside the summer season. Across the street from the superb *Mike and Tony's* restaurant. ④.

Mount Shasta Ranch B&B, 1008 W A Barr Rd (☎530/926-3870). A stylish ranch house with spacious rooms and a great view of Mount Shasta. ③.

Stoney Brook Inn B&B, 309 W Colombero Drive, McCloud (☎1-800/369-6118 or 530/964-2300). Affordable retreat close to the ski park with comfortable rooms and an outdoor hot tub. Double rooms cost ③ with shared bath, ④ without.

Travel Inn, 504 S Mount Shasta Blvd (☎530/926-4617). Decent, clean motel with basic rooms. ②.

Camping

The most picturesque campground in the area is the woodland *Lake Siskiyou Camp Resort* ($18; ☎530/926-2618), four miles west of town on a lake of the same name, where you can picnic, bathe and go boating. More **primitive sites** tend to be free if there is no piped drinking water, though creek water is often available. The most useful of these is the walk-in *Panther Meadows* (7400ft, closed in winter), high up on the mountain at the end of the Everitt Memorial Highway, though McBride Springs ($12; 5000ft) being lower down the same road tends to be open for longer. The fully equipped KOA, 900 N Mt Shasta Blvd (☎1-800/736-3617 or 530/926-4029), two blocks from downtown, charges $19 per site.

The Town and around

Quite rightly, few people come to Mount Shasta for its museums, but in bad weather you might visit the otherwise missable **Sisson Museum**, 1 N Old Stage Rd (June–Aug daily 10am–4pm; Sept–May daily 1–4pm; donation; ☎530/926-5508), with a few examples of Native basketware, a fair bit on pioneering life in the region, and some more diverting material on the mountain itself. The brown, rainbow and eastern brook trout in the **fish hatchery** outside (daily April–Sept 8am–4pm; free) can be fed on food from a vending machine.

A couple of New Age **bookstores** along N Mount Shasta Boulevard provide the key to some of the town's more offbeat activities. Golden Bough Books at no. 219 (☎1-800/343-8888 or 530/926-3228), for example, has active bulletin boards and stacks of publications exhorting you to visit a sweatlodge or discover your inner goddess. The visitor's center provides an ever-changing list of metaphysical, astrology and alternative healing options as their practitioners and followers migrate in and out of the town.

Mainly, though, Mount Shasta is full of outfits hoping to help you into the **outdoors**, from trout fishing to dog sledding to, of course, mountain climbing. Competition keeps prices reasonable and the options wide open. Obviously, there are a thousand ways to climb Mount Shasta, and these are covered in the box on p.640. Otherwise, Shasta Mountain Guides, 1938 Hill Rd (☎530/926-3117), arranges jeep trips up the mountain and conducts rock- and ice-climbing courses for all levels from $65. For real thrills, **whitewater rafting trips** on the churning Upper Sacramento are offered by Turtle River Rafting (☎530/926-3223) and River Dancers (☎530/926-3517), both starting at $80 a day. Train enthusiasts should check out the elegant **Shasta Sunset Dinner Train**, which departs from the nearby town of McCloud, 10 miles southeast of Mount Shasta city on Hwy-89. Cars constructed in 1916 clack along east and west-bound routes while you sit back and enjoy a full course meal (3 hours; $70; ☎1-800/733-2141).

Eating

Aside from a rash of fast-food outlets towards I-5, Mount Shasta's **eating** options are largely health-conscious, with vegetarian dishes featured on almost every menu. Hardy mountain types are amply catered for, too, with plenty of opportunities to stoke up on hearty fare before hitting the mountain heights.

The Bagel Café and Natural Bakery, 105 E Alma St (☎530/926-1414). A favorite with Mount Shasta's spiritual community, serving moderately priced soups, sandwiches, great *huevos rancheros* and, of course, bagels.

Lily's, 1013 S Mount Shasta Blvd (☎530/926-3372). Moderately priced and consistently good restaurant serving California cuisine, vegetarian and Mexican dishes. Mains cost $12–15, sandwiches around $6.

Mike and Tony's, 501 S Mount Shasta Blvd (☎530/926-4792). It may not look like much, but this excellent Italian restaurant specializes in homemade ravioli. Fresh flowers decorate the tables, and the owner usually comes out to ask how you like the food. Good wines, figs and goat cheese; great martinis. Dinner only; closed Tues and Wed.

Serge's, 531 Chestnut St (☎530/926-1276). Moderately priced and informal French dining at lunchtime and evenings. Several vegetarian plates are featured, and the Sunday brunch is something of a local tradition.

Simply Vegetarian, at the *Stoney Brook Inn*, 309 W Colombero Drive, McCloud (☎530/964-2300). The only fully vegetarian place around, twelve miles away in McCloud. There's a lunchtime soup and organic salad bar, and $8 full dinners, most of them vegan, in the evening. Closed Mon & Tues.

Willy's Bavarian Kitchen, 107 Chestnut St (☎530/926-3636). The pick of the town's restaurants, serving sauerbraten and wiener schnitzel alongside tasty vegetarian dishes inside or on the deck. Wash your dinner down with German beer, local microbrews or fabulous fruit shakes.

Around Mount Shasta

Five miles north of town, the treeless cone of **Black Butte** (2.5 miles; 2–3hr; 1800ft ascent), offers a more modest alternative to climbing Mount Shasta. The switchback trail to this 6325ft volcanic plug dome is hard to find without the leaflet available from the ranger station or Visitors' Bureau.

If you have time, you'd also be well advised to explore the beautiful trails that climb 4000ft up to the 225-million-year-old glacier-polished granite crags at the aptly named **Castle Crags State Park** (☎1-800/444-7275 or 530/235-2684), thirteen miles south of Mount Shasta along I-5. Campgrounds with full amenities are available for $16 per night in the often deserted 6200-acre forested park.

Mount Shasta Ski Park (☎1-800/SKI-SHASTA), near McCloud on Hwy-89, has yet to establish itself on the ski circuit, so its rental charges ($17) and lift tickets ($29) are quite reasonable. **Snowboarding**, on the other hand, has created quite a scene around here – you can rent equipment at House of Ski in Mount Shasta, but the requisite baggy pants are up to you. In summer, it transforms into some of the best **mountain biking** territory in the region, with marked trails following the ski runs. A pass is $12, and bikes can be rented for $16 a day. There's also an artificial tower for climbing ($10/day) and chairlift rides ($8).

After a day or two trudging around or up Mount Shasta, **Stewart Mineral Springs** (Sun–Thurs 10am–6pm, Fri & Sat 10am–8pm; ☎530/938-2222) at 2222 Stewart Springs Rd off I-5 just north of Weed, provides welcome relief. Individual bathing rooms in a cedar and pine forest glade soothe your aches away for $15, less if you stay in the very affordable cabins, dorm units, tepees or campground here.

Dunsmuir

One example of how the Shasta area looked in the past can be seen in the hamlet of **DUNSMUIR**, which is even quainter than Mount Shasta City. Situated ten miles south of Mount Shasta on a steep hill sloping down from I-5, Dunsmuir's downtown was bypassed by the freeway, essentially freezing the community in time. Now it makes its living as a historic railroad town, and the main drag, **Dunsmuir Avenue**, is lined with restored hotels and shops, many of them taking the train theme a bit too far; expect to see shopkeeps dressed as train engineers and restaurant names like the *Choo-Choo Café*. Amtrak stops here, its last California stop before continuing north to Oregon.

Dunsmuir used to bill itself as a daytrip from Shasta, but recently realized that it had a quietude and natural wonders of its own. Foremost among these are the Mossbrae

CLIMBING MOUNT SHASTA

Even if you are only passing through the region, you'll be tempted to tackle Mount Shasta. Ambling among the pines of the lower slopes is rewarding enough, but the assault on the summit is the main challenge – and it can be done in a day with basic equipment and some determination.

Every year several deaths occur and numerous injuries are sustained through inexperience and over-ambition. The wise will stick to the routes prescribed by the **Mount Shasta Ranger District Office**, 204 W Alma St (summer daily 8am–4.30pm; rest of year Mon–Fri 8am–4.30pm; ☎530/926-4511), who will insist that you obtain a **wilderness permit** (also self-issued outside the office when closed and at the trailhead, $15) and enter your name in the **voluntary climbers' register** before and after your ascent.

The mountain's isolation creates its own weather, which can change with alarming rapidity. In early summer, when most novice attempts are made, the snow cover is complete and crampons and an ice axe are a requirement to get a good grip; later during the season, as the snow melts, patches of loose ash and cinder appear, making the going more difficult and the chance of rockfall greater. Only at the end of summer, with most of the snow melted, is there a chance of climbing safely without equipment. There are countless equipment rental agencies in town, such as Fifth Season, 300 N Mount Shasta Blvd (☎530/926-3606), which can fit you out with boots ($20 for two–three days), crampons and ice axe ($16 for two–three days) and camping gear ($28 for two–three days), and provide a mountain weather forecast on ☎530/926-5555. House of Ski, 316 Chestnut (☎530/926-2359), offers much the same at very competitive rates.

Even for fit, acclimatized climbers **the ascent**, from 7000ft to over 14,000ft, will take eight to ten utterly exhausting hours. The easiest, safest and most popular way up is via **Avalanche Gulch** – just follow the footprints of the person in front of you. Drive up the mountain on the Everitt Memorial Highway to the Bunny Flat trailhead at 7000ft. A gentle hour's walk brings you to **Horse Camp**, 7900ft, a good place to acclimatize and spend the night before your ascent – there's drinking water, toilet facilities and a knowledgeable caretaker who can offer good advice about your impending climb. The return trip is done in four or five hours, depending on the recklessness of your descent: Mount Shasta is a renowned spot for **glissading** – careering down the slopes on a jacket or strong plastic sheet – a sport best left to those proficient in ice-axe arrests, but wonderfully exhilarating nonetheless.

On the lower slopes, keep your eyes skinned for the inedible **watermelon snow**, its bright red appearance caused by a microbe which flourishes here. Most importantly, be prepared for storms on the mountain. Bring extra food, stove fuel, a good, wind-resistant shelter, and plenty of warm clothing. And if the weather does take a turn for the worst, don't hesitate to head back down the mountain – high elevation storms sometimes last for days, with little or no visibility.

---

and Hedge Creek **waterfalls**, along the Sacramento River canyon, beautiful spots for walks and picnics. To reach Mossbrae, drive north on Dunsmuir Ave to Scarlet Way, crossing the bridge and railroad tracks to the parking area. Follow the walking trail along the train tracks for one mile until you get to the railroad bridge. Don't cross, but continue on the train through the trees and the falls are ahead. Hedge Creek Falls are accessible via the parking area at the north Dunsmuir exit on I-5.

The Visitor's Bureau, on Pine Street under the Timberline Bank (Mon-Sat 10am-4pm, Sun 12pm-4pm; ☎800/DUNSMUIR), has updated train and STAGE schedules. On Dunsmuir Ave, the *Cornerstone Bakery Café*, no. 5759, sells all the fixings needed for a **picnic**, and several **B&Bs** ply their trade nearby, including *Castle Rock Inn*, 5829 Sacramento Ave (☎888/382-ROCK; ③), which has rooms near the fishing-friendly river. *Espee Dave's Trains-n-Things*, 5815 Dunsmuir Ave, sells electric and model trains if you'd like to take home a piece of the railroad atmosphere.

Weed

A gateway town to Klamath Falls, Oregon and the Lava Beds National Monument, **WEED** can't compete with Mount Shasta City's hip charm. But, perhaps in a form of karmic justice, it gets the better view of the peak during the summertime. Too bad the tourism board couldn't leave it at that, instead of dressing up the place as a "historic lumber town" with the groaner of a slogan, "Weed love to see you." Despite this, there's two good budget **hotels** and a pleasant **café** in town, as well as the **College of the Siskiyous**, which is certainly California's prettiest campus for its views of the peak. In town, the *Hi Lo Travelers Complex*, 88 S Weed Blvd (☎530/938-2731; ②) has decent rooms and a café that slings hash and eggs. On the northern end of Weed Blvd, at no. 466, *Motel 6*'s new spread includes a nice outdoor pool and stunning sunrise views of Mount Shasta (☎530/938-4101; ②).

Five miles outside of town, north on US-97 on the way to Oregon and Lava Beds, the **Living Memorial Sculpture Garden** experience (unrestricted entry; donation) is an intriguing remembrance of the Vietnam War. Artist Dennis Smith has created ten metal sculptures illustrating different aspects of an American soldier's experience in the war. Surrounding the art are about 53,000 pine trees, one for every American killed in Vietnam. The trees, art, silence and position under Mount Shasta add up to a very moving experience.

Yreka

There's little to justify more than an hour or two in quiet, leafy **YREKA** (pronounced "Why-reeka"), fifteen-odd miles north of Weed on I-5, but it makes a pleasant break. Most people come here to ride the Yreka Western Railroad, better known as the **Blue Goose** (mid-June to Aug Wed–Sun; late May to mid-June & Sept–Oct Sat & Sun only; ☎1-800/973-5277 or 530/842-4146), a 1915 Baldwin steam engine pulling attractive carriages to and from the nearby historic town of **Montague**; the three-hour excursion costs $9 and includes an hour in Montague – all very agreeable. The **Siskiyou County Museum**, 910 S Main St (summer Tues–Sat 9am–5pm; donation) deserves some attention, particularly the outdoor section (closes 4pm) with its historic buildings – church, houses and shops – transported here from around the county. Finally, there's a paltry collection of gold nuggets in the **County Courthouse**, 311 Fourth St (Mon–Fri 8am–5pm; free).

The **Chamber of Commerce**, inside *Sue's Coffee and Cones* at 117 W Miner St (summer Mon 9am–5pm, Tues–Fri 9am–7.30pm, Sat 10am–6.30pm; rest of year Mon–Fri 9am–5pm; ☎530/842-1649), issues maps for a self-guided **Historic Walking Tour** around Yreka's numerous Victorian homes. It can also help you find **accommodation**, not difficult with dozens of chain motels and the *Thunderbird Lodge*, 526 S Main St (☎1-800/554-4339 or 530/842-4404; ②). The *Heritage Inn*, 306 N Main St (☎530/842-6835; ①), is cheap and surprisingly adequate. **Eating** is best done along the street at *Nature's Kitchen*, 412 S Main St (☎530/842-1136; closed Sun), not at the cutesy *Grandma's House* which has an unfathomable, statewide appeal to elderly Americans whose RVs fill the parking lot. Yreka can be reached by STAGE **bus** (☎1-800/24-STAGE or 530/842-8295) from Mount Shasta and Dunsmuir. If you're here on a Saturday, fancy a drink and don't mind backtracking a little, head twenty miles south of Yreka along Hwy-3 to charming, turn-of-the-century **ETNA**, home to the *Etna Brewing Company*, 131 Callahan St (Sat 1–5pm; ☎530/467-5277), a tiny micro-brewery producing just three-hundred barrels a year for local distribution. There are usually four or five of the malty real ales and other beers available to taste, each and every one a beer drinker's dream. While here, check out the Fifties soda fountain in the Scott Valley Drugstore at the top of Main Street. And if you're really struck by the place, you can **camp** for free in the town park on Diggles Street.

Lava Beds National Monument and around

After seeing Mount Shasta you should push on to the **Lava Beds National Monument**, which commemorates a war between the US and Modoc Indians in the far northeastern corner of the state. Carved out of the huge **Modoc National Forest**, it's actually a series of volcanic caves which you can explore and huge black lava flows with a history as violent as the natural forces that created it.

Lava Beds is one of the most remote and forgotten – and beautiful — of California's parks, with pungent yellow rabbit brush blooming around the burnt rocks in autumn. It's in the heart of Modoc country, a desolate outback where cowboys still ride the range, and where, as the territory of one of the last major battles with the Native Americans, there is still a suspicious relationship between the settlers and the native peoples. Until the 1850s Gold Rush it was home to the Modoc tribe, but after their repeated and bloody confrontations with the miners, the government ordered them

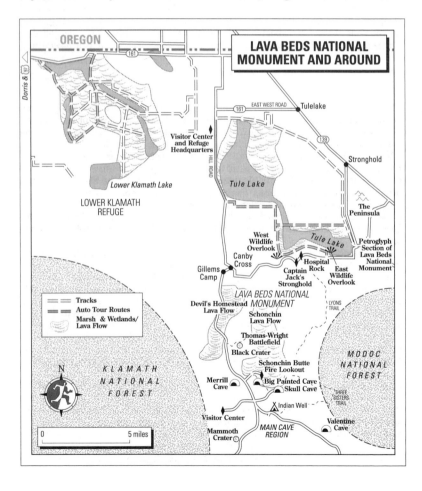

into a reservation with the Klamath, their traditional enemy. After only a few months, the Modoc drifted back to their homeland in the lava beds, and in 1872 the army was sent in to return them by force to the reservation. It was driven back by 52 Modoc warriors under the leadership of one Kientpoos, better known as "Captain Jack," who held back an army of US regulars and volunteers twenty times the size of his for five months, from a stronghold at the northern tip of the park (see overleaf).

Eventually Captain Jack was betrayed by a member of his tribe, captured and hanged and what was left of the tribe sent off to a reservation in Oklahoma, where most of them died of malaria. Today the lava beds region is inhabited only by the wild deer and three million migrating ducks who attract the trickle of tourists that make it this far.

To the west and north, the **Klamath Basin National Wildlife Refuge** spreads over the border into Oregon. This stop on the Pacific Flyway draws birders and hunters alike for its millions of migratory guests.

Practicalities

Lava Beds National Monument ($4 per vehicle for seven days) is 160 miles northeast of Redding, and inaccessible without a **car**. It's a day-trip from Mount Shasta, one-and-a-half hours away, but can be combined with camping, spelunking and birding for a much longer stay. The most tortuous route follows Hwy-89 to Bartle, then passing Medicine Lake (see p.645); the approach via Hwy-139 is easier, but the best and fastest is from Weed, following US-97 through Dorris and then via Hwy-161 through the Klamath Basin National Wildlife Refuge (see p.645).

Pick up an excellent **map** of the monument from the **visitor center**, just inside the southwestern entrance (summer daily 8am–6pm; rest of year Sat & Sun 8am–5pm and sporadic weekdays; ☎530/667-2282). Close by, at Indian Wells, is the park's one **campground** ($10 in summer, $6 in winter). All **wilderness camping** throughout the monument is free and no permits are necessary, but campers must pitch at least a mile from any road, trail or camping area, and fifty yards from any cave. Be warned, though, that elevation throughout the park ranges from 4000 to 5700 feet and there's snow and freezing nights for most of the year, which can make camping uncomfortable.

The only **accommodation** center in the area, and the one place to pick up supplies (the monument can only muster a soda machine), is **TULELAKE**, 25 miles north. The near-deserted main street (Hwy-139) holds the *Tulelake Hotel,* 156 Main St (☎530/667-5190; ②) and a few restaurants. Nearby is the **Modoc Ranger Station** (Mon–Fri 8am–4.30pm; ☎530/667-2248) with general information on the Modoc National Forest.

The monument

A day spent in the **Lava Beds** is akin to exploring the innards of a volcano, scampering down hollow tubes through which molten lava once coursed. The youngest of them were formed 30,000 years ago when volcanic upwellings sent molten, basaltic magma careering across the Modoc Plateau. As the magma came into contact with cool air, it solidified, leaving a flowing molten core feeding the expanding lava field downhill. In time, the magma flow stopped and the molten lava drained out, leaving the world's largest concentration of such hollow tubes. Most remain unexplored, but where the casing has collapsed, access is possible and you are free to scramble through. Some of the caves are so small that you have to crawl along on all fours, while others are an enormous 75 feet in diameter. Some contain Native American **petroglyphs** – not to be confused with the names painted on the cave walls by J.D. Howard, one of the first white men to explore and name the caves.

Pick up the free loaner flashlights from the visitor center and begin your explorations of the caves just outside. Initially, though, entering the darkness alone can be an unnerving experience, so most people prefer to take the **free guided ranger walks** (daily Memorial Day, late May–Labor Day, early Sept). Two-to-three-hour morning walks (9am) leave from the visitor center and explore little-known sections of the monument; afternoon tours (2pm) concentrate on ninety-minute guided cave trips, and in the evening (9pm) rangers lead hour-long campfire talks and slide shows.

If you insist on eschewing ranger guidance, you must abide by a few rules. Don't go alone, wear decent shoes, and take two flashlights each. Borrowed flashlights must be returned by nightfall to ensure no one goes missing. For night explorations (the caves remain open), you'll need your own light source. Hard hats are strongly advised and available for $3.50 at the visitor center.

If caves don't do it for you, the other attraction of Lava Beds is its well-documented history. Begin at the visitor's center for an exhibit on the Modoc War, including photos of its chief participants, including Modoc leader Captain Jack, and scathing editorials from national papers condemning the US Army over its mission. You'll need a car to get to the northern reaches of the park, around **Captain Jack's Stronghold**, a natural fortress of craggy lava flows and shallow caves on the shores of the Old Tule Lake. When you arrive, pick up a trail book ($.25) from the parking lot and enjoy one of two well-narrated **self-guided trails** (one half a mile, the other 1.5 miles) through a war that in many ways typ-

---

EXPLORING THE LAVA BEDS

Most of the interest in Lava Beds lies around the visitor center, where the largest concentration of caves can be visited on the short **Cave Loop** access road. For a confidence-building handle on your location in the twenty-five "developed" caves – less than a tenth of the known total – get the *Lava Caves Map* ($4.50) from the visitor center. New ones are discovered all the time, so the possibilities are almost endless, but for the moment, the tried and tested caves below should be enough to be going on with.

Catacomb Cave At over a mile long, this is the longest open tube in the monument, though you need perseverance, a slim body and a cool head to get anywhere near the end. The profusion of interconnecting passageways make it one of the most confusing; keep track of whether you are heading up or downhill.

Fern Cave Full of ferns growing in patches of light where the roof has fallen in, with Native pictographs on the walls.

Labyrinth Striking geological features – lava pillars and lavacicles – and evidence of Native American habitation.

Mushpot Cave Right by the visitor center, this is the most developed of the caves. It provides a good introduction, is lit during center opening hours, and has interpretive panels highlighting key features.

Skull Cave Named for Bighorn skulls found when the cave was discovered by early explorer E.L. Hopkins, this has the largest entrance of any of the lava tubes and contains ice all year round.

Symbol Bridge and **Big Painted Cave** (1.5-mile round-trip; almost flat). Two very worthwhile caves adjacent to each other on a trail north of the visitor center. No flashlight is needed though one could come in handy. Some of the best examples of pictographs in the Monument – tentatively dated between 1000AD and 1500AD – show up as different angles of sunlight catch the rocks beside the entrance. Respecting Modoc sensibilities, make two clockwise turns before descending into a large cave, open at both ends (hence the "bridge" name), in which zigzags, squiggles, sunbursts and human figures are picked out in grease and charcoal on pumice-washed background. Make a single anti-clockwise turn on departure for Big Painted Cave, where the pictographs are less impressive. In the mid 1920s J.D. Howard excavated a small tunnel at the very back of the cave to reveal an ice flow in a cavity fifteen feet down: with a flashlight you can scramble down there.

ified the conquest of the West. When you get here you'll see how the Modoc managed to hide and move around through the passageways of the hills. Two miles west, **Canby's Cross** marks a turning point in the war, when Captain Jack, coerced by the man who would later betray him, drew a gun during a council and murdered US General Canby and a pastor. Two miles east, the shallow lava bowl of **Hospital Rock** marks the point where one Lt Sherwood, wounded by the Modoc, was unsuccessfully tended in a makeshift field hospital towards the end of the siege on the stronghold.

Around the monument

Small volcanic craters, buttes, spatter cones and chimneys dot Lava Beds, but the flows which produced most of the lava tubes came from **Mammoth Crater** on the southern perimeter of the monument, where a short path leads to a viewpoint overlooking the deep conical crater.

Underlying the most recent of Lava Beds' fabulous creations is a bed of basalt, the product of a huge shield volcano with a profile so flat it is barely noticeable. Its core is now filled by the sub-alpine **Medicine Lake**, ten miles southwest of Mammoth Crater. Formerly a Modoc healing center, the only therapies on offer today are fishing and swimming from the $7 **campsites** along the north shore. It's accessible via an unpaved road closed November to mid-May.

More volcanic spectacle lies just west at **Glass Mountain**, made almost entirely of glassy, black obsidian – source of Modoc arrowheads – but covered in fluffy, white pumice quarried for stonewashing jeans. A short and fairly easy trail leads in from the road. Just beyond the monument's northeast corner, a small outlier known as the Petroglyph Section contains **Petroglyph Point**, a three-hundred-yard-long cliff face made of "tuff," volcanic rock formed when lava flows hit Old Tule Lake. The soft rock offers some fine, but cryptic, examples of ancient art: shields, female figures and a series of small circles thought to represent travel. Pick up an interpretive leaflet at the visitor center.

East of the Petroglyphs Section, the road continues to Hwy-139 and the town of **NEWELL**, site of the **Tule Lake Camp**, where 110,000 people of Japanese descent, many of them American citizens, were interned without charge or trial between 1942 and 1946. Many of the camp buildings have been sold off to local farmers, but the wooden-sided police and military barracks remain.

Perhaps the most rewarding excursion from the monument, though, is to the **Klamath Basin National Wildlife Refuge** (open daylight hours), just to the north along Hill Road (Hwy-161) leading to US-97 and spreading into Oregon. One of the last wetlands in California, with swathes of open water and emerging vegetation on the shoreline, it attracts an estimated eighty percent of birds following the Pacific Flyway, the major migration routes from Alaska and northern Canada to Baja California in Mexico. In spring and fall, almost a hundred species are present and the population tops a million. Bald eagles appear January to March, bringing out hundreds of photographers trying to navigate the snowy road. The most accessible reaches of the reserve are the **Lower Klamath Refuge** and **Tule Lake**, an open body of water surrounded by reeds (*tule* in Modoc). At the northwestern corner of the latter, the **visitor center** (Mon–Fri 8am–4.30pm, Sat & Sun 10am–4pm; ☎530/667-2231) issues permits for the birdwatching and hunting blinds ($5): call ahead to be sure of getting one. Surprisingly, the best way of spotting the wildlife is by driving along designated routes ($3): getting out of the car and walking scares the birds off.

Heading south back towards Mount Shasta on US-97, your car will be stopped in otherwise droll **DORRIS** by agriculture agents checking to see if you're transporting fruit or vegetables from out of state. Say "No" and they'll give you a nice color map to welcome you to California.

travel details

Trains

Oakland to: Chico (1 daily; 4hr 30min); Dunsmuir (1 daily; 7hr, 30min); Redding (1 daily; 5hr 44min).

Buses

Combined Greyhound and Amtrak Thruway schedules.

Arcata to: Crescent City (2 daily; 1hr 30min); Garberville (2 daily; 1hr 30min).

Chico to: Redding (4 daily; 1hr 30min).

Eureka to: Crescent City (2 daily; 1hr 50min); Garberville (2 daily; 1hr 30min).

Mount Shasta to: Yreka (3 daily; 50min).

Redding to: Chico (5 daily; 2hr); Mount Shasta (4 daily; 1hr 30min); Sacramento (7 daily; 4hr); Yreka (3 daily; 2hr 15min).

San Francisco to: Chico (4 daily; 5hr); Redding (5 daily; 6hr); Santa Rosa (2 daily; 1hr 30min).

Santa Rosa to: Arcata (2 daily; 6hr); Crescent City (2 daily; 8hr); Eureka (2 daily; 4hr 40min); Garberville (2 daily; 4hr); Leggett (2 daily; 3hr 30min); Willits (2 daily; 2hr).

PART THREE

THE
CONTEXTS

THE HISTORICAL FRAMEWORK

To many people, California seems one of the least historic places on the planet. Unburdened by the past, it's a land where anything seems possible, whose inhabitants live carefree lives, wholly in and for the present moment. Its very name, appropriately for all its idealized images, is a work of fiction, free from any historical significance. The word first appeared as the name of an island, located "very near to the terrestrial paradise" and inhabited entirely by Amazons "without any men among them," in a popular Spanish picaresque novel of the early 1500s, *Las Sergas de Esplandián* by García de Montalvo.

NATIVE PEOPLES

For thousands of years prior to the arrival of Europeans, the **aboriginal peoples** of California flourished in the naturally abundant land, living fairly peacefully in tribes along the coast and in the deserts and the forested mountains. Anthropologists estimate that nearly half the native population then living within the boundaries of the present-day US were spread throughout what's now California, in small, tribal villages of a few hundred people, each with a clearly defined territory and often its own distinct language. Since there was no political or social organization beyond the immediate level of the tribe, it was not difficult for the coloniz-

ing Spaniards to divide and to conquer, effectively wiping them out – though admittedly more died through epidemics of disease than outright genocide.

Very little remains to mark the existence of the Californian Native Americans: they had no form of written language, relatively undeveloped craft skills, and built next to nothing that would last beyond the change of seasons. About the only surviving signs of the coastal tribes are the piles of seashells and discarded arrowheads that have been found, from which anthropologists have deduced a bit about their cultures. Also, a few examples of **rock art** survive, as at the Chumash Painted Cave, near Santa Barbara on the Central Coast. Similar sorts of petroglyph figures were drawn by the Paiute Native Americans, who lived in the deserts near Death Valley, and by the Miwok from the Sierra Nevada foothills.

DISCOVERY AND EARLY EXPLORATION

The first Europeans to set foot in California were Spanish explorers, intent on extending their colony of New Spain, which under the 1494 Treaty of Tordesillas included all the New World lands west of Brazil and all of North America west of the Rocky Mountains. In 1535, **Hernán Cortéz**, fresh from decimating the Aztecs, headed westward in search of a short cut to Asia, which he believed to be adjacent to Mexico. Though he never reached what's now California, he set up a small colony at the southern tip of the Baja (lower) California peninsula. He thought it was an island, and named it Santa Cruz, writing in his journals that he soon expected to find the imagined island of the Amazons.

The first explorer to use the name California, and to reach what's now the US state, was **Juan Cabrillo**, who sighted San Diego harbor in 1542, and continued north along the coast to the Channel Islands off Santa Barbara. He died there six months later, persistent headwinds having made it impossible to sail any further north. His crew later made it as far north as what is now the state of Oregon, but were unable to find any safe anchorage and returned home starved and half-dead from scurvy. It was fifty years before another Spaniard braved the difficult journey: **Juan de Fuca**'s 1592 voyage caused great excitement when he claimed to have discovered the Northwest Passage, a potentially lucrative trade route across North America. It has long since turned out that there is no such thing as the Northwest Passage (de Fuca may have discovered the Puget Sound, outside Seattle), but Europeans continued to search for it for the next two hundred years.

The British explorer **Sir Francis Drake** arrived in the *Golden Hind* in 1579, taking a break from his piracy of Spanish vessels in order to make repairs. His landing spot, now called Drake's Bay, near Point Reyes north of San Francisco, had "white bancks and cliffes" that reminded him of Dover. Upon landing, he was met by a band of native Miwoks, who feted him with food and drink and placed a feathered crown upon his head; in return, he claimed all of their lands – which he called Nova Albion (New England) – for Queen Elizabeth, supposedly leaving behind a brass plaque that's now on display in the Bancroft Library at the University of California.

Setting sail from Acapulco in 1602, **Sebastián Vizcaíno**, a Portuguese explorer under contract to Spain, made a more lasting impact than his predecessors, undertaking the most extensive exploration of the coast, and bestowing most of the place names that survive. In order to impress his superiors he exaggerated the value of his discoveries, describing a perfect, sheltered harbor which he named **Monterey** in honor of his patron back in Mexico. Subsequent colonizers based their efforts, 150 years later, upon these fraudulent claims (the windy bay did not live up to Vizcaíno's estimation), and the headquarters of the missions and military and administrative center of the Spanish government remained at Monterey, 100 miles south of San Francisco, for the next 75 years.

COLONIZATION: THE SPANISH AND THE BRITISH

The Spanish occupation of California began in earnest in 1769 as a combination of military expediency (to prevent other powers from gaining a foothold) and Catholic missionary zeal (to convert the heathen Native Americans). Father **Junipero Serra** and a company of three hundred soldiers and clergy set off from Mexico for Monterey, half of them by ship, the other half overland. In June 1770, after establishing a small mission and *presidio* (fort) at San Diego, the expedition arrived at Monterey where another mission and small *presidio* were constructed.

The Spanish continued to build missions all along the coast, ostensibly to Catholicize the Native Americans, which they did with inquisitional obsession. The mission complexes were broadly similar, with a church and cloistered residential structure surrounded by irrigated fields, vineyards, and more extensive ranchlands. The labor of the Native American converts was co-opted: they were put to work making soap and candles, were often beaten and never educated. Objective accounts of the missionaries' treatment of the indigenous peoples are rare, though mission registries record twice as many deaths as they do births, and their cemeteries are packed with Native American dead. Not all of the Native Americans gave up without a fight: many missions suffered from raids, and the now ubiquitous red-tiled roofs were originally a replacement for the earlier thatch to better resist arson attacks.

Most of the mission structures that survive today were built to the designs of Serra's successor, Father **Férmin de Lasuén**, who was in charge of the missions during the period of their greatest growth. By the time of his death in 1804, a chain of twenty-one missions, each a long day's walk from its neighbors and linked by the dirt path of *El Camino Real* (The Royal Road), ran from San Diego to San Francisco.

During this time the first towns, called **pueblos**, were established in order to attract settlers to what was still a distant and undesirable territory. The first was laid out in 1777 at San Jose, south of the new mission at San Francisco. Los Angeles, the second *pueblo*, was established in 1781, though neither had more than a hundred inhabitants until well into the nineteenth century.

One reason for Spain's military presence in California – which consisted of four *presidios* all told, with twelve cannons and only two hundred soldiers – was to prevent the expansion of the small **Russian** colony based in Alaska, mostly trappers collecting beaver and otter pelts in the Northwestern states of Washington and Oregon. The two countries were at peace and relations friendly, and in any case the Spanish *presidios* were in no position to enforce their territorial claims. In fact, they were so short of supplies and ammunition that they had to borrow the gunpowder to fire welcoming salutes whenever the two forces came into contact. Well aware of the Spanish weakness, in 1812 the Russians established an outpost, called **Fort Ross**, sixty miles north of San Francisco. This further undermined Spanish sovereignty over the region, though the Russians abandoned the fort in 1841, selling it to John Sutter (who features prominently in later California history; see overleaf).

THE MEXICAN ERA

While Spain, France and England were engaged in the bitter struggles of the Napoleonic Wars, the colonies of New Spain rebelled against imperial neglect, with Mexico finally gaining independence in 1821. The Mexican Republic, or the United States of Mexico as the new country called itself, governed California as a territory, though none of the fifteen distinct administrations it set up – lacking the money to pay for improvements and the soldiers needed to enforce the laws – was ever able to exercise any degree of authority.

The most important effect of the Mexican era was the final **secularization** in 1834, after years of gradual diminution, of the Franciscan missions. As most of the missionaries were Spanish, under Mexican rule they had seen their position steadily eroded by the increasingly wealthy, close-knit families of the *Californios* – Mexican immigrants who'd been granted vast tracts of ranchland. The government's intention was that half of the missions' extensive lands should go to the Indian converts, but this was never carried out, and the few powerful families divided most of it up among themselves.

In many ways this was the most lawless and wantonly wasteful period of California's history, an era described by **Richard Henry Dana** – scion of a distinguished Boston family, who dropped out of Harvard to sail to California – in his 1840 book *Two Years Before the Mast*. Most of the agriculture and cottage industries that had developed under the missionaries disappeared, and it was a point of pride amongst the *Californios* not to do any work that couldn't be done from horseback. Dana's Puritan values led him to heap scorn upon the "idle and thriftless people" who made nothing for themselves. For example, the large herds of cattle that lived on the mission lands were slaughtered for their hides and sold to Yankee traders, who turned the hides into leather which they sold back to the *Californios* at a tidy profit. "In the hands of an enterprising people," he wrote, "what a country this might be."

THE FIRST AMERICANS

Throughout the Mexican and Spanish eras, foreigners were legally banned from settling, and the few who showed up, mostly sick or injured sailors dropped off to regain their health, were often jailed until they proved themselves useful, either as craftsmen or as traders able to supply needed goods. In the late 1820s the first **Americans**, males without exception, began to make their way to California. They tended to fit in with the existing Mexican culture, often marrying into established families and converting to the Catholic faith. The American presence grew slowly but surely as more and more people emigrated, still mostly by way of a three-month sea voyage around Cape Horn. Among these was **Thomas Larkin**, a New England merchant who, in 1832, set up shop in Monterey, and later was instrumental in pointing the disgruntled *Californios* towards the more accommodating US; Larkin's wife Rachel was the first American woman on the West Coast.

The first people to make the four-month journey to California overland – in a covered wagon like in so many Hollywood Westerns – arrived in 1841, having forged a trail over the Sierra Nevada mountains via Truckee Pass, just north of Lake Tahoe. Soon after, hundreds of people each year were following in their tracks. In 1846, however, forty migrants, collectively known as the **Donner Party**, died when they were trapped in the mountains by early winter snowfall. The immense difficulties involved in reaching California, over land and by sea, kept population levels at a minimum, and by 1846 just seven thousand people, not counting Native Americans but including all the Spanish and Mexicans, lived in the entire region.

THE MEXICAN-AMERICAN WAR

From the 1830s onwards – inspired by **Manifest Destiny**, the popular, almost religious belief that the United States was meant to cover the continent from coast to coast – US government policy regarding California was to buy all of Mexico's land north of the Rio Grande, the river that now divides the US and Mexico. President Andrew Jackson was highly suspicious of British designs on the West Coast – he himself had been held as a (14-year-old) prisoner of war during the Revolutionary War of 1776 – and various diplomatic overtures were made to the Mexican Republic, all of which backfired. In April 1846, Jackson's protégé, President James Polk, offered forty million dollars for all of New Mexico and the California territory, but his simultaneous annexation of the newly independent Republic of Texas – which Mexico still claimed – resulted in the outbreak of war.

Almost all the fighting of the **Mexican–American War** took place in Texas; only one real battle was ever fought on Californian soil, at San Pasqual, northeast of San Diego, where a roving US battalion was surprised by a band of pro-Mexican *Californios*, who killed twenty-two soldiers and wounded another fifteen before withdrawing south into Mexico. Monterey, still the territorial capital, was captured by the US Navy without a shot being fired, and in January 1847, when the rebel *Californios* surrendered to the US forces at Cahuenga, near Los Angeles, the Americans controlled the entire West Coast.

Just before the war began, California had made a brief foray into the field of self-government: the short-lived **Bear Flag Republic**, whose only lasting effect was to create what's still the state flag, a prowling grizzly bear with the words "California Republic" written below. In June 1846, American settlers in the Sonoma Valley took over the local *presidio* – long abandoned by the Mexicans – and declared California independent, which lasted for all of three weeks until the US forces took command.

THE GOLD RUSH

As part of the Treaty of Guadalupe Hidalgo, which formally ended the war in 1848, Mexico ceded all of the *Alta California* territory to the US. Nine days before the signing of the accord, in the distant foothills of the Sierra Nevada mountains, flakes of **gold** were discovered by workmen building a sawmill along the American River at Coloma, though it was months before this momentous conjunction of events became known.

At the time, California's non-Native American population was mostly concentrated in the few small towns along the coastal strip. Early rumors of gold attracted a trickle of prospectors, and, following news of their subsequent success, by the middle of 1849 – eighteen months after the initial find – men were flooding into California from all over, in the most madcap migration in world history. **Sutter's Fort**, a small agricultural community, trading post and stage stop which had been established six years earlier by John Sutter on the banks of the American River, was overrun by miners, who headed up into the nearby foothills to make their fortune. Some did, most didn't, but in any case, within fifteen years most of the gold had been picked clean. The miners moved on or went home and their camps vanished, prompting Mark Twain to write that "in no other land, in modern times, have towns so absolutely died and disappeared as in the old mining regions of California."

STATEHOOD

Following the US takeover after the defeat of Mexico, a **Constitutional Convention** was held at Monterey in the autumn of 1849. The men who attended were not the miners – most of whom were more interested in searching for gold – but those who had been in California for some time (about three years on average). At the time, the Territory of California extended all the way east to Utah, so the main topic of discussion was where to draw the eastern boundary of the intended state. The drawing up of a state constitution was also important, since it was the basis on which California applied for admission to the US. The constitution contained a couple of noteworthy inclusions. To protect the dignity of the manually laboring miners, **slavery** was prohibited; and to attract well-heeled **women** from the East Coast, California was the first state to recognize in legal terms the separate property of a married woman. In 1850, California was admitted to the US as the thirty-first state.

THE INDIAN WARS

Though the US Civil War had little effect on California, many bloody battles were fought throughout the 1850s and 1860s by white settlers and US troops against the various Native American tribes whose lands the immigrants wanted. At first the government tried to move willing tribes to fairly large reservations, but as more settlers moved in the tribes were pushed onto smaller and smaller tracts. The most powerful resistance to the well-armed invaders came in the mountainous northeast of California, where a band of **Modoc** fought a long-running guerrilla war, using their superior knowledge of the terrain to evade the US troops.

Due to a combination of disease and lack of food, as well as deliberate acts of violence, the Native American population was drastically reduced, and by 1870 almost ninety percent had been wiped out. The survivors were concentrated in small, relatively valueless reservations, where their descendants still live: the Cahuila near Palm Springs, the Paiute/Shoshone in the Owens Valley, and the Hupa on the northwest coast continue to reside near their ancestral homelands, and are quite naturally defensive of their privacy.

THE BOOM YEARS: 1870–1900

After the Gold Rush, **San Francisco** boomed into a boisterous frontier town, exploding in population from 500 to 50,000 within five years. Though far removed from the mines themselves, the city was the main landing spot for shipborne argonauts (as the prospectors were called), and the main supply town. Moreover, it was the place where successful miners went to blow their hard-earned cash on the whiskey and women of the **Barbary Coast**, then the raunchiest waterfront in the world, full of brothels, saloons and opium dens. Ten years later, San Francisco enjoyed an even bigger boom as a result of the silver mines of the Comstock Lode in Nevada, owned in the main by San Franciscans, who displayed their wealth by building grand palaces and mansions on Nob Hill – still the city's most exclusive address.

The completion in 1869 of the **transcontinental railroad**, built using imported Chinese laborers, was a major turning point in the settlement of California. Whereas the trip across the country by stagecoach took at least a month, and was subject to scorching hot weather and attacks by hostile natives, the crossing could now be completed in just five days.

In 1875, when the Santa Fe railroad reached Los Angeles (the railroad company having extracted huge bribes from local officials to ensure the budding city wasn't bypassed), there were just ten thousand people living in the whole of **Southern California**, divided equally between San Diego and Los Angeles. A rate war developed between the two rival railroads, and ticket costs dropped to as little as $1 for a one-way ticket from New York. Land speculators placed advertisements in East Coast and European papers, offering cheap land for homesteaders in towns and suburbs all over the West Coast that as often as not existed only on paper. By the end of the nineteenth century, thousands of people, ranging from Midwestern farmers to the East Coast elite, had moved to California to take advantage of the fertile land and mild climate.

HOLLYWOOD, THE WAR AND AFTER

The greatest boost to California's fortunes was, of course, the **film industry**, which moved here from the East Coast in 1911, attracted by the temperate climate that enabled films to be shot outdoors year-round, and by the incredibly cheap land that allowed large indoor studios to be built at comparatively little cost. Within three years, movies like D.W. Griffith's *Birth of a Nation* – most of which was filmed along the dry banks of the Los Angeles River – were being cranked out by the hundred.

Hollywood, a suburb of Los Angeles that was the site of many of the early studios, and ever since the buzzword for the entire entertainment industry, has done more to promote the mystique of California as a pleasure garden landscape than any other medium, disseminating images of its glamorous lifestyles around the globe. Los Angeles still dominates the world film industry, and, increasingly, is an international center for the music business as well.

This widespread, idealized image had a magnetic effect during the **Great Depression** of the 1930s, when thousands of people from all over the country descended upon California, which was perceived to be – and for the most part was – immune from the economic downturn which crippled the rest of the US. From the dust bowl Midwest, entire families, who came to be known as **Okies**, packed up everything they owned and set off for the farms of the Central Valley, an epic journey captured by John Steinbeck's best-selling novel *The Grapes of Wrath*, in the photographs of Dorothea Lange, and in the baleful tunes of folk singer Woody Guthrie. Some Californians who feared losing their jobs to the incoming Okies formed vigilante groups and, with the complicity of local and state police, set up roadblocks along the main highways to prevent unemployed outsiders from entering the state.

One Depression-era initiative to alleviate the poverty, and to get the economy moving again, were the US government-sponsored **Works Progress Administration (WPA)** construction projects, ranging from restoring the California missions to building trails and park facilities, and commissioning art works like the marvellous Social Realist murals in San Francisco's Coit Tower.

Things turned around when **World War II** brought heavy industry to California, as shipyards and airplane factories sprang up, providing well-paid employment in wartime factories. After the war, most stayed on, and still today California companies — McDonnell Douglas, Lockheed, Rockwell and General Dynamics, for example — make up the roll call of suppliers to the US military and space programs.

After the war many of the soldiers who'd passed through on their way to the battlegrounds of the South Pacific came back to California and decided to stay on. There was plenty of well-paid work, the US government subsidized house purchases for war veterans and, most importantly, constructed the **freeways** and Interstate highways that enabled land speculators to build new commuter suburbs on land that had been used for farms and citrus orchards.

The **Fifties** brought prosperity to the bulk of middle-class America (typified by President Eisenhower's goal of "two cars in every garage and a chicken in every pot"), and California, particularly San Francisco, became a nexus for alternative artists and writers, spurring an immigration of intellectuals that by the end of the decade had become manifest as the **Beat generation**, pegged "Beatniks," in honor of Sputnik, the Soviet space satellite, by San Francisco columnist Herb Caen.

THE SIXTIES AND SEVENTIES

California remained at the forefront of youth and **social upheavals** into and throughout the **Sixties**. In a series of drug tests carried out at Stanford University — paid for by the CIA, who were interested in developing a "truth drug" for interrogation purposes — unwitting students were dosed with **LSD**. One of the guinea pigs was the writer Ken Kesey, who had just published the highly acclaimed novel *One Flew Over the Cuckoo's Nest*. Kesey quite liked the experience and soon secured a personal supply of the drug (which was as yet still legal) and toured the West Coast to spread the word of "acid." In and around San Francisco Kesey and his crew, the Merry Pranksters, turned on huge crowds at **Electric Kool-Aid Acid Tests** — in which LSD was diluted into bowls of the soft drink Kool-Aid — complete with psychedelic light shows and music by the Grateful Dead. The acid craze reached its height during the **Summer of Love** in 1967, when the entire Haight-Ashbury district of San Francisco seemed populated by barefoot and drugged flower children.

Within a year the superficial peace of Flower Power was shattered, as protests mounted against US involvement in the **Vietnam War**; Martin Luther King and Bobby Kennedy, heroes of left-leaning youth, were both gunned down — Kennedy in Los Angeles after winning the California primary of the 1968 presidential election. The militant **Black Panthers**, a group of black radical activists based in Oakland, terrorized a white population that had earlier been supporters of the Civil Rights Movement. By the end of the Sixties the "system," in California especially, seemed to be at breaking point, and the atrocities committed by **Charles Manson** and his "Family" proved what the rest of the US had known all along: that California was full of madmen and murderers.

The antiwar protests, concentrated at the University of California campus in Berkeley, continued through the early **Seventies**. Emerging from the milieu of revolutionary and radical groups, the Symbionese Liberation Army, a small, well-armed and stridently revolutionary group, set about the overthrow of the US, attracting media (and FBI) attention by murdering civil servants, robbing banks and, most famously, kidnapping 19-year-old heiress **Patty Hearst**. Amid much media attention Hearst converted to the SLA's cause, changing her name to Tanya and for the next two years — until her capture in 1977 — she went underground, provoking national debate about her motives and beliefs.

After the unrest of the previous decade, the **late Seventies** were decidedly dull. The one interesting phenomenon was the rise of **cults**, among them LA's Scientology Church, megalomaniac L. Ron Hubbard's personality-testing sect; the Moonies, who pestered people at airports and public places all over the coast; and San Francisco's People's Temple, of which over a thousand members died when their leader, Jim Jones, dosed them with cyanide in a religious service held at their commune in Guyana. The most public and visible of the lot were the followers of the **Bhagwan Shree Rajshneesh**, clothed entirely in shades of red.

Californian **politics**, after Watergate and the end of American involvement in Vietnam, seemed to lose whatever idealistic fervor it might once have had, and popular culture withdrew into self-satisfaction, typified by the smug harmonies of musicians like the Eagles and Jackson Browne. While the Sixties upheavals were overseen by California Governor Ronald Reagan, who was ready and willing to fight the long-haired hippies, the 1970s saw the reign of "Governor Moonbeam" Jerry Brown, under whose leadership California enacted some of the most stringent **anti-pollution** measures in the world – one of which pays environmental activists to expose corporate polluters, offering a 25 percent commission on the multi-million-dollar fines imposed by the courts. The state also actively encouraged the development of renewable forms of energy such as solar and wind power, and protected the entire coastline from despoilation and development. California also decriminalized the possession of under an ounce of **marijuana** (though it remains an offense to grow or sell it), and the harvesting of marijuana in both states continues to account for over $1 billion each year, making it the number-one cash crop in the number-one agricultural region in the US.

CONTEMPORARY CALIFORNIA

The easy-money **Eighties** crash-landed in a tangled mess, with LA junk-bond king Michael Milkin convicted of multi-billion-dollar fraud and the S&L banking scandals enmeshing such high-ranking politicos as California Senator Alan Cranston, and the **Nineties** kicked off with a stagnant property market and rising unemployment.

In **Los Angeles**, the videotaped beating of black motorist Rodney King by officers of the LA Police Department, and the subsequent acquittal of those officers, sparked off destructive **rioting** in April 1992. State and federal authorities, forced into taking notice of LA's endemic

poverty and violence, promised all sorts of new initiatives – with, as yet, few concrete results. The race issue also dominated the year-long trial of black former football star **O.J. Simpson** – accused and finally acquitted of murdering his ex-wife and a male friend – splitting public opinion into directly opposed camps of black and white.

All these factors combined to make the first five years of the 1990s perhaps the bleakest since the Great Depression, and **natural calamities** – regional flooding, Malibu fires and mudslides, and two dramatic earthquakes – only added to the general malaise. Mike Davis' *City of Quartz*, despite its flaws and inaccuracies, served as a secular bible for the time, an artfully written work based on the inevitable doom LA was facing. And with LA's chronic inter-ethnic hatred, natural disasters, bureaucratic inaction, and general public pessimism, it seemed that Davis was probably right.

For now the jury is out. Current mayor **Richard Riordan**, a multimillionaire technocrat, has presided over a major **revival** in the city's economic fortunes and a restructuring of its economic base – aerospace and automotive industries are dead, having been replaced with tourism, high-tech, and as always, Hollywood. New property developments look favorable, and even crime and violence have tailed off marginally. However, both economic and crime rates probably owe more to changes and improvements at the national level than they do to any real local factors, and racial hostilities are never far away.

San Francisco was also hit hard in the early nineties; on top of AIDS-related illnesses stretching health services, the area was hit by a series of natural disasters. An **earthquake** in October 1989 devastated much of the San Francisco Bay Area, followed two years later by a massive **fire** in the Oakland Hills which burned over two thousand homes and killed two dozen people – the third worst fire in US history.

But even more so than LA, San Francisco's economic upswing has turned the city around, replacing pre-millennium jitters with Information Age optimism. The **Silicon Valley** industries are booming, with companies scrambling to find high-paid workers to fill their constantly growing rosters. San Jose, San Francisco's southern neighbor, now has a larger population than the

Golden Gate city, and even Oakland, the gritty East Bay port-town, is in the midst of a much needed face-lift. Still, not everyone in the Bay Area is happy. **Gentrification**, the hot-button issue of the moment, is threatening to turn San Francisco from a province of activism into a playground for Silicon Valley's rich young things. Housing prices are sky high, and tenancy at 99 percent full, forcing out not only the city's poor but middle class, as well.

Throughout all of these changes, California still clings on to its aura as something of a Promised Land. Barring its complete destruction by the **Big One** (the earthquake that's destined one day to drop half of the state into the Pacific and wipe out the rest under massive tidal waves), the state seems set to continue much as it is, acting as the cornerstone of the mythical West and as the place where America reinvents itself.

WILDLIFE

Though popularly imagined as little more than palm trees and golden sand beaches, for sheer range of landscape, California is hard to beat. With glaciated alpine peaks and meadows, desolate desert sand dunes and flat, fertile agricultural plains, it's no wonder that Hollywood film-makers have so often and successfully used California locations to simulate distant and exotic scenes. These diverse landscapes also support an immense variety of plant and animal life, much of which – due to the protection offered by the various state and national parks, forests and wilderness areas – is both easily accessible and unspoiled by encroaching civilization.

BACKGROUND: LANDSCAPES, GEOLOGY AND EARTHQUAKES

California's landscape has been formed over millions of years through the interaction of all the main geological processes: Ice Age glaciation, erosion, earthquakes and volcanic eruptions. The most impressive results can be seen in **Yosemite National Park**, east of San Francisco, where solid walls of granite have been sliced and shaped into unforgettable cliffs and chasms. In contrast, the sand dunes of **Death Valley** are being constantly shaped and reshaped by the dry desert winds, surrounded by foothills tinted by oxidized mineral deposits into every color of the spectrum.

Earthquakes – which earned Los Angeles the truck driver's nickname "Shakeytown" – are

the most powerful expression of the volatile unrest underlying the placid surface. California sits on the Pacific "Ring of Fire," at the junction of two tectonic plates slowly drifting deep within the earth. Besides the occasional earthquake – like the 1906 quake which flattened San Francisco, or the 1994 tremor which collapsed many of LA's freeways – this instability is also the cause of California's many **volcanoes**. Distinguished by their symmetrical, conical shape, almost all of them are now dormant, though Mount Lassen, in Northern California, did erupt in 1914 and 1915, destroying much of the surrounding forest. Along with the boiling mud pools that accompany even the dormant volcanoes, the most attractive features of volcanic regions are the bubbling **hot springs** – pools of water that flow up from deep underground, heated to a sybaritically soothing temperature. Hot springs occur naturally all over the state, and though some have now been developed into luxurious health spas, most remain in their natural condition, where you can soak your bones *au naturel* surrounded by mountain meadows or wide-open deserts. The best of these are listed throughout the Guide.

Though some of the most fantastic **wildlife**, like the grizzly bear – a ten-foot-tall, two-ton giant that still adorns the state flag of California – and the California condor – one of the world's largest birds, with a wingspan of over eight feet – are now extinct in their natural habitats, plenty more are still alive and thriving, like the otters, elephant seals and gray whales seen all along the coast, and the chubby marmots – shy mammals often found sunning themselves on rocks in higher reaches of the mountains. Plant life is equally varied, from the brilliant but short-lived desert wildflowers to the timeless Bristlecone pine trees, which live for thousands of years on the arid peaks of the Great Basin desert.

Below you will find details of the major **ecosystems** of California. The accounts are inevitably brief, as the area encompasses almost 320,000 square miles (ranging from moist coastal forests and the snow-capped Sierra Nevada peaks to Death Valley, 282 feet below sea level with an annual rainfall of two inches), and is inhabited by a multitude of species. Native to California are 54 species of cactus, 123 species of amphibians and reptiles, 260 species of birds, and 27,000–28,000 species of insects. See "Books" for recommendations of more specific habitat guides. Bear in mind, also, that museums all over the state examine and exhibit the natural world in depth, notably Monterey's superb Aquarium – see p.392 for details.

THE OCEAN

The **Pacific Ocean** determines California's climate, keeping the coastal temperatures moderate all year round. During the spring and summer, cold nutrient-rich waters rise or well up to produce cooling banks of fog and abundant crops of phytoplankton (microscopic algae). The algae nourishes creatures such as krill (small shrimps), which in their turn provide baby food for juvenile fish. This food chain provides fodder for millions of nesting **seabirds**, as well as harbor and elephant **seals**, California **sea lions** and whales. **Gray whales**, the most common species spotted from land, were once almost hunted to the point of extinction, but have returned to the coast in large numbers. During their southward migration to their breeding grounds off Mexico, from December to January, it is easy to spot them from prominent headlands all along the coast, and most harbors have charter services offering whale-watching tours. On their way back to the Arctic Sea, in February and March, the newborn whale pups can sometimes be seen playfully leaping out of the water, or "breaching." Look for the whale's white-plumed spout – once at the surface, it will usually blow several times in succession.

TIDEPOOLS

California's shoreline is composed of three primary ecosystems: tidepools, sandy beaches and estuaries. To explore the **tidepools**, first consult a local newspaper to see when the low tides (two daily) will occur. Be careful of waves, don't be out too far from the shore when the tide returns, and also watch your step – there are many small lives underfoot. There are miles of beaches with tidepools, some of the best at Pacific Grove near Monterey. Here you will find **sea anemones** (they look like green zinnias), hermit crabs, purple and green shore crabs, red sponges, purple sea urchins, starfish ranging from the size of a dime to the size of a hubcap, mussels, abalone and chinese-hat limpets – to name a few. You may also see black **oyster-catchers**, their squawking easily heard over

the surf, foraging for an unwary, lips-agape mussel. Gulls and black turnstones are also common, and during the summer brown pelicans dive for fish just offshore.

The life of the tidepool party is the **hermit crab**, who protects its soft and vulnerable hindquarters with scavenged shells, usually those of the aptly named black turban snail. Hermit crabs scurry busily around in search of a detritus snack, or scuffle with other hermit crabs over the proprietorship of vacant snail shells.

Pacific Grove is also home to large populations of **sea otters**. Unlike most marine mammals, sea otters keep themselves warm with a thick, soft coat rather than blubber. The trade in sea otter pelts brought entrepreneurial Russian and British fur hunters to the West Coast, and by the mid-nineteenth century the otters were virtually extinct. In 1938, a small population was discovered near Big Sur, and with careful protection otters have re-established themselves in the southern part of their range. They are charming creatures with big rubbery noses and Groucho Marx moustaches. With binoculars, it's easy to spot them amongst the bobbing kelp, where they lie on their backs opening sea urchins with a rock, or sleep entwined within a seat belt of kelp which keeps them from floating away. The bulk of the population resides between Monterey Bay and the Channel Islands, but – aside from Pacific Grove – the best places to see them are Point Lobos State Park, the Seventeen-Mile Drive and the Monterey Wharf, where, along with sea lions, they often come to beg for fish.

Many of the **seaweeds** you see growing from the rocks are edible. As one would expect from a Pacific beachfront, there are also **palms** – sea palms, with four-inch-long rubbery stems and flagella-like fronds. Their thick root-like holdfasts provide shelter for small crabs. You will also find giant **kelp** washed up on shore – harvested commercially for use in thickening ice cream.

SANDY BEACHES

The long, golden **sandy beaches** for which California is so famous may look sterile from a distance. However, observe the margin of sand exposed as a gentle wave recedes, and you will see jetstreams of small bubbles emerge from numerous clams and mole crabs. Small shore birds called **sanderlings** race amongst the waves in search of these morsels, and sand dollars are often easy to find along the high tide line.

The most unusual sandy-shore bathing beauties are the **northern elephant seals**, which will tolerate rocky beaches but favor soft sand mattresses for their rotund torsos. The males, or bulls, can reach lengths of over six meters and weigh upwards of four tons; the females, or cows, are petite by comparison – four meters long, and averaging a mere two thousand pounds in weight. They have large eyes, adapted for spotting fish in deep or murky waters; indeed, elephant seals are the deepest diving mammals, capable of staying under water for twenty minutes at a time, reaching depths of over four thousand feet, where the pressure is over a hundred times that at the surface. They have to dive so deeply in order to avoid the attentions of the great white sharks who lurk offshore, for whom they are a favorite meal.

Like otters, elephant seals were decimated by commercial whalers in the mid-nineteenth century for their blubber and hides. By the turn of the century less than a hundred remained, but careful protection has partially restored the California population, which is concentrated on the Channel and Farallon Islands and at Año Nuevo State Park.

Elephant seals only emerge from the ocean to breed or molt; their name comes from the male's long trunk-like proboscis, through which it produces a resonant pinging sound that biologists call "trumpeting," which is how it attracts a mate. The Año Nuevo beach is the best place to observe this ritual. In December and January, the bulls haul themselves out of the water and battle for dominance. The predominant, or alpha, male will do most of the mating, siring as many as fifty young pups, one per mating, in a season. Other males fight it out at the fringes, each managing one or two couplings with the hapless, defenceless females. During this time, the beach is a seething mass of ton upon ton of blubbery seals – flopping sand over their back to keep cool, squabbling with their neighbors while making rude snoring and belching sounds. The adults depart in March but the weaned pups hang around until May.

Different age groups of elephant seals continue to use the beach at different times throughout the summer for molting. Elephant seals are completely unafraid of people, but are huge enough to hurt or even kill you if you get in their way, though you're allowed to get close, except during mating season, when entry into the park is restricted to ranger-guided tours.

ESTUARIES

Throughout California, many **estuarine** or river-mouth habitats have been filled, diked, drained, "improved" with marinas or contaminated by pollutants. Those that survive intact consist of a mixture of mud flats, exposed only at low tide, and salt marsh, together forming a critical wildlife area that provides nurseries for many kinds of invertebrates and fish, and nesting and wintering grounds for many birds. Cord grass, a dominant wetlands plant, produces five to ten times as much oxygen and nutrients per acre as does wheat.

Many interesting creatures live in the thick organic ooze, including the fat **innkeeper**, a revolting-looking pink hot dog of a worm that sociably shares its burrow with a small crab and a fish, polychaete worms, clams and other goodies. Most prominent of estuary birds are the **great blue herons** and **great egrets**. Estuaries are the best place to see wintering shore birds such as dunlin, dowitchers, eastern and western sandpipers and yellowlegs. Peregrine falcons and osprey are also found here.

Important Californian estuaries include Elkhorn Slough, near Monterey, San Francisco Bay and Bolinas Lagoon.

COASTAL BLUFFS

Along the shore, **coastal meadows** are bright with pink and yellow sand verbena, lupines, sea rocket, sea fig and the bright orange **California poppy**, the state flower. Slightly inland, hills are covered with coastal scrub, which consists largely of coyote brush. Coastal canyons contain broadleaf trees such as California laurel, alder, buckeye and oaks – and a tangle of sword ferns, horsetail and cow parsnip.

Common rainy-season canyon inhabitants include four-inch-long banana slugs and rough-skinned newts. In winter, orange-and-black **Monarch butterflies** inhabit large roosts in a few discreet locales, such as Bolinas, Monterey and Pacific Grove. Coastal thickets also provide homes to weasels, bobcats, gray fox, raccoons, black-tailed deer, California quail and garter snakes. **Tule elk**, a once common member of the deer family, have also been reintroduced to the wild; a good place to view them is on Tomales Point at the Point Reyes National Seashore; see p.536 of the Guide.

RIVER VALLEYS

Like most fertile **river valleys**, the Sacramento and Central (San Joaquin) valleys have both been greatly affected by agriculture. Riparian (streamside) vegetation has been logged, wetlands drained and streams contaminated by agricultural run-off. Despite this, the riparian habitat that does remain is a prime wildlife habitat. Wood ducks, kingfishers, swallows and warblers are common, as are gray foxes, racoons and striped skunks. The Sacramento National Wildlife Refuge has one of the world's largest concentrations of **snow geese** during winter months. Other common winter migrants include Canada geese, green-winged and cinnamon teals, pintail, shovelers and wigeon. These refuges are well worth a visit, but don't be alarmed by large numbers of duck-hunters – the term "refuge" is a misnomer. However, most have tour routes where hunting is prohibited.

Vernal pools are a valley community unique to California. Here, hardpan soils prevent the infiltration of winter rains, creating seasonal ponds. As these ponds slowly evaporate in April and May, sharply defined concentric floral rings come into bloom. The white is meadowfoam, the blue is the violet-like downingia, and the yellow is goldfields. Swallows, meadowlarks, yellowlegs and stilts can also be found. Jepson Prairie Nature Conservancy Reserve is the easiest to visit, south of Sacramento near the small town of Rio Vista.

FORESTS

Perhaps the most notable indigenous features of Californian forests are the wide expanses of **redwood** and **sequoia trees**. It's easy to confuse the coastal species, *Sequoia sempervirens*, or redwood, with the *Sequoiadendron giganteum*, or giant sequoia (pronounced *suk-oy-ah*), as both have the same fibrous reddish-brown bark. Redwoods are the world's tallest trees, sequoias have the greatest base circumference and are the largest single organisms on earth. Both species can live for over two thousand years, and recent research now indicates a maximum age of 3500 years for the sequoia.

Their longevity is partially due to their bark: rich in tannin, it protects the tree from fungal and insect attack and inhibits fire damage. In fact, fire is beneficial to these trees and necessary for their germination; prescribed fires are set and controlled around them. The wood of these great trees is much sought after both for its beauty – near any forest you'll see signs advertising redwood burl furniture – and its resistance to decay (the bark continues to protect the tree for several hundred years after felling).

They are the only surviving members of a family of perhaps forty species of trees which, fossil records show, grew worldwide 175 million years ago. Now just a few pockets remain, and a tremendous battle between environmentalists and loggers is being waged over the remaining acres. These **virgin forests** provide homes to unique creatures such as the spotted owl and marbled murrelet.

Redwoods are a relict species, which means that they flourished in a moister climate during the Arcto-Tertiary (just after the golden age of the dinosaurs), and now occupy a much-reduced range. As the weather patterns changed, redwoods slowly retreated to their current near-coastal haunts. Today, they are found from the border with Oregon to just south of Monterey.

The floor of the redwood forest is a hushed place with little sunlight, the air suffused with a rufous glow from the bark, which gives the trees its name. One of the commonest ground covers in the redwood forest is the redwood sorrel, or oxalis, with its shamrock leaves and tubular pink flowers; ferns are also numerous. Birds are usually high in the canopy and hard to see, but you might hear the double-whistled song of the varied thrush, or the "chickadee" call from the bird of that name. Roosevelt elk, larger than the tule elk, also inhabit the humid northwest forests. Prairie Creek Redwoods State Park, near the border with Oregon, has a large herd.

Sequoias are found on the western slopes of the Sierra Nevada, most notably in Yosemite and Kings Canyon National Parks – though saplings given as state gifts can be found growing to more modest dimensions all over the world.

The sequoia forest tends to be slightly more open than the redwood forest. Juvenile sequoias – say up to a thousand years old – exhibit a slender conical shape which, as the lower branches fall away, ages to the classical heavy-crowned shape with its columnar trunk. For its bulk, its cones are astonishingly small, no bigger than a hen's egg, but they live on the tree for up to thirty years before falling.

THE SIERRA NEVADA

In the late nineteenth century, the environmental movement was founded when John Muir fell in love with the **Sierra Nevada** mountains, which he called the Range of Light. Muir fought a losing battle to save Hetch Hetchy, a valley said to be more beautiful than Yosemite, but in the process the Sierra Club was born and the move to save America's remaining wilderness began.

The Sierra mountains, which run almost the entire length of the state, have a sharp, craggy, freshly glaciated look. Many of the same conifers can be found as in the forests further west, but ponderosa and lodge-pole pines are two of the dominants, and the forests tend to be drier and more open. Lower elevation forests contain incense cedar, sugar pine (which has the longest pine cones – over eighteen inches – in the world) and black oak. The oaks, along with dogwood and willows, produce spectacular autumnal color. The east side is drier and has large groves of aspen, a beautiful white-barked tree with small round leaves that tremble in the wind. **Wildflowers** flourish for a few short months – shooting star, elephant's head and wild onions in early spring, asters and yarrow later in the season.

The dominant campground scoundrels are two sorts of noisy, squawking bird: Steller's jays and Clark's nutcrackers. Black bears, who may make a raid on your campground, pose more danger to iceboxes than humans, but nonetheless you should treat them with caution. The friendly twenty-pound pot-bellied rodents that lounge around at the fringes of your encampment are **marmots**, who probably do more damage than bears: some specialize in chewing on radiator hoses of parked cars.

Other common birds include mountain chickadees, yellow-rumped warblers, white-crowned sparrows and juncos. Deer, golden-mantled ground squirrels and chipmunks are also plentiful.

THE GREAT BASIN

The little-known **Great Basin** stretches from the northernmost section of the state down almost to Death Valley, encompassing all of Nevada and parts of all the other bordering states. It's a land of many shrubs and few streams, and what streams do exist drain into saline lakes rather than the ocean.

Mono Lake, reflecting the 13,000-foot peaks of Yosemite National Park, is a spectacular example. Its salty waters support no fish but lots of algae, brine shrimp and brine flies, the latter two providing a smorgasbord for nesting gulls (the term "seagull" isn't strictly correct – many gulls nest inland) and migrating phalaropes and grebes. Like many Great Basin lakes, Mono Lake has been damaged through diversion of its freshwater feeder streams to provide water for the city of Los Angeles.

Great Basin plants tolerate hot summers, cold winters and little rain. The dominant Great Basin plant is **sagebrush**. Its dusky green leaves are very aromatic, especially after a summer thunderstorm. Other common plants include bitterbrush, desert peach, junipers and piñon pines. Piñon cones contain tasty nuts that were a mainstay of the Paiute diet.

The **sage grouse** is one of the most distinctive Great Basin birds. These turkey-like birds feed on sage during the winter and depend on it for nesting and courtship habitat. In March and April, males gather at dancing grounds called leks, where they puff out small pink balloons on their necks, make soft drum-banging calls, and in general succeed in looking and sounding rather silly. The hens coyly scout out the talent by feigning greater interest in imaginary seeds.

Pronghorns are beautiful tawny-gold antelope seen in many places in the Great Basin. Watch for their twinkling white rumps as you drive.

Other Great Basin denizens include golden eagles, piñon jays, black-billed magpies, coyotes, feral horses and burros, black-tailed jackrabbits and western rattlesnakes. Large concentrations of waterfowl gather at Tule Lake in northeastern California, where hundreds of wintering **bald eagles** gather in November before the cold really sets in.

THE MOJAVE DESERT

The **Mojave Desert** lies in the southeast corner of the state, near Death Valley. Like the Great Basin, the vegetation here consists primarily of drought-adapted shrubs, one of the commonest of which is creosote, with its olive-green leaves and puffy yellow flowers. Death

Valley is renowned for its early spring wild-flower shows. The alluvial fans are covered with desert trumpet, gravel ghost and pebble pincushion. The quantity and timing of rainfall determines when the floral display peaks, but it's usually some time between mid-February and mid-April in the lower elevations, late April to early June higher up.

Besides shrubs, the Mojave has many inter-esting kinds of **cactus**. These include barrel, cottontop, cholla and beavertail cactus, and many members of the yucca family. Yuccas have stiff, lance-like leaves with sharp tips, a con-spicuous representative being the **Joshua tree**, whose twisting arm-like branches are cov-ered with shaggy upward-pointing leaf fronds, which can reach to thirty feet high.

Many Mojave desert animals conserve body moisture by foraging at night, including the kit fox, wood rat and various kinds of mice. The **kangaroo rat**, an appealing animal that hops rather than runs, has specially adapted kidneys that enable it to survive without drinking water. Other desert animals include mammals such as the Mojave ground squirrel, bighorn and coyote; birds like the roadrunner, ash-throated flycatcher, ladder-backed woodpeck-er, verdin and Lucy's warbler; and reptiles like the Mojave rattlesnake, sidewinder and chuck-walla.

CALIFORNIA
ON FILM

In the early 1910s, attracted by the endless sunshine, the cheap real estate and the rich variety of landscape throughout the state of California, a number of independent movie producers left the East Coast and the strangle-hold monopoly of the Motion Picture Patents Company, and set up shop in a small Los Angeles suburb called Hollywood. Within a decade Hollywood had become the movie capital of the world and Southern California, by default, became the setting for everything from Keystone Cop car chases to low-rent Westerns, not to mention the odd Biblical epic or old-world romance shot on studio lots.

But, as the movie industry grew, Hollywood's films about California – as opposed to those that just happened to be set there – began to take on a special sheen, whether presenting the state as the kind of idyllic El Dorado beloved of the pioneers, or, more commonly, as a state of mind. Much has changed on the long road between John Farrow's **California** (1946), in which Ray Milland leads a wagon train to the Promised Land during the Gold Rush, and Dominic Sena's **Kalifornia** (1993), in which David Duchovny unwittingly invites a serial killer along for the cross-country ride, but both films posit California as the answer to everybody's problems. ("If it wasn't OK there, then it probably wouldn't be OK anywhere" says Duchovny).

Transcendence used to be what California was all about, and it's still a major theme in Californian films. But more and more California – or more specifically Los Angeles – seems to be turning into not an answer, but simply a problem. The City of Dreams is becoming the City of Recurring Nightmares, a locus of vapid consumerism, rampant crime and racial division, trembling on the verge of **apocalypse**. Or so the movies tell us.

Hardly surprisingly, the list of movies set in California, and especially Los Angeles, is endless. What follows is a roll-call of the most significant movies, those that make the most original use of Californian locations (from the vertiginous streets of San Francisco, to the breakers of Monterey, from the dust bowls of the Mojave to the storm drains of LA), as well as those that reflect California's navel-gazing fascination with itself.

HOLLYWOOD DOES HOLLYWOOD

The Bad and the Beautiful (Vincente Minnelli 1952). Made just as the studio system was beginning to come apart at the seams, Minnelli's bitter insider tale of the rise and fall of a ruthless Hollywood producer (Kirk Douglas) is told in flashbacks by the star, the writer and the director he launched and subsequently lost.

Ed Wood (Tim Burton 1994). The ragged low-budget fringes of Fifties Hollywood are beautifully recreated in this loving tribute to the much-derided auteur of *Plan Nine from Outer Space* and *Glen or Glenda*. Gorgeously shot in black and white, and with a stunning performance by Martin Landau as ailing Hollywood habitué Bela Lugosi.

Get Shorty (Barry Sonnenfeld 1995). When movie-loving Miami loan shark Chili Palmer (John Travolta) is sent to Hollywood to collect a debt from schlock-horror auteur Harry Zim (Gene Hackman), he sees his chance to pull a fast one on a gang of drug-smuggling mobsters and get his name in lights. Faithfully based on the Elmore Leonard novel.

Gods and Monsters (Bill Condon 1998). An interesting tale of 1930s horror-film director James Whale's (masterfully portrayed by Ian McKellen) final days, ignored by the Hollywood elite and slowly dying of malaise by his poolside. The title refers to a memorable Ernest

Thesiger line from Whale's classic *The Bride of Frankenstein*.

Hurlyburly (Anthony Drazan 1998). David Rabe's acidic play about Hollywood players and hucksters is rendered in celluloid as a prattling pathos-fest, with much angst for Sean Penn and Chazz Palmenteri and much ironic detachment for Kevin Spacey and Garry Shandling.

In a Lonely Place (Nicholas Ray 1950). A glamor-less Hollywood peopled with alcoholic former matinee idols, star-struck hat-check girls and desperate agents forms the cynical background for this devastating doomed romance between Humphrey Bogart's hot-tempered screenwriter and his Beverly Hills neighbor Gloria Grahame.

The Player (Robert Altman 1992). Tim Robbins is perfectly smug as an egocentric studio executive getting away with murder. Peopled with movie stars playing themselves, and packed with movie-biz in-jokes, Altman's tour-de-force is a wickedly accurate depiction of Hollywood's lowered expectations and diminishing returns.

Singin' in the Rain (Stanley Donen & Gene Kelly 1952). The eternally popular, lovingly made song-and-dance satire about Hollywood's fraught transition from silents to talkies. With great songs, perceptive gags, and the unforgettable title sequence, the film is pure pleasure.

A Star is Born (George Cukor 1954). The best of many versions of this classic Hollywood weepie, in which Judy Garland is given a hand up the ladder by James Mason, an alcoholic former star very much on the way down.

Sunset Boulevard (Billy Wilder 1950). The darkest of the many mirrors Hollywood has held up to itself, Wilder's acerbic classic about an impoverished screenwriter (William Holden) who falls into the clutches of an aging silent film star (Gloria Swanson) posits Hollywood as a nightmare world of vanity, illusion and decline.

Who Framed Roger Rabbit? (Robert Zemeckis 1988). This eye-popping fusion of live-action and animation imagines a Forties Hollywood in which cartoon characters inhabit the same universe as humans, but only as second class citizens forced to live in the crime-ridden cartoon ghetto of Toontown.

LA CRIME STORIES

American Gigolo (Paul Schrader 1980). LA is at its glossiest and most vacuous in this arty,

muted, pulp thriller about a high-class, Armani-clad male prostitute (Richard Gere), framed for murder and searching for grace.

Chinatown (Roman Polanski 1974). One of the most memorable cinematic marriages of story and setting, Polanski's classic neo-noir stars Jack Nicholson as a private eye adrift in the moral desert of late Thirties LA, when real estate was booming, water scarce, and corruption at every level a given.

Double Indemnity (Billy Wilder 1944). The definitive LA noir, in which traveling insurance salesman and all-round fall-guy Fred MacMurray provides us with an incidental tour of Forties LA as he winds himself ever more tightly into Barbara Stanwyck's devastating web of duplicity.

Heat (Michael Mann 1995). The urban architecture of LA has rarely been more beautifully filmed than in this criminally underrated face-off between Robert De Niro's master-thief and Al Pacino's dogged detective which plays out against a stunning Antonioniesque backdrop of shimmering cityscapes, spaghetti-looped freeways, and the runways of LAX.

He Walked By Night (Alfred Werker 1948). This verité-style crime story set in "the fastest growing city in the nation" starts with a random cop-killing in Santa Monica and ends with a manhunt though the 700-mile subterranean city storm drain system, stunningly shot by torch-light by peerless noir cinematographer John Alton.

The Killing of a Chinese Bookie (John Cassavetes 1976). Strange and self-indulgent, but perfectly evoking the sleazy charms of the Sunset Strip, Cassavetes' behavioral crime story about a club-owner (Ben Gazzara) in hock to the mob is just one of his many great LA-based character studies.

LA Confidential (Curtis Hanson 1997). A sizzling epic of police corruption and Tinsel-town sleaze in Fifties Los Angeles – a city swarming with unscrupulous tabloid journalists, venal bureaucrats, racist cops and movie-star-looka-like whores. Superbly done.

The Long Goodbye (Robert Altman 1973). Altman's masterpiece updates Raymond Chandler's shadowy Forties noir to sun-drenched Seventies me-generation LA. Elliot Gould's disheveled Philip Marlowe lives in the Hollywood Hills with a bevy of hippy chicks for neighbors and a bushel of problems that take him from Tijuana to Malibu and back.

Point Blank (John Boorman 1967). Though it begins and ends at Alcatraz, Boorman's virtuoso avant-garde thriller, in which a poker-faced Lee Marvin seeks revenge for an earlier betrayal, is most effective imagining Los Angeles as an impenetrable citadel of concrete and glass built on the wages of corporate crime.

To Live and Die in LA (William Friedkin 1985). The glossiest and flashiest of LA policiers, Friedkin's updating of his *French Connection* formula to the Eighties and the West Coast follows two FBI agents on the trail of a master counterfeiter, and features another of his trademark spectacular car-chases – this time LA-style on a major freeway at rush hour.

APOCALYTPIC LA

Blade Runner (Ridley Scott 1982). This brilliant combination of sci-fi and neo-noir envisions the Los Angeles of 2019 as a depopulated, crime-ridden metropolis of towering skyscrapers, sprawling street-markets, and perpetual darkness, where Harrison Ford's gumshoe tracks renegade replicants through the never-ending acid rain.

Escape from LA (John Carpenter 1996). In Carpenter's alternative vision of the future, Los Angeles has been cut off from the mainland by an earthquake and declared so "ravaged by crime and immorality" that it has been turned into a deportation zone for undesirables. Sent in to uproot insurrection, Kurt Russell battles psychotic plastic surgeons in Beverly Hills and surfs a tsunami to a showdown in a netherworld Disneyland.

Falling Down (Joel Schumacher 1993). Mad as hell, and unable to tolerate the height-of-summer LA traffic jam in which he finds himself, Michael Douglas abandons his car and goes on the rampage through some of the city's less picturesque neighborhoods, railing at petty injustices and wreaking havoc with every step.

Kiss Me Deadly (Robert Aldrich 1955). Aldrich's no-holds barred apocalypse-noir follows proto-fascist private eye Mike Hammer on a punch-drunk tour of LA in search of a deadly Maguffin – from boarding houses to the mansions of Beverly Hills to a Malibu beach house where, quite literally, all hell breaks loose.

1941 (Steven Spielberg 1979). "This isn't the State of California, this is a state of insanity," yells Robert Stack's General Stillwell as LA prepares for a Japanese invasion at the height of post-Pearl Harbor paranoia. Spielberg's joylessly frantic epic comedy begins with John Belushi crash-landing in Death Valley and ends with a submarine attack on the Santa Monica Pier.

The Rapture (Michael Tolkin 1991). Mimi Rogers plays an LA telephone operator who abandons her hedonistic lifestyle when she hears a fundamentalist group talking about the impending "Rapture," and becomes born again, ultimately heading into the desert to await Armageddon. Michael Tolkin's wonderfully literal film takes his premise just as far as it can go, and then some.

Strange Days (Kathryn Bigelow 1995). In this visceral, millennial joy-ride by one of LA's most visionary auteurs, Angelenos party like it's 1999, and Ralph Fiennes' Lenny Nero fiddles while his racially-sundered city burns. Surrogate thrills, in the form of virtual reality tapes of someone else's private heaven or hell, are the illegal drug of choice as the century goes out with a bang.

Terminator 2: Judgment Day (James Cameron 1991). As in Cameron's impressive first *Terminator* (1984), the machines in charge of the future have sent a cyborg back in time to assassinate a future resistance leader. This time, however, the film makes even more memorable use of LA locations, with a thrilling truck chase along the concrete bed of the Los Angeles River and a spectacular visualization of the city's apocalyptic destiny.

They Live (John Carpenter 1988). In this ludicrous but entertaining horror flick, a drifter living in a shanty town pitched on the outskirts of LA discovers a pair of sunglasses that allow him to see that skull-faced aliens in positions of wealth and power are subliminally encouraging the city's rampant consumerism.

MODERN LA

Boyz 'n' the Hood (John Singleton 1991). Singleton's influential debut film, a sober portrayal of life in South Central LA, highlights the odds against success or even survival in a community riddled with drugs, poverty and violence.

Clueless (Amy Heckerling 1995). As exemplary of LA in the Nineties as *Boyz 'n' the Hood*, Heckerling's Girls in the Mall comedy made a star of Alicia Silverstone, who guides us through the empty heads of shopaholic Beverly Hills High schoolgirls and their Valley-inflected, rich-kid lingo.

The End of Violence (Wim Wenders 1997). Bill Pullman plays a successful schlock-movie producer obsessed with violence who finds redemption after he is nearly murdered himself. Wenders' existential thriller is preposterous and po-faced but he films end-of-the-millennium LA with a hypnotically other-worldly beauty and his typically quizzical outsider's gaze.

The Glass Shield (Charles Burnett 1995). Institutionalized racism in the LAPD is brought under the harsh glare of Charles Burnett, who, with his masterpieces *Killer of Sheep* (1977) and *My Brother's Wedding* (1983), has long been one of the great chroniclers of LA's black urban underclass.

Go (Doug Liman 1999). A kinetic joy-ride through LA's rave subculture told from three perspectives, including Sarah Polley's botching of an aspirin-for-Ecstasy drug sale, and Jay Mohr and Scott Wolf – as two TV soap stars – stuck in a police sting operation.

Magnolia (Paul Thomas Anderson 1999). Anderson's darkly affecting travelogue of human misery staring, amongst many others, Jason Robards and Tom Cruise. The San Fernando Valley serves as an emotional inferno of abusive parents, victimized children, haunted memories, plaintive songs, and a curious plague of frogs.

Pulp Fiction (Quentin Tarantino 1994). Tarantino's electrifying roundelay of stories about sudden deaths and second chances is set in a depopulated, down-at-heel Los Angeles of kitsch diners and low-rent motels, store basements and funereal saloons – a deliberately bland backdrop against which his fast-talking hustlers and half-hearted hit-men seem all the more vivid.

Short Cuts (Robert Altman 1993). Transposing the stories of Raymond Carver from Washington to LA, Altman's haunting, bluesy city symphony brilliantly knits together the parallel universes inhabited by a gaggle of suburban Angelenos whose lives are interlinked by small disasters and surprising moments of grace.

Speed (Jan De Bont 1994). In a city in which public transportation is little more than a utopian ideal, and in which bumper-to-bumper traffic clogs the freeways from morning till night, the idea of a city bus primed to explode if its speed drops below 50mph was the perfect LA joke, as well as the excuse for a thrilling travelogue of the city's transit system.

Star Maps (Miguel Arteta 1997). A *telenovela*-esque melodrama of immigrant life on the fringes of Hollywood. Carlos, who has grandiose dreams of movie stardom, is doing time in his father's prostitution ring, standing on street corners ostensibly selling maps to the homes of the stars, in reality selling his body for cash.

Swingers (Doug Liman 1996). Modern-day cocktail culture is skewered in this hilarious cult favorite about a couple of dudes who spend their nights in Sunset Boulevard lounges and swing clubs eyeing up the "beautiful babies" and shooting the breeze like Rat-Pack-era Sinatras.

IF YOU'RE GOING TO SAN FRANCISCO...

The Conversation (Francis Ford Coppola 1974). Opening with a mesmerizing sequence of high-tech eavesdropping in Union Square, Coppola's chilling character study of San Francisco surveillance expert Harry Caul (Gene Hackman at his finest) is one of the best films of the paranoid Watergate era.

Dim Sum: A Little Bit of Heart (Wayne Wang 1985). Set among San Francisco's Chinese community, Wayne Wang's appealing comedy-of-manners about assimilation and family ties is a modest and rewarding treat. His earlier sleeper *Chan is Missing* (1982) also shows a Chinatown tourists don't usually see.

Dirty Harry (Don Siegel 1971). Based on the infamous case of the Bay Area Zodiac Killer, Siegel's morally debatable, sequel-spawning, catch-phrase-begetting thriller casts Clint Eastwood in his most famous role as neo-fascist San Francisco cop who'll do anything to get his man and make his day.

Escape from Alcatraz (Don Siegel 1979). Though evocatively portrayed in *The Bird Man of Alcatraz*, *Point Blank*, *The Rock* and many others, this is the ultimate movie about San

Francisco's famously unbreachable offshore penitentiary. Starring Clint Eastwood (again) as a most resourceful con.

Greed (Erich von Stroheim 1924). This legendary silent masterpiece about the downfall of Polk Street dentist Doc McTeague was shot mostly on location in the Bay Area, and remains, even in its notoriously truncated version, a wonderful time capsule of working-class San Francisco in the 1920s.

Petulia (Richard Lester 1968). Julie Christie is dazzling in this fragmented puzzle of a movie about a vivacious and unpredictable married woman who has an affair with a divorced doctor (George C. Scott). Set against the wittily-described background of psychedelic-era San Francisco, and superbly shot by Nicolas Roeg, *Petulia* is a forgotten Sixties masterpiece.

Play It Again, Sam (Herbert Ross 1972). A strike in Manhattan led to one of Woody Allen's rare visits to the West Coast, for this hilarious film about a neurotic San Francisco film critic in love with his best friend's wife and obsessed with Humphrey Bogart in *Casablanca*.

The Times of Harvey Milk (Robert Epstein 1984). This powerful and moving documentary about America's first openly gay politician chronicles his career in pre-Aids-era San Francisco and the aftermath of his 1978 assassination.

Vertigo (Alfred Hitchcock 1958). Hitchcock's somber, agonized, twisted, tragic love story is the San Francisco movie nonpareil. From James Stewart's wordless drives around the city to the film's climax at the San Juan Bautista mission, Hitchcock takes us on a mesmerizing tour of a city haunted by its past.

What's up Doc (Peter Bogdanovich 1972). This madcap homage to the heyday of Hollywood screwball comedy stars Ryan O'Neal as a hapless stuffed-shirt musicologist and Barbara Streisand as the kook who drives him around the bend, and features, next to Steve McQueen's *Bullitt*, one of the great vertiginous San Francisco car chases.

"WAY OUT" WEST

Bob & Carol & Ted & Alice (Paul Mazursky 1969). This once-daring, now dated, but still funny zeitgeist satire about wife-swapping and bed-hopping in late Sixties Southern California,

starring Natalie Wood, Robert Culp, Elliott Gould and Dyan Cannon as the titular foursome.

Boogie Nights (Paul Thomas Anderson, 1997). Eddie Adams from Torrance meets stroke-movie auteur Jack Horner in a San Fernando Valley nightclub and is reborn as porn-star "Dirk Diggler" in this delirious ode to Seventies excess and Eighties redemption in sexy, swingin' Southern California.

California Suite (Herbert Ross 1978). "It's like paradise, with a lobotomy" snarls Jane Fonda's hard-bitten East Coast journalist when faced with ex-husband Alan Alda's new Californian lifestyle in the best of these four Neil Simon stories about out-of-towners at the Beverly Hills Hotel.

LA Story (Mick Jackson 1991). Steve Martin's sentimental, only-in-LA love story is laced with in-jokes about automobile dependence, health-obsession, and double-decaf lattes, and filmed by British director Jackson with an outsider's tolerant delight.

Modern Romance (Albert Brooks 1981). Brooks – the Woody Allen of the West Coast – stars in this hysterical comedy about a neurotic film editor who dumps his girlfriend and instantly regrets it. Full of early Eighties LA signifiers from quaaludes to jogging suits to off-Hollywood parties with B-movie stars.

Point Break (Kathryn Bigelow 1991). If any film captures the sun-drenched, free-spirited élan of California, it's this slightly preposterous but thrillingly kinetic crime story starring Patrick Swayze as a bank-robbing, sky-diving New Age surfer dude and Keanu Reeves as his straight-arrow FBI nemesis significantly named Johnny Utah.

Rebel Without a Cause (Nicholas Ray 1955). The seminal LA youth movie in which James Dean, at his most perfectly iconographic as the new kid in town, kicks over the traces at Hollywood High School and falls in with disaffected rich kid Sal Mineo and mixed-up school sweetheart Natalie Wood.

Safe (Todd Haynes 1995). In Haynes' brilliant tale of millennial unease and corporeal paranoia, Julianne Moore plays a San Fernando Valley homemaker with seemingly little inner-life and an opulent outer one, who is diagnosed with environmental sickness and finds refuge at a New Age desert retreat.

Sex: the Annabel Chong Story (Gough Lewis 1999) An unblinking documentary that reveals some of the seediest aspects of LA's porn business, starring Annabel Chong, porn star and avowed feminist who set out to break the world "gang bang" record by having sex with 251 men in front of a camera, all in the space of ten hours. A complex and riveting portrait, though not for the easily offended or disgusted.

Shampoo (Hal Ashby 1975). Great cast in a spot-on adult comedy, which sees LA as a big bed on the eve of the 1968 presidential election. Co-writer Warren Beatty has one of his best roles as an inarticulate, confused, priapic Beverly Hills hairdresser.

Slums of Beverly Hills (Tamara Jenkins 1998). Traveling back to the 1970s, troubled teen Natasha Lyonne deals with growing pains in a less glamorous section of town, far from Rodeo Drive, where a pill-popping cousin, manic uncle, weird neighbors, and her own expanding bustline are but a few of her worries.

Valley Girl (Martha Coolidge 1983). Southern Californian cultures clash in this sweet romance between the eponymous Valley Girl Deborah Foreman and "Hollyweird" punk Nicholas Cage. The *Clueless* of its day.

OFF THE BEATEN TRACK

Bagdad Café (Percy Adlon 1988). Lovable, inspiring fable about a German tourist (the incomparable Marianne Sagebrecht) who arrives at a dusty roadside diner in the Mojave Desert and magically transforms the place with her larger-than-life charm.

The Birds (Alfred Hitchcock 1963). Set in Bodega Bay, just north of San Francisco, Hitchcock's terrifying allegory about a small town besieged by a plague of vicious birds, features indelible bird's-eye views of the Northern Californian coastline.

California (John Farrow 1946). Ray Milland leads a wagon train to the Land of Milk and Honey only to find the land ruled by greed and graft, in this elaborate paean to the pioneer spirit and the founding of the state. Worth seeing for its ecstatic opening montage of

Californian vistas and aphorisms about the approaching Promised Land.

Faster, Pussycat! Kill! Kill! (Russ Meyer 1965). Meyer's wonderfully lurid camp action flick unleashes a trio of depraved go-go girls upon an unsuspecting California desert. One of a kind.

Fat City (John Huston 1972). Stacy Keach and Jeff Bridges star in Huston's poignant, evocative, beautifully paced portrait of barflies, has-beens and no-hopers on the small-time boxing circuit in Stockton, Northern California.

One-Eyed Jacks (Marlon Brando 1961). Set, unusually for a western, on the roaring shores of Monterey, where Brando tracks down Karl Malden – the bank-robbing partner who betrayed him five years earlier in Mexico – only to find him reformed and comfortably ensconced as sheriff.

Play Misty for Me (Clint Eastwood 1971). Another Monterey movie, Eastwood's directorial debut, a thriller about the consequences of a DJ's affair with a psychotic fan, was shot in Clint's home town of Carmel, and on his own two hundred acres of Monterey coastland.

Shadow of a Doubt (Alfred Hitchcock 1943). Urbane Uncle Charlie (Joseph Cotten) comes to stay with his sister's Santa Rosa family and seems to be the answer to his bored niece's prayers, until she starts to suspect that he might be a mass murderer. Hitchcock's brilliantly funny and enthralling film is a perfect depiction of life in small-town Northern California.

Three Women (Robert Altman 1977). A fascinating, hypnotic and utterly unique film in which Sissy Spacek and Shelley Duvall, co-workers at a geriatric center in Desert Springs, mysteriously absorb each other's identity. A film brilliantly imbued with the woozy spirit of Southern California.

Zabriskie Point (Michelangelo Antonioni 1970). Though it opens with student sit-ins at UCLA, Antonioni's gorgeous, too often derided homage to Flower Power disaffection is most famous for its Death Valley love-in and the stunningly voluptuous explosion in the desert, that blows the lid off Southern Californian consumerism.

CALIFORNIA IN FICTION

While California may be mythologized as the ultimate stimulant for the imagination, it has inspired comparatively few travel writers, an exception being Robert Louis Stevenson, whose lively description of the Napa Valley and Mount St Helena is printed below. In contrast, floods of fiction have poured out of the state, in particular Los Angeles, over the last few decades, not only shaping perceptions of the region, but often redefining the whole course of modern American writing.

The contemporary writers featured here – Amy Tan and T. Coraghessan Boyle – are both concerned with newcomers to the state, Amy Tan with the interaction of an older generation who grew up in China with their sophisticated San Francisco daughters, and T.C. Boyle with the explosion of the Mexican population in LA, and its uneasy impact on the white elite.

ROBERT LOUIS STEVENSON

Robert Louis Stevenson was born in Edinburgh in 1850, and was educated at the academy and university there. He became an ardent traveler, writing *An Inland Voyage* and *Travels with a Donkey* about his journeys through France, where he fell in love with a married American woman, Fanny Osbourne. She obtained her divorce in 1879 and Stevenson, battling with ill-health, sailed to America to marry her. They took their honeymoon in the mountains of San Francisco. The result of this happy period in Stevenson's life is *Silverado Squatters*, a charming if occasionally slight volume about the landscape and characters of the mountains, already inflected with Stevenson's vigorous descriptive powers – and love of a good yarn. In this extract, Stevenson sets the scene of his book, and interestingly prefigures how development will change the area.

THE SILVERADO SQUATTERS

The scene of this little book is on a high mountain. There are, indeed, many higher; there are many of a nobler outline. It is no place of pilgrimage for the summary globe-trotter; but to one who lives upon its sides, Mount Saint Helena soon becomes a centre of interest. It is the Mont Blanc of one section of the Californian Coast Range, none of its near neighbours rising to one-half its altitude. It looks down on much green, intricate country. It feeds in the springtime many splashing brooks. From its summit you must have an excellent lesson of geography: seeing, to the south, San Francisco Bay, with Tamalpais on the one hand and Monte Diablo on the other; to the west and thirty miles away, the open ocean; eastward, across the cornlands and thick tule swamps of Sacramento Valley, to where the Central Pacific railroad begins to climb the sides of the Sierras; and northward, for what I know, the white head of Shasta looking down on Oregon. Three counties, Napa County, Lake County, and Sonoma County, march across its cliffy shoulders. Its naked peak stands nearly four thousand five hundred feet above the sea; its sides are fringed with forest; and the soil, where it is bare, glows warm with cinnabar.

Life in its shadow goes rustically forward. Bucks, and bears, and rattlesnakes, and former mining operations, are the staple of men's talk. Agriculture has only begun to mount above the valley. And though in a few years from now the whole district may be smiling with farms, passing trains shaking the mountain to the heart, many-windowed hotels lighting up the night like factories, and a prosperous city occupying the site of sleepy Calistoga; yet in the meantime, around the foot of that mountain the silence of nature reigns in a great measure unbroken, and the people of hill and valley go sauntering about their business as in the days before the flood.

To reach Mount Saint Helena from San Francisco, the traveller has twice to cross the bay: once by the busy Oakland ferry, and again, after an hour or so of the railway, from Vallejo junction to Vallejo. Thence he takes rail once more to mount the long green strath of Napa Valley.

In all the contractions and expansions of that inland sea, the Bay of San Francisco, there can be few drearier scenes than the Vallejo Ferry. Bald shores and a low, bald islet enclose the sea; through the narrows the tide bubbles, muddy like a river. When we made the passage (bound, although yet we knew it not, for Silverado) the steamer jumped, and the black buoys were dancing in the jabble; the ocean breeze blew killing chill; and, although the upper sky was still unflecked with vapour, the sea fogs were pouring in from seaward, over the hilltops of Marin County, in one great, shapeless, silver cloud.

South Vallejo is typical of many Californian towns. It was a blunder; the site had proved untenable; and, although it is still such a young place by the scale of Europe, it has already begun to be deserted for its neighbour and namesake, North Vallejo. A long pier, a number of drinking saloons, a hotel of a great size, marshy pools where the frogs keep up their croaking, and even at high noon the entire absence of any human face or voice – these are the marks of South Vallejo. Yet there was a tall building beside the pier, labelled the *Star Flour Mills*; and seagoing, full-rigged ships lay close along shore, waiting for their cargo. Soon these would be plunging round the Horn, soon the flour from the *Star Flour Mills* would be landed on the wharves of Liverpool. For that, too, is one of England's outposts; thither, to this gaunt mill, across the Atlantic and Pacific deeps and round about the icy Horn, this crowd of great, three-masted, deep-sea ships come, bringing nothing, and return with bread.

The Frisby House, for that was the name of the hotel, was a place of fallen fortunes, like the town. It was now given up to labourers, and partly ruinous. At dinner there was the ordinary display of what is called in the west a *two-bit house*: the tablecloth checked red and white, the plague of flies, the wire hencoops over the dishes, the great variety and invariable vileness of the food and the rough coatless men devouring it in silence. In our bedroom, the stove would not burn, though it would smoke; and while one window would not open, the other would not shut. There was a view on a bit of empty road, a few dark houses, a donkey wandering with its shadow on a slope, and a blink of sea, with a tall ship lying anchored in the moonlight. All about that dreary inn frogs sang their ungainly chorus.

Early the next morning we mounted the hill along a wooden footway, bridging one marish spot after another. Here and there, as we ascended, we passed a house embowered in white roses. More of the bay became apparent, and soon the blue peak of Tamalpais rose above the green level of the island opposite. It told us we were still but a little way from the city of the

Golden Gates, already, at that hour, beginning to awake among the sand-hills. It called to us over the waters as with the voice of a bird. Its stately head, blue as a sapphire on the paler azure of the sky, spoke to us of wider outlooks and the bright Pacific. For Tamalpais stands sentry, like a lighthouse, over the Golden Gates, between the bay and the open ocean, and looks down indifferently on both. Even as we saw and hailed it from Vallejo, seamen, far out at sea, were scanning it with shaded eyes; and, as if to answer to the thought, one of the great ships below began silently to clothe herself with white sails, homeward bound for England.

For some way beyond Vallejo the railway led us through bald green pastures. On the west the rough highlands of Marin shut off the ocean; in the midst, in long, straggling, gleaming arms, the bay died out among the grass; there were few trees and few enclosures; the sun shone wide over open uplands, the displumed hills stood clear against the sky. But by-and-by these hills began to draw nearer on either hand, and first thicket and then wood began to clothe their sides; and soon we were away from all signs of the sea's neighbourhood, mounting an inland, irrigated valley. A great variety of oaks stood, now severally, now in a becoming grove, among the fields and vineyards. The towns were compact, in about equal proportions, of bright, new wooden houses and great and growing forest trees; and the chapel bell on the engine sounded most festally that sunny Sunday, as we drew up at one green town after another, with the townsfolk trooping in their Sunday's best to see the strangers, with the sun sparkling on the clean houses, and great domes of foliage humming overhead in the breeze.

This pleasant Napa valley is, at its north end, blockaded by our mountain. There, at Calistoga, the railroad ceases, and the traveller who intends faring farther, to the Geysers or to the springs in Lake County, must cross the spurs of the mountain by stage. Thus, Mount Saint Helena is not only a summit, but frontier; and, up to the time of writing, it has stayed the progress of the iron horse.

AMY TAN

Amy Tan was born in Oakland in 1952, and first visited China in 1987. Her father, who was educated in Beijing and worked for the United States Information Service after the war, came to America in 1947. Her mother came to the United States in 1949, shortly before the Communists seized control of Shanghai. Amy Tan now lives in San Francisco and New York. Her first work of fiction, *The Joy Luck Club*, explores the nuances of Chinese-American identity through the relationships between four Chinese mothers and their American daughters, each of whom narrate their own stories, rich in detail and atmosphere. Each character's story carries inflections of their cultural identity, which is both a barrier to understanding between the two generations, and a source of shared strength. Here junior chess champion Waverly Jong takes a plunge into San Francisco's Chinatown.

THE JOY LUCK CLUB

My mother imparted her daily truths so she could help my older brothers and me rise above our circumstances. We lived in San Francisco's Chinatown. Like most of the other Chinese children who played in the back alleys of restaurants and curio shops, I didn't think we were poor. My bowl was always full, three five-course meals every day, beginning with a soup full of mysterious things I didn't want to know the names of.

We lived on Waverly Place, in a warm, clean, two-bedroom flat that sat above a small Chinese bakery specializing in steamed pastries and dim sum. In the early morning, when the alley was still quiet, I could smell fragrant red beans as they were cooked down to a pasty sweetness. By daybreak, our flat was heavy with the odor of fried sesame balls and sweet curried chicken crescents. From my bed, I would listen as my father got ready for work, then locked the door behind him, one-two-three clicks.

At the end of our two-block alley was a small sandlot playground with swings and slides well-shined down the middle with use. The play area was bordered by wood-slat benches where old-country people sat cracking roasted watermelon seeds with their golden teeth and scattering the husks to an impatient gathering of gurgling pigeons. The best playground, however, was the dark alley itself. It was crammed with daily mysteries and adventures. My brothers and I would peer into the medicinal herb shop, watching old Li dole out onto a stiff sheet of white paper the right amount of insect shells, saffron-colored

seeds, and pungent leaves for his ailing customers. It was said that he once cured a woman dying of an ancestral curse that had eluded the best of American doctors. Next to the pharmacy was a printer who specialized in gold-embossed wedding invitations and festive red banners.

Farther down the street was Ping Yuen Fish Market. The front window displayed a tank crowded with doomed fish and turtles struggling to gain footing on the slimy green-tiled sides. A hand-written sign informed tourists, "Within this store, is all for food, not for pet." Inside, the butchers with their bloodstained white smocks deftly gutted the fish while customers cried out their orders and shouted, "Give me your freshest," to which the butchers always protested, "All are freshest." On less crowded market days, we would inspect the crates of live frogs and crabs which we were warned not to poke, boxes of dried cuttlefish, and row upon row of iced prawns, squid, and slippery fish. The sanddabs made me shiver each time; their eyes lay on one flattened side and reminded me of my mother's story of a careless girl who ran into a crowded street and was crushed by a cab. "Was smash flat," reported my mother.

At the corner of the alley was Hong Sing's, a four-table café with a recessed stairwell in front that led to a door marked "Tradesmen." My brothers and I believed the bad people emerged from this door at night. Tourists never went to Hong Sing's, since the menu was printed only in Chinese. A Caucasian man with a big camera once posed me and my playmates in front of the restaurant. He had us move to the side of the picture window so the photo would capture the roasted duck with its head dangling from a juice-covered rope. After he took the picture, I told him he should go into Hong Sing's and eat dinner. When he smiled and asked me what they served, I shouted, "Guts and duck's feet and octopus gizzards!" Then I ran off with my friends, shrieking with laughter as we scampered across the alley and hid in the entryway grotto of the China Gem Company, my heart pounding with hope that he would chase us.

My mother named me after the street that we lived on: Waverly Place Jong, my official name for important American documents. But my family called me Meimei, "Little Sister." I was the youngest, the only daughter. Each morning before school, my mother would twist and yank on my thick black hair until she had formed two tightly wound pigtails. One day, as she struggled to weave a hard-toothed comb through my disobedient hair, I had a sly thought.

I asked her, "Ma, what is Chinese torture?" My mother shook her head. A bobby pin was wedged between her lips. She wetted her palm and smoothed the hair above my ear, then pushed the pin in so that it nicked sharply against my scalp.

"Who say this word?" she asked without a trace of knowing how wicked I was being. I shrugged my shoulders and said, "Some boy in my class said Chinese people do Chinese torture."

"Chinese people do many things," she said simply. "Chinese people do business, do medicine, do painting. Not lazy like American people. We do torture. Best torture."

Reproduced by kind permission of The Putnam Publishing Group.

T.CORAGHESSAN BOYLE

PEN/Faulkner Award winner **T. Coraghessan Boyle** was born in Manhattan, but now lives in California; his sixth novel, *The Tortilla Curtain*, is pure LA. Its protagonist, prosperous and peaceable Delaney, lives on the leafy fringes of the city and spins out his nature column "Pilgrim at Topanga Creek," while his dynamic wife Kyra shifts real estate. Meanwhile another pilgrim has come to the creek: Cándido, an illegal Mexican immigrant, who is trying to protect his young pregnant wife América from the natural and unnatural forces around them. The initial violent encounter between the two men precipitates events that both tear at the veneer of Delaney's liberalism, satirized with easy precision by Boyle, and expose the vulnerability of LA's legions of have-nots. In this extract, Delaney's incipient fear of invasion is realized, in an unexpected and dramatic form.

THE TORTILLA CURTAIN

High up in the canyon, nestled in a fan-shaped depression dug out of the side of the western ridge by the action of some long-forgotten stream, lay the subdivision known as Arroyo Blanco Estates. It was a private community, comprising a golf course, ten tennis courts, a community center and some two hundred and fifty homes, each set on one-point-five acres and strictly conforming to the covenants, conditions and restrictions set forth in the 1973 articles of incorporation. The houses were all of the Spanish Mission style, painted in one of three prescribed shades of white, with orange tile roofs. If you wanted to paint your house sky-blue or Provençal-pink with lime-green shutters, you were perfectly welcome to move into the San Fernando Valley or to Santa Monica or anywhere else you chose, but if you bought into Arroyo Blanco Estates, your house would be white and your roof orange.

Delaney Mossbacher made his home in one of these Spanish Mission houses (floor plan #A227C, Rancho White with Navajo trim), along with his second wife, Kyra, her son, Jordan, her matching Dandie Dinmont terriers, Osbert and Sacheverell, and her Siamese cat, Dame Edith. On this particular morning, the morning that Cándido Rincón began to feel he'd lost control of his wife, Delaney was up at seven, as usual, to drip Kyra's coffee, feed Jordan his fruit, granola and hi-fiber bar and let Osbert and Sacheverell out into the yard to perform their matinal functions. He hadn't forgotten his unfortunate encounter with Cándido four days earlier – the thought of it still made his stomach clench – but the needs and wants and minor irritations of daily life had begun to push it into the background. At the moment, his attention was focused entirely on getting through the morning ritual with his customary speed and efficiency. He was nothing if not efficient.

He made a sort of game of it, counting the steps it took him to shut the windows against the coming day's heat, empty yesterday's coffee grounds into the mulch bucket, transform two kiwis, an orange, apple, banana and a handful of Bing cherries into Jordan's medley of fresh fruit, and set the table for two. He skated across the tile floor to the dishwasher, flung open the cabinets, rocketed the plates and cutlery into position on the big oak table, all the while keeping an eye on the coffee, measuring out two bowls of dog food and juicing the oranges he'd plucked from the tree in the courtyard.

Typically, he stole a moment out in the courtyard to breathe in the cool of the morning and listen to the scrub jays wake up the neighborhood, but today he was in a rush and the only sound that penetrated his consciousness was a strange excited yelp from one of the dogs – they must have found something in the fenced-in yard behind the house, a squirrel or a gopher maybe – and then he was back in the kitchen, squeezing oranges. That was what he did, every morning, regular as clockwork: squeeze oranges. After which he would dash round the house gathering up Jordan's homework, his backpack, lunchbox and baseball cap, while Kyra sipped her coffee and washed down her twelve separate vitamin and mineral supplements with half a glass of fresh-squeezed orange juice. Then it was time to drive Jordan to school, while Kyra applied her makeup, wriggled into a form-fitting skirt with matching jacket and propelled her Lexus over the crest of the canyon and into Woodland Hills, where she was the undisputed volume leader at Mike Bender Realty, Inc. And then, finally, Delaney would head back home, have a cup of herbal tea and two slices of wheat toast, dry, and let the day settle in around him.

Unless there was an accident on the freeway or a road crew out picking up or setting down their ubiquitous plastic cones, he would be back at home and sitting at his desk by nine. This was the moment he lived for, the moment his day really began. Unfailingly, no matter what pressures were brought to bear on him or what emergencies arose, he allotted the next four hours to his writing – four hours during which he could let go of the world around him, his fingers grazing lightly over the keyboard, the green glow of the monitor bathing him in its hypnotic light. He took the phone off the hook, pulled the shades and crept into the womb of language.

There, in the silence of the empty house, Delaney worked out the parameters of his monthly column for *Wide Open Spaces,* a naturalist's observations of the life blooming around him day by day, season by season. He called it "Pilgrim at Topanga Creek" in homage to Annie Dillard, and while he couldn't pretend to her mystical connection to things, or her verbal virtuosity either, he did feel that he stood apart from his fellow men and women, that he saw more deeply and felt more passionately – particularly about nature. And every day, from nine to one, he had the opportunity to prove it.

Of course, some days went better than others. He tried to confine himself to the flora and fauna of Topanga Canyon and the surrounding mountains, but increasingly he found himself brooding over the fate of the pupfish, the Florida manatee and the spotted owl, the ocelot, the pine marten, the panda. And how could he ignore the larger trends – overpopulation, desertification, the depletion of the seas and the forests, global warming and loss of habitat? We were all right in America, sure, but it was crazy to think you could detach yourself from the rest of the world, the world of starvation and loss and the steady relentless degradation of the environment. Five and a half billion people chewing up the resources of the planet like locusts, and only seventy-three California condors left in all the universe.

It gave him pause. It depressed him. There were days when he worked himself into such a state he could barely lift his fingers to the keys, but fortunately the good days outnumbered them, the days when he celebrated his afternoon hikes through the chaparral and into the ravines of the mist-hung mountains, and that was what people wanted – celebration, not lectures, not the strident call to ecologic arms, not the death knell and the weeping and gnashing of environmental teeth. The world was full of bad news. Why contribute more?

The sun had already begun to burn off the haze by the time Jordan scuffed into the kitchen, the cat at his heels. Jordan was six years old, dedicated to Nintendo, superheroes and baseball cards, though as far as Delaney could see he had no interest whatever in the game of baseball beyond possessing the glossy cardboard images of the players. He favored his mother facially and in the amazing lightness of his hair, which was so pale as to be nearly translucent. He might have been big for his age, or maybe he was small – Delaney had nothing to compare him to.

"Kiwi," Jordan said, thumping into his seat at the table, and that was all. Whether this was an expression of approval or distaste, Delaney couldn't tell. From the living room came the electronic voice of the morning news: *Thirty-seven Chinese nationals were drowned early today when a smuggler's ship went aground just east of the Golden Gate Bridge* . . . Outside, beyond the windows, there was another yelp from the dogs.

Jordan began to rotate his spoon in the bowl of fruit, a scrape and clatter accompanied by the moist sounds of mastication. Delaney, his back to the table, was scrubbing the counter in the vicinity of the stove, though any splashes of cooking oil or spatters of sauce must have been purely imaginary since he hadn't actually cooked anything. He scrubbed for the love of scrubbing. "Okay, buckaroo," he called over his shoulder, "you've got two choices today as far as your hi-fiber bar is concerned: Cranberry Nut and Boysenberry Supreme. What'll it be?"

From a mouth laden with kiwi: "Papaya Coconut."

"You got the last one yesterday."

No response.

"So what'll it be?"

Kyra insisted on the full nutritional slate for her son every morning – fresh fruit, granola with skim milk and brewer's yeast, hi-fiber bar. The child needed roughage. Vitamins. Whole grains. And breakfast, for a growing child at least, was the most important meal of the day, the foundation of all that was to come. That was how she felt. And while Delaney recognized a touch of the autocratic and perhaps even fanatic in the regimen, he by large subscribed to it. He and Kyra had a lot in common, not only temperamentally, but in terms of their beliefs and ideals too – that was what had attracted them to each other in the first place. They were both perfectionists, for one thing. They abhorred clutter. They were joggers, nonsmokers, social drinkers, and if not full-blown vegetarians, people who were conscious of their intake of animal fats. Their memberships included the Sierra Club, Save the Children, the National Wildlife Federation and the Democratic Party. They preferred the contemporary look to Early American or kitsch. In religious matters, they were agnostic.

Delaney's question remained unanswered, but he was used to cajoling Jordan over his breakfast. He tiptoed across the room to hover behind the boy, who was playing with his spoon and chanting something under his breath. "Rookie card, rookie card," Jordan was saying, dipping into his granola without enthusiasm. "No looking now," Delaney warned, seductively tapping a foil-wrapped bar on either side of the boy's thin wilted neck, "right hand or left?"

Jordan reached up with his left hand, as Delaney knew he would, fastening on the Boysenberry Supreme bar just as Kyra, hunched over the weight of two boxes of hand-addressed envelopes – Excelsior, 500 Count – clattered into the kitchen in her heels. She made separate kissing motions in the direction

of her husband and son, then slid into her chair, poured herself half a cup of coffee lightened with skim milk – for the calcium – and began sifting purposively through the envelopes.

"Why can't I have Sugar Pops or Honey Nut Cheerios like other kids? Or bacon and eggs?" Jordan pinched his voice. "Mom? Why can't I?"

Kyra gave the stock response – "You're not other kids, that's why" – and Delaney was taken back to his own childhood, a rainy night in the middle of an interminable winter, a plate of liver, onions and boiled potatoes before him.

"I hate granola," Jordan countered, and it was like a Noh play, timeless ritual.

"It's good for you."

"Yeah, sure." Jordan made an exaggerated slurping sound, sucking the milk through his teeth.

"Think of all the little children who have nothing to eat," Kyra said without looking up, and Jordan, sticking to the script, came right back at her: "Let's send them this."

Now she looked up. "Eat," she said, and the drama was over.

"Busy day?" Delaney murmured, setting Kyra's orange juice down beside the newspaper and unscrewing the childproof caps of the sturdy plastic containers that held her twelve separate vitamin and mineral supplements. He did the little things for her – out of love and consideration, sure, but also in acknowledgment of the fact that she was the chief breadwinner here, the one who went off to the office while he stayed home. Which was all right by him. He had none of those juvenile macho hang-ups about role reversal and who wore the pants and all of that – real estate was her life, and he was more than happy to help her with it, so long as he got his four hours a day at the keyboard.

Kyra lifted her eyebrows, but didn't look up. She was tucking what looked to be a small white packet into each of the envelopes in succession. "Busy?" she echoed. "Busy isn't the word for it. I'm presenting two offers this morning, both of them real low-ball, I've got a buyer with cold feet on that Calabasas property – with escrow due to close in eight days – and I'm scheduled for an open house on the Via Escobar place at one . . . is that the dogs I hear? What are they barking at?"

Delaney shrugged. Jordan had shucked the foil from his hi-fiber bar and was drifting toward the TV room with it – which meant he was going to be late for school if Delaney didn't hustle him out of there within the next two minutes. The cat, as yet unfed, rubbed up against Delaney's leg. "I don't know," he said. "They've been yapping since I let them out. Must be a squirrel or something. Or maybe Jack's dog got loose again and he's out there peeing on the fence and driving them into a frenzy."

"Anyway," Kyra went on, "it's going to be hell. And it's Carla Bayer's birthday, so after work a bunch of us – don't you think this is a cute idea?" She held up one of the packets she'd been stuffing the envelopes with. It was a three-by-five seed packet showing a spray of flowers and printed with the legend *Forget-Me-Not, Compliments of Kyra Menaker-Mossbacher, Mike Bender Realty, Inc.*

"Yeah, I guess," he murmured, wiping at an imaginary speck on the counter. This was her way of touching base with her clients. Every month or so, usually in connection with a holiday, she went through her mailing list (consisting of anyone she'd ever sold to or for, whether they'd relocated to Nome, Singapore or Irkutsk or passed on into the Great Chain of Being) and sent a small reminder of her continued existence and willingness to deal. She called it "keeping the avenues open." Delaney reached down to stroke the cat. "But can't one of the secretaries do this sort of thing for you?"

"It's the personal touch that counts – and moves property. How many times do I have to tell you?"

There was a silence, during which Delaney became aware of the cartoon jingle that had replaced the voice of the news in the other room, and then, just as he was clearing Jordan's things from the table and checking the digital display on the microwave for the time – 7:32 – the morning fell apart. Or no: it was torn apart by a startled breathless shriek that rose up from beyond the windows as if out of some primal dream. This was no yip, no yelp, no bark or howl – this was something final and irrevocable, a predatory scream that took the varnish off their souls, and it froze them in place. They listened, horrified, as it rose in pitch until it choked off as suddenly as it had begun.

The aftereffect was electric. Kyra bolted up out of her chair, knocking over her coffee cup and scattering envelopes; the cat darted between Delaney's legs and vanished; Delaney dropped the plate on the floor and groped for

the counter like a blind man. And then Jordan was coming through the doorway on staccato feet, his face opened up like a pale nocturnal flower: "Delaney," he gasped, "Delaney, something, something—"

But Delaney was already in motion. He flung open the door and shot through the courtyard, head down, rounding the corner of the house just in time to see a dun-colored blur scaling the six-foot chainlink fence with a tense white form clamped in its jaws. His brain decoded the image: a coyote had somehow managed to get into the enclosure and seize one of the dogs, and there it was, wild nature, up and over the fence as if this were some sort of circus act. Shouting to hear himself, shouting nonsense, Delaney charged across the yard as the remaining dog (Osbert? Sacheverell?) cowered in the corner and the dun blur melded with the buckwheat, chamise and stiff high grass of the wild hillside that gave onto the wild mountains beyond.

He didn't stop to think. In two bounds he was atop the fence and dropping to the other side, absently noting the paw prints in the dust, and then he was tearing headlong through the undergrowth, leaping rocks and shrubs and dodging the spines of the yucca plants clustered like breastworks across the slope. He was running, that was all he knew. Branches raked him like claws. Burrs bit into his ankles. He kept going, pursuing a streak of motion, the odd flash of white: now he saw it, now he didn't. "Hey!" he shouted. "Hey, goddamnit!"

The hillside sloped sharply upward, rising through the colorless scrub to a clump of walnut trees and jagged basalt outcroppings that looked as if they'd poked through the ground overnight. He saw the thing suddenly, the pointed snout and yellow eyes, the high stiff leggy gait as it struggled with its burden, and it was going straight up and into the trees. He shouted again and this time the shout was answered from below. Glancing over his shoulder, he saw that Kyra was coming up the hill with her long jogger's strides, in blouse, skirt and stocking feet. Even at this distance he could recognize the look on her face – the grim set of her jaw, the flaring eyes and clamped mouth that spelled doom for whoever got in her way, whether it was a stranger who'd locked his dog in a car with the windows rolled up or the hapless seller who refused a cash-out bid. She was coming, and that spurred him on. If he could only stay close the coyote would have to drop the dog, it would have to.

By the time he reached the trees his throat was burning. Sweat stung his eyes and his arms were striped with nicks and scratches. There was no sign of the dog and he pushed on through the trees to where the slope fell away to the feet of the next hill beyond it. The brush was thicker here – six feet high and so tightly interlaced it would have taken a machete to get through it in places – and he knew, despite the drumming in his ears and the glandular rush that had him pacing and whirling and clenching and unclenching his fists, that it was looking bad. Real bad. There were a thousand bushes out there – five thousand, ten thousand – and the coyote could be crouched under any one of them.

It was watching him even now, he knew it, watching him out of slit wary eyes as he jerked back and forth, frantically scanning the mute clutter of leaf, branch and thorn, and the thought infuriated him. He shouted again, hoping to flush it out. But the coyote was too smart for him. Ears pinned back, jaws and forepaws stifling its prey, it could lie there, absolutely motionless, for hours. "Osbert!" he called out suddenly, and his voice trailed off into a hopeless bleat. "Sacheverell!!"

The poor dog. It couldn't have defended itself from a rabbit. Delaney stood on his toes, strained his neck, poked angrily through the nearest bush. Long low shafts of sunlight fired the leaves in an indifferent display, as they did every morning, and he looked into the illuminated depths of that bush and felt desolate suddenly, empty, cored out with loss and helplessness.

"Osbert!" The sound seemed to erupt from him, as if he couldn't control his vocal cords. "Here, boy! Come!" Then he shouted Sacheverell's name, over and over, but there was no answer except for a distant cry from Kyra, who seemed to be way off to his left now.

All at once he wanted to smash something, tear the bushes out of the ground by their roots. This didn't have to happen. It didn't. If it wasn't for those idiots leaving food out for the coyotes as if they were nothing more than sheep with bushy tails and eyeteeth . . . and he'd warned them, time and again. You can't be heedless of your environment. You can't. Just last week he'd found half a bucket of Kentucky Fried Chicken out back of the Dagolian place – waxy red-and-white-striped cardboard with a portrait of the grinning chicken-killer himself smiling large – and he'd stood up at the bimonthly meeting of the property owners' association to say something about it. They wouldn't even listen. Coyotes, gophers, yellow jackets, rattlesnakes even – they were a pain in the ass, sure, but nature was the least of their problems. It was humans they were worried about. The Salvadorans, the Mexicans, the blacks, the gangbangers and taggers and carjackers they read about in the Metro section over their bran toast and coffee. That's why they'd abandoned the flatlands of the Valley and the hills of the Westside to live up here, outside the city limits, in the midst of all this scenic splendor.

Coyotes? Coyotes were quaint. Little demidogs out there howling at the sunset, another amenity like the oaks, the chaparral and the views. No, all Delaney's neighbors could talk about, back and forth and on and on as if it were the key to all existence, was gates. A gate, specifically. To be erected at the main entrance and manned by a twenty-four-hour guard to keep out those very gangbangers, taggers and carjackers they'd come here to escape. Sure. And now poor Osbert – or Sacheverell – was nothing more than breakfast.

The fools. The idiots.

Delaney picked up a stick and began to beat methodically at the bushes.

Reproduced by kind permission of Bloomsbury Publishing Plc and Viking Penguin.

BOOKS

In the following listing, wherever a book is in print, the publisher's name is given in parentheses after the title, in the format: UK publisher; US publisher. Where books are published in only one of these countries, we have specified which one; when the same company publishes the book in both, it appears just once.

TRAVEL AND IMPRESSIONS

Tim Cahill *Jaguars Ripped My Flesh* (Fourth Estate; Vintage). Adventure travel through California and the world, including skin diving with hungry sharks off LA and getting lost and found in Death Valley. Thoughtful and sensitive yet still a thrill a minute.

Jan Morris *Destinations* (OUP). Of the essay on LA in this fine collection of essays written for *Rolling Stone* magazine, Joan Didion said, "A lot of people come here and don't get it. She got it."

Mark Twain *Roughing It* (Penguin; University of California Press). Vivid tales of frontier California, particularly evocative of life in the silver mines of the 1860s Comstock Lode, where Twain got his start as a journalist and story-teller.

John Waters *Crackpot* (Fourth Estate; Random House). Odds and ends from the Pope of Trash, the mind behind cult film *Pink Flamingos*, including a personalized tour of LA.

Edmund White *States of Desire* (Picador; Plume). Part of a cross-country sojourn that includes a rather superficial account of the gay scene in 1970s LA.

Tom Wolfe *The Electric Kool-Aid Acid Test* (Black Swan; Bantam). Take a trip with the Grateful Dead and the Hell's Angels on the magic bus of Ken Kesey and the Merry Pranksters as they travel through the early days of the psychedelic 1960s, on a mission to turn California youth onto LSD.

HISTORY

Walton Bean *California: An Interpretive History* (McGraw-Hill, US). Blow-by-blow account of the history of California, including all the shady deals and back-room politicking, presented in accessible, anecdotal form.

Gary Brechin *Imperial San Francisco* (University of California Press, US). A myth-shattering look at the genesis of the Golden Gate city, complete with close looks at the elite families who shaped San Francisco.

Daniel Boorstin *The Americas 2: The National Experience* (Random House; Cardinal, US o/p). Heavy going because of the glut of detail, but otherwise an energetic appraisal of the social forces that shaped the modern USA, with several chapters on the settlement of the West.

Carey McWilliams *Southern California: An Island on the Land* (Peregrine Smith, US). The bible of Southern Californian histories, focusing on the key years between the two world wars. Evocatively written and richly detailed.

Kevin Starr *Inventing the Dream* (OUP). One of a series of captivating books – the other two are *Material Dreams* (OUP) and *Americans and the Californian Dream* (OUP, US o/p) studying the phenomenon known as California. Cultural histories written with a novelist's flair.

Dale L. Walker *Bear Flag Rising: The Conquest of California, 1846* (Forge). An entertaining and painstakingly detailed account of how the US, in the name of Manifest Destiny, acquired California from Mexico.

POLITICAL, SOCIAL AND ETHNIC

Jean Baudrillard *America* (Verso). Scattered thoughts of the trendy French philosopher, whose (very) occasionally brilliant but often overreaching exegesis of American pop culture, especially in LA, is undermined by factual inaccuracy.

Mike Davis *Ecology of Fear* (Picador; Vintage). As in his previous book, *City of Quartz: Excavating the Future of Los Angeles*, Davis writes a compelling account of LA's apocalyptic style, focusing on the gloom and doom in movies and literary fiction, the danger of earthquakes and fires, mountain lion attacks, and unrecognized threats like tornadoes.

Joan Didion *Slouching Towards Bethlehem* (Flamingo; Noonday Press). Selected essays from one of California's best journalists, taking a critical look at Sixties California, from the acid culture of San Francisco to a profile of American hero John Wayne. In a similar style, *The White Album* (Farrar Straus & Giroux, UK) traces the West Coast characters and events that shaped the Sixties and Seventies, including The Doors, Charles Manson and the Black Panthers.

Frances Fitzgerald *Cities on a Hill* (Picador; Simon & Schuster). Intelligent and sympathetic exploration of four of the odder corners of American culture, including San Francisco's gay Castro district.

Maxine Hong Kingston *China Men* (Picador; Vintage). A compelling history dealing with the various waves of Chinese immigrants to America, but specifically California. Interwoven with fact and myth, *China Men* examines the nature of being an American.

David Koenig *Mouse Tales* (Bonaventure Press, US). All the Disneyland dirt that's fit to print: a behind-the-scenes look at the ugly little secrets – from disenchanted workers to vermin infestations – that lurk behind the happy walls of the Magic Kingdom. Enough to fill a second recent volume, *More Mouse Tales*.

Russel Miller *Barefaced Messiah* (Sphere; Holt both o/p). An eye-opening study of the rise and rise of L. Ron Hubbard and his Scientology cult, who have their HQ in LA and their devotees lurking everywhere.

Jay Stevens *Storming Heaven: LSD and the American Dream* (Flamingo; Groundwood Books). An engaging account of psychedelic drugs and their relationship with American society through the Sixties, with an epilogue to bring things up to date with "designer drugs" – Venus, Ecstasy, Special K and others – and the inner space they apparently help some modern Californians chart.

Danny Sugarman *Wonderland Avenue* (Abacus; Bullfinch). Publicist for The Doors and other seminal US rock bands from the late Sixties on, Sugarman delivers a raunchy autobiographical account of sex, drugs, and LA rock'n'roll.

ARCHITECTURE

Reyner Banham *Los Angeles: The Architecture of Four Ecologies* (Penguin). The most lucid account of how LA's history has shaped its present form; the author's enthusiasms are infectious.

Philip Jodidio *Contemporary Californian Architects* (Taschen). This glossy trilingual (English, French and German) book argues that the public and private buildings of Frank Gehry, Eric Owen Moss, Frank Israel and Michael Routundi, among others, are strongly influenced by the state itself. The gorgeous photographs strengthen the case.

Sam Hall Kaplan *LA Lost and Found: An Architectural History of Los Angeles* (Random House, US). The text is informative but dull, though the outstanding photos vividly portray the city's growth and the trends in its design.

Richard Meier *Building the Getty* (University of California Press; Knopf). If you're a fan of this hilltop art colossus in West LA, you'll want to pick up this highly readable account of the conception and creation of the Getty Center, as told by its architect, the high prince of modernism.

Charles Moore *The City Observed: Los Angeles* (Random House, US). The best book to guide you around the diffuse buildings and settings of LA, loaded with maps, illustrations and historical anecdotes.

HOLLYWOOD/THE MOVIES

Kenneth Anger *Hollywood Babylon* (Arrow; Bantam). A vicious yet high-spirited romp through Tinseltown's greatest scandals, although the facts are bent rather too often. A rarer second volume covers more recent times, but was hurriedly put together and shoddily researched.

Peter Bogdanovich *Who the Devil Made It* (Random House, US). Acclaimed book of conversations with the great Hollywood filmmakers.

David Bordwell, Janet Staiger & Kirstin Thompson *The Classical Hollywood Cinema* (Columbia UP). Academic handbook aimed at the serious student, but still a generally interesting account of the techniques used in the best-known Hollywood movies up to 1960.

Kevin Brownlow *Hollywood: The Pioneers* (Knopf, US). History of the founding of Hollywood by one of the great historians of the early days of cinema. (Brownlow and David Gill's 1980 TV documentary *Hollywood* is available on video.)

Otto Friedrich *City of Nets* (Headline o/p; University of California Press). A rich and colorful social and cultural history of Hollywood during its golden age in the Forties.

Clayton R. Koppes & Gregory D. Black *Hollywood Goes to War* (I.B Tauris o/p; University of California Press). Masterly examination of the influence of World War II on the film industry – and vice versa.

Barry Norman *Talking Pictures: The Story of Hollywood* (Arrow; NAL-Dutton o/p). The most accessible mainstream outline of the growth of movies in Hollywood, informative and pleasantly irreverent in tone.

Julia Phillips *You'll Never Eat Lunch in This Town Again* (Mandarin; Signet). From the woman who became a Hollywood somebody by co-producing *The Sting*, a diary of drug abuse, spouse abuse and film-business bitching.

SPECIFIC GUIDES

Bicycle Rider Directory (Cycle America, US). Low-cost guide to do-it-yourself bicycle touring around the Bay Area and Napa and Sonoma valleys, with good fold-out route maps.

Tom Kirkendall and Vicky Spring *Bicycling the Pacific Coast* (Mountaineers Books). Detailed guide to the bike routes all the way along the coast from Mexico up to Canada.

National Audubon Society Nature Guides: *Western Forests*; *Deserts*; *Pacific Coast*; *Wetlands* and others (Random House; Knopf). California has six of the world's seven major ecosystem types, and between them, these immaculately researched and beautifully photographed field guides, though not specific to California, cover the lot.

National Geographic Society *A Field Guide to the Birds of North America* (National Geographic). Self-explanatory – and thoroughly useful.

Peterson Series Field Guides: *A Field Guide to Western Reptiles and Amphibians*; *A Field Guide to the Insects of America North of Mexico*; *A Field Guide to Pacific State Wildflowers* (Houghton Mifflin). Excellent general field guides to the flora and fauna of California and the West Coast.

For guidebooks of specific relevance to travelers with **disabilities**, see p.47 of "Basics."

Jeffery Schaffer *The Pacific Crest Trail: California* (Wilderness Press). A guide to the southern section of the trail that leads all the way from Mexico to Canada through the Sierra Nevada range.

David & Kay Scott *Guide to the National Park Areas: the Western States* (Globe Pequot). How to get around and camp in the West's National Parks, including Yosemite and the Kings Canyon.

Tom Steinstra and Ann Marie Brown *California Hiking: The Complete Guide* (Foghorn Press, US). Dense 700-page tome detailing over 1000 hikes, from hour-long strolls to the 1700 Californian miles of the Pacific Crest Trail. Unfortunately, the trail notes and maps are limited, and the text is hardly inspirational.

Walking the West Series: *Walking Southern California*; *Walking the California Coast*; *Walking California's State Parks* and others (HarperReference). Well written and produced paperbacks, each covering over a hundred excellent day walks from two to twenty miles. They're strong on practical details (maps, route descriptions and so on), and boast inspiring prose and historical background. Recommended.

CALIFORNIA IN FICTION

James P. Blaylock *Land of Dreams* (Grafton o/p; Ace Books). A fantastic tale spun out as the twelve-year Solstice comes to a Northern Californian coastal town.

T. Coraghessan Boyle *The Tortilla Curtain* (Bloomsbury; Penguin). Set in LA, this novel boldly borrows its premise – a privileged white man running down a member of the city's ethnic underclass – from Tom Wolfe's *The Bonfire of the Vanities*, and develops its plot with a similar pacey intensity. See p.672 for an extract from the novel.

Ray Bradbury *The Martian Chronicles* (Flamingo; Bantam). Brilliant, lyrical study of colonization, of new worlds and new lands – it's very easy to read the Martian setting as a Californian one. Bradbury's first, and still best, book.

Scott Bradfield *What's Wrong With America* (Picador). Humor and idiosyncratic absurdity combine as Bradfield explores America's malaise through an elderly woman's slide towards mental breakdown. Southern California provides the backdrop and its people the caricatured bit players.

Richard Brautigan Born in Tacoma, Brautigan is more often associated with the California Beat writers of the Fifties and Sixties. His surreal fable-like work seems overtly simple, but is overlaid with cultural references which question the direction the country was traveling in. His most successful book, *Trout Fishing in America* (Vintage; Dell o/p), although designed as a fishing handbook, stealthily creates a disturbing image of contemporary life. Other novels include *A Confederate General from Big Sur* (Houghton Mifflin), *In Watermelon Sugar* (o/p), and he also wrote a fine book of poems, *The Pill Versus the Springhill Mine Disaster* (Dell, US).

Charles Bukowski *Post Office*; *Women* (Black Sparrow). Three-hundred-hangovers-a-year Henry Chinaski (the author, thinly veiled) drinks and screws his way around downbeat LA, firstly as a misfit mailman, then as a moderately successful writer with his own tab at the local liquor store and an endless supply of willing female fans. Savage and quite unique. See also *Factotum* (Black Sparrow), which recounts Chinaski's early days.

James M. Cain *The Five Great Novels of James M. Cain* (Picador, UK); *Double Indemnity*; *The Postman Always Rings Twice*; *The Butterfly*; *Mildred Pierce*; *Love's Lovely Counterfeit* (all Vintage, US). Haunting stories of smoldering passion told with clipped prose and terse dialogue.

Raymond Carver *What We Talk About When We Talk About Love* (Harvil; Knopf); *Where I'm Calling From: New and Selected Stories* (Harvill; Vintage). Set mostly in the Northwest and Northern California, Carver's deceptively simple eye-level pictures of plain-dealing Americans, concise and sharply observed, are difficult to forget.

Raymond Chandler *Three Novels* (Penguin, UK); *The Raymond Chandler Omnibus* (Random House, US). Essential reading, some of the toughest and greatest LA crime fiction of the Thirties and Forties – including *The Big Sleep*, *The Lady in the Lake*, and *Farewell My Lovely*, to name only the best.

Philip K. Dick *A Scanner Darkly* (Voyager; Random House). Of all Dick's erratic but frequently brilliant books, this is the best evocation of California. Set in the mid-1990s, when society is split between the Straights, the Dopers and the Narks, it's a dizzying study of individual identity, authority and drugs. Among the pick of the rest of Dick's vast legacy is *Blade Runner/Do Androids Dream of Electric Sheep?* (Voyager; Ballantine), set (unlike the movie) in San Francisco.

Joan Didion *Run, River* (Vintage, US). Focuses on the Sacramento Valley of the author's childhood and follows its change from agriculture into a highly charged consumer society. In contrast, but just as successfully done, *Play It As It Lays* (Flamingo; Farrar Straus & Giroux) is an electrifying dash through the pills, booze, and self-destruction linked with the LA film world.

Bret Easton Ellis *Less Than Zero* (Picador; Vintage). Numbing but readable tale of wealthy LA teen life. A classic brat-pack tome, with influence and fame far in excess of its worth.

James Ellroy *White Jazz* (Arrow; Fawcett). The final instalment of Ellroy's quartet of LA books exploring, in nail-biting noir style, the mind-set of corrupt LA cops and psychotic criminals over three decades. The series began with *The Black Dahlia* and continued with *The Big Nowhere* and *LA Confidential* (all Arrow; Warner).

F. Scott Fitzgerald *The Last Tycoon* (Penguin; Macmillan). Fitzgerald died before he completed his Hollywood novel, but what remains is executed in glittering prose, with passages of deep poignancy and tenderness, as well as Fitzgerald's trademark conjuring of glamorous decadence. The complex portrait of the brilliant, melancholy film producer Monroe Stahr is peculiarly memorable.

David Freeman *A Hollywood Education* (Michael Joseph o/p; Carroll & Graf). Cumulatively powerful collection of short stories concerning a writer's lot in Hollywood.

James Gardner *Fat City* (University of California Press). A beautifully precise, poignant account of small-time Stockton boxing, following the initiation and fitful progress of a young hopeful and the parallel decline of an old contender. Painfully exact on the confused, murky emotions of its men as their lives stagnate in the heat of the town and the surrounding country. Brilliantly filmed by John Huston, with a script by Gardner himself.

Ursula le Guin *Always Coming Home* (Gollancz; Bantam). Impressive "archeology of the future," describing the lifestyles and culture of a mysterious race living in Northern California.

Dashiell Hammett *The Four Great Novels* (Picador; Vintage); *The Maltese Falcon* (Random House, US). The former is a volume of seminal detective novels starring Sam Spade, the private investigator working out of San Francisco; the latter is probably Hammett's best-known work. See also the absorbing biography of Hammett: Diane Johnson's *Dashiell Hammett: A Life* (Picador; Fawcett).

Joseph Hansen *The Dave Brandstetter Omnibus* (No Exit Press, UK o/p); *Death Claims* (Holt; No Exit Press); *Gravedigger* (Holt; No Exit Press); *Skinflick* (Holt; No Exit Press); *Troublemaker* (Holt; No Exit Press). Entertaining tales of Dave Brandstetter, a gay insurance claims investigator, set against a vivid Southern California backdrop.

Aldous Huxley *Ape and Essence* (Flamingo; I.R. Dee); *After Many a Summer Dies the Swan* (I.R. Dee, US). Huxley spent his last twenty years earning a crust as a Hollywood screenwriter, and both these novels are a product of that time. The first chronicles moral degeneracy and Satanic rituals in post-apocalyptic Southern California; the latter, based on William Randolph Hearst, concerns a rich, pampered figure who surrounds himself with art treasures and dwells on the meaning of life.

Jack Kerouac *Desolation Angels* (Flamingo; Riverhead); *The Dharma Bums* (Penguin).The most influential of the Beat writers on the rampage in California. See also his first novel *On The Road* (Penguin), which has a little of San Francisco and a lot of the rest of the US.

Elmore Leonard *Get Shorty* (Penguin; Bantam). Ice-cool mobster Chili Palmer is a Miami debt collector who follows a client to Hollywood, and finds that the increasing intricacies of his own situation are translating themselves into a movie script.

David Levien *Wormwood* (Allison & Busby; Hyperion) Get a glimpse of the seamier side of the contemporary movie biz, following an up-and-coming story editor through the corporate ranks until he achieved utter exhaustion, and

curiously, an addiction to absinthe.

David Lodge *Changing Places* (Penguin). Thinly disguised autobiographical tale of an English academic who spends a year teaching at UC Berkeley and finds himself bang in the middle of the late Sixties student upheaval.

Jack London *The Call of the Wild* (Penguin); *White Fang and Other Stories* (Penguin); *Martin Eden* (Penguin); *The Iron Heel* (Wordsworth Editions; Dugan). *The Call of the Wild*, a short story about a tame dog discovering the ways of the wilderness while forced to labor pulling sleds across the snow and ice of Alaska's Klondike, made London into the world's best-selling author almost overnight. Afterwards, frustrated by the emptiness of his easy fame and success, the young, self-taught author wrote the semi-autobiographical *Martin Eden*, in which he rails against the cultured veil of polite society. Besides his prolific fiction, London also wrote a number of somewhat sophomoric political essays and socialist tracts; the most effective was *The Iron Heel*, presaging the rise of Fascism.

Ross MacDonald *Black Money* (Allison & Busby; Vintage); *The Blue Hammer* (Allison & Busby; Vintage); *The Zebra-Striped Hearse* (Allison & Busby o/p; Knopf o/p); *The Doomsters*; *The Instant Enemy* (Allison & Busby, US). Following in the footsteps of Sam Spade and Philip Marlowe, private detective Lew Archer looks behind the glitzy masks of Southern California life to reveal the underlying nastiness of creepy sexuality and manipulation. All captivating reads.

Armistead Maupin *Tales of the City*, *Further Tales of the City* (both Black Swan; HarperCollins); *More Tales of the City* (Corgi; HarperCollins). Lively and witty soap operas detailing the sexual antics of a select group of archetypal San Francisco characters of the late Seventies and early Eighties. See also *Babycakes* (Black Swan; HarperCollins) and *Significant Others*, which continue the story, though in more depth, and *Sure of You* (last two Black Swan; HarperCollins) – set several years later and more downbeat, though no less brilliant.

Brian Moore *The Great Victorian Collection* (Flamingo; Acacia Press). A professor dreams up a parking lot full of Victoriana, which becomes the biggest tourist attraction of Carmel,

California.

Walter Mosely *Devil in a Blue Dress* (Pan; Pocket Books). The book that introduced Easy Rawlins, a black private detective in late-1940s South Central LA, the central character in an excellent portrayal of time and place. Easy gets further into his stride in the subsequent *A Red Death* and *White Butterfly* (both Pan; Pocket Books).

Thomas Pynchon *The Crying of Lot 49* (Vintage; HarperPerennial). Follows the hilarious adventures of techno-freaks and potheads in Sixties California, and reveals the sexy side of stamp-collecting.

Richard Rayner *Los Angeles without a Map* (Flamingo; Mariner Book). An English non-driving journalist goes to LA on a romantic whim and lives out movie fantasies made even more fantastic by the city itself.

Theodore Roszak *Flicker* (Bantam, US o/p). In a tatty LA movie house, Jonathan Gates discovers cinema, "like a bewildered neophyte wandering into the dark womb of an unformed faith." His particular obsession is the director Max Castle – a genius of the silent era who disappeared under mysterious circumstances in the Forties – and it leads Gates into a labyrinthine conspiracy with its roots in medieval heresy. Unlikely, disturbing and immensely readable, *Flicker* deserves to be a Hollywood classic.

Danny Santiago *Famous All over Town* (New American Library, US). Coming-of-age novel set among the street gangs of East LA, vividly depicting life in the Hispanic community.

Vikram Seth *The Golden Gate* (Faber; Vintage). A novel in verse which traces the complex social lives of a group of San Francisco yuppies.

Mona Simpson *Anywhere But Here* (Faber; Vintage). Bizarre and unforgettable saga of a young girl and her ambitious mother as they pursue LA stardom for the daughter.

John Steinbeck *The Grapes of Wrath* (Mandarin; Penguin). The classic account of a migrant family forsaking the Midwest for the Promised Land. For more localized fare, read the light-hearted but crisply observed novella, *Cannery Row*, capturing daily life on the pre-war Monterey waterfront, or the epic *East of Eden* (both Mandarin; Penguin) which updates and resets the Bible in the Salinas Valley and depicts three generations of familial feuding.

Robert Louis Stevenson *The Silverado Squatters* (Everyman; Tuttle). Stevenson vividly describes the splendor of the San Francisco hills and the cast of eccentrics and immigrants who populate them, as well as the strange atmosphere of Silverado itself, a deserted former gold-rush settlement, where the last trace of the mine is "a mound of gravel, some wreck of a wooden aqueduct, and the mouth of a tunnel, like a treasure grotto in a fairy story." For an extract, see p.669.

Amy Tan *The Joy Luck Club* (Mandarin; Putnam). The premise of this novel is that four Chinese women, new arrivals in San Francisco in the 1940s, come together to play mahjong, and tell their stories. They have four daughters, divided between Chinese and American identities, who also tell their stories, from childhood and from their often troubled present. The format of the novel is over-complex so that it often reads like a book of unconnected short stories, but there are passages of brilliant prose, and the evocation of childhood fears and perceptions is wonderful. For an extract, see p.670.

Michael Tolkin *The Player* (Faber; Grove Atlantic). Convincing, multi-layered story of a movie executive using his power and contacts to skirt justice after committing murder.

Nathanael West *Complete Works* (Picador, UK o/p). Includes *The Day of the Locust*, an insightful and caustic tale that is *the* classic satire of early Hollywood.

MEXICAN-SPANISH TERMS

California is bound to its Spanish colonial and Mexican past, a fact manifest in the profusion of Spanish place names, particularly in the south of the state. Today large numbers of people living in California speak Spanish as their first language, so it can be useful to know a few terms. Note that the double-L is pronounced like a "Y" and an "Ñ" sounds like an N and a Y run together.

ABIERTO	open	**MAR**	sea
AGUA	water	**MESA**	high plateau, literally "table"
ALTA, ALTO	high		
ANGELES	angels	**MONTE**	mount(ain)
ARROYO	canyon or gully	**NEVADA**	snowy
AVENIDA	avenue	**NORTE**	north
BUENA, BUENO	good	**OBISPO**	bishop
CALIENTE	hot	**ORO**	gold
CALLE	street, pronounced "ka-ye"	**PARQUE**	park
		PESCADERO	fisherman
CERRADO	closed	**PLAYA**	beach
COSTA	coast	**REY**	king
CRUZ	cross	**RIO**	river
DE	of	**SAN, SANTA, SANTO**	saint
DEL	of the	**SIERRA**	mountain range
DORADO	golden	**SOL**	sun
EL	the	**SUR**	south
ESCONDIDO	hidden	**TAQUERIA**	taco stall or shop
GRANDE	big	**TIENDA**	shop
HERMOSA	beautiful	**TIERRA**	land
JOLLA	jewel, pronounced "hoya"	**TRES**	three
LAS, LOS	the (plural)	**VERDE**	green

For the basics, the most useful language book on the market is *Mexican Spanish: A Rough Guide Phrasebook* (Rough Guides); £3.99/$5, which covers the essential phrases and expressions, as well as dipping into grammar and providing a fuller vocabulary in dictionary format.

INDEX

ROUGH GUIDES: Travel

Amsterdam
Andalucia
Australia

Austria
Bali & Lombok
Barcelona
Belgium &
  Luxembourg
Belize
Berlin
Brazil
Britain
Brittany &
  Normandy
Bulgaria
California
Canada
Central America
Chile
China
Corfu & the
  Ionian Islands
Corsica
Costa Rica
Crete
Croatia
Cyprus
Czech & Slovak
  Republics
Dodecanese &
  the East Aegean

Dominican
  Republic
Ecuador
Egypt
England
Europe
Florida
France
French Hotels &
  Restaurants
  1999
Germany
Goa
Greece
Greek Islands
Guatemala
Hawaii
Holland
Hong Kong &
  Macau
Hungary
India
Indonesia
Ireland
Israel & the
  Palestinian
  Territories
Italy
Jamaica
Japan
Jordan

Kenya
Lake District
Laos
London
Los Angeles
Malaysia,
  Singapore &
  Brunei
Mallorca &
  Menorca
Maya World
Mexico
Morocco
Moscow
Nepal
New England
New York
New Zealand
Norway
Pacific Northwest
Paris
Peru
Poland
Portugal
Prague
Provence & the
  Côte d'Azur
The Pyrenees
Rhodes & the
  Dodecanese
Romania

St Petersburg
San Francisco
Sardinia
Scandinavia
Scotland
Scottish
  Highlands &
  Islands
Sicily
Singapore
South Africa
South India
Southwest USA
Spain
Sweden
Switzerland
Syria

Thailand
Trinidad &
  Tobago
Tunisia
Turkey
Tuscany &
  Umbria
USA
Venice
Vienna
Vietnam
Wales
Washington DC
West Africa
Zimbabwe &
  Botswana

AVAILABLE AT ALL GOOD BOOKSHOPS

ROUGH GUIDES: Mini Guides, Travel Specials and Phrasebooks

MINI GUIDES

Antigua
Bangkok
Barbados
Big Island of
  Hawaii
Boston
Brussels
Budapest

Dublin
Edinburgh
Florence
Honolulu
Jerusalem
Lisbon
London
  Restaurants
Madrid
Maui
Melbourne
New Orleans
Rome
Seattle
St Lucia

Sydney
Tokyo
Toronto

TRAVEL SPECIALS

First-Time Asia
First-Time
  Europe
Women Travel

PHRASEBOOKS

Czech
Dutch

Egyptian Arabic
European
French
German
Greek
Hindi & Urdu
Hungarian
Indonesian
Italian
Japanese

Mandarin
  Chinese
Mexican
  Spanish
Polish
Portuguese
Russian
Spanish
Swahili
Thai
Turkish
Vietnamese

ROUGH GUIDES:
Reference and Music CDs

REFERENCE
Classical Music
Classical:
  100 Essential CDs
Drum'n'bass
House Music
Jazz
Music USA

Opera
Opera:
  100 Essential CDs
Reggae
Reggae:
  100 Essential CDs
Rock
Rock:
  100 Essential CDs
Techno
World Music
World Music:
  100 Essential CDs
English Football
European Football

Internet
Millennium

ROUGH GUIDE MUSIC CDs
Music of the
  Andes
Australian
  Aboriginal
Brazilian Music
Cajun & Zydeco

Classic Jazz
Music of
  Colombia
Cuban Music
Eastern Europe

Music of Egypt
English Roots
  Music
Flamenco
India & Pakistan
Irish Music
Music of Japan
Kenya & Tanzania
Native American
North African
Music of Portugal

Reggae
Salsa
Scottish Music
South African
  Music
Music of Spain
Tango
Tex-Mex
West African
  Music
World Music
World Music Vol 2
Music of
  Zimbabwe